INTRODUCTION TO

INTRODUCTION TO
PSYCHO

LOGY

Melvin H. Marx

PROBLEMS, PROCEDURES, AND PRINCIPLES

Macmillan Publishing Co., Inc.
NEW YORK

Collier Macmillan Publishers
LONDON

Macmillan Publishing Co., Inc.
866 Third Avenue, New York, New York 10022

Collier Macmillan Canada, Ltd.

Library of Congress Cataloging in Publication Data

Marx, Melvin Herman.
  Introduction to psychology.

  Includes bibliographies and index.
  1. Psychology. I. Title. [DNLM: 1. Psychology.
BF121 M392i]
BF121.M38   150   75–2349
ISBN 0-02-376850-9
Printing: 1 2 3 4 5 6 7 8   Year: 6 7 8 9 0 1 2

Credit to the following individuals and organizations is gratefully given for materials included in this text:

Psychological Abstracts, for permission to reproduce the table of contents that appears on page 10.
Macmillan Publishing Company, Inc., New York, for Figure 1–10 adapted from Penfield, W., and Rasmussen, T.: *The Cerebral Cortex of Man,* 1950, 214–215.
Sperry, R. W., for Figure 4-4 from "Hemisphere deconnection and unity in conscious awareness," *American Psychologist,* **23** (1968), 723–733. © 1968 by the American Psychological Association.
Scott, Foresman and Company, Chicago, for Figures 5-10 and 6-18 from Ruch, F. L.: *Psychology and Life,* 7th ed., pp. 278 and 307.
Eastman Kodak Company, Rochester, New York, for permission to reproduce Plate 1.
Inmont Corporation, New York, for permission to reproduce Plate 2.
American Optical Corporation, Southbridge, Massachusetts, for permission to reproduce Plate 8.
Attneave, F., for Figure 6-6 from "Multistability in perception." *Scientific American,* 1971, **225** (6), 62–71.
NASA, for Figure 6-8.
Neisser, U., for Figure 6-11 from "The process of vision." *Scientific American,* 1968, **219** (3), 204–214.
Liveright Publishing Company, New York, for Figure 6-19 adapted from Kohler, W.: *Gestalt Psychology,* 1947.
Barron, F., for the Breather material on p. 195 adapted from "The psychology of imagination," *Scientific American,* **199** (1958), 150–166.
W. B. Saunders and Company, Philadelphia, for Figure 7-4 from Hebb, D. O.: *Textbook of Psychology,* 1972, p. 283.

Harper & Row, Publishers, New York, for the Breather material on pp. 232 and 236 adapted from Werthheimer, M.: *Productive Thinking,* 1959, pp. 266–268.

Prentice-Hall, Englewood Cliffs, N.J., for Figure 9-3 from Dethier, V. G., and Stellar, E.: *Animal Behavior,* 3rd ed., 1970, p. 91.

John Wiley and Sons, New York, for Table 10-2 from Wright, H. F.: "Observational child study" in Mussen, P. H. (Ed.): *Handbook of Research Methods in Child Development,* 1960, p. 74.

Holt, Rinehart, and Winston, New York, for Figure 10-5, adapted from McCandless, B. R.: *Children: Behavior and Development,* 1967.

Lenneberg, E. H., for Table 10-3 from "On explaining language," *Science,* **164** (1969), pp. 635–643.

Perkins, F. T., for Figure 12-3, adapted from "Symmetry in visual recall," *American Journal of Psychology,* **44** (1932), pp. 473–490.

Bell Telephone Company, for the Breather material on p. 377 adapted from Karlin, J. E., *Bell Laboratory Records,* **36** (1958), pp. 284–288.

Peterson, L. R., and Peterson, M. J., for Figure 12-7 adapted from "Short-term retention of individual verbal items," *Journal of Experimental Psychology,* **58** (1959), pp. 193–198.

King, R. A., for Figure 12-8 from "Consolidation of the neural trace in memory: Investigation with one-trial avoidance conditioning and ECS," *Journal of Comparative and Physiological Psychology,* **59** (1965), pp. 283–284.

University of Minnesota Press, Minneapolis, for permission to reproduce the Breather material on p. 475 from Palermo and Jenkins: *Word Association Norms: Grade School Through College.* © 1964 by the University of Minnesota Press.

Harvard University Press, Cambridge, for permission to reproduce Figure A-13.

Houghton Mifflin Company, Boston, for permission to reproduce Figure A-15 from Terman, L. M., and Merrill, M. A.: *Measuring Intelligence,* 1937, p. 37.

Harrell, T. W., and Harrell, M. S., for Figure A-16, adapted from "Army general classification test scores for civilian occupations," *Educational Psychological Measurement,* **5** (1945), pp. 229–239.

Aldine Atherton, Chicago, Ill., for Table A-2, reprinted from Page, J. D.: *Psychopathology: The Science of Understanding Deviance,* © 1971 by Aldine Atherton Company.

Guilford, J. P., for Figure A-17, from "Intelligence: 1965 model," *American Psychologist,* **21** (1966), Figure 1, p. 21. © 1966 by the American Psychological Association.

Osgood, C. E., and Luria, Z., for Figure B-1, from "A blind analysis of a case of multiple personality using the semantic differential," *Journal of Abnormal and Social Psychology,* **49** (1954), pp. 579–591. © 1954 by the American Psychological Association.

Thigpen, C. H., and Cleckley, H. M., for Table B-2, adapted from "A Case of Multiple Personality" appearing in *The Journal of Abnormal and Social Psychology,* **49** (1954), pp. 135–151. © 1954 by the American Psychological Association.

The C. V. Mosby Company, for Table B-3, adapted from Cleckley, H. M.: *The Mask of Sanity,* p. 265. © 1964 by the C. V. Mosby Company, St. Louis.

To Kathleen,
Diana,
Christine,
Ellen,
James

Certain features of this book seem to justify its appearance, at a time when there would hardly appear to be a crying need for another introductory psychology text.

My intention in first planning this book, a good number of years ago, was to counter the tendency to make such introductory texts increasingly encyclopedic. I planned to employ two techniques to accomplish this admirable objective. First, the book was to be selective rather than exhaustive in its treatment of fundamental psychological problems. Second, it was to stress concepts and principles rather than accumulate a mass of fact and data.

Looking now at the final product, I must admit that this objective has been only partially accomplished. In sheer size, the book has far exceeded my expectations. The sharp contrast with the typical encyclopedic text that I had anticipated did not materialize. Nevertheless, I think that there are some crucial differences, in emphasis and organization, between this book and others of comparable scope. For one technical point, approximately one fifth of this text consists of supplementary materials; if these are not included, the hoped-for size contrast does become apparent. More importantly, I believe that I have substantially achieved my primary objective of concentrating on problems and concepts rather than facts. And it is my strong conviction that in thus trading off attention to facts for attention to concepts the student is far more likely to engage in learning that will stick with him and transfer to future situations; he may even develop some lasting interests in psychological matters in the process.

The focus of this book is on basic issues and problems, the procedures by which they can be attacked, and the general principles that have been or are being developed to deal with them. The major objective of the book is to give the reader sufficient information about these and related psychological issues so that he can form some of his own tentative judgments. Perhaps the reader will also be in a better position to evaluate other proposed solutions than if he memorizes a host of names and a mass of experimental results for examination purposes.

This book is organized around three enduring problem areas: (1) the relationship of conscious experience to brain and behavior; (2) the relationship between heredity (nature) and learning (nurture) as determinants of behavior; and (3) the theoretical controversy over the roles of action (organism-induced) and reaction (environment-elicited) as factors in behavior. A separate chapter, introducing each of the three major parts of the text, is devoted to each of these issues.

The temerity of any single author in attempting to cover all the manifold subject matter of contemporary psychology may be questioned. For a book of this kind, with selective emphasis on problems and concepts, this question does not appear to me to be well taken. It requires no undue modesty for me to assume that I, or for that matter any reasonably well-trained professional psychologist, either already knows or can readily learn a sufficient amount about the major topics of psychology to provide an *introduction* to the subject. As suggested above, this text is designed to be such an introduction and not the kind of handbook for which the question would indeed have relevance.

The core topics are covered in the seventeen chapters of the text proper. Certain additional information is provided in two sets of supplements (on research methods and applied problems) that can be selectively assigned by the instructor or read by

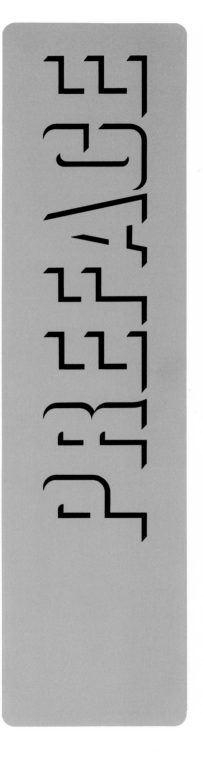

the student on his own. Several functions are served by this optional material. Some of the supplements provide fundamental background information of an essentially nonpsychological sort (e.g., the biological contributions of Darwin and Mendel, the nature of measurement and statistics); some provide methodological backgrounds more distinctly psychological in nature (e.g., opinion-poll methods, intelligence testing); some consist of more extended and in-depth treatment of major topics (e.g., learning, motivation, personality, problems of social interaction); and some are concerned with special topics of more than ordinary interest to the student (e.g., human love, psychosomatic illness, behavior disorders).

In an effort to treat mainly the more significant problems of psychology, and not to distract the reader from these matters by continuous naming of (to him) relatively unimportant experimenters or writers and by describing empirical details, all the references to the work described are placed in a notes section at the end of each chapter (except for citations of direct quotations). These sections also contain a number of additional comments that might interest the potential psychology major but are not as likely to interest the typical reader, as well as some suggestions for further reading. Experiments are described in the text where appropriate in terms of their significance for problems.

In each of the substantive chapters, beginning with Chapter 4, a section called a breather has been inserted to give the reader a place to pause. In addition to providing a brief diversion, the breather also serves as a convenient breaking point when the text is used with unit mastery systems of instruction.

Completion of a task of the magnitude of an introductory text in a field as broad as psychology necessarily enlists the aid of a great number of people, only some of whom can be explicitly thanked. My thanks go to a large number of colleagues and students whose critical reading of selected parts of the manuscript have immeasurably strengthened it: Lee Becker, Bruce Biddle, Sam Brown, Marion Bunch, June Chance, John Farbry, Donald Kausler, Robert Leeper, William Lichte, Marjorie Marlin, David McDonald, John Mueller, Jim Nelson, Steve Richards, Ernest Sears, Lottie Sears, and David Witter. Thanks are due Robert Daniel, Fred McKinney, and Mike Nawas for graciously providing useful background materials, and to Robert and Beatrice Gardner, Harry Harlow, David Premack, Duane Rumbaugh, and Fred Skinner for kindly supplying photographic materials. I am most grateful also to the hardworking students on whom drafts of these chapters were tried and whose frank critiques helped to remove much verbiage and simplify construction, and to River Ridgers Diana, Christine, Ellen, and James for their very helpful services through the last years of the preparation of the manuscript.

I am deeply indebted to Charles Cole for his critical reading of the entire manuscript and his many constructive suggestions. I acknowledge also the vital assistance of two Macmillan Company editors in this project: Joseph Britt, who was instrumental in its initiation, and T. P. McConahay, who was instrumental in its completion and who contributed illuminating artwork as well as excellent editorial assistance. Finally, the largest debt of all is due Kathleen Marx for her unflagging efforts on all aspects of this work throughout the years of its development.

Columbia, Mo. 1976   M. H. M.

CONTENTS

PART V

Supplements

INTRODUCTION TO

PSYCHOLOGY

This 1885 illustration, called the pictorial head, is from a popular health book of the period. It is particularly appropriate to use to begin our discussion because it illustrates a conceptualization of psychology that prevails even today. The artist has depicted twelve areas of human activity and represents these as the major products of the various "faculties" shown indelibly stamped upon the individual. Modern scientists still hold the study of psychology to be, in the broadest sense, the study of the organism's activities and endeavors as manifestations of its biology and environment.

Interspersed throughout this book we have used eighteenth- and nineteenth-century illustrations. The intent is in part to entertain with their quaintness, but more importantly, to project a sense of continuity of the human condition. The objectives of psychology are the same today as they were in the past; the science employed to further these objectives is of the present and future.

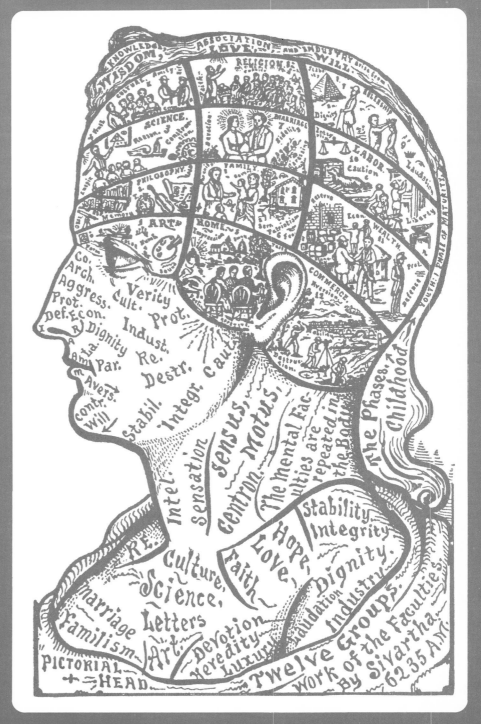

The Study
of Psychology

his introductory part attempts to lay the groundwork for the wide range of topics that follow in the main body of the book. The general nature of psychology is discussed in Chapter 1, and a brief description of the most psychologically relevant biological equipment of the organism is given.

The focus of the book is on psychology as a science, rather than on any of the alternative guises in which the same subject matter (briefly, subjective experience and behavior) may be viewed. Chapter 2 therefore describes some of the fundamental characteristics of science. Much of this material will be familiar to many readers from previous course work or their general background. However, it is likely that additional review will do no harm. It is even conceivable that the material presented here may correct earlier misconceptions as well as fill in gaps in background information.

The systematic overview of psychology provided in Chapter 3 is designed to give the reader a fuller picture of the underlying forces that have shaped contemporary American psychology than is ordinarily offered in an introductory textbook. This material is provided on the assumption that supplying at least some knowledge of such fundamental forces is a more important objective of the introductory course than merely adding to the store of facts on this or that topic. Moreover, some of the discussion will serve the function of setting the stage for the first chapter in Part II, where the key problem of consciousness (subjective experience) is directly attacked.

The Discipline and the Individual

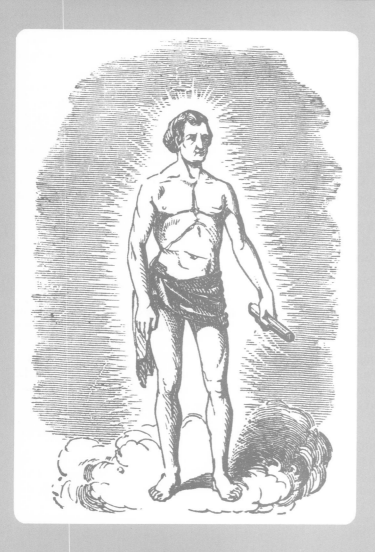

In this chapter we deal with the ways that the individual interacts with his environment. The nineteenth-century wood engraving shown here illustrates a then popular conception involving this theme. The aura surrounding the person has been called by a variety of names, among them, "nerve-ether," "nerve-atmosphere," and "animal magnetism." This electromagnetic field was thought to have profound effects on other individuals and objects, and it was believed that impairments in a person's nerve forces would often result in physical or mental disease.

his introductory chapter provides a brief preview of the field of psychology, with special reference to the way in which it is perceived in the organization of the book. First, a selection of salient questions from the chapters that follow is presented to suggest the great breadth of psychology and to indicate some of the more enticing issues with which it deals. Psychology is identified in terms of its major concerns. These concerns are the behavior and the subjective experience of the organism. The study of psychology has two broad objectives: first, and of most immediate import to the typical student, an improved understanding of one's own feelings and behavior; second, and of greatest concern to the student interested in learning more about the scientific nature of psychology, a more objective appreciation of how these processes function in all organisms.

The bulk of the chapter provides a brief but fundamental look at the organism, with special reference to man and his environmental sensing and reacting systems. This basic biological information is provided at this point so that the reader will have a minimum amount of knowledge concerning the equipment that the organism has at its disposal in its attempts to arrive at an optimal adjustment in a continuously changing and hostile environment. The nature of the structural unit in the nervous system, the neuron, and the major structural and functional divisions of the nervous system are described. The discussion includes a brief description of the primary functions of the brain as well as an outline of the salient features of the autonomic nervous system and the endocrine gland system, all of which are intimately involved in biologically equilibrating man with his environment.

The chapter concludes with a categorization of primary and secondary behavioral processes, and an indication of where these are treated in the book.

The Scope and Breadth of Psychology

The questions posed below are examples of the kinds of issues and problems about which the psychologist is concerned and which are treated in this book. The variety of questions should suggest the very wide range of topics with which contemporary psychology is concerned. Indeed, it is probably true that no other single scientific field spans so broad a spectrum of problem areas. This breadth is one reason for the difficulty psychologists have in agreeing on a single definition of psychology. (Location of text discussion is indicated by page numbers.)

1. Under what conditions does one's left hand *literally* not know what his right hand is doing? (P. 87.)
2. Why does a mother often sleep through all sorts of loud sounds and normally distracting noises only to awaken to the much softer cry of her baby? (P. 144.)
3. Which organism is able to smell as little as .00004 milligram of musk in 1 liter of air? (P. 130.)

4. Why did some fighter pilots during the war wear goggles with red lenses at all times while on duty? (P. 115.)
5. Why do so many psychologists fail to accept the inherited nature of differences in intellectual ability among social classes and races as well as among individuals within one social class or race in spite of so much evidence of such differences? (P. 277.)
6. How are bats able to locate insects in flight in total darkness? (P. 129.)
7. If science is unable to explain how "mind" is generated by bodily processes, how can psychologists hope to understand mental functions and related behaviors? (P. 97.)
8. Why are psychologists so generally unenthusiastic about the various claims for extrasensory perception (ESP) when they are presented in a normal scientific manner? (Pp. 175–176.)
9. What objections are there to a fully controlled society of the sort that has been advocated by some psychologists in which the overall objective is the happiness of all people? (P. 411.)

As a science, psychology attempts to deal with these and other questions by applying the general methodology characteristic of all science. However, because psychology has a rather unique subject matter, it has become necessary to develop its own unique or individualistic methodological techniques. In other words, psychology has *adapted* the scientific procedures that it has inherited from older disciplines rather than merely transferring them all intact. Despite the fact that many of the older psychological techniques can still be usefully applied to study current problems, man's behavior is a dynamic topic. Therefore, in order to deal adequately with its subject matter psychology also needs to develop some new methods and procedures. Misunderstanding on this mix of old and new methodology within psychology has troubled a large number of persons, both professionals and laymen, and has encouraged criticism, much of it unfair, of the more orthodox branches of experimental psychology.

Psychology has its nonscientific as well as its scientific aspects. In particular, those psychologists who have been influenced by the so-called humanistic movement in psychology appear to be little concerned with scientific methodology as a way of gaining understanding, or with the use of controlled observation and the collection of empirical data. This is because the primary motivation that inspires such movements is the serving of human interests. Humanistic psychologists therefore are prone to look with favor on whatever procedures seem to offer immediate help in solving human problems. Because they are less concerned with the purely intellectual process of discovery and confirmation, they are less interested in the use of strictly scientific techniques.

This book, however, is about psychology as a science and its bias is therefore experimental. Its objective is the development of understanding, that is, a conceptually clear appreciation of the problems, procedures, and principles of contemporary psychology. It is necessary to keep this kind of objective assessment separate from one's personal beliefs. Each of us tends to bring to any new study a host of prior beliefs and attitudes, many of which prove to be inconsistent with the orthodox messages of authorities in the field. This situation is particularly acute in psychology because we all have enjoyed continuous opportunities to experience, to observe, and to speculate about behavior. For example, all of us at one time or another have no doubt speculated on the "dynamics" (motivation) of a friend's behavior. Although it is necessary for each student to divest himself of enough of these prior speculations and belief systems to permit some genuine learning of new ideas, a diversity of opinion on any topic is to be encouraged. Fresh points of view are especially necessary in a fast-growing field such as psychology. It is anticipated that the student's willingness to entertain alternative conceptual systems will facilitate that understanding of scientific psychology which is the primary goal of the book.

DEFINITION: IDENTIFICATION

The problem of defining a science, or any other subject matter, is one that plagues instructors as well as textbook writers. The problem is aggravated when tendencies toward rigidity in thinking demand too much precision in such definitions. Here no attempt to define the subject matter will be made in any systematic way. Rather, we will attempt to identify the *nature* of psychology as it has developed and is developing. The important distinction is that this kind of description follows actual usage—describes what it is that psychologists are investigating—rather than delineates what they should be or might be studying. It is, in a sense, a "definition" of psychology in terms of the activities of which it is composed.

Two Subject Matters: Experience and Behavior

Identification of the nature of psychology reveals at once the existence of two great arrays of subject matter. One of these is centered around the subjective experience of man—his thoughts, perceptions, feelings, and the like. Analysis of such mental phenomena was the initial objective of psychology as it split off from philosophy. The other central concern, a more contemporary one, is the behavior of organisms, lower animals as well as man.

Investigation of one's mental phenomena or private experiences is difficult because they are essentially *covert,* hidden to outside observers. *Overt* behavior, on the other hand, is directly observable by an outside observer and so can be more readily, and more objectively, studied.

The relationship between these two seemingly disparate subject matters has long been a major problem within psychology (cf., for example, Chapter 4).

IDENTIFICATION BY VARIABLES. Examined more closely, the field of psychology may be identified, like any other science, in terms of the *variables,* various aspects of behavior, it measures. This criterion is the most accurate means of differentiating the various sciences. For example, the chemist typically measures properties of substances, such as their acidity–alkalinity; the physicist typically measures somewhat different kinds of properties of objects, such as the pressure of a gas as it is enveloped within a membrane and subjected to temperature variations; the physiologist typically measures still other properties of the functioning of specific organ systems within an organism, such as variations within the red-cell count of the blood; and the psychologist typically measures some aspect of the behavior of the whole organism. He may be concerned with such large-scale (molar) and complex behaviors as speech or written discourse, each sample of which may reflect the operation of a host of diverse variables. On the other hand, he may be concerned with such simple and seemingly uncomplicated behaviors as the reflexive approach response of an insect to a light stimulus. He may infer subjective experience in others on the basis of their behavior, and of course can always directly observe his own subjective experience.

Useful as this kind of differentiation may be as a means of approximately locating psychology within the spectrum of science, it is at the same time quite clear that no hard-and-fast lines can be drawn to separate the field from all others. Just as physics and chemistry share a common and often ambiguous border area, so psychology merges imperceptibly into such neighboring disciplines as physiology, on the one hand, and sociology, on the other hand. As a matter of fact, it is in just such borderline areas that many of the more interesting problems lie and the more productive investigations proceed—for example, historically, the emergence of such major fields as biochemistry, physical chemistry, physiological psychology, and social psychology. Each of these has resulted from the combination of fields that were formerly adjacent but more or less separated. There are many contemporary cases of similarly fruitful joint ventures that are now actively in the process of "spinning off" new areas of inquiry. Two recent illustrations are the application of genetics to psychology and the utilization of computer functions as a means of studying human problem-solving behavior. All such changes reflect the progress of science. Boundaries between areas are arbitrarily established, from ignorance, or convenience, or simply by historical accident. We need to underscore the fact that nature knows no such boundaries, or artificial divisions of knowledge, even though they have traditionally been used to separate scientific disciplines and, perhaps with even less justification, college and university departments.

The science of psychology has concentrated mainly on behavior, but consciousness, subjective experience, has always hovered in the background. Psychology has therefore been a notorious and in some ways unique straddler of subject matters. Straddling follows also from the nature of the relationships among behavior and its determining conditions. The behavior of organisms is the complex product of an immense number of factors. Psychology is both a biological and a social science for the simple and unassailable reason that behavior is determined by both *biological* and *social variables*. Individual psychologists, or even subfields within psychology, do of course often lean one way more than the other. But at least for human psychology this kind of leaning can be permitted only to a limited extent. Willful disregard or ignorance of either aspect can be disastrous. No account of man's behavior that aspires to be complete can afford to neglect either one of these two major influences.

DIVERSITY OF PSYCHOLOGY. A more concrete idea of the diversity and scope of the field of psychology can be gleaned from the organization of the *Psychological*

Abstracts, the monthly publication that attempts to keep up with the world's literature in psychology. The table of contents from a recent issue of that periodical is reproduced below. This outline provides merely the skeleton within which over 40,000 professional psychologists are now actively engaged in research, in teaching, and in application of psychological principles to everyday problems. More than 20,000 separate published items are abstracted each year. In the chapters that follow this broad outline will be filled in with the concrete problems as selected instances of these manifold activities are described.

Table of Contents from
Psychological Abstracts, February, 1975

GENERAL

PSYCHOMETRICS AND STATISTICS
  Test Construction & Validation
  Mathematical Models & Statistics

PERCEPTION AND MOTOR PERFORMANCE
  Perceptual Processes
  Auditory Perception
  Visual Perception
  Motor Processes & Performance

COGNITIVE PROCESSES AND MOTIVATION
  Learning & Thinking & Conditioning
  Attention & Memory
  Motivation & Emotion

NEUROLOGY AND PHYSIOLOGY
  Neuroanatomy & Electrophysiology
  Physiological Processes
  Genetics

PSYCHOPHARMACOLOGY AND PHYSIOLOGICAL INTERVENTION
  Brain & Electrical Stimulation & Lesions
  Drug Effects

ANIMAL PSYCHOLOGY
  Learning & Motivation
  Social & Sexual Behavior
  Sensory Processes

DEVELOPMENTAL PSYCHOLOGY
  Cognitive & Physical Development
  Emotional & Personality Development
  Social Behavior & Family Relations
  Adult Development & Aging

CULTURAL INFLUENCES AND SOCIAL ISSUES
  Culture & Ethnology & Race Relations & Religion
  Social Issues & Social Processes

SOCIAL BEHAVIOR AND INTERPERSONAL PROCESSES
  Group Dynamics & Interpersonal Processes
  Social Perception & Motivation & Attitudes

COMMUNICATION AND LANGUAGE

PERSONALITY

PROFESSIONAL PERSONNEL

PHYSICAL AND PSYCHOLOGICAL DISORDERS
  Mental Disorders
  Behavior Disorders
  Learning Disorders & Mental Retardation
  Speech Disorders
  Physical & Toxic Disorders

TREATMENT AND PREVENTION
  Psychotherapy & Psychotherapeutic Processes
  Drug Therapy & Drug Rehabilitation
  Behavior & Group Therapy
  Psychoanalysis
  Counseling & Community Mental Health & Crisis Intervention
  Physical Treatment
  Social Casework & Rehabilitation
  Hospital Programs & Hospitalization & Institutionalization

EDUCATIONAL PSYCHOLOGY
  School Administration & Educational Processes
  Curriculum Development & Teaching Methods
  Academic Learning & Adjustment & Achievement
  Special Education
  Counseling & Measurement

APPLIED PSYCHOLOGY
  Occupational Guidance & Personnel Selection & Training
  Job Performance & Satisfaction
  Management & Leadership
  Organizational Structure & Climate
  Human Factors Engineering & Safety

Before proceeding to the subject matter of psychology, more attention needs to be paid to one fundamental issue that will continue to divert the student's attention from other problems if not placed in a proper perspective from the outset. This issue concerns the reasons for the study of psychology.

There are two fundamental reasons for anyone to study psychology: (1) *a personal self-help interest,* and the hope that one will gain from the study new insights into his own personality and so improve his adjustment to and his satisfactions from life; and (2) a *general intellectual interest,* with respect to the improvement of one's understanding of how psychology functions as a science, what it can tell us about man and animals, and how it can contribute to solving social as well as personal problems.

Both of these objectives are quite legitimate. I hope that each of them will be at least partially achieved by reading this book and taking a formal course in psychology. Nevertheless, there are certain serious roadblocks in this process, and it is best that they be honestly posed by the writer and squarely faced by the reader.

Fundamental problems arise with regard both to the first objective (personal improvement itself) and to its relationship to the second objective (general understanding). Unfortunately, the study of psychology bestows no magic wand with which personal difficulties can be mysteriously waved away. Most behavioral difficulties are too deeply ingrained to be easily eliminated, even with the strongest of motivation. It is true that gaining insight into one's difficulties, and learning that they are shared by other people, can be an important first step in the right direction. But psychology should not be oversold, and the student should be warned not to expect miracles.

Psychologists seem to operate under a handicap that may not affect other professionally trained persons. Should a psychologist be any better than anyone else in managing people? Certainly many people expect him to be—for example, with respect to the rearing of his own children! But look at a similar situation in some other fields. Take chemistry, for example. Should a professionally trained chemist be expected to be, say, a better cook than anyone else merely because he might be able to explain some of the chemical processes involved in preparing foods? Hardly. The reason that a chemist is not likely to be any better or any worse than anyone else as a cook is that expertise in cooking requires more than a simple intellectual understanding of chemistry. It requires experience and/or training in cooking itself. Similarly, the psychologist whose field is behavior need not be expected to be able to *apply* behavioral principles unless he is specifically trained and experienced to do so.

There is another subtle difficulty produced by the relationship between the two objectives in the study of psychology. The stronger one's motivation is for personal improvement, or some other particular relevant application from psychology, the more this motivation is likely to interfere with his gaining a general understanding of the field. In part this is because thinking and performance are more likely to be hindered than helped by strong emotional arousal of the sort that is typically, if not necessarily, associated with the consideration by an individual of his own problems.

For the same reason, it may be noted, a surgeon does not operate on members of his own family.

Apart from this kind of interference, there is the problem of maintaining the student's interest in introducing and discussing fundamental scientific materials. Many of these are intrinsically uninteresting to the typical student, and few have much direct applicability to real-life problems. Some such material is presented in these three introductory chapters. Nevertheless, many students recognize the necessity of learning basic methodological procedures and new vocabulary, as well as factual and theoretical propositions of various sorts. As one student aptly put it in a written critique of a draft of these chapters, "I am looking forward to the end of basic concepts. They tend to be dull, although deep down I know they are necessary to prepare for a good foundation."

The dilemma faced by the author of an introductory psychology textbook is thus to be able to take advantage of the high interest and enthusiasm that students bring to the study of psychology and at the same time present the subject in a reasonably sound scientific manner. On the assumption that in this case to forewarn is to disarm, these comments are intended to encourage the reader to regard psychology in the same manner as he would any other science and not to allow a preoccupation with the more intrinsically interesting aspects of the subject to blunt his overall appreciation of its scientific aspects.

Excessive concern with personal insights as a consequence of the study of psychology is doubly unfortunate: first, it reduces one's achievement of the general understanding itself, and second, it is likely to reduce his chances of personal improvement. This latter point is certainly arguable, but it does seem that one's personal insights are more likely to be substantial and to persist and be effective in personal improvement if they are based on a solid base of general understanding than if they are centered too narrowly on one's immediate problems.

Our discussion to this point has concerned *every* student of introductory psychology regardless of his occupational objective. A third, less general, purpose of studying psychology is to prepare for a career either in psychology itself or in some related field. It is expected that this book will provide sufficient basic material to help such students gain a sound foundation from which further study can proceed. However, the book has been prepared primarily for the general student, who may or may not take additional formal course work in psychology. It is intended to provide all readers with sufficient background to gain a good picture of what scientific psychology is all about.

The Organism

The focus in psychology is on the individual organism and its adjustment. An *organism* is a living entity, plant or animal, that is composed of interrelated and interdependent organ systems, each with a different function but sharing the common task of the maintenance of the integrity of the organism. Generally we are more interested in the higher, mammalian forms, and most of all of course in the human being. But before we can begin to appreciate the full complexity of man's adjustment to his environment we need to know something about the equipment with which he must make these adjustments. As part of the present preview of the field of psychology, therefore, we take a very broad overview of the main resources that enable man to adjust to the stresses and strains that confront him as an organism required to make a continuous adjustment to the environment.

THE ENVIRONMENT

The *external environment* consists of the sum of all factors and forces existing outside the body of the organism that exert an influence on the organism. Quite obviously the list of such factors is voluminous. Everything from the quantity of oxygen in the air we breathe to the temperature of the room and the level of noise therein must be included. Included also as a part of the external environment is the constant onslaught upon the organism by bacterial and viral agents as well as the wide variety of physical and chemical compounds introduced by way of the organism's alimentary system.

Although not as readily apparent, each organ system within the organism (and indeed each cell within an organ) exerts its influence upon the whole organism. Profound effects upon the animal may be produced by relatively minor changes in the functions of the cardiovascular system or the gastrointestinal system, for example. These organ systems may be thought of as the *internal environment*.

Like all other organisms, man must make a more or less continuous adjustment to both internal and external environmental changes. Figures 1-1 and 1-2 illustrate the organism's link with its environments.

Two broad types of adjustment to environmental change occur in the organism: biological adjustment and behavioral adjustment. Biological adjustment occupies a good percentage of the organism's total time and effort, but for the most part a discussion of the biological adjustive responses of an organism falls outside the scope of this book.

Just as the internal physiological functions need to be maintained continuously, adjustments in overt behavior are also required on almost as continuous a basis. Most of these adjustments, physiological as well as behavioral, consist of relatively small and routinized changes, but occasionally substantial threats or challenges occur and more radical behavioral as well as physiological adjustments are required.

BEHAVIORAL ADJUSTMENT

As conventionally seen, there are three major sets of structures involved in behavioral adjustment. Stimulation, from within as well as outside the organism, is detected by means of the *sensory system*. Experiencing these stimuli, storing the information for future use, and integrating the information within the totality of other mental experiences as well as the various behaviors exhibited is the function of the *nervous system*. The behaviors themselves, and other forms of reactivity, are made possible by *effectors*, for the most part either muscles or glands.

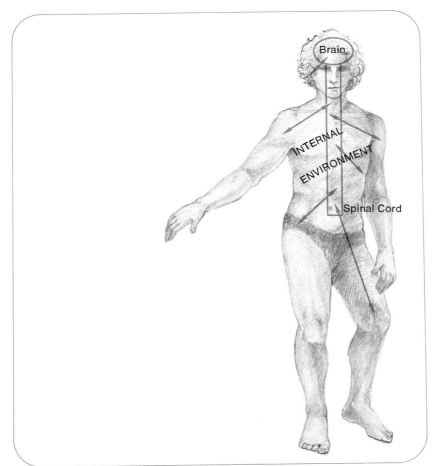

Brain

INTERNAL

ENVIRONMENT

Spinal Cord

1-1 The organism monitors changes in the external environment by way of the classical five senses: taste, touch, hearing, sight, and smell. The sensing of these changes in the environment, as well as the organism's adjusting response, be it biological or behavioral, is mediated by the nervous system.

Under normal conditions man's behavior, like his experience, is integrated. The organism typically focuses attention on one kind of experience at a time (e.g., reading a book or listening to music) and his responses are similarly channeled into a single main type of action (e.g., baking a cake or tossing a basketball). Under conditions of extreme stress, fragmentation of both experience and behavior can occur, and may become chronic in the case of serious behavior disorder. Thus, for example, a normal person under conditions of emotional stress or intense concentration may show some disorganization in his behavior, such as failing to hear questions directed at him. The psychotic or seriously disturbed person, to take a much more extreme example, characteristically shows fragmented behavior, appearing to live in a world of his own making and only upon occasion reacting "normally" to social stimulation. The organism is usually able to select relevant stimulation from the host of environmental changes that are impinging upon his sense organs (partly by means of exquisitely tuned *filtering* mechanisms in the

1-2 The organism monitors changes in the internal environment by means of temperature, chemical, and pressure-sensitive sensors located at various points within the cardiovascular, respiratory, gastrointestinal, and genitourinary systems of the body. Once again, the nervous system is the mediating system for both the sensing and adjustive responses of the organism.

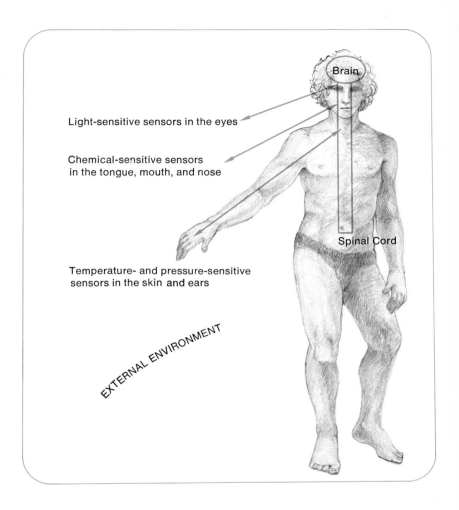

Brain

Light-sensitive sensors in the eyes

Chemical-sensitive sensors in the tongue, mouth, and nose

Spinal Cord

Temperature- and pressure-sensitive sensors in the skin and ears

EXTERNAL ENVIRONMENT

nervous system) and to coordinate his overt responding so as to achieve effective performance.

We will discuss the sensory system and many of the particulars of the effectors much more fully at later points in this text. At this time we are concerned only with providing a broad, general description of the mechanisms within the nervous system and with giving some indication of how the process of selecting and integrating stimuli and storing and retrieving information is achieved.

THE REFLEX ARC

Psychologists, like physiologists, have characteristically used the concept of the reflex arc as a convenient simplification in their description of organismic adjustment. If not taken too literally, the reflex-arc concept has value in pointing up the fundamental kinds of structures and functions that are necessarily involved in organismic adjustment. Environmental energy changes are conceived as stimuli, and the organism's reactions to them as responses. According to the reflex-arc concept, there exists a chain of reactivity from the stimulus to the response. Figure 1-3 illustrates the concept. There are five parts of the chain: sense organs, sensory nerve fibers, connecting nerve fibers, motor nerve fibers, and effectors. In this general scheme, the stimulus is detected by an appropriate sense organ, which passes information concerning it on by means of the sensory nerve fibers to connecting or association nerve fibers; these in turn are in contact with motor nerve fibers that directly activate effectors, the muscles and/or glands, by means of which the response is made.

The reflex-arc concept has long been recognized as of limited applicability to the behaviors of the higher, more complex organisms. Even when the simplest reflexes in the simplest animals are involved, there are many interrelated nerve fibers activated by a stimulus event. Moreover, both sense organs and effectors are complex structures. In higher organisms a great variety of neural activities intervene between stimulus and response—again, even in the simpler types of behavior—so that a literal interpretation of adjustment in terms of the reflex-arc concept is deceptive. The nervous system is now known to consist of a vast array of complexly organized systems and to take a much more active initiating and organizing role than was once believed.

SENSORY FUNCTIONS. The functional part of a sense organ is called the *receptor.* Each receptor is sensitive to a particular type of energy change, such as the electromagnetic waves (visible light) that serve as stimuli for seeing or the waves of mechanical pressure in the air (audible sound) that are the stimuli for hearing. The essential function in all cases is the *transducing,* or converting, of the environmental energies detected by the receptors into nervous impulses. The various forms of sensory function, called sensory modalities, are discussed in detail in Chapter 5.

ASSOCIATION FUNCTIONS. The three types of association or connecting functions attributed to the nervous system in the reflex-arc scheme are accomplished by three types of nerve fibers, or neurons. *Afferent* fibers carry information from the sense

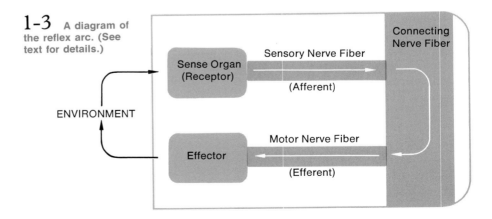

1-3 A diagram of the reflex arc. (See text for details.)

organ toward the central nervous system. Within the central nervous system there are a variety of *connecting fibers,* intricately associated in clusters, which not only tie the afferent to the efferent fibers but also mediate most of the higher mental processes. *Efferent* fibers carry information in the form of nerve impulses from the central nervous system to the effectors.

RESPONSE FUNCTIONS. *All* overt responses are made by muscles or glands. The muscles of higher organisms are of two types. Skeletal muscles, striated (striped) in appearance, are attached to various parts of the skeleton and are the means by which voluntary actions are taken. Smooth muscles, activating the inner organs (viscera), are mainly involved in physiological maintenance (vegetative) functions, such as digestion and respiration, which are involuntary.

THE NERVOUS SYSTEM: ANATOMY AND PHYSIOLOGY

Rudimentary information about the nervous system of man and all the higher mammalian forms can be presented in terms of the structure and function of the basic cellular unit in the system, the neuron, and of the major parts, central and peripheral, of the system considered as a whole.

The Neuron

The neuron is a cell that is specialized to accept, pass on, and transmit the special kind of electrochemical energy called the nerve impulse. Anatomically, all neurons consist of three parts, a central cell body and two elongated connective parts (fibers), one extending one way and the other the opposite way from the cell body. Figure 1-4 depicts a typical neuron with its constituent parts.

The cell body contains the nucleus, which controls both the development and the continued metabolic (vital) functions of the cell; if it is detached from the other parts they die. Each neuron has multiple dendrites and a single axon. *Dendrites* are the short, branched, receiving ends of the neuron; they are connected either to the receptor cells of a sense organ (afferent fiber) or other neurons (connecting fiber). The *axon* is the very long extension of the neuron; as the transmitting end of the cell it is attached to either an effector (motor fiber, for muscle attachment) or other neurons (connecting fiber).

Varying numbers of nerve fibers run together in the form of a *nerve* or *nerve tract.* The cell bodies of the separate fibers are typically clustered together in centers. When these are within the nervous system they are called *nuclei;* when in other parts of the body, they are called *ganglia.*

Transmission of the Nerve Impulse

The nerve impulse itself is a wave of electrochemical energy that when measured with the proper equipment is recorded as a wave of negative electricity. This change in voltage that occurs as the nerve fiber transmits an impulse can be detected by means of a microelectrode (approximately one-millionth of a meter in diameter) implanted in the nerve fiber and connected to a voltmeter recorder. This change in electrical potential that accompanies nervous discharge by a fiber

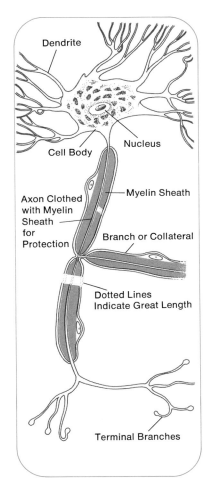

1-4 Diagram of a motor neuron from the ventral gray area of the spinal cord. To coordinate this with Figure 1-3, consider the neuron to reside in the efferent side of the reflex arc. Many such neurons together make up the motor nerve fiber.

produces a "spike" in the recording, as shown in Figure 1-5. The electrical record itself is called an *action potential*.

Each neuron is surrounded by a cell membrane, the inside of which is normally electrically negative with relation to the outside because of the presence in the intercellular fluid of a high quantity of positively charged sodium ions. The passage of a nerve impulse past the point at which the microelectrode is implanted is then marked by a sharp swing in the needle of a voltmeter recorder, which results in the spike or action potential recording marking this momentary change in potential. The entire process lasts usually less than one millisecond.

The actual mechanism by which this voltage potential (nerve impulse) is propagated along a nerve fiber is not completely understood. However, it is known that the movement of the nerve impulse along the fiber is accompanied by a change in the status of the cell membrane. The cell membrane suddenly "allows" a rapid influx of positively charged sodium ions from the intercellular fluid into the interior of the nerve fiber. This process is represented by the steep upward spike of the

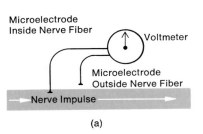

(a)

1-5 (a) Method for measuring and recording of the action potential in a nerve fiber. (b) The recording or action potential.

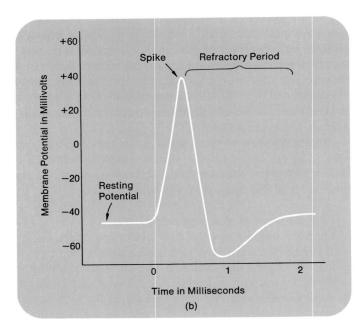

(b)

action potential. This sodium influx is immediately followed by the movement of positively charged potassium ions outward from the fiber, resulting in the downward slope in the action potential. Typically, this precipitous flux of potassium ions carries the membrane potential well past the resting level. A reversal of the sodium and potassium movement and return to the resting potential level indicate a restoration in the membrane's integrity.

Immediately after the spike of the action potential, the nerve fiber is insensitive to further stimulation for a brief period of time. This period, called the *refractory period,* is important because it imposes a limit on the frequency of nerve impulses that can be transmitted along the fiber, and hence limits the role of temporal summation.

The speed of the nerve impulse varies markedly, in accordance with the size of the conducting fiber. The range is from approximately 1 meter per second for very small fibers to 100 times or more that rate for very large fibers.

The Synapse

The connection between neurons is called the synapse. Much experimental and theoretical attention has been paid the synapse on the assumption that very important functions (e.g., learning) are somehow determined by it. However, only a few very important conclusions regarding the synapse can be asserted with reasonable confidence. It is definitely a traffic control device. Nerve impulses can be shown to proceed either way in the nerve fiber but can cross a synapse only from axon to dendrite; that is, there is *one-way* conduction across the synapse. The width of this space is only about $\frac{1}{500,000}$ centimeter. Certain chemical transmitters (e.g., acetylocholine) are passed between neurons at the synapse and mediate the transfer of nerve impulses. The action in the synapse is inhibited by other chemicals, such as acetylcholinsterase, that deactivate the chemical transmitters.

Recent experimentation has indicated that there are two fundamentally different types of synapses, one excitatory (facilitating impulses) and the other inhibitory (suppressing impulses) in function. Because any one neuron is likely to have both excitatory and inhibitory connections, its rate of discharge and consequently its contribution to summation function can be influenced by various other parts of the nervous system. In its own integrating of such positive and negative factors it also contributes to the remarkable way the nervous system is able to generate patterned responses of graded intensity to a great variety of complex stimuli. As the ever-increasing sophistication of microelectrical techniques produces more knowledge of synaptic functions we can expect to obtain a more adequate factual basis for our theories of behavioral functions.

CENTRAL NERVOUS SYSTEM

It has been estimated that the many varied structures of the human central nervous system are comprised of a total of about 10 billion neurons. The two main structures are the brain and the spinal cord, as shown in Figure 1-6, along with the spinal nerves of the peripheral nervous system.

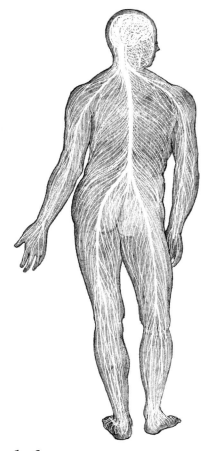

1-6 Diagram illustrating the brain, spinal cord, and spinal nerves.

The Brain

The human brain is a massive network of neurons. It is a large handful of a jellylike substance weighing about 3 pounds. Approximately 70 per cent of its surface is hidden in deep fissures (convolutions). The elaboration of this organ through primate evolution seems to be responsible for the spectacular ability of man to learn new ways of behaving. To explain this advantage, we must look to the nature of the internal system of communications mediated by the human nervous system. The superiority of the human brain appears to be largely a function of the amount and the organization of this complex network of nerve fibers rather than of any qualitative differences in the neural material itself. The sheer number of possible interconnections in a human brain is well beyond the capacity of the imagination to comprehend. Some nerve cells are connected to as many as 60,000 other nerve cells. With the total of about 10 billion neurons, each with multiple relationships throughout the nervous system, an enormous number of potential routes exist for the impulses generated by any particular stimulus. It has been estimated that there is a total of around *500 trillion* neuronal connections available for the transmission of information. This simple fact alone permits the establishment of an immense number of complex behavioral repertoires. Because of his brain, man is probably the least stereotyped of all living things.

For gross anatomical discussion it is convenient to divide the adult human brain into three major parts: the *midbrain,* the *hindbrain,* and the *forebrain.* These structures develop early in the embryonic period. Figure 1-7 shows an overview of the brain. Most of what appears from such an external view is part of the *cerebrum;* this is the great mass of nervous tissue that lies to the front of the brain and is the major part of the forebrain. Other important structures in the forebrain are the *thalamus* and the *limbic system,* which because of their interior location are not shown in the figure. The function of these structures is described in later sections of this chapter.

The midbrain mainly consists of a diffuse bundle of nerve tracts, usually referred to as the *reticular activating system* (RAS). The RAS is perhaps the most important filtering device in the brain. It serves as a kind of "gatekeeper" for incoming stimuli, thereby controlling attention, arousal, alertness, and quite possibly even consciousness itself. The relaying of sensory impulses to the higher brain centers in the cerebral cortex is influenced by the tracts in that part of the RAS called the ascending reticular activating system (ARAS). Because efferent impulses are also sent back to the RAS from the cerebral cortex, the other part of the RAS, which has the function of monitoring these messages, is called the descending reticular activating system. Again, because of its interior location, the RAS is not shown in the figure.

The hindbrain consists of the *cerebellum,* the *medulla,* and the *pons,* all shown in Figure 1-7. Anatomically, the cerebellum is similar to the cerebrum, with an exterior (cortex) of gray matter and an interior of white matter; the white appearance is derived from the myelin sheaths that characteristically cover the axons. The cerebellum is the main brain center for control of motor activities, as well as body balance and posture. It is served by the pons, which is a kind of relay station

1-7 Lateral view of the brain.

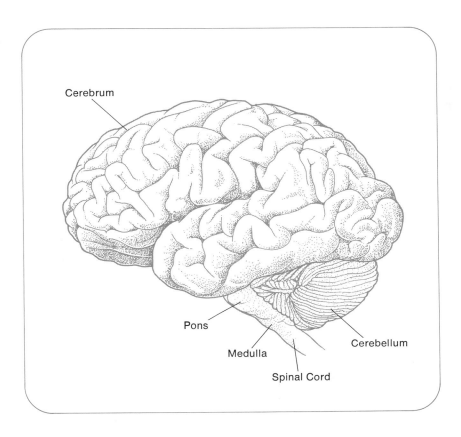

Cerebrum

Pons

Medulla

Spinal Cord

Cerebellum

between the cerebellum and the cerebrum. The medulla, which merges into the spinal cord, contains centers for control of vital functions like breathing and heartbeat as well as for relay of sensory impulses on their way to the higher brain centers.

The forebrain consists of several functional regions. The *thalamus* functions in part as a relay ("way") station. The sensory nerve tracts that have thalamic centers generally provide specific service to one or another of the sensory systems (e.g., vision, via the lateral geniculate body), in contrast to the more diffuse action of the ARAS. The *limbic system* is a complex structure with a variety of nerve tracts and centers. Many of these have close relationships with significant behavioral processes, mainly of a motivational and emotional nature. Prominent in this respect are the *hypothalamus,* the *hippocampus,* and the *septal area.*

Although the full story cannot be told here, some idea of the remarkable properties that have been revealed by recent research on the limbic system can be suggested. Experimental destruction of a small part of the hypothalamus in rats, for example, can produce compulsive, uncontrolled eating behavior, which results in the subject offered unlimited food growing to enormous proportions. Control of both the initiation and the cessation of eating behavior is apparently in separate "centers" within the mammalian hypothalamus. Even more interesting are the

21

effects that can be produced by very small amounts of electrical or chemical stimulation of different parts of the septal area. Thus a rat or a monkey whose response (usually the convenient one of pressing a bar in his cage) is followed immediately by a momentary electrical charge in microelectrodes properly implanted will continue to respond, thousands and thousands of times, until quite literally exhausted; response until actual death from exhaustion has occurred.

Presumably the part of the brain stimulated in these cases acts as a kind of "reward center," and the external application of electrical stimulation short-circuits the usual more elaborate process within the brain by which various responses are rewarded and so tend to be repeated. Tiny hollow cylinders can be permanently implanted into sections of the limbic region to receive chemical stimulation, another research technique. When the appropriate chemical (e.g., a sex hormone) is injected, responses normally occurring in such primary behaviors as eating, drinking, or sexual activity can be directly elicited. These and other similar illustrations of recent neuropsychological research have pointed the way in which researchers can work to increase our understanding of how the brain functions, but before definitive and comprehensive principles are developed a great deal of hard but fascinating and rewarding research must be done.

1-8 Gross anatomy of the cerebrum, showing four lobes and the major fissures.

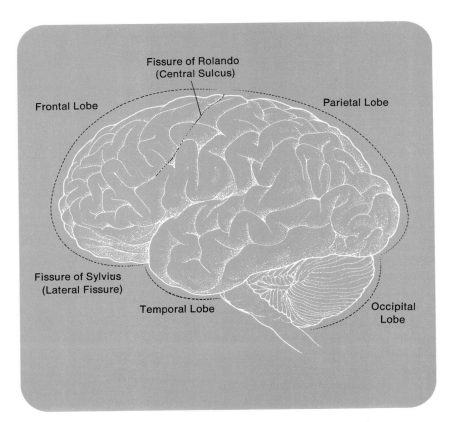

Fissure of Rolando
(Central Sulcus)

Frontal Lobe

Parietal Lobe

Fissure of Sylvius
(Lateral Fissure)

Temporal Lobe

Occipital
Lobe

1-9 Cortical function, some hypothetical (e.g., the elaboration zones), others firmly established.

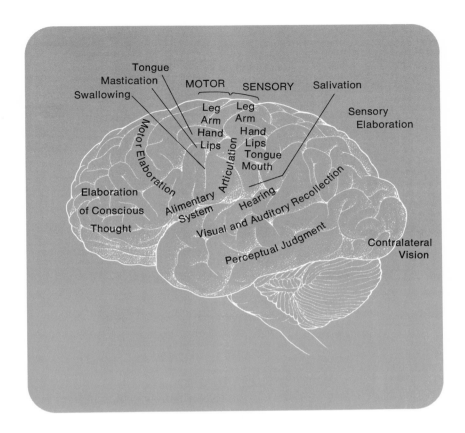

The great mass of neurons in each of the two cerebral hemispheres have their dendrites and cell bodies in the tortuously convoluted exterior, called the *cerebral cortex* ("bark"). Anatomically, the hemispheres appear to be mirror images. The left hemisphere controls the right side and the right hemisphere controls the left side of the body. This reversal is a result of the crossing over of nerve tracts as they make their way to and from the brain. Functionally, however, there are some important differences between hemispheres, mainly in that the left hemisphere usually controls speech functions—a fact that can be dramatically demonstrated in patients whose hemispheres have been surgically separated by cutting of the corpus callosum, which contains the connecting tracts; such "split-brain" effects are described in detail in Chapter 4.

The four anatomical divisions of the *cerebrum* are shown in Figure 1-8. The temporal lobe contains the major centers for hearing, the occipital lobe the major centers for vision, the parietal lobe a variety of sensory and motor functions, and the frontal lobe the centers for speech and thinking functions.

The more behaviorally significant functions of the cerebral cortex are shown, diagrammatically, in Figure 1-9. Most of the functions labeled are firmly established; one exception is the "elaboration" zones indicated. The evidence for this function in those areas is mainly conjectural, and seems to be based largely on the

23

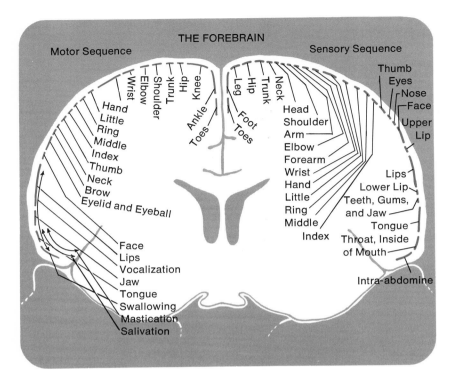

THE FOREBRAIN

Motor Sequence

Hand
Little
Ring
Middle
Index
Thumb
Neck
Brow
Eyelid and Eyeball

Wrist
Elbow
Shoulder
Trunk
Hip
Knee
Ankle
Toes

Foot
Toes
Leg
Hip
Trunk
Neck

Sensory Sequence

Thumb
Eyes
Nose
Face
Upper
Lip

Head
Shoulder
Arm
Elbow
Forearm
Wrist
Hand
Little
Ring
Middle
Index

Lips
Lower Lip
Teeth, Gums,
and Jaw
Tongue
Throat, Inside
of Mouth

Face
Lips
Vocalization
Jaw
Tongue
Swallowing
Mastication
Salivation

Intra-abdomine

1-10 Cross section of the cerebrum through the sensorimotor region with the motor and sensory sequences indicated. The lengths of the solid bars represent an estimate of the average relative cortical areas from which the corresponding responses were elicited. (Adapted from W. Penfield and T. Rasmussen, *The Cerebral Cortex of Man.* Courtesy of Macmillan Publishing Co., Inc.)

absence of more specific functions for them in conjunction with the felt need to pinpoint some areas as a center for what are often called the "higher mental functions." Figure 1-10 shows in more specific detail the sensorimotor functions by means of a cross section through that region of the cerebrum.

The Spinal Cord

Just as the brain is enclosed within the protective cover of the skull, so the spinal cord is within the protective encasement of the spinal column. Thirty-one pairs of spinal nerves, each consisting of thousands of axons, connect the central nervous system to the various parts of the body via the spinal cord. Bilaterally arranged, they enter the cord at regular intervals from the neck, where the lower brainstem merges into the spinal cord, to the lumbar region in the lower back. The inside core of the spinal cord consists of cell bodies and is therefore gray, whereas the exterior part consists of the connecting axons and is therefore white, because of the color of the myelin sheaths that cover them. The sensory (ascending) tracts are clustered in the dorsal (back) side and the motor tracts in the ventral (front) part of the H-shaped core. Reflex actions not involving the brain can be effected entirely within the spinal cord and its conducting peripheral nerves. However, this is the exception rather than the usual case. For the most part, brain connections of various sorts are activated as the organism responds to stimulation from its internal and external environment. These arrangements are shown schematically in Figure 1-11.

24

THE PERIPHERAL NERVOUS SYSTEM

The peripheral nervous system consists of two main parts. First, there are the thirty-one pairs of *spinal nerves* that connect to the spinal cord, as already described. Each spinal nerve has both afferent and efferent functions. Second, there is the very important *autonomic nervous system,* which also consists of nerves coming off the spinal cord but which services the viscera, or vital organs of the body. These nervous structures are outside the central nervous system in the periphery of the body; hence the collective name.

Autonomic Nervous System

The autonomic nervous system has two divisions, the *sympathetic* and the *parasympathetic,* each with its own set of nerve fibers and ganglia. As described in Chapter 15, the sympathetic system is mainly activated in strenuous bodily activity and in emotion; it is the emergency system that prepares the organism for adjustment to stress. The parasympathetic system, on the other hand, operates mainly to maintain the internal, vegetative functions of the body. In general, the two systems have antagonistic effects on the various organs they serve; sympathetic stimulation, for example, speeds up the heart, whereas parasympathetic stimulation slows it down. But there are certain behaviors in which they are nicely balanced and cooperative rather than antagonistic in function, most notably sexual behavior. In this case sexual arousal is mediated by the sympathetic but sexual climax (orgasm) by the parasympathetic system.

The Endocrine Gland System

The ductless, or endocrine, glands are of major significance to both physiology and psychology. Their chemical secretions, the hormones, are major agents (along with the nervous system) in the internal regulation of body functions as well as in the embryological development and subsequent growth of the organism. Throughout development, the hormones exercise vital regulatory functions.

With regard to behavioral processes, the most important endocrine glands are the *gonads,* the *adrenals,* the *thyroid,* and the *pituitary.*

THE GONADS. The gonads, or sex glands (male testes, female ovaries), are prime movers of sex behavior and also affect many sex-related body features and behaviors. In addition, these glands produce the gametes, or reproductory cells (spermatazoa and eggs). The main male hormone, testosterone, and the main female hormone, estrogen, are produced in accordance with the production of stimulatory hormones from the anterior part of the pituitary gland. This fact suggests the very complex manner in which the endocrine glands constitute a highly coordinated, self-regulatory system. Characteristic male and female sexual responses, although subject to enormous variation from cultural and other learning factors, are correlated with the presence in the bloodstream of one or the other of these sex hormones.

THE ADRENAL GLANDS. Attached to the end of each kidney is an adrenal gland, with different hormones produced by its cortex (outer layer) and its inner core, the adrenal medulla. The cortical secretions are influential in maturation. The hor-

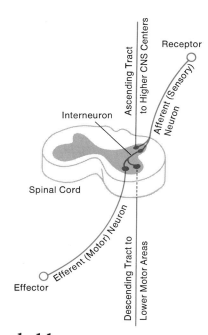

1-11 Schematic representation of a spinal cord, in cross section, and spinal nerves. As can be seen from this diagram, information coming from the receptors through the afferent neurons may be acted upon directly at this spinal level through the interneuron and efferent neuron, or may be sent upward through the ascending tract for integration with other sensory input. By the same scheme, an integrated message may be sent down the descending tract for a modified effector response.

25

mones of the medulla are instrumental in preparing the individual for emergency reactions and so are involved in emotion; these hormones are adrenalin and noradrenalin (also called epinephrine and norepinephrine). They have, in general, the same effects upon the body as activation of the sympathetic division of the autonomic nervous system.

THE THYROID GLANDS. The thyroid glands in the neck produce the hormone thyroxin, which controls the general level of bodily activity as well as the rate of physical growth, including that of the nervous system. Persons with low levels of thyroid function (hypothyroid) tend to be sluggish and apathetic, unless aided by thyroxin supplements. Persons with overactive thyroid glands (hyperthyroid) tend to be excessively active and excitable. The thyroid gland may thus have an important input into personality structure and needs to be considered whenever unusual deviation from normal activity level is found.

THE PITUITARY GLAND. The pituitary is a small, unobtrusive, single unpaired structure that lies just beneath the brain in the center of the head. Because of the many regulatory hormones it secretes it is sometimes considered the "master" gland. Its hormones are essential to growth and to maintenance of the vegetative functions of the body. The pituitary secretes hormones that directly affect each of the three other endocrine glands just cited for their behavioral influences, so that it must also be mentioned in this connection.

Behavioral Processes of the Organism

There are many ways in which behavior can be categorized. Division of behavioral processes into *primary* and *secondary* has been selected on the ground that the continuum from simple to complex behavior can more simply be understood in this context. The distinction does not mean that processes labeled primary are in any ultimate sense elementary or that they are any more important than those labeled secondary. Rather, it means that the primary processes represent essential functions that all organisms must use in order to adjust and survive and that the processes labeled secondary tend to be elaborations of the primary ones.

PRIMARY PROCESSES

There are three sets of primary behavioral processes that must be included in any study of organismic behavioral adjustment.

Sensation and Perception

The organism must be able to obtain information about the world around him (and inside him); sensation is thus a necessary starting point for any study of behavior and experience. When the sensory process is elaborated by prior sensory experiences and other mental activities, the term *perception* is used to describe the more meaningful events that ensue. These topics are treated in Chapters 5 and 6.

Emotion and Motivation

The disruption of smoothly organized behaviors by frustrating events of various sorts produces that state of mind, physiological condition, and pattern of behavior classified as *emotion*. The broader problem of why organisms behave as they do constitutes the subject of *motivation*. Each of these topics is treated in a separate chapter. Emotion appears in Chapter 15. Motivation, whose scope ranges from the simplest of behaviors to the most complex, is discussed in Chapter 14 after the methodological treatment of the action–reaction issue (Chapter 13).

Learning and Memory

One of the most striking facets of human behavior is the extent to which it is molded by environmental events. The changes in behavior that occur as a function of such events, and as a function also of the behaviors resulting from them, are generally categorized under the topic of *learning*. When learning occurs it must be because these experiences have left some kind of residual effect in the organism; the study of memory, representing that effect, is thus fundamental to an understanding of learning and an important problem in its own right. These topics are considered in successive chapters (Chapters 11 and 12) in the part of the book concerned with hereditary and environmental determinants of behavior; Chapter 9 tackles this problem directly, with special reference to the controversial issue of intelligence and intelligence testing.

SECONDARY PROCESSES

As here conceived, there are three crucial secondary processes in behavior: (1) thinking, (2) personality, and (3) social interaction.

Thinking

The human organism is a pre-eminent manipulator of concepts and symbols that substitute, in his covert experience, for real things and events; the topic of *thinking* encompasses the great variety of such manipulations as they occur in man. The topic of thinking is covered in Chapter 7, immediately following the treatment of sensation and perception, which provide the raw materials for thinking.

Personality

Each human individual has a unique organization of traits, attitudes, and behaviors. This organization is usually referred to as personality. The concept quite clearly is dependent upon a host of genetic and environmental conditions. More specifically, it may be considered to be a function of all the primary processes already mentioned. Personality is covered in Chapter 16.

Social Interaction

Social interaction, the last of the secondary behavioral processes, which refers to the relationships among organisms, is perhaps the most critical for the human organism. Although social interaction is considered in Chapter 17, it is of prime importance for many of the processes treated earlier, and especially for personality. The influence of the social interaction process, however, may also be regarded as mediated by means of some of those more primary processes, such as learning, emotion, and motivation.

INTERACTIONS

Behavioral processes can also be studied within other, alternative frameworks. These alternative methods of study cut across most or all of the individual processes themselves, from different vantage points. For example, we can ask questions about the processes in terms of their incidence and functioning in different forms of animals, the body functions involved in their operation, or how they develop during the growth of the individual. These problems constitute the subfields known as *comparative, physiological,* and *developmental* psychology, respectively. The former two subjects are treated at various places throughout the book. Development is covered in Chapter 10, following the methodologically oriented problem chapter on heredity and environment, because in many respects it is a joint expression of the interaction of genetic with environmental variables.

Notes

The *notes* that follow the text in each chapter have three main functions: (1) They serve as a depository for all the references cited except where direct quotations are used; thus only the major names, with whom the student may reasonably be expected to become familiar, are used in the text. (2) They provide a set of suggestions for further readings for the various topics treated in the chapter; these are worked into the discussion, under each topic treated, with such annotation as seems appropriate, rather than formally listed together at the end of the chapter, as is usually done. (3) They contain miscellaneous pieces of information and occasional elaborations of points in the text that the interested reader may find informative and perhaps even entertaining.

All the publications cited by name and year of publication in text or notes are fully referenced in the list at the end of the book.

Scope of Psychology

A good idea of the scope of psychological research can be gleaned from the many collections of readings that have been designed for a general audience. Somewhat different kinds of approach to the scope of psychology are provided in Pronko's innovative *Panorama of Psychology* (1973), which consists of various reprinted and rewritten as well as specially prepared reports, and Berelson and Steiner's *Human Behavior: An Inventory of Scientific Findings* (1964), which is a compilation of more than 1,000 statements for which reasonable scientific support seems to be available. The former book is paperback; the latter is hard-cover.

For general experimental psychology a basic reference work is Kling and Riggs's huge and authoritative handbook (1971). Helson and Bevan's *Contemporary*

Approaches to Psychology (1967) emphasizes research methodology, and Gilgen's *Contemporary Scientific Psychology* (1970) offers a collection of essays by active researchers. Wolman's *Handbook of General Psychology* (1973) is, as its title suggests, a more comprehensive treatment of the field. Readings on other more specific topics, in all the fields of psychology, will be found in the notes at the end of the respective chapters.

Of the many periodical publications in psychology, a few of the most general interest may be mentioned. The official publication of the American Psychological Association (APA), the *American Psychologist,* is a monthly journal that contains many articles of general scientific and professional interest. The association started in 1892 with a handful of members and at this writing has a membership exceeding 39,000 (not counting a good number of doctoral psychologists who have never become members or have allowed their membership to lapse). Although most of the other APA journals are specialty journals (e.g., the *Journal of Comparative and Physiological Psychology,* the *Journal of Abnormal Psychology*), two others deserve mention. These are *Contemporary Psychology,* which is entirely devoted to reviews of current books, and *Psychological Bulletin,* which publishes long articles summarizing the literature (which means the more or less scholarly publications of various sorts) on particular topics.

Outside the APA group of journals periodical publications of diverse sorts appear in ever-increasing number. Two are of general interest: *Psychology Today,* a popular (mainly nontechnical) and highly pictorialized monthly, probably already familiar to many readers, and the *Annual Review of Psychology,* which contains long review articles of the major areas of psychology at a rather technical level.

Careers in Psychology

Of all the sciences, psychology is probably the most severely handicapped with regard to the picture ("image") that high school graduates have of it as they enter college and begin to make decisions not only about courses but also on majors and occupations. Few students entering college really have an accurate notion of the nature of psychology *as a science.* Partly this deficiency occurs because of distorted press coverage, but more particularly it is a function of the fact that there is such a large gap between high school and college courses. Most other sciences, such as chemistry, physics, biology, and geology, are taught in substantially similar manner in high school and college. But psychology, on the other hand, is still taught in high school with much less frequency, and when it is offered is rarely taught by a teacher with much training in scientific psychology. The result is that prospective majors, especially those with a genuine scientific bent, are much less likely to consider psychology than they would be if more adequate factual information had been made available to them.

Although it might be just a bit premature at this point, at least for most readers, some information concerning professional careers in psychology is discussed here briefly. The best general source for this information is probably the pamphlet prepared and distributed by the American Psychological Association, *A Career in Psychology.* One of the nicer aspects of this publication is that a single copy will be sent without charge if requested by an individual; write the American Psychological Association, Inc.; 1200 Seventeenth Street, N.W.; Washington, D.C. 20036.

Professional careers in psychology almost all require at least the M.A. and preferably the Ph.D. degree (requiring usually two years and four or more years of graduate training past the bachelor's degree, respectively). Apart from graduate study preparation, an undergraduate major in psychology is mainly of general cultural value, like most other liberal arts' majors, or helpful as an adjunct to professional training in some related field, such as medicine or law. There are, however, a few exceptions to this generalization, notably, for example, the field of child care, with training and degree often given in a school of home economics, and personnel psychology, with a heavy dose of business courses mixed in with psychology.

The Organism

Any of the more recent textbooks in physiological psychology are good sources for further information on anatomical and physiological details. For somewhat less technical materials, Luria (1970) has prepared an interesting and informative account of brain functions, and Crombie (1964) provides an entertaining account of some of the (to us, with hindsight) quaint notions of sensory and nervous functions from early history. A special series of articles in *Life*, fortunately published in 1971, the year before the magazine ceased operations, offers a superb graphic and modern account of the brain and its functions. A more recent account is available in the August 9, 1975, issue of *Saturday Review*.

Techniques and Tools

This nineteenth-century engraving of Gulliver in Brobdingnag is appropriate at this point because we now turn to the ways and means that psychology has employed to study the individual. Unlike the Brobdingnagians, scientists do not enjoy the luxury of having a "laboratory-sized" human for observation purposes, but must devise elaborate experiments to examine the nature of human behavior.

Psychology shares with all other sciences certain fundamental methodological characteristics. Some familiarity with these is essential for the fullest appreciation of both science in general and psychology in particular. This chapter is therefore concerned with science as a method and emphasizes certain of the more controversial issues concerning science and psychology.

The chapter opens with an overview of science as consisting of three major facets: knowledge, method, and attitude. Two fundamental dichotomies within science (discovery vs. creativity, and discovery vs. confirmation) are examined, with Freud and Einstein cited illustratively. Comparison of the three great knowledge-seeking enterprises of religion, philosophy, and science is made, focusing on the attributes of rationalism, skepticism, and empiricism. The differentiation of the various sciences from philosophy in the Western world is then discussed in a historical overview.

The unique characteristics of the scientific method are discussed. The three major types of variables used in experimentation—independent, dependent, and controlled—and the key role of the principle of control are discussed at length because of their central significance for science.

The end products of science are categorized as laws and theories. Laws represent the empirical relationships that are established among variables. Theories represent the more abstract attempts to provide underlying order to our data, and so explain them.

The important matter of scientific attitude is treated in the next section of the chapter. In addition to skepticism and empiricism, we select tolerance for error and ambiguity, propensity for creativity and imagination, and curiosity and intellectual challenge as crucial attributes. The implications of the latter attitudinal attribute for the distinction between basic and applied science are indicated in the final section, and the role of the scientist is compared with that of the engineer (or technician).

Measurement and statistics are treated, in Supplement A-1 of Part V, in a preliminary description of their functions in science.

General Overview

A major force in the contemporary world, science is nonetheless not well understood by many citizens, including a discouragingly large proportion of those who have been exposed to higher education. The public has a particularly distorted view of the psychologist as a scientist. How many times are experimental psychologists, for example, asked if they can "psychoanalyze" someone? Or, on the other side of the coin, how many times are clinical psychologists asked if they conduct experiments on, say, animal behavior? The former event far exceeds the latter in frequency, reflecting the distorted picture that laymen seem to have of both psychologists in particular and scientists in general.

Apart from the identification problem with which psychologists must contend, the general lack of understanding of science stems from two major factors. First, the public is very inadequately served by the popular media. Most newspapers and magazines, as well as radio and television, concentrate upon the superficial aspects of science. Thus the white coat that symbolizes "doctor" in the television commercial or serial program misrepresents medicine in much the same way as the more sensational, albeit often trivial, science feature stories misrepresent science. Second, even in colleges and universities there tends to be an inadequate classroom presentation of fundamental methods and objectives. Science courses all too often require much memorizing of "facts" and an undue emphasis on the end products of scientific research. This applies to material as well as theoretical products; our legitimate concern with the products of scientific technology has been allowed to overwhelm the less utilitarian intellectual interest in how scientists actually operate.

FACETS OF SCIENCE

For a more adequate overall picture, three different facets of science as a human enterprise must be distinguished. With regard to its end product, science consists of a *body of knowledge.* This knowledge has been obtained by a particular kind of methodology, usually called the *scientific method,* which has as we shall shortly see some most important and unique features. Finally, scientists typically work with a more or less characteristic set of *attitudes* that tend to set them off in some important ways from most other people.

The order in which these three facets are described above follows their visibility, but to discover the way scientific work is actually performed, the reverse order is more meaningful. That is, the scientist is a person who has a certain set of motivations and attitudes, mainly related to the achievement of understanding of some part of the world. He then proceeds to make some observations of the phenomena in which he is interested and to attempt to interpret the results of those observations so as to make them understandable. The results are usually collected as *data,* in ordered and as far as possible quantified form. The heart of the scientific method is the *experiment,* which is a special kind of observational procedure to be described in detail below. The cumulative products of this combination of empirical (that is, observational) and theoretical (that is, interpretive or inferential) process is scientific knowledge in the form of *laws and theories.*

Discovery vs. Creation

One of the more deep-seated misconceptions of the scientist's role is that he simply discovers natural laws that are already in existence. Now it would be foolish to deny that there are in existence certain regularities in the way in which natural phenomena operate; on the contrary, such an assumption is made, implicitly if not explicitly, by every working scientist. But it would be almost as foolish to overlook the equally significant if less often appreciated fact that the scientist needs to *create,* conceptually in his theoretical constructions, the order he imposes upon his subject matter. In other words, he must play an active role in making sense—law and theory—from the complex and often jumbled form in which observations typically occur.

The distinction between sheer discovery and active creation of scientific principles may be difficult to grasp, and sometimes in fact only a fine line can be drawn between them. But it might be helpful to consider an analogy from the field of archeology. Let us suppose that we are digging carefully on a site that we suspect has been covered by some ancient volcanic eruption, such as the sudden flow of lava that buried the city of Pompeii centuries ago. As we remove layer after layer of earth we may uncover, as in the dramatic case of Pompeii, a complete scene from the past, with people and objects remarkably preserved more or less as they were at the moment of their almost instantaneous engulfment by the volcanic eruption. Some scientific uncovering may approximate this kind of situation, but only very rarely. Much more characteristic of science would be the partial uncovering of only very limited clues to the past, such as the finding of a part of a jawbone or a tooth or two from some prehistoric creature. Now it is quite clearly the job of the physical anthropologist to construct, on this very fragmentary basis, a representation of the kind of complete animal that much earlier included the present fragment. A similar creative task is faced by the archeologist who uncovers merely a fragment of a vase or bowl, or some other partial artifact, from which he wishes to construct a picture of the life of the people of that time.

Naturally, anthropologists and archeologists with this kind of objective are going to utilize as many cues from other finds and other sources of information as they possibly can. So, and for the same reasons, is the scientist who is able to obtain comparable regularity in the form of his own observations. Thus science consists of an accumulation of facts and interpretations concerning some phenomena that is built up in a more or less piecemeal manner from bits of observations as well as related facts and theories. But in most respects the fabrication of scientific knowledge is much more like painting a picture than it is like simply uncovering a picture that is already there, or taking a photograph of some existing scene.

Discovery vs. Confirmation

Considered in a somewhat different perspective, discovery is more often contrasted with confirmation within the scientific enterprise. As used in this context, discovery is a creative (artistic) rather than a reproductive (photographic) activity. The distinction between this kind of creative discovery and confirmation of hypotheses reflects differences between two kinds of scientific activities, or two kinds of scientists.

The scientific discoverer is the brilliant and inspired innovator, the man whose shrewd hunches and educated guesses lead to great advances. Without such men the progress of science would be intolerably slow and tedious. But they represent only one side of a two-sided enterprise. Realization of scientific advances requires more than shrewd hunches and deep insights. As a matter of fact, any imaginative person has a great number of such hunches and insights. Unfortunately, most of them turn out to be wrong. Therefore it is absolutely necessary in science that all ideas be carefully evaluated. Certainly the ideas are necessary, and the more the better, but by the same token so is their sorting out and evaluation. Here is where the confirmer enters; and here, rather than in its generation of insights, is where science differs most significantly from all other human intellectual activities. The confirmation process is by its very nature less glamorous and less exciting than the creative discovery, but without it the house of science would be built upon shifting sands rather than a solid bedrock of fact.

FREUD AND EINSTEIN. Our distinction between discovery and confirmation can be clarified by some illustrations from the recent history of science. Consider the question, "Was Sigmund Freud a scientist?" This question is answerable in either the affirmative or negative, depending upon whether one emphasizes the discovery or the confirmation aspect of science. On the one hand, Freud was without a doubt a tremendously ingenious and highly successful discoverer. His work opened up new fields of investigation and was extremely stimulating to countless subsequent investigators. On the other hand, Freud does not stand out as a confirmer. Scientifically he was not a good model in this respect. He took the position that there was no need for further testing of his ideas, because they had been sufficiently confirmed in his own (and perhaps others') experience.

Albert Einstein, although unquestionably an outstanding scientist, was not himself directly concerned with the confirmation of his revolutionary theories of relativity. But there was an important difference between Freud and Einstein on this issue. Unlike Freud, Einstein was quite emphatic in his recognition of the need for testing and confirmation of his ideas. That is, Einstein was himself a theoretical physicist and did not conduct experimental research, but he saw clearly the need for evaluation of his theories by experimental physicists.

However we view the relative merits of these two great men and however we tend to emphasize one or the other of the two contexts of discovery and confirmation, it should be made quite clear that *both* activities are indispensable to science. Furthermore, it will be helpful to appreciate the futility of the question cited above for illustrative purposes. Arguments raised by such questions can only be settled in terms of one's prior biases, or his relative preference for one context or the other; moreover, engaging in them is not conducive to any improvement in scientific understanding. In practice, it is quite possible to find substantial achievements of both discovery and confirmation in a single scientist, although more commonly any given scientist is likely to favor one or the other of them.

Viewed historically, in the long perspective of man's cultural development, science may be usefully contrasted as a social and intellectual enterprise with religion and philosophy. These three important human achievements are here compared in order to delineate the general structure of science. No value judgment as to overall or general superiority of science is intended. Rather, each as a way of interpreting the world has its own unique function and should be judged on that basis; difficulties arise when overzealous proponents of one or the other of these factions (usually, science or religion) seek to extend its domain so as to encroach on the other.

For our present purposes, the essence of religion may be assumed to be postula-

Historical Overview

tion and acceptance of some kind of supernatural force or entity. Similarly, the essence of philosophy is assumed to be a concern for the interpretation of reality. As outlined earlier, the essence of science is seen as the systematic effort to understand all phenomena, including man, by a unique combination of empirical investigation and inference. It is recognized that each of these complex enterprises has multiple facets, each with the potential for stimulating interminable disputation, but here we are concerned only with core meanings.

COMPARISON OF RELIGION, PHILOSOPHY, AND SCIENCE

Before attempting to differentiate religion, philosophy, and science, their common objectives should be recognized. All represent efforts both to impart *meaning* to life and to provide *support* for man in his continuing need to sustain himself in a world of unpredictable dangers and threats to his very existence. This objective is perhaps most evident in religion, with its direct appeal to superhuman force. But it is also a potent motivation for philosophy and science. In science, for example, the latter half of the dual objective (support for man in his struggle with an ever-hostile environment) is directly involved in technology and applied science. Philosophy and that part of science called basic or pure science are more directly concerned with the meaningfulness aspect of the common objective.

The comparison of these three kinds of human enterprise can be most effectively done in terms of specific characteristics. Three such characteristics have been selected as most instructive when applied to these activities: rationalism, skepticism, and empiricism.

RATIONALISM. As the term is being used here, all three enterprises are clearly rational; that is, they all involve a reasoned attempt to interpret man and his universe. In this respect they are separate from superstition, a kind of thinking in which causal relationships between conditions are inferred (implicitly at least) from mere coincidence of the conditions in time or space. It might be mentioned that traces of superstitious thinking can be found in all three activities, in science as well as in religion and philosophy. But in terms of their more sophisticated versions all three activities clearly qualify as rational.

SKEPTICISM. Although particular religious thinkers may show skeptical elements, doubt is generally eschewed in formal religious institutions. Here religion parts company with philosophy and science. Skepticism, or the tendency to question authority, is a keystone of both philosophy and science. Nevertheless, it may be remarked that individual philosophers and scientists are more likely to be skeptical about someone else's views than about their own, just as theological dogma is designed to maintain faith in itself and reserve questions for alternative positions.

EMPIRICISM. The faith that the scientist has, and in large measure, is reserved for his method. That is, he has faith in his own sensory observations as the base of his reasoning. Dependence on sensory observations is the heart of empiricism. Here science parts company with philosophy as well as religion: with philosophy because the philosopher is not likely to make the kind of empirical measures that the scientist does (and to the extent that he does he moves away from pure philosophy and toward science), and with religion because faith rather than fact is the keystone of religious belief.

Both philosophy and religion tend to engage in what is sometimes labeled "arm-chair speculation," by which is meant essentially nonempirical reasoning, or thinking that is loosely tied to an observational base. Intuitive insights, characteristic of science as well as philosophy and religion, are much more likely to be based upon strictly nonempirical bases in the latter cases. In religion, for example, interpretation of one's own inner experiences, as in religious conversion, usually has a powerful emotional component but little basis in ordinary kinds of sensory observation. "Arm-chair speculation" within science, and especially within psychology, is still frowned upon by some, but it can also play an important role in the context of discovery. The difficulty with it in science develops when it is not joined by an adequate empirical complement.

Science as a way of building knowledge thus depends upon empiricism as well as reason and skepticism. Moreover, it uses a special kind of empiricism—experimentation. The essence of the experimental method is the concept of *control,* or the deliberate manipulation of conditions in the observed situation, as described in detail below. The success of science in developing its own kind of knowledge of the world is basically due to the special way it has learned to make observations so that a more secure empirical base is available for drawing inferences.

DIFFERENTIATION OF SCIENCES

The development of the various sciences has been by means of progressive proliferation (or the breaking off as separate scientific disciplines of the newer branches) from the nucleus of knowledge initiated within ancient Greek society. This story is diagrammatically shown in Figure 2-1.

Fundamentally, the Greeks were rationalists rather than empiricists. That is, they tended to rely for their knowledge more upon their reasoning than upon new observations; an important exception was Aristotle, who did pursue original empirical investigations in a number of areas. In spite of this restriction to reason alone the Greeks did succeed in creating an intellectual base of great scope and outstanding sophistication, even by modern standards, so that to this day they are generally recognized as the forebears of modern science in the Western world.

As Figure 2-1 indicates, all knowledge during the Greek period could be encompassed within the single, undifferentiated label of "philosophy." Even at the peak of Greek culture, around the fourth or third century B.C., the totality of such knowledge was sufficiently small that it could be substantially mastered by a single man within his lifetime (Aristotle, for example). Contrast that situation with contemporary science, when a single man has great difficulty in mastering even the relatively restricted domain of his own immediate subsection of some discipline, not to mention his difficulties in attempting to keep up with new developments as they occur!

2-1 Historical development of sciences as differentiations from philosophy.

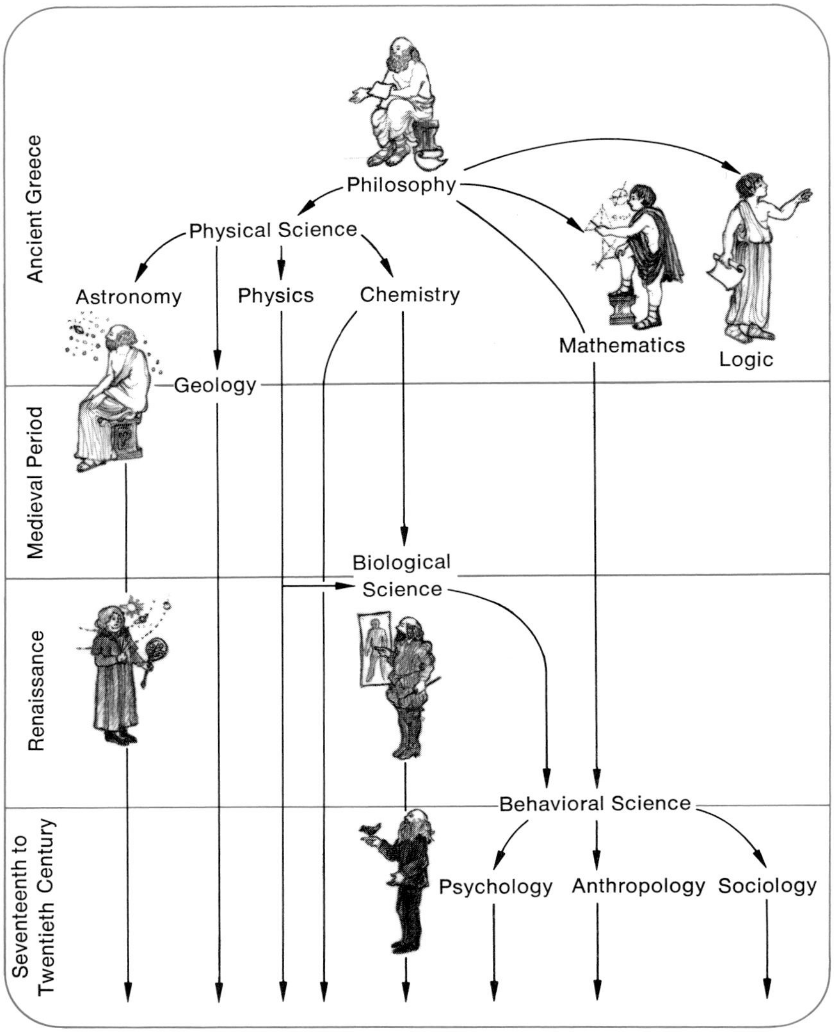

During the Dark Ages the development of science was painfully slow. The contrast with the great acceleration of science during recent history is especially sharp, as shown in Figure 2-1. However, there are certain other important aspects of the development of science, not shown in the figure, that should be emphasized. For example, each new discipline has tended to break up into subfields as it developed, much in the way that the major sciences themselves emerged from philosophy. This process exemplifies the continuous change that is the very essence of science. Moreover, as suggested in Chapter 1, the most interesting new developments tend to be at the junction between old and established fields. It is the active pursuit of these junctions or interfaces that produces strong new disciplines, such as biochemistry and neuropsychology. The fact that psychology is experiencing a number of fruitful interdisciplinary developments (with engineering, for example, as well as neurophysiology) is one of the more hopeful marks of its increasing maturity as a science.

There are many characteristics of science that help to make it such a successful means of accumulating knowledge. We have already emphasized empiricism as a crucial feature that tends to distinguish it from religious and philosophical procedures. But an appreciation of science requires a much more refined examination of its empirical method, and specifically a very close look at the nature of experimentation as the keystone of that method.

The Experimental Method

THE LABORATORY

According to popular interpretation, a scientific laboratory is some particular place, generally isolated and well equipped, where experiments are performed. Of course, there are many laboratories that fit this picture. More importantly, however, a laboratory is *any* place where variables can be scientifically manipulated and related, or ideally, where experiments can be performed. Such a broadened view emphasizes the process rather than the physical setting and is in keeping with a dynamic picture of science.

The overemphasis on the physical setting of the laboratory comes partly from popularizations, as in the press and periodical literature, where elaborate equipment and sophisticated measuring devices are easier to portray than the more elusive procedural niceties that underlie scientific advances. An essentially static view of science is fostered not only by the popularizations in the press and magazines but also by scientific textbooks and even by scientific reports themselves. All of these give a distorted picture of the true process of science. They all tend to emphasize the successes and ignore the failures—the false starts, the blind alleys, the pet theories that we all tend to hold on to so tenaciously. The true process of science is marked more by errors, from which scientists learn, than by successes—by zigs and zags rather than by straight lines. It is important that the citizen as well as the neophyte scientist recognize this fact of scientific life.

THE EXPERIMENT

Briefly, an experiment is a *specially contrived situation* in which the investigator so arranges the conditions of observation as to make possible a *relatively unbiased determination of the relationships among the particular variables or factors* in which he is interested.

The Concept of Variable

The key to understanding an experiment is the concept of *variable*. A variable is any factor, an attribute of organisms or objects or events, that occurs in different forms or amounts; for example, height, weight, skin color, hair color, and body temperature are all variables. Sometimes the variable is primarily qualitative; that is, it consists of difference in kind but the differences are not quantified. A variable must have at least two categories, such as maleness and femaleness in the sex variable. Skin and hair color are common examples of qualitative variables with greater numbers of categories. These qualities can be changed into a quantitative scale to refer to the amount of the particular quality (such as degree of darkness of skin or of blondeness of hair). When possible, a variable is directly measured in quantitative units with, in theory at least, an infinite number of values; height, for example, can be expressed in various units of measurement capable of indefinite fractional refinement.

Types of Variables

In an experiment there are three different types of variables. The *independent variable* is the condition that the experimenter manipulates directly, if possible; it is the variable whose effect is at issue. In most experiments the independent variable can be directly manipulated at the hands of the experimenter, but in certain situations these changes are not under direct experimental control. Then the investigator must wait for them to occur, in what is often called a "natural experiment." For example, in astronomy one may wish to study some effect of a particular condition, such as an eclipse of the sun; because this condition can be predicted with a high degree of accuracy, it is possible to arrange the observations well in advance and so take maximal advantage of the natural occurrence of the event. In other kinds of situations, such as a neurophysiologist's desire to study the effects of a particular type of brain lesion in human subjects, the availability of such subjects (as from accidental wound or tumor) cannot be predicted very far in advance.

The second kind of variable in an experiment is the *dependent variable*. This is the condition or factor that is directly measured. In other words, the dependent variable is that condition that is observed to change as a result of the change in the independent, or manipulated, variable; an experiment is thus essentially a situation in which the *observations are arranged so as to assess the effect of changes in the independent variable upon the dependent variable*. In simple experiments only one independent and one dependent variable may be involved, but in more sophisticated experimental designs, such as the kind called multivariate, more than one variable of each kind is involved.

The Principle of Control

Our discussion to this point is correct but incomplete because we have not yet introduced the third type of variable. Yet it is this third type of variable that is the most crucial in experiments and that is responsible for differentiating experimental from all other kinds of observations. This is the *controlled variable*. The controlled variable is one whose influence is *not* under investigation, and which is therefore eliminated. It is the operation of an indeterminate number of such *un*controlled variables, whose influence is not desired but which may nonetheless be functioning along with the independent variable to affect the dependent variable, that makes nonexperimental observations suspect. *When uncontrolled variables are allowed to operate, unambiguous relationships between independent and dependent variables cannot be established.* Thus the experiment is successful to the extent to which it is able to control unwanted variations in the measured variables from extraneous conditions, and this is accomplished by controlling as many such variables as can be identified.

AN ILLUSTRATIVE EXPERIMENT. For a simple example of the way in which these three types of variable function in psychological experimentation, suppose that the investigator is concerned with determining the relationship between age and speed of learning a motor skill (see Figure 2-2). Age would be the independent variable and speed of learning the skill would be the dependent variable as measured, say, by number of darts on target per trial. What would the controlled variables be? Here the answer depends upon a large number of factors, prominent among which are the degree of prior knowledge about the situation possessed by the investigator, his level of experimental and theoretical sophistication, and the particular requirements under which he is conducting the experiment (for example, the degree of exactitude required). In other words, there is no simple answer to this question. But as already mentioned, the success of an experiment will vary directly with the success of the experimenter in eliminating extraneous variability so that he can thereby attribute his results (the variations in the dependent variables) to his manipulations (the variations in the independent variables).

To return to our simple illustrative experiment, one obvious variable that might be controlled is sex. Sexual differences may be quite significant for the motor skill our hypothetical experimenter is investigating. To be on the safe side therefore he

2-2 Hypothetical experiment in which the age of the dart thrower is the independent variable, the number of successful throws in each "round" is the dependent variable, and such factors as sex of the dart thrower, general physical health, and environmental distractions are the controlled variables.

may decide to restrict his experiment to one sex only, thus controlling (by eliminating the variability in) sex as a factor.

It should also be noted that there are always a large number of procedural variables the control of which the experienced experimenter takes for granted but which the less experienced experimenter might ignore and therefore allow to vary and contaminate the results. These are such straightforward matters as keeping the number of trials and various other conditions affecting learning equal among the subjects.

Typically groups of subjects in a psychological experiment are arranged to represent varying degrees of the independent variable. Thus in the present illustration, each age level would be represented by a certain number of subjects (called treatment groups) of that age. Because there are always practical limitations in the number of subjects that can be "run," that is, experimented upon, some selection is almost always involved, and herein lies a large number of risks. For example, it would be natural for the subjects from the different age groups to be taken from different grades in a school. The experimenter must see to it that the selection of subjects is done on an objective basis rather than, say, by the teachers or school authorities. If the latter procedure were adopted it is quite possible that the particular classes selected might not be comparable in ability or general motivation. Or if only a small number of subjects from any one class could be used, the teachers might vary in their propensity to select the more capable representatives, either deliberately or unconsciously, so that the experimenter may unwittingly be investigating this characteristic of teachers as well as the age of the subjects as a determinant of test response. Use of some random scheme of drawing subjects helps to eliminate (control) this kind of unwanted variability.

EXPERIMENTER BIAS. Subtle biases in the experimenter himself can also intervene to produce unwanted variability in experiments. The resolution of this problem lies mainly in insuring that the person who does the actual collecting of *data* (the technical and commonly used term for the experimental records or results) does not himself know the purpose of the experiment, the groupings of the subjects, and the like; the experimental aid is, in this sense, "blind." As far as possible, then, the experimenter utilizes technical devices, which may usually be assumed to be relatively free of bias, and similarly "ignorant," unbiased, aids in the actual execution of the experiment.

PASSIVE CONTROL. There is a distinction between the active application of experimental control, as described, and more passive application, of the kind that is necessarily utilized in the typical conduct of certain kinds of scientific endeavor. In astronomy, as already mentioned, the investigator is seldom able to effect the same kind of direct manipulation of variables that other scientists are accustomed to arrange. He must patiently wait for certain kinds of events to occur, whereupon he makes the relevant observations. In the social sciences, also, it is usually not possible to effect the kind of social manipulations the investigator desires; here, however, he is less likely to have the kind of prior knowledge that permits the same kind of exact prediction of when his "natural experiment" will occur.

Within psychology, such passive application of control is necessary for certain kinds of observations within, for example, the fields of personality and psycho-pathology. A clinician who wishes to ascertain the relationship between a particular set of symptoms and some antecedent conditions must usually await the accumulation of a reasonably large number of this kind of case; furthermore, and more critical, he must also obtain cases that are equivalent except for the particular conditions in question and observe these as controls. This kind of research requires not only a high degree of sophistication but also a great deal of patience and strong motivation on the part of the investigator.

Measurement and Statistics

Before very much in the way of scientific laws or theories can be developed, even with the most carefully designed experiments, an investigator needs to apply at least some simple principles of measurement. It should help our understanding of the principles underlying measurement if the various forms of measurement are explicitly stated. Also, few experiments give perfectly clear answers without some kind of treatment of the data. This is especially true in behavioral research, where there are so many different kinds of variables that can have important influences on our measures. Thus it is almost always necessary to subject the numerical data obtained from experiments or other types of observations to statistical analysis. Again, our understanding of the rudimentary principles of statistical analysis will help to prepare us for the variety of statistical treatments that have been developed and are in common use in psychology.

The role of numerical as opposed to purely verbal manipulations merits some attention. The reason that numbers are so widely used in science is simply that there is no substitute for their exactness. If one picture is worth a thousand words, as the ancient Chinese maxim holds, then a few well-chosen numbers are worth several thousand ordinary words. It is also important, however, that we not allow these tools to become our masters. Except perhaps for the special case of mathematics and associated enterprises, all scientific investigations start and end with verbal formulations. Numerical operations are introduced as tools. Numbers, and possibly even relatively sophisticated mathematical expressions, may persist into the ultimate formulations of laws and theories, but in such cases they are supports for the ideas represented by the words rather than substitutes for them. Over-emphasis upon the role of numerical operations, so that they are prized more than the ideas they should serve, has no place in any empirical science.

Exposition of the topics of measurement and statistics necessarily involves a certain amount of technical information. Instructors vary widely in their feelings as to how much of this kind of material should be presented to their introductory students. The detailed discussion of these matters has therefore been placed in Supplement A-1, where it can be assigned by the instructor if he pleases and where any reader can use it or ignore it if that option is left to him. Nevertheless, every reader is urged at least to skim and sample the discussion, and especially the latter part, where some of the abuses of statistics are outlined, for his own general information.

The ordered, systematically arranged knowledge that is produced by scientific effort mainly culminates in one or the other of two main categories of verbal statement: law or theory. A scientific law is in general concerned with direct empirical relationships that have been observed and confirmed among variables, whereas a scientific theory is concerned with the more abstract (that is, less concrete or empirical) underlying relationships that are presumed to account for lawfulness. Theories are thus the main way in which scientific interpretations, or attempted explanations, are developed.

LAWS

Within psychology and the other behavioral sciences the development of a body of scientific laws is just beginning. Regular, predictable relationships between independent and dependent variables of the sort that the more mature sciences call law seem to be somewhat more difficult to establish when so many interlocking variables are influential and effective controls cannot easily be applied. It is therefore important that in their haste to acquire true laws psychologists not waste the partial laws they have. In other words, the development of laws is not an all-or-none process, and the gradual achievement of increasingly reliable relationships must be accepted as the normal manner in which fully accepted laws are obtained. From this point of view, half a law may be regarded as significantly better than none at all, especially if its incomplete nature is recognized.

The relative nature, as opposed to the absolute, of scientific laws is further indicated by the fact that no matter how firmly established a law may be it can never be regarded as beyond question. This fact has been repeatedly demonstrated in the history of science, and most persuasively perhaps in the field of physics, unquestionably one of the most mature of the sciences. A good recent illustration is the discovery of a fundamental assymetry in the arrangement of the nucleus, where symmetry had been long assumed without question. It is always possible that new ways of looking at phenomena or new techniques of observation will force modifications in even the best established principles. Such changes are the very stuff of which science is made and are to be welcomed and regarded as a mark of a successful science. It is this openness to change and encouragement of revision that further tends to separate typical scientific from ordinary religious and philosophic ways of thinking.

The changes that are demanded by new ideas in science do not always merely contradict old laws. More often they provide important new perspectives that change our perception of the place that the old laws play in the total picture. Again, consider an example from physics. When quantum or nuclear physics was developed, the older principles of mechanics were not contradicted. Rather, a new domain of investigation was initiated. The lawfulness of the lever, for example, still holds, but we now look at mechanical principles in a somewhat different light. A similar shift in perspective may be seen to have accompanied the even more recent and very rapid emergence of molecular biology; older ("classical") forms of biology, such as taxonomy, have not been discarded but are now necessarily regarded as having a different role in the total scheme of the life sciences. Examples of similar shifts in perspective within the history of psychology, such as the sudden emergence of behaviorism or psychoanalysis, are described in the next chapter.

LAWS, VARIABLES, AND DISCIPLINES. The nature of the laws toward which any given scientific discipline works is determined by the particular variables it investigates. As a matter of fact, it is precisely this matter, and more particularly the *dependent* or measured variables, that delimits any field of science. A science may thus be said to be known by the variables that it measures.

Note that it is only the dependent, measured variables that have this role. Both independent and controlled variables tend to cut across disciplines. Thus the psychologist as well as the biologist studies the role of age, or sex, or drug dosage as independent variables. But he studies their effects on behaviorally relevant variables, such as learning or personality. The biologist studies the effects of these same manipulated variables on more biologically relevant measures, such as physical growth or the functioning of some particular organ system. It should be just as evident that many extraneous variables (e.g., environmental variables such as temperature, noise, and the like) will need to be controlled in research of quite different objectives, although naturally their degree of relevance will often vary with the nature of the dependent variables.

It is an encouraging sign that in contemporary science the artificial boundary lines between disciplines are weakening, and scientists with widely varying training and experience find themselves converging on common problems. This development is important because researchers with such different backgrounds usually have much to offer each other. The boundaries are essentially artificial and too much importance has been attached to them. When they become hardened and inviolate, as sometimes seems to occur within university departmental systems, fruitful interchange of ideas and techniques is hindered. Moreover, some of the most absorbing problems are to be found in the interfaces between disciplines. The emergence of new fields has been one important byproduct of interdisciplinary research, as has already been emphasized.

THEORIES

Our discussion of laws has led us to a consideration of interpretations and directly into the realm of theory. This is hardly surprising because it is the interpretation, and the consequent understanding that is thereby achieved, that is the ultimate objective of most scientists. Laws are necessary, both as a basis for theory and as useful aids to prediction in their own right. But even when laws are apparently used by themselves in this way, in the apparent absence of theory, their interpretation is by no means automatic. There are always many hidden assumptions, relating to methodological points if nothing else, which if followed up must bring questions of interpretation.

Within the confines of this introductory chapter it will be possible to do little more than sketch some central aspects of theory construction. Any theory is an orderly interpretation of some set of data (ideally, experimental results). Scientific theories range in scope from very narrow hypotheses (which are more or less formalized guesses) concerning a limited set of data to the broadest of cosmological interpretations (of, say, the origin and fate of the planetary system in our universe). For this reason as well as many other differentiating attributes of scientific theories, it is difficult, and risky, to generalize meaningfully about them. Nevertheless, it can be said that any theory is broader than the data it attempts to incorporate. In the main, theories attempt to "explain" data by attributing them to some more fundamental kind of orderliness. All theories have a gap-filling function, in that they make explicit some more complete orderliness than is usually evident in the data themselves. When there are obvious gaps within the data, or between different sets of data, the invitation to fill them by theory is especially, and often inescapably, powerful.

TESTABILITY. Any good scientific theory—or to put it more modestly, hypothesis—must first be testable. This attribute is more important than its plausibility, or the degree to which it seems to fit the data, or even its ultimate correctness. The reason for the importance of this essential attribute has already been suggested (e.g., in the comparison of Freud and Einstein as scientists). It is simply that there can be no scientific way of determining the value of a hypothesis until it has been tested. Then, even if it is found wanting—that is, even if it is discarded—it has played a vital role. The scientific theories that we honor today have been built upon the dead and usually forgotten bodies of countless disconfirmed prior theories, without which today's theories would not have been refined and sharpened. Unfortunately, there are also about in science, and especially in that near science that psychology must always contend with, a host of theories apparently viable but actually untested because they are untestable. This type of theory has an unusual longevity, for the very good reason that it is not capable of disconfirmation. Add to it the closely related type of theory that is purposely kept so broad as to be able to elude disconfirmation, or the theory that means all things to all men—that is, is not presented with sufficient clarity to permit agreement about what test results mean. Now it should be apparent that at least some of psychology's troubles come from this overabundance of theoretical richness; too many broad and essentially untestable propositions have been retained because they are difficult or even impossible to disconfirm.

Properly used, theories thus play a dual role in science. Not only are they the ultimate objectives of our research and interpretative efforts, but they are also the tools that we commonly use to direct our empirical investigations. Although all viable theories contain some element of each of these functions, the relative weighting usually varies in accordance with the intent of the theorizer.

FACTS

The relationship of theory to data, or to "facts," is especially interesting and important. Although at first it may appear that theories and facts are cut from entirely different cloth, they do share some common ground. This statement follows from the recognition that fact, *as the term is most commonly used,* does have an important element of faith or trust, much in the same sense as theory. Thus, contrary to some popular opinion, facts are not objects or events, but are rather statements *about* objects and events. When one says therefore, "Let us get down to the facts," what is meant is, "Let us attempt to see how much *belief* about some kinds of objects and events we *share*." Any fact is relative to a particular time and place, and most importantly to a particular population of believers. Although the degree of acceptance concerning certain kinds of "factual statements," such as those concerning the weather outside at any given moment, is very great, once one leaves such immediately "obvious" situations for, say, the realm of politics or religion, he immediately enlarges the range of acceptability and the element of belief emerges as a predominant factor. In between these two extremes, however, there is a very wide sector of observation, containing most scientific situations, in which belief, although not so obvious, is nonetheless present.

It is instructive, in discussing the nature of facts, to ask some critical questions that stimulate lively, and often surprisingly heated, discussion. For a starter, one may inquire whether, in days when the earth was generally believed to be flat, it was indeed a "fact" for such believers that the earth was flat. Discussion of this simple question can be used to point up the relative nature of factualness as opposed to a more absolute view.

Throughout this chapter we have had many occasions to refer to various attitudes that are characteristic of the scientist (e.g., his empiricism and skepticism). Here some of the most important of the personal characteristics of the scientist will be discussed in generalized terms. More specifically, we are referring to the *idealized* scientist; these characteristics do not apply to each and every scientist, nor even to each highly successful scientist. Nevertheless, the scientific population will average out much higher on these attitudinal characteristics than will the nonscientific, so that we are justified in labeling them as attributes of scientists. It must be remembered, also, that these characteristics are ones that fit the scientist, at least collectively, in his professional life; they do not automatically transfer to other spheres. In his personal life he is just as likely as the next man to show the typical human weaknesses.

Beyond his skepticism and empiricism, already sufficiently emphasized, the scientist typically evidences some attitudinal characteristics that are in no way unique but that, rather, are shared by many other individuals.

TOLERANCE FOR ERROR AND AMBIGUITY. The scientist's skepticism is tempered by an unusual degree of tolerance for error and for incorrect theories. In fact, the scientist is even prone to welcome errors, in his research results, because he knows that he can learn from them. Also, it is simply too much to expect error-free advances in science. His objective is to *reduce* the error in his observations and his theories and to guard against the kind of bias that results from premature acceptance of premises not actually warranted by data or theory. He also tends to be tolerant of ambiguity for similar reasons. Most of the data and theories with which he is in contact have substantial proportions of ambiguity. The scientist must learn

Scientific Attitudes

to live with these, even as he attempts to reduce the ambiguities. That is, the scientist tends to work in the border area between relatively established knowledge, or hard "facts," and complete ignorance. He must, therefore, be comfortable with something less than black and white answers; he must learn to tolerate the grayness that is associated with ambiguity.

CREATIVITY AND IMAGINATION. Because these important ingredients of scientific success are relatively less emphasized, the attributes of creativity and imagination are discussed here, in spite of their earlier mention and their much fuller treatment in Chapter 8.

To many the scientist is not seen as a creative person. Moreover, it is true that many aspects of science involve routine functions that require little in the way of imagination. But this is certainly not true of certain other aspects of science, particularly those having to do with the kinds of intellectual activities already briefly discussed. In a very real sense, the scientist may be just as creative, in his construction of theory and design of experiments and measuring devices, as the graphic artist or the musical composer. As emphasized earlier, scientific laws are not really "discovered" in that they are lying somewhere out in the real world waiting for someone to come along and find them. They are constructed by man, just as are the more broadly based scientific theories. The fact that the scientist must keep his construction tied to reality, perhaps to a greater extent than the artist or the novelist, certainly does not lessen the degree to which imagination and creativity are needed, but does seem to make his job a somewhat more difficult one.

CURIOSITY AND INTELLECTUAL CHALLENGE. Allowing free play of imagination in the service of creativity is clearly the hallmark of a great scientist. The key factor that underlies the dedicated behavior of so many scientists is, quite simply, curiosity. More specifically, it is the intellectual challenge the scientist finds in his work. Much as the expert chess player or bridge player is challenged by the subtle problems he faces in these games, the scientific researcher is challenged by the equally fascinating and much less formalized kinds of intellectual problems he faces every day in his work. These problems concern especially the interrelationships between theory and data. For example, how can one best conceptualize the so-called intervening variables that operate within the organism to facilitate his behavior in various problem-solving situations? What processes operate to strengthen errors in learning situations in spite of clear "wrong" signals, or for that matter to reinforce such socially and personally undesirable habits as nail biting and cigarette smoking? Are there any general behavioral principles that underlie all these error-strengthening tendencies? These are all examples of the kinds of problems that are constantly posed by the inquiring scientist.

The design of experiments to test hypotheses about such problems, and the interpretation of results of such experiments, or others not expressly designed to bear upon the problems, are among the most fascinating aspects of the work of the scientist. Moreover, the interplay of data and design is never finished, because each new set of data collected and reported bears upon the theoretical constructions under consideration and new experimental designs are thereby suggested. As a matter of fact, it is often easy for the scientist to concern himself too exclusively with this interplay and with the design of new experiments, so that his data-collection activities may tend to lag seriously.

Pure and Applied Science

Our discussion of the curiosity motive as a central factor in scientific motivation brings us close to a particularly lively and significant contemporary issue. This is the opposition of applied and basic (or "pure") science. Such an opposition is unfortunate. Not only are these two activities closely related, and at times indistinguishable, but they are essentially complementary to each other. Nevertheless, the dichotomy has been sharpened and exaggerated recently because of the emphasis on relevance. Clarification of the basic issues is therefore especially desirable.

DISTINCTION. Basic science is intended to develop knowledge for its own sake. It is thus closely related to theory construction, although more strictly empirical endeavors are also included in this category. Applied science, on the other hand, is intended to develop knowledge, both theoretical and empirical, with a particular practical application in mind (e.g., the cure for some disease, such as cancer).

This difference in intention, or motivation, is the *only* way these two nominally contrasted scientific endeavors can be fundamentally distinguished. *All science utilizes the same procedures, such as those described previously in general terms, regardless of the intent of the investigator.* Normally, the kind of problems attacked will vary with the intent of the investigator, but even here a distinction between pure and applied science cannot always be safely made; and there are many borderline cases, where the motivation of the investigator is not clear. Finally, much pure knowledge of broad scope and fundamental character has been gained from primarily applied efforts (e.g., the germ theory of disease, initiated by Pasteur's applied medical efforts) and many important practical applications have stemmed from pure scientific efforts (e.g., the development of atomic weaponry during the World War II, based on fundamental discoveries in physics by Einstein and others). It is this close interrelationship between the two kinds of science that makes especially unfortunate continuing attempts to emphasize their distinction.

JUSTIFICATION OF BASIC RESEARCH. From a strictly utilitarian point of view, basic research is generally regarded as groundwork for applications and practical developments; when basic research is stifled or for some reason fails to proceed, there tends to be a corresponding weakening of the applications to real problems. From a more theoretical or knowledge-centered point of view, man is first and foremost an unusually curious animal and seems to have a strong "need to know"; fundamental knowledge about the world in which he lives therefore has an especially high motivational priority, particularly when the more urgent biological needs, such as those for food and security, are reasonably well taken care of.

To apply these arguments to a specific case, consider the problem of cancer. Decades of effort and many millions of dollars have been expended upon applied efforts to discover methods of stopping the unwanted growth of body cells. It is now generally agreed that curing cancer will be possible only when we have

Form, Language, and Function in Science

developed more effective general principles of cell growth, so that cancer research funds are being increasingly alloted to fundamental cytological research projects (perhaps even to researchers who have little immediate professional interest in the cancer problem per se) as well as to researchers who are directly interested in cancer as a problem.

COMMITMENT. The key to understanding the importance of pure research, as contrasted with applied research, is the concept of commitment. Scientists are unusually curious men who have a strong commitment to know more about their subject matter, to solve their immediate research problems, and to develop some higher-order abstractions in theories that will enable them and their fellow men to account better for some part of the real world. But in basic science, scientists have learned that other, more practical commitments so curtail their freedom of inquiry as to retard seriously the development of fundamental knowledge. Unlike the task of the engineer and the developer, where the objective is relatively clear and the procedural problems, no matter how difficult, usually relatively straightforward, the pure scientist has no clear guidelines to knowledge. He works best if allowed to follow his hunches and his research leads. It is impossible to predict in advance which particular directions will turn out to be the most profitable. Thus if he has to be concerned with research plans that seem to be directed toward resolving practical problems, such as that of curing cancer, he is correspondingly restricted in his work. It is for this reason that research-fund-granting agencies have generally felt that as few commitments as possible should be placed on a scientist's work, once his general competence and the quality of his provisional research plans are assured, and that he should be given a very wide latitude in changing direction as he sees fit in processing his research. His basic motivation, curiosity, is thus assured.

ENGINEER AND TECHNICIAN. The fundamental role of the scientist, in contrast to that of the engineer and the technician, needs to be clarified. The scientist's role is to cut through the manifold complexity of everyday living and work with such underlying conceptualizations and correlated empirical observations as he can. He should not be expected to be an engineer and a technician at the same time. The psychologist in particular is subjected to such expectations. Do we expect a competent chemist to be also a first-rate cook? Why not? Obviously because the kind of variables he manipulates and the rules he develops (laws, theories) as a chemist cannot be directly translated into the practical prescriptions of the kitchen, even though the latter are entirely subject to the former. Why then expect the qualified research psychologist always to be a first-rate parent? He may be, but for other reasons than his scientific psychological background. And he may not be, but again for other reasons.

The engineer, like the physician and lawyer, is a *practitioner;* his primary objective is to solve practical problems of the everyday world. Like any citizen, he may also be interested in knowledge for its own sake, but this interest goes beyond his engineering per se and is not necessary for it, just as it is not necessary that the scientist be concerned with the applications of his work in order to do it effectively. As a citizen, of course, he should be so concerned, but again that concern goes beyond his purely scientific activities.

The important job of translating basic principles in some field of knowledge into practically usable prescriptions, for child rearing as well as cooking, is thus within the province of applied science and engineering. The challenge is both an exciting and an important one. In practically all fields of knowledge we know more in theory than we do in practice. We should be spending more time and energy in attempting to bridge this gap, but not at the expense of forsaking basic science, as some politicians and social theorists would do.

In science, the emphasis is more on asking the fruitful *question* and less on getting the right answer. This difference from everyday life, and technical and engineering functions, is difficult for the layman to appreciate. Especially perhaps in our own culture, the layman wants the right answers and tends to equate science with success; that is, to focus on the solutions rather than the processes that produce them. What is not appreciated is that science must proceed by finding the right questions to ask before solutions can be obtained.

Distinguishing between answers that are *useful* and those that are *right* is another, related difficulty. The scientist realizes the tenuous nature of his knowledge; he is humble. Having learned from centuries of hard experience that even the most rock-ribbed and apparently secure beliefs can be toppled, he is always likely to show at least a hint of insecurity in his thinking. This the layman is prone to interpret as weakness, as he would when it occurs in, say, a politician or a labor negotiator. It is hard for him to see the scientist as a different breed of animal. But unless he is so seen, and social and political decisions are made accordingly, support for his crucial contribution to society is likely to be weakened and his contribution correspondingly reduced, which is a consequence that thoughtful observers will find disturbing at a time of great social and intellectual flux, when both science and engineering contributions to society are becoming ever more necessary.

Some of the more important and more interesting scientific issues within psychology will be discussed.

TERMINOLOGY

One of the upsetting discoveries that students make as they start their study of psychology is that psychologists, like other scientists, tend to use a different vocabulary than that of the layman. Each field of study has its own jargon. It would be nice if this were not the case, that is, if exactly the same set of words could be used throughout all fields of study with exactly the same meanings. Unfortunately, however, such a large vocabulary would be required, with some words restricted only to certain fields, as to defeat the purpose of the attempted simplification.

Within psychology the semantic problem is aggravated by the complexity of the subject matter. The same word is often used with multiple meanings. It is necessary for the student to keep these meanings separate, in accordance with the context in which they are used. A single example should clarify this. Consider *frustration*. This word is taken from the common language and used by psychologists in

Scientific Issues Within Psychology

essentially a conventional manner. Nevertheless, in experimental work by psychologists there are at least three distinct usages of the word. First, *frustration* can mean a particular *operation* or manipulation, which may be made by the experimenter or in real life by anyone. So used, the term refers to some kind of blocking operation that prevents a motivated organism from obtaining a goal or persisting in goal-directed behavior. Second, *frustration* can mean the *behavior* that is evidenced when the organism is thus blocked; for example, a child whose toy is kept from him may react with such "frustrated" behavior as screaming or attacking some one in the vicinity. Third, *frustration* can be used to mean some hypothesized internal state or *process* presumed to underlie the overt behavior that occurs after blocking. Thus, for example, the college student who has failed an important course and is thereby blocked from achieving an occupational objective may verbally attack the instructor or take his complaint to some administrative official. Such frustrated behavior can be attributed to the inner state of frustration that is assumed to exist.

Operational Definitions

It is clear that each of the preceding different usages of the same word is necessary for one purpose or another if we are to treat *frustration* adequately in its various facets. But what is of crucial importance is that the user explicitly make clear which use he intends. Defining words or concepts in terms of the operations that produce them is called *operational definition*.

Much controversy has been generated within psychology as well as other fields by confusion about the so-called operationism movement. Some of this confusion has resulted from an early overselling of the movement, within philosophy and science, but much has also arisen from a reluctance of writers to be pinned down by the demands of the movement. Without getting into this controversy, let us be clear about the fundamental issue. Stated most simply, operationism merely requires that a communicator be explicit about the meaning intended for his terms. Because this is such a big issue within science generally, and because it has not always been clearly presented within psychology, it is important that the student begin the study of scientific methodology with an appreciation of the role of operational definitions. Operationism thus deals only with clarity of communication and has nothing to say about the accuracy or validity of the empirical or theoretical statements themselves. Moreover, adherence to operational definitions cannot be held responsible for a dearth of ideas, and there is no incompatibility between the free use of one's imagination and operational clarity in communication.

Because words are such important tools in science, unnecessary ambiguity in their use compounds the difficulty that one's audience has in understanding scientific communications. Even at the risk of seeming stilted and mechanical, it therefore behooves scientific writers to be as clear and explicit as possible with regard to the fundamental meanings of their terminology. Once this basic matter is settled, there is plenty of opportunity for imagination and creativity to be evidenced in the substance of the ideas expressed, and these virtues can be better appreciated when words are operationally defined from the start and such meanings are maintained throughout the discussion.

PARSIMONY

The principle of parsimony relates to the *evaluation* of theoretical principles within science. In this usage, *parsimony* means "simplicity," and the principle asserts that the simplest of alternative theoretical accounts is to be accepted whenever the alternatives are equally consistent with the empirical data.

The basis for the wide acceptance of the principle of parsimony is largely in the historical experience of scientists. Scientists have learned that unnecessarily complicated explanations are more likely to be in error than simpler ones. Analogically, the more that one embellishes a lie, the more likely he is to be caught up in it; the simplest lies are generally the most effective ones. In general, the greater the elaboration of any explanatory network, the greater the probability of error.

How can the principle of parsimony be reconciled with the fact that the scientist deliberately sets up his experiments to determine the degree of his error? Very simply. The principle of parsimony has nothing to do with the testing of hypotheses or theories; it concerns only their acceptance on the basis of evidence currently available. Parsimony thus relates more closely to the use that is made of scientific data than to the actual conduct of research. When one is faced with the need to decide whether a new social or educational or military program should be adopted, making and implementing an unparsimonious decision can be disastrous, in terms of loss of time, money, and even lives.

It is necessary to emphasize that the principle of parsimony in no way prevents any proponent of a more complex hypothesis or theory from producing data to support it and thereby give it an advantage over its simpler competitors. The principle cannot therefore be blamed for retarding the advance of scientific knowledge, as its detractors sometimes claim. On the contrary, the principle is a very strong positive force in this direction, for the very simple reason that it does put the burden of proof on such proponents. If they do not then succeed in obtaining such evidence in support of their own positions, they and not the principle of parsimony are responsible.

Within psychology the best-known instance of the application of parsimony is with respect to the interpretation of the behavior of infrahuman animals. Consider some common examples, such as certain tricklike responses of pets (e.g., the regular return of the evening newspaper by a dog, or more interestingly, the dog's carrying the newspaper through a rail fence by holding it in a horizontal position). Most pet owners have interpretations of such behaviors that stress high intelligence and other humanlike attributes; this tendency to attribute human characteristics to animals is called *anthropomorphism*. Application of the principle of parsimony to such behaviors requires that simpler theoretical accounts, such as conditioning (Chapter 11), be accorded a greater degree of confidence until and unless they are unable to explain all the observations equally well. Questioning of the more complex account, and the refusal to accept it as long as the evidence does not so demand, is not equivalent to any absolute denial of it. Rather, this parsimonious stance is to be regarded as a kind of working position that both safeguards the practical application of scientific principles and encourages the active seeking of new experimental evidence.

One of the aspects of contemporary psychology that many students find most difficult to comprehend, although they accept it in medical or other biological research programs, is the widespread use of animal subjects in research. The picture of psychology that many students bring to its study is apparently centered upon man and his problems of adjustment; the relevance of animal research is not readily grasped. The justification for the use of animal subjects within psychology is simply that they are organisms and they behave. Hence if we are concerned as psychologists with the observation and interpretation of behavior, infrahuman as well as human organisms are feasible subjects.

The special advantages of animal subjects are clear. They are relatively cheap, are more or less readily available, are in no position to raise objections to their service as subjects in the way that humans characteristically do, and above all can be subjected to many conditions (e.g., surgical operations on brain structures, long periods of food deprivation) that are not permissible with human subjects. More-over, their entire lives can be controlled to a degree that is impossible with human subjects.

The most serious objection to the use of animals in psychological research probably concerns the question of generality: Can results obtained with animal subjects be generalized to humans? There are a number of cogent reactions to this question. First, it should be understood that the issue is fundamentally empirical: to what extent can the results of animal research be generalized? There is and can be no simple and unequivocal answer to this question. Rather, each instance must be evaluated in its own right. However, it is safe to say that the psychological literature is full of instances in which animal subjects of various sorts have been effectively used in the development of general behavioral principles.

Secondly, the problem of generality is by no means restricted to the animal–human dichotomy. Even when only human subjects are used, the problem of generality is always with us. As a matter of fact, there is sometimes good reason to doubt that the data collected on an individual at any given time and under some particular conditions can safely be generalized to even the *same* individual at some other time and under different conditions. In other words, generalizability is a relative matter and not merely a question of the kind of subject used.

Thirdly, the generalization issue is only relevant if a comparative objection is involved; that is, if the purpose of the research is to compare various animal forms, and ultimately relate them to man. However, it is also possible to study animals in their own right, for their own sake; their behavior is then clearly one of the crucial features of such study. Behavioral investigations of animals are thus just as legitimate as any other types of biological research.

Study of the behavioral capacities of animals often pays unexpected dividends, quite apart from the contribution to basic knowledge that they make. Consider one humorous illustration. During the Vietnam War of the 1960's the U.S. Army developed a most interesting device designed to detect enemy personnel in a thick jungle. This device consisted simply of a few hungry bedbugs enclosed within a tube with air circulation only at one end. When air currents brought human scent into the tube the bedbugs began to move about quite energetically. Thus this device could be pointed at suspicious-looking areas in order to detect hidden enemy soldiers, who were able to escape detection by visual inspection even at very close range.

Psychologists have designed and performed numerous animal experiments bearing on fundamental behavior problems. Consider some recent research on the effects of dominance in rats. Laboratory rats were first trained individually to turn a wheel in order to avoid or escape electric shock (applied through a floor grid). When two rats were placed together there was severe disruption of the avoidance behavior (turning the wheel before the shock came on, at a light signal). Moreover, and more interestingly, there was a peculiar effect on escape behavior (turning the wheel to stop the shock after it started). Although most of the wheel turning was performed by the submissive rat, the dominant rat often actively prevented its submissive partner from making this response, even when both were being shocked, and attacked aggressively even after the wheel was turned and the shock stopped.

Regardless of how this preliminary experimentation is interpreted (and a definitive interpretation obviously requires much more data), it should be clear that social variables are crucial even at the relatively "low" level of the rat and that these subjects can be fruitfully used in research designed to tease out fundamental behavioral principles that have potentially wide applicability over animal species. Moreover, most psychologists who utilize rats, pigeons, monkeys, or other animals as subjects do so because they are primarily interested in an analysis of some behavioral *process*, rather than in the animal itself or in the comparison of various animal species, including man. Choice of an appropriate organism for any given study must thus be made on the basis of a number of important factors related to the particular behavioral problem being investigated. Certain species offer advantages for particular problems; for example, the pigeon has excellent visual learning ability and so is a much better subject than the rat in studies involving discrimination of visual cues. There is no good reason for excluding any particular species because of preconceived notions of the nature of psychology. Investigation of the behavior of various animal forms along with that of man is necessary if psychology is to prosper as a fully developed science.

Experimentation and Control

For illustrations of experimental control Valentine and Wicken's 1949 book is still a good introductory treatment. Sidman's *Tactics of Scientific Research* (1960) is a provocative, advanced discussion from a special point of view (positivistic, with formal use of theory minimized).

A comment concerning the dual use of the term *control* is in order. The term is often used along with *description* and *prediction*, as in the common statement that it is the task of science to "describe, predict, and control." In this usage *control* means "to manage objects and events" in a very practical sense. This usage may be remotely related to the use of the same term in *principle of control*, in the sense that

Notes

the latter type of (experimental) control of variables does make possible effective management. Nevertheless, the two meanings are, in terms of the operations they identify, really quite distinct with quite different objectives—experimental, as contrasted with practical—and so should not be confused.

For more general treatments of scientific procedure, there are recent paperback books on science as a "game" (e.g., McCain and Segal, 1973). Standen's older *Science Is a Sacred Cow* (1950) is entertaining and does make some telling points; it can be faulted, however, for exaggerating the abuses and excesses of science and scientists without presenting a balanced account in which the solid achievements of science are recognized. The main source on experimenter bias is Rosenthal (1966); for a critical treatment, see also Barber and Silver (1968). A subsequent volume by Rosenthal and Jacobson (1968) is also of interest; it purports to demonstrate the way the performance of schoolchildren tends to follow their teachers' a priori expectations, indicating a substantial influence of bias in this everyday activity.

Measurement and Statistics

With regard to psychologist's attitudes toward statistics, that of the behaviorist B. F. Skinner deserves mention. Skinner (1972) has persistently refused to acknowledge that statistics is as useful as most psychologists seem to think. He feels that it is often used as a substitute for careful experimental controls, which are thereby discouraged. Skinner has also insisted on the primacy of the single subject and argued that averaged data, from groups, give a misleading picture. This general point of view is well represented by Sidman (1960).

A comment on the extremely commonplace abuse of the term *normal* is also in order. Consider, for example, weather data. We are constantly given the "normal" rainfall for the year to date, with the implication that anything below that figure is somehow inferior or unusual, disregarding the obvious fact that approximately 50 per cent of the cases have fallen below! Use of the normal curve as a framework rather than the simple mean would require very little in the way of added learning but would add a great deal to the accuracy and even a little to the sophistication of much information presentation.

Laws and Theories

An excellent introduction to the philosophy of science and scientific methodology in general is provided by an early "classic" on this topic by Cohen and Nagel (1934). With regard to psychology, Turner (1967) has written a philosophically oriented but excellent advanced treatment. Marx's 1970 book on learning theory contains papers reviewing theories in that field as well as a general treatment of formal theory construction and more informal theorizing.

History of Science

For science generally, authoritative and readable sources of historical fact and interpretation are available in books by Conant (1947), Sarton (1952), and Butterfield (1957). More recent treatments are by Daniels (1971) and Burnham (1971). The classic treatment of the history of psychology is by Boring (1950).

Contemporary Science

Science is currently undergoing a searching re-examination as our society struggles to adjust to fast-moving social changes. The intellectual ferment that accompanies this process is represented by numerous articles. For example, the chemist Blackburn (1971) has proposed that sensuous and intellectual activities be regarded within science as complementary, reflecting the revolt of the counter-culture against an exclusively intellectual stance.

In the light of so much questioning and criticism, it is reassuring to learn, from a 1972 poll, that approximately half the populace still regards science and technology with "satisfaction and hope," whereas only a very small percentage (6 per cent) of those queried expressed either fear or indifference. Nevertheless, doubt that basic science is generally understood is raised by the very low rating given to the objective of "discovering new basic knowledge about men and nature."

The role of basic science in technology and application of scientific principles has been researched in several investigations. Project Hindsight, conducted by the U.S. Department of Defense, raised questions about the extent of this role. A subsequent study by the National Science Foundation, however, indicated that the earlier study had not gone back far enough in its search for relevant basic research; about 90 per cent of such research was found to have occurred at least one decade prior to the development of technological devices. This study was called *Technology in Retrospect and Critical Events in Science,* abbreviated TRACES. A further study sponsored by the National Science Foundation, *Interactions of Science and Technology in the Innovative Process: Some Case Studies,* consisted of a more intensive analysis of eight technological innovations and gave further support to the interplay of basic science and technological innovations.

Operationism

Benjamin's 1955 book is a good introduction to this topic; Steven's 1939 paper remains a meaty evaluation of the role of operations, and more generally positivism, in psychology.

Parsimony

Other names for the principle of parsimony are *William of Occam's razor* (named for an early proponent) and *Lloyd Morgan's canon* (used when it is applied specifically to the problem of interpreting animal behavior).

Animal Subjects

There have been occasional protests against the excessive use of certain favored animal forms, mainly the rat, in behavioral research (e.g., Lockard, 1971). The research on dominance–submission in avoidance performance was reported by Logan (1972). A further explanation of the widespread experimental use of animals in psychology (e.g., rats and pigeons in learning research) is provided in Supplement A-3.

Precedents and Procedures

3

Unlike this artist's interpretation of the state of French law in the 1830's, psychology is in no immediate danger of perishing under the weight of its own body of knowledge. The scientific study of behavior, however, has amassed certain procedures and precedents and these historical antecedents are the subject of this chapter.

his chapter briefly reviews the systematic movements that have been of greatest significance in the development of American psychology. Some appreciation of these movements is necessary as a basis for understanding contemporary psychology.

These movements have been mainly in the form of "schools" or "systems." Within psychology, a school is a group of individuals who share certain fundamental methodological or theoretical points of view. A system is similar in that it is a particular conceptual framework within which the problems of psychology are viewed and basic principles are developed. Systems differ from schools in that they are less likely to involve continuity of individuals.

The first important movement, *associationism,* was a product of philosophy. Although in some ways now mainly of historical interest, its influence persists in a variety of contemporary forms.

The first school in American psychology, *structuralism,* was initially a joint product of European philosophy and German psychology. It was brought into this country by an Englishman, E. B. Titchener, whose name is most closely associated with its refinement. Structuralism concerned itself exclusively with a study of mental experience using a rigorous form of introspection and is of limited direct influence today.

Two of the most generally influential systems, functionalism and behaviorism, were almost entirely American made.

Functionalism, which emphasizes utility, has a scope as broad as that of structuralism was narrow; it grew from Darwinian evolutionary theory and the consequent interest in animal behavior as well as the American pragmatic philosophy. Never a highly formalized or strongly proposed system, functionalism nonetheless represents the way in which a great number of psychologists, perhaps a majority, actually go about the business of researching and theorizing. In refusing to make a clean break with the philosophic past, however, and in insisting on the use of introspection as one of its methods, functionalism failed to satisfy John B. Watson, who proceeded to proclaim the virtues of a completely objective psychology.

Watsonian *behaviorism* was essentially an attempt to apply the objective techniques used in studying animal behavior to human problems. Under the pressure of polemic competition and criticism from various sources, Watson proceeded to deny the existence of consciousness as an entity and the causal significance of mental processes (thus leading to the witticism that psychology first lost its soul, then its consciousness, and finally its mind). The more moderate form of behaviorism has been and continues to be enormously successful in shaping American psychology particularly.

Several systems of European origin have been transplanted to the United States and have helped to modify the behavioristic revolution in psychology. *Gestalt psychology,* initiated in Germany by the powerful triumvirate of Max Wertheimer, Kurt Koffka, and Wolfgang Köhler, emphasizes perceptual rather than learning factors; its major tenets have been more or less integrated within modern psychology. Kurt Lewin's *field theory,* a close relative to Gestalt theory, which was also imported from Germany, has been significant mainly in the areas of social psychology and personality. Of greater general influence, outside psychology as well as within, has been *psychoanalysis,* a product of the Austrian physician Sigmund Freud. Psychoanalysis has had questionable scientific status but unquestionable scientific impact. There are signs now that its impact is waning within both general psychology and clinical psychology, but its complete demise is probably well in the future.

Schools and systems no longer play a directly active role in psychology, but there is still a great deal of ferment and controversy. Much of this is today centered around the humanistic, or "Third Force," movement. Proponents of this view hold that orthodox psychology, as represented by the traditional forces of behaviorism and psychoanalysis, has failed to present an authentic and truly human picture of man. The chapter is concluded with a brief examination of this movement and an explanation of why it is best regarded as complementary to rather than a replacement of experimental psychology.

Schools and Systems

This review of systems in psychology is presented as a means of orienting the reader to the field, not because systems are currently highly significant within psychology, but because their historical influence is still evident within most psychological research and practice. More important, they offer an excellent opportunity to review the history of psychology, or at least of the American psychology upon which we shall concentrate, and thereby to gain a valuable framework into which the more detailed picture of various aspects of psychology can be fitted.

A *school,* as used in the present context, is a collection of scholars and/or researchers who may or may not be physically together or contemporary with each other but whose work and whose underlying point of view share salient features. A *system* is a correlated phenomenon but differs from a school in that there is less emphasis on the persons involved and more on theoretical principles.

Historically, schools and systems have had more influence in the development of psychology than is true of most of science. Their role has been, in the main, to facilitate concentrated but broadly based work on a relatively narrow set of problems, or conversely, to stimulate an intensified but narrow approach on a broad set of problems. This they have accomplished mainly by instilling in their adherents the kind of zeal that is associated more often with religious and political endeavors than with scientific efforts. This strong motivation, combined with the school's provision of a common framework for and impetus to research and conceptualization, has resulted in a number of growth spurts within psychology, as detailed in Table 3-1.

Such enthusiasm does not come without a price. The price that psychology has paid for its schools is an overemphasis on the personal element, on the personalities of the systematizers, and the rightness or wrongness of their efforts.

Table 3-1 Systematic Phases in American Psychology

System	Date of Major Activity	Key Proponents (Univ. Affiliation)	Subject Matter	Primary Research Technique
Structuralism	1880–1920	Wilhelm Wundt (Leipzig) E. B. Titchener (Cornell)	Normal adult human mind	Introspective analysis
Functionalism	1900–	Harvey Carr (Chicago) Robert Woodworth (Columbia)	Organism's adjustment to environment	Experimentation to develop functions among behavioral variables
Behaviorism	1915–1960	John B. Watson (Chicago) B. F. Skinner (Harvard)	Overt behavior, external environmental variables	Relating behavior to environmental factors and prior behavioral variables
Gestalt Psychology	1915–1960	Max Wertheimer (Frankfurt, Berlin) Kurt Koffka (Frankfurt, Giessen, Smith College) Wolfgang Köhler (Frankfurt, Swarthmore)	Visual perception, properties of patterns	Phenomenological (naive and untrained) observation
Field Theory	1920–1950	Kurt Lewin (Berlin, Iowa)	Motivation, personality, group dynamics	Experimentation in social settings
Psychoanalysis	1900–1950	Sigmund Freud (Vienna)	Unconscious motivation, sexuality in maladjustment	Free association, dream analysis

The major systematic phases in the development of contemporary American psychology are brought together in Table 3-1. Associationism is omitted because of the inclusion of the fundamental principles of association in other, more clearly delineated systems (for example, behaviorism); field theory is presented separately from Gestalt psychology, in accordance with its origin, although the text treats them together. A considerable amount of arbitrary judgment has necessarily been exercised in connection with the selection of names and dates, with the latter especially to be considered an approximation. This table should be consulted as our discussion of the various systems proceeds.

Major Theme	Major Criticism	Enduring Contribution
Psychology is the study of the normal adult human mind—and nothing more	Narrowness of method, artificiality and barrenness or results	A thorough test of one kind of strict scientific introspective analysis
Psychology should study functional relationships in the organism's adjustment to his environment	Too electric, lacking theoretical salience	Many specific contributions to substantive issues, mainly learning and motivation, with variety of investigative techniques
Strict objectivity, ignoring or denial of mental phenomena	Ignoring of many basic (covert) psychological functions; overdependence on strict experimentation and gadgetry	Demonstration of importance of usual scientific objectivity in psychology (overt behavioral measures, even for covert functions)
Primacy of the whole, of patterns (Gestalts)	Insufficient precision in experimental demonstrations, too much speculation	Centrality of patterns in visual perception particularly and behavior generally
An individual behaves in accordance with the psychological rather than the physical nature of his environment (his "life space")	Looseness of fit between theory and data	Ingenious experimental indicants for key psychological processes; group dynamics movement
Maladjustment is produced by repression of early emotional experiences, mainly of a sexual nature	Nonexperimental methodology, exclusive dependence on clinical validation of highly speculative and questionable theory	Pointing to critical role of unconscious motivational factors in behavior, especially maladjusted; centrality of sex and defense mechanisms, importance of early years for personality

ASSOCIATIONISM

Associationism is not so much a school or a system as it is a general principle around which psychologists and others have long concentrated a variety of theoretical efforts. The principle, simply stated, is that ideas or events that occur together in time or space become related in memory, so that on future occasions the recurrence of one member of such an association tends to produce the other members; the word *table*, for example, suggests *chair*, and hearing a class bell sound ordinarily leads to such behaviors as opening notebooks, looking forward, and the like.

63

Associationism is included here because of its ancient origin and persisting influence up to and including the contemporary scene. Indeed, philosophical precursors to psychology used it more than any other single explanatory principle; an account of its history is therefore at the same time an account of much of the history, and the prehistory, of psychology.

STRUCTURALISM

In contrast to the amorphous character and long history of associationism, structuralism was a closely knit system that flourished for a relatively brief period around the turn of the twentieth century. In spite of its short time span, it is important because it arose in connection with the formal initiation of psychology as a science separate from philosophy and was important in the early development of psychology in the United States.

Structuralism represents the culmination of a highly sophisticated kind of introspectionism, or systematic concentration upon self-observation of consciousness. Introspection, as the structuralist used it, consisted of an intense effort by a thoroughly trained investigator to study his own conscious experience. In this process the observer was expected to learn to ignore extraneous, distracting stimuli and to concentrate upon the conscious elements that the structuralist felt to be the central subject matter of psychology.

Structuralism as a school was largely the work of one prominent and energetic psychologist, E. B. Titchener. His training had been in the laboratory of Wilhelm Wundt, at Leipzig, Germany. Wundt's formal establishment of this psychological laboratory in 1879 is generally recognized as marking the more or less official birthday of psychology as a separate discipline (separate, that is, from its two "parents," philosophy and physiology). Titchener brought Wundtian psychology to this country, got it established and accepted as a new field of study, and carried on a variety of introspective studies.

The first three decades of this century witnessed a vigorous attempt, by Titchener and his associates, to maintain the pristine quality of an introspectionistic science. Nevertheless, structuralism failed to survive as a system. Its demise was almost as rapid as its rise.

FUNCTIONALISM

We turn now to the mainstream of American psychology. Associationism, with its historical roots in antiquity and its philosophical and early behavioral development in Europe, and structuralism, with its methodological roots in Germany, were essentially transplants to this continent. Functionalism was and is basically an American system.

Functionalism was never a strongly self-conscious or systematic school. It was partly a reaction against the self-declared exclusiveness of Titchenerian psychology in this country and partly a matter of many pioneer psychologists engaging in a variety of new activities (e.g., devising and administering tests of ability, studying children by asking them questions, or experimenting on the learning of animals). Functionalism thus represented a wide and variegated process, or set of processes, in American psychology.

Insofar as there really is any basis for *a* functional system, it is that functionalists generally have been concerned with the behavioral adjustment of the organism to his environment. Because this adjustment may take many forms and be studied in many different ways, there have been many different kinds of functional psychology. More specifically, the functionalist tends to be concerned with dependency relationships—that is, "function" in the sense of the dependence of one variable or process upon another. This is what science is all about. The functionalist in psychology has gained systematic prominence more from his opposition to, or failure to identify with, some *other* school or system, such as, initially, the structuralist or, more recently, the behaviorist, the Gestalt, or the psychoanalytic.

Functionalism as a school culminated in two particular locations: the University of Chicago, where it reached its most vigorous activity under Harvey Carr, and Columbia University, where its spokesman was Robert Woodworth. But the heart of the functional movement was and is the systematically unpretentious researcher who continues to experiment on a variety of behavioral and experiential problems and to interpret his results without benefit of any particular overreaching theoretical framework. Because this kind of scientific activity promises to be with us for an indefinite period the prospects are good that functionalism too will remain a systematic trend with high viability but low visibility.

BEHAVIORISM

Although trained as a functionalist, John Watson felt that the functionalist position did not go far enough in the direction of objectivity to insure full scientific respectability. Watson felt that the earlier concern with subjective matters, as exemplified in the structuralist introspection technique, should be discarded.

In place of such study psychology was to use a strictly objective approach, depending only on directly observable factors. In proposing behaviorism Watson intended to apply the objective techniques that had been developed for studying animals to human psychology. This was the message of the early behaviorist position.

A more radical form of behaviorism developed gradually over the ensuing years as Watson took a more extreme and negative position, largely it seems as a function of his running arguments with numerous critics. The upshot was that he, and other more radical behaviorists, came to deny, sometimes explicitly and sometimes by implication, the existence of "mind" or "consciousness." However, in thus attempting to refute his critics Watson painted himself, so to speak, in the very corner that he initially asked psychology to avoid, by taking an extreme metaphysical position on an essentially philosophical problem whose direct relevance for psychology is questionable. In any case, it was his early methodological behavioristic position that won for him great support, especially among the younger breed of psychologists, and that is much more readily defended.

The most Watsonian of all present-day behaviorists is B. F. Skinner. Skinner's continuing insistence on a strictly objective and behavioral psychology is generally recognized as representing the closest approach to the fundamental Watsonian position. Like Watson, Skinner has worked within a stimulus-response (S–R) framework. Skinner's own research program has concentrated mainly upon the operant conditioning technique (described in Chapter 11); associated techniques have been developed in education and therapy. Skinner's many and varied research projects are tied together by a common theme—*reinforcement* (or the strengthening of responses by positive aftereffects, such as rewards)—and an apparent extension of Watson's radical form of behaviorism; he has persistently refused to consider nonobservable factors in the determination of behavior. Skinner's general position is discussed in depth in Chapter 13.

GESTALT PSYCHOLOGY AND FIELD THEORY

Gestalt psychology and field theory are two rather closely related but independently developed systems. Both arose in Germany during the second decade of this century. Because they share certain fundamental assumptions and general perspectives, they are treated together in this section, but their independent origin and their important differences should not be overlooked.

The basic tenet of these systematic positions is that in perception especially, but also in behavior generally, it is necessary to consider the *context* in which particular stimuli occur. In other words, the total *pattern* or configuration of stimulation is more important than the individual stimuli that are emphasized in other systems, notably structuralism (for perception and thought) and behaviorism (for behavior).

Gestalt Psychology

The Gestalt psychology movement actually began with an experiment, and its interpretation. Max Wertheimer, with the aid of Kurt Koffka and Wolfgang Köhler, tackled the problem of explaining the phenomenon of perceived movement. One important kind of such movement, named the "phi phenomenon" by Wertheimer, is produced by presenting a series of still stimuli. How can motion in perception be produced by stimuli that themselves do not move? This question was addressed by Wertheimer.

This phenomenon will be recognized as precisely the same process as that which occurs in the motion picture. Presenting a series of *still* pictures at an appropriate rate, usually sixteen frames per second, provides a remarkably smooth flow of *movement* in the objects photographed. Why? There is movement in the objects as perceived, but no movement in the pictures themselves.

The interpretation of the phi phenomenon that was advanced by Wertheimer was deceptively simple. Rather than attempt to explain apparent motion in terms of some other processes, such as Wundtian sensations, or some internal functions, he simply accepted it, as a given, or as a phenomenon; in other words, his conclusion was that it did not need explanation! This view is a good illustration of the approach to perception called *phenomenology,* which stresses untrained observation and acceptance of the consequent experiences. Phenomenological observation contrasts vividly with the highly trained, artificial kind of introspection that was advanced by the structuralists.

From this modest but quite significant beginning Gestalt psychology extended into many fields of perception and ultimately into other fields, such as learning. The significance of this kind of attitude was in large part a result of its running counter to the dominant positions and procedures of the time. The emphasis in all the

Gestalt work was on configurations (*Gestalten*) and the importance of the whole, which was held to be more than merely the sum of the component parts. Determination of some of the salient principles of visual perception, which relate to how the whole is organized, was an early, primary task tackled by Gestaltists, and some illustrations of this work are provided in later parts of this book.

Field Theory

Although there is considerable question as to the appropriateness of the analogical use, within psychology, of the term *field theory*, borrowed from physics, there is no question about the efficacy and meaningfulness of some of the work that has been performed under this rubric. The research and conceptualizing of Kurt Lewin is pre-eminent in this respect. Although Lewin was in no direct way identified with the Gestalt psychologists, his underlying point of view shared a number of common aspects. The basic tenet of field theory is that it is the pattern and organization of the situation that are the determining factors in behavior rather than the elements of stimulus and response. Also, like the Gestalt psychologists, Lewin emphasized perceptual and cognitive conditions in his research. Psychological rather than physical determinants are stressed throughout his work, which ranged from memory to personality and social psychology.

The positive contributions of these movements have been significant in psychology generally as well as in such subareas as perception and personality theory. Most generally, they have served to provide an important balance to the S–R theoretical notions, as well as a refutation of much of the elementaristic character of the structuralist. The Gestalt psychologists and the field theorists thus have served psychology very well, even though they may not have won over nearly as many adherents as the more influential systems. The frequency with which their particular contributions are cited is further evidence of the excellence of their contribution.

PSYCHOANALYSIS

Psychoanalysis was the product of an Austrian physician and medical researcher, Sigmund Freud. Psychoanalysis is both a particular kind of psychotherapy and a loosely organized set of theoretical principles, which were more or less continuously subjected to revision as Freud's thinking developed. It is important to keep these two roles separate, for conclusions drawn concerning one of them may or may not be relevant to the other; not only were the theoretical propositions themselves loosely connected, but their relationship to the actual therapeutic practice was equally ambiguous.

Freud took his medical degree, specializing in neurological factors, but preferred to continue in research rather than practice. It was his association with an older physician, Josef Breuer, which led to the actual founding of the psychoanalytic school. Their publication *Studies in Hysteria*, in 1895, was an account of the extended treatment by Breuer of the hysterical symptoms of one patient, the now famous "Anna O." Breuer had used hypnotism in treating her and during the course of the therapy discovered that allowing the patient to talk about the origin of her symptoms while under hypnosis led to the disappearance of the symptoms.

This latter technique, which is not dependent for its effectiveness upon the use of hypnosis, was labeled the "talking cure," or somewhat more technically, "catharsis" (meaning "a cleansing out"). Freud himself was extremely interested in this case and especially in the implications of the therapy that was developed, and he encouraged Breuer to proceed with the report. Breuer in the meantime had acquired a strong affection for the patient, and terminated the treatment.

Largely as a result of his finding that not all patients could be successfully put into a hypnotic trance, Freud gradually modified the therapeutic procedure to concentrate upon a free and uninterrupted opportunity for the patient to talk. This is the *free-association* technique. Along with an analysis of the dreams reported by patients, it became the major tool in the psychoanalytic armentarium. However, Freud consistently found that symptoms expressed by patients seemed to be related to events in their past that they apparently could not recall. Hence his interest in unconscious motivation developed. Moreover, he was more convinced than Breuer of the centrality of sexual factors in the genesis of the kind of symptoms (e.g., paralyses and anesthesias) with which he was mainly concerned, those of patients with a classification of hysteria. He finally concluded that traumatic sexual experiences, mainly in childhood, were at the basis of most if not all neurotic disturbances.

Our discussion thus far has mentioned the major themes Freud emphasized in his theoretical interpretation of psychological disturbance: (1) the importance of *unconscious motivation,* (2) the predominance of *sexual* experiences, (3) the critical role of *childhood* and even infancy. Freud proceeded to put these three potent ingredients together in a theoretical mix that he propounded in various forms and with various ramifications throughout the remainder of his long and illustrious career.

Freud's contributions to psychology were enormous. However, from the point of view of the typical contemporary psychologist, they look somewhat different than they do to the nonpsychologist. The latter might be inclined to attribute to Freud a much higher degree of success in his interpretative and explanatory endeavors. The psychologist, on the other hand, would be more inclined to give Freud unstinting praise for opening up important new points of view—critical variables (infancy and childhood), the role of sex and the unconscious, the defense mechanisms (not mentioned above but to be discussed in Chapter 16 in detail)—and in general for illuminating dark areas of human motivation and behavior disorder. But he would be equally strong in his criticism of the general looseness with which Freud's basic principles were related to the empirical evidence, if any, and his persistent refusal to admit the need for any kind of scientific (that is, controlled) evidence to test his ideas.

A good example of this theoretical inadequacy is the Freudian construct of *psychic apparatus* (the conscious, unconscious, and preconscious), which has been well received and endlessly circulated, especially in lay circles and literature, but which is without any kind of substantial empirical underpinnings. Freud's dependence upon *clinical validation,* or the attempt to confirm a proposition by piling up additional reports allegedly showing the same relationship as originally observed (in the absence of anything like the usual scientific attempts at control of variables), is completely unacceptable on strictly scientific grounds.

THE DECLINE OF SYSTEMS

The significance of systems in American psychology has been steadily declining. Partly this is a result of the great loss of confidence that psychologists have had in the major theoretical and systematic positions and their turning more and more to narrower and more circumscribed theoretical efforts (for a time called "miniature systems," although this particular term does not appear to have retained favor). Partly the decline is a function of the increasing numbers of psychologists and the burgeoning variety of research and practitioner roles that they are playing; psychology in this sense has burst the bounds of the old prescriptions and formulations. And partly, perhaps, the decline in systems is a reflection of the growing scientific maturity of psychology; as science advances it tends to reshape its perspectives and its problems.

CONTRASTING PERSPECTIVES

Psychology has been the product of two great historical traditions. The first of these and historically the oldest is philosophy; the second is physiology. Modern psychology emerged during the nineteenth century as a consequence of the joining of philosophy, which provided mainly the problems, and physiology, which provided mainly the methods of study. In contemporary psychology versions of each of these traditions can be observed. The present-day counterpart of philosophy may be seen, by and large, in the humanistic and in the clinical type of interest. The present-day counterpart of physiology may be observed in more strictly scientific or experimental psychology.

The humanistic and clinical view looks at behavior mainly from a molar, or large-scale, perspective; the scientific point of view is mainly from a more analytic perspective. That is to say, the emphasis in humanistic and clinical psychology is on man and his feelings, his social relationships, his personality and its development. The emphasis in scientific psychology tends more to be on the particular mechanisms and processes involved in behavior. Humanistic and clinical psychology want solutions to practical problems, want psychology applied to life. Scientific psychology wants solutions to fundamental theoretical problems; its objective is scientific order. The humanistic and clinical psychologist looks at man as he is. The experimental psychologist tends more to abstract man and other organisms, to utilize "artificial" types of situations.

The Clinical–Experimental Schism

The recent history of psychology has been marked by a fundamental cleavage in point of view and method between the clinical and the experimental perspectives. Although there are many facets to this divergence of opinion, it has been, at heart, a methodological disagreement. Some clinicians have held that adequate knowledge can be acquired about behavior and its manifold determinants, especially those of a subjective (mental) nature, by clinical techniques (e.g., Freudian). Experimentalists have typically insisted on the necessity of the more orthodox, controlled kinds of observations. It must be noted that exceptions have occurred in both

69

directions, but perhaps most frequently in the case of clinicians, who have tended to agree in essence with the experimental position.

The Humanism–Experimentalism Schism

In contemporary psychology the clinical–experimental schism has been largely superseded by somewhat different sets of opposed values. The values offered by a diverse set of humanists have been set against the orthodox views of scientifically oriented psychologists. Here we will first examine the humanistic movement as it has attempted to influence psychology and then explain why it has failed to generate as much enthusiasm within psychology as it has outside the profession.

THE THIRD FORCE. The contemporary humanistic movement in psychology is now often called the *Third Force*. In this way it is contrasted with the first two forces of behaviorism and psychoanalysis. From the perspective of the Third Force, these earlier forces are now seen as inadequate to meet the demands that modern society places upon psychology as a science of the human organism.

As expressed by one of its leading proponents, an important objective of Third Force psychology "is to present a more accurate picture of mankind—one that does not conflict with the way we experience ourselves and others" (Severin, 1971, p. 2).

The unity of the person, autonomy of the individual (cf. Chapter 13), human goals and values, and the uniqueness of man are some of the other positive concerns of the Third Force.

METHODS: THE BASIC ISSUE. It would be difficult indeed to disagree with many of the objectives of the Third Force psychologists. Who among us does not want more authentic models for living, or more adequate understanding of the integrity of the person? The fundamental issue remains how these are to be achieved. Third Force psychology is, in essence, "an *orientation* to psychology—a way of thinking about man and the whole scientific enterprise that modifies our image of human beings and frees psychology from several artificial restrictions placed upon it by theories that now appear to be outmoded" (Severin, 1971, p. 11).

In their insistence upon new techniques of study the Third Force psychologists make much of certain new developments within the philosophy of science that stress the role of subjective factors in science. In the main these new arguments deal with the context of discovery, as earlier described, rather than with the context of confirmation.

The contrasting points of view about method can be illustrated by the statement quoted earlier that an accurate picture of mankind is one that does not "conflict with the way we experience ourselves." The whole history of science points in the other direction; it is when scientists have deliberately chosen new and different ways of picturing their phenomena in contrast to the way they appear to us as laymen, that they have most often been able to develop an adequate understanding of them. For example, visual experience tells me that the world is flat; Columbus's voyages showed that not to be true. Ultimately the scientific picture needs to be translated back into the language and the imagery of the layman so that it can be incorporated into his own framework; this process results in an enrichment both of the ordinary view and the scientific view, because these are complementary to each other.

There does not seem to be any good reason for holding that psychology is in essence different from the other sciences, biological as well as physical (often classed together as "natural," to contrast with human sciences; are the latter, then, by implication "unnatural"?). The pivotal distinction here is that between method and technique. It is certainly true that the human sciences require unique techniques, because they, like all sciences, deal with a unique subject matter and constitute unique problems. On the other hand, it is the general experimental position that these techniques must all fit under the broad umbrella of scientific method, as this has been described in Chapter 2. Thus Third Force psychology, although of value for calling attention to certain deficiencies in prior work and perspectives, has not itself offered much in the way of new positive methodology. Moreover, if and when it does so, it may be expected to converge with the mainstream of experimental psychology, if it really means to stay with a scientific approach to psychology rather than one of the alternatives.

A COMPLEMENTARY RELATIONSHIP. As suggested above, the humanist and the experimentalist positions are not mutually contradictory. In general, the humanistic position provides important problems for the experimentalist to resolve but is itself incapable of providing scientifically acceptable answers. The experimentalist, on the other hand, has the tools to attack the problems but is less likely to use them effectively unless he has important problems. For its fullest advance, therefore, psychology will ultimately need to combine the richness of problems offered by the humanistic and clinical approach with the experimental analysis offered by the scientific approach.

There are now encouraging signs that this process is beginning. For example, experimentalists at long last are taking seriously an obvious but exceptionally difficult problem that has been generally skirted or deliberately ignored: the relationship of conscious experience to overt behavior, which is the central topic of Chapter 4. It is important that development of research on this topic be accelerated.

Schools and Systems

For the history of psychology, Boring's classic treatment (1950) is indispensable. Heidbreder's *Seven Psychologies* (1933) remains an excellent discussion of the basic schools. Historical information is also available in Watson's *Great Psychologists from Aristotle to Freud* (1971). Systems are critically reviewed in Marx and Hillix's *Systems and Theories in Psychology* (1973), and Hillix and Marx's reader (1974) provides selections from the original sources.

The Third Force

Severin's description of the Third Force movement from which the quotations in the text were taken is his 1971 essay. A good overview of the movement is provided by Bühler and Allan (1972).

Notes

This nineteenth-century engraving of an earlier painting by the Dutch artist Van Hoogstraten is entitled "Curiosity" and serves to introduce the subject of this next section of the text. The old man looking through the window is symbolic of the constraints placed on all of us; for we too must view the world through the window of our consciousness. The extent to which we are limited in our ability to perceive and the consequences of these limitations on our behavior are the concerns of the following five chapters.

Conscious Experience and Behavior

PART II

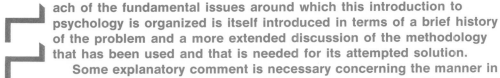

ach of the fundamental issues around which this introduction to psychology is organized is itself introduced in terms of a brief history of the problem and a more extended discussion of the methodology that has been used and that is needed for its attempted solution.

Some explanatory comment is necessary concerning the manner in which these key problems will be presented in this book. The major solutions to them that have been advanced will be presented and evaluated, but in most cases there will be little attempt to decide which of these solutions must be accepted as "correct." In other words, the emphasis will be on the formulation of the problems; the objective will be to have the reader understand not only the nature of the problem, but also the principles that underlie the attempted solutions of it. This procedure is based on the assumption that if the reader really has a good grasp of these problems and of the way in which they have been and can be approached, he will be in possession of fundamental and long-lasting knowledge—and he will have the necessary tools for some evaluation of both current and future attempts to resolve the issues.

The maintenance of intellectual tolerance is particularly necessary in psychology. For many problems final answers are simply not available on the basis of our present knowledge. The working scientist, in his quest for new knowledge and understanding, maintains a tolerance for ambiguity and uncertainty. Premature emphasis on final solutions or premature acceptance or rejection of proposed solutions may have the effect of stifling future scientific work.

No issue has a more complex and extended history or a more difficult methodology than that of the role of consciousness in behavior. The difficulty in the comprehension of this problem is matched by its importance. Few psychological issues have greater interest for many students or, ultimately, greater implications for all psychology. Chapter 4, which tackles the problem of handling consciousness scientifically, is thus an appropriate starting point for our study of psychology.

The remaining chapters in this part all deal with other fundamental facets of conscious experience. Chapter 5 is concerned with the primary way in which sensory processing of incoming information is accomplished by the various receptors, with varying degrees and kinds of conscious experience. Chapter 6 is concerned with the crucial topics of attention, or focusing of consciousness, and perception, or the manner in which the organism actually interprets as well as senses stimulation. The next two chapters deal with thinking; Chapter 7 takes up the more basic issues and Chapter 8 concentrates on problem solving, an activity for which the human organism is beautifully equipped.

The Problem of Consciousness

4

This illustration by John Tenniel from the original version of Alice in Wonderland *is very appropriate to open our discussion of consciousness. In this scene the caterpillar has just asked, "Who are you?" Alice's reply is, "I hardly know . . . I know who I was when I got up this morning, but I think I must have been changed several times since then." Alice's reaction to the conscious experience of changes in her physical size and to the odd assortment of characters that she encounters illustrates a fundamental relationship between conscious experience and behavior. Has her ability to perceive, feel, think, and will been altered by her adventure, or has such an alteration, in fact, produced her adventure?*

his chapter presents first a brief summary of the meanings of the terms *consciousness* and *mind*. Consciousness is the name ordinarily given to describe our subjective, private experiences. When one is conscious, he is *subjectively experiencing*—that is, perceiving, feeling, thinking. A conscious individual is normally responsive to stimulation. Consciousness thus refers to the condition of the organism in which subjective experiences occur. The introspectively given functions of consciousness are described as perceiving, feeling, thinking, and willing.

Two roles for consciousness in behavior are considered. The *active-role* hypothesis sees consciousness as playing a vital part in determining behavior, even while it is a function of neural activities in the brain. The *passive-role* hypothesis sees consciousness as having no causal significance for behavior, but occurring merely as a function of brain processes. The interpretation of the results from behavioral testing of "split-brain" human subjects is a pivotal issue in this discussion. Imagine an adult human with the two halves of his brain surgically separated. What might be the effects of such a separation on his conscious experiences? Would the normal unity of his consciousness be retained, or would he now experience two sets of conscious states, one for each half of the brain?

Some partial answers to these intriguing questions can now be advanced. Split-brain human subjects have been produced by neurosurgeons in an effort to relieve the debilitating effects of severe epileptic conditions and have been carefully studied by psychologists. The present chapter focuses on this research and the implications of the results thus far obtained.

The chapter continues with consideration of other lines of evidence on both of the alternative views on the role of consciousness. It is concluded that consciousness as a phenomenon is like flame and electricity in that its relationships to other variables may be scientifically determinable even though any *ultimate* understanding, in a philosophical or metaphysical sense, of its essential nature is unattainable.

Overview of Consciousness

IDENTIFICATION OF TERMS

There are two commonly used terms requiring identification: *consciousness* and *mind*. Because these are frequently confused and treated as synonymous, it is important to point out their somewhat different meanings.

In its most fundamental meaning, *consciousness* refers to the way an organism typically processes information or stimulation from the environment. Conscious experiences are therefore always processes, even though we often think of them in terms of states. Such fundamental experiential processes are typically taken for granted, until such time as a stark contrast is provided by sudden losses of consciousness, as from a blow to the head.

Like many terms used in psychology, *consciousness* is a *construct*, which means it is a kind of abstraction, based upon the processes observed, and in this instance directly experienced. There is a strong tendency to treat constructs as though they are things in and of themselves, and are somehow more than the processes upon which they are based. This tendency, already noted for its troublesome effects with regard to psychoanalysis, is a dangerously misleading one that needs to be constantly combatted. Speaking and thinking of consciousness (or even more often, mind) as though there exists some superordinate entity is therefore to be discouraged. Such explicit caution is necessary in view of the common tendency toward this kind of *reification*, as the process is usually called. However, we all do have conscious experiences, as processes, and it is these that we are emphasizing even when, for the sake of convenient communication, we use the term *consciousness*.

At some time during his life the typical human organism becomes aware of the fact that he is able to process stimulation in this way, that is, his consciousness itself becomes an object of consciousness. In other words, the person becomes aware of his consciousness, or of his awareness. Paying attention to conscious processes by conscious processes obviously sets the stage for a great deal of puzzlement and confusion and has helped to keep laymen as well as philosophers and psychologists busy for a long time. In spite of these various confusions, the fact that the human adult at least is capable of such sophisticated use of his consciousness must be reckoned with in any complete survey of human capacity and potential, and is especially crucial for a full development of psychology.

Mind is a much broader and less precise term than *consciousness*. In its most common usage, *mind* is a construct that refers to the totality of conscious experiences. It is thus a more abstract as well as more inclusive term than *consciousness*. Moreover, *mind* is also often used in an even broader sense, to refer to adaptive behavior generally. In this usage it would of course encompass much more than would the term *consciousness*.

Because the term *mind* is so much more ambiguous than *consciousness* the latter term will be used throughout this chapter to refer to subjective experience. When the term *mental* is used, however, it is intended to refer to conscious processes rather than to the more vague concept of mind from which it was derived; this usage of *mental* is a common one.

TREATMENT OF CONSCIOUSNESS IN THE STUDY OF PSYCHOLOGY

Within psychology there has been a curious tendency to downplay the significance of consciousness. Only recently has there been a widespread renewal of interest in problems directly relating to it. The lag in general recognition of and attention to problems involving consciousness is understandable in terms of the history of American psychology. As the discussion in Chapter 3 indicates, the major force toward greater objectivity in psychology has been the behavioristic system. In the process of arguing for objectivity behaviorists at first minimized consciousness and ultimately, in the radical behavioristic version of the system, came to deny consciousness any role at all.

THE CONTEMPORARY SITUATION. None of the various mind–body solutions advanced by philosophers has captivated the psychological public. As a result it is the fashion in psychology today to deny the reality of the metaphysical problem —that of the ultimate nature of reality—at least as a problem for empirical science. Probably a majority of psychologists if given the opportunity would gladly vote to return this legacy to the philosophers from whom it originally came.

Is this really a desirable solution to this age-old puzzle? Yes and no; yes because we can certainly do without the metaphysics in psychology, but no because the complete refusal to consider mental–physical relationships leaves psychology cut off from some of its most basic and challenging problems. Let us be more specific on the stance that we as psychologists need to adopt on this fundamental issue, or set of issues. (1) It is quite apparent to all but the most metaphysically biased persons that so-called mental experiences not only exist but are nearly constant companions of even the least mentally active human beings, so that consciousness along with overt behavior is indeed a quite legitimate and necessary subject matter for science. (2) It also seems that the metaphysical solutions thus far offered have little if any direct contribution to make to science. (3) It seems probable that the ultimate resolution of the relationship between our mental experiences and our brain processes, upon which most of us agree the former depend, must be worked out on the basis of a great deal more empirical data and theoretical orderliness than we now possess; until these are achieved the only reasonable position is simply to suspend judgment as to which if any of the solutions advanced is in fact correct.

We need to pursue a large number of investigations both on mental phenomena, as these are behaviorally expressed, and on correlated overt behaviors. The neuropsychologist and the neurophysiologist, working directly on brain–behavior relations, will then have increasing amounts of usable grist for their theoretical mills.

Psychologists are in a good position to provide an ever-increasing number of potentially relevant observations, both objective and subjective, for neurophysiological consideration. The remainder of this chapter will provide examples of both kinds of observations. Some of the basic issues relating to the tripartite relationship between consciousness, body (brain, mainly), and behavior will be outlined with a minimum of metaphysical assumptions and implications.

The content and organization of the following treatment are based primarily upon the kind of naive introspective procedure that is usually called *phenomenological;* that is, it is essentially untrained, in contrast to the structuralist, or Titchenerian, procedure and is similar to the procedure adopted by the Gestalt psychologists. It is, as far as possible, without philosophical or metaphysical biases and is a procedure that anyone can utilize.

Accepting Consciousness

We may best begin by recognizing the reality of consciousness, as a kind of "given" (meaning that it is to be simply accepted, without question). As a matter of fact, consciousness may be accorded a unique status: for the human being it is *the* given. As a variety of scholars and thinkers have said, in one way of another, if there is anything that man can be certain of, that one thing is his own consciousness. However, this does not mean that its status as a construct, as discussed earlier, can be ignored. Moreover, simply accepting the reality of conscious experiences does not require that any particular philosophical position about its relationship to brain processes also be accepted.

Conscious experiences occur in nearly infinite variety. It has been estimated, for example, that the human eye is capable of discriminating 1.5 million different hues, or color variations. Subtle shadings and nuances in, say, emotional feelings are also possible in almost infinite variety. How does the investigator cope with such a great range of experience? It is apparent that pure description, although valuable and even necessary as a first step, is still just a first step. The scientific account depends upon cutting through the manifold complexity of everyday life to a set of useful abstractions so that predictable underlying regularities can be found. One such example, for the case of consciousness, might well be the positive–negative (or approach–avoid) dimension along which feelings appear to be basically orderable. Another, more obvious dimension would be the modality, or sensory mode, along which incoming stimulation is received.

FUNDAMENTAL PROCESSES IN CONSCIOUSNESS

Four fundamental mental processes—perceiving, feeling, thinking, and willing —are described in Table 4-1. The fact that they are listed as separate and independent functions does not of course mean that they always occur that way in consciousness. On the contrary, our conscious experiences are more typically mixed, consisting of combinations of both these fundamental processes and their elaborations, as described in the table. Also, this kind of categorizing, like any based primarily upon introspective evidence, is arbitrary. Its value is as a preliminary but not exhaustive survey, showing some of the organizational conditions in consciousness, as well as a kind of starting point from which further deductions can be made and new inquiries launched.

Perceiving may be regarded as the fundamental conscious process. It represents the direct apprehension of the environment, or put another way, it is the immediate consequence of the functioning of the various sensory receptors, or specialized body structures that are sensitive to particular environmental energies and are appropriately connected to the brain by neural pathways. The variety of sensations and perceptions in the normal human subject is treated elsewhere. Perception is characterized as "primary" because it seems to be a natural and inevitable concomitant of consciousness. *Images* are the conscious experiences that replicate the prior sensations or perceptions upon which they are based; they occur in the

Table 4-1 Fundamental Processes in Consciousness

Process	Character	Elaboration	Psychological Subject Matter
Perceiving	Primary	Imaging, remembering	Sensation and perception
Feeling	Primary; accompanying sensation, perception, or thought	Mood; temperament	Emotion; affect
Thinking	Secondary; reflective	Problem solving, planning, decision making; reverie	Cognition; thought; higher mental processes
Willing	Secondary; product of thinking or of habit	Overt voluntary actions	Motivation; volition

absence of the original external stimulus and differ from the original experience in generally being less vivid (for example, less deeply saturated in color) and distinct.

Feeling is the name given to the emotional aspect of conscious experiences. Like sensations and perceptions, feelings must be experienced to be appreciated. Although there are many subtle variations, most feelings can be conveniently classified as either positive (pleasurable) or negative (painful or unpleasant); by definition it would be impossible to have a strictly neutral or indifferent feeling (as indicated in the idiom to "feel nothing" or "have no feeling" for something or someone). Feelings, again like sensations, always appear to be primary in the sense of being immediate and not derived from other experiences. They can, however, accompany secondary or derived experiences, such as perceptions or thoughts, and so may then appear to lose some of their primacy. Thus some feelings seem to be inherently positive or pleasurable (e.g., sexual orgasm) whereas others seem to be inherently negative or unpleasant (e.g., nausea). Feelings may develop more slowly than sensations, especially when they are produced at least in part as a consequence of thought; moreover, they are unlike sensations also in being subject to dissipation if not kept free of distractions. (This point includes the distraction of one's own introspection; it is impossible to maintain a high degree of anger, for example, while attempting introspectively to inspect it.)

When feeling tones persist and tend to color one's thought and behavior they are usually referred to as "moods." Chronic feeling tones, which are integral aspects of one's personality, are instrumental in determining an individual's "temperament" —the name for an individual's characteristic emotional coloring as seen by others.

Thinking is the generic or class name given to the process in consciousness by which the several kinds of other experiences are manipulated. For this reason it is here categorized as "secondary." "Thoughts" are thus usually complexes of sensations, perceptions, feelings, and various kinds of images, including those representing previous thoughts.

Few terms in psychology cover a broader range and scope of functions. For this reason it is especially important to make clear the way in which thoughts can vary. For present purposes we may look briefly at some of the key dimensions—variables with continuous and more or less measurable values—along which thoughts can be placed.

1. *Reality orientation:* here the extreme positions are represented by problem solving, which is directly oriented to the real, external world, and reverie, which consists of a flow of imaginatively produced thoughts, as in dreaming (or, even more extremely perhaps, as in hallucinatory and similar experiences of the psychotic patient).
2. *Temporal orientation:* extreme positions would be represented by planning future actions, on the one hand, and reminiscing, on the other hand, with most thinking probably being somewhere in between with regard to the time dimension (and often restricted simply to present situations).
3. *Emotional involvement:* minimal intrusions of feeling would be found in pure reasoning, whereas a maximum degree of feeling would occur in impulsive thoughts, such as those relating to aggression, personal violence, and the like.
4. *Conscious sufficiency:* extreme positions on this continuum would be represented by deliberate decision making, with fully conscious manipulation of thoughts, on the one hand, and the kind of unconscious contribution called incubation, on the other hand. Incubation refers to the production of solutions to problems in the absence of any apparent thinking of the usual sort; the person simply ceases to think about the problem, usually after a considerable expenditure of effort. Then the solution occurs suddenly, presumably as a result of "unconscious thinking." Obviously this term refers to basic brain functions occurring in the presumed absence of consciousness. The role of unconscious functions in determining the structure and direction of cognitive processes has long been recognized by psychologists, after Freud. This was particularly true in early research on problem solving, in which mental sets and hints apparently not noticed by the subject were shown to be effective factors in solution achievement.

These few dimensions and illustrations barely scratch the surface of the thinking phenomenon but must suffice for the present. Many other illustrations of the richness of thinking will occur throughout the major sections of this book, as well as in Chapters 7 and 8. The human ability to form concepts—symbolic representations of abstract relationships among things and events, such as justice, loyalty, and friendship—is especially significant and is mentioned here as illustrative of the many processess whose detailed examination is deferred.

Willing typically seems to be a product of thinking and so is here regarded as secondary. However, it is such an important phenomenon, and often appears to be of primary behavioral significance, that it is included as a fundamental conscious process in spite of its clearly derived nature. Willing refers to any conscious determination and is of course elaborated in terms of such so-called voluntary actions.

THE NATURE OF CONSCIOUSNESS

As we develop from infancy all of us tend to take the fact of our sensory and intellectual experiences—our "mind"—for granted. Moreover, it seems clear to us that mental experiences—sensations, emotions, ideas, wishes, intentions—are extremely potent factors in the determination of behavior. It often comes as something of a shock, then, to learn in high school or college that the significance of such mental phenomena, if not their very existence, can be seriously questioned.

The most serious challenges to the role of mind have come, as we have seen in the last chapter, from the psychological school of behaviorism. Although in its most extreme form (radical or metaphysical behaviorism) this system seems to deny the existence of mental phenomena, in its more moderate form behaviorism simply denies the efficacy of mental phenomena as determinants of behavior. The apparent power that wishes and intentions exercise, for example, is held to be illusory.

In this chapter we examine some of the major facets of the ancient problem of the role of mind as it relates to body and the behavioral manifestations of body. Our examination must of necessity be restricted to the highlights of the problem. Our basic assumption is that mental experiences, whatever their ultimate nature, do play some kind of a role in human life. But it is the nature of their relationship to physical variables (brain physiology) and to behavior that constitutes the heart of the problem. Our purpose is neither to argue for any one version of the mind–body relationship nor to attempt any kind of final resolution of the problem. Rather, our purpose is to clarify as far as possible the fundamental issues so that the student will at least have a better idea of these issues and perhaps can develop some form of perspective on them for himself if he so chooses.

A simple analogy may be helpful in providing a perspective on this problem of the nature of consciousness. Consciousness, as each of us knows it, has one characteristic that stands out from all others. This is its searching nature. It is very much *as if* man were housed in a small capsule with a kind of reversible searchlight that can be used either to probe the world outside of the capsule or to turn inside and probe the searching processes themselves.

The purpose of this representation of the pivotal, searchlight character of conscious processes is simply to provide the reader with an orientation to the problem. The representation is strictly analogical, and is *not* to be taken literally; psychologists as well as laymen have already populated man's body with far too many "inner men." If the temptation to look for such inner men can be successfully resisted, then this kind of figurative representation may well be of service in illuminating some of the fundamental properties of human consciousness.

Consciousness and Brain Functions

A KEY ISSUE

We are now ready to look at the key question in the entire array of mind–body problems: Does consciousness have a causal relationship to behavior, or is its apparent active role merely illusory? In other words, do conscious processes play any essential part in influencing brain processes?

Figure 4-1 provides a simplified, schematic representation of what may be called the consciousness–brain–behavior triangle. As here conceptualized, there are two fundamental lines of influence. The solid lines, running from brain to consciousness, from brain to behavior, and from behavior (including of course perceptual response) to brain, indicate those about which there is little or no disagreement. The single broken line, from consciousness to brain, poses the big question mark. If consciousness does indeed play an active role, then this line should really also be drawn solid, representing a true interaction of mental and neurophysiological processes. If, on the contrary, consciousness is restricted to a purely passive role, then this line represents an illusory, nonfunctional interaction and should really be erased.

The possibility of some kind of direct but nonphysiological connection between consciousness and behavior, as postulated by some proponents of *extrasensory perception* (ESP), would be shown by a direct connection in the diagram. It is omitted here in the absence of any positive theoretical or empirical position advanced by such proponents. Other similar conjectures have involved the direct relationship between the consciousness of two different organisms (*telepathy*), the direct (nonperceptual, in any known sense) influence of physical objects on consciousness (*clairvoyance*), and the opposite process, the direct influence of consciousness on physical objects (*psychokinesis,* or PK). All of these must be recognized as interesting suggestions as possibilities for specific mediating functions. They will need to be seriously considered when such proposals are made in an empirically testable manner. The psychological problem of evaluating them is considered in the notes to Chapter 6.

ACTIVE AND PASSIVE ROLES OF CONSCIOUSNESS

With direct conscious-behavior and conscious-conscious connections ignored, for present expository purposes, Figures 4-2 and 4-3 present a somewhat more simplified version of the two alternative views of the function of consciousness. The *active* theory is depicted in Figure 4-2, which shows a succession of brain and consciousness states and their running interaction. The *passive* theory is depicted in Figure 4-3, where the one-way traffic between brain and consciousness is apparent; successive brain states are directly influenced only by the brain states themselves

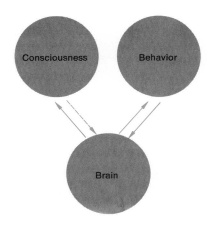

4-1 The consciousness–brain–behavior triangle. Generally accepted relationships, such as the behavioral input into the brain and vice versa, are shown by solid lines. The most controversial relationship, consciousness to brain, is shown by a broken line.

4-2 Schematic representation of an active role of consciousness. Consciousness is assumed to be an active, casual influence on behavior, as indicated by the two-way interaction.

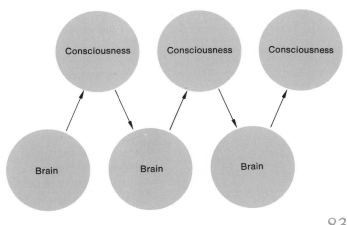

Time ⟶

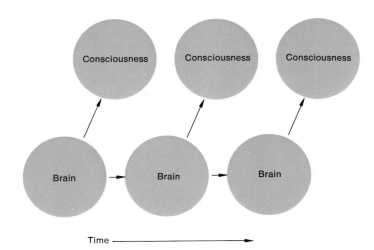

4-3 Schematic representation of a passive role of consciousness. Brain processes are assumed to produce conscious processes, but the reciprocal relationship is denied.

(ignoring the role of behavior as an active factor on the brain), and mental states and processes exist strictly as functions of concurrent brain activities.

A variety of arguments in support of each of these two alternative accounts will now be summarized so that the reader will have them available for his own judgment, to be made or remade, tentatively, in the light of the quite tenuous support that can be mustered at present for either view.

THE CASE FOR THE ACTIVE ROLE OF CONSCIOUSNESS

Four major types of evidence may be summarized as support for the case of an active role of consciousness: this evidence is introspective, experimental, theoretical, and neurophysiological. Rebuttal of these various arguments, as made by those who refuse to accept them, will be offered as a part of the next section on evidence for a passive role of consciousness.

EVERYMAN'S INTROSPECTION. Here we may consider briefly the layman's typical position on the problem of consciousness. It is that consciousness must play an active role because his introspections indicate quite clearly that what we *perceive* affects our decisions and what we *will* normally determines our actions (except of course in certain extreme cases that can be categorized as "abnormal"). This position is mentioned here because of its frequency of occurrence and its legitimate and useful role as a starting point for scientific investigation. In its unadorned state, however, it is obviously quite unsophisticated, relying primarily upon relationships that *seem* to exist, and requires no further comment at this point with regard to its bearing as evidence on the primary issues.

EXPERIMENTAL INTROSPECTIVE EVIDENCE: IMAGERY. Of all the kinds of experimental introspective evidence that might be brought to bear upon this problem the most impressive is that relating to the relatively recent demonstration of the potency of the *imagery* operation in learning and memory. An image is an inner-

84

determined replication of some earlier perceptual experience, such as the visual perception of a particular person or event, in the absence of the external stimuli that initially produced the experience. In general, it seems to be quite clearly established that learning and memory are markedly facilitated when human subjects use images of concrete things (i.e., *elbow, hat, dog,* and the like) as aids, as compared with the learning and memory that occurs when this procedure is not used. That is, subjects whose task is to memorize certain relationships between words (e.g., *elbow* and *hat*) do so more quickly if they are instructed to visualize the words as concrete objects (i.e., form images of both *elbow* and *hat* and "see" them together). It has also been suggested that images are instrumental in the learning of language, a problem that is currently under investigation by psychologists as well as linguists.

The conclusion that can be drawn from this rapidly growing field of research is that the active use of images is a most important human function, with extensive contributions to behavioral efficiency. The experiments that have been reported are well controlled.

Imagery concreteness has clearly been shown to be a much more effective factor in verbal learning than such other meaningfulness variables as frequency of occurrence. The potency of the perceptual experience was recently brought home to me when, after failing completely to recall the name of an acquaintance in spite of a variety of verbal cues, the sight of his face produced an immediate recall of the name. Apparently this kind of experience, which may be fairly common, is based upon a process very similar to that by which images when added to perception of words alone can result in critically different, and generally more effective, behavioral functions.

Theoretical Treatments

The important role of *attention,* or the focusing of consciousness (see Chapter 6), generally has been pointed out by many writers. William James, for one prominent instance, stated that, "Only those items that I *notice* shape my mind" (1890, p. 402). More surprisingly, a very similar statement has recently been made by a long-time behaviorist whose learning theory represents the purest form of a strict associationism: "What is being *noticed* becomes a signal for what is being done" (Guthrie, 1959, p. 186; emphasis added).

Emphasizing the *utility* of consciousness, William James argued that if consciousness had not played an important role, it would not have survived in human evolution. This role, according to James, is that of choice: as a selective agent, consciousness enables man to adapt to changing conditions more effectively.

The significance of *empathy* (sympathetic feeling) in consciousness has been emphasized. According to this argument, it is only when one has already himself had a particular kind of experience that he is able to appreciate the attitudes and behaviors of others. Each of us can probably think of at least some occasions in which this has been true, occasions when a new experience (say, for example, being the object of a certain teacher's sarcasm for the first time) has given us a better appreciation of, and often sympathy for, someone else's situation. In this process the role of conscious deliberation is central.

It is instructive to consider further the behavioristic argument on empathy. The behaviorist would take the position that when he "feels" something for someone else, he is simply responding to the cues in that person's situation that were associated with his own prior negative or positive experiences. He responds with some fraction of whatever type of feeling may have been elicited in the original situation. Indeed, he may have some better understanding of what that other person who is now surrounded by such cues is feeling, but there is no way in which he is actually privy to the other's emotional response. He feels an emotion that he infers is similar, and it may be, in fact, some sort of rough approximation of that other's feeling. Such a response to learned cues of course does not require that he possess any sort of conscious awareness; however, consciousness would seem to be required for his contemplation of the event, for his appreciation of the dynamics of his own behavior (why he is responding as he is), and perhaps for the integrative processes that come into play as he decides what to do about it.

Somewhat similar but more elaborated theoretical arguments have been advanced by an eminent cognitive psychologist to demonstrate the potential value of conscious processes. This writer makes four main points, in developing an alternative to the methodological behaviorists' exclusive dependence upon objective, overt behaviors.

1. Subjective experience, such as the consciousness of pain, can itself serve as a kind of dependent variable. Thus, "A person with intractable pain from neuralgia is not concerned primarily whether he expresses this pain in overt behavior and whether it could be inferred from objective evidence; he is concerned with the fact that the pain exists as subjective fact" (Leeper, 1963, p. 380).

2. In real life, people often make predictions from their own subjective experience as well as from objectively observable facts; consciousness can thus serve also as a kind of independent variable.

3. People often formulate and test hypotheses concerning both objective (overt behavioral) and subjective (experiential or conscious) facts, and their relationships; an example given is the writer's own discovery, as a graduate student, that colors can be generated in subjective experience as a function of the speed of rotation of a wheel containing only black and white discs.

4. The functional relationships discovered in this way can be effectively transmitted to other persons; the writer cites the discovery of the differential loss in brightness of flowers of various colors in his garden at twilight, a discovery that could obviously be passed on to others and that led to the important functional distinction between rods and cones in vision. These various arguments clearly constitute a viable alternative to the methodological behavioristic view that the raw data of psychology can only be strictly objective.

Neurophysiological Considerations: Sperry's Position

The most dramatic of all investigations of conscious awareness in relation to the brain is the research initiated by psychologist R. W. Sperry with "split brain" human subjects. After considerable experimental research on animals, mainly cats,

Sperry intensively studied a large number of human patients requiring drastic neurosurgery for control of severe epileptic seizures. The operation used in these patients consists of the disconnecting of the two cerebral hemispheres, or halves of the brain, including the complete separation of the corpus callosum, the main connecting structure. Sperry was primarily interested in investigating what happens to conscious experience, as reflected in the verbal reports and other behaviors, when the two halves of the cerebral hemisphere have been surgically disconnected.

The behavioral results of this operation are fascinating. Let Sperry summarize the results in his own words:

One of the more general and also more interesting and striking features . . . may be summarized as an apparent doubling in most of the realms of conscious awareness. Instead of the normally unified single stream of consciousness, these patients behave in many ways as if they have two independent streams of conscious awareness, one in each hemisphere, each of which is cut off from and out of contact with the mental experiences of the other. In other words, each hemisphere seems to have its own separate and private sensations; its own perceptions; its own concepts; and its own impulses to act, with related volitional, cognitive, and learning experiences. Following the surgery each hemisphere also has thereafter its own separate chain of memories that are rendered inaccessible to the recall processes of the other [1968, p. 724].

This conclusion is based upon a large variety of behavioral observations. The basic testing situation is shown in Figure 4-4(a). This set-up permits the separation, for testing purposes, of left and right visual fields and also the separation of the left and right hands and legs. For visual lateralization the subject has one eye covered and fixates with the other eye on some point on the translucent viewing screen. Visual stimuli are then projected for .1 second or less, which is too short for eye movements to occur and enable the subject to shift the visual material into the "wrong" half of the field. The eye–brain connections are shown in Figure 4-4(b). Visual materials on the left side of the field of either eye are projected to the right hemisphere, and vice versa, with little overlap.

Evidence for assuming two separate visual worlds comes from experiments involving speech and writing. The brain mechanisms controlling the verbal functions are in the dominant hemisphere (normally the left hemisphere for a right-handed person). Now when the experimenters present visual stimulation to the right half of the visual field, which is served by the left-hemisphere optical system because of the crossing of most of the optical nerve fibers (not affected by the operation), the right-handed split-brain subject speaks and writes in the normal manner. But when the very same material is shown on the left side, thus activating brain centers in the right hemisphere for the right-handed subject, either nothing is reported as seen or at best a "flash of light" is reported. Nevertheless, the same subject when shown either the same object or a pictorial representation of it can point to it appropriately with his left hand.

The limitations of the split-brain subject when tested under special conditions are indicated in the situation depicted in Figure 4-4(c). If a picture of some common object, such as a pear, is shown on the left visual field, and so to the minor (nondominant) hemisphere (for the right-handed subject), the subject can succeed

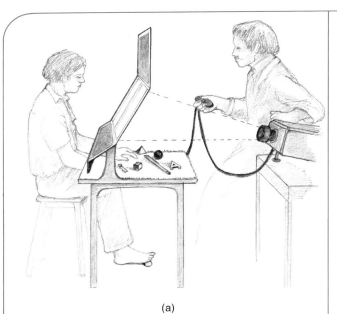

(a)

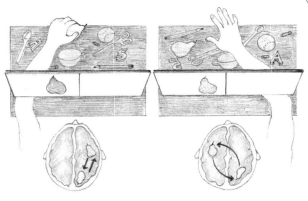

(c)

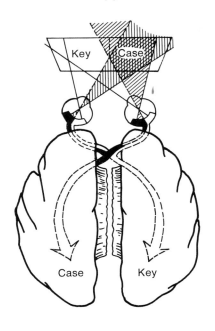

(b)

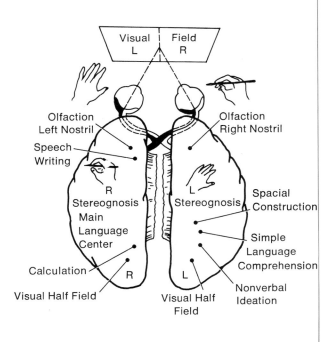

(d)

in locating the appropriate object by blind touch, but only when using the left hand. Apparently the right hand "does not know what it is looking for" in the absence of hemispherical connection, and cannot identify the appropriate object even though the subject is able to identify each object the right hand feels by calling out the correct name for it. The more general situation in such tests is shown, schematically, in Figure 4-4(d).

Other functions of the minor, or nondominant, hemisphere are especially interesting. According to Sperry, the nondominant hemisphere is "observed to demonstrate appropriate emotional reactions as, for example, when a pinup shot of a nude is interjected by surprise among a series of neutral geometric figures being flashed to the right and left fields at random. When the surprise nude appears on the left side the subject characteristically says that he or she saw nothing or just a flash of light. However, the appearance of a sneaky grin and perhaps blushing and giggling . . . belies the verbal contention of the speaking hemisphere. . . . Apparently, only the emotional effect gets across . . ." (Sperry, 1968, p. 732).

Supporting evidence for this conclusion comes from observations of the reactions of split-brain subjects to the presentation of various odors through the right nostril to the minor hemisphere. Subjects are unable verbally to identify the source of the odor (garlic, cheese, perfume, and so on) but can make strong aversive responses, such as "phew," to a particularly noxious stimulus. Moreover, as in the case of the tactual identification of objects described above, they are able to identify the appropriate source of the odor with their left hand, indicating that the corresponding detailed information is present in the right hemisphere, in the absence of any verbal or symbolic representation.

Even in normal testing, split-brain subjects are observed to show affective sensitivity in minor hemispheric stimulation. Sperry comments that, "This is evidenced in the frowning, wincing, and negative head shaking in test situations where the minor hemisphere, knowing the correct answer but unable to speak, hears the major hemisphere making obvious verbal mistakes" (1968, p. 732).

SPERRY'S THEORETICAL INTERPRETATION. After his long study of split-brain behaviors, Sperry has concluded that "the conscious phenomena of subjective experience do interact on the brain process, exerting an active causal influence . . . consciousness is conceived to have a directive role in determining the flow pattern of cerebral excitation" (1969, p. 533).

Although the precise factors underlying the development of this theory are not

4-4 Details of procedure and results of Sperry's split-brain research. (a) The experimental apparatus. The projector is used to block out the right or left visual field. (b) Objects seen to the right of a central fixation point with either eye are projected to the left hemisphere and vice versa. (c) An object projected to the right hemisphere (left visual half field) may be located by the left hand because the functional control of the left hand is also located within the right hemisphere. Failure occurs when the subject is asked to locate the object with the right hand. In this case, the right hand "doesn't know what it is looking for." (d) The localization of various functions as determined by Sperry's studies. (Adapted from Sperry, 1968.)

spelled out, and it is advanced on a quite provisional basis, it does appear that the repeated observation of dual consciousness was an important consideration. Applying a kind of "Gestalt theory," Sperry suggests that consciousness is a "dynamic emergent property of cerebral excitation"; in other words, conscious processes are somehow produced by special kinds of cerebral functions in much the same way as water is produced by the combination of two hydrogen and one oxygen molecule (a favorite Gestalt example of an "emergent" process, one that cannot be predicted in advance of its occurrence).

An important property of consciousness, as conceived by Sperry, is that it *supervenes*, rather than *intervenes*, in brain physiology. By this he means that conscious processes play an autonomous independent role as superordinate, co-ordinating processes, even though they are themselves products of cerebral mechanisms and they do not directly influence specific brain processes. Thus conscious processes serve more as regulatory or moderating devices (supervening) than as directly causal agents (intervening) according to this view. The precise manner of formation of such conscious processes from cerebral functions remains to be determined, but Sperry thinks that this new way of conceiving them will be helpful in stimulating the development of new measuring devices; at present, he has asserted, the only way of direct plugging into one consciousness by another is the normally intact corpus callosum (the subbrain structure that is surgically separated in the split-brain operation).

EXPERIMENTAL TESTS. Sperry's interesting theorizing has begun to influence research and interpretation. In one laboratory study, for example, the subjects' heart rates were recorded as they were preparing either to make an overt response (lever press) or a covert response (thinking the word *stop*, according to the instructions).

The experimenters report that in either case a quite reliable preparatory heart rate change occurred, developing in accordance with the temporal pacing required but not differing for the two types of response, and conclude that their results support Sperry's theoretical position. An alternative view, of course, would be that whatever basic brain functions underlie consciousness and overt responding can just as easily account for the autonomic (heart rate) effect.

Apart from its potential value as a stimulator of new measuring techniques and new experimental observations, Sperry sees his position as having certain other advantages. For one, it puts consciousness to work, giving it a reason for existence and for its evolutionary persistence (following William James's much earlier argument). For another, the view occupies an intermediate position between the familiar extremes of a pure mentalism, on the one hand, and a pure physicalism, on the other. It recognizes the transcendental properties of mind, and so shares the advantages of mentalism to that extent, but at the same time it also recognizes the fundamental dependence of mind on brain matter, and so shares likewise certain of the advantages of the physicochemical, materialistic account. In any case, whatever its ultimate fate, Sperry's view deserves attention if for no other reason than the fact that he has opened up such an intriguing field of research and produced so many provocative experimental results.

The case for a passive role for consciousness depends in part upon a rebuttal of the arguments for the active role as summarized above as well as upon the development of effective positive arguments for the passive role itself.

Rebuttal

Everyman's introspection, although it may be valuable as a starting point for scientific investigation and is of course also of some value in its own right, is still hardly sufficient to weigh very heavily on scientific scales. If observations were generally accepted at face value as demonstrating what they *seem* to mean, then science would hardly have progressed to its present state. It is of course precisely because man has refused to accept such meaning and has delved more deeply into problems posed by the initial observations that science has advanced.

The evidence of the research on imagery is indeed important, but is it convincing with regard to the active role of consciousness? Only in a very limited way, because there is still no question but that the use of imagery is itself based upon corresponding, and presumably fundamental, brain processes. In other words, images are *functions* of brain events, and it may well be the underlying brain events upon which the images depend that are actually responsible for the superior learning and memory that has been demonstrated. Some contemporary researchers have expressed the opinion that there is a serious question as to whether or not images need to be consciously reportable in order to be effective. The problem appears to be difficult if not impossible to resolve on introspective evidence alone. In any event this line of investigation cannot be considered as giving unequivocal support to the active-role position, valuable as it may be on other grounds.

The various arguments for the utility of consciousness can be rebutted on the basis of their questionable causal relationship to the problem at issue. That is, they do not differentiate between the two roles assigned to consciousness. The evolutionary persistence argument is especially questionable, not only on the same grounds but also because there are a number of animal characteristics that have persisted for long periods of time in spite of their apparent inutility and even their occasional negative value (for example, the human vermiform appendix).

Sperry's fascinating research has not yet produced data that bear directly on the key issue of an active role for consciousness, as we have posed the problem. Sperry's results show very nicely that cortical activity in the left hemisphere can gain control of the organ of speech and thus lead to verbal reports, and that cortical activity in the right hemisphere can enable the subject to answer questions that call for a left-hand overt response but *not* questions that call for a verbal response. The right hemisphere can make a *nonverbal* language response, as indicated in the description of the research.

As for the interesting theoretical account developed by Sperry, it must be regarded as provocative but without substantial support at the present time. As Sperry himself notes, his account is advanced "on a tentative and speculative basis for its consideration alongside the alternative theories for explaining mind and consciousness available to date" (Sperry, 1969, p. 533). Sperry's suggestion quite obviously requires extensive elaboration and refinement as well as experimental testing, but in this need is little different from its long-honored competitors.

In sum, it does seem that all the various arguments that have been reviewed as supportive of the active role for consciousness can be questioned on the grounds that the fundamental operations may still be the primary brain processes that underlie *both* the behavioral and the experiential effects.

Behavioral–Introspective Observations

There are a large number of various types of behavioral–introspective situations that suggest the passivity of consciousness as a process. Foremost among these is the phenomenon of human speech. Although each of us may on occasion carefully plan what he says, more often oral speech is, or seems to be, entirely spontaneous. That is, we find ourselves saying things that may, on occasion, surprise even ourselves. And this statement does not apply merely to extremely impulsive or unusual situations. Characteristically there is little conscious planning in human discourse. Each of us often finds himself more or less in the role of a spectator, or auditor, of his own behavior (both covert and overt, it may be noted). Support for this assertion is not difficult to find in the literature. For example, there is the response of Alice in Wonderland to the admonishment that she think before she speak: "How can I know what I think till I see what I say?" More prosaically, there is the forthright admission by an experimental psychologist that, "None of us is very close to an understanding of how people create and understand sentences" (Osgood, 1968, p. 519).

The clear implication from this kind of easily obtained evidence is that conscious control, although frequently appearing to be central with regard to the direction and flow of behavior, is certainly not essential for either the creation or the maintenance of smooth and well-organized sequences of responses.

The essential passivity of human consciousness is also suggested by certain phenomena of memory. For example, most students have had the experience of an immediate impression of trueness or falseness in recognition on a particular test item, and of then attempting to bring to recall relevant information, on the basis of which the answer is changed. The consensus of experts seems to be that first impressions in such cases are more likely to be correct than not, so that first answers should not be changed in the absence of reasonably clear contradictory information. A parallel situation holds in more controlled, laboratory research. Thus as a leading researcher on consciousness has noted, "In judgmental tasks requiring difficult discimations it is not uncommon to find that subjects can make above-chance discriminations or show above-chance accuracy although they report a subjective feeling of 'pure' guessing" (Erikson, 1962, p. 24).

We may also experience in recall some bit of information—such as a name or a meaning—that is only vaguely familiar or may actually seem to be incorrect but that on closer inspection is ultimately shown to be correct, whereupon the feeling of rightness may also suddenly appear. One such experience recently occurred to me, when the meaning of the negative power (x^{-10}) was queried by an occupant of the household then enjoying the initial benefits of high school mathematical training. It had been some time since I had occasion to interpret this simple symbol and I was momentarily stymied. Very soon, however, an answer suggested itself: the reciprocal function $(1/x^{10})$. This recall came without any recognition of "rightness" but turned out to be correct.

Such vagaries of recall and recognition, coming from both directions (that is, recognition in the absence of recall, and recall in the absence of recognition), appear to be largely independent of consciousness as an active determinant. They thus add to the introspective evidence, of a gross but common nature and cumulatively persuasive, that consciousness plays more of a passive role than an active role in cognitive as well as other behavioral processes.

Experimental–Introspective Evidence

Suggestive as common introspective observations may be, they are no substitute for properly controlled, experimental evidence that can also be brought to bear, at least tangentially, on this problem. The nonessential role of consciousness in at least some phases of certain important functions, such as thinking and problem solving, is well attested. John Dewey's theory of problem solving emphasized the *incubation* period, during which nonconscious thought processes are assumed to operate to produce a number of alternative solutions. Experimental evidence for the role of presumably nonconscious factors in problem solving has been reported. For example, in one study subjects were presented with a difficult problem and then provided a subtle cue (such as the assistant's accidentally starting a string to swinging, when this operation was part of the solution of the problem). Subjects so aided preponderantly proceeded to solve the problem but generally did not report in subsequent questioning that they had noticed the cue.

Behavior and Awareness

A patent weakness in any research that attempts to assess learning in the absence of consciousness is the difficulty of making accurate inferences concerning consciousness or awareness on the basis of a subject's retrospective verbal reports. At some level, the behaving organism is always aware.

There are, however, experimental procedures relating to the present problem that do not entirely depend upon so slender a reed. Three types of such experimentation will be discussed: (1) learning without awareness, utilizing different experimental approaches; (2) verbal encoding, in which extremely rapid and presumably more or less "automatic" processing of words seems to occur; and (3) neurophysiological correlates of conscious and unconscious processes.

LEARNING WITHOUT AWARENESS. Because of the difficulty of eliminating consciousness as a potential factor in the normal human subject's behavior, as suggested above, there are relatively few reasonably clear-cut demonstrations of this phenomenon. In order to circumvent the typical subject's exceedingly effective perceptual and cognitive abilities an experimenter needs to resort to unusual research strategies.

One such strategy was devised to measure the dependence of performance on reinforcement (reward) of one response (eye blinking) when the subjects were told that they would be reinforced, and actually were initially reinforced, for another response (lever pressing). The pennies initially earned by the subjects for lever pressing continued to be paid, but now for eye blinking, which was covertly observed and recorded by an experimenter observing behind a one-way mirror. Changes in the eye-blinking response occurred in the usual manner observed to result from reinforcement in this kind of operant-conditioning situation; according to the experimenters, the subjects "never became aware of this change."

This study was criticized on the ground that the assumption of nonawareness in this experimental situation was unwarranted in the absence of specific experimental evidence. The same basic experimental procedure was applied to additional college students, ambulatory retarded subjects, and severely defective infants. Nine of the total of ten such subjects showed an increment in blinking in accordance with the reinforcement schedule. The results were considered particularly significant because three of the four retardates and both of the retarded infants, who were reinforced with food, demonstrated the learning. In the latter case especially there would seem to be little basis for assuming conscious control, because these severely retarded infants (who typically die before reaching the age of one year) have no visual motor control, although they do blink.

A more straightforward demonstration of effective conditioning of a small, covert response, of which conscious awareness could scarcely be expected, has been reported. Invisibly small thumb twitches were conditioned as responses that were effective in temporarily turning off or postponing a noise stimulus.

More recently, conditioning of a single motor (muscular) unit in young male subjects has been reported. Postconditioning questioning again indicated that most of the subjects were unaware of the reinforcement procedure actually used. Moreover, several had apparently adopted behavior patterns that they felt were effective but that, in many cases, did not even involve the muscle whose covert responding was actually conditioned. Consciousness can thus scarcely be posited as a very effective factor in this experimental demonstration of learning. It has recently been convincingly demonstrated that the involuntary musculature (e.g., heart and stomach walls), of which human subjects at least seem to have little conscious awareness, is sensitive to the same principles of instrumental (or reward-mediated) learning. This work also leaves little room for questioning that effective learning can occur in the absence of consciousness. The conclusion, therefore, seems justified that at least some kinds of learning, as well as many kinds of performance of previously learned behaviors, can occur in the absence of conscious control and direction.

VERBAL ENCODING. When a human perceives a word it seems to be immediately encoded, transformed, into a rich network of categories, but with a minimum of conscious effort. Such categorizations, according to one researcher on the process, "are achieved with very little conscious awareness of the subject of what he is doing" (Wickens, 1970, p. 12). Consequently, "subjects were usually unable to verbalize the encoding categories which they used" (Wickens, 1970, p. 13). It is assumed, for example, "that when a person hears the word 'horse,' it is encoded into the broader categories of beasts of burden, four-legged creatures, warm-blooded animals, and finally of animals in general" (Wickens, 1970, p. 1).

The data collected in such research indicate the operation of some extremely rapid and largely unconscious encoding mechanism: "We are unaware intellectually of the richness of the encoding of a single word. If we were to consciously recognize this richness, then so much time would be required for the perceptual ingestion of a single word that we could find it next to impossible to listen to a series of words and remember but the first and last of them" (Wickens, 1970, p. 1).

NEUROPHYSIOLOGICAL CORRELATES. Although new and interesting neurophysiological research techniques have been and are being developed in great variety, a single illustration will suffice. The problem of subliminal (below conscious threshold) perception has been a central and controversial one in psychology in recent years. The question is, "Does a subject 'perceive' some aspects of stimulation that are not sufficiently strong to result in conscious experience?" The methodological difficulties in determining whether or not perception is really subliminal are substantial, and there are theoretical difficulties to match. One way around some of these difficulties is to use very brief stimulus presentation durations to insure that there is little question as to the subliminal nature of the presumed perception.

Brain processes are measured directly at the time of stimulation by electrical potential-detecting apparatus. An experiment with this design showed clear evidence of electrocortical discrimination that was related to differences in stimulus content. Corresponding differential responses were revealed in verbal associations. These evidences of brain and behavioral differentiations were obtained in the presumed absence of any relevant conscious experience.

Advance of Physicochemical Explanation

Perhaps the most telling argument in favor of the passive view of consciousness is simply the manner in which the physicochemical interpretation has succeeded in storming, one by one, the various citadels of popular belief and mythology regarding the human body and its functions. Starting with the demonstration early in the seventeenth century that hydrostatic principles can explain the previously mysterious pumping of the blood from the heart through the body, the scientist, by applying similar ordinary engineering principles and sometimes more refined physicochemical knowledge, has been able similarly to fathom the mysteries of the other basic physiological systems. Production of "test-tube" babies, discovery of the secret of coding of heredity in the chromosome, even synthesis of simple forms of life all produce headlines in current newspapers. The nervous system and the mind remain as the one last fortress not yet successfully captured; even here tremendous progress has been made. One last major hurdle, perhaps the most difficult of all, is the very instrument by which science itself seems to operate —human consciousness. But the momentum is quite clearly on the side of the scientist who adopts the passive rather than the active view of the role of consciousness.

The basic care for a mechanistic, or physicochemical, interpretation of consciousness can be supported by certain observations by brain surgeons. In the course of surgery on human patients for the removal of brain tumors, electrical stimulation of various brain centers was found to be an effective means of determining the boundaries of the defective tissue. This technique also produced some interesting results with regard to the patient's ability to name objects and otherwise utilize thinking processes. For example, during electrical stimulation of a particular area of the cortex he might be able to describe the use of an object shown in a picture, such as a shoe, without being able to give its name; but such naming would immediately recover upon cessation of the electrical stimulation. More remarkable long-term memory effects were accidentally discovered when one patient was stimulated to an apparent reliving of some experience from childhood. This result has subsequently been confirmed in many other patients. The experience is very detailed and vivid to the patient and is entirely dependent upon the electrical stimulation. If it is stopped and started again in the same brain location the patient reports that the entire episode is again initiated, from the beginning. This result is referred to as *double consciousness* because it appears to coexist with the normal operating-room consciousness of the patient. Because no pain receptors are present in the brain tissues, there is no need for an anesthetic.

Such observations as these constitute undeniable evidence of the dependence of at least some form of consciousness, and by implication of all forms, upon the physical structures and functions of brain tissue. However, they are by no means the whole story. Probably the most critical development has been the demonstration of the central significance of the neurological network in the brainstem that is generally referred to as the *reticular activating system* (RAS). As already suggested (Chapter 1), this system has been shown to have some very important communicating functions. The RAS acts as a kind of switching device, controlling to some extent the information that is passed on to the higher brain centers in the cerebral cortex. Moreover, and most important for our present problem, it seems to serve as a switch for consciousness. Sleep can be experimentally induced in laboratory animals by the appropriate stimulation of a part of the RAS. Moreover, experiments have also suggested that there may be no difference in the pattern of electrical response in the cerebral cortex that results from external stimulation whether the animal is in a waking state, with a normally functioning RAS, or in an apparently unconscious state, with the RAS deactivated by general anesthesia. Thus it appears that the crucial determination of conscious states may somehow be located in the RAS rather than the cerebral cortex. This latter fact is of special importance because it touches most directly upon the key question of the role of consciousness. If it can be shown to be generally true—if, in other words, no difference can be demonstrated in brain activities as a function of the presence or absence of consciousness—a very strong presumptive case can indeed be made for its essentially passive role.

CONCLUSION

The case for a merely passive role for consciousness is persuasive, but it is not yet completely proved. We remind the reader that this survey of the problems of consciousness was initiated with the caution that no *ultimate* solutions are in sight, and that its objective was mainly to orient him with regard to the fundamental nature of the problems and the lines along which their resolutions may be expected. Moreover, it is quite possible, as proponents of the passive view have argued, that an ultimate understanding of the *essence* of consciousness may be forever beyond man's capacity—just as other phenomena of the real world may be (e.g., gravity, electricity, fire). That is to say, even though scientists understand how to manipulate and use such phenomena, what they "really" are, in the sense of fully understanding their causes and their origins, remains and may always remain obscure. If such ultimate mystery continues to shroud the phenomenon of consciousness, this does not mean that a useful set of laws concerning it cannot be developed, just as they have been for other natural phenomena. This kind of restricted understanding is the objective of the scientist, even if it may not satisfy all the demands of the philosopher.

One of the more interesting, and informative, collections of essays on the brain-consciousness-behavior issue is the volume *Brain and Conscious Experience,* edited by Eccles (1966). Among its many provocative papers by the most distinguished men in the field, the contribution of D. M. MacKay is especially noteworthy. His ingenious theory of the role of consciousness manages to maintain both free will and determinism—an achievement of immense significance regardless of its ultimate fate. (These topics are treated in Chapter 13.)

Notes

Mind

The term *mind* is usually defined rather loosely in terms of the "totality of conscious functions." However, alternative definitions of *mind* have been offered that can be strongly supported. Perhaps the most satisfactory of these is the definition of the functionalist school (Carr, 1925). The following commentary, for the substance of which I am indebted to Marion Bunch (personal communication, 1972), will be of interest to those who are concerned with this problem and wish to explore it further.

For Carr, mind was simply a group name for the main activities studied by psychology: perception, learning, memory, thinking, emotions, personality, and the like. The distinctive feature that all these activities have in common (and because of which they are called mental) is that they are reactions of the subject made in the light of his own past experiences. Elementary mental activities would thus be perception (getting information from the environment) and learning and memory (subsequent utilization of the information obtained by perception); these are seen as the basic concepts underlying most of the operational definitions of *mind.*

Consider the complete ament (a person with no "mind" at all). He has no ability to profit from past experience, although his nonmental physiological functions may be adequate (as seems to be true in the case of some of the vegetative organisms who can be found in chronic mental hospitals). The dement (a person who is mentally deviant) would, on the other hand, be described as one who has lost the capacity to behave in a socially acceptable manner, or to utilize his past experience properly. For the functionalist theory, *mind* is a generic term for a group of activities and is not merely synonymous with consciousness. For this reason the term *mind* when so defined has little direct bearing on the "mind"–body issue, which really deals with consciousness and its relationship to bodily processes.

Imagery

The rapidly burgeoning literature on imagery is highlighted by Paivio's 1971 book, which is a comprehensive coverage of the role of images, as in language; see also Segal (1973) and Sheehan (1972).

Altered States of Consciousness

Altered states of consciousness, mainly but not entirely involving use of drugs, have been critically examined by Tart in a book of readings (1969) and a comprehensive review article (1972). Tart argues for the importance of recognizing the role that state of consciousness plays in the development of scientific laws, and the consequent necessity for "state-specific sciences." He also points out the inadequacy of the assumption, apparently commonly made, that normal states of consciousness are essentially similar in all people. On the contrary, Tart thinks that very great *normal* individual differences occur, and are concealed by the commonalities of language. As he says, "For example, some people think in images, others in words. Some can voluntarily anesthetize parts of their body, most cannot. Some recall past events by imaging the scene and looking at the relevant details; others use complex verbal processes with no images" (1972, p. 1208).

Teyler's (1972) *Altered States of Consciousness* offers additional readings. An especially interesting version of the many ascientific efforts to impart meaning to life is Watts's *On the Taboo Against Knowing Who You Are* (1967). This book presents a popular adaptation of Hindu Vedenta philosophy. It eliminates all apparent dichotomies, such as that between mind and body, by regarding all the elements of the universe as united. Wallace and Benson (1972) review the physiological research on altered states of consciousness and conclude that significant bodily changes do occur in them.

Theory of Consciousness

Sperry's (1969) "emergent" theory of consciousness was attacked by Bindra (1970) on the grounds that (1) he had really proposed two old and independent propositions, the one concerning the emergent phenomena of cerebral functioning, the other presuming a causal influence by consciousness on neural activity and behavior, and (2) there is no evidence for the latter. Sperry's detailed rejoinder (1970) to this critique notes that it is the combination of these two ideas that is new and stresses the "mutual interdependence" of consciousness and brain processes, denying that either is primary. He compares his hypothesis with a number of more familiar, competing interpretations (e.g., epiphenomenalism, with which his hypothesis most directly contrasts because of the causal role it assigns to consciousness acting on neural processes).

Sperry's interpretation can also be attacked on the ground that he has allowed traditional language to influence his thinking unduly. For example, it can be maintained that what he has shown has little to do with consciousness but does show, rather, that cortical activity in the left cerebral hemisphere can control the organ of speech and thereby lead to verbal reports to the experimenter, whereas cortical activity in the right hemisphere can mediate answers to questions that call for a right-hand response but *not* questions that call for a *verbal* response.

Schwartz and Higgins (1971) performed the experiment on change in heart rate described in the text.

Verbal Learning and Awareness

The application of reinforcement operations to human verbal learning progressed through three more or less clearly definable stages. In the first of these, positive results were obtained, presumably demonstrating learning in the absence of conscious determinants. When responses of a certain type, such as plural nouns, were made, the experimenter "reinforced" them by saying, for example, "good" or merely "hmmm"; the number of such responses relative to other response categories was then found to increase, often markedly. In the second stage, more careful assessment of possible awareness factors led to the general conclusion that *only* those subjects who had actually been aware of the response contingencies (that is, which type of responses would be followed by "reinforcing" stimulus events) did in fact show the predicted increment in response strength; it was therefore concluded that the early positive results had been prematurely hailed as evidence for conditioning without awareness. In the third, contemporary stage much more refined experimental techniques are being applied with a number of interesting developments.

Experiments have been reported in which the relationship between response strengthening and awareness of the response-reinforcement contingency is more carefully assessed. One has shown that when assessment of awareness is made on *every* trial *during* training (rather than only after the conclusion of training, as was originally done, or even after each block of, say, twenty-five training trials, as was later done), there is evidence for performance gains made prior to reported awareness. The interpretation was advanced that the reported awareness in such situations may be a function of the prior performance gains but would not be detected unless frequent assessment were made. The experimental question thus remains an open one, subject to the kind of continuing improvement in experimental technique that is characteristic of the advance of an active science.

The use of postexperimental questionnaires is illustrated by studies of "motivated forgetting." Subjects were instructed to attempt to forget selected verbal cues presented during a memory session. They were then shown to be less able to recall such cues. In a final experiment in the study the subjects were given an intensive questionnaire. On the basis of their answers to this questionnaire eleven subjects were classified as "suppressors"; there was evidence that they had in some way deliberately or consciously tried less hard to recall. Another twenty-two subjects were classified as "repressors" because of the lack of such evidence. The retention scores of these two classes of subject were compared, and a very similar pattern of results was found. It was concluded that conscious cognitive processes are not necessary in this kind of motivated forgetting.

A major development in the contemporary stage of research on this problem concerns the finding that awareness is itself an important experimental problem. As had earlier been noted, "Awareness should enter into lawful relationships no less fundamental than any other, and we may have been throwing away the best part" (Dulany, 1962, p. 113).

The preceding research has been reported as follows. Greenspoon (1955) and Taffel (1955) performed the paradigmatic early experiments. The basis for concluding, in the second phase of the verbal conditioning research, that awareness is necessary is summarized by Spielberger (1962). Kennedy (1970, 1971) reports the research with more frequent assessment of awareness by verbal report. The recent research on "motivated forgetting" was by Weiner and Reed (1969).

Conditioning Without Awareness

The first research described, on eye blinking, was by Keehn et al. (1965). The subsequent research, utilizing the retarded subjects, was by Keehn (1967). Conditioning of the minute and invisible thumb twitches was reported by Hefferline and Perera (1963) and Hefferline and Keenan (1961). Lloyd and Leibrecht (1971) performed the research on conditioning of single motor units in human subjects, and Miller (1969) has reviewed the research on instrumental (reward-mediated) conditioning of autonomic functions; that research is described in more detail in Chapter 11.

The best single comprehensive source of material on this complex problem is a set of papers (by F. H. Kanfer, I. Maltzman, D. E. Dulany, and H. H. Kendler) in *Verbal Behavior and General Behavior Theory,* edited by Dixon and Horton (1968). An earlier volume, *Behavior and Awareness* [see Eriksen (1962)], is also still quite useful. The cognitive position is well represented by Spielberger (1965) and Spielberger and DeNike (1966). Among the more recent experimental research that indicates the great complexity of the problem is research by Uleman (1971) in which the conclusion is drawn that whether awareness (the cognitive position) or conditioning (the behavioristic position) comes first depends upon which of several types of awareness is measured.

Wickens (1970) summarizes the research on encoding of words that was described in the text. The early research on awareness of cues in problem solving was reported by Maier (1931). Shevrin and Fritzler (1968) performed the experiment on "electrocortical discrimination" described in the text.

Neurophysiology of Subjective Experience

Recent research reviewed by John (1972) suggests one direction in which the identification of special correlates of subjective experience may proceed. Johns cites evidence from both human and animal subjects that "indicates that when a specific memory is retrieved, a temporal pattern of electrical activity peculiar to that memory is released in numerous regions of the brain" (p. 862). He concludes as follows: "These findings suggest that the subjective experience of remembering is correlated with [this] release . . . and provide some basis for the speculation that coherent temporal patterns in the average activity of anatomically extensive neural ensembles may constitute the neurophysiological basis of subjective experience" (p. 863).

Other recent research on humans has revealed the existence of so-called associative cortex potentials. There are signals from the points of the cerebral cortex generally identified as the neural seat of mental functions, such as language. Exciting research results like these are discussed in books on evoked brain potentials by Regan (1972) and Shagass (1972).

Subliminal Perception

An unusually broad conceptualization of the problem of subliminal perception is provided by Hilgard in an essay appropriately entitled "What Becomes of the Input from the Stimulus?" (1962). A more recent comprehensive treatment is offered by Dixon (1971).

The Physicochemical Position

Wooldridge, in his two books *The Machinery of the Brain* (1963) and *Mechanical Man* (1968), has been a leading spokesman for the view that mental phenomena, including consciousness, are functions of physical and chemical (brain) processes, nothing more. These books are fascinating reading regardless of one's own opinions on the matter and can be profitably examined by persons with unsympathetic views to their theme.

An Ultimate Explanation of Consciousness?

Wooldridge (1968) has suggested that an ultimate explanation of consciousness may be out of reach. Turning of attention to the nervous system, now that the genetic code has been "broken," is sometimes suggested as the next major phase in the research efforts of molecular biologists (e.g., Stent, 1968). This author suggests that "the inability to even imagine any reasonable molecular explanation for conscious life still offers some hope that 'other laws of physics' may yet turn up through study of the nervous system" (p. 395). Although this kind of suggestion seems to be more impressive when the brain is considered as the judge of its own products, the same statement can be made with regard to the other phenomena mentioned (that is, flame, electricity, gravity) so that the brain–brain confrontation is not different in principle.

Sensation

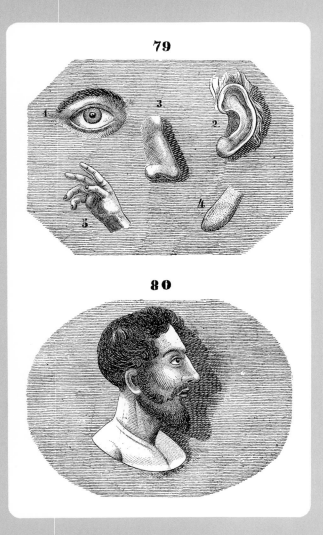

The classical five senses shown on this page are from an eighteenth-century Italian book. Seeing, hearing, smelling, tasting, and touching are the ways we gain information about the world around us, and the subject of the following chapter.

n this chapter we begin our consideration of the orthodox subject matter of psychology. Appropriately, we begin with the topic that initiated psychology as a science—sensation.

Discussion of general problems of sensation precedes that of any particular sensory system. The fundamental role of sensory processes, the nature of the environmental energies that are effective stimuli, the role of the receptors in transducing and decoding energy are among these topics. The last general topic is that of the concept of the threshold, or the amount of energy change in the stimulus necessary for a sensory response. Discussion here includes a description of signal detection, a recent theory that has threatened the concept of the threshold.

The bulk of the chapter is concerned with the important sensory modalities. For each modality there is some description of the anatomy and physiology of the sense organs, the physical correlates of sensation, and then a discussion of the major facets of the sensations themselves.

Our discussion emphasizes the four great sources of environmental stimulation: electromagnetic waves (light and heat), mechanical pressure (sound and tactual stimulation), chemical substances (smells and tastes), and temperature (heat and cold).

Vision, as the primary sense in man, is the first sense treated, and also receives the greatest amount of attention. Audition is next, followed by the chemical senses (olfaction and gustation), the skin senses (touch, pain, warmth, and cold), and the body senses (vestibulation and kinesthesis).

Types of Sensory Processes

Sensory processes provide the only means of contact between the organism and his environment, internal as well as external. External environmental events (those occurring outside the organism) are sensed by means of specialized receptors called *exteroceptors* (e.g., the eye and the ear), and internal environmental events by *interoceptors* (e.g., pressure-sensitive receptors within the viscera, or inner organs, such as the intestinal tract and the circulatory system). Movements of the body itself are sensed by *proprioceptors* (e.g., the semicircular canals in the inner ear).

Because of their prominence in human experience and behavior, seeing and hearing are sometimes referred to as the major senses; the remaining senses are then placed in the minor category. The sense organs involved in seeing and hearing are more usefully distinguished from the other exteroceptors by the fact that they function as *distance* receptors; that is, they operate quickly and efficiently when the initiating physical events (the stimuli) are at some distance from the organism. The biological utility of this feature lies in the fact that it enables the organism both to find prey and to escape from danger more effectively. The skin senses, on the other

Table 5-1 Human Sensory Modalities Categorized by Type of Receptor and Physical Stimuli

Type of Receptor	Physical Sensitivity			
	Temperature-Sensitive	Pressure-Sensitive	Light-Sensitive	Chemical-Sensitive
Exteroceptors				
Vision			X	
Audition		X		
Olfaction (smell)				X
Gustation (taste)				X
Touch		X		
Pain	X	X		X
Warmth	X			
Cold	X			
Proprioceptors				
Body erectness		X		
Movement and awareness of body position		X		
Interoceptors				
Heart rate		X		X
Blood pressure		X		
Oxygen content of blood		X		X
Relative acidity of blood				X
Breathing rate		X		
Chemical composition of blood				X
Satiation		X		
Excretory function		X		
Core body temperature	X			

hand, operate relatively inefficiently, or not at all, when the initiating stimuli are at a distance.

Table 5-1 provides an overview of some of the various human senses. They are categorized into three sets according to their locus of operation, and the correlated physical changes that serve as stimuli are also indicated.

The significantly exclusive role of the senses in establishing and maintaining contact between an organism and his environment is convincingly indicated by imagining a man to be enclosed by successive layers of sensory receptors. As each such layer is removed, less sensory function remains, until finally all avenues of sensory contact with the environment are gone. What is left? A purely rational being, with absolutely no sensory contact with the environment or with his own body function, is almost impossible for us to conceive. The evidence from sensory impoverishment research, discussed below, suggests that an unusually severe degree of sensory reduction produces disorientation and bizarre experiences and behaviors.

SELECTIVITY OF SENSORY SYSTEMS

Man's sensory systems detect only a very small proportion of the great variety of physical energies in his environment. A frequently cited illustration of this fact is the electromagnetic energy spectrum, shown in Figure 5-1. The human eye is sensitive to only a very small part of this system, those energy waves possessing a length that ranges from approximately 400 nanometers (or millionths of a meter), the violet end of the visual spectrum, to 700 nanometers, the other, red end. Except for heat (from infrared radiation), the other kinds of electromagnetic energy can be detected by various devices that man has built but not by any of his own sensory receptors. These forms of energy differ quantitatively from light energy in terms of wavelength and wave frequency, which are inversely related; that is, because the speed of all the waves is the same (186,000 miles per second), the shorter waves have higher frequencies, and the longer waves lower frequencies.

In general, physical stimuli that are most important in the adjustment of any given species, in terms of evolutionary survival (Supplement A-2), are detected. Thus man is primarily a seeing and hearing organism, with functional but relatively poorly developed chemical senses (e.g., smell and taste); the dog, on the other hand, is primarily a smelling and hearing organism, with vision less well developed.

SENSATION AND PERCEPTION

Gathering information from the environment is sometimes regarded as the fundamental function of perception. Perception is commonly distinguished from sensation as being in one way or another a more inclusive function. Perception thus

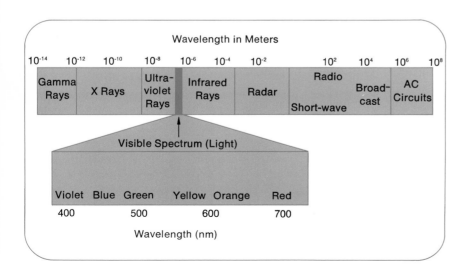

5-1 The electromagnetic spectrum has an enormous range. Wavelengths vary from the extremely short gamma rays (measured in billionths of an inch) to the radio waves and AC waves (measured in miles). The visible spectrum, shown below, constitutes a tiny fraction of the total energy spectrum.

usually refers to the overall apprehension of the environment, whereas sensation refers, more narrowly, to the specific ways in which different kinds of environmental energies are detected and processed. However, perceptual function does not necessarily consist of merely adding meaning to sensory experience; as a matter of fact, conscious sensory experiences may not even be involved. Rather, the organism is conceived to be an active seeker of information, utilizing any cues from the environment that promise to be useful and combining sensory contacts of various sorts. It is interesting that the five traditional senses are used in this kind of active searching; the organism looks, listens, touches, smells, and tastes. From the totality of sensory contact thus established it is able to construct a perceptual representation of environmental objects and events that enables it to avoid danger and secure food and security for itself.

There are any number of ways in which perception does not simply follow sensory capacity. Illusions, described in Chapter 6, constitute one common example of this failure of correlation. More generally important, there is the pervasive slanting of perception by such conditions as expectations and other forms of learning. This failure of perception to be completely veridical (true) with respect to the physical dimensions of the environment constitutes an additional kind of restriction on man and other organisms. Not only does the sensory apparatus of any species fail to respond to a very high percentage of environmental energies, but what is within the range of sensory capacity is often represented incorrectly by purely physical standards.

THE STIMULUS

The concept of stimulus is a deceptively simple one. Psychologists have offered all sorts of definitions, in accordance with their own special interests. Most often a stimulus is defined as a kind of spur to experience (sensation) and/or behavior. But even this apparently straightforward view can be qualified so as to complicate matters. Watson himself, in proposing the fully objective system of psychology he called behaviorism, was careful to broaden the meaning of stimulus (and response) to include large-scale as well as small-scale units of description. It is quite apparent that as any organism matures it learns to attend to increasingly finer gradations in the environmental energies that surround it, so that the effective stimulation for it becomes accordingly more and more subtle. This is true of social stimuli—cues produced by other organisms—as well as stimulation from inanimate objects and events. Thus a man may respond to slight variations in female speech that as a boy he would not have noticed, and a woman to surreptitious male glances that as a young girl she might have overlooked.

The concept of stimulus, no matter how defined, cannot be understood without reference to the environment, and particularly to the environmental energies that constitute the main external stimulating forces that act upon the organism. Before proceeding to outline some of the manners in which stimuli are studied, therefore, the major sources of environmental energy change will be briefly surveyed.

ENVIRONMENTAL ENERGIES

All the animals on earth are immersed either in the layer of air that surrounds the planet or the bodies of water that lie upon it. Except for external sources of stimulation from space (the most obvious of which are the sun, the moon, and the stars), all external stimulation comes from objects and events on the land or in the atmosphere or water. The physical nature of land, atmosphere, and water thus underlies much of the stimulation that is perceived by earth-dwelling creatures, and has been therefore a potent factor in the evolution of sensory as well as response systems.

Physical Energies

Several major categories of stimulation can be identified: electromagnetic, mechanical, chemical, and thermal. These are summarized in relation to the various sensory receptors in Table 5-1. Figure 5-1 shows the range of physical energies in the electromagnetic spectrum; for man the visual light band and the infrared (heat) band are most important as sources of stimuli. Mechanical stimulation comes primarily in the form of pressure on the skin, from solid bodies mainly, and vibrations of the compressible medium, mainly air, in which man lives; the former stimuli mediate tactual sensitivity, the latter auditory. Chemical volatility of substances such as foods produces molecules that are propagated through the surrounding medium to stimulate the chemical senses of smell and taste. Temperature effects in the surrounding medium, normally air, and contiguous objects produce thermal sensitivity.

Social Stimulation

Stimulation from other living organisms constitutes a most potent source of energy change. Nevertheless, all such social cues must operate via one or more of the physical energies described above; there is no other, more direct way for one organism to stimulate another. (The problem of extrasensory perception, or ESP, is discussed in another chapter.)

The special significance of social stimuli is a consequence primarily of the crucial role that other organisms play. For example, they serve as sexual partners and parents, insuring propagation and the preservation of the species. They are also potential predators, able and willing to convert other living things to foodstuff, or may themselves be food sources. The higher animals especially have evolved in such a manner that visual and auditory displays, as well as chemical messages sent by means of special odors, mediate these various roles. The animate world is full of announcements of sexual readiness; familiar examples are the striking visual display of the peacock and the splendidly varied auditory productions of the songbirds.

Apart from these special functions, the animate environment offers certain other distinctions from the inanimate. For example, animals are spontaneously active, unlike inanimate objects, and so produce more variable and less predictable stimulation. Moreover, they grow and develop, so that changes in their bodies and their behavioral potential must be accommodated by other animals. For all of these reasons social stimuli come to play key roles in the lives of all animals, including the lower as well as the so-called higher (that is, more complex) forms.

Cultural Stimulation

The incredibly complex environment of the human animal is due to his production and maintenance of various "artifacts"—both "material," in the form of physical objects such as tools and sculptures, and "immaterial," in the form of signaling behaviors and symbolic systems such as religion, music, and language. The latter type of artifact, especially, underlies most if not all of man's cultural environment. His ability to use vocalizations as substitutes for actions, and to build upon this base an enormously complex system of coded meanings, most clearly distinguishes man from all other animals. Although various other forms of expressive behavior, such as gestures, are important, it is man's communication with man that produces most of the cues each of us must learn to respond to as stimuli.

SENSORY TRANSDUCTION AND ENCODING

All stimulation consists of changes in energy. Each sensory system, or *modality*, is specialized to react to a particular form of energy change. When this energy change is effective, it may be referred to as an *adequate stimulus*. However, a further change in energy is also involved in the process of detection by the sensory receptors; such energy change, from the environmental energy to neural excitation, is called *transduction*.

Various types of transduction are involved in the different reception processes. For example, vision is dependent upon photochemical changes in which the chemical substance in the retinal receptors (rhodopsin, or visual purple) decomposes when the retina is stimulated by electromagnetic energy within the light spectrum. Receptors for hearing, touch, and the body senses (kinesthesis and proprioception) transduce mechanical energy into electrical. Chemical energy is transduced into electrical by the olfactory and gustatory (smell and taste) receptors in the nasal cavity and on the tongue.

Once the energy has been converted into neural impulses by the transduction process within the receptors, the information concerning the environment that is contained within the stimulus needs to be maintained and transmitted. The process by means of which this information is thus preserved and passed on by the nervous system is called *stimulus encoding*. The whole story is by no means clear, but some of the major steps in stimulus encoding have been worked out. Part of this process consists of specialization within the receptor itself. For example, the retina of the eye has now been shown to contain three different kinds of color receptors so that the distribution of primary colors in the stimulus can be represented by the degree of stimulation of the differentially sensitive receptors. Similarly, the thermal receptors in the skin are differentiated in accordance with their sensitivity to warm or cold temperatures.

Another part of the process involves complex interactions within the nervous system that operate to encode stimulus information at later stages in the total process. Much still remains to be discovered about these mechanisms, but reciprocal facilitation and inhibition can be mentioned as one of the more prominent mechanisms involved. For example, it has been shown that certain vision nerve fibers not only are excited by one type of color receptor but are also inhibited by another. That is, a receptor cell that is stimulated by light in the red range of the spectrum not only will excite certain nerve fibers but will at the same time inhibit certain others. In general, the synchronized operation of sensory receptor and nervous system has evolved to insure a reasonable degree of fidelity in both the detection and the transmission of the information available in the environment by means of these fundamental transduction and encoding processes.

Receptors

Receptors are cells that are specialized to detect some kind of energy change. Such sensory cells are found throughout the body, in various kinds of tissue, and in the muscles, joints, and tendons. More importantly they are found concentrated in special body structures called sense organs. The more obvious examples of these organs, such as our own eyes and ears, are quite familiar to all of us, but some of the less well-known sense organs that have evolved in certain animals are indeed remarkable. For example, consider the surface-dwelling fish that preys on marine organisms at the surface of the water. It has a specialized sense organ on the top of its head that is sensitive to ripples in the surface of the water produced by potential prey. Mechanical stimulation by the ripples is sensed, and the direction of the source determined. Apparently the distance as well as the direction of the ripple-producing object can be detected in this way.

The Threshold

As psychology emerged from physiology and philosophy, the relationship of stimulus and response was a critical problem. Discrete stimuli, unlike the flux of energies of various sorts that characterize the everyday world, were used in the laboratory studies. This procedure—the isolation of a stimulus event—has been characteristic of much psychological research and practically all research in sensory physiology.

One of the first questions raised in such analytic study of sensation concerns how much stimulation is required for the various sensory responses. This is the problem of the *threshold*, defined as the amount of physical energy required either to produce a sensation from a particular stimulus or to cause a change in sensation by a stimulus that has already been detected. The former function is generally labeled the *absolute* threshold, the latter function is referred to as the *difference limen*.

The threshold is usually defined in terms of the physical value for which an observer is able to detect stimulation or a change in stimulation on half of the test trials.

Signal Detection

By far the most influential of all recent stimulus measurement techniques has been that of *signal detection*. The major advantage of this technique is that it takes into account important factors other than just the strength of the physical stimulus. For example, the standard or classical methods have no way of taking motivational variables into account.

The success of signal-detection methodology is a result of the separation of the concept of *signal* from that of *noise,* which is the random and unpredictable stimulation that is always assumed to be present in some degree. The subject's task is to decide whether the noise has in fact been exceeded by the typically very weak true signal that is used in determination of absolute threshold.

In signal detection research the emphasis is on the *criterion* that the observer uses in deciding whether or not a signal is present on any particular trial. Signal-detection theory assumes that a strongly motivated observer or an observer who is more willing to take risks will use a lower criterion for deciding whether or not a signal has occurred—that is, such observers are more likely to report signals even when they were in reality not presented. This outcome, called a *false alarm,* is one of four possible outcomes in the typical signal-detection situation. The observer might also fail to report a real signal (a *miss*). He can also, of course, report a signal that has occurred (a *hit*) or correctly not report one when none has really occurred (a *pass*).

By varying the reward (e.g., money) associated with hits, or the punishment (e.g., loss of money) associated with false alarms, the experiments can effectively alter the subject's criterion and strikingly modify his signal-detection behavior.

Signal-detection methodology and theory have tended to supplant the more traditional psychophysical methods because they bring the important motivational and personality variables that contribute to sensory function into the open and make them available for investigation. The concept of a fixed threshold, with some single "true" value independent of experimental conditions, can no longer be defended. The concept of threshold itself can of course be accommodated within the signal-detection framework, but account must be taken of the relevance of other various external factors.

No sense is more important to man than vision. Identification and location of objects in the environment are mainly accomplished visually. Our treatment of visual sensation will cover only the highlights of this vast subject. The major topics treated, for each of the other sensory modalities as well as vision, are the sense organ (or receptors), the physical energy correlates of the major sensory attributes, and the more important sensory functions, including some attention to sensory defects and theories of how the transduction process operates.

Vision

THE EYE

ANATOMY. The gross anatomy of the human eye is diagrammatically shown in Figure 5-2. Superficially at least, the spherical eye is comparable to a camera in both its structure and its function. The essential parts of a simple camera, therefore, are also shown, for comparison, in Figure 5-3; the analogy is instructive but it must be remembered that the eye is not the same as a camera.

STRUCTURE OF THE RETINA. The actual visual receptors, the *rods* and the *cones,* are located at the far end of the retina, behind several layers of neurons that gather

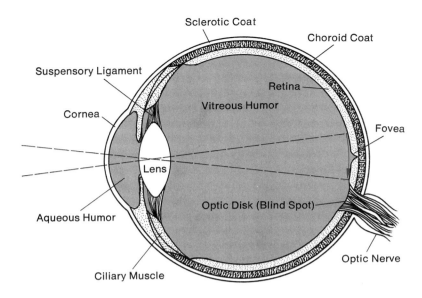

Sclerotic Coat

Choroid Coat

Suspensory Ligament

Retina

Vitreous Humor

Cornea

Fovea

Lens

Aqueous Humor

Optic Disk (Blind Spot)

Ciliary Muscle

Optic Nerve

5-2 Cross-section view of the human eye. As light rays pass through the cornea and the lens of the eye they are bent (refracted) and focused on the retina, normally on the fovea. The lens is an elastic body that changes shape—accommodates—in accordance with the distance of the object being looked at; near objects require a thicker and far objects a thinner lens for proper focusing. The common visual defects of *nearsightedness* and *farsightedness* are the consequences of a poor fit between the ability of the lens to accommodate and the distance between the retina and the cornea-refracting system.

together into the *optic nerve.* The optic nerve from each eye is split at the optic chiasma, with fibers from the same side of each retina rejoining on the way to the higher brain centers. The retinal structures and the optic nerve are all embryologically actually part of the brain itself, so that the complex interrelationships among them may in one sense be considered to be like internal brain connections.

The retina contains two other features of special interest. The *blind spot,* or optic disk, which has no rods or cones, occurs at the point where the optic nerve enters the eye, somewhat below and to the nasal side of the center; its existence can be easily demonstrated by means of Figure 5-4. The more centrally located *fovea* contains only cones and is the fixation point for normal vision because it is the most sensitive area for acuity and color vision. The approximately 5 million cones in each eye are concentrated in the fovea and the immediately surrounding area, falling off in frequency as the periphery (outside) of the retina is approached.

Rods and Cones

The two types of receptor cells, the rods and the cones, play differential roles in visual function. The more numerous rods function only in brightness vision and are especially sensitive both to low intensities of light and to movement. We can see better out of the "corner of the eye" (the outside or periphery) both at night and for the detection of movement, because the rods are more thickly concentrated around the periphery of the retina. A simple way to verify this fact is to pick out a fairly faint star in the evening sky. Looking directly at it, with its image fixed on the fovea and therefore activating cones, is much less effective than looking at it through the side of the eye. When one does look to the side of the object, it becomes much clearer and steady, because it is seen by means of the rods, which function better in dim light.

The cones function for color vision (*memory hint:* co nes = co lor) and are efficient

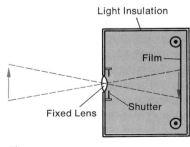

Light Insulation

Film

Fixed Lens

Shutter

5-3 Schematic cross section of a simple box camera. Note that the optics of focusing is similar to the human eye in that the image is cast on the sensitive surface (retina or film) upside down.

5-4 Demonstration of the blind spot. Close your left eye and fixate with your right eye on the hat at approximately 12 inches distance. As you move the paper closer the rabbit will momentarily disappear and then reappear, its disappearance indicating the point at which it is focused on the blind spot.

for seeing details under strong illumination. Both color and fine detail are best seen when objects are looked at directly, because this places the focus on the fovea.

The biochemistry of rod function has been especially well detailed in recent research. A major role in rod vision is played by the chemical compound *rhodopsin* (also called visual purple). It is bleached by light and transformed into other chemical substances. Vitamin A is intimately involved in this action; a deficiency of it thus leads to failure of rod function and poor night vision (hence the admonition to eat foodstuffs with large amounts of vitamin A, such as carrots, for improving visual function under conditions of low illumination). These chemical processes somehow transduce the light energy activating the receptors into neural energy transmitted over the optic nerve to various brain centers, ultimately to the *occipital cortex*, at the rear of the head, which is the major visual center in the brain. The photochemical processes are reversible so that rhodopsin is reconstituted from the components produced in its breakdown.

PHYSICAL CORRELATES OF VISUAL SENSATION

The three major experiential (sensory) attributes of vision are *brightness, hue,* and *saturation* (amount of hue). Their physical correlates—the particular energy changes with which each is associated—are listed in Table 5-2. As already indicated

Table 5-2 Quality, Intensity, and Composition Attributes of Visual and Auditory Sensations with Correlated Physical Energies

	Vision		Audition	
	Sensory	Physical	Sensory	Physical
Receptor / Energy	retina	electromagnetic radiation	cochlea	mechanical pressure
Attribute				
Quality	hue	wavelength (400–700 nm)	pitch	wave frequency (20–20,000 Hz)
Intensity	brightness	wave amplitude	loudness	wave amplitude
Composition (purity)	saturation	wave complexity	timbre	wave complexity

(see Figure 5-1), the visual light spectrum is a very tiny fraction of the total spectrum of electromagnetic energies. These range from waves as short as .00000000000001 meter to some as long as 1 million meters, with the light spectrum running only from about 400 to 700 millionths of a meter (nanometers). Immediately below the light spectrum, in terms of wavelength, is the ultraviolet range, and the infrared rays are immediately above it. Still shorter radiations are cosmic rays, gamma rays, and X-rays; radiations involved in radar, FM and AM radio broadcasting, television, and AC electrical circuitry are among the higher wavelengths.

Differences in hue are associated with differences in wavelength, with the shortest radiations producing violet and the longest red sensations. Differences in amplitude of radiation (intensity) are associated with experiential differences in brightness. The saturation dimension refers to the deepness (purity) of hue; highly saturated colors are produced by relatively homogeneous wavelengths. This fact is obviously related to the composition of sunlight (white light), which contains all the spectral wavelengths. Use of a prism, as shown in Plate 1, readily demonstrates the heterogeneous nature of sunlight, broken down into its component spectral wavelengths (and the corresponding colors thus experienced). The degree of heterogeneity of wavelength, and the corresponding degree to which white light is approximated, thus determines the amount of saturation in a visual sensation.

BRIGHTNESS

Brightness is the most primitive attribute of visual sensation. Some very simple organisms, whose visual sense organ is merely a collection of light-sensitive cells, are able to detect the presence or the absence of light. In the higher organisms, with the duplex (rod and cone) system of light receptors, brightness is a much more complex function. This conclusion follows from the fact that the rods and the cones each have separate sensitivity curves for brightness; that is, the relationship between experienced brightness and wavelength is different for them. One way of measuring sensitivity is in terms of absolute thresholds—the minimum amount of light energy needed to produce a visual sensation.

Separate visibility curves for rod vision (technically called *scotopic*) and cone vision (technically called *photopic*) are shown in Figure 5-5. Two features of these curves are noteworthy. First, the rods are much more sensitive to small amounts of stimulation, as indicated by the considerably lower threshold values for the scotopic curve. Second, the point of greatest sensitivity—the lowest threshold value for each curve—varies, with the rods most sensitive at about 511 nanometers and the cones most sensitive at about 555 nanometers.

The absolute threshold for brightness is dependent upon the state of the eyes, or more precisely, upon the degree of dark adaptation of the rods and the cones. The duplex curve shown in Figure 5-6 is a function of *dark adaptation* (allowing the eyes to remain in the dark for some time) first for the cones and later for the rods. The curve is obtained by repeatedly testing a subject for the weakest light stimulation that he can detect (the absolute threshold) without regard to wavelength, as his

5-5 Relative brightnesses of equally intensive lights of different wavelengths for (a) scotopic (rod) vision and (b) photopic (cone) vision. Note that the two curves have different peaks; the brightest light for scotopic vision has a wavelength of around 511 nm, the brightest light for photopic vision a wavelength of around 555 nm.

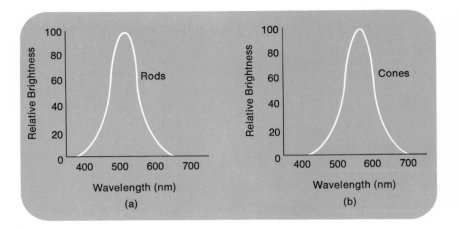

eyes are maintained in a completely darkened room and so allowed to adapt over a relatively long period of time. Full adaptation of the cones occurs quickly, after approximately five minutes in a dark environment, and the initial decline in threshold thus reflects their progressively more sensitive condition. The rods adapt much more slowly but also to a much greater degree, so that the very much greater improvement in sensitivity shown in the second decline in the threshold curve is a function of their adaptation; it is estimated that after complete adaptation the rods are able to detect light intensities only one ten-thousandth as great as those detected before dark adaptation was started.

Light adaptation of both rods and cones also occurs, but at a more rapid rate. Rods stimulated by high levels of light simply fail to function, so that the entire burden of seeing is thus taken over by the cones.

The facts of dark adaptation, especially with regard to night vision, have interesting and important implications for behavior. For example, during wartime fighter pilots needed to stay alert for night-time duty at all times. Moreover, if they were to function most efficiently, and most safely, they needed to be able to see the bombing planes that were their target under conditions of very low illumination. For this reason it was necessary to keep their eyes as dark adapted as possible in order to save the valuable time that would be necessary for effective dark adaptation after the bombing raid was first discovered. But keeping all these men permanently in dark rooms to maintain dark adaptation in their rods was not feasible because it would have deprived them of visual sensitivity for unpredictably long periods of time.

An ingenious solution to this problem was worked out as the result of the suggestion of an experimental psychologist familiar with the kind of facts of dark adaptation. The rods are very slightly stimulated by the long wavelengths, around 700 nanometers, whereas the cones are strongly stimulated by these wavelengths. The fighter pilots were therefore equipped with goggles with red lenses, transmitting only wavelengths above 620 nanometers and allowing the rods to remain unused and ready for service in the dark. This device enabled the men to lead

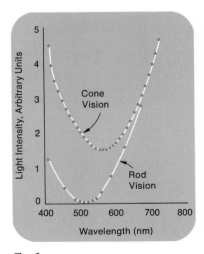

5-6 Photopic (cone) and scotopic (rod) visibility (spectral luminosity) curves compared. Each point on each curve represents the minimum amount of light of a given wavelength that can be detected.

5-7 Brightness contrast. Do the two stars appear equally bright? They would if brightness sensation were determined only by the actual physical intensity, which is equal. The fact that these stars are seen as different in brightness illustrates the operation of the brightness contrast phenomenon.

normal visually oriented lives, utilizing cone vision at usual illumination intensities, and at the same time to keep their rods in a highly advanced state of dark adaptation while they waited for the call to duty. A similar treatment was used by sailors in advance of their night look-out duties.

One other important determinant of brightness remains to be described. This is the context around the object whose brightness is being evaluated. Figure 5-7 demonstrates the role of context. First compare the relative brightness of the two medium-gray stars, one surrounded by a dark and the other surrounded by a light gray context. It should be quite apparent that the star with the darker context is perceived as brighter, although the two stars are of exactly the same intrinsic brightness.

HUE AND SATURATION

The facts of color vision are shown diagrammatically in Figure 5-8 and also in the color solid of Plate 2. The hue and saturation dimensions are represented along the circumference and radius of the circle, respectively, and brightness is represented by the vertical axis of the cone.

The 7.5 million different colors that the human observer is theoretically capable of distinguishing are dependent upon the various combinations of wavelength, intensity, and purity (saturation), the three dimensions varied in the double cone shown. A color wheel is a horizontal slice through the color solid. Because it is at a right angle to the brightness dimension (vertical axis), brightness is not varied. Pairs of colors opposite each other on this wheel are called complementary; when mixed they produce brightness only (gray).

The main discriminable colors are shown in the color wheel of Plate 3. When noncomplementaries are mixed, the resulting hue is always between the two original hues, such that a straight line between their position on the color wheel will indicate its position; exactly where the new hue is on this line depends on the proportion that each hue contributes.

The hue of any object depends upon the wavelengths that it reflects, from the white light that is normally incident upon it. Most light stimulation is reflected in this way from objects, in contrast to the relatively few objects that are themselves luminant, such as the sun, incandescent light bulbs, and the like.

The most saturated (deepest, or purest) colors are those of medium intensity, represented by positions around the outside circumference of the color circle shown in Plate 3. The brightest and the darkest colors are essentially achromatic; that is, really not hues at all, in a technical sense, but rather very bright (white) or very dark (black) grays.

We can obviously discriminate many more hues than we have names to identify. Actually, people learn a surprisingly small number of names for colors and tend to speak of "shades of red" and the like. This situation causes no serious problem in communication and is therefore likely to persist until some real need for more refined verbal tagging of color sensations develops.

COLOR DEFICIENCIES. Between 5 and 10 per cent of human subjects seem to have

Plate 1

Courtesy of Eastman Kodak Company.

Courtesy of Inmont Corporation, New York, N.Y.

Plate 2

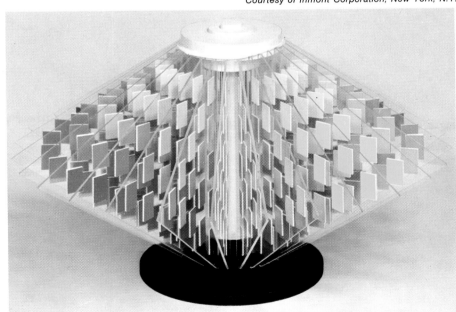

Plate 3

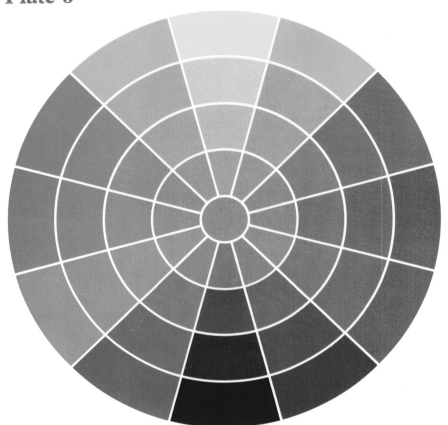

Plate 4

Normal

Plate 5

Red-Green Weakness

Plate 6

Blue-Yellow Weakness

Plate 7

Monochromatic Vision

Plate 8

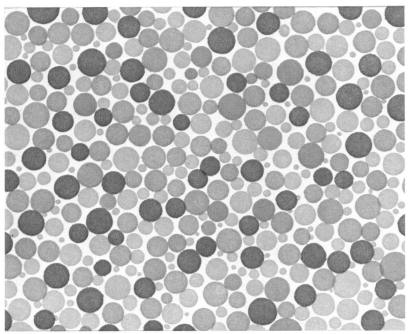

Courtesy of American Optical Corporation, Southbridge, Massachusetts. This reproduction does not present true testing conditions and cannot be used as a color vision deficiency test.

Plate 9

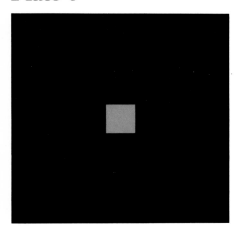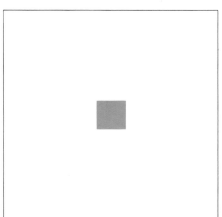

some difficulty in color sensation. This genetic defect is carried by the Y-chromosome and is therefore much more common in males. Although the term *color blindness* is in common use, the great majority of color deficiencies are partial; such subjects are said to suffer from *color weakness*.

The occasional person who is completely color blind is called a *monochromat*, because he sees in only one color dimension; actually he sees no hue at all but only various shades of brightness. The monochromat sees only with his rods. Moreover, his foveal vision is poor or absent, and he depends mainly or entirely upon peripheral vision. As a result, he tends to move his eyes, in order to take advantage of the ability of the rods to detect movement, much more than the normally sighted person. Even the normal person, it should be noted, keeps his eyes moving most of the time, but the eye movements of the monochromat may be so excessive as to be classified as nystamic. *Nystamus* is an almost constant and involuntary back-and-forth movement of the eyes.

Much more common are the two types of color weakness in which either the red-green or the blue-yellow sensations are poorly developed or absent. Such individuals are called *dichromats*. Plates 4 to 7 illustrate these two types of dichromat vision and, for comparative purposes, monochromat and normal color vision.

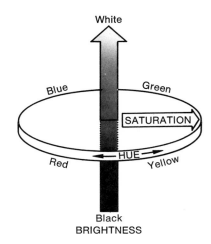

5-8 The color solid. The three dimensions of brightness (vertical axis), hue (circumference of circle), and saturation (radius of circle) are shown in relation to selected colors.

CONTRAST EFFECTS

Color sensation is especially sensitive to context effects, similar to that shown in Figure 5-7 for brightness. *Color contrast* is easily demonstrated, as shown in Plate 9, where the same orange square acquires a different saturation effect when it is viewed in different background situations.

Aftereffects or *afterimages* are color sensations produced immediately after color stimulation. Gaze steadily at the orange square on the black background in Plate 9 until the orange loses saturation and bits of brownish cast appear around the edges. Then shift your gaze to the center of the white square at the right. You should shortly experience a dark square image in the middle of the black background. This kind of negative afterimage always involves the complementary hue, in this case, blue-green.

Positive afterimages can also occur, in which case the same hue rather than its complementary will reappear after a time interval. This experience is especially common following a strong visual experience such as a glance at a very bright luminous object (e.g., the sun or a light bulb). An especially vivid experience is the *flight of colors,* in which a succession of color experiences follows such stimulation (e.g., a flashing bulb).

THEORIES OF COLOR VISION

There are two classical theories of color vision. The older of these is called the *Young-Helmholtz* theory. It assumed three kinds of cones in the human eye, one for each of the three primary colors seen in normal (trichromatic) color vision. White

117

light is a consequence of the equal stimulation by each of these primaries (in the red, blue, and green spectral areas). The facts of color mixture are in general quite consistent with this kind of theory, and it has been supported also by recent physiological evidence for three differentially sensitive types of cones. But it does have a number of difficulties. For example, the theory did not handle very well the facts of complementary colors, or color zones.

These difficulties were well handled by the alternative theory, initially introduced by the physiologist *Hering* and given his name but more recently renamed the *opponent processes* theory. This theory assumes the operation of three separate color systems, one for red and green, one for blue and yellow, and one for black and white. The Hering theory was primarily designed to account for the fact that certain pairs of colors, such as blue and yellow or red and green, cannot be combined. There is no way to obtain a blue-yellow or a red-green hue; mixtures either simply reduce the saturation of one or the other of these particular complementaries or reduce entirely to the achromatic gray. The facts of afterimages and contrast effects, described briefly above, are also quite consistent with this view.

VISUAL ACUITY

Visual acuity can be defined in terms of the absolute threshold, or in terms of the smallest stimulus that can be identified at some standard distance. By these criteria man's visual system is indeed a powerful one. For example, it is estimated that the normal eye under optimal conditions can detect a candle flame at a distance of 30 miles. This kind of sensitivity is believed by some physiologists to reach the theoretical limit of visual capacity, because a single quantum (energy unit) of light radiation can be detected.

More commonly, however, visual acuity is defined in terms of the resolving power of the eye. The question here is how far apart two lines, for example, must be in order to be seen separately. Here a wide range of visual acuities exists among people. The standard device for testing visual acuity quickly but crudely is the familiar *Snellen chart.* This consists of lines of letters of varying sizes placed at a standard distance of 20 feet, at which point the light rays are approximately parallel when they reach the eye. The subject is asked to read letters from successively smaller lines until he clearly is unable to identify them. The line that the average individual is able to read at 20 feet is used as a standard against which each subject is rated. If one can also read this line he is said to have 20/20, or normal, vision. Persons with inferior visual acuity are rated by the smallest line that they are able to read. Thus if one is said to have 20/40 vision, this statement means that at 20 feet he is only able to read the line that the average person can read at 40 feet; a similar interpretation applies to even poorer ratings, such as 20/100 or 20/200.

The Snellen chart is obviously a very rough and easily abused device (e.g., subjects can easily memorize certain lines to inflate their acuity rating). However, it offers such a convenient and simply obtained estimate that it is in wide use in spite of the existence of more sophisticated and generally superior techniques. Moreover, it utilizes the ability to detect letters of print, which in our word-dominated world affords a quite representative sample of the kind of visual acuity that we are all called upon to make almost constantly.

Visual acuity is best in the fovea, with its heavy concentration of tightly packed cones. Very small details are more readily resolved by the eye when they activate such larger numbers of closely packed receptors. It is now believed that the separation of two or more lines can be seen only when there is a kind of "dead space," so to speak, lying between activated receptors; in other words, there must be some *nonactivated* receptor units separating activated receptors in order for linear separation to be detected. Moreover, the effective unit in this process is not the receptor cell itself (that is, the cone), but the group of receptors connected to one nerve fiber. The number of such functional receptor–nerve units is much less in the periphery of the eye, and the retinal distances that any one such unit covers is therefore much greater. These facts explain the inferiority of peripheral vision relative to foveal vision under normal illumination.

Visual acuity is strongly influenced by various kinds of eye movements as well as by the distribution of the actual receptors and associated nerve fibers. For one thing, there is the crucial role of the lens as it accommodates to objects at varying distances from the eye. Opening and closing of the pupil is also involved in acuity. The pupil shuts down quickly and involuntarily in a reflex reaction to strong light. This action has an obviously protective function for the delicate structures within the eye, but it also serves to improve detail vision by improving lens function.

Beyond these quite involuntary movements of lens and pupil, there are a number of movements of the entire eyeball that are necessary for proper fixation of images and therefore good visual acuity. Some of these have to do with maintaining orientation to the object being expected, so that light from it falls upon corresponding areas in the two retinas; examples of such movements are the *convergence* of the two eyes (turning in toward each other) for looking at objects closer than 20 feet and the twisting or rotational movement of each eye independently around its own axis. Finally, searching movements, partly voluntary and partly involuntary, are made by the two eyes together. Called *conjugate movements,* these consist of relatively smooth gliding of the eyes, as when one is tracking or pursuing a moving object, and more jerky, jumplike movements of varying degrees of magnitude and speed.

The explanation of the role of these movements in improving visual acuity is that they enable the stimulus to affect different sets of receptor cells, and associated neural connections, so that more time is permitted for registration of finer details and subsequent identification of objects. Eye movements thus help one to see detail better as well as to detect very small objects and movement and the eye is a generally more effective instrument when it is scanning and roving.

Animal Vision

Our emphasis throughout this chapter is on human sensory and perceptual experience, but some mention should be made of animal sensory capacity. Great variety of visual capacity is found through the animal species. Some kind of light-sensitive sense organ is found in practically all the "higher" organisms exposed to light radiation. These range from the simplest of brightness receptors to the finely structured eyes of such birds as hawks, some of which have been found to have visual acuity several times as great as that of the human organism.

Color vision is sporadically distributed among the species. Insects and birds seem to be well but by no means universally endowed in this respect. Some organisms are able to detect radiation of shorter wavelengths than those man can detect (e.g., ultraviolet light by some insects) and some can detect longer wavelengths than man can detect (e.g., infrared radiation by some snakes). Many of the more common mammals (e.g., dogs) have either no color vision or so few cones that only the strongest stimuli may be presumed to be effective for color. In general, in accordance with expectation from evolutionary theory, nocturnal animals (e.g., owls) have well-developed systems of rod vision, whereas diurnal animals (e.g., most other birds) have well-developed systems of cone vision.

Audition

For man audition is second in importance only to vision. We use visual cues where possible to detect and identify objects, and especially to determine the finer details of their structure (such as facial features). Audition is generally a poor substitute for vision; however, although auditory cues may be utilized for some of these functions, audition is pre-eminent as a means of direct *social communication*. The relative inefficiency of using written signs or sign language, such as hand signals, is quickly evident to anyone who tries such techniques. Audition also provides us with important danger signals (the raucous honk of a horn in a city street or the muffled padding of a large animal moving through the forest) as well as the very considerable esthetic enjoyment of music.

Physically, sound is the cyclic production of mechanical pressure in some medium surrounding the organism, usually the atmosphere. A body that vibrates in such a medium produces cycles of alternative compression and decompression that are propagated through the medium. The various attributes of sound as a sensory phenomenon are correlated with the major characteristics of sound as a physical energy.

THE EAR

A schematic diagram of the major parts of the human ear is given in Figure 5-9.

Sound waves in the air normally enter the ear canal and transmit their mechanical vibrations to the fluids in the cochlear canals by means of the tympanic membrane, the three small connected bones in the middle ear, and the oval window. Mechanical vibrations of the head bones can also transmit sound waves to the inner ear, although this route is ordinarily (assuming a fully functional ear system) not very important. The hair cells lying on the basilar membrane of the organ of Corti

5-9 Schematic drawing of the anatomy of the human ear. Sound is gathered by the pinna, and travels through the canal to the eardrum, which it causes to vibrate. This vibration is transmitted by the bones of the middle ear to the basilar membrane across the entrance to the cochlea. Vibration of the eardrum is thus transmitted to the fluid of the cochlea and then travels the length of the cochlea, eventually stimulating the sense organs that transduce the mechanical energy into electrical energy.

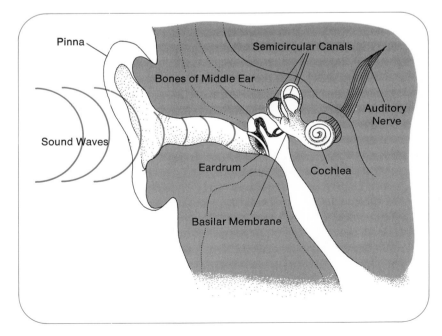

are then excited by the movements of the cochlear fluids. In some way yet to be fully determined the auditory nerve is stimulated to transmit this information to the hearing centers of the brain, where the sound sensation is produced. Auditory nerve fibers make connections at several "way stations" before reaching the cortical hearing centers in the temporal lobe, and in the process may cross to the other side, as in the case of vision.

AUDITORY SENSATION

Physical Correlates

The three fundamental sensory attributes of sound are *pitch, loudness,* and *timbre.* The pitch of a sound (its subjectively experienced "highness" or "lowness") is correlated primarily with the physical dimension of wave frequency. Loudness is correlated with the physical intensity, or amount of energy in the mechanical vibrations of the medium. Timbre is determined by the composition of the sound wave pattern, that is, by the distribution in the complex sound of different pitches. These three correlated dimensions may be considered to represent, respectively, quality (what *kind* of energy change and sensation?), quantity (*how much* energy change and sensation?), and complexity (*how pure* an energy change and sensation?).

PITCH. Like color, *pitch* must be consciously experienced to be appreciated. There is simply no substitute for direct experience. The pitch of a tone is commonly described in terms of the frequency of the sound waves that produce it; the older term for such frequency is *cycles per second* (cps), but the term *Hertz* (Hz) is now more commonly used. Because sound travels in a medium as alternating mechanical compressions and decompressions, both its wavelength (distance from one crest or trough to the next) and its frequency (number of crests or troughs passing a certain point each second) can be measured. As in the case of light waves, these are reciprocals, with the shorter waves having the higher frequencies and the longer waves the shorter frequencies. For sound, frequency rather than length is the preferred measure.

The concept of mechanical wave energy is more readily understood if other, more directly observable forms of such energy are used as illustrations. Consider the waves produced by wind energy in an ocean, or more simply, the wavelike ripples that are produced by dropping a stone in a quiet pond. In each of these cases the main movement of the medium (water, rather than air) is *not* in the same direction as the wave of mechanical energy itself; that is to say, if one were to plot the actual movement of the water molecules he would find that they mostly move up and down in the ocean or the pond, with very little horizontal movement. Nevertheless, the wave itself does move horizontally. This fact can also be more simply noted by watching some small object, such as a piece of wood, that is floating on the surface of the water when one tosses the stone. As each wave passes, such an object will be observed to bob up and down (in the same manner as a "bob" or float used in still fishing) but to move only a short distance horizontally along with the wave.

The limits of human pitch sensitivity are usually placed at approximately 20 to 20,000 Hertz, if sufficiently intense stimuli and sufficiently young subjects are used. The ability to hear extremes of very low and very high frequencies suffers from various diseases (such as scarlet fever) as well as the ravages that accumulate with age, especially in our own quite noisy society. The middle frequencies are the most important, however, because it is in that range that most of the sounds that we experience occur. Probably the most important frequencies are those used in human conversation, running mostly from 2,000 to 4,000 Hertz; maximum sensitivity occurs at about 3,000 Hertz. Musical appreciation requires a considerably greater auditory capacity, for the higher tones particularly (as discussed below under the topic of timbre).

LOUDNESS. The difference in pressure between the compressed and the decompressed phases of the sound wave—or the intensity of the wave—determines the *loudness* of the experienced sound. To some extent also, however, loudness is determined by frequency, because low frequencies typically show higher absolute thresholds than high frequencies. The ear is so sensitive an instrument that the ratio of the highest sound energy that can be heard to the lowest detectable sound energy is on the order of several million to one. At the higher energy levels, however, pain begins to supersede sound.

The unit commonly used to measure intensity ratios is the *decibel*. The decibel scale is a logarithmic one, in which the numbers express relative or proportional rather than linear relationships, and is based upon a zero point. The approximate decibel values of some common sources of sound are listed in Figure 5-10, along with hearing and pain thresholds.

TIMBRE. The *timbre* of a sound sensation is its characteristic quality that differentiates it from other sounds, including those with the same basic pitch. Understanding of timbre depends upon understanding of the concept of fundamental frequency and partial frequencies, or overtones.

Envision, if you will, a string attached on both ends, like a guitar or violin string. Assume that it is 24 inches long. When it is picked up and released it will produce a sound wave proportional to its full length of 24 inches, with a correlated frequency. This frequency is its *fundamental frequency*. Such frequencies are all that pure tones have (hence the label *pure*) because their vibrating sources have been designed to vibrate only in their total length.

Such pure tones are rare in everyday life. All musical instruments and practically all other commonplace sound sources also produce vibrations of their partial lengths, with correspondingly higher frequencies, called *overtones*. Thus our 24-inch string when plucked will vibrate in waves of one half its length, one third its length, and so on, as diagrammatically shown in Figure 5-11.

The sine wave, shown at the top of Figure 5-11, is a graph of a pure tone or an overtone. Production of a pure tone requires special apparatus, such as a tuning fork, and pure tones rarely occur outside the laboratory. The flute is one musical instrument whose tones approximate purity more closely than most.

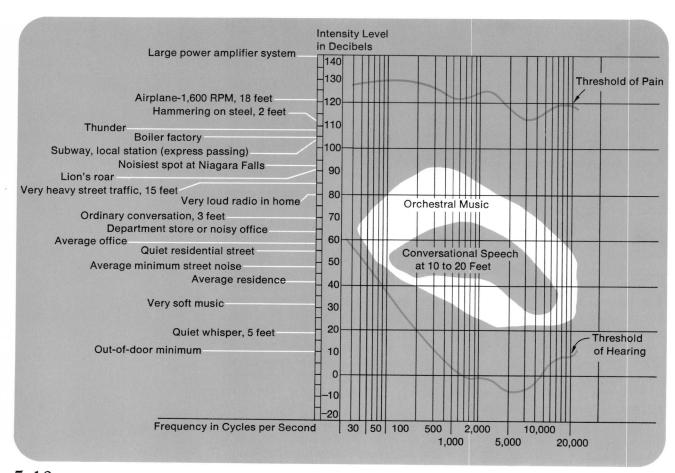

5-10 The comparative loudness in decibel units of some common sounds. Note also the thresholds for hearing and pain. [From Floyd L. Ruch, *Psychology and Life*, 7th ed. (Chicago: Scott, Foresman, 1967) p. 278.]

When the various partial vibrations are added to the fundamental vibration of any vibrating body, a more complex tonal pattern emerges. Any complex wave form can be physically analyzed into its various pure tone components (Fourier analysis, technically). A trained musician, or an experienced music lover, is able to hear the higher overtones especially, and so can perform a kind of sensory or experiential analysis. A tone-deaf person, on the other hand, is one who seems to be incapable of distinguishing between simple differences in pitch; it is unclear as to how much improvement can be effected by the proper training of such persons, but it is quite likely that motivational factors and habits of not discriminating as well as sensory ability are involved.

5-11 Fundamental and overtones. Panel (a) illustrates the fundamental or sine wave of a "pure" tone. Panel (b) shows the fundamental (broken line) with an overtone of twice the frequency of the fundamental. Panel (c) shows an overtone of three times the frequency of the fundamental.

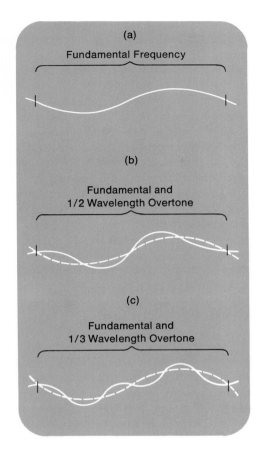

(a)

Fundamental Frequency

(b)

Fundamental and
1/2 Wavelength Overtone

(c)

Fundamental and
1/3 Wavelength Overtone

Hearing Deficit

There are two main categories of hearing deficit. One is called *conduction deafness.* It is a result of some kind of blocking of the mechanical transmission system through the middle ear. For example, the vibrations in the ear may be slowed or blocked entirely by a bonelike growth; this can be surgically removed, and the stapes replaced by a prosthetic device if necessary, often with remarkable hearing improvements. If the conduction block is of another type, an electronic hearing aid may be of considerable help. As a matter of fact, a surprisingly high number of partial hearing deficits are due to such prosaic matters as the accumulation of wax and dirt in the external ear; the cure of such blocks is self-apparent, once the condition is suspected or properly diagnosed.

The other most common kind of hearing deficit is called *sensorineural,* or sometimes simply *neural,* deafness. This is usually a more serious condition and one that is much more difficult to treat. Damage to the cochlea or the auditory nerve is typically irrevocable. Moreover, it is extremely unfortunate that people in our society are exposed to so continuous a barrage of high-intensity noise—some of which, it must be admitted, they actually bring on themselves (e.g., rock-music noise).

Persons whose occupation exposes them to such high levels of noise are commonly found to suffer progressive deterioration of their hearing; it is hardly surprising that so delicate and sensitive a receptor system as that of the cochlea should be subject to such abuse. The term *boilermaker's disease* was formerly used to refer to such a deficit. More recently, airplane pilots and artillerymen have been found to suffer similarly from partial deafness. A more or less continuous ringing in the ear (technically, *tinnitus*) is also characteristic of this kind of case; severe symptoms can be medically corrected. When sudden very loud noises, such as explosions or gun discharges or rocket firings, can be anticipated, their effects can be reduced by appropriate protection of the ears. A special precaution adopted by the military forces has also proved effective; this is the deliberate activation of the *acoustic reflex*, which involves a contraction of small muscles to clamp down the vibratory transmission of the ossicles of the middle ear, by the production of a more moderate noise just before the explosive stimulus.

AUDITORY THEORY

Theories of hearing have concentrated on the problem of pitch. (Loudness is generally considered to be a function of the total number of sensory cells activated and has not figured prominently in the theoretical endeavors.) The theories have tended to cluster into two major types: (1) those that look to the *place* of the cochlear membrane that is stimulated to account for pitch and (2) those that account for pitch in terms of the *frequency* of stimulation. An early place theory was offered by Helmholtz, who attributed pitch sensation to the area of the basilar membrane that is stimulated. Helmholtz's notion of resonance, by which the hair cells at different parts of the basilar membrane were assumed to vibrate in tune to different mechanical vibration frequencies, has not been confirmed. However, the facts of auditory sensation do seem to require place theory for frequencies above 5,000 Hertz; up to that point some modern version of a frequency theory, such as the volley theory, can handle the data very nicely.

The evidence that strongly supports a place theory for the higher frequencies is both clinical and experimental. Clinical evaluations of persons with high-pitch deficiences have shown damage to the basilar membrane in the region of the base of the cochlea. Moreover, movements of the various parts of the basilar membrane under conditions of artificial stimulation by different sound frequencies have been actually observed using high-powered microscopes; again the higher frequencies produced the greatest disturbance at the basal end of the membrane, with the point of maximal agitation moving progressively up toward the apical end as the stimulating frequencies were lowered.

The simplest form of frequency theory held that the pitch sensation is mediated directly in terms of frequency of neural impulses; in other words, the basilar membrane was supposed to function in much the same manner as a telephone transmitter in passing on the frequencies it receives (turning mechanical into electrical neural frequencies). Evidence initially interpreted as strongly supporting a frequency theory was obtained in some interesting and ingenious research utilizing cats as subjects. In essence, the cat's cochlea was used as a kind of microphone, with electronic connections taken directly off of it. Words then spoken into the anesthetized cat's ear were heard on speakers in another room. The electrical potential produced by the cochlea, called *cochlear microphonic potential,* follows the frequency pattern of the physical stimulus very closely. Although this phenomenon was believed by some to represent the critical element in the transduction process whereby the mechanical energy is transformed to neural impulses, more recently many questions have been raised concerning its interpretation. It is not now generally accepted as crucial support for a simple frequency theory.

A simple version of frequency theory, such as the *telephone* model mentioned above, has been found to be inapplicable; for one thing, no single nerve fiber is able to respond at a rate even approaching the higher frequencies of sound energy (neural frequencies of no more than 1,000 per second seem to be maximal). This fundamental objection is circumvented by the modified frequency theory called *volley theory.* According to this version, *different* nerve fibers, each responding at its own rate, can together account for the necessary correlation of mechanical and neural frequencies. It is as though a large number of riflemen were assigned the job of matching some very rapid rate of signal with rifle shots. Even if no single rifleman were able to fire at so high a rate, by staggering their firing, the group would make sure that each signal was matched by some rifle fire. The very large number of receptor cells and nerve fibers available makes such a theory at least plausible, and the volley theory is at present given strong support for the lower frequencies.

Some attempts at combining these two types of auditory theory have been made. For example, a place-frequency version has been suggested which would account for tones up to about 400 Hertz on the basis of frequency alone, tones between 400 and 5,000 Hertz by both frequency and place, and all higher tones by the place principle alone. More knowledge about the neurophysiology of the hearing mechanism, and especially about the contribution of the higher nerve centers to pitch sensation, is needed before any further development of these classic theories or some new and more satisfactory ones can be expected.

Auditory Sensitivity Thresholds

A plot showing the absolute threshold of human hearing as a function of frequency is given in Figure 5-12. It can be seen that the ear responds most sensitively to tones of intermediate frequency, as already suggested.

Clinical determination of individual hearing sensitivity can be very useful. The result of this kind of testing is the *audiogram,* a sample of which is shown in Figure 5-13. The audiogram shows tonal gaps in a person's hearing capacity, as well as his overall sensitivity. It is especially important in the case of children where partial deafness is suspected or older persons who suspect that their hearing has deteriorated.

PERSONALITY EFFECTS OF HEARING LOSS. Because of its role in social interaction,

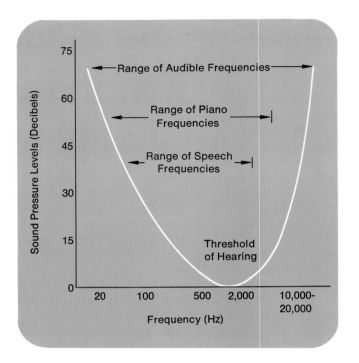

5-12 The absolute threshold of hearing for sine waves, or pure tones, of different frequencies. The tones most people hear best are frequencies between 1,000 and 4,000 Hertz.

5-13 Representative audiograms for normal hearing at 20 years and 60 years and for the two major forms of deafness (conduction and nerve).

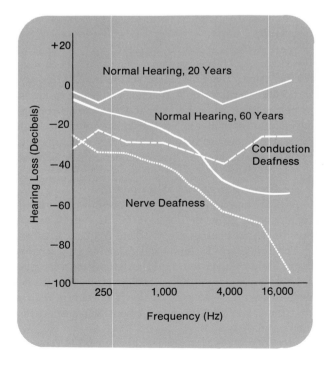

hearing when partially lost in an adult is more likely to result in serious personality disturbances than is vision when partially lost. The hard-of-hearing person at worst develops paranoid tendencies (e.g., excessive unfounded suspicions that people are talking about him "behind his back" and the like) and at best suffers the embarrassment of having to inconvenience his associates by asking them to repeat what they have just said. These developments are most likely to occur in the case of recently deteriorated hearing, before adjustments have been made. Recognition of the deficit and correction of it as far as is possible will of course improve the probability that the adjustments made will be socially and personally desirable ones.

The partially deaf child whose defect is not recognized runs the risk of being diagnosed as retarded because of his inferior school work, apparent inattentiveness and similar behaviors. Once the diagnosis of hearing deficit has been made appropriate steps can be taken to correct at least the mistaken notions concerning his intellectual capacity. Again, unfortunately, the longer the deficit remains unnoticed the more likely his own adjustments to the world will harden and become permanent. A child who is hard of hearing is not likely to recognize this fact himself; the way people sound is probably the way they have always sounded to him and he is not in as good a position as the adult with deteriorating hearing to appreciate the difference. For this reason he is even more at the mercy of others, such as parents, schoolteachers, and administrators, with regard to proper diagnosis of his difficulty. These facts underscore the importance of universal tests of hearing as well as seeing capacity early in the primary grades.

Sensitivity in Animals

The range of human response to sound frequency is exceeded by a number of animals, such as moths, dogs, porpoises (which may respond up to 80,000 Hertz), and bats (sensitive up to 98,000 Hertz). Bats have been shown to locate objects in flight on the basis of the return of their very high-pitch emissions. This ability, called *echolocation,* enables these organisms to catch flying insects in the absence of any visual sensitivity. A more commonplace application of supersonic ability is the use of the high-pitched whistle to call dogs; the fact that the frequencies used are above the upper threshold for humans reduces the annoyance that they would otherwise occasion.

Man has two senses that are responsive to chemical substances: olfaction and gustation. *Olfaction* (smell), like vision and audition, involves distance reception; smells from many miles off can be detected by some animal forms as diverse as dogs and moths, even when the odiferous stimuli are present in fantastically small amounts. Functionally, *gustation* (taste) is more perceptual than sensory, insofar as these two concepts can be usefully distinguished; in other words, what we call taste ordinarily includes a number of other diverse sensory experiences, such as smell, touch, temperature, and even vision. Here, however, only the fundamental taste receptors themselves will be considered.

Chemical Senses: Olfaction and Gustation

OLFACTION

RECEPTION. Smell stimuli activate the olfactory epithelium, high up in the nasal passages, in the form of molecules of gaseous substances. In order to activate the millions of *hair cells*, which are the actual chemical receptors, a substance must therefore be volatile (i.e., capable of being transformed from solid or liquid state to gaseous). Unbelievably small amounts of the more odiferous chemical substance in air can be detected, even by the relatively undeveloped human olfactory sense; for example, only .00004 milligram of artificial musk in a liter of air can be an effective stimulus. The hair cell receptors transduce the chemical energy to electrical energy, which is then transmitted in the form of neural impulses in afferent fibers. These gather together as the olfactory nerve, which runs into the olfactory bulb of the brain.

SENSATION. In the so-called smell prism six distinctive primary or pure smell sensations are assumed: flowery, putrid, fruity, spicy, burned, and resinous. All odors can theoretically be accounted for in terms of either one or several of these fundamental types of smell in combination. Other simpler schemes have also been suggested—e.g., acid, burnt, fragrant, and sweaty—but there is no general agreement. The lack of a satisfactory account of the stimulus dimensions along which olfactory substances vary makes it difficult to suggest physical correlates for these or any subjective descriptions of odors.

The most important thing about human smell sensations is their rapid adaptation. One needs only to contemplate what life would be like in, say, an active packing plant if smell adaptation were not rapid!

In man the sense of smell is not particularly relevant to survival, and smells are generally less important for man than they are for many lower animals. Nevertheless, odors have been viewed as useful to those persons concerned with the desirability of certain types of products. For example, leather scents are sometimes used by the manufacturers of plastic products, and new-car scent can be purchased by any car owner who wishes to revive the odors originally placed there by the marketeers of the auto industry. Scents may also have more directly obvious motivational properties. The deliberate blowing of the aroma of hot bread or doughnuts onto the nearby street may be frequently used to attract customers; and, presumably, the various perfumes worn by females and males are intended to serve a similar function.

GUSTATION

RECEPTION. The taste receptors are called *taste buds,* which are collected in clusters called *papillae.* They occur mainly on the dorsal surface of the tongue, but can be found scattered in smaller numbers throughout the oral cavity. Again, the receptor is a kind of hair cell, with associated nerve fibers. The hair cells are stimulated by chemical substances in water solution—normally dissolved by the saliva of the mouth; to be tasted, therefore, substances must be watersoluble, much as they must be volatile in order to be smelled.

Taste buds appear to have an unusually short life and are constantly replaced by new ones. The replacement rate falls off rather sharply with increasing age, so that food seasoned enough for an adult is disliked by a child. Also, older persons justifiably often complain that food does not taste as good as it used to; the change in taste sensitivity may well be at least part of the basis for the nostalgic recall of the superiority of "mother's cooking."

SENSATION. There is much more agreement on the primary taste than on the primary smell sensations. Subjectively, taste appears to be *sour, salty, bitter,* and *sweet,* or some combination of these qualities. Either concentrated stimuli of an appropriate type or direct electrical stimulation of the appropriate part of the brain can be shown to produce one of these fundamental subjective tastes. There are characteristic differentiations of the taste buds on the tongue. The tip of the tongue is most sensitive to sweet stimuli, the back of the tongue to bitter stimuli, and the sides of the tongue to sour stimuli; salt sensitivity seems to be somewhat more widely distributed, with salty substances being most readily tasted on the tip and parts of the sides of the tongue.

Taste sensitivity is not nearly as acute as smell sensitivity, in terms of the amount of chemical substance required for detection (absolute threshold). Generally, acid and bitter stimuli seem to be more readily detected than sweet and salty stimuli.

As mentioned earlier, what we call taste in everyday life is really a very complex phenomenon. Taste depends on odors, as well as on temperature, touch, and vision. Much of our subjective experience attributed to taste is really the result of olfactory stimulation, as can be shown experimentally by controlling smell; when this is done many of the correct identifications of common "tastes" are no longer possible. Simple "natural experiments," such as head colds, which reduce olfactory reception but leave gustatory reception relatively unimpaired, also demonstrate the strong dependence of taste sensitivity on odors. Food in particular often becomes relatively tasteless at this time. When the sense of smell has been eliminated, tomatoes and oranges taste alike. So do apples and potatoes.

As a complex sense organ, the skin has separate receptors for sensitivity to pressure, physical insult such as cutting or bruising, and either high or low temperature. These four sensory modalities utilize separate receptors, which are differentially distributed.

Skin Senses: Touch, Pain, and Temperature

Touch

The effective stimulus for touch is either movement of the hairs that cover much of the human body or, more commonly, active displacement or deformation of the skin itself. The adequate stimulus in the latter case is not pressure per se but rather a *gradient* of pressure; uniformly distributed pressure is not effective. Moreover, we adapt relatively rapidly to skin disturbance of this kind, as is suggested by the fact that the new pressure patterns of a new pair of shoes, for example, are usually noticed only for a short time (unless accompanied by pain).

Because of the great superiority of distance receptors such as the eyes and the ears we do not normally cultivate our sense of touch. Some indication of its potential, however, may be seen in the effective use of Braille for reading by blind persons.

Pain

The receptors for pain seem to be the nonspecialized *free nerve endings* that abound in the skin and especially in places that are most pain-sensitive. Pain is induced by a variety of types of insult to the skin. Radiant heat, which produces first warmth then pain, is the stimulus most commonly used in laboratory research.

Because the skin is readily available to manipulation for research purposes, pain reception in it has been most thoroughly examined in research. Pain also occurs, but under less well-understood conditions of stimulation, in the deeper areas of the body. Gaseous or other pressure in some of the viscera can apparently produce pain, but many of the more important body organs are surprisingly free of pain (the brain, for example, which can be operated upon with no direct discomfort to the subject, as mentioned in Chapter 4). Pain from the inner parts of the body is subjectively dull, in contrast to the sharp ("bright") pain that ordinarily results from insult to the skin.

As a biological danger signal, pain serves an obviously crucial role in survival. The much-cited case of a small girl who had no pain sensitivity demonstrates this role quite dramatically; she accumulated great numbers of body injuries, from such behavior as remaining in contact with a hot stove until the smell of her burning flesh alerted her parents.

As a sensory modality, pain is especially susceptible to "psychological" influences, such as those from suggestion. Pain thresholds can be readily manipulated in suggestible subjects by hypnotic techniques, but they also show great variability in the everyday life of us all.

Temperature Sensitivity

The effective stimulus for the temperature sensations of warmth and cold is a difference between the temperature of the outer layers of the skin and the temperature of the inner layers resulting from the circulation of the blood. The normal temperature of the skin is 32° centigrade, and this is called *physiological zero;* temperature stimuli close to this value do not induce any temperature sensations when applied to the skin. Stimuli of higher temperatures induce warmth sensations and those of lower temperatures induce cold sensations. The distribution of both kinds of temperature-sensitive receptors may be measured by point-to-point stimulation over an area of skin. Separate receptor systems are therefore assumed. Thus far, however, only the free nerve fibers have been implicated as temperature receptors.

The interesting phenomenon called *paradoxical cold* also suggests that different receptors are involved in the two temperature sensations. Paradoxical cold is the subjective experience of coldness that is sometimes felt when a skin location already demonstrated to contain only receptors for cold sensation is stimulated by a very warm stimulus. This experience indicates that the usual stimulus for warmth, high temperatures, is ineffective as far as warmth is concerned in the absence of warmth receptors, but can under some conditions trigger the cold receptors.

The dependence of temperature sensations upon the *relative* rather than the absolute temperature of the skin—that is, upon the relationship between the ambient (surrounding) temperature and the skin temperature—can be readily demonstrated by placing the two arms in water solutions with different temperatures. Suppose that one solution is higher and the other lower than 32° centigrade. Accommodation of the temperature of the skin in each arm occurs quickly, and the same previously neutral stimulus (say, 32° centigrade) will now be felt as warm by the arm in colder water and cold by the arm in the warmer water.

The sensation of heat seems to be a function of no single receptor but rather of the simultaneous activation of cold and warm spots. How such fusion occurs, so that these points act together to produce the integrated sensation, is not yet understood.

Two major systems of body sensation underlie our reactivity to positional and movement factors in our own bodies. These are sometimes combined under the term *proprioception.* The *vestibular* sense tells us the orientation of our body. *Kinesthesis* provides us with information concerning movements of the various parts of our bodies.

Body Senses

Vestibular Sense

The vestibular sense is the sense of balance, or body orientation. In spite of its importance in helping us maintain body orientation, both under static (fixed) and dynamic (moving) conditions, the vestibular sense modality does not give us any direct conscious experiences. The vestibular sense organ is closely associated with the cochlea, sharing a location in the inner ear. Its main structure consists of three channels of fluids lying at right angles to each other, the *semicircular canals.* The actual receptors in these canals are, again, *hair cells.* They are responsive to movements of the endolymph, the fluid in the canals. The vestibular nerve is formed from these receptors and joins the auditory nerve to compose the VIIIth cranial nerve.

Vestibular functions are obviously crucial in certain occupations, such as tight-wire balancing acts in a circus, where the relationship to gravity is delicate, or more recently, under space ship conditions in which persons must function in the absence of gravitational force. Most of us are more familiar with the vestibular sense, however, because of those (fortunately) rare occasions when it produces some form of motion sickness. Car, air, and sea sickness are probably the most common forms of this affliction. It can be countered, in advance, if the contradiction of sensory modalities is reduced. This can also be accomplished behaviorally, as it is, for example, by the skilled ballet dancer, who keeps the eyes fixated on one object as long as possible even while the body is spinning. Dizziness and nausea occur when there is a marked contradiction between what we see and what we feel, by means of the vestibular sense. Thus whirling about rapidly and watching the fixed environment spin by is inconsistent with the stable report of balanced equilibration; similarly, the persistent vestibular change resulting from steady movement in a vehicle, while visual cues remain relatively unchanged (as in, say, an airplane), can produce nausea.

Kinesthesis

The muscle sense, kinesthesis, is probably the least heralded of our major sensory systems. Yet it is of profound importance, because it tells us how our body parts are functioning. Because it carries no corresponding sensory experience, however, it is a generally unrecognized modality.

Kinesthesis functions by means of nerve endings in the muscles, the tendons (which tie the muscles to bone), and the joints (connections of bony parts). It works with the vestibular sense and with vision to provide the information we need to maintain balance and perform skilled activities.

Like other crucial but generally underestimated functions, kinesthesis is most appreciated when it fails. A striking kind of such failure is the *tabetic* patient. A victim of *tabes dorsalis,* resulting from an advanced case of syphilis, this person has lost the use of the sensory pathways from his muscles. He therefore has little or no kinesthetic sensitivity. He can perform even the most simple motor skills, such as walking, only by visual observation of the position of his appendages. The absence of "feedback" in the form of afferent stimulation indicates the crucial role that such stimulation plays in the maintenance of normal behavior.

Notes

For general sources on sensation, Geldard's *The Human Senses* (1972) remains a classic. Day's 1969 paperback is titled *Human Perception* but contains information on animal as well as human sensory systems. Sensory coding is well covered in a book with that title, edited by Uttal (1972).

Role of Senses

The account of the marble statue with its sensory layers as originally conceptualized by Condillac, and similar theorizing by La Mettrie and others, is well told by Boring (1950); Boring's 1942 book is perhaps the best overall historical account of sensory research. Crombie's 1964 historical treatment is both informative and entertaining.

The remarkable career of Helen Keller may also be mentioned here. In spite of the handicap of being both blind and deaf from a very early age she rose, with the aid of a most effective and dedicated teacher (Anne Sullivan), to a position of high achievement and national prominence. Miss Keller's autobiography, *The Story of My Life,* first published in 1902, is a fascinating document.

Receptors

Sensory receptors are of course described in the general sources mentioned above, as well as in Butter's 1968 paperback and Thompson's 1973 book, and in much greater detail in the various sections of Kling and Riggs's 1971 handbook. The water-ripple sensory receptor described in the text was reported by Schwartz (1965). Hubel (1963) reported the results of research on the highly specific types of visual receptor cells and their relationship to the visual cortex.

Vision

Gregory's *Eye and Brain* (1973) is a good general introduction to vision. Hering's theory has been most actively championed, and revised, by Hurvich and Jameson, whose 1974 paper is a recent statement. MacAdams's *Sources of Color Science* (1970) contains key contributions by sixteen scholars over a span of twenty-three centuries.

A commonly accepted belief is that such birds as eagles have visual acuity vastly superior to man's—as much as eight times greater. Recently, however, this belief has been questioned (e.g., Schlaer, 1972); the newer estimates, based on actual measurement of the retinal image rather than anatomical examination of the retina by means of a microscope, reduce the difference by approximately half. (The eagle is now estimated to have visual acuity from 2 to 3.6 times greater than man's.)

Terminology in vision is especially confusing. The term *color*, for example, is sometimes used as essentially synonymous with *hue*, to refer strictly to the wavelength variable per se; by this usage black and white would be purely brightness experiences in view of their lack of specificity of wavelength. A more generally accepted usage, however, regards *color* as a complex term in which hue, brightness, and saturation are all involved; by this usage black and white qualify as colors. *Chroma* is then used to refer to the combination of hue and saturation.

Audition

The direct observation of differential mechanical vibration in the basilar membrane was reported by von Bekesy and Rosenblith (1951). The telephone version of frequency theory was proposed by the British physicist Rutherford. Wever and Bray (1930) did the classic research on cochlear microphonics and suggested the volley theory. Research with bats demonstrating the echolocation phenomenon was first reported by Griffin (1958a and 1958b). A recent report on echolocation in bats (Suga and Schlegel, 1972) is of special interest in that it indicates the attenuation within the nervous system of the intensity of self-generated vocalizations (as compared with the same sounds played back to the bat). This mechanism permits the more effective discrimination of echoes and, like the acoustic-defense mechanism in man, is obviously of adaptive value. Human echolocation ability is reviewed in a comprehensive article by Rice (1967).

Minor Senses

The German chemist Henning proposed the olfactory prism. The case of the girl without pain sensitivity was described by Boyd and Nie (1949). Dethier (1971) discusses the remarkable efficiency found in the coding of sensory information in the relatively simple gustatory and olfactory systems of insects. Harper's *Human Senses in Action* (1972) is unusual in that it emphasizes smell and taste, allotting them more than twice the space given vision and audition. The behavioral significance of pheromones (chemical influences) is reviewed by Gleason and Reynierse (1969).

Attention and Perception

This eighteenth-century engraving of the "Isle of Dogs" is a fitting opening illustration for our discussion of attention and perception. This and several other kinds of illusions will be discussed.

137

here is no easy way to distinguish between sensation and perception. Very often perception is simply assumed to be sensation plus meaning. That is to say, when an organism establishes a meaningful contact with the environment he is said to be perceiving, and perception always occurs by means of one or more of the sensory modalities. However, this distinction is regarded as too artificial by some psychologists. They hold that *all* apprehension of the environment is meaningful, in adult higher organisms at least, and that pure sensory functions therefore exist mainly in theory. Nevertheless, there is in fact a continuum with "pure" sensory functioning at one end and the more meaningful perceptual functions at the other.

However one wishes to look at perception, there is no doubt that it is of central significance in all behavioral processes as well as practically all areas of conscious experience. For the most effective functioning, perception is dependent upon the prior and concomitant process of attention. Whatever else it is, perception is first and foremost a *selective* process; if it were not, the organism would be simply overwhelmed with the sheer mass of sensory input and would be utterly incapable of handling it. Perceptual selectivity depends primarily upon mechanisms of attention. Our discussion of perception therefore starts with attention and includes a survey of a variety of topics in this general category.

Hypnosis and sleep are among the more prominent and attention-getting of these topics. The more important perceptual phenomena are then considered, focusing on the ways in which perception is both *stable* (e.g., the various *constancies,* which permit that perceptual consistency which is necessary for effective behavioral adjustment) and *unstable* (e.g., the *illusions,* or perceptions that are not in accord with the physical characteristics of the stimulus). We use mainly visual perceptual illustrations, with other modalities touched upon only occasionally; this concentration upon vision reflects not only the more central role of this modality in human experience and behavior but also the fact that most of the research has been concerned with it.

Attention

The concept of attention is an especially broad one. Attention may refer to the clarity of *consciousness,* in an introspective sense. It may also refer to the predisposition of the organism to *concentrate* upon one sensory modality, or some one aspect of that modality, and *screen out* most of the remaining sensory input. Finally, attention can refer to *motor predispositions* (sometimes called motor sets) that facilitate responding. We shall deal only briefly with the first and the last of these facets of attention, concentrating upon the sensory-selection aspect.

Many introspective studies were performed on attention within the framework of the structuralist school. Introspective evidence was consistent in agreeing that consciousness has a clear, central focus upon which sensory experience is fixed (in somewhat the way that light rays reaching the retina are physically fixated on the fovea by the lens of the eye). The fuzzier peripheral aspect of conscious experience was even resolved into varying numbers of levels of diminishing clarity in some of the more refined introspective analyses.

Two of the more lasting introspective contributions involving attention and consciousness may be briefly described. One was a theory of meaning, emphasizing conscious experience, and the other a stress on the role of certain less salient conscious experiences.

Titchener himself developed a *context theory of meaning.* According to this view, the meaning of any conscious experience is whatever accompanies it in consciousness—that is, its subjective or experiential context. Thus if one is looking at some object in the environment—attending closely to it, so that it occupies the central focal position—its meaning to the organism can be determined by examination of the various other, less well-focalized conscious experiences that accompany it. For the most part these would be images or other memorial representations, which would presumably carry the main burden of meaning for the object, although peripheral environmental objects and events might also be present.

The other contribution was by William James. He pointed to the ordinarily unnoticed importance of many less well-attended and consequently vague conscious processes. Transitional experiences and similar "fringe sensations" really serve a most significant function as a kind of experiential glue that serves to tie together the more sharply focused conscious experiences to which the organism typically attends. One example of such a transitional experience is the feeling of familiarity each of us experiences at some time or the other. Although difficult to tie down, by their very nature, such conscious experiences are indispensable in maintaining what James so aptly called the *stream* of consciousness.

EXTERNAL DETERMINANTS OF ATTENTION

The stimulus features that attract attention have been the subject of extensive research. In part this research has been encouraged by the desire of advertising agencies in Western society to find more effective means of making their products more alluring. There are a small number of principles generally agreed to be effective attention getters. Usually included in any such listing are movement, novelty (or contrast), stimulus size (e.g., loudness or some other facet of intensity), and repetition.

MOVEMENT. Like most other higher organisms with well-developed visual systems, humans are visually attracted to moving objects. The fact that movement detection is primarily a function of rods, as described in Chapter 5, makes movement an especially effective stimulus feature at night, when the rods are generally more efficient. Walking or driving down many urban thoroughfares at night usually means exposing oneself to a succession of garish moving advertising signs of almost unbelievable variety. Flashing arrows, blinking lights, and various sorts of animated figures abound, as we are all well aware. In the field or the forest, to which we may turn for a moment of relief, movement is no less effective, even if less extreme in appearance. Thus the moving mouse is more likely to be seen and caught by the stalking cat, just as the carelessly active cat is more likely to be detected by the mouse and so avoided by "freezing" (a reaction to fear that occurs in many animals).

NOVELTY. Experiments have demonstrated that the more novel of two otherwise equivalent stimuli is more likely to engage the attention of the organism. Evidence on this point ranges from measurement of the eye movements of human observers, as they scan visual materials of varying degrees of familiarity and complexity, to determination of the behavioral preference of rat subjects in mazes where they are permitted access to reward via a short and familiar alley or a longer and less familiar pathway. The preference of rat subjects for the latter alternative may also be attributed to their curiosity, but this may simply be another way of expressing the attention-getting property of novel stimuli.

Attention is more quickly directed toward the unusual stimulus. Such a stimulus tends also to be learned more quickly; the latter fact may of course be at least partly dependent upon the attention-attracting property. For example, if one word of a series to be memorized is printed in some contrasting color, it will generally be both noticed and learned first.

The novelty factor seems upon occasion to counter the force of certain of the other stimulus features used (by advertisers, for example) to attract attention. Thus when practically all the neon signs on a street or in a shopping center are of the garishly flashing variety, the appearance of a single simple and nonmoving sign may stand out; similarly, the more straightforward and unembellished statement of fact now used in an occasional advertisement may stand out by contrast with the more extravagent typical version.

SIZE. Sheer size is also a most effective way to attract attention. Fortunately, however, sheer size without additional redeeming virtues is more or less readily adapted to; thus the full-page newspaper advertisement run for the first time is likely to attract much more attention than the identical advertisement run for the fifth or tenth time.

REPETITION. Repetition is most effective in attracting attention when it occurs with at least some slight variation in theme or mode of presentation. Nevertheless, not only commercial advertisers but also politicians have learned that it pays to run the risk of the contempt that familiarity is alleged to breed. The familiar name, whether of an advertised product or a much-publicized politician, is more likely to be selected when the purchase is made or the voting lever is pulled. There may be some justification for this kind of action, if the alternative product or politician is unknown; on the other hand, in certain cases one may well elect to take his chances with the unknown product or office seeker.

Perceptual familiarity results from repeated or continuous stimulation in providing behavioral support; this has been demonstrated in a variety of experimental situations. The laboratory rat, for example, commonly "hoards" food pellets; that is, from a storage bin it carries away many more food pellets than it can possibly eat in any reasonable time. But it returns them only to a home cage with familiar odors from shavings and other cage features; changing these may prevent or seriously disrupt this behavior. Also, laboratory rats reared in cages with certain geometric patterns are later found to learn to discriminate these forms more rapidly than control rats not so reared.

INTERNAL DETERMINANTS OF ATTENTION

INTERESTS. The immediate or long-term interests of an individual, and his various dominant motivational systems, are clearly potent internal determinants of attention for him. To some extent the attention he pays to environmental objects and events, in accordance with such interests and motives, results from perceptual habits. Thus, for example, a hair stylist will most likely notice quite different aspects of a person to whom he is being introduced than will the voice teacher.

THE PUPILLARY RESPONSE. One of the more interesting of the various measures of internal determinants of attention is the pupillary response. The size of the pupil of the eye normally decreases in strong light, thereby protecting the retina, and increases in dim light so as to permit more light to enter the eye. The size of the pupil can also increase quite markedly when an individual's attention is engaged by a visual stimulus. Pupil size also increases when the individual is attending to certain nonvisual stimuli, as in mental problem-solving activity.

The data of Figure 6-1 represent the reactions of male and female subjects to

6-1 Differential reactivity in the pupillary response. A person's pupils enlarge when his interest is engaged. Males (shaded bars) and females (open bars) respond differently to the various stimuli. (Adapted from data in Hess, 1965.)

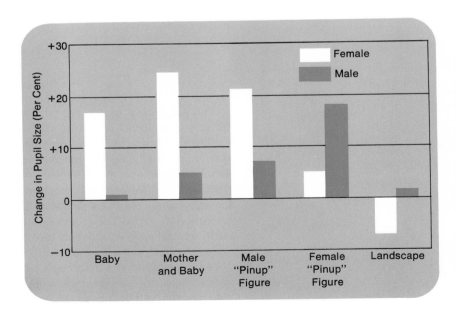

pictures designed to arouse differential amounts of interest in the two sexes. The pupillary measurements were made photographically by a camera taking pictures every .5 second. In accordance with our commonsensical expectations, men responded actively to female figures, and vice versa. The expected positive response of women to baby pictures and to mother and baby pictures was also obtained. The fact that constriction occurred in women to a landscape picture suggests that this supposedly "neutral" stimulus may have some slight aversive property for them; pupillary constriction can be shown to occur regularly with a stimulus that has negative feeling tones.

DISTRACTION

The most notable fact about attention may well be its fluctuation. A shift in attention is likely to be attributed to distraction, to some new stimulus acquiring sufficient potency to gain the limelight. Sometimes attention shifts when some particular behavior episode is completed, such as may occur when goal-directed behavior results in the satisfaction of a motive or even when a person is bored. In such cases the person may actively search for a new perceptual focus rather than be led there by some new stimulus.

One is usually said to be "distracted" when he is concentrating so intently upon a particular train of thought or attending so closely to something happening that he becomes oblivious to stimuli that would otherwise be noticed. On such occasions we may drive past familiar corners without turning, as we would if we were properly "paying attention," or we may make the accustomed turn when in fact we had this time not intended to do so. People are also unusually distractable when under severe emotional tension. Attention then tends to fluctuate much as it does under conditions of boredom, although for quite different reasons.

TRAINING ATTENTION

The inadequacy of the typical untrained person in attending to the crucial features of incidents witnessed, especially when he is not given prior warning, is readily demonstrated. In a common demonstration, an intruder bursts into a classroom, briefly accosts the instructor, and then hurriedly leaves. When the members of the class are subsequently quizzed about the details of what happened, the answers given are usually more notable for their variety than for their validity. Details of all sorts—of the intruder's dress, physique, and facial features as well as his behavior, verbal and otherwise—are very poorly reported. Perception under such circumstances is extremely incomplete and inaccurate, in large part probably because of faulty attentive mechanisms.

Less significant stimulus details may be assessed, as is sometimes done by the college instructor who includes on an examination a question about the color of the covers of the textbook. Even students who rarely open the pages of their text, thus leaving the covers more or less continuously open to observation, are likely to fare poorly on this item.

Difficulties in perception associated with inadequate habits of attention are compounded by poor registration in memory of what was actually observed, and subsequently also by poor recall of what was actually registered. Training observers to attend carefully to central aspects of things and events thus needs to include attention to memory. For this reason police officers are often trained to provide solid support for their memory by making a permanent *written* record of all pertinent information and observations as soon as possible after the observed event.

SELECTIVE ATTENTION AND DISCRIMINATION

Selective attention is critical to the development of discrimination among various stimulus objects and events. Some of the most thoroughgoing training in discrimination has been accomplished with animal subjects, mainly using the experimental techniques of operant conditioning (Chapter 11; A-3). For example, pigeons can be trained to respond to slight deviations in, say, the roundness (or some other stimulus feature) of small white objects by pecking, for which they are reinforced (given food reward), while allowing the normal (uniformly round) objects to pass by. Such birds have actually been "employed" on assembly lines in which pills were being examined for quality in drug plants; employers of course are delighted to pay off their labor in "chicken feed." The dismissal of these birds was due not to any performance inadequacy on their part but rather to the vociferous complaints of supplanted human employees!

An even more startling utilization of this same animal was made by B. F. Skinner, the leader of the American operant-conditioning movement. During World War II, Skinner trained pigeons to peck at a projected image when it went slightly off the center of a target area. The idea was to use such pigeons as unwittingly expendable bombardiers. The bomb was to be rigged to a gyroscopic directional device and a visual display of the target continuously presented to the harnessed pigeon. Appropriate pecking at the target, in the manner in which the pigeon had been trained, would then correct the face of the bomb so as to keep it on target. The degree of practicability of this device in actual use will probably never be known, because the final operational tests were reportedly blocked by an unbelieving and recalcitrant admiral. (The project was sponsored by the U.S. Navy.) Shortly thereafter the development and initial application of the first nuclear bomb, with greatly reduced need for pinpoint accuracy of delivery, rendered Skinner's project superfluous.

PHYSIOLOGICAL BASIS OF ATTENTION: ARAS

One of the more significant physiological breakthroughs of the past two decades has been the discovery of the sensory screening function of the reticular activating system (RAS). As described in Chapters 1 and 4, the reticular formation is a thick

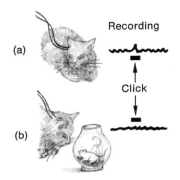

6-2 Neural activity of the cochlear nucleus in a cat is shown. (a) Response to an audible click sounded nearby while the cat is in repose. (b) Response in the same nerve to the same click while the cat is looking at the mice. (Adapted from Hernandez-Péon et al, 1956.)

neuronal network running from the lower part of the brainstem up into the thalamus. This network exercises some control over efferent (motor) functions, particularly with regard to maintenance of bodily sets and postures. It also has intimate connections with the association centers in the cortex. It is best known, however, for its role in filtering afferent (sensory) channels and so providing the basis for much of what we categorize as "attention." This function is performed by the *ascending* reticular activating system (ARAS), so named because of the ascending orientation—from lower to higher brain centers—of the sensory tracts.

The filtering of sensory input by the ARAS is well illustrated by one of the most famous recent experiments in neurophysiological research. In this experiment the neural activity of the cochlear nucleus (auditory nerve) of a cat subject was electronically monitored, as shown in Figure 6-2. Regular auditory stimulation by a clicking sound elicited a corresponding sharp uptake in neural activity, as expected on the basis of the afferent function of this sensory system. When the cat was shown two live mice within a glass jar, however, the sensory input from the click stimulus was clearly dampened, as evidenced by the reduction of the concomitant voltage spikes in the lower curve of Figure 6-2. Removal of the distracting (attention-getting) stimulus resulted in a resumption of the passage through the auditory nerve of the clicking stimulus, as shown at the top of the figure. (Some more recent critical treatments of the research and its interpretation are cited in the notes at the end of this chapter.)

This kind of evidence forced a reappraisal of the role of the nervous system with regard to the processing of sensory information from the environment and helped to clarify the determining factors in attention. It is quite clear that the ordinary afferent pathways from sense organ to brain are not the only determiners of sensory input. More generalized facilitation and inhibition can be attributed to the ARAS as a major system involved in the filtering of sensory information through the nervous system. The ARAS thus accounts for momentary fluctuations in attention, at least insofar as attention is a function of environmental factors.

Attenuation of potentially distracting stimulation from the same sensory systems is also achieved by means of the ARAS, as seen in the phenomenon of *auditory shadowing*. In this experiment different auditory inputs are provided the two ears separately. The subject is instructed to ignore the input to one ear while paying attention to the input to the other ear, which he is to repeat ("shadow"). The incompleteness of the effect is indicated, however, by the fact that unusual cues, such as hearing one's own name, do tend to attract attention and disrupt the shadowing performance, just as they do under more usual perceptual circumstances.

A similar process occurs during sleep. The sleeping mother, for example, may be quite oblivious to all the usual attention-getting cues in her environment but nonetheless awaken immediately to the cry of her baby. Differential perceptual sensitivity of this kind is evidently attributable to the differential selectivity of the sensory filtering mechanisms of the ARAS working in conjunction with higher cortical centers.

Overall, the picture that has emerged suggests that the detailed patterns of sensory input that are coded in the nervous system after their transduction and then transformed somehow by the brain into conscious experience are normally handled by the specialized afferent nerves of the central nervous system. The controlling attentional mechanisms that determine the flow of this information are largely under the control of the ARAS.

SENSORY DEPRIVATION

The way in which deprivation of one particular sensory modality can have dramatic behavioral effects has been indicated in the discussion of the tabetic patient (Chapter 5, p. 134); visual controls are poor substitutes for the normal kinesthetic feedback from limb movements. Persons deprived of normal vision and hearing are of course much more common. Adjustments can be made, within limits, to such unfortunate sensory losses. The remarkable career of Helen Keller attests to the extent to which such adjustments are possible. Although blind and deaf—and as a result also mute—Miss Keller, with the help of a gifted and devoted teacher, was able to learn to express herself effectively and become a most respected and productive member of society.

Reduction in Sensory Input

Another approach to the general problem of sensory function is drastically to reduce the total sensory input to normal human subjects. A number of such experiments have been performed, with interesting and instructive results. Perhaps the most dramatic results occurred in the very first such experiment. College students were hired at a reasonable rate of pay ($20 a day). They were required simply to remain comfortably reclined on a bed except for brief periods allowed for eating and elimination. The bed was in a small, lighted compartment. Light stimulation thus occurred but details of even the bare visual environment could not be perceived because the subjects wore translucent goggles. Auditory stimulation was minimized by the masking noise from an exhaust fan, which also provided adequate ventilation in the compartment. Tactual stimulation was reduced by having the subject wear gloves over the hands and cuffs over the forearms.

The perceptual and behavioral consequences of this severe reduction of normal sensory stimulation were profound. Perceptually, marked spatial and temporal disorientation occurred. Hallucinations, both bizarre and dreamlike, were common. (Hallucinations are perceptual experiences that seem quite real to the subject but are without any corresponding basis in actual external stimulation, at least as far as other observers can detect.) Behaviorally, ability scores on intellectual tasks declined and the subjects showed poor concentration when work requirements were imposed by the experimenter. The strange environment became intolerable. Two or three days of the experiment were all that most of the subjects could manage.

Subjects' verbatim descriptions of hallucinatory activity have been reported. For example:

The herd of elephants. Oh, that was pretty. That came very spontaneously. It was just sort of elephants in back, with pink and blue and purple. . . . They were moving. The elephants themselves weren't moving, the picture was moving as if it were a close-up, sort of a backdrop . . . the elephants were gray . . . the background was pink . . . they weren't real elephants, because they were more like cutouts [Freedman et al., 1961, p. 68].

The general conclusion from this kind of research is that the normal person depends to a very great degree on the variety of sensory stimulation that he is constantly receiving, although this dependence is not always realized. Just as each sensory system maintains a more or less continuous, albeit low-level, input from the sense organ to the brain, so the higher nervous centers apparently maintain a continuous monitoring of the various sensory inputs. The central role of attentional mechanisms in these processes is evident.

SLEEP AND DREAMING

The important and interesting phenomenon of sleep is one which has recently enjoyed a revival of experimental and theoretical attention. Although popularly regarded as a state in which behavior is absent, sleep is more often regarded by psychologists as an active state. Certainly it poses an important behavioral problem, even apart from the phenomenon of dreaming. Sleep constitutes a significant problem because, if for no other reason, it fills so large a proportion of a human's time, roughly one third of the day for each of us. With regard to attention, sleep is clearly a state of markedly reduced alertness, even though selective attention may be maintained, as illustrated in the earlier example of the mother's being so readily awakened by even the low cry of her baby.

One of the relatively recent results of sleep research has been the experimental confirmation of the everyday observation that there are more or less distinct stages in sleep. Neurophysiologically, the gradual reduction of arousal and alertness—of attention—can be measured in terms of changes in brain waves, measured by the *electroencephalogram*, or *EEG*. The sleep process begins with the *alpha* rhythm (with frequencies of about 10 cycles per second). This is gradually superseded by slower wave frequencies as alertness diminishes, with the delta rhythm (1 to 3 cycles per second) characteristic of very deep sleep.

The most interesting of the various stages of sleep that can now be distinguished is that of *paradoxical* sleep, in which the person seems to be fast asleep by behavioral and attentional standards (because he is not easily awakened and is not likely to respond to stimulation) yet shows the fast waves characteristic of the waking state. The paradox produced by the apparent contradiction between evidence from behavioral observation (deep sleep) and electrophysiology (waking state) is resolved by the fact that this is the stage during which rapid eye movements also occur (hence the term *REM stage*) and very active dreaming can be readily demonstrated. The brain may thus be presumed to be extremely active during the REM stage of sleep, but with attention turned inward rather than outward.

Sleep and waking are now believed to be at least partially under the control of specific brain centers. There is at present good evidence for a waking center, related closely to the reticular system (and the ARAS mechanisms); experimental destruction of this presumed center has been shown to result in continuous sleep over prolonged periods (up to a week or more) in monkeys. There is also suggestive evidence for a sleep center. (Sleep can be induced on demand in cats appropriately wired by electrical stimulation of implanted electrodes.)

There is no question but that humans do vary quite markedly in their sleep needs, or conversely, in their ability to sustain waking activity with minimal amounts of physiological recovery from sleep. Nevertheless, humans are also notoriously inaccurate in their claims concerning their own lack of sleep. Those persons who claim to sleep for some extraordinarily low number of hours (or minutes) per day may not be counting all the time; they are most likely to overlook so-called catnaps or other short periods of light rest, perhaps verging into sleep.

HYPNOSIS

The most dramatic manipulations of attention are probably found in the phenomenon of hypnosis. Although superficially resembling sleep, hypnosis is quite another matter. It is generally agreed to be a result of profoundly heightened *suggestibility*. The hypnotic subject has voluntarily reduced his attention at the request of the hypnotist. The hypnotized subject is thus a very alert subject, but he is alert mainly to this one source of external stimulation, the hypnotist. Under these conditions the skilled hypnotist is able to manipulate the subject's perception and behavior to a remarkable degree.

HYPNOTIC INDUCTION. The crux of hypnotic induction is the progressive reduction of attention by the subject to external stimulation other than the hypnotist's voice and any special auxiliary aids that he may use (e.g., a small bright object such as a bead). The particular details of procedure can and do vary considerably but in all cases the (usually quite willing) subject is made as relaxed as possible, with a deliberate reduction of external stimulation, and instructed to concentrate on the hypnotist's voice. The voice is ordinarily kept low and monotonous as the hypnotist proceeds to instruct the subject to carry out some simple action, such as crossing his legs. He may also make categorical statements, such as that the subject is being very quiet (which he obviously is), so as to win confidence and gain additional respect. Gradually as the session proceeds the hypnotist leads the subject into accepting increasingly radical, and ultimately quite untrue, statements and performing very unusual kinds of behavior.

HYPNOTIC BEHAVIOR. The fully hypnotized subject is capable of some incredible perceptual responses. For example, he can be made functionally blind, or deaf, or anesthetic (unfeeling), in accordance with the suggestions advanced by the hypnotist. These very dramatic perceptual changes are the basis of the use of hypnosis as an anesthetic technique; although the first such use, in the nineteenth century mainly, was for surgical operations, today the most popular application is in connection with dental work.

Behaviorally, the hypnotized subject is equally susceptible to the suggestions of the hypnotist. One of the more common of these involves age regression; the subject is told that he is five years old, for example, and he may then behave accordingly (e.g., write his name in a childish hand). In general, such behaviors are in accordance with the subject's present *conceptions* of behavior at such an earlier age rather than with the actual behaviors that then occurred.

The typical hypnotic session ends with an instruction by the hypnotist to "wake up" at a signal, such as the count of 3. In the meantime, however, the subject may have been given some particular instruction to follow after he awakens from the trance. For example, he may have been instructed to rise and leave the classroom when the teacher (who may or may not have also been the hypnotist) looks at him directly, rather than waiting for the usual bell and leaving with the rest of the class. When this cue is delivered, the subject, now fully awake, may rise, perhaps looking rather puzzled, and leave the room with a short excuse of one kind or another. This kind of behavior, which can be fully as impressive as the perceptual phenomena that occur during the trance itself, results from *posthypnotic suggestion*.

USES OF HYPNOSIS. Scientific opinion is somewhat divided on the practical value of hypnosis. Apart from its use as an anesthetic, hypnosis can be used in psychotherapy. Hypnosis is most effective in treating patients with the symptoms of hysteria (e.g., functional sensory loss or paralysis). This is not surprising, because these symptoms are generally believed to be the result of suggestibility. Freud was trained in hypnosis and used it in therapy until he found that a substantial proportion of even his own patients showed great resistance to it.

Hypnosis is also occasionally used for other miscellaneous purposes, such as attempting to change some undesirable habit (e.g., smoking) or to enable the subject to recall some important but forgotten fact. In the former case, unfortunately, it has not been shown to have any more lasting efficacy than any of the many other techniques tried. In the latter case it is often claimed that inducing the subject to relax and concentrate his attention on the matter to be recalled (both features present in the typical hypnotic session) can be just as effective without the hypnosis. One exception to this statement is the situation where the original learning had itself been under hypnosis; there is some evidence that retention under hypnosis is better for learning that also occurred under hypnosis. In this respect, however, there is no need to assume anything special about the hypnosis, because the same statement can be made generally about all learning and memory cues; retention is usually best when it is tested under conditions similar to those in which the learning occurred.

DANGERS OF HYPNOSIS. Because of the danger of triggering serious emotional episodes in chronically or acutely disturbed individuals, the detection of which in advance is not always easy, hypnosis is not generally recommended as a parlor game. There is still some difference of expert opinion as to whether or not one can really be hypnotized "against his will," and whether it is possible to induce the hypnotized person to do something that he would not do under normal circumstances, such as commit a crime. Nevertheless, the difficulty of determining motivational factors and the ease with which the hypnotized individual can be perceptually misled suggest that extreme caution be exercised in the use of the technique. The advance detection and "screening out" of individuals who may be harmed in some way by the hypnotic process is neither easy nor certain. Hypnosis is definitely not something to be casually engaged in, either by the experienced hypnotist or by the amateur.

Of the many ways in which attentional processes interact with overt behavior, three in particular may be singled out for a brief description and comment: the orienting reaction, reaction time, and vigilance.

The Orienting Reaction

Initially emphasized by Pavlov, the Russian physiologist who did the first systematic research on conditioning, the orienting reaction (OR) is basically a mechanism of attention, a readying of the organism for perception as well as action. It occurs in response to stimulation whose exact nature the organism is not quite able to identify. Novel stimuli, for example, are quite likely to elicit the OR. It takes characteristic form in different species; for example, the dog, the most favored subject in Pavlov's conditioning research, visibly perks his ears and takes a generally ready posture when so stimulated.

In humans, there is the predictably greater variety of physiological and behavioral changes to novel stimuli, but OR's do occur.

The OR is behaviorally important in that it prepares the organism for more effective perception and performance. By improving attentional functions it facilitates learning as well as perception and performance. It has therefore been thoroughly analyzed, with respect to its psychophysiological as well as its more overt behavioral correlates.

The OR has been shown to consist of changes in the following organs: *sense organs* (e.g., pupillary dilation) and their *orientation* (e.g., eyelids opening, ears pricking up), *skeletal musculature* (e.g., increase in muscle tone), *central nervous system* (e.g., slower brain waves, or EEG, replaced by faster), and *circulatory system* (heart rate decelerates, blood tends to leave the limbs and concentrate in the head). All these changes will be recognized as improving the perceptual adjustment of the organism.

Reaction Time

Reaction time (RT) is the amount of time required for a response to be made following some appropriate cue. Studies of RT are older than the formal science of psychology. Individual differences in this type of reactivity are quite marked, within the limits of the very small intervals of time (e.g., .001 second) in which RT's are usually measured. The theoretical significance of RT research involves mainly the dependence of RT on attentional mechanisms and the implications for neurophysiology. Practically, RT is perhaps of somewhat greater significance; the ability to respond quickly is crucial in such commonplace skills as rapid braking of automobiles and a large number of similar behavioral requirements of our machine-oriented and gadget-dominated culture.

Much of the theoretical interest in RT and attention has been concerned with the question of whether a motor set or a sensory set is most efficient. A *motor set* is defined as concentrating on making the reaction; a *sensory set* is defined as concentrating on perceiving the cue. The question is whether one improves the speed of reacting better by adopting a motor or a sensory set during the foreperiod (the time preceding the signal). The more recent evidence on this question tends to support the sensory set as more facilitative, but there is really no single simple answer; many factors, such as degree of training and past experiences, play a part in determining RT.

From a practical point of view, there are several facts of general significance concerning RT. For example, measurements of RT are essential in determining the guidelines relating distance between vehicles and safe braking practice. That is, we need to know how quickly the typical driver is able to make a braking response to a danger signal before we can work out safe following distances for various automobile speeds. The speed with which braking occurs is directly dependent upon RT.

Other applicable results from RT studies concern the differential speed of reaction to various sensory modalities, and to combinations of sensory stimulation. Generally auditory cues are responded to most rapidly. Also it is better to use more than one modality for cuing if improved speed of RT is desired.

With regard to experimental procedure, there have been two main forms of RT testing. *Choice reaction time,* in which the subject must decide which of two (or more) responses to make as a result of which cue is given, is much more difficult than *simple reaction time,* in which only a single cue and a single related response are involved. The brief comments concerning RT in this section have concerned the simple type of situation. In the next section we turn to a related form of performance test in which a continuing discrimination must be made, but the emphasis is not so much on speed as on accuracy.

Vigilance

In many situations an observer must maintain a close watch on environmental events over very long periods of time. Such a task is called *vigilance* when some particular type of event is to be detected and reported. Vigilance tasks are most common in military operations but occur also in certain peacetime occupations (e.g., fire watcher, sailor on watch). If equipment is to be observed, such as a radar screen, the term *monitoring* is usually applied.

The crucial problem in all vigilance tasks is maintenance of attention over extended time periods. Detection of signals typically diminishes as time passes, presumably because of the great difficulty of sustaining high degrees of attentiveness. Superior performance results from giving the observer adequate feedback (knowledge of results), giving him sufficient interpolated rest periods even if they are very brief, and providing him with some sort of signal even if not all of them are to be reported. The latter procedure in particular would seem to operate by helping him maintain interest and thereby attentiveness. Further, there is some indication that the deliberate provision of "distracting" stimuli (e.g., comic books, pictures of girls provided Navy sonar men) improves signal detection under at least some work conditions.

The most familiar need for vigilance, and one that touches in one way or another practically all of us, is associated with automobile driving. With the advent of the U.S. interstate highway system of freeways, highway driving became so attractive that increasing numbers of people began to drive long distances. The new national freeway system, with smoothly paved, divided four-lane roads and limited access, seemed to assure improved traffic safety. Before long, however, highway traffic engineers discovered some unanticipated negative features. For one thing, they noted a strong tendency for drivers to develop a kind of self-hypnotic (trancelike) condition after several hours of more or less continuous driving. The boredom associated with the long stretches of uninterrupted pavement, enhanced by the hum of the tires on the pavement (a cue similar to that deliberately used by the hypnotist, as described above), seem to lull a driver into a severe condition of *nonvigilance*. The consequent lack of attention to new cues, such as those related to a sudden emergency situation, poses a threat to safety.

This threat can be avoided only if positive steps to maintain vigilance are taken (e.g., listening to the radio, engaging in conversation). It is ironic that the very characteristic sought by the highway planners, namely, the reduction of presumably unnecessary distractions such as those associated with intersecting roads or intrinsically undesirable billboard advertisements, would now be seen to constitute in itself a new kind of risk. The situation indicates that applications of knowledge are not unlike experimental research in that unplanned consequences can often necessitate a revision of a practical program in much the same way as unanticipated results can change the direction of a research program.

Take a Breather

FOOLING THE MIND'S EYE

The three curious figures shown on this page are all physically impossible; that is, they could not exist *as objects*. Nevertheless, they are perceptually quite possible. For example, try running your eye up the inclines in figure (c); the perpetual incline is perceptually but not logically real. Similar contrasts between perception and reason can be experienced with figures (a) and (b).

Why do these contrasts exist? Simply put, they result from the need of the perceptual system to establish a three-dimensional world on the basis of essentially two-dimensional information. The visual system is thus unable to resolve the contradiction between its usual two-dimensional framework and the fundamentally incompatible information provided by the third dimension.

In any event, quite apart from their theoretical implications, "impossible objects" afford a fascinating sidelight on the functions of our visual perception system.

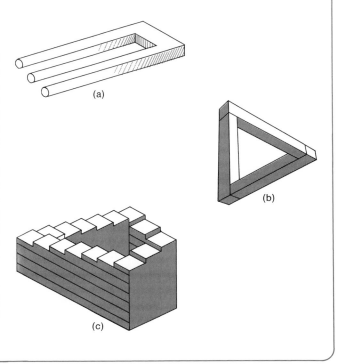

PERCEPTUAL CONSTANCIES

The processes by which the organism is able to perceive objects as stable in spite of the very great variation in the actual sensory patterns are called *perceptual constancies*. The most important of these involve shape, size, and brightness.

Shape Constancy

Once an object is identified as a familiar one, it is perceived as having its characteristic shape. The typical dinner plate is round and is so perceived in spite of the fact that it very seldom presents a perfectly or even approximately round retinal image. Most commonly, in fact, the angle at which we see a dinner plate dictates some degree of ellipticity for its retinal image. Similarly, a door is known to be rectangular and is so perceived in spite of the fact that it is most commonly represented by a trapezoidal retinal image.

Size Constancy

The perceived size of an object is an inverse function of its distance from the observer, as long as stimulus distance perception is all that is involved. This relationship occurs because the farther away an object is from the eye, the smaller will be the size of its retinal image. However, when one recognizes the object as a familiar one whose size is known—e.g., a friend—then the perceived size is constant regardless of the distance of the object and the actual size of its retinal image. The greater distance is perceptually registered; that is, we do not assume that our friend has suddenly become very small.

Because perceived size is closely related to distance perception, it is easy to make mistakes about one or the other or both. Under conditions of poor visibility (e.g., heavy fog or twilight) or extreme emotional state (e.g., one is very anxious to see the friend) the figure identified as one's friend may turn out to be something quite different (e.g., a small boy or a post light). As soon as this mistake is recognized, a new perceptual adjustment occurs with regard to both size and distance (e.g., the small boy, now clearly seen as such, is also recognized as being much closer than originally perceived).

Brightness Constancy

If the brightness of some object is known previously, and the object is identified, it is perceived as being of that brightness in spite of the great variations that occur in the actual amount of light that is reflected to the eye. Thus a white or gray cat will be seen as white or gray, and brighter than a black cat, even when appearing in much weaker illumination than the black cat and thus actually reflecting less light to the eye. Perceived brightness is reconciled with the degree of illumination much as perceived size is reconciled with distance.

Brightness constancy can be eliminated, or at least greatly reduced, if one is deprived of perception of the actual illumination incident upon the object. This is most readily done, in the laboratory, by means of a *reduction screen*. For example, a subject will be shown two pieces of paper, one white and one black, and will have no difficulty in selecting the brighter when requested to make this judgment. Now his perception and his judgment remain the same even if the illumination of the white paper is greatly reduced and the illumination of the black paper is greatly increased. If the reduction screen is used, however, the perception changes. A simple form of this device is merely a tube through which only a part of the object can be seen, with no way of detecting the illumination. Under this condition the black paper under very strong light will be judged as brighter than the white paper under very dim illumination, in accordance with the retinal realities. Brightness constancy is thus subject to the same limitations as the other types of constancy, such as size, when the usual relevant perceptual cues are removed.

Similar types of constancy occur with color, spatial location, and a variety of similar perceptual processes. This discussion should suffice to indicate the generality of the constancy effect and its dependence upon normal perceptual functions involving the stimulus as well as the perceiver and his personal characteristics.

PERCEPTUAL INSTABILITIES

In general, perceptual instability reflects the equivocal character of the stimulus as it appears to the subject. Three kinds of illustrative materials will be examined: object and figural instability, reversibility related to learning, and motion instability (the autokinetic effect).

Object and Figural Instability

The figures shown in Figure 6-3 are all well-known examples of visual fluctuation. Each of them can be reversed with respect to orientation; in the case of the staircase (c), for example, one can see it either as the topside or the bottomside of a staircase whose treads rise from right to left, or as an upside-down view of such a staircase. If this reversal is difficult to achieve, and it typically occurs rather unpredictably as one stares at the figure, try the simpler truncated pyramid, book, or pipe. The truncated pyramid is perhaps the easiest of all to reverse, because it is apparent that the small central square can be seen either as near or far from the observer. Similarly, the central line of the book figure can be viewed as near or far. The pipe, which is more objectively a cylinder formed by interlacing concentric circles, can be seen as pointing off to the far left or the far right.

All these figures, and many more, share the property of presenting quite ambiguous orientational cues to the retina. Eye movements were once suggested as an explanation of the reversal in perception, but this explanation was contradicted by the fact that when eye movements are directly measured they are found to *follow* rather than precede the reported fluctuations. Moreover, the fluctuations have been found to occur even when the retinal image is itself stabilized. The mechanism by means of which this kind of perceptual fluctuation operates is presumably some kind of brain function that remains to be discovered.

The reversals that are demonstrated by the drawings in Figure 6-3 can be seen as well with two eyes as with one. Because they are two-dimensional they provide very little in the way of cues for depth perception. However, if the *objects* themselves are shown to an observer, whether the reversals occur depends largely upon

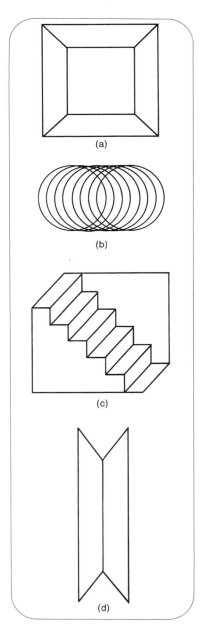

(a)

(b)

(c)

(d)

6-3 Reversible figures. Each of these well-known figures represents a familiar object, the perceptual orientation to which reverses spontaneously as one looks at it steadily.

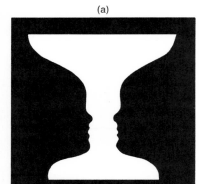

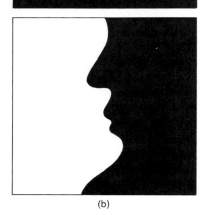

6-4 Reversible figure–ground. Perceptual reversibility in these drawings consists of shifts in the figure–ground relationship. In (a) seeing the vase—as a figure—makes the two facing profiles impossible to see, at that time. In (b) seeing the left (white) figure as a girl precludes seeing the right profile as a man—simultaneously, that is—and vice versa. Spontaneous shifts are likely to occur in these figure–ground relationships much as they do in other reversible perceptions.

whether he is viewing with one or two eyes. With one eye, and practically no cues for depth, the reversals would occur much as they do for the two-dimensional drawings. With two eyes, however, powerful depth perception cues are effective, as explained below, and a high degree of perceptual stability is achieved.

Additional examples of reversible figures are shown in Figure 6-4, which illustrates the figure–ground principle of perception, discussed later under organizational processes.

Reversibility and Learning

Perceptual instability is very largely a function of ambiguous stimulus representation. It is reasonable therefore that when one has a substantial bias resulting from his past experience (learning) it is likely to be even more effective in determining perception of reversibility of normal stimuli. Look at and identify item (c) in Figure 6-5. What is it? The figure readily reverses from human profile to rat, or vice versa, for most people, but what did you see first? The bias produced in many psychologists by their years of "running" laboratory rats very likely influences them to see the rat much more often than the "average" person. The human faces seen in part (b) of Figure 6-5 also fluctuate. Which of these two women did you see first?

Now try to recall how the reversible staircase in Figure 6-3 first appeared. Did it first appear as the top or the bottom of the staircase? The chances are that it appeared first, and remained longer, as the top, because that is the way most of us most often see staircases.

The progressively modified figure shown in Figure 6-6 illustrates the immediate effect of expectations induced by the sequential changes in the drawing. Besides the exercise suggested in Figure 6-6, asking a friend to say what he sees when the figures are shown singly, starting at one end or the other or in the middle, may also be an instructive means of demonstrating the bias that is immediately developed when the extreme figures (man or girl) are seen first.

Instability of Motion: The Autokinetic Effect

Our final example of perceptual instability is of a somewhat different nature from those preceding. The autokinetic effect refers to the perceived motion of an actually fixed light in an otherwise completely darkened room. The autokinetic effect can be diminished and ultimately eliminated by the gradual introduction of a visual framework.

The fact that the visual autokinetic effect is sensitive to suggestibility indicates that cortical mechanisms are involved. Experience with visual movement or even the suggestion of movement (e.g., an arrow pointing in a certain direction) prior to being placed in the darkened chamber with the small stationary light is very likely to result in reported movement consistent with the direction and velocity of the light movement previously perceived. In the absence of such experimental manipulation the light is reported to wander aimlessly around a point, once a period of no perceived movement has passed.

Although the visual autokinetic effect has received the most attention, a corresponding type of autokinesis has also been reported for audition and touch.

PERCEPTION OF FUNDAMENTAL PHYSICAL DIMENSIONS

Our discussion has already touched upon some of the ways in which the human organism perceives the fundamental physical dimensions of his environment (e.g., his perception of distance as it relates to size perception). Now we look more closely at the perception of several of these dimensions.

Visual Depth Perception

How one perceives visual distance is a very old problem in philosophy and physiology, preceding the formal origins of psychology as a science. It has continued to attract much experimental attention within psychology. Further, depth perception is one of those problems that concern a number of practitioners as well as scientists; in addition to physiologists, psychologists, and philosophers, these include graphic artists, athletes and coaches, automobile safety engineers, and military scientists.

The basic problem in visual depth perception relates to the fact that the retinal light-sensitive layer does not itself have a depth dimension. Depth must therefore somehow be developed on the basis of indirect cues. These are customarily divided into two categories, those dependent upon two eyes (binocular cues) and those requiring only one eye (monocular cues).

BINOCULAR CUE: RETINAL DISPARITY. Retinal disparity is probably the major cue normally used in producing visual depth effects. This cue depends upon the fact that the two eyes, separated by 2 inches or more, receive slightly different perspectives of the same view. These slightly different retinal representations are somehow translated, by the visual brain centers, into perceived depth. Retinal disparity is the basis for the stereoscopic effect of depth achieved when two such pictures are shown separately, one each to the appropriate eye. This kind of photograph can be made by a stereoscopic camera equipped with two lenses set approximately as far apart as the human eyes. A very vivid experience of visual depth is possible upon the basis of this cue alone, although if other cues also contribute the effect can be enhanced.

BINOCULAR CUE: EYE CONVERGENCE. The role of eye convergence, the second binocular cue, in visual perception of depth is much more questionable than that of retinal disparity, but it is believed by most authorities to play at least a minor part. As the eyes look at far-off objects they are looking along essentially parallel lines of sight. As the object viewed comes closer, however, the eyes must turn toward each other more and more—converge—in order to focus the light rays it reflects. Kinesthetic cues from the eye musculature are thus thought to be the basis of some of the perception of depth, although in keeping with kinesthesis generally they are not represented by any correlated conscious sensations.

MONOCULAR CUES IN DEPTH PERCEPTION. Experiencing depth in a single eye is multiply determined, as indicated by the long list of monocular cues listed below.

Interposition refers to the blocking-out effect that occurs when a nearer object intrudes between the eye and a farther object. With this powerful cue, the eye

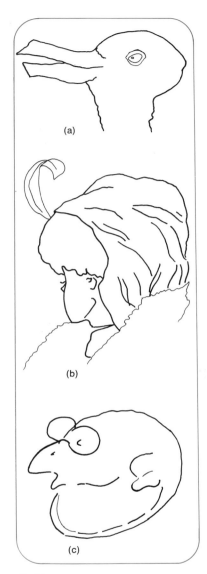

6-5 Ambiguous (reversible) figures. (a) Rabbit–duck; the rabbit face looks to the right, the duck face to the left; (b) young girl–old woman; the girl's chin is the woman's nose; (c) rat–man; since both rat and man look left this figure may have to be looked at steadily for both to occur.

155

6-6 A progressively modified figure. To check the influence of expectation on perception, try showing *either* the top row *or* the bottom row to some friends, asking each to concentrate on the two most ambiguous figures (x or y) and then to tell you what they see. It is more difficult to see the girl at x and the man at y than when both rows are shown together and the entire sequence is evident. (From Attneave, 1971.)

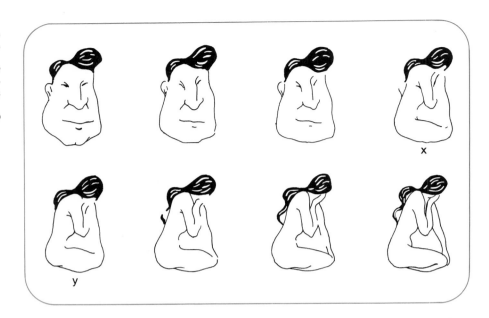

interprets the object that does the blocking as closer in accordance with the ordinary physical state of affairs that produces such an effect.

Clarity refers to the sharpness with which an object can be seen. It is a distance cue because far-off objects are normally much fuzzier than close-up ones. However, it can be a very misleading cue upon occasion; for example, an urban resident unaccustomed to the relatively clear atmosphere of the rural countryside or the desert may grossly underestimate the distance of a mountain range he is able to see very clearly even though it is many miles away.

Linear perspective depends upon the fact that far-off objects not only project a smaller image on the retina but are separated from other objects by smaller retinal distances. Consider the way railroad tracks appear closer together as they recede into the distance (shown in Figure 6-7) or how objects at the far end of a tunnel are framed by similarly converging walls as seen from the near end of the tunnel.

Movement cues in visual depth perception depend upon two main features of objects in relation to the observer. First, far-off moving objects seem to move much slower than near ones actually moving at the same rate of speed; they cover the same retinal distance in much longer time. This effect can be obtained with the head held steady. When the head is moved, the second cue may operate. Now the nearest objects seem to move in a direction opposite to the actual movement of the head; far-off objects seem to move in the same direction as the head. These two cues produced by movement either in the objects or in the observer contribute to his ability to estimate distance visually.

Shadows contribute significantly to the depth effect, although again not in a directly conscious manner. Look at the view in Figure 6-8. We normally see the figures as holes or craters, because we are accustomed to having light appear from overhead and shadows therefore appear on the upper part of concave surfaces.

6-7 Linear perspective. Note how the rectangles, actually of equal size, appear to differ in size as a function of their placement along the converging lines.

When the view is turned upside down, however, the figures are seen as protuberances, rather than as holes lighted from below. (To achieve this latter effect the illumination source from below would need to be shown explicitly, because it is normally not so inferred.) Convex surfaces usually show the shadow effect indicated by the inverted perspective, so that one perceives depth accordingly.

Figures 6-9 and 6-10 demonstrate the operation of *texture gradients*. In a manner somewhat analogous to the linear effect mentioned above, any texture tends to show a progressive diminution as one looks at it at increasingly greater distance. Depth effects are produced by geometric drawings as well as actual photographs.

Relaxation of the ciliary muscles, which control the shape of the lens, allows the lens to flatten and adjust the focus of light rays coming from a distance. As an object moves closer these muscles contract, making the lens bulge and so continue to focus the light rays appropriately. This *accommodation* process is believed to contribute to the depth effect, at least up to about 20 feet (which is as far as much contraction is required). The presumption is that the kinesthetic feedback operates as it does in the binocular convergence process. The direct evidence for this effect, however, is even less convincing than that for the convergence effect. Nevertheless, it is possible that both make some kind of indirect contribution to the visual perception of depth.

157

6-8 View of moon craters. Invert the view and note that the craters seem to be hillocks, indicating the important role that shadows play in depth perception. (Photo courtesy of NASA.)

DEVELOPMENTAL FACTORS IN DEPTH PERCEPTION. There has been an unusual amount of interest within psychology in the problem of development of visual depth perception. The central issue has been whether or not experience is required. The experimental question as to whether a naive organism, usually a very young mammal, can perceive depth has been asked of a variety of animal forms, including human babies.

An ingenious testing device, called the *visual cliff*, was invented in an effort to obtain experimental answers to this question. Essentially, the visual cliff consists of a heavy sheet of glass on which the subject is placed and under which a textured surface appears at varying distances. The assumption is that if a very young and visually relatively inexperienced baby or animal avoids crawling on the side with the apparent fall-off, it is utilizing an innate ability to perceive depth. Figure 6-11 shows some of the crawling behavior of a baby. Like most of the other young

6-9 Depth from textured surfaces. The five disks shown in panel (a) are of obviously different sizes and appear to lie on the same plane surface. In panel (b), however, with the addition of the latticework texture, exactly the same five disks now appear to lie on different planes and also appear to be of the same size but at different distances.

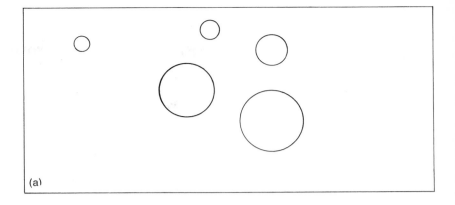

(a)

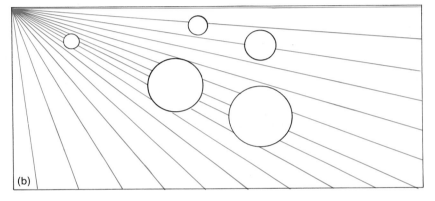

(b)

organisms tested, the baby typically does in fact avoid approaching the superficially dangerous end of the test surface. The presence of the solid glass plate is apparently not sufficiently reassuring! The conclusion that at least some ability to perceive depth visually is innately determined and so independent of visual experience is therefore generally drawn from these studies.

Localization

Under normal conditions one can utilize visual distance cues to help in the visual location of objects. Location by sound, however, is necessary under many conditions (e.g., temporary or permanent impairment or loss of vision, partial or complete darkness, objects out of sight). There are three major cues used in the localization of sources of sounds. They all depend upon binaural stimulation and reflect differences in reception of sound by the two ears. One cue is the difference in *time of arrival* of the sound, if the source is closer to one of the two ears. The second cue is a slight difference in *intensity,* because the ear that is farthest removed from the sound source will receive a signal that has been partially blocked out by the head. The third cue is a difference in *phase* of the sound cycle. Very slight differences in timing and intensity are sufficient to mediate this kind of localization.

Another kind of object localization is used by the blind. Blind individuals are

159

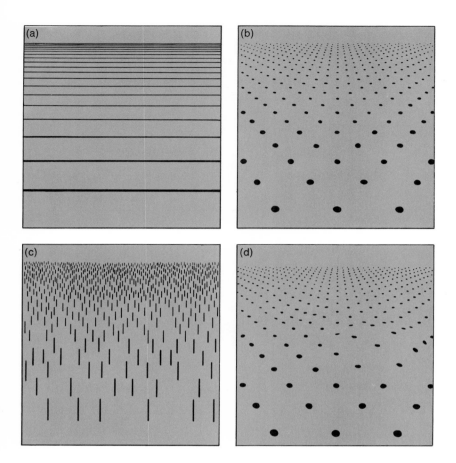

6-10 Depth from density gradients. Panels (a) and (b) appear as smooth and flat surfaces, (c) as a rough and flat surface, and (d) as a surface with varying elevation. All panels show how direct depth perception can be achieved by varying density of texture. (From Ulric Neisser, *The processes of vision*, *Scientific American*, 1968, **219**, 204–214.)

capable of avoiding obstacles in walking to a much greater degree than sighted individuals who are temporarily deprived of visual cues by blindfolds. Blind persons, and normally sighted persons who have been appropriately trained, are able to localize and avoid obstacles by listening carefully for the echoes of sounds they produce, such as the sound of their own footsteps. Their tapping with canes provides another source of such sounds. Various devices are being worked on that will provide improved echolocation for blind individuals, although as yet none of these has been widely marketed. This kind of localization ability is a counterpart to the remarkably well-developed ability of bats, which have no visual receptors, to localize objects by reflected sound waves of a very high pitch that they emit.

Localization of objects in space by means of the third distance sense, olfaction, is relatively poor. Sources of smells can ordinarily be located only after a considerable amount of sniffing and even then locomotion is usually aided by visual cues.

Movement Perception

Experimentation on visual perception of real movement has uncovered some interesting facts. At the upper threshold of movement some blurring occurs, as would be expected. However, strange and quite unexpected perceptual effects have been reported around the lower threshold of real motion of an object; that is at the speed of real movement of the object that is just barely sufficient for the object to be perceived as actually moving. At very slow rates, for example, the observer may experience an apparent *backward* movement of the object, and sometimes also an apparent *duplication* of the object.

Time Perception
The ability of an organism to "tell time" is apparently a function of one or the other internal body processes. Infrahuman organisms, such as bees, have been found to have much more precise time-measuring mechanisms than those man has. Humans show wide individual differences in their time-telling ability. A progressive improvement in this ability has been found with increasing age. Monotonous tasks, which readily induce boredom and reduce motivation, tend to make time pass more slowly, as is commonly noted. Variations in apparent time passage are also reported to be the result of some drugs, the general perceptual effects of which are discussed below. Finally, a very marked telescoping of the apparent passage of time is also commonly experienced in dreaming.

The "biological clock," or internal timing mechanism, that humans, like other animals, seem to possess has received attention lately. The apparent disorienting effect of rapid travel around the world is one practical problem that man has had to face with the arrival of the "jet age." When several time zones are passed through very quickly the traveler is often unable to function properly for a day or two and is well advised to refrain from taking on too many responsibilities until recovery has occurred.

6-11 The visual cliff. Babies or young animals are placed on a thick glass sheet with a drop-off underneath. Avoidance of the apparent drop-off is held to be evidence for depth perception in such young and presumably inexperienced organisms.

ILLUSIONS

Illusions are perceptions that are contradictory to the physical arrangements of the stimulus situation. Illusions may be regarded as occupying the opposite end of a continuum from perceptual constancy. Whereas constancy produces accurate perception in spite of various transformations of reality in the sense organ, an illusion is produced by perceptual processes in spite of truthful representations of reality in the sense organ.

Geometric Illusions of Size
Some of the better-known visual illusions of size are shown in the panels of Figure 6-12. The lines or small circles are in each case of the same size, although size differences typically appear and are difficult to eliminate even after they are pointed out to the observer.

Panel (a) shows the Müller–Lyer figure, perhaps the best known of all the visual illusions. Its generality has been indicated by the fact that under appropriate testing arrangements it can be demonstrated in subhuman forms as lowly as the chicken. The magnitude of the illusional effect is measured by having observers adjust one or the other of the lines until the two appear subjectively equal. The magnitude of

161

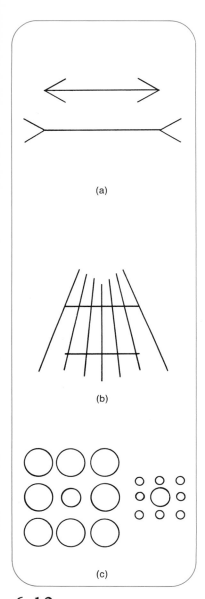

(a)

(b)

(c)

6-12 Some common illusions of size. Compare the pairs of horizontal lines in panels (a) and (b) and the two central circles in (c); each member of these pairs is equal in size to the other but one appears to be larger.

the illusory effect has been found to decrease with age, suggesting that experience with geometric representations is not the basis of the illusion. The effect can be demonstrated by showing *both* inward and outward arrows in the *same* figure. Therefore movements of the eye muscles, once thought by some to be the basis of the illusion, can also hardly be responsible.

A closer relationship of distance perception cues to apparent size is suggested in the illusion shown in panel (b) of Figure 6-12. Here the converging lines are characteristic of increasing distance, so that the line crossing the lines closer to their convergence point should be perceived as larger than the apparently closer line when the two retinal images are actually the same length. Unlike the Müller–Lyer illusion, this linear effect does seem to increase with age and experience.

An illusion like that illustrated in panel (c) can be obtained with successive presentations of a small circle and a large circle. When the small circle is presented surrounded by large circles, it appears to be smaller than when it is presented surrounded by smaller circles.

The Moon Illusion

An ancient visual size illusion involves our most prominent celestial body. For centuries the moon has been seen by men as appearing much larger when it is at the horizon than when it is at its zenith. Photographs of the moon at these two positions reveal no difference whatsoever in size. Nevertheless, experimental measurements of similarly placed optical disks indicate that a disk is perceived to be about 30 per cent larger when it is at the horizon. Generations of men have apparently puzzled over the explanation of this striking phenomenon. It is indeed curious that recent experimental evidence supports one of the most ancient theoretical interpretations, that offered by the Greek astronomer Ptolemy two millennia ago. Ptolemy's hypothesis was that the moon at the horizon seems so much larger than the moon at its zenith because it is perceived in relation to various features of the surround rather than against the empty sky of the zenith moon. Objects perceived over such "filled" space are seen as being farther away than the same object perceived without intervening or surrounding stimuli. But inasmuch as the retinal images in the two cases are the same size, the visual perceptual system is presumed to interpret the horizon moon as larger—if it is farther away and yet projects the same size retinal image, it must be larger. In the recent experimental test of this hypothesis, the optical disk seen close to the landscape appeared larger than the same artificial "moon" seen with the landscape features masked.

Although this research has satisfied some, with regard to the problem of the moon illusion, it must be said that psychologists are nowhere near agreement on the explanation. Other viable interpretations have also received support, and very likely the daily movements of the moon with its changing apparent size will continue to entertain amateur and professional alike for many years to come.

The Ames Distorted Room

Unlike the moon illusion, which requires no special props at all, the Ames distorted room is an elaborately contrived situation. However, it can produce a startling effect. Moreover, it demonstrates with great clarity the intimate relationship between size and distance cues in producing illusional effects.

In brief, the Ames room illusion involves the *actual preparation* of a room with quite unusual proportions, as shown in (b) of Figure 6-13. The left corner of the room is actually much farther away from the observer than the right, but when the observer is given only a peephole view from the front he cannot detect the irregular angles of the corners. The room therefore appears to be normal, with the usual square corners. Now, if human figures of normal size are placed at the far left corner and the close right corner, they produce retinal images markedly differing in size. The interpretation of such retinal differences would ordinarily be consistent with the true distance of the objects, in accordance with the size constancy effect described above; that is, the person on the left would be seen as of normal size but much farther away than the normally sized person on the right. In this special case, however, with the room appearing quite normal and the corners equally close, distance differences are not perceptually registered. Instead, the two individuals are perceived as of markedly different size, as shown in (a) of Figure 6-13.

It is interesting that if either of the human figures used is very well-known to the observer, so that his true size cannot be readily falsified, the illusional effect is eliminated. This elimination has been shown to result, for example, when a wife perceives her husband in such a distorted room; the room is seen to be distorted rather than the husband (or wife). But under the specially arranged viewing conditions that ordinarily hold, and with unfamiliar humans occupying the corner positions, the illusion of difference in size is a very powerful one indeed.

6-13 The Ames room. Panel (a) shows the apparently rectangular room, with figures perceived to be of different sizes. Panel (b) shows the geometry of the actual room. The figure on the left is thus really farther away than the one on the right but the eye normally perceives the figures as of different sizes and the same distance off, because the room is assumed to have its usual rectangular shape.

(a)

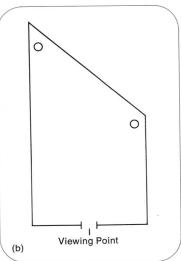

Viewing Point

(b)

Geometric Illusions of Shape

The relationship between distance and size cues is by no means the only determinant of visual illusions. Figure 6-14 shows some common illusions of shape into which that relationship does not enter. The perceptual resolution of the retinal image in each case is a kind of mismatch with the physical properties of the stimulus. Shape perception is especially subject to illusional effects because of its very close dependence upon the tilt of the perceived object, relative to the position of the observer. Shape constancy factors are strong determinants of perception, as emphasized earlier, but only when the observer is able to perceive the degree of tilt. Illusional effects can readily be produced, as in (b) of Figure 6-14, when this information is not available and only the retinal image is used; two-dimensional representations are especially prone to yield illusions of shape because they involve a reduction of perceptual information. The close relationship between size and distance cues that is involved in illusions of size thus has a counterpart in the relationship between shape and tilt cues in the production of illusions of shape.

Many illusions of shape can be explained on the basis of relatively simple mechanical factors, such as the blunting of acute angles. The most popular theoretical framework in which interpretations are attempted is that developed by Gestalt psychologists (cf. Chapter 3) to account for dynamic processes in the brain.

Gestalt Principles

The organizational factors in visual perception have been most vigorously studied by the Gestalt psychologists who tend to interpret perception as a function of the way the brain is made and operates, rather than in terms of past experience.

GROUPING. Consider the patterns of dots in Figure 6-15. Certain "natural" groupings into figures will be immediately apparent. The major more particular stimulus determinants of this kind of perceptual patterning are (a) *proximity:* dots that stay close together seem to belong together; (b) *similarity:* dots that look alike also seem to belong together; and (c) *directionality* (sometimes called *common fate*): dots that move alike seem to belong together.

The latter principle can be simply illustrated, as shown at the left.

Illusions of Brightness

Look carefully at the gray ring shown half in a black surround and half in a white surround in Figure 6-16. Is the brightness constant throughout the ring? The difference in brightness of the two halves of the ring is clearly seen by most observers. This difference can be explained in terms of the brightness contrast that operates when the visual system is apparently able to register the two ring parts separately, so that the context or surround can operate on each independently. A further discussion of this kind of phenomenon is offered below in connection with organizational properties in perception.

Illusions of Movement

The visual autokinetic phenomenon described earlier in this chapter occurs only under a rather special set of circumstances, but apparent motion of quite another sort is a very commonplace experience in today's world. Both motion picture and

There is likely to be nothing especially eye-catching about a

dancer

or about a group of dancers

but let one leave the group

and stand alone

or

be different in some way

or be going in the wrong direction

and the grouping is violated; the violator will be noticed!

television screens show what appears to be the motion of people and objects. Actually, however, this motion is only apparent—and therefore illusory—because it is not really present in the physical stimuli at all. What is present is a series of still pictures taken at a rapid rate (usually 16 frames per second, for the motion picture). The same kind of effect can be produced by flipping a series of slightly different pictures, or even more simply by the successive flashing on of lights in a given direction at an appropriate rate (as is done, of course, in the electric signs that are so common in our urban environment).

ORGANIZATIONAL FACTORS IN PERCEPTION

Besides the constancy and illusional phenomena just considered, there are various other fundamental ways in which human perception operates in accordance with the physical properties of the stimulus situation. The processes involved are called *organizational* because it is the *patterned structure* of the stimulus that determines the perceptual response.

Although learning cannot be entirely ignored, the processes to be described appear to be primarily dependent upon certain normal, presumably inherited, functions of the perceptual systems. Survival value in evolution has apparently been responsible for most of the organizational functions. Just as the retina is sensitive to the electromagnetic energies that are most abundant in our atmosphere, so the visual perceptual system is sensitive to those features of the environment that are both most common and most critical in the adjustment of the organism to that environment.

Figure and Ground
Perhaps the most nearly universal aspect of the environment is that objects stand out from the context in which they appear. They must be perceived as objects, as separate from their background, if appropriate responses to them are to be made. It is hardly surprising therefore that the ability to see figures as separate from ground is a fundamental characteristic of the visual system, and to some extent of the other perceptual systems as well.

The vase-profile illustration in Figure 6-4 is a special case, designed to show the ambiguity of the figure–ground relationship under certain conditions. But there is always some part of the visual field that takes on the property of a figure (that seems to stand out) as compared with the ground (which appears to recede). Very brief exposures of visual stimuli demonstrate this fact. The observer may be unable to identify what he saw but he is almost certain to make some kind of guess. In such guesses a figure of one kind or another is quite likely to be involved.

The figure–ground relationship is by no means restricted to the visual modality. Consider a melody. It stands out, as a kind of auditory figure, even when in the presence of extremely high levels of noise or conversation. Or consider other salient sensory experiences, such as a pungent odor, a sharp pain, or a sudden tactual pressure, as from a pinch; each of these is figurelike in that they are sensations that quite clearly stand out. Moreover, shifts in attention can produce

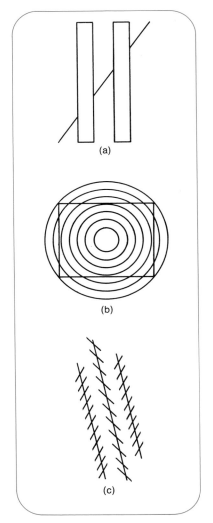

6-14 Illusions of shape. In panel (a) the actually straight line appears to be deflected by the vertical bars. In panel (b) the perfectly square figure is perceived as slightly concave because of the varying surround produced by the geometric curves. In panel (c) the parallel lines are seen to tilt, again because of the varying angles of the connecting lines.

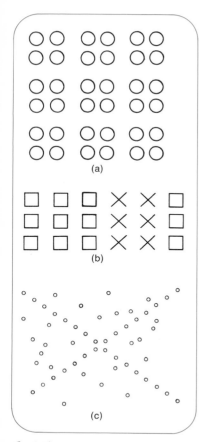

6-15 Gestalt principles of visual grouping. Some of the more important principles are (a) proximity, (b) similarity, and (c) directionality.

the same basic kind of reversibility in the other modalities as occurs in vision, particularly as adaptation occurs or interest flags. At a cocktail party, for example, one's attention can shift from this to that conversation, without noticeable changes in the intensity or other physical characteristics of the stimuli involved.

An implication of this cross-modality generality of the figure–ground phenomenon is that it may represent simply an extreme case of the normal situation that holds in all sensory function; that is to say, the figure, which stands out so vividly, can be regarded as an event of maximal sensory clearness, as a function of an unusually sharp focusing of attention, whereas the ground represents moderate or faint attentional processes. By this account, the visual modality is most amenable to figure–ground phenomena not because of any unique features of the visual processing system but rather because vision affords a greater abundance of distinctive cues.

Closure

The good figure is a complete figure. Small gaps in such figures are not likely to be seen, particularly if only very brief visual stimulation occurs. A stimulus that may have independent existence and even be quite familiar when appearing by itself, as a figure, will usually not be readily perceived when it appears as part of a larger good figure where it is required for perceptual closure. Hidden figures, such as those shown in Figure 6-17, illustrate this proposition.

The closure principle, like that of grouping, is held by the Gestalt psychologists to be a directed and fundamental property of the manner in which the brain functions. Thus, for example, a small gap in a circle is ordinarily not noticed, especially if only a very brief presentation of the stimulus is provided. The Gestalt interpretation of this failure of perception is that there are in the brain energies that actually take the shape of a circle. Because a circle is a "good" figure these energies are strong. They therefore tend to form a complete circle, and there is a correspondingly strong perceptual tendency to see the circle as complete, or closed.

The Gestalt theory of brain–perception relationships is a tempting interpretation of the facts of visual perception, and may very well be essentially correct. Nonetheless, the hard neurophysiological evidence which such a hypothetical extension of the perceptual data needs for firmer support has not yet been obtained.

Context

The context in which a given figure occurs is always a potent factor in its perception. For example, consider the figure at the lower right corner of both (a) and (b) in Figure 6-18. It is identical in both versions but because of the varying nature of the context it will ordinarily be seen, along with its confreres, as a bird in (a) and an antelope in (b). This example offers a useful complement to the hidden figure illustration of Figure 6-17, in which a different role for context (closure) is indicated.

More natural contextual effects are to be observed in our everyday perceptual responses to jokes, to interpersonal situations, and in casual conversation. In all these commonplace situations the exact physical character of a particular stimulus (such as some simple declaratory statement) is often of much less importance in its interpretation than the nature of the context in which it is made.

SENSORY INTERACTION: SYNESTHESIA

The normal human is almost constantly exposed to simultaneous stimulation from several sensory modalities. However, little basic research has been performed with regard to the interactions between modalities. Some attention has been given to the relationship of auditory and visual senses, particularly in regard to educational problems.

A better-known phenomenon is *synesthesia*. This term refers to a type of interaction in which perception in one modality follows stimulation in some *other* modality. "Colored hearing" is perhaps the most common form of synesthesia; some subjects seem consistently to "see" specific colors when certain sounds are presented.

Less striking but more commonly experienced is the use of a descriptive attribute from one sensory modality to refer to some other kind of sensation. For example, we speak of a "bright" tone and a "dark" smell. A number of similar types of descriptive interactions may well occur to the reader. Figure 6-19 illustrates the interaction of verbal and pictorial cues; see how many of your friends associate the rounded-line figure with Takete and the jagged-line figure with Maluma! Research on this problem is handicapped by the difficulty of obtaining objective and replicable introspective accounts of such phenomena. What one "really" perceives is strictly a private matter and its translation into verbal behavior always entails methodological difficulties, as we have seen in Chapter 4. Resumption of more active interest in such problems may be anticipated, however, in light of the contemporary revival of psychological concern with conscious processes.

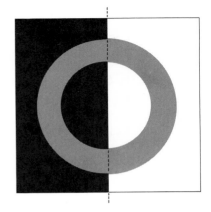

6-16 Simultaneous brightness contrast. Observe the difference in apparent brightness between the two halves of the ring. (The effect can be enhanced by placing a pencil between the two halves.)

6-17 Hidden figures. There are in this picture a number of hidden animals that require some effort to find. Once found, however, these animals become quite prominent, and one may wonder why they were missed for so long. The illustration is a Currier and Ives lithograph published in 1872. You should find a horse, a wild boar, and several human faces.

167

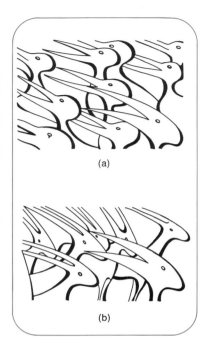

6-18 Context and perception. Note the lower right-hand figure in both panels. In the context of birds, in panel (a), this figure assumes a birdlike appearance, whereas in the context of antelopes, in panel (b), this same figure seems to take on a more antelopelike appearance. From Floyd L. Ruch, *Psychology and Life,* 7th ed. (Chicago: Scott, Foresman, 1967), p. 307.

PERCEPTION AND LEARNING

The relationship between perception and learning is a close and mutually influential one. On the one hand, learning as we ordinarily know it (Chapter 11) would be impossible without the stimulus input that is perceptually mediated. On the other hand, perception depends to a very great extent upon experience; even if certain key perceptual processes, such as visual depth perception, are essentially unlearned, the way in which these processes are actually used is a function of learning.

In this section certain of the more crucial interactions between perception and learning are reviewed. No effort at a complete coverage or even a full survey of this broad and pervasive relationship is attempted. However, the problems sampled should suffice to suggest both the breadth and the depth of the relationship.

Adjustment to Perceptual Modification

A favorite experimental device used by those interested in the role of learning in perception has been to alter the sensory input in some radical manner and then observe the perceptual consequences. If satisfactory perceptual adjustments are made to the new sensory input, then the role of learning in that case at least is presumed to have been indicated.

A pioneer effort along these lines was the application of special goggles to experimental subjects. Lenses in the goggles inverted the fundamental orientational dimensions. Both right and left and up and down were reversed. The general result of this kind of radical modification of visual input is that it takes only a few days of constant wearing of the reversing goggles before things no longer look abnormal. That is, the subject reports that at first an object that he knows to be on his right—and whose right-handed position he can verify by, say, touch—appears to be on the left. Perceptual and motor processes are accordingly quite confused, and the subject makes nearly constant blunders as he attempts to walk to and around objects or touch them. Gradually, however, his psychomotor behavior improves and he is able to carry out these same tasks in substantially a normal manner. For example, he reaches to the right for objects actually on the right, and up for objects above him.

Introspective reports from such subjects, however, indicate that the perceptual experience itself is less well stabilized. For example, if the subject stops to think about rightness and leftness, some of his earlier bewilderment may return.

Less radical alterations of visual perception have been achieved by having subjects wear so-called squint spectacles. These consist of prisms designed to produce various aberrations of shape and color, an effect similar to the large amusement park mirrors of concave or convex design that produce images of grotesque shape. Little adaptation to certain of these effects, especially those involving color, has been reported. In general, however, the prismatic spectacles when worn for several weeks result in a return to normal perceptual organization. For example, the geometric distortions, such as straight lines seen as curved and vice versa, gradually disappear, and a physically "straight" line is again perceived as straight.

It is interesting that in these experiments the removal of the distorting lenses typically triggers a period of new perceptual confusion, but one in which the *opposite* distortions to those first experienced occur (for example, really straight lines are once again perceived as curved). This revived perceptual confusion is presumably the result of the new perceptual habits acquired during the wearing of the "squint" spectacles still functioning, but now inappropriately. Counteradjustments are required in the perceptual organization processes, and these normally are quickly made.

Although a great deal remains to be learned about the exact ways in which such perceptual organization occurs, the net result of these experiments is to demonstrate a remarkable resiliency in human visual perception, and to indicate a fundamental role for learning in the perceptual processing of sensory input.

Adaptation Level

Adaptation level refers to the way in which perceptual judgment depends upon standards that to a great extent are determined by the context in which the judgments are made. For example, the mediocre card player will usually be rated as superior by persons with even worse skill of this type and as inferior by expert players; similarly, an adolescent will be rated as young by adults and as quite grown up by his more youthful acquaintances.

The concept of a standard was originally introduced to account for some of the bias found in making simple perceptual judgments, such as those of size of visual cues or weight of various test objects. It was found that judgments of this sort were quite markedly biased in accordance with whatever standards of comparison were provided. These standard stimuli apparently served as *anchors* against which comparative perceptual judgments were made. In more common language, they provided a frame of reference for the observer.

Adaptation quite clearly depends upon prior experience for its functioning and so constitutes an additional source of evidence for the active role of learning in perception.

Perceptual Defense

Perceptual defense is an unconscious protective process that is supposed to occur as part of a person's response to stimulation. Presenting very brief exposures of visual stimuli, various investigators have attempted to demonstrate that perception in human subjects involves a prior unconscious screening mechanism that in some way evaluates the meaning of the stimuli and serves to impede the conscious recognition of certain threatening or socially embarrassing cues. Any such evaluation and differentiation of stimuli according to their meaningfulness must be based on the individual learning experiences of the subject.

The most common procedure used in this research has been to present college students with various verbal stimuli, some of which are socially taboo (e.g., words with sexual connotation, such as *rape* or *penis*) for a fraction of a second and then measure the time required before the word is successfully identified. The first results showed reliably slower recognition times for the taboo words compared with neutral control words. These early positive results were criticized on a number of counts (such as the possibility that the taboo words used were actually less

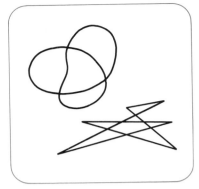

6-19 Which of these figures is *maluma* and which is *takete?* In spite of the essentially meaningless character of both the names and the line drawings, practically everyone asked this question identifies the rounded figure as *maluma* and the sharply angular figure as *takete,* suggesting some intrinsic sensory processing equivalence between visual and verbal stimuli. [Adapted by permission from W. Kohler, *Gestalt Psychology* (New York: Liveright, 1947).]

169

frequently encountered than the more common control words so that frequency alone may have produced the effect). Subsequent experiments included additional controls with a tendency toward continued positive results, but the subject remains a somewhat controversial one. (The reader may wonder whether under contemporary relaxation of old moral standards and increased freedom of expression it would be possible to find sufficiently "taboo" words to test college students in this kind of experiment; research interest in the problem has been dormant recently so that this problem may not have been met.)

A more subtle criticism of this kind of experiment has been that the effect if genuine may not really be perceptual at all but rather on the response itself; in other words, subjects may actually perceive the taboo words equally well but merely hesitate to report them. Although this is an interesting and basic point, it really raises the question of defining perception and in particular of separating it from overt responding. Such questions as these will require for full resolution more sensitive measuring devices and experimental designs than are now available. In the meantime, we have plenty of evidence for unconscious inferences of a variety of sorts (e.g., the distance cues apparently integrated in the visual system to produce depth perception). Thus the kind of filtering mechanism presumed to occur in perceptual defense experiments is at least quite feasible.

Personal Values in Relation to Perception

The theoretical issue raised by the perceptual defense research just described suggests the broader role that personal values and biases play in perception generally.

An objective appraisal of human behavior in any culture will indicate the remarkable extent to which perceptual processes are dependent upon the acquisition of various value systems, particularly those relating to religious, political, and social issues. It is reasonably clear that each of us learns to perceive essentially in accordance with his own personal value systems. We all may be said to go through life wearing goggles (if not blinders) that distort the visual world and require perceptual readjustments.

Social values cannot easily be separated from one's own special goggles. Nevertheless, there are classic experiments that have attempted to bridge this gap and that have provided interesting data.

Perhaps the best known of this type of experiment is that which relates the perceptual judgment of physical size to social class. In the original experiment, children of differing socioeconomic class were asked to equate the physical size of circles to coins of varying value. The hypothesis that poorer children, for whom the coins presumably had considerably greater value than rich children, would make larger size estimates than rich children was confirmed. In one of the many subsequent experiments of this kind subjects were hypnotized and instructed either that they were poor or that they were rich. Under the "poor" simulation white spots of substantially greater size were again rated as equal to coins of four values (pennies, nickels, dimes, and quarters). Although the ultimate interpretation of these data will not be as simple as any single conclusion, they do suggest the potency of learned social norms in perceptual functions.

The relationship between perception and learning is quite clearly multifaceted. Here two of the more interesting and more important facets of this relationship will be discussed.

Several theorists have pointed out the reinforcing (response-strengthening) role of perception. Reinforcement, more popularly translated as "reward," is considered by many to be a key factor in learning. Thus perception would become one of the determinants of learning. The general idea behind these various suggestions is that organisms are motivated to perceive—or more broadly, to *know*—and that successful perception is therefore intrinsically rewarding.

The second way in which perception functions within the learning process has been much less publicized. What we perceive, especially under consistent or chronic conditions, seems to be somehow incorporated within our personal value systems. In other words, we tend to *learn the standards that we experience.* Such learning by means of perception would seem to be the basis of many of the effects that we have already noted; for example, the crucial role of the religious and social standards to which one has been exposed in providing guidelines that bias subsequent behaviors, including perceptual processes.

In this connection attention should be called to experiments that demonstrate the importance of perceptual familiarity in learning. As mentioned earlier, rats exposed to certain geometric figures in their home cages were found to be superior in discrimination learning when these figures were used as cues. Apparently the familiarity that is engendered by such a simple procedure is helpful to the rat. Exactly why this effect occurs is a more difficult question, the answer to which has yet to be provided. In any event the generalization is suggested that perceptual familiarity produces superior learning.

Before leaving the topic of perception–learning relationships one *ineffective* application of familiarity, on a very short-term basis, may be mentioned. This is the attempt to influence people by subliminal stimulation. Flashing the name of a product on a movie or television screen for such a brief exposure that it cannot be consciously identified does not seem to do very much one way or the other. This type of presentation has not proved successful when tried as an advertising technique.

ANIMAL PERCEPTION

We conclude this chapter by briefly pointing out some of the special perceptual performance of infrahuman animals. Among the many verified accounts of truly extraordinary perceptual and motor abilities of infrahuman animals the phenomena of migration and homing stand out. Although recent research on bird navigation suggests that there might be some common orientational factor in these two behaviors, it is still best to treat them separately because their determinants and at least some of their characteristics are quite different.

Migration

Migratory behavior is a response to seasonal changes, such as the regular increments in light that stimulate gonadal changes in birds during the springtime. The distances that may be traversed, by water-living organisms as well as by birds, are truly enormous. Trips of several thousand miles—for example, from the upper parts of North America well into South America—are not uncommon for birds. The Alaska fur seal, which breeds only in the Bering Sea, is particularly interesting in that there is a sex distinction in its migratory behavior. Males make a short winter journey to the Aleutian Islands, whereas females and their young swim all the way to southern California!

The perceptual problem involved in migration is the determination of what cues and what sensory capacities are used. Tracking by means of small radio transmitters implanted in certain animals (e.g., the green turtle, which makes a very long migratory journey) has helped to establish the routes taken but does nothing to inform us about the basic perceptual process.

Perhaps the most intensive research has been with the salmon. These economically important fish return to fresh water to spawn after several years in the ocean. Considerable information has been amassed concerning the various sensory cues they use—temperature gradients, chemical composition of the water, and the like.

Birds appear to use surprisingly sophisticated navigational devices, involving the sun, in determining their flight patterns. A fuller account of the precise perceptual mechanisms involved in the various migratory behaviors may be only slowly achieved, because of the great difficulties of performing controlled research, but the search promises to be an intellectually most rewarding one.

Homing

Homing behavior, much more than migration, is susceptible to anecdote, and the usual kind of error that accompanies anecdotes (faulty memory, unconscious exaggeration, especially if one's own pet is involved, and the like). Nonetheless, there is experimental evidence that land-living animals as well as birds do manage to return home, sometimes over remarkably long and arduous paths. Dogs and homing pigeons, nevertheless, home more effectively when they are first trained to make short trips of progressively wider range, so as apparently to establish landmarks that can be used later on more extensive forays. Most dogs seem to train themselves, by their straying habit. Releases of homing pigeons at increasingly great distances serves as an effective training device. Pigeons, like other birds, may be presumed to use visual landmarks chiefly. The recent suggestion that they also use for homing navigational devices similar to those utilized in migration will require a considerable amount of careful checking but does open up what may well be a whole new chapter in this fascinating story.

Notes

A good introduction to perception may be obtained from Rock's *An Introduction to Perception* (1975), or in shorter paperback form from Leibowitz's *Visual Perception* (1965).

The information pick-up view of perception has been most convincingly advanced by Gibson (1966). Among the more important emphases of this point of view is the reminder that sequential properties of stimuli are often more important than they are given credit for; thus, for example, veridical perception may only be possible when the sensory system is allowed sufficient time to register and interpret more aspects of the stimulus than is possible when it is only presented briefly, as by a tachistoscope.

Coherence in the stimulus has also been shown to be a crucial factor in perception. In a recent experiment (Biederman, 1972), for example, it was shown that the accuracy with which single objects were identified when shown in real-world visual scenes was greater for coherent than for jumbled pictures. This result held even when the subject knew in advance *where* to look as well as *what* to look for.

Attention

James's comments on attention are in Chapter 11, Vol. I, of his *Principles of Psychology* (1890). Gibson and Walk (1956) reported the research demonstrating superior discrimination in rats tested with the geometric test patterns earlier maintained on walls in their home cages. The pupillary changes as a function of attention have been described by Hess (1965); the data presented in the text were reported by Hess and Polt (1960). Training and employment of pigeons in visual quality control tasks are described by Verhave (1966). Skinner has reported his research on training pigeons as bombardiers, following the removal of security classification, in his 1960 paper. The research showing the direct influence of the ARAS on auditory receptivity in cats was reported by Hernandez-Péon, Scherer, and Jouvet (1956); subsequent criticisms of the research and the interpretation of the data have been reported by Worden (1966). The early research on sensory deprivation, conducted in the McGill University laboratory, was reported by Bexton, Heron, and Scott (1954). Visual disturbances in particular were later described by Heron, Doane, and Scott (1956). A more recent comprehensive review appears in a book by Zubek (1969).

Sleep and Dreaming

An elementary introduction to recent sleep research is available in a paperback by Webb (1968). Evidence for a waking center in the brain has been presented by Ranson (1939) and Nauta (1946); the posterior hypothalamus is the brain area implicated. The evidence mentioned for a sleep center in the anterior hypothalamus has been reported by Clemente and Sherman (1963).

An especially interesting experimental result has been recently reported (Pessah and Roffwarg, 1972). Middle ear muscular activity (MEMA) was found to occur spontaneously in sleep. Approximately 80 per cent of this kind of middle-ear activity occurred during the rapid eye movement (REM) phase of sleep. These authors also noted a preliminary suggestion that subjects reported more auditory imagery when they awakened after a sleep period in which MEMA had been observed.

Hypnosis

Hull's classic *Hypnosis and Suggestibility* (1933) remains a readable and instructive work. A more recent general introduction to this topic is the book by Moss (1965). Barber (1969) has attacked the notion that the hypnotic trance represents a special behavioral condition, and Hilgard (1968) has defended the more orthodox position that it does.

Orienting Reaction

Research on the orienting reaction (OR) is reviewed by Gormezano and Moore (1969).

Reaction Time

The importance of reaction time was initially pointed out by the Dutch physiologist F. C. Donders in 1868. Sternberg (1966) demonstrates the extremely elaborate manner in which mental operations can be measured by means of this "subtractive" technique.

The major theoretical positions on choice reaction time are reviewed from a more modern point of view by Smith (1968). The controversy between Titchener and Baldwin as to whether sensory or motor RT's are faster can have no simple resolution; if naive observers are used, motor set is superior, as Baldwin claimed; but if trained observers are used, in accordance with Titchenerian practice, sensory set is superior, as Titchener claimed.

Vigilance

The experiment on vigilance indicating that superior performance is maintained when more signals are provided, even if they are sometimes irrelevant, was done by Lawson (1959) and that showing the efficacy of pinup pictures of girls under at least some conditions by McGrath (1961).

Perceptual Constancy

The leading research in and spokesman for perceptual constancy research was Egon Brunswik (1956). Unfortunately, Brunswik is not easy reading; a more readily understood introduction to the topic may be found in the interesting account of Bower (1971) of his constancy research with human infants.

Perceptual Instability

The research mentioned on reversible figures and eye movements was done by Pheiffer, Eure, and Hamilton (1956) and Pritchard (1958). The initial research relating the autokinetic visual effect to social suggestibility factors was reported by Sherif (1958). Matin and MacKinnon (1964) performed research on the autokinetic effect that suggested some role for eye movements. Auditory and tactile autokinesis were reported by Kleint (1937).

Illusions

Good introductions to the topic of illusions are in Gregory (1966, 1968) and Day (1969, 1972). Attneave (1971) reports on spontaneous reversibility in visual perception. Warren and Warren (1970) describe auditory illusions.

Kaufman and Rock (1962) reported the recent research suggesting the distance perception interpretation of the moon illusion.

The finding that a wife will distort the Ames room before she distorts the size of her husband was reported by Wittreich (1952, 1959). The "impossible objects" in the Breather are from Penrose and Penrose (1958).

Organizational Factors

The significance of the figure-ground phenomenon was first noted by Danish psychologist Rubin in 1915. Because this phenomenon fits in so well with the Gestalt psychological emphases, it was quickly embraced by the pioneer Gestaltists and is often included as a part of that system. The principles of grouping in visual perception are mainly attributable to Max Wertheimer, the leader of the original triumvirate who "founded" the Gestalt school.

Visual Depth Perception

An early theory of depth perception was suggested by the British philosopher Berkeley. The visual cliff test was devised by Gibson and Walk (1960).

Localization

Supa, Cotzin, and Dallenbach (1944) reported the first experimental determination of the auditory echo cue used by blind subjects in their avoidance of obstacles. Worchel and Dallenbach (1947) later showed that blind and deaf subjects did not have this ability, indicating that the auditory modality is indeed involved.

Perception and Learning

The pioneer use of inverting goggles was by Stratton, in 1897, and the more recent use of prismatic spectacles was by Ivo Kohler (1964). Adaptation level is a contribution mainly of Helson (1964). The perceptual defense research described was reported in a series of studies by McGinnies (e.g., 1949). Bruner and Goodman (1947) reported the classic, and quite controversial, research on estimation of size as a function of economic level. The use of age-regressed subjects on this problem was by Ashley, Harper, and Runyon (1951). Woodworth (1947) made the provocative suggestion of "re-enforcement of perception."

Migration

Problems of orienting cues in bird migration are discussed by Wiltschko and Wiltschko (1972). The less familiar topic of insect migration is treated in a review by Dingle (1972). Movements of turtles, penguins, and salmon are discussed by Carr (1965), Emlen and Penney (1966), and Hasler and Larson (1955), respectively.

Extrasensory Perception

Without making any judgment on the reliability or the validity of the experimental demonstrations of extrasensory perception (ESP), it is nonetheless very difficult to see how the issue can be seriously entertained with regard to the general problem of sensation and perception. This conclusion follows from the essentially negative character of so much of the standard ESP research and theory. The experiments are typically designed and interpreted to show some perceptual effect in the absence of the usual sensory channels, but the kind of mechanism that might mediate such an effect is seldom suggested. Until a more positive approach is developed, at least with regard to this particular issue, it is hard to see how a significant contribution can be made by ESP research. If some new channel of influence on an organism can be suggested, and reasonably strong positive evidence in its support generated, then of course psychologists will need to examine the proposals much more seriously than they have to date. If substantiated, such data would presumably add to our knowledge of sensory capacity, and perhaps require the addition of some new sensory channel. But in the absence of this kind of more positive evidence and theory, a skeptical silence is the most likely response by most psychologists to the claims ordinarily advanced.

The issue of the validity of ESP phenomena is treated elsewhere in this book (Chapter 8).

Unidentified Flying Objects (UFO's)

The problem of identifying UFO's is essentially one of perception, although there is always also involved a good amount of theoretical interpretation. In general scientists have tended to regard UFO's as instances of faulty perception and/or theoretical overinterpretation. However, a small number of the vast number of instances reported have proved less amenable to such interpretation, and it is there that considerable controversy has ensued. An official report of a federal government committee chaired by Edward U. Condon, and edited by Gillmor (1969), concluded that there was insufficient basis for any continued scientific inquiry of these phenomena. The interested reader might also consult the more recent book by J. Allen Hynek (1972), an established astronomer who takes an opposite view; the review of this book by Murray (1972) offers a different perspective in which both of the extreme pro and con positions are briefly evaluated.

It is suggestive that reports of UFO's typically occur in spatial and temporal clusters. That is, there will be a sudden onset of sightings, followed by a flood of additional reports, mostly centered in the same geographical area. This fact is consistent with two interpretations. First, it can be assumed there has been some kind of centralized activity in that area at that time, such as an invasion of earth by foreign objects or organisms—a very popular conclusion—for which, however, there is little if any hard evidence. Second, it can be assumed, more simply, that people have at that time and place a heightened sensitivity to unusual perceptual experience, as well as unusual interpretations of such experiences, because of the generalized expectations that have developed—a view that most scientists hold.

Thinking and Decision Making

Our Three Wise-Men of Gotham, from the eighteenth-century nursery rhyme, have taken a direct approach to accomplishing their objective; that is, capturing the moon. Chapter 7 deals with the thinking processes that enable us to make productive decisions such as this.

his chapter initiates our consideration of the complex phenomenon of human thinking. It is his thinking ability that, more than anything else, sets man off from the "lower" animals. In this chapter we outline the major components of thinking and discuss in detail the role of language and concepts. Determinants of thought, such as attitudes and beliefs, are examined, and the chapter closes with a brief review of the attempts to determine the neurophysiological bases of thinking. The next chapter continues our treatment of thinking, concentrating upon man's problem-solving processes.

When one "thinks," he is able to deal with external objects and events by means of their *symbolic* representatives—mainly the images and words that have come to "stand for" them. He does not therefore need to be stimulated by the actual objects and events themselves. It is this feature of thought that makes it so effective, however it is otherwise defined or interpreted. At the same time, the essentially private and covert character of thought renders it more difficult to investigate by means of objective scientific techniques and helps to account for much of the mystery and controversy surrounding the topic.

So much of our thinking is essentially language that it is difficult to separate the two processes. The modern student of language, the *linguist,* is concerned with how the developing human organism is able to generate and comprehend sentences even in the absence of specific grammatical tutoring. Although the linguists have been able to raise serious questions concerning the applicability of orthodox learning interpretations to language functions, they have not as yet been able to provide any very definitive explanatory concepts of their own. In this work the interdisciplinary field of *psycholinguistics,* in which psychology is combined with linguistics, offers much promise for future research.

Unlike language, concept formation has long been an orthodox problem in experimental psychology. The essential question here is how one learns to abstract the properties of objects and events according to which they are the same, which is what a concept does, in spite of all the dissimilarities that exist among them. Intimately involved in this problem is the process of *generalization,* by which one tends to make the same response (such as verbal naming) to different objects and events on the basis of some commonality. Also considered is the antagonistic process of *discrimination,* by which the differences among objects and events are recognized and differential responding made possible.

Of more practical importance, although thus far receiving proportionately small experimental attention, is decision making, or how one attempts to translate into action the concepts and knowledge that he has acquired. Contradictions among belief systems, or between beliefs and behaviors, are a central focus of this discussion. Research on the ways in which humans attempt to resolve such contradictions under the label of *cognitive dissonance* is examined in some detail.

Research on the neurophysiological basis of thinking has historically concentrated on the opposing views that thinking is in essence a *peripheral* (muscular) or a *central* (brain) phenomenon. The development of highly sophisticated electronic testing devices has opened up new means of experimenting on this old problem.

Thinking deals in essence with covert or implicit processes. It is a way in which the human is able to manipulate objects and events, not in the real world but by means of their representatives, the symbols that stand for them in mental processes.

In addition to being the most uniquely "psychological" subject, thinking is possibly the broadest concept in all psychology. In this respect it rivals, and may even in some respects surpass, "behavior." The variety of ways in which thinking occurs is emphasized by contrast with the difficulty of objective assessment of it. The single term *thinking* thus covers a multitude of different internal representative functions, ranging all the way from the most mechanical rote memorizing to the most imaginative fantasizing, all expressed in a great variety of overt behaviors.

IDENTIFICATION OF TERMS

The one feature of thinking that is common to all its various forms is its subjectivity. Whatever else it may be, thinking as here viewed is always covert and private. It differs from other subjective processes, such as sensing and feeling, in that it is more likely to be separated from external stimulus or response relationships. In sensation, for example, we concentrate upon manipulation of the external energy change, and in feeling we are likely to look closely at the accompanying behavioral or physiological changes. Thinking, on the contrary, is most likely to be identified by the apparent *absence* of any such stimulus or response relationships. In other words, one is *most likely* to be said to be thinking when one is *least overtly* active, that is, when one is "doing nothing"; the inference of thought is thus essentially negative, at least insofar as any immediate behavioral product is concerned. But much thought is judged in terms of its ultimate consequences, which are often productive, in the sense of being effective in solving problems.

Basic Functions

Thinking may thus be distinguished from other private mental processes, especially sensory and emotional experiences, in terms of its function. Basically, all thinking tends to involve some degree of *manipulation of representative processes*, such as images or ideas. Thinking thus tends to be *relational*, in that it is very largely concerned with the relationships among objects and events, especially when these objects and events are not physically present in the environment.

> *Thinking*

Equivalences

When one says, "I think," he usually means one of two major equivalences:

1. "I *am concerned with*," in the sense of mental manipulation of associated images and other representative processes; "I think of you often" and "I think of Mother whenever I hear that song" illustrate this usage.
2. "I *believe*," suggesting an evaluation of some kind; thus, "I think it is time to go" or "I think you are wrong."

Beyond these two fundamental equivalences, the term *thinking* is used to refer to intention or anticipation, to reasoning, to memory, to realization, to judging and decision making, and of course to imagination and creativity. The variety of such meanings is so great as to defy adequate description in any such brief treatment as is here intended. Rather, some of the more significant ways in which thinking varies will be examined.

METHODS OF APPROACH

The study of thinking can take many forms. The subjective character of thinking imposes some obvious restrictions upon its scientific analysis, while at the same time inviting a variety of approaches of a less scientific type. In studying thinking directly, one must either examine one's own thought processes, introspectively, or examine the overt expressions, verbal or otherwise, of someone else's thinking. A different type of approach is to examine the presumed neurophysiological bases of thought, perhaps attempting to correlate these with one or the other of the direct methods of study.

The methodology used in thinking research can also be categorized according to the nature of the type of analysis. In common with other psychological problems, thinking can either be studied from a *molar* (overview) approach, which tends to be associated with an introspective methodology, or from a *molecular* (analytic) approach, which breaks the problem into components for behavioral and neuro-physiological types of analysis.

COMPONENTS OF THOUGHTS

There are two major components of thoughts about which there is little, if any, question: *words* and *images*. Whether thinking can occur in the absence of these components was once a controversial question in psychology, resolved more or less in favor of the positive answer. There does not seem to be any generally accepted name for the kind of thought element that is independent of words and images; perhaps the term *idea* is as good as any. Ideas, as a kind of general and inclusive label for all thoughts that appear to have some direction or structure, most commonly utilize both words and images. Although each of us can probably recall instances of thinking in which words and images seemed to play at best a minimal role, the great part of our thinking does seem to depend upon words or some similar kinds of symbols, and a lesser part upon images.

Signs and Symbols

As the terms are used here, a *symbol* is any stimulus or other kind of cue that *stands for* (represents) something else. A *sign* is a stimulus that indicates the impending occurrence of some other object or event. A sign is thus a kind of symbol, but one that is itself a physical object or event. The kind of symbols that are more often instrumental in thinking are those that are mediated by internal processes rather than external objects or events.

Consideration of some common object—say, a mouse—can serve as a stimulus. When such a stimulus acquires some kind of meaning for any given observer, it can be called a sign, meaning that it serves as a signal. *What* meaning is signaled by any particular object will of course vary from one observer to another, and even within the same observer from one time to another. A mouse may thus signal a meal to a cat, assuming proper culinary training, and at the same time produce a highly emotional and traumatic reaction in a person.

The processes described above would ordinarily be classified as perceiving, not as thinking; but the mouse once experienced can be *represented* in the subsequent experience of the observer so as to become an object of thought when it is not physically present. It is then represented by a *symbol*, something that stands for it in its absence. The mouse can be experienced as an image—*re*-presented, as it were. The observer thus experiencing the mouse in its absence can be said to be "thinking" of it, or seeing it in the "mind's eye." More complexly, the mouse can be represented by a surrogate (substitute) stimulus of one kind or another; the English word *mouse*, the German word *maus*, and the French word *souris* are examples of such symbols.

An analogy that utilizes some commonplace processes may clarify the distinction between the sign (the direct stimulus) and the stimulus representations (the image or other type of symbol that substitutes for the stimulus). In telecasting of sports events, recourse is frequently made to the so-called instant replay, of some action in a football or baseball game. Here the replay is based upon a stored or taped record of the action. This essentially perfect reproduction of previous perception is in effect similar to the much less accurate "replay" that each of us can generate ourself by means of our own visual images of past events. Thus an image replaces the actual event.

When the sportscaster uses proper names to identify the players in his commentary on the action just completed, he is of course employing the kind of symbols, or object surrogates, that are characteristic of human communication. In this case words (names) stand for the players themselves. The action sequence can thus be "replayed" either by images, quite faithfully when actually given physical existence on tape rather than only physiological representation in the brain, or by verbal or other symbols, customarily carried by brain processes.

Covert manipulation of symbols which represent real objects and events is the hallmark of human thinking. Once an organism overcomes the need for an object to be physically present in order to be related to other objects and events, in consciousness, the possibilities for such manipulation are almost unlimited. Indeed, our Western society is characterized by many persons who deal almost exclusively with symbols of one kind or another in their business if not their personal lives. For example, consider the businessman who deals in, say, wheat futures; his buying and selling of grain may well be carried on without his ever seeing the wheat itself. Similarly, the homemaker is besieged by endless exhortations to use this or that product, on television or in newspaper or direct mail advertisments, where symbols of one kind or another are presented.

The flood of symbolic stimulation is so great that when advertisers occasionally offer small samples of their products they are likely to facilitate sales appeal, perhaps because of the contrast that the real object offers with the more common symbols. Nevertheless, children may become so accustomed to symbolic representations of various sorts that they often seem to prefer them to the real thing; witness, for example, the child who daydreams about playing with children rather than actually doing so, or the child with a live horse who prefers to watch cowboys on television rather than ride his own horse. In this latter instance the viewer is not even supplying his own symbols, as does the daydreamer, but rather is exercising visual perception. It is hardly an exaggeration to say that we live in a world in which symbols predominate; their exclusive use is by no means restricted to schoolteachers and professors.

DO ANIMALS THINK?

As is the case with all such questions, the answer is entirely dependent upon the way in which terms are used; unfortunately, the urge to ask the question and receive an answer of some kind is ordinarily much greater than the urge to define such terms. Recent work with chimpanzees, described in more detail below, indicates clearly that these primates can learn to use a *kind* of language when their efforts are not restricted to human type vocalizations. The higher animals must thus be granted the ability to think, as long as thinking is equated with the covert use of language. All the lower animals that have been investigated have been found capable of responding to signs, such as the sound of their master's voice or the rattling of a food dish, and so show at least the simplest form of learning. But how often and to what extent they can generate their own symbols or images, and so think in a humanlike sense, are not known. There is no easy way of investigating this problem. As a matter of fact, thought is difficult enough to investigate in the human organism itself, with all its verbal facility.

Classic Experimental Tests

In the early literature on animal behavior there are a number of studies attempting to determine the presence of symbolic processes in nonverbal organisms. The two most frequently cited behavior tests are the *delayed-reaction* and the *double-alternation* techniques.

DELAYED REACTION. In the delayed-reaction experiment the animal subject is allowed to see where food reward is placed (as, for example, behind one of two spatially separated doors). A time interval is then interpolated between baiting and allowing the response; if the animal is permitted to respond immediately it will ordinarily go directly to the food. The assumption is that if the animal is able to bridge the time gap and reliably select the correct alternative, it must be using some kind of substitute or symbolic internal activity that might be properly classified as thinking.

In the course of this experimentation it has been found necessary to control for bodily orientation and any other stimulus that is associated with the correct response. Rats, for example, were able to "remember" the correct response in some of the early research for relatively long periods if they were permitted to hold a position pointing to the baited alternative. If a present stimulus is arousing the correct response, one does not need to assume that a symbol is functioning for it. When forced to give this orientation up and move about the chamber in order to test for a true symbolic process, the rats were found to be able to remember the correct alternative for only a few seconds. Raccoons and dogs have been found to be much more capable, however, in this test. Raccoons are able to bridge intervals of at least 15 seconds and dogs can bridge intervals of up to several minutes, even while moving about the apparatus. Young children, of course, are capable of bridging temporal gaps of 15 or 20 minutes with little difficulty.

DOUBLE ALTERNATION. The double-alternation technique utilizes a somewhat simpler apparatus but more complicated procedure. The subject in this experiment must generate the internal (symbolic) cues entirely on his own, not having the kind of stimulus help provided in the delayed-reaction situation by the baiting of one alternative. The double-alternation task requires the subject to make two right turns followed by two left turns; the subject is required to keep the record of such responding in his own head, so to speak.

Figure 7-1 shows, diagrammatically, the kind of test device used in double-alternation research. The problem consists of making at the choice point first two successive right (R) turns, then two successive left (L) turns, then two more R turns, and so on. The animal is rewarded following the completion of the correct *double* response—both turns made without error. The difficulty of this task is in large part due to the fact that the first R turn follows an L turn, whereas the second R turn follows an R turn; the same is true for the two L turns. In other words, the same multiple stimuli at the choice point must arouse an R turn on one occasion and an L turn on another. For such to occur, some symbolic process is necessary to signify the differentiating cue of alternation. Rats do very poorly on this problem and have difficulty in achieving even the first four turns (RRLL). Raccoons are able to extend their successful performance somewhat past the first four turns and monkeys can do considerably better than that. Human subjects, with the aid of their symbolizing ability ("take two rights, then two lefts, and so on") are able to perform the task, once learned, as long as they and the experimenter wish.

The research just described offers an approximate answer to the question of animal thinking. There is no question at all but that animals do "think," if we define thinking in a sufficiently broad manner—for example, as the use of symbolic processes in reacting to situations. For any more precise answers to this question, more precise formulations of the question are necessary.

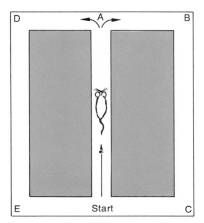

7-1 Floor plan of the apparatus used in the double alternation experiment. Rats are started as indicated and left or right turns are measured at point A.

IMAGES

Take 10 seconds out from reading and *think* of what you had for breakfast this morning (assuming that you are not reading this chapter before breakfast—if so, please think of your most recent breakfast). Did you *see* (or *taste*, or maybe *hear*) your food? (Crunchy cereal, for example, or coffee being slurped.) If so, you were probably using images. On the other hand, if you thought of breakfast exclusively or mainly in words (e.g., "orange juice, cereal, toast with grape jelly, coffee"), you were using language processes as symbols rather than images.

Experimental research on imagery was initiated by Sir Francis Galton. He asked his subjects questions similar to the one just asked and carefully collected and interpreted their responses. Galton's data indicated that images of various kinds are indeed commonly experienced but that they are by no means universally reported, nor are they apparently essential to efficient and productive thought. Scientists, for example, often report very little in the way of images, and some subjects even claim to have none at all.

As indicated in our discussion in Chapter 4, research on images has developed remarkably within psychology in the last few years. A favored procedure has been to compare the effect of imagery with that of meaningfulness, which is mediated primarily by verbal symbols. Here some interesting results have emerged. For example, the use of imagery by subjects facilitates learning more when the imagery is applied to the stimulus than when it is applied to the response, whereas exactly the opposite relationship holds when the meaningfulness variable is manipulated. In other words, subjects learn to respond with some particular word as a response to another word as a stimulus more readily when they are instructed to try to imagine the stimulus (e.g., "see" some particular face for the stimulus *face*) than when they are similarly instructed to imagine the response. But when subjects are instructed to attach some meaningfulness to the word (e.g., think of *face* as the front part of the head), they learn more readily by attaching meaning to the response member of the pair to be associated rather than the stimulus member.

LANGUAGE

Although verbal symbols are not the only kind that humans use, they are by far the most common kind of symbols used in thinking. Regardless of the extent to which words as opposed to images are themselves used in thinking, they are the medium by which one expresses his thinking to others. Language thus plays a dual role: it not only provides an excellent *internal* (mental) means of thinking, but is the only practicable means of *external* (social) communication of that thinking.

THE STUDY OF LANGUAGE. The most important approaches used to study language are the linguistic and behavioral (psychological), and their hybrid off-spring, psycholinguistics, which has only recently come to receive the attention it deserves in the light of its focal role in understanding both experience and behavior. The various other ways of looking at language, such as the clinical, the biological, the humanistic, and the artistic, all have an important place in the attempt of man to understand and appreciate what many claim to be his most valuable and unique ability, but they are more tangential to the central interest of the psychologist.

Linguistics

Contemporary linguists focus on the *capacity* of man to *generate* language. That is, they attempt to understand how it is that the typical human can demonstrate so remarkable a facility in his native tongue. They probe beneath the surface of what most of us tend to take for granted, our largely untutored ability to communicate and thereby use some kind of grammar. The grammar, or rules of sentence structure, that we use may be implicit rather than explicit; in other words, it may be quite different from the grammar that schoolteachers strive to impose on their pupils. But it is nonetheless real and effective. A good example is the language of black Americans in the inner cities. Studies by linguists have clearly demonstrated the independent grammatical status of this language, which is passed on from one generation to another by actual usage rather than formal instruction. The fact that almost all white-oriented American social and business life utilizes the English that is taught in the schools handicaps most black Americans and accounts for a substantial amount of their difficulties in academic and occupational adjustments. But the fact remains that the grammar they have learned to use is real and viable, although markedly different from that used by the majority of Americans, and is therefore worthy of serious study in its own right.

Linguists have generally been greatly impressed by the fact that grammar is used quite effectively in the apparent absence of any tutoring, and by the apparent inapplicability of certain classical learning theories. Accordingly, they have come generally to interpret language ability as a *native* or inherited rather than an acquired property of man. However, this view is as one-sided as the opposite position, which would deny any inherited basis for language and stress only the learning aspect. Both native capacity, in which man clearly excels all other known species, and the opportunity to learn are involved in all language performance.

Psycholinguistics

In studying language the psychologist has tended to concentrate upon actual verbal *performance,* which is usually imperfect and incomplete relative to linguistic capacity. The psycholinguist then attempts to bridge the gap between linguistics and psychology by focusing on both verbal performance and capacity, and especially on the relationship between them. Like all such interdisciplinary efforts, psycholinguistics demands competence in both of the two disciplines involved. It is nevertheless a growing field of investigation, with strong empirical as well as theoretical components. Its objective, simply and generally stated, is to determine how humans *understand* and *generate* sentences.

INFLUENCE OF LANGUAGE ON THOUGHT AND PERCEPTION. There are a number of ways in which the study of psycholinguistics is being fruitfully pursued, but most of these would require a lengthy and complex description. The potential value of this general approach may be best illustrated by the *Whorfian hypothesis,* that cognition (knowledge) generally is organized in accordance with one's linguistic organization. In a very real sense, one's cognitions are held to be limited by the meaning and the structure of his language, and such limitations are not easily overcome.

Whorf was a student of American Indian language and culture. He was impressed greatly by the way in which linguistic differences seemed to organize thinking and perception. For example, the Navaho Indians have no words to distinguish between blue and green hues; such distinction is apparently not an important matter in their lives and so the linguistic differentiation that we take for granted in English and other languages simply does not exist. The result, according to anthropological observations made by Whorf, was that Navahos do not distinguish between these two hues in practice. In a later study monolingual Zuni Indians, bilingual Zunis, and English-speaking college students were compared for color recognition performance. Monolingual Zunis tended to confuse yellow and orange, for which there is only a single term in their native tongue; bilingual Zunis showed a much greater ability to pick out yellows and oranges, but not as much ability as the college students.

For another example, consider snow. Most of us recognize that various types of snow exist but we are not very likely to notice these differences unless they are pronounced (very wet snow, very powdery, and so on). Eskimos, on the other hand, have at least three distinct words for snow. They thus learn to recognize much more subtle distinctions, in accordance with the importance of this kind of differentiation in their everyday lives.

The examples just described are relatively simple. When we extend our analysis of meaning to more abstract problems, however, the true significance of this general position becomes more apparent. For example, the American meaning of *freedom* is hardly likely to be completely consonant with, say, the Russian meaning for the same word. American and Russian interpretation of the very same events and situations will therefore vary accordingly. Linguistic differences play a pivotal role in helping to determine some of our most cherished beliefs, such as those involving religion and politics. Improving our understanding of the fundamental psycholinguistic functions should therefore help considerably in our attempts to understand these focal aspects of our behavior and experience.

INFLUENCE OF GRAMMAR. The examples briefly provided above all relate to the meaning of words as symbols. Grammar, as a set of rules that govern the operation of language, is more concerned with the structural relationships of words within sentences. In this respect too language has been found to influence thought. Our own language, English, is but one of a large group of Indo-European languages. The differences of grammar within this category tend to be slight, in spite of the difficulties that some of us may experience in learning such "foreign" languages. But there are at least fifteen separate categories of languages in the world, classified by their operational grammars.

The importance of grammatical variations for thought can be indicated by another illustration from Whorf's work. Whereas in English a sharp distinction is made between objects and events, this dichotomy is by no means common to all languages. Some American Indian grammars (notably the Hopi) emphasize other dimensions, such as that of duration of action; fast-acting events (e.g., lightning, wind) are given verblike status, and more stable features (e.g., forests, houses) have nounlike status. (It should be mentioned that American Indian languages do *not* belong to the Indo-European class.) Differences of this kind contribute to the difficulties of communication between persons with widely different native tongues, beyond the more obvious problem of meaning.

ENCODING. The codeability of an object (e.g., a chair or a dog) or a property of an object (e.g., height or color) refers to its susceptibility to verbal or some other form of identification. Thus a pure-bred dog is generally easier to encode (e.g., as a collie or a boxer) than a mongrel (e.g., small and brown). Identification of a particular breed carries with it a great deal more information. The relationship between a perception (or its more purely central subsequent representation, the image) and verbal coding has been studied in many experiments. In one such study the investigators first presented the subjects with a series of twenty-four colors and asked them to name each. They then ranked the colors in terms of their codeability; those which were given the same name by a high proportion of the subjects were placed high on the codeability scale, those which received a wide variety of different names were placed low on this scale. The researchers then had a separate set of subjects look briefly at each color (without anything being said about naming) and later select it from a large set of colors. The latter recognition task either came immediately or after a considerable time delay.

The results of the experiment were quite different for the two conditions of recognition. When the subjects were able to look at the colors again *immediately* they recognized colors with low codeability values about as well as they did those with high codeability values. When their recognition was *delayed,* however, a clear relationship between codeability and successful recognition was found; the more codeable colors were more often recognized. These results have important implications. With an immediate test the imaginal representation of the colors was presumably still sufficiently vivid to permit effective recognition performance. After the delay, the images themselves were apparently insufficient to mediate adequate performance; the more readily named colors (high codeability) were assumed to be remembered better because their representation consists of a complementary verbal tag. In other words, they were more likely to have been verbally encoded, and the verbal tag could thus be used as a basis for comparison of colors and selection of the one previously seen from among the set.

ASSOCIATIONS AND MEANINGS OF WORDS

Most psychologists now seem to agree that an understanding of language will require more than the simpler associationistic types of learning theory. Nevertheless, there are ways in which such simple associationistic principles do apply to language problems.

WORD FREQUENCY. One of the more important facts concerning the use of words is the enormous variability in frequency of use. A word count investigation, utilizing almost 20 million words from actual English prose of various sorts, showed this very clearly. The pronoun *I,* for example, occurred at a rate of nearly

20,000 times per million words spoken. Many words (e.g., *titular*) occurred only at a rate of 1 per million words. Everyone understands many more words, in his native language, than he normally uses in his active vocabulary. And within that active vocabulary, as the above illustration suggests, each of us tends to depend upon a relatively small number of words for most of our communicating.

WORD ORDER. Closely related to the problem of word frequency is the question of the sequential ordering of words. Words are selected for use in terms of the context of other words (or ideas) that have already been used. Some words thus tend to follow others, independently of their absolute frequency.

WORD-ASSOCIATION TESTS

The earliest empirical research on associations seems to have been undertaken by Sir Francis Galton. His first procedure was to walk along a busy street, noting each object that caught his attention and attempting to bring up some associations for it. He later modified this procedure, making it more amenable to laboratory conditions. He prepared a large number of words (up to seventy-five) as cues, with each one written on a separate sheet of paper. A subject was then asked to respond to each word with one or more ideas that the cue word elicited. These were recorded and later analyzed. Also recorded was the amount of time required for a first response to each cue word.

These simple procedures provided the basis for the later development of word-association tests. In these tests the subject is provided each word, one at a time, and asked to report the first word that comes to mind (or to tongue). This simple procedure has been applied in a variety of research and practical settings, ranging from language studies to lie-detection tests in crime detection (where the procedure is usually complemented by a number of physiological measures, such as of heart rate, galvanic skin response, and the like). Some of these applications are described elsewhere in this book (e.g., lie detection and diagnosis of emotional problems in Chapter 15).

From the standpoint of language and thought, the most interesting aspect of word-association tests is the remarkable similarity of most responding. So-called common responses (e.g., *white* to *black, chair* to *table*) account for the majority of responses given to high-frequency words; "idiosyncratic" responses (e.g., *tie* to *black, meat* to *table*) account for a tiny percentage of the responses. Speed of responding is also positively correlated with frequency; that is, the words that are most often given as responses are generally given more rapidly than the more idiosyncratic, or individualistic, verbal responses. Also, when more than one response is required, the words given after the first ones tend to come with progressively reduced speed.

It is quite clear that exceptionally strong associations between words are developed by most people in the normal practice of their native tongue. Some data concerning the tendency to make common verbal responses in word association tests illustrate this point nicely. In one group of 1,008 college students, for example, over half (647), when presented with the stimulus word *light*, responded with the word *dark.* The next most common response was *lamp* (only 78). Some of the more unusual responses, in terms of their very low frequency (each given only once), were *look, high, out, awaken, sunshine, hand, love, eyes, dirt, easy, year, boat, daytime, earth, path, air, glow, head.*

The Semantic Differential

The semantic differential test is one of many verbal probing techniques designed to get at the structural dimensions involved in the meaning of concepts. It is particularly concerned with the *affective* meaning (emotional tone) of words or concepts. A subject is asked to rate each of a series of words on several dimensions. Extreme positions are identified by a pair of polar adjectives: for example, *weak–strong, good–bad* (Figure 7-2). A seven-point scale is used for each dimension. The result of a subject's evaluating the concept words is a kind of semantic (or meaning) profile, determined by the ratings on the three independent dimensions. Such data are valuable in detecting and measuring the affective concomitants of words, especially for comparative purposes in research, but are more restricted than the free-association tests in that only a limited set of dimensions is tapped.

Individual Differences

Before leaving the topic of verbal associations, some attention needs to be given to the problem of individual differences in language production. Here there is an apparent paradox. On the one hand, we have just noted the predominant tendency of most people to respond with pretty much the same words to certain cue words (e.g., *table* to *chair, white* to *black*), thus suggesting a high degree of commonality in verbal associations. On the other hand, most people seem to have quite characteristic ways of speaking and writing; once we come to know a person well and

7-2 An example of a semantic differential test for the word *son.* The actual test would have many adjectives listed; a numerical scale is applied to compare results among individuals.

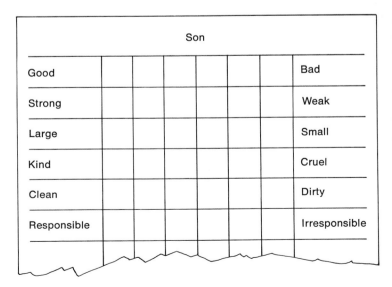

are accustomed to his own individual linguistic style, it is often easy to identify him from a sample of speech or writing.

How can these seemingly contradictory facts be reconciled? For one thing, each individual has his own "voice print" (now capable of being expressed in graphic form, similar to finger prints). The characteristics of vocalization are of course independent of the meanings of the words used and are probably the main contributors to the successful identification of the voice. Even when these are eliminated, however, as in typed or printed prose passages, we can often identify the writer from his style (especially if the choices are limited and there are secondary cues available). We apparently do so on the basis of characteristic individual modes of expression. It seems that each of us has to some extent his own individualistic "grammar" as well as the grammar common to the language he uses.

ANIMAL "LANGUAGE"

We have occasion at various other places in this book to refer to the problem of animal "language." Here we may summarize the problem and evaluate its present status.

Communication by animals occurs at a number of different levels of complexity, with different sets of mediating mechanisms.

Reflexes

The simplest forms of communication, nicely exemplified by the so-called social insects, such as bees and ants, consist of reflexive reactions, both behavioral and chemical (called pheromones). The behavioral forms are especially interesting. The biologist Von Frisch has provided a fascinating account of the way in which both the direction and the distance of food objects are communicated by the worker bee upon return to the hive. Her "dance" tells the story. The angle at which she climbs the comb is related to the orientation of the food source to the sun. The distance of the food source is expressed in terms of the number of rotations in the dance, with short distances represented by fewer rotations or turns.

These signs are quite effective in directing other workers to the food found by the forager, but there is no reason at all for considering them to be anything more than exceedingly interesting reflexive behaviors that have been built into the bee by evolution over many generations. The entire set of complex social relationships observed in insects like bees and ants can best be similarly interpreted; the term *language of the bees* that is sometimes used to describe the "dance" behavior may have more poetic than scientific significance.

Nonreflexive Communication

At a higher level of complexity, animals express what might be considered true communication. The term *true* is intended to convey the nonreflexive character of the signs demonstrated. The animal that is signaling is responsive to the reception of the sign by the receiver; for example, begging behavior by a dog or other pet signals a request for, say, food or perhaps coddling or petting. Moreover, this kind of signaling behavior varies in accordance with the behavior of the receiver, unlike the dance of the worker bee. The dog starts his begging behavior only under certain circumstances and he increases or decreases it in accordance with the results it achieves. It can in this sense be called *purposive,* although the implication that such a label has for the "mental" correlates is unclear.

Most of the higher animals, such as mammals, exhibit this form of communication (among themselves perhaps more commonly than in relationship to humans). However, this fact does not mean that they do not also have more strictly reflexive forms of communication. Pheromones, chemical signals, are quite common among mammals. It is noteworthy that within recent years the laboratory rat's ability to respond to odor trails in a maze has been demonstrated and the implications of this form of previously unsuspected behavior for certain problems in learning and motivation are only now being developed.

Language

The complexity of ordered relationship among signs or symbols is the critical feature that elevates language to a position above simple communication by signs. The organism that uses a language must be able to make combinations of symbols to at least some degree and then express these combinations to other organisms.

Two lines of research have recently demonstrated true if rudimentary language ability in subhuman animals. In both cases chimpanzees have been the subjects. In both cases also the experimenters have bypassed vocalization, so readily adopted by the human but apparently relatively difficult for the chimpanzee to use as a means of expressing ideas and communication. In one case vocalization was replaced by the use of hand signals, in the other by plastic forms to be placed on a magnetized slate or by visually differentiated keys to be pushed on a computer console.

AMERICAN SIGN LANGUAGE: WASHOE. Washoe, a young female chimpanzee, has been intensively trained to communicate with humans by means of a slightly modified form of the American sign language widely used by deaf persons to communicate among themselves. In the chimpanzee, hand gestures are naturally much more common than vocalizations (occasional chirps and screams). Washoe learned to use approximately 160 different signs. Moreover, she learned to combine these signs appropriately (e.g., "Washoe wants food") so as to express her needs and desires effectively as well as understand the signs made to her.

In an extension of this research various other young members of a colony of chimpanzees have been trained in the same system of hand signs, demonstrating the ease with which the chimpanzee can acquire this form of communication. It is interesting that Washoe continued to use her well-learned signs when placed in this colony of untrained chimpanzees, even though they were not able to understand or respond appropriately to them. Spontaneous use of certain signs, such as that for *tickle,* was frequently observed to occur in two young male champanzees serving as subjects in this colony. Another young female chimpanzee in training has been observed to entertain herself by signing the question, "What that?" while watching herself in a mirror and then answering this question herself by making the appropriate sign for whatever object she was handling. An incidental but highly suggestive observation concerns the use by Washoe of the sign *dirty* (normally referring to soiling) before the sign of the name of a person who has just refused to honor one of her requests, a most interesting indication of an apparently spontaneous form of symbolic simian insult.

PLASTIC FORMS AND KEYS: SARAH AND LANA. While Washoe was engaged in learning American sign language, another young female chimpanzee, Sarah, was learning to communicate with her human associates by placement of differentially shaped plastic forms. Sarah developed a vocabulary of about 140 words, was able to form short but complete sentences, and in general according to the experimenter showed linguistic ability superior to that of the average two-year-old child.

In a subsequent adaptation of this kind of language training a third female chimpanzee, Lana, has been more recently instructed to read and write short but complete sentences. In this case, the "words," or symbolic units, are represented by various visual patterns. Utilizing the plastic keys of an appropriately prepared computer console, Lana first learned the meaning of noun symbols for such objects as *apple, drink*, and *window*. After about one year of this rote memory she began to put the various words together in strings to express her motives.

To insure that Lana was really using the visual patterns as communication units, and not merely memorizing the location of the various patterns on the keyboard, the experimenters scrambled the location of the patterns on the console daily without disturbing her performance. Moreover, when Lana did make an error, such as hitting the wrong key, she proceeded to erase it, providing further evidence of the degree of her understanding of the "word" meanings.

Utilization of a grammar, or set of rules for constructing and understanding sentences, is a crucial linguistic feature that is clearly demonstrated by both Sarah and Lana. Lana, for example, carefully punctuates her sentences either with a period, following a declaration, or a question mark, following a query. It is their ability to demonstrate mastery of a functional if rudimentary grammar by constructing real sentences that is the most impressive linguistic achievement of the chimpanzees serving as subjects in these recent researches on subhuman language. (Sarah and Lana are shown communicating in Figure 7-3.)

COMPARISON WITH HUMAN LANGUAGE. Although the significance of the chimpanzee language demonstrations and their implications for linguistic ability in subhuman primates are not to be denied, the results also highlight the remarkably superior linguistic capacity of the human organism. It is only by the most intense training program that a very few chimpanzees have thus far been able to show the simplest forms of symbolic manipulations of the sort that the typical child readily develops in the absence of any special tutoring. Moreover, human language is enormously more complex than anything yet attempted in any subhuman program. Whether these differences are regarded as truly qualitative or merely quantitative depends of course upon how one wishes to set up his scheme of classification, but however categorized they constitute extremely impressive evidence of human thinking capability. This conclusion follows from the assumption, which is commonly made and seems to be essentially sound, that overt language performance provides at least an approximate mirror for covert thinking processes.

(a)

(b)

7-3 Chimpanzees communicating by means of visual shapes. (a) Sarah communicates with human assistant. (b) Lana works at computer console, selecting appropriate visual patterns. (Photos by the University of California at Santa Barbara and Yerkes Primate Center, Emory University.)

Without some kind of ordering, it would be impossible for any complex organism to deal with the bewildering array of stimulation that impinges on him. Effective use of symbols (mainly images and words) would also be impossible in thinking without some such means of ordering objects and events. The fundamental operation of this kind that organisms use is the formation and utilization of concepts (also called, with increasing frequency in the psychological literature, concept attainment; these terms are now used interchangeably).

A concept may be defined as a *property of objects and events that is common to some of them;* it is thus a symbolic means of both integrating and differentiating our experiences, and it is a fundamental step in higher forms of thinking. A concept defines the properties that all objects or events of a given category have in common; for example, the concept of *Father* and *Daddy* includes those properties that fathers have in common with each other, regardless of size, color, personality, and so on. Concepts are also of course closely related to language problems, because they are ordinarily given verbal status, and most of the research on them has utilized verbal terms.

Concept Formation

In the growing child, concepts are formed on the basis of his learning experiences. In this process two simultaneous and diametrically opposed processes, generalization and discrimination, play important roles. *Generalization* refers to the tendency for an organism to respond to a stimulus that is in some way similar to an earlier stimulus in the same manner as it had to the earlier stimulus; the very young child's calling "Daddy" to a variety of men other than the father after learning to make this response to the father is an illustration of this phenomenon. *Discrimination* refers to the distinguishing between stimuli, by making different responses to them, *even when* they are in some way similar; once the child learns to discriminate between people, it will stop calling all other men "Daddy" and reserve the term for the father.

The illustration cited shows these two processes in unusually bald fashion but the same fundamental processes operate, albeit more subtly, in organisms of various types and ages. One experiment in which two-year-old children were pitted against rats and chimpanzees gave instructive results. The problem was one of visual form discrimination. The subjects were required to select the triangle form. The two-year-old children not only learned this simple discrimination problem readily, as would be expected, but when tested on a variety of other triangular forms (as shown in Figure 7-4), selected them also, indicating that they had by generalization developed a true concept of triangularity. The rats learned the original problem more rapidly than the chimpanzees but were unable to demonstrate, in this case, generalization to the other triangles. The chimpanzees were able to respond appropriately to the first two of the test triangles, suggesting the existence of greater conceptualization of the basic properties of triangularity.

7-4 Perception of the concept of triangularity. Trained to respond to the top figure, the rat makes random responses to items 2 and 3; the chimpanzee recognizes item 2 as a triangle and responds selectively to it but makes random responses to 3; the two-year-old human child recognizes the training figure in all three test figures. It has been concluded that these three kinds of subjects differ in the cerebral processes that were involved in the original training to respond to the triangle. (Adapted from Hebb, 1972.)

1

2

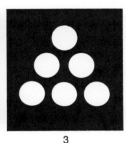
3

Take a Breather

STYLE OF THINKING

Below are eight questions* that have been found to differentiate individuals with respect to one facet of their style of thinking. Answer them for yourself, pondering each one carefully, before turning to p. 198, where an interpretation is provided. Indicate, on a sheet of paper, true or false for each question in accordance with your own most honest answer.

1. I like to fool around with new ideas, even if they turn out later to be a total waste of time.
2. The best theory is the one that has the best practical application.

*From Frank Barron, "The Psychology of Imagination," *Scientific American,* 1958, **199,** 150–166.

3. Some of my friends think that my ideas are impractical, if not a bit wild.
4. The unfinished and the imperfect often have greater appeal for me than the completed and the polished.
5. I must admit that I would find it hard to have for a close friend a person whose manners or appearance made him somewhat repulsive, no matter how brilliant or kind he might be.
6. A person should not probe too deeply into his own and other people's feelings, but take things as they are.
7. Young people sometimes get rebellious ideas, but as they grow up they ought to get over them and settle down.
8. Perfect balance is the essence of all good composition.

In this section we will first take an overall look at decision making generally, attempting to bring into focus some of the more significant determinants, and then a small number of closely related areas in which more active research has been carried out will be surveyed. Subsequent sections of the chapter will take up certain of the major determinants of decisions (for example, attitudes and stereotypes) as topics of broad significance in their own right.

DECISIONS

Each of us is called upon to make decisions throughout the course of our everyday lives. Some of these decisions are truly significant; they have far-reaching influences on our own as well as others' futures. Other decisions are trivial; their effects are unimportant even at the moment they are made. Decisions thus come in many forms and sizes, but they have certain features in common.

First, decisions are typically the result of a certain amount of *intellectual effort;* reflex or automatized habitual responses clearly do not qualify, but so-called snap judgments might be considered to be decisions of a sort. The critical variable is the amount of deliberation required; the more deliberation, assuming some outcome, the more likely a given process is to be considered a decision.

Second, decisions always involve the *choice* of one or more *alternatives* as an answer to an explicit or implicit question of some sort. The minimal number of alternatives is of course two, as represented by the relatively simple yes or no decision.

Third, most decisions have more or less immediate implications for *overt action* of one kind or another; such actions may or may not be taken but they are generally implied in a decision.

The more significant decisions of course are ones in which overt action (beyond the expression of the decision itself) is taken, especially when the ramifications are far-reaching and long-lasting. The selection of a major in college, for example, carries with it a host of subordinate decisions (such as which specific courses to take). At the same time, it at least partially resolves additional issues (such as foreclosing certain occupational choices, even while leaving others still open as alternatives).

Determinants of Decisions

In the absence of very much in the way of theoretical, let alone experimental, analysis, the process of decision making as here defined remains almost a complete mystery. However, lack of knowledge concerning the exact thinking mechanisms that are involved in making decisions need not keep us from examining the input variables that seem to be effective. Three major categories of such determinants seem to be involved in decision making: cognition, motives, and attitudes. Treatment of these variables as distinct categories may do some injustice to the facts, in that they may actually be difficult to separate in practice; nevertheless, this logical procedure has the merit of highlighting the more critical factors.

COGNITIONS. A variety of *cognitive* processes are quite obviously involved in any decision making. The problem or question itself depends in its recognition upon some degree of cognition or knowledge; that is to say, some kind of appreciation of the question must be present, even when it is posed by others or directly imposed upon one from outside. In general, then, the quality of decision making may be presumed to vary, first and most directly, with the *quality* of the *information* concerning the various alternatives available to the decision maker.

Another special problem relating to cognition as a determinant of decisions is posed by the frequent need for the decision maker to evaluate his own capabilities. Such considerations are important in a substantial number of personal decisions. An accurate assessment of oneself is of course often difficult to achieve, and failure to do so may be presumed to underlie many poorly made decisions. Actively soliciting objective assessment, with regard to the specifics of a particular situation, is one relatively simple way of circumventing this roadblock, but it does require the proper attitude on the part of the individual concerned. He must not be so over-confident as to disregard the more objective views of others; at the same time he must not be so lacking in confidence as to seek too many such views or depend too heavily upon them.

MOTIVES. The second class of determinants is the *motives* of the decision maker. How the various alternatives that he sees as open to him in the situation relate to his own motivation will be a most potent, and sometimes clearly *the* most potent, factor in his decision making. Anticipated consequences (which are a subvariety of cognition) are usually assessed in relation to the relevant motivational conditions. The complexity of motivation is treated at length in a later place (Chapter 14) but here one fundamental complication should be mentioned. This is the fact that much of one's motivation is unconscious. The consequence of this most important fact is that interpretation of the true bases of decisions is often extremely difficult, especially for the decision maker himself. It is also difficult for an objective observer to determine where lack of awareness of motives leaves off and deliberate deception begins.

ATTITUDES. The third major class of determinant for decisions is closely related to motives. It is the set of attitudes, or the underlying belief systems, that each of us acquires. Attitudes, which are considered at length in a later part of this chapter, differ from motives in that they are *generalized predispositions,* which usually entail a positive or negative feeling, rather than specific dispositions toward some action or the other. In other words, it is our attitudes that lay the groundwork for many of our more particular motivations or objectives. For example, a person may be strongly *motivated* to work for civil rights and as a result make a *decision* to enlist in some particular movement because of his positive *attitude* toward the *concept* of equality of opportunity. Here the attitude has set the stage for both the more particular motive and the still more particular decision. The concept is of course a part of the person's cognitive structure, and as such is the basis upon which the more affectively tinged attitude is built.

Postdecision Processes

When a person has to choose among equally attractive alternatives, such as from among the numerous makes and models of new cars available, choosing one of the alternatives may produce some degree of a dilemma because of the need to reject the other, equally attractive alternatives. The *cognitive dissonance* that produces this dilemma is the contradiction between the fact that some alternative is desirable and the fact that it has nevertheless been rejected. Thus after a person has committed himself to one among a number of such desirable alternatives, he may regret not having chosen one of the rejected alternatives. He can bolster his decision by emphasizing, on the one hand, both the good qualities of his chosen alternative and the bad qualities of the rejected alternatives and by minimizing, on the other hand, the bad aspects of his chosen alternative and the good aspects of the rejected alternative. The extent of the bolstering of the original decision that occurs after the decision has been made is assumed to be related to the magnitude of the cognitive dissonance produced by the decision. Other cognitive dissonance processes are discussed in a later section of this chapter.

ATTITUDES, BELIEFS, OPINIONS

We have already had occasion in this chapter to use the concept of attitude as a major determinant in decision making. Now we consider attitudes more generally, along with two closely related concepts, beliefs and opinions.

Because these are topics that are customarily treated under social psychology, some explanation of their inclusion at this point is required. Consider attitudes. There are three critical questions relating to attitudes:

1. How are they *formed?*
2. How are they *changed?*
3. How do they function to *influence* behavior?

It is of course the third issue that we have already met and that we are now concerned with primarily. The first two issues belong more properly in the province of social psychology, because it is almost entirely via social influences that attitudes are formed and changed. These two questions are considered in detail in Chapter 17. Not all attitudes relate to social variables, however, and all attitudes, social and nonsocial, play crucial roles in our thinking; hence we will take up here those functional aspects of attitude that are relevant to thought.

Attitudes, beliefs, and opinions all involve some aspect of an individual's cognitive organization of his world. They vary mainly along two dimensions, the degree to which they are *explicitly expressed* and the amount of *affective tone* they contain. Underlying attitudes themselves are usually expressed only indirectly (as by statements of belief, or in motivated behaviors); they are necessarily inferred from observations of behavior. Although a great variety of definitions of attitudes can be found in the psychological literature, the most frequently occurring features are the positive or negative (affective) tone and the postural characteristic; that is, an attitude always *pre*disposes its holder toward one posture or the other. As the often hidden but nonetheless fundamental source of so much of our behavior, especially our social behavior, attitudes have been accorded a great deal of attention by psychologists.

Like attitudes, beliefs tend to be indirectly expressed in behavior, usually in verbal behavior. They may be more specifically directed toward particular problems. Thus one may have a negative attitude toward members of some particular group, such as an ethnic class (say, blacks or Jews) or an occupational or economic category (say, professors or wealthy persons) that is expressed in a number of beliefs (say, that blacks are intellectually inferior or Jews are sharp businessmen, to take two common examples). Beliefs are more often neutral in affective tone than attitudes, even though they involve acceptance of a proposition. When they do have heavy affective loading, it can usually be attributed to some more fundamental and longlasting attitude.

Opinions are verbally expressed beliefs or attitudes. Opinions are by definition explicit. They are more likely than beliefs to have a strong affective tone, perhaps partly because when one expresses an idea he tends to vest in it a personal (ego) factor. Adoption of some position on a given issue normally leads to an opinion. Generation of at least a minimal amount of affect seems to be an inevitable concomitant of opinion making. Most of us have experienced the kind of argument (involving, say, political issues) in which the emotional level of the disputants, and the strength of their attachment to their own opinions, seems to rise markedly as those opinions are expressed and, especially, defended from attack. A very good way of insuring that beliefs become more vigorously and emotionally held is to force their overt expression as opinions and then attack them, even implicitly.

Attitudes; Prejudices

Attitudes with strong negative tones may become prejudices, especially when they are formed on the basis of relatively restricted information concerning the people, objects, or activities involved. A prejudice is, literally, a *pre*judgment. Like all attitudes it reflects a generalized posture or orientation, and it is very often sufficiently subtle to resist detection.

Few of us are likely to deny that we have attitudes (any more than that we have correlated beliefs and opinions). But not many of us will admit to having prejudices. The only important factor that would produce a substantial reduction in such attitudes being properly classified also as prejudices would be the development of the attitude on the basis of a sufficiently broad experiential basis to justify its existence on objective grounds. Thus the student who has suffered at the hands of four or five professors of some subject presumably has more objective grounds for expressing a negatively toned opinion of that subject than the student who has suffered through only one or maybe two such courses. When adverse opinions are advanced by the latter, he is therefore more likely to be accused of being prejudiced.

The point made in the last paragraph reflects an important recent development, namely, the growth in the United States particularly of a more negatively toned attitude toward being identified as prejudiced. The newly found (and hard-earned, legally and morally) respect for various minorities, chiefly black citizens, is mainly responsible for this change.

It is impossible for any of us to avoid developing both positively and negatively tinged attitudes toward the various groups and institutions that we encounter. However, allowing such attitudes to operate without checks is not inevitable. This is important because prejudices allowed free rein can have remarkably pervasive effects. Most of us who have lived in anything but the most monolithic society can recall incidents that illustrate how influential and pervasive a prejudice can be; a single stimulus signifying some socially stigmatized condition (e.g., blackness, Jewishness, womanhood) can under the appropriate circumstances cue a remarkably wide assortment of behaviors.

Touching the sensitive ethnic or similar nerve of an individual afflicted with a strong prejudice can thus effect an instantaneous change in his thinking mechanisms as well as his perceptions and his behavior. It is for this reason that identification of prejudices is so important; a recognized prejudice is a better target for countermeasures, should one wish to apply them. (Discussion of ways in which attitudes can be changed is postponed until Chapter 17, because almost all strong prejudices are socially oriented, and the measures used are socially mediated.)

Thus far in the discussion of attitudes we have stressed their affective content. Now it should be mentioned that not all attitudes, or covert predispositions of a generalized sort, are emotionally toned. Affectively neutral attitudes do occur (e.g., one of curiosity, or questioning, or respect); in these there is no necessarily strong affective component. Other types of attitudes occur in which affective components are more likely to develop (e.g., attitudes of defiance, or defensiveness, or quarrelsomeness) but where the focus is on the particular behavioral process rather than the affect. These are all important behavioral and experiential determinants and like other attitudes tend to have pervasive influences. But they are less likely to have as dramatic effects or be as resistant to change as those attitudes, such as strong prejudices, in which the affective component alone is involved.

BELIEFS AND FACTS

Like so many of the words in common use in psychological problems, the word *belief* has significant multiple dimensions. Basically, beliefs are those propositions about the world for which one has some degree of conviction. They are composed of the various concepts that have been acquired, and they organize the concepts in ways that seem to make sense out of the manifold complexities of experience. They are obviously highly correlated with one's attitudes because they have come from the same background of experience. Beliefs and attitudes are mutually self-supportive and sometimes rather difficult to disentangle.

How, then, do facts enter into this picture? Are not facts related to the way in which the world *really* exists, rather than to the way each of us from his own perspective develops his belief systems?

Ask someone what a "fact" is. You are likely to get an answer that says, in effect, either that facts *are* events or that they describe the way things *really* are. These are the two most common interpretations of the term *fact*. They sound alike but the similarity is deceptive. Anyone is free of course to use either of these, or any other interpretation, that he wishes, but this is really beside the point. The significant question is how this term, or any other term for that matter, is most often used and how it is most usefully interpreted.

Look again at the two meanings just mentioned. What is the critical element of the first, which tends to equate facts with things and events? It is the emphasis upon a presumed real state of affairs. But how do we achieve an understanding of this real world? Unless we hold to some supernatural capacity we must depend upon our perceptual mechanisms. And that is exactly what the second meaning is trying to tell us, namely, that *facts are propositions about the world upon which we can agree.* The connection between the two meanings is their common *empirical* referent. In the first meaning, however, such an empirical referent is only implied, whereas in the second meaning not only is it explicated, but it is the very essence of factualness. False beliefs that are maintained in the face of contradictory evidence as judged by others are classified as delusions.

Consider what people really do when they "get down to the facts." They try to find a *common basis* upon which to proceed. In other words, they look for propositions on which they can *agree.* Such propositions of course are beliefs. They are certainly not the things or events themselves (the absolute view of facts), but are rather the way in which people perceive and interpret those things and events (the relative view of facts).

Consider some examples of facts. Is it a fact that the earth is flat or that the sun revolves around the earth? Few people today, in our society at least, would care to affirm either of these statements about the earth. Why not? It is not because very many can themselves directly perceive the roundness of the earth or the revolution of the earth around the sun. Rather, each of us is able to perceive a number of partial implications of each of these propositions that fit together in a consistent pattern. More important, however, we accept authority on such questions. In other words, facts are in the long run primarily a matter of the kind of belief that each of us more or less implicitly invests in propositions about the world.

Now think back a few centuries. Was it ever a fact that the earth was flat or that the sun revolved around the earth? The answer is no if, by today's standards, we accept the view that facts *are* things and events and their relationships. It is yes of course if we accept the view held here that facts are rather the *limited* and *changeable* verbal statements that man makes about such matters. That is to say, a fact as we think the term is most usefully identified is always *relative* to a particular time and place and population of people. So the propositions cited were facts for most people at some time and place in the past but are not facts for many people today. Who can say that a similar fate will not befall many of today's "facts" in the future? Indeed, the advance of science makes such a fate inevitable for most of today's facts. But there is no way to tell in advance which of today's facts will be tomorrow's superstitions. If we were really concerned with maintaining as beyond question the factualness of our beliefs, we would hardly want to develop science as a very vigorous intellectual enterprise, because plowing under old facts and developing new facts is exactly what scientists must do if they are to make effective progress.

The discussion thus far has focused on verbal propositions that are, in principle, more or less directly testable empirically. We have concluded that these facts contain a high component of belief. It should hardly surprise us therefore that as we turn to a consideration of facts that have higher proportions of opinion in them, and are much less empirically testable, we should find increasingly higher degrees of the belief component accompanied by correspondingly greater emotional involvement. Good examples can be found in practically any political or religious issue. Whether or not this kind of proposition should be labeled as fact, and it is hard to see where a dividing line can be drawn in view of the continuous nature of the dimension, the need for agreement about meanings of concepts and propositions becomes increasingly crucial as their amenability to external verification decreases.

OPINIONS AND STEREOTYPES

If attitudes are usually inferred from behavior and beliefs are sometimes inferred and sometimes directly expressed, opinions stand clearly at the expressed end of this covert-overt continuum. They are by definition *expressed beliefs* that state relationships of some kind or the other about the world and are identified as one's own. Opinions therefore share all the characteristics of beliefs and so are subject to all the same functional relationships. Moreover, as indicated earlier, they tend to contain more affective tone (positive or negative feeling), perhaps because of the personal investment that is necessarily generated when one's name is attached, even if implicitly, to an idea. Opinions are thus indexes of a predisposition to behave in a relatively consistent way. They are also indexes of the acceptance or rejection of propositions (i.e., beliefs). Of course they are not always a valid index; in some cases people behave quite differently from their expressed opinions.

Opinions even more than unexpressed beliefs seem to be influenced by some additional kinds of thinking mechanisms. Formation of opinions in people is remarkably influenced by certain special forms of categorizing. The term *stereotype* is one prominent example. We are stereotyping when we select a relatively small number of characteristics of some category of people or things and use these characteristics as representative of the category, and then usually proceed to provide a verbal tag or label to them. For example, viewing Southerners as bigots, farmers as uneducated, women as nonrational, men as sexist, long-haired youths as "hippies," or police officers as despots are common stereotypes, obviously closely related to the prejudices mentioned above. As a matter of fact, stereotypes can be readily considered as forms of prejudice, should we care to extend the meaning of that term, because they involve *pre*judgment. They are discussed here, in relationship to opinions, because they do seem to be especially closely related to the way in which opinions operate, as can be seen in the examples provided.

Stereotypes have the apparent advantage of all categorizing in that they simplify things. Certainly we all need simplifying devices; they facilitate perception and thought. But each such device must be evaluated on its merits, in regard to its other features; in this respect stereotypes are quite clearly real and lasting hazards to effective thought processes, and behaviors. Most of the hazard can be summarized in the statement that stereotypes *exaggerate*. They do so both with regard to errors of omission and commission. On the one hand, they ignore many significant attributes of the subjects while focusing on the alleged crucial features. On the other hand, they ignore exceptions to the stereotyped perspective, and these can of course be not only frequent but also to others without the stereotyping tendency, quite obvious. In spite of these shortcomings, stereotypes persist because they are fed by more basic beliefs and attitudes and in turn feed these systems.

A more extended treatment of techniques by which stereotyped thinking, along with its underlying attitudes, can be changed must await our later discussion (Chapter 17). But we can look briefly at one interesting aspect of stereotypes. All of us tend to stereotype objects that are unfamiliar. The common American opinion that, "All Chinese look alike," is a direct reflection of this; so do all Indians (American or Asiatic), all blacks, or all whites—*if* one is seeing them for the first time. Under such conditions we all tend to see only the most prominent of features—the skin color, in this example—and ignore other perhaps more important features. But this kind of perceptual selectivity need not be carried over into later phases of greater familiarity. Nevertheless, many people continue to "see" only the skin color, or at best that plus some small number of similar characteristics, and to identify all members of the category by these restricted features. This fact indicates the persistent intervention of fixed attitudes that serve to inhibit normal perceptual learning in some social situations.

An interesting illustration of the persistence of naive perceptual categorizing is afforded by the frequently cited comment of a prominent politician that once you have seen one Redwood tree, you have seen them all. Of course in a way you have if you are only concerned about the grossest features of the trees, such as their size and height. But if you are at all sensitive to slightly more complex matters, such as the variety of growth patterns exhibited in different settings (with or without direct monetary value), then you may want to take a few more looks. As a matter of fact, you may want to make the Redwood the target of a lifetime of study; there is no object so simple that it cannot be infinitely analyzed, scientifically or otherwise.

One last point can be made in regard to this kind of perceptual categorizing, and corresponding oversimplification of intellectual processes. This concerns the role of the "image" (not the perceptual image we have already met, of the Titchenerian variety). An "image" is said to be projected by, say, a politician or statesman, or perhaps even the name of an automobile. Advertisers and public relations experts spend much time and even do some empirical research trying to improve such "images" in order better to "sell" their products. The "charisma" of the politician and the "sexiness" of the car name (related to virility) usually are examples of their objectives.

Efforts such as these are clearly designed to tune into existing stereotypes. The hair style of the politician, for example, will be examined closely to keep it in tune with whatever current styles exist. The choice of a new name for an automobile will be researched, with respect to which names most effectively suggest a male phallic symbol. The recipients of all this careful work are assumed to perceive selectively, by such stereotypes, and then form their opinions, in voting or buying, accordingly. Unfortunately, there does seem to be sufficient empirical basis for these expectations; such efforts seem to pay off handsomely in both votes and dollars. Whether the payoffs would significantly decline with increased sophistication of the public, and the presumed reduction of stereotyped perceiving and thinking, is a moot point on which there does not seem to be any directly relevant empirical evidence.

The illustrations cited are relatively subtle in their operation. Much more blatant appeals to stereotypelike behavioral processes can be evoked by means of simple symbols like flags or religious objects. The amount of emotion aroused by such symbols is indeed remarkable, indicating the great depth of the belief systems that are tapped in this way. "Waving the flag" is a pretty sure way of eliciting more or less stereotyped patriotic responses in many appropriately conditioned people. We have thus gone full circle, from consideration of the nature of symbols through various complicated thinking processes and now back to a reconsideration of relatively simple symbols as elicitors of some of those processes. One might of course question whether this kind of response (e.g., removing one's hat and standing as the flag passes by) is properly classifiable as *thinking*, in the light of its relatively automatic, and often autonomic, character. But regardless of how it is classified, this kind of function is clearly continuous with other behaviors in which some thinking is more readily evidenced.

Aided by sudden squalls in the often quite variable winds of public opinion, symbols with little initial affective tone can sometimes very quickly develop into "scare words" with real clout. For example, in the furor over the ending of the long Vietnam war by the United States, the word *amnesty* (relating to those opponents of the war who had evaded the draft by leaving the country) rapidly acquired strong emotional tinges. Another recent example, with two vigorously contending but opposed factions, is the abortion issue. Although the development of *abortion* into the same kind of scare word was not quite so abrupt, emotionality increased as legislative campaigns heated up. These illustrations from recent events in the United States provide a clear picture of the way in which emotionally tinged issues transfer their emotional meanings to initially relatively neutral verbal symbols, showing the reciprocal influence of thinking and perception on each other.

CONTRADICTORY ATTITUDES AND BELIEFS

There are a number of different kinds of reactions made to contradictory attitudes and beliefs when these occur within an individual. These range from those of the scientist, who is trained to be tolerant of ambiguity and contradictions even while he seeks to reduce them, to those of the paranoiac, who apparently resolves the conflict by fixating certain of his own interpretations (called delusions by others) and blocking out all opposing views. With this breadth of behaviors there is almost certainly a large number of different kinds of mediating mechanisms. Unfortunately, we are not yet in a position to make definitive identification of many of these, let alone relate them to their own determining variables. We must therefore be content with tentative and preliminary descriptive statements. Here we look at a number of what appear to be modal types of reactions to contradictions among attitudinal and belief systems, pointing out the more salient characteristics of each and such implications as are indicated.

Contradictory Attitudes

Most authorities agree that when one has markedly different kinds of experience with a particular attitudinal object, he tends to develop either an "averaged" attitude or a compromised attitude that varies with the occasion. In other words, the affective value, positive or negative, that a group of people or an institution or an activity has for an individual may be regarded as essentially the algebraic sum of all his relevant affective experiences. Some interesting interactions occur. Consider the girl who thoroughly dislikes some game, say football. Now assume that she acquires a new boyfriend (or, worse still, a new husband) who is extremely fond of football. The chances are that her attitude toward the game will change for the better, even though her positive regard for the boyfriend may be correspondingly reduced.

Although it may well be true that this kind of averaging-out process does generally occur to produce a reasonably persistent overall attitudinal value, there nonetheless seem to be persistent occurrences of more particular positive and negative reactions. Thus the typical child will have strong positive affectional bonds with both parents and siblings but at the same time will demonstrate on occasion equally strong negative reactions (after, say, punishment or quarreling). There is also clear evidence of such love–hate combinations in many adult relationships, such as between husbands and wives. In some such instances the negative factor can of course be stronger and more pervasive than the positive, producing an overall negative attitude, although more often fortunately the opposite is true.

Considering the complexity of human interactions, it does seem that there is room for comparably complex behavioral mechanisms. Hence the acceptance of both specific negative and positive components and an averaging-out process in attitudes is theoretically defensible as well as empirically indicated.

LOGIC-TIGHT COMPARTMENTS. When the factor of belief systems is added to the contradictory attitudes, a more complex situation develops. It is not possible simply to average beliefs in the way that attitudes can be averaged. Also, reconciling beliefs not only is hard work but often has unpleasant consequences. For example, having to make difficult decisions is usually decidedly unpleasant. A solution that is commonly resorted to in such conflict situations is simply to ignore the contradiction: the two (or more) contradictory belief systems are thus all maintained, just as though they were not logically inconsistent. Such *logic-tight compartmentalizing* of thinking processes is especially likely to occur when the belief systems are invested with strong affective components (that is, they consist of powerful attitudes).

Examples of this illogical but adjustive mechanism are easy to find, once one is alerted to it. Thus the businessman whose practices may be dishonest on weekdays may have little trouble professing Christian doctrine on Sundays; the gangster whose mere suggestion condemns men to death may show tenderness and compassion to his family; and the scientist who insists upon the strictest of logical reasoning in his laboratory may reveal no respect for what others see as logical analysis in his personal interactions. All these illustrations depend upon the failure of the persons involved to apply the same rules of thinking to the different aspects of their lives. They can thus, in a sense, both have their cake and eat it too. Calling attention to the apparent logical contradictions is not likely to do more than force the individuals into one or more of the more common *defense mechanisms* that are discussed in Chapter 16, such as rationalization.

The prime example of logic-tight compartmentalizing may be seen in the tendency that each of us exhibits to some degree to have a double standard of morality and general behavioral evaluation. The code we apparently use for evaluating our own conduct is typically (but not always) milder than the one we use for evaluating the conduct of others.

Failures to relate factual information in a reasonable manner, perhaps produced by mechanisms similar to those operating in logic-tight compartmentalizing on a more chronic basis, are rather common. The strength of habitual arrangements is often so strong that changes in such routines necessitate special attention. The frequency with which we all on one occasion or another fail to put 2 and 2 together, because we do not even try, suggests some fundamental continuity with logic-tight compartmentalizing as a "normal" human thinking process.

DELUSIONS. The development of delusional systems (beliefs that are inconsistent with those of the majority of the people in one's society) is another way in which contradictions between one's attitudinal and belief systems are apparently resolved. Unfortunately, very little is known about the causal conditions. The paranoiac is a person who is "normal" except for the irrational delusional system he has developed. Characteristically, his delusions are of one or two main types: delusions of *grandeur,* in which he claims to be a famous person, or delusions of *persecution,* in which he sees himself persecuted and threatened.

Delusional systems of this sort tend to be intricately elaborated, woven into most of the major threads of the individual's life. When such a system becomes sufficiently prominent, an individual is likely to be classified as "mentally ill" and may be legally committed to an institution. If his behavior in reference to his delusional system becomes dangerous to others, he is then labeled as a *paranoiac.* No one has ever devised any kind of effective treatment for a paranoiac. The most commonly used therapeutic effort, direct argumentation, is least likely to succeed. By the time the person is identified as paranoid he has lived with his delusional system so long that it is too much a part of him to be dislodged by logic; in a very real sense, it is nonnegotiable. Direct argumentation might have some chance of success, although probably a rather slight one, if it could be used early in the development of the delusion. This is rarely possible, however, because the serious nature of the thinking ailment is seldom noticed at this time, especially because the person shows no other symptoms of psychosis. Moreover, mild delusions of all sorts are quite common in all people and as a result go virtually unnoticed. By the time his associates realize that there is more to this particular delusion than there should be and call it to the attention of professionals, it is generally too late to do much about it. The prognosis (anticipated future course) of this condition is of course very poor.

Ideally, therapy would involve whatever emotional problems presumably underlay the delusional system. But these are hard to uncover, particularly after the length of time that the delusion has had to grow and mature. Most experts do believe that there are crucial unresolved emotional problems that have been responsible for the paranoiac's taking this particular way out of his conflict situation. They also believe that the particular details of the irrational belief systems are of symptomatic and more or less accidental rather than truly causal significance. But all of us have unresolved emotional problems of one kind or another, just as we tend also to have at least minor instances of irrationality in our thinking.

Figure 7-5 shows a hypothetical frequency distribution of delusions in terms of their intensity. In the absence of real data no values are filled in; the figure is intended to be suggestive only.

There are two noteworthy aspects of this hypothetical J-curve (so named for its shape) distribution. First, the great majority of people are presumed to be free from any serious delusions, at least as far as can be determined. Second, the number of serious delusions is assumed to decrease more or less regularly in frequency as their intensity increases. And third, there does not seem to be any clear-cut dividing line between "normal" serious delusions and those found in paranoia.

As already suggested, it is generally believed that a substantial number of otherwise "normal" people in our society have delusional systems as well developed as many of those who are institutionalized as paranoiacs. Why are they not also institutionalized? For one thing, they have probably managed to contain their delusions so as not to allow them to dominate their lives. For another, the delusions

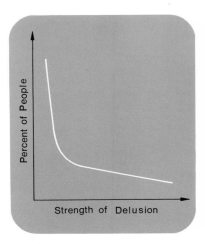

7-5 Hypothetical distribution of people according to the depth of their delusions. Most people have very mild delusions, with decreasing proportions having increasingly severe delusions.

may not be in any apparent way dangerous to others; many apparently harmless individuals are merely considered to be "eccentric," even though the logical content of their pet ideas may be quite at variance with public belief systems. But most important of all, the chances of any individual remaining at large in society in spite of extreme, well-developed delusions vary directly with his social and economic position in that society. Delusions that would quickly result in legal commitment if occurring in a person of low economic and social standing are often tolerated without much ado in persons of high standing. I can well recall an internationally well-known professor (from a sister field, not psychology) who had a number of fairly well-developed delusional systems, including strong delusions of persecution related to the administrator of his department. Among his minor aberrations was the peculiar notion that unless a student could demonstrate greater knowledge than his own, that student should not be given a top grade; as a consequence, for some reason, he had trouble filling his courses, and they were especially shunned by graduate students concerned about their transcripts. Behaviors that are simply not accepted from lesser persons may be condoned, and covered up when noticed, in persons with sufficient social status.

The power over both thinking and behavior that can be gained by basically irrational intellectual procedures is attested in many diverse ways. Witness the popularity, for example, of astrology. The popularity of astrology as a kind of "parlor game," like the ouija board, may well be matched by the degree to which many quite normal and reasonable people actually believe its propositions, in spite of the complete lack of any formal scientific support. Another example is provided by the powerful hold that various superstitions acquire over many people; devious justifications of their behavior are often provided by superstitious persons, to complement the superstitious behavior itself. In the light of these commonplace concessions to irrationality it is not hard to understand how delusions can develop, presumably in some similar fashion, and insidiously move the individual across the thin and variable line that separates normality from abnormality.

Cognitive Dissonance

How does the normal person handle newly developed contradictions among his belief systems? This problem has received considerable experimental attention, within the field of social psychology, and some answers are available. It is possible that they can be of help in suggesting the differentiation between maintenance of normality and development of severe and irrational delusions.

Within the framework of this research the existence of logically contradictory beliefs is assumed to create a condition called *cognitive dissonance.*

A common experience may help to illustrate the dissonance phenomenon. Suppose that one has purchased an item that turns out not to be as effective as expected. What are the chances that the item will be used anyway? It is generally much better if the item is expensive. The reason for this difference is, according to cognitive dissonance theory, that there will be a greater contradiction in not using an expensive item than there will be in not using an inexpensive one. In other words, not to use something that was costly, in money or otherwise, produces dissonance; and people seem to feel more obligation to use such items than they would if the items were easy to come by.

The condition of dissonance is held to be unpleasant, so that the individual is motivated to reduce it. The normal reaction to cognitive dissonance is to change one or the others of the beliefs so that they are more nearly consonant with each other. Several examples will help to clarify the rationale behind the theoretical interpretation.

DISSONANCE FROM EFFORT. High school girls volunteered for an experiment allegedly on study techniques. They were signed up for a two-hour session but were told that only half of them would actually be used for the second hour. During the first hour one group was instructed to memorize a great deal of specific information for possible use if they were selected to take the intelligence test; the other group was simply instructed to look over this material briefly. The independent variable was thus a substantial difference in the amount of effort expended during the first hour. At the end of this time all subjects were asked several questions and then dismissed without any further test actually being administered.

The dependent variable was the response to this question: "Do you believe that you are one of the people that have been selected to take the test?" Remember, all the girls had been told earlier that only half of them would be kept for the second hour of testing, so that the chances of any one being selected would presumably be 50 per cent. However, 92 per cent of the group that had done the hard preparation answered this question affirmatively, as compared with 60 per cent of the low-effort group. This result was predicted on the basis of cognitive dissonance theory, on the assumption that the girls who had expended more effort would feel less dissonance if they felt they were going to have an opportunity to use what they had worked so hard to learn.

How often in nonexperimental circumstances are we similarly motivated to use what we have prepared and disappointed not to be able to do so, even when release from such an obligation is otherwise satisfying? Situations that come readily to mind range from a student's discomfiture at not having to take an expected test, especially of course if he has prepared well for it, to what some critics feel is too often the military's apparent dissatisfaction at not being able to try out in actual warfare the powerful devices it has prepared.

DISSONANCE FROM DISCREPANT ACTIONS. Another experiment of a somewhat different design involved asking male undergraduate students to volunteer for one further experiment after they had already endured some severe electric shock in the course of earlier verbal learning trials. They were told that the same shock would be used. The independent variable was manipulated in relation to the purpose of the further experiment. Half of the subjects were given a very elaborate justification for it, emphasizing its importance in the space program as well as its general scientific significance, whereas the other half were given no explanation. Subjects who volunteered to remain for the additional trials behaved in accordance with the predictions from dissonance theory. Those who had been given adequate justification for staying, and so would presumably have low dissonance, reported pain from the shocks and showed the same interference in learning as control subjects given the same shock treatment in the absence of any explanation or opportunity to volunteer. Subjects who volunteered without the justification provided, and who therefore presumably would show high disonance because they had done so, not only reported less pain from the shocks but also learned the new list without showing the interference. As a matter of fact, they performed at the same level as control subjects who were given this last trial with markedly reduced shock intensity. These last results were interpreted as demonstrating attempts to reduce the much greater dissonance assumed to have been developed in these subjects when they volunteered to take further shocks, presumably on the basis of some kind of social motivation, such as a disinclination to displease the experimenter.

DISSONANCE AND "FREEDOM." It is only when the person feels that he is free to act or not to act that discrepant actions lead to cognitive dissonance and the resultant restructuring of attitudes. If a person's volition is reduced by external pressures and justifications such as the "scientific importance" of acting, high monetary incentives, or merely being told that one "must" act, then little dissonance is experienced. One implication of this volition effect is that people come to evaluate their actions positively when they engage in them for small incentives or justifications, that is, when they engage in acts because they feel free to do so.

For example, if one wants his child to like spinach after he eats it, then he should be offered the *minimal* incentive necessary to get him to try it. Threatening strong punishment or offering $5 for eating his spinach will both produce eating, but neither is likely to produce a liking for spinach. On the other hand, if one offers only a penny, then eating is more likely to result in liking. This result may seem inconsistent with what many people commonly believe to be the effect of incentives; we usually feel better about our actions when we receive large rewards than when we receive small rewards.

This inconsistency between these two incentive effects can be resolved by noting *when* the incentive or reward is offered. If it is offered *prior to the act* or decision, then high rewards or justifications decrease the amount of volition and little cognitive restructuring occurs. The person can rationalize his behavior by saying that he did it for the money or because he felt otherwise obligated to do so. If the incentive comes *after the act* or decision, then it becomes a reward for having acted and the degree of positiveness toward the act is directly related to the amount of reward.

DISSONANCE AND VOLITION. Cognitive dissonance has also been studied in a variety of other (nonexperimental) settings. Cigarette-smoking students, for example, have been shown to be less accepting than nonsmokers of reports concerning the relationship of cigarette smoking to lung cancer. Moreover, the percentage of subjects questioned who expressed the opinion that the linkage of cigarette smoking and lung cancer was adequately proved was inversely related to the amount of smoking reported. Although these results are consistent with both common sense and cognitive dissonance theory, they have been criticized on the grounds that the initial decision to smoke or not may have been based to some extent on belief in the cigarette–cancer relationship; if so, the results are to that degree spurious.

The fact that this last illustration, although of interest and relevance to most people, can also be so readily faulted suggests the superiority of the experimental method when matters of theoretical interpretation are concerned. Before leaving the description of this generally interesting area of research, however, one distinctly nonexperimental but especially interesting report can be mentioned.

DISSONANCE AND PROPHECY. A naturally occurring instance of cognitive readjustment to dissonance that has been closely observed was the prediction of the end of the world by a small religious group. Needless to say, the prediction in this particular instance was not fulfilled; it may therefore be assumed that cognitive dissonance developed. This dissonance was apparently resolved by the report of a new extraterrestrial message explaining that the doom had been postponed because of the faith demonstrated by the group. Although this dissonance-reducing step may seem a bit extreme to nonbelievers, it is basically similar to the kind of "explanations" that are regularly provided under more mundane circumstances and that may be assumed to have important functions in cognitive readjustment to traumatic events.

IMPLICATIONS OF RESEARCH. We may now return to the question with which our discussion of cognitive dissonance started, namely, the implications these results have for the more general question of what determines the nature of one's reactions to various kinds of contradictory information and belief systems. We have seen that one solution is simply to retain all of them, keeping them, however, in quite carefully segregated ("logic-tight") compartments and generally behaving as though there was really no contradiction at all. A great many well-adjusted persons seem to behave in this way; perhaps all of us do to some degree. The cognitive dissonance research has demonstrated over quite a wide variety of experimental settings that there is a very pervasive tendency to reduce the unpleasant feeling that seems to be produced by the recognition of inconsistency or contradiction between beliefs and behaviors.

NEUROPHYSIOLOGICAL BASIS OF THINKING

Having now surveyed a very wide variety of thinking processes, we may conclude this chapter by taking a brief look at the problem of the bodily basis of thought. Historically, within psychology, there have been two general theoretical explanations of thought processes. One position has assumed that thinking is in essence a *central* (brain) phenomenon; this is probably close to the man-in-the-street view. The other kind of interpretation has emphasized *peripheral* (muscular response) conditions as essential components of thinking; the significant role played by human language in thought has been a major stimulus to this position.

PERIPHERAL VS. CENTRAL THEORIES. The early behaviorist John Watson (Chapter 3) was perhaps the most influential exponent of a peripheral view of thinking. Watson held that thinking is condensed, silent speech. He pointed to the fact that all normal children do much of their "thinking" aloud during the early childhood period and that only under strong social pressure in our society is this tendency progressively diminished (although we can find occasional evidence in adults of such "thinking out loud"). Watson concluded that language processes are thus gradually made covert, or implicit, but that they remain the basis of thought, along with associated motor behavior, both covert and overt.

Although some crude attempts were made under the Watsonian behavioristic influence to test the motor theory of thought, as by measuring the presumably crucial responses during thought, the equipment then available was simply not sufficiently precise to permit an adequate test. Nonetheless, Watson's position was not simply one undertaken for polemic reasons. He developed a thoughtful generalized account as to how unverbalized thinking could be mediated by visceral reactions, which are poorly connected to laryngeal responses. In his later interpretation, he concluded that we think with our whole bodies. The resulting quip that Watson "made up his larynx that he had no mind" is amusing even though somewhat unfair.

As electronic measuring devices became increasingly sophisticated, experimental tests were conducted with results surprisingly supportive of the general peripheralistic position. Thus subjects instructed to "think of" specific actions, such as tossing a football, are found to have corresponding bursts of implicit activity ("action currents") in the appropriate muscles. More impressive is the later finding that deaf mutes, whose laryngeal musculature is presumably quiescent in thinking, show the predicted implicit responding in their fingers (used in sign language) when they are instructed to think. In all these cases there is a close correspondence between the frequency of action currents as well as the amount with the presumed thought processes; that is to say, if a subject is instructed to imagine that he is pumping water or hammering nails, the corresponding covert musculature activity will occur in the appropriate member (i.e., right of left arm, according to the individual's normal preference) and with a frequency that matches the number of overt responses suggested.

The net result of this kind of research is generally assumed to be that there is indeed a very close association between thought processes and peripheral muscular activity. However, the fundamental question of the presumed causal relationship —that is, whether peripheral activity of this kind is *essential* to thinking—is left unanswered by these data.

A negative answer to this question, and support for the central theory of thinking, is provided by two more recent experiments in which total paralysis of the body has been achieved by injection of the drug curare. In the first such experiment, an anesthesiologist was the subject. During the 10 minutes of his complete paralysis he remained fully alert and was later able to report accurately the details of his sensory experience. The subject in the second experiment was a student who volunteered because of his strong interest in the problem. He was also totally paralyzed, in two separate sessions, and was given a series of simple reasoning problems to solve, in order to assess the efficacy of more complex thinking that was attempted in the earlier study. In each session this subject was able to report correct answers for most of the problems presented to him during his period of total paralysis, thus indicating that thinking of this nature is not dependent upon musculature activities.

The subject's reports in each of these unusual experiments are of considerable interest. Thus, the subject given the reasoning problems reported in part as follows:

My perception of the things going on around me was fuzzy. I seemed to be drifting. I was still this way when the first problem was given to me. When I was working on this problem I seemed to get a better grip on what was going on around me. . . .

By the third problem, I had even less trouble solving it. . . . Now, I had plenty of time and concerned myself with trying to move, which I couldn't, and listening to what was going on in the room around me. . . . I felt that I could think, solve problems, do any mental operations just as quickly, efficiently, as when I am in a normal state [Leuba, Birch, and Appleton, 1968, p. 853].

BRAIN MECHANISMS IN THINKING. Neurophysiologists have to date been unable to offer very much in the way of verifiable theories as to the mechanisms that are involved in the central brain functions assumed to mediate thinking. Beyond certain gross measures, such as "brain waves," there has been little achieved in the way of measuring brain functions. The complexity and delicacy of these functions, as well as their relative inaccessibility to observation, have inhibited research on lower animals as well as human subjects.

It is generally agreed that the cerebral cortex is the major base for most if not all of the so-called higher mental functions. Within the cortex the association areas are believed to be primarily responsible for thought, but exactly how is not known. The various types of electrical activities cumulatively categorized as *EEG* (for *electroencephalogram*) have provided a disappointingly small amount of information concerning the more discrete underlying functions. *Evoked potentials*, so called because they are produced by specific sensory events in contrast to the spontaneous potentials generated in the EEG, have proved to be of somewhat greater experimental utility; they offer the opportunity of more exact relating of experimental variables, but they still offer little in the way of direct value to interpretations of thinking.

DEVELOPMENTAL STUDIES. A more hopeful report than the preceding one can be given with regard to manipulations that seem to affect development and function of the brain. In one long-term research program, with rats exposed to environments of varying degrees of complexity, it has been shown that both the size of the cerebral cortex and certain biochemical functions in it can be markedly influenced. Rats maintained in the more restricted environments (such as the bare and isolated cages customarily used) show less brain development than those given "toys" such as wheels, platforms, boxes, ladders, and the like. Extrapolation of these results to the human case must of course be done with considerable caution but they do offer promise of some interesting possibilities.

ULTIMATE UNDERSTANDING. In concluding this extended account of thinking in its various manifestations and roles it may be well to reaffirm a point that was made in Chapter 4 with regard to consciousness. The question, "What *is* a thought?" may be interesting and productive of at least much philosophic thought and discussion. However, it does not require an answer for the advance of understanding of thinking, any more than the corresponding biological question, "What *is* life?" needs to be answered before scientific advances are possible in biology. Definitions of this sort can be expected to develop on the basis of the accumulation of understanding of the multiple processes and their complex interrelationship. An overemphasis on premature attempts to answer such global questions can only hinder the scientific progress that may ultimately make it possible to provide more adequate answers.

Notes

General references on thinking of a scientific quality have been surprisingly scarce in psychology. Classic treatments covering a very broad spectrum of theoretical perspectives are available in Mandler and Mandler's 1964 paperback *Thinking: From Association to Gestalt* and in *Thinking: Studies of Covert Language Processes*, edited by McGuigan (1966). Readings of a more distinctly experimental and contemporary sort are collected in another paperback volume edited by Duncan (1967). Bruner, Goodnow, and Austin's *A Study of Thinking* (1956) was a landmark in the recent surge of renewed interest in the topic. More recent textbook treatments are by Johnson (1972) and Bourne, Ekstrand, and Dominowski (1971).

Language

The case for the independent grammatical identity of black English in the United States is convincingly made in a book edited by Baratz and Shuy (1969). The pervasive role of cultural factors generally is reviewed by Cole and Bruner (1971). The paperback by Slobin (1971) offers a good introduction to recent work by linguists and psycholinguists. Whorf's ideas are presented in his *Language, Thought and Reality* (1956). For more specific reports of some of the research described briefly in the text, see Lennenberg and Roberts (1956) for the experiment on Zunis, Carroll and Casagrande (1958) for work with the Hopis, and Brown and Lennenberg (1954) for the research on encoding of color names.

A good example of how communication between scientists can also be thwarted by conceptual misunderstandings is seen in Chomsky's 1959 review of B. F. Skinner's *Verbal Behavior* (1957). Skinner has never replied, because in his opinion Chomsky did not understand the book. An enlightening paper detailing alleged misunderstandings by Chomsky is MacCorquodale's "On Chomsky's Review of Skinner's 'Verbal Behavior'" (1970). A recent clarification of the radical behaviorist position can be found in Catania (1972).

Semantic Differential

The semantic differential is described by Osgood, Suci, and Tannenbaum (1957). An interesting application of this technique to an unusual psychiatric phenomenon may be noted. The case of multiple personality that was made into the popular movie "The Three Faces of Eve" yielded quite different semantic profiles for the different personalities. The contrast was especially striking between Eve White and Eve Black, the two most bipolar personalities. See Thigpen and Gleckley (1957) for a discussion of this case, which is also described in Supplement B-2.

Animal Language

The discussion of animal communication in the text follows that offered by Hebb (1972, p. 255 ff.). The fascinating account of communication among bees is provided in von Frisch's 1950 book. The role of pheromones, or chemical signals, in vertebrates is described by Gleason and Reynierse (1969). Nonverbal communication is treated by Hinde (1972). Kellogg (1968) has reviewed the early attempts to teach chimpanzees to use language.

Washoe was trained by Gardner and Gardner (1969, 1971) at the University of Nevada and was later moved to the University of Oklahoma. Fouts (1972) has described Washoe's training as well as the subsequent training of the additional chimpanzees at Oklahoma (Fouts, 1973); his 1974 article, in which appears some of the incidental results mentioned in the text, is an especially comprehensive review of the relevant research on chimpanzee learning of language. Sarah was trained by Premack (1971; Premack and Premack, 1972) at the Santa Barbara campus of the University of California. Lana was trained by Rumbaugh, Gill and von Glaserfelds (1973) at the Yerkes Regional Primate Center in Atlanta.

In an interesting but quite different research project, Ferster and Hammer (1966) have taught chimpanzees complex numerical concepts using operant techniques. Their chimps learned to count and to respond to the number of objects in a pattern by "writing" the correct binary number.

Do Animals Think?

The early research on delayed reaction testing was initiated by Walter Hunter; comparative results are reviewed by Munn (1950).

Images

The resurgence of research on imagery and related topics has been accompanied by the sudden appearance of a number of books (e.g., Paivio, 1971).

Early research on the neurophysiological correlates of imagery was conducted by Walter (1953) in Britain. Walter has found that people who use extensive visual imagery in their thinking exhibit a very low incidence of one particular type of EEG (the alpha waves). People that do not think with images have a high incidence of these waves. He intimates that personality conflicts between people may be partially due to differences in thinking style, i.e., visual image thinkers (low alpha) have a difficult time communicating with abstract thinkers (high alpha).

Volition and Decisions

If we knew more about the mechanisms of decision making we could make some enlightening statements about "will power" (volition). As it is, however, we can probably do little better than the early behaviorist A. P. Weiss. He saw the problem as one of determining the kind of behavior that is associated with the apparent exercise of volition or will power. When there are several equally strong alternative courses of action, requiring a difficult decision, Weiss felt that the basic brain processes (which would actually do the "deciding") are likely to "spill over" into motor tensions not allowed immediate outlet. The resulting condition would then be recognized as one involving "will power" but the fundamental decision-making processes are no different from those employed in simpler situations. Those not satisfied with this kind of "explanation," which allots a descriptive but not a causal significance to the will power concept, will need to probe more deeply into volitional functions to fill the gap that now exists in knowledge of their operation.

A very comprehensive review of this problem is available in Kimble and Perlmuter's 1970 paper. *Plans and the Structure of Behavior* by Miller, Galanter, and Pribram (1960) provided a provocative cognitive account of decision making that helped to fill the gap left in orthodox S–R type theory and prepare the way for the present-day emphasis on mental operations.

Tversky and Kahneman (1974) report some interesting observations on how judgment varies under conditions of uncertainty; it is more research of this kind on biases affecting decision making that is needed. Decisions within the information-processing framework are intensively and insightfully considered by Broadbent in his *Decision and Stress* (1971).

Attitudes, Beliefs, Opinions

Attitudes, beliefs, and opinions are ordinarily placed under the heading of social psychology, partly because they typically involve social influences and perhaps partly because that is where they have been placed before. More detailed treatments of them and suggestions for further readings can therefore be found in any text on social psychology. Guthrie's 1946 paper contains a useful discussion of the nature of "facts," along the line adopted in the text.

Mayr's 1972 review of evolutionary theory should be consulted for its impressive account of the way in which scientific beliefs inhibited the pre-Darwinian acceptance of evolutionary hypothesis. The concept of image was introduced by the economist Kenneth Boulding (1956).

Cognitive Dissonance

Cognitive dissonance was first advanced by Festinger (1957). With regard to the specific experiments in the text: the "study techniques" experiment was by Yaryan and Festinger (1961), and the electric shock experiment was by Zimbardo et al. (1966). *When Prophecy Fails,* by Festinger et al. (1956), is the account of the religious group's adjustment to the failure of their prediction that was observed at close hand by these social psychologists.

Neurophysiological Basis of Thinking

Jacobsson (1932) reported the early research relating thought processes and implicit musculature changes. His *Progressive Relaxation* (1938) remains a useful guide to practical steps toward relaxation and release from tension. The work on thinking in deaf mutes was reported by Max (1937). Shaw (1940) also reported that the amount of muscular tension varied with the magnitude and vividness of imagining specific performances. The two reports of thinking in fully curarized subjects were by Smith et al. (1947); the report for the problem-solving test was by Leuba, Birch, and Appleton (1968). An early report of the research on changes in rat brain structure and function was provided by Krech, Rosenzweig, and Bennett (1966). Recent research and theorizing on the psychophysiology of thinking are treated in a recent book of readings edited by McGuigan and Schoonover (1973).

Problem Solving

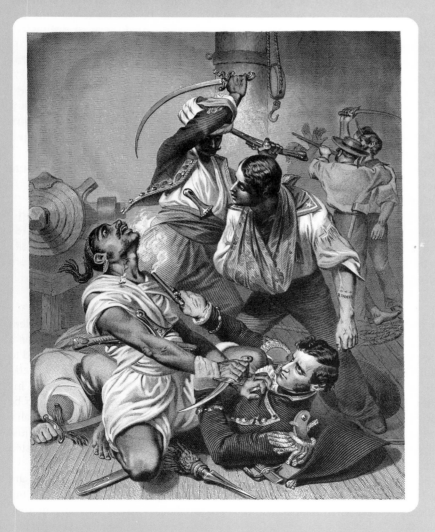

The response of Commander Decatur to his dire predicament at the hands of the Tripoli pirates is not the subject of this chapter. Decatur's reaction in this illustration is primarily a hormonal one. Our concern here is with the decision-making processes that led Mate Reuben James to interpose his head between the pirate's blade and his fallen commander. Leaving aside questions regarding James's values and judgment, we now turn to a discussion of problem solving.

217

Problem solving represents the peak of human thinking. The one feature that all difficult and complex problems have in common is that they stimulate man to think, to manipulate symbols covertly.

The range of problems that confront a complex organism such as man is enormous. Some problems are personal, involving one's interpersonal relationships; others may be regarded as more strictly intellectual, with a minimum of personal reference. Some problems demand immediate, or nearly immediate, attention; others are long-range and chronic, eliciting only occasional effort distributed over a long period of time.

The roadblocks in the path of effective problem solving are many and varied; prominent among them are insidious biases and assumptions, as well as more outright emotional conditions. But man's ability to think, mainly but not entirely in terms of his language mechanisms, gives him at least the potential ability to tackle problems of amazing difficulty and variety.

In addition to the description and illustration of puzzles and laboratory research on problems, including a discussion of obstacles in, theories of, and stages in problem solving, the chapter is concerned with creativity and reverie (daydreaming), which may be regarded as a kind of back-door entry to problem solving. The chapter then considers the difficulties that science generally and psychologists in particular have with parapsychological phenomena, which by definition are alleged to operate outside the realm of orthodox known psychological processes. Extrasensory perception (ESP) and the activities of mediums are among the parapsychological phenomena described. Parapsychological phenomena provide some of the more interesting problems faced by psychologists, albeit some of the more difficult to handle. The chapter is concluded with a discussion of the steps that can be taken in attempting to improve the clarity of thinking in problem solving generally.

Problems

The first thing that strikes us when we contemplate problems and problem solving is the ubiquity of problems. Life for any organism can be viewed as a succession of problems; the organism is almost constantly required to adjust and to readjust to changing conditions. How long any organism is able to remain relatively inactive, with no immediate problems to resolve, varies of course with his species. Some species, especially the "higher" or more complex ones, seem to be beset by more frequent and more serious problems than others. This varies also with the individual's own particular good or bad fortune in life. The need to adjust does not cease until death; it has been noted that the only perfectly adjusted organism is a dead one.

These comments should not be interpreted as meaning that all problems are aversive. On the contrary, most of the higher organisms appear to seek out problems, at least when their basic needs are satisfied. A strong curiosity motive, for example, has been demonstrated in laboratory rats as well as monkeys and other higher primates. Of all the organisms studied, the human is by far the most adept at making problems for himself, as we shall see when we consider his personality and his social interactions.

DIMENSIONS OF PROBLEMS

Ubiquitous as problems are in human life, it is hardly surprising that they come in a great variety of types. Here we can indicate only a few of the many dimensions along which problems can be ordered, especially with relevance to the type that has been mainly studied in the laboratory, as diagrammatically indicated in Figure 8-1.

Problems vary markedly with regard to the amount of *structured information* provided. Most laboratory problems are highly structured. Many real-life problems, on the other hand, can be almost completely unstructured, or open-ended. An

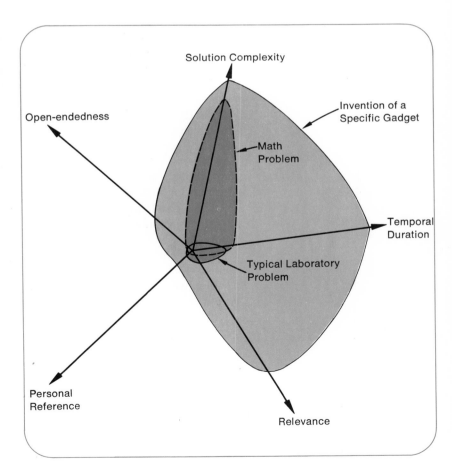

8-1 Schematic illustrating three kinds of problems analyzed along five dimensions. These are hypothetical analyses and are intended only to show that typical laboratory problems, often by design, tend toward the low end of each of the five analytical dimensions.

inventor, for example, may be told simply to try to work out a device of some kind to fill a certain need and be given wide latitude in how to proceed.

The *complexity of the solution* is a somewhat related dimension along which problems vary greatly. Again, laboratory problems tend to have relatively simple, single solutions, whereas many real-life problems are not so simply resolved. The inventor, for example, may have a succession of separate problems to solve before he is able to implement his ideas completely and develop a final product. Many other kinds of problems met in real life tend to resist ultimate solution and may require a series of partial solutions before they are finally resolved. Moreover, many real-life problems have no solution at all, at least no single solution comparable to the logically derived solution characteristic of laboratory problems; again, an invention would most often be only one solution among many possible ones.

The last comment suggests another important dimension along which problems can be seen to vary. Some are more or less quickly solvable (again laboratory problems tend to be of this nature, for obvious reasons), whereas others may engage the attention of the problem solver for quite extended periods of time. Not all of this *temporal extension* can be attributed to the complexity of the problem (that is, its having separate subproblems requiring solution, as described above). Some relatively simple problems, simple in the sense of having single solutions, may nevertheless be so difficult as to require years of intermittent effort for solution; examples would be problems of a mathematical sort, which can keep mathematicians occupied for such extended periods.

The degree of *relevance,* or applicability to the real world, is still another variable on which problems differ. To some extent, relevance, like beauty, may be said to be in the eye of the beholder. Consider the mathematical problems just mentioned. Are they relevant to the real world? Yes, if we include the world of the mathematician as real (as it certainly must be regarded, it would seem). But no, if we are looking for some more direct applicability to, say, pressing social, economic, or political problems of our society. The type of intellectual exercises used by psychologists in studying problem solving typically have little relevance outside the laboratory. Nevertheless, it is assumed that the basic principles underlying laboratory problem solving are essentially the same ones that operate in real-life problems.

A subvariety of the relevance discussion would be the degree of *personal involvement* or reference in problems. Here the question is the extent to which the welfare of the problem solver himself is contingent upon how the problem is resolved. This characteristic is clearly one of the main factors in real-life problems, where personal relationships are often potent ingredients of the problem, but it is ordinarily minimal in the laboratory problem.

EXPERIMENTAL ANALYSIS OF PROBLEM SOLVING

To bring the discussion to a focus on the matter of thinking, we will look more closely at a special kind of problem that has been studied in the laboratory and whose solutions have been experimentally and theoretically analyzed. Like all problems, this laboratory variety is produced by the interpolation of a gap between the stimulus situation confronting an organism and the behaviors that are immediately available to him in his response repertoire. Discovery of the appropriate gap-filling behavior constitutes solution of the problem. Typically, the solution is achieved not by overt behavior, although some of this may be involved in the solution, but rather by thinking—covert manipulation of symbols and concepts that render unnecessary the making of their overt counterparts.

Because problem solving is continuous with "learning," and is often classified as such, how to relate these two topics poses something of a problem for exposition. An arbitrary decision has been made to include in this section only discussion of human problem solving. Animal studies are discussed under learning (Chapter 11). The discussion there of insight learning is essentially continuous with the present discussion.

Some Typical Laboratory Problems

Having thus surveyed the general nature of problems both inside and outside of the laboratory, we are in a position to look at some examples. Two of the more instructive problems that have been used by psychologists are presented in Figures 8-2 and 8-3. Try to solve these before reading ahead and taking advantage of the further hints supplied.

The trick in the problem shown in Figure 8-2 is to make the top triangle look exactly like the bottom triangle by moving only three of the component circles to new positions. Give this a good try before looking at the box on p. 224 for a hint that should lead to a solution. This problem is representative of a very great variety of puzzles that have been invented and that appear in books, magazines, and newspapers to entertain readers.

The problem presented in Figure 8-3 is deceptively simple. It is of a type that has been gainfully employed in research. The problem is to discuss the proof or disproof of the following statement concerning four two-sided cards, each of which has on one side either a large or a small triangle and on the other either a large or a small circle: *Every card that has a small triangle on one side has a large circle on the other side.* The problem is to indicate *which cards* must be turned over in order to determine the truth or falsity of the statement. This problem merits your close attention. You should work out an answer, noting your reasons, before turning to the box on p. 224 for the correct answer.

The discussion immediately following concerns some implications of common student (and other) reactions to these problems and so should not be read until you have made a serious effort to solve both problems.

Implications of Attempts to Solve the Sample Problems

The triangle problem is typical of many intellectual puzzles; it has a single, relatively straightforward solution, which is nonetheless peculiarly difficult to achieve for some people (and even sometimes difficult to remember subsequent to success, a rather unusual feature for this kind of "insight" problem). The most interesting question about it is why so many people seem to have so much trouble

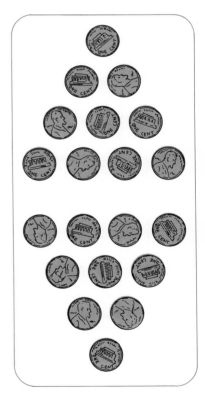

8-2 A representative problem. Try to convert the top triangle to the same shape as the bottom triangle by changing the positions of only three of the component circles. See the box on p. 224 for a helpful hint, but only after making a serious effort to solve this problem.

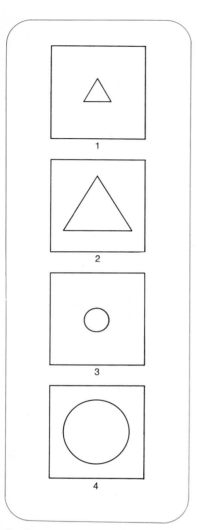

8-3 Another representative problem. Each of the four cards has either a large or small triangle on one side and either a large or small circle on the other side. The problem is to decide *which two cards must be turned over* in order definitely to prove or disprove the following statement: *Every card that has a small triangle on one side has a large circle on the other side.* See the box on p. 224 for the correct answer but only after you have made a careful effort and produced what you think is the solution to the problem. [Adapted with permission from Wason (1969).]

solving it. One suggestion has been that the solution is retarded by the implicit assumption that one should work *down* from the row of four circles; there is no logical reason why this should be so, and of course it is not so. (It has been assumed that the reader knows the answer by now; however, if he did not solve this problem by himself or with the aid of the boxed hint and was not given the answer by anyone else, by now he will have additional hints to use!) Attempting to move the entire row of three circles is apparently a natural, but of course quite ineffective, first response; the successful pattern of moves usually falls quickly into place once the technique of moving only parts of a line is tried.

As suggested earlier, there are important implications for problem solving in the card problem. The most common response is cards 1 and 4. But suppose that card 4 does in fact have a small triangle on the other side; one would still not know whether there is a small or a large triangle on the back of card 3; hence the statement would still be in doubt. The statement *can* definitely be disproved, however, if a card is found that has *two small* figures, such as either card 1 or card 3 could have. The only sure way of answering the question is therefore to check these two cards.

The experimenter who reported the use of this simple but ingenious reasoning test made a special interpretation of the frequency of the 1–4 error and the fervor with which this mistaken answer was often defended even after the explanation described above was given. These results were attributed to the strong tendency in people to search for evidence supporting their initial hunches or inferences and to disregard opposing evidence. It might also be noted that the layman, unlike the (ideal) scientist, is typically more concerned with *proving* than with *disproving* hypotheses; he will be more likely, therefore, to turn over a card that can support the hypothesis rather than one that can disprove it. Nevertheless, the scientific method depends upon disproof more than proof. This is true because, as in this simple reasoning problem, one can be logically certain with a single disproof, whereas positive instances merely build up additional probabilities, always short of certainty. In scientific problem solving, moreover, hypotheses are deliberately set up to encourage disproof, so that they can be more rigorously tested and discarded or modified as necessary. Failures to disprove hypotheses are thus more impressive than merely adding further proofs, especially when such proofs are open to alternative interpretations.

OBSTACLES IN REASONING

The difficulty that so many people seem to have with the card problem just described exemplifies one type of obstacle to efficient reasoning. There are of course a great many other types, some of which have been discussed in Chapter 7. With special regard to laboratory problem solving, as a form of reasoning or thinking, several major kinds of handicaps commonly found in human subjects will be discussed. Although these handicaps are in some respects all related, they do have sufficiently different determining variables to merit their separation.

Atmosphere Effects

The potent influence that emotional biases, as reflected in attitudes, can have on thinking is easy to demonstrate. These influences are sometimes called *atmosphere effects,* because they seem to be mediated more by the atmosphere in which his thinking occurs than by any specific operations of the experimenter or the interviewer.

An early study on reactions to political platforms as a function of the party label attached to them is instructive. Subjects were asked to evaluate the platform that had been prepared by a political party. In one condition it was accurately labeled. In a second condition it was not. It is hardly surprising that the platform was generally unacceptable when presented as a socialist product but was generally accepted when presented as a product of one of the dominant political parties. Apparently the evaluations that most people make depend more upon their affective arousal than upon their dispassionate analysis of the issues.

Judgment of propositions about economics yielded another demonstration of the susceptibility of ratings to the attitude of the judge toward the source of the proposition. Favorable judgments were made when the propositions being rated were attributed to such Americans as John Adams or Abraham Lincoln, whereas unfavorable ratings of exactly the same propositions were recorded when they were attributed to such foreign revolutionaries as Karl Marx or V. I. Lenin.

Halo Effect

An effect similar to atmosphere effects is commonly observed in personal evaluation, where it is sometimes called the *halo effect.* For example, a teacher who grades papers with knowledge of who wrote the paper runs the risk of awarding higher marks on the basis of the teacher's expectation rather than on the basis of the student's answers. Similarly, inferior students (and perhaps troublemakers or others with negative valence for the teacher) are likely to be downgraded unfairly, in a kind of negative halo effect. For these reasons teachers often are careful to use blind grading, in which the identities of the writers are concealed. In an effort to reduce the influence of similar biases experimenters are typically kept in the dark as to the experimental group into which the subjects have been placed.

Logical Fallacies

Logical reasoning, in the formal sense, is rarely used in productive problem solving, by scientists or laymen (with the possible exception of some specialized kinds of problems, such as mathematical ones). Nevertheless, it is sometimes possible to clarify the operation of thinking processes by referring to their logical properties. Consider the following propositions, put in a logical form, called a syllogism:

All conservatives are capitalists.
All businessmen are capitalists.
Therefore all businessmen are conservatives.

And

Hint for the triangle problem, Figure 8-2, p. 221: Try moving only the three circles at the corners of the triangle.

Solution to Figure 8–3 card problem. p. 222: Cards 1 and 3. See text for explanation.

All drug users are hippies.
All long-hairs are hippies.
Therefore all long-hairs use drugs.

Does either one of these conclusions follow logically (that is, necessarily) from the two premises? Do both?

Now try the following syllogism, of exactly the same logical status:

All x is z.
All y is z.
Therefore all y is x.

Does this conclusion follow logically from the two premises? Hardly! It is quite clear that the conclusion does not *necessarily* follow from the two premises, as can be readily demonstrated by means of a simple diagram such as that in Figure 8-4. Nevertheless, people will frequently affirm that conclusions do follow logically from such premises when they are consistent with existing attitudinal and belief systems. It has been experimentally demonstrated that such affirmations are much more likely with meaningful subject matters of that sort than when a strictly logical form is used. Once the validity of the premises is accepted, some quite illogical (as well as some logical) conclusions are often reached, and unfortunately may become firmly entrenched in the belief systems of the individual.

Sets

A very similar process occurs under some naturally occurring and some experimentally contrived conditions. It can be generally characterized as a *set*, a strong tendency to think along a certain path. Research on sets differs from research on atmosphere effects in that the experimenter devises a procedure to induce a particular set, and in that sets ordinarily are relatively devoid of affect.

The most commonly cited illustration of a set in problem solving is probably the *water-jug problem.* This is a simple reasoning or mental calculation problem, adapted from the Stanford–Binet intelligence test. The subject is told that a mother has sent her son to the well for water, and is given a series of questions concerning how each combination of different sizes of water jugs can be used to produce a specified amount of water. Table 8-1 shows some typical problems that were posed in one experiment. The procedure in this experiment was to have an experimental

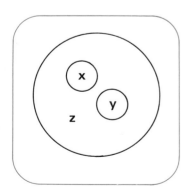

8-4 Diagrammatic representation of a possible relationship between the *X, Y,* and *Z* categories in a syllogism. (See text for explanation.)

Table 8-1 The Water-Jug Problem[0]

Problem	Size of jars (in quarts)			Quarts of Water Needed
	A	B	C	
1	29	3	–	20
2	21	127	3	100
3	14	163	25	99
4	18	43	10	5
5	9	42	6	21
6	20	59	4	31
7	23	49	3	20
8	15	39	3	18
9	28	76	3	25
10	18	48	4	22
11	14	36	8	6

* The problem is to measure out the number of quarts of water in the final column, using jars of the sizes shown in columns A, B, and C. In problem 1 the solution is to fill jar A, then remove nine quarts from it by filling jar B three times.
Adapted from A. S. Luchins, Mechanization in problem solving. *Psychological Monographs,* 1942, **54,** 248.

group perform all the problems, in order, while a control group rested in another room during the first five problems (after all subjects had been given the same practice problem to indicate the procedure).

Note that the first five problems all have one characteristic in common: they require that water be poured *from* the filled largest jug into the smaller jugs, in various combinations, in order to get exactly the amount specified. Problems 6 through 8 can be solved in a simpler, more direct manner (and problem 8 can be solved *only* in that more direct way).

In general, the experimental subjects continued to use in the last three (test) problems the same subtractive method they had found successful in the first five, even when it could not be applied to problem 8; as a result many of them failed to solve that one. Control subjects, without experience with the first five problems, generally used the more direct procedure and did not find the last problem at all difficult.

These results (and many others like them) can be nicely explained by postulating the rapid building up of a particular set, or specific thinking mechanism, in the experimental subjects. It is generally believed that the operation of similar sets in real life plays a large part in human problem solving and accounts for much of the difficulty that people have in this kind of thinking.

Functional Fixedness

A special kind of set has been vividly demonstrated in certain experimental research on problem solving, especially in that conducted by the Gestalt psychologists. *Functional fixedness* (or *fixity*) refers to the strong tendency to think of objects in terms of their normal function, and thus to have difficulty in envisioning their utilization in new and unfamiliar ways. When such utilizations are necessary to the solution of a problem, and when the normal function of the object has been recently emphasized, subjects are seriously retarded in their problem-solving ability.

In one frequently used experimental demonstration of the potency of functional fixedness, the subjects are given the task of mounting three lighted candles onto the side of a door. They are supplied with the following objects: three candles, some matches, some tacks, and some pasteboard boxes. To solve the problem the boxes have to be mounted on the door with the tacks, after which the candles can be lit by the matches and some wax melted onto the boxes in order to form a base for the candles.

There is an important difference in how the subjects are given these materials. In one condition they are given all the materials scattered on a table; these subjects typically solve the candle problem within a short time. In the other condition the candles, matches, and tacks are all placed inside the boxes; these subjects typically have considerable difficulty with the problem, and some never manage to solve it at all. The presumption is that the subjects given the *filled* boxes continue to think of them essentially as boxes rather than potential *platforms* for the candles; in other words, they show functional fixedness with regard to the boxes. The subjects given the empty boxes apparently are able to perceive them as platforms much more readily and so were able to solve the problem without undue difficulty.

The problem, and variations of it, have subsequently been employed in research with generally consistent results, indicating the efficacy of this kind of set. In one interesting extension, for example, it was found that the solution was more rapidly achieved when the filled box was labeled separately—and thus given individual identity—during the instructions.

THEORETICAL APPROACHES TO PROBLEM SOLVING

Thus far in our treatment of problem solving we have stressed the inhibitory factors that distract and interfere with effective thinking. These are of great importance in understanding the problem-solving process, but they do not tell us how problem solving works when it is not so seriously inhibited. In other words, how do people solve problems? The answers to this question have largely come in the form of various theoretical attempts to explain productive thinking generally. Three main classes of such theories may be detected.

Stimulus–Response and Associative Theories

The theme that is common to these various theories is that problem solving, like all thinking, is a function primarily of the associations that have been established in the experience of the organism. Thinking is basically no different from overt responding. Implicit responding is subject to the same general laws as explicit, or overt, responding. It is granted that these laws are more difficult to study in the case of covert responses such as thinking, but it is believed that once such difficulties are surmounted and the relationships among variables established, there will be no need for assuming any unique functions.

In stimulus–response (S–R) theorizing, the concept of *mediation* is a key one. A mediator is an inferred process (a symbol, or in more common language, an idea) that links a stimulus and a response. The concept of *mediated generalization* is a good example of how such mediation is presumed to operate. Generalization is the tendency for a new stimulus, similar in some way to one that has already been used in training, to elicit the response formerly made to the original stimulus. According to the notion of mediated generalization, a new stimulus may elicit some old response implicitly without any overt expression. The covert response can then serve as a stimulus to evoke an overt response, and therefore play a mediating role. In this way new combinations of S–R associations can be produced and can account, at least theoretically, for the novel behaviors that appear to be involved in productive problem solving.

Another key concept in S–R theory has been that of *habit-family hierarchies.* This is the notion that a stimulus can elicit a number of different responses, in anticipatory as well as overt form, and that these response categories are ordered in terms of their associative strength in relation to the stimulus. Suppose, for example, that one is faced with the problem (stimulus) of a nonstarting automobile. Suppose, further, that the last few times this happened the battery turned out to be dead and the automobile was started by pushing it. Arranging to get another push would therefore be most likely to represent the strongest habit family in the various hierarchies of habit available (another response category or habit family might be attempting to have a mechanic check the motor, which could be resorted to in case the push failed to solve the problem). Deciding on a push would constitute a new problem (stimulus) situation, which itself would be linked to a variety of habit families; one might try to push the car oneself, attempt to enlist the aid of other persons to help in the pushing, or perhaps try to engage a passing motorist to use his car to push. Which of these would be strongest in the hierarchy, and therefore tried first, would depend upon a number of secondary stimulus characteristics, such as the slope of the roadway, the number of passersby, and the like. This everyday kind of situation should suffice to indicate the way in which habit families arranged in hierarchical orders can operate in thinking as well as overt behavior.

Gestalt and Cognitive Theories

Gestalt theories have emphasized perception as the key process in problem solving. The concept of *direction* in behavior, exemplified in the functional fixedness experiments described above, is one particular way in which perceptual processes are believed to operate. Solution of problems by *insight*—interpreted as a kind of perceptual restructuring—has been emphasized; this concept is discussed in Chapter 11 in some detail.

A cognitive theory is one in which central brain processes are stressed, rather than environmental cues and overt responses (as in the S–R type of theory).

The cognitive perspective can be illustrated by its early application to laboratory rats. In one ingenious experiment insight was demonstrated by rats who ignored the next shortest open path to the goal, normally taken, when they were blocked from the preferred shortest path but had also experienced a block at a further common part of the two shortest paths; their selection of the longest path was then attributed to the function of a *cognitive map* of the test apparatus.

Although the cognitive theories have not produced as much research as the S–R theories, the research that is available is among the most ingenious and provocative in the field. Many of the concepts introduced by cognitive theorists have become integrated into the generally accepted body of fact. Moreover, the criticisms of simple associative theories offered by cognitive theorists have forced the S–R theorists into progressively more refined formulations, so that the distinctions between these two great classes of theory have been consistently diminished. This reduction of theoretical distinction must be regarded as a measure of growing maturity. Nevertheless, the fundamental problems (such as specifying in advance which mechanisms will operate in particular situations) have been resolved by neither class of theory.

Information-Processing and Computer Simulation Theories

The most recent entry into the theoretical arena is a type of theoretical and research program which focuses on the information-processing properties of the human organism particularly (cf. Chapter 12) and uses the simulation of these properties made available by modern digital computers.

Before surveying some of the successes already achieved by this fresh approach to an old problem it is well to rid ourselves of some common misconceptions about the approach. For one thing, there is no intention of equating the hardware of the computer with the capabilities of the human brain; rather the relationship that is critical is the comparison between the software of the computer (its programming) and the processes the brain utilizes in its problem-solving behavior (its own software). The computer is thus a tool, or a testing device, by which the information-processing functions evident in human thinking can be simulated. The extremely rapid calculating properties of the computer, which enable it to complete within seconds massive numerical tasks that would require the human brain very much longer, are not ordinarily involved in this type of research.

The early research involving computer simulation of human thinking demonstrated that relatively simple computer programs could be devised with the capability of solving problems that typically gave human subjects considerable trouble. Further, these programs utilized only a few fundamental capabilities—the reading, writing, storing in memory, erasing, and comparing of patterns that human subjects characteristically evidence in their thinking. Comparison of the computer program with the verbal descriptions of their own thinking processes, obtained from human subjects engaged in problem-solving experiments, indicates a considerable correlation between these two processes.

The most important such correlation, and a central concept in the simulation research to date, has been the commonality of heuristics. A *heuristic* is any procedure that directs the search for solution along specific paths, severely reducing the number of alternatives. An *algorithm*, in contrast, is a procedure in which every possible alternative is systematically checked out. With limited numbers of alternatives, algorithms may be quite adequate, but when the range of possible responses is very great, as in the game of chess, heuristics markedly improve the speed of problem solving. The problem-solving programs that have been written for computers in efforts to simulate human performance have focused on selectivity of response, by means of heuristics; they have thereby managed to "capture" this pivotal feature of human thought. The success of this research is suggested by the fact that chess-playing programs have been written and put into use against expert players; only the very best have succeeded in beating the computers. In the game of checkers, with drastically reduced response alternatives, the computer program is in fact unbeatable.

Methodologically, computer simulation of the information-processing capabilities of the human problem solver has the very great advantage of precision. Before any computer program can be written one must be able to specify every step in detail. Simulation of any process by a computer thus requires much more attention to detailed, step-by-step theorizing than is required in alternative endeavors. It also prevents leaving crucial functions to unspecified inner forces. As two of the pioneer workers in this field recently put it, "The programmability of the theories is the guarantee of their operationability, an iron-clad insurance against admitting magical properties into the head. . . . They may be empirically correct theories about the nature of human thought processes or empirically invalid theories; they are not magical theories" (Simon and Newell, 1971, p. 148).

The computer simulation research offers a nice combination of the advantages of both the S–R and the cognitive approaches to problem solving; its emphasis upon precise mechanisms is similar to S–R theory and its attention to direction and pattern mimics cognitive theory. Computer simulation theory is not likely to replace either of these older types of theory, but it has already more than earned its keep as a new and most promising tool for the analysis of distinctly human thinking. Although we can hardly predict today just how far toward simulation of human thinking this kind of research will ultimately proceed, it is worth noting that some surprising achievements have already been recorded. For one example, an early experiment in logical programming actually managed to produce a more "mathematically elegant" proof for one of the mathematical theorems than had the mathematicians who devised the original proof.

STAGES IN PROBLEM SOLVING

Apart from the theoretical approach that one takes with regard to problem solving, there has been a lively and continuing interest in a descriptive account of what appear to be describable *stages* in the process. Such descriptions have leaned heavily on introspective accounts of actual problem-solving experiences as well as objective accounts of the overt behavior, including verbalizations, of problem solvers not instructed to introspect. Although details differ somewhat, there has been a substantial amount of agreement about the major stages. This information is summarized in the discussion that follows.

Preparation

Recognition of the problem and arrangement of the necessary materials for its attack are the essential achievements during this initial phase. The importance of these steps is often overlooked. Well begun is indeed half done, in problem solving as in many other more routine activities. Much of the inefficient problem-solving behavior that is so commonly observed in "real life" as well as academic situations is largely a function of inadequate preparation. Milling about with woefully incomplete understanding of the essential aspects of the problem is characteristic of those whose motivation to gain some objective (e.g., a passing grade in a course) far exceeds their interest in the problem itself (e.g., the subject matter at hand).

One of the more instructive lessons that we can learn about problem solving comes from scientific work. Here the way in which the question is posed usually helps to determine the ultimate success of the problem solver. As a matter of fact, the ability simply to ask the "right" questions is generally recognized as a mark of scientific genius. If genius is 99 per cent perspiration and 1 per cent inspiration, as some have said, most of the perspiration must flow during the preparatory phases of problem solving.

Incubation

The incubation stage of problem solving is marked by the development of potential solutions to the problem. Usually these are in the form of hypotheses, or tentative guesses. It is of course difficult to draw any hard-and-fast line between this stage and that of preparation. It is equally difficult to pinpoint the source of good ideas. Intuition is just as important in scientific work, for example, as it is in any other form of creative endeavor, but no one has yet come up with a satisfactory account of how intuition works.

Once the problem solver has immersed himself sufficiently in his problem, ideas seem to incubate spontaneously. Most of these ideas will be fruitless, but there is no way of determining this in advance. No potential solution, regardless of its apparent absurdity, should be dismissed out of hand. Many people consider the incubation period to be one in which all sorts of novel and apparently wild ideas are to be deliberately encouraged, even solicited. *Brainstorming,* which was in vogue for a time with business executives, was designed to do just that. In a typical brainstorming session a variety of business employees are brought together to work on some particular problem. They are instructed to voice any and all ideas that occur to them, no matter how outlandish they might seem. The rationale is that a small number of really valuable ideas are likely to emerge from this kind of social effort; the vast amount of useless material that is produced is felt to be a fair price to pay for the insights that may be achieved.

The feature of brainstorming that appears to be common to most efforts to encourage creativity is the removal of the problem solver from the restrictions of his customary stimulus situation, which has spawned thus far only ineffective solutions. Providing a new stimulus situation is supposed to encourage the incubation of new ideas by releasing one from the bonds of his previous thinking. In this respect merely relieving the pressure for a solution, and allowing a respite from thinking of the problem, seems to be about as effective a step as can be taken to encourage incubation of fresh approaches. This statement assumes that the preparation has been adequate of course.

Illumination

As already suggested, there does not appear to be any good way of predicting when the ultimately successful idea will emerge. Often it seems to pop up after the person takes a rest from the problem. Thus the French mathematician Henri Poincaré indicated that one of his major mathematical discoveries came to him as he boarded a bus to take a vacation from his long and drawn-out efforts to solve the problem. This frequently cited instance of sudden illumination, or insight, should not be regarded as demonstration that most problems are solved so dramatically. As a matter of fact, successful solutions are more often a function of successive approximations, with lots of hard work behind each advance; illumination can be the result of a slow, steady process as well as a flash of insight.

Verification

Often the final checking out of an insight, or a more prosaically developed hypothesis, is straightforward; the key can be put into the lock and it can be quickly determined whether it fits. But more often there ensues a long and difficult period of verification. The latter situation is more likely to exist in science. We have already had occasion to identify the experiment, with its control of extraneous variation, as the hallmark of science and the major single basis of the distinction between scientific and nonscientific thinking. But few single experiments are crucial, in the dramatic sense that they can "prove" the correctness of some scientific hypothesis. Rather, positive support is built up slowly, as the growing number of positive results gradually increases our confidence in the hypothesis. The sudden decisions are typically negative ones, or disproofs, as we have indicated in the earlier discussion of the card problem (p. 222). Verification is thus not only a critical stage of problem solving but also one in which a great deal of perspiration, sometimes even more than is shed in preparation, is involved.

A particularly good example of just how drawn out verification of a scientific problem solution can be is given by the history of Darwin's theory of evolution. Even today, more than a century after its initial promulgation, it remains shrouded in political and legal entanglements; for example, the state of California recently proceeded with an official recommendation of a state commission that the alternative special creation account of the origin of life, as recounted in the Bible, be accorded a full treatment in any biology textbooks used through the secondary school level. The fact that the special creation view emerged from a different type of discourse, and is neither a scientifically testable account nor a logical complement to evolutionary theory, did not dissuade the State Board of Education from taking this giant step backward in time.

There are of course other situations in which verification is not as drawn out as it is in science. Inventions, or technological advances generally, can often be more quickly evaluated. And solutions to contrived problems, developed for research or entertainment purposes, can usually be quickly evaluated. But there is always some engagement of effort in verification and the bloom of new insights more often fades than persists when all instances of illumination are considered.

Take a Breather

THE ALTAR WINDOW

Here is another problem. It is one of many that Max Wertheimer worked with during his long-continued investigation of human problem solving. It should prove instructive as well as entertaining. Please give it a very thorough try before turning to p. 236 for Wertheimer's account of some sample efforts, in the course of which the solution becomes apparent. The solution is really very simple and well within the capacity of every reader:

"Painters are at work, painting and decorating the inner walls of a church. Somewhat above the altar there is a circular window. For decoration the painters have been asked to draw two vertical lines tangent to the circle, and of the same height as the circular window; they were then told to add half circles above and below, closing the figure. The area between the lines and the window is to be covered with gold. For every square inch, so much gold is needed. How much gold will be needed to cover this space (given the diameter of the circle)? Or, *what is the area between the circle and the lines?*

"Before reading further, try to get the solution. (Not much mathematics is needed.) After you have the solu-

tion, it may be of interest to you to read the kinds of reactions one gets in experiments with this task. They are on p. 236, but should not be read until a thorough effort has been made to solve the problem."

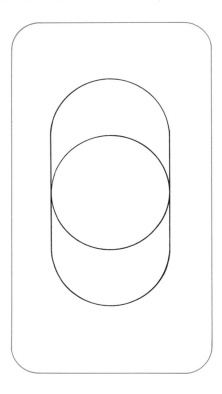

From Max Wertheimer, *Productive Thinking,* enlarged edition, Appendix 2 (New York: Harper & Row, 1959), pp. 266–268.

CREATIVITY

The emphasis upon creativity, as contrasted with conformity in thinking, is a healthy and relatively new development in our society. One of the most telling criticisms of our educational system has been that it overstresses conformity and stunts rather than encourages individuality. Creativity in thought and behavior can be regarded as a major product of individuality. It is the unique individual, in science as well as in other forms of creative endeavor, who is likely to be the most effective and successful.

The relationship between general intelligence, as measured by a standardized intelligence test, and creativity is especially important. Most creative persons in science are also persons of relatively high general intelligence, but by no means all persons with the highest intelligence ratings are also creative. This situation occurs because the intelligence test measures, in a sense, the degree of conformity to thinking norms that one has evidenced, and such conformity may not be a valid index of the individuality that must be expressed in creative acts. The relationship between creativity and general intelligence may not be high in special fields like music and art, because here there is less need than in science for the learning of standardized facts and procedures that require thinking. The fact that the intelligence test does not tap the roots of creativity and may even emphasize as virtues features that are antagonistic to creativity has only recently been recognized.

Training in Creativity

Measurement of creativity and methods of encouraging creativity have been in the forefront of recent psychological concern with educational problems. In general, the measurement of creativity has focused on the degree of uniqueness, or individuality, evident in verbal output (e.g., uncommon associations). Whether one believes that creativity can be trained depends in part upon his position on the essential aspect of problem solving. If "unconscious thought" is seen as the critical factor in creative thinking, there is at present little that can be done to manipulate this factor. This is because we are still largely in the dark as to its nature. On the other hand, if changes in set are seen as the critical factor, then various training devices can be developed in an effort to encourage this tendency. There is some evidence that creativity scores, as measured by quantity and quality of ideas, can be improved to some extent by this type of special training.

One of the generally overlooked aspects of training for creativity is the importance of encouraging students, as well as others, to ask the "right" kind of questions. In other words, it is just as important to *find* problems as to solve them, mainly because if they are not found they are not likely to be solved. As a matter of fact, a good case can be made for the proposition that there has been too much emphasis in the past on the solutions of problems and too little attention paid to the *problem-locating* and *question-posing* functions necessarily involved in creativity.

Despite the clear significance of the problem, there are a number of warnings that need to be given in connection with the training of creativity. For one thing, so much of our educational system is deliberately slanted toward increasing conformity rather than individuality that merely adding some special training at some stage is unlikely to have a prominent effect. For another, there is need in science as well as all other spheres of activity for steady, undramatic work as well as creative and inspirational efforts. Moreover, not everyone is suited to creative thinking, nor is there any good reason why everyone should be so suited. There is thus some danger of an overstimulation of ambition with regard to creativity, especially perhaps with regard to scientific training. There is therefore cause for moderation in attempting to redress the years of neglect of this important problem.

In spite of these warnings, there is no reason why everyone cannot be stimulated to express his individuality and to see through specious reasoning and premature categorization regardless of his potential for creative thinking. The forces that lead to undue conformity are many and varied and are potent within science as well as elsewhere. For example, there is a strong tendency among professional psychologists to categorize new ideas in terms of their own already established belief systems. Dismissal of novelty unless it smacks of something with which one is already familiar results in the premature rejection of many ideas and a consequent failure to explore their implications.

Serendipity

An overriding consideration in support of establishing early and continuing efforts within our educational system to encourage independence of expression and creativity in thinking and problem solving is that it is impossible to say in advance where the most productive ideas are going to come from. One of the more emphasized processes whereby unexpected ideas are produced is *serendipity,* or accidental discovery. As usually defined, *serendipity* refers to the finding of some important or interesting procedure or principle while looking for something else.

A commonly cited instance of serendipity within psychology is the discovery of the efficacy of partial reward (providing food, for example, only occasionally after the organism makes the required response) by B. F. Skinner when his equipment worked inefficiently (failed to provide food reward after each response, as it was supposed to do). Organisms that are rewarded only occasionally consistently respond more when reward is wholly withdrawn (extinction procedure; see Chapter 11, p. 350). Other less well-known instances of serendipity within psychology, as they have been noted in one treatment, include the following: the discovery of the "reward" centers in the brain by investigators seeking to relate arousal and learning; the finding of pronounced hallucinations in normal college students who had been perceptually isolated by investigators initially concerned with motivation and intelligence; and the discovery of various personality deviations in Scottie pups reared in isolation by investigators interested in learning deficiencies. This list could be extended indefinitely, because so many scientific discoveries are of this general nature.

One of the frequently neglected aspects of serendipity is the fact that important discoveries are made by researchers who are prepared to take advantage of the opportunities that come their way. In other words, being "lucky" is not the entire story; if one is not able to see the significance of an "accident," it is not likely to be celebrated as an instance of serendipity. The investigator must be able to change set and notice that some unexpected result has occurred. Uncounted numbers of potentially serendipitous events doubtless occur, but remain unrecorded because nothing much is made of them. How many dirty culture dishes were there before Sir Alexander Fleming happened to observe, *and* correctly assess the significance of, the flowering that led to the discovery of penicillin?

INTUITION

All the efforts to understand creativity, whether mediated by serendipity or in a more direct manner, seem to focus on the process called *intuition.* As some authorities have observed, discoveries are by definition at variance with established systems of knowledge; intuition is an inductive step by means of which a radically new point of view is obtained and a new insight thereby achieved. The only other aspect of intuition about which there seems to be quite general agreement is that it is a kind of reasoning in which the most crucial facets are simply not evident; in other words, it is in essence unpredictable, at least in terms of any known measures. But it does depend upon both a strong motivation and a thorough grounding in the essentials of the problem. Also, it is undoubtedly true that for each successful insight there are many false leads generated, all of which look equally promising at first. It is only through the verification procedures that scientific methodology has sharpened to a remarkably keen edge that the wheat of genius can be distinguished from the chaff of more ordinary intuition.

REVERIE

Reverie, more popularly called daydreaming, is a kind of thinking in which there is no apparent problem to be solved. It is true that motivation for reverie is often inferred, and some underlying problem may then be inferred, but there is certainly no such motivation evident in at least some reverie. One simply gives his thoughts free rein, as it were, and enjoys the full play of his thinking processes.

Children's play has been likened to adult fantasy, or reverie production. The two processes seem to have much in common. Both consist of fragmented sequences, of behavior or thoughts, that have been previously experienced and now recur, although often in new arrangements. Both seem often to be pursued in the absence of any external instrumental motivation (although, as suggested, some such motivation may be present); each process seems to carry within it sufficient satisfaction to justify its continuation and renewal.

In spite of the self-sustaining basis, reverie, like play, does have important instrumental functions. It has, for example, been implicated as a crucial element in the incubation and illumination stages of problem solving. Certainly in fantasy one is not required to think along the customary grooves. The seemingly illogical and contradictory nature of fantasy is thus clearly conducive to the kind of thinking that is needed for inspiration.

Reverie has many interesting facets. For example, distinguishing between dreamed (or imagined) experiences and "real" ones is often retrospectively difficult. One way of doing so is to utilize concomitant states of consciousness that we all tend to take for granted and so fail to appreciate. For example, suppose that one has had a dream that is unusual and perhaps shocking but yet not quite impossible. Later the question may arise of whether it was "just" a dream or was actually experienced. If its recall is not accompanied by an appropriate sense of shock or at least surprise, the chances are very good that it was indeed a dream, because such concomitant auras do characteristically accompany real memories more than dreams. It is only by means of this kind of "unconscious response" that many of our everyday dreams are made, and some introspective effort is necessary to detect them. New research on the long-neglected problem of reverie has only recently begun to appear and is to be encouraged. Apart from its intrinisic interest there is

THE ALTAR WINDOW: SOME ATTEMPTED SOLUTIONS

An example, in the words of one highly educated subject: "Of course, I must be able to do this. Let's see . . . which theorems about the computation of areas do I need here? Surely I must be able to recall them. . . . If this were only a real ellipse (pause) . . . but it isn't. . . . If I divide it, then these parts are very easy. At the bottom and at the top I have half circles—and the area of half circles I can easily calculate. But there are also these funny remainders. . . . What theorems do I know about such 'quasi-triangles,' which have, instead of a straight side, such a circular segment? . . . I do not recall any. . . ." And then, after a period of hard thinking, he gave up.

Another subject, similarly intelligent, and with a good deal of geometrical training, went about it in a similar way. When he came to the four strangely shaped remainders, though, he said: "The area of these four is equal to the area of the square minus the area of the circle inscribed in the square. . . . The area of each

From Max Wertheimer, *Productive Thinking,* enlarged edition, Appendix 2 (New York: Harper & Row, 1959), pp. 267–268.

remainder is $(a^2 - \pi a^2)/4$; this is equal to a^2 times $(4 - \pi)/4$. . . . Or is it? . . . Is that correct? (This took half an hour.)

A third subject started by computing the area of the circle, and cried suddenly: "How blind I was! How simple it is! It is the area of the circle plus—what? Square . . . circle; it is simply the area of the square! Excellent problem!"

A ten-year-old child, with no geometrical training to help him, said: "Now, how can you expect me to do this? I can't. I have no idea how one does such things." He looked intently at the figure, and then said quietly: "The two half-circles must fit into the window. . . . It is—the whole square!" (He did not use the term "square" but traced the figure with his finger.) The whole thing took about one minute.

A fifth subject, another boy, twelve years old, without training in geometry, started boasting about how good he was in such problems, and made wild guesses with great assurance. For example: "The four remainders are a quarter of the circle." I said to him, "Don't talk nonsense. Think a bit." He was silent half a minute and then said, "If you move both upper remainders up, and have them fit the upper semi-circle, and if you do the same with the two lower remainders, both things taken together make a square. That's it."

the possibility that more will be learned about intuition and creative thinking through this more or less indirect (back-door) approach than through a direct attack upon productive thinking itself.

PARAPSYCHOLOGICAL PHENOMENA

Parapsychological phenomena are those events, such as extrasensory perception, that are alleged to occur outside the orthodox, generally accepted boundaries of psychological science. They thus pose a dual problem for the orthodox psychologist. First, there is the question of their validity: Do they really occur as claimed? Second, there is the issue of the interpretation: How can they be explained?

It is but a short step from reverie to various forms of parapsychological phenomena, or so it seems. But there is one very important difference. All of us at one time or another engage in reverie and fantasy, with a suspension, *for that time,* of normally ordered (logical) rules of procedure. Parapsychological phenomena, however, are alleged to operate with a more or less chronic suspension of the rules of normal scientific thinking. In the light of our previous discussion concerning creativity we cannot afford to dismiss such phenomena out of hand; however, we are not bound to accept them merely because they offer various propositions that are at odds with, say, those of the scientific community. Like any other proposals, the propositions advanced on the basis of parapsychological procedures need to meet the usual tests of scientific verification before they are accepted as permanent residents in the scientific community.

The study of parapsychology seems to belong in the mainstream of a number of historical, and still quite active, ways of explaining and manipulating events that are without apparent physicalistic components. Astrology, for example, is still a preoccupation of many people. Its popularity continues in spite of the clear lack of any real evidence for it as an explanation of individual differences, similarities among people, and even future human events. Witchcraft, in one form or another, is still a widely practiced art, and one that is apparently increasing in popularity even among the more educated classes (witness the development of new courses, especially in "free universities"). In large measure a reaction to Christian mythology, witchcraft ordinarily depends upon various spells and incantations to produce changes in the physical world. As in the case of the more commonplace magician, these arts rely heavily upon suggestibility, expectancy, and selective perception. The tendency of the human organism to construct after-the-fact (ad hoc) explanations has created many internally consistent but externally questionable theoretical systems. For those who adhere to any such system, the will to believe, rather than suspend judgment, is crucial to the potency of the system. This relationship is especially marked in the various parapsychological phenomena and the great belief many people have in them despite objective contradictions of various kinds.

Spiritistic Phenomena

Here we can sample only a small part of the very great variety of parapsychological phenomena that one finds on all sides in contemporary society. Spiritistic phenomena are those physical events alleged to represent communications from departed organisms (spirits). The "medium" is the vehicle by means of which the spirits are supposed to express themselves. These phenomena present two sets of problems for psychologists. First, there is the question of the reality of the alleged phenomena themselves. Second, there is the problem of why so many people (including some scientists themselves) are convinced of that reality in the absence of what appears to the typical scientist to be anything like adequate supporting evidence.

There is probably no problem in psychology that has such a variety of alleged manifestations, ranging from the common parlor games using ouija boards through automatic writing to seances by professional mediums of one kind or another. The result is a great mass of anecdotal, uncontrolled data, the net scientific value of which is very slight.

Scientists generally are incredulous as to the "evidence" typically submitted in support of spiritistic phenomena. Not only has there been a steady stream of negative results once adequate controls are introduced, but cases of outright fraud, well witnessed and often admitted, have been numerous. Astute and sometimes quite eminent observers, even scientists, have on occasion pronounced these very same events as genuine. Moreover, they occasionally persist in their belief even when well aware of the negative results and reports of others and the difficulties of objective observations. The rigor with which a physical scientist evaluates the theoretical interpretations of data collected in his own laboratory often seems to dissipate when he turns to a consideration of allegedly spiritistic phenomena.

Table 8-2 provides a comparison of the conditions under which laboratory (experimental) observations are made with those typically obtaining in the seance (the "sitting" that the medium arranges for manifestation of communication from spirits). It is quite apparent that the conditions of the seance are made to order, and often deliberately so, for all sorts of illusions, errors of observation, and the like.

TRICKS OF THE TRADE. Some of the techniques used by fraudulent mediums, or by entertainers posing as mind readers or "mentalists," are of interest. A few samples will suffice to show the way in which allegedly supernatural phenomena are readily produced. Take the matter of answering questions, which so often mystifies an audience (usually live, but now also occasionally reached via television). Questions or commentaries are obtained in various ways by the performer, often by sending attendants out into the audience. The performing medium, in or out of a trance (which may be real), then proceeds to pick up the cards or envelopes and answer the questions. There are two fundamental requirements for successful performance of this kind. First, there must be some way of perceiving the question; this is the key problem. Second, the medium needs a facile imagination, so that he

Table 8-2 A Comparison of Laboratory and Seance Conditions

Laboratory	Seance
1. Selection of simple phenomena	Multiplicity of phenomena
2. Provision of a definite time of occurrence of phenomena	Unpredictable schedule of events
3. Exclusion of distractions	Many distractions, including conversation
4. Limited time for concentrated observation	Close attention required for long periods, often many hours continuously
5. Provision of lighting favorable for visual observation	Typical curtailment of lighting
6. Utilization of all essential instruments (e.g., cameras)	Lack or denial of essential instruments
7. Complete control of conditions by observer	Lack of control of conditions by observer
8. Exclusion of emotionality	Accentuation of highly emotional atmosphere
9. Adequate recording immediately after phenomena	Inadequate recording
10. Verification of events through repetition	Repetition typically not possible on demand

can impressively embellish his answers; here experience is a great aid in polishing performance. Figure 8-5 depicts a closely related type of performance.

With regard to the key problem of perceiving the question, which may be in a tightly sealed envelope, ingenious performers have developed a very large number of techniques. One of the oldest and simplest is also one of the most effective. This is merely working "one behind"; that is, the performer consistently answers the question he has looked at in the immediately *preceding* envelope, which was opened up for reading to the audience immediately after his pretended answer. All he has to do, then, is remember the wording so that he can pretend to read it off as he opens

8-5 This nineteenth-century engraving illustrates the fortuneteller plying her trade. From the expression on the face of her client, the fortuneteller is obviously telling the client just what she wants to hear.

the next envelope; he can get one behind in various ways, such as by evading an answer to the first envelope—feigning illegibility, for example, or using some more subtle trick. Slick performances are quickly achieved with practice.

There are other ways of answering questions from the audience. For example, an attendant may substitute blanks for the questions, then retire to an anteroom from which he communicates questions to the performer by means of telephonic or now wireless electronic techniques; or an attendant may simply use a large blackboard in the wings of a theatre, out of sight of the audience, to communicate the questions. Slightly more subtle techniques include various ways in which the writing on the paper inside the envelop can be exposed, as by moistening chemically treated materials with a sponge. There is no limit to the ingenuity of performers, who are in a crude sense magicians. Many members of the audience, left in the dark as much as possible, are not likely to detect the trickery and so are inclined to attribute supernatural abilities to the clever performer instead of suspecting their own judgment, as they would do under different circumstances. If, for instance, the performer is billed as a magician, then one may still marvel at his performance, be clearly incapable of explaining it, but not be likely to attribute it to supernatural powers. One knows that tricks are involved and that if he could look more closely at the performance he would probably be able to figure out how it was done. But magicians are notoriously and understandably reluctant to reveal their secrets, even when they freely admit that they are tricks, as the best magicians customarily do.

Similar interpretations can be made of the other common phenomena of the seance. For example, raps, movements of tables, various noises, and the like, can be produced by clever performers who slip their hand or foot out of a glove or a shoe, or who replace one hand or foot by another when hands and/or feet are connected to the next person in the circle. Another very common device is the slate with the false front, on which a person is asked to provide some information, say in advance of the performance. This ploy is frequently used with especially eminent persons, who are then duped into expressing their conviction as to the authenticity of the alleged supernatural phenomena; they are not told that the slate provides a copy of their information, so that rubbing it off and allowing the person to keep the original is no guarantee that the performer will not have access to the information.

Appeal of the Supernatural

The lure of the magical and the supernatural is a very strong one for the human organism. Lurking close beneath the surface of even the most sophisticated adults are strong tendencies to believe. Nature appears to abhor a theoretical vacuum. In this respect, if no appropriate belief system is inherited as part of the cultural legacy of an individual, he is very likely to adopt one, or perhaps several, from those available in his environment, or even to invent one. The security afforded by a belief system—religious, magical, scientific, or otherwise—is a major factor in the behavioral adjustment of most people.

How does the psychologist explain the remarkable appeal of the supernatural, and the ability of so many mediums and stage performers alike to convince their audiences that they are using supernatural powers? Many specific factors are involved, beyond the strong and generalized desire to believe in supernatural events, and thus to require very little in the way of "proof" to jump to positive conclusions. In the case of seances and similar events particularly, those in attendance are likely to be in an unusually emotional, and therefore receptive, frame of mind. (They may have recently lost a loved one, for example.) Objective observation and critical interpretation are not traits that occur in high degree in very many people even under normal circumstances. As the comparison in Table 8-2 indicates, the circumstances of the seance are designed to discourage these thinking facilities and to encourage illusions. In addition, there are the general tendencies in all people to look for external explanations rather than internal ones and to seize upon and enlarge slight effects. Finally, the emphasis on successes, with failures ignored, is a very potent factor of widespread significance in thinking, beyond the situations we are considering here. We tend to remember the occasional hit and to forget the much more numerous misses, as, for instance, when we have a premonition of danger to an absent relative. How many people *count* their premonitions that are *not* confirmed? Very few indeed. But let one experience a *single* confirmation and he is not likely to allow his friends to forget it. The chance baseline that is necessary for an objective evaluation of the significance of such occasional bits is seldom even recognized, let alone computed. Here we see again the overemphasis on confirmation of propositions and underevaluation of failures to confirm that were noted earlier in the chapter when we discussed inhibitions in problem solving.

Extrasensory Perception

The parapsychological phenomena we have thus far discussed are of a quite different nature from those being investigated in contemporary scientific research programs. Under the direction of J. B. Rhine at Duke University the modern parapsychological movement has succeeded in subjecting a variety of alleged extrasensory and similar capacities to more extensive tests than have heretofore been applied. Here we shall not be able to analyze these experiments in any detail, but we can say by way of summary that many of the early methodological errors (e.g., the use of playing cards with designs that could be seen through the back) have been corrected and sophisticated statistical analyses have been applied to the results. But granting the existence of a presumably solid residue of positive results in some experiments that cannot be readily explained away on the grounds of more or less apparent errors, one is left with the problem of how to interpret such data within a scientific framework. A number of alternative postures have been suggested. These can be summarized as follows:

1. Adequate empirical evidence should be required for all propositions, regardless of their nature, with the phenomena that cannot now be explained simply left to the unknown.
2. We should admit the incompleteness of present scientific knowledge and trust that many of our current puzzles, including parapsychological phenomena, will someday be better understood in the light of additional scientific studies.
3. We should welcome the persistence of mystery, such as that suggested by ESP, and should assume that the physical determinism of science simply is not capable of dealing with all the phenomena of human life.
4. Parapsychological phenomena such as ESP should be accepted, even in the

absence of the kind of solid empirical evidence required of other scientific propositions, along with religious conceptualizations (e.g., God) and hypotheses (e.g., immortality) that cannot be readily subjected to empirical proof.

Scientists mostly fall into one of the first two categories, whereas laymen are more likely to be found in the last two categories. The major reason that such a high proportion of scientists is disinclined to be concerned about parapsychological phenomena is partly historical: so many phenomena once alleged to be evidence for parapsychological functions have subsequently been found to be perfectly explicable in terms of previously established scientific principles.

CLEVER HANS. The role of unconscious cues is especially significant in the kind of event exemplified by the case of Clever Hans. Clever Hans was a German horse that early in this century was hailed throughout Europe as capable of at least simple arithmetic calculations. It was not until careful observation of his abilities under controlled conditions was finally achieved that a more scientifically adequate explanation of his behavior was advanced. Hans was apparently capable of solving various arithmetic problems, such as simple addition or subtraction, and gave his answer by stamping his paw the appropriate number of times. It was found, however, that this ability to "count" was dependent upon the trainer's inadvertently giving the horse a signal when the answer was reached in his pawing. What the horse had learned was simply to observe the trainer carefully and stop pawing when some characteristic change occurred in his behavior (such as a nod of the head or even a slight relaxation after the correct number had been reached). There are many more subtle examples of unconscious cuing, but the case of Clever Hans remains one of the more dramatic in the history of man's efforts to cope with mysterious performances and is representative of the historical reasons for the general distrust by scientists of occult and supernatural hypotheses.

THE FUTURE OF PARAPSYCHOLOGY. Whether or not the data on parapsychological phenomena now being collected under scientifically rigorous conditions will be incorporated into the body of scientific knowledge is impossible to predict. The alternative is that bit by bit they will be discovered to be artifacts (that is, functions of conditions other than those their proponents claim), and so, like many other less well-controlled data similarly advanced in the past, will be disregarded. In any event, it is their interpretation that is ultimately at issue. As we have already indicated (in the notes to Chapter 6), a big stumbling block in this respect has been the persistent failure of the proponents of parapsychological phenomena to offer scientifically verifiable hypotheses. It is one thing to point to the incompleteness of scientific knowledge (few scientists would really care to argue with that position), but it is quite another to specify the exact ways in which those gaps can be filled. If parapsychologists succeed not merely in pointing to the mysteries of behavior and experience but also in indicating how those mysteries can be reduced, their role in science will be assured. In the meantime, one is well advised to maintain a skeptical view of parapsychological claims, in light of the susceptibility of this kind of behavioral process to very subtle and unsuspected variables and the methodological uncertainties still surrounding its investigation, and to suspend judgment concerning theoretical interpretations.

A good number of suggestions for improving the clarity, or objectivity, of thinking are implicit in the discussions already presented in this chapter and in Chapter 7. Here some of the more significant of these, and a few additional ones, will be more explicitly identified and briefly evaluated.

Inhibitory Factors

The many factors that contribute to a lack of clarity in thinking can be classified in various ways.

ERRORS OF LOGIC. Some logical errors are normal in childhood and simply persist as hangovers to cloud and distort adult thinking; for example, children normally think in an egocentric, or self-centered, fashion, confuse correlation and causation (assuming that because one event precedes another it is an essential condition, or cause), and show a number of logical weaknesses of the kind that Piaget has probed (discussed in Chapter 10). There are also a number of more typical adult errors in thinking, such as the tendency to jump too quickly to conclusions and misapply formal logical processes.

EMOTIONAL FACTORS. Another large class of contributors to cloudiness in adult thinking relates to the involvement of emotional factors. The role of prejudice and stereotypes in thinking and the generally significant influence of affect have been stressed earlier. Chronic emotional defects in some people intensify the normal tendencies that all of us show to allow our emotions to dominate our intellectual processes.

It is particularly important that we keep separate our emotional and our intellectual satisfactions, especially when dealing with the different issues posed by parapsychological phenomena. In other words, we must guard against allowing any emotional satisfaction that such experiences may provide to influence our intellectual or scientific evaluation of the same phenomena. Failure to keep these two processes separate no doubt accounts for much of the strong support given parapsychological interpretations.

FAULTY INFORMATION. A third category of conditions contributing to inefficiency in thinking concerns the lack of appropriate information on which to base sound conclusions. Sometimes this lack is recognized, but more often it seems to be ignored and conclusions are formed on the basis of scanty facts or facts of questionable relevance to the issues at hand. Astonishingly small amounts of information are sometimes discovered when objective measures are made of various samples of a population. In a recent questionnaire study of 3,000 adults conducted for the U.S. Food and Drug Administration, a surprisingly large number of misconceptions about health were uncovered. For example, extra vitamins were believed to be responsible for added physical vigor by three fourths of those questioned, and fully one fifth expressed the conviction that cancer is at least in part associated with vitamin and mineral deficiency. Beliefs such as these, which have no medical or scientific support, can be accounted for on the basis of the high proportion of the population that apparently assumes that advertisers are so closely monitored that they would not risk false claims.

ACCEPTANCE OF AUTHORITY. Finally, there is the all too frequent uncritical acceptance of authority, in one form or another. Statements made by recognized experts in one field are frequently influential even though they concern affairs that are unrelated to the person's area of competence, as we have just noted with regard to the testimony of, say, physical scientists on issues of immortality and spiritistic manifestations, and as can be seen in the interminable appearance of celebrities testifying on television about the unexcelled quality of this shampoo or that hair dressing.

Positive Steps

Obviously, correction or reduction of the various inhibitory factors already discussed, or any of the many other such factors not mentioned, will serve to improve the clarity and efficiency of one's thinking processes. The emotional facets, especially when they are not recognized as such, are generally the most insidious in their operation and the most difficult to remove. Here a few specific positive steps toward improved clarity in thinking can be briefly reviewed.

By far the most important single step in this direction is the determination to open all aspects of one's thinking to *objective scrutiny*, and the serious attempt to provide this scrutiny as well as solicit it from others. The premises on which conclusions are based are in this respect more important than the conclusions themselves, and more important than the formal logical steps by which the conclusions have been reached. More heat, with insignificant amounts of light, has been produced by unrecognized differences in assumptions than by any other single factor. If one habitually keeps his premises in mind and open to scrutiny, he is much more likely to avoid the emotional involvements that tend to freeze opinion and discourage the re-examination of premises.

Raising questions about premises and assumptions generally, as well as about conclusions, need not be restricted to one's own thinking. All sources of information should be treated with reasonable skepticism. No authorities must be taken for granted, unless one does so deliberately and with an open commitment, in which case there is little point in arguing about *those* premises at least (although one may still wish to question the reasons for making such a commitment). The relativity of facts, as discussed in Chapter 7 (p. 201), is relevant to this point. There are so many subtle ways in which perspectives differ that it is hardly surprising to find honest men differing over what appear to be identical stimulus situations.

The major molders of public opinion or attitudes are popular media such as newspapers, magazines, and television. It is well to look carefully not only at editorial opinions, but at "facts" as reported in the media. Reporters are under considerable pressure to meet time deadlines and are not always able to check their sources carefully; publishers have business as well as social or political relationships with advertisers and other institutions with an interest in how the news is interpreted. Although many reporters and editorial writers strive to maintain a high standard of accuracy and objectivity, these cannot be assumed to hold in all cases. Moreover, the formation of the crucial attitudes that underlie so much of our thinking is mediated in a much more insidious manner than simply accepting stated opinions. Thus the constant barrage of physical violence to which children are exposed in television programs is believed to have cumulative attitudinal effects, although it is difficult to show conclusive evidence of direct behavior influence at the time. Similarly, frequent reports of political skullduggery seem to have raised the threshold of public indignation to such an extent that increasingly bizarre events, such as those occurring during the presidential campaign of 1972 in the United States, seem to have little effect upon the electorate. These attitudinal changes in the frame of reference that people use to form their conclusions are much more difficult to detect, but each of us needs to guard against them in his own thinking, or at least to be aware of their potential function in his decision making.

Finally, we may point to one particularly pervasive error in thinking and interpretation that can be more readily checked than can attitudinal change. This is the tendency that we all have to *select* data. That is, we all tend to notice things that fit in with our preconceptions and to ignore things that do not. Drawing conclusions that are plausible for only part of the data and ignoring failures of predictions while concentrating on successes (as discussed above in connection with spiritistic phenomena) are common examples of this kind of selectivity in thinking. Again, we can point to the importance of examining our preconceptions and our assumptions, not only for their intrinsic merit but also with regard to the role that they play as determinants of our perceptions and our interpretations of what we perceive.

Selection of data is often associated with what is called the *hidden agenda*—the real reason for decisions and actions, in contrast to the rational façade that is usually offered. Such hidden agendas, although perhaps most blatant in politicians, are common in various corners of everyone's behavior.

All the preceding points suggest the conclusion that it is not the thinking processes themselves as much as their auxiliary conditions that we need to watch closely if we wish to improve the clarity of our thinking. Formal logic is in this respect of limited value. Its main role seems to be as an aid in point out the errors that we may make in reasoning (as was illustrated on p. 224). But the wishfulness in our thinking comes from other than logical considerations and so requires other types of correctives and precautions if a reasonable degree of clarity is to be maintained.

Laboratory Problems

Morton, cited by Kimble and Garmezy (1968), reported the research on attitudinal systems and logical reasoning. Errors in formal logic, like those described in the text, are labeled "psycho-logic" by Abelson and Rosenberg (1958). The four-card problem illustrated in Figure 8-3 and discussed in the text has been intensively investigated by P. C. Wason (1969; see Wason and Johnson-Laird, 1972 for a more extended discussion).

Set and Functional Fixedness

Two classic papers concerned with set (*Einstellung*) are Luchins's 1942 report of his water-jug research and Duncker's 1945 research and theorizing within the Gestalt psychology framework, with special reference to the concept of functional fixedness. Adamson (1952) reported that the candle problem was easier when an

Notes

empty box was presented. Glucksburg (1964) found that subjects who had not solved this problem also showed no evidence of having perceived the box as a separate object when asked to describe the materials. The finding of faster solutions to the candle problem when subjects were asked to label each material separately before attempting to solve the problem was reported by Glucksburg and Weisberg (1966).

Theories of Problem Solving

The application of S–R theory to thinking, in terms of such concepts as the habit-family hierarchy, has been vigorously attempted by Maltzman (1955); Wertheimer's 1945 book and Maier's 1940 theoretical paper represent applications of Gestalt theory.

With regard to the application of the habit-family hierarchy concept to problem solving, it should be noted that variable (or trial-and-error) behavior occurs when the subject does not have the correct response at his command. The stimulus situation is likely to be quite complex, consisting of multiple cues, including those generated by the subject's own trial-and-error behavior. The extent to which various response sets of the habit-family sort are actually hierarchically arranged, as the S–R theory assumes, is not clear, and some theorists would question whether habit families are really a valuable concept. The cognitive map concept was developed by E. C. Tolman; the rat experiment described in the text was performed by Tolman and Honzik (1930).

Computer Simulation

A recent review of the computer-simulation research and theory has been published by Simon and Newell (1971); Simon's *The Sciences of the Artificial* (1969) and Newell and Simon's *Human Problem Solving* (1972) are more detailed, book-length presentations. The early comparison of mathematical proofs by the Logical Theorist with those actually done by Whitehead and Russell is in the report by Newell, Shaw, and Simon (1958).

The relationship of motivational and emotional controls to cognition generally is considered by Simon (1969), in the context of computer research, and the same problem is the subject of a small volume edited by Tomkins and Messick (1963); Tomkins's introduction to this book is especially interesting. (He reminds us that adding drive and emotional determinants to computers can be done in their programming, and may be worthwhile from a scientific-research point of view, but that this will seriously detract from their efficiency as computers. It is exactly their disinterest, their general invulnerability to bias and breakdown or disturbance from such factors as emotions, that makes them such admirable tools of man.)

Creativity

The characteristics of college teachers who have been identified as instrumental in the training of creative researchers have recently been analyzed in a large-scale study utilizing factor analysis of a number of personality inventories (Chambers, 1972). The results indicated that such teachers, as compared with controls who were matched on relevant variables, tended to be more introverted (oriented towards oneself), dominant, and self-sufficient. Some support was also found for the proposition that they are more sensitive to esthetic factors and less likely to conform to social mores.

Mackworth (1965) has stressed the importance of problem finding. The research on improvement of creativity scores was reported by Meadow and Parnes (1959) and Parnes and Meadow (1960). Koestler's *The Act of Creation* (1964) is an attempt by this erudite scholar and long-time critic of orthodox science to interpret creativity as the combination ("biosociation," in his terminology) of normally disparate ideas. Innovation as a byproduct of the dialogue between science and technology is discussed by Price and Bass (1969), and the limitation of most scientific progress to the contributions of a relatively small number of scientists is argued by Cole and Cole (1972). Hebb (1972, p. 265) has provided the list of examples of serendipity within psychology from which several examples were drawn in the text.

Intuition

Wilder's 1969 paper on intuition stresses mathematical research and teaching methods. Greene's 1969 edition of Polyani's essays, *Knowing and Being* concentrates on the *tacit knowing* concept. The incident involving Poincaré is described in his 1913 report.

Reverie

Comparison of children's play and adult reverie has been made in detail by Klinger (1971). Harlow, McGaugh, and Thompson's 1971 text provides a readable and informative discussion of play, with special reference to its instrumental role in such functions as sexual adjustment.

Parapsychology

The Case for and Against Psychical Belief, edited by Murchison (1927), contains some interesting discussions of classical cases. Pfungst's 1965 account of the horse Clever Hans appears in a book of the same name. Ebon (1971) has written a popular account of the way in which many prominent men (e.g., William James, Mark Twain, Sigmund Freud) have been concerned with parapsychological phenomena in their own lives. Rhine (1971) has presented a historical review of the contemporary research program pioneered by her husband at Duke University. In addition to the classical phenomena of *clairvoyance* (the ability to perceive by means other than the known sensory channels) and *telepathy* (the ability to communicate with another mind outside of the known sensory channels), the new concept of *telekinesis* or *psychokinesis* (PK) has been advanced; this is the ability to determine physical events, such as the roll of dice, by thought processes. Critical evaluations of this work have been published by Gardner (1957) and Hansel (1966). (Methodological questions concerning ESP are raised in Chapter 6.) Also of interest is the symposium "Science and the Supernatural" edited by Soal (1956) with contributions by several prominent persons, including J. B. Rhine, physicists Soal and Bridgman, and psychologist Meehl.

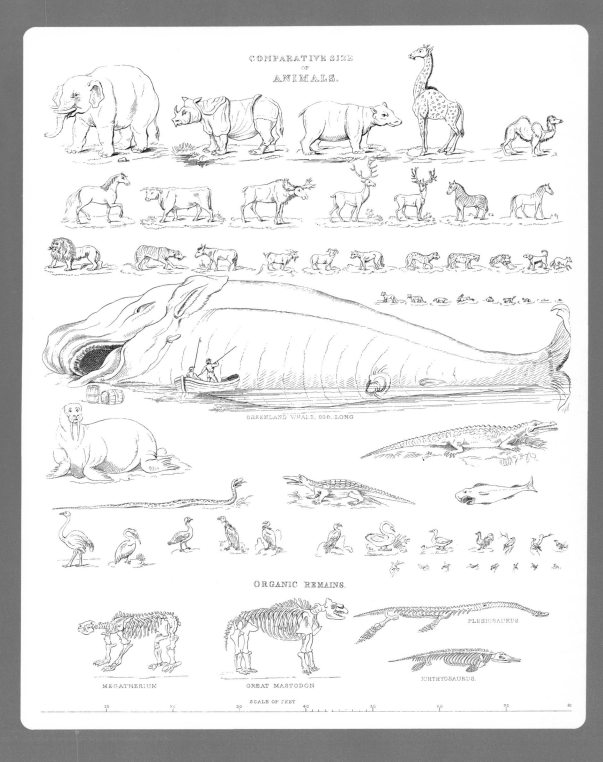

COMPARATIVE SIZE
OF
ANIMALS.

GREENLAND WHALE, 60 ft. LONG.

ORGANIC REMAINS.

MEGATHERIUM

GREAT MASTODON

PLESIOSAURUS

ICHTHYOSAURUS.

SCALE OF FEET

10   20   30   40   50   60   70   80

Heredity and Environment

PART III

This page from an early nineteenth-century book sets the stage for a discussion of heredity and environment. The subject of what we are and why we are as we are has always occupied scholars and scientists. The relative competence of species and of individuals within species, as well as the factors that contribute to the development of these abilities, is the subject of the next section.

he relationship between inherited and environmental factors in the determination of behavior ranks as one of the most enduring and pervasive issues in psychology. Its ramifications throughout psychology are probably as extensive as those of the consciousness–brain–behavior relationship. Moreover, they tend to arouse much emotion (witness the issue of racial differences in intelligence, for one instance). The questions associated with this issue, however, give somewhat more promise of at least partial resolution, as should be evident in the following chapters.

The first chapter of this part is again a combination of methodological and substantive treatments, with the objective of providing a fundamental basis for understanding the issues as well as setting the stage for the exposition of the closely related subject matters. The latter are contained in three following chapters on development, learning, and memory. Chapter 10, on development, emphasizes strictly maturational (that is, primarily inherited) conditions as well as environmental influences that are not commonly attributed to learning (for example, nutritional factors). Chapter 11, on learning, emphasizes the standard types of tasks that have been used but considers also the now more widely recognized limitations of some of the orthodox problems and theories. Chapter 12, on memory, focuses on that fundamental process as perhaps the most critical one for an understanding of human behavior and conscious experience.

Individual Potential

This nineteenth-century lithograph pokes fun at the then contemporary theories of Charles Darwin. Despite the whimsey of this illustration, the topic of the individual's potential and the relative impact of environmental factors upon its development is a serious concern to modern scientists and educators.

his chapter deals with the ancient "nature–nurture" problem, the question of the relative contributions to animal development and behavior made by inherited factors ("nature") and of those made by environmental or learned factors ("nurture"). The theme of this chapter is that the dichotomy between hereditary and environmental influences is misleading. The most acceptable contemporary position is one of *interaction* between the two fundamental types of determinants.

Interaction is illustrated, in the introductory sections, by certain classic biological demonstrations of the dependence of genes, or inherited factors, upon the environment even in what appear to be simple anatomical matters (e.g., the number of eyes in fish). Three types of methodological approach to the general problem are then described: statistical, experimental, and genetic. A historical overview of the problem is provided, focusing on the "instinct" controversy and describing some classic behavioral research.

The discussion of "what is inherited" leads into a description of ethology, the study of the natural behavior of organisms, and an analysis of the interaction position. It is pointed out that there is an increasing dependence upon environmental (learned) mechanisms as compared with inherited behavioral mechanisms as one ascends the phylogenetic scale (that is, as one considers increasingly complex forms of animal life).

For those who are not sufficiently familiar with either evolutionary theory or the fundamental mechanisms of heredity, Part V provides an account of these two topics. It concentrates on the achievements of Charles Darwin and Gregor Mendel, two scientific giants of the nineteenth century whose work has laid the foundation for modern behavioral science as well as modern biology generally.

The last part of this chapter is concerned with the more difficult problem of tracing hereditary and learned influences in human behavior. After a survey of the major types of behavior, the problem of intelligence is considered in depth. On this issue there has been a running controversy between proponents of a fundamentally hereditarian viewpoint and proponents of a fundamentally environmentalistic point of view. Moreover, both positions have serious and far-reaching political and social implications. The evidence for hereditary influence centers upon an analysis of test scores of identical twins, who share the same hereditary materials, and fraternal twins, who have differing hereditary materials but tend to have the same environment. In view of the complexities of this problem, which are summarized in the discussion, it is impossible to draw any hard-and-fast conclusions, but recent research does support, again, an interaction position in which both hereditary and environmental factors and their interrelationship are emphasized. Certainly neither of the two extreme positions, which would deny the influence of one set of factors while stressing the primacy of the other, is justified by available or foreseeable evidence, nor can any particular program of a social or political nature be justified on the basis of such evidence.

253

INDIVIDUAL POTENTIAL

THE PROBLEM

The nature–nurture problem has generated so much misinformation that it may be well to start with a brief consideration of some general cautions. In spite of common assumptions to the contrary, the basic problem cannot be usefully regarded as an "either-or" proposition. Neither hereditary nor environmental influences can be emphasized to the detriment of the other; both are essential. Moreover, it is impossible adequately to assess the influence of one factor without some knowledge of the other. Heredity never operates in a vacuum; environmental variables always operate on and by means of inherited structures. Although the latter point may be regarded as self-evident, the former may require some elaboration.

Interaction of Heredity and Environment

Even with respect to the biological inheritance of purely physical characteristics, it is always necessary to take into account the kind of environment in which the genetic determinants, the genes, operate. When the environment is radically changed, striking differences in genetic effects may occur. An early demonstration of this principle was provided by an experiment on fish development. By adding magnesium or lithium chloride to the water in which the fish *Fundulus* was developing, it was possible to produce cyclopean (one-eyed) offspring from "normal" parents. Various degrees of eyedness could be produced by varying the amount of chemical added to the water, as indicated in Figure 9-1; the same results were obtained with other animals, such as frogs.

This relatively simple demonstration has enormous implications for the interpretation of the role of the gene in hereditary transmission. For example, one may raise a question as to the nature of the *genotype*, as the presumed genetic characteristic is called. Are there genes for two eyes, for one eye, and for some particular degree of separation or fusion of the eyes? Yes, and no. Yes, because obviously the genes have all these potentials. No, because they are all the same kind of gene. The major conclusion to be drawn is that, with regard to the *phenotype* (as the expressed bodily characteristic is called), the gene has no inevitable or intrinsic result. Its action depends upon the particular environment in which it operates, and this condition therefore also needs to be specified.

Subsequent experiments with the vinegar fly, or fruit fly, *Drosophila*, a favorite subject of geneticists since early in this century, amplify this conclusion. Two kinds of experiments may be noted. First, there are genes for defective phenotypes that will produce such defects only in a particular kind of environment; for example, supernumerary (extra) legs can be produced if the eggs are hatched and raised in low temperatures, and certain abnormalities in the joints and abdomen will occur only if the eggs are in the usual moist environment.

Heredity and Environment

	Environment	
Genotype	Normal	Modified
Normal	Phenotype normal	Phenotype defective ("phenocopies")
Defective	Phenotype defective	—

Table 9-1 Relationship Between Genetic Constitution (Genotype) and Environment in Production of Body Structure (Phenotype)

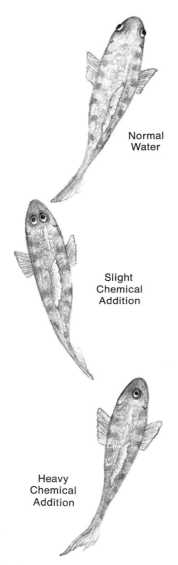

Normal Water

Slight Chemical Addition

Heavy Chemical Addition

9-1 Eye development of *Fundulus* as a function of the amount of chemical additive in its water environment during early growth.

A second type of experiment involves "normal" genes but radical environmental changes during a critical period in development. Certain of the naturally occurring birth defects of the fruitfly (such as vestigial, or undeveloped, wings) usually attributed to a defective genotype were exactly duplicated in flies with "normal" genotypes by modifications of the temperature and moisture conditions for relatively short time periods during the development of the egg. These phenotypes —that is, the birth defects that resulted—could not be distinguished from the phenotypes resulting from the development of flies with defective genotype raised in the usual "normal" environment. Apparently the action of the defective gene could be simulated, or copied, by appropriate environmental manipulation, hence the term *phenocopies* for this kind of genetic product. The basic results are shown in Table 9-1.

The implications of these relatively simple demonstrations, with relatively simple kinds of organisms, are great. For one thing they raise the question of what is "normal," particularly with regard to the environment. More specifically, they indicate that gene action can be meaningfully described only in relation to certain specified environmental conditions. In other words, genes do not carry any necessary determiners of specific body characteristics *independent* of developing conditions. Rather, they must be viewed as producers of certain developmental events mainly involving biochemical processes within cells. These processes then interact with both other genetically determined processes and a whole host of environmental factors to produce such body characteristics as normal or vestigial wings in Drosophila.

A large number of other, more complex demonstrations of the complementary character of inherited and learned variables can be described. But the fundamental point can be made on the basis of these classic and readily duplicated observations.

NEW APPROACHES TO THE PROBLEM

As a result of the increasing acceptance of relativistic thinking about heredity and environment, there has been a growing tendency to dismiss the entire nature-nurture problem as a "pseudoproblem." It is important to recognize the implications of this position, which are *not* that the problems posed are unimportant, but rather that the ancient solutions, especially any kind of simplistic solution, are misguided and essentially fruitless. Such severely simplified attempts at solutions have been generated by posing hereditary and environmental influences as antagonistic alternatives rather than necessarily complementary factors. It is apparent that the problem needs a radical reformulation.

A number of alternative positions have been developed. Some researchers have attempted to retain the problem as initially posed but have modified the methodology. There has been a fairly common tendency to attempt to allocate proportions of responsibility, as in terms of percentages developed on the basis of sophisticated statistical techniques. This *statistical* procedure has been frequently applied to the problem of intelligence, which is treated in detail later in this chapter. For example, it might be concluded that 70 per cent of the variance (variation in measurements of intelligence) is due to heredity and 30 per cent to environment, or vice versa. Such allocations, however, must be done with extreme caution because of the subtle ways in which all behavioral data are sensitive to variations in the interacting factors. Moreover, the procedure is open to the serious risk of asserting more than is justified by the data and consequently of being misinterpreted. The quantitative results may be distorted and used in support of one or another doctrinaire position. Degeneration into this kind of a "numbers game" is difficult to discourage. Although admittedly an improvement over earlier methodologies, this procedure leaves the fundamental difficulty—an implicit assumption of antagonistic rather than complementary factors—substantially untouched. Thus it cannot be regarded as entirely satisfactory.

In dealing with the nature–nurture interaction a more generally useful *experimental* procedure is to investigate each specific situation in terms of its own determining conditions, regardless of how they are classified. As sufficient factual ("lawful") information is accumulated, higher-order generalizations concerning the relative contribution of nature and nurture variables to various classes of behaviors may become possible. But in this case they will be based upon a solid empirical foundation, rather than the kind of a priori generalizations, one way or the other, that all too often have been made on mainly theoretical assumptions.

The two alternatives just discussed—that is, the statistical and the experimental approaches—may be regarded as contributions to the study of *individual differences*. A third, considerably more sophisticated, position has been developed on the basis of modern genetic theory. In essence, this genetic procedure views the contribution of heredity (via the genotype) as accounting for the *differences* among *populations*, rather than merely the more orthodox production of some phenotype in the individual animal. As one behavior geneticist has recently put it,

There is always a spectrum of genotypes throughout a population—what we call individual differences. I have come to realize that it is impossible to study the genetics *of* a behavior. We can study the behavior of *an* organism, the genetics of *a* population, and individual difference in the expression of some behavior by the members of *that* population. Therefore, we now speak of behavior-genetic analyses, understanding by that expression simultaneously the experimental analysis of well-defined behaviors into their sensory and

Table 9-2

Approach	General View	Specific Rationale	Procedure and Product
Statistical	Heredity and environment are *antagonistic* factors	Behaviors can be attributed to heredity *or* environment	Allocation of *percentage* of influence to each factor is by statistical analysis
Experimental	Heredity and environment are *interacting* factors	Each behavioral situation needs to be examined *separately*	Responsibility in terms of heredity and environment should be made only *after specific causal factors* in each case have been *identified*
Genetic	*Genotypes* in a *population* always *vary*, producing individual differences	Heredity accounts for differences among *populations*	Experimental breeding or analysis of human pedigree is used in conjunction with *behavior analysis*

response components, the reliable and valid measurement of individual differences in the behaviors and in their component responses, *then* subsequent breeding analysis or, for man, pedigree analysis by the methods of genetics over a specified set of generations in the history of a given population under known ecological conditions [Hirsch, 1967, p. 121].

The highlights of these three prototypic approaches to the nature–nurture problem are summarized in the chart in Table 9-2. Although there is some overlap of functions (e.g., the appearance of experimentation in both the experimental and the genetic approaches), the emphasis varies (e.g., experimentation is the central concern in the experimental approach but is supplementary to population genetics for the genetic approach).

THE INSTINCT CONTROVERSY

Perhaps the best example of the general tendency to attribute causal relationships to heredity has been the use of *instincts* as explanations of an increasingly large proportion of human behavior. An instinct is defined as a complex behavior that

1. Occurs universally in a species.
2. Is inevitable under the appropriate stimulating conditions.
3. Achieves some kind of objective generally important to the organism.
4. Is not dependent upon practice or learning.

During the early part of the twentieth century it became fashionable in some psychological circles to use the instinct concept to attempt to counteract the environmentalistic bias of some prominent systematists (notably certain of the behaviorists). This trend culminated in the appearance of an influential textbook on social psychology in which practically all human behavior was accounted for by one instinct or another. The list had become so long as to render the concept almost meaningless, especially in view of the lack of anything like appropriate empirical support. As a result the instinct bubble burst, partly under the attack from the environmentalists but primarily as a consequence of its own overextended condition.

Instinct was replaced, in part, by *drive*. This new concept assumed the existence of internal motivational factors, such as hunger and thirst, and was eagerly embraced by some experimentalists. But it too began to proliferate unduly and soon came under strong critical attack.

The heart of the objection to both of those nativistic concepts is not that heredity is unimportant but rather that the concepts have been used indiscriminately and in the absence of adequate empirical supports. Drive as a concept was initially in a position somewhat superior to that of instinct; the simpler drives, such as hunger and thirst, could be manipulated by straightforward deprivation of environmental materials. But the concept was extended to more abstract, presumed "needs" of the organism. Some critics felt that drive theorists were willing to attribute internal motivational properties for *any* behavior exhibited by an organism and then account for it by assuming an appropriate drive.

This kind of use of both drive and instinct can be criticized as essentially "circular," especially if explanatory powers are attributed to the concept. In the case of instinct, for example, man was said to be gregarious—meaning simply that he tends to live in groups—and such behavior was then explained on the basis of a "gregarious instinct." The question as to the basis for assuming such an instinct might be answered by pointing to the fact that man does live in groups. Similar *tautologies* (circular arguments) were also evident, although not quite so glaringly, in the case of some of the drive conceptualizations.

Beyond the circularity involved, the use of such concepts as instinct for explanations is objectionable because it is very likely to stifle further investigation. That is, those who use such concepts in this way are very likely to be satisfied with them and so unlikely to feel the need for an analysis designed to determine specific causal factors in the behavior at issue. Such dependence upon essentially verbal explanations in the absence of supporting evidence is sometimes called word magic.

Dismissal of the instinct concepts as an explanatory factor was appreciably facilitated by certain experimental research. For example, Zing Yang Kuo made extensive observations on the developing chick embryo by replacing a section of the egg shell by a transparent window through which developing behaviors could be closely watched. Kuo demonstrated the *continuity* of the development of stepping behavior, which was generally considered to be instinctive because it occurred shortly after hatching in the absence of any apparent practice. The critical phases that Kuo noted were as follows:

1. Head turning, at fifth day of incubation.
2. Forelimbs flapping, from eighth to tenth day.

3. Trunk wiggling, on twelfth day.
4. Alternate stepping, progressively occurring until hatching at twenty-first day.

When this sequence was observed during incubation, the chick invariably walked. However, if one or the other of these phases failed to occur, the chick was crippled at hatching.

Kuo's theoretical interpretation, which was ingeniously related to his observations, stressed mechanical factors; he felt that it was basically the developing structure interacting with the environment that determined the behavior. He accounted for the initial head turning on the grounds of its weight; the neck musculature had not kept up with head growth, and so the first side-to-side movements started. The forelimbs similarly flapped from side to side because there was no room for any other kind of movement. The trunk wiggling was likewise a function of space limitations; there was no room within the cell for full movements. Finally, and most important, the alternate stepping that was observed during the later days of incubation was clearly due to the fact that free movement was only possible with one limb at a time, again owing to the crowded condition of the rapidly growing chick embryo within the shell. Thus a considerable amount of "practice" and integration of these various reflexive movements had already occurred within the shell at the time of hatching, so that the normal alternate stepping behavior of the newly hatched chick was simply an extension of these earlier behaviors.

Kuo's theoretical interpretation is important because it stressed the interaction of inherited structural conditions with environmental factors as an explanation of this particular kind of behavior. Such an analysis clearly left little need for any kind of direct and inevitable hereditary influence upon behavior, such as was assumed to occur via instincts as they were then viewed. Although more recent research has required some modification in Kuo's interpretation of embryo chick behavior, mainly in that a greater degree of control of developing behaviors by neurological structures is indicated, the descriptive value of these early observations and the main thrust of Kuo's interaction position remain.

Naturalistic Studies

A marked renewal of interest by psychologists in the hereditary determinants of behavior has been evident within recent years. Very largely this trend has been stimulated by the researches of a small group of zoologists who have specialized in naturalistic studies of animal behavior. The ethologists, as these animal observers are called, were initially concerned mainly with the behaviors of birds and fish in their natural environment but have more recently extended their studies to a much wider variety of animal forms, even including man himself.

The most prominent ethologists have been Konrad Lorenz and Niko Tinbergen. These men have led the movement in Germany and England, respectively. Lorenz's studies of *imprinting* in ducks—with widely circulated newspaper pictures of imprinted ducklings following him in preference to ducks—are the most famous illustration of classic ethological research. Tinbergen's description of the fighting of the male sticklebacks, small and widely distributed freshwater fish, is almost as well known.

Some of the more important ethological concepts may be reviewed to show something of the nature of their contributions. *Species-specific behavior,* a kind of modern counterpart of the earlier instinct, refers to a behavior pattern that is highly specific to a given type of animal in contrast to those that are developed on an individual basis. For example, all birds of a particular species tend to build the same kind of nest and to sing the same kind of song, more or less independently of their environment (although the latter behavior is definitely dependent upon experience in some species). Both nest building and singing, then, are considered species-specific behaviors.

The fighting behavior of the male stickleback provides an especially interesting illustration of ethological research. During the mating season the underbellies of these male fish turn bright red. At this time they attack any other male stickleback that happens to approach their nest. Tinbergen's observations demonstrated that the stimulus for this kind of species-specific behavior is the redness of the belly. As a matter of fact, it is the redness alone that triggers the attack because when a variety of models is shown to a male fish in breeding condition practically any kind of red spot will serve as a stimulus, quite apart from its resemblance to a fish.

One major result of the success of the ethologists in re-emphasizing the hereditary components in behavior has been a renewed interest in evolutionary theory as it applies to behavior. Although psychologists have generally recognized the significance of evolutionary theory as a historical factor in the development of psychology, its direct applicability to contemporary problems has until recently been neglected. Now, however, one hears more frequent reference to the evolutionary "niche" occupied by some particular animal species; when used with special reference to psychology, this term refers to the constellation of adaptive behaviors that have developed in that particular form during the course of its evolution.

The key question in the behavior-heredity issue is, "How do the genes operate to produce behavior patterns?" It is clear that behavior cannot be inherited, it must be transmitted via some kind of anatomical structure. Put another way, the question becomes, "What structure or process is inherited that mediates the expression of particular behavior patterns?" Although it is quite possible that there is no single simple answer to this question, and certainly none is possible on the basis of the evidence now available, some of the major alternatives can at least be described and tentatively evaluated.

> *Behavior and Heredity*

WHAT IS INHERITED?

The most straightforward answer to the question, and the one that seems to have been more or less implicitly assumed in connection with the instinct doctrine, is that specific *neural connections* or *patterns* within the nervous system are inherited. Historically, this has been a relatively safe assumption to make because we knew so little about how behavior patterns are in fact mediated by the nervous system. The general consensus among scientists is that such "wired-in" connections are most probable for some of the more reflexlike behaviors characteristic of the lower organisms.

A second major class of heritable factors that may predispose the organism toward particular behavior patterns consists of the anatomical and physiological properties of the *sensory* and *motor* equipment. An animal's behavior is obviously circumscribed by the kind of *motorium,* or complex of potential movements, it inherits, and we have already seen how the *sensorium,* or complex of receptor capacity, is also involved in the organism's behavior. We noted earlier the dependence during breeding of the male stickleback's fighting response upon its perception of a spot of red, normally appearing on the belly of an intruding male fish but just as effective in eliciting a fighting response when presented in other, unfishlike ways. Nest building of birds, where each kind of bird tends to build a nest more or less peculiar to the species, very nicely illustrates the dependence of some behavior upon both sensory and motor properties. Careful study of the type of nests built by a particular bird shows this relationship. Thus certain birds appear to be more attracted by some colors than others, as in the bits of straw or grass available, and are more capable of picking up certain types and sizes of such materials and depositing them in a particular manner. These sensory and motor predispositions can often be correlated with differential sensitivity to wavelength and with the anatomical properties of the claw with regard to picking up objects.

The ethologists have provided us with a rich diversity of interesting and challenging behavioral data. The "hawk–goose phenomenon" nicely illustrates the apparent dependence of basic behavioral processes upon inherited factors. This phenomenon consists of the escape reactions shown by certain birds when the silhouette of a hawk passes overhead and the failure of these reactions to occur when exactly the same silhouette passes overhead but in the opposite direction, simulating a goose. The situation is illustrated in Figure 9-2.

Presumably the fear reaction to the hawklike stimulus has been selected and fixed in the course of evolution of these birds because of the great survival value of the response. The use of simple triangles moving with apex forward or backward does not differentially excite the birds, and the response does not seem to depend on prior experience. It does appear that there is some inherited tendency in certain birds to react with fear to the particular silhouette produced by a predatory hawk flying overhead and not to that produced by a harmless goose, but the basic mechanism of this behavior—that is, precisely *what* is inherited to mediate it—remains to be determined.

CHEMICAL MESSAGES: PHEROMONES. Within recent times research on animal behavior has demonstrated the existence of a new type of behavior determinant. The *pheromone* is a chemical produced by one organism that serves as an indicator or provides a "message" for other members of the species. A good example is the production of certain chemicals by fearful animals, the detection of which by other organisms can produce a similar fearful reaction, even in the absence of the initial alarming stimulus. The production of the pheromone is a hormonal rather than strictly a motor phenomenon, so that its inclusion within the present section really requires a broadening of the present category to "effector" rather than merely

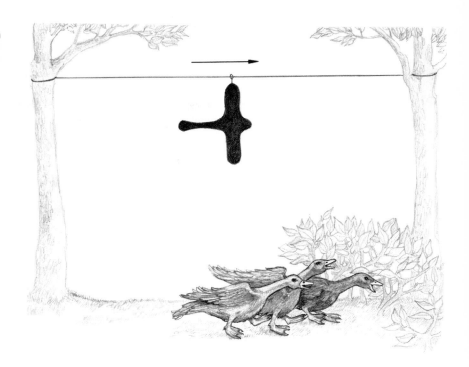

9-2 Hawk–goose phenomenon. When the silhouette is moved in the indicated direction, it resembles a hawk in flight and birds on the ground exhibit alarm. When the silhouette is moved in the opposite direction, it resembles a goose in flight and the ground birds ignore it.

motor processes. On the reception side, the detection of and response to such chemicals may be viewed as clearly sensory in function, much in the way the red spot operates to trigger responses in the male stickleback. The role of chemical communication in the insect world has been studied intensively, and chemical factors have also been recognized in reptiles and fish. However, the discovery of increasing numbers of this kind of chemical messenger in mammalian forms opens up the prospects of a new and potentially quite important kind of primarily "innate" behavior determinant for the higher animals and one in which the influence of environmental variation is normally relatively small.

THEORETICAL POSITIONS

It would be only a mild exaggeration to say that almost as many different points of view exist on the issue of "innate" behavior as there are "experts" of various kinds who have adopted theoretical positions. Rather than attempt to tease out the often subtle differences among these many and varied positions we may briefly describe two of the more extreme views, one from each end of a kind of continuum. We will then present a generalized compromise view that would be at least approximately representative in its major tenets of a majority of the biologists and psychologists who have recently concerned themselves with this basic issue.

INNATE EMPHASIS. The continuum that we are here using is the degree to which the particular theoretical account gives explicit acceptance to the proposition that

261

hereditary (genetic) and environmental (learned) components in behavior can indeed be separately identified. Perhaps the most extreme acceptance of this orthodox position is represented by Konrad Lorenz, the eminent German ethologist. Lorenz holds that there are only two ways in which information about the environment can be provided to the organism: (1) via evolutionary adaptation as this is recorded in the gene pool of the species and (2) via the learning of the individual organism from its sensory experience. Both types of information inputs are always present in the organism, but Lorenz believes that these two sources of information are differentially and often exclusively associated with different kinds of responses. He acknowledges the interplay of sensory input with genetic disposition but still feels that the role of certain unlearned "chunks" of behavior remains, as in the so-called vacuum responses. There are certain presumably "inherited" reactions, such as some of the mating responses in male birds (strutting, for example), that animals exhibit in the absence of the usual stimulating conditions. Among the major ethologists Lorenz thus stands as the strongest proponent of the singularity of hereditary and environmental factors in the determination of behavior.

ENVIRONMENTAL EMPHASIS. The end of the continuum opposite that occupied by Lorenz is occupied by the American-trained Chinese behaviorist Zing Yang Kuo. Kuo saw no need for attempting to sort out alleged "innate" from "acquired" behaviors. Although generally referred to as an extreme "environmentalist," Kuo himself disclaimed this role. Rather, he regarded himself as an "epigenetic behaviorist," by which he meant to convey the general notion that understanding behavior development is dependent upon the analysis and synthesis of a number of different kinds of more molecular approaches. These more basic approaches that contribute to an understanding of behavior are summarized by Kuo as (1) morphological factors, (2) biophysical and biochemical factors, (3) stimulating objects, (4) developmental history, and (5) environmental context. Kuo's epigenetic position stresses the continuity of behavior, as expressed in the phrase "a continuous stream of activity from fertilization to death" (Kuo, 1965, p. 13). His own research has documented the behavioral continuity that is the keystone of his theory.

Kuo borrowed the term *epigenetic* from embryology. It refers to development that is considered to be new, and essentially independent of prior determination; the epigenetic position contrasts with the *preformation* position, according to which development is fixed in advance, or fully determined by genetic blueprints. On the negative side, Kuo objected to many of the observations and conclusions of the ethologists, and in particular Lorenz, on the grounds that they have ignored too many of the behavioral deviations that actually occur. His own long-time observations of fighting in chow dogs, for example, failed to corroborate the generally harmless ending of fights between such dogs in which the dominant dog allows the weaker one to survive unscathed if it lies on the ground and exposes its throat. This presumably innate behavior pattern, more clearly evident in wolves, was seen by Lorenz as evidence for evolutionary adaptation being transmitted through the genes and acting to help preserve the species. Kuo objected that Lorenz overlooked too many other fighting patterns, and remarks that in his own experience "there are also many circumstances in which such a response is an invitation to certain death, as it gives the top dog an opportunity to grab the underdog's throat and shake it until the underdog is dead or at least shows no sign of bodily movement" (Kuo, 1967, p. 20).

INTERACTIONIST POSITION. The more typical position on the nature-nurture issue, and the one that is most often adopted by both English-speaking ethologists and American comparative and experimental psychologists, is essentially an *interactionist* point of view. It holds that all behaviors are joint functions of hereditary (genetic) and environmental (learning) factors. Although for certain purposes one or the other of these two factors may be stressed, their opposition is a remnant of old and misguided assumptions, and neither one can be dispensed with in consideration of any behavior. The behavior geneticists point out that behavior, like all phenotypical features, is of course influenced by genes, but that it is the *differences* in behavior, rather than the behavior itself, that can properly be attributed to genetic control.

Another way of putting this point is to refer to the gene pool of a given population, in accordance with the general position of behavior genetics described earlier in this chapter (cf. Table 9-2). Viewed in this way, heredity certainly imposes some stringent limitations upon behavior. That is, there are no doubt genetically imposed limits upon behavior beyond which environmental variations, no matter how beneficial, cannot push an organism; for example, consider the great difficulty of teaching a chimpanzee to use vocal speech, in contrast to the relative ease of teaching him sign language, as described in Chapter 7, p. 191. This fact suggests that the gene pool from which these organisms have been produced is restricted more with regard to oral mechanisms than with regard to symbolic functions of the kind that underlie language.

Environmental conditions are also capable of imposing limits on behavioral potential. Thus a very poor environment can impose practical limits beyond which an organism's genetic endowment, no matter how rich, cannot go. This issue is especially relevant to the problem of intelligence, and will be treated in depth as a key problem in the heredity–environment interaction.

An informative way of looking at the relationship between hereditary factors and behavior is to correlate particular types of behavior with the phylogenetic level. One such correlation is reproduced in Figure 9-3. The extent of the various modes of adaptive behavior among the invertebrate and vertebrate phyla is schematically indicated. Increasing dependence upon learning and a correspondingly decreasing dependence upon heredity is evident as behavior patterns become more complex. *Taxes,* also called tropisms, are whole-body orientations or forced movements to particular environmental forces (e.g., the flight of a moth into a light source and the climbing response of a young rat up an incline). Taxes are primarily determined by genetic factors. *Reflexes* are defined as relatively simple movements of body parts under appropriate stimulation, and are also generally regarded as primarily genetically determined, but with a greater degree of environmental involvement. *Instincts* differ from reflexes in being more complex, often consisting of rather elaborate chains or patterns of specific behaviors and serving some more important biological function, such as reproduction and thereby survival of the species, as in

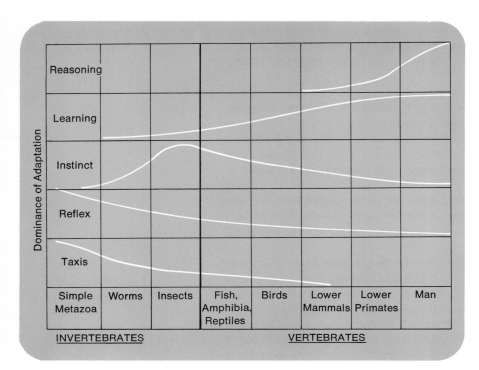

9-3 Schematic portrayal of the changes that take place in the major modes of adaptive behavior in phylogeny. (From Dethier & Stellar, 1970.)

the case of the so-called sexual instincts. Instincts are like reflexes in that they are characteristic of the species (and are perhaps better termed species-specific, in contrast to individual-specific, behaviors). But as we have already seen in our earlier consideration of instincts the role of the environment in such behavior has been shown to be much more extensive than was initially believed, so that they may be regarded as clearer evidence of interaction than either taxes or reflexes. Both *learning* (briefly defined as the change in behavior attributable to behavior itself) and *reasoning* (briefly defined as the solving of problems by manipulation of symbols; cf. Chapter 8) are clearly products of interaction between heredity and environment but with increasing dependence upon the opportunities available in the environment.

HUMAN BEHAVIOR

Man is the most interesting and at the same time the most difficult organism in which the heredity-environment interaction can be studied. He occupies a unique position with regard to this problem not only because of his greater learning and reasoning abilities but also because of the infinitely greater opportunities for learning that are made possible by culture. Alone among animals the human species has produced a substantial cultural heritage that, like genetic or biological heritage, is passed along from one generation to the next. The task of teasing out innate and acquired determinants in human behavior thus becomes correspondingly more difficult.

Taxes, the most relatively "innate" category, do not operate in man, as far as we can now see. Reflexes do play a small and sometimes important part. The role of *instinct* category is shown as minimal, in Figure 9-3, but this estimate is really of limited significance because of the ambiguity of the instinct concept, even with regard to a strictly descriptive usage of the term. Both learning and reasoning, with preponderant contributions from the environment, play obviously maximal roles.

Reflexes

All reflexes have a clear biological basis and may well be considered as essentially "innate." Most vital reflexes (those necessary to life, such as breathing, heartbeat, and the like) as well as some with less significant roles (e.g., sneezing) clearly fit this description. With certain other apparently similar reflexes, however, the picture is not nearly so clear.

The difference seems to lie mainly in the extent to which the given reflex becomes embedded in cultural factors. The prime example here is probably sexual experiences and individual behavior, and specifically the reflexes involved in the sexual act. Even before these were so intensively studied by interview and in the laboratory, the fact that there is an amazing variety of sexually stimulating cues in humans was well established; for example, sexual "fetishes," or quite unusual individualistic kinds of sexually arousing objects (e.g., shoes) were fairly commonplace in the clinical literature. With the new openness in Western society, and particularly in the United States, with regard to sexual matters, the extent of the variation from "normal" sexual practice has become more apparent. Although there is no general agreement among scientists as to the effective determinants in, for example, homosexuality, most authorities leave room for substantial contributions of both the genetic and the environmental sort.

Basic Psychological Processes

Although it would be foolhardy indeed to attempt any very meaningful generalization about all the basic psychological processes with regard to the heredity-environment problem, it is nonetheless quite clear that both factors play a substantial role. The details of this role are treated in other chapters. For example, visual research has demonstrated evidence for functions that are sometimes independent of and sometimes dependent upon experience (cf. Chapter 6). In the study of motivation (Chapter 14) it has long been customary to distinguish between "primary" and "secondary" needs on the basis of a dichotomy between inherited and learned conditions. And learning itself (Chapter 11) has been shown to have restrictions imposed by genetic determinants that can be quite striking.

Complex Psychological Processes

Formerly labeled "higher mental processes," complex psychological processes were for a time largely ignored by American psychology. As the influence of the early Watsonian behaviorism, and the subsequent positivistic movement colorfully referred to as "dust-bowl empiricism," waned, renewed interest generally developed in such problems as thinking and cognition. The research of Piaget on cognitive development began to receive more respectful attention, and it was generally regarded as providing support for the critical contribution of innate factors. Psychologists began to look more closely at the fascinating problem of human language, partly in collaboration and partly in competition with linguists. Because the controversy concerning language is in certain ways highly instructive for the heredity-environment problem, we digress at this point to treat it in more depth.

Language

The history of the psychological approach to the problem of language can be summarized quite briefly. For the behaviorists, language has typically been viewed as learned through a form of conditioning. Watson early advanced an interpretation that involved simple classical conditioning whereby the infant's early babbling sounds are repeated back to him by parents and other adults and associated with the appropriate objects in the environment. More recently Skinner has offered a much more refined theoretical account in which language learning is held to be in essence no different from other kinds of behavior. As the study of linguistics developed, however, these conditioning views were rejected as too simplistic, first by linguists and later by psycholinguists (the name used for those who are trained in one or the other of the two disciplines but are substantially at home in each and concentrate on the study of language). The linguist Noam Chomsky in particular was widely influential in his attack upon Skinner's views as being totally inadequate to account for the subtlety and intricacy of grammar. Chomsky and a great many experts in the field have concluded that language is not learned and hence must be in some way an inherited function.

It is no tribute to psychology that this latter position, which at best must be regarded as essentially negative in character, was so long allowed to stand substantially unrebutted. Only recently have effective rebuttals been presented. The gist of these is that cognitive learning rather than conditioning can be utilized to help account for the acquisition of language and that prematurely attempting to separate out the contribution of inherited and experiential factors in this kind of behavior is inadvisable. The interaction position has been wisely expressed in the following passage:

> It is clear that man is born to talk, innately provided both with the capacity and with a motivation, almost a *need*, to learn, at least in the case of native language. . . . In behavior that depends on perception and thought, the relation of constitution to experience is multiplicative rather than additive; to ask which is more important is like asking which contributes more to the area of a field—its length or its breadth. . . . Both are of 100 percent importance, even when one is a greater source of variance than the other, and their relation is such that one must understand both to understand either [Hebb, Lambert, and Tucker, 1971, pp. 213-214].

Hebb et al. proceed to discuss the manner in which certain of the major problems in language learning might profitably be attacked. The value of this kind of interpretation lies not in the fact that it has succeeded in providing irrefutable evidence of learning of language, but in the fact that it is a more realistic and potentially profitable point of view that is clearly expressed as an alternative to the extreme environmentalism of some of the learning theorists and the mystic acceptance of a crude nativism by so many linguists. Working out the details of acquisition of language will not be an easy task but at least the scientist should be pointed in a direction that offers some promise of ultimate success.

Personality and Social Interaction

Again the interactionist position is essential to a clear understanding of the basic problem presented by personality and social interaction. It has been succinctly expressed as follows:

We do not propose that genetic transmission determines specific form of detailed social interaction. The problem is not that simple and the answer is predictably multifactorial. We do assert that we can now begin to know—not what the human animal is going to do—but what it is likely to do. Because of the animals we are, we can try to predict what is easy for human animals to learn; and because of what we are not, we can try to outline what is difficult for us [Tiger and Fox, 1971, p. 27].

With regard to some of the more specific problems in this area, at least one personality factor is usually accorded a broad constitutional basis. This is temperament, the chronic emotional level of an individual. On the other end of the heredity–environment continuum, the host of specific details of attitude and belief (political, religious, and the like) must, like the details of whichever language is learned, be granted a heavy environmental determination. In between, there are many personality traits in which the relative contributions of innate and acquired factors are evident but not easily separated. Indeed, one of the more fascinating general problems in this particular area concerns whether peculiar modes of response (as in thinking) are in fact substantially transmitted genetically, as casual observation of familial similarities often suggests. The many difficulties of performing the experimental research required for a solution of this problem, with adequate control and manipulation of environmental as well as genetic variables, preclude any quick and easy answer and suggest that the problem will be with us for a long period of time.

INTELLIGENCE

From the standpoint of contrasting the roles of heredity and environment, there are few problems as relevant as intelligence and its testing. This problem has probably aroused more emotion, with no clear signs of abatement, than any other single issue in psychology. Intelligence testing is an especially controversial matter because of its ramifications in political and social, ethical and educational, and legal and economic matters. The recent emphasis upon minority rights has spotlighted the use of intelligence tests as selection devices in education especially and intensified the question of whether the presently available instruments can ever be fairly

Take a Breather

THE CHITLINGS INTELLIGENCE TEST

Most authorities now agree that it is impossible to devise an intelligence test that is completely free of bias and equally fair to all social and cultural groups. The bias occurs because all test materials must use items of information with which various cultural groups are differentially familiar. Because most test constructors and most of the subjects tested have been from the white middle class, the typical intelligence test is generally assumed to be relatively biased against the blacks in American society.

To demonstrate how difficult it is to make a reasonably accurate showing with unfamiliar test materials, regardless of how intelligent one might be, try answering the following test items. They are taken from the Dove Counterbalance Intelligence Test, devised by a social worker in a black community. Write your answers on a scrap of paper and refer to the box on p. 270 for the scoring key. (This exercise assumes that the reader is unfamiliar with black ghetto culture; otherwise, obviously, its impact is likely to be substantially reduced.)

1. Which word is out of place here? (a) Splib, (b) Blood, (c) Grey, (d) Spook, (e) Black.
2. A "Handkerchief head" is (a) a cool cat, (b) a porter, (c) an "Uncle Tom," (d) a hoddi, (e) a "preacher."
3. Cheap "chitlings" . . . will taste rubbery unless they are cooked long enough. How soon can you quit cooking them to eat and enjoy them? (a) 15 minutes, (b) 2 hours, (c) 24 hours, (d) 1 week (on a low flame), (e) 1 hour.
4. Hattie Mae Johnson is on the county. She has four children and her husband is now in jail for nonsupport, as he was unemployed and was not able to give her any money. Her welfare check is now $286 per month. Last night she went out with the biggest player in town. If she got pregnant, then, nine months from now, by how much will her welfare check change? (a) $80 more, (b) $2 less, (c) $35 more, (d) $150 more, (e) $100 more.
5. "Hully Gully" came from (a) "East Oakland," (b) Fillmore, (c) Watts, (d) Harlem, (e) Motor City.

applied to persons who have not had the advantages offered by the middle-class white environment from which have come the majority of the subjects on whom these instruments were developed.

The controversy has been stirred anew within recent years by the publication of a particularly provocative scholarly article, by an educational psychologist, Arthur Jensen. After a thorough review of the voluminous literature on the issue of genetic transmission of intelligence, with special regard to white-black differences in American culture, Jensen concluded that the black population is probably about 15 IQ points inferior, on the average, and should possibly be provided with a different kind of educational program. This conclusion was vehemently opposed by large numbers of psychologists, among others, and the result has been a considerable airing of the issue and a reconsideration of many of its manifold facets.

The present discussion begins with a consideration of the problem of defining intelligence. After a brief account of the history of intelligence testing, it will proceed to the various kinds of evidence in support of heritability, and the criticisms of this evidence, before closing with a consideration of the theoretical and practical implications of all these matters. As suggested above, this problem is explored in depth not only because of its intrinsic importance but also because of the way in which it permits a full analysis of the intricacies of the heredity-environment interaction. Only those technical aspects of intelligence testing that are directly relevant to the present concern are considered here; the remaining aspects, and a more thoroughgoing treatment of testing generally and other types of tests, are presented in Supplement A-5.

Definitions

"Intelligence is what the intelligence test measures." This prime example of an "operational" definition is among the most ridiculed, if occasionally defended, of all definitions in psychology. Most such ridicule is misplaced. Any operational definition has one, and only one, purpose: clarity of communication. Thus although it may be rightfully accused of being tautological, the operational definition quoted is nonetheless correct. It is used so commonly mainly because it is needed as a reminder of the facts of scientific life. The major reason for objecting to this definition is the perfectly correct belief that there is more to "intelligence" than what is measured by any test. As most of us ordinarily think of the term, *intelligence* refers to the *relative* quickness with which an individual organism *understands,* especially but by no means exclusively with regard to problem situations with symbolic representation. Colloquially, the ability to "catch on," assuming adequate sensory functions and background experience, is what is involved. More broadly, intelligence relates to an individual's ability to solve problems, especially again with reference to reasoning or the use of symbolic operations. Finally, in its broadest usage, intelligence refers to an organism's generalized adaptive ability (although this usage clearly involves a number of processes, such as sensory and motor functions, which are not normally included in the sharper definitions).

There is nothing "wrong" about these various definitions, as long as one can make clear to others how he is using the term. Their weakness is in relation to their measurement and their utility in the development of scientific propositions. It is at just this point that the more prosaic but more exact operational definition comes into the picture; we need to measure intelligence, or any other organismic variable, by particular empirical situations. Just as the experiment is a specific kind of controlled observation, so the test is a specific type of highly circumscribed observational situation. It is necessary to sample a person's behavior in order to estimate his intelligence (or some other trait) because we simply do not have the time needed to make the long-term observations on individuals that will tell us more fully than most tests what we want to know about them. There are just too many individuals to be evaluated, and too few psychologists, or other appropriately trained professionals, all with limited working time.

Viewed in this way, defining intelligence as what is measured by one's test instrument is fairly obvious but certainly not foolish. Moreover, it does not mean that the tester or the scientist using test results believes that this is all there is in intelligence. He knows, or should know, as well as anyone else that he is working with only one segment of a very broad and pervasive concept. But if understandable scientific propositions are to be developed and critically evaluated by others, as they must be if science is to advance, then the narrow but empirically and conceptually manipulable operational definition must be used as a complement to the more commonsensical but less usable ordinary definition.

Breather Interpretation

THE CHITLINGS INTELLIGENCE TEST

All correct answers are (c).

Testing Intelligence

If intelligence *is* (for certain scientific purposes at least) what the intelligence test tests, then just what is it that is tested?

The first widely used intelligence test was devised by the French psychologist Alfred Binet, in collaboration with a French physician, Theodore Simon, in the early 1900's. Their Binet-Simon scale was the result of the formation of a commission, of which Binet was a member, whose charge was the development of techniques that could be used in the diagnosis of mental retardation in French school-children.

Discarding the use of simple sensorimotor tasks and instrumentation then popular in the psychological laboratory, Binet and Simon worked up a *battery* of graded problems whose presentation and solution required mainly paper and pencil and some common objects. They also developed a scoring technique by means of which an individual's successful performances on the various test items, graded according to age normally required for success, were accumulated to produce a "mental age" representing his overall achievement.

This age-scale concept was quickly adopted in other countries. In the United States L. M. Terman at Stanford University produced an American version, the Stanford–Binet Scale, which has proved to be both the most popular individually administered intelligence test and the prototype from which most other tests, both group and individual, have been developed.

Several fundamental characteristics of this type of intelligence test need to be reviewed. First, like any behavior sample, the typical intelligence test is a direct measure of *achievement;* it measures in essence what the testee has learned. As a kind of general aptitude test, however, it differs from an achievement test per se in that its objective is to predict from selected small behavior samples the much wider behavior potential of the individual testee. Second, to be generally useful it must have the twin properties of *reliability* and *validity*. A reliable test is one that can be depended upon to give at least approximately the same result on successive administrations, assuming no significant changes in the testee or the testing conditions. A valid test is one that in fact measures what it purports to measure. Reliability is most simply evaluated by repeating the test (or by somewhat subtler devices, such as correlating one half of the items with the other half, called the split-half measure). Validity is usually evaluated by correlating test results with some independent criterion; in the case of intelligence, teacher's ratings or school grades might be used. The procedure by which test reliability and validity are developed, along with the selection of items to be used in the final test, is called the *standardization* of the test. Once a particular test, such as the Stanford–Binet, has been developed and accepted it can be used as a criterion against which other new and different tests (e.g., group rather than individual) can be evaluated. It is important to keep this description of the intelligence test well in mind, because some of the most trenchant criticisms of the alleged misuse of intelligence tests depend upon a clear grasp of these simple characteristics.

AN ANALOGY: MEASURING HEALTH. It may be helpful at this point to digress a bit and consider a somewhat analogous problem in the field of biology, that of estimating the general health of an individual. The fact that many of the particular problems connected with the measurement of health as a general concept are essentially the same as those found in estimating intelligence as a general concept should facilitate the understanding of the basic difficulties in the latter case.

Like the intelligence of an individual, his health cannot be adequately indicated by any single empirical measure. This fact tends to make health, like intelligence, an elusive but important concept. The solution is to use a battery of measures (e.g., pulse, blood pressure, body temperature, and the like). General health, like general intelligence, is a relative rather than an absolute concept. That is, for the great majority of individuals, in whom there is no overwhelming injury or disease present, a physician uses norms, or standards based upon a frequency distribution of results, much as the psychologist uses norms in working up a single test score, or a group of test scores, related to his subject's performance. There is a greater tendency in the case of health to apply absolute standards (such as a pulse of 72 heartbeats per minute), but this is really done in a rough and approximate manner. The more exact biochemical measures, such as are now often obtained in automated analyses of the blood, must still be evaluated as a part of the overall picture by the physician.

Like most analogies, this analogy breaks down in numerous respects, such as with regard to the dependence in medicine on negative cases, such as serious disease, to which severe mental retardation does not seem comparable. But for the majority of persons both of these important generalized concepts can only be evaluated by specific empirical samplings, so that predictions as to future conditions can be reliably made in the absence of continuous expert observation, which is not feasible. Dependence upon friends and relatives, who are in the position of being able to make long-term, continuing observations, is also not feasible. In either case, the operation of biases of various sorts makes conclusions suspect, although it is true that much more than chance success should be achieved in this way. For the more exacting quantitative demands of scientific experimentation and theorizing, however, more specific data are needed.

Evidence for Heritability

In lieu of the direct breeding manipulations that are not feasible for human subjects the researcher interested in assessing the contribution of heredity to intelligence has tended to utilize the "natural experiments" involving twins. A careful distinction between the two major kinds of twins is necessary in this research. *Fraternal* twins come from two eggs, which happen to be fertilized independently. They are no more closely related genetically than any pair of siblings and are just as likely to be of opposite sex as of the same sex. *Identical* twins, on the other hand, are the result of the complete separation of the two cells produced at the first cell division (mitosis) of the fertilized egg or shortly thereafter. Identical twins therefore have exactly the same hereditary makeup and are always of the same sex. Because they come from two fertilized eggs, or zygotes, fraternal twins are technically referred to as dizygotic, whereas identical twins, coming from a single egg, are called monozygotic.

Fraternal and identical twins can be separately identified on the basis of various anatomical and physiological measures. Comparison of the two types of twins has consistently indicated that identical twins resemble each other more closely on intelligence test scores (as well as on a number of other behavioral samples) than do fraternal twins. Such evidence suggests the importance of hereditary determinants in intelligence, but it cannot be regarded as conclusive, because of the fact that identical twins also seem to share a more similar environment than fraternal twins. That is, because they usually look so much more alike they tend to be treated more similarly (as, for instance, by being dressed in an identical manner). This kind of comparison therefore cannot be accorded the kind of confidence that it might at first glance appear to merit, and other more subtle kinds of comparisons must be made to evaluate the role of heredity in intellectual functioning.

In one early study nineteen pairs of identical twins who were raised in separate homes were tested. The results were compared with those from both identical twins and fraternal twins raised together. In general, it was found that the earlier the separation and the greater the difference between the environments in which the two twins were raised, the greater the deviation in intelligence test scores (to a maximum of twenty-four IQ points for two girls separated at eighteen months into very different home settings). Even so, the mean difference was only eight IQ points, compared with means of approximately six IQ points for identical twins reared together and ten IQ points for fraternal twins reared together.

The conclusion that is usually drawn from data of this sort, where relationships among intelligence test scores are higher for closely related than they are for more remotely related individuals, is that heredity plays a more important role than environment in accounting for the variation in intelligence. But most of these studies are limited in that they do not really include an adequate measure of environment, so that conclusions concerning its role cannot be drawn with much confidence.

REBUTTALS TO HEREDITARIAN ACCOUNTS. The main burden of the argument against the typical evidence for hereditary influence in intelligence is that the intelligence test scales that have been most commonly used are not appropriate for certain social classes and racial groups. They were almost without exception standardized on groups of middle-class white children; minority groups were unrepresented. Thus the content of the test items is drawn exclusively from the life experiences of middle-class white children and so is distinctly unfamiliar to lower-class children, particularly if they are black and have been reared in a different subculture. The assumption of the test that all the testees have had approximately equivalent opportunity to learn to do the things that are asked by the test is not met.

Some efforts have been made to develop and use culture-free or culture-fair tests, particularly those involving performance (that is, nonverbal responses). But those have thus far been used only on a limited basis. There is certainly a need for a black intelligence test, and with the new emphasis on black studies some such instrument seems destined to appear.

Certain lines of evidence are commonly used in support of the general position that the tests in use are heavily biased against minority groups, particularly blacks. During the World War I, when the testing movement was given its first impetus, the Army Alpha was developed as a quick test of general intelligence for use in the classification of recruits. Black soldiers from Northern states actually made higher average scores than white soldiers from Southern states (with Northern whites at the top and Southern blacks at the bottom). The clear implication of these data is that they reflect the environmental differences then existing between North and South with respect to educational opportunities.

Gains in intelligence test scores occurring as a function of the length of time spent in presumably superior Northern schools have also been cited as evidence of the substantial role of environmental factors. In the Philadelphia schools, for example, the test scores of Southern-born black schoolchildren were found to improve regularly with increasing years of attendance. Thus black children showed IQ's averaging, from lower grades through grade 6, 85.5, 89.3, 91.8, and 93.3. The conclusion that there is a substantial environmental contribution is inescapable.

Evidence of Interaction

A recent investigation that has utilized at least gross measures of environmental as well as hereditary variables has produced results that help to clarify their respective roles insofar as the usual intelligence test is concerned. Because this study delineates some of the ways in which hereditary and environmental variables interact, the procedure and the interpretation of results will be reviewed in depth.

The study surveyed more than a quarter of a million schoolchildren enrolled in April, 1968, in the first twelve grades of the public school system in Philadelphia. The researcher identified 3,042 as twins (when they had the same last name, birth date, and home address) and proceeded to carry out a thorough analysis of their aptitude-test performance and their home environment as related to their status as monozygotic (identical) or dizygotic (fraternal) twins, and race (about two-thirds black, and one-third white).

The study was designed to evaluate two contrasting contemporary theoretical accounts of the commonly observed difference in intelligence test scores between relatively high and relatively low socioeconomic classes and between whites and blacks. One of these was designated as the "environmental disadvantage hypothesis [which] assumes that lower-class whites and blacks live under suppressive . . . conditions for the development of IQ," and the other as "the genetic differences hypothesis [in which] social class differences in mean IQ are assumed to be principally genetic in origin and to result from the high heritability of IQ throughout the population. . . . [with] environmental differences between social class groups [and races] . . . seen as insignificant in determining total phenotypic variation in IQ" (Scarr-Salapatek, 1971a, p. 1286).

Although the details of the statistical treatments utilized are well beyond the scope of this book, we can summarize the manner in which this investigator obtained data from the formidable number of subjects used. Because of the practical difficulties in direct determination of zygosity in the twins, this key characteristic, which was used as a direct measure of the heredity factor, was estimated by a commonly used statistical procedure based upon the proportions of same-sex to opposite-sex frequencies in the various groups studied. Standard educational aptitude and achievement tests, with nonverbal as well as verbal components, were available in the school records. Finally, each pair of twins was assigned to a relatively advantaged or disadvantaged environmental category. This environmental measure was derived by an evaluation of home addresses in terms of the 1960 U.S. Census information for the various urban tracts involved without regard to race. Each pair of twins was assigned to one of three socioeconomic groups: a below-median group, in which both educational and income levels for their neighborhood were below the median of all the census tracts used in the study; a median group, in which one or the other of these two measures was below the median; and an above-median group, in which both measures were above the median.

The results of this comprehensive study do not provide unambiguous support for either of the opposing hypotheses outlined above. They are especially embarrassing to an extreme view of either type: a naive hereditarian view, which holds the IQ or similar ability measure to be a fixed product of one's heredity and essentially unalterable by environmental variations, or an equally naive environmentalistic view, which holds environmental variation to be the exclusive determinant. However, the results are extremely valuable in that they indicate clearly an important *interaction* between the effects of hereditary and environmental determinants: *the role of heredity becomes increasingly significant as the environment improves.* That is, the variance attributable to genetic differences is very slight in the disadvantaged groups, both white and black, but relatively substantial in the advantaged groups. The author's conclusion is, "If all children had optimal environments for development, then genetic differences would account for most of the variance in behavior . . . equality of opportunity leads to bigger and better genotype–phenotype correlations" (Scarr-Salapatek, 1971a, p. 1294).

In buttressing her interpretation of these illuminating results, this investigator cites several earlier reports. A number of these deal with an analysis of the disadvantaged environment as it relates to racial differences. The gist of these is that the relevance of the home environment for scholastic work is significantly greater in the white culture than in the black. In other words, black children are typically more dependent for intellectual stimulation and support upon their classroom than are white children.

Research on animals is relevant to these issues. For example, it has been shown that "suppressive" environments (normal unadorned cages) for mice reduce not only performance scores but also phenotypic variability and genetic variance. Mice with "enriched environments" showed both much superior learning and four times as much variance attributable to heredity. The parallel with the human intelligence data is apparent.

SOME PRACTICAL IMPLICATIONS. In a controversial review paper by Jensen it was suggested that if, in fact, black genetic potential is inferior to white in the United States—that is, if the typical group difference averaging about 15 IQ points is accepted as reflecting a true population difference—then perhaps we should accommodate our educational program to the realities of intellectual function. Black students, only 15 per cent of whom surpass the mean white score by the reviewer's estimate, might be offered less abstract and more practical educational fare.

This suggestion was based upon postulation of two levels of intellectual functioning. Level I consists of relatively straightforward formation of associations, such as that involved in memorizing or in simple trial-and-error learning. This kind of cognitive activity is typical of the lower primary grades, where black–white differences are relatively small. Level II includes various forms of more complex symbolic learning in which stimulus transformations are required. This is the kind of cognitive activity required in the higher school grades, where black–white IQ differences typically are found to widen. The suggestion was that we adjust our educational programs to the genetic potential of individuals by training blacks primarily at Level I, on the assumption that they are probably less able to cope satisfactorily with Level II kinds of problems.

This facet of the report has stirred up more emotional reaction than the more cautious suggestion that we accept the face validity (appearances) of the white-black IQ comparisons as probably indicative of an underlying genetic difference. The proposal has been vigorously refuted, for one instance, by a former student of the famous Swiss psychologist Jean Piaget. This application of Piagetian principles to the heredity–environment issue not only serves to refute the hereditarian thesis but, in a more positive way, also provides a radically different approach to the problem. It thus merits careful consideration.

The heart of the Piagetian approach is to emphasize the development of certain key cognitive (thinking) processes as functional bases of intellectual activities. It was pointed out that within Piaget's framework "if we really want children to learn it is the *process* of interacting with the environment which must be emphasized rather than a specific response already decided upon by the teacher" (Voyat, 1969, p. 86). When these fundamental cognitive processes (described in detail in Chapter 10) are tested in experiments in countries outside the Western world, the same developmental sequence is found regardless of cultural and racial differences. Thus it was observed that, "the stages are respected in their succession and do not permit, even in a theoretical continuum, division into the type of level differences that Jensen describes, and they most strongly suggest the irrelevance of these genotypically distinct basic processes" (Voyat, 1969, p. 75).

Persuasive as these observations may be with regard to the theoretical interpretation of racial dichotomies, the fact remains that scores on the more static type of task used in the ordinary intelligence test correlate very substantially with success in the higher educational and professional tasks of the white affluent culture upon whose children the tests were originally developed. This fact poses a serious dilemma for black educators and others who are sympathetic to the plight of the minority groups. Even if they are correct in condemning the severe bias built into the testing instruments, some way must be found of improving both the educational and the selection procedures for minority groups so that the more capable individuals can more effectively compete for the rewards of higher-level professional training in our society. Those who feel that an individual is to be treated in accordance with his own achievements and potential regardless of his racial or national origin are not likely to be sympathetic toward any such racially bound scheme as Jensen's proposal described above, even if really controlled evidence in support of its underlying propositions were available.

One last practical implication remains to be discussed. This concerns the dire prediction, emphasized especially by proponents of the genetic-deficit hypothesis, that because of the significantly higher birth rate ordinarily found in the lower socioeconomic classes and the allegedly inferior races, there will be a progressive reduction in the intellectual potential of our society. Happily, such predictions seem unwarranted. Empirical determinations of average IQ's in school populations in various places have generally shown increments rather than decrements. For example, one of the more outspoken advocates of the genetic-deficit position predicted the average loss of approximately one IQ point per decade, characterized as a "galloping plunge toward intellectual bankruptcy" (Cattell, 1937). Some thirteen years later, however, he himself reported data showing an average gain of more than one IQ point (Cattell, 1950).

A related "natural experiment" has been cited as providing strong evidence against any easy eugenic approach to human ability. Thus an eminent geneticist has made this comment on the caste system in India:

India has performed the grandest genetic experiment ever attempted with human materials. For possibly as long as 100 generations, people were bred for genetic specialization in different occupations. . . . It appears . . . that the "experiment" turned out to be a failure, in the sense that the castes have not become genetically specialized for their respective occupations. Modern India has discovered that the low castes contain at least some individuals capable of performing quite creditably the functions heretofore reserved for the high ones; and it has also discovered that the converse is true [Dobzhansky, 1962, p. 113].

The Fundamental Problem: A Summing Up

By way of summing up the relationships in the heredity-environment issue as it relates to intelligence we may now look more closely at some of the measurement problems involved in any empirical attempt to produce definitive data. These problems are so immense that one researcher has stated that "there is little to be gained from approaching the nature-nurture problem of race differences in IQ directly" (Scarr-Salapatek, 1971b, p. 1226).

The problem can be made more manageable, with respect to understanding the fundamental difficulties (a major objective of the present treatment), by looking at each of the major variables separately.

1. The *behavior sample,* or test. If our measure of intelligence is to correlate satisfactorily with external criteria (that is, have adequate test validity), then it almost certainly must be broadly based and must sample a variety of behavioral situations. But as has been pointed out by the behavioral geneticists, such broad-spectrum measures cannot at the same time be "very precise measures of biological differences, which . . . should prove to be relatively fine grained" (Hirsch, 1967b, p. 127).

2. The *genotype*. Any broadly based behavioral function must be polygenic, as just indicated. In other words, it will be determined by a large number of separate genes. The fact that certain severe intellectual deficits (e.g., mongolism, a form of retardation) are monogenic is to be accounted for on the basis of specific metabolic abnormality in these unfortunate cases and seems to have no implication for the problem of variations in "normal" intellectual function.

3. The *environment*. Although we can make some very rough guesses about the kinds of environmental variables that are favorable to optimal intellectual growth, we have not yet been able to pinpoint the exact conditions that are most effective in this respect. Until and unless we can do so, assessment of environmental adequacy cannot readily advance beyond very gross estimates, such as the trichotomy (above, at, or below median) described earlier. Furthermore, as long as our behavioral samples remain broadly based, it seems most probable that the correlated environmental variables will also be correspondingly broad, so that a large number of different kinds of determining conditions, rather than one or two, can be anticipated.

From this summary it can be seen that each of the three major variables involved in this problem is likely to be composed of a blend or mosaic of many specific factors. The difficulties of measurement are compounded when an equally complex dimension, such as "race," is introduced into the problem, because of the mixture of gene populations resulting from interbreeding.

Only one remote possibility may be envisioned at present for breaking through the complexities of this situation. This would be the discovery of one or more fundamental modes of intellectual function that can be directly attributed to specific types of brain structure or function, which in turn might each be associated with a relatively small number of single genes. But this possibility must be regarded as extremely remote.

In the meantime less than perfect approximations to regular relationships can be developed, as evidenced by the recent study by Scarr-Salapatek, and more definitive experimental and conceptual attacks upon circumscribed facets of the basic problem can be anticipated. Practically, however, we may expect that *euthenic* (environmental improvement) programs will not prove to be any easier to apply (although socially perhaps more respectable) than *eugenic* (genetic improvement by selected mating) programs. Recent experience with the short-term Head Start project demonstrates this point; disappointingly small gains in IQ occurred. Those familiar with the underlying complexities of this problem should not expect too much in the way of truly definitive conclusions and should be able to resist the strong pressure from diverse political and social forces to adopt an absolute theoretical position one way or the other. On this point we can do no better than to end our treatment of this important social issue by quoting an already much-quoted comment: "to assert, despite the absence of evidence, and in the present social climate, that a particular race is genetically disfavored in intelligence is to scream 'FIRE . . . I think' in a crowded theater. Given that so little is known, further scientific study seems far more justifiable than public speculations" (Scarr-Salapatek, 1971b, p. 1228).

Notes

Dichotomizing "nature" and "nurture" has been strongly opposed as unduly restrictive and misleading by many writers (e.g., Lehrman 1970). Much of this criticism has been directed against the ethologist Lorenz, whose comprehensive statement of a theoretical sort appears in his 1965 book. Lorenz has been the target for this criticism because of his long-standing position that complex behavior can be broken up into components that are clearly identifiable as either inherited or learned. The opposing and more generally acceptable position argues that both hereditary and environmental factors typically contribute to the same components at all stages of development. Hailmon's 1969 essay, describing the development of feeding behavior in the sea-gull chick, illustrates such interaction very nicely. Greenough's 1973 reader on nature and nurture focuses on developmental biology.

Classic Experiments
Stockard performed the early (1909) cyclopean manipulation of fish; more recently Rogers (1957) has demonstrated that such eyes are functional. Gold-schmidt performed the early research on phenocopies.

Instincts and Drives
The book by McDougall that marked the culmination of the instinct-listing movement was his *An Introduction to Social Psychology* (1923). The instinct doctrine as applied to human behavior was vigorously and effectively attacked by the behavioristically oriented sociologist L. L. Bernard, in his *Introduction to Social Psychology* (1926). Woodworth's classic work, which helped to stimulate use of the drive concept, was *Dynamic Psychology* (1918). A comprehensive attempt to revive instinct theory in the light of contemporary comparative psychology and ethology has been made by Fletcher in his *Instinct in Man* (1957).

Biological contributions to human psychology in which genetic determinants are stressed have recently become popular. The best known of these, and the one that was mainly responsible for starting the vogue, is Desmond Morris's *The Naked Ape* (1967a). Although not well received by many biologists, who objected particularly to its immoderately speculative aspects, it was nevertheless immensely successful as a popular book. Several similar books by Robert Ardrey have also achieved best-seller status, most recently his *Social Contract* (1970). His earlier work was focused on the concept of territoriality, *Territorial Imperative* (1966). Morris has also recently edited a book on primate ethology (1967b), a topic that has begun to enjoy popular as well as scientific attention; another collection of such papers is available in *Man and Beast* (Eisenberg and Dillon, 1971). Authors with the unlikely names of Tiger and Fox have produced a similar but less objectionable approach to human behavior, *The Imperial Animal* (1971), written from an anthropological vantage point. Fox (1973) has also edited a reader.

The various attempts to reduce complex human social behavior to basic biological determinants have been much more influential with the general public than they have been with the scientific community. Singling out Lorenz, Ardry, and Morris, for example, the anthropologist Alland, in his *The Human Imperative* (1972), has attempted to provide a better balance in the picture by demonstrating the force of the cultural determinants overlooked by the popularizers; cf. also Montague's 1970 book. Lorenz himself (1970), in the introduction to the first of three projected volumes translated into English, has strongly attacked Morris and Ardrey, among others. A refreshing essay by the psychiatrist Eisenberg (1972) is worth consulting for its succinct yet effective rebuttal of the contemporary instinctivists who overlook the human (cultural) and the environmental contributions to human behavior. Two popular books stressing cultural factors have been published by the social psychologist Aronson, *The Social Animal* (1972) and a reader (1973) on the same topic.

Sexual Behavior

The classic works on this topic are Kinsey, Pomeroy, and Martin, *Sexual Behavior in the Human Male* (1948) and Masters and Johnson, *Human Sexual Response* (1966), which utilize the interview and the direct laboratory technique, respectively. Frank Beach's *Sex and Behavior* (1956) offers a broader look at the great variety of behavioral variations involving sex in man and infrahuman animals. In spite of its suggestive title, *Intimate Behavior,* the most recent book by Morris (1971), touches on a broad range of tactually related topics beyond the obvious sexually relevant ones. Additional comments and references related to sexual behavior can be found in Chapter 15 and Supplement B-6.

Heritability of Attitudes

The Swiss psychiatrist Carl Jung (1956) developed what is probably the most elaborate account of inherited attitudinal predispositions in all of psychology. Reasoning mainly from his analysis of the commonalities found in myths and artistic productions of many various cultures, Jung postulated that each man carries within him a kind of "collective unconscious." This heritage has been shaped by man's evolution. It is mediated by what Jung labeled "archetypes," which are universally observed and symbolically represented tendencies to perceive and act in specific ways. Examples are vital stages, such as birth and death, and such concepts as God, hero, and the like. Jung felt that the striking commonalities among the symbolic expressions of isolated cultures required the assumption of evolutionary influence, somehow acting upon man's genetic heritage. An alternative point of view, of course, is to point to the fundamental similarity in man's experience in all societies, his propensity for cultural transmission by oral if not written symbol. (It is interesting in this respect that very little in the way of even the simplest cultural inheritance has been observed in the other higher primates; the best and most frequently cited instance would possibly be the sweet potato washing and similar food-related behaviors that have been observed to be socially transmitted after incidental individual development in various free-ranging troops of Japanese macaques; see Kawamura, 1959.) Although Jung's work has never exactly caught on with the mainstream of behavioristically oriented American psychology, he has nonetheless had considerable, and increasing, popular influence as well as some strong support in clinical circles as a psychoanalytic alternative to Freud.

Ethology

The initial naturalistic observations that led to the modern ethology movement are often reported to be those made around 1900 by such zoologists as Charles Whitman in this country and Oskar Heinroth in Europe. The two men given most credit for the modern movement, however, are Konrad Lorenz, a German zoologist, and Niko Tinbergen, a Dutch zoologist who has spent most of his career in England. Lorenz is internationally known for his pioneering work on imprinting in birds and is familiar to newspaper and magazine readers in many countries because of the widely circulated photographs of him being followed by ducks that have been imprinted on him. The books in English most relevant to the text discussion of Lorenz's views on heritability of behavior are his *Evolution and Modification of Behavior* (1965) and the 1970 volume mentioned earlier. Lorenz's most popular book is *The Study of Instinct* (1951); his 1970 book is the first volume of a projected set, and Hall's (1974) "conversation" with Tinbergen is interesting and informative. It is worth remarking that the first Nobel prizes ever awarded for behavioral research were given in 1973 to Lorenz and Tinbergen, along with the German biologist von Frisch for his work on communication among bees.

The experiment that demonstrated the inefficacy of the triangle stimulus as compared with the hawk–goose silhouette was reported by Green, Green, and Carr (1966).

Genetics and Behavior

Useful reference sources on behavior genetics, although of a technical rather than practical character, are *Behavior-Genetic Analysis* by Hirsch (1967a) and *Genetic Diversity and Human Behavior* by Spuhler (1967). Books by Manosevitz, Lindzey, and Thiessen (1969) and Lindzey and Thiessen (1970), and an essay by Vale (1973) are also instructive. Ludmerer (1972) has provided a historical appraisal of genetics, showing its amenability to social influences. A number of other treatments of contemporary genetics, with considerable relevance for psychology, are noted at the end of Chapter 13 and in Supplement A-2.

Kuo's Epigenetic Behaviorism

Kuo's *The Dynamics of Behavior Development* (1967) is the best single source of his theoretical notions and description of his many ingenious and interesting empirical researches. It contains references to the early chick-embryo and rodent-killing projects as well as the observations of dog fighting that are described in the text.

Language

Skinner's behavioristic treatment (1957) was scathingly reviewed by Chomsky (1959), who has elsewhere (1972) published his own views on grammatical transformation. A defense of Skinner has recently appeared (MacCorquodale, 1970), as has a "behavioral translation" of Chomsky (Catania, 1972).

Language is also discussed in Chapters 7 and 10.

Interaction: Two Meanings

The term *interaction* is commonly used in two different ways, which should be kept separate. The first meaning refers to the joint determination by two or more factors of some product. Thus the interaction (perhaps better called *interactionism*) point of view with regard to heredity and environment as determinants of intelligence is that they act jointly. This is clearly the preponderant view today on this and most related behavioral issues. J. McV. Hunt (1969), who has been one of the more forceful proponents of this position, credits the Danish geneticist Johannson with its initial general development, pointing out that he has been virtually ignored by psychologists. Johannson was also the scientist who distinguished genotype and phenotype and performed some of the first research demonstrating the influence of environmental factors on the phenotype. The second meaning for *interaction* refers to the way in which the operation of one variable is dependent upon the operation of one or more variables in producing some observed effects. This usage, which comes from the statistical meaning of *interaction* as in the analysis of variance (cf. Supplement A-1), is illustrated by Scarr-Salapatek's (1971a) finding that heredity interacts with environment in producing aptitude differences in that it becomes a significant factor only when the environment is more favorable, as described in the text.

Intelligence

The recent controversy was initiated by Jensen (1969a) in a provocative article in the *Harvard Educational Review*, where key responses to it also appear, as well as Jensen's rebuttal (1969b). Jensen's 1973 book is a subsequent assessment. Scarr-Salapatek's review (1971b) should also be consulted; it covers in addition a recent popular book by Eysenck (1971) and a magazine article by Herrnstein (1971). Layzen (1974) has criticized the heritability estimates. Haller's 1971 historical summary of scientific attitudes toward racial intellectual inferiority is interesting in that it shows clearly the unanimous scientific assumption of black inferiority that existed at the end of the nineteenth century, which contrasts with the predominant view of equipotentiality today. Hunt's 1969 book is an excellent source of historical fact and contemporary interactionism on the basic problem, with special reference to counteracting the depressive effects of poverty. Burt's 1972 article is a thorough historical review of work on genetic components in intelligence; if it is assumed that much of the research, for example, that on schoolchildren, has involved subjects with favorable environmental backgrounds, the relatively substantial greater influence found is generally consistent with Scarr-Salapatek's of greater variance in test scores attributable to heredity under superior environmental conditions.

The early study of intelligence in twins was reported by Newman, Freeman, and Holzinger (1937). The improvement in test scores of Southern-born black children was reported by Lee (1951); Scarr-Salapatek (1971a) performed the research on the Philadelphia schoolchildren. The study indicating markedly superior learning and greater influence of heredity with enriched environments was reported by Henderson (1970). Voyat (1969) wrote the rebuttal to Jensen based on Piagetian principles and data.

With regard to some of the more practical implications of testing and racial or socioeconomic differences, McClelland (1973) has mounted a vigorous attack on testing generally and has argued for more direct measures of competence. Stanley (1971), on the other hand, has argued that minority groups, such as American black college students, must be evaluated on the same criteria as other students because the same predictors of academic success (test scores, high school grades) operate for both kinds of subjects. Jencks et al. (1972) have argued that schooling and presumably improved intellectual functioning among minority groups are much less important than generally assumed, especially when compared to familial factors, with regard to occupational and economic benefits. Williams (1974) represents the antitest position, and Cleary et al. (1975) provide an exhaustive treatment of the problem of testing disadvantaged students.

Vandenberg (1968) has suggested the need for breaking down the gross concept of intelligence and looking more analytically at different components that seem to be differentially heritable. The genetecists Bodner and Cavalli-Sforza (1970) review the evidence on black–white differences in intelligence test scores and conclude that the issue cannot be resolved on the basis of present evidence; see also Johnson and Mihal (1973) for a review of interpersonal effects in intelligence testing. A short and nontechnical book by Baughman (1971) on the psychology of black Americans is useful in pointing up the complexity of the problem of apparent black–white differences in intelligence; motives and attitudes are implicated as key determinants of performance differences. Cronbach (1970) presents a historical review of half a century of controversy over mental testing.

Development

The extremes in development have always captured the imagination of the public, as shown in this eighteenth-century broadside of Mr. Patrick O'Brien, The Irish Giant. In this chapter we deal with the normal course of development and the factors that influence its progression.

his chapter begins by identifying developmental psychology within the context of the major approaches to its study. The overview of development through the entire life-span includes physiological development as well as the development of basic behavioral processes, such as language, cognition, and general intelligence. Included in this discussion is the work of Piaget, who has been particularly influential in the study of language and cognition.

The final section of the chapter covers the effects of the various socializing agents in our culture—home, family, school, and the community as it represents the culture. Consideration is given to the manner in which moral and social values are inculcated.

Methods of Study

Developmental psychology is best identified as the study of an individual organism throughout its growth process. Generally, the organism shows increasing complexity of both structure and function as it develops. Developmental psychology is distinguished from the study of separate stages of development, such as childhood or old age, by its more comprehensive perspective and its focus on the continuity of changes throughout the lifetime of the individual.

To be completely comprehensive, developmental psychology must also be comparative. That is, it must include various animal forms as well as the human organism. Most animal development shows at least some of the basic principles and often in a simpler and more readily studied manner than human development; nevertheless, even though the developmental study of animals has intrinsic theoretical and often practical significance, our emphasis in this chapter will be on the human organism.

Man as the most complex form of animal life known affords the greatest scope for developmental variables. Investigation of how each of the fundamental behavioral processes initiates and progresses as the organism ages is thus an integral part of each subfield of psychology. Man is born in an essentially helpless condition; for a period of some years he is dependent upon other people for nurturance. This dependence means that from the beginning man must be a social organism and passes through a long series of developmental stages within a social environment.

APPROACHES TO CHILD STUDY

Several of the more important methodologies that have been applied in child study are briefly surveyed here. This treatment will serve as both a brief historical overlook and a framework within which the substantive empirical and theoretical contributions of child psychologists and others can be viewed.

Psychoanalysis

Initially attention was directed toward infancy and early childhood by Sigmund Freud in his psychoanalytic emphasis upon these early years as the source of fundamental disturbances in the adult human. Although the impact of these ideas left Western society, including science, in a permanently changed condition (that is, shook Western man at least out of his previously naive conception of the essential innocence of childhood), there was great resistance to acceptance of Freudian notions, particularly because of what was regarded as his overemphasis upon the sexual aspects of development and adjustment. In part the recent renewal of interest in developmental problems has stemmed from the recognition that all that matters in development need not be Freudian. In other words, there is plenty of room in the study of development for other conceptual modes as well as strictly empirical approaches.

Although Freud first called attention to the primary formative influences of the early years, orthodox Freudian psychoanalysis is theoretical and speculative rather than empirical, in the sense that the analyst simply takes the word of the subject concerning his childhood experiences instead of directly investigating such experiences. Freud himself was basically concerned with the biological, instinctual factors, although he did leave some room for the role of experience. One of his emphases in the latter respect was with regard to the interpersonal relationships within the family. In spite of these limitations, and the general scientific inadequacy of his theorizing, Freud must be credited with a truly revolutionary achievement in opening up the field of child study and development generally. Moreover, the neoanalysts, as certain of his successors are usually called, have moved toward an even greater emphasis on familial and related social, as opposed to strictly biological, variables.

Normative–Maturational Study

The first stage of any discipline, or subdiscipline, tends to be essentially descriptive. Developmental psychology is no exception. Simply observing and recording the succession of behaviors, as in the normal infant or child, preceded any experimental study. The *age norms* thus produced are of some utility in their own right and are useful as necessary points from which more analytic and controlled observations can start.

A normative-maturational investigation is one that endeavors to establish the ages—norms—during which certain kinds of behaviors mature in typical children. This descriptive study of children's behavior patterns as they develop over the years was one of the early alternatives to psychoanalytic interpretations. Such study is generally atheoretical, being concerned primarily with a straightforward account of the developing behavior systems. This research is *normative,* in that it provides age standards or norms for various behaviors, and generally *longitudinal,* in that it tends to involve continuous study of the same subjects for as long a time as possible.

There are several weaknesses in the normative-maturational approach. Basically, it usually assumes the overriding influence of maturational (internally and presumably genetically determined) development. As a consequence of this focus, little effort is made to investigate interactions with environmental variables or to develop external explanations of the developmental patterns observed. Furthermore, although its data are fundamentally useful and even essential as a base from which further investigations can start, when age norms are presented as guidelines to parents and teachers they can be quite harmful. Although it is useful from a diagnostic point of view to know that an individual deviates from a norm in some way, it is not useful to base therapy on that one aspect. For example, there may well be nothing at all wrong with a child who does not walk at the time projected in these maturation tables; if he is treated as a problem, however, a real problem can be generated. On the other hand, if there is an anatomical or physiological reason for his slow rate, the maturation tables may prove to be useful in helping to detect such a defect.

In the absence of appropriate caution, unthinking application of age norms all too often occurs. The normative approach thus tends to be not only theoretically sterile but also practically risky; child psychology has therefore moved well past this kind of research, even while recognizing its contributions. Table 10-1 provides an illustration of the products that ensued from this kind of approach.

Cross-Sectional and Longitudinal Study

Two special methods have been widely employed in developmental research: the cross-sectional and the longitudinal. Each has certain advantages and disadvantages.

Cross-sectional research attempts to select representative individuals from each age or developmental level to be studied and then subjects them all to some kind of behavioral inquiry. Scores thereby collected are compared, as on graphs plotting

Table 10-1 Relationship Between Age and Performance as Shown by Selected Items in Gesell and Thompson (1934)

Behavior Items	Age in Weeks											
	12	16	20	24	28	32	36	40	44	48	52	56
Accepts strangers	100	80	61	52	59	41	39	39	26	18	18	14
Withdraws from strangers	0	19	8	24	16	47	42	19	48	44	30	9
Adjusts to words		0	8	12	16	47	68	75	94	82	89	73
Responds to "bye-bye"		0	3	3	3	13	35	53	63	38	59	27
Adjusts to commands		0	0	0	3	22	23	31	55	56	73	50
Responds to inhibitory words		0	0	0	3	25	23	28	45	44	52	23
Responds to "So big"		0	0	0	0	6	7	8	26	18	34	0
Elicits attention		0	0	0	0	9	16	24	26	27	53	50
Plays pat-a-cake		0	0	3	6	19	23	25	42	27	50	9
Plays peek-a-boo		0	0	6	0	9	13	11	13	9	25	9
Has regular toilet training	3	12	35	48	47	59	71	83	86	90	96	90
Says one word or more				0	7	12	21	34	69	77	88	95

Numbers refer to the percentages of subjects showing the various behaviors.

some behavior against age levels, and conclusions are drawn concerning the development of some behavior or its relationship to a manipulated variable. Cross-sectional research is restricted usually to rather gross comparisons and does not take account of the manner in which behaviors develop. Moreover, it is liable to underestimate and fail to control for important interactions; for example, if older individuals are being compared on learning with younger ones, it may be very difficult to equate motivation for the two groups. Nevertheless, cross-sectional studies have most of the typical advantages of scientific experimentation and form an indispensable part of the research techniques of the developmental scientist.

Piecing together cross-sectional samples to provide a kind of longitudinal picture can be extremely misleading. For example, consider the problem of performance on verbal or other tests as a function of age. The simplest procedure is to take cross-sectional samples from the various ages at a given time; this enables the investigator to collect his data and complete his study within a reasonable amount of time. However, the results he obtains in this way may be strikingly different from those obtained when the same individuals are studied longitudinally over the same developmental period. This is mainly because physical growth as well as cognitive and similar psychological processes are heavily influenced by changes over generations in nutritional, cultural, and other stimulating conditions. Children of more recent generations generally tend to have more stimulating and facilitating environments; hence the younger samples tend to be relatively favored. Parenthetically, it may also be noted that in spite of this disadvantage, an encouraging tendency has been found for measured verbal ability to hold up very well throughout adulthood, showing very little decline until the ages of fifty-five to sixty. In any case it is reasonably clear that the apparent rapid decline of human abilities in the late teens or early twenties that was reported in many cross-sectional studies cannot be taken at face value.

The longitudinal preceded the cross-sectional method in the form of such naturalistic (descriptive) techniques as baby biographies or the study of diaries. In longitudinal research the same individual is studied over various times. The technique thus has the great advantage of staying close to development as it occurs and so not being as likely to miss the more subtle changes. It is limited, at least in the relative primitive form of its earliest applications, by inaccuracy of recording and intrusion of bias. If more sophisticated observers, such as developmental researchers themselves, are involved, the technique is enormously time-consuming. It has therefore been more prominent in observations of the investigator's own children, who tend to be at hand (if not under foot); the best-known example of effective use of such home-bred subjects is Piaget's insightful discoveries of cognitive processes. Even at its best, however, it is difficult to apply longitudinal study over more than a relatively short time period and it is not well suited to provide adequate controls. Nevertheless, the few major longitudinal studies that have been carried out in this country have provided significant results and indicate the great value of the technique.

The relationship between longitudinal and *idiographic* techniques should be noted. Idiographic research is that in which a given individual is studied intensively, with a view to the full understanding of him as a unique person; it is thus a kind of subvariety of the longitudinal technique. Idiographic study is most often contrasted with the so-called *nomothetic* approach, whose purpose is the production of general laws, most often but not necessarily by the comparison of groups of individuals; this approach is thus related to the cross-sectional technique. There should really be no conflict between these two approaches. They are complementary, just as longitudinal and cross-sectional techniques are. If one insists on the primacy of the individual, without regard for the nomothetic character of the general laws that he exhibits in becoming unique, then there is likely to be some conflict. Such conflict is unnecessary because there is plenty of room for idiographic endeavors associated with scientific (nomothetic) as well as practical (clinical) efforts.

LIFE-SPAN STUDIES. Several long-term longitudinal studies have been and are being performed. In 1921, for example, approximately 1,500 California schoolchildren were selected on the basis of their extremely high IQ scores. They have been observed periodically, as they have progressed through the various developmental stages. Achievement tests and personality inventories have been administered, and a large number of other measures relating to their occupational status, personal life, and the like have been taken; some of the results from this study are described elsewhere in this chapter.

Observational and Experimental Study

A large variety of observational types of study have been employed with subjects of various ages. Table 10-2 presents a digest of some that have been used with children. Subjects of various ages can be used in many kinds of experiments. When the emphasis in the research is upon a comparison of ages, or upon developmental processes, the results may be interpreted within the framework of developmental psychology. One of the more encouraging signs of the last two decades or so of experimental research has been the increasing use of subjects of a wide range of ages and status so that a truly experimental base for developmental psychology is emerging.

Developmental Stages

EMBRYOLOGICAL DEVELOPMENT

THE GERMINAL PERIOD. For the first two weeks of its new existence the human organism is said to be in the germinal period. The first cellular differentiation occurs, and the clusters of cells from which the various body parts will form are organized.

THE EMBRYO. The embryo proper takes form from about the second week after conception. The various rudimentary body structures begin to form. In this process three cellular layers first emerge, and from these the various organ systems and body parts develop. These are (1) an outer layer, the *ectoderm*, from which comes the skin, the sensory organs, and the nervous system; (2) a middle layer, the *mesoderm*, which produces blood, muscle, and skeleton (bone); and (3) an inner layer, the *endoderm*, the precursor of the intestinal tract and digestive system.

Table 10-2   A Digest of Methods in Observational Child Study

Methods		Sampling Plan		Recording Technique	Analysis Procedure
		Continuum Coverage	Material Coverage		
O P E N	Diary description	More or less regular day-to-day intervals	Successive steps in behavioral growth and associated life episodes	Itemization of growth changes and summary narration	Classification and interpretive study
	Specimen description	Continuous behavior sequences	"Everything" of ongoing behavior and situation	Detailed sequential narration	Interpretive study or coding, scoring, and statistical analysis
C L O S E D	Time sampling	Intermittent short and uniform time units	Selected variables of behavior or situation or both	On-the-spot coding or narration or both	Scoring and statistical analysis
	Event sampling	Event time spans	Behavioral events of a given class (as arguments)	On-the-spot coding or narration or both	Scoring and statistical analysis
	Trait rating	Continuous behavior sequences	Selected dimensions of behavior	Rating based on cumulative direct observation	Scoring and statistical analysis
	Field unit analysis	Successive behavior units	Selected variables of behavior or situation or both	On-the-spot coding	Scoring and statistical analysis

Reprinted from Wright, 1960.

Figure 10-1 shows the development of a human embryo, from about three through eight weeks, and of a fetus of three and four months.

THE FETUS. By about the ninth week sufficient differentiation of the body parts has occurred that the organism begins to take on a humanoid appearance. It is then called the fetus. Birth, at approximately forty weeks after conception, ends the fetal period.

Fetal Behavior

Fetal behavior has been studied, for the most part, in prematurely delivered organisms, and thus under unusual conditions. Nevertheless, some conclusions can be drawn from these observations concerning development and behavioral capacity in the fetus.

A variety of spontaneous behavior is evident, mostly in the form of slow, sluggish movements of body parts and reflexes such as grasping and sucking. The latter reflex is an especially well-developed one in all mammalian forms, and for good reasons; tenacious sucking is necessary at birth if the organism is to survive. Fetuses also show reactivity to external stimuli, and are capable of at least primitive learning. Classical conditioning of the intact fetus has been demonstrated, using

289

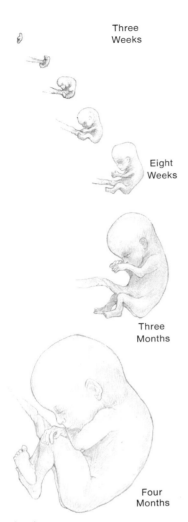

Three
Weeks

Eight
Weeks

Three
Months

Four
Months

10-1 Growth stages in prenatal development.

stimuli such as loud sounds and vibrations applied to the mother's abdomen. Generally, however, the sensory system of the fetus is probably of limited utility during this developmental period and is not much needed as long as the organism remains within the shelter of the mother's uterus.

Deleterious physiological effects on the fetus have been demonstrated shortly after birth, caused by a disturbingly large number of environmental conditions acting upon the pregnant mother. Most dramatic of these was the production of severely deformed babies, with missing appendages, that resulted from use of the sedative thalidomide (which is now banned by federal drug regulations). Large doses of radiation can also produce a high rate of physical abnormality, and even the much smaller normal rate can result in a detectably greater frequency of some abnormalities. More prosaically, and perhaps more important in the long run, such commonplace practices as cigarette smoking and the routine use of presumably milder drugs have been associated with higher rates of premature delivery. Pregnant mothers who are addicted to the "harder" drugs also subject their fetuses to undesirable physiological strain; these babies may show withdrawal symptoms after birth, and physiological measures may need to be taken accordingly. Within recent years more attention has been paid to the ill effects of chronic malnourishment, now known to be surprisingly widespread even in such a generally affluent country as the United States. Malnutrition can retard fetal growth; babies whose mothers are malnourished are likely to be premature or if full-term are more likely to be either stillborn or immature than are babies of well-nourished mothers.

The nervous system in particular is most vulnerable to the severely harmful effects of malnutrition during the prenatal (and neonatal) period, when it is most actively growing. As one neurobiologist has said, "Inadequate nutrition in newborn mammals results in slowing of the rate of neurological development; if the duration and severity of malnutrition are sufficiently great, it may cause a permanent reduction in brain weight and . . . lead to mental retardation in man" (Jacobson, 1970, p. 196). On a more hopeful note, however, it should be added that there is evidence that some restoration of behavioral functioning and presumably of underlying neurological structure is believed to be possible in the human child if adequate feeding is provided within the first four years of life.

THE POSTNATAL PERIOD

Observation of prenatal development of the embryo and the fetus is, of course, handicapped by the location of the organism inside the mother. After birth the human organism is clearly in a better position to be subjected to all kinds of study, behavioral included. As a result, a vast amount of data has been accumulated on the new organism.

Within the postnatal period it is customary to call the developing organism first a *partunate* (after *parturition*, the technical name for *birth*) for the first few hours following birth; then a *neonate*, for the first two weeks to four weeks of postnatal life; and finally an *infant*, until approximately two years have passed.

290

Needless to say, neither these age phases nor those of later years to be discussed below should be considered as more than arbitrary temporal labels within which the important developmental processes operate. Although age stages are convenient tags, and even play more substantive roles in certain theories, they should not be allowed to draw attention away from the more significant maturational and behavioral functions that underlie development.

The Partunate

Birth is indeed a traumatic event, for baby as well as mother. For the first forty weeks or so of its existence, the organism has been completely dependent upon its mother for all its needs. The fetus has been connected to the mother's physiological systems by means of the umbilical cord, through which all its oxygen and food needs are supplied and its waste products passed out. It has been safely shielded within the amniotic sac, and further cushioned from physical shock by the amniotic fluid. Rudely thrust into a strange new environment, the partunate must make some immediate physiological adjustments and not too long thereafter must also begin to initiate behavioral adjustments, which are necessary throughout the life-span.

The most immediate physiological need is for oxygen. The well-developed but until now completely nonfunctional lungs must be inflated with air and breathing must be initiated. The initiating stimulus is normally applied by the attending physician, nurse, or midwife. The well-developed sucking reflex must soon be put to work on breast or bottle. The partunate has been described as an elongated intestinal tube; once breathing starts, most of its time is spent in feeding (when it is not sleeping).

The Neonate

Physically, the neonatal period is mainly a holding operation. The baby is hard-pressed to maintain its birth weight. Deprived of the dependable food supply it has enjoyed throughout the fetal period, and so forced now to obtain its own food, the neonate typically loses some weight before beginning to show the weight gain that marks much of the remainder of its period of growth.

Even after recovering from its initial shriveled appearance as a partunate, the neonate is not a very impressive physical specimen (splendid as it may appear to the proud parents). Its head is disproportionately large (approximately one quarter of the total length, compared with one seventh in adulthood). Its stomach is large and its musculature is understandably small and flabby. The changes in anatomical form and body proportion that occur from birth to physical maturity, about twenty-five years, are shown in Figure 10-2. Sensorily, the neonatal equipment is usually intact but some of its functioning is in doubt (mainly because of a lack of reliable subjective reports). William James's famous conjecture that the baby's early experience is "one great blooming, buzzing confusion" seems as apt today as when first offered. Apart from the predominant sucking and crying responses, most of the early behavior still consists mainly of diffuse, generalized movements of larger parts of the body or simple reflexes. Behaviorally, the neonate is in little better shape, although evidence on this point is considerably harder to obtain.

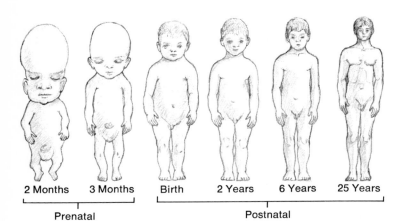

2 Months   3 Months   Birth   2 Years   6 Years   25 Years

Prenatal   Postnatal

The Infant

The two years or so of infancy see the very definite beginnings of the basic behavioral functions as well as the continuing differentiation of physical structures and the refinement of physiological functions. The more important of the beginning behavioral processes will be briefly discussed.

Sensory Exploration. Infancy is a time of intensive sensory exploration. Indeed, most of the responses of the infant (beyond those required for feeding and defensive reactions) are related to its attempts to explore the world that is now emerging with ever-increasing sensory clarity. The baby reaches out for nearby objects, touching and grasping those it can reach. Two-week-old babies will respond to objects when the baby is upright. Babies of sixteen to twenty-four weeks respond more generally to objects; shortly after this period they are able to identify their mother.

By the end of the infancy period at two years of age the typical infant has achieved sufficient locomotor and manipulative ability to make possible exploration of a substantial number of objects in his environment. Experimental evidence has accumulated concerning the effectiveness of the various sensory systems, mainly vision and hearing. The infant's world is beginning to show the differentiation characteristic of all the later developmental stages.

Thinking. It has been hypothesized that infants begin to generate hypotheses —to think—as early as eight to nine months. This development may reflect a critical period for changes in the central nervous system, although these have not yet been documented.

Locomotion. Among the most prominent of the infant's behaviors are his attempts to move himself about his environment. Beginning early in infancy with the first crib movements, such as raising his head to examine things better, the infant progresses through a series of quite individualistic locomotor responses until he has succeeded at last in walking. A typical sequence of postural and locomotor development is shown in Figure 10-3. Although most children will certainly approximate this sequence, it should not be taken too literally. The one generalization that seems justified with regard to this development is that it is indeed individualistic: the particular steps through which one baby goes seem to be relatively unique. Infants can walk as early as nine months, or as late as eighteen or even twenty or more months. Each infant has his own developmental rate as well as pattern, and these seem to be more a function of maturation of his physical effector system as well as his nervous system than of his actual experiences.

Readiness

The concept of readiness has recently been emphasized. *Readiness* refers to the proposition that some particular function, such as talking or toilet training, cannot be effectively learned until the child is anatomically and physiologically equipped, and that then its acquisition is relatively quick and straightforward. Readiness is related to the critical period concept in that it specifies a time of optimal introduction of some kind of training or experience and is presumed to depend upon maturation. Thus, for example, it is only at the very end of the infancy period, at age two years, that the baby is said to be ready for toilet training. Attempting to train him earlier than this time is likely to lead not only to repeated failure, but also to persistent emotional upset.

The research that is probably most often cited with regard to the readiness concept is that involving Hopi Indian children. Normal Hopi practice is for the mothers to carry Hopi infants on their backs in various kinds of cradleboards in which their legs are so restricted as to make movements nearly impossible. When another (experimental) group of infants was allowed full locomotive freedom during these early months, they nevertheless did not begin to walk any earlier than the (control) children who had been bound in their usual cradleboards. Readiness resulting from maturation was apparently the main determining condition in this situation. Experience prior to the point at which the child has the physical and nervous system equipment for walking appears to make very little difference in his later mastery of the task.

To mention another example from a later developmental period, some authorities feel that the optimal time to train children to swim is about eight years. Fear of the water has not yet developed and the child is sufficiently mature physically to insure a very good prospect of successful training. Of course, earlier swimming training can also be effective, but it would then require more effort and be somewhat less likely to succeed.

The readiness concept can be misused by parents or teachers when it is too slavishly followed. There must be due regard for individual maturational differences among children or emotional factors that may complicate learning. The fact that growth typically takes place in spurts, which cannot be reliably predicted for any given child, makes it imperative that the readiness rule, based upon averaging growth rates from many children, be applied with care. It is important that failures of training not simply be attributed to a child's not being "ready" for some training, such as reading; this may often be the case, but an individual analysis should be made.

Critical Periods

The concept of critical periods has already been discussed (Chapter 9) with reference to embryological research. Although most of the evidence on this topic is

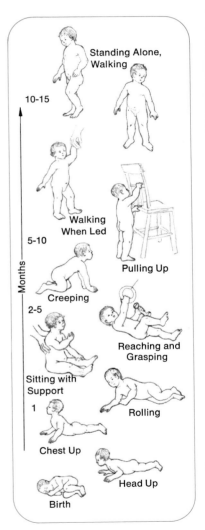

Standing Alone, Walking

10-15

Walking When Led

5-10

Pulling Up

Creeping

2-5

Reaching and Grasping

Sitting with Support

1

Rolling

Chest Up

Head Up

Birth

Months

10-3 Postural stages in motor development. (Based on data in Shirley, 1931.)

from animal research, the concept may well have some pertinence, albeit reduced in significance, for human development. The best-known illustration of a critical period is the *imprinting* phenomenon. Imprinting consists of exposing very young organisms to some particular stimulus objects. If this exposure occurs during the critical period, the imprinted organism will become attached to the stimulus object and remain so attached ("imprinted") throughout their lives. Good examples of this phenomenon are the ducklings that were imprinted on Lorenz, and will therefore follow him rather than the mother duck upon whom they would normally be imprinted.

A lesser-known but perhaps more practically important critical period involves dogs and their relationships to people. If a puppy passes through the period of the second to the third month of life with only limited human contact, his relationships with humans will always be strained, no matter how sympathetic and friendly his later masters may be. On the other hand, once he is adequately stimulated by humans during this period (rather than merely earlier or later) a permanently close relationship with people is established (and seems often to persist in spite of some very adverse experiences the dog may suffer at the hand of later masters).

Restricted environments in general are probably important factors in growth during infancy. Thus dogs raised in restricted environments from seven to ten weeks of age showed less activity, less intellectual ability, and less sociability than ones in a stimulating environment.

CHILDHOOD

The childhood period starts at the end of infancy, at about two years, and continues to puberty, or sexual maturation, at around twelve years. This period sees not only the continued development of all the important behavioral functions begun in infancy but also their proliferation into many new channels and the initiation of a number of new problems, mainly having to do with social relationships. These crucial problems of socialization are left for subsequent discussion in this chapter; here we are concerned with biological rather than psychological or social growth.

Figure 10-4 shows the typical course of growth patterns for boys and girls from birth through eighteen years of age. Note that the early slight height advantage of boys is offset by the end of childhood, with girls growing faster than boys and actually exceeding them in height. The adult height difference is gained during the adolescence period.

ADOLESCENCE

The onset of puberty initiates the adolescence period. Again, the psychological and psychosocial problems that mark this transitional period are its most crucial features, and it is difficult to discuss primarily biological changes without mentioning them. This is because so many of the matters that concern the adolescent are

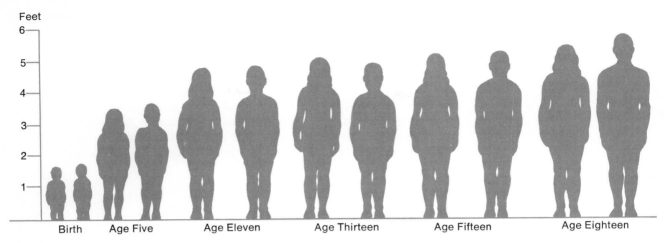

10-4 Average growth in males and females from birth to maturity. Note the periods of slow and fast growth and the sex differences.

more or less directly related to the biological changes that have occurred and are occurring, often without his having had adequate prior preparation for them.

Onset of Puberty

Such evidence as is available to us indicates very clearly that with each succeeding generation pubescence occurs at a slightly earlier average age. It is estimated that today puberty starts at least four years earlier than it did a century and a half ago. A correlated increase in physical size has occurred, with today's adolescents reaching approximately 4 inches greater height than their counterparts of a century ago. It is generally believed that improved nutrition and health care are largely responsible for both of these changes; whether other factors are also responsible is difficult to determine.

Sexual Development

Sexual maturation is the defining criterion of puberty. A distinction needs to be made between primary and secondary sexual characteristics. *Primary* sexual characteristics relate directly to the reproductive organs (gonads), the testes in the male and the ovary in the female, and their associated structures (e.g., penis, vagina). *Secondary* sexual characteristics are those correlated changes in body parts that are effected by the gonadal organs, or more properly by their hormonal products, but that do not themselves play any direct role in reproduction.

Figure 10-5 offers some interesting contrasts in growth patterns during adolescence. One curve shows *neural* growth, an index of increases in physical size mainly of the brain and spinal cord. Note the rapid acceleration during infancy, the slowing down during childhood, and the very slight further development during adolescence. The development of primary sexual characteristics (gonads) is shown in a second curve. A very slight early development is followed by a long period of no growth during childhood, after which the precipitous growth of the puberty period occurs. The contrast with the neural growth pattern is quite apparent.

A similar contrast may be seen between reproductive growth and general body, or *somatic,* growth, shown in Figure 10-5. This measure is an index of physical size changes in such measures as arm and leg length, body girth, height, and weight. Again, as in the case of neural growth, there is a fast rate of change during infancy and some slowing down during childhood. Unlike neural growth, however, there is also a marked growth spurt just before and during puberty, far less spectacular than the reproductive growth explosion but nonetheless substantial. This adolescent growth spurt usually occurs one or two years earlier in girls than in boys (as is also suggested by Figure 10-4).

Self-concepts

Adolescence represents the period during which the developing human must at least begin to come to grips with adult responsibilities and expectations. This places many demands upon this age group, including the problem of formation of a reasonable self-concept (view or "image" of oneself) that can help the individual to cope with these demands. Although there are naturally many other considerations than sexual matters, these are certainly among the prime determinants for most adolescents, which is hardly surprising in view of their defining role for adolescence. What is somewhat surprising, and is quite variable among cultures, is the contribution of secondary sexual characteristics. Most prominent among these in our own culture are breasts for girls and hair for both girls and boys. These

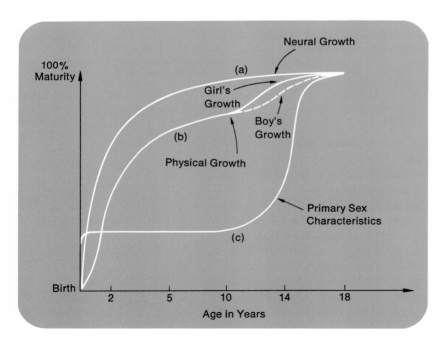

10-5 Differential rates of growth can be seen in (a) neural tissue, including the brain; (b) body dimensions, including some of the major internal organs; and (c) the development of primary sex characteristics. [Adapted from B. R. McCandless, *Children: Behavior and development* (New York: Holt, 1967).]

characteristics may play a very active part in shaping the self-concepts of adolescents.

Another extremely important factor in the formation of adolescent self-concepts is physical size and associated aspects of body structure. Although many detailed factors are important in this respect, two important generalizations should be emphasized. First, the way in which various body attributes are regarded is relative to a given culture and given period in that culture. Thus, extreme height in males, not long ago generally considered to be a serious handicap, has recently become in some ways an advantage (e.g., in basketball, which increasingly has become a tall man's game). Our culture idealizes the female who has certain body proportions, thus making life hazardous for the female who is over- or underweight or ill proportioned.

A second generalization is that the initial self-concept that one forms is, unfortunately, very resistant to change. Here the individual variations in growth rate are important. For example, the boy whose eventual overall physique is quite satisfactory but who developed slowly may have considerable difficulty in shedding the self-concept (and associated attitudes) of a short, thin, physically unimpressive individual. A similar persistence in self-concepts may occur with regard to such temporary but embarrassing matters as skin blemishes, early social ineptitude, or clumsiness arising from inexperience in sexual advances. It is therefore extremely important that adults not only maintain a basically tolerant attitude toward adolescents as they begin to take on adult roles but also actively endeavor to soften the potentially debilitating effects of initial failures and inadequate self-concepts by specifying appropriate and adjustable standards and objectives.

MATURITY

Once sexual maturity has been attained further development is largely a social process. The most notable physiological changes during this period concern the female, who must cope with changes during pregnancy and/or with birth control devices and their physiological effects. Cessation of menstruation, which occurs between the ages of forty and fifty (with great individual differences) marks a significant physiological change. During this menopause period most women find their physical and emotional health improved by the taking of hormones to replace those that are no longer produced. Evidence at present is inconclusive as to whether there are significant hormonal changes in the male, but most authorities assume at least the possibility of a slight "change-of-life" phenomenon.

The mature individual in our society is indeed a neglected person—psychologically speaking, at any rate. Once the rigors of adolescence are surmounted, psychologists tend to lose interest in human development, as far as experimental or even simple observational studies of mature persons are concerned. These are very scarce indeed. Interest is revived again in their psychological concern for the elderly.

Physical maturity, in terms of the most commonly used growth measures, occurs in the mid-twenties. This age period represents the peak of physical development

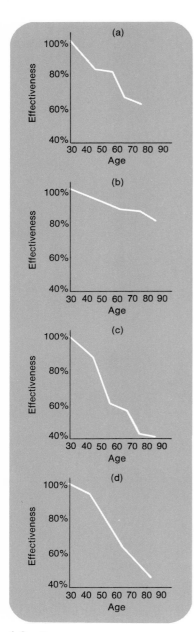

10-6 **Decline in vital functions with increasing age: (a) heart, (b) nervous system, (c) lungs, (d) kidneys.**

and vitality. Thereafter, the catabolic (break-down) functions in body metabolism begin to predominate the anabolic (build-up) functions, although both processes occur simultaneously throughout each lifetime. Weight increments tend to continue throughout maturity, unless carefully guarded against by appropriate dietary concern and physical activities. Only as middle age is passed does the trend reverse, with the aged being relatively thin. The overweight problem is indeed a serious one in the United States, as it tends to be for middle age especially in any society where there is a good supply of food available to most people. From early maturity on, changes in skin texture are liable to be unhappily noticeable. Wrinkling appears as the skin loses elasticity. Hair becomes progressively more gray and less abundant. The various kinds of cosmetic "cure" of these conditions that are so commonly attempted in our own society may do more harm than good; again, as in the case of adolescence, social norms have a great deal to do with how effectively one adjusts to these inevitable bodily changes. Certainly the adolescent has no monopoly on overreaction to bodily conditions!

The more crucial decline with age in selected vital functions is portrayed in the four curves of Figure 10-6. A fairly regular decline in each of the functions considered can be seen from the age of thirty onward.

OLD AGE

As Figure 10-6 indicates, from age sixty on there tends to be some acceleration of the decline in vital functions (especially in heart and lung). These progressive changes demand appropriate adjustment, in terms of, say, type and amount of physical exercise. Although it is very difficult to make any fixed and all-embracing generalizations, because of the great individual differences that exist in prior habits as well as rates of decline, it is nonetheless quite clear that older men and women must face up to the unavoidable toll that aging takes.

The aging problem has been increasingly in the news, mainly because we are rapidly becoming a nation of older people. This is not because very many of us are living unusually longer than before, but rather because relatively fewer of us are dying at earlier ages (mainly because of improvement in the management of the major diseases). At the present time, about 10 per cent of our population is over sixty-five. The science of *gerontology,* or study of aging, and the associated medical practice of *geriatrics,* or treatment of the aged, have accordingly become very prominent.

A study of exceptionally old people has yielded some very interesting results. Persons between eighty and 130 years of age were interviewed in three areas of the world where great longevity is supposed to be unusually common. Their attributes can be roughly sorted into biological and psychological categories. On the biological side, they tended to consume markedly lower amounts of food than the "average" American, to stay physically active, and to come from families with a history of longevity. On the psychological side, they were esteemed for their age and their presumed wisdom, were considered to be useful members of society, and were expected to live to 100 years. Many of them were members of an extended household, which includes several generations or age groups.

The dietary factor is especially suggestive because it has been shown to be effective in animals raised under carefully controlled conditions. (Rats raised on severely restricted diet have been found to live substantially longer than litter-mate controls given as much food as they wish.) Also, the dietary factor, compared to heredity in particular, is one that can be socially and personally manipulated.

Malnutrition of the aged has become a problem in the United States for several reasons. For the elderly on low incomes there is not enough money to purchase the necessary food. Some are not able to prepare their own food. A government-sponsored program, "Meals on Wheels," was designed to alleviate this problem by bringing prepared food to the elderly in their homes. Another problem for those who live alone is the lack of desire to prepare a nutritious meal to eat alone.

Concentrated research on the aging process as a natural phenomenon has only recently been seriously started and it is too early to say whether biological manipulations can be found that will significantly increase longevity. The best guess at this time is that the symptoms of old age can be postponed for at least a decade or more, on the average, simply by improved treatment of the major diseases that now run largely unchecked and that attack older persons especially (e.g., cancer and diseases of the kidney and circulatory system). The failure of medical service to check the ravages of these diseases is indicated by a comparison of some life-expectancy statistics. Although life expectancy of the average American has improved by twenty-three years (to about seventy years) since 1900 —mainly because of the control of such fatal childhood diseases as bacterial pneumonia and diphtheria—once an American reaches the age of sixty-five he can today look forward only to two more years of life than he could in 1900 (fifteen years against thirteen years). If basic research on aging discovers why aging occurs, perhaps effective countersteps could be taken to prolong maturity and middle age and so produce more dramatic improvements in life expectancy.

Chronological age has been found to be a poor indicator of an individual's cognitive and emotional characteristics. Paramount among the problems of the aged are housing, social role, use of time, and segregation from society as a whole. In this respect the aged share the same problems as youths, who are segregated by their life in schools and colleges. The solutions of these problems of the aged may lie in their ability to form a power structure of their own to force needed changes in society.

LANGUAGE DEVELOPMENT

The crucial role that language plays in behavior has already been indicated (e.g., Chapters 7, 8, and 9), as have some of the problems associated with language functions. Here we concentrate on outlining some of the research and thinking that have gone into the problem of the development of language in the normal human.

Development and Behavior

Because the basic linguistic functions are clearly formed by the end of the child-hood period, our present discussion is restricted to infancy and childhood.

Infancy and Childhood

We disregard nonverbal forms of communication in infants and describe only the first attempts at "true" communication by means of sounds.

BABBLING. Speech commences in the infant in a relatively meaningless manner. The infant's earliest language activities are generally called "babbling." This term refers to the production of relatively pure (that is, essentially meaningless) sounds, seemingly produced for their own sake. In spite of its apparently inauspicious debut, language is quite dependent upon babbling for its subsequent development. Babbling provides the infant with valuable experience in manipulation of lips and tongue, in relation to breathing. When children do not babble normally (e.g., congenitally deaf children), they are extremely unlikely to learn to speak normally. As a matter of fact, such children require intensive and prolonged special training to learn to speak at all (in spite of the intact and normal nature of their vocal mechanisms). Deaf children often seem to start to babble, indicating the normality of their speech apparatus, but they do not continue because they lack the kind of persistent sensory stimulation that the normal child enjoys.

Table 10-3 presents a comparison of verbal with motor "milestones" for the first few years of development. Note that babbling develops out of the first "cooing" sounds emitted by the baby and stops about the end of the infancy period, when

Table 10-3 Correspondence in Chronological Development of Motor and Language Behaviors

Age (years)	Motor Milestones	Language Milestones
0.5	Sits using hands for support; unilateral reaching	Cooing sounds change to babbling by introduction of consonant sounds
1	Stands; walks when held by one hand	Syllabic reduplication; signs of understanding some words; applies some sounds regularly to signify persons or objects, that is, the first words
1.5	Prehension and release fully developed; gait propulsive; creeps downstairs backward	Repertoire of 3 to 50 words not joined in phrases; trains of sounds and intonation patterns resembling discourse; good progress in understanding
2	Runs (with falls); walks stairs with one foot forward only	More than 50 words; two-word phrases most common; more interest in verbal communication; no more babbling
2.5	Jumps with both feet; stands on one foot for 1 second; builds tower of six cubes	Every day new words; utterances of three and more words; seems to understand almost everything said to him; still many grammatical deviations
3	Tiptoes 3 yards (2.7 meters); walks stairs with alternating feet; jumps 0.9 meter	Vocabulary of some 1,000 words; about 80 per cent intelligibility; grammar of utterances close approximation to colloquial adult; syntactic mistakes fewer in variety, systematic, predictable
4.5	Jumps over rope; hops on one foot; walks on line	Language well established; grammatical anomalies restricted either to unusual constructions or to the more literate aspects of discourse

Reprinted with permission from Lenneberg, 1969, p. 636.

two-word phrases have become common and an interest in more meaningful communication has developed.

CRITICAL PERIOD FOR LANGUAGE. Perhaps the most extended critical period to which attention has been directed concerns language development. In normal humans, the left cerebral hemisphere contains the center for control of speech, as was first demonstrated by the French physician Broca (for whom the center was named) in the nineteenth century.

There are indications that language learning must occur relatively early in children's development for maximum facility. Data from aphasic children (those who are without speech) who recover speech functions suggest that the normal differentiation of speech control within the brain is complete some time during the teens. Up to this point children who recover from aphasia, as by means of an operation on the left hemisphere, can still relearn language in the usual manner, with the right hemisphere taking over control. From this time on, however, such relearning is progressively more difficult, much as is the learning of a second language. Evidence from other sources, such as language development in retarded children, also points to the early or mid-teens as the approximate end of a rather loose kind of critical period for language development.

Theories of Language Development

The big question concerning language is *how* it develops. Here we review two of the more popular viewpoints. The older one is the S–R theory, early embraced by the behaviorist John Watson and consisting in essence of an elaboration of Pavlovian (classical) conditioning. The newer type of theory stresses the essentially unlearned nature of language, especially as it consists of grammar rather than vocabulary. This viewpoint is, in one form or another, accepted by most linguists and psycholinguists.

S–R THEORY. As Watson and other behaviorists have interpreted language, it is simply another form of conditioning. The concept of "circular conditioning" was early invented to account for the manner in which vocabulary develops. For example, the infant hears some wordlike sound, such as *da*, as he himself emits it; so if an object, such as a doll or a dad, is presented at the time he is both saying and hearing the sound, emitting it can be conditioned both to the sight of the object and (circularly) to the sound itself. In this way an adult can emit the same sound, or an approximation thereto, and so elicit it in the infant, much as the object itself also does.

The contemporary behaviorist B. F. Skinner has presented a much more sophisticated behavioristic version of the S–R point of view. For Skinner language is essentially the same as any other kind of behavior. Words are responses and as such are subject to all the fundamental laws of learning. One of the more fundamental distinctions made by Skinner is that between *mand* and *tact*. Verbal behavior that is in some way demanding or commanding is called a *mand*. *Gimme da* would be an early example of a mand by a child who wants the doll. When verbal behavior is elicited by environmental objects, it is labeled a *tact*. *Da gone* would be an example of a tact elicited in the child who notes the absence of a plaything.

This simple description can do no more than impart the flavor of the Skinnerian approach to language. It contrasts most sharply with that developed by the linguists, which assumes an entirely different kind of internal framework for language and emphasizes presumably innate (unlearned) processes in its development.

PSYCHOLINGUISTIC THEORY. The psycholinguist tends to follow the linguist in postulating that there is an internal system of rules that serve to guide language development and expression in the child. As we have already discussed (Chapter 9), this system is presumed to be genetically programed, but there is no direct positive evidence for such a presumption.

Combining two words ordinarily begins at about eighteen months of age. Usually there will be one or more pivotal words, around which secondary words tend to cluster. A small number of new pivotal words enter the child's active vocabulary each month. Typical pivotal words are *night-night, all-gone, my, see.* Most of the secondary words are nouns, such as *boy, boat, house.* Functions such as demanding, negating, describing, and the like are served by such simple combinations of words.

As more complex patterns of language develop, they do so in a distinctly hierarchical manner. That is, a two-word demand may be followed by a more complete three-word utterance. Hesitations in speech are especially common at this stage and play a meaningful role in the child's expression of his ideas and intentions in language.

The prominence of grammatical rules that seem to be developed in the absence of any explicit training is suggested by a number of regularities in early language behavior. For example, the child may learn the correct forms of some irregular verbs, such as *came* and *broke.* Once he also learns the regular past-tense form, however, he is quite likely to change *came* to *comed,* and *broke* to *breaked.* He thus follows a simple but self-determined rule, which he is now overapplying. The same kind of error may occur with plurals (e.g., *foots*).

The key emphasis in this linguistic interpretation of language is on the *transformations* among sentence parts. When these occur they are produced by the child in his own way. They are not simply copies of adult transformations. Thus, when he repeats a sentence like, "Which toy do I get?" it is likely to be transformed into, "Which toy I do get?" There are so many regularities of this kind that the linguist has come to call this general theoretical framework *transformational grammar,* and has developed it as a quite viable alternative to the older and psychologically more orthodox S-R type interpretation.

It is apparent that to some extent at least these two contrasting points of view concentrate upon different facets of the most complex realm of language behavior. There is certainly room for each point of view at the present time, and only future theory and research can determine which view will ultimately be most favored.

COGNITIVE DEVELOPMENT

Piagetian Stages in Cognitive Development

Our discussion of intellectual development has thus far been concerned with essentially structural, or cross-sectional, approaches. An alternative approach to the

Take a Breather

SOME EXAMPLES OF IRREVERSIBILITY

One of the most impressive of the principles of cognitive development in children that have been worked out by Piaget is that of irreversibility. Briefly, this term refers to the inability of the young child to reverse his thinking, or "to return to the point of origin." Consider the following two examples:

1. Identical plasticene balls are shown to the child: He is asked if they are the same size, or if they contain the same amount of plasticene. He states that they are the same size.

Then, as he watches, one of the balls is molded into a different shape, say a sausage shape:

The child is again asked to compare their size, and he will usually state that there is a difference. (Most often the sausage is judged to be larger.) Apparently he is unable to return to the point of origin in his thinking.

2. The child is given a pile of beads and asked to place them, one at a time, in two glass containers of different shapes:

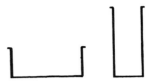

He is instructed to put one bead in each hand at the same time and drop each into one of the glasses. After they are well filled, he is asked which one contains the larger number of beads:

Generally his answer will be that the taller but thinner one does, again because of an inability to reverse his thinking. (This same experiment can be done with amounts of liquid but is probably simpler—and certainly less messy—with beads.)
If you have access to a four-year-old, try one of these for yourself.

study of intellectual function is that provided by the Swiss psychologist Jean Piaget. Piaget has been by far the most influential researcher utilizing the concept of age stages in development in relation to the development of cognitive processes. Much emphasis has been placed not only on the discontinuity of the various stages of intellectual functions but also on their dependence on chronological age. Although he and his collaborators and adherents have been criticized for overemphasizing age as a determining factor and underplaying individual differences, they have been extraordinarily productive and have produced highly provocative data and theory. Moreover, Piaget has recognized the interplay of experiential and maturational factors and has thus adopted a much more flexible position with regard to hereditary determination than is implicit in the typical normative research described above.

Piaget has interpreted intelligence dynamically, as cognitive activity involving organization and adaptation. *Schemata* are behavior patterns of thinking that are instrumental as cognitive tools. They are characteristic ways of adapting (assimilating and accommodating) and are thus "tools" for coping with the environment. *Assimilation* consists of the child's incorporating within his cognitive functioning the structures that he finds in the environment. *Accommodation* consists of the modification of old cognitive structures or the acquisition of new ones as the individual copes with new demands of the environment.

Piaget's stages, like those of Gesell and other normative thinkers, represent qualitative changes. However, he has worked from an essentially epigenetic point of view that puts a great deal more stress on the environment, and the child's active interaction with it, than does the typical normative position. Although new schemata develop for each stage, they do so on the basis of the old schemata and as a result of the pressures of the environment as well as the maturational forces within the child.

The Sensorimotor Period: Birth to Two Years

During the earliest developmental period the schemata consist of primarily congenital behavior patterns. The stage roughly corresponds to the infancy period (up to two years of age). On the basis of extended semiexperimental observations on his own three children, Piaget distinguished six substages in the sensorimotor period. Samples of these will be described.

The first substage involves only the inherited behaviors, such as sucking, looking, listening, and the like, which are at first directly under the influence of external stimulation. Gradually, however, the infant shifts to a more active "groping," or trial-and-error type behavior in which these schemata are applied in new situations.

The last two substages, appearing during the second year, involve elaboration and invention. For example, the child will try out some new procedures, as by deliberately allowing a familiar object to drop to the floor and then observing it intently. It is during this substage that appropriate toys, or other objects not intended as toys by adults, are vigorously subjected to shaking, throwing, and so on. The final substage involves the conceptual, or mental, representation of such activities as new and complementary schemata. Rather than actually groping with objects, the infant now begins to foresee the consequences of some of these activities without actually needing to test them empirically. These important new schemata, like all the preceding ones, are thus built upon the basis of the old patterns and continue to complement rather than replace them.

The sensorimotor period, with its quite limited and preliminary use of symbolic and representational processes, brings the infant approximately to the highest level of intellectual function reached by subhuman animal forms. The child has a more or less stable perceptual perspective and conceptual basis for viewing the world, in contrast to the early infantile stage in which a succession of sensory impressions occur but in a more detached manner. The stage is thus set for the enormous intellectual advance made possible by the child's more extensive utilization of both signs and symbols, mainly in the form of words and images.

Preconceptual Thought: Two to Four Years

Piaget has advanced the notion of the preconcept, which is somewhere between the particularity of the object itself and the generality of a class of objects, to account for the child's cognitive behavior during the transitional stage between two and four years of age. The child is said to reason *transductively*, from one particular object or situation to another, rather than either deductively (from general to particular) or inductively (from particular to general) as the adult does. The three-year-old child, for example, would not be sure whether the taxicab that he sees parked on the street as he drives through the city is the same one or a series of different ones. In general, he may be said, during this period, to be relearning on a conceptual level the lessons earlier acquired on a sensorimotor level. His cognitive processes, although clearly exceeding those of the infant, are therefore of a fumbling and inefficient nature.

Intuitive Thought: Four to Seven Years

The four- to seven-year-old child, who has now mastered concepts, still functions cognitively in a distinctly limited manner. Piaget's most widely cited experiment illustrates some of the deficiencies of the intuitive thinking that characterizes this stage. (See "Take a Breather," p. 303.) The child is shown some substance, such as water or beads, being poured from one glass container to another that is, say, taller and thinner than the first. He is assured that all the material from the first container is in the second, with nothing added or subtracted. He is then asked whether there is now more of the material in the second container than there was in the first. A typical response at this age is that there is now more, because the level has risen. (Or sometimes the child may respond that there is less, because of the lesser width of the container.)

The fundamental reason for the intuitive character of cognitive functions during this stage is the continued dominance of perceptual over thought processes. The notion of *conservation*, which Piaget has emphasized as underlying a correct answer in the test situation just described and as generally critical in thinking, has not yet developed. Conservation of such properties of objects as their quantity, weight, or volume depends upon one's *conceptual* maintenance of these properties in spite of the apparent changes that are perceived.

In another experiment stimulated by Piaget's work, children from three to six years were first shown a cat, then they were shown the same cat wearing realistically molded rabbit and dog facial masks. Emotional reactivity measures indicated that the older children responded to the later stimuli as a cat, thus indicating conservation of its identity, but that the younger children did not. Conservation is thus based essentially on thought or representational processes. It is the child's focusing on (perceiving) the physical dimensions of the containers in contrast to invoking the conceptual nature of the conservation of the substance (thinking) that accounts for his error in the experiment described. During this intuitive period, however, the child's behavior is still dominated by the perceptual processes that underlay his earlier cognitive functions. These are notoriously more subject to distortion and therefore less reliable than the conceptualization involved in thinking (although the way in which the latter are used can also introduce a substantial amount of distortion).

A related factor in intuitive thinking is its tendency to focus on a single aspect of a situation rather than adopt different perspectives. This tendency is also characteristic of perception. For example, visual attention is attracted by the sheer size of parts of the visual field. Moreover, visual perception is always clearer in the center of the field and progressively less clear as the periphery is approached. The use of concepts in relational thinking can overcome these shortcomings and distortions of perception, but only when thought comes to be regarded as more stable than perception, as it is by the normal adult under most conditions.

Concrete Operations: Seven to Eleven Years

Logical operations, regarded as internalized responses, become functional between the ages of seven and eleven. Operations involving *classification, relational ordering,* and *numbering* of objects occur. However, these are effectively applied only to concrete objects; the child still has difficulty with more abstract situations. For example, he is likely to have trouble deciding which boy is older when the relative ages of the boys are given in pairs: "Ed is older than John, Bill is older than Ed. Is John or Bill older?"

The child in this stage is able to use the two key concepts of *conservation* (as described above) and *reversibility.* Thinking is reversible in the sense that it can return to an earlier condition: the examples given earlier in the "Breather" indicate the failure of young children to make this kind of conceptual somersault. There is a considerably greater degree of fluidity and flexibility associated with thinking than there is with perception. Hence children who have reached this stage and are emphasizing thought processes independent of perceptual processes are much more capable of solving intellectual problems and responding effectively in a larger variety of practical situations. As mentioned, however, they are still limited to operations that involve concrete, readily perceived objects and events.

Formal Operations: Eleven to Fifteen Years

Abstract thought processes characteristic of the normal adult are acquired between the ages of eleven and fifteen, the final stage of cognitive development. The restriction of operations to concrete situations no longer holds. Full freedom from the kind of errors resulting from uncritical acceptance of the way things appear to be (perception) rather than the way they can be conceived to be (thought) has now been won. Arguments can be made and problems solved purely in words and images. The adolescent now can concentrate upon the *form* of a proposition independent of its content.

Piaget's Contribution

Perhaps the most important contribution that Piaget has made is to counteract the strictly cross-sectional and essentially static view of intellectual function that has characterized most of the work done on intelligence testing. The more functional approach emphasized and popularized by Piaget is certainly a needed corrective to what was previously a badly unbalanced situation. Moreover, he has continued to emphasize the essential unity of the behaving organism, as evidenced by his somewhat less-well-known research on affective development.

Piaget's persistent efforts to make understandable the development of cognition in children have won him increasing recognition. Although this was initially confined mainly to developmental psychologists, and by no means all of them, he has been regarded with more interest and respect by increasing numbers of experimentalists, particularly as the rigor with which he has collected and analyzed his data as well as formulated his theories has increased over the years. Problems of translation slowed the initial propagation of his ideas in this country, but these have now been largely overcome; in addition, a good number of secondary sources reporting and interpreting his work and some of his original publications are now available in English.

Piaget has not been concerned with age, except as an index of sequence in development, nor has he ever evidenced any concern about the problem of individual differences. The principal reason for his later popularity on this continent is that he has emphasized cognitive development and a view of it that describes qualitative change. In contrast, American views of cognitive development have been pretty well cemented into the quantitative increase of a faculty, conceptualized along the lines of the psychometric measures of intelligence. Piaget's methods also happen to be alien to most American-trained psychologists, because he employs neither statistics nor experimental manipulation in the sense that we understand them. Because his techniques were so "unorthodox," few American psychologists could bring themselves to trust him until it became very clear that he knew more about cognitive development than anyone else did.

Piaget has often been compared with Freud and with the Gestalt psychologists. He shares with Freud some of the characterization as a brilliant innovator and also certain ideas concerning the origins of developmental functions. But he has been quite unlike Freud in that he has appreciated the need to buttress his theories by empirical support, and as far as possible with experimental (even if nonstatistically treated) data. Similarly, although he has emphasized the fieldlike basis of experience in common with the Gestaltists, he has not evidenced their disinclination to analyze patterns into components. On the contrary, he has made such an analysis a central part of his research. Moreover, he has been careful to take into account environmental learning as well as inherited factors, and has been concerned with their interaction in development.

Learning psychologists have recently become more interested in Piaget's work. It has been noted, for example, that some of his key concepts are basically similar to orthodox concepts in learning. Thus assimilation seems to be substantially what learning researchers call generalization (cf. Chapter 11, p. 350) and accommodation is closely related to response differentiation as well as acquisition of new responses. Such correlations have helped to orient more orthodox experimentalists with regard to Piaget's thinking by providing some familiar landmarks. They have thereby contributed to his growing acceptance in spite of the somewhat unorthodox character (by American experimental standards) of his research.

Apart from the intrinsic merit of his research and theorizing, which must be regarded as very considerable, Piaget has been a major factor in the ever-increasing flood of research activity involving children. Although his influence is only one factor in the total situation, it has been significant. Piaget's ideas of the direction of behavior as moving toward ever-increasing organization and of the human child as an active organizer, maker, and discoverer of his own experiences are fundamentally different from those of other psychologists. Since 1950 research on developmental topics has increased at a remarkable rate, perhaps reflecting the long underdevelopment of this most important field. It is a rare research project on children's cognition that has not been in some way significantly affected by Piaget's highly ingenious and original work. We have therefore presented his developmental model in summary form because some knowledge of it is needed if one is to appreciate the full flavor of contemporary work on children, from a practical as well as an experimental or theoretical point of view.

DEVELOPMENT OF COMPETENCE

Probably no topic in psychology is as controversial as that of competence (or as more specifically considered, general intelligence). Our extended discussion of this issue in Chapter 9 has indicated the extent of this controversy. Only very recently have psychologists begun to turn away from some of their earlier fixed notions concerning the measurement of intellectual capacity. Apart from the role of the environment in determining the relative degree of intellectual achievement there is the more basic issue of *what* we should test for. There is a strong and growing tendency to look more broadly at human performance and to downgrade the traditional concept of general intelligence. The growing influence of Piagetian conceptualizations has helped to accentuate this trend, as has the stress on creativity, which does not correlate very much with general intellectual capacity as measured by standard tests.

In the light of these newer views, and the stress on the more dynamic Piagetian principles that have just been considered, our technical discussion of the orthodox tests of general intelligence is presented as a supplement in Part V, where it can be more readily assigned and/or studied as an option. This discussion focuses on the Stanford–Binet intelligence test, not because of any marked current superiority to other competing forms but because of its historical significance in the field of intelligence testing and its pre-eminent position as a kind of prototypic test. The developmental aspects of intelligence testing are emphasized in the supplement and some attention is also paid to alternative forms of tests and to testing theory.

Socialization

The process of socialization of the human organism is practically as broad and multifaceted as that of human behavioral development itself. There is no important behavioral process that is free of social influences in human development. In part, this fact results from the condition of utter helplessness into which all humans are born. Their emancipation is an arduous and gradual process that takes place over a number of years as the individual becomes less dependent on those who have sustained him. In this process other humans become not only the most significant stimuli in the environment but also the mediators of the underlying cultural values and expectations (the cultural heritage) that are insidiously but inevitably built into each of us.

Our treatment in this section can only provide samples of the multiple ways in which the socialization process occurs, with a focus on the crucial childhood period. Other developmental processes relating to socialization are treated elsewhere (for example, the origin of children's fears, in Chapter 15).

One methodological point seems in order. Not only are children important to study for their own sake—to provide pivotal information on various developmental processes—but they also make excellent subjects for those who are primarily interested not so much in development as in the particular kind of process that is developing (say, learning, perception, language, and the like). This conclusion follows both from the fact that the origins of these processes are often critical to their understanding and from the fact that children typically show basic processes in a relatively clear and uncomplicated manner. They are complex enough to permit investigation of most of the commonly studied functions but not yet so complex as to hide them under the various layers of cognition and affect that are characteristic of most adults. Children can as a result be refreshingly frank, and sometimes perhaps disturbingly so, as in their answers to questions asked after experiments. Moreover, they are less likely than adults to bring their own interpretations into the instructions provided by the experimenter. For all these reasons they have become increasingly popular as experimental subjects, so much so as to tax the patience of some of the schoolteachers and administrators confronted with requests for their use in investigations.

MAN'S BEHAVIORAL PLASTICITY

An important implication of man's socially dependent condition at birth is the remarkable plasticity of his behavioral potential. There has been endless argumentation as to whether man is born with inherent "good" or "bad" tendencies. Such argumentation is groundless; there is no objective basis for making this kind of moral or value judgment about man. Such judgments must be regarded as based primarily upon the moral premises of the judger; that is, they are always relative, rather than absolute. They are clearly inapplicable unless used relative to the framework from which they come.

If man is born morally neutral, then what is it that normally produces the behavioral qualities that result in his being morally judgable as he matures? Here a second kind of legacy from his ancestors needs to be invoked, to supplement the biological inheritance, in his genetic programming, that each man has. Man's *cultural legacy* shapes him more or less in the form of his more immediate ancestors. The process of socialization, accentuated in man because of his long period of dependence upon others for his very life, thus accounts largely for the direction that his behavioral development takes. Because it is impossible for any organism to retrace his steps completely, in spite of the most extreme countermeasures, we tend to accept the form of each person's behavior and personality as fixed and often fail to recognize the constant but quite insidious action of social forces in molding him in the image of his society.

From a somewhat more analytic point of view, man's behavior is remarkably influenced by his learning to respond emotionally and otherwise to certain symbolic cues characterizing great institutional forces, such as family, school, and community. Man's development during his life-span is thus a combination of his biological inheritance and his responses to social forces and culture.

THE INFANT AS A SOCIAL ORGANISM

The infant, though dependent upon others for nurturance, is born with a very capable sensorimotor system. He can hear, see, smell, and feel cold, heat, or pain. He can cry, turn, suck, and kick. By crying he can summon his mother or other caretaker to tend to his needs. Very early the infant smiles, another social communicator. Thus a social relationship is established between the infant and his caretaker, with each having an effect upon the other.

Some important individual differences have been identified in infancy. For example, temperament is apparently differentiated from birth on. One group of researchers was able to categorize different temperaments in babies from early years until childhood, finding some "easy" or "difficult," others "slow to warm up," and so on. Recognition of these persistent differences should be a consideration in evaluating the effects of all the socializing environments, such as the home and school.

Among the objects most frequently explored visually and often reached for physically are the faces of the children and adults who inhabit the infant's world. Although in very early infancy there is little reason to believe that a human face is an especially outstanding stimulus, by about four months human faces and human actions have clearly begun to acquire special significance. Psychologists have come to believe that a substantial part of the organism's subsequent reactions to people depends upon the kind of social relations that he first experiences in the infancy period. By the end of the first year mother and child usually have developed a stable interaction pattern. Patience in such necessary processes as weaning and toilet training and a generally affectionate and sympathetic set of attitudes seem to be especially critical with regard to the healthy subsequent development of the infant's personality.

One of the most important results of the observational studies of infants and children as they interact with parents and other adults is the increased awareness on the part of psychologists of the fact that the interaction is two-way. That is, the child and/or infant maintains and shapes the responses of those with whom he interacts by selectively reinforcing their behaviors. For example, the infant's crying gains attention from attendants, and infants use this behavior to make demands on parents or other adults.

Role of the Mother

MATERNAL SEPARATION. A special problem in socialization concerns the role of the mother. Maternal separation has been studied intensively in recent years, with empirical observations replacing the theoretical speculations and home-spun wisdom of previous generations. Analysis of these studies indicates that the detrimental effects of maternal deprivation so often described are by no means automatic or inevitable. Rather, the nature and degree of such effects depend upon a very large number of subsidiary conditions, such as the duration of the separation and especially the kind of replacements that are provided. Moreover, the separation of infant and mother is seldom an isolated event, but occurs within a context of other, frequently disturbing events, so that it is not easy to isolate its influence.

An early analysis of the case histories of a group of forty-four convicted thieves is illustrative of the kind of result that kindled interest in this problem. A subsample of fourteen of these was selected as "affectionless characters." There was evidence in their biographical material that at least twelve of the fourteen had been separated from their mothers during infancy. Other disruptive experiences had followed, including institutionalization and numerous changes from one foster home to another. Thus it was impossible to pinpoint the determining factor in their subsequent antisocial behavior, if indeed any one factor could be so isolated. The difficulties of applying experimental controls to this kind of problem are self-evident.

ANIMAL STUDIES OF MATERNAL DEPRIVATION. Experimental studies of maternal deprivation have been carried out in a well-known series of researches in the Wisconsin primate laboratory by Harry Harlow. The results generally indicate that permanent psychological effects can ensue unless adequate substitutes for the mother are provided. So-called *surrogate mothers* made of inanimate materials produced rhesus monkeys that did not show normal sexual behavior at maturity and that, when finally bred, failed to exhibit normal maternal behavior themselves.

Because both heat (from an electric light bulb) and food (from a nursing bottle with the nipple protruding through a hole) were provided by the surrogate mothers, these satisfactions do not appear to be sufficient to produce normally behaving offspring. Harlow's baby monkeys definitely preferred the surrogate mother with a body of terry cloth over sponge rubber to the simpler wire-frame model, although each presented the same heat and food. Apparently the monkey affectional system is dependent upon contact stimulation provided by the terry cloth, which encourages cuddling; there is more to even monkey motherhood than warmth and hunger satisfaction. Figure 10-7 shows a representative infant monkey response to the surrogate mothers.

ATTACHMENT BEHAVIOR. A variety of observational researches have been performed on the problem of affective attachment of infant and child to mother. Attachment is evidenced by the child's remaining near the mother and is strong until about three years of age. This behavior is not dependent only on activities relating to physical needs. For example, in an Israeli kibbutz, attachment to parents is maintained even though physical needs are met by other persons.

As the infant becomes able to move about by himself to explore his environment,

10-7 Harlow's baby monkey with surrogate mother. (Photo by The University of Wisconsin Primate Laboratory.)

he becomes progressively able to be separated for longer periods. In one observational study the researcher watched children in a park and recorded their approaches and leave-takings of their mothers when the mothers were stationary and when they were moving. At the age of two-and-one-half the child has difficulty in following its mother, but after the age of three it can follow her and will accept hand holding until about seven years of age. Other studies have shown the progress from attachment to mother and separation from mother by measuring the amount of time the child will be separated from its mother in a controlled situation. It is hardly surprising that the amount of time the child can readily be separated from the mother increases with increasing age. It is also true that the child will stay separated from the mother longer when the area he is exploring while away from her has more stimulus objects, such as toys or toylike materials.

Attachment behavior was exhibited in the report of one researcher who raised a monkey in his household. The monkey began discriminating individual members of the household between five and fourteen days of age. Subsequently he became attached to the experimenter and up to the age of three-and-one-half months still showed a preference for the experimenter, despite his absence during the intervening period.

CHILDHOOD SOCIALIZATION

Children's Play

The significance of children's play, particularly with regard to their subsequent socialization, would be very hard to exaggerate. As every observant parent knows, play is indeed serious work and often hard work for children. But it is also the means by which enduring patterns of social interaction are initiated. Experimental documentation of this crucial role of play has been reported by Harlow and his co-workers using infant rhesus monkeys. These investigators have found that effective adult sexual interactions are almost impossible to achieve unless normal heterosexual affective patterns have been established. This occurs primarily through playful interactions of the young monkeys. Monkeys that have been socially isolated and so have missed these early play experiences strongly resist subsequent therapeutic efforts to induce them to mate.

Beyond its crucial role in socialization, play serves more broadly to increase the developing organism's competence. Here games with more or less established rules serve as the nucleus around which various kinds of competence develop. An important factor in the development of such competencies is the repetition of activities. Seemingly endless repetition, even to the most minute detail, is quite boring to the adult but needs to be understood in relation to the child's need both to form effective habits and to build confidence in his own abilities. It is extremely difficult for the sophisticated adult to put himself in the child's place, in games as well as other kinds of situations, but what appears to be senseless repetition of behaviors to the adult may in fact permit improved understanding of procedures as well as consolidation of skills for the child.

The fantasy that functions in so much play (of a make-believe nature, in contrast to more formally established games) also has an important role. Among other things, it permits the child to practice adult roles, often explicitly, as when the little girl plays "Mother" with her dolls, but also in more subtle ways. A variety of roles, assertive and demanding as well as meek and compliant, can be exercised in play when they would not be permitted otherwise by adults or perhaps even peers.

Traditional cultural norms are important informal regulators of play activities. For example, little girls are typically discouraged from activities involving rough, physical contact ("tomboys" are in the minority) and little boys are usually discouraged from playing with dolls ("sissies" are likewise in the minority and socially frowned upon). The significance of these early social roles in determining later behavior patterns and attitudes has been effectively pointed out by advocates of women's liberation.

Finally, play is probably the major means by which the surprisingly potent motivational factors involved in one's "peer culture" develop. The need to conform to one's peers' behavior, especially strong during the adolescent period, may well have its origins in the give and take of social interactions molded during the play periods of childhood. The fact that peers are accepted more readily than most adults seems to encourage the development of this kind of motivation. The segregation of the young from adult activities also encourages reliance on peers.

Child-Rearing Practices

Child-rearing practices constitute one topic on which many parents appear eager to receive instruction. Unfortunately, clear-cut and foolproof rules for child rearing in the home are not available. In general, the same overall statement can be made with regard to effective parenthood as can be made for effective psychotherapy: the specific form of the activities practiced is less important than the personality of the parent or the therapist.

Child-development researchers have tended to be descriptive and explanatory in their reports. Changes that have occurred in child-rearing practices over the past three decades may be attributable to exponents of such practices or may simply reflect changes that have already taken place.

The major changes, mostly apparent in middle-class homes, have been in the direction of (1) freer expression of affection; (2) increased permissiveness, especially with regard to spontaneous expressions of childish wishes; and (3) decreased dependence upon physical techniques of discipline, such as spanking, and greater dependence upon reasoning and explanation, as well as withdrawal of affection and arousal of guilt. Major changes associated with parental sex have also been noted. The father has become less authoritarian and more likely to show affection, and the mother more likely than heretofore to serve as a disciplinarian agent, especially for boys. Finally, the class differences that previously appeared to be distinct have greatly diminished, with lower-class families tending to approximate the middle-class practices.

The products of these trends in child-rearing practice are generally agreed (by child psychologists at least) to be superior in socially desirable characteristics such as self-control and leadership as well as generally more satisfactory adjustment. These features are reported most often for middle-class children, because it is in this large social category that the changes described have been most pronounced.

Some socially undesirable personality changes have been produced by the newer types of child rearing. Interactions with sex of child and of parent are especially complex. Girls are in general more likely to receive affection and less likely to be punished than boys; they are also more likely to become more anxious and more dependent. That this is not simply a matter of genetic sex-related differences is indicated by observation of the same pattern of parental treatment and personality outcome tending to occur when first-born are compared with later-born children, with sex controlled. Thus first-born children of both sexes are more likely to receive affection and less likely to be punished and tend overall to be more anxious and dependent.

It must be emphasized that all these trends are tendencies, based on means of relatively large numbers of subjects, and that the individual variations are really more important when any one person is concerned than the group averages. Also, further complications are involved. For example, extremes of either affection or

DEVELOPMENT

strong discipline have been found to be detrimental to the development of both sexes; whereas more girls than boys seem to show susceptibility to the deleterious effects of overprotection, boys suffer more from insufficient discipline. Finally, all these trends are clearest at the lower social levels, where sex roles are still most clearly distinguished; they are obscured in the upper and the upper-middle classes, where the sexes tend to be treated more equally.

In sum, a balance between affection, discipline, and so on, appears to be crucial in the optimal development of children. Unfortunately, there is no simple way of expressing this kind of relationship, nor is there any simple way of telling parents just *how much* discipline is optimal, or of relating various kinds of standards across families. It bears repeating, therefore, that although the overall effects of the contemporary movement toward greater affection and less rigid discipline are seen as beneficial, there seem to be certain risks associated with these child-rearing practices, as there are with others. Furthermore, if we want to continue to encourage certain personality differences between the sexes, then we will need to be careful to continue to differentiate their treatment; if, on the other hand, we want to obliterate personality differences between the sexes, perhaps in accordance with some contemporary proponents of "women's liberation," then we should reduce even more the differential treatment that boys and girls receive as children.

School

The more formalized social requirements of the child's first schooling constitute a radical, and often quite traumatic, break with his previous social interactions in the home. The child's role in the home is to a degree at least independent of his behavior, for he enjoys a certain role and status merely as a member of the family. In school, on the other hand, he is one of a large and probably heterogeneous group. He will be judged, especially by his teachers, by the effectiveness of his behavior rather than by virtue of his pre-established role. He loses much of his individuality, and it is up to him to re-establish it. Many new roles appear and offer the child both an opportunity to develop new skills and social relationships and, too often unfortunately, an occasion to hold back and fail to cope with these new challenges.

There are of course a great number of conditions in the school and in the parents' reactions to the child's new life in the school that affect how he seizes these opportunities. One of the less often emphasized of these factors is sheer physical size. The differences in size that exist within the classroom can work to improve or worsen a child's adjustment in school. For example, early or late physical maturity can be a significant factor in a boy's athletic competency, so highly regarded in our culture. The social experiences of the early maturers, who tend to have correspondingly advanced athletic skills, have been shown to be consistently more cordial. The typical late maturer, on the contrary, has been described as more dependent on others, impulsive, self-indulgent, and rebellious.

As a miniature social representation of the larger world, the school thus provides during middle and late childhood the seething cauldron of social forces out of which the adolescent and the mature individual will emerge. Its place as an initial and continuing contact point of the child and his all-encompassing culture gives it a significance approaching and sometimes surpassing that of the home with respect to the nature and direction of the child's socialization.

As the child passes from the informal training of the home and community into the formal training situation of the school, he will encounter differences based on the aims of these types of training. The informal training has concentrated on individualistic personal values; the formal will concentrate on universal values. Learning in the formal situation will be ordered and to a great degree abstract, consisting of the manipulation of symbols rather than objects. Language becomes the transmitter of information. These changes in the learning environment will be troublesome for some children, who are handicapped in school because they are not accustomed to dealing with symbols in this abstract manner.

One of the aims of the Head Start program was to make this transition easier for the socially or culturally deprived child. In working with such children it was found that verbal skills were directly related to socioeconomic background. It was necessary to develop innovative programs to stimulate language growth. These innovations involved pacing materials, teaching teachers, and bringing families into the programs. Under the proper conditions children were able to progress. Some Head Start programs were held to be of dubious value because the improvement disappeared when children were placed in a regular classroom. Optimal results can only be obtained if the home environment is also modified so that the informal training more nearly matches the formal training. Because of the pervasive influence of the home, it is unrealistic to expect instant success from all programs, nor should the value of enrichment programs be denied because some of them failed.

Because schools are such an important factor as a socializing agent, it might be well to take a look at what happens in the twelve or more years that an individual attends. The student is measured within that system in some terms of "achievement" of set items—reading, arithmetic, and so on. He is also evaluated in other ways by the teacher, who is an adult representative of the society. Such evaluations may include components of "good behavior" involving conformity to set standards of society. These "achievement" records, whether they be intelligence tests, which are one tool used in measurement, or standard achievement tests, also serve a selective function. By the time an individual is in junior high school the selection process is sealed in terms of selecting who will and who will not be able to do college work. There has been recent concern about the fact that students' records are passed on from year to year. Thus a teacher with access to these records has to a degree already formed an opinion of a child before he or she enters the classroom. A teacher's attitude toward a child reinforces certain behaviors; thus a teacher who treats a student as though he were stupid to some extent has a "stupid" student even though the student may actually be intellectually capable. The same thing is true for "good" or "bad" behavior.

Classrooms are operated in such a way that aversive reinforcement, such as fear of failure and other kinds of social punishment, are used extensively. Reinforcement of certain behaviors by teachers and peers may teach the student that (1) going beyond the assignment does not pay off, (2) the rewards of the school may be obtained in easier ways than by academic performance, (3) he should avoid excellence, (4) conformity is rewarded, (5) curiosity is irrelevant. Current educational practice is keyed to the middle-class children who come from an environment which enables them to adapt. Some other groups cannot adapt to the middle-class achievement ethic and the deferral of rewards. Individualized prescribed instruction has been suggested as one means by which individuals may be taught subject matter so that the preceding problems are minimized. This adaptive mode of education "assumes that the educational environment can provide for a wide range and variety of instructional methods and opportunities for success. Alternate means of learning are adaptive to and are in some way matched to knowledge about each individual . . ." (Glaser, 1972, p. 6).

SPECIAL PROBLEMS IN SOCIALIZATION

Inculcation of Moral and Social Values: Conscience

Among the more fascinating and challenging problems faced by psychologists is that of the development in the child of values of various sorts, especially those relating to moral standards. It is clear that moral values or standards of social acceptability in behavior are learned from the social environment of the child, but the manner in which this occurs remains obscure.

One of the more interesting facets of moral attitudes is that they are so unlikely to be questioned by those who hold them. They tend to be accepted as absolutes, in spite of their unmistakably relative character, as demonstrated by cultural anthropologists in the many observations of societies other than our own. Ethnocentrism, or the tendency to adopt the perspective of one's own culture as central, is such a strong and pervasive factor as to suggest the unusual strength and persistence of the underlying learning and motivational conditions.

Moral values can be studied directly, in terms of the behavioral processes themselves, or indirectly, in terms of the intervening variable usually labeled *conscience*. Here we shall point to some of the more interesting and provocative work of both types. Our treatment cannot be complete, nor can we point to more than the initial stages of the experimental and theoretical analysis of the problem.

An early, classic study on moral behavior demonstrated very clearly its specific nature. Honesty, which we assume to be a generalized kind of behavior that parents and others attempt to instill in children, was studied in a variety of settings. No generalized trait of honesty was found. For example, a given child was observed to be scrupulously honest when, say, he was tested in the home but quite dishonest when tested in school. Thus he might persistently refuse to take money left on dressers at home but regularly take advantage of apparent errors in examination grading at school; some other child might show exactly the opposite pattern. Such specificity suggests corresponding specificity in the learning factors that underlie these behaviors, and a failure of moral exhortation to produce generalized moral behavior. This research also seems consistent with the variability observed in the behavior of adult models, whose actions may be presumed to be influential in children's learning, and the inconsistency between adult behavior and adult verbalization that has led so many of our contemporary youth to voice disenchantment with our social system.

Moral codes, whether generalized or specific, are clearly potent factors in our behavior. The interesting internal function called conscience is usually given credit for the strength of moral values in children and adults. But so labeling this function hardly explains it, and our understanding of conscience and how it develops has not proceeded very far. A variety of mechanisms (identification, internalization, introjection) have been suggested to account for the manner in which the moral code of a society comes to be inculcated into the conscience of a child, but these terms do little more than rename the phenomenon. Moreover, their usage varies so markedly from one writer to the next that even the definition of the term *conscience,* let alone its experimental analysis, can hardly be considered adequate.

A useful definitional analysis has been advanced by one set of workers. Three criteria for recognizing the functioning of conscience in young children were suggested. These are (1) resistance to temptation, (2) self-instruction to obey rules, and (3) evidence of guilt feelings and guilty behavior after violation of rules. Conscience is thus defined by the appearance of these three kinds of behavioral manifestations.

An especially provocative experimental analysis of resistance to temptation has been reported using young beagles as subjects. In this study the dogs were first made very hungry by reducing their food intake over a period of time. Then they were given access both to their normal dry meal and an especially appetizing meat dish. However, they were punished by the experimenter (by being swatted on the nose with a rolled-up newspaper) if they attempted to eat the meat dish. The independent variable was the delay between their starting to eat the meat and the onset of punishment; this was immediate for one group, was several seconds delayed for a second group, and was delayed a longer time for a third group. All the dogs learned to ignore the meat and eat the less attractive dry food. Then, in the test of resistance to temptation, they were all given access to both foods in the absence of the experimenter and the amount of time and number of trials required before they began eating the meat was measured.

The major results were that the dogs given the immediate punishment during training both stopped trying to eat the meat in training and resumed eating it in test more quickly than the others. Moreover, they showed many less obvious signs of emotionality. The dogs with the longest delay between onset of meat eating and punishment had the most difficulty, both with regard to their eventual eating of the tabooed meat and the vacillation and emotionality they exhibited. This study thus provides good support for the generally accepted proposition that when punishment is used, it should be immediate and clear-cut. Moreover, it suggests the utility of animal subjects for even such human problems as resistance to temptation in the development of conscience.

Shifting attention to the second criterion for conscience, self-instructions, we may tentatively conclude that clear evidence of this aspect of conscience can be found only in human subjects. The manner in which young children customarily accompany their overt behavior with overt verbalizations ("Johnny runs," "Mary throws ball," and the like) suggests that there is nothing unusual about this development; negative admonitions (e.g., "Johnny not run," "Mary not throw") are in no fundamental way different from positive ones. Moreover, this kind of overt vocalization normally diminishes as the child matures so that covert verbalization of prohibitions as well as positive actions would be expected to continue. Their ultimate transformation into self-instructions to conform, or not to transgress social rules, would constitute one basis for conscience.

The third criterion, that of guilt feelings and behaviors, poses more of a theoretical problem. The self-sacrificial aspects of guilt are especially difficult to interpret on the basis of normal learning and motivational principles. Moreover, this aspect of conscience, like self-instructions, appears to be a strictly human phenomenon. Animals may behave in a way to suggest a kind of "shame," but this behavior may merely reflect fear of punishment for their transgressions. The expiation of guilt through the active seeking out of punishment seems to be uniquely human. This aspect of conscience thus not only makes it more difficult to relate to other kinds of learning and behavior but also may help to account for the great strength of moral factors once established. However, the analysis of guilt as a quite complex phenomenon in its own right remains to be done.

ADOLESCENCE

Adolescence is the period from the onset of puberty, roughly at twelve years of age, until adult responsibilities are taken on. This latter event occurs at varying ages for individuals within our culture (with either eighteen or twenty-one years, and increasingly the former, marking the age at which such formal functions as voting or buying liquor are legally sanctioned).

The cross-cultural variation in the adolescent period is even more striking than the interindividual variations within the United States. Thus in some cultures anthropologists have reported absolutely minimal attention to this period; there may be a simple ceremony marking sexual maturity, or the pubescent may be almost immediately accepted into adult society. Other cultures have more elaborate and sometimes temporally extended ceremonies and tests of various sorts. But no culture allows adolescence to be as indefinitely continued or to be emphasized as much as ours.

Much of this obsession is probably attributable to the highly unrealistic set of contradictory attitudes and practices that exist with regard to sexual expressions, especially heterosexual activities. Adolescence is by definition a time of sexual maturity. The turmoil accompanying this important transitional period is aggravated by attempting to enforce sexual inactivity at a time of greatest biological urge. It is small wonder that the present generation of adolescents have generally refused to listen to adult moralizing on sexual expression. Newer social attitudes, plus the timely introduction of "the pill" by means of which girls are able to utilize a simple contraceptive device, have combined to produce the contemporary movement toward freer sexual expression in youths. The consequences of this freer expression in Western society are indeed serious for the family as a social structure, especially when combined with concern about population growth, more personal freedom for women, and changing attitudes toward marriage.

In addition to the obvious sexual adjustment issue, faced particularly by adolescents in their late teens, there are related problems of social interaction. At a time when new social skills, of a youth–adult as well as a boy–girl variety, are needed, all kinds of distractions and diversions are needlessly introduced. For example, the normally socially sensitive adolescent is made even more so by the flood of advertisements that threaten him with dire social effects unless he hurries out to buy this antiperspirant or that toothpaste, or hastens to reduce skin blemishes or remove undesirable hair. Overemphasizing such normal problems as acne is bad enough but fabricating new ones is even worse; the fast bucks that are thus made by enterprising salespeople and advertising agencies may increase the gross national product but they hardly contribute to the emotional or social maturity of our nation's youth.

Adolescents in our culture have an uncommonly long transitional period during which they can accommodate to the adult role, but by the same token they are likely to face many frustrating delays in actively taking up that role. Much of this delay is occasioned by the extended educational process they undergo, particularly in the middle class but increasingly in the lower class as well. Further, although extended upper-class educational careers are not likely to have associated financial problems, middle- and lower-class adolescents, with few financial resources of their own, are quite likely to have financial problems. Overstimulation of educational and occupational objectives by a culture with too much concern for college education, regardless of its appropriateness, is very largely to blame. The correlated slighting of technical training further aggravates the situation. Occupational as well as sexual problems of adolescents need to be more squarely faced by adults in our society.

Adulthood is not dependent upon leaving all adolescent traits at one time. There are dimensions along which individuals vary quite markedly with regard to their rate of maturation. Thus some of us never really quite "grow up" emotionally, remaining in our so-called adolescent stage throughout our remaining years, although perhaps being economically self-sufficient, and therefore on this dimension adult. Others may be socially mature long before they gain economic independence. Furthermore, in contrast to the clear-cut legal dates mentioned earlier, there are no absolute standards by which we can neatly categorize an individual as adolescent or adult; the process of maturing tends to be a continuous one, or perhaps one in which such sudden changes as physical growth spurts are interpolated between periods of little change (plateaus). Recognition of these facts of individual variations and offering adolescents the opportunity to shorten their period of overlong dependency are among the social problems our society needs to resolve.

One solution that has been proposed is that adolescents be given work experience as an integral part of their educational training as early as high school. The arguments in favor of this plan are that the pay would make the adolescent more independent, he would become responsible as a person for the work performed, and he would have an opportunity to have an adult model as he works. Some colleges now require work experience as part of their training. Practical application at an earlier level would cause problems of scheduling, finding appropriate work, and fixing pay schedules. Some high school students, usually those who do not intend to go to college, are now allowed this opportunity.

MATURITY

The mature adult is likely to have his or her time occupied in some kind of occupational setting. Societal adjustments during this period are those related to acquiring financial security, becoming part of a community, and so on. When a family is started, adjustments must be made with regard to care of the child; usually the mother in our society is responsible for child care. If the mother prefers to work, other means of child care must be found. At any rate, the ages twenty to forty constitute a period with strong ties to home and community.

As the individual enters middle age (usually considered to be ages forty to sixty) he may encounter new social adjustment problems. For the male they may involve such things as his perceived success in his career, or his concern over sexual functioning or physiological changes connected with aging. If he is economically secure he is likely to have an increasing amount of leisure time and must decide how to spend that time. Typically adjustment for women has been considered most difficult during this period. Aside from the physiological adjustments to the menopause and loss of ability to bear children, the woman now has increasing amounts of leisure time. The children she has cared for are leaving home and becoming independent. At this age it is difficult for women to return to a career and many turn to volunteer work as a means of adjusting to this change in life. How these problems are handled by the middle-aged will determine to a large extent how successful and satisfying the subsequent years are likely to be. Very little literature is available on these problems or their solutions, although it has been pointed out that those who are financially secure have an easier time with these adjustments.

THE AGED

A great deal of research is going on in the medical field in attempts to isolate the factors that cause aging and to find methods of interfering with these factors and thus prolonging life. However, physiological and biological factors are not the only ones that influence aging. In observations of the aged who are over 100 years old, one common factor was that they are still productive and respected members of a household that might include three generations.

The elderly have reported that in old age they become more socially detached, having fewer social interactions and less intimate ones. Many elderly are detached in other ways; they are detached from their jobs, detached from part of their income, and possibly detached from their home, for economic or health reasons. This problem of the aged is aggravated when it is no longer possible for the individual to care for himself and he must either go to live with relatives or move to a nursing home.

Changes that the elderly dread are the loss of significance and loss of independence. Anxiety neurosis is provoked by lack of security, circumstances where the older person is less welcome, less valued, and more dependent on others than in his earlier years. It is not surprising, then, to find that the elderly who have sufficient income have a good advantage in terms of adapting to change. As evidence of the importance of having sufficient income to the well-being of the aged it is interesting to note that among the records of individuals over sixty who were admitted to mental hospitals for the first time, only 20 per cent were admitted for physical disability. Moreover, those who were admitted were overrepresented by certain groups as compared to total population. These groups are (1) residents in an urban area, (2) widowed or divorced, (3) low in educational attainment, (4) low in economic status, (5) blacks and foreign whites.

Most of the evidence available indicates that psychological functions are not as likely to deteriorate during these later years as had previously been assumed. Of course sensory deficit is common, and motor abilities also decline at an accelerated rate. This decline varies, depending on whether the individual has a good genetic background, for protection from physiological deterioration, and beneficial environmental experiences. Learning and memory functions do not decline as precipitously as some observations earlier suggested; senescence (senility) is by no means inevitable. With proper control of motivation and related factors—so that the older subject is almost equally motivated as younger persons to learn and remember such meaningless materials as nonsense syllables, for example—some decline is usually found, on the average. However, this decline is by no means so much that new tricks are no longer teachable. Again, the older subject's motivation to cut through habits of a lifetime is a major factor in determining the degree to which he can learn. There is some reason to think that older subjects are less likely to remember new materials, especially on a short-term basis and if much interference in the way of extraneous stimuli and responses is present.

Some attitude scales have shown that the elderly are more rigid than other age groups, though this is modified by the possession of a high intellect; are less confident of their abilities; and are more cautious. Because the latter two attitudes were measured on the basis of a performance test of aiming ability, it is possible that the decreased confidence and more cautious attitude constituted a realistic appraisal.

Researchers have concluded that although proper health care, such as medication and proper diet, have their place in the probability of living a long time, the other important factor is the individual's actual desire or expectation of doing so. It is especially important that aged persons do not fall victim to the belief, now all too prominent among youth, that there are inevitable generalized decrements in capacity accompanying old age. Correction of this myth will become increasingly necessary as the age proportions of our population change. It has been predicted that if present population trends continue, by the year 2000 fully one half of the population of the United States will be over fifty years of age and one third will be over sixty-five years of age. Black power and women's power, presently social forces of substantial import, may pale before the power of the aged. In any event it is highly desirable that some accurate appraisal of the true capability of the aged be widely circulated among all age levels of society if appropriate social adjustments are to occur.

Notes

There are many useful books of a general nature concerned with developmental psychology. Goulet and Baltes's *Life-span Developmental Psychology* (1970) and *Human Development* by Lugo and Hershey (1974) present a current approach to development that takes into account the entire life-span of the human organism.

Methodology in Research

Recent reports based on longitudinal studies are by Jones, Bayley, and Mac-Farlane (1971); McCall, Hogarty, and Hurlburt (1972); and Kagan (1971). The Jones et al. study is based on data from 500 individuals continuously recorded at the University of California at Berkeley. These records succeeded in predicting physiological factors as the individual aged, predicted to a lesser degree mental test performance, but failed entirely to predict the adaptation and achievement attained in adult life. The McCall et al. study is a report from longitudinal records kept at Fels Institute and concludes that early IQ tests have little predictive value. Kagan's report involves the longitudinal study of 180 infants.

An example of the extensive collection of individual records on infants is contained in Church's *Three Babies* (1966). Ethological studies of children are collected in the reader edited by Jones (1972) and in McGrew's 1972 book.

The psychoanalytic approach to child study is represented by Kris (1950), Hartman (1958), and Anna Freud (1952), Sigmund's daughter. Gesell's normative methodology is applied in Ilg and Ames's *Child Behavior* (1955). Flavell's *The Developmental Psychology of Jean Piaget* (1963) is a good introduction to Piagetian stage theory of cognition. Bijou and Baer's *Child Development* (1965) is a thorough Skinnerian treatment.

An important type of descriptive research was initiated by the pioneer child psychologist in the United States, G. Stanley Hall. He developed the questionnaire technique, in which information on what children of various ages are thinking, how they feel about various issues, and the like, is obtained by asking them standardized questions under relatively objective conditions.

Maturation of Physiological Systems

Spelt (1948) reports some of the early research on fetal learning, and Kagan (1971) emphasizes the functional condition of most of the neonatal sensory systems. Bower (1971) concentrates on infant vision. Deleterious effects of nutritional deprivation are discussed with regard to the nervous system in Jacobson's *Developmental Neurobiology* (1970). Kaplan (1972) discusses the detrimental effects of malnutrition on intellectual ability, concluding that these are irreversible if adequate nourishment is not furnished in the first four years of life. Warren (1973) questions on methodological grounds such studies as Kaplan's that show strong effects. He argues that the question of irreversible effects remains open pending results of longitudinal research now under way.

The discussion of adolescent growth is largely based upon McCandless's 1970 book. Tanner (1968) discusses the earlier age at which puberty occurs in the context of man's increase in physical size over the past 100 years.

Language

Brown's *Words and Things* (1958) and Smith and Miller's *The Genesis of Language: A Psycholinguistic Approach* (1966) are good introductions to the problem of linguistic development. Slobin's 1971 paperback is an excellent introduction to the psycholinguistic point of view on this problem. Bruner et al. (1966) and MacNamara (1972) relate language and cognitive development. Chomsky's views are expressed in his *Language and Mind* (1972). Cultural determinants of language are discussed by Cole and Bruner (1971). The critical period for language development is discussed in Lenneberg's 1969 paper.

Stages of Cognitive Development

Piaget's work is presented by himself in English in his 1961 paper and his book *The Language and Thought of the Child* (1959). The experiment on the cat turned into a rabbit or dog was reported by DeVries (1967). The older review paper by Berlyne (1957) is also still valuable. Flavell (1963) and Phillips (1969) offer good introductions to Piaget's work. Changes of cognitive functioning in the aged are discussed in Botwinick (1967).

Conscience

The tripartite definition of conscience was advanced by Sears, Macoby, and Levin in their *Patterns of Child Rearing* (1957). The early study on honesty was by Hartshorne and May (1928). The experiment on resistance to temptation in puppies was reported by Solomon, Turner, and Lessac (1968).

Evidence reported by Maslow (1963) suggests that morals shift in accordance with reality and achievement. Work on cognitive dissonance has shown attitudes to change so that what succeeds is "good" and what "is" is what ought to be.

Child-Rearing Practices

Sears, Macoby, and Levin (1957) and Miller and Swanson (1960) are good introductions to this vast literature. A review paper by Bronfenbrenner (1961) documents the changes that have occurred in child-rearing practices in the United States over the three preceding decades.

Attempts to deal with physical abuse of children by their parents reflect an unfortunate social problem. Discussion of personality factors in such parents can be found in Spinetta and Rigler (1972). Rheingold (1973) proposes a program for more effective child rearing relating the program to all socializing agents.

Play

Harlow's 1962 paper reports on his research on development of the heterosexual affectional system in monkeys. White's 1959 seminal paper introduced his concept of competence. A good review of the subject of the child's world of play is in Singer (1973).

Socialization

Infant and child. The deleterious effects of restrictive environments has been shown by Thompson and Melzack (1956) and Scott (1963), using dogs as subjects. The Wisconsin studies on social deprivation in monkeys are described in Harlow (1962) and in Harlow and Harlow (1962). Kagan and Klein (1973) report that the effects of deprivation of stimuli on infant humans is not irreversible because cognitive development allows some catching up. Kagan (1972) has suggested that infants begin to form hypotheses at about the age of eight to nine months, indicating early cognitive development. The Kagan and Klein study (1973) touches on the concept of competence; these authors point out that "There are few dumb children in the world if one classifies them from the perspective of the community of adaptation, but millions of dumb children if one classifies them from the perspective of another society" (Kagan and Klein, 1973, p. 961). Similarly, Ladner (1971) has viewed classification of young adult black women from the point of view of competence in relation to social adaptation and has held that behavior viewed as aberrant by the white middle class may well be a technique for survival in the ghetto.

An experiment in which young monkeys were placed with dogs following one to ten months with cloth maternal surrogates has been reported by Mason and Kenney (1974). All the monkeys formed close filial attachments to the dogs. These results suggest that filial attachments in primates are much more flexible than has been assumed and are contradictory to the critical-period hypothesis for filial attachment.

The early work on the effects of maternal separation on the infant was reported by Spitz (1945), Bowlby (1951), and Yarrow (1963). An overall view of socialization in the infant is presented by Rheingold (1969). Rheingold and Eckerman (1968) describe experiments on separation from the mother. A study analyzing early differences in temperament was done by Thomas, Chess, and Birch (1970). The studies describing experimental work on attachment behavior are reviewed in Bowlby (1969), which also reports the study on children in the park, and the measurement of attachment in play sessions. Spiro (1958) describes attachment behavior in an Israeli kibbutz.

Schools. An analysis of the school as a social class system can be found in Parsons (1959). Skinner (1968) and Marx and Tombaugh (1967) point to some of the adverse effects of misapplication of known principles of learning within the school system. The article proposing the giving of work apprenticeships to young people as an aid to maturation is by Harris (1961). Bruner (1972) suggests induction to maturity by allowing youth to serve as helpers in the educational process itself. Work with the socially disadvantaged at the New York University Institute for Developmental Studies is described by Deutsch (1967).

Adolescence. Early adolescent development is the topic of a reader by Kagan and Coles (1972). See also McCandless (1970). Conger's 1973 book focuses on the adjustments required by rapidly changing social and moral standards.

The Mature. Very little research is reported on studies of the mature person. However, Schmeck (1972) discusses the crises of the mature.

The Aged. Schaie's 1968 reader discusses the psychological aspects of aging. Baltes and Schaie's 1974 article provides a very good introduction to the problem of aging and ability, with special reference to the need for more careful methodology, such as longitudinal rather than merely cross-sectional data. They do not find any good evidence for the generalized decline in ability that is commonly assumed to occur. Looft (1972) reinterprets the rigidity that is traditionally identified with aging as a manifestation of increasing egocentricy, in part attributable to a shrinkage of life space in later years, which may be a purposeful way of conserving energy. A nurse, Sharon Curtin, has written a popular book called *Nobody Ever Died of Old Age* (1972), which points to the sociological factors that hasten aging; she suggests that the elderly form a power structure to change these societal problems. The problems of housing, education, and transportation were also noted by the 1971 White House Conference on aging, to which an APA task force contributed; the report was edited by Eisdorfer and Lawton (1971). All contributors agreed that chronological age is a poor indicator of an individual's cognitive and emotional characteristics.

Learning

The processes that allow the organism to acquire a repertoire of behaviors are the subject of this chapter. Perhaps the individual is not capable of extending its learned behavior to the somewhat exaggerated degree shown by these animal performers; however, we shall see that training can indeed result in some remarkable accomplishments.

327

here are relatively few distinctly inherited patterns of behavior in the higher organisms, and especially in man. Moreover, those behaviors that do have primary and clearly identifiable hereditary components, such as the sexual responses, are also markedly subject to modification as a function of environmental differences. Such modification, usually called learning, has particularly great significance for the understanding of human behavior and its determinants.

Learning as a technical term in psychology is most often defined as that change in behavior that is a direct result of prior behavior. This usage excludes a number of behavioral determinants, such as motivation and fatigue. It is always necessary to measure learning by means of performance. However, one cannot conclude that learning has not occurred simply because it is not being expressed in performance; unless an organism is appropriately motivated, for example, its performance will not adequately reflect its learning. Actual behavior is thus always a joint function of both learning and motivation.

Learning processes are categorized into five focal types, ordered by their decreasing involvement of overt behavior: *motor skill, conditioning, verbal learning, cognition,* and *insight.* In brief, a *motor skill* is any pattern of movements that enables one to cope with some environmental demand (e.g., stroking a tennis ball, threading a needle, typewriting). *Conditioning* refers to the predictable occurrence of a response in a stimulus situation where it had not previously occurred with any regularity. Conditioning is of two major types. *Classical* conditioning is produced by the pairing in time of a previously ineffective stimulus (e.g., the sight and sound of a dental drill) with a stimulus (e.g., the actual feeling of the dental drill on the tooth) that already elicit some response (e.g., pain and fear). The consequence of such pairing is that the new stimulus comes to elicit the response even in the absence of the one that originally elicited it. *Instrumental* conditioning is produced by the rewarding and punishing of responses that are emitted by an organism in a learning situation; the particular response that is followed by satisfying consequences ("rewarded" or positively "reinforced") becomes predictably more probable in that situation and the nonrewarded responses tend to disappear (e.g., the child whose crying or temper tantrum is unintentionally rewarded by increased parental attention is likely to continue to use such behavior when attention is desired, because it has proved to be instrumental in achieving that objective). *Verbal learning* refers to any new combinations of responses involving words (e.g., memorizing a list of unrelated words or a poem). *Knowledge* is the symbolic representation (covert or implicit, as in thinking) of some aspects of the world; knowledge can be translated into the slightly more technical term *cognition. Insight* refers to a type of problem solving in which a solution or principle is achieved, usually quite suddenly and without any apparent preliminary stage of partial solution; it is one kind of understanding and a special form of knowledge.

Two fundamental types of underlying mechanisms for learning are identified: *reinforcement*, which refers to the strengthening of habits, and *cognition*, which refers to the acquisition of knowledge. Learning theories are discussed with reference to conditioning and verbal learning, the two most active areas of current learning research. The chapter then provides a description of some of the more important learning functions, which cut across the major types of learning process, and concludes with a discussion of certain limitations on learning.

Attention is also directed to the more extended treatment, in Supplement A-3, of the basic experimental procedures in learning research and of some of the special problems involved in understanding that research (e.g., the use of animals as subjects).

IDENTIFICATION OF TERMS

> ### *Characteristics of Learning*

Lay definitions of learning tend to focus either on improvement, with practice, of some behavioral function or on acquisition of knowledge. There are some serious limitations to such notions; for example, it is unfortunately true that undesirable as well as desirable habits are learned.

More technical definitions of learning tend to concentrate on the relatively permanent character of behavior changes that occur as a function of behavior itself. Thus I have elsewhere defined *learning* as "*a relatively enduring change in behavior which is a function of prior behavior* (*usually called practice*)" (Marx, 1969, p. 5).

This definition, focusing on overt behavior, is typical in that it does not explicitly recognize the knowledge-acquisition aspect of learning. Such an emphasis on behavior rather than subjective experience is characteristic of the bulk of the research in the field, and especially of that which has been concerned with some of the more popular theoretical interpretations of learning. The definition itself, however, is theoretically neutral; that is, it is consistent with a variety of interpretations, of the sort considered later in this chapter.

DEFINITIONAL EXCLUSIONS. There are a number of other behavioral functions that produce progressive changes in behavior that are easily confused with learning changes. It is customary to exclude these from the definition of learning on the ground that identifiable mechanisms other than the prior behavior itself are responsible for them.

Maturational changes, considered in Chapter 10, are among the more prominent of such progressive changes; growth is presumed to be in essence the result of innate determinants. Similarly, behavioral changes that are due to *fatigue, drug* and *dietary* treatments, the effects of *disease processes*, and *adaptation* are generally excluded. Fatigue effects operate by means of the accumulation of lactic acid in the musculature; drugs, as well as dietary and disease processes, more or less directly affect the various body systems in a manner that is not dependent upon prior behavior.

Adaptation effects may be either sensory or motor in character, depending upon location of the effect. *Sensory* adaptation refers to the gradual loss of effectiveness in stimulation that is due to adjustments in the sense organs to continued stimulation (such as the loss of effectiveness of some kinds of extremely noxious odors, as in packing houses, with continued stimulation). *Motor* adaptation, more often called *habituation,* refers to the progressive decrement in responsivity to some particular stimulation that occurs with continued or repeated exposure to that stimulation (e.g., the reduction in the startle response to repeated stimulation with loud stimuli, such as fire crackers). Although there is some question as to how closely the latter phenomenon is related to learning, in general these progressive adaptation effects are considered sufficiently distinct from the more typical learning processes to merit a separate classification.

LEARNING DISTINGUISHED FROM PERFORMANCE. Although not strictly a definitional exclusion of the sort just considered, the distinction between learning and performance is a key one. It may best be introduced by an example. Consider the young child who has learned to recite a difficult poem, or to perform a difficult piece on some musical instrument. His mother is understandably proud, and when company comes she calls upon him to "perform." Now, unfortunately, he often fails to satisfy this request. Perhaps he remains silent, or perhaps he performs in an inadequate manner, making errors of the sort his mother knows he has earlier eliminated by practice.

It is clear from illustrations such as this that performance depends upon a number of factors other than training, or learning. College students who suffer from acute "examination anxiety" will also appreciate the crucial role that emotional distraction can play. In summary, performance depends upon both motivation and freedom from interfering conditions. Learning is therefore a necessary but not a sufficient condition for adaptive behavior.

Learning Processes

Our treatment of learning begins with an overview of the variety of different kinds of learning processes that have been investigated. Here our emphasis is upon the empirical rather than the theoretical aspect of learning. The five major types of learning process that are distinguished are motor skills, conditioning, verbal learning, cognition, and insight. Certain limitations to this, and any similar classification scheme, should be noted. Keep in mind that these labels refer to *focal* types of learning, processes that have many common features (such as dependence upon muscular responses for expression) and are thus not mutually exclusive categories. There are many further subdivisions that could be made within these relatively gross categories, as well as any number of alternative ways of slicing up the behavioral complex. Moreover, certain important concepts clearly entail more than one category; attitudes, for example, are combinations of verbal learning and cognitions.

Although learning processes may be organized around a number of different dimensions, the one that is perhaps most instructive is that of the degree of overt (vs. covert) response. Figure 11-1 presents our five major classes of learning process ordered on this dimension. These are first ordered in accordance with their respective focal positions on the overt-covert dimension. Then their various presumed underlying strengthening (reinforcement) mechanisms will be compared.

The two extreme types, motor skills and insight learning, represent processes with maximal expression of either overt or covert functions. Thus motor skills are almost purely overt. They obviously depend upon some kind of sensory cuing, and also upon internal (covert) associations of the various responses themselves. However, the visible (overt) expression of this kind of learning is maximal, in the sense that an external (objective) observer can sense all that is meant by the terms *swimming, golfing, bicycling,* and the like.

In clear contrast, the heart of what is presumed to occur in insight learning is not visible to an external observer. It is true of course that once a problem is solved by insight, some overt behavior must be exhibited in order to demonstrate to others the occurrence of the learning. But the crux of this kind of learning process is apparently some sort of internal function, generally called thinking. In our examples, described below, we will see that the overt expression, although necessary, is incidental to and really quite unimportant in relation to the covert functions.

The other three types of learning process occupy intermediate positions on the overt-covert dimension. Conditioning processes are toward the center of the dimension but are more overt because they do involve an explicit dependence on the stimulus as well as upon the presumed associative or connective relationships of stimuli to responses (hence the stimulus-response, or S-R, orientation of most of them). However, categorizing all conditioning processes together, for purposes of this overall comparison, obliterates some important distinctions, which we will discuss later.

"Verbal learning" also covers a multitude of different procedures. Covert mechanisms are commonly presumed to underlie verbal learning: however, an overt stimulus is typically involved (seeing or hearing the materials to be learned). Thus verbal-learning processes may be considered to be somewhat toward the covert end of the dimension, relative to "conditioning."

Cognitive learning processes, on the other hand, clearly belong toward the covert end of the dimension. However, because their dependence upon overt expression is

11-1 Five major types of learning process ordered in accordance with their position on the overt-covert behavior dimension.

often somewhat more substantial than that of insight learning (which may be considered an extreme example of cognitive processes), they are here given the slightly interior position.

MOTOR SKILLS

Motor skills are the complexes of sensorimotor responses that each of us learns in order to cope with the constant demands of bodily adjustment to the physical environment. Walking, running, climbing, handling utensils, such as knives, forks, and spoons, are all everyday examples of simple motor skills. More elaborate skills, such as toe dancing or skiing, usually require longer and more elaborate training and are acquired by relatively small numbers of people.

Motor skills were among the first type of learning to be scientifically investigated; for example, learning of telegraphy was investigated in a truly pioneer piece of research in the nineteenth century. Nevertheless, the topic has been generally relegated to a distinctly secondary position within the psychology of learning. Perhaps this has occurred mainly because of the lack of very much theoretical interest in motor learning, especially as contrasted with conditioning. In any case, it remains a practically important problem area and there have been some recent signs of a renewal of interest in it (for example, the establishment of a psychological journal specifically and exclusively devoted to motor skills). The applications of motor skills research include such diverse activities as teaching disabled children to walk and designing space craft for optimal human performance.

Sample Tasks

Motor skills that have been investigated vary from the very simple, such as merely drawing a line of a specified length, to the exceedingly complex, such as those involved in the performance of various musical instruments. Favorite laboratory devices have been the pursuit rotor, in which the subject is required to respond continuously in the tracking of a target moving in an erratic circular manner, and a variety of tasks in which the subject is required to make some particular discrete response (e.g., pressing a button) to each of several discrete stimuli (e.g., light bulbs in various positions flashing on). Motor skills have been almost exclusively studied with human subjects, perhaps reflecting the primary utilitarian interest motivating this research as well as the more limited capacity of many animal forms when judged by human standards.

Because of the emphasis on "perfection" of performance in many motor skills, measures of errors and time on (or off) target are commonly used. More positive measures may also be used, such as numbers of "hits" in dart throwing, or the number of steps a disabled child takes.

Representative Research Results

In the acquisition of a skill, *knowledge of results* (usually abbreviated KR), or feedback, is of special importance. Moreover, the immediacy with which KR occurs is also usually of critical importance, especially for tracking tasks such as learning to follow the highway by turning the steering wheel of a car. The role of KR was first demonstrated convincingly in experimentation in which human subjects were asked to draw lines of specified lengths. Blind-folded subjects were given KR immediately after they drew 3-, 4-, 5-, or 6-inch lines. They improved their performance from a median of 34.5 per cent correct (so judged when drawn within $\frac{1}{8}$ inch of 3 inches and $\frac{1}{4}$ inch of the longer dimensions) to 54.5 per cent correct in a seventh session (with a total of 600 lines drawn per session). Control subjects, in contrast, failed to show any improvement even after 5,400 lines were similarly drawn but in the absence of KR.

Motor skills often seem to improve over long periods of no practice. This phenomenon is labeled *reminiscence*. William James expressed this relationship well by stating that we learn to play tennis during the winter and ice skate during the summer.

CONDITIONING

Conditioning refers to a form of learning in which a response or complex of responses that has previously not occurred in a particular stimulus situation now comes to occur with a predictable degree of regularity. The emphasis is upon the stimulus–response relationship, rather than upon the responses themselves, as in motor skills. Two broad categories, classical and instrumental, are generally subsumed under the single term *conditioning*. The two kinds of conditioning are similar in that each involves the selective response strengthening, by a kind of "reinforcement" process. They are fundamentally different in that both the nature of the "reinforcement" and its contingency, in relation to the learned response, differ.

Crucial distinctions among learning concepts need emphasis. The most important of these is the distinction between classical conditioning and instrumental conditioning. In classical conditioning, on the one hand, the conditioned (learned) response is *elicited* by a conditioned stimulus; in Pavlov's original experiments, for example, powdered meat was directly applied to the dog's tongue in order to elicit salivation. The reinforcement, or strengthening of the new stimulus–response connection, is by presentation of an unconditioned stimulus that is provided regardless of whether or not the conditioned response occurs. In instrumental conditioning, on the other hand, the learned response is *emitted* by the subject; the cat in the puzzle box, for example, emits a variety of different responses, such as pushing on or scratching at the bars, climbing up the sides of the cage, pulling on wire loops, and so on. The instrumentally conditioned response is reinforced by presentation of the rewarding stimulus *only* when it occurs.

Classical (Pavlovian) Conditioning

The classical conditioning process is sometimes referred to as *stimulus substitution;* this term describes what appears to be happening. A response becomes conditioned to a new stimulus if it can be made to occur repeatedly after presentation of that new stimulus. Such occurrence is made possible by the use of an already effective stimulus to elicit the response. The classical conditioning process thus seems to involve the substitution of a new, or conditioned, stimulus (CS) for an old, unconditioned stimulus (UCS). The adaptive importance of classical conditioning is illustrated by an example of a stimulus substitution that has probably occurred for all of us. If one is stung (effective stimulus–UCS) by a bee, the innate response will be flinching and pain. When the stimulus (sting) and the response (flinch) are preceded by the sight of the bee (initially a neutral stimulus), the sight of the bee will become a conditioned stimulus for the flinch response. Even years later, being surprised by the sight of a bee may result in a conditioned flinch. Thus we react to the bee very adaptively and do not have to experience the sting again.

The classical conditioning process is shown schematically in panel (a) of Figure 11-2. The orienting response (OR) that is included in the diagram is the most common initial (unconditioned) response to the usual CS; a dog, for example, may prick its ears and look around when the sound is first presented, as though to ask, "What's that?" When a CS is presented in sufficiently close temporal relationship to the unconditioned or eliciting stimulus, optimally, approximately .5 sec., with the CS preceding the UCS, conditioning generally develops in a more or less regular manner. The response comes to occur to the CS in advance of the occurrence of the UCS and even eventually in its absence (as on test trials). The OR is, typically, a

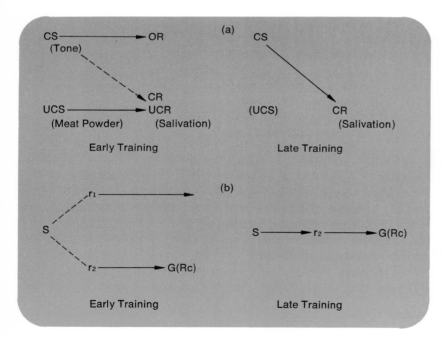

11-2 Basic relationships in two types of conditioning. These schematic diagrams are to be used in conjunction with the text description of classical and instrumental conditioning. (a) Classical (Pavlovian) conditioning. CS = conditioned stimulus; UCS = unconditioned stimulus; CR = conditioned response; UCR = unconditioned response; OR = orienting response. (b) Instrumental (operant) conditioning. S = stimulus situation in which responses are emitted; r_1 = emitted response not followed by any rewarding after effort; r_2 = emitted response followed by a rewarding after effort. For example, the stimulus may be food presented behind a screen. r_1 would be the animal's response in scratching at the screen. r_2 would be the animal's response in opening the screen's hinged door, and the goal object (G), food, is the reinforcement for the consummatory response (Rc) of eating. Note that in classical conditioning the reinforcing UCS occurs on every trial in early training but is no longer necessary on every trial after control has been achieved by the CS (that is, after it has become an elicitor of the CR); whereas in instrumental conditioning the reinforcement provided by the goal object occurs only when the appropriate response (r_2) occurs.

vague and weak response and is easily replaced by the much stronger CR as conditioning develops. The classical-conditioning procedure is to present the UCS independently of the occurrence of the CR; that is, the new response is not necessary for the reinforcement. It is this feature that is must often pointed to as the crucial distinction between classical and instrumental conditioning.

Instrumental Conditioning

In instrumental conditioning the reinforcement is not given unless the response to be learned, the *instrumental* response, does in fact occur. Reinforcement is thus said to be contingent upon the occurrence of the response. In other words, the response has an effect, whereas it has no effect in classical conditioning. Certainly this is an important difference. Not to be overlooked, however, and probably equally important, is the fundamental difference in the nature of the reinforcement operation itself. In instrumental conditioning there is always a consequence of the response: food for a hungry animal, money for a college student, smiling for a human infant, and the like. In classical conditioning the reinforcement operation may involve a similar consequence, such as meat powder for a hungry dog, but it does not need to be so; weak acid is also an effective UCS for the salivation response. The only necessary condition of the reinforcement operation in classical conditioning is that the UCS be an effective stimulus for the dependable elicitation of the UCR, which is then transformed into the CR in the course of conditioning.

There is another crucial feature of instrumental conditioning that distinguishes it from classical conditioning. This is the fact that the instrumental response (e.g., a lever press by a rat or the recitation of a poem by a child) is *emitted* by the organism rather than elicited by some particular stimulus. The term *operant* conditioning is often used as a synonymn for instrumental conditioning or learning, reflecting the fact that the organism is presumed to "operate" on the environment; when this term is used for instrumental conditioning classical conditioning is referred to as *respondent* conditioning, to indicate the fact that the CR is a response to the CS.

An example of how the consequences of an instrumental response reinforce the response can be given by the bee sting of a few paragraphs earlier. If we see the bee (stimulus) and then run (instrumental response), we are reinforced by attaining safety far from the bee. If we are successful (reinforced) we will have learned to escape from bees by running.

An example of instrumental learning that is not as painful as association with bees is the reinforcement (money) that we receive for working (instrumental responses). When we work we are reinforced with money, and the probability of working then increases. To illustrate how important reinforcement is, consider what most people would do if their boss stopped paying them. The consequences (reinforcement or punishment) of what we do (responses) determine the future probabilities of the responses. The basic relationships in instrumental conditioning are shown in (b) of Figure 11-2, where the contrast with classical conditioning is indicated.

There are some other important differences between the two kinds of conditioning. For example, the elicited responses in classical conditioning tend to be relatively fixed and stereotyped; such innate behaviors as reflexes are commonly elicited and conditioned in this way (for example, the knee jerk and the eyelid-closure or blinking reflex in humans). Also, the same stimulus tends to elicit the same response in all members of a species. Respondents, moreover, are not ordinarily affected by their consequences; thus shock elicits hand or paw flexion even though the flexion does not terminate the shock. Finally, operant responses are readily modified (can be "shaped," in operant terminology, as described in Supplement A-3). Most of the socially important responses that humans make—in walking, talking, working, playing—are operants; they are emitted rather than elicited, and are subject to instrumental conditioning in that their consequences are important. This fact accounts for the great variability in operant behaviors, in contrast to respondents; their sensitivity to environmental conditions helps to account for the great significance of learning in everyday life.

One or Two Fundamental Conditioning Mechanisms?

There is little agreement at the present time as to whether instrumental and classical conditioning are in fact based upon the same fundamental learning mechanisms. There are both similarities and differences that have not been mentioned. For example, the two procedures are similar, in that effective conditioning occurs in either case only when the organism is adequately motivated. They differ, for another example, in that classical conditioning frequently requires the harnessing of the organism, such as the dog, so that it can be appropriately stimulated and its response adequately measured without interference from other responses. Also, the response measured is typically a part reaction (such as secretion of a gland, or movement of a paw) rather than a movement of the entire body (such as movement down a runway and into a goalbox), as is likely to occur in instrumental conditioning.

For many years it was generally held that classical and instrumental conditioning were fundamentally dissimilar because they seemed to involve a different class of musculature. Thus it was pointed out that classical conditioning utilizes visceral functions and involuntary musculature, as in the case of glandular secretions or reflex actions, whereas instrumental conditioning involved voluntary musculature, such as that concerned with running or making various movements with hand, paw, or beak. Only recently has this neat distinction been blurred. It has been shown that under the appropriate learning arrangements a variety of visceral, involuntary reactions, such as heartbeat or intestinal contractions, can be instrumentally conditioned; they can be made to vary in accordance with the rewarding operation, as is generally true of instrumental learning. The question of the relationship between the two basic classes of conditioning remains an open one and affords a fertile field for theoretical speculation. Moreover, the distinction between the two kinds of conditioning in terms of skeletal and visceral processes, although now known not to be an absolute one, still has some validity. That is, it is still generally true that operant conditioning is relatively easy with skeletal responses and difficult with glandular responses, whereas the opposite relationship tends to hold for classical conditioning.

Verbal learning refers to learning in which either words or a similar type of symbol are acquired in some new kind of combination. In everyday life verbal learning is involved in a tremendous variety of different kinds of situations, running from the relatively simple matter of telephone numbers to the vastly more complicated arrangements of verbal symbols employed in poetry or similar forms of artistic expression. In the laboratory, stimuli of a much narrower range, such as discrete words or specially contrived verbal materials, are customarily used.

Contemporary research on verbal learning tends to focus on one of two alternative paradigms; the *paired-associates* technique, in which the materials to be learned are presented as explicit stimulus and response terms, and the *free-recall* technique, in which the subject is allowed to impose his own organization or structure on the materials.

PAIRED ASSOCIATES. Until the relatively recent advent of the free-recall technique, there was evident in the field of verbal learning a growing tendency for research to converge on what is now a still powerful but no longer dominant technique, that of paired associates. Although various refinements of the basic procedure are used, the unit for learning is generally a pair of verbal items, one in the stimulus position and the other in the response position. The learner's task is to learn to associate the two, so that when the stimulus term is presented, usually in a series of similar terms, he can quickly and accurately give the proper response term.

It is apparent that paired-associates research, involving the explicit use of stimulus and response items, can in theory be related to the basic conditioning procedures. Some early attempts to interpret human verbal learning were adapted from conditioning theories developed on the basis of animal research. Verbal learning, occupying an intermediate position on the overt-covert dimension, permits ready postulation of two kinds of functions—the more or less direct operation of rewards on overt responding and the active intervention by the learner on the basis of his memory of past events and his motivation (as demonstrated in the free-recall process, for example). Laboratory investigations designed to tease out the interrelationships between these two fundamental types of function are becoming more popular and should be in the forefront of learning research on human subjects for some time.

FREE RECALL. Investigations of information processing and various other related problems involving human memory have generally helped to expand the boundaries of research on human capacity. More specifically, they have led to the intensive utilization of a relatively new technique for investigation of verbal learning, that of free recall. In free recall a subject is first provided the essential materials to be learned (e.g., a list of unrelated words) and then is permitted to use his own organizing tendencies in attempting to demonstrate his acquisition during the test (that is, he can put the words together in whatever groups or clusters he prefers). This method represents a combination of acquisition (learning) and recall (retention); because it is in essence a retention measure, however, it is treated in depth in the following chapter.

COGNITIVE LEARNING

The category of behavior known as cognitive learning is not ordinarily included as a form of learning. Nevertheless, some of our most important types of learning, in the popular sense, produce knowledge and should be so recognized. However knowledge is acquired the process may be called cognitive learning.

The scope of cognitive learning is obviously very great. The category includes many instances in which verbal materials are directly involved, and so may be regarded as encompassing much of verbal learning. Nevertheless, there are other, more subtle forms of knowledge in which verbalization plays a minimal role or even no role at all (e.g., imagery). It is the acquisition of knowledge that is most stressed by the layman when he thinks of "learning." Thus a "learned man" is one who has achieved a high degree of cognitive acquisition, mainly but perhaps not exclusively, by reading as well as the ability to utilize this knowledge.

Basically, knowledge is the result of perception, modified especially by emotional and rational functions. The fundamental problem with this kind of learning is how knowledge gets translated into action. Certainly behavior can change—habits can be energized—strictly on the basis of knowledge and the appropriate motivation. As a matter of fact, there is even some suggestive evidence that motor skills can be improved on the basis of imagery alone. But the question as to whether habits can really be developed by cognition, in the absence of overt responding, remains. It is doubtful that anything near the strength customarily achieved on the basis of conditioning can be attained through cognitive functions alone.

11-3 Solution of a multiple-stick problem by a chimpanzee. The chimpanzee first obtains a long stick by means of a short stick, then is able to reach the piece of fruit with the long stick. Presumably this kind of problem-solving behavior depends upon understanding the relationship among the various items involved.

INSIGHT

An insight is a new appreciation of how to solve some problem. Insight typically comes suddenly and often without prior warning, as exemplified by the expression *flash of insight*. In popular language, an insight is most readily identified as a form of understanding. The insight solution to a problem usually constitutes a general principle of some scope. Insight learning is, in essence, a function of the reformulation of ideas (or perhaps, as the Gestalt psychologists held, of perceptions). However it is interpreted, an insight solution of a problem is one that can occur in the apparent absence of any overt behaviors, on the basis of thinking alone (see also Chapter 8, on problem solving, for much relevant discussion). Learning by insight represents the culmination of the use of reasoning, imagery, and other cognitive processes in the achievement of the solution of problems. In some celebrated early research chimpanzee subjects were found to be capable of solving a variety of difficult problems. The chimpanzee Sultan was the most gifted learner in this group. Sultan's best-known achievement was probably his learning to insert one pole into another and thereby reach an incentive, such as a banana, that either pole separately was too short to reach. A similar problem that was also solved by insight was the use of a short stick to obtain a longer stick, which could then be used to obtain a desired incentive. Figure 11-3 illustrates this kind of learning.

A simpler but basically similar set of problems have been collectively labeled

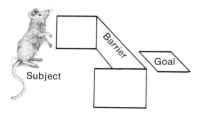

11-4 The Umweg problem. The subject's task is to learn to go away from the goal object in order to reach it.

Umweg (meaning "roundabout" or "detour"). A stripped-down version of this class of problem is diagrammed in Figure 11-4. Here the subject can be an organism as intellectually gifted as a small human child or as intellectually limited as a hen. This simple test provides a useful comparative measure. The subject's problem is to learn to go directly to the goal object, which is clearly visible through the barrier. The solution is necessarily a roundabout one, in that the subject must temporarily turn his back on the goal object. The goal objects used are appropriate to the species tested (for example, a toy for a child, banana for a chimpanzee, meat for a dog, grain for a hen). It is assumed that the task is really a new one for the subject and that he doesn't have available any pattern of responses that can be directly applied to the problem without the occurrence of learning.

The results of experimentation on this problem may be summarized by the statement that it is relatively simple for the higher organisms, such as human children and the other higher primates, moderately difficult but solvable by various forms of intermediate intellectual capacity, such as dogs and cats, and extremely difficult if not impossible for such more lowly forms as hens. The behavior of the latter is especially instructive. Typically the hen will spend a great deal of time at the barrier, attempting to get directly at the goal object. Eventually she will tire of this ineffective activity (technically, it will "extinguish," from lack of reinforcement). Once the hen wanders off and happens to achieve a direct visual line in relation to the goal object she will be able to see it and go directly to it. On subsequent trials such so-called trial-and-error or apparently random behavior will recur. Gradually the solution is achieved with decreasing time required. This kind of behavior is illustrated in panel (a) of Figure 11-5.

Panel (b) of Figure 11-5 shows the true insight solution achieved by, say, a chimpanzee subject. The critical difference is in the timing and character of the behavior in relation to the goal. The chimpanzee subject is also likely to spend a certain amount of time at the barrier, attempting to get at the goal object directly. However, if he solves the problem by insight, he will *suddenly* leave the barrier and go as *directly* as possible to the goal as indicated by the path shown in Figure 11-5. Such a solution, once it occurs, generally results in *relatively smooth* and *enduring behavior patterns;* that is, on subsequent trials in the same situation the organism that has solved the problem by insight will go quickly and directly (as directly as possible, as indicated by the smoothness of the path) to the goal. Moreover, this kind of solution is marked by extreme durability, in that it is much less likely to be forgotten than the typical trial-and-error solution, such as that exhibited by the hen.

Such sudden solutions of problems have been experienced by most if not all humans and are often referred to as "aha" experiences. They are clearly *thinking* rather than habit or response solutions, in that once achieved the particular kind of response used is relatively trivial. That is, in the *Umweg* problem illustrated, the important thing is to leave the goal and proceed *around* the barrier; how one proceeds—left or right, crawling, hopping, running, and so on—is relatively unimportant, with respect at least to the basic problem.

The Gestalt interpretation of this kind of learning emphasizes what is called the restructuring of the visual field. This means that the organism has to "see" the

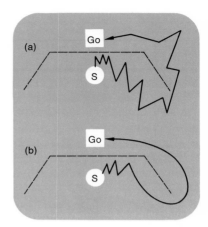

11-5 Two kinds of solutions to the Umweg problem: (a) trial-and-error solution by a hen; (b) insight solution by a chimpanzee. Go = goal object; S = subject.

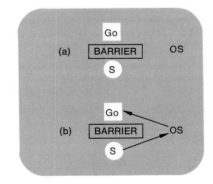

11-6 Gestalt interpretation of an insight of the Umweg problem. (a) Presolution perceptual field, representing environmental relationships; (b) perceptual field reordered, constituting insight solution. Go = goal object; B = barrier; S = subject, OS = open space.

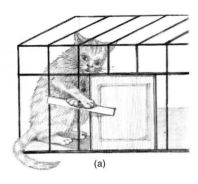

(a)

(b)

11-7 Two views of the cat in the puzzle box. Panel (a) shows subject performing the necessary instrumental act that opens the door; panel (b) shows the escape response. This response enables the cat to obtain the incentive (not shown), which was generally placed outside the box in the early research.

Learning Mechanisms

problem elements in a new light; he has to rearrange the relationships, or reorder his perception. A rough illustration of what is meant in this interpretation is provided in Figure 11-6. The critical aspect of the successful restructuring of the field is to see the open space behind and around the barrier in a new way: as a means to the goal object. Piecemeal thinking is then not necessary. Apparently the hen is insufficiently equipped with perceptual ability to permit this kind of restructuring, and so is restricted to trial-and-error learning, whereas the higher forms are capable of such functioning and so are able to solve problems insightfully.

An important implication of the insight problem is that the particular responses used are unimportant. The control is cognitive. In other words, once the proper cognition occurs, such as the organism seeing the open space in a new relationship to the goal, the appropriate motor responses will be made and this response is less important than the fact that he has solved the problem by acquiring an effective *idea*.

COMPARISON OF INSIGHT AND TRIAL-AND-ERROR LEARNING. It is instructive to compare insight learning with the instrumental learning procedure originally developed for research on animal learning. Consider the puzzle box, shown in Figure 11-7. The puzzle box is essentially a cage in which an animal such as a cat is placed with a goal object or appropriate incentive outside. The essential difference between the two learning situations lies in the fact that solution to the puzzle box is *necessarily* by trial and error; that is, the subjects' responses are initially a matter of "chance." There is no way by which the cat can be expected to solve the puzzle box problem by insight, or any other similar kind of higher-level intellectual activity. This conclusion follows from the fact that the experimenter always makes an arbitrary response, such as pulling on a loop of wire, the one to be learned—that is, the one that is followed by the "satisfying after-effect," such as the door opening.

Should the experimenter make the necessary response one that is more closely related to the situation—for example, simply pushing open the door that forms the barrier—then to that extent he has moved the problem closer to the insight type. But this step is seldom taken by experimenters interested in trial and error, or reinforcement, learning processes. They generally prefer to have the organism start with a minimal ability to solve the problem on the basis of any a priori intellectual activities, so that the learning process itself is more completely encompassed within the training session. The contrast with the Gestalt position is quite marked.

Insight learning, as the epitome of cognitive learning, has been treated in this chapter somewhat more fully than the other types of learning because it is important to recognize the role of cognition, which has often been overlooked by conditioning researchers and theorists.

The five basic types of learning just reviewed reveal two major types of mechanism: habit formation (or reinforcement) and cognition (or acquisition of knowledge). Table 11-1 presents a summary of the five types of learning processes together with some indication of how the reinforcement and the cognition variables seem to be involved in each process. The most critical relationship, with regard to the

INSIGHT LEARNING

Following is an example of a type of problem that has been extensively used in research on reasoning with human subjects and that illustrates the features of *insight* learning. *After* you have solved this problem turn to the box on p. 344 for further instructions.

Imagine that there is some simple organism that divides into two identical organisms once every three minutes. Each new organism in turn divides into two once every three minutes. Now assume that *one* such organism is placed into an empty jar, which is completely filled within one hour. How much time would be required to fill the jar if originally there were *two* such organisms so placed?

formation of habit or the operation of cognition, is also suggested, on the basis of presently available evidence, for each basic process.

Inspection of Table 11-1 reveals that habit formation is regarded as the fundamental mechanism only in the two classes of conditioning. Even here cognition plays some role. The exact locus of the essential reinforcement mechanism differs for the two classes of conditioning, as indicated by the bracketing of the CS–UCS relationship for classical conditioning and the R–G (response–goal) relationship for instrumental conditioning. Placing the feedback (knowledge of results) function in the cognitive category for motor skills and verbal learning indicates the more deliberate (that is, consciously directed) manner in which this variable is now believed to operate in these learning processes.

Table 11-1 Five Major Types of Learning Process, with Role of Reinforcement (Habit-Strengthening) or Cognition (Knowledge-Acquisition) Indicated

Type of learning	Reinforcement	Cognition
Motor skill	(S)–R	Provides knowledge of results (KR)
Conditioning		
Classical	$\begin{cases} \text{CS} \rightarrow \text{CR} \\ \text{UCS} \nearrow \end{cases}$	Auxiliary role
Instrumental	S--r--G(R) (Law of effect)	Expectancy (Knowing what leads to what)
Verbal learning		
Paired-associates	S–R (Law of effect)	KR
Free-recall	Questionable	Information processing
Cognitive learning	Questionable	Perception and memory
Insight learning	Questionable	Perceptual restructuring

(S)–R = (stimulus)–response; CS = conditioned stimulus; CR = conditioned response; UCS = unconditioned stimulus; S = stimulus; r = instrumental response; G(R) = goal response.

As already emphasized, cognitive learning processes do not depend upon the strengthening of any particular responses, and so are independent of the reinforcement mechanism, as here defined. Although the cognitive mechanism is shown to have at least a potential role in each of the major types of learning process, it is clearly most intimately involved in knowledge and in insight learning.

The omission from our discussion of certain important processes, such as affective and attitudinal processes, does not mean that learning is not believed to be involved in them. They are regarded as more complex, rather than elementary, processes in which learning depends on some combination of both conditioning and cognition. Moreover, it should be recognized that many other commonplace and important kinds of learning are also complex combinations of two or more of these basic processes (e.g., musical performance as a joint product of motor skills and cognitive function).

Learning Theories

A fundamental problem in attempting to interpret learning is that we are dealing with an unobservable, intraorganismic variable. That is, learning is a process that we assume occurs within the organism but that is only measured in terms of overt behavior, or performance. Performance is quite clearly determined by more than the learning process itself. Hence we have basic difficulties in both measurement and interpretation, apart from those produced by the issue of one or multiple underlying mechanisms.

THEORIES OF INSTRUMENTAL CONDITIONING

Learning theorists have focused on the problem of instrumental conditioning. Three distinct kinds of theoretical position have been developed. These may be briefly identified as (1) *reinforcement theory*, (2) *cognitive theory*, and (3) *contiguity theory*. A fourth position, which was initially relatively *atheoretical* in character, has been developed within the *operant conditioning* movement led by B. F. Skinner.

REINFORCEMENT THEORY. The heart of reinforcement theory is the proposition that S–R connections are formed and strengthened during the course of learning. Early versions of this position stressed the role of reward as a necessary part of the reinforcement process but later, more sophisticated versions either ignore or play down this aspect of the theory. Classical conditioning processes are often included as crucial elements in these later versions. However, the concept of S–R reinforcement remains the basis of instrumental learning and serves to differentiate this theoretical position from the others.

As already indicated (Table 11-1), the reinforcement position concentrates on the S–R relationship, or the *habit*. Reinforcement *is* the direct strengthening of such S–R relationships.

COGNITIVE THEORY. According to the position taken by cognitive theory, what is learned is not so much an S–R connection, or habit, as a kind of idea, an expectancy. The animal whose turning left into a goalbox or whose bar-pressing is followed by reward comes to expect the reward when such responses are made. Other responses, such as turning right into the goalbox or sniffing at the sides of the cage, are not followed by reward and so a different set of expectancies develops for them. Because of its emphasis upon "what leads to what," this cognitive framework has been labeled S–S (stimulus–stimulus) theory. One of the more interesting and suggestive products of this theoretical stance is the notion of the *cognitive map*, which refers to the complex interlocking expectancies that one forms as bits of knowledge are gained in a new environmental situation, such as a strange city. (See also the discussion in Chapter 8, p. 228.) This cognitive position has generated many provocative experiments and proved to be a worthy adversary for the more orthodox S–R reinforcement position.

CONTIGUITY THEORY. The contiguity position is a much simpler one than either the S–R or the S–S theories. In essence, it holds that learning is associative but that the association is always between particular stimuli and the movements that occur in their presence. In other words, this theory is really a form of classical conditioning applied to the instrumental conditioning problem. It is the contiguity of stimulus and response that accounts for learning; no additional assumptions, such as the reinforcement effect that reward is supposed to exercise, are needed.

In spite of its simplicity the contiguity position has interesting and useful implications. One much-cited illustration of its applicability to everyday life will illustrate its potential utility. Suppose that a child has the habit of entering the house and dropping his coat on the floor. Further suppose that the parent wishes to change this habit and encourage the child to place his coat neatly upon its appointed place on a hall rack. What is the parent most likely to do in an attempt to rectify the situation? Most often the parent will use some form of verbal plea, perhaps embroidered with veiled hints of punishment or even open threats. But these are seldom very effective. Suppose that instead the parent forces the child to behave in accordance with his own wishes; normally this would take the form of the child's being instructed to pick up the coat and place it in its proper place. But, according to the contiguity theorist, such a course is likely to be of little more value than the verbal entreaty or threat. The reason is that the child has formed no really appropriate habits in either case. What the parent is encouraging, by his requiring the child to pick the coat up after dropping it, is simply more of the same; that is, the child will probably pick it up more quickly as learning occurs, but he will also be dropping it after he enters the room, in accordance with his earlier behavior. In order to break this habit the child must be sent out of the house, instructed to re-enter the room with his coat and then place the coat on the rack. In accordance with contiguity theory (and some other forms of learning theory as well, it should be noted) this procedure is more likely to result in the desired behavior.

Within recent years the basic contiguity position has been given new life by being incorporated in a mathematical learning theory. It is admirably fitted to this kind of framework. It remains a viable alternative to the other more complex theoretical positions and one that is especially difficult to embarrass by experimental evidence.

OPERANT CONDITIONING. B. F. Skinner has consistently opposed the elaborate and systematic theoretical efforts of most other psychologists. He has proposed,

Breather Interpretation

INSIGHT LEARNING

Now that you have solved the first problem presented, try this one: Suppose that a college student living in a dormitory starts a rumor and passes it on to two new students in the dormitory every day. Suppose further that each of these two students in turn passes the rumor on to two other new students in the dormitory every day and that within one week the entire population of students in the dormitory has been given the rumor. How many days would be required for the rumor to reach the entire student population of the dormitory if the rumor had been started by *two* students on the first day?

After you have solved this problem, consider the following points:

1. Was this second problem much easier to solve than the first? Why? The ease with which such a comparable form of the problem is typically handled following a prior solution illustrates the relative permanence and ready transferability of insight learning.
2. Did you solve the first problem quickly and directly? Most solutions occur only after a variety of false starts have been made. These typically may appear to be obviously inappropriate and even stupid when viewed with the perspective of hindsight. However, such trial-and-error efforts are characteristic of most problem-solving behavior and play an important part in facilitating the development of hypotheses that lead to solutions and general principles.
3. Suppose that the question in these problems had been phrased in terms of how long it would take to half-fill the jar or to reach half of the dormitory population. Would this have made the problem easier? Why?
4. Suppose that the rumor problem had been posed in terms of a certain number of students in the dormitory (say, sixty-four) rather than a time measure. Would this have made the problem appreciably more difficult?
5. Suppose that each student passed the rumor on to *three* other students each day. What other changes in the problem would need to be made in order to maintain the applicability of the general principle to a single statement of the problem?

---

instead, a primarily descriptive and inductive approach to behavior (cf. Chapters 3 and 13), with little concern for theoretical mechanisms. Nevertheless, Skinner has developed a quite systematic position, focusing on instrumental—for him, operant —conditioning.

The first operant research was performed in a very simple chamber—a "Skinner box"—in which the behavioral alternatives available to the organism were severely limited. A rat subject was offered a simple lever or bar, the pressing of which was followed by a reinforcing event, the presentation of a food pellet. Such variables as time between reinforcements and the number of lever presses required for reinforcement could then be manipulated to determine their direct effect on the lever-pressing response.

Operant conditioning emphasizes the contingencies of reinforcement; emitted responses—operants—are selectively strengthened by reinforcement. That is, operant responses made in various stimulus situations are strengthened or weakened in accordance with their consequences. The behavior modification movement, described in Chapter 16 because of its essentially clinical character, is a more recent application of this general systematic framework in which behavior is directly manipulated by positive and negative consequences.

Skinner sees three major roles for the stimulus in learning. First, it *elicits* responses, as in classical conditioning (which Skinner prefers to call respondent conditioning in order to contrast it with operant conditioning). Second, it "sets the occasion for" responding; for example, a pigeon may be reinforced (by being allowed to feed from a supply of grain) when it pecks in the presence of a green light but not when it pecks in the presence of a red light. The green light would then be called a *discriminative* stimulus because it enables the responding organism to differentiate his behavior and thus learn. When an organism is consistently rewarded in the presence of some particular stimulus, that stimulus becomes a discriminative stimulus for the response, and operant conditioning can be said to have occurred. Third, a stimulus can be an incentive or a goal object, such as food for a hungry organism, and its presentation is then said to be *reinforcing;* this statement simply means that when this kind of stimulus follows a response, the response becomes progressively more probable, as compared with other possible responses.

In keeping with his general positivistic (descriptive) approach, Skinner has refrained from making any guesses about the nature of the reinforcing mechanism. He feels that top priority must be given to the accumulation of facts and lawful relationships among behaviorally relevant variables; the most effective theory will thereby emerge as sufficient facts are developed and ordered into meaningful relationships. In other words, Skinner feels that theories are more useful as products of than as guides to research, and he has arranged his interpretations of behavior accordingly.

HUMAN VERBAL LEARNING

Until recently, theoretical efforts directed at interpreting human learning were quite limited. In earlier times most such theorizing was centered around the Thorndikian principles; then as other theoretical positions were developed, mainly on the basis of animal research, these tended to be carried over, sometimes bodily, to the human learning situation. Within the past decade, however, there has been a vigorous questioning of these concepts, and new views, mainly focused on cognitive assumptions, have begun to emerge.

The major questioning has been of the *automaticity* of response strengthening assumed by the law of effect, an earlier version of what is now called the principle of reinforcement. Several theorists have developed similar notions. The crux of these is that the human learner is an active transformer of information (feedback), rather than a more or less passive reactor to such effects. Thus in the traditional verbal learning situation, the learner is now seen as actively utilizing his memories of past trials. The contrast with reinforcement theory is clear-cut. For example, suppose that on the previous trial the subject had responded to the stimulus word *lake* (one of a large number of such stimuli presented in series) with the number 2 (from a set of numbers 1 through 10 at his disposal) and that this response was called right (by the experimenter directly perhaps, or by means of some signaling device, such as a green light flashing on). Reinforcement theory assumed that a connection, or bond, was thereby established between the stimulus *lake* and the number response 2, so that on subsequent trials that response would be more likely to be given.

According to the newer views, the subject now retrieves from his memory storage (as described in Chapter 12) at least two pieces of information when he is again presented with the stimulus *lake*: (1) the *identity* of the particular number response that he gave on the prior trial and (2) the *outcome* of that response, in terms of the right or wrong signal that followed it. He then decides whether or not to repeat the response, in accordance with these memories (and his motivation, which has not yet been actively worked into all these new theoretical formulations).

Learning Functions

Our discussion now centers upon the most important learning functions that have been identified in experimental and theoretical work. The functions described generally cut across the bounds of the various learning processes, as already discussed, but are most relevant to the conditioning process, and especially to instrumental conditioning. In keeping with the basic approach of this book, the emphasis will be on problems and procedures, as well as principles, with illustrative experimental designs and results presented where they seem to be indicated.

In our discussion thus far we have assumed the operation of what is commonly regarded as a positive reinforcer, an incentive or goal for which the appropriately motivated organism will actively work. The counterpart of the positive reinforcer is the negative reinforcer, defined as a noxious condition that the organism will actively work—and thus learn—to remove or avoid. Excessively loud noise, electric shock, and very bright light are all examples of the kind of noxious environmental situations that serve as negative reinforcers for an organism such as the laboratory rat.

There is no absolute distinction between such external environmental cues and the internal conditions, such as hunger and thirst, which are commonly used to motivate the organism in a learning situation. Both types of noxious conditions are obviously ones the organism seeks to remove. However, they differ in the degree to which they are objectively evident. External cues are typically more acute and demanding forms of stimulation.

AVERSIVE CONDITIONING

Aversive stimuli are most often used to train the organism in one of two major research paradigms, escape or avoidance training.

Escape Training

In escape training the subject is permitted to eliminate the noxious stimulation, either by turning it off (through manipulation of some such device as a lever) or by removing himself from it (as by leaving the area). The latter alternative has been more frequently used, especially with animal subjects such as rats or cats. Thus the *two-way shuttle box* is simply a double cage arrangement in which the subject must learn to leave each side alternatively as it becomes noxious (normally the grid floor is electrified to produce some degree of unpleasant but nonlethal shock). Latency of escape responding is usually the major measure taken over acquisition trials of this sort.

Avoidance Training

In avoidance training the subject is allowed to respond instrumentally *in advance of* the appearance of the noxious stimulation so that it can be avoided. The distinction between these two basic kinds of aversive conditioning, escape training and avoidance training, thus depends upon whether the noxious stimulus is present and is turned off or left (in escape conditioning) or is prevented from occurring (in avoidance conditioning).

All avoidance conditioning experiments start out as escape conditioning, as far as the subject is concerned. This follows from the fact that on the first few trials at least, while the subject is learning about the noxious state of this new environment into which he has been placed, he will invariably experience the noxious condition and then escape from it. Typically a neutral stimulus (tone, light) will precede the shock; the subject then will come to respond during the tone, thus avoiding the shock. Once the subject begins to make the required response during the preshock stimulus (tone or light), such as leaving one cage for the other in the simple shuttle box or pressing the lever in the Skinner box, he is able to prevent the occurrence of the noxious stimulus completely. Avoidance conditioning is said to be achieved when some criterion, such as three or five successive avoidances, is reached.

SIDMAN AVOIDANCE. A special kind of avoidance schedule, named after Murray Sidman, its originator, has been developed and used extensively. Unlike the ordinary avoidance experiment, which typically has a signal of some sort to indicate the initiation of a trial (a light change or a buzzer being common examples), the Sidman avoidance situation is completely unsignaled. That is, the noxious stimulus, such as shock, comes on a temporal schedule without any advance warning, as by a light change or a tone. The subject thus has to learn for himself just how much time he has to make the required response and thereby avoid the noxious stimulus.

Sidman avoidance procedures are used within the free-operant experimental situation described in A-3 (p. 633), and have been especially popular for use with monkey subjects. A familiar sight in the apparatus company exhibition booths at the psychology conventions has been the bored-looking monkey who periodically and ever so nonchalantly pauses in his peering at the passing human parade to push one panel or the other on the device to which he is harnessed, thereby avoiding shock.

Punishment

By far the most common form of aversive conditioning is that labeled by the popular term *punishment*. Unfortunately, in addition to being quite common, and very easy to apply, punishment is also perhaps the least effective of the aversive control techniques. Moreover, it is very likely to have quite serious and long-lasting concomitant emotional consequences, presumably established by classical conditioning of the fear produced by the punishing action to the punisher. This is seen commonly when a child comes to fear the parent that delivered the punishment rather than fearing the act for which he was punished. Such fear conditioning is extremely difficult to remove, as we shall see (Chapter 15), no matter how good the intentions of the punisher.

Punishment refers to the situation in which a noxious stimulus of some kind is presented following the occurrence of a response whose frequency we wish to decrease. It is thus a logical counterpart to the positive reinforcer, which follows the desired response. For this reason a punishing stimulus is sometimes called a negative reinforcer. However, this usage simply tends to make for terminological confusion, in view of the other, and probably somewhat more common, meaning of negative reinforcement already described.

Conditioned Emotional Responses

Another form of aversive conditioning involves the association of some cue, such as a tone, with a noxious stimulus, such as an electric shock. Here the originally neutral cue tends to acquire behavior-suppressing properties, much as does the noxious stimulus itself, again presumably on the basis of classical conditioning. This *conditioned emotional response* (CER) was initially demonstrated and is most commonly used in the operant-conditioning research framework.

SECONDARY REINFORCEMENT

A secondary reinforcing stimulus is one that, though originally neutral with respect to some response, comes to serve as a reinforcer, or strengthener, of that response as a result of its relationship to the primary reinforcing process. For example, consider a black-and-white-striped goalbox in which a hungry rat is repeatedly fed. Prior to the feeding, this empty goalbox would have little attraction for the rat; subsequent to the primary reinforcement in it, however, the black-and-white striping, either in the same goalbox or in some other context, would be likely to show definite reinforcing capacity for the animal. Such reinforcement is called *secondary* because it is apparently dependent upon some more primary reinforcement. The two ways in which secondary-reinforcing properties of a stimulus are normally tested are (1) to determine whether it slows down the extinction process (discussed below) when it is presented in the absence of primary reinforcement and (2) to determine whether it will reinforce some new learning response.

Secondary reinforcers are generally found to be weak. To maintain their reinforcing powers they must be periodically associated with primary reinforcement. They would thus seem to offer relatively little as an explanatory mechanism or theoretical resource. Nevertheless, the principle is very frequently applied to important problems, such as that of explaining the powerful effects of such presumed "secondary" reinforcers as money. To explain this powerful property of certain stimuli, resort may be made to the concept of a "generalized reinforcer"—a stimulus whose potency is maintained across a variety of different situations.

Secondary reinforcement is a behavioral function that is itself in need of clarification. Superficially it would seem to resemble the classical conditioning paradigm, in that the temporal contiguity of primary and secondary cues is involved. However, the secondary reinforcer may probably be better viewed as a kind of subgoal, or motivation arouser and maintainer for the organism, generally weaker and less persistent in its effects than the primary reinforcer but nonetheless at times a potent factor in behavior.

EXTINCTION

As an experimental operation, extinction refers simply to the *withholding* of the reinforcer in a situation in which reinforcers have been previously offered on some schedule. As a behavioral function, however, the term refers to the progressive *decrement* in responding that typically occurs when reinforcement previously offered is now consistently withheld. The operation and its behavioral result are both extremely important in learning research and theory. The extinction operation has a variety of uses in experimentation (for example, in discrimination learning, discussed below) and the behavioral decrement has proved quite useful in theoretical interpretations.

A typical reinforcement and extinction combination is shown in Figure 11-8 for the bar-pressing response in the rat. Note the marked but temporary increment in responding that is the first consequence of withdrawal of the reinforcement. Such

11-8 Idealized acquisition, extinction, and spontaneous recovery in a typical instrumental learning situation. (a) = acquisition; (b) = extinction; (c) = measure of increased vigor and presumed frustration; (d) = measure of spontaneous recovery.

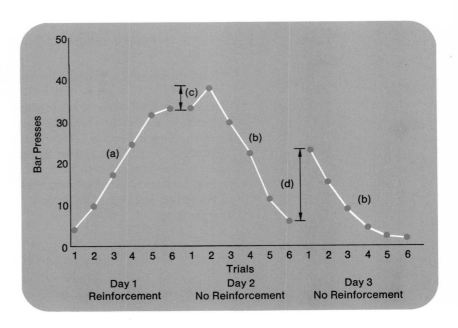

increased vigor in responding can be viewed as a function of the emotional arousal produced by the extinction procedure, and a sign of frustration in the subject.

THE PREE. Empirically, the most important phenomenon relating to extinction is the influence on it of a partial, as opposed to a consistent or continuous, reinforcement schedule. Such partial scheduling almost invariably results in markedly increased resistance to extinction. The *partial reinforcement extinction effect* (PREE, or sometimes just PRE) is one of the most pervasive and most strongly established lawful relationships in the learning area.

Ratio schedules of reinforcement applied to free operants produce some of the most dramatic illustrations of the PREE. A ratio schedule of reinforcement occurs when a number of responses are required for reinforcement, as opposed to continuous reinforcement, where each response is reinforced. The ratio schedules (e.g., one in which on the average every tenth response is reinforced) generate behavior that persists long after reinforcement has stopped. An unhappy and all too common illustration of this effect is provided by the gambler; slot machines are deliberately programmed to offer a sufficient number of payoffs (reinforcements) to maintain the money-inserting response at a fairly high rate, but an insufficient number of payoffs to insure the financial prosperity of the persistent player. Similar but more mundane illustrations of this same principle abound; for example, consider the fisherman who happens to catch a "big one" of a certain hard-to-catch type and then spends an inordinate amount of time, money, and effort in an entirely unsuccessful effort to repeat this feat. Or consider the slightly talented but highly enthusiastic young writer among whose plentiful rejection slips there are just enough encouraging letters if not outright acceptances to keep him hoping and producing magazine manuscripts. Few principles in all of psychology are as well founded and as liberally illustrated as the partial reinforcement extinction effect.

SPONTANEOUS RECOVERY

First intensively researched by Pavlov in his development of the classical conditioning field, spontaneous recovery refers to the commonly observed tendency of an extinguished response to show renewed strength (recovery) over a period of no practice and in the absence of any further reinforcement (therefore, spontaneous). A typical result is shown in Figure 11-8.

Although possibly of greater theoretical than practical interest, spontaneous recovery does not seem to have attracted very much in the way of intensive experimental attention subsequent to its early identification. It nevertheless remains an interesting and potentially important process and awaits adequate analysis and interpretation.

STIMULUS GENERALIZATION

When a response is conditioned to a particular stimulus other similar stimuli also seem to acquire a certain amount of response-eliciting power. This phenomenon is

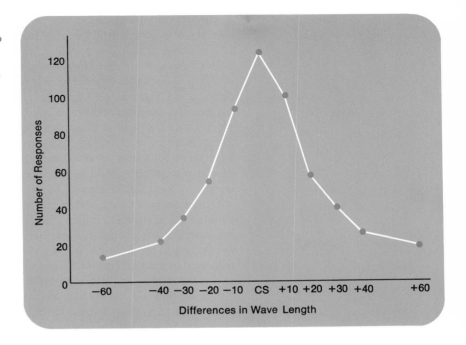

11-9 Generalization gradients. Pigeons, conditioned to peck in response to colored light of a particular wave length, also pecked when the light wave length was altered slightly. As can be seen here, the pigeons responded more frequently when the light was closer to the conditioned stimulus in color.

called stimulus generalization, referring to the extension of the response-eliciting property beyond the particular stimulus that was used in the training. As Figure 11-9 indicates, the degree of generalization typically falls off as the difference between test stimulus and training stimulus increases.

The widespread distribution of stimulus generalization in behavioral phenomena has suggested its importance as an explanatory concept. It is particularly well fitted as an explanatory concept with regard to the extension of fear-producing properties in emotional learning. Thus, as is described in Chapter 15, when Watson conditioned a child to fear a furry animal, such as a rabbit, he found that the fear generalized to various other small animals, such as a rat. A single occurrence of such emotional learning may thereby have results that are especially difficult to remove. Both the original training stimulus and various other stimuli related along a number of dimensions (sometimes seemingly unimportant) may need to be considered for the complete removal of the emotional response.

DISCRIMINATION

The phenomenon of stimulus generalization needs to be offset if behavioral precision is to be developed and maintained. Thus the young child will sooner or later need to cease calling men other than one "Daddy." Similarly, the adult will need to tell apart strangers all of whom share some prominent characteristics, such as skin color, and so tend to be responded to alike. The learning process by which this kind of differential responding is acquired is called *discrimination*.

351

Discrimination learning takes many forms. It is sometimes regarded as the most fundamental process in all learning. For instance, discrimination is an ultimate base of definition. When two people agree on the differentiation of one stimulus or object from another they have the basis for the development of a common understanding. They can then proceed to build on this basis with regard to more complex definitions. Contrariwise, when one is having trouble in explaining the meaning of his terms to someone, perhaps an individual who speaks a different language, he can regress until the point-at stage mentioned above is reached and the two agree that a given object is *dog* or *food* whereas some other objects are not. The nearly universal head signs for assent (vertical head movements) and negation (horizontal head movement) are very useful in this respect, as many people who have had to attempt communication in the absence of a common language can attest.

Operant-conditioning techniques are especially useful for studying animal discrimination abilities. In this kind of research the animal is first trained to make some particular response to a given stimulus, then differentially reinforced so that responding to other similar stimuli is extinguished. This discrimination training is then used to test the limits of the animal's ability to discriminate between the initial positive stimulus and other negative stimuli that are relatively close on some dimension that is being studied, such as frequency of sound. Similar techniques are also useful in testing human discrimination, even though the human subject normally has available a language response that enables him to tell the experimenters more directly whether or not he "sees" a difference.

Limitations on Learning

Learning is a most pervasive variable that can be shown to have at least potential ramifications in all behavioral functions. Nevertheless, various kinds of limiting conditions have been suggested as restricting the role of learning. Two major limitations are imposed by biological and by motivational factors.

BIOLOGICAL LIMITATIONS

Constraints on learning imposed by the biological nature of the organism are the most obvious of the various restrictions. Here the clearest illustrations have been provided by two experimental psychologists in the course of their successful business enterprise involving the training of performing animals. A single example taken from their own account should suffice to illustrate this point. Describing their difficulties in attempting to maintain a certain kind of reinforced operant response in the pig, they found that certain learned responses could not be maintained because of the great natural strength of certain other responses that interfered with the new behavior. Thus:

The last instance we shall relate in detail is one of the most annoying and baffling for a good behaviorist. Here a pig was conditioned to pick up large wooden coins and deposit them in a large "piggy bank." The coins were placed several feet from the bank and the pig required to carry them to the bank and deposit them, usually four or five coins for one reinforcement. (Of course, we started out with one coin, near the bank.)

Pigs condition very rapidly . . . they have ravenous appetites (naturally), and in many ways are among the most tractable animals we have worked with. However, this particular problem behavior developed in pig after pig, usually after a period of weeks or months, getting worse every day. At first the pig would eagerly pick up one dollar, carry it to the bank, run back, get another, carry it rapidly and neatly, and so on. . . . Thereafter, over a period of weeks the behavior would become slower and slower. He might run over eagerly for each dollar, but on the way back, instead of carrying the dollar and depositing it simply and cleanly, he would repeatedly drop it, root it, drop it again, root it along the way, pick it up, toss it up in the air, drop it, root it some more, and so on.

We thought this behavior might simply be the dilly-dallying of an animal on a low drive. However, the behavior persisted and gained in strength in spite of a severely increased drive—he finally went so slowly that he did not get enough to eat in the course of a day. Finally it would take the pig about 10 minutes to transport four coins a distance of about 6 feet. This problem behavior developed repeatedly in successive pigs [Breland and Breland, 1961, p. 683].

This kind of evidence indicating a basic restriction on the conditionability of some behavior is especially convincing not only because of its intrinsic merit, but also because it comes from two very dedicated researchers who were early indoctrinated with the persuasive enthusiasm of Skinnerian behavioral engineering. Moreover, they started their animal-training efforts with the conviction that *any* operant response could be successfully conditioned in accordance with the assumption commonly made in this learning system.

A second example of biological constraints is provided by some recent research on what seems to be aversive conditioning from toxic stimulation. This research involves long periods of exposure of animals to some noxious stimulation such as radiation or toxin (UCS) in the presence of a particular sensory cue such as saccharine (CS). The aversion (UCR) has been shown to become conditioned (as a CR) to the CS in such experiments. The temporal intervals involved may be minutes or hours rather than seconds, as in the orthodox conditioning paradigm. Conditioned aversion has been repeatedly demonstrated. Moreover, it is specific to the substance consumed (food or water) and the related sensory components; that is, the aversion is difficult to condition to the usual external cues relating to the spatial location. In this respect the phenomenon is very similar to that reported for animals, such as wild rats that have been poisoned but survived; their aversion is almost entirely to the particular food substance in which the toxin was contained rather than the location in which it was found. Such "bait-shy" behavior makes some animals difficult to poison more than once.

As a counterpart to this kind of aversive conditioning, positive conditioning has also been reported. Rats given a distinctive flavor during their *recovery* from illness were subsequently found to have developed a distinct liking for that particular flavor. Rats deprived of certain vitamins will respond to obtain those vitamins even though they cannot taste them.

Because phenomena of this sort seem to conform to the basic classical conditioning paradigm, they have raised some serious questions concerning the theoretical interpretation of conditioning. One pioneer researcher has pointed especially to the extension of the temporal relations and the differential involvement of the internal digestive mechanisms, as contrasted with relatively unaffected exteroceptive cues, as posing important problems for traditional conditioning theory. Either these data and the biological factors they imply must be accommodated within an enlarged theoretical framework for classical conditioning or some very clear demarcation of its boundary conditions must be indicated.

MOTIVATIONAL CONSIDERATIONS

A number of recent developments within learning theory suggest the necessity of attributing an increasing amount of behavioral variance to what may be more properly identified as motivational, or activating, variables rather than purely associative, or learning, factors. Perhaps the most instructive illustration of such predominance of motivational factors within "learning" is afforded by the operant-conditioning movement. Operant-conditioning experiments customarily begin experimental manipulations after a stable behavioral baseline ("operant rate") has been determined; for example, a certain number of lever presses made by a rat subject under standardized training conditions during a set time period would constitute such a baseline, once the number stabilized. It is during the establishment of this behavioral baseline that most of the basic acquisitions occur, but this phase of the research is seldom even measured, much less emphasized, in such experiments. The reinforcement operations that are emphasized, and that account for most of the behavior then measured, may well be regarded as differentially motivating the organism, in spite of the fact that this particular term may not be used by the researcher.

Laboratory and theoretical considerations aside, it is apparent from even a casual observation of everyday behavior that most of the behavioral variance found in the higher organisms can be attributed to motivational factors. Although learning deficiencies definitely circumscribe one's behavior, and often markedly so, the major learning dimensions of a human are laid down relatively early in life, so that more adult behavior is clearly attributable to what the individual wants to do than is attributable to what he is learning to do. The picture is complicated by the fact that so much of our motivation is itself learned (Chapter 14). Nevertheless, habit provides a kind of upper limit within which motivational variables operate to account for most of our behavior, much as in the manner that heredity serves to provide limitations within which learning variables operate.

<table>
<tr><td>Notes</td></tr>
</table>

Motor Skills
Bilodeau's *Principles of Skill Acquisition* (1969), in paperback, is a good book-length introduction to the research literature. The research on line-drawing described in the text was reported in Thorndike (1935).

Classical Conditioning

The main source for Pavlov is Anrep's translation (Pavlov, 1927). The more recent work is covered in a symposium report, with contributions by active researchers (Black and Prokasy, 1972).

Instrumental Conditioning

Thorndike's writings on the law of effect cover a range of publications, from his *Animal Intelligence*, an 1882 account based on his doctoral research, to his posthumous *Selected Writings from a Connectionist's Psychology* (1949).

Biofeedback

Self-control of visceral processes by means of biofeedback techniques has become a popular application. Jones (1973) reviews Neal Miller's pioneering work on the instrumental conditioning of visceral functions as well as the biofeedback by-product of that research. Miller's own publications (1971) are now collected into two volumes. A popular article by Lang (1970) and the more technical and authoritative handbook edited by Barber et al. (1970) are good sources for biofeedback. Schwartz's 1973 review contains references to more recent reports.

Classical and Instrumental Conditioning Compared

One difference between classical and instrumental conditioning deserves special mention. B. F. Skinner, the developer of the operant conditioning variety of instrumental conditioning, early emphasized the differential role of the stimulus. In distinguishing between respondent classical conditioning, in which a stimulus elicits the response, and operant instrumental conditioning, in which the organism simply emits the response, Skinner (1938) held that the latter function occurs in the absence of any determinable stimulus. Strictly speaking, this may well be so, but from a broader point of view it is quite apparent that the experimental context provides the "stimulus" for the conditioned response. Such a context might better be termed a *situation* than a *stimulus;* it seems that what is involved is a continuum of the degree to which a specific stimulus is effective, as contrasted with a more generalized situation, rather than a dichotomy between stimulus and no-stimulus conditions.

On the issue of the separability of the two varieties of conditioning, Black and Prokasy, in their 1972 editing of the most recent contemporary publication available at this writing, make clear their preference for the orthodox assumption of continuity: "we prefer to avoid the assumption, at least to begin with, that classical conditioning is a special kind of learning which is clearly different from other types of learning, such as operant conditioning" (1972, p. xi).

Verbal Learning

The older literature on human learning is comprehensively covered by McGeoch and Irion (1952); this book is also noteworthy for its exposition of the role of dimensions in learning. The newer problems outlined are treated in a number of sources, including recent books by Kintsch (1970) and Kausler (1974).

Insight Learning

Köhler's major book on chimpanzee research is *The Mentality of Apes* (1925).

The conclusion seems inescapable that there are two important and substantially different kinds of learning functions. Conditioning research focuses on one type, which seems to be characteristic of all organisms in situations where they either have no reasonable way to use any higher intellectual processes they might have or are somehow inhibited, as by set (Chapter 7) or emotion (Chapter 15), from using them effectively. The Gestalt psychologists (e.g., Köhler) made a most significant contribution in pointing out the role of insight learning as a complement to conditioning; they criticized procedures such as Thorndike's puzzle box or the maze vigorously for not allowing the organism to make maximal use of its intellectual powers. This is done in the insight type of problem by arranging the situation appropriately. Nevertheless, the instrumental conditioning type of learning situation, in which random responding is necessary if the solution is to be achieved, seems to be characteristic of many situations in everyday life as well as the laboratory. Moreover, most learning situations require multiple responses, sometimes complexly organized, rather than the single and often relatively simple response required in the insight problems typically used in research.

Learning Functions

The books edited by Campbell and Church (1969) and Brush (1971) are devoted to the general topic of aversive conditioning. The Sidman avoidance technique is described in Sidman (1953). Estes's original report on punishment is his 1944 paper, and the Estes and Skinner 1941 paper covers their CER work.

Biological Restrictions

The Breland and Breland quotation is from their 1961 paper. A more general treatment of this problem has recently been offered by Seligman and Hager (1972). The research on toxic conditioning is reviewed by Garcia, McGowan, and Green (1972); the experiment demonstrating the enhancement of a flavor fed during recuperation from illness was reported by Green and Garcia (1971).

Memory

12

*"Doctor Laft, what's the news?
Oh, I'm come for my shoes."*

*The puzzlement expressed by this poor
fellow indicates a lapse of memory. The
factors that influence retention of information are discussed in this chapter.*

n this chapter we look at the major ways in which the effects of learning are expressed after the learning has occurred. This expression is mainly measured by the *persistence* of learning in the *same situation* (*retention measures*) or in a deliberately *altered situation* (*transfer measures*).

Each of the five focal types of learning process described in Chapter 11 is evaluated with respect to retention. Standard measures of retention (*recall, recognition,* and *relearning*) are then discussed, and some attention is given to organizational factors in recall, particularly in the *free recall* process. Qualitative changes that occur continuously in retention are described; these are mainly *leveling* (the tendency to reduce differences) and *sharpening* (the tendency to accentuate differences).

The major theories of retention are then discussed. In the *disuse* account, whatever neural changes underlie learning simply are assumed to deteriorate with aging; in the *interference* account, forgetting occurs because of confusion between different learning experiences. Although the interference theory has largely supplanted the older disuse theory, it in turn has more recently been challenged by the newer emphasis on organizational factors in learning; the implication is that much forgetting occurs because of a failure of appropriate organization.

Transfer of training is a more significant function than is often recognized. From one point of view, all subsequent expression of learning can be viewed as essentially transfer, because of the fact that some changes necessarily occur in both situations and subjects with time. The measurement procedures used in transfer research are reviewed, as are the major determining variables; the most important of these is the type and degree of *similarity* between training and test (transfer) situations. This section concludes with a consideration of a number of special transfer phenomena, notably *learning set* and *warm-up.*

The next section of the chapter is concerned with the basic nature of memory. The stress is on *information processing.* A key facet of this conceptual framework is the distinction between *short-term memory* (STM) and the more traditional *long-term memory* (LTM). A detailed description is provided of the stages of (1) *sensory reception* (by perception), (2) *registration* (by attention), (3) *memory storage* (by rehearsal, which transfers items from STM to LTM), and (4) *memory retrieval* (by active search of memory stores).

Once items are established in LTM (that is, are stored), they are indefinitely maintained. It is this LTM that is the concern of traditional research on retention, reviewed in the first part of the chapter. Within the information-processing framework, however, the problems of memory storage and retrieval can also be attacked. Although not much has yet been done with the storage problem, which cannot be readily researched, there are many interesting results on retrieval.

This problem also lends itself nicely to personal observations anyone can make; a number of illustrations of this kind are described.

The chapter ends with a review of some miscellaneous topics (such as memory aids, amnesia, idiot savants), and a description of the present situation with regard to the neurophysiological interpretation of memory; here two especially important research areas involve *consolidation* (the notion that a certain amount of time is required to transfer items from STM to LTM) and *transfer of memory* (the phenomenon in which animals have been found to learn more rapidly after they have been fed homogenized bodies or brains of other animals that had previously been trained on the problem, thus suggesting the transfer of some kind of molecular structure that is presumably involved in the learning-memory process).

RETENTION AND TRANSFER

By convention, retention is distinguished from acquisition (learning) by the time interval that intervenes between the end of training and the test of persistence of the effects of that training. But this is strictly an arbitrary distinction. All learning obviously depends upon the retention from one trial to the next of the effects of previous trials, and so is intimately tied in with retention. Moreover, as we shall see in our treatment of short-term memory (STM), some of the retention intervals used are shorter than the usual intertrial intervals used in learning, thus further tending to obscure the distinction between learning and retention.

Nevertheless, as a practical matter for research and theory construction, the study of retention focuses on the investigation of those variables that mainly operate during the time interval between reaching some criterion of mastery in training and a subsequent, and normally relatively delayed, testing of the persistence of this learning. The measure of the strength of training, or the amount of learning achieved, thus becomes a particularly critical problem for the investigator of retention; essential equivalence of training level in the subjects whose retention is to be compared is necessary before reliable conclusions can be drawn concerning the effects of other manipulated variables on retention.

In transfer of training, the subsequent test of the effects of training is in terms of the influence that such acquisition has on some *other* learning. All situations necessarily change; if nothing else the subject changes. All subsequent tests may therefore be considered transfer tests. Practically, again, as in the case of the learning-retention distinction, recourse is made to an arbitrary distinction. To differentiate among acquisition, retention, and transfer, we consider the experimenter's intention and manipulation; if no change is manipulated from the training to the test situation, subsequent tests are considered either acquisition or retention, depending upon the time interval involved (and the nomenclature adopted by the investigator); if a deliberate change is made from the training to the test task, so

Retention

that new learning is required, the test is customarily considered one of transfer of training.

From a practical point of view, both retention and transfer are more important than acquisition. That is, what really counts in everyday life is a person's ability to use what he acquires, either in substantially the same situation (retention) or in new situations (transfer). Consider education, for example. This vast enterprise is based almost entirely upon the assumption of effective transfer from classroom to everyday life. Seldom is one called upon to repeat exactly what he has learned in the classroom. Rather, in functions varying from the most elementary of the language and arithmetic skills to the most complex professional training, one is expected to be able to apply what is learned in new and sometimes quite different situations. Thus transfer is, ultimately, the crucial test of education. Indeed, the early research on transfer was mainly carried out by educational psychologists, and it was done in the classroom rather than the laboratory.

RETENTION AND MEMORY

The terms *retention* and *memory* are often used synonymously and refer to the same basic function. However, the contexts in which they are customarily used differ. *Retention* is usually applied to laboratory or similar testing procedures designed to measure the persistence of learning. *Memory* is a more specific yet more general term. This paradox is created by the fact that the term is customarily used in two contexts: first, specifically with regard to deliberate attempts to retrieve information, mostly of a cognitive sort, which has been obtained at some past time and is presumably still available; second, generally with regard to the problem of the persisting influence of past experience on behavior and with special regard to the neurophysiological mechanisms that are assumed to underlie all retention.

Another difference between the two terms involves the kind of research that is done in connection with each concept. Memory research largely relates to sensory processing of information; retention research is more often that which is performed in the traditional manner of the learning laboratory. Separation of these two great streams of ongoing research in the present discussion by using the terms *retention* and *memory* does not mean that the fundamental mechanisms are presumed to be necessarily different; they are separated for convenience of exposition and for emphasis on the varying operational procedures.

TYPES OF LEARNING

To begin our treatment of retention we may look at each of the fundamental types of learning process that were described in Chapter 11. This overview will then be followed by a more specific description of the major methods of measuring retention and some of the more prominent problems and principles.

Motor Skills

Once well learned, motor skills are generally quite resistant to forgetting. They require a surprisingly small amount of occasional practice to maintain a high level of proficiency. Thus individuals who master such games as tennis, golf, or handball are often able to continue to participate in such sports at a level of proficiency consistent with their general physical well-being throughout their lifetime.

Motor skills often show improvement over a period of no practice whatsoever; the examples given in Chapter 11 were "learning" to ice skate during the summer or play tennis during the winter. The technical term for such improvement without practice is *reminiscence;* although the phenomenon was first detected in verbal learning, and has been most systematically investigated with such materials, it is probably more marked in motor skills.

Very little direct experimental evidence is available for long-term retention of motor skills in human subjects. One psychologist, however, has provided the following typical and "relatively reliable anecdotal evidence":

When inducted into the Air Force in 1942 I stopped playing tennis and did not have a racket in my hand until my son urged me to play with him in 1963. Although speed and endurance were reduced by increased age and weight, when I stepped onto the court for the first time in 21 years, I found to my delight that there had been very little deterioration in the complex skills involved in the basic strokes which could not have been practiced during the intervening time without court, ball, or racket [Miller, 1967, p. 321].

A similar illustration from my own recent experience concerns an interesting facet of the relationship between motor and verbal processes in memory. After a lapse of quite a few years I had occasion to resume a motor skill—pitching horseshoes. The motor skill itself was relatively resistant to forgetting (although not quite as resistant as I would have preferred) but some of the associated verbal materials, mainly concerning the rules of competition, were disturbingly absent. For example, I was particularly baffled by not being sure whether the winner of a round then pitched first or last the next time. Because I was playing with a beginner, the rules were up to me. I had the winner pitch last, but I did not feel very confident of the procedure. The most impressive aspect of the incident occurred on the next occasion; I found myself pitching first after winning, and then quite suddenly recognized that this was in fact the correct procedure—a clear case of superior *nonverbal* (habitual) recall!

As a sideline to this incident, it should be noted that verbal recall can be interfered with by thought processes. One often thinks about a number of alternative courses of action, before actually choosing and carrying out one of them; consequently he is likely to have some subsequent difficulty in remembering which alternative was actually adopted. This is especially true if the action has not been sustained in further usage and also if some other alternative was actually preferred but not selected. For example, a student might vacillate between two (or more) sections of a course for which he is preregistering, undecided as to whether to take the early-morning class with the reputedly good teacher or the late-morning class with the reputedly poor teacher. He is forced to elect one or the other, but later, before classes start, may be confused about which has been selected.

The reason usually given for the relatively high degree of retention of motor skills is that they tend to consist of highly specific responses that are not very similar to many other response patterns, and hence are not subject to much of the kind of response interference that typically produces forgetting in some of the other types of learning process. The contrast with verbal materials, which are subject to marked forgetting, is consistent with this view; the letters or words that ordinarily make up the learned verbal passages are used in many other passages so that the response confusion, and thereby interference, that is believed to underlie much forgetting is more likely to occur. Moreover, a high degree of similarity exists among verbal passages, and this variable is the major one that facilitates interference and negative transfer.

Conditioning

Classically conditioned responses are generally well retained. This is especially true, unfortunately, of emotional conditioning (cf. Chapter 15); fear responses particularly seem to be very slowly forgotten and extremely resistant to even more active techniques of elimination. Again, this fact may in part reflect the rather unusual, highly specific character of many CS–CR relations and hence their resistance to interference from similar relationships. It is also possible that such learning is intrinsically more powerful and therefore more resistant to forgetting than nonemotional types, because of its closer involvement with autonomic functions.

Retention measures are not ordinarily applied to instrumental conditioning. This is particularly true of animal instrumental conditioning; until recently, the problem of animal memory, especially over longer periods of time, has had little attraction for experimenters. Because control of the activities of the subject is much more difficult for human than for animal subjects, this long-standing omission has been unfortunate.

Where measured in instrumental conditioning, forgetting seems to be relatively rapid, perhaps reflecting the greater sensitivity to interference of some of the responses typically acquired. For example, the running response most often used for rat subjects is apparently one that is used continuously by the animal in all sorts of other situations. Common human responses, such as talking or walking, are similarly subject to much interference, and learning that is based upon them may often be forgotten for the same reason.

Verbal Learning

This type of learning process, restricted to human subjects, is by far the most commonly used variety for retention studies in the laboratory. As indicated in Chapter 11, retention and acquisition may often be difficult to separate in such situations (e.g., the free-recall technique). Most of the principles relating retention to such variables as interference of intervening activities have come from verbal learning investigations. Some later discussions will therefore develop this topic in depth.

Cognition

Cognition has recently been the focal point of a whole new approach to the study of human retention (here usually called memory), involving the serial processes of information processing, coding, and various stages of memory (short-term to long-term). This research, described in some detail below, offers an important complement to the traditional laboratory research utilizing more formally "learned" materials.

Whereas verbal-learning research has traditionally focused on neutral (relatively meaningless) kinds of verbal materials, following the Ebbinghaus tradition, the research on sensory processing and consequent memory functions emphasizes the meaningfulness of materials. Nevertheless, commonality between these two research procedures is suggested by the great dependence in each of certain fundamental functions, for example, rehearsal, which is generally recognized as a crucial variable for investigation or control.

The principles of memory that have thus far resulted from the sensory or information-processing (cognitive) approach will be considered below. Here they may be summarized in the statement that only a limited number (five to seven) of items can be carried at any one time in short-term memory, whereas a practically unlimited number can be carried in long-term memory. Items seem to enter long-term from short-term memory either directly through rehearsal or indirectly through repeated practice over successive trials, as in the traditional laboratory procedure used to establish "learning."

Insight Learning

The discussion in Chapter 11 indicated that insight solutions once achieved are extremely durable; under anything like normal conditions they are well remembered for indefinite periods. Such permanence of learning is partly a function of the extreme simplicity of most of the solutions applicable to the insight situations used in experimentation and partly also a function of the uniqueness (and consequent resistance to interference) of the situational context as well as the solution. The *Umweg* problem used to illustrate the discussion in Chapter 11 (p. 339) obviously fits both of these criteria, and especially the former. Again, there may well be other factors involved in such superior retention (perhaps relating to the underlying neurophysiological functions) but there is little evidence available on this point.

MEASURES OF RETENTION

There are three fundamental measures used in retention experimentation with human subjects: recall, recognition, relearning. Because these measures give substantially different results, even when applied to precisely the same learning, the conclusions one draws about retention must obviously be linked to the particular method of measurement used. The major distinguishing characteristics, and strengths and weaknesses, of each of these measures will be considered before attention is directed toward matters of more empirical and theoretical substance.

Recall

The method of recall is perhaps the most basic of the three commonly used. Here the subject is given a minimum of cues; he is simply asked to provide the materials he has learned. Actually the nature and number of cues provided by the experimenter does vary in practice; thus, for example, in paired-associate recall testing the stimulus term of each pair will normally be given, with the subject required to provide the response term he has previously learned. In *free recall,* on the other hand, the subject is usually left to his own devices in terms of organization of recalled materials; he can list items, for example, in any order that he wishes to use.

The recall measure is generally considered to be the most difficult of all retention techniques and this presumption is supported by the fact that it typically provides the smallest amount of retention, as indicated by the early results plotted in Figure 12-1.

Relearning (Savings)

The relearning method puts the subject back into the same learning situation as he was in originally and has him continue to practice (relearn) to the same criterion of mastery as in training. Relearning is also called the *savings method* because the measure it provides is computed by comparing the number of trials required to relearn with the number required to learn; the difference is expressed then in percentage and called a savings score. This is done on the assumption that relearning will require less trials than learning, as is normally the case.

One difficulty with the relearning method is that the subject may change over the retention interval; for example, a student may become much more proficient with verbal materials as a consequence of school experiences. Thus there is some danger that part of his "savings" may actually be due to this kind of extraexperimental factor. Caution must therefore be exercised, especially when the relearning method is used for long retention intervals and there is some likelihood of such changes occurring in the subjects. Another more practical disadvantage is the amount of time and effort required of both subjects and experimenters, as compared with the other two basic methods, both of which are easier to administer.

Recognition

The recognition method is the simplest of those used to measure retention. The subject is merely asked to indicate, for each item presented, whether or not it was previously learned, or to select one item as correct from each set of several items (as in the familiar multiple-choice-type objective test). This method is by far the least demanding of the subject, as every student who has experienced an objective-type examination can attest. Moreover, it usually provides much more apparent evidence of retention, and thus is a relatively sensitive measure.

The weaknesses of the recognition method mainly revolve around the use of alternatives, technically called *distractors.* Varying their nature and number can easily change the amount of retention shown and can eliminate and even reverse the superiority of the method compared to recall. Students object to the objective examinations that are based upon recognition on several grounds. Many of these are related to the fact that the questions asked do not provide sufficient opportunity

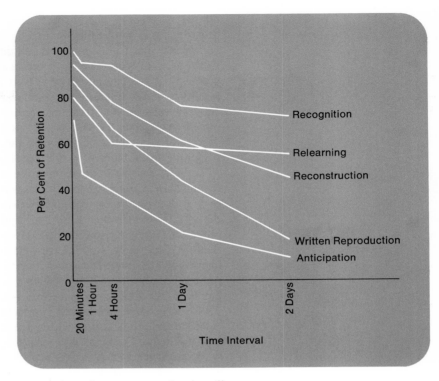

12-1 Retention curves obtained by five different methods of measurement. (From Luh, 1922.) Reconstruction, written reproduction, and anticipation are special forms of recall.

for complete display of what has been learned, as does the essay question (recall method of measuring of retention). In addition, a sophisticated examination taker with a minimal amount of knowledge can frequently outscore a student with greater actual knowledge of the subject matter but less experience with the examination technique. Both of these objections can be at least partially met by sufficient care in the preparation of the examination, and especially by the manipulation of the distractor items. This requires both ability and patience on the part of the instructor or experimenter.

FACTORS INFLUENCING RETENTION

Here we review briefly some of the major variables that have been shown to influence retention scores in experimental work, mainly that using human subjects and verbal learning materials. Our coverage is necessarily limited to the more important generalizations that may be safely asserted and therefore does not reflect the depth and variety of the numerous ongoing research projects in this very active field.

Learning Variables
In consideration of learning variables, the overriding variable is *amount of original learning*. It is necessary to control this variable before evidence can be

365

offered in support of any direct effect upon retention of some other variable. Suppose, for example, that an investigator wishes to test for the influence of such variables as speed of learning and meaningfulness of materials on retention. Both of these variables operate first to produce a greater amount of learning; it is therefore very difficult to manipulate (vary) them in a learning situation without at the same time varying the amount of original learning. If this factor is also allowed to vary between experimental treatment groups, no conclusion about the effects of the other two variables themselves and retention can safely be made. This confounding of variables complicated many of the earlier experiments, although it is now beginning to be more generally recognized as a problem.

The fact that amount of retention varies positively with amount of original learning has a simple but nonetheless very important practical implication. This has to do with overlearning. Because overlearning is a relative concept, depending upon the criterion of mastery arbitrarily adopted, it is also positively related to amount of retention. In general, to insure good retention, the best procedure is to overlearn in the first place. However, one runs the risk of sharply diminishing returns and of incurring undesirable consequences (such as neglect of some other study) without reasonable advantage if too much overlearning is attempted. Overlearning is therefore not a principle to be followed blindly.

One other important learning variable for which there is experimental evidence in relationship to retention, with amount of learning controlled, is that of *distribution of practice*. For recall and relearning, and in short-term and long-term situations, distributing practice over several sessions has been found to produce superior ultimate retention to massing practice in a single session. The implication of this result for such common student practices as "cramming" for examinations is quite apparent.

Interference: Retroactive and Proactive Inhibition

Interference from other learning is a major variable that has been implicated in forgetting. In general, verbal-learning researchers have employed two basic experimental designs to produce interfering effects on retention: *retroactive inhibition* and *proactive inhibition*. The experimental designs for these two procedures are shown in Table 12-1.

Retroactive inhibition refers to the interfering effect that subsequent learning (B) has upon the retention of previous (original) learning (A). The necessary control, against which the interfering effect of such interpolated learning can be assessed, must be equivalent in original learning and have no interpolated activity (be "rested" at this time). The retention of original learning (A) is then measured for both groups. Any net decrement in the retention of A shown by the experimental group is then attributed to interference in memory produced by B.

Assume that a student first studies one foreign language (e.g., French) and later studies a second foreign language (e.g., Spanish). There are almost certainly going to be difficulties with recall of some of the French words learned that can be clearly attributed to interference from Spanish words (e.g., confusing *oui* and *si*). Such memory interference is what is meant by the technical term *retroactive inhibition*.

Proactive inhibition refers to the interfering effect on the retention of original

Table 12-1 Experimental Designs for Retroactive Inhibition and Proactive
Inhibition in the Study of Interference in Forgetting*

367

MEMORY

	Learn	Learn	Retention Test
Retroactive inhibition			
Experimental	A	B	A
Control	A	(rests)	A
Proactive inhibition			
Experimental	B	A	A
Control	(rests)	A	A

*Task A is in each case used for training and the testing of retention of training; task B is the inter-
fering (retention-inhibiting) task.

learning (A) that *prior* learning (B) can be shown to exert. Here the control group
again is "rested" during the time the experimental group learns B. Both groups are
then treated the same for the learning and retention testing of A, as is shown in
Table 12-1.

A real-life example of proactive inhibition would be the reduced retention of
Spanish produced by the prior learning of French; whether retroactive or proactive
inhibition is involved depends upon which of the two learning tasks is measured for
retention. Whenever two tasks are successively learned, the conditions are present
for either or both types of interference; which is measured depends upon the nature
of the retention test.

These two types of interference show similar detrimental effects in retention.
Although there are a number of variables that have been shown to influence the
amount of interference in retention, two of these are of such overriding importance
that this discussion will treat them only. These are the variables of similarity and
degree of original learning.

SIMILARITY. Unfortunately, the relationship between degree of similarity of
learning materials (in A and B tasks) and amount of interference in retention is not
a simple one. As a matter of fact, the similarity variable is generally found to have
complex interactions with learning and retention functions. Part of the complexity
arises from the differentiation of stimulus and response terms, as in the paired-
associates design (described in Chapter 11, p. 337); manipulation of similarity has
different effects, depending upon whether the stimulus or the response items are
involved. The total picture not only is complex but also is not yet completely
defined to everyone's satisfaction. However, we may mention the classical generalization, called the *Skaggs–Robinson* hypothesis (after two early researchers who
suggested it). As shown in Figure 12-2, this hypothesis holds that the amount of
retroactive inhibition in retention is negligible when the two tasks (A and B) are
identical (in which case task B is merely additional practice of task A). Interference
increases rapidly, approaching the maximum with slight departures in the degree of
similarity; at much lower degrees of similarity between the two tasks, correspondingly low amounts of interference in retention occur.

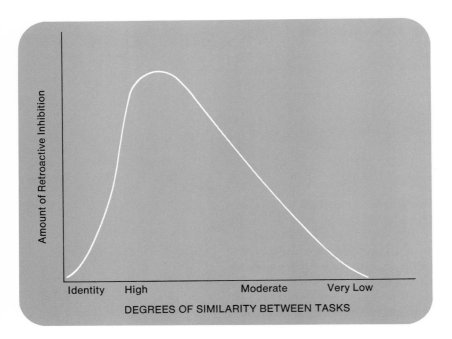

12-2 Schematic representation of the Skaggs–Robinson hypothesis, relating amount of retroactive inhibition in retention and degree of similarity between learning tasks.

Amount of Retroactive Inhibition (vertical axis)

Identity   High   Moderate   Very Low

DEGREES OF SIMILARITY BETWEEN TASKS

Original Learning

Fortunately, original learning, the second of the two major variables related to interference effects in retention, offers a simpler and more optimistic picture. Over a variety of tests it has been found that the greater the amount of original learning is, the less the retroactive inhibition is likely to be. This reasonably uniform result thus helps to strengthen the conclusion drawn earlier from studies in which explicit attempts at interference were not made: if one wants to *remember* well, even in the face of deliberate attempts at confusion, he should *learn* well. Although this can scarcely be regarded as a revolutionary principle, relative to common sense, it is nice to know that there is such strong scientific support for what parents and teachers have been preaching (and students have often known if not admitted).

A large number of experiments have also manipulated the amount of learning of the interfering task (B). Here, again quite generally, subjects tend to show progressively reduced amounts of retention as the amount of interfering activity is increased. The evidence for interference in retention from various retroactive sources is so great that the interference theory has for some time been the dominant theory of forgetting. It is only now being challenged by another type of variable, the factor of organization in recall.

ORGANIZATIONAL FACTORS IN RECALL

Although the existence of various kinds of organizational factors in recall of verbal learning has been experimentally demonstrated for more than two decades (it was first demonstrated in the early 1950's), interest in this variable has accelerated rapidly within the past few years. Partly this acceleration is the result of the convergence of other lines of research, particularly those having to do with coding processes in learning (discussed below, in relation to sensory processing and memory). In any case there is now clear recognition of the empirical importance, if not agreement on the theoretical significance, of this variable.

When subjects are given a free-recall type of test they generally tend to report the response items they have learned in *clusters* of related items. It appears that materials or tasks that are potentially arrangeable by the subject will be readily recalled. Most of the research results indicate that the associative strength of the interitem relationships is the major determining variable. Superordinate relationships, in which the various items are categorized under some central theme (such as various flower names all categorized under color, or names of animal forms categorized under reptile), are also helpful in recall.

SUBJECTIVE ORGANIZATION. More importantly, when clusters are *not* provided by the experimenter, in any obvious way, the typical subject himself tends to produce his own organization in the material by various forms of coding and recoding. Thus, for example, a subject provided the trigram *MUN* as a stimulus term in a retention experiment might code it into *Monday* or *money,* or given the trigram *RZL* might encode it as *razzle-dazzle* for the purpose of recalling the letters. Such more familiar individualized cues then serve as mediators on which the trigram can be pegged and its relationship with other trigrams better recalled. Although such associations might well be considered a function of learning rather than recall, and so operate by means of the amount-of-learning variable already discussed, they can be demonstrated in a single presentation; thus they are, in terms of operations at least, not measured in the same way as the amount of original learning, that is, by traditional number-of-trials technique.

QUALITATIVE TREATMENT OF VARIABLES

Researchers in the S–R associationistic tradition have consistently attempted to quantify their data, to provide numerical values for variables rather than simply relationships among them. A different approach has been traditional within the Gestalt conceptual system (Chapter 3). Here the emphasis has been primarily upon qualitative treatment of variables, on attempting to discover first the more crucial processes. The assumption is that the important variables need to be identified before effective quantification can be carried out.

The problem of retention was early attacked in this manner. In one experiment, for example, subjects were shown geometric forms with various irregularities. They were then asked to reproduce the figures (a form of recall test) on a succession of occasions. Three main distortions of the original figure were observed in the reproductions. As illustrated in Figure 12-3, subjects tended to reproduce the figures as more regular than they actually were, a process called *leveling* (or reduction of differences); to exaggerate some salient feature of the form, a process known as *sharpening;* or generally to reproduce the forms more in accordance with their usual appearance, which is called *normalization.*

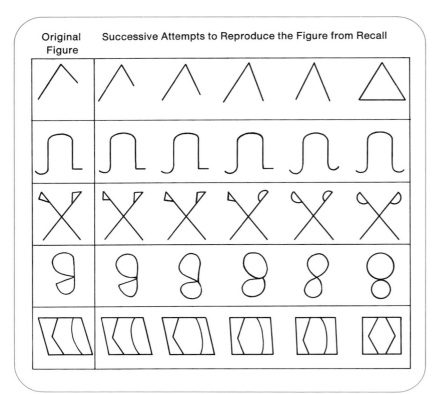

Original Figure	Successive Attempts to Reproduce the Figure from Recall

12-3 Examples of successive reproduction of visual recall (reading from left to right). Look for evidence of leveling, sharpening, and normalization, as these processes are described in the text. (Adapted from Perkins, 1932.)

Subsequent research on the problem of retention of visual shapes has sometimes used so-called nonsense figures (a term that parallels the nonsense syllable devised by Ebbinghaus and widely used in verbal learning research). Generally the results have confirmed the early ones reported, but again, the interpretations may differ. Thus the associationistic psychologist can point to the prominence of experiential factors as possible explanations for the distortions found.

Meaningful materials, such as stories, have also been used in a well-known series of experiments. Similar changes were found in retention, namely, the tendency to regularize (level) as well as differentiate (sharpen) when attempting to recall a story. Much of the early research in this area was beset with methodological problems, such as the use of the same subject in successive tests, so that new learning experiences were possibly confounded with the presumed autonomous neurological changes advocated by Gestalt interpretations. The use of recognition rather than reproduction tests and application of quantitative scaling techniques have helped to improve the methodology of the more recent research.

THEORIES OF FORGETTING

Most theoretical accounts have tended to concentrate on forgetting as the other side of the coin from retention. Why do organisms forget? The most obvious answer to this question would seem to be that with time and disuse of learned materials there is a natural kind of decay, and eventual failure, in the retention system, presumably neurophysiologically mediated. Such an answer was commonplace in the early days of experimental psychology, but little evidence of a completely acceptable sort has been obtained in support of it. The most prominent support for the decay hypothesis is indirect. The apparent interference with the *consolidation* of the learning process that is produced by electroconvulsive shock is an example of this indirect evidence, but even this relationship is still controversial.

What is left? Within the framework of "traditional" associationistic learning research, from which most of the results discussed in this section have come, the role of interference in retention has been overwhelmingly accepted. As we have seen, there is no doubt as to the empirical reality of the interference variable. Interpolated learning, that is, learning materials or tasks of a similar sort, is the surest way to produce forgetting.

Outside the verbal-learning research framework some attention has been directed toward evaluation of the role of activity as a critical factor in forgetting. Here two techniques of eliminating, or at least greatly reducing, overall retention ability have been used. With human subjects, learning has been followed, in one group, by the normal waking activities of the day (with no further exposure to materials of the experimental task); in a second group, equated for learning scores with the first, the subjects were allowed to sleep for eight hours immediately after learning. Retention tests were then given both groups. The critical parts of the stories earlier read (the learning task) were equally well recalled by both groups. However, the sleep group remembered about twice as many of the more trivial or incidental items, thus providing suggestive evidence in support of the proposition that any activity tends to produce some interference with prior learning.

Another technique used to eliminate activity has been the complete anesthetization of the organism immediately after acquisition. Retention of such subjects is then tested immediately after their awakening and compared with the retention of control subjects allowed to engage in their normal waking activities during the same interval. When cockroaches were treated in this way it was found that the active (control) group retained less than the inactive (anesthetized) group, thus again suggesting the important role of intervening activities as inhibitors of memory.

There has been a somewhat unfortunate tendency among psychologists to regard decay and interference hypotheses strictly as competing accounts. More realistically, however, it is probable that some compromise solution of the problem will be found, and that some role can be accorded to each of these factors. Forgetting is too widespread to depend upon a single determining factor.

Transfer of training is defined as the influence that prior learning has on subsequent learning. The fundamental question asked in transfer research is, "Will a subject's learning of one task be different—improved or worsened—because of some other previous learning?"

Transfer obviously plays a continuing and crucial role in the behavioral adjust-

Transfer of Training

ment of all organisms. It is especially important in the higher organisms, such as man, where the more complex forms of learning are common. The fact that transfer experiments always involve a combination, or interaction, between at least two different learning tasks or situations complicates matters for the transfer researcher. The great variablity in tasks and learning situations, already a problem in learning and retention research, is further compounded in transfer research by the interaction necessarily involved. One consequence of this situation is that comprehensive conclusions and generalizations applicable over the total range of transfer relationships are extremely difficult to obtain.

CLASSICAL THEORIES OF TRANSFER

Historically, transfer research has been related to educational problems. There was much interest in the doctrine of *formal discipline,* which holds that mental functions can be generally improved by experience with the training provided by such studies as mathematics and logic. These studies are supposed to discipline the mind because of the rigorous thinking they require. This doctrine has now been largely discarded. An associationistic alternative to the formal-discipline hypothesis has been the *identical-elements* hypothesis of transfer, which attributes transfer phenomena to the commonality of specific elements of S–R relationships in the original and the test learning situations. Although not universally accepted, this view has persisted, perhaps in part because it fits nicely into the general associationistic approach of verbal-learning research.

MEASUREMENT OF TRANSFER

Transfer is typically measured in terms of the *net* effect obtained; in other words, the investigator asks the question whether the overall new learning is more efficient (*positive* transfer), less efficient (*negative* transfer), or not particularly affected (*zero* transfer) by the prior learning. Determination of the net effect is made against a control-group base. Control subjects are presumed to be equal in motivation and learning capacity to the experimental (transfer) subjects; an independent measure of learning by both groups is desirable for such matching. Controls either lack the prior training provided the transfer subjects or are given a different (and presumably innocuous) prior learning task in order to equalize such factors as time required to "warm up." This precaution is especially important when there is only a short time interval between training and test tasks, because then the transfer subjects are already warmed up when they start the test. All groups are treated the same way in the test. The simple transfer paradigms are shown in Table 12-2.

The group that receives the transfer (experimental) treatment first learns task A, then is tested on the learning of task B; the nontransfer (control) group is rested (or given some time-filling activity such as task C) before learning B. The difference between the groups in learning B is then attributed to the prior learning of A and constitutes the transfer effect.

Table 12-2 Basic Experimental Paradigm for Transfer of Training Research

	Learn	Test
Experimental (Transfer group)	A	B
Control group	"rest" or learn C	B

DETERMINING VARIABLES

The influence on transfer of a small number of the more relevant determining variables will be reviewed. The most important of these is similarity; next in importance are the amount of original learning, various task characteristics, and temporal interval between training and test.

Similarity

Similarity is not really a simple variable. Learning tasks have so many different dimensions along which their similarity can be varied that it is difficult to make any overall evaluation of this variable. Similarity is clearly the most relevant variable determining the amount and direction of transfer effects. Most of the more recent research has specified the locus of the similarity. The chart in Table 12-3 contains two generalizations. Thus *positive* transfer generally occurs when the *same responses are involved in the transfer* (test) task but must be made to *new stimuli*, whereas *negative* transfer (interference) most commonly occurs when *new responses are required in the transfer task* but the *same stimuli* are used as had been present in the training task.

Some illustrative instances drawn from automobile driving may help to clarify this experimental paradigm. When a driver has learned the appropriate responses in one type of road situation, they generally can also be used in other types (say, a gravel country road as compared with a city street or a freeway). The varied stimuli require the same responses and positive transfer typically occurs when situations change. Assume that a driver trained in the United States is driving in England or Australia. Even though the road stimuli are generally similar, a radically new response—driving on the *left* rather than the right side of the road—is now required. Negative transfer may now be anticipated. Learning to make so different a response to similar cues can be very troublesome and even quite dangerous (especially in the absence of new cues, such as actually seeing cars driving on the left side).

This generalization about positive and negative transfer seems to hold, but only in a very gross manner. Later research has been more analytic. For example, stimulus similarity has been systematically varied between learning and transfer tasks, with responses kept the same; then positive transfer is generally greater with the higher degrees of similarity.

Temporal Interval

Varying the time interval between training and transfer test has revealed some important relationships in the transfer situation. For example, when rats who have previously been trained to turn right upon being placed in a T-maze are put into a second T-maze and trained to turn left, the result is a high degree of negative transfer. As increasingly long intervals were employed between original (right-turn) training and transfer (left-turn) training in separate groups of subjects, net transfer effect first turned to zero and later became clearly positive. These results are shown in Figure 12-4.

The interpretation of this interaction between transfer effect and interval is

Table 12-3 Typical Transfer Results from Changing Stimuli and/or Responses Between Training and Transfer Test*

Transfer Result	Stimuli	Responses
Positive	New	Old
Negative	Old	New

*"New" stimuli and/or responses are changed from those in the training task; "old" are the same.

373

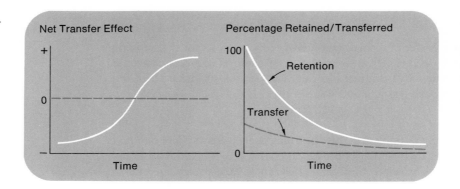

reasonably straightforward, and of considerable general significance in the analysis of transfer phenomena. It is the contradiction between the specific response details (right versus left turn) that would be expected to produce a strong negative transfer contribution to the net effect. These details should gradually be "forgotten" as the time interval increases. However, the more general learning factors—adapting emotionally, avoiding the immediate repetition of errors, and the like—are better remembered over longer time intervals. Hence the *relative* contribution to the net transfer effect of these general factors is greater for the longer intervals. These general factors for the most part can be expected to produce a strong positive effect over time.

Other early research related transfer-time to retention-time functions. These results were consistent in supporting the distinction between specific and general learning components in transfer effects. Idealized results are shown in Figure 12-5 based on the data from a study involving paired-associate nonsense syllables. The stability of the transfer effect over the various time intervals suggests the prominence of general factors (the S and R elements were not varied along a similarity dimension), whereas the marked and systematic decline in retention scores over time suggests the gradual loss of the specific details of learning. Thus the transfer subjects were essentially as capable as the retention subjects at the longest test interval, which suggests that the general learning component in both cases was about the same and that the advantage accruing to the latter subjects' having had identical syllables in both cases had disappeared.

Amount of Learning

The results relating the variable of amount or degree of original learning to transfer effect are fairly consistent, at least for the transfer paradigms shown in Table 12-2. They show that with a very small amount of original task learning negative transfer is likely to occur; with somewhat greater amounts of original-task learning, transfer tends to approximate zero; and with increasing amounts of original-task learning, progressively greater amounts of positive transfer are found.

These results confirm those based upon retention research in that they demonstrate the value of a reasonable amount of practice if one wishes to benefit adequately from learning whether retention or transfer is involved. The implication is that it is probably better not to start a learning process unless adequate training can be attained. Here again, the disadvantages of such partial and sketchy study procedures as "cramming" become apparent.

Characteristics of the Task

Attention has been paid mainly to two task variables, variety and difficulty, in transfer research. In general, the results seem to show that more positive transfer results from greater variation in the initial training. The theoretical interpretations of these results have focused on the increased attention subjects learn to pay to stimuli when variations in tasks occur. There is also some evidence that discrimination ability (as between relevant and irrelevant cues) is improved when approximately equal (and optimal) amounts of training are allowed on each of several tasks. This result is in contrast to that produced by a disproportionate amount of practice on one task; then there is a tendency to stamp in the particular S–R associations, or specific factors, but to neglect the more general factors.

With regard to the difficulty variable, experimental attention has concentrated on the question of whether it is preferable to start with a hard or an easy task when transfer to a difficult test situation is involved. The relevance of this issue for practical affairs is widespread. Although there are certain problems of the usual sort associated with scaling of difficulty and complex interactions among the variables, the general result is that transfer in *discrimination learning* at least is *facilitated* when one starts with the *easier* discrimination. This result is commonly explained on the basis of the greater ease of discovery of relevant stimulus dimensions made possible by the easier task. The picture is not so clear, however, when other types of learning are considered (e.g., motor skills).

LEARNING TO LEARN

The ability to learn new tasks more rapidly as a result of the cumulative transfer from a sustained series of learning experiences has been called *learning to learn*. This is clearly the kind of transfer that is of greatest generalized benefit to the learner. In one extensive set of studies Harlow's monkeys were trained on relatively simple discrimination problems. The monkey subject would be given two objects, such as a cube and a triangle, with the incentive invariably placed under one of them. The right–left position of the two objects was randomly varied. Following mastery of this problem a second one of the same sort would be presented, one involving, say, discrimination between two sizes of cubes. Monkeys so trained were found to become progressively more efficient at learning over successive blocks of problems. As a matter of fact, the minimum number of errors was often reached and maintained over a succession of trials. This means that the subject learned that if the incentive is under his first choice he repeats it on each trial, and if not he simply switches to the other choice. This level of performance indicates the operation of a learning set in the problem situation.

More recent learning-set research involving verbal learning and human subjects has been carried out, with analysis of a variety of subproblems peculiar to that kind of learning.

WARM-UP

Warm-up refers to the commonly observed fact that a certain amount of effort is necessarily devoted to various preliminary types of behavior during the early phases of any practice session. The *warm-up* effect is well known to a wide range of performers (for example, athletes, musicians, and so on). It is related to learning set but is a much more transitory phenomenon. Until the performer has thus "warmed up," his performance will not be as fast, smooth, and error-free as it would otherwise be. Much of the research on warm-up has been done with verbal materials, where we might expect the effect to be less pronounced than in motor skills. The facilitation that seems to occur when one learning session follows another with a relatively short interval (say, within one hour for verbal learning) is usually attributed to such general factors as postural and orienting adjustments, efficient selection of relevant cues, and the like. These adjustments to the learning situation are assumed to transfer from one learning session to the next but can be substantially lost if long periods of time intervene between sessions.

Thus a college student may have learned to warm up effectively when taking examinations (for example, by going quickly to the questions so as not to waste time, avoiding spending too much time on any one question, and so on); however, some of these adjustments may be lost over a summer vacation or, even more naturally, when examinations are again taken after a year or more away from school.

MISCELLANEOUS PHENOMENA

An early and somewhat persistent interest has concerned the problem of *bilateral transfer*, the extent to which learning involving one side of the body (say, one arm or eye) is transferred to the other side's performance. Typically, such bilateral transfer is found, and in substantial amounts.

Transfer from one *sensory modality* to another has also been demonstrated in a number of studies. Auditory and visual modalities have been the most commonly used, as in the learning of verbal materials. This sort of intersensory transfer has obvious practical implications, especially with regard to the usual school learning situation.

Also closely related to the school learning process is the problem of the *transfer of general principles,* as contrasted with particular S–R units of the type more commonly employed in research. In one study, for example, retention of card tricks learned by high school subjects was essentially equal over one night, whether the tricks had been learned by rote or by general principle (which, incidentally, required more time). When a subsequent transfer test was administered, however, the subjects trained to understand the principles showed faster learning of new tasks in which certain of the old principles were involved.

Take a Breather

MEMORY FOR TELEPHONE NUMBERS

Before reading the explanation of this exercise on p. 380 take a few minutes to make the following test on yourself. First, copy the prefixes shown in column II on a clean sheet of paper, then study the ten telephone numbers listed in column I for *three minutes*. Attempt to memorize as many as you can. Use any method of memorizing that you wish, but distribute your effort over all the numbers.

At the end of this period, close the book and write down as many of the numbers as you can after the prefixes on the test sheet.

I	II
544-8561	DE 4-
422-4471	FO 4-
GI 3-2643	824-
DE 4-2424	AX 0-
814-3498	GI 3-
PA 2-7167	544-
824-8667	337-
AX 0-8138	PA 2-
337-2360	422-
FO 4-1394	814-

From J. E. Karlin, All-numerical dialing: would users like it? Bell Laboratory Records, 1958, **36**, 284–288.

When you have completed your recall test turn to p. 380 for instructions on how to score the results.

Our treatment of the phenomenon of persistence of learning now shifts to the closely related topics of sensory processing and memory. The phenomena to be considered are in no real sense discontinuous from those already considered; as a matter of fact in some cases they are identical. However, the research has been directed from a different set of assumptions and interests and to some extent also by different operating procedures.

The Memory Process

From the point of view of the learning processes schema developed in Chapter 11, the focus in this research is on cognitive learning. A major operational difference from the traditional learning–retention research is that ordinarily only a single exposure of the test material, and sometimes a very brief one at that, is provided to the subject; this technique is in marked contrast to the multiple trials customarily offered subjects in the usual "learning" experiment, with retention then tested following some resting interval. The focus in the present procedure is thus on *how information is processed, then maintained, and eventually retrieved in memory.*

OVERVIEW OF MEMORY PROCESS

An overview of the total memory process is presented in Figure 12-6. Although this overview is useful in giving a picture of the whole process, the division of the process into stages of this sort must be recognized as arbitrary. The memory process is actually one in which the organism is constantly making use of all these phases.

Information processing consists mainly of sorting out, by attentional mechanisms, particular sensory impulses from the vast amount of stimulation that the organism is constantly receiving. Once this stage of information processing is

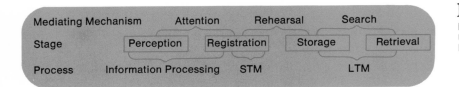

12-6 The four stages of memory processing and associated mediating mechanisms. STM = short-term memory; LTM = long-term memory.

successfully passed, the sensory information appears to go into a kind of primary memory stage, in which it is consciously registered. This stage is usually now referred to as *short-term memory* (STM). This is a most interesting process, in which a kind of instant playback of selected information is available on demand, but for a very short time only (a few seconds) and for only a limited number of items (generally considered to be five to nine) at any one time. Items of information may next enter the relatively permanent stage of memory, called *long-term memory* (LTM); the mechanism that seems to account most often for this major step is rehearsal, or repetition of the item before it has "left" STM (that is, become unavailable for "replay"). The final stage is the ultimate retrieval, upon demand, of items from LTM, mediated by *memory-search* mechanisms.

Before discussing the two fundamental memory stages, we should point out that the typical learning and retention experiment concentrates on the LTM stage (assuming the various earlier stages), whereas the research that we are now considering tends to focus on the STM stage, with attention also directed toward the retrieval stage of LTM. The apparent discontinuity between the two kinds of research effort can thus be seen to be in large part a result of their focusing on different segments of the total learning–memory process.

SHORT-TERM MEMORY (STM)

The STM phenomenon has long been known to psychologists as well as laymen, but has only recently received experimental attention in relation to learning and memory functions. The memory span item in the intelligence test battery is one example of the earlier utilization of this phenomenon by psychologists, mostly those interested in the capacity of the human organism and in individual differences. Memory span is determined by requiring a subject to repeat a string of individual items, such as digits, that are called out to him, usually at a rate of about one item per second. The memory span for a given individual is the number of such items that he is able to reproduce correctly immediately after hearing them.

STM Research Paradigm

Once STM functions were investigated within the traditional associationistic learning paradigm, research on the phenomenon accelerated rapidly. The procedure by which STM data are collected may be indicated by a brief description of a classic experiment on this problem. The subject was given one stimulus item at a time (a three-consonant trigram, such as *CKM*), and then asked to recall it after an interval of 3, 6, 9, 12, 15, or 18 seconds. In order to prevent rehearsal and the passage of the item into LTM, the experimenters required the subject to count backward by 3's from some number provided him during the retention interval. They then measured the number of successful recalls. Each subject had eight trials at each of the time intervals, with an average trigram used only once.

The results, shown in Figure 12-7, are quite regular, indicating a progressive and surprisingly rapid decline in recall over the relatively short temporal intervals used. Subsequent experiments have generally confirmed this general result.

Meaningfulness

A critical feature of STM is that items that have successfully survived the attentional mechanisms in sensory informational processing are likely to have some degree of meaningfulness for the subject. In fact, if they do not enjoy this property intrinsically, or enjoy it because of their context, the subject is likely to work at providing them with it. In this process the subject is said to "search" LTM stores for aids, in order to increase the meaningfulness of sensory information in STM.

CODING AND DECODING. The process by which some degree of organization or meaningfulness is provided to such neutral items as nonsense syllables or visual forms is generally called *coding;* items so treated are said to be encoded. Subsequently, in the memory search that occurs in the retrieval stage, a *decoding* process is required to return the original neutral items to the learner.

Some of the basic principles now starting to emerge from contemporary research on coding may be indicated. One of the more important mediators, used to provide meaning to neutral cues, is that of ordinary language; a popular name for this kind of transformation of cues is *natural language mediator.* Examples of natural language mediators from one experiment are *DUP-TEZ* transformed to the single word *deputize, CEZ-MUN* transformed to the phrase *says man,* and *GEY-NUR* transformed to the phrase *gray nurse.* Obviously, the range of possible language mediations is practically unlimited, and much more abstract and fragmentary transformations than these relatively concrete examples are frequently reported by subjects.

The role of decoding is closely related to that of coding. It is apparent that the longer and more elaborate the coding mechanism has been, the greater the amount of material that must be stored and the more difficult and more time-consuming the decoding—the retrieval—is likely to be. Even relatively simple coding devices are subject to error in decoding. For example, assume that the nonsense syllable *DEV* is coded into the natural language mediator *DIVIDE;* if a decoding error occurs, however, the syllable might be incorrectly recalled as *DIV.* Correct recall in this instance depends upon both the retention of the natural language mediator *and* the fact that it is not a perfect mediator (that is, that the letter *E* rather than the *I* occurs in the middle of the syllable). The more elaborate mediators themselves often tend to be forgotten, sometimes leaving the subject worse off than he was before he attempted the transformation. A balance thus needs to be maintained between improvement in meaning and complexity of mediation for optimal efficiency in memory.

There is a second major kind of mediator into which both verbal and nonverbal materials are often transformed: images. For concrete items (e.g., *chair, egg)*

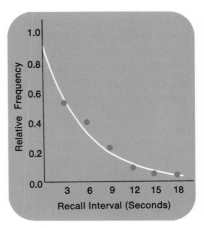

12-7 Correct recalls as a function of recall interval. (Adapted with permission from Peterson and Peterson, 1959.)

MEMORY FOR TELEPHONE NUMBERS

(Before reading this page complete the exercise on p. 377).

Interpretation

Individual telephone stations were originally identified by two letters and five digits. When the telephone company changed this system to the present all-digit system it received a number of complaints that seven digits are harder to learn and remember than two letters and five digits. One basis of many of the arguments against the new system was that seven digits in a string are more difficult to organize for recall. Because seven items is about the most that most people can hold in short-term memory, the all-digit numbers tax memory more severely than the mix of letters and digits.

Scoring

The simple exercise that you have performed enables you to make a comparison of the two styles for yourself. Prepare a table such as that shown below on your test sheet. The ten hypothetical telephone numbers consist of five old-style (two letters and five digits) and five new-style (seven digits) numbers. Now make two simple counts of your test responses from p. 377: (1) tally the number of correct *answers* for each style number; (2) tally the total number of *errors,* again separately for the two styles, in terms of incorrect digits. Insert these data in the table.

	Old Style (two letters, five digits)	New Style (seven digits)
Correct Numbers	_____	_____
Incorrect Digits	_____	_____

Class means can be computed for the two styles using the individual data supplied by each student to see if the class as a whole is better able to learn and remember the old-style numbers. Statistical treatment of the data can then be applied to determine the reliability of the difference.

especially, images seem to provide a more efficient mediation device than verbal tags. Moreover, they have one marked advantage over words in that they are less likely to require the complexity of relationship that can entangle a subject using strictly verbal transformation. As "conceptual" pegs, images are especially effective for encoding. The encoding process is likely to be more rapid, and memory thereby more efficient, when images are used as associative mediators for initially meaningless materials. "Seeing" a friend's face in connection with some particular trigram that reminds one of his name would be a means of combining both verbal and imaginal factors in the coding.

Transfer from STM to LTM: Rehearsal

Unfortunately, there is very little that can be said at this time about the pivotal process of passage of items from STM into LTM. The role of rehearsal, or deliberate repeating of an item or association in STM, seems to be crucial. Rehearsal usually refers to the subject's own covert repetition, in contrast to the more orthodox experimentally manipulated repetition subsumed under the term *practice.* As we have already noted, it is very difficult to prevent covert rehearsal by subjects in learning experiments. A major function of rehearsal may well be to keep an item in STM until some kind of consolidation process is completed and it has been moved into LTM.

Like so many other problems in this area, rehearsal is just now beginning to enjoy experimental attention. For example, subjects' rehearsal strategies are being experimentally manipulated. One interesting experimental result can be described to impart some of the spirit and substance of this kind of research. Clear-cut evidence for the crucial role of rehearsal during the retention interval was obtained by an ingenious data-processing technique. The experiment utilized the STM procedure in which subjects were required to count backward as a filler task during the 30-second retention interval. However, they were also asked to report each occasion on which they "practiced the trigram" or it "came to mind" by pressing a button. The experimenters found a positive relationship between number of rehearsals reported and efficiency of recall. More important, however, they analyzed the data with respect to each individual's own rate of rehearsal report. This measure, which varied quite widely over the subjects, provided an indication of individual differences in rate of reported rehearsal. Most of the reported rehearsals (button presses) came within a few seconds of the initiation of the retention interval.

This direct empirical evidence of rehearsal is subject to some distortion because it is dependent upon the learner's motivation and ability to report rehearsal. It nonetheless fills a gap in the experimental design typically used. Covert rehearsals have too often simply been assumed to occur during retention. As data of this kind accumulate we may confidently anticipate a corresponding improvement in our understanding of this crucial memory function.

LONG-TERM MEMORY (LTM)

Storage

After memories have passed into LTM they are said to be in "storage." This means that they are then accessible to the subject, on a more or less enduring basis. Unfortunately, very little is presently known about the nature of this kind of storage function; it is mainly inferred to exist from the clear-cut evidence that items that have been, say, sufficiently rehearsed are at some subsequent time available for recall.

The major factor now believed to be involved in the human storage function is that of organization. Stored materials seem to be organized categorically and probably in various hierarchical arrangements. This fact, again, is inferred mainly on the basis that item recallability seems to be so strongly influenced by such organizational structure and that learning enjoying a similar organizational structure seems to be better remembered.

There is one caution to be remembered when considering the LTM storage question. This involves the reliability of the storage, when only the terminal, or output, evidence is available. Thus, for example, an individual may be able to recount in vivid terms some childhood experience or other long-term memory, but how can the correct recall of this experience be established? For this reason full confidence in such evidence of extreme long-term memories is inadvisable.

A kind of evidence for faithful LTM storage that would seem, on its face, to be free of this kind of particular problem is the successful reproduction of some lengthy piece of prose or poetry that is said to have been memorized at a much earlier age and never since practiced. The adult performance can be accepted as incontrovertible evidence that the passage was in fact once learned. The problem in this kind of case concerns the "never-since-practiced" aspect. Again we have the problem of verification. When such long intervals are involved, and when memory is notoriously unreliable on this kind of event, the best we can say is that these accounts offer highly suggestive but not completely convincing support for the indefinite storage potential of LTM.

Retrieval

Unlike storage, where experimental manipulations are limited, the retrieval stage of the memory process is ripe for experimental analysis. The new emphasis on organizational factors in recall is beginning to influence experimentation on retrieval. Moreover, retrieval of memories is a problem each of us faces in our everyday life, so that we necessarily are exposed to much food for thought about the vagaries of recall.

One of the most important and interesting questions concerning the memory process generally and the retrieval process particularly has been virtually ignored to date, insofar as direct experimental attack is concerned. This is the question of how cues operate to produce recall. Experimental emphasis has been placed on the question of how learning occurs, how memories are encoded and stored, and how straightforward retrieval of these memories is managed from storage; and there is general agreement that maintaining the same *context* from learning to retention test is an important consideration in effective recall. But the complex relationships between cues and recall have received only slight experimental attention. This relationship, nevertheless, has significant neurophysiological as well as purely behavioral implications.

There has been considerable recent interest in a two-phase interpretation of retrieval. By this view search and recognition functions are considered to be separate components of retrieval. This seems to be a most reasonable assumption on logical as well as more formal theoretical grounds, and is either assumed in or more or less directly implicated by some of the personal observations noted below.

"TIP OF THE TONGUE." One of the more intriguing memory problems concerns the role of verbal tags, such as names, in relation to other more general cues. The so-called tip-of-the-tongue phenomenon is the inability, for varying periods, to recall exactly the right word, usually a name of a person, in spite of the feeling that it is just about to appear. In an experimental analysis of this commonly experienced memory phenomenon, subjects were read dictionary definitions of words and asked to respond with the word so defined. On those occasions when they were not able to give the exact word they were often nevertheless able to approximate it in various ways (e.g., give the first letter or the number of syllables, or provide a word equivalent in sound or meaning). These and many other results from verbal learning and memory studies indicate quite clearly the multiplicity of dimensions along which particular items are retrievable in recall.

VERBAL TAGS AS MEMORY CUES. Many other facets of the relationship between a name or other verbal tag and the more general retrieval cues remain to be investigated. It is interesting that the dimensions along which retrieval cues operate may frequently be affective as well as cognitive. Thus, I recently recalled a statement made by an acquaintance concerning the short-lived nature of the long-hair fashion then quite evident in male youths. Although I was unable to recall the particular person who had made the statement I did have a very strong impression that it was someone about whose opinions I was not as concerned as I might have been (presumably because of the overall low esteem in which he was held). In a similar way the positive or negative feeling tones that so often accompany our "picture" of individuals or institutions sometimes get detached in memory and we may recall them with regard to a remembered event in the absence of some other, ordinarily more prominent cue, such as a name.

Sometimes when one has difficulty in a more or less straightforward or direct recall of a particular verbal tag it helps to use a "side door," where resistance to recall is not yet strongly set. For example, I have noted a momentary failure to recall the last name of a certain "Bill . . ." and the achievement of full recall of the name by reposing the question in terms of a particular geographical location that I knew to be named for the man. The latter association was probably a stronger one than the man's name, because more commonly used perhaps. This incident thus illustrates the successful retrieval by means of a stronger cue whose application was initiated by failure of a weaker cue.

FALSIFICATION IN RECALL AND RECOGNITION. The term *retrospective falsification* is sometimes used to refer to the variety of ways in which recall is frequently blurred and incomplete but nonetheless treated as faithful (that is, recognition memory is also faulty, with regard to the recalled materials). Most of the errors of this sort are likely to involve various transpositions, as of numbers or people's names, and other confusions in the organization of the memory systems. Such common human weakness is the major reason why observers of accidents and the like are cautioned to make written records as soon as possible of their observations. Gaps in attention, and thus registration and consequently memory storage, are often supplemented by faulty recall, so that we may well wonder why testimony of complex and unexpected events is ever deserving of our full confidence.

Failures in recognition memory, although perhaps neither as common nor as impressive as failures in recall, nonetheless occur. For example, I am confused as to whether or not I have actually met a particular psychologist, whose latest book I recall looking over, on a previous trip to his institution. I can recall quite clearly a number of the salient features of the visit, as well as some events associated with the man himself, but I am not at all certain about an actual meeting. This incident reflects the gradual loss in details in memory, amid the endurance of certain more prominent features. The question may be asked as to whether this process repeats, but in a reverse direction, the gradual building up of solid memory that seems typical of certain very well-established associations.

AGE AND MEMORY. A question that has been experimentally tested concerns the differential recallability in children and college students of (1) actual objects, (2) pictures of these same objects, and (3) names of the objects. College students were found to have recall superior to that of the children for the latter two categories, but their recall was not superior for the objects themselves. This result suggests that the greater experience of the older subjects with representative symbolic functions facilitates their establishing and retrieving memory for pictures and names but is of more limited use for remembering the objects themselves.

It would be interesting to extend this kind of experimental memory test to subjects over a wider age range. There are a great many experimental questions concerning aging and memory that require experimental answers. These have to do, for example, with differential forgetting of important ideas versus trivial details (or ideas versus names), with the number of cues required for recall, and with changes in STM capacity as a function of number of cues. It is quite possible that significant interactions between age and some of these variables exist (such as older persons requiring a greater number of cues for effective recall of recently learned materials) and have important theoretical and practical ramifications.

SPECIAL PHENOMENA

This section is concerned with a brief review of some of the more unusual phenomena associated with memory. These range from some not so very special, such as the memory aids (technically, mnemonics) first discussed, to the quite spectacular feats achieved by the so-called idiot savant, which must be considered as something very special indeed.

Mnemonics

A variety of special devices have been developed for improving the storage and retrieval functions in memory. Most of these depend upon the utilization of some already learned, and well remembered, framework as a basis for learning and remembering new materials. Memory aids of this sort may be grouped into three large categories. First, there are those that depend upon *rhymes* of one sort or another. Second, there is the very ancient method of *places,* or loci, which uses the framework of a known building, such as your own house, within which the items to be memorized are imagined. Third, there are various schemes in which an *established chain,* such as of numbers (e.g., 1, 2, 3 . . .) or letters (e.g., a, b, c, ...), is used as the stimulus part of a kind of paired-associates procedure.

RHYMING. The first category, rhyming, is a familiar one. A well-known example is the ditty that begins, "Thirty days hath September . . ." with which so many of us have been introduced to the vagaries of our calendar.

PLACES. The second system, that of places, may not be as familiar as the first, although it is indeed an old system and one that has been long used by orators. There is an interesting story about its origin in ancient Greece. According to this account, the poet Simonides was invited to a banquet. During the course of the banquet he was called outside. In his absence the building collapsed, killing all the occupants. Simonides is supposed to have been able to identify all the guests by imagining where each had been sitting around the banquet tables. In its oratorical application, this system involves the speaker's imagining that he is strolling through such a familiar setting and encountering the various ideas or objects that he wishes to remember in succession as he passes from one place to another.

CHAINS. The category of key words or other serial items simply involves using these as pegs upon which to hang the various new items to be memorized. A great variety of forms of this general procedure is of course possible; some include simple rhyming devices somewhat similar to the calendar ditty already mentioned.

All of these memory aids have in common the effective use of organization in memorizing. They tend to require more time and effort in the acquisition phase but pay off in reduced effort in retrieval. For instances where the latter is crucial, as in the orator's performance or that of the schoolchild who has memorized a poem, they seem to work very well indeed. They thus represent the generalization that most new material is best learned in relation to some already established system of organization, so that its meaningfulness is not strictly dependent upon its own intrinsic structure.

Eidetic Imagery

The phenomenon of "photographic memory," more technically referred to as eidetic imagery, represents the opposite end of the effortfulness dimension from the mnemonic systems just discussed. Persons with this visual-memory ability simply have it, from birth on, and need expend little effort applying it. It does appear to peak in childhood, however, and decline with further aging. Such "human cameras," as we may consider eidetic imagers to be, can remember exact details of, say, a page of print merely by taking a good look at it. Although this ability may occasionally be of significance for special assignments, and if properly utilized can also be a considerable aid in reducing the effort required in many kinds of memorizing, it is of no direct value with respect to the more meaningful aspects of learning and memory, such as those involved in comprehension and the building up of cognitions. It does pose an interesting problem for the neuropsychologist as an extreme example of a special relationship between the visual sense and the memory system.

The Idiot Savant

The idiot savant is generally a person of rather low general intellectual status, as measured by intelligence tests or as evaluated on the basis of even casual observation, who has nonetheless managed to achieve some monumental feats of memorizing. The secret to this success is hard, persistent effort (thus placing this phenomenon back at the high-effort end of the continuum). The low general level of intellectual status of idiot savants appears to be an important feature of their development; it leaves them essentially uninterested in many of the activities that occupy most other persons so that they gladly take the time to develop their memories. Unlike the individual with eidetic imagery, the idiot savant thus has no special natural talent; rather, he has a lack of it.

Typically, some special feature is selected for memorizing. A very popular item is calendar memorizing, in which some persons become so proficient that they can readily tell you the day of the week on which you were born (which you presumably have handy in your own memory also for a check) when you tell them the month, day, and, year of your birth. The well-trained idiot savant is usually correct. This feat appears all the more remarkable because of his generally low intellectual status and because the audience for whom he is performing commercially is not aware of the great effort he has made in almost constant practice.

Dual Personality

The phenomenon known as split or dual personality is especially interesting with respect to memory because it involves one individual with what appears to be two separate memory systems. Experiences that the individual has when he is in one of the two (or sometimes more) personalities apparently enter a separate memory storage system from those he has while in the other personality.

A similar but much less chronic separation of memory systems is readily induced during hypnotic states. What the subject learns while under hypnosis, for example, does not seem to be effective while he is in a normal, unhypnotized condition, and vice versa. The split-personality phenomenon, which to some extent at least may be presumed to be based on similar mechanisms, does not seem quite so mysterious. Or, to put the matter a little differently, both phenomena may be equally mysterious, because little is known about the underlying processes, beyond the apparent fact that separate memory-storage systems are involved. These phenomena will pose interesting problems also for neurophysiology, once that field is ready to tackle them. The experimental separation of conscious and sensory functions in the split-brain subject, described in Chapter 4 (p. 87), is probably a different kind of phenomenon, because it is so clearly based upon an anatomical operation.

Motivated Forgetting

Recently there has been a sudden spate of research on the interesting phenomenon of "motivated forgetting." In this procedure the subject is instructed that he is to remember certain of the presented items and that he can forget others. Such cuing can occur at different stages of the learning–memory process but usually occurs immediately after an item or block of items. In general the results indicate that subjects so instructed forget the selected items, at least as far as the usual retention test is concerned. Moreover, they are able to remember the other items correspondingly more efficiently, presumably because of reduced interference from the "forgotten" items. However, subjects in several experiments have also been able to identify "forgotten" as well as "remembered" items in a subsequent recognition test, thus indicating that the basic mechanism involved in the selective forgetting process is differentiation of the items into two sets: (1) to be remembered and reported and (2) not to be remembered. It is thus doubtful that either true erasure of some items or superior rehearsal of other items can account for the usual data.

One of the underlying interests in this research in motivated forgetting has been its relationship to the psychoanalytic defense mechanism of *repression*. Memories are said to be repressed, or forced from consciousness, when they arouse emotionally disturbing feelings. This mechanism has long been well regarded but without much in the way of direct experimental verification, let alone analysis. The continuity evident between these two types of selective forgetting promises a more fruitful future for the Freudian hypothesis. There is one fundamental question concerning all these phenomena, namely, "Have these subjects really forgotten, or simply learned not to report?" No easy way of answering this question is apparent.

Amnesia

Systematic and extensive memory losses are technically called *amnesia* (meaning "without memory"). Fortunately, they are uncommon, but they are obviously troublesome when they occur. Some amnesia appears to be based upon *emotional trauma* and may involve selective forgetting. For example, a soldier who has had an extremely frightening combat experience is unable to recall details of military procedures in which he was trained. Such dissociation of memory is functional rather than organic (physical) in nature and therefore is readily reversed; the lost memories are likely to be recovered after the emotional trauma is reduced.

Other amnesias are produced by *physical insult,* such as severe blows to the head, which presumably disrupts memory-storage systems. If immediately preceding events are forgotten, this condition is called *retrograde amnesia;* it is perhaps the most common of the various amnesias. If events that occur immediately after the physical insult are forgotten—or more likely, not adequately registered or stored— then *anterograde amnesia* is involved.

Experimental production of amnesia is also sometimes accomplished with animal subjects, using such physical procedures as electroconvulsive shock, in order to test the so-called *consolidation theory* of memory; these tests are described in the section on neurophysiology of memory.

NEUROPHYSIOLOGICAL BASIS OF MEMORY

The bodily mechanisms underlying learning and memory continue to elude scientific determination in spite of the accelerated pace of research utilizing a variety of new electrophysiological and biochemical techniques. Needless to say, practically all the experimental research on this problem has been performed with animal subjects. Their expendability and the possibilities of extreme treatment (such as cannabalism, as described below) leaves little question of the advisability of this procedure.

Search for the Engram

The continuity of learning and memory functions, emphasized throughout this chapter and the previous one, is pointed up by the clear trend of neurophysiological thinking. Little distinction has been made between the two functions. Historically, the search for the neurophysiological basis of learning and memory has centered on the concept of the *engram,* the hypothetical change in the nervous system that is believed to result from learning experience and thus mediate memory. The engram has most often been sought in the form of some kind of structural modification in the nervous system. A favorite location has been the synapse, the structural connection between neurons. Unhappily, however, little progress in this direction has occurred, although some of the theories are still said to be viable. But the major fact contraindicating any kind of structural hypothesis, and particularly those that invoke particular brain locations, is the remarkable plasticity shown by the brain in retaining learning ability in the face of massive insult and removal of extremely large parts. Lashley's well-known experiments, based upon rat research and involving removal of varying amounts and sections of tissue, have established the principles of mass action and equipotentiality. The principle of *mass action* holds, in brief, that learning generally depends upon the *total amount* of brain tissue available to the organism. The principle of *equipotentiality* states that in learning phenomena all parts of the brain are *equally functional* (in other words, that there is no one "learning" center). Although some restrictions must be made for the latter generalization, these mainly have to do with special sensory or motor conditions.

In the light of the consistent failure of the structural-modification hypothesis, more recent efforts at research and theorizing have turned to more molecular and essentially biochemical factors. Our discussion revolves around four more or less distinct research areas, mainly involving the newer type of research.

Disruption of Consolidation

An active neurophysiological research area has been concerned with the presumed consolidation process in LTM. The consolidation hypothesis holds that establishment in LTM requires a certain period of time during which permanent modifications in the brain are being made. The experimental technique typically used in this kind of investigation of the storage process is to attempt to interfere with such consolidation of memory by some disruptive event. If the disruptive event results in reduced retention of the learning that preceded it, this outcome is regarded as evidence in support of the consolidation hypothesis on the grounds that memory storage was at least partially prevented. Electroconvulsive shock (ECS) has been the most popular disruptive intervention, but various drugs or chemicals are also used.

A typical result of disruption is shown in Figure 12-8. Rat subjects first received a foot shock after a running response. They were then given one ECS at varying times after the foot shock. Their running latencies were subsequently measured as a function of the time interval between the foot shock and the ECS. The presumption in such experiments is that with increasing temporal delay of the ECS, increasing strength of the memory for the foot shock will result, because of the greater amount of memory consolidation permitted. The results clearly support the theory. Moreover, the two control groups, one given only foot shock and the other only ECS, show the expected behavior; rats given only the foot shock showed relatively good retention, as evidenced by their very slow running on the test trial, but were approximately at the same level as the longest interval (1 hour) used in the experimental groups. Rats given only the ECS showed relatively quicker running, but were only slightly superior to the experimental group with the shortest delay of ECS after footshock. This result indicates that the memory of the foot shock in that group was substantially if not completely impaired.

These results are typical for the ECS experimental paradigm. Moreover, relatively long-lasting impairment in memory has been reported; in one study, for example, mice given a single foot shock as they stepped down from a platform, and received the ECS a few seconds later. Mice so treated stepped down almost as quickly as unshocked controls as long as one month later. Nevertheless, some other studies have reported only a temporary impairment in memory. Such varied results and experimental conditions permit the entertaining of a variety of hypotheses with

12-8 A test of memory consolidation. Rats trained to run on an electrified wheel were individually tested by administering a foot shock and measuring the length of time the rat would run after the shock. The foot-shocked rats ran for a significantly longer period than did a group of similar rats who were not shocked. If a single electroconvulsive shock (ECS) was then administered to the rats at certain time intervals following the foot shock, a pronounced change in their running behavior was noted. As can be seen from this graph, when the ECS stimulus to the brain occurred at short intervals following foot shock the rats' memory of the foot shock was obliterated and the running times were low. As the interval between foot shock and ECS was lengthened, the rats seemed to remember the foot shock and their running times were much longer. With a one-hour interval there was no difference between ECS subjects and controls that received only foot shocks. (From King, 1965.)

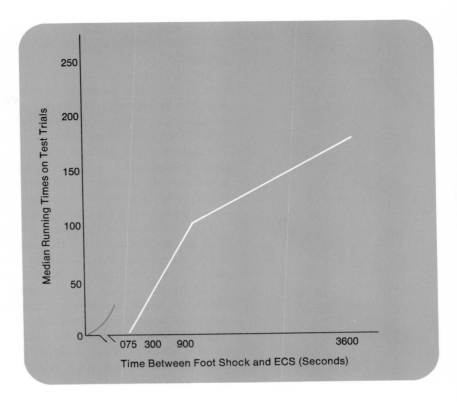

regard to even this fundamentally rather simple operation and its complex interactions with variables that have been manipulated.

Because ECS is so traumatic and widespread a treatment, efforts have been made to utilize more specific single electric shocks to isolated parts of the brain. This more discrete procedure avoids the massive disruption of bodily functions produced by ECS and promises to produce more definitive results.

Facilitation by Drugs

The experimental counterpart to the consolidation-disruption procedure is to attempt to improve LTM storage, as by means of drugs. The presumption is that consolidation processes require a relatively long period of time; the administration of drugs known to stimulate central neural functions during that period should produce a corresponding improvement in memory. Some positive results have been reported, with the greatest effects found if the drug administration occurs shortly before or shortly after training. Only small facilitation in memory occurs when the drug is given as long as one hour before or two hours after daily training.

Transfer of Memory

Perhaps the most dramatic of all the recent neurophysiological research on memory is that in which first flatworms and subsequently higher forms have been fed to one another to determine whether chemical changes produced by learning

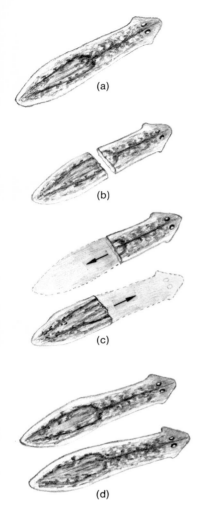

12-9 Experimental bisection of planarian (flatworm): (a) intact organism; (b) experimentally bisected organism; (c) regeneration of missing head and tail parts in two segments of bisected organism; (d) two new intact animals that result from regeneration after bisecting.

can be thereby transferred. Like most of the other current projects described, this one is still controversial, but there are sufficient positive results to justify our attention.

The planarian is a small and simple flatworm that inhabits freshwater bodies all over the earth. It is distinguished by a very active regenerative ability: cut in half, as shown in Figure 12-9, each half regenerates completely so that a new intact animal develops. Moreover, the planarian can be trained by classical conditioning or instrumental (avoidance) techniques. Its most remarkable feature is that when it is trained and then cut in half the new head part, with a completely new head ganglion (representing a very rudimentary kind of "brain"), now shows the effects of the previous training as well as the old head. Moreover, cutting the original worm up into even smaller bits has the same result: each piece fully regenerates and shows the effects of the previous learning.

The implications of these facts for the memory problem are indeed exciting. They indicate that memory in the planarian is carried in some kind of modification that is present throughout the body, rather than localized in the nervous system proper. They thus suggest a chemical carrier.

The further research has been even more intriguing. It occurred to some experimenters that the apparent chemical organization of memory might well be transferred to other, experimentally naive planarians if parts of the trained worms could be transferred. Again the planarian made an excellent subject: he would accept as food bits of cut planarian. Experimental subjects so fed were found to learn significantly faster than controls fed only on uneducated worms. Almost immediately this experiment was replicated at other laboratories, and later ground rat brain from trained or untrained animals was fed to naive rats in a similar design. Mixed results occurred; some laboratories reported failures to replicate the results, others reported partial replications, and still others reported satisfactory confirmations. It is still too early to permit definitive conclusions but the prospects for further research and theory are certainly exciting. In any case, laboratory animals the world over can look forward to more varied diets than they have enjoyed in the past.

The RNA Hypothesis

Implications of ribonucleic acid (RNA) in the memory process is another facet of the planarian research. Extraction of this chemical from trained planarians and its injection into untrained worms seemed to produce the same kind of memory transfer as feeding of the worm itself. This result, like the others, remains controversial. However, it fits in with some neurophysiological research and theory. It has been suggested that electrophysiological events in the brain underlie STM processes, at least for the first few seconds after the learning experience; temporary synaptic changes are implicated for this function. Following consolidation, however, more enduring biochemical modifications are suggested as the basis for LTM. Here the role of RNA and "information-rich" proteins with which it is associated is seen as central.

Although the biochemical details of this very complex research are beyond our present scope, the theoretical framework that is emerging must be regarded as extremely promising. Moreover, the very recent involvement in this problem of large numbers of molecular biologists, looking for new fields to conquer now that the genetic code has been broken, insures a high level of continued research activity. Regardless of the success of such biological research, direct behavioral measures and experimentation on memory functions will continue to play an essential role in our efforts to understand this extremely important behavioral problem.

Books on human memory by Adams (1967) and Cermak (1972) offer good introductions to that general topic. Authoritative but more advanced treatments are offered by Tulving and Donaldson (1972), Norman (1970), and Murdock (1974). The relatively neglected problem of animal memory is covered in Gleitman (1971) and James and Honig (1971).

Notes

Types of Learning Processes

The standard older book on human retention is McGeoch and Irion (1952); Kintsch (1970) and Kausler (1974) cover the more recent work.

Retention Methodology

Melton's *Categories of Human Learning* (1964) contains material of methodological interest. Luh's 1922 paper is a report of his classic comparison of the various retention measures.

Factors Influencing Retention

The demonstration of the relationship between distribution of practice and retention, with amount of learning controlled, was reported by Keppel (1964). The original research leading to the Skaggs-Robinson hypothesis was by Skaggs (1925) and Robinson (1927).

Investigators differ as to whether the various forms of organizational factors in recall can be entirely accounted for by the traditional associative-strength concepts of verbal learning research or whether they require some additional assumptions. Like many theoretical controversies, this one may well be resolved by a progressive reduction in the distinction between the two initially polar concepts as more refinement of one or the other of them, or both, occurs. Wallace (1970) states the contiguity view and Postman (1971) the traditional S–R account.

Qualitative Variables

The pioneer study described was by Wulff (1922). Bartlett's classic work is described in his *Remembering* (1932).

Recognition memory is often said to involve a rapid searching of LTM storage to provide criteria against which the new item can be checked in order to determine its familiarity or unfamiliarity; this step is made explicit in some theoretical treatments. Introspective evidence available to each of us, however, would seem to be in direct contradiction to this position. Rather, on the basis of such evidence recognition seems to be so rapid, instantaneous in many instances, that some more primitive and direct mechanism, possibly unique to STM, must be involved. The nature of such a mechanism remains to be determined by future research, but in the meantime the introspective evidence is persuasive indeed.

Transfer and Stimulus Generalization

Stimulus generalization (see Chapter 11, p. 351) is frequently stated to be the basis for positive transfer effects, because a particular response once conditioned to a particular stimulus can be shown to occur to other stimuli as a function of their similarity to the conditioned stimulus. The explanatory value of stimulus generalization in the transfer phenomenon is, however, somewhat limited. For one thing, there are many cases of transfer in which stimulus generalization is simply not applicable. Beyond that, stimulus generalization itself can be considered one kind of transfer phenomenon and is itself in need of explanation. Nevertheless, the two phenomena are obviously related and some explanatory power may be gained by reinterpreting certain gross transfer effects in terms of the more analytic stimulus–generalization process.

Theories of Forgetting

The classic research on sleep and retention was by Jenkins and Dallenbach (1924); the study described in the text is that reported by Newman (1939). The cockroach study was by Minami and Dallenbach (1946).

Theories of Memory

A number of recent and comprehensive books survey the various theories of memory. Among these are Norman's *Models of Human Memory* (1970) and the collections by Melton and Martin (1972) and Tulving and Donaldson (1972).

Transfer of Training

The early identical elements theory was proposed by Thorndike and Woodworth in 1901. The first suggestions of the relationship between S–R variation and positive or negative transfer were by Wylie (1919) and Bruce (1933). The T-maze study described was by Bunch (1939); the comparison of transfer and retention curves over time in verbal learning was by Bunch and McCraven (1938). Mandler (1962) treats the relationship between amount of learning and transfer. Harlow's basic report on learning sets was in his 1949 paper. The more recent research on learning sets in verbal learning has been reported by Postman (1964, 1968). The mediation interpretation of the positive transfer sometimes found when new responses are required to old stimuli was by Barnes and Underwood (1959); Postman (1962) has presented supporting evidence. The experiment on transfer of general principles was reported by Hilgard, Irvine, and Whipple (1953).

Memory for Telephone Numbers

The initial research comparing all-digit numbers with letter-and-digit combinations was performed in the Bell Telephone Laboratories and was reported by Karlin (1958). These results indicated that all-digit numbers were both more rapidly and more accurately dialed as well as somewhat easier to remember. However, subsequent research (e.g., Brautman, 1972) has consistently yielded an opposite result on memory.

STM

The paradigmatic experiment by Peterson and Peterson was reported in their 1959 paper; Peterson's 1966 paper provides a more recent theoretical interpretation of STM. The active role of the human subject in coping with materials to be learned and remembered is treated in a variety of recent sources, among them the book by Paivio (1971). The experiment illustrating language mediation was by Bugelski (1962). The experiment illustrating empirical measuring of rehearsal was by Hillix and Peeler (unpublished ms.).

STM and Decay Theory

Much of the interest in STM has been with regard to the issue of whether the rapid forgetting typically found occurs because of a natural decay of the neuro-physiological "traces," as contrasted with such impaired factors as interference from other learning. In this respect a major methodological limitation in STM research is that in order to prevent rehearsal, and thus insure the measurement of STM functions without serious contamination by LTM functions, some kind of activity has to be required of the subject. The interference theorist has been quick to point out that it is not safe to assume, as some theorists have, that such activities do not involve retroactive inhibition and so reflect decay of memory. Moreover, the use of multiple tests (eight at each interval in the early study described above) with different stimulus items may well lay the basis for proactive inhibition (that is, the interference in recall of later test items resulting from the accumulation of interfer-ing associations during the early test trials).

Although these considerations are certainly relevant to the issue of decay versus interference, they by no means negate the easily experienced impermanence of the STM function; most of us have had too many experiences with quickly forgotten telephone numbers or names to question this crucial facet of STM, however it may be interpreted.

LTM

The tip-of-the tongue analysis was published by Brown and McNeill (1966). Bevan (1971) reported the research on recall of objects, pictures, and names.

STM and LTM

A persistent and as yet unresolved theoretical issue concerning STM is whether it is fundamentally different from LTM. Most researchers now consider it to be distinctive, mainly because certain variables seem to have different effects on STM and LTM. The issue remains an active one in which attention has mainly been concentrated on whether such variables as interfering activities have the same effect on STM and LTM. Recency has been pointed to as a potentially distinguishing variable, because it would be expected to operate maximally within STM but not LTM; that is, as time passes within the very short temporal span used in STM experimentation, the effect of recency would be expected to decline rapidly, accounting for the temporal effects found in STM functions without the need to invoke the differential operation of interference.

Depth of Processing

A relatively new alternative to the STM-LTM dichotomy has been developed, also out of the information-processing framework. This view, first emphasized by Craik and Lockhart (1972), holds that the STM-LTM dichotomy should be replaced by the assumption that all memories are processed, but to varying depths or levels. Ease of retrieval varies with the depth of processing; thus memories that remain at the purely sensory level are not readily retrieved, whereas those that are processed more deeply, with semantic (meaningful) relationships, are more easily retrieved. A continuum of depth of processing on which all memories can be placed would therefore replace the more orthodox distinction between STM and LTM.

Mnemonics

Papers by Bower (1970) and Wood (1967) concern mnemonic systems. Yates's *The Art of Memory* (1966) is a somewhat more general treatment.

Idiot Savants

Luria's 1968 book concerning one case of exceptional memory is an especially thorough and interesting treatment of this topic.

Motivated Forgetting

The experiments mentioned in the text were reported by Block (1971), Woodward and Bjork (1971), and Davis and Okada (1971).

Neurophysiological Basis of Memory

The consolidation experiments described were by King (1965) and Luttges and McGaugh (1967), respectively. The newer technique of using single, more isolated direct shocks to the brain has been reported by Peeke and Henry (1971). McGaugh and Merz (1967) have described the facilitative effects, along with the other facets of the general problem. The early work on memory transfer in invertebrates is reviewed by the pioneer researcher, McConnell (1966); an example of more recent research yielding positive results is the report by Smith, DeVietti, and Gaines (1973), and Smith (1974) has reviewed the literature on the problem. The RNA hypothesis with related research is described by Hyden (1967), who is responsible for the basic notion.

Dependence of memory formation on a small part of the limbic system, the hippocampus, has been dramatically demonstrated by a famous case in recent medical history. Publicly referred to only as "H.M." in order to preserve his privacy, this person underwent a lobotomy in 1953 in which the hippocampus in both hemispheres was removed. Since then he has retained perfectly all prior memories but has been completely unable to form any new memories. The case is described in detail in the nontechnical book *The Brain Changers* by Pines (1973).

Consolidation and Drugs

The results described in the text serve to complement those reported for interruption on consolidation and help to strengthen the general consolidation hypothesis. However, they offer little further, more specific clues as to the locus or nature of memory storage itself. One possible exception to this conclusion is suggested by research on two facilitatory drugs, megimide and strychnine (Luttges, 1968; Andry and Luttges, 1971). These have quite different mechanisms of action on the central nervous system. Moreover, each has been shown to disrupt memory if used in massive doses. Nevertheless, some degree of commonality of action was found for them; with facilitative doses, each seemed to activate the posterior hypothalamus, whereas with disruptive doses both the reticular formation and the hippocampus appeared to be activated. It was therefore suggested that facilitative doses of either drug may increase the activation state of the organism in the absence of the increased level of stimulation normally required for such an effect; the net result would then be improved learning and memory consolidation without the interfering effect of increased stimulus input. This hypothesis is of course quite speculative but respresents the kind of result and interpretation that gives promise of producing interesting and informative research and interpretations in the future.

There is a newer tendency to regard the consolidation data as irrelevant to the issue of forgetting, on the grounds that retrieval difficulties are really responsible for the apparent failure of memory (Miller et al., 1974). This argument is a part of the more general view that memories are never lost, except for operations like radical surgery, and that amnesia does not actually occur.

"All the world's a stage, and all the men and women merely players; they have their exits, and their entrances, and one man in his time plays many parts." **These words from** *Shakespeare's* **As You Like It** *frame the discussion for the next section of the book. To what extent is the individual free to act out, to determine his own course of behavior, and to what extent is that behavior only a reaction to environmental forces and unseen manipulators?*

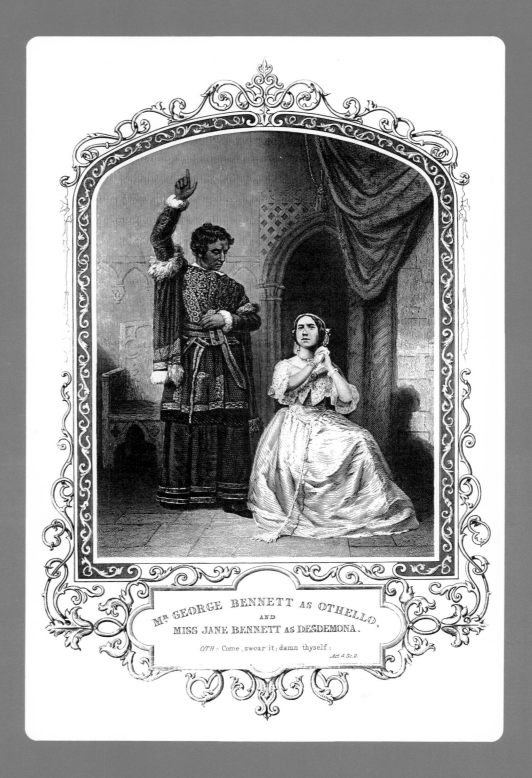

MR GEORGE BENNETT AS OTHELLO,
AND
MISS JANE BENNETT AS DESDEMONA.

OTH: Come, swear it; damn thyself:

Act 4. Sc. 2.

Man: Actor
and Reactor

n this last of the three major parts of the book consideration is given to problems that bear more directly upon the central concern of most people. The central question is, "What is man?" More precisely, to what extent and under what conditions does man react to his environment? To what extent and under what conditions does he act upon or control his environment?

Man is clearly *both* an actor and a reactor. He is an actor in that he has the capacity to make and act upon his own decisions, as seemingly demonstrated by many of the phenomena of motivation and emotion. But he is also quite plainly a reactor, responding to myriad environmental forces, some obvious and some subtle, again as demonstrated by the phenomena of motivation and emotion. The general question of how much of his active decision making is really environmentally determined cannot now be fully answered. Determination of how much real internal responsibility is granted to man will depend on much more scientific data than are presently available. As long as there is evidence for both acting and reacting, both need to be theoretically maintained. Dismissal of one or the other of these key functions may be dictated by one's fundamental theoretical bias, but that choice should be recognized as being an arbitrary theoretical preference rather than a scientific conclusion demanded by the evidence.

How the organism (O) can be included within the basic S–R formulation, and some of the problems that psychologists who attempt to do so must face, are among the key issues treated in this section. A substantial part of our attention is also given to the general problem of behavior controls.

The questions raised here involve the convergence of many disciplines and many points of view, ranging from philosophy and religion to the most empirically based sciences. They are certainly relevant. They are just as controversial as the problems of consciousness and heredity and equally in need of clarification. Like the previous parts of the book, therefore, this one begins with a key methodological chapter. One of its major objectives is to cut through the emotionalism that surrounds this basic issue of action–reaction, in all its ramifications, to help the reader appreciate what are now seen as the fundamental features of the central problem. Subsequent chapters in this part deal more specifically with the pervasive problems of motivation and emotion, and with the details of personality and social interaction.

Behavioral Controls

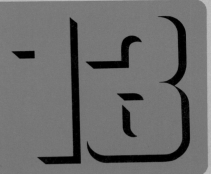

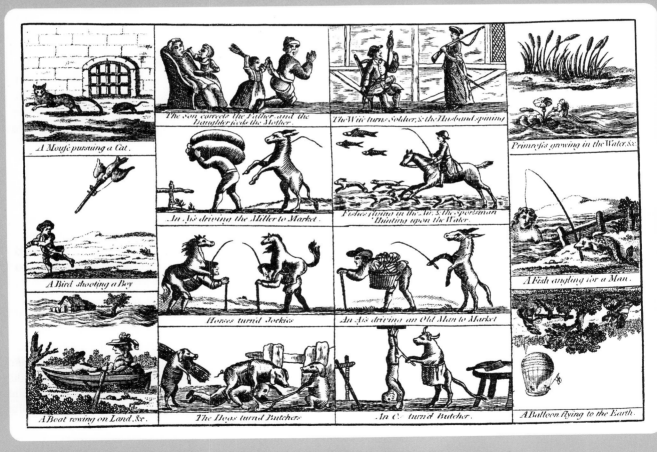

13

A Mouse pursuing a Cat.

The Son corrects the Father, and the Daughter feeds the Mother.

The Wife turns Soldier, & the Husband spining.

Primroses growing in the Water. &c.

A Bird shooting a Boy

An Ass driving the Miller to Market.

Fishes flying in the Air, & the Sportsman Hunting upon the Water.

A Fish angling for a Man.

Horses turnd Jockies

An Ass driving an Old Man to Market

A Boat rowing on Land. &c.

The Hogs turnd Butchers

An Ox turnd Butcher.

A Balloon flying to the Earth.

The topsy-turvy activities illustrated in this eighteenth-century engraving provide a whimsical introduction to our discussion of behavior controls. In this chapter we shall explore the question of whether we are in control of our environment or are, in fact, controlled by it. Are we masters of our fate or servants of our circumstances?

an's ability to determine his own fate seems to have grown enormously within recent years. So much so, as a matter of fact, that dire predictions as to that fate are being issued with distressing frequency. This chapter attempts to take a closer look at the fundamental problem of determination of and responsibility for behavior. Consideration is given the two extreme positions: the view that man is fully autonomous, self-directing (an actor), and the opposing view that man is entirely dependent on environmental forces (a reactor).

After a statement of the problem and a historical overview the chapter considers selected clinical and experimental procedures that have attempted to open the "black box"—the organism viewed without regard for its internal mechanisms. These procedures may also be considered as attempts to interpolate an O (for *organism*) between the traditional S (stimulus) and R (response) of the typical behavioristic framework.

The focus of this chapter is on the provocative proposals advanced by behaviorist B. F. Skinner in his controversial book *Beyond Freedom and Dignity*. Skinner makes a strong case for the reactor view, arguing that the notion of an "autonomous man" is illusory. The environment ultimately controls all of man's behavior, according to this view; it therefore follows that deliberate social controls, such as those in the "controlled society" Skinner proposes, would be an improvement over the present situation in which the actual controls are often hidden and frequently adventitious, if not sinister.

The major criticisms of Skinner's position are described, and some suggestions are made for the case for man as an actor. The probabilistic nature of scientific law is emphasized and related to the problem of determinism and the actor–reactor issue. The chapter concludes with a discussion of some of the more important ways in which behavioral controls function and some of the even more startling ways—such as the various genetic interventions now regarded as possible—in which future controls may be anticipated.

The Nature of Man

As science progresses, moving from the inanimate to the animate world, the physiological mechanisms underlying the vital functions of the higher forms, including man, are being discovered and thoroughly analyzed. The nervous system and especially the associated behavioral processes of man have been among the areas most resistant to this kind of analysis. Replacement of ancient myths and folklore by scientific propositions has been significantly slower for behavioral problems than for other aspects of man's adjustment.

In the absence of anything approaching an adequate understanding of human neurological functioning, behavioral scientists have been prone to rely on the kinds of measurements that can be reasonably well achieved *outside* of the organism. The S–R (stimulus–response) formulation has been especially influential, in part because it focuses on directly observable input and output processes. Certain specifiable stimulus inputs may be measured, and a behavioral history of the organism is observable. To researchers and theorists working strictly within this framework, man, like other animals, may be considered to be a kind of "black box," that is, an amalgam of various internal processes whose nature is best left unspecified (at least until such time as the fundamental neurophysiological functions are better known).

It is apparent that a great deal of scientific research and even theorizing can be accomplished with such a working assumption. Nevertheless, many scientists are not satisfied with this kind of incomplete methodology; they feel that we can profitably make some assumptions about what is happening inside the "black box." As a matter of fact, many feel that these internal, or intraorganismic, functions offer not only the most challenging, but also the most important problems for the psychologist, and that therefore they should not be ignored while we wait for the neurophysiologist to provide more complete information. Such a position is often referred to as S-O-R, with the O representing the organism, which is left out of the simpler formulation.

HISTORICAL OVERLOOK

Most philosophies and religions see man as an actor, as a shaper of his environment, as master of his fate. Within psychology, however, there has been no unanimity on the issue of action-reaction. Insofar as psychology derived from philosophy, sharing certain of its problems and approaches, early psychologists mainly seemed to accept the typical philosophical view of man's self-determinism. In the United States, with the advent of behaviorism early in this century, a strong counterargument developed. John Watson, stressing the role of the environment, popularized the emphasis on the S-R formulation. Its most outspoken contemporary proponent is B. F. Skinner, with his emphatic dismissal of the notion of the "autonomous man." Quite apart from the merits of his case, Skinner has done psychology a great service by so vividly drawing attention to salient issues and stimulating their thorough airing.

More remote from the mainstream of American experimental and theoretical psychology, but much closer to the mainstream of general and popular psychology, various clinicians and personality theorists have never lost sight of what to them is clearly the central role of man as an initiator of behavior. Their stress is firmly on man's essential capacity for initiative and determination of his fate. As therapists they tend to call upon his inner resources for improved adjustment in his social world. It would be difficult to imagine a sharper contrast than that between this kind of position and the Watson-Skinner account.

OPENING THE BLACK BOX

Clinical Procedures
To delineate the salient positions on the action-reaction issue, three of the most influential clinical procedures can be contrasted. These are the nondirective therapy

developed by Carl Rogers, the psychoanalytic therapy of Sigmund Freud, and the behavior modification procedure developed within the framework of the Skinnerian operant conditioning movement. Here only those aspects of these three types of therapy that are needed to accentuate the important contrast they offer will be covered. Also, it should be pointed out that the respective successes—or failures—of the therapies have little real bearing on the adequacy of the theories advanced; for the latter purpose direct empirical observations are necessary.

ROGERIAN NONDIRECTIVE THERAPY. Nondirective therapy is clearly an attempt to utilize the self-actuating capacity of the client. Rogers feels that the client himself must produce both the motivation to change and the ability to reshape his own self-structure. The role of the therapist is on the surface at least a truly minimal one. Mainly he *reflects* the client's own attitudes and emotional expressions, using noncommital verbal responses designed to elicit further expressions. The assumption is that only by the client's coming to understand himself can true improvement be gained. Although Rogers based much of his therapy on the psychoanalytic writings of Otto Rank, he disagreed with the Freudian emphasis on the all-pervasive role of the unconscious. Regardless of the extent of the operation of unconscious mechanisms, it is up to the client to take an active role in the therapeutic process, and without this, little lasting change is believed to be likely.

FREUDIAN FREE ASSOCIATION. The free-association technique, in which the client is encouraged to express whatever happens to come into his mind, represents a midway position on the act–react dimension. Although Freud and Rogers differed on the role of the unconscious, they agreed on the value of the client's achieving conscious recognition of his problems. For Freud, this is accomplished by breaking down the various unconscious defense mechanisms as the client gains insight into his problem. In this process the therapist, as an environmental (stimulating) agent, plays a much greater role in Freudian than in Rogerian procedures. He is extremely directive once he thinks he detects the source of the difficulty, and to some extent the client may be said to be encouraged to reflect the therapist's not-so-subtle suggestions, rather than vice versa as in nondirective therapy. In any event, it is clear that Freud's biological determinism and the mixed nature of his therapy, in which both therapist and client have active roles, occupy an intermediate position on the dimension under consideration.

SKINNERIAN BEHAVIOR MODIFICATION. Behavior modification developed as a direct attempt to apply Skinnerian operant-conditioning techniques, initiated with rats and pigeons as subjects, to the clinical problems of human clients. On the one hand, a basically passive role on the part of the client, or subject, seems to be assumed. Thus the behavior modifier places all his confidence in his ability to induce behavior changes by means of appropriate environmental manipulations, mainly through reinforcement, and makes no assumptions whatever about the client taking any kind of active role in this process.

On the other hand, and somewhat paradoxically, in light of this view of man as a reactor, it is the basic objective of behavior modification to teach clients to control themselves. This self-control does not rely on "will power" or other active internal processes. Instead the client is taught to identify and change those environmental influences that are assumed to control his behavior. An example of environmental self-control can be seen in the case of an overweight person who controls his eating of sweets by not buying sweets (it helps to shop with a full stomach). If sweets are not present, the cues for eating them will not be as strong.

The contrast between behavior modification and Freudian technique and theory is quite sharp, hinging mainly on contrary views about the role of the underlying mechanisms and the nature of the symptoms treated. With regard to underlying mechanisms, Skinnerians again make no presumptions as to the internal processes and profess to see little merit in those made by others. Behavior modifiers feel that it is the *overt behavior* that needs to be treated directly, rather than some hypothetical inner disorder of which the overt behavior is merely a "symptom" or reflection. This symptomatic view is held by the psychoanalysts and most of the other alternative theoretical positions.

Behavior modification thus occupies an extreme position on the act–react continuum, attributing no fundamental responsibility to the person in the therapeutic process. The person is taught that his behavior is controlled by his environment. This extreme reactive role is seen as an asset, in that if controlling variables can be identified, the person can try to change them and thereby indirectly change himself.

Experimental Manipulations

Research in this area requires the use of conceptual aids known generally as "intervening variables." An intervening variable is a process, such as hunger or guilt or loyalty, that is presumed to occur within the organism so as to account for the particular behaviors that are produced by specific environmental stimuli. It is so named because the hypothesized process is defined as intervening between the overtly observable stimulus inputs and response outputs of the S–O–R formulation.

As an illustration of how the assumption of such intervening constructs can lead to fruitful research and theory, when combined with appropriate empirical operations, some experiments utilizing laboratory rats as subjects will be described.

Helplessness and/or Control Concepts

Psychologist O. H. Mowrer has devised a number of ingenious animal research designs to test theoretical notions derived from human clinical problems. One much-cited experiment offers a good illustration of this kind of research. The problem was to determine whether effective learned behavior would occur under noxious test conditions more often in animals given an opportunity to influence the environment than in matched control subjects whose behavior had no effect on the environment.

Matched experimental and control rats were placed in contiguous cages with the same floor containing a metal grid through which electric current could be sent. Both of the rats had been deprived of food. They were offered wet mash through the floor of their cage and 10 seconds after they started eating and at regular intervals thereafter the animals were shocked. Each experimental subject was able to turn off the shock himself by making an appropriate instrumental response. Because of the common metal floors, each control subject received exactly the same duration of shock as the experimental subject with which it was matched, but it was unable to do anything about controlling the shock. Under these conditions the amount of physical stimulation from the shock was exactly the same in both animals, but the ability to affect the situation varied. The experimental subjects not only learned to make the instrumental shock-terminating response but also returned to eating much sooner and ate for much longer periods of time than their matched controls. This result permits the conclusion that there was some intra-organismic process that differentiated the two groups, and that could reasonably be assumed to be related to their differential behavior.

The results of these and various other experiments may be generally interpreted as demonstrating the utility of positing an intervening variable to describe the difference in results between experimental and control groups. Although Mowrer referred to a "sense of helplessness" as being responsible for the failure of the control animals to eat as quickly or as much as their experimental subjects, researchers in later experiments preferred to look at the same kind of difference in results as the product of something added in the experimental animals rather than as something subtracted from the control animals. They attributed the superior performances shown by their experimental rats to a "sense of control."

The Behavioristic Proposals of Skinner

AUTONOMOUS MAN

B. F. Skinner has mounted a major attack upon the time-honored concepts of personal freedom and dignity. In his book *Beyond Freedom and Dignity* Skinner's main theme is that freedom and dignity are illusory and that, like it or not, all men are fully controlled by environmental forces. He holds that it would be better to accept this fact and channel these controls into socially acceptable forms rather than to continue to give lip-service to outmoded concepts. The latter practice simply allows unscrupulous men, historical accidents, and chance events to determine the lot of millions of people.

Man as a Reactor

The major thrust of Skinner's argument is against the notion that man is free to act in accord with his expressed motives. He refers to this traditional notion as the assumption of "autonomous" man. Skinner wants to emphasize behavior—in its own right and not merely as a manifestation of some kind of assumed inner world. This is done, in the "experimental analysis of behavior," the commonly used name for the Skinnerian research program. Skinner believes that lawful relationships between behavior and environmental events can be developed in this way, and that only then can psychology as a science proceed properly. This view is obviously an extreme expression of the position that man is a reactor rather than an actor.

Skinner attributes to the environment responsibility for *both* genetic and behavioral determination. Genetically, evolution has proceeded via the natural selection of best-fitting characteristics; feedback from the environment is thus responsible for the shape of populationwide genetic determinants. Behaviorally, within the lifetime of the individual, the environment also supplies constant feedback, "reinforcement," to account for the selection of some behaviors and the elimination of others. In each case, Skinner points out, the effect is insidious (and also temporally drawn out in the case of evolution) so that it requires careful scientific inspection and analysis for its detection and description.

A less emphasized but somewhat more unusual kind of argument is offered with regard to man's "dignity." Skinner objects to giving a person credit for achievements, and thereby providing dignity, only when we feel that he has somehow *overcome* the environment, and not when the environment has obviously helped him to achieve. Skinner holds that such credit is misplaced, because in these cases we simply have not noticed the environmental determinants that have really been responsible for the behavior. Again, autonomous man is falsely credited.

SKINNER'S POSITIVE PROGRAM: EXPLICIT CONTROLS

In place of this misguided double standard for behavioral achievements, Skinner feels that we should manipulate the environment so as to utilize positive reinforcements (rewards) and in the process dismiss dignity, along with freedom. *Changing* controls is the heart of Skinner's positive program. There is no place in his social scheme for punishment or any other kind of aversive control. He has long argued against the nearly exclusive dependence, in the traditional schoolroom in our society, on the various forms of punishment and threats of punishment that are used to control behavior. He argues for greater use of positive reinforcement.

As an illustration of his rejection of autonomous man, Skinner uses the common procedure of offering prisoners an opportunity to volunteer for service in experiments designed to test the effects of potentially dangerous new drugs, in return, say, for shortened sentences or improved living conditions. Do these offers really provide prisoners with a true "choice"? No, says Skinner. Such freedom is illusory. The dice are too heavily loaded in one way. "Everyone would protest if the prisoners were forced to participate, but are they really free when positively reinforced?" he asks (Skinner, 1971, p. 39).

In the place of such rigged "choices" Skinner opts for "control which does not have aversive consequences at any time. Many social practices essential to the welfare of the species involve the control of one person by another, and no one can suppress them who has any concern for human achievements" (Skinner, 1971, p. 41).

It is important to distinguish Skinner's positive proposal from the mere absence of aversive control. Permissiveness is seen by Skinner as seeming to have a number of advantages (such as the saving of supervisory labor and reduced antagonisms between successive generations). However, he points out that permissiveness is not a policy but is rather "the abandonment of policy, and its apparent advantages are illusory. To refuse to control is to leave control not to the person himself, but to other parts of the social and nonsocial environments" (Skinner, 1971, p. 84).

Take a Breather

THE AIR CRIB

One of the most interesting and controversial implementations of behavior control and environmental manipulation was B. F. Skinner's putting his own newly born daughter into a specially designed environment—the famous "baby box."

The box was heat controlled and sound attenuated, and the large window allowed the baby to see out. The baby was clad only in a diaper and thus was free to move about and exercise without the constraints of clothing and blankets. The principal benefit ("reinforcer") for Skinner and his wife was the elimination of most crying and dirty clothes, blankets, or sheets.

When the baby first came home from the hospital, the temperature in the box was set at 86°F. Skinner discovered that raising or lowering the temperature in the box only a degree or two resulted in marked behavior changes. When the baby cried or fussed, lowering the temperature slightly stopped the crying. Be-

cause the baby did not lie in wet clothes and blankets it did not suffer from diaper rash. The filtered air eliminated the sniffles and colds common in babies. Except for play periods Skinner's daughter spent her entire first year in the box.

Here are a few questions designed to make the reader (and his or her friends) think about some of the problems of controlling the environment in this unusual situation. After deciding on the answers that seem most reasonable, turn to the box on p. 410 and see how Skinner handled the question for his daughter.

QUESTIONS

1. When shifted from four to three feedings a day, Skinner's daughter began to wake up an hour earlier than usual and cry for breakfast. Not being pleased with his organic alarm clock, Skinner

With regard to the problem of "changing minds," Skinner states:

It is a surprising fact that those who object most violently to the manipulation of behavior nevertheless make the most vigorous efforts to manipulate minds. Evidently freedom and dignity are threatened only when behavior is changed by physically changing the environment. There appears to be no threat when the states of mind said to be responsible for behavior are changed, presumably because autonomous man possesses miraculous powers which enable him to yield or resist [Skinner, 1971, pp. 91–92].

Skinner also points out an interesting difference in the susceptibility to change of the behaviors themselves and the beliefs that support them:

Where it is not too difficult to change informal instruction . . . it is nearly impossible to change an educational establishment. It is fairly easy to change marriage, divorce, and child-rearing practices as the significance for the culture changes but nearly impossible to change the religious principles which dictate such practices. It is easy to change the extent to which various kinds of behavior are accepted as right but difficult to change the laws of government [Skinner, 1971, p. 155].

Skinner concludes: "The intentional design of a culture and the control of human behavior it implies are essential if the human species is to continue to develop. Neither biological nor cultural evolution is any guarantee that we are inevitably moving toward a better world" (Skinner, 1971, p. 175).

made a simple adjustment that resulted in one more hour of sleep. Skinner
a. made the box more soundproof.
b. conditioned the baby to wake up 5 minutes later each morning.
c. put a lever in the box so the child could press the bar and feed herself.
d. raised the temperature in the box.

2. According to Skinner does a baby need to cry?
a. Yes, regularly, because otherwise it could not learn to speak properly.
b. Very seldom, if ever.
c. Only when it is physically mistreated.
d. Only when it is psychologically mistreated.

3. Was Skinner's baby isolated in the box?
a. Only in a physical sense, and then not completely.
b. As completely as possible, for as long as she could stand it without crying.
c. Rarely, because there was usually someone there.

d. Never, in order to avoid undesirable antisocial behaviors.

4. In order to provide proper stimulation for the baby in the box, Skinner
a. added levers to press, to permit the baby to obtain her own food.
b. gave the baby various playthings.
c. maintained a fully lighted environment at all times.
d. markedly varied such conditions as temperature, light, adult attention.

5. When the baby graduated from the box, she was
a. totally unprepared for the real world.
b. primarily prepared for artificial environments, only partially prepared for life outside the box.
c. reasonably prepared for the shift to life outside the box.
d. perfectly prepared for any and all environments.

Skinnerian Treatment of Organismic Variables

The major categories of variables within the organism (O) of the S–O–R paradigm are three in number: conscious processes, physiological functions, and intervening constructs. These will be described in terms of their Skinnerian treatment.

CONSCIOUSNESS. Conscious processes, which are strictly private experiences (and as such are extremely important to each of us), are of limited scientific utility. Skinner accepts them as events and as worthy of study but does not think any use can be made of them scientifically; certainly he rejects the notion that they have any direct causal significance for behavior. (Chapter 4 provides a more thorough discussion of this problem.)

NEUROPSYCHOLOGY. Physiological processes Skinner recognizes as scientifically important—but not for an analysis of behavior. He thinks that behavior laws must stand on their own, independent of physiological assumptions. When sufficient neurophysiological information is available, then it can be integrated with behavior laws to help provide a more complete picture of the organism in its environment. In the meantime Skinner does not see that neuropsychology, in spite of its recent dramatic breakthroughs, has any necessary contributions to offer the scientific study of behavior.

INTERVENING CONSTRUCTS. It is this third category, the intervening constructs, that constitutes the main battleground for alternative conceptualizations and procedures. These are the internal processes that the orthodox theorist, along with the man in the street, attributes to the organism; habit, intelligence, anxiety, and a great number of personality traits and characteristics are among the many and varied types of intervening constructs.

Skinner's basic objection to this use of constructs is that they do not really have causal or determining influence and that the real determinants are in the environment. In addition to this criticism, they may be objected to on more fundamental methodological grounds: they often do not have the tight logical relationship to empirical measurement that permits them to be unambiguously understood. In other words, they are not "operationally" defined to a sufficient degree.

EVALUATION OF SKINNER'S PROPOSAL

Skinner's program has been subjected to as searching and widespread an attack as anything in psychology. There has been a great number of reviews in the popular press and in periodicals as well as in scientific journals. Many of the criticisms represent defensive reactions from the guardians of traditional social values and orthodox institutions. These range from relatively mild strictures to the comment by one professor of religion that "Skinner's utopian projection is less likely to be a blueprint for the Golden Age than for the theory and practice of hell" (Rubenstein as quoted in *Time*, September 20, 1971, p. 53).

Two kinds of critical question concerning the Skinner program are here selected for discussion, one theoretical and one practical. The theoretical issue concerns the problem of determinism: Are all human actions strictly determined by environmental stimuli as Skinner's proposal seems to assume, or is there in behavior some degree of freedom or unpredictability? The practical issue concerns the question of responsibility for controls: Who decides what is good for society and how are such decisions reviewed by those to whom they apply? The difficulty of achieving agreement on social objectives has been dramatically pointed up recently by the variety of attacks upon "the establishment." In the absence of any new and generally acceptable solution to these twin problems of power and responsibility within society, early large-scale acceptance of such a program as Skinner's seems unlikely. "Muddling through" by means of piecemeal adjustments of traditional procedures seems a much more probable prospect in our own society at least.

The Problem of Determinism

Although this is not the place to present any kind of detailed analysis of the complex problem of determinism, certain fundamental conceptualizations and perspectives can be suggested. Determinism is the view that all events have *causes,* that is, are determined by prior events. The relationship between the cause (prior event) and the event is called a functional relationship.

A functional relationship exists when changes in one variable result in ("cause") changes in another variable. For example, large changes in temperature result in changes in the type of clothing worn. Wearing shorts is thus determined by (is a function of) the temperature. However, some people wear shorts when it is freezing and not everyone wears shorts even in the warmest weather. These contradictory facts illustrate the *probabilistic* nature of causation (determinism). High temperatures only increase the probability that people will wear shorts, they do not predetermine that above 95°F we will all wear shorts.

Scientific laws, which relate empirically observed variables, are essentially statements of probabilities. Similarly, sociological and economic predictions can be made, and laws of a sort achieved, on the basis of probability statements that encompass the cumulative behavior of large numbers of individuals.

This kind of summary or probability statement can be contrasted with the immediate observation of what appear to be direct causal sequences (determination) in everyday physical events. Thus we can predict with considerable precision the consequences of various antecedents (e.g., the falling of an object dropped from a tower, the rebound of a ball propelled against the cushion of a billiard table). There is a much greater immediacy in the experiencing of this kind of sequence, in which the antecedent event is commonly said to be the "cause" of the subsequent event.

With these two seemingly diverse types of relationships in mind consider the role of an organ such as the brain, which we may regard as a prime determinant of most human behavior. From one point of view it is certainly true that insofar as there is predictability in the brain's operation, and in the corresponding behaviors that we assume to be causally related to brain functions, the laws involved are probabilistic. For example, knowing something of both the genetic background (as influenced by environmental events in the past) and the stimulation in the present environment, one can often make reasonably accurate probability statements about the behavior of various organisms. In this sense Skinner is certainly correct in emphasizing the controlling role of the environment.

Such statements remain, however, probability statements. Moreover, they relate peripheral variables—stimuli and responses. They do not tell us anything about how the brain operates.

Consider the operation of a complex computer program. Once such a program (say, how to play chess at an advanced level) is set into the computer system, many of the moves made may be more or less predictable, but not all. The degree of uncertainty may in part be introduced by various "random" events; the programmer himself may not be able to take into account the exact way in which all the inputs are handled by such a program. When such a complex program begins to make "decisions"—perhaps in a manner analogous to the human brain—adventitious ("chance") conditions come prominently into play. That is, the effect of some particular stimulus input is crucially dependent on the time of its occurrence. The importance of this kind of timing of stimuli is clearly apparent in everyday life situations; for example, a new job offer will be more tempting if a worker has just been severely criticized by the boss, and a new girl or boy will be viewed with more interest if a college student has just quarreled with his or her current boy or girl friend.

The human brain is certainly far more complex than any computer program thus far developed, so that there are in its operations vastly greater margins for error— or opportunities for an apparent "freedom." Whether or not increased knowledge

Breather Interpretation

THE AIR CRIB

1. **(d)** Slightly raising the temperature in the box during the night resulted in the baby's sleeping for another hour. The evening meal lasted longer apparently because the baby did not use as much energy to keep itself warm during the night.

2. **(b)** Skinner thinks that the only time a baby should cry is when it is hungry, wet, or injured. After three months Skinner's daughter cried only when distressed by such things as inoculations. Properly adjusting the temperature of the box, providing a regular feeding schedule, and allowing the baby freedom in the box eliminated crying.

3. **(a)** The baby was isolated in the sense that noise and light that would ordinarily disturb or waken a baby were stopped by the box. In another sense the baby was exposed to much more stimulation than normal. When the box is kept where the family's activity is centered the baby can see the activity, and the baby's babbles and rattles do not disturb the occupants of the room.

4. **(b)** The Skinners did not require their daughter to work for her supper. But they did provide manipulable objects and toys before they became popular in child rearing. For example, their daughter learned to play "Three Blind Mice" by rapidly pulling a ring with her toes.

5. **(c)** Because the baby was healthier (no cold, rashes, bumps, or bruises) and more active (no clothes), it was reasonably well prepared for outside living. The baby was also adapted to the outside world by gradually increasing its play time outside the box.

and ever-narrowing probability statements will ultimately remove all such uncertainties from human behavior cannot now be said with any assurance.

A crucial distinction that must be kept in mind when considering the problem of determinism and freedom is that between the *generalized* scientific law, which is as we have seen essentially a probability function that makes possible highly accurate predictions, and the *specific* cause–effect chain of events of the sort involved in some particular behavioral process. Much as it is not possible to predict the path of any particular molecule in a diffusing chemical on the basis of a generalized scientific law concerning diffusion, so it may well not be possible to predict with accuracy all the behavior of an organism even when the generalized laws underlying behavior are fully developed. This state of affairs would not necessarily mean that the behavior is not lawful or determined, but would indicate rather that behavior is "emergent," in the sense that new and essentially unpredictable patterns can occur.

It is necessary also to distinguish between determinism and *predestination*. Predestination, which is a form of fatalism (the general view that attributes everything to suprahuman forces), is the belief that there is some *pre*determined pattern that events must follow.

It is conceivable that on a probability basis responses are predictable and thus "determined" even while the *specific* processes of an organ such as the brain are essentially unpredictable. They would then not be *pre*determined. In this sense the processes of the brain may be crucial in the instigation of behavior—in the making of decisions, for example—in a way that really merits the designation of a truly "active" role for the organism. Of course major determinants of these processes are various environmental events: those that account, as Skinner has pointed out, for its evolutionary history and thus its present genetic "programming" as well as those that were involved in the past experiences of the organism and those that are presently stimulating it. Nevertheless, it is possible that some *new* and to some degree unpredictable products occur even when a reasonably complete account is available of such environmental determinants.

For example, an individual suddenly decides that he has "had it" and informs his boss of his resignation, effective immediately; or a long-time friend unexpectedly turns on one and heaps on abuse in a most unfriendly manner. What induces such decisions and actions? Some answers can be suggested, especially if an investigator or clinician is familiar with the personalities and environmental stresses involved. But these are basically just guesses. Moreover, they are post hoc (after the fact), explanations, rather than predictions. The brain plays a central role in such matters but we do not know the extent to which its operations are independent of environmental events or, to put it another way, the extent to which its operations once active can generate new outcomes. The possibility that such self-actuating processes occur cannot be denied on the basis of generalizations that are themselves little more than presumptions.

The Problem of Who Controls

The second category of critical reaction to Skinner's *Beyond Freedom and Dignity* is by far the most significant from a practical point of view. This is the raising of the question of *who* is to be given the ultimate authority to decide on the desired behaviors if explicit social controls of the sort Skinner envisions are in fact to be instituted. A fundamental difficulty is that not enough of us can agree on what kind of society we want; if sufficient agreement could be reached the problem of controls would be greatly reduced.

Clearly, there is no easy and satisfactory way to answer this all-important question. Skinner has provided a dual answer. First, he has pointed out that his own proposal by no means generates the problem; there *are* already many sources of personal control in society. Second, he has observed that if his program of explicit controls were to be instituted it could include a set of checks and counterbalances that would serve to make the controllers responsible to the people. Unfortunately, implementing this desirable objective would obviously be a great deal more difficult than accepting its reasonableness in principle.

Society's failure to accept the Skinner proposal in its entirety should not mean that all the various subsidiary points made by Skinner, such as those about reducing the use of aversive motivation in the educational system, need also be ignored or postponed. On the contrary, if some of them are reasonably applicable and sufficiently acceptable, they can be implemented to the extent that the persons now in control can be convinced and their constituency accedes. Such partial implementation of Skinner's proposals carries no corollary acceptance of other aspects of his program, much less the entire program. These various subsidiary facets must all be evaluated on their own merits.

Skinner's proposals have spotlighted some of the critical problems of social organization and have especially called into question the whole problem of social controls. From the point of view of the act–react continuum, one may well ask, "How much individual control does the person actually have in contemporary Western society?" "What are the prospects for change in the situation?" These two questions will be briefly answered by surveying first present controls and then prospects for future controls in American society.

Present Controls

Restrictions on the freedom of action of the individual in society are many and varied. The more prominent are discussed in the following sections.

LEGAL CODES. All societies have some form of more or less explicit rules for behavior, enforcement of the rules, and prescribed punishments for violations. The ability of a society to live by these legal codes depends on the degree to which its members agree that they are desirable. The battleground over many legal questions, particularly in the United States, is in the area of individual liberty versus societal regulation. A pertinent example is the debate over legalizing abortion. Is the mother's desire to abort a lawful and necessary individual freedom for her? Does the fetus have an individual right? If so, at which stage of development? Another important area of current debate is the degree to which society should prosecute so-called victimless crimes, such as gambling, prostitution, or use of drugs. Some believe such prosecution is an unnecessary violation of the individual's right to engage in behavior that does little social harm to others. Some argue that society receives less protection from "victimful" crimes, such as personal assault and robbery, because so much law enforcement time is taken up in prosecuting the former type of crime. These groups want current laws changed; other groups do not. The degree of compliance with legal codes and the frequency with which they are changed obviously varies widely; but all legal codes are restrictions on individual behaviors and do not permit absolute freedom.

MORAL CODES, MORES, SOCIAL ROLES. These are somewhat more subtle but nonetheless powerful forms of behavior control, mediated within families, educational institutions, and religious groups. Peer cultural controls are especially powerful, particularly among the young. Remarkably rapid changes can occur in social roles, as evidenced by recent changes in life styles related to the family structure (e.g., group living in communes, living together of heterosexual pairs without marriage, and so on). Social changes are occurring as a result of emphasis upon various forms of "liberation," as for women, homosexuals, and minority ethnic groups whose rights have in the past been severely curtailed in practice apart from legal infringements.

PHYSIOLOGICAL CONTROLS. There are varying degrees of directly physiological control, as in addiction to the "hard" drugs or dependence on some forms of medicinal treatment involving drugs. The degree to which tobacco and alcohol usage develops true physiological addiction over and above psychological or habitual factors remains in question; in any event, the psychological controls they exert are certainly formidable enough. The extent to which individuals in Western society within recent years have been "willing" to subject themselves to drug addiction, with all its attendant long-term miseries to offset any short-term pleasures, is indeed remarkable and raises a number of questions concerning the way in which personal freedom functions in practice. Controls exercised by primary physiological needs—in particular, food, water, and sex—are obvious.

HABITUAL CONTROLS. Habit is the most subtle form of behavior control and the one that is basic to many of the controls described earlier. As we have already seen in Chapter 11, habit is a central concept in all human behavior and in the molding of personality. One simple example of the way in which habit exerts a powerful controlling influence on behavior may be cited. Chronically unemployed and therefore economically disadvantaged people are not accustomed to early rising, and in the absence of alarm clocks they often have difficulty in getting up and out to go to work; seeing that they receive employment is therefore not sufficient—one must also see that they take advantage of such opportunities. That such a seemingly small problem, and one that could be so readily remedied, should have caused even enough difficulty to be noted is symptomatic of the pervasive role that habitual forms of behavior play in controlling our lives.

There is little doubt that Skinner is correct in assuming that behavior processes of the sort he is attempting to influence do play the central role in the variety of social problems for which controls are normally used, regardless of how one otherwise views his program or his theoretical position.

Future Shocks

Present problems involving social control, such as the few examples given (e.g., abortion, drugs, life-styles) seem large enough, and require a great deal more than they have thus far received in the way of intensive, enlightened public discussion. These problems, however, pale into insignificance when compared with some that are in the offing. The startling advances now being made in, for example, genetics promise to pose new and exceptionally difficult ethical questions for all segments of society. These ethical issues are too important to be left to the traditional guardians of the public conscience, such as religious and political leaders, alone. All of us must engage in continuing serious discussion and decision making on these issues.

A taste of what is to come has already been experienced in the matter of certain medico-surgical interventions, such as organ transplants (eye, heart, and the like) from persons who have recently died. A host of new questions have arisen concerning not only who decides on the recipients, but also, more basically, such issues as exactly when death occurs, in a legal sense. The determination of when death occurs is important because of the very short time interval during which a viable organ can be obtained and transplanted successfully. Brain transplantation, in spite of an occasional hint in the popular press, remains unfeasible because of the vast number of connections that would need to be made (compared, say, with the heart, which requires only a small number of connections).

Much more disturbing are the great number of genetic interventions now becoming increasingly feasible. Gene transfer techniques are almost certain to be developed with ever-increasing scope and refinement. Specific eugenic interventions for man are therefore now well within the realm of the possible, even the probable. Genetic intervention raises such practical societal questions as whether "supermen" or "superwomen" should be bred; or whether defective individuals should be eliminated before birth; or whether more females or more males should be produced for future society.

Future Insulations

Shocks such as these will require substantial insulation. The problem is cogently expressed in the following comment by a staff member of the National Heart Institute:

> The point which deserves special emphasis is that man may be able to program his own cells with synthetic information long before he will be able to assess adequately the long-term consequences of such alterations, long before he will be able to formulate goals, and long before he can resolve the ethical and moral problems which will be raised. When man becomes capable of instructing his own cells, he must refrain from doing so until he has sufficient wisdom to use this knowledge for the benefit of mankind. I state this problem well in advance of the need to resolve it, because decisions concerning the application of this knowledge must ultimately be made by society, and only an informed society can make such decisions wisely [Nirenberg, 1967, p. 633].

The sooner that considerations such as these are seriously applied in an analysis of our multitude of social problems, the more likely we are to find answers that do more than postpone the day of reckoning. Certainly one does not need to agree with Skinner as to the kind of controlled society that is most desirable in order to recognize the urgency of the problem and the compelling need for re-evaluating the role of behavioral controls.

Notes

The act–react variable is not to be confused with the superficially similar but actually different dimension of physical activity. A person who is physically very active may not be "acting" in the present sense of initiating behavior and thereby influencing his environment, rather than merely being influenced by it. On the one hand, a person who shows a high degree of sheer physical activity may simply be reacting to a high degree of environmental stimulation. On the other hand, an apparently passive receiver of stimulation may be actively engaged in implicit responding ("thinking") by means of which important actions are subsequently initiated. The variable of overt physical activity is thus by no means a reliable measure of action in the present usage.

Clinical Interventions

Rogers's nondirective therapy is described in his *Client-Centered Therapy* (1951). Psychoanalytic techniques are most generally described by Freud himself in his *A General Introduction to Psychoanalysis* (1943). The much newer behavior therapy movement is described by Franks and Wilson (1974). All of these topics are treated more intensively in Chapter 16.

Helplessness and Control Concepts

Mowrer and Viek (1948) reported the experiment described. The further experiments (on control of audiogenic seizures) were reported by Marx and Van Spanckeren (1952) and Goodson and Marx (1953). Joffe, Rawson, and Mulick (1973) have reported an interesting experimental demonstration of the effectiveness of environmental control in reducing emotionality. Experimental rats were reared from birth in a "contingent environment" in which food, water, and lighting were dependent on their own behavior; matched controls had the same food, water, and light given to them. The experimental rats were more active and showed less defecation (a standard measure of emotionality) in an open-field test (being placed in a strange open area for observation).

Control: Two Meanings

In view of its prominence, within the present chapter especially, the word *control* needs to be examined closely. It is used with two essentially different meanings. As used in the present context, *control* means "to influence or manage." This usage applies both to the *sense of control,* the construct designed to identify certain presumed intervening functions, and to the more general usage of the term by Skinner.

The second meaning is with reference to the elimination of the influence of a variable in observation, as in an experiment. This usage of control is similar to the other in that it also implies a kind of management, but its objective is quite different: to make possible an unambiguous assessment of some manipulated ("independent") variable(s), rather than to have any "practical" impact on events.

Skinner on Freedom and Dignity

Skinner's much-discussed *Beyond Freedom and Dignity* (1971) represents an updating and elaboration of his earlier introductory text, *Science and Human Behavior* (1953). The basic issues in the problem of controlling human behavior were argued by Carl Rogers and B. F. Skinner in an early symposium (Rogers and Skinner, 1956). Skinner's utopian novel, *Walden Two* (1948), approximately 1 million copies of which have now been sold, includes leading characters (Burris and Frazier) who voice some of the dual opinions of the author himself (humanistic and scientific) as well as his basic formulation of the ideal society.

It is interesting that Skinner has recently succeeded in implementing his theories in the establishment of a rural commune in Virginia. Twin Oaks at the present writing is a struggling, financially insecure commune that is attempting to put into practice Skinner's behavioral engineering notions with the supervisory assistance of some trained psychologists. Kinkade (1973) has reviewed Twin Oaks's first five years. Another source of information on Skinner's brand of social engineering is *Control of Human Behavior,* edited by Ulrich et al. (1968). The relatively new Skinnerian periodical, *Journal of Applied Behavior Analysis,* publishes articles concerned with a variety of behavior control techniques. Skinner's views on education are presented in his *The Technology of Teaching* (1968).

For critical reactions to Skinner's proposal, consult Wheeler's 1973 reader, which contains some of the most thoughtful analyses from a variety of perspectives and is balanced by a cumulative rejoinder by Skinner himself. Skinner's more recent *About Behaviorism* (1974) should also be consulted.

Permissiveness

Although barely mentioned in the text in relation to Skinner's views, the issue of permissiveness has recently received increasing attention in the light of contemporary protest movements, in educational circles as well as elsewhere. Most of the attention has been directed at the famous Summerhill school in England. A book by Summerhill's founding headmaster and guiding light, A. S. Neill (1972), should be consulted, along with Popenoe's *Inside Summerhill* (1970).

Future Shocks and Insulation

The best-selling book from which the section title has been borrowed is Toffler's *Future Shock* (1970). It is only one of the many recent book-length sociological essays designed to review and interpret some of the critical social changes that are either occurring or are anticipated in the relatively near future.

With regard to the intriguing yet disturbing prospects of genetic intervention, authoritative and enlightening papers have been published by Davis (1970) and Friedman and Roblin (1972).

The behavior demonstrated in this nineteenth-century engraving is familiar to us all, yet less frequently witnessed in its same form today. Why we are compelled or propelled to behave in certain ways, be it fighting a duel or making love, is the subject of this chapter. Once you have studied this material see if you can describe the type of psychological conflict that each of the participants in this event must be experiencing.

417

otivation is clearly one of the most pervasive topics in psychology. Few behavior problems can be approached without at least some concern for the motives of the organism. However, because motives, like habits and similar psychological concepts, must be inferred from behavior, there has been a wide range of conceptual approaches to the problem.

From the present point of view motives are explicitly recognized as crucial elements in behavior. A motive is defined as a complex construct that includes both *directional* (associative) and *energizing* (activating) components. The directional component is usually called habit and the energizing component is often called drive.

In this chapter certain of the more prominent dimensions along which motives can be regarded and some of the major categories into which they can be classified are described. There is a discussion of biological motives—defined as motives in which the determining mechanisms are clearly of more or less immediate physiological character (e.g., hunger and thirst). Psychological motives, with less directly relevant biological determinants, are surveyed; these are categorized as organismic (curiosity, competence, achievement) or social (affiliation, power, independence).

Motives as *processes* are then emphasized, in contrast to the more common emphasis on motivational content (e.g., the "instinct" approach). The important distinction between instrumental and consummatory motives is discussed. The origin and the transformation of motives are treated, with consideration of such problems as conflict (the clash of motives).

The chapter concludes with sections on the neurophysiology of motivation (emphasizing research on drug addiction using animal subjects) and the significance of motivation (utilizing the concepts of self-actualization and the central organizing motive as illustrative of the centrality of motives).

Supplement A-4 contains brief discussions of techniques of research on motivation.

Characteristics of Motives

Motivation is a concept that has long been used to account for the direction and the intensity of behavior. Like learning and memory, motivation is inferred from behavior. In addition, each of us is consciously aware of a variety of motives, or intentions, in himself.

There are two major reasons why the motivation concept has been inferred from observations of behavior. First, goal-directed and clearly motivated behavior is both extremely commonplace and remarkably persistent, suggesting the operation of some equally persistent underlying force. Second, responses frequently fail to follow directly from stimuli; this fact suggests that there are internal determinants that select particular responses and influence the direction of behavior.

Psychologists use the same terms as everyone else to describe the various facets of motivation. However, they tend to give these terms a somewhat more precise meaning. Some of the more important of these concepts will be briefly distinguished.

Key Concepts

The key concept, *motive,* typically is used to refer to the presumed internal condition that organizes and energizes behavior in some particular direction, accounting thus for both the selection of responses and the vigor with which they are made. The term *purpose* is frequently used to express the idea of goal-directedness that marks so much of our normal ongoing behavior; some behavioristically oriented psychologists have objected to this term because it carries implications of consciousness, but as we have seen in Chapter 4 these objections are now weakening. The term *intention* has an even more avowed conscious referent; it is used to refer to a motive that one has expressly recognized in consciousness and, usually, also formulated for others in overt verbal communication.

Biological Referents

All the terms thus far mentioned are typically used with respect to socially determined forms of motivation. When the simpler biological motives are considered, a different set of terms tends to be used. *Drive* refers to this kind of motive, as expressed in the common terms *hunger drive* and *sex drive.* As discussed in Chapter 13 (p. 403), drive is an intervening construct used to refer to internal processes that mediate the behavior that typically accompanies certain stimulus manipulations; for example, the increased activity correlated with increasing hours of food deprivation is related to a hypothetical motivating condition, the hunger drive.

An *incentive* is a particular goal object, such as food or water or a sexually receptive mate, that is sought by the organism with an active drive.

The term *drive* has been applied to more complex forms of motivation than the relatively simple biological conditions described above. There is less question about its use, however, when it is applied to the biological conditions from which it originated. When it is used to explain complex behavioral sequences such as might be observed in interpersonal encounters, the term becomes less precise and, consequently, less scientifically profitable.

Relationship of Motives and Habits

The relationship of motives to habits is an intimate one. The two concepts have frequently been confused in formal theory as well as in more informal interpretations of behavior. We can here make a basic distinction between these two fundamental concepts. Habit refers to the *strength* of the behavioral tendency, usually assumed to have been developed as a function of the reinforcement process (see Chapter 11); in other words, the concept of habit is concerned with behavioral *potential.* The motive concept usually focuses on the degree to which a habit is actually energized. A motive can be regarded as a kind of *activated habit*—a learned behavior in operation.

A simple example may be helpful in clarifying this distinction between the two concepts of motive and habit, as delineated above. Suppose that a hungry rat has been trained to press a bar for food reward, and later is brought into the classroom for a demonstration. If all goes well the trained rat will probably deliver an adequate bar-pressing performance when presented to the class. But suppose further that someone has accidentally fed the rat shortly before the demonstration. The satiated rat is not likely to be a very good performer. As a matter of fact, it may well be content to groom itself, lie sleepily in the cage, or merely look tauntingly at the frustrated instructor. In order to account for the marked difference in behavior under these two conditions we do not need to assume that the rat has forgotten or somehow otherwise lost his bar-pressing habit; rather we can simply interpret his lassitude to a loss of motivation. The general rule is that performance depends not only on capacity (habit), but also on the energization of that capacity; it is the energizing or activating of the habit that constitutes the motive.

Within psychology, and especially within experimental psychology, more attention has been given to the problem of learning than to motivation. Lately, however, there has been increasing recognition of the more crucial role that motivation plays in most behavior. Variations in the learned behavior of most people, in whom learning is substantially complete, tend to be relatively slight, whereas motives are subject to a great deal more variability. Fluctuations in motivational states give rise to variability in behavior across superficially similar situations.

DIMENSIONS OF MOTIVES

Confronted with the great variety of motives, it is necessary to order them in some fashion. The following discussion therefore focuses on important dimensions along which motives can be most meaningfully described.

Temporal Duration

The temporal duration of motives is one of the most strikingly varied of all the dimensions that can be used to describe them. On the one hand, some motives are extremely short in duration—for example, the gentleman hastens to open a door for his female companion (in the old days, anyway) or the student feels compelled to compliment the instructor for an especially interesting lecture. Once these immediate motives are satisfied, they disappear. On the other hand, there are persistent and long-lived motives that may represent life-long objectives—an individual's ambition to move up the social and economic ladder through success in business and social affairs or the novelist's desire to complete a set of interlocking stories. The latter motives are obviously complex, with many behavioral ramifications, as well as long-lasting. In between these two extremes there is an infinity of types of motive with varying degrees of temporal extension, and such motives are by far the most common.

421
MOTIVATION

types of motive with varying degrees of temporal extension, and such motives are by far the most common.

Cyclic Character

The cyclic character of many motives is one of their most visible properties, and this periodic recurrence is most clearly seen in the biologically based motives. All organisms must ingest food materials on a regular basis in order to survive, and most organisms need to take in water also on a regular basis. It is therefore easy to understand why the motivation to eat and drink should be recurrent, or cyclic, in organisms. Susceptibility to sexual arousal is also cyclic, even though satisfaction of sexual motivation is not necessary for survival. Recurrence of sexual interest following sexual activity usually follows a period of sexual quiescence. The resumption of sexual motivation is then a function both of physiological factors (in the mammalian male, for example, the renewal of appropriate hormonal supply) and psychological conditions (revival of interest following satiation).

The psychological determinants of motivation related to satiation are not restricted to biologically based motives. A kind of boredom sooner or later develops in many organisms after sufficient satisfaction of any motive, and some interval of time must pass without further such activity before the motivation begins to recover strength.

The cyclic character of some motivated behavior is directly imposed by the cyclic controlling factors in the environment. An example with which college students are all too familiar is the schedule of examinations in a course. The sudden increase in course-related activities as examinations approach represents a corresponding increase in motivation. The close relationship of the two events seems hardly coincidental.

Dormancy

Some motives appear to be completely inactive for long periods of time yet they can reappear suddenly, often in great strength, when conditions become appropriate. They thus show both considerable temporal extension and a kind of modified, or highly irregular, periodicity. For example, a man who is envious of the position in the company that his boss enjoys may give occasional signs of antagonism but on the whole manage to restrain himself until circumstances appear propitious (such as the company's having financial difficulties or the boss's falling into disfavor with higher officials for one reason or another). Observation of this kind of behavior suggests that the motive to oust and replace the boss was actually dormant (i.e., not manifest in overt behavior) throughout the period of time during which few observable aggressive responses occurred.

Scope

Our discussion has already suggested that motives vary greatly in their scope, in the extent of their comprehensiveness. It is not always possible to determine the true scope of the motive from the motivated behavior alone. A young child's fumbling attempt to feed himself may serve merely his food motive (especially if adult help is not readily forthcoming) or it may in addition be an expression of his broader motivation to do things by himself (and so occur even when adult help is offered and perhaps rejected—as by pushing back the hand that tries to feed him).

CATEGORIES OF MOTIVES

Motives, which can be assumed by definition to cover practically all human behavior, can be categorized in any number of different ways. One of the more familiar of these categories is the distinction between biologically determined and psychologically determined motives. Another important distinction is that between instrumental and consummatory motives. An *instrumental* motive is one that is more or less clearly subordinate to some other motive; in other words, its primary function is to make possible satisfaction of the other motive. A *consummatory* motive is one whose primary objective is the actual satisfaction of the motive itself; in other words, the important thing is the consummation, as in the literal consuming of food or water. Implications of this distinction are developed later in the chapter.

From still another point of view, motives can be categorized according to their focus. Table 14-1 shows one such summary. According to this scheme, motives are assumed to focus on the body and thereby contribute to the regulation of physiological functions. This type of regulation is often called *homeostasis*. Motives also focus on one's self-perception, by means of various mental operations, and so produce the level of *self-esteem* with which one regards himself. And finally, motives may focus on social relations and mediate the development of personality or character.

Within this framework, motives are further divided in accordance with whether they involve avoidance or approach behavior. The avoidance category is associated with so-called deficiency motivation, which is produced either by the absence of a

Table 14-1 Focus of Human Motives

	Avoid	Seek
Homeostasis (body functions)	Hunger, thirst, loss of oxygen supply, fatigue, illness	Sexual satisfaction, pleasurable sensory and satisfying motor experiences generally
Self-esteem (mental functions)	Inferiority, feeling of failure, shame, guilt, loss of orientation or identity	Self-respect, self-expression, meaningful role in life, self-confidence, accepting and satisfying challenges
Social relations (interpersonal functions)	Hostility, aggression, too much dependence on others	Affection, group identification, enjoying social interaction, helping others, dominance and power

needed or desired substance or activity or by the presence of an unwanted condition; in either event the organism strives actively to eliminate the condition. The approach category consists of active searching for positive incentives and conditions. Biological drives like hunger and sex are good examples of the way in which one's point of view can determine the category in which a given motive is placed.

Although this system of categorizing motives is useful in providing an overview of the various types of motives important in human behavior, it should not be considered as a hard-and-fast means of characterizing these processes. For one thing, certain motives can be placed in either the avoid or the seek category. Thus hunger can be interpreted, as in Table 14-1, as the avoidance of the "tissue tensions" associated with the absence of food or, alternatively, it can be considered as the active searching for food as incentive. Similarly, sexual motivation can be considered as an active searching for sexual satisfaction or as the avoidance of the unpleasant tensions of sex drive. Placement of motives in the table is therefore to some extent a result of arbitrary decisions, but the tabulation is nonetheless useful in indicating the major classes of motives, if not their exact theoretical location in a systematic scheme.

> ### *Biological Motives*

The marvelously balanced manner in which the brain and various other body structures interact to maintain the physiological integrity of the organism is just beginning to be fully appreciated. The general concept of *homeostasis,* which is the name usually applied to the maintenance of such physiological balance, is by no means new; however, as our description of the major motivational systems will indicate, the intricate interrelationships among brain centers and organ systems are still being discovered. In the following paragraphs we concentrate upon the major biological motives of hunger, thirst, and sex.

HUNGER

In spite of a long history of research and the recent focusing of several separate lines of attack upon this problem, the precise mechanisms by means of which the hunger motive functions are far from clear. Nevertheless, a great deal is known, much of it only recently discovered.

Two major types of physiological processes mediate hunger and control eating. These are the direct monitoring of the *eating behavior* itself and the indirect monitoring of the *state* of *food supply* in the body. Beyond these mechanisms, *learned controls* of eating also operate to complicate the picture.

Direct signals to initiate or to stop eating behavior are apparently produced in the hypothalamus (cf. Chapter 1, p. 21). The evidence for these relationships is mainly from research analyzing the effects of various brain lesions on eating behavior. The general picture that has emerged from these studies is that initiation and persistence of eating results from neural signals coming from the ventromedial nucleus of the hypothalamus.

Widely varying mammals have been experimentally studied, including rats, cats, and monkeys. The center for inhibition of eating, the so-called satiety center, has been found to reside in the lateral nuclei of the hypothalamus, not very far from the feeding center.

Loading of the stomach from intake of food is perhaps the most common event that activates the hypothalamus to inhibit the further intake of food. The initiation of eating was at one time commonly attributed to "hunger pangs"—the conscious feelings that are supposedly associated with an empty stomach. Research has shown, however, that these are not reliable cues. For example, contractions have been found to occur more often *after* eating than before, when they were directly measured in human subjects by means of inflated baloons in the stomach; also, hunger pangs have been reported by subjects whose entire stomachs were surgically removed.

It is the signals that come from various monitors of body state that have been increasingly implicated as the more crucial determinants of hunger. Feedback from stores of *body fat* and *blood sugar* is the most important type thus far demonstrated. Information concerning these conditions is transmitted to the hypothalamic feeding centers. There they apparently help to set food intake levels, which then serve to trigger initiation and cessation of feeding behavior. In other words, these centers do not function in any absolute manner to start and stop eating; they are part of a complex neural network in which a variety of different sources all contribute to help determine the level of eating exhibited by the organism.

The evidence for the conclusion that the hypothalamic nuclei function in a relative rather than an absolute manner has come in part from experiments on rats that were first underfed or overfed before being subjected to hypothalamic lesions. Consider overfed rats. When lesions were made in their ventromedial nuclei, the usual effect—overeating—did not occur. Instead when these rats were placed on a strictly free diet, their weight fell somewhat. Underfed rats with lesions in their lateral nuclei, which normally produce cessation of eating, gained weight when allowed to eat as they pleased. The interpretation usually made of these interesting results is that the nuclei in the hypothalamus that have been shown to control eating behavior do so by integrating information from many sources and that they tend to set target weight levels toward which eating behavior is adjusted.

Learned Controls

There are many ways in which learning contributes to the control of eating and, thereby, to body weight. Here we cite as illustrative one experimental observation with animal subjects.

Some early observations on eating in chickens provide clear evidence of how social, and thus presumably learned, conditions control this behavior. A hen was permitted to eat from a large pile of grain until she ceased. Then a second, hungry hen was introduced into the test chamber. When she started eating from the grain pile, the first hen also resumed pecking—and ate as much as 60 per cent additional food. Introduction of more than one hen (say, three) resulted in even greater amounts of additional food being eaten. The importance of the social variable is further suggested by the fact that a reversal of the procedure did not give comparable results. That is, when three hens were allowed to eat until they stopped and then a *single* additional hungry hen was introduced, its eating did not induce the three hens to resume eating.

The way in which learned biases of various sorts influence human eating behavior is well known to all of us. Religious proscriptions of certain foods are common. Even more prevalent and therefore more influential are certain less obvious prejudices that we all tend to acquire as a part of our social heritage. Consider, for example, the eating of horsemeat as compared with that of the cow and pig. In the United States, at least, few people would prefer it to beef or pork. Why? Most answers would involve its quality or flavor, but these are obviously subjectively determined to a very large extent. And if cleanliness were considered, the horse would probably be rated well above the cow and the pig.

A recent anecdotal account suggests how people react to horsemeat when unaware of its nature. Horsemeat was obtained from a local pet store and served in successive meals as fillets to twenty people, all of whom had previously indicated an aversion for this type of food. These people not only ate all the meat offered but made favorable comments upon its tenderness, and even inquired as to where it had been obtained. It requires little imagination to predict how these same persons would have reacted had they been told in advance where the meat came from, or for that matter had they been told after they ate it.

Weight Control: Human Obesity

Overeating and consequent obesity is a serious problem that has attracted a great deal of attention. This is especially true in our "affluent society." Two sets of interesting experimental data indicate the scope of the problem and some of its more important determining variables.

Under conditions of "normal" activity the human organism tends to eat in accordance with the energy requirements set by the amount of physical exertion expended. This relationship is shown very nicely in the data graphed in Figure 14-1. The data are especially reliable because they were collected from a racially homogeneous group (Bengalese Indians) of a single sex (male). The open bars in the graph plot daily caloric intake as a function of amount of work. It is evident that there is a regular relationship between these two variables, *but* only to the right of the graph, where there are four degrees of physical exertion related to type of job. Sedentary (management) personnel eat far more than is justified by the kind of work they do.

The results of this situation are shown in the solid bars of Figure 14-1. The body weights of the various kinds of workers on the right side vary little, indicating that the additional caloric intake of the more active workers is effectively utilized in their work. The shop owners and supervisors, however, are overweight, indicating that they have not worked off the excess food they eat.

Careful observations and experimental studies have begun to provide some insights into the human obesity problem. Some of these were based upon comparisons of animals that had been made experimentally obese (by hypothalamic lesion).

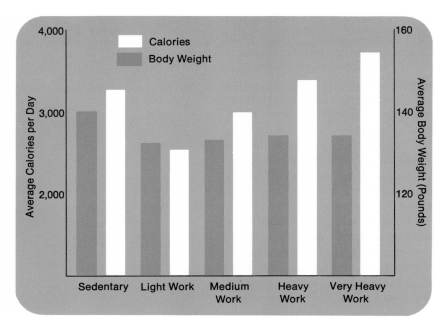

14-1 Food intake and work. The open bars of this graph show the relationship between food intake and type of work; the solid bars show the relationship of body weight and work. People in sedentary occupations such as shop owners and supervisors show both high food intake and correspondingly high body weight. The differences in body weight are minimal, despite a regularly increasing food intake, in people engaged in light to very heavy work. (Adapted from data in J. Mayer, P. Roy, and K. P. Mitra. Relation between caloric intake, body weight and physical work: Studies in an industrial male population in West Bengal. *Americal Journal of Clinical Nutrition,* 1956, **4,** 169–175.)

Obese humans were found to show the same major behavioral characteristics as obese rats: much greater than normal or necessary total food intake but *fewer* meals, faster eating and more taken per meal, and less physical activity.

Obese organisms are less likely than normals to eat if effort is required to obtain the food or if the food is a bit unusual or offtaste. One especially ingenious experimental study supports the notion that obese people are less dependent upon their own internal food-related tendencies. In this experiment a bag of almonds was left on a desk while the student subject was filling out a questionnaire, which was the purported objective of the experiment. After helping himself to a nut and inviting the student to take one also, the experimenter left the room for fifteen minutes. The experimental variable was the kind of almond left in the bag; half of the students had shelled and half had unshelled nuts. It was found that students of normal weight ate unshelled as much as shelled nuts, but a strikingly different result occurred for the forty obese subjects: nineteen of the twenty given shelled nuts ate them, but only one given unshelled nuts did so.

The practical implication of this study and the general framework in which it was performed is clear: obese people who want to reduce their weight must see to it that extra eating is not easy. In other words, they should dispose of the open candy dish, the full cookie jar, and all the other between-meal snack materials. This step is only a part of the story and the treatment indicated, but it is an important and relatively easily arranged part. In general, overeating can be reduced if not eliminated by reducing the number and strength of environmental cues to eating; obese persons have been shown to be more sensitive to these cues, such as clocks, announcements of meals, and the like, than persons with normal weight.

At the other end of the eating spectrum from obesity is *anorexia,* the complete failure to eat. This relatively rare condition occurs when an individual stops eating, presumably from loss of appetite, and begins to starve. Anorexia is generally treated as a kind of behavior disorder, requiring psychiatric and/or psychological attention, because if it persists forced feeding may be required to avoid slow death from starvation.

Specific Hungers

A variety of situations in which some particular food or substance is craved have been reported. The classic case of specific hungers concerns pregnant women who may suddenly develop a powerful yearning for some unexpected type of foodstuff, often to the consternation of husbands who may not understand this (to them) quite bizarre behavior. Although it is of course possible that some cases of craving for special foods are "psychological," investigations of many such conditions in humans and animals have uncovered a dietary deficiency sufficient to account for the specific hunger evidenced.

One procedure that has been used in much research on food selection is the so-called cafeteria-style experimental setup. In this procedure a subject is offered a variety of foods and allowed to select how much of each he wishes to eat. The general result of these experiments is that subjects achieve a reasonably balanced diet even though specific foods may be preferred in great quantity for short periods of time (eating jags) to the virtual exclusion of other types. In these experiments, especially when children are subjects, much care is taken to ensure that only safe foodstuffs are offered.

THIRST

Dryness in the throat appears to be the effective stimulus to thirst and drinking, at least on a conscious level, much as hunger pangs in the stomach appear to be associated with eating. The effective stimulation of drinking behavior, however, has been shown to be a function of two physiological measures with separate monitoring systems: *osmotic pressure* in the blood and *volume of fluid* in the body.

Specialized cells in the hypothalamus have been implicated as the agents in the monitoring of the osmotic pressure level. It has been shown, for example, that drinking behavior is quickly induced in experimental animals by the injection of salty solution directly into this region of the brain (via surgically implanted tubes). No drinking occurs from the injection of fluids with significantly less salt content and consequent lower osmotic pressure level. The feedback loop for monitoring of body fluid involves the flow of blood through the kidney, which is related to body fluid level, and the adjusted release of chemicals into the bloodstream; these same chemicals have been shown to evoke drinking when directly injected into appropriate parts of the brain.

The ways in which social learning factors influence liquid preference and intake are quite comparable to those influencing eating. Excessive intake of, say, alcoholic beverages for social and/or psychological reasons is one of the more unhappy demonstrations of this fact. Concern has been evidenced about advertising that encourages children to consume nonnutritional foods such as soft drinks and sugar-coated cereals.

AIR HUNGER

Although lack of adequate oxygen has no conscious correlate, it involves an obviously vital need. The brain, for example, can remain unimpaired for only a very short time in the absence of fresh oxygen; even one minute without oxygen can produce irreparable damage. Some cases of mental retardation are the result of such temporary *anoxia* (absence of oxygen) during childbirth. This result may occur when the partunate's breathing apparatus fails to function promptly.

Air hunger as an experienced phenomenon is associated with the collection of carbon dioxide in the lungs, and not simply with the lack of the critical oxygen. This is why some anoxic conditions (e.g., holding one's breath) produce air hunger whereas others (e.g., moving into a pocket of marsh gas in a mine) do not. The need to breathe can thus suddenly produce a prepotent motive, even though under normal conditions with adequate air supplies available it is of small moment.

FATIGUE

The fatigued body can exert a powerful motive to rest. The major physiological change that has been related to fatigue is the accumulation of lactic acid in the blood. Although it is known that lactic acid is produced by muscular contraction, exactly how this and other changes are translated, neurophysiologically, into rest and sleep motives is not yet known.

The effect on behavior of extreme fatigue varies with the kind of behavior required. Efficiency of simple tasks is little affected, even by periods of enforced sleeplessness up to 100 hours. The performance of more complex tasks, however, has been shown to be seriously disturbed by much shorter periods of sleeplessness.

Some individuals seem to be tired all the time. In such cases, fatigue is not simply a function of physical exertion or sleeplessness. It has emotional origins; and in these cases fatigue is much more difficult to manage. Merely resting, for example, will do little to improve one's tiredness because it leaves untouched the real sources of the fatigue.

SEX

Because it is so closely related to various social and moral factors, and because its satisfaction in many cultures is so tightly supervised, the sex drive accounts for a much greater proportion of the variance in behavior than the other biologically based motivational systems. This fact is all the more impressive because, unlike other biological drives, the sex drive does not need to be satisfied to maintain the individual's life.

Inasmuch as emotional aspects of sexuality are thoroughly treated subsequently (Chapter 15 and Supplement B-6), we shall confine our discussion here to the strictly physiological determinants. These have been demonstrated to be the production of the primary sexual hormones by the gonads. The male testes secrete mainly *androgen;* the female ovaries secrete mainly the *estrogens,* which mediate the sex drive, and *progesterone,* which is instrumental in pregnancy.

The extent to which habit and psychological factors contribute to sexual behavior varies directly with the phyletic level of the species concerned. Thus the simpler mammalian forms have been shown to engage in sexual behavior that appears to be closely related to the amount of sex hormone present at the time, whereas the higher forms, and notably the primates, show sexual behavior that is much less closely tuned to this underlying physiological condition. Rats raised in isolation, for example, typically show normal sexual behavior when tested with appropriate sexual partners, but monkeys so reared are extremely ineffective in their sexual behavior (cf. discussion in Chapters 10 and 15). Elimination of the normal production of the sexual hormones, as by castration, also has much more seriously disruptive effects on sexual behavior in rats than in primates. Castrated rats will not mate unless the sexual hormones are artificially provided, whereas primates may show strong sexual motivation even with very low levels of sex hormones.

Some observers have emphasized the learned or habitual facets of sexual motivation in the human, and propose that much of sexual motivation is really a kind of learned appetite, much like the preference for specific foods or drinks. Certainly past sexual experiences have a great deal to do with the amount and type of subsequent sexual motivation. Descending the phyletic scale, sexual behavior is increasingly determined by genetically arranged hormone cycles. In man, however, and particularly in middle and late adulthood, sexual behavior is almost totally determined by prior learning experiences. As the human organism matures, the kinds of sexual experiences it elects to have become increasingly critical to subsequent sexual adjustment.

Sexual behavior in humans often seems to satisfy other motives than the purely sexual (e.g., the need for a man to express his power or for a woman to verify her attractiveness or desirability). Thus biological and psychological factors interact in sexual motivation in multiple ways as they do in the development of other complex behavioral phenomena such as general intelligence or language. It is impossible to understand either of these interacting components without taking account of the other.

MISCELLANEOUS BODY DRIVES

Our discussion of biological motives would not be complete without some mention of certain other ways in which bodily functions can be potent sources of motivation. Among such factors are pain, extreme temperatures, and urges to eliminate body wastes. More generally, however, it may be said that any physical discomfort or physiological tension can serve to motivate an organism. The more prominent tissue needs that we have discussed have generally attracted the greatest amount of attention, in psychologists as well as in laymen, but they by no means exhaust the list of biological sources of motivation.

Psychological Motives

The term *psychological motives* is used here to categorize a broad class of motivational conditions having one feature in common: they do not involve in any direct manner the biological integrity of the organism. Thus these motives may be contrasted with the ones described earlier in that their physiological basis is less clear and their physiological consequences are not as important as their behavioral consequences.

There are a vast number of motivated activities that can be broadly labeled as psychological. Here we discuss briefly six such categories. The first three—curiosity, competence, and achievement—are primarily personal, or *organismic,* in the sense that they relate to intrinsic functions of the organism and social interactions. The last three—affiliation, power, and independence—are definitely *social;* they depend upon relationships of the organism to other people.

ORGANISMIC MOTIVES

Curiosity

Interest in curiosity as a motivating factor is a relatively recent development within psychology. It reflects the broad trend away from the earlier nearly exclusive concern with deprivation of biologically useful incentives in psychological thinking about motivation.

Curiosity is readily demonstrated in lower animals as well as in man. Numerous experiments have been performed with laboratory rats to determine the ways in which stimulus change and novelty motivate these organisms. When given a choice between two responses, each of which is appropriately rewarded, rats generally alternate their choices. That is, they are more likely to turn left on the trial immediately following a right turn, and vice versa. Experiments have indicated that it is the different stimulus that mediates this alternation behavior, rather than the making of different responses; this conclusion is drawn on the basis of the rats' responding to changed stimuli in preference to changing their responses when the two factors are experimentally separated.

Research specifically directed at the stimulus change factor has confirmed its effectiveness. For example, rats in one experiment were shown both black and gray panels at the end of a T-maze and were later given the opportunity to go to one of two white panels which replaced the black and grey ones. They predominantly chose the previously black side at test, presumably because the substitution of white for the previously presented black panel provided the greater stimulus change. In other research rats were offered a choice between a long, circuitous path and a short, direct path to the same end box. The animals typically preferred the long and presumably more interesting path. There seems to be little question but that curiosity plays a significant role in the behavior of even so lowly a mammalian form as the rat.

Monkeys have proved to be especially susceptible to the manipulation of novel stimuli. Even more or less familiar stimuli, such as that provided by a brief look at laboratory activities as viewed through a window, are sufficient to motivate monkeys. After they have been deprived of such visual stimulation, they will work hard for this opportunity to look. On the motor side, manipulation of simple mechanical devices, such as hasps, will keep monkeys occupied for a considerable period of time.

Human subjects are prime candidates for research on curiosity motivation. Even infants have been found to prefer to look at more complex patterns, as measured by the duration of their visual fixation.

Information itself is also a potent incentive for the higher animals. They seem to have not only an interest in strange objects and places but also, somewhat more specifically, a *need to know*. The kinds of knowledge that are desired vary along a very wide spectrum and across numerous dimensions. The human may be motivated merely to identify a sound or a sight, and once he is satisfied that he has done so with reasonable accuracy may lose interest in the situation. Or he may be motivated to acquire a complex network of information about some other individual, or organization, or subject matter of one kind or another. The former motivation may require but a few seconds, whereas the latter may keep one occupied for an entire lifetime (e.g., a scientific problem or a hobby).

It should be mentioned that the power of these motivational factors seems to be negatively correlated with the degree to which the more immediately biological motives are satisfied. Thus when one has reasonably satisfied vital needs one can afford the luxury of responding to stimuli for curiosity or of engaging in an extended search for knowledge for its own sake.

Competence

Closely related to the processes involved in curiosity and perceptual functioning are those that enable the growing organism to develop and perfect its ability to cope with the environment. The motivation to use sensory and motor processes effectively is called the *competence* motive. In most mammals these skills are developed during the periods of play that seem to be universally present. But motivation for competence is not restricted to the young. Mature organisms also seem to be generally strongly motivated by a desire for effective performance, over and beyond the immediate instrumental value that such behavior may have in obtaining other incentives.

The concept of competence is sometimes considered to belong in a broader category and to encompass some of the more specific motives, such as curiosity. Regardless of how we categorize them, the effective performances of both perceptual and motor sorts as well as the more abstract information-seeking activities, all seem to motivate organisms to a very great degree. It is unfortunate that as a consequence of persistent frustration some mature organisms seem to lose this kind of intrinsic motivation. It is even more unfortunate that such strong and apparently unlearned motives are not utilized to a greater extent in our educational systems, so that a higher proportion of developing human organisms can be encouraged to maintain their interest in competence as their formal education proceeds.

Achievement

The final example of our three personally oriented types of psychological motives is that of achievement. Unlike curiosity and competence, *achievement* is presumably restricted to human organisms. Surprisingly, it has been the subject of more research than either of the other two described.

The distinction between competence and achievement is mainly one of scope. That is, competence motivation refers to the exercise of specific skills of a perceptual, motor, and intellectual sort. Achievement refers to more complex and long-lasting endeavors, such as those relating to academic or occupational affairs. Running behavior, for example, might by itself be considered a case of competence motivation, but when it is placed in a competitive situation, as in a track meet or a football game, it is transformed into achievement motivation. In our society achievement motives are generally related to competitive situations, but competition with others (and thereby direct social involvement) is not essential to the concept. It is possible to achieve in relation to a set of internalized standards.

A group of psychologists has developed a measure of achievement motivation that utilizes the subject's fantasy production. The subject is asked to make up a story based on each of a number of drawings. The degree to which he introduces achievement-related topics into his stories determines his level of achievement motivation. (See Supplement A-5, on the TAT, for details of this procedure.)

A large number of relationships have been reported between achievement motivation as measured by this kind of test and various other variables. For example, first-born children, middle-class children, and boys all tend to have higher achievement motivation scores than later-born, lower-class children, and girls.

The dependence of high achievement motivation upon social conditions has been empirically demonstrated. In one study, for example, nursery school children were studied both at home as they were interacting with their mothers and at school. Children whose mothers were observed to praise them and reward them frequently and strongly were found to show much more interest in activities that required competence and were aimed at mastery (e.g., modeling clay, painting).

One of the more interesting applications of the achievement-assessment technique was an attempt to improve achievement motivation in business executives. Small groups of business managers in the United States, Mexico, and India were given courses lasting from one to three weeks. In essence, the training consisted of sensitizing the managers to achievement motivation by the application of various psychological principles; for example, the trainees were instructed to advance as many reasons as possible in support of the attempt to increase achievement motivation, to conceptualize particular means of achievement through various kinds of associations, and to link such achievement-related associations to specific actions.

The initial evaluation of this program was that it resulted in no more behavioral change than the typical "therapy" (estimated at about two thirds of the subjects or clients changed and the remaining one third essentially unaffected). Nevertheless, some striking changes were reported in individual cases. On the one hand, for example, a man decided early in the course that he was not and did not want to become an achievement-minded person; he therefore resigned his managerial job (in which he had not been effective apparently) and became a chicken farmer. On the other hand, an Indian businessman suddenly resigned from his very good public relations job with an oil company and was immediately successful in the construction business, which afforded him more distinctly achievement-related opportunities.

SOCIAL MOTIVES

Three sets of motives that focus directly on relationships with other people are discussed in this section: affiliation, power, and independence. The first two of these, affiliation, and to a lesser extent, power, are shared with infrahuman organisms, whereas the last tends to be more a uniquely human characteristic.

Affiliation

There is no question but that for human organisms other humans constitute peculiarly powerful stimuli. Infants, for example, seem to be unusually attracted to faces as a special kind of stimulus. There is nothing magical or even surprising about this, nor is there any need to appeal to any special inherited factor for an explanation. People in general, and their faces in particular, are normally among the most active and the most expressive of all the objects that one encounters.

A variety of specific conditions have been suggested as contributing to the development of the strong incentive value that one human has for another. Research with infant monkeys has indicated the significant role that physical contact (as expressed in the infant's clinging to the mother) can have in the development of affectional response. Resort to other humans as a means of emotional support, as in a situation where anxiety reduction is sought, is a commonly observed process and one that has also been psychologically studied. Beyond these examples, human organisms are clearly the most significant features of our environment with respect to the many satisfactions of all sorts that all of us seek. It is hardly surprising that affiliation motivation in the form of human attachments and human-oriented behaviors is so powerful a factor in our lives. The prevalence of such motives has made a significant contribution to the survival of the species.

Measurement of the degree to which affiliation motivation is present has been accomplished in the same way as for achievement motivation. Imaginative productions in the form of stories made up about pictures are scored for their affiliative content. Joining a club, meeting with people, and helping the needy would all score high in affiliative content. This measure has been shown to be related to the tendency to perceive faces rather than things, to do well when social approval is involved, and to be more socially conforming when one's real friends rather than strangers make the requests.

Persons who are especially high in affiliation motivation run the risk of setting such high standards for themselves that rejection is more likely to be detected. All of us must be prepared to experience some social rejection at some time or other. But for those with high affiliation needs, rejection, whether real or fancied, may initiate a vicious circle. This process occurs when the rejected person intensifies his efforts to become acceptable, even though such efforts are likely to irritate and alienate others more than attract them. The other extreme, a tendency toward self-imposed isolation, is no better; such failures to make social contact lead to others responding in kind. One's social isolation is thereby likely to be worsened. The only resolution of this dilemma is for the socially sensitive person to strike a happy medium—and obviously this is much easier to say than to do. Social acceptance, like learning, is easy for some to achieve, quite difficult for others. There is no easy way for those unlucky ones whose motivation exceeds their natural social gifts. But the situation is never hopeless, and a realistic appraisal of one's problem is generally a good starting place.

Take a Breather

HUMAN MOTIVATION

The following questionnaire is a slightly abridged form of one devised and used by one of psychology's most productive and ingenious pioneers, E. L. Thorndike (1935, pp. 80–81). Its purpose was to make possible a comparison of the strength of certain aversive motivations. In his usual manner, Thorndike attempted to quantify motivation by having the rater use a common measure, the amount of money estimated as necessary to compensate for each of the conditions indicated.

The reader should find it interesting to try answering the questions himself and perhaps have friends do so also, indicating how strongly the various deprivations and inconveniences are regarded. Then, for comparison with how some young people of that time responded, turn to p. 438.

For how much money, paid in cash, would you do or suffer the following? You must suppose that the money can be spent on yourself only and that whatever you buy with it is destroyed when you die. You cannot use any of it for your friends, relatives, or charity.

1. Have the little toe of one foot cut off.
2. Become unable to chew, so that you can eat only liquid food.
3. Become unable to taste.
4. Become unable to smell.
5. Require 25 per cent more sleep than now to produce the same degree of rest and recuperation.
6. Fall into a trance or hibernating state throughout October of every year.
7. Fall into a trance or hibernating state throughout March of every year.
8. Be temporarily insane throughout July of every year (manic-depressive insanity, bad enough so that you would have to be put in an insane asylum, but with no permanent ill effects).
9. Same as 8 but for two entire years now, with no recurrence ever again.
10. Have to live all the rest of your life in New York City.

Power

The power motive was stressed by the psychoanalyst Alfred Adler (Chapter 3). Adler felt that power was even more important than sex as a kind of master motive in human life. He also emphasized the *inferiority complex*—the emotional response made by the individual to a real or imagined deficiency—as a crucial element in personality organization. The fact that this concept has been overused and abused by many persons should not be allowed to detract from its significance.

Experimental approaches to this problem have followed the thematic analyses of achievement and affiliation motivation. Power motives can also be assessed by means of content analysis of the thematic-apperception test (TAT)—the imaginative stories provided by subjects on the basis of pictures they are shown. In scoring this particular test, power is defined in terms of one's ability to influence other people; thus stories about social influence provide higher degrees of power content and, therefore, higher power motivation scores.

Among the more common examples of powerful agents in our society are parents, teachers, police, and politicians. The last occupation may well be considered one in which the purest expression of power motivation is likely to be found.

Persons who score high in power motivation have been found to be more

11. Have to live all the rest of your life in Boston, Mass.

12. Have to live all the rest of your life on a farm in Kansas, ten miles from any town.

13. Have to live all the rest of your life shut up in an apartment in New York City. You can have friends come to see you there, but cannot go out of the apartment.

14. Eat a dead beetle 1 inch long.

15. Eat a live beetle 1 inch long.

16. Eat a dead earthworm 6 inches long.

17. Eat a live earthworm 6 inches long.

18. Eat a quarter of a pound of cooked human flesh (supposing that nobody but the person who pays you to do so will ever know it.)

19. Eat a quarter of a pound of cooked human flesh (supposing that the fact that you do so will appear next day on the front page of all the New York papers).

20. Drink enough to become thoroughly intoxicated.

21. Choke a stray cat to death.

22. Let a harmless snake 5 feet long coil itself round your arms and head.

23. Attend Sunday morning service in St. Patrick's Cathedral, and in the middle of the service run down the aisle to the altar, yelling ''The time has come, The time has come'' as loud as you can until you are dragged out.

24. Take a sharp knife and cut a pig's throat.

25. Walk down Broadway from 120th Street to 80th Street at noon wearing evening clothes and no hat.

26. Spit on a picture of Charles Darwin.

27. Spit on a picture of George Washington.

28. Spit on a picture of your mother.

29. Spit on a picture of a crucifix.

30. Suffer for an hour pain as severe as the worst headache or toothache you have ever had.

31. Have nothing to eat but bread, milk, spinach, and yeast cakes for a year.

32. Go without sugar in all forms (including cake, etc.), tea, coffee, tobacco, and alcoholic drink, for a year.

33. Lose all hope of life after death.

argumentative in classrooms, to prefer leadership roles, and to chafe under close supervision. None of these findings is surprising, of course. What may be considered more surprising is the finding that fathers who are high in power motive tend to be more affectionate to their sons; mothers with high power scores, on the other hand, have not been found to be more affectionate to their children. One interpretation of this difference is that fathers are using affection to maximize their power motive, whereas mothers are more likely to use affiliation in this way.

The source of high power need is usually said to be the consequence of some condition of deprivation. Socially deprived and relatively less powerful social groups have been found to score high on the power motive. Because persons in these groups are also less likely to have access to the power positions in society, their power aspirations are difficult to implement. Improving the education of socially deprived persons has been seen as one step toward improving their power position; but, although "knowledge is power," it is only one of several types of power that can be identified and it by itself is not likely to prove entirely satisfactory. The use of aggression (coercive power) has therefore been more popular, as exemplified by the riots and demonstrations of the late 1960's. This behavior may produce quick results but it triggers counterattack and more suppressive measures. It also produces concern in those who recall that the Nazi movement originated with young people who sought extreme solutions to social problems. A balanced approach to the problem of improving the power position of such relatively powerless groups as students and minority peoples must therefore be seen as offering more promise than dependence upon any one avenue.

Independence

Independence motivation may be defined as a desire to do things by oneself. It is most clearly evidenced in the young child who is beginning to appreciate the need for autonomous existence. It can be found at all age levels, however, and in a large variety of situations.

It is apparent that the motive to be independent often conflicts with the other strong motives that we have been discussing. A drive for independence may lead to the expression of a kind of counteraffiliative motive, and may also force one to forego a considerable amount of achievement (insofar as achievement is aided by others' helping).

Males in our society have traditionally played more independent roles than females. A marked change in this situation is taking place as women express their right to certain behaviors long considered male prerogatives. We may expect to see gradual changes in such secondary characteristics as independence as the sex roles change.

Motivational Processes

In this section we examine some of the processes involved in the origin and transformation of motives. The emphasis is on the mechanics by which motives originate, develop, and are transformed. Unfortunately, not much is known about these mechanics, in part because in spite of the great importance of the problems relatively little research on them has been done. Rather the stress has been largely on content of motives, as the following discussion indicates.

Content of Motives

Much attention has been devoted, both within and outside psychology, to the content of motives at the expense of processes and mechanisms. Of course, a certain amount of attention must be paid to matters of content. Knowing which motives are active at any given time in a particular individual is especially valuable in clinical situations. When we are concerned more with practical than with theoretical matters in motivation, we tend to concentrate on which motives are functioning, rather than on how they developed.

Historically, there have been many listings and categorizations of human motives (sometimes identified as interests, or instincts, or drives). None of these has been particularly successful in achieving more than a moderate degree of acceptance, even for a limited time. As a matter of fact, it was the overextension of these lists that more or less directly led to a decline in interest in them and a turning to other schemes and concepts. Thus the excessively long listing of human instincts, in which practically every aspect of human behavior was ultimately included, was eventually regarded by many as having rendered essentially meaningless the whole endeavor and so helped to discredit the instinct concept for several decades within psychology.

Consider Table 14-2, which is a relatively restricted tabulation of the instincts as conceptualized by one social psychologist. Although suggestive of the kind of thinking that the instinct view led to regarding motivation, this simple tabulation does not really reflect the way in which instinct concepts were worked into explanations of complex phenomena. In describing the instincts supposedly underlying religion, for example, the author gives due credit to fear and focuses on the web of associated emotions that he finds included. He then brings in a number of other, less crucial but nonetheless pertinent instincts (e.g., self-display and submission). A major methodological objection that developed to this kind of view related to the way in which such new concepts were readily introduced, purely on a verbal basis, to cover logical gaps in the interpretation. In other words, whenever there seemed to be the need for postulating some additional concept to account for some facet of behavior, a new "instinct" could be introduced. But this practice came to be regarded as scientifically logically unacceptable—a kind of "word magic" lacking an adequate observational basis. Thus the instinct type of interpretation lost its scientific appeal and remained dormant until recently revived within the framework of ethology.

Although no one can accuse Freud of being unconcerned with process, his focus was also to a large extent on content. The continuing overemphasis in man on content (on *what* one is supposed to want to do) has been especially unfortunate. This is so partly because of the disguised nature of so much of human motivation, as Freud himself was first able to argue convincingly. One of the many advantages of investigating behavioral processes generally and motivational processes particularly in animals and young children is the presumed absence, or near absence, of such disguised motives (e.g., the power motive).

Table 14-2 Human Instincts

I. Principal instincts (and associated primary emotions)
   Flight   (fear)
   Repulsion   (disgust)
   Curiosity   (wonder)
   Pugnacity   (anger)
   Self-abasement (subjection)
   Self-assertion (elation)
   Parental   (tenderness)
II. Lesser instincts (with less well-defined associated emotions)
   Reproduction
   Gregariousness
   Acquisition
   Construction
III. Pseudo Instincts (nonspecific innate tendencies)
   Sympathy
   Suggestibility
   Imitation
   Play

Conceptualized by William McDougall, *An Introduction to Social Psychology* (Boston: John W. Luce & Co., 1923).

Although knowledge of specific motivational content (or, at least, the patient's labeling of his motives) is of great importance to professional psychologists who are involved in the analysis and treatment of problems, such an approach has not seemed to produce concepts useful for either theory building or research. This section is therefore designed to help redress the relative lack of attention accorded motivational processes by outlining some of the more significant problems and achievements relating to them.

Breather Interpretation

HUMAN MOTIVATION

On p. 439 are averages for some of the data collected by Thorndike (1935, p. 181) from forty unemployed young people (twenty to twenty-nine years of age) responding to the questionnaire reproduced on p. 434. It should be noted that Thorndike was well aware of the verbal nature of the data. He commented, "The replies cannot, of course, be taken at face value. . . . But differences between the replies of young and old seem likely to run parallel to what tests of the real behavior of young and old would reveal" (1935, p. 79). (As far as is known, Thorndike did not actually make the "real" tests.) With regard to the young–old difference, much higher amounts of money were generally listed by the older (over forty years of age) than the younger (under thirty years of age) subjects. For example, one third of the older subjects said that no amount of money (indicated by the infinity sign) would induce them to eat any of the objects in items 14 to 17, as compared with one seventh of the younger subjects. Also, for items 26 to 27 averaged, two thirds of the older subjects and only one tenth of the younger subjects gave answers over $10,000; half of the young and none of the old indicated that they would perform the task for $10 or less.

When motives are viewed as processes, an important distinction is that between instrumental and consummatory types mentioned earlier in the chapter. An *instrumental motive* is one relating to behaviors that serve some function in carrying the organism in a definite direction but that are not themselves the ultimate objectives of the behaviors; a *consummatory motive* is one in which the behavior itself

The Reported Strength of Various Aversions: Prices Reported for Enduring Various Sufferings and Deprivations by Unemployed Young Men and Young Women

Item	Estimates of Money Equivalent			
	20 Men: Age 20–29		20 Women: Age 20–29	
	Median	Range	Median	Range
1. Lose one toe	$ 50,000	$ 500 to ∞	$500,000	$ 500 to ∞
2–4. Unable to chew, taste, smell	∞	125,000 to ∞	∞	35,000 to ∞
5. Need $\frac{1}{4}$ more sleep	500,000	20 to ∞	10,000	500 to ∞
6–7. Trance 2 months of the year	2 million	5,000 to ∞	200,000	1,500 to ∞
8–9. Insane temporarily or periodically	95 million	26,000 to ∞	$4\frac{1}{2}$ million	200,000 to ∞
10–11. Live in New York, Boston	40,000	0 to ∞	30,000	0 to ∞
12. Live on Kansas farm	1 million	0 to ∞	55,000	10,000 to ∞
13. Confined to apartment	10 million	0 to ∞	$62\frac{1}{2}$ million	50,000 to ∞
14–17. Eat beetle, earthworm, etc.	48,000	4 to ∞	950,000	2,200 to ∞
18. Secret cannibalism	50,000	40 to ∞	750,000	500 to ∞
19. Public cannibalism	260 million	250 to ∞	$1\frac{1}{8}$ million	5,000 to ∞
20. Intoxicated	25	0 to ∞	98	0 to ∞
21–24. Choke cat, cut pig's throat, etc.	2,500	2 to ∞	105,000	25 to ∞
22. Let snake coil around	100	0 to ∞	400	10 to 7 million
23. Create disturbance in church	1,250	20 to ∞	1,000	15 to ∞
25. Act the fool on the street	125	3 to 1 million	75	5 to 100,000
26–27. Spit on pictures of Darwin and Washington	30	0 to ∞	20	0 to 475
28. Spit on picture of one's mother	25,000	1 to∞	500,000	5 to ∞
29. Spit on crucifix	60	0 to ∞	5	0 to ∞
30. Hour of severest pain	250	3 to ∞	325,000	10 to ∞
31. Restricted diet for one year	50,000	100 to ∞	10,000	100 to 750,000
32. No sugar, tea, coffee, tobacco, alcohol for one year	5,000	4 to ∞	1,000	1 to 500,000
33. Lose all hope of life after death	1,000	0 to ∞	10	0 to ∞

∞ = infinity.

From E. L. Thorndike, *Adult Interests* (New York; Macmillan, 1935).

constitutes a terminal stage in the behavioral process. The prototype of consummatory motivation and behavior is hunger and eating. The act of eating is consummatory in a very direct and real sense; the organism literally consumes the incentive.

Some idea of the complexity of the interactions that exist among various sets of instrumental and consummatory motives is provided by Figure 14-2. Instrumental

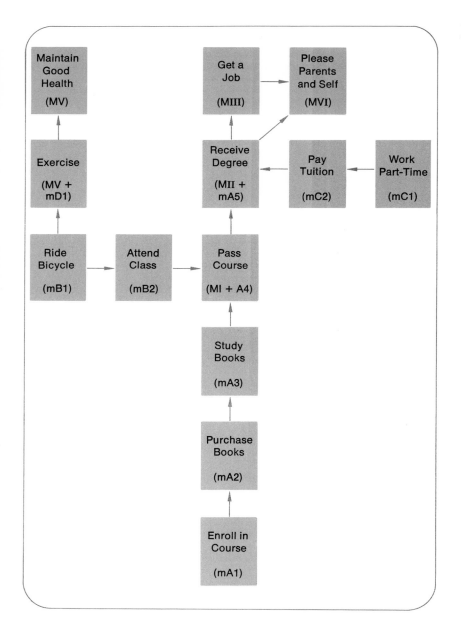

14-2 Diagrammatic representation of interactions among instrumental (m) and consummatory (M) motives. For example, there are several chains of instrumental motives shown leading to the consummatory motive MI. See text for additional discussion.

motives are depicted by lower-case *m*'s, consummatory motives by upper-case *M*'s. Several chains of instrumental motives are shown, and related to a number of consummatory motives. The various motives indicated in the figure are of course merely illustrative of the vast number that operate in this manner in everyday life; each reader can fill in a different set of names to represent the instrumental–consummatory interplay as well as the chaining of instrumental motives. The question is simply, "What objectives are important and which intermediate behaviors contribute to those outcomes?"

A few general principles can be readily adduced from the conceptual framework represented in Figure 14-2. First, multiple *m*'s serve a single *M*; this is perhaps the most important single generalization that can be developed from the instrumental–consummatory distinction. Moreover, these instrumental motives are related to the consummatory motives they serve in both a serial (chained) and a parallel (multiple inputs) manner. Second, the same *m* or instrumental motive can serve more than one *M*; thus *m BI* is a participant both in the *B* chain that feeds into the *M I* consummatory motive and in the more direct service of the *M IV* consummatory motive. Third, a given consummatory motive can also serve as an instrumental motive; *M IV*, physical exercise, for example, is an objective in its own right as well as instrumental to the long-range maintenance of good physical health.

Origins of Motives

Where do our motives come from? This question is one of the more intriguing of all of psychology's fundamental problems. Here we suggest a few of the more promising major lines of attack on the problem.

INNATE MOTIVES. The most logical place to start is with the wiring or programming that each organism inherits from his ancestors. There is, of course, no simple way of separating this source of directed behavior from the more immediate environmental (learning) influences. The field of ethology, emphasizing the naturalistic study of animal behavior, has supplied some interesting and suggestive evidence concerning the role of inherited factors in energizing and directing many forms of behavior.

Two ethological principles are of special relevance for this problem: the innate releasing mechanism and vacuum activity. The notion behind the *innate releasing mechanism* (IRM) is that the appropriate stimulus will often elicit ("release") a particular response in the absence of any opportunity to learn. A famous example we have already cited is the red abdomen that elicits the fighting response of the male stickleback when it is mating. Courting behavior, on the other hand, is elicited at this time by any swollen object similar to the shape of the egg-laden female.

A corollary theoretical proposition is that the basis of such instinctive behaviors is neural energy that is action-specific; that is to say, such energy is discharged only in the typical actions. *Vacuum activity* is the appearance of instinctive actions in the absence of the appropriate eliciting stimulus. It is assumed that the action-specific energy in the nervous system is finally released, even in the absence of the normal IRM, because of the great neural excitation that builds up in the organism. Thus courting behavior may appear in the absence of any apparent stimulus, appropriate or inappropriate; or the bird that has had its food supplied may sometimes exhibit complex fly-catching behavior even in the absence of the fly. Sexual responses as well as other less striking types of behavior often resemble vacuum activities, in man as well as infrahuman organisms.

CULTURAL HERITAGE. The great majority of human motives can probably most safely be attributed to the social environment that is "inherited" by each of us and to which we are constantly exposed. The behavior is not "wired in" but is transmitted by the culture. In other words, most human motives—especially, of course, those that deal most directly with other people—are absorbed from our culture. The learning process by means of which this process occurs may be direct, as when social imitation of a model is involved, but more often it is devious, as when social motives such as power or affiliation are involved.

Perhaps the most interesting general facet of the problem of the origin of motives is that relating to the manner of interaction between such cultural or socially learned motives and the basic biological drives. Although no great unifying principle is yet at hand to resolve this problem, certainly much if not most human motivation is a blend of biological drive and social learning.

EXTEROCEPTIVE STIMULATION; INTELLECTUAL FUNCTIONS. Two great sources of motivation that are not closely tied either to biological drive states or cultural factors are those related to exteroceptive stimulation and intellectual processes. Curiosity, as noted, seems to be a very strong and fundamental motivational condition in many animals as well as man. It can be invoked both by stimulus conditions (e.g., experiencing a novel object) and intellectual functions (e.g., being challenged by a puzzle). Sensory satisfactions, on the other hand, are more strictly related to exteroceptive stimulation (e.g., the enjoyment of graphic art or music). These sources of human motives are recognized as potent factors in modern life and constitute, therefore, a predominant source of motivation.

THE ROLE OF REASON. To what extent does reason, or cognitive control, operate to produce motives? This question will be recognized as a variation of a fundamental issue that cuts across many areas of psychology, as described, for example, in Chapter 13. Introspectively, there seems to be little doubt that one can consciously and deliberately formulate intentions and implement them by motivated behaviors. There also seems to be a very good basis for questioning both the extent and the persistence of the motivational influence of many such intentions. Nevertheless, conscious intention must be accorded a significant role in human motivation, at least until more evidence to the contrary is collected. Underemphasized by some (e.g., the strict behaviorists) and overemphasized by others (e.g., certain clinical theorists), this source of motivation is certainly more important than its severest critics suggest and yet less important than its most enthusiastic proponents assert.

Cognitive control may well be as important for its organization of motivational factors as for its creation of them. As many students could testify, wishing oneself to be motivated to study is usually markedly ineffective. One can, however, consciously place himself in surroundings in which studying behavior is more likely to occur. Such a maneuver will affect one's behavior and one's motivational state as well. One can use his intellectual capacities to arrange his stimulus

MOTIVATIONAL MECHANISMS

We now consider some of the more prominent of the various mechanisms by means of which motives are modified and transformed.

Increments and Decrements in Strength

The simplest mechanism by which motives are modified is that which leaves the motive essentially intact but elevates or depresses its intensity. One of the surest ways of increasing motivational strength is by *depriving* the organism of the usual incentives that satisfy the motive. The role of deprivation is most apparent in such biologically based drive conditions as hunger and sex, but it is probably equally if less visibly effective in more subtle socially based motives (e.g., deprivation of Father's usual easy chair or, more seriously, deprivation of his salary or other rewards—including even social approval—for work).

If deprivation acts to increase motives, so does motive satisfaction, or reward. The trend in psychological theory in recent years is strongly toward attributing motivational, rather than associative, properties to the general *reinforcement* process (cf. Chapter 11). In other words, it is now believed that many S–R associations, or habits, are quickly brought to a maximal or nearly maximal level and that what is really happening when performance improves with further practice is that the activational component of the motive is progressively strengthened. Thus increments in motivation would be a consequence of the reinforcement (reward) process as well as the deprivation process.

How, then, do motives ever weaken? In the case of instrumental motives especially, persistent failure to keep the instrumental behavior chain going and ultimate failure to achieve consummation will eventually, and sometimes rather quickly, reduce the motivational strength of some particular behavior to a very low level. More often, however, motives are simply transformed, or are "lost," so to speak, in the shuffle of continuing development. This latter process is most evident, of course, during periods of greatest change, such as late childhood and adolescence, but it can also occur in more mature individuals. All of us have had favored activities in which we sooner or later lost interest—ranging from physical participation in sports (where reduced physical vigor and skill may be an important consideration) to more purely intellectual pursuits, such as bridge, chess, or checkers. New interests are often developed to supplant the old. Of course, the loss of interest in an activity may reflect a change in motive or the discovery of a better vehicle for its satisfaction.

Functional Autonomy

Some psychologists have stressed that instrumental motives that have long served consummatory motives may themselves eventually take on true consummatory properties, that is, become objectives in their own right. This concept, called *functional autonomy of motives,* is illustrated by the so-called busman's holiday—occupying oneself during leisure time with the very same activity that has been instrumental in earning a living. The bus driver who on his day off rides the bus, perhaps for want of something better to do, is in this respect much like the professional lawyer who argues his cases over at home with his friends or neighbors, or the sailor who stays with the sea long after the end of his productive seamanship, or any other persons who continue to practice their occupation in some manner long after their earlier satisfactions (salary, for example) have been discontinued.

It is clear in such cases that new satisfactions, presumably relating to the instrumental activity itself, have taken over as reinforcers. Some suggestive experimental support for this proposition is available. Animals and children may continue to make responses that have been instrumental in obtaining an incentive even when they are offered the same incentive on a free basis.

Displacement

Displacement is a common motivational mechanism in humans that is similar to the vacuum activity described earlier in that it represents making a strongly motivated response to an inappropriate stimulus. In the case of displacement a person does not, for some reason, involve the normal target of the motivated behavior. In the example mentioned earlier, a person may not be willing to vent his anger against his boss, who provoked it. He may instead "take it out" on peers or his subordinates, his wife, or his children, all of whom are safer targets. The scapegoat is a victim of such displaced aggression on a more persistent basis.

When the fundamental motivation underlying displaced motivation is understood, persons associated with the displacer are more likely to be sympathetic with the problem and the behavior exhibited and thereby avoid worsening the situation by their own behavior (such as retaliations that are likely to be made when the dynamics of the behavior are not understood). The more subtle and difficult to uncover kinds of personal interaction in which displacement is actively involved are more likely to produce serious inflammation of interpersonal relations and thereby cause irreparable damage to most or all the participants.

Secondary Reinforcement and Motivation

Secondary reinforcing and motivating stimuli are those that themselves did not initially have these properties, but have acquired them by association with objects and cues that did have them. Some experimental and everyday examples should indicate at least the main outlines of this kind of mechanism, by means of which potent motivational conditions can operate.

Consider first the negative case. Cues associated with punishing or otherwise aversive situations can quickly acquire secondary negative properties. The classic experiment demonstrating this used albino laboratory rats. Each rat was placed in a white box with a grid floor that could be electrified to shock the animal. After a 1-minute period during which no shock was applied, the rat was shocked briefly once every 5 seconds, for a second 1-minute period. Then a door leading to another compartment, painted black, was opened, and the shock was turned on continuously.

It does not require an expert to predict what the rat did under these conditions. Because there was no shock in the black box, the rat entered it with reasonable quickness, especially during the latter part of the ten trials given each subject. But of course this demonstration of escape learning was not the objective of the experiment. The purpose was to determine whether the fear that was presumably produced by the shock experience would be sufficient to motivate subsequent instrumental learning, even in the absence of any further shock. Each subject was therefore given further trials by being placed in the white box. No further shocks were administered. Nevertheless, it was found that the typical subject would not only move into the black box, but would also learn to turn a wheel and later to depress a lever in order to open the door when it was closed at the start of the trial. The conclusion was drawn that the white box had become a potent negative secondary reinforcer by virtue of its association with the shock, and that the learned fear could motivate a variety of subsequent responses that served to reduce fear by permitting the subject to leave the aversive area.

The best example of a positive secondary reinforcer is money, or any other medium of exchange. Tokens have been widely used in research with both mental patients in hospitals and laboratory chimpanzees. The human patients are allowed to earn tokens for good behavior (e.g., coming to meals, eating properly, and the like) and then to spend them for hospital privileges (e.g., seeing movies, being granted late hours or passes, and the like). The chimpanzees will work for tokens that can then be used to obtain goal objects, such as fruit, made available in automatic vending machines. Here the token is strictly a secondary reinforcer, because its only value is that it can be exchanged for some object or opportunity that satisfies a consummatory motive. When the value of the secondary reinforcer decreases, its motivational power is weakened correspondingly and the subject eventually ceases working to obtain it.

Conflict

A *conflict* can be simply defined as a situation in which there are contradictory motives, both (or all) of which cannot be satisfied. Conflicts have been analyzed in terms of their approach and avoidance components. Three fundamental patterns of conflict so analyzed have been defined: approach–approach, approach–avoidance, and avoidance–avoidance, as shown in Figure 14-3.

An *approach–approach* conflict occurs when one has two positive goals but is not able to achieve both of them. That is to say, in obtaining one he must forsake the other. Most such conflicts are more or less readily resolved, because one of the goals is clearly more attractive, or is much easier to achieve. Sometimes, however, the goals are very similar in strength, and considerable vacillation may then ensue. One cannot, for example, decide which of two movies to attend on some given night, or which of two equally interesting courses to take when they are offered at the same time, or, to illustrate the general principle with even more significant matters, which of two persons to marry or which of two careers to follow.

It is characteristic of approach–approach conflict that most of the vacillation and

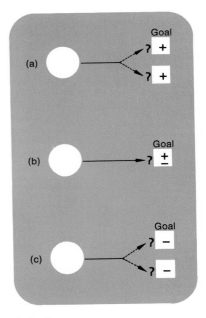

14-3 Conceptual classification of conflicts. Contradictory and incompatible responses are involved in each of three types of conflict. In the *approach-approach* conflict [panel (a)], the organism is positively attracted by each of two goals, only one of which can be attained; in *approach-avoidance* conflict [panel (b)], the organism has only one goal by which it is simultaneously attracted and repelled. In *avoidance-avoidance* conflict [panel (c)], the organism is repelled by both goals but is forced to respond to one. (Based on Lewin, 1935.)

indecisiveness occur early in the decision-making process. Once at least a tentative start has been made in one direction or the other it becomes easier to continue with that choice. The goal itself may become more attractive. In any event, the more time and effort one invests in, say, a given career, the easier it becomes to continue in the same direction. If a person is fundamentally dissatisfied with his choice, however, the sooner he forsakes it and starts in a new direction, the better.

An *approach-avoidance* conflict occurs when a single goal entails both positive *and* negative features. For example, a student takes a college course that he wants and needs, but must work long and hard. The young man realizes that if he marries the girl of his choice, he is acquiring also a new association with her family; or the girl, for her part, appreciates that if she marries the man of her choice, she is going to have to put up with his personal habits of smoking or drinking or his lack of money and occupational opportunity.

This kind of conflict is likely to engender even more vacillation and agitation than the others. Only one direction is involved and it is not possible to relieve the conflict as readily as in the approach-approach situation. Moreover, as the goal is approached, the negative factors are likely to become accentuated in much the same way as the positive. As a matter of fact, they can even be more strongly affected. Experimental support for this statement comes from some early experiments with laboratory rats in which careful measurement of motivational strength of positive and negative processes was made by means of a harness arrangement. The force with which the rat pulled either *away from* an electric shock or *toward* a food incentive was thus measured. The results, shown in Figure 14-4, indicated clearly that a much more marked gradient of motivational force exists for the avoidance component. It is apparent that in this situation at least the organism's motivation increases much more sharply as the goal is approached for the negative component.

Although these results cannot be translated bodily into the human situation, with which we are likely to be more directly concerned, there is some reason to think that human subjects respond similarly. Figure 14-5 depicts a situation that is frequently offered as an illustration of approach-avoidance conflict.

An *avoidance-avoidance* conflict is defined as a situation in which one is forced to choose between two negative courses of action. Neither of the available alternatives is desirable, but circumstances dictate the selection of one or the other. A common example of this kind of conflict occurs frequently in college work; a student who is definitely interested in majoring in, say, psychology finds that a choice must be made among laboratory courses, none of which is really desired. Or the young lady who wishes to attend an important social affair is forced to choose between two or more gentlemen for her escort when she does not really wish to go with any of those available. In all such cases it is apparent that some additional motive is sufficiently overriding to keep the individual moving in the same direction; in the examples cited, the student must remain sufficiently motivated by psychology as a major and the young lady motivated to attend the social affair to require that the unpleasant decision ultimately be made. When this strong motivation does not exist, however, a decision may not be made. The person may simply give up on the goal; this kind of behavior is sometimes referred to as "leaving the field."

These types of conflict are much more clear-cut as they have been described—as

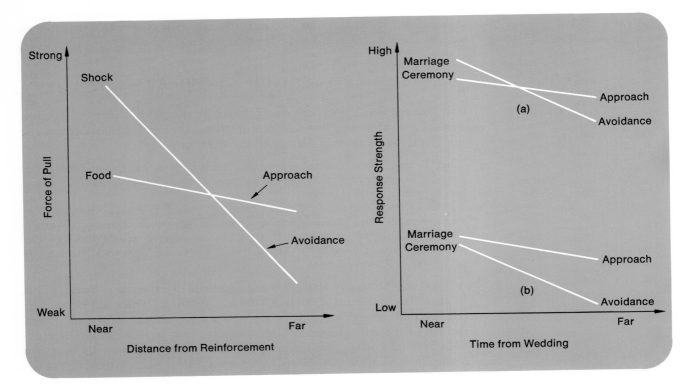

14-4 Gradients of approach and avoidance. The strength of the positive and negative reinforcements (food and shock) is measured by the amount of pull toward or away from reinforcement that the rat applies to a restraining harness. Note that the avoidance gradient is steeper than the approach gradient. See Figure 14-5 for a more realistic version of this same relationship in a human situation. (Adapted from Brown, 1948.)

14-5 Approach-avoidance conflict applied to a prospective marriage. When one both desires and fears marriage his avoidance tendency is likely to be steeper, in relation to the time of the wedding, than his approach tendency. Panel (a) depicts the case of one for whom the relative positions of the gradients are so close that considerable vacillation, and ultimate refusal to wed, may be anticipated; panel (b) shows the happier outcome in which approach tendencies triumph over avoidance and the wedding occurs. (Based on theoretical analysis in Miller, 1944.)

"textbook cases"—than their real-life representations are likely to be. Most conflict situations are complex mixes of a great variety of interacting conditions. It may be helpful, nonetheless, to treat them in terms of the basic pattern they most closely approximate, so that some appreciation of their structure can be achieved.

We have already considered, in our discussion of biological motives, some of the physiological mechanisms that have been identified as underlying such relatively simple processes as hunger and thirst. In several earlier treatments of various topics we have had occasion to describe the functions of the important neurophysiological filtering system, the RAS (Chapter 6), which has direct implications for motivation, and to mention some of the brain structures. Now we complete our consideration of

Neurophysiology of Motivation

the neurophysiological basis of motivation by describing in somewhat greater detail certain research that seems to be most relevant and exciting.

ELECTRICAL STIMULATION OF THE BRAIN (ESB)

In the early 1950's two young postdoctoral psychologists who were collaborating on RAS research made a very fortunate mistake—they misplanted an electrode. As one of them later described it, the results were "amazing":

When the animal was stimulated at a specific place in an open field, he sometimes moved away but he returned and sniffed around that area. More stimulation at that place caused him to spend more time there.

Later we found that this same animal could be "pulled" to any spot in the maze by giving a small electrical stimulus *after* each response in the right direction. This was akin to playing "hot and cold" game with a child. Each correct response brought electrical pulses which seemed to indicate to the animal that it was on the right track. [Olds, 1955, pp. 83–84].

From this fortuitous accident many hundreds of experiments have ensued. Implanted electrodes have been widely used in animals from mice and rats through dogs and cats to monkeys, and even, with a small number of chronic mental patients (diagnosed as incurable schizophrenics), man himself. Practical applications have been sought; for example, dogs with implanted electrodes have been used as subjects in army-sponsored experiments to determine the feasibility of this technique operated by means of a teledirecting (wireless radio) system in the field.

Although the theoretical understanding of this phenomenon is not complete, it appears possible that the ESB technique allows short-circuiting of the usual motivational mechanisms in the brain. When certain areas of the limbic system are electrically stimulated, whatever response the animal has just made is repeated. The suggestion is that this direct "reinforcement" process is functionally similar to the motivational process that occurs when the organism receives a more usual reinforcer such as a food pellet immediately following an instrumental response. Because of this functional similarity it is often assumed that the ESB procedure activates a kind of "reward center" in the brain.

In contrast to the theoretical interpretation, which will require much more research for clarification, there is no doubt at all about the empirical power of the technique. Some of the results that have been obtained with it are indeed awesome. Monkeys have been observed to make as many as seventeen bar presses per second. Rats have been induced to work at an even more fantastically high rate—up to 8,000 bar presses per hour—until they literally drop with fatigue. Whatever its ultimate theoretical explanation, the ESB technique is clearly a powerful one that must be involving equally powerful brain functions. In contrast with the technique of ablation (surgical removal of tissue), it does not produce a diffuse effect on neighboring tissues and it is reversible. Moreover, if the organism is left intact, the ESB procedure can be supplemented by another similarly precise and even more flexible technique utilizing chemical stimulation. This is done by implanting extremely small tubes into the brain and then injecting selected chemicals (e.g., sex hormones). The main advantage of this technique is that it permits the continuing test of the implanted brain area by a variety of different chemical substances. The combination of electrical and chemical means of stimulating pinpointed brain structures has already paid great dividends in research results and offers a research tool for future investigations of truly enormous promise.

DRUG ADDICTION

The currently controversial topic of drug use, abuse, and addiction has many facets. Here we consider the motivational basis of addiction, on which some interesting and suggestive research has been performed.

Research on Chimpanzees

An early experiment on addiction used chimpanzees as subjects. Morphine was injected by hypodermic syringe twice daily for from six weeks to thirteen months. The first signs of a true physiological dependence upon the drug began to appear from three to seven weeks after the onset of the experiment. The chimpanzee subjects began to show the same symptoms commonly reported for human addicts as the hour of the regular morning or afternoon injection approached. These symptoms are increased irritability and restlessness, salivation, and crying. The apparent need for the drug deepened as the injections proceeded. The subjects attempted to escape the cage as the time for injection neared; after being released from the cage, they would sometimes attempt to lead the experimenter to the injection room and when there would get on the table voluntarily and assume the usual position for the injection. As soon as they had been injected their behavior changed and the symptoms indicating need did not reappear until the time for the next injection approached.

This same experiment also offered the addicted chimpanzees an opportunity to choose between a black box with food in it or a white box containing the hypodermic syringe. The chimpanzees predominantly chose the food box if they had just been injected. However, after eighteen hours of deprivation of *both* food and morphine, they predominantly selected the morphine box. Moreover, they not only spent more time in attempting to get at the morphine box than the food box when blocked from either, they worked more effectively to obtain the white morphine box than the black food box when one or the other of these was presented as a reward in problem-solving tests.

Research on Rats

A more recent experiment with rats as subjects is important in that it demonstrates the complexity of the addiction situation and points to certain psychological variables as crucial even in this kind of fundamentally physiological process in relatively simple animals. The rat subjects were first given twenty-five days of preliminary morphine injections. They were then given a choice of morphine or water, and none chose morphine. Half of the rats, selected randomly, were then placed in an experimental group permitted to drink morphine solution, voluntarily, every third day; the control rats were then given water to drink for two days of each three-day cycle and were injected passively with morphine on the third day. The amount given each control rat was the same as that drunk by the experimental rat with which it had been arbitrarily matched. The same amount of morphine was thus taken by each pair of rats but no opiate-directed behavior was permitted in the controls.

Choice tests pitting water against morphine solution were then administered to all the rats. The self-serving, experimental rats markedly increased their consumption of morphine on these tests, even when water was also available to them. The control rats took very little morphine. More important, in terms of generalization to real-life situations, the experimental rats maintained their opiate-directed behavior even after their withdrawal symptoms had subsided, as indicated by the results of retention tests administered two and seven weeks after the end of the training. This result contrasts with the finding that the chimpanzees that passively ingested the drug in the earlier experiment showed no interest in morphine once their withdrawal symptoms had subsided.

The significance of these results is that they strongly suggest that drug addiction is in part a function of the reinforcement of particular behaviors; in the rat experiment, the drinking behavior is reinforced by the opiate incentive. In any case, it is clear that more than purely physiological factors are involved in morphine addiction—as is suggested by the behavior of "cured" addicts, off the drug, who nonetheless continue to inject themselves with water or jab themselves with needles.

From the standpoint of the personal and social problems posed by drug addiction, the implications of this experiment are instructive. It is not merely the morphine-obtaining behavior itself that can be reinforced by the reduction of stress produced by the morphine; other behaviors, not originally connected with morphine, can also be reinforced by it. Sex drive stimuli, for example, can be responded to by taking morphine rather than finding an appropriate sexual outlet; so can the tensions associated with the office or social affairs. In this way the internal drive conditions that in the nonaddict are associated with a variety of different behaviors can all become dependent on a single, relatively simple response: the injecting of the opiate.

A comparison of opium with alcohol addiction is also instructive. Briefly, opiate addiction is much faster than alcohol, and therein lies its greatest danger, even though the ultimate consequences of long-continued alcoholism are more severe and the prospects of recovery less promising. The development of dependence upon additional intake as a single cure-all for one's problems is even more common in extreme alcohol addiction than it is in opiate addiction. From a motivational point of view, alcohol is easier to resist early in addiction but harder to resist later in addiction. Moreover, the periodic improvement (relief from withdrawal symptoms) that occurs in opiate addiction is less likely to be evident with alcohol.

Significance of Motivation

The crucial function of motivation in all behavior should by now be evident. As emphasized in the discussion of learning (Chapter 11), most of the actual variance in behavior is associated with motivational factors rather than the more stable learning factors. In this concluding section we turn to a brief consideration of certain ways in which the centrality of motivation can be more specifically identified and evaluated.

The *self-actualization* concept is typical of a number of attempts, mainly by personality theorists, to take a broad look at the long-term dimensions of human motivation. In one treatment of the concept, man is assumed to have a fundamental need to express his potentialities as completely as he can. This scheme holds that there are five different levels of needs, which may be listed in the following order beginning with the more basic ("lower"):

1. Biological needs (e.g., food, drink, sex).
2. Security or safety needs (e.g., shelter, stability).
3. Affectional needs (e.g., affiliation, acceptance).
4. Esteem needs (e.g., self-respect, prestige).
5. Self-actualization needs.

According to this proposal, the basic needs are prepotent and must be satisfied before the higher ones can operate to produce appropriate motives. For example, unless one's biological needs are satisfied, one is not likely to be concerned with safety, let alone affection, esteem, or self-actualization. And when security is questionable, the higher needs are unlikely to be very strong. But when all the various basic needs are relatively satisfied, the self-actualization need functions.

The developmental aspect of this grand scheme is important. Each fundamental need tends to be met at a successively later age. Moreover, it is not necessary that each lower need be completely satisfied before a higher need begins to function. For one thing, as we have seen, the biological needs in particular are cyclic; they must be periodically satisfied. To some extent this is also true of the other needs. Motivation always presents a dynamic and changing pattern of needs.

Many persons, because of unfavorable environment or perhaps genetic factors, may never be sufficiently free from hunger or danger to permit concern with what others of us see as the finer things of life. To a chronically hungry or hunted man, self-actualization is not likely to be of much concern. But for most people in our culture the more fundamental needs are sufficiently satisfied to permit at least some concern with higher needs; in these cases the focus of the predominant motives that concern the individual may be seen to change progressively as maturity is reached. This change occurs more or less in accordance with the scheme described.

THE CENTRAL ORGANIZING MOTIVE (COM)

Another way of looking at the dynamic organization of motivation and motive systems is to search for some central theme(s) in the life of the individual. This kind of theme has been noted by many biographers and by some psychological theorists, but this idea does not seem to have been given as much formalization as the self-actualization concept. Because there does not seem to be a better term already in use, this central motivational theme is here labeled the *central organizing motive* (*COM*).

The *central* aspect of the COM reflects the predominance of the motive system among all the motives expressed by the individual. The *organizing* aspect refers to the superordinate status of the motive system in a network of interlocking instrumental and consummatory motives (refer back to Figure 14-2, p. 440, for a simplified illustration). The term *motive* represents the dual associative (directive) and activating (energizing) properties of the concept.

COM's may reflect the successive needs of an individual as these are schematized in the self-actualization hierarchy just described. But the intent of the COM concept is to identify more specifically the particular motives that concern the person. These may be multiple, although at any given time one will usually predominate. They will ordinarily change over a lifetime, and often quite markedly, although in some few cases an interest or a "cause" once developed may remain throughout a lifetime.

COM's come in all sizes and types. Some common examples would be religion, drama, music, and science, or more prosaic interests such as golf and gardening. All these motive systems vary along a great variety of dimensions—as do all motives. Breadth, temporal duration, degree of social involvement are just a few of the dimensions along which COM's can be described. The manner in which COM's develop and function to organize subsidiary motivational (instrumental) systems needs to be directly investigated, experimentally as well as theoretically.

Striking examples of COM's coming to dominate an individual's life are not hard to find. During the turbulent 1970's, for instance, suicidal missions by terrorists were common as a part of the political strife in Ireland and the Middle East. The suicidal missions of these terrorists were reminiscent of the Japanese kamikaze pilots during World War II, who dive-bombed their planes on target, sacrificing themselves for the greater good of their country. The power of ideological commitment in all these cases is awesome. Similar commitment, although not ordinarily expressed in so dramatic a form, is responsible for the religious orientation of many people, and is perhaps most marked in those who forsake the lay world for a monastery or a cloister.

On the basis of presently available knowledge a few comments about COM's can be offered. It is particularly important that long-term goals as well as short-term goals be reasonably achievable, and be recognized as such by all the persons involved (e.g., parents or teachers as well as children). Behaviors instrumental to these goals can often be specifically trained. If the child is to be capable of making reasonable choices, he must be given the opportunity to choose rather than trained merely by proscriptions laid down by his society. But this objective would probably require some radical changes in our educational program to ensure that broad exposure to more aspects of contemporary life be made available to more students. The curiosity that motivates the typical young child needs to be encouraged rather than blunted by the educational endeavor. The motivation of many in the educational system could no doubt be remarkably improved by providing a school environment that rewards individuality and creativity throughout all grades and by making available more effective vocational training to those not willing or able to take advanced academic and college-preparatory course work in the secondary schools.

COM's of course are not restricted to educational practices. Occupational and social restrictions, especially for clearly defined minority groups, tend to stunt aspiration and deflect COM's from socially sanctioned channels. Expecting ghetto youth to develop the usual middle-class motives is foolish; the appeal of the various protest and militant organizations that have recently flourished is precisely that they do offer alternative and more viable COM's to people who have been effectively if not always legally disenfranchised in terms of economic and social objectives.

How markedly new motivational factors can improve the behavior of disadvantaged persons was effectively illustrated by the experience of a small engineering business in a large American city. This organization began training and hiring black drop-outs as draftsmen (an occupation in which the necessary skills seemed to be relatively independent of intellectual activities of the sort in which the drop-out was likely to be deficient). Although not every young man succeeded, a reasonable proportion did. Moreover, the relatively small weekly payroll had a social spin-off whose value could not be readily measured in dollars. For example, profound changes were noted in these young men as they began to acquire technical proficiency and thereby to build up their earnings. The draftsman who was already earning a relatively high hourly wage became a model to be followed. He typically dressed neatly and carried a small briefcase for his tools. The neophyte draftsman was observed not only to begin to dress more neatly and carry his own briefcase but also to show improved manners and greater alertness as his salary increased. These personal and social gains apparently were associated with the improvement in motivational conditions made possible by the employment situation.

Difficulties with COM's are by no means restricted to socially and economically disadvantaged groups or individuals. Many children from the middle or upper socioeconomic levels of our society suffer crucial motivational deficits. Searching for some "reason" for continuing education, for example, is a common and understandable phenomenon among today's youth. Rapid social changes of the sort our society is experiencing are almost certain to raise such doubts and disturb developing motivational systems.

Another developmental phase where COM's are crucial is that of old age. The transition from full occupational activity to partial or complete retirement obviously involves the need for changing COM's. If new positive motivations are not available, withdrawing those long connected with an occupation and associated activities is very likely to have such undesirable consequences as apathy and general loss of interest, too often observed in the aged.

A final comment is in order concerning the relationship of the COM to emotional problems, especially as these relate to disease. Loss of hope has been implicated as a critical accompaniment of susceptibility to certain diseases. Here it may simply be pointed out that throughout life having an effective set of COM's will help ensure the maximal utilization of personal and social resources in making one's life as fulfilling as possible.

Standard textbooks on motivation have been published by Atkinson (1964), Cofer and Appley (1964), and McTeer (1972). The annual publication *Nebraska Symposium on Motivation* is a valuable source.

English and English's standard dictionary of psychological terms stops at thirty-three for motivation, clearly one of the more ambiguous words we have to deal with in psychology.

Biological Motives

Social facilitation of eating in chickens is among the topics reviewed by Zajonc (1972). The anecdote on human eating of horsemeat is from Cox (1973, p. 365). The research on eating of almonds by normal and obese subjects is described by Schacter (1971). Schacter and Rodin's *Obese Human and Rats* (1974) is more up-to-date and popular. Use of the self-feeding "cafeteria" technique to test food selection in children was first reported by Davis (1939). Rosenzweig (1973) has provided an excellent review of the biological events that have been implicated in thirst. Sexual function in the male rat has been studied intensively by Beach (1971).

Motivational Processes

Tinbergen (1952) has popularized the mating behavior of the stickleback, and his 1972 book is a good introduction to classic ethology. Berne's *Games People Play* (1964) is a popular account of interpersonal dynamics related to such mechanisms as displacement; see also the Notes on Social Traps in Supplement B-1. Miller (1948) performed the classic experiment on secondary motivation, utilizing rats in the black and white chambers. Brown (1948) reported the experiment on approach-avoidance conflict in which positive and negative forces were directly measured by means of a harness on the rat subject. Zimbardo's 1969 book concerns the cognitive control of motivation. Singh (1970) has reported an apparent preference for bar pressing to obtain rewards over being given the same rewards directly ("free-loading") in both rats and children

Neurophysiology of Motivation

The initial report of the ESB research was made by the two pioneer investigators, Olds and Milner (1954). Subsequent research is detailed in Olds and Olds (1965) and in most of the standard texts on physiological psychology. Spragg (1940) reported the early experiment demonstrating drug addiction in chimpanzees. The more recent experiment with rats was performed by Nichols (1965).

Significance of Motives

Marx and Tombaugh (1967) indicate the significance of motivational processes, with special reference to education. The self-actualization concept is forcefully presented by Maslow (1962) in the developmental framework described in the text. Irwin (1971) emphasizes the role of choice, intention, and volition in human motivation. Dember (1974) has pointed out the great potency of ideological motives, which he feels have not been given sufficient attention.

Emotion

15

This distressed young man opens our discussion of emotion. The complex psychological and physiological components of emotional behavior are of significant personal interest to all of us because they are often the basis for evaluation of the quality of existence.

motion is a particularly broad and multifaceted psychological phenomenon. It has *experiential* (conscious), *behavioral,* and *physiological* facets, all of which must be considered for an adequate appreciation. Emotions range from purely sensory experiences with minimal cognitive or situational content to complex social interactions. Because of this great scope definitive generalizations that apply to all emotions are difficult to obtain.

This chapter concentrates on the primary interpersonal emotions of love and hate, fear and anger. The growth, expression, control, and personal and social effects of these emotional processes are described. It is emphasized that repeated occurrences of emotional reactions tend to build up areas of sensitivity of varying degrees of specificity. Although these "sore spots" may not often surface and may remain undetected and even unsuspected by one's associates, they stay dormant, in a state of readiness, until triggered, perhaps by some thoughtless comment or act. Emotion-precipitating responses may seem quite innocuous to the offender, who receives the brunt of an unexpectedly strong and emotional reaction, to which he may then respond emotionally himself. Such reciprocal attacks, with neither of the two (or more) antagonists ever really appreciating the perspective of the other(s), constitute the basis of many interpersonal problems (e.g., in marital incompatibility, sibling rivalry).

This chapter concludes with a discussion of the physiology of emotion and the major theories of emotion, in which recent experimental demonstrations of the key role of cognition are stressed.

Two supplements are of special relevance to emotion: B-6, which provides a detailed account of certain dimensions of human love, and B-3, which surveys the problem of psychosomatic (emotionally induced) illness.

Characteristics of Emotions

Emotion is another of those concepts, so common in psychology, that practically everyone more or less understands but that is nevertheless extremely difficult to define exactly. Most often emotion refers to a generalized disturbance or "stirring up" of the organism, with characteristic *conscious, behavioral,* and *physiological* concomitants. Which of these three concomitants is most centrally associated with emotion is a question that has long occupied theorists, as we shall see later in this chapter. Placement of the treatment of emotion in this part, rather than with other major conscious phenomena, does not mean a commitment to the behavioral component as being any more essential than either of the other two components. The organism is by definition an integrated entity and it is only for purposes of investigation that any generalized process, such as emotion, can be theoretically divided into separate components. Moreover, any investigator is free to emphasize whichever type of definition he chooses; emotion *is,* therefore, whichever component process one wishes it to be. However, a full understanding of emotion and its contributions to both behavior and experience can be fully achieved only when all the component features are given adequate attention.

Unfortunately, there has been a tendency to treat emotion as an undesirable problem, as a hindrance to maximal intellectual functioning. Indeed, as we have seen in our consideration of clear thinking, it is often just that. But emotion is also a very desirable feature of life. It is emotion that adds flavor to living; life without emotion would be peculiarly dull and tasteless. The heights of man's experience—his joys and his ecstasies—are just as important a part of his emotional life as are the depths of grief and despair to which he can descend.

These comments suggest one of the major problems that the scientist meets in attempting to cope with emotion: it is so broad and multifaceted a set of phenomena that few definitive statements can be made to fit all its aspects. Treating emotion as an entity, although necessary for textbook exposition, can only compound the difficulties of understanding unless its complexity and breadth are fully recognized. In this respect, again, emotion is no different from other global concepts, such as learning or personality. In order, therefore, to permit some kind of toehold on this vast and slippery subject we start our consideration of emotion with a brief survey of the ways in which it can be dimensionalized, rather than with any attempt to provide a precise definition.

DIMENSIONS OF EMOTIONS

The dimensions along which emotions can be most meaningfully ordered seem to be *affective tone* (pleasantness or unpleasantness), *intensity, temporal duration,* and *complexity*.

AFFECTIVE TONE. The pleasant or unpleasant character of an emotion may well be its most important characteristic. Certainly this seems to be the most fundamental characteristic. Much of the motivating power of emotions is mediated by means of the apparent attractiveness of the positive emotions or the apparent repulsion of the negative emotions. The affective tone of an emotion refers directly to its introspective, or conscious, pleasant or unpleasant quality. Although organisms generally seem to be attracted to pleasant qualities and repelled by unpleasant ones it is not always easy to distinguish clearly between these qualities, especially in cases of relatively mild emotional arousal. For example, we may be attracted by a mild sense of danger, finding it stimulating and exciting (especially after a period of relative boredom), whereas the same stimulus as it increases in intensity may become distinctly unpleasant; thus the black bear ambling peaceably along a path is quite a different emotional stimulus from the same bear up close and moving more determinedly.

It is often difficult to separate causal relationships in emotional situations. Do we move toward a positive stimulus, such as the bear at a distance, because we experience a pleasant conscious state, or do we experience the pleasantness because we are moving toward the positive stimulus? This will be recognized as the same type of question William James asked with regard to the conscious feeling in an emotion and the stirred-up physiological reaction, as we shall see later in this chapter. How we answer the question will likely be in accordance with our own view of the role of consciousness in emotions. Nevertheless, it should be noted that the positive–negative dichotomy of stimuli functions at the lowest levels of animal life; for example, it may even occur in the approach or avoidance movements of a single-celled amoeba or paramecium to different stimuli. The kind of consciousness with which humans are familiar can hardly exist in such simple organisms. It thus appears to be safe to assume that the positive–negative dimension is a most primitive one. What is added to it by the emergence of pleasant and unpleasant conscious experiences remains to be seen.

INTENSITY. The intensity of emotions can be manifested in any of the three component processes mentioned—consciousness, behavior, or physiological reaction. The correlation among the vigor of these different kinds of processes is far from perfect. Thus, for example, the seemingly inert man who has just been insulted by his boss may be seething inside (both consciously and physiologically), although giving no overt behavioral indication of such strong emotion. Or, on the contrary, the vigorously reacting individual (even when not "acting") may actually be very little disturbed, either consciously or physiologically. But these extremes are exceptional instances, and often the degree of emotional excitement is reflected with reasonable fidelity in vigor of overt behavior and physiological reactivity as well as in disturbance of consciousness.

TEMPORAL DURATION. Emotional reactions vary widely in their temporal duration. Some are very brief. A pain reaction, for example, may be momentary and have no lasting effects. Most emotional reactions tend to persist over longer times, and indeed may have permanent consequences (witness the psychosomatic symptoms considered in Supplement B-3).

Two special categories of temporally prolonged emotional states, mood and temperament, are generally recognized. A *mood* is an emotionally tinged affective condition that lasts for hours or even days; one is said to be "moody" when he is subject to such long-lasting emotional states. A moody person typically expresses his emotionality in a generalized manner—the grumpy individual is likely to be negative to most social contact as long as the mood lasts, and the extremely happy (euphoric) individual is generally positive in his reactivity. Like other emotional conditions, moods vary markedly in intensity. A moody individual can be violent in his overt behavior (and presumably in his inner experience also) but more often the mood is expressed in a relatively low-key manner. When some particular type of emotional state becomes more chronic, and seems to be characteristic of an individual most of the time, it is referred to as *temperament*. This is an important dimension of personality, and so is discussed at more length in Chapter 16; the term *trait* refers to this kind of condition.

COMPLEXITY. One of the most striking aspects of emotions is their diversity. Psychologists have lagged far behind novelists and poets in their delineation of the great variety of combinations of separate kinds of feelings that are involved in emotions. The pure emotion, such as sheer rage or pure fear, is probably less common than the more subtle reactions called remorse or jealousy. Indeed, some have asserted that we can describe as many emotional experiences as we can identify types of stimulating situations. Whether or not it is necessary to accept this extreme position it is certainly true that the subtlety of emotional reactivity, in its conscious and behavioral aspects probably more than its physiological, is sufficient to test the resources of the most gifted artist. The psychologist will need to introduce a degree of clarifying simplicity, as he attempts to impart some order into this magnificently confused picture. The classification of emotions that follows is a first step in that direction.

TYPES OF EMOTIONS

Verbal labels are especially inadequate as representations of the salient features of emotions, let alone the more subtle nuances. The situation is basically like that which obtains in the naming of colors, as discussed in Chapter 7, but here it is aggravated by the more volatile character of the phenomena. Nevertheless, we can at least categorize the major types of emotions by their *origin* and their *objects*. Using these criteria, we can isolate two major sources of emotion—situations and organisms (mainly human)—and then make some further subdivisions according to objects of the emotions within each of these categories.

Table 15-1 provides a summary of the various types of emotion in this classification as they are discussed in the following paragraphs.

Situational Emotions

Emotions aroused by situations can be broken down into those initiated by the immediate stimulus situation by means of direct sensory effects and those related to the more long-term motivational or other characteristics of the situation.

DIRECT SENSORY EFFECTS. The sensory basis of some emotional reactions is

Table 15-1 Classification of Types of Emotion According to Origin and Object

Emotion	Origin	Object
	Situational	
Pleasure Pain	Sensory	Approach stimulus Withdraw from stimulus
Joy Sorrow Fear Anger	Cognitive	Approach Quiescence Flight (escape) Fight (attack)
	Social	
Pride Shame Guilt, remorse	Self-referral	Oneself
Love Hate	Interpersonal	Significant others

exemplified best by pain. Any severe stimulus that damages bodily structure, especially at the periphery of the body, is likely to elicit a pain reaction. Whether the pain response leads to anger (attack) or fear (withdrawal) depends upon the nature of the situation, and the organism's awareness of it. Thus although the initial emotional reaction of pain is largely unconditioned, what follows is very largely a function of learning; in other words, it is a function of how the organism perceives the situation. Thus it is impossible to make any absolute, hard-and-fast distinction between strictly sensory and situational determinants, although pure types can be conceptually distinguished.

Positive or pleasurable responses to sensory stimulation, sometimes referred to as delight, usually attract less attention than the negative reactions. "Creature comforts," such as warmth and food, represent situations that are associated with pleasurable emotional responses. The variety of such responses is very great; any sensory modality can provide some degree of emotional satisfaction. Here again, however, it is impossible to make an absolute distinction from the broader motivational properties of the situation; how much of an individual's pleasurable reaction to the soft feel of mink is produced by the sheer sensory response to the fur itself and how much by the more complex motivational satisfactions associated with the gift? Similarly, how much of the home-run hitter's satisfaction comes from the solid feel of the bat on the ball and how much from the effects thereby produced, or at least the increment in the statistical achievements of the batter? Obviously both types of situational emotion are involved in many such instances and there is no simple way of separating them.

PRIMARY EMOTIONS. We have already introduced the topic of motivation, as separate from the immediate sensory experience. Most emotions are aroused by the way in which the organism perceives the stimulus situation, with respect to its own motives of various sorts. Four fundamental types of emotional reaction, which are sometimes referred to as primary emotions, can be distinguished.

HAPPINESS. By whatever name (e.g., joy, delight, ecstasy), a happy response is the product of satisfaction of a motive. The stronger or deeper the motive, and the more adequate the consummation, the greater the happiness.

SORROW. At the other end of the affective continuum from happiness is the emotion called sorrow, which results from the loss of a goal or a desired object. In its extreme form, sorrow turns into severe grief and even depression and is characterized by a markedly reduced level of overt activity and a tendency to dwell upon the loss. Although there are various forms that this negative emotion can take, it is always basically unpleasant to some degree; we can disregard some of the apparent exceptions, such as the person who seems to enjoy attending funerals, on the ground that true sorrow has not been experienced to any substantial degree, but it is also true that sorrow can be tempered by ameliorating processes, such as deep religious convictions attendant upon the loss of a loved one.

FEAR. Also at the other end of the affective continuum from pleasure, but not quite so squarely opposed to happiness, is the emotion of fear. It is no more possible to characterize the felt emotion of fear (or any other of the primary emotions, for that matter) to the uninitiated person in verbal terms than it is to tell him what the sensation of red or blue is like. But each of us has experienced the emotion of fear, as a conscious response to real or fancied danger or threat. Basic to fear is the realization that one is not able to ward off the danger that threatens. For example, approaching traffic at an intersection as one's automobile coasts down a steep hill constitutes very little of a fear stimulus to a driver, until he finds that his brakes have gone out and that he has no control over his automobile.

ANGER. Blocking of some goal-directed activity, either real or fancied, is the normal stimulus for the anger reaction. Whether anger or fear results in this kind of frustration situation depends, again, upon the organism's perception of the situation. There are numerous situations in which a delicate balance exists between fear, or withdrawal, and anger, or attack, tendencies. Consider the automobile driver who has just been struck from behind by another automobile. After the initial emotional shock has disappeared, he may become very angry indeed, until he observes that the other driver is (1) exceptionally large and/or menacing, perhaps carrying a weapon; (2) a police officer; or (3) a friend. In most of these cases the anger is quite likely to dissipate rapidly and even turn into mild fear, or apprehension.

Like other primary emotions, anger shows an enormous variation in intensity, ranging from the mildest exasperation to the most violent rage. Also like the other emotions, it mixes in many subtle ways with a variety of other feelings. It should also be mentioned that by no means all frustrating situations produce anger or fear, or necessarily any emotion for that matter. Aggression, which is the most common form of persistent anger, is discussed in Supplement B-5.

EVALUATIVE EMOTIONS. There is another type of emotional reaction to situations that seems to be sufficiently different from either the sensory or the primary emotions to merit special attention as a separate category. These emotions involve evaluation or appreciation of situations. Examples of this kind of relatively mild emotional response are esthetic reactions to artistic performance or production, in which the sensory element is likely to be pronounced, and responses to humor, in which the cognitive element is more important. Awe, as of the wonders of nature (or man), and religious emotions of various sorts are other instances of this kind of response to situations. These reactions are labeled as emotions because the organism is quite clearly stirred up, as evidenced both by his introspective reports and his overt behavior, but the emotional arousal is to a lesser degree than typically occurs in other types of emotional situations.

Social Emotions

Emotions directly relating to people can be divided into two major classes, those of self-referral and those involving reactions to others. It is obvious that there will be much overlap between social emotions and situational emotions, in that practically all the former will involve situations. The distinction hinges upon the degree to which the *focus* in the emotional reaction is on the particular person or persons in the situation rather than on the situation. Because our classification and description is for expository rather than research or theoretical purposes the fact that the categories indicated are not neatly separable need not be a matter for serious concern.

SELF-APPRAISAL EMOTIONS. The capacity of the human organism to appraise himself is certainly one of man's most significant features. Here the broad outlines of the more important self-referral emotional reactions will be indicated; in Chapter 16 a more detailed exposition of these conditions and factors in personality organization is given.

SELF-ESTEEM: PRIDE AND SHAME. The esteem in which one holds himself is a function of many social and personal variables. Among the more important of these are the kinds of standards, with regard to various performance categories, such as academic, athletic, economic, and the like, observed in the society in which one lives. But more important than such external, social standards are one's own personal standards, which are determined by the complex interaction between various aspects of personality and the social standards. One's level of aspiration, with regard to each of the performance tests faced, is a potent determinant of self-esteem. Thus the objective nature of one's performance—how poorly or how well one does by the usual standards of society—is a less significant factor than one's relative achievement—how well one does with respect to the level of aspiration that he has set for himself, either explicitly or more likely implicitly.

GUILT AND REMORSE. Whereas shame refers generally to lowered self-esteem in one form or another, *guilt* is a more specific emotional reaction to a particular violation of a code of ethics or moral behavior. The stress in our culture upon sin and consequent guilt, with respect to a variety of behaviors, has exaggerated the problem. Religious dogma provides the most obvious example of the kind of code that invites violation and guilt, but there are other less explicit codes that make significant contributions; for example, the strong personal moral code of an autocratic father may have little or nothing to do with religion but can serve to intimidate and distort the emotional development of the entire family. Any rigid code of behavior invites violation and can contribute to the arousal of guilt feelings that have deep and pervasive consequences on personality development.

Remorse may be recognized as an explicit and extended variety of guilt feeling. Dwelling upon moral violations is characteristic of many segments of our culture. The implications that such needless exacerbation of guilt have for self-esteem and personality development are quite apparent.

INTERPERSONAL EMOTIONS: LOVE AND HATE. The affective continuum, with strong positive feelings on one end and strong negative feelings on the other end, is nowhere more evident than with respect to our reactions to "significant others" in our lives. We need not dwell long on these two extremes, love and hate, because they are familiar to everyone and they are treated more elaborately in other places. Here we may simply identify *love* as a more or less intense emotional attachment for other individuals—with many subvarieties, such as romantic love, parental love, and the like—and *hate* as a more or less intense feeling of emotional repulsion toward other individuals—with varying degrees of fear and anger being most prominent in the emotional mix. Both love and hate tend to be persistent or enduring emotional conditions; further, both show characteristically periodic increments and decrements, which are mostly associated with the presence or absence (or more accurately, the proximity in reality *or* imagination) of the target individuals. If absence does in fact "make the heart grow fonder," it is because the physical removal of the loved individual is offset by an increased amount of thought and fantasy, so that the linearity of the relationship between proximity and emotional intensity is maintained.

Effects of Emotional Arousal

The important relationship of emotional arousal to other behavioral processes is far too complex to be neatly and fully described in a simple manner, but some of the more prominent processes can be briefly described.

SHORT-TERM EFFECTS. Emotional arousal has certain contradictory effects. On the one hand, it is often disruptive of performance (e.g., "stage fright"), and on the other hand, emotional arousal can be an important factor in organizing behavior and in the mobilization of resources brought to bear on a problem. Although some degree of exaggeration must be admitted, there is nontheless good reason to accept the essential accuracy of the many stories that demonstrate the extraordinary feats, as of physical strength or endurance, that can be achieved by persons under sufficient emotional arousal. In large part, these achievements must be credited to the high degree of motivation produced by such emotions.

Normally the disruptive effects of emotional arousal are more evident; the indecision or vacillation and the precipitate actions often evidenced by persons in acute emergencies, such as being trapped in a burning building, are dramatic illustrations.

In general, a moderate degree of emotional arousal is believed to be optimal for efficiency of behavior. Figure 15-1 represents this generalized relationship. However, quite different kinds of relationships from the hypothetical one shown there can be anticipated under various circumstances. Thus highly trained skills may be expected to show both quicker facilitation and delayed disruption as the degree of emotional involvement increases; nevertheless, even well practiced acts, such as

15-1 Hypothetical generalized relationship between degree of emotional arousal and efficiency of performance.

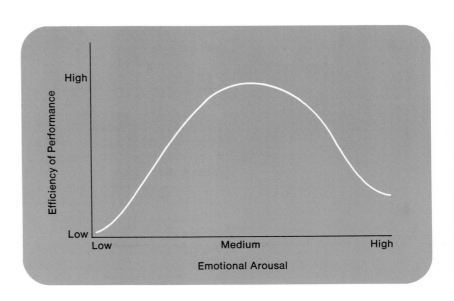

providing one's own address or telephone number, can be momentarily "forgotten" under conditions of sufficient duress or terror and consequent emotionality. Complex tasks requiring, say, fine sensory discriminations may be expected to be much more susceptible to disruption by emotional arousal than relatively gross responses utilizing sheer physical force.

The relationship between emotionality and behavioral efficiency may be demonstrated even when indirect measures of emotionality are used. Various types of personality inventories designed to assess the level of chronic anxiety have been developed. When subjects in learning experiments are categorized according to their scores on these measures, highly anxious individuals are found to perform better on simple tasks, but more poorly on complex ones.

ROLE OF CONFIDENCE. The disruptive emotionality that interferes with efficiency of performance in such phenomena as stage fright can be prevented, under normal circumstances, by sufficient prior practice and experience. Such experience not only helps to perfect the particular skills needed but also builds self-confidence. This last factor may be of greater importance than the skills themselves, granted some minimal level of proficiency, because the performer with adequate confidence is not likely to be emotionally upset.

The role of confidence is often quite subtle. Consider, for example, the rash of 4-minute-mile runs that occurred once the first such mile had been run. Breaking of the imaginary "barrier" by that first runner apparently gave other runners of that same general caliber sufficient confidence that they were able to put forth the extra effort that pushed them past the magic number. Although such auxiliary conditions as improved training techniques may have had something to do with the improved performances, the major factor must be regarded as the knowledge that the feat not only *could* be done but actually *had* been done.

LONG-TERM EFFECTS. The disruptive effects of emotionality thus far described are immediate and readily identified. More chronic or long-term effects are less readily identified but are generally believed to be even more serious in terms of personality development and deterioration. These are described in Supplements B-2 and B-3.

GROWTH AND CONTROL OF EMOTIONS

In this section we start our more detailed consideration of emotions, with some generalized observations concerning their development in infancy and childhood. We review the problem of discrimination of emotions, looking at some of the work done on their expression. We then look more closely at some of the more prominent emotions, notably love, fear, and anger, and comment on the important personal and social problem of emotional control.

EMOTIONAL DEVELOPMENT IN INFANCY. There seems to be general agreement that the earliest expression of emotion in the human infant is diffuse and not restricted to any clearly identifiable mode of expression. This generalized excitement begins to differentiate, about three months of age, into positive and negative emotions, approach (joy and delight), and then into avoidance (mainly fear and anger) by six months. Joy subsequently differentiates into situational delight and personal affection, attached first to adults and then to children.

The most detailed account of the development of affection has been provided by Harry Harlow and his associates, working on rhesus monkeys at the Primate Center at the University of Wisconsin. They have identified a heirarchical system of affectional stages, with each new stage dependent for its full development on the consummation of the previous stage. Although monkey love may not be exactly the same as people love, the broad outlines of this research are probably reasonably representative of human emotional development. Descriptions of these stages follow (pp. 467 ff.).

Some of the most influential early research on infantile emotional expression was conducted by John Watson, the founder of the behaviorism school. Watson was concerned with the nature of the first stimuli that are effective in producing emotional responses in the infant. He decided that each of three primary emotions had a characteristic type of eliciting stimulus in the newborn. *Love* (cooing, expansive behavior) was elicited by stroking and petting, including stimulation of the erogenous (pleasurable) zones. *Fear* was elicited by loud sounds and sudden loss of support (dropping baby, or pulling out crib mattress); fear was expressed by crying and generally disturbed behavior. *Anger* was elicited by physical restraint of the movement of the baby (as by binding its arms with cloth) and was expressed, in a manner that is all too familiar to parents, by crying, holding of breath, and thrusting out of legs. (Apparently Watson regarded crying associated with wetness and lack of food as sufficiently normal to require no emotional classification!)

In general, as the child ages, emotional expressions become less frequent. Those that occur, however, tend to be more differentiated—that is, more specific to situations as well as more clearly identifiable behaviorally. Further comments on the developmental aspects of emotional behavior are provided later in this chapter, under the specific emotions described.

DISCRIMINATION OF EMOTIONS. Popular opinion notwithstanding, experiments have consistently demonstrated that people are remarkably inefficient in judging emotions by observing behavior, *unless* they are also allowed to observe the stimulating situation. In experimental situations people serving as judges are consistently unable to discriminate emotions from facial expressions alone. Even with characteristic facial expressions designed to express particular emotional states—as stylized in acting, for example—such judges will typically confuse the emotions that are represented. In general, the more subtle emotions (e.g., pity, disdain, sympathy, suspicion) are more difficult to identify; the more common and the relatively simpler emotions (e.g., happiness, fear, anger, surprise) are easier to detect.

There are reliable differences between various cues with respect to their contribution to emotional discrimination. Consider Figure 15-2. It is apparent that the mouth contributes much more strongly to our overall impression of emotionality than the eyes, thus accounting for the fact that composite photographs (c) and (d) resemble more closely original photographs (a) and (b), respectively.

Accurate discrimination of emotions, especially of the more subtle ones, is often of considerable practical importance, as for instance in business operations like

(a)

(b)

(c)

(d)

selling, or in clinical interviews. Improvement in emotional discrimination does of course occur with practice, but rarely approaches maximal efficiency. The best insurance against making serious interpretive mistakes, which can be socially embarrassing as well as professionally or financially unsettling, is to have long experience in observing the behavior of the individual who is under observation; characteristic modes of emotional response are gradually learned by one's spouse, parent, sibling, or close friend. But such advice is of little value to the salesman or the clinician, who must most often make decisions regarding emotionality in people who are complete strangers, whose basic motivations and stimulating situations are unclear.

Love, fear, and anger in their various manifestations are generally regarded as the most important of the major emotions. Each will be considered with respect to some of the more important conclusions that can be drawn on the basis of contemporary scientific knowledge.

> ## The Major Emotions

LOVE

Monkey Love

Harlow's long-term research program on rhesus monkeys is by far the most comprehensive experimentally based attempt to conceptualize and analyze the positive affectional systems in primates. The five interlocking affectional systems that have been identified in monkeys are, in order of appearance: maternal love, infant love, peer (age-mate) love, heterosexual love, and paternal love. The systems overlap temporally. Moreover, they do seem to be functionally interdependent. Unless the infant primate has experienced the comfort and security of the mother, or some surrogate, it is unlikely to develop its own love potential for the mother. Thus maternal love and infant love are reciprocally related; love of the infant for the mother is dependent upon the prior love of the mother for her infant.

MATERNAL AND INFANT LOVE. Some interesting if anecodotal bits of evidence on the reciprocity of maternal and infant love in monkeys have been reported. In one case a young kitten was substituted for the monkey infant. The monkey mother accepted the kitten and tried valiantly to be a real mother to it. For example, she began to nurse it. Unfortunately, however, she failed as a mother and eventually lost interest in the kitten, but only for a simple but fundamental reason: the kitten was unable to cling, like the monkey infant, to the body of the mother. The failure was really in the kitten, or in the kitten's inherited behavioral repertoire. The normal monkey infant spends many hours each day clinging tightly to the ventral

15-2 Two photographs (a) and (b) of the same individual with the eyes interchanged in versions (c) and (d). How significantly do eye cues contribute to our perception of this individual's emotional state? How important are mouth cues?

part of the mother's body, suitably positioned for periodic breast feeding. In a second instance a monkey mother after a few days of preliminary effort lost interest in a badly disturbed monkey infant that engaged in autistic behavior, such as clinging to itself rather than the potential mother. The same mother later accepted completely and successfully a blind but normally clinging orphan.

As mentioned in Chapter 10, surrogate mothers of various sorts were devised in the Wisconsin Primate Laboratory to determine the maternal stimuli that are most effective in turning mother love into infant love. Wire surrogate mothers and terry-cloth surrogate mothers with wooden faces were made available to large numbers of infant monkeys, both with and without fountain service (that is, milk-producing nipples). The results of these experiments may be summarized by saying that the biological need reduction provided by the nipple is of relatively small emotional value, contrary to the presumed implications of some of the more popular psychological views on motivation, whereas the cutaneous contact provided by the cloth surrogate mother is quite clearly more effective than the austere stimulation of the wire surrogate mother. Infant monkeys, which would normally snuggle against their mother and so obtain warmth and coddling, definitely prefer the terry cloth substitute, even without milk, to the wire surrogate, even when milk and heat are also provided (see Figure 15-3).

If real or surrogate monkey mothers are not provided, so that neither of the first two types of affection develops normally, the maturing monkey is forever stunted in his emotional development. Lacking the initial affectional impulses that are normally elicited by the mother, or mother surrogate, the infant monkey is not prepared to cope with the stresses and strains of playful age mates, as its dependence upon the mother is gradually reduced. The *basic trust* that has been learned in prolonged contact with mother now apparently serves to maintain the infant's newly emerging social contact. Moreover, the body contact that the infant has long enjoyed with mother also seems to transfer to the play activities, in which substantial amounts of physical contact are inevitable.

PEER AND HETEROSEXUAL LOVE. The heterosexual stage, including sexual relationships, develops on the basis of physical contacts and emotional relationships established in play with age-mates of both sexes. The best evidence for the powerful role that prior affectional systems play in heterosexual adjustments is the utter failure in this sphere shown by monkeys that have been raised in isolation or have otherwise not enjoyed the usual give and take of peer play. Male and female monkeys reared in individual wire-mesh cages were unable to develop either infant love or peer love. Despite normal hormonal development, as measured by direct tests, and the normal occurrence of masturbatory behavior in both sexes, no heterosexual mating occurred. The damage to the affectional bonds was especially evident in the deprived males, which were unable to suppress their aggressive tendencies toward the female. They would show obvious signs of sexual arousal but were apparently then able only to engage in diffuse groping. The females, with a less active sex role, were able to display the usual sexual-presentation posture but were not able to support the mounted male; apparently they were turned off rather than on by body contact.

Thus maturation of the gonads and their hormonal stimulants is by itself

15-3 Choice of surrogate mother by baby monkey. It is clear that the baby monkey prefers the soft cloth "mother" to the wire mother even when the nursing bottle is attached to the wire surrogate. (Photo by Sponholz for The University of Wisconsin Primate Laboratory, Madison, Wisconsin.)

insufficient to insure adequate heterosexual behavior. Experimenters in the Wisconsin Primate Laboratory have identified the particular muscular components used in adult heterosexual behavior in the normal play activities of prepuberal rhesus monkeys of both sexes. These are mainly the penile erection of the male (and the corresponding but much less prominent clitoral erection of the female) and pelvic thrusting. Components of the more complex posturing required for monkey coitus have also been identified in the threat, passivity, and rigidity that are common in infant monkey play. Moreover, there are consistent sex differences with regard to the relative frequencies of these three behaviors; threatening is found to be a male prerogative and passivity and rigidity female characteristics, in keeping with the distinctly different behaviors required of male and female in sexual intercourse.

PATERNAL LOVE. The final stage of monkey affection is that of paternal love. This type of affectional bond is quite clearly more sensitive to learned than strictly biological variables. The close association between father and offspring that leads to paternal affection is apparently a by-product of the conjoint operation of maternal and heterosexual bonds; that is, it is mother love that keeps the offspring nearby during infancy; and the presence of the father is insured by the heterosexual bond between him and the mother. The mother is thus the pivotal influence in this affectional relationship, although she herself is not directly involved.

IMPLICATIONS FOR HUMAN AFFECTION. There is at least a very gross parallel between these stages of monkey affection and those of the human. Nevertheless, it is apparent that many of the details described in the monkey research cannot be carried over totally to the human case. For example, the specific components of sexual intercourse differ. In general, human affectional relationships show a great deal more variability and a far greater susceptibility to the influence of learning and culture.

Human infants are of course just as capable of love for mother and other attending adults as monkey infants, provided that the necessary stimuli are present. Moreover, they are apparently more prone to accept surrogates than monkeys, perhaps because they are less dependent upon body-contact stimulation. Observations of human infants and children at play have in one case led to the conclusion that almost identical *patterns* to those reported for monkeys do in fact occur, although the specific behaviors differ. A major difference is the much greater involvement of cognitive factors, mediated by the extensive verbalization typically occurring in human play. Moreover, the effective mediators of the transfer from peer to heterosexual affection in the human would be a very wide variety of different kinds of social behaviors and attitudes. Underlying all of these, however, the basic trust that is generated by successful interpersonal relationships is probably even more essential for humans than for monkeys; its absence in many cases of chronic maladjustment may be regarded as a prime determinant of social and personal failure, both in life generally and in sexual adjustment.

One interesting difference between monkey and human infants relates to the nature of the sensory modality that mediates effective social contact. In place of the clinging behavior that is so important to monkey infants, visual contact appears to be the effective means by which the human infant establishes social relationships. That there is also some influence of tactual sensation and clinging responses, however, is indicated by the persistence in many human infants and even children of close physical attachment to favorite blankets and teddy bears.

A more extended discussion of human love is presented in Supplement B-6.

HATE

The emotion of hate is identified as an extreme antipathy combined with an element of malice or destructive intent. The normal target of hate is some other person, or group of persons, or institution, but occasionally a person may turn this extreme aversive response upon himself; in such cases severe behavior disturbance may ensue, even to the point of suicide.

GENESIS. The effective determinant of hate is generally a frustration of one kind or another, with the intense dislike or aversion focused upon the person(s) seen as the major agent(s) in the thwarting. Thus one may come to hate one's boss, for real or imagined blocking of occupational advancement; one's sibling for excelling in studies, sports, or social attractiveness; or one's spouse for a great variety of reasons. Hate is typically combined with one or more discernible other emotions of a negative sort, such as the jealousy implied in the sibling illustration just mentioned. Most often hate seems to be mixed with anger, and to a lesser degree with fear. The former fact would of course account for the observation that hate typically involves some degree of aggressive motivation. The complexity of emotional mix that is associated with hate is suggested by some of its main synonyms, each of which carries a slightly different connotation: *loathe* (extreme dislike and disgust but minimal aggression), *detest* (violent antipathy), *abhor* (maximal repugnance, without active enmity), and *abominate* (profound detestation, with a strong hint of inability to tolerate a shameful object).

The most critical aspect of hate is its development. Rarely does so strong an emotion develop quickly, in the absence of previous emotional reactions. Typically hate grows in intensity from the accumulation of small irritations and resentments. Sometimes these resentments are harbored within a person and allowed to accumulate with little mutual animosity; that is, the hate that develops is essentially a one-sided affair. An employee, for example, may be quite careful not to allow his enmity toward his tyrannical boss to show. More often, however, there is a reciprocal development of negative emotionality. The hate of one sibling for another, or of an individual for his or her spouse, is likely to be of this mutual type.

The most important feature of such situations is the fact that *each of the participants perceives and interprets the situation from quite a different vantage point, and generally does not recognize this fact.* Thus the husband's apparently innocuous and trivial comment at the breakfast table may have no malicious intent but may be taken in quite a different manner by the wife. Should several such comments follow, the accumulation of resentment can be very rapid, with each successive comment requiring less in the way of perceived insult to arouse an emotional reaction—and eventually therefore an overtly angry retort. Receiving this kind of emotional attack in the apparent absence of any reasonable basis is of course one of the surer ways to elicit a counterattack, and a shouting match can very quickly ensue. The major ingredient for this unfortunate and all too common development is the cumulative buildup of emotional sensitivity on the basis of the mutually aggravating stimulation.

Probably the best general insurance against the development of psychologically debilitating hatred and associated aggressive behavior is the maintenance of as much openness in communication as possible, along with a studied effort to see the other side of questions and arguments. If these safeguards can be developed the mutual antagonisms, and the consequent accumulation of resentments, can be attenuated.

It should be pointed out, however, that "bringing things out in the open" is not a panacea for interpersonal friction. Some deliberately contrived communication meetings held among people who are having relationship problems do not work; in fact, the result may be to make the participants more aware of the actual reasons for their poorly articulated dislike of one another. The moral is that to understand is not necessarily to forgive or to like, but probably there is some sort of gain to be derived from placing even hostility on a realistic basis. If people are not getting along, they should at least be aware of the reasons.

ANGER

Of the various emotional states on the unpleasant side of the affective continuum, anger is possibly the least unpleasant. Perhaps the relatively mild unpleasantness associated with anger is a reflection of its typically transient character. All emotions tend to dissipate when introspectively analyzed, but none any faster than anger; it is simply not possible to remain thoroughly angry when one is simultaneously attempting to examine his emotional state. Under normal (that is, nonintrospective) conditions also, anger tends to rise and fall rapidly, as suggested by the idiomatic term *fit of anger*.

As indicated earlier, the fundamental stimulus condition eliciting anger is some kind of frustration, and especially any kind of personal attack upon oneself or a valued object. By no means all frustrating situations lead to anger, however. The responses to frustration and attack are often unpredictable, even when some knowledge of the personal characteristics of the reacting individual is available. Because of its centrality in behavioral adjustment generally as well as its central role in eliciting anger, the problem of frustration and the reactions to frustration will be considered here in some detail.

Frustration Situations.

Inevitable as it is in life, frustration as a basic process occurs in an amazing variety of forms. There are of course many ways of categorizing frustrating, or blocking, situations for human organisms. Here we select four prototypic kinds of blocks of ongoing, motivated behavior as representative of the great variety of frustrations that all of us face at one time or another.

PHYSICAL BLOCKS. This type of blocking is clearly the most primitive; frustration in such situations can be mediated by objects (e.g., the barrier imposed in the *Umweg* reasoning problem illustrated in Figure 11-4) or by living organisms, including people. In this type of frustrating situation the human thus is a blocking agent because of his *physical* presence—especially in the case of infants and children, where sheer size is a powerful determinant of behavior—much in the same way as, for example, a threatening watchdog.

SOCIAL BLOCKS. The effective block can be an institutional rule or practice of one kind or another (e.g., the requirement of a particular grade-point average or a certain sum of money for fees before admission to a course of study by a college, or the presence of a first-string football player who keeps one from playing regularly in his desired position throughout a season, or the sudden appearance of one's parents during a musical or dramatic performance). Social blocks in general are more likely to arouse emotional reactions than physical blocks, in part because of the prior opportunity one has had to develop such reactions with respect to the social agents.

PERSONAL BLOCKS. Frustration resulting from personal inadequacy, either real or imagined, is a very common phenomenon in our society. There are so many standards of various kinds to which we are exposed, and against which our performance is measured, that some degree of such frustration is inevitable.

SITUATIONAL BLOCKS: CONFLICT. The final category of frustrating modes is one that has to do directly with the situation (and often the social and personal factors in the situation) itself. When there are strong but incompatible motives acting on the individual, *conflict* is generally the outcome. Conflict is a potent frustrating condition. However, it tends to be resolved by deep-seated and often quite habitual modes of responding (such as the "defense mechanisms" first identified by Freud). Further pursuit of this topic is therefore deferred until the subject of personality (Chapter 16) can be fully treated. Although emotional reactions are of course important parts of conflicts, no unique forms appear to be involved.

Reactions to Frustration

The range of reactions to frustration is almost as great as the diversity of frustrating situations. Physical blocks or attacks (e.g., sudden intense pain produced in a caged or harnessed animal by electric shock) tend to evoke primarily physical attack or *aggression* responses (e.g., violent biting by the shocked animal, even though it is normally quite docile). More subtle types of frustrating conditions or attacks (e.g., barbed comments by one's age mates concerning inappropriate behavior) are likely to evoke reciprocating responses; the socialization process is generally quite effective in reducing the physical dimensions of aggression, although the price that is ultimately paid for such suppression of emotional expression may be much higher than is normally assumed.

Among the more common versions of the subtle, socialized response to frustration, with or without an anger component, is that of *displaced aggression.* Displacement of aggression occurs when an initially irrelevant and logically unrelated target bears the brunt of the aggressive counterattack; it is more likely to occur, of course, when the relevant and logical target, the initial attacker or frustrating agent, is either too big and powerful to be effectively counterattacked or social pressures prevent a direct response. The *scapegoat* is such a substitute target for aggression (e.g., the Jews in Germany after the defeat by the Allied powers in World War I). A complex fabrication of justifications sometimes accompanies scapegoating behavior. When anger is turned inward much in the way that hate can be under seriously disturbed emotional conditions, *suicide* is a possible consequence of displaced aggression. If no such definite targets are attacked, completely innocent victims are apparently sometimes hit after a long period of brooding; the occasional shooting sprees of persons who go berserk and strike out at groups of strangers in explosive rage reactions may be regarded as possible occurrences of such *chronic anger.* The variable and unpredictable character of such outbursts is illustrated by the two mass murders of the summer of 1966 (eight girls at a student nursing home in Chicago and the shooting spree at the University of Texas in which sixteen persons were killed and an additional thirty wounded).

A variety of other types of reactions to frustration and attack can occur, with varying degrees of emotional involvement but without either direct or indirect attack or aggression. *Fixation,* represented by stereotyped and often repetitive behavior, may occur, especially when there is a substantial element of surprise in the attack. *Regression,* which is a return to earlier and often childlike behavior, is another type of response. *Withdrawal,* or retreat, can also occur but has many diverse means of expression: for example, *fantasy,* in which substitute satisfactions and victories may be won without the risks of battle in the real world; or, more positively, the attacked organism may simply accept defeat by showing *submission*. Ceremonial forms of submissive behavior are common ways of ending combat in the animal world and serve the important function of settling disputes over mates and territories without the risk of serious physical damage; in humans submissive postures and crying are human counterparts.

More positive responses to frustration and attack are also quite possible and much to be desired. They may be considered as types of problem solving, with objective analysis of the situation and the roles of the participants.

Control of Anger

Although no precise set of directives can be provided for the effective control of anger a few broad guidelines and some comments about common social practices can be offered.

The most commonly used social technique is punishment, which is a form of counteraggression. It would be foolish to hold that punishment does not afford some deterrent to the undesirable behavioral products of anger (direct aggression, especially), but there is little evidence that its efficacy is even approximately equal to that often assumed for it. Moreover, fear is an almost inevitable and usually quite undesirable concomitant of punishment. Thus in spite of the ease of its application, which helps to account for its popularity among controlling agents such as parents and teachers, punishment is best used sparingly for control of anger as well as other proscribed behaviors.

The objective analysis mentioned above as a positive, socially effective reaction to frustration and attack is, ideally, the best way to handle anger. Unfortunately, however, not only is it difficult to instill in people as a habitual response, it is unlikely to be employed during the peak of the anger reaction. It follows that any way that the anger response can be managed without potentially self-defeating counterattacks will help to enable one to survive this critical initial period. Because the peak of an anger reaction usually passes rather quickly, such popular maxims as "count to ten" before taking action or making irrevocable decisions have considerable merit. Indulging in physical action of an innocuous sort, such as simply taking a walk, permits one to work off some of the emotional tension (and may have the additional function of removing one at least momentarily from the emotion-eliciting stimuli and targets of aggression). The "cooling-off" period thus provided is an indispensable prerequisite to the development of sober second thoughts and the application of reasonable objectivity.

Like other emotions, anger is best prevented, rather than "cured," although it must be admitted that under some stimulating conditions a certain amount of anger is not only justifiable but personally therapeutic. The vast majority of anger reactions, nonetheless, are events without which one would probably be much better off. How to avoid such unnecessary anger? Here we can make two sorts of general comments.

First, with regard to the critical problem of how to handle anger and temper tantrums in children, the best advice is to ignore them (which is, unfortunately, very difficult for many parents to do, even if they "know better"). This avoids giving the child the attention that he is often after. In other words, parents and other controlling adults need to avoid the reinforcement of anger outbursts. Simply ignoring them, as far as possible, while attempting to insure that no physical damage is done to the child or any targets of his anger, is generally the most effective procedure. Attempting to replace the anger outburst by a socially more desirable behavior is even better but this course runs more risks. For example, if one offers the angry child another plaything, to replace the one he just hurled against the wall (or against baby brother), he may be able to elicit more satisfactory responses to it but at the same time he may have reinforced the temper tantrum itself.

Second, with regard to adolescent and adult anger the best insurance would seem to be avoidance of the prior annoyances and resentments that accumulate to produce the "chips" on the shoulder that predispose one to real anger. If one can keep such sensitive issues from smouldering into the ultimate flames of anger and rage by means of open communication and objectivity his chances of mature emotional status are immeasurably enhanced.

FEAR

More attention has probably been paid by psychologists to the fear emotion than to all the other emotions combined, and with good reason. By all odds, fear in its various forms is the most chronic and the most difficult emotion to control, and may very well do more psychological harm than all the other emotions combined. Theoretically, fear has been generally identified as the flight or withdrawal component of the "flight-fight" dichotomy of emotional reactivity. The primitive character of this kind of behavior is suggested by zoological research indicating that for each of the common mammalian species there exists a characteristic "flight distance," a distance within which a wild animal will not permit another animal, such as a human, to approach without taking flight. Although such primitive and

---

Take a Breather

WORD ASSOCIATIONS

One of the oldest and simplest of the tests of emotionality is that of word associations. Here are some sample items from one well-known set of word association norms based on a sample of 1,000 students in an introductory college psychology class.

Copy the list of words below on a sheet of paper, writing after each stimulus word the *very first word* that comes to mind. After you have completed this task turn to the box on p. 477 for instructions on the interpretation of your responses.

bitter	wish	river
chair	this	spider
dream	street	joy
king	scissors	guns

presumably innate tendencies are overlaid in adult humans with learning, a somewhat similar phenomenon may be observed in the fact that an infant or young child will generally permit a strange (and potentially fear-producing) stimulus to be brought to within a certain distance, but only to that point, before his curiosity is suddenly overcome by withdrawal.

Sources of Fear

INFANCY. The classical research on fear during infancy was performed by the behaviorist John Watson in the 1920's. Watson's conclusion was that in the infant, fear reactions could be produced by two types of stimulation, removal of physical support and a sudden loud noise. He therefore concluded that fear has a very limited inherited basis and that most if not all adult fears are attributable to learning. Moreover, the kind of learning involved was, according to Watson, a straightforward form of classical conditioning, as described below (and in Chapter 11).

MATURATION. As the child matures a great variety of new sources of fear emerge. Whether these can be entirely attributed to learning, as Watson thought, or whether inherited factors are also directly responsible cannot be determined readily. Certainly some fears are quite clearly due to the special circumstances of an individual's experience and so may be said to be learned; but even in such cases the contribution of biological inheritance cannot be disregarded, as is pointed out in the consideration of the so-called nature–nurture problem (Chapter 9). In any event it seems best to acknowledge that the emotional reactions of the maturing individual, and in particular the fear reactions, are a complex product of both biological and experiential conditions.

The major component in the increased susceptibility to fear that accompanies maturation is cognitive. More specifically, one increasingly realizes the nature of various kinds of threatening conditions that must be coped with as he matures intellectually. Thus the essentially fearless infant or young child tends to develop first caution and eventually fear as he ages.

One particularly important source of fear in the developing animal is visual novelty; unfamiliar objects and organisms constitute fear stimuli for many organisms. In animals, also, there seems to be a fear of approaching objects.

LEARNING. Watson performed the first systematic research on the learning of fear. In a famous experiment he trained an eleven-month-old infant, named Albert, to fear a white rat. Prior tests demonstrated that Albert, who was an unusually calm and generally happy little boy, had no apparent fear of the rat or a wide range of similar stimuli. Fear training consisted of the experimenter presenting the white rat to Albert. As he reached out for it, a metal bar was struck behind his head, making a loud sound. When this first trial did not produce fear in Albert a second trial was administered. Now Albert showed a strong startle reaction and whimpered. After a week interval subsequent trials were given and Albert then cried whenever he was shown the rat.

The demonstration of the acquisition of fear-producing properties by a number of objects that were similar in some way to the white rat was an important secondary result of this early research. Watson found that after the training Albert

Breather Interpretation

WORD ASSOCIATIONS

In the table below are listed some of the more common responses that college students make to the stimulus words listed on the Breather. The appearance of a very idiosyncratic response (highly individualistic or unusual) is *suggestive* of *potential* emotionality relating to that stimulus. However, it should be apparent that such individualistic responses are also characteristic of highly creative persons. Definitive interpretation of this kind of response data therefore requires additional information, such as that provided by the "complex indicators" (see p. 485), which cannot be measured in this simple exercise.

The four most common responses of 500 male and 500 female college students are given. Note that the predominant responses tend to be words that represent synonyms (e.g., *street–road*), opposites (e.g., *bitter–sweet*), properties (e.g., *scissors–cut*), familiar pairs (e.g., *king–queen*), or simply common sequences (e.g., *this–is*).

If class norms are prepared from the distribution of all of the individual scores (total number of common responses) each student can obtain some idea of his own relative standing on that measure.

Stimulus Word	Most Common Responses (Male frequency on left, female on right)			
bitter	sweet 277, 267	sour 56, 93	taste 25, 18	lemon 11, 10
chair	table 190, 238	sit 122, 102	seat 32, 16	soft 13, 20
dream	sleep 247, 238	night 24, 28	wish 18, 29	nightmare 11, 20
king	queen 301, 350	crown 29, 19	ruler 8, 13	England 5, 9
wish	want 54, 95	dream 60, 66	hope 50, 38	will 41, 29
this	that 188, 256	is 128, 124	thing 21, 10	here 11, 10
street	road 58, 60	car 50, 49	avenue 38, 42	cars 25, 34
scissors	cut 352, 326	sharp 53, 51	paper 16, 23	cloth 14, 21
river	water 156, 130	stream 79, 75	Mississippi 42, 47	lake 36, 44
spider	web 203, 175	bug 63, 73	insect 69, 49	legs 26, 25
joy	happy 132, 128	happiness 81, 105	sorrow 72, 62	Christmas 14, 21
guns	shoot 102, 99	bullets 38, 53	fire 29, 34	ammunition 17, 19

From D. S. Palermo and J. J. Jenkins, *Word association norms: Grade school through college* (Minneapolis: University of Minnesota Press, 1964).

showed fear reactions to such initially innocuous stimuli as a dog, a rabbit, a fur coat, and a wool or cotton object; like the white rat, these had been shown to be neutral or even positive stimuli. It was clear that the emotion of fear could not only be very quickly learned, with appropriate arrangements of stimuli, but that such learning could also readily involve, through the process called *generalization* (cf. Chapter 11), a very broad spectrum of other similar stimuli.

PUNISHMENT. Of all the sources of fear in our society one of the most significant is punishment. A great deal of attention has been paid to this particular operation within recent years because of its prominence as a means of behavior control. In the home and the school punishment is likely to be used in a direct and explicit manner, whereas in many other facets of society it is more likely to be manipulated through threat (as in the business world, for example, where the threat of loss of occupational status may be much more potent than any actual losses). In any event fear is an almost inevitable concomitant of punishment and threat of punishment.

Because of the ethical problems associated with the application of strong, persistent punishment to humans, most of this kind of research has been performed with animal subjects. One such experiment, which was described in Chapter 10, is especially noteworthy because it suggests the range of problems that are susceptible to experimental attack with animals. In this experiment eighteen-month-old beagle dogs were trained to discriminate between two kinds of food, a highly preferred food (canned meat), which they were punished for eating, and the customary dry laboratory chow, which they were permitted to eat. The punishment consisted of a smart swat on the snout with a tightly rolled newspaper, administered by the experimenter from his position on a nearby chair. The main variable manipulated was delay of the punishment. One group of dogs was punished immediately, as soon as their mouths touched the tabooed meat. Other groups were punished after 5 or 15 seconds of eating the meat. The experimenters were interested in studying the effects of delays of punishment. Their dependent variable was the dogs' resistance to temptation, as measured by their eating the meat in test sessions during which the experimenter was absent from the room.

The main results of this experiment were that the longer intervals of delay of punishment during training resulted in substantially less resistance to temptation in this group of dogs, even though they were just as effective in training the dogs to avoid the tabooed food during training as the immediate punishment. Furthermore, the immediate-punishment dogs showed a much greater level of fearfulness in training *before* beginning to eat the dry chow, even backing off from it repeatedly at first. Once they started to eat, however, they did so quite normally, gulping down the food with head in dish and tail vigorously wagging. The long-delay dogs, on the contrary, showed no signs of fear as they entered the room or approached the food but became quite fearful, completely in accord with the punishment conditions of their training, after they had snatched a few pellets from the dish; they would characteristically crawl behind the experimenter's chair, urinate and defecate, and circle the room on their bellies before returning to snatch a few more pellets from the food dish. In general, the fear evidenced by these animals during training persisted into the test sessions; and the researchers reported that they seemed to behave then as though the experimenter were still actually in the room.

The immediate-punishment animals, on the other hand, ate the tabooed horsemeat voraciously and with no signs of fear once they broke the taboo during the test.

Control of Fear

A certain amount of fear, or at least caution, is obviously desirable, in view of the multiple hazards that exist in even the most stable society. As suggested, however, the amount of fear that many individuals exhibit is disproportionately large in relation to the actual dangers, as well as to a great extent inappropriately related to objects in the real world. Apart from the very serious personality disturbances that can be aggravated if not entirely produced by such emotional reactions, considered in Chapter 16, the typical individual pays a very high price in personal happiness and general adjustment for his excessive fear. The fearful child, for example, is simply unable to develop his potential, intellectually or otherwise. Moreover, unreasonable fear, once established, can have pervasive and far-reaching future effects long after the initial fear has been lost and forgotten; a slow start in arithmetic, for example, apparently correlated with fear of numerical operations, can permanently cripple a student insofar as subsequent appreciation of mathematical achievements is concerned.

COUNTERCONDITIONING. For these many reasons psychologists have long been concerned with the problem of how to eliminate or at least reduce unreasonable fears. Watson himself turned to this problem in his research after demonstrating how readily fear conditioning can occur. He found the method of *counterconditioning*—or replacement of the aversive fear response with a positive response—to be the most effective means of eliminating fear. To illustrate, we may return once more to Albert, Watson's favorite subject. By keeping the aversive stimulus, the white rat, at a relatively safe distance Watson was able to keep the conditioned fear reaction from occurring. Then he introduced, in the presence of the white rat, an extremely positive stimulus, a chocolate bar. By gradually bringing the white rat closer while the child was reacting positively to the chocolate bar Watson was able to reduce the amount of fear it produced. But this process is a slow and difficult one, especially as contrasted with the speed of the emotional conditioning; it therefore requires much more patience and skill. There is always the danger that the conditioning process will go the wrong way. If the white rat, or other fear stimulus, should be brought too quickly up to the subject (as many parents and teachers would be tempted to do), the resulting fear reaction can quickly transfer to the positive stimulus itself, and a new fear stimulus be produced rather than an old one eliminated.

Counterconditioning requires a high degree of knowledge and skill, and a carefully contrived situation. This technique is therefore of restricted practicality. Unfortunately, however, most of the other more commonly used attempts to reduce fear are almost uniformly ineffective.

DISUSE. The simplest procedure is that of *disuse*—the fear stimulus is avoided so that it does not have the opportunity to acquire renewed vigor. Put more positively, the subject either actively attempts to avoid the fear object or others attempt to shield him from it. Suppose that, for one reason or another, an individual has a strong and unreasonable fear of elevators or escalators. Suppose further that he is able to avoid these objects, by regularly using stairs, so that the vigor of the emotional fear reaction is not renewed. Does it decrease over time? Unhappily, no. Not to any significant extent, at least. Emotional conditioning seems to be remarkably resistant to forgetting; merely avoiding relevant stimuli without taking more positive steps to eliminate them as fear stimuli rarely results in any substantial reduction of their effectiveness.

The persistence of emotional reactions of this kind was demonstrated in an early study of conditioning of the *galvanic skin response* (GSR). This is the change in electrical conductivity of the skin produced in emotional arousal and measured by electronic devices. Certain words used as stimuli in a free-association situation were associated with electric shock. Although these words were subsequently recalled less often than control (nonshocked) stimuli, they continued to produce an unmistakable GSR in the subjects. This result occurred not only after a short interval (5 minutes) but also after a much longer interval (2 weeks), and subsequent research has indicated a much longer, almost indefinitely prolonged persistence of such emotional reactivity.

OTHER ATTEMPTS AT CONTROLLING FEAR. Another commonly attempted technique is just the opposite of disuse; *frequent application* of the feared stimulus may be tried in an effort to extinguish its effectiveness. Some amelioration may occur with this technique, but it comes only slowly and after a very long period of stimulation. Moreover, there is some danger that strengthening rather than weakening of the fear will occur, especially with younger subjects.

Perhaps the least effective of all techniques, but at the same time unfortunately one of the most commonly attempted, is that of *verbal appeal*. A parent, for example, will simply appeal to the child, by saying that he or she "shouldn't" be afraid of such and such an object. Needless to say, the value of such an approach is essentially unrelated to the magnitude of effort expended. Moreover, such verbal appeals may serve to aggravate and intensify the fear, by calling attention to it and arousing cognitive factors related to it; at best, they prevent more effective measures from being taken.

A related but potentially even more damaging technique is that of *ridicule*. Especially when combined with sarcasm, as by parents or teachers, ridicule is likely to be harmful. It is intrinsically ineffective for the same basic reasons as verbal appeal, because it attempts to invoke the purely cognitive and voluntary aid of the subject in what is fundamentally an involuntary, autonomic function. Moreover, there is again a serious risk of conditioning going the wrong way; thus, for example, other persons with whom one is scornfully compared may become fear stimuli themselves, as a result of the emotionality elicited in connection with their naming.

A somewhat more hopeful technique is to bring in *social models*—nonfearful individuals whose normal reactions to the fear stimulus might be copied by the fearful child. Certainly this behavioral technique is far safer than the verbal comparison, even when scorn and ridicule are not involved, because it allows the subject to experience, along with the model whom he is supposed to imitate, the reality of the feared stimulus. Like counterconditioning, however, this technique requires a high level of skill and much patience and is also subject to a reversal of conditioning (that is, if the undesirable emotional response occurs it may transfer to the model).

Finally, it should be noted that anything that will help an individual to acquire *improved skills* with which he can cope with problems generally is likely to aid in the reduction of his fearfulness. Although this point does not address itself directly to any particular fear stimulus, the inappropriateness of fear responses to many stimuli is much more likely to be appreciated by secure and otherwise well-adjusted individuals. This point is especially relevant to young children; preschool nursery experience, for example, may so improve the coping skills of a child that many of his previous fears appear to diminish more or less of their own accord. And this desirable result is much more likely to occur, given the suggested improvement, if the fear reactions themselves have not been aggravated by the well-meaning but misdirected corrective efforts of adults.

Worry and Anxiety

Thus far in the discussion of fear as a primary emotion we have focused on emotional reactions to more or less specific stimuli. In humans especially, however, there are various related forms of negative emotionality that have less definite stimuli and more cognitive involvement, especially over a relatively long temporal span. Worry and anxiety are the most prominent of the labels given these attenuated forms of fear and associated emotions.

Worry can be identified as a kind of self-torment in which anticipation of unpleasant consequences predominates; the degree of specificity can vary over an enormously wide spectrum in worry, from highly specific distress concerning a particular physical symptom to the vaguest of premonitions of evil. *Anxiety* refers to a much more diffuse and highly generalized distress in which the source of fear is sometimes not at all identifiable; the term *free-floating anxiety* is often used to describe this extreme form. Anxiety seems to be a product of unresolved conflict and is characteristically marked by prolonged, intermittent arousal of some degree of tension. Because there are so many sources of conflict in any complex society anxiety is a most prevalent emotion of adult humans. Unhappy humans are thus much more frequently the victims of their own worries and anxieties than of more specific fears.

The origins of anxiety in particular can be traced to infancy. During the sixth month of human life the sight of a strange face typically produces a diffuse distress reaction called *stranger anxiety.* The infant may cry at the strange face, stop when it disappears, and begin again as soon as it reappears. Fortunately, by the twelfth month or so this kind of anxious reaction has usually weakened, soon to disappear. Lest the prospective parent who reads this rejoice too soon, however, attention must be called to another form of infant anxiety, which typically becomes evident around the tenth month. This reaction is called *separation anxiety.* It characteristically occurs whenever the infant's mother leaves him, or even appears to be about to do so. Its occurrence in monkeys, even those whose mothers have been surrogate, suggests a high degree of incidence among higher mammalian forms at least. Again, crying and general agitation are typical of separation anxiety, and these symptoms begin to diminish once the infant begins to develop increased perceptual and motor controls of his own.

One of the more interesting features of anxiety in adult humans is its negligible occurrence under conditions of strict regimentation. Thus prisoners, who have few important decisions to make, are frequently found to be relatively free of anxiety. The same thing can be said of many mental patients, once their initial entry into an institution is completed. Anxieties begin to develop, however, if the regimentation is relaxed and the patients are given more latitude in making choices of various kinds. All these observations support the general conclusion relating anxiety to unresolved conflicts.

The Physiology of Emotion

We have had numerous occasions to refer to the physiological bases of emotionality throughout this chapter because of the intimate relationship between these changes and emotional reactivity. In this section we take a closer look at two particularly important facets of the physiology of emotion. These are the preparatory reactions associated with the sympathetic branch of the autonomic nervous system and the problem of detection of emotionality by physiological measures, popularly but inaccurately called lie detection. In Supplement B-3 we pursue the related matter of excessive emotionality and its ultimate disturbance of personal adjustment by means of physiological changes: the topic of psychosomatic illness.

EMERGENCY REACTIONS: THE SYMPATHETIC PATTERN

Physiological reactions of the body in emotion are in general concerned with preparation of the body for physical action. Arousal of the sympathetic division of the autonomic nervous system accounts for these effects. The major physiological changes are the following: The arteries in the large skeletal muscles relax, thus permitting an increased flow of blood, at the same time as the arteries supplying the digestive tract contract, reducing the blood flow; the net effect is to shunt increasing amounts of blood to the large muscles, an action that is facilitated by the immediate increase in both heart rate and blood pressure (subjectively felt as a "pounding heart"). The respiration rate also increases, resulting in faster acquisition of fresh oxygen. The improved circulation to the large muscles thus makes possible a higher and more efficient level of physical activity by bringing in more oxygen and removing fatigue products more quickly. The same effect is achieved by the breaking down of stored sugars in the liver, and their transport to the muscles by the bloodstream. Another change is faster clotting time of the blood, an effect that helps to insure recovery if serious wounds occur. Other changes less directly related to physical activity but potentially of value include the raising of hairs (hackles, in dogs or cats, which are more visible than the weaker effect in man), increased sweating, and enlargement of the pupils of the eyes.

The changes described as a function of the sympathetic division of the autonomic nervous system are in general opposite to those induced by action of the parasympathetic division of that system. Whereas the sympathetic system is activated as part of the preparation of the body for action, the parasympathetic system is concerned with maintenance of the basic physiological functions that may be classified as vegetative in nature. The two systems for the most part innervate the same organs, and their action is generally reciprocal rather than merely antagonistic; increased sympathetic activation, as in a typical state of emotional arousal, is accompanied by reduced parasympathetic function. The beautifully precise manner in which these various internal regulatory processes are normally adjusted to keep the organism in tune with external environmental forces has led to the concept of *homeostasis,* which refers to the reciprocal or compensatory bodily adjustments made on the basis of feedback mechanisms.

An interesting aspect of the emotional emergency process is that it is impossible, on the basis of the physiological effects themselves, to discriminate between emotional and nonemotional determinants. In other words, the same physiological changes appear to occur in emotion as in normal physical activity. Thus, for example, whether one is running from sheer fright or as a part of preplanned action in a contest cannot be determined from any differences in the visceral or autonomic patterns themselves.

Although it was long believed that different emotional states could not be differentiated on the basis of any discriminable patterns of physiological function, some results are now beginning to appear that suggest such differences might be eventually demonstrable. Thus far the differences have been measured mostly as differential excretions of two of the hormones secreted by the adrenal gland. For example, greater amounts of norepinephrine have been reported in hockey players in active competition and in psychiatric patients showing aggressive outbursts, whereas greater amounts of epinephrine have been found in nonparticipating hockey players and in psychiatric patients merely attending staff conferences. Thus the suggestion is that norepinephrine is produced in greater amounts under anger (fight) conditions and epinephrine in greater amounts under fear (flight) conditions. Subjects watching films designed to evoke emotion (comedies, tragedies) excreted more of both hormones when compared to those watching documentary films.

Indirect support for the differential effect of these two hormones is also available from pharmacological studies. In general, those drugs that inactivate norepinephrine in the brain produce sedation or depression, whereas those drugs that potentiate norepinephrine generally have an opposite, excitatory effect in man. As indicated later, it is possible by injection of these hormones to mimic the various autonomic functions normally produced by emotion or physical activity.

Simulation of the autonomic changes in emotion can also be produced by electrical stimulation of appropriate parts of the brain. Activation of the hypothalamus results in either emotional (sympathetic) or vegetative (parasympathetic) simulation, depending upon which part is stimulated; the back half is associated with sympathetic and the front half with parasympathetic functioning.

"LIE DETECTION": THE POLYGRAPH

What popularly passes as a "lie detector" is really, as suggested earlier, nothing of the sort. The term is a misnomer because lies cannot be directly detected. Rather, what is done is to attempt to detect undue emotional arousal in connection with certain kinds of stimuli; the presumption is that when emotionality occurs under the appropriate circumstances lying is one of the determinants that can be inferred. But this procedure is, at best, inferential and circumstantial and for this reason is not ordinarily admitted as legal evidence.

Because multiple physiological indicants are used, and simultaneous records are recorded automatically by a polygraph, the term *polygraph* is preferable to the less accurate term *lie detector*. The emotional changes that are most apt to accompany lying, and thus are most often measured by the polygraph, are galvanic skin response (GSR), respiration rate, heart rate, and blood pressure. In addition, measures of generalized skeletal muscle tension may be taken.

When properly administered, by a well-trained practitioner, the polygraph can be extremely useful as a diagnostic aid in various kinds of investigations. Let us suppose, for example, that a robbery has occurred in a small store and that the circumstances are such that the prime suspect is one or more of the employees who had access to the materials stolen. Suppose further that only the employer, the police, and the guilty employee(s) know exactly what was stolen. By subjecting each of the employees to a polygraph test in which the names of some of the items actually stolen are mixed in with a number of otherwise comparable but nonstolen (control) items, the investigator has a good chance of obtaining fairly suggestive evidence. The extent to which any one of the employees evidences an unusual amount of emotionality when given the names of the stolen items *as compared with the other items* constitutes the extent to which suspicion points to him. The implication is that he has a degree of guilty knowledge that must be accounted for somehow; the most plausible explanation is that he is indeed implicated in the robbery.

The more such crucial items can be used as stimuli, the greater the likelihood that significant information will be uncovered, because any one item, like any one physiological measure, cannot be given as much weight as a pattern of items, or of measures. For these reasons a battery of indicants as well as a variety of items is used; sometimes one and sometimes the other physiological measure will prove most useful. There are wide individual differences in the degree to which people show emotionality. Some, for example, with relatively higher natural levels of emotionality require much more preliminary work, so that a "normal" baseline of emotional expression can be determined before the real stimuli are interpolated among the neutral items. Hardened criminals, or just plain citizens with low levels of emotional expressibility, may be much more difficult as subjects. There are enough technical problems associated with the operation of the polygraph to require a considerable amount of expertise in the investigator who is responsible for its use.

In spite of these problems and the various uncertainties connected with its application, the polygraph has proved to be a useful investigative device. The extent to which normal subjects cannot "beat" it when motivated to do so is suggested by the results of one experiment. Twenty subjects from a medical school were each offered a reward of $10 if they could avoid detection of guilt when only their GSR was taken. After the principle of the device was explained they were given practice trials. They were even instructed as to the best way of avoiding detection (i.e., giving high GSR's to false stimuli). They were then given questions of simple facts, with only one alternative of four being true. Not a single one was able to avoid revealing his knowledge, as measured by a stronger GSR to the crucial items. This result suggests the difficulty of practicing deception even when the subjects are strongly motivated and relatively knowledgeable.

The most common use of the polygraph in police investigative work is as an aid in obtaining confessions when the suspect is confronted with the results of the tests. The false aura of invulnerability that is popularly associated with lie detection devices is probably responsible for a large part of this success.

Emotion Indicators

Although more applicable to research utilization than investigation of guilt, word-association tests by themselves provide another useful way to detect emotionality. When free association is used, so that the subject is told simply to respond with whatever comes to mind as each verbal stimulus is given, there are a number of fairly reliable indicators of emotion (sometimes called *complex indicators,* in psychiatric jargon). The value of these lies in their ease of application, so that even relatively untrained persons can use them; as will be evident from the examples given, these behavioral indicators of emotion are commonly identified by many persons with no special expertise but simply some experience with emotionality. All that is required to make this technique scientifically useful is some regularity of stimulus presentation and careful recording of responses, most notably the use of a timer.

Among the more important behavioral indicators of emotionality in word association testing are the following. Any failure to respond (or a very slow response) suggests emotion. The subject may then attempt to cover up this cue by such artifices as pretending he did not hear the word, saying he thought it was really a different word, and asking a question, relevant or irrelevant. Even more obviously, of course, any overtly emotional behavior, such as blushing, lowering the eyes, or stuttering, points clearly to some emotional connection, or affective loading for the item. Perseveration in responding, such as giving the same response as has just been given to another word, is another suggestive sign. Variations in reaction time are also suggestive; even slight hesitation, coming after a succession of rapid responses, or perhaps an unusually rapid response, are cues. These require especially careful scrutiny and perhaps even statistical analysis of the data. Finally, the nature of the responses themselves may be examined, although this kind of analysis (typically used in psychoanalytic techniques) must be done with great caution. The most common method is to score the degree of commonality of responses, basing such scoring on well-established norms of word frequencies for a given population; very unusual words, those with high idiosyncratic value, are perhaps the most frequent indicators of potential emotional connections.

Although the word-association test has proved extremely useful in research, its utility is greatly enhanced when it is combined with a more direct physiological assessment, such as that provided by the polygraph. Overt behavioral cues and differential visceral reactivity can then be jointly assessed and more accurate estimates of emotional involvement thereby obtained.

Major Theories

In describing representative samples of the major theories relating to emotion we shall categorize the classical theories in terms of their focus—experiential, behavioral, or physiological. We shall then describe some versions of the more recent cognitively based interpretations.

THE JAMES–LANGE THEORY. The American psychologist-philosopher William James and the Danish physiologist Carl Lange independently proposed a kind of visceral-feedback theory of emotion (in 1884 and 1885, respectively). Because of its contradiction of the common-sense view this theory attracted a great deal of attention. Moreover, a considerable amount of scientific support was developed for the theory and it continues to be a viable even if now overshadowed interpretation. Fundamentally, the James–Lange theory holds that felt emotion is a direct reflection of body responses, and especially the reactivity of the visceral organs affected by the autonomic nervous system. James's famous example was the stimulus of meeting a bear in the woods. His theory of the emotional arousal in this kind of situation is that *"the bodily changes follow directly the perception of the exciting fact, and that our feeling of the same changes as they occur is the emotion"* (James, 1905, p. 448). Thus it is the trembling and associated visceral responses that cause the fear rather than vice versa.

Many objections have been raised to the James–Lange theory. For one thing, visceral responses are extremely slow in developing and could not possibly therefore be the sole direct determinant of fast-developing emotional feelings. For another, there is the generally diffuse state of visceral reactivity in emotionality, with no specific patterns associated with different emotions. By including proprioceptive feedback from the skeletal (voluntary) musculature, however, as a complement to visceral changes the weight of these criticisms can be reduced. Not only are skeletal muscular changes very rapid (tightening up immediately to a startle stimulus, for example), but they do display a considerable degree of patterned specificity in different kinds of situations.

BEHAVIORAL THEORIES. No single behaviorally oriented theory has succeeded in attracting as much attention as the James–Lange theory. Emotion is said by some behavioral theorists to be caused by conflict that is aroused when an organism is stimulated to make incompatible responses. Other theorists define emotion in terms of the disruption of organized behavior. These theories suffer from difficulties in operational specification of conflict as well as a bias toward a particular kind of emotionality (that is, conflict theories are most directly applicable to anxiety arousal, as we have already noted). Disruption-of-organization theories of emotion also stress the behavioral measures and can each account for a certain type of data. But neither of these behavioral theories is generally recognized as complete.

PHYSIOLOGICAL THEORIES. In response to the James–Lange theory the physiologist W. B. Cannon enumerated a large number of objections and then proposed his own theory of emotions. Sometimes known as the Cannon–Bard theory, this view holds that emotional *feeling* is a result of stimulation of the dorsal *thalamus* and emotional *behavioral expression* a function of the *hypothalamus*. (See p. 21 for a review of these anatomical structures.) The major experimental support for this theory is the fact that "sham" behaviors (overt emotional expressions in the apparent absence of any appropriate stimulation) can be produced in cats whose cerebrum has been removed, but not in cats whose thalamic structures were also removed. Electrical stimulation of these parts of the brain in experimental animals produces both visceral and overt behavioral responses characteristic of normal emotion. Further, clinical evidence from human patients with thalamic damage indicates unusual reactivity to quite trivial stimulation, such as pinpricks, suggesting a close relationship to emotionality.

THE LIMBIC THEORY. A more recent neurophysiological theory of emotion holds that emotion is a function of the activation of the limbic area of the forebrain. The theory is largely based on the relationship between the limbic area and visceral responsivity that has been demonstrated by means of modern sophisticated electronic technology. This theory is able to incorporate portions of the earlier leading neurophysiological theories, the James–Lange (which left out the brain) and the Cannon–Bard (which identified the wrong part of the brain).

One more recent entry of a neurophysiological sort deserves mention. This is the application of the activation theory, involving the ascending reticular activating system (ARAS; see also p. 143 ff.) to the problem of emotion. When stimulated, the lower brainstem reticular formation seems to produce emotional-type responses in both the skeletal musculature and the viscera; its close connection with the hypothalamus is also suggestive of a relationship to emotionality. Further, chronic apathy is produced in an animal whose anterior reticular formation is removed, indicating the possibility of its participation in emotional arousal. These observations and theoretical suggestions help to implicate the brainstem as a critical agent in emotionality, but the complete interpretation of emotion remains a task for the future.

THE ROLE OF COGNITION. A recent series of experiments has helped to fill in the gap left in all of the physiologically oriented theories and supporting experimental research. In brief, emotional expression is quite possible in the absence of any truly emotional feelings (e.g., by an accomplished actor or actress). Research using epinephrine injected into human subjects demonstrated this possibility. Most of the subjects (71 per cent in this study) reported no emotion but only a stirred-up internal condition. Of the remainder many reported a "cold" kind of emotionality as a result of the visceral reactivity produced by this hormone; it was "as if" the subject were experiencing or about to experience an emotion, but not at all the same as in fact experiencing some emotion.

The most notable recent experimental attack upon this problem has been performed by a group of social psychologists. Intrigued by the fact that such a variety of reports of feeling states could result from exactly the same dose of epinephrine, these psychologists proceeded to explore the way in which cognitive determinants interact with physiological factors in producing emotionality.

The rationale underlying this research program is that a human subject will label any state of emotionality produced by physiological arousal in accordance with the cognitions that he has available. Control subjects received placebos (innocuous injections) and experimental subjects were actually given an injection of epinephrine so as to produce the full set of physiological events associated with activation of the sympathetic nervous system. Some of the experimental subjects were informed of the "side effects" of the injection that they should expect (shaking hands, pounding heart, and so on); others were not informed of these effects. Each subject was then placed alone in a room with a stooge who demonstrated either extreme euphoria (flew paper airplanes, kept up a constant patter, and so on) or extreme anger (tore up an irritating questionnaire on which he had been working and stalked out of the room in a rage). During this period the subject was observed by means of a one-way vision screen. He was subsequently asked to answer standardized scales to assess his degree of anger or euphoria.

The prediction made by the experimenters was that subjects given epinephrine and so aroused physiologically but without anticipation of any such effects would be more acutely influenced by the mood of the stooge than either the control subjects, with no internal activation, or experimental subjects who were told to expect some side effects. This is essentially what happened. Both anger and euphoria were clearly evidenced to a greater degree in the experimental subjects without cognitive structure. In other experiments different emotional states, such as amusement and fear, were readily induced by the combination of epinephrine injection without appropriate information as to its consequences.

One final example of this kind of recent experimental research may be described because of its variance with the common-sense interpretation. The subjects were all persons bothered by insomnia. They were asked to take a pill shortly before retiring in order to assess its influence on their dreaming. Actually the pill was a placebo, perfectly harmless and with no particular effect. Half of the subjects were told that the pill would keep them intensely aroused, the other half that it would relax them. Although the common-sense interpretation mentioned would predict that the subjects who expected to be aroused had more difficulty in sleeping, because of suggestibility, the results were actually in the other direction, and in accordance with the prediction based upon the cognitive view of emotionality. The presumption is that the subjects who were expecting to be aroused were able to attribute their normal tension to the pill, and so were able to relax more quickly and sleep, whereas the subjects who were led to expect relaxation were more likely to attribute their keyed-up feelings to their own emotionality and so had greater trouble in sleeping.

It is clear that no one of the various classes of theories yet proposed is sufficiently broad and complex to encompass all of the manifold empirical evidence now available, but certainly full recognition must be paid to the role of cognitive as well as physiological determinants in emotional arousal.

Notes

Emotions in Infancy

Bridges (1932) reported the pioneer investigation of expression of emotionality in human infants. Watson's (1926) report concerns his classical studies of infant emotion. Harlow's long-term study of the positive affectional systems in the monkey, mainly centering on infancy, is described in several reports (e.g., Harlow, 1973).

Discrimination of Emotions

The early work described was reported by Sherman and Sherman (1929), Feleky (1922), and Kanner (1931). Research suggesting the predominance of the mouth in facial expression of emotion was performed by Dunlap (1927) and Plutchik (1962). Some recent cross-cultural research (including that dealing with preliterate peoples) reported by Ekman, Sorenson, and Friesen (1969) suggests that certain facial muscular movements are universal to some degree as agents of emotional expression, although cultural differences are pronounced. These results are interpreted by the researchers as contradicting the orthodox view of no innate pattern of emotional expression and supporting the very early evolutionary interpretation advanced by Charles Darwin in his classic book *The Expression of the Emotions in Man and Animals* (1872). Ekman's reader, *Darwin and Facial Expression: A Century of Research in Review* (1973), affords a comprehensive treatment of how Darwin's views have been treated over the past century.

Anger and Hostility

Moyer's *The Physiology of Hostility* (1971) covers biological bases of extreme anger. Cook's *Interpersonal Perception* (1971) is a soft-cover treatment of this important topic. For a comprehensive treatment of the blaming tendency (technically referred to as "causal attribution") Kelley's 1973 article may be consulted. The topic of aggression is treated more thoroughly in Supplement B-5 as a social problem, and those notes and references contain additional sources.

Love

The story of mammalian love relationships is charmingly told in Harlow, McGaugh, and Thompson's *Psychology* (1971), with a focus on monkey love but frequent generalizations to humans. Harlow's more recent *Learning to Love* (1973) is another source for this material. The concept of basic trust is elaborated by Erikson (1950). Paternal love in nonhuman primates is discussed by Mitchell (1969) and the theoretical interpretation of paternal affection as nonbiologically based is described by Adams (1960). Observations of play in human and monkey are reported by Jones (1967); Beach (1947) has collated the evidence on male sexual inadequacy over various vertebrate phyla; and Rheingold (1961) discusses the role of sensory modalities in human and monkey infants.

The biological bases of sexual behavior are treated by Bermant and Davidson (1974), the social dimensions by Bell and Gordon (1972), and the differentiation of sex identity throughout human development by Money and Ehrhardt (1973). The physiology of sexual arousal is reviewed by Zuckerman (1971). A number of books concerning the "new sexuality" and its relationship to old "myths" about human sexuality have appeared (e.g., Kennedy, 1972; Gagnon and Simon, 1973). Kaplan (1974) describes the new sex therapy, and Burton (1973) examines marital adjustment.

Fear

The initial experimental work on fear by Watson and his associates is described in Watson and Rayner (1920) as well as in Watson's (1926) paper. Hediger (1964) describes the flight distance shown by wild animals. Bronson (1968) summarizes the work on development of fear of novel stimuli, especially of a visual sort, in man and animals. The early research indicating the difficulty of conditioning some objects as fear stimuli was reported by Valentine (1930).

Punishment

The experiment on the varied resistance to temptation evidenced as a function of the delay of punishment was by Solomon, Turner, and Lessac (1968).

Anxiety

"Stranger anxiety" in human children is described by Schaffer and Emerson (1964). Peters (1963) refers to the reduced anxiety shown by prisoners and mental hospital patients, apparently as a result of his own clinical experience. Brady (1958) reported the original research on the "executive monkey" and ulcer formation; the subsequent discovery that this phenomenon could only be produced by the particular (6-hour) intertest interval that initially happened to be used restricts the generality of the finding but not its primary import.

Cognitive Factors

Marañon's influential research on the subjective effects of epinephrine injection is described in his 1924 article. Schachter (1967) reviews the development of the research on cognition as related to emotion; more specific accounts of the research described in the text appear in the following separate reports. Schachter and Singer (1962) report the important early study purporting to investigate effects of the vitamin supplement; the insomnia study is described by Storms and Nisbett (1970); the study on tolerance of pain is in Nisbett and Schachter (1966); and the two studies mentioned incidentally are reported by Schachter and Latane (1964) and Schachter and Wheeler (1962), on fear and amusement, respectively. The Russian research on interoceptive conditioning is entertainingly and instructively reviewed by Razran (1961).

Physiology of Emotion

In addition to the various sources mentioned, a comprehensive review of the biochemical influences on affective state is available in Schildkraut and Kety (1967). The various empirical researches described in the text (e.g., the urinanalysis of active and inactive hockey players) are cited in that review. The experiment designed to determine whether knowledgeable subjects can "beat" the polygraph was by Lykken (1960); Lykken (1974) provides a more recent review of the problems encountered in using "lie detectors."

Theories of Emotion

The treatment of some of the basic problems in theorizing about emotion leans heavily upon Peters's insightful 1963 essay. Emphasis upon the inherited ("instinctive") relationships of emotionality may be found in Darwin's 1872 book and in McDougall's 1923 work; a more recent comprehensive review appears in Fletcher (1957). James's original statement of his visceral-feedback theory was in his 1884 paper; the *Principles* (1890) contains a later version. Cannon's critique of the James-Lange theory is in his 1927 article. Fehr and Stern (1970) have recently "reinitiated" the James-Lange theory in a comprehensive review article. Cannon's own homeostatic research on the autonomic system is described in his 1915 report; Bard's contribution, emphasizing the sham-rage phenomenon, appears in his 1928 paper. The more recent limbic theory is described in separate papers by Papez (1937) and MacLean (1949), and is therefore often called the Papez–MacLean theory. *Neurophysiology and Emotion,* edited by Glass (1967), provides a good, broad overview of most of the important theoretical facets of the relationship of physiological variables to emotion.

Personality

16

This seventeenth-century engraving shows Christ exorcising a possessed man. The demons are seen fleeing through the mouth of the afflicted individual. This illustration is of interest as we open our discussion of personality because until the nineteenth century, any unusual or bizarre behavior was considered to be the work of demons who had gained possession of the unfortunate person's body.

493

he study of personality is the study of man's *individuality,* of the unique way in which his behaviors and their underlying determinants are organized. Each of us shares certain characteristics with all other human organisms but at the same time is unique in the way those characteristics are organized.

This chapter contains a consideration of some key methodological issues, such as the type of general approach to personality used in research and practice. Certain fundamental questions on which researchers hold widely divergent views are also discussed. For example: Is it more important to achieve a thorough understanding of particular individuals (the clinical objective) or to work out general laws about how personality develops and is modified (the more usual scientific objective)? Is the consistency that we commonly observe in a given individual's behavior more appropriately attributed to generalized habit systems, usually called *traits,* or to underlying consistencies in the environment?

Some of the more prominent determinants of personality are first reviewed. The type of body physique as related to personality and the role of population (technically, *demographic*) variables such as birth order are discussed.

The problem of personality *assessment* is considered next. Nonscientific varieties of personality and scientific techniques are discussed. Some of the individual differences that emerge as a result of the application of assessment techniques are reviewed briefly.

Scientific types of personality assessment are described in Supplement A-5. These include the interview, rating scales, personality inventories and interest inventories, and various forms of tests, ranging from direct samples of real behavior to the most subtle kind of projective test materials (e.g., inkblots, ambiguous pictures) for which the subject is asked to "make up" explanations or stories. (In the accomplishment of this task, he is presumed to impose upon the unstructured test stimuli certain of his own fundamental personality tendencies and problems.)

This chapter continues with a look at the major theories of personality. Some psychologists question whether there is any real need to have a special form for personality theory. They assume, rather, that general behavior theory when adequately developed will cover personality sufficiently; but this is not the majority view and there has been no dearth of interpretive efforts. The theories reviewed are Freudian psychoanalysis, trait theory, and learning theory.

The chapter continues with a review of the problem of behavioral deviancy. The major types of behavioral aberrations are *neuroses,* more or less chronic emotional disturbances revolving around anxiety and seldom resulting in complete social disability, and *psychoses,* major behavior disorders in which disorientation in time and space and marked disturbances in thought and speech generally leave the person so afflicted that he is unable to function normally in his usual social environment. In "functional" psychoses (schizophrenia, affective or manic-depressive disorder, and paranoia) no organic basis for the disabled behavior has been implicated. A detailed but introductory account of the major forms of neurosis and psychosis is provided in Supplement B-2.

There are several major types of treatment of behavior disorder. *Somatic* treatment is now mainly by means of drugs, especially the tranquilizers, which alleviate symptoms by relaxing the patient but do not get at the basic determinants of the disorder. *Psychotherapeutic* treatment includes such individual one-to-one procedures as psychoanalysis and client-centered therapy as well as the somewhat newer and quite promising group techniques, such as family therapy or encounter groups. *Behavioral* therapies are now usually some form of behavior modification, in which an attempt is made to change behavior itself and such underlying personality characteristics as traits are virtually ignored.

We conclude our discussion of personality aberrations with an evaluation of the associated therapeutic endeavors and some indication of the main lines along which more desirable mental health may be developed.

There is no easy way to achieve the objective of considering man as an integrated living system, of putting the bits and pieces of human behavior together, as must be done in the study of personality. Psychologists have not agreed about the proper way to comprehend man's personality any more than they have agreed about how best to comprehend learning or motivation or emotion. Nevertheless, there is a certain amount of general agreement about some of the basic concerns in the study of personality. These will be emphasized before we turn to the diversity of approach that marks so much of the problem of personality.

The Study of Personality

IDENTIFICATION

If a single synonymn were to be selected for the concept of personality that term would most probably be *individuality*. Personality is unique to the individual. More broadly, personality refers to the unique organization of one's tendencies in thinking, feeling, and behaving. The *pattern* of these covert and overt responses is what is meant by the term *personality*. There is assumed to be a certain degree of *consistency* in this pattern, so that knowledge of a personality organization makes possible better-than-chance predictions about future behavior.

The focus of personality is generally on interpersonal relationships. That is, one's personality is mainly defined in terms of how one relates to other persons. The word *personality* itself reflects this central aspect; it comes from *persona*, or "mask." In the Roman plays different facial appearances could be readily assumed merely by putting on different masks. Those most usually seen are the masks symbolizing comedy and tragedy. Emphasis on social role is still reflected in contemporary thinking about personality. However, some persistent internal pattern of behavioral tendencies is usually assumed to function in addition to whatever superficial appearances may be present.

DETERMINANTS OF PERSONALITY

In a sense, all the processes investigated by psychologists can be considered to be, in principle at least, potential determinants of personality. Although defensible perhaps on theoretical grounds, this point of view provides little aid in the important matter of pinpointing those variables and conditions that are of greatest relevance in the formation of personality. Some of these have already been considered—for example, the socialization process in development (Chapter 10) and many of the emotional functions (Chapter 15). The present discussion is thus aimed at illustrating by means of selected factors the manner in which personality is now believed to be shaped.

Genetic and Constitutional Factors

The role of genetic and constitutional factors in personality has been persistently emphasized throughout the history of science. The most influential of the many attempts to relate constitutional factors, which are assumed to be based on genetic conditions, to personality types will be described.

On the basis of a detailed examination of many thousands of photographs of nude male bodies physician William Sheldon and psychologist S. S. Stevens postulated three basic types of physique: the *endomorph,* or fatty; the *mesomorph,* or muscular; and the *ectomorph,* or lean. It was recognized that every individual has some tendency toward each of these types of physique, with only the very rare person being predominantly one or the other. Each body was therefore rated, by a seven-point scale, on the degree to which it approximated each of the three physiques, and the resulting *somatotype* was expressed as a three-digit number. A "pure" endomorph would thus get a somatotype rating of 7–1–1; similarly, extreme mesomorphs and ectomorphs would be rated, respectively, 1–7–1 and 1–1–7. Most people, of course, are mixed, but one or the other of the three primary types of physique predominate (e.g., 2–6–4 for a mesomorph with some endomorphic but still more ectomorphic tendency or 1–3–7 for an ectomorph with no fatty tendency but some muscular prominence).

Figure 16-1 provides a representation of the basic idea of the relationship between these various body types. The blending of types of physique that occurs in this particular body typing avoids the most common pitfall of most typologies, namely, the failure to realize that a mixture of conditions, rather than pure types, is characteristic.

The next step in the development of this personality typology was the crucial one of relating physique to personality. Personality was defined in terms of *temperament,* or chronic emotional condition, which had been long believed to be more susceptible to genetic influence than most of the other facets of human behavior. Three clusters of temperamental features were described, and each individual was rated on each cluster using the same seven-point scale as had been used for rating physique. The three clusters were *viscerotonia,* with an emphasis on body comforts, such as eating, a need for sleep, ready relaxation; *somatotonia,* with an emphasis upon body movement, a love of adventure, a readiness for physical competition; and *cerebrotonia,* with an emphasis upon fast but limited physical movements, an inhibition of social response, chronic fatigue, poor sleep habits.

Now it was hypothesized that a single set of genetic factors accounted for *both* physique and temperament, recognized as clusters of traits or tendencies rather than absolute factors. According to this system, the person with a tendency toward

16-1 Three basic types of physiques as conceptualized by Sheldon (1954).

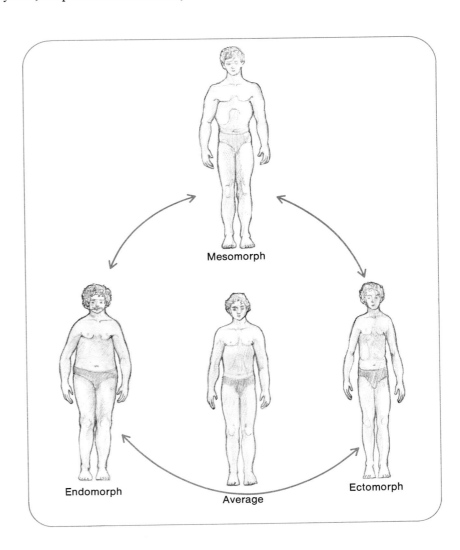

endomorphy tends also to have the viscerotonic temperament, the person who is predominantly mesomorphic tends also to show features of the somatotonic temperament, and the person who is predominantly ectomorphic inclines toward the cerebrotonic temperament. These correlations are very similar to many of the old stereotypes about people that have survived in the folklore—the fat jolly person, the thin thoughtful and worrisome individual, and so on. But the difference is that the present typology not only achieves a blending of both physical and temperament factors but also has in its support a certain amount of reasonably well-controlled empirical evidence.

In the first empirical study designed to test this hypothesized relationship between physique and temperament remarkably high correlations were found. The somatotype ratings of 200 college men were correlated with temperamental ratings based on intensive behavioral observations. Positive correlations were found for endomorphy and viscerotonia (.79), mesomorphy and somatotonia (.82), and ectomorphy and cerebrotonia (.83). Critics quickly pointed out that the same investigator had made both sets of ratings, so that there was an unknown but possibly quite substantial amount of unconscious bias in favor of the hypothesis. Subsequent investigations run by others under very tightly controlled conditions have in the main confirmed the theory; however, there have been some exceptions and the correlation coefficients have been much smaller than those initially reported. Certain of these studies will be described as representative of the more objective research on the problem.

In a study of 100 college women the somatotype ratings were done under highly objective conditions and temperament ratings were based entirely on the self-ratings of the subjects. The resulting correlations were all positive and statistically reliable.

It can be argued that even one's self-ratings may reflect some of the cultural stereotypes that relate physique and temperament, and so may also be in error. Research with children, where the influence of such cultural stereotypes on behavior generally may be considered to be minimal, offers a more promising line of experimental attack. Such evidence as has been reported with children has tended to confirm the proposed relationships, but again with markedly less statistical support than originally found.

On the basis of the existing evidence it seems safe to conclude that some fundamental relationship between *tendencies* toward particular physique and particular temperaments does exist, and this relationship is presumably mediated as theorized by inherited factors. The relationship is a tendency, however, and not as clear-cut as stereotyped cultural notions imply.

Demographic (Population) Determinants

Demographic conditions, those relating to the characteristics of populations, represent the other side of the coin from the genetic factors just considered. All cultural conditions clearly have enormous potential for influencing personality. The extent to which any particular ones actually do, and under what circumstances they do so, poses a set of research questions that should suffice to keep socially oriented investigators quite busy for some time.

The range of cultural conditions is almost as great as the scope of their influence on personality. The most direct factors are probably those of the immediate family, and especially of the parents (see Chapter 10). Here we select for discussion two of the more general and less direct factors, birth order and sex, as illustrative of the way in which demographic conditions can influence personality.

BIRTH ORDER. The psychoanalyst Alfred Adler was among the first to emphasize the significance of birth order as a psychological variable. His emphasis was strictly rational and was based on clinical rather than controlled empirical data; hence his speculations were accorded progressively less attention by behaviorally oriented psychologists and this variable was relatively neglected for many years. Recently, however, there has been a renewed interest in ordinal position of birth as a determinant of personality.

The initial empirical observation that seems to have stimulated the contemporary revival of interest in this variable was made during the course of a social-psychological investigation of affiliation. Young women who were either first-born or only children seemed to prefer to wait for a painful event (an electric shock administered in the experiment) while in the company of others more than later-born children of otherwise comparable demographic characteristics. Subsequent research confirmed this relationship and extended the range of situations in which ordinal position of birth seems to make a difference.

Affiliation motivation has been measured directly in first-borns as compared with later-borns by means of the Thematic Apperception Test; the stories "made up" by first-borns were found to contain more affiliation-related materials. Less obviously, the birth-order variable has also been found to differentiate fighter pilots in terms of their effectiveness: first-borns were rated below later-borns, presumably because they become more anxious and thus less capable of performing well when subjected to periods of social isolation.

The general conclusion that can be drawn from these relatively recent observations is that first-borns as a group are more susceptible to social influences and have a greater need for security, such as that offered under some circumstances by the social presence of others. This personality attribute is believed to result from the fairly obvious fact that first-borns get much more social attention from their parents than later-borns. Later-borns are allowed to fend for themselves to a much greater extent either because they are more likely to be taken for granted or because their parents simply have less time for them, owing to the pressure of other matters and possibly the growing number of siblings. Also, the mother is much more likely to be anxious in dealing with a first-born, and more likely to make a variety of mistakes, ranging from such trivial matters as applying diaper pins into flesh instead of cloth to being oversolicitous, which can produce high levels of social anticipation in the child.

Other aspects of being first born have been noted. For example, first-borns are more likely to achieve eminence in scholarship, but are less likely to be rated as attractive by their peers (perhaps because of the greater social demands they make), and they are more likely to become psychiatric patients. All of these differences represent statistical trends only with a great deal of overlap among the various groups. In as far as they do represent trends, they can be theoretically attributed to the especially intensive relationship that first-borns have with their parents; they both benefit from the unusual degree of verbal interchange they have with their parents and suffer from their greater exposure to parental peculiarities.

SEX. Male and female roles are changing so rapidly, in the United States at least, that it is dangerous to draw any hard-and-fast distinctions. In any case, it is difficult to separate out any genetic or constitutional differences between sexes that influence personality from the vastly more numerous cultural and social distinctions that are drawn. Some indication of the latter can be given, with due regard for the active state of flux that exists.

Some distinctions of sexual roles in other cultures have been provided by the anthropologist Margaret Mead in a classic study. Mead studied three primitive tribes in New Guinea. She found clear-cut and striking differences in sex role. Two of these tribes, the Arapesh and the Mundugumor, made relatively small distinctions but held generally different expectations for the sexes. The Arapesh dictated for both males and females a role that is close to the traditional female role in our culture; the Mundugumor expected both sexes to behave more like the males in our own culture. But the third tribe provided the eye-opener, at least for western eyes: the Tchambuli had expectations for the two sexes that were very similar to our own—but in the opposite direction! The females were far more aggressive and dominated in the running of the tribal affairs, whereas the males were not only more passive and compliant but were also more artistically inclined. Clearly the biological differences that exist do not dictate any necessary cultural role for the two sexes.

An interesting observation from the contemporary scene may be cited as illustrative of the way in which personality features and expectations vary. Moreover, the results would hardly seem attributable to biological factors, so that they offer a clear demonstration of the potency of cultural learning. In this recent investigation educated women were found to be biased in the same way as the "male chauvinist." A group of 120 college women were asked to evaluate the work of artists on the basis of some abstract paintings. They were given personality profiles for each artist. Each profile appeared in two forms, one with a female name and the other with a male name, with no other changes. The women rated each artist on technical competence and probable future success. When they were informed that a given artist had won a prize there was no difference in their ratings according to sex, but when they were informed that the judging had not yet occurred the women actually rated the productions by alleged male artists significantly higher!

Consistent sex differences have been observed in one experimental situation. This involves the personality attribute initially called *field dependence* or *field independence* but more recently labeled *psychological differentiation*. Subjects are placed in a darkened room. They are shown both a luminous rod and a luminous square frame, which may be independently rotated around the vertical axis. The subjects' task is to align the rod with the vertical, as it would be, say, if they were permitted to use a surveyor's plumb line. Then they are tested under various conditions of vertical distortion involving both the frame and the rod itself. A field-dependent subject is defined as one who consistently follows the frame in aligning the rod, even when it is severely distorted from the vertical; a field-independent subject is one who is able to use his own self-produced alignment cues and so tilt the rod properly, with respect to the vertical, regardless of the rotation of the frame.

Females have been found to be in general more field-dependent than males. It is difficult to say whether this result is to be attributed to some fundamental hereditary sex difference or, more plausibly perhaps, to subtle differences in sex roles and expectations and learning from birth onward (with boys having the advantage of more mechanical learning about the environment). In any event, this example represents the kind of result that has been reported and the problems that are associated with separation of biological and cultural determinants.

PERSONALITY ASSESSMENT

Assessment of personality needs to be considered in terms of both the non-scientific and the scientific approaches. Our discussion starts with the more familiar nonscientific type of assessment.

Nonscientific Types

Nonscientific and common-sense means of assessing personality tend to be holistic, or based upon the total impression gained by the observer. Scientific, or formalized, means of assessment tend to be more analytic, or based upon particular kinds of observations, such as items in a test of one kind or another. But this is not an absolute distinction; much common-sense assessment is actually based upon a very small number of salient cues and is thus quite particularistic.

Although nonscientific assessment may be extremely misleading, it is sometimes actually very effective. An astute and experienced observer can become a surprisingly accurate assessor; skill in personality evaluation is by no means restricted to scientific techniques. Indeed, each of us tends almost daily to make at least some form of personality assessment, especially if we meet many new people, and we are likely to improve to some extent in our ability to "size up" people.

OBSERVATION OF BEHAVIOR: FIRST IMPRESSIONS. Most nonscientific assessment is like scientific assessment in that it is based upon observations of behavior. The main difficulty with this behaviorally based assessment is that evaluations are apt to be made upon a very scanty observational basis. "First impressions" are especially liable to error and distortion. One cannot tell whether the behaviors observed are truly characteristic of the individual observed or whether they have been "put on" to serve some special purpose. Also, unusual circumstances, such as severe fatigue or extreme nervousness, can alter normal behavior so markedly as to make observations highly unreliable.

The safest precaution to take with regard to first impressions is firmly to consider them as tentative and thereby reduce their tendency to exercise undue influence upon subsequent observations. Of course, this is much easier said than done. A related precaution is to attempt to broaden one's observational base as much as possible and to supplement those observations with other forms of information.

The greater the variety of situations in which one has the opportunity to observe a person, the more likely the resulting assessment is to be accurate.

THE INTERVIEW. A special form of observation is the interview, a deliberate and contrived effort to obtain information by asking selected questions in an interpersonal setting. Interviews come in varying degrees of structuring, or formality. The major advantage of the interview is that it provides an opportunity to focus on presumably crucial points in a relatively short time. When standardized questions are provided, and these can be informally presented, the interview procedure seems to be most effective and can be applied by relatively untrained persons. Again, there is no real substitute for experience, and skill at interviewing improves with practice. The interview is dependent upon first impressions in terms of the evaluations that ensue, and is not immune from the difficulties described. When it is supplemented by other techniques for obtaining information, such as objective test scores or autobiographical statements or letters of recommendation, the interview is likely to have much improved reliability.

BODY LANGUAGE. A form of observation of behavior that has been much emphasized in recent years as a means of personality assessment is so-called expressive moments or body language. These terms refer to largely unconscious ways each of us has of expressing ourselves by means of nonverbal behavior. Although there is certainly some value to this method, the degree to which it can be accepted as a useful supplement to other more orthodox means of obtaining information in personality assessment cannot be stated until it has been subjected to adequate experimental tests.

PHYSIOGNOMY. The use of facial features, or physiognomy, to assess personality is so common as to require some special mention. No experimental support has been reported for the popular belief that certain facial features are consistently associated with personality characteristics. Nevertheless, the stereotyped beliefs persist. Figure 16-2 shows one scheme of historical interest.

It should be noted that there is one way in which an indirect association between some facial feature and some personality characteristic can be formed. This occurs if a sufficient number of people come to accept the association, say that allegedly found between red hair and temper. Thus, although there is no real evidence for any necessary relationship between these two features, some association may be observed if red-haired individuals take the notion seriously.

PHRENOLOGY. The study of configurations of the skull as determinants of personality, phrenology, has a long history. At one time phrenology was a highly respected scientific field of investigation. It seemed a reasonable assumption that differential protuberances in the skull were associated with exceptional development of the underlying brain centers—hence such commonplace names as the "bump of knowledge," so called because of its position on the head outside of the presumed center for cognitive functions. As neurological knowledge grew, however, it became apparent that centers for various brain functions simply do not exist in the simplistic manner assumed by the early phrenologists. Moreover, to the extent that centers do exist there is no evidence whatsoever that their functional efficiency is correlated with gross physical size. Finally, even if physical size were somehow related to superior function it is by no means clear that the hard bony structure of the skull would conform to such differential development of the very soft brain material. Thus no scientific evidence has been obtained in support of phrenology and it has consequently been left to unscrupulous peddlers of pseudo-scientific personality systems for exploitation.

ASTROLOGY AND PALMISTRY. A variety of systems of personality assessment are to be found in all societies. The fact that many and varied procedures are used attests to the great popular demand for quick and easy methods of personality assessment. The most popular of the pseudoscientific systems in our society are probably astrology and palmistry. The astrologer purports to use birth dates as the key to personality assessment, the palmist the pattern of lines on the palms. These systems offer no scientifically acceptable evidence to explain the alleged relationships. However, they are simple and they are "fun" and so appeal to a wide variety of people. They represent a currently quite popular alternative means of acquiring knowledge, and their success depends in large part upon the relatively poor understanding of basic scientific procedures and objectives in the general public.

One of the more discouraging aspects of this whole problem is the extent to which such systems appeal even to highly educated segments of the populace. How many newspapers, for example, are without the standard astrology column, even when the editors know much better? The presumption is that this kind of feature helps to sell newspapers (or magazines or radio and television programs).

Very often clever practitioners of these systems are able to make reasonably accurate personality judgments. They do so in the course of their work, but from an orthodox scientific point of view by quite different means than those they allege to use (such as lines in the palm, astrological codes, and the like). They may be astute

16-2 A representative effort to evaluate personality by means of physiognomy. The five drawings were presented by French writer Johann Kaspar Lavater over two centuries ago. For example, Lavater held that a perpendicularly protruding forehead (as in faces 1 and 5), a gaping mouth (as in 2 and 4), and a small eye and wrinkled skin (as in 3) are unfailing signs of stupidity, weakness, and indolence. Offsetting features, however, also need to be considered. Thus the nose in face 1, if viewed alone, was said to represent brightness. Generally the five faces depicted were believed to predispose their owners to increasing degrees of retardation, from left to right.

observers of behavior, and by noting a few crucial items they can be surprisingly accurate and thereby impress clients.

Outright deception is, unhappily, common in some of these persons. Sometimes such normal observations are supplemented by surreptitiously obtaining information, as by scanning the contents of purses or coats left obligingly available, and so they are able to achieve even more striking successes with unsuspecting and gullible clients. The resemblance of these practices to those of the medium (Chapter 7, p. 238) are evident, and again they are successful for the same reasons (the failure to look closely and think objectively about such matters).

While recognizing that some practitioners are sincere in their belief in their systems, it is important to recognize also that the client's belief and willingness to behave on the basis of that belief makes the systems appear valid. The fact is, however, that assessments of personality based on astrology and palmistry have no demonstrated scientific value. Their acceptance therefore depends upon the acceptance of scientifically questionable procedures and is, in the last analysis, simply a matter of personal preference.

Scientific Types

Scientific efforts to assess personality cover a very wide spectrum of measures. Not all efforts are equally "scientific"; the degree to which effective and scientifically validated assessment is achieved varies not only with the type of testing instrument but also with the user. Nevertheless, although there is no guarantee of scientific success, all of these efforts are similar in that there is at least some effort made, in a more or less objective and controlled manner, to evaluate the degree to which the measure succeeds in living up to the claims made for it.

Like their nonscientific counterparts, scientific efforts at personality assessment are primarily concerned with speed. There are many situations in which important decisions about people can be more objectively made if quick measures of one or more aspect of personality can be made available. The educational setting will be the most familiar to readers of this book; from the earliest school years teachers and administrators depend upon a variety of tests, mainly of capacity and achievement, to help them sort and select students for various purposes. The fact that tests in school settings are sometimes abused and may also be utilized carelessly has tended to give them a bad name, but their positive contributions should not be overlooked.

Personality evaluations are even more necessary in the clinical setting, where behavior disorders are diagnosed and treated, as well as in certain specialized business and military settings when the prediction of future behavior may be of considerable practical importance. In all of these usages, speed is likely to be a key consideration.

STANDARDIZATION OF PERSONALITY MEASURES. Unlike their nonscientific counterparts, the scientific assessment techniques undergo varying degrees of examination. A test, for example, must be standardized before it is put on the market for real-life application. Standardization consists of an objective and intensive effort to determine the reliability and validity of the test as well as to weed out the ineffective parts and provide a set of norms, or standards, and a detailed instruction booklet.

It must be remembered that a test is simply a tool. Some are perhaps better tools than others (with reference in particular to validity and reliability); however, whatever the merits of any particular test, it can be neither better nor worse than the person using it. Like a scalpel, it can repair or destroy, depending upon the skill of the user. Furthermore, the results of any test must be interpreted. The interpreter must be skilled in giving test scores their most appropriate meaning, just as the test administrator must be skilled in taking those measurements of which his instruments are capable. When a carpenter's tool is inappropriately used, the consequences are soon apparent. The misuse of psychological instruments (tests) is more likely to persist, because the negative consequences are less immediately apparent. The damage, if any, is not grossly physical.

The problem of standardization and some of the more common forms of scientific personality assessment are described in Supplement A-5.

Individual Differences

Personality has been identified as, in essence, individuality. If personality tests have achieved anything they have demonstrated anew the tremendous amount of individuality that people show. The many different kinds of tests that we have just reviewed produce such a diversity of different results that psychologists are forced to recognize individual differences as a key feature in all human behavior.

The study of individual differences has a relatively long history. The exceptionally talented English scientist Sir Francis Galton stimulated interest in this topic during the latter part of the nineteenth century. As a result of his interest in heredity and the role that it plays in familial achievement, Galton made a great number of quantitative measurements of human characteristics—anatomical, physiological, and behavioral—and even invented measuring instruments for sensory testing. His work helped to insure the general recognition, as the science of psychology was just beginning, of the central fact of individual differences in all the various measures that he made.

TEMPERAMENTAL DIFFERENCES. Individual differences appear from the very first postnatal days and even during the fetal period. Babies vary markedly, for example, in the vigor and amount of physical activity. Some are extremely placid, others extremely vigorous; boys generally show higher levels of physical activity than girls. Later, when it is possible to measure temperamental differences more meaningfully, a wide range of results is obtained.

In one longitudinal study, beginning at two or three months of age and continuing through ten years of age, three basic types of temperament were identified. In a sample of over 100 children studied through this age span, approximately 40 per cent were categorized as of "easy" temperament, meaning that they showed regular eating and sleeping characteristics, quickly adapted to changes in routine, and were generally happy and cheerful. Another 15 per cent were classified as of "slow" temperament; they were less active, seemed to be more negative, especially about changes in routine, and were in general slow to warm up in new situations.

An additional 10 per cent were categorized as "difficult"; these children had marked difficulties in eating and sleeping, adjusted poorly to new experiences, and in general were quite negative. The other children in the sample (35 per cent) showed some combination of these three patterns of temperament and could not be simply categorized. The value of this early categorization is suggested by the follow-up observations made on these children. For example, by the age of ten, 70 per cent of the "difficult" children had been referred to professionals for their behavioral problems, compared to only 18 per cent of the "easy" children.

ANATOMICAL AND PHYSIOLOGICAL DIFFERENCES. A very wide range of individual differences has been found in anatomical and physiological measurements in adults as well as children. The endocrine gland system shows very great individual differences with regard to function as well as gross size. Pituitary glands, for instance, have been found to vary in their output from 250 to 1,100 milligrams, thyroid glands from 7 to 20 grams. The role of individual differences with regard to emotional responsivity has already been stressed, as evidenced by the differential susceptibility to psychosomatic symptoms, for example. There is hardly any fundamental way in which human organisms can be measured that does not reveal a substantial range of individual differences.

It is interesting that differences among the individuals of a species seem to be associated with their point of emergence on the scale of evolution; that is, the range of behavioral individuality appears to increase as we consider animals of "higher" physiogenetic status. This is hardly surprising in view of the increasingly large number of variables that determine the behavior of organisms with increased complexity of sensory, motor, and associative neural functions. When we consider man, also, there does seem to be a marked positive correlation between the range of individual differences exhibited and the complexity of the social environment.

So many variables contribute to personality and there are such a variety of different ways of studying man as a functioning organism that it is hardly surprising to find a corresponding diversity of theoretical interpretations. Here we consider the more important of these various theoretical views. Our discussion begins with the psychoanalytic conception of personality. We then briefly describe some alternatives to psychoanalysis; self-theory and personal construct theory are the two types selected for description. The last theories treated are more strictly psychological developments, trait and factor theory and learning theory approaches to personality.

PSYCHOANALYTIC THEORY

Foremost in their influence, and to some extent the focus around which competing theories have centered, have been the psychoanalytic theories of Freud and his successors.

Mental Function

LIBIDO. By libido Freud meant the fundamental drive for pleasure and biological satisfaction (mainly sexual) that motivates all human organisms throughout life. Freud assumed that there was a certain amount of libidinal energy inherited by each developing organism and that this energy could be attached to various objects, varying with the psychosexual stage of the organism. Fixation of too much libidinal energy on objects at any particular stage was felt to account for many adult personality disturbances because there was not enough energy left for normal mature relationships.

Society by its various rules and codes prevents the direct expression of libidinal energies, and personality disturbances were seen as a common consequence. Aggressive impulses as well as sexual ones were included within the libidinal concept. The psychoanalysts have therefore argued that society must provide safety valves to allow more socially satisfactory releases of libidinal energy and to prevent the disturbances in personality (behavioral symptoms) as well as antisocial behaviors that otherwise result. War and military actions generally provide one such release, but athletic competition and participation in various "causes" are socially preferable alternatives.

DEFENSE MECHANISMS. The inevitable resistance to libidinal forces imposed by society results in both frustration and guilt, frustration from blocking some of the antisocial impulses and guilt produced by the impulses themselves as well as the actual violations of the social code that occur. To account for the successful coping by the human organism with these stresses and strains Freud emphasized a number of basic *defense mechanisms,* unconscious ways in which each of us adjusts to the realities of our lives without constantly ravaging our personalities and reshaping our self-concepts.

The fundamental defense mechanism in the psychoanalytic theory is that of *repression.* Repression refers to the more or less automatic (that is, nondeliberate) "forgetting" of socially and personally unacceptable impulses and memories. It was

507

this concept that led Freud to his development of the elaborate theory of the unconscious.

Repression is both a necessary process and, in extreme form, a most harmful one. On the one hand, it serves a most useful role because it relieves one of constant harassment by many petty irritations and unacceptable libidinal impulses; these are simply forced into the unconscious where they usually remain without undue disturbance of the personality. On the other hand, repression can keep one from seeing the source of some of his problems—such as socially unacceptable impulses relating, say, to his parents—and in the psychoanalytic theory it is a major factor in development of severe behavior or personality disorders.

The many other major defense mechanisms stressed by Freud and other psychoanalysts may be more briefly identified.

Denial is closely related to repression in that it consists of the "forgetting" of information concerning some particular threat to the person. For example, the aging professional athlete whose career is about to end may refuse to accept this fact, disregarding evidence, such as his manager's warnings, to the contrary; or the student who is about to fail a course may reject the objective evidence offered by friends and instructors.

A special form of denial occurs when an individual refuses to admit the existence of socially undesirable behavior or impulses in himself but instead refers them to others. This mechanism is called *projection*. Guilt is prevented by attributing the negative tendencies in oneself to others. The classic example of projection is provided by the avid reformer, such as the axe-wielding destroyer of saloons. According to the psychoanalytic theory such a person is likely to be projecting his own impulses, unacceptable to himself; his fervor results from redirecting his own exceptionally strong motivations.

A functionally similar mechanism is that of *reaction formation*. In this process an individual's own undesirable or unacceptable impulses are countered by the assumption of the opposite characteristics, and often to an extreme degree. Again the fervent reformer is interpreted by the psychoanalyst as an illustration of reaction formation as well as projection.

Regression refers to the return to an earlier stage of behavior, such as childhood. It occurs when the person is overwhelmed by seemingly impossible demands and represents a search for the security and protection offered by the earlier stage of life. Excessive drinking is sometimes regarded as a regressive mechanism in that it involves a reversion to a kind of bottle feeding; infantile mannerisms and childish speech are less damaging forms of regressive behavior.

Rationalization refers to the giving of socially acceptable reasons for behavior that is actually more personally motivated; in the classic example of the "sour grapes" form, for example, a person who has been unable to obtain a prized objective (such as the desirable grapes sought by the fox in Aesop's fable) says that he did not want them anyway because they really are not very desirable (the grapes are sour, not tasty). The "sweet-lemon" counterpart to this process involves the making the best of a bad situation; the lemon that one is forced to take becomes a delectable and desirable object.

It is important to note that the person who rationalizes in this way is not lying or purposely transforming the affective character of the situation. Rationalization is a defense mechanism because it protects one's ego by fending off the necessity of admitting failure. Of course, a little rationalization goes a long way, and people who rationalize too much, like those who protest too much, merely succeed in calling attention to their own shortcomings.

A related but much more socially desirable defense mechanism is that of *compensation*. In this process one endeavors to make up for a weakness in one function by excelling in some other. The boy whose athletic ambitions are stymied by inadequate physique may compensate by directing exceptional energy into his studies and becoming a successful scholar; or the girl whose home-making motivation is thwarted by a lack of appropriate suitors may compensate by working hard to become a success in the business world.

When compensation is combined with denial, a mechanism called *overcompensation* is likely to occur. In this process the individual refuses to recognize some particular shortcoming and expends great energy in attempting to excel in some manner related to that shortcoming. The classic example here is the political dictator whose need for power is attributed in part at least to his own physical limitations. Thus Napoleon, Hitler, Mussolini, and Stalin were all men of short physical stature who nonetheless achieved and exercised tremendous powers.

Finally, the mechanisms of displacement and sublimation operate to rechannel libidinal energies in more acceptable directions. In *displacement* the new goal is one that does not have the social stigma of the initial goal (e.g., drinking tea instead of an alcoholic beverage). In *sublimation*, which is typically related to redirecting sexual energies, socially desirable activity (e.g., athletic competition, a formal religious career) is substituted for libidinal urges.

It should be emphasized that the defense mechanisms represent personally and socially desirable processes that in general enable the biologically driven human organism to maintain a reasonable degree of personal comfort while accommodating his libidinal impulses to social restrictions and conventions. As conceptually developed within the psychoanalytic system, defense mechanisms without doubt

Breather Interpretation

PERSONALITY APPRAISAL

Did you think that the personality sketch in the Breather on p. 506 applied to you (rating 1 or 2)? If so, join the club. Most people do! And for a very good reason: the appraisal is so general as to apply to most if not all people.

The point of this exercise is to demonstrate how easy it is to produce and "sell" such highly generalized accounts and how useless they are. Similarly vague and deliberately all-encompassing characterizations are offered by many persons, such as fortunetellers, who feed upon the naiveté of the public in order to make a living as well as by many other well-intentioned persons who use some pet notion or special system. This kind of assessment is just one of the pitfalls all of us need to guard against in the important but difficult matter of appraising personality.

reflect the realities of personality dynamics and have probably been the most readily accepted feature of Freudian theory.

Mental Structure

In his dynamic conceptions (e.g., the libido as a physical force) Freud necessarily adopted the biological assumptions of his time (that is, the assumption of energy as a constant factor that could not be completely suppressed). In his conceptualizing of the structure of the mind, Freud tended to think in terms of physical analogue. This has had the unfortunate consequence of misleading many of his supporters into taking the structural analogue too literally, into *reifying*, as the process is usually called, processes and regarding them as things. Avoidance of this error is important if the value of Freud's ingenious theorizing is to be maintained. Thus although the language that he used is that of structures, it must be remembered that he was actually observing behaviors and forming conceptualizations about the mental processes that might underlie them. Casting these into the form of a "mental structure" is only a useful expository device. The process may exist; the structure does not.

The Psychic Apparatus: Id, Ego, Superego. According to the Freudian conception the so-called psychic apparatus or, more simply, the personality, is composed of three more or less distinct parts.

The core of personality for Freud is the *id*. This is the genetically determined receptacle of all psychic energy, or libido. The id is constantly seeking to discharge its (primarily sexual) energies. When it does so tensions are reduced and pleasure is experienced. The id thus operates on the so-called *pleasure principle*, and in terms of *primary processes*.

The *reality principle*, by which the social demands of the culture and the more immediate personal demands of other individuals are met, is the basis of a second part of the personality, the *ego*. It is the ego that acts to permit fulfillment of the impulses of the id, or more commonly in most societies to delay or block them. The ego operates by means of so-called *secondary processes*, which mediate the relationship of id impulses to reality. An important function of parental and educational training is to develop strong ego functions so that an individual is able to cope with developmental crises and build and utilize his own inner resources effectively.

The final part of the psychic apparatus as Freud initially conceptualized it is the *superego*. The superego represents the incorporation within the developing child of the host of social conventions and restrictions expressed by the adults with whom he interacts. The *conscience* is the internalization of the inhibitions the child experiences, the violations of which are usually punished. Adult values, or *ego ideals*, are similarly internalized as part of the superego. The developing human organism is thus motivated to avoid guilt, which results from the violation of the internalized social code or conscience, and to achieve pride and self-esteem, which are produced by approximations of the ego ideals.

In the normal healthy personality these three components all work smoothly together, with a minimum of disharmony. In severely disturbed individuals, however, one or the other of the three systems is disproportionately undeveloped or overdeveloped, and personal crises of the kind described later in the chapter therefore occur.

LEVELS OF CONSCIOUSNESS. In recognizing for the first time the crucial role of the unconscious factors in personality and adjustment, Freud posited three more or less distinct levels of consciousness, or mind.

The *conscious* level is defined as that of which the person is immediately aware. It is the arena in which the ego mainly operates. As we have emphasized, a major contribution of Freud's was to downgrade the actual significance of this kind of rational function. Prior to Freudian emphasis on man's nonrational processes, the majority of philosophers and psychologists had been concerned with rational, conscious factors in their interpretations of behavior and personality.

The *preconscious* level is composed of experiences and memories that can readily be brought into consciousness. The mechanism of attention (Chapter 6) serves to transfer memories between conscious and preconscious levels, with relatively little difficulty.

Finally, and most importantly, there is the *unconscious* level. This consists of the vastly greater number of experiences that are not readily available to awareness. They are brought into consciousness only under unusual circumstances. But it is the unconscious level that contains not only all of the id (libidinal) impulses but also many other less emotionally toned mental phenomena that underlie our interpersonal relationships and our decisions in all areas of life (e.g., vocational choice, social attitudes, hobbies).

The ferreting out of crucial unconscious memories was regarded as a major function of the psychoanalytic procedure. Some of Freud's most brilliant insights involved this problem. For example, he observed how assumption of unconscious motivation could account for commonplace slips of the tongue (e.g., one of the more notorious of such errors occurred several years ago when a radio announcer who was supposed to read, "the best in bread," inadvertently blurted out, "the breast in bed!"). The significance of such errors had not been previously recognized.

Although Freud sought at first to utilize hypnosis as the major avenue into the unconscious, he later turned to free association and dream analysis as more reliable techniques. In analyzing the *manifest content,* as of dreams, in order to uncover the *latent content,* or true meaning, recourse to some means of translation is necessary. That is, because of the restrictions of the ego the impulses of the id are ordinarily indirectly expressed, as *symbols.* Although the translation and reinterpretation of such symbols is sometimes relatively straightforward, this is an exercise that invites the use of imagination, and some of the more doubtful features of psychoanalysis are directly attributable to fanciful excesses in these interpretations.

Evaluation of Psychoanalysis

Any exact assessment of the psychoanalytic theory of personality is difficult to make. This is partly because of the great scope and complexity of the theory and partly because of the mix of extremely valuable and scientifically questionable features. The Freudian language system, being largely nonempirical, appeals to the layman and is possibly of clinical relevance but does not lend itself readily to scientific analysis. Freud's own contributions were of course immense and he clearly rates as one of the intellectual giants of all time. Moreover, there are important new trends within psychoanalytic theory itself, as his successors continue to work out new directions (e.g., with regard to ego functions, which Freud regarded as essentially derived from the id but which are now more often treated as at least partly autonomous). Nevertheless, few psychologists today would accept the orthodox Freudian theory of personality as sufficient, and the alternatives to which we now turn were developed to stress facets of personality that he neglected or minimized.

SELF THEORY

Self theory represents, in essence, an attempt to restore to the individual some of the dignity and self-determining properties of which he had been relieved by psychoanalytic theory. Self theorists focus on the organism (hence their theories are sometimes called *organismic theories*) as the source of its own fate. Moreover, they tend to stress consciousness as crucial in this process. They are in this respect closely allied to the contemporary existentialists, who also stress the primacy of conscious functions.

The self as a concept has been variously defined, but in general the most acceptable definitions regard it as the conscious picture or image that each of us tends to have of himself. This picture is constantly changing. Moreover, self theorists emphasize that these changes are not simply those directly imposed by environmental forces, but rather are deliberately effected, by a continuing series of more or less conscious decisions, by the individual himself. *Self-actualization* is the key word here; it describes the way in which an individual is believed to develop his *real* self from his *ideal* self.

Most self theorists accept some role for unconscious processes but not the all-important role that Freud proposed. The primary factor in self-actualization, or realization of one's true potential, is rather the love and respect of others. Of course, one must also have a reasonable amount of self-regard—love and respect for oneself—as a necessary condition for personal growth.

One version of self theory is that man is inherently "good" and that his development is essentially a matter of his own self-fulfillment. In this process the role of special conscious experiences, called *peak experiences*, is held to be crucial. The contrast of this and the other self theories from psychoanalysis is obviously quite marked, not only with respect to the role of the unconscious but also, and even more significantly, with respect to the nature of the instinctive forces that are presumed to underlie behavior and personality development.

PERSONAL CONSTRUCT THEORY

Personal construct theory holds that the key to one's personality is the particular set of constructs that one uses to represent the people and things that play important roles in his life. Personal construct theory is similar to self theory in that it places the controls for each personality in the hands of the individual and stresses rational rather than irrational functions as the source of this control. Thinking and judgment, not growth or self-actualization, are accorded the key role in personality.

Personal construct theory is more phenomenological than self theory. It is based on the assumption that certain core concepts, relating to how the person sees himself and "significant others" in relationship to himself, are instrumental in personality formation and maintenance. The role of motivation is resolved simply by circumventing it. As the author of personal-construct theory put it in rejecting both "push" (drive—e.g., putting a pitchfork to the recalcitrant donkey) and "pull" (purpose—e.g., enticing the donkey by dangling a carrot in front of it) factors of the usual motivation theory, "Our theory is neither of these. Since we prefer to look at the nature of the animal himself, ours is probably best called the jackass theory" (Kelly, 1958, p. 50).

It seems fair to say that personal construct theory has neither overwhelmed the competing viewpoints on personality nor threatened to do so at any time in the future. Nevertheless, it offers an interesting alternative to the psychoanalytic and other theories, a refreshing reminder of the potential of strictly cognitive features in personality, and some evidence that even a common-sense approach may have something of interest to offer in this difficult field.

TRAIT AND FACTOR THEORIES

Apart from psychoanalysis, the type of approach to personality that seems to have most attracted psychological attention is that of *trait theory*. Trait theory focuses on those persistent characteristics of an individual that are assumed to underlie a variety of seemingly disparate overt behaviors. The concept of trait is thus a broader one than either the overt response or the hypothesized habit that produces it. Responses and habits can be viewed as manifestations of traits; traits in turn are less broadly conceived than self or, ultimately, personality. They thus offer a moderate amount of scope and significance and, according to the trait theorists, are at the level at which personality can be most profitably investigated.

Implicit in the development of trait theory is the notion of a hierarchical structure in behavior. The simplest variable is that of the reflex or the conditioned response; habits and attitudes fit in between that level and the trait. The self-concept resides at a somewhat higher level of the hierarchy. The trait approach lends itself nicely to a dimensional analysis, implemented by tests and scales and graphically represented by personality profiles.

Factor theory is a logical, mathematized offshoot of trait theory. In one version a distinction is drawn between two kinds of traits, surface and source. *Surface traits* are identified in terms of clusters of specific traits resulting when individuals are evaluated in terms of a large number of variables. Thus if specific traits are found to be highly intercorrelated (to a correlation index of .60 or more), they are presumed to be manifestations of the same surface trait (e.g., the trait represented by the paired opposites of boldness and shyness). The term *surface* is used because the clusters are based upon the raw data and do not require additional mathematical treatment for discovery.

When such additional treatment is applied, in the form of factor analysis (cf. Supplement A-1), different sets of uniformities emerge and are given the label *source traits* (e.g., dominance-submissiveness). Presumably the interrelationships thus uncovered represent a more profound kind of uniformity than that evidenced by the simpler cluster of variables identifying surface traits.

The success of these methods will depend upon how effectively the experimental and quantitative techniques can be combined. Regardless of the degree of mathematical precision their promise will not be realized unless at least an approximate degree of experimental, and conceptual, treatment can be developed.

LEARNING THEORY APPROACHES

Learning theory approaches to personality tend to be elaborations of general behavior theory rather than special theories expressly designed to handle the facts of personality. Thus there were early efforts to develop stimulus–response interpretations, including some endeavor to wed this approach to the psychoanalytic, and there is today the rapidly growing application of operant conditioning. But the learning theory that has been most influential with regard to its implications for personality is social learning theory.

Social Learning Theory

A major objective of social learning theory is to describe the way in which personality is learned and the environmental circumstances under which it is subsequently modified. The primary process that has been investigated is imitation. The necessary condition for this kind of learning is observation of behavior. The consequences, rewarding or punishing, that follow imitation of observed behaviors then determine the extent to which the behavior persists.

Models can be either symbolic or exemplary. Symbolic models are presented in such media as movies and books. Exemplary models are usually well-known figures, such as political leaders, famous athletes, student leaders in college, and the like. They are instrumental in providing social norms that are learned.

This form of social learning theory is close in spirit and technique to Skinnerian operant conditioning. Reinforcement schedules are used in explaining the effects of social reinforcers; variable schedules seem to be especially prominent, and they produce long-lasting behavioral effects (cf. Notes, Supplement A-3).

Social learning theory has called attention to the actual behaviors of the human participants in interpersonal relationships as causal factors in personality development. Although cognition plays some part in the theory, there is no assumption of mysterious inner determinants or symbolic transformation of overt behavior. The theory has thus provided a refreshing, behaviorally oriented alternative to the other theoretical formulations. Moreover, it has made important contributions to therapy, discussed later in the chapter.

Although there can be no real question raised about the significance of personality as a psychological problem some question can be raised concerning the efficacy of personality theory as a means of attacking the problem. The central force in personality theory, psychoanalysis, has been steadily losing influence, until today there are many who see it as essentially a dead issue. The more recent theoretical contributions of psychologists have had varying degrees of success in attracting and holding adherents, but none has demonstrated clear superiority to all of the other alternatives.

It is quite possible that the central issues in personality will ultimately be resolved by the accumulation of data and theory on specific problems rather than by the demonstrable superiority and general acceptance of any global theory of personality. This possibility exists even if important, but partial, contributions are sometimes made by the global theories. To require that any single psychological theory explain personality is almost like asking for a biological explanation of life; both concepts represent such a broad scope of scientific problem as to defy complete interpretation.

There is a wide range of deviation in behavior and hence, presumably, in personality. Several major types of behavioral deviancy can be distinguished. Clearly, antisocial behavior, such as delinquency and crime, is a major category, but this kind of behavioral deviancy is primarily a function of social factors (Chapter 17). Mental retardation, a second major form of behavioral deviancy, has been considered in Supplement A-6. The third category is behavior disorder, also sometimes called mental disorder, mental disease, or psychopathology. It is this form of personality variation that is psychologically most intriguing and accounts for the lion's share of clinical and theoretical attention; consequently we shall spend most of our time in this section on abnormalities in behavior.

> *Behavioral Deviancy*

BEHAVIOR DISORDERS

A great variety of frameworks, or models, have been utilized to define behavior disorders. A historical overview may help to orient the reader with regard to this problem.

Historical Perspective

In ancient times, and in the Western world until relatively recently, behavior disorder was explained by assuming that the deranged individual was possessed by evil spirits. Accusations of witchcraft were also commonly made against persons who exhibited bizarre behavior, and during the Middle Ages many women with psychotic symptoms were burned at the stake as witches. Less severe efforts to purge afflicted persons of the presumed agents of the devil were prayer and flogging—the latter designed to drive the demons out of the body (cf. the motion picture *The Exorcist*). Mentally ill persons were also subjected to hot irons and electric shock. They were generally kept in crowded, hopelessly confined quarters. Often they were chained and were even exposed to public display, sometimes for a fee.

Around 1800 improvements in treatment of the mentally ill began to appear. Hospitals were cleaned up and reorganized, attendants were cautioned to treat inmates as patients rather than as animals, and individual records began to be kept; and there was some attempt at simple diagnostic classification. From that time improvements in treatment have been generally, if sporadically, maintained, although even today mental hospitals leave a great deal to be desired.

Focal Issues

DEFINITION OF NORMAL: STATISTICAL OR FUNCTIONAL? There are two major and contrasting ways of defining normality, hence abnormality, of behavior. One is in terms of a frequency distribution of relevant behaviors. By this *statistical* criterion the abnormal is simply any marked deviation from the most common, modal types of behavior. A minor difficulty with this definition is that logically it entails two directions: lower as well as higher frequencies are abnormal. As a practical matter, however, only the least desirable tail of the distribution is considered abnormal, at least for the purpose of defining behavior disorder. Thus a person who shows an extremely low frequency of movement, sitting for hours on end in one place and refusing to respond to conversation, is likely to be considered abnormal.

Let us suppose, however, that the individual who sits quietly for long periods of time is in a monastery. There this behavior may be quite normal, at least under the special circumstances that involve long periods of meditation. This illustration points up the necessary consideration of cultural norms and values—the statistical definition of normality is necessarily used within some cultural framework; by itself it is of limited utility.

The *functional* definition of normality disregards the statistical criterion and concentrates upon the consequences of the behavior. If it works well and helps the individual adjust, behavior is by this definition normal. Again, however, note the essential interactions with the culture: what works well in one culture will simply not do in some other; hence the function of behavior is also necessarily tied in with the cultural framework in which people live and behave.

Historically, behavior disorder was primarily if crudely defined in terms of a combination of the statistical and the functional criteria; people whose behavior was sufficiently different from the social norm were suspect, and if, in addition, the form of the behavior did not enable the persons to adjust reasonably well to their environment (again mainly a matter of social expectations), they were doubly suspect and quite likely to be regarded as disordered and requiring custody and whatever treatment might be in vogue at the time.

THE APPROPRIATE MODEL: MEDICAL OR BEHAVIORAL? One of the great advantages of the new outlook on behavior disorder that arose around 1800 in Europe was the shift from a mystico-religious to a medical conception. In other words, behaviorally disordered persons were now regarded as sick and in need of medical treatment, in much the same way as a patient with a physical illness. As a matter of fact, behavior disorder was beginning to be regarded as one form of physical illness, with determining conditions in the body that were simply more subtle and therefore more difficult to uncover than those of the ordinary physical illnesses.

This view was obviously based upon an application of the functional definition of normality. An organ is normal if it functions properly, regardless of how common such proper function may be. Psychologists generally recognize the great historical contribution of the application of this *medical model*, as it is now called. Many psychologists, however, feel that the medical model as applied to behavior disorder has outlived its usefulness and that it is now time to apply a different kind of functional approach. The most popular such approach is sometimes called the *behavioral model*. This model focuses upon how well the behavior in question enables the individual to adjust in his social and cultural setting; it discards the notion of sickness and concentrates upon purely behavioral determinants and therapies. The same principles that account for normal behavior are assumed to hold also for abnormal behavior, without any special features required. It seems safe to predict that the behavioral model will become increasingly influential. It has crucial implications for therapy as well as for diagnosis and this feature in particular has infused a new enthusiasm into the clinical aspects of psychology.

Diagnosis of Behavior Disorders

There are two great classes of behavior or mental disorder, which need to be kept separate. *Neurosis* (or psychoneurosis) refers to the less severe yet on occasions personally most debilitating variety of behavioral deviation. *Psychosis,* popularly termed insanity, refers to the much more severe type of behavioral disorder in which there is a more or less chronic disorganization of personality sufficient to require radical treatment and usually hospitalization. Table 16-1 summarizes the salient distinctions between neuroses and psychoses.

Practitioners

It may be useful, at this point in our discussion, to distinguish among the major types of practitioners who deal with behavior disorder. The main disciplines that are involved are psychiatry, a branch of medicine; clinical and counseling psychology; and psychiatric social work.

The psychoanalyst is usually a specially trained psychiatrist. However, so-called lay analysts are not medically trained. Freud himself was extremely dubious as to the value of medical training for the practice of psychoanalysis, and so encouraged lay analysis. Today, however, the number of lay analysts is steadily declining, and the M.D. degree is required for all psychiatric practice, including psychoanalysis.

The psychiatrist is thus an M.D., and the clinical and counseling psychologist a Ph.D. Further details covering these various practitioners are provided in the notes at the end of the chapter.

Table 16-1 Major Distinctions Between Neuroses and Psychoses

Distinction	Neurosis	Psychosis
Intensity of symptoms	Relatively mild; contact with reality and social functioning maintained	Severe disorganization; reality orientation and social functioning disturbed
Nature of symptoms	Wide range of mental and psychosomatic complaints, but no hallucination, delusion, or marked behavioral deviancy	Generally chronic, often progressive hallucinations and delusions; speech and thought impairments common
Orientation to environment	Rarely disturbed	Frequently lost
Insight	Commonly but not always present	Rare, as far as can be determined
Social relations	Physical injury to self or society rare	Occasional danger of injury to self or others; social maladjustment common
Causal factors	Faulty emotional adjustment; ineffective handling of anxiety	Largely unknown; two major conditions hypothesized; organic factors (e.g., syphilis, alcoholism) and grossly inadequate emotional adjustment
Therapy	Hospitalization uncommon; counseling or psychotherapy	Hospitalization usual; somatic (drug, electric shock) treatment and psychotherapy

SCOPE OF BEHAVIOR DISORDER

With regard to the question of whether every society has its share of behaviorally disordered persons a study of the Hutterites offers valuable information. In 1951, at the time of the study, the Hutterites were a small German religious sect with approximately 9,000 people living in 100 colonies scattered across the upper Midwest states and the prairie provinces of western Canada. It had been stated that there was a "complete absence of mental disease" in these people, who live a secluded, simple, rural life and seem to be relatively untouched by much of the turmoil of life around them. For example, they have no television, movies, or even radios, and stop schooling after the primary grades. A team of one sociologist, one psychiatrist, and two clinical psychologists made an exhaustive investigation of these people. Obtaining the full cooperation of the Hutterite people they were able to prepare a census of every person who then was or at one time had been disordered. The results of this census were most interesting. A substantial amount of behavior disorder was discovered, but much less than the amount expected on the basis of the overall American and Canadian rates. A total of 199 persons either had or had recovered from some variety of behavior disorder. The distribution of diagnoses was unusual; all but five of the fifty-three psychotic cases were functional. No cases were found of disorder resulting from alcoholism, drug addiction, or syphilis, reflecting the ascetic character of the society. The investigators concluded that immunity to behavior disorder was not provided even by this secure and stable social order. An equally plausible interpretation would be that even in so stable a social structure there is plenty of room for interpersonal conflict, so that emotional factors could well also account for the disorders. Perhaps a more important implication of these data is the contribution toward recovery (a total of forty-nine persons were regarded as recovered) of that social order. Support was apparently offered by the entire community to people with behavior difficulties, and no stigma remained after recovery. Even this conclusion must be tempered, however, by the fact that over half of the recoveries were classified as manic-depressive (twenty-seven of thirty-nine so classified had recovered) and this disorder has an unusually favorable prognosis.

The Neuroses

Inadequately controlled anxiety is the central feature of neurosis. Or it might be more accurate to say that the symptoms of the neurotic represent, essentially, ways in which he has learned to cope with stress and contain anxiety. All of us utilize various defense mechanisms, as described above, in this way. But we become neurotic, or can be labeled as neurotic, when these mechanisms fail to function efficiently, and we adopt ways of coping that are essentially maladaptive. The general assumption seems to be that anxiety blocks adjustive learning. The anxiety in turn is believed to be produced by unresolved conflicts, another instance of ineffective learning.

The symptoms in neurotic reaction show tremendous variability. In general, the person is well aware of his disturbance but not of its causes. Neurotic symptoms are usually disturbing, primarily to the individual suffering them but also to some extent to his associates, especially if they are concerned (and often overconcerned) about him.

The prognosis, which is the prospect for recovery, tends to be better for neurosis than for the more severe and disabling psychotic reaction. Indeed, most of the therapies to be described are mainly effective for neurotic reactions. Moreover, neurosis does not seem to lead to psychosis, as is sometimes mistakenly assumed; neurotic patients who worsen typically remain neurotic, commonly showing intensification of their initial difficulty, sometimes to the point where hospitalization is required.

Brief descriptions of the major diagnostic categories of neurosis are presented in Supplement B-2. It should be remembered that there is a great deal of individual variability in neurotic reaction and the pure clinical type is relatively infrequent.

The Psychoses

Compared with the neuroses, where actual frequencies of occurrence are almost impossible to estimate, the psychoses can be counted with reasonable accuracy. Because the victims of psychosis exhibit such socially and occupationally disabling behavior, they typically receive some kind of professional attention and are usually hospitalized. The general extent of the problem can therefore be assessed from hospital records.

The enormity of the problem can be suggested by some of the statistics commonly cited and generally accepted. For example, it is estimated that in the United States fully 10 per cent of the population will receive psychiatric attention at some time during their lives and half of these will be hospitalized.

The United States is by no means unique in this sorry record. Psychoses with essentially similar symptoms are recorded in all times and cultures. There is no real evidence that they are increasing in frequency, as is sometimes believed. Hospitalization rates vary with such things as economic conditions, but actual increases in long-term base rates can usually be attributed to such factors as more extensive reporting of psychotic behavior, reduced social stigma attached to treatment and hospitalization, and improvement of facilities and treatment (e.g., tranquilizing drugs, which give symptomatic relief and permit shorter hospital stays). As a matter of fact, when careful checks of hospital records have been made, little change has been found over a century (1840 to 1940, in one study).

Very recently, however, a trend seems to have developed in many states toward marked reductions in both the number of patients in state hospitals and the mean length of stay in the hospital. Central Islip State Hospital in New York, for example, was at one time the second largest in the country, with 9,500 patients, but the number had dropped to about 3,500 by 1973. This general reduction in hospitalization statistics has been produced by many factors, including financial and political pressures, the more extensive use of drugs (in particular the tranquilizers), and the growth of effective community psychology and short-term treatment programs.

The term *insanity,* which has legal but not psychiatric meaning, is a popular synonym for psychosis. The usual legal criterion of insanity is whether the patient can tell right from wrong; this test, however, is of little psychiatric value. The problem of assigning legal responsibility, as in crimes, is an extremely difficult one, but attempting to assign responsibility can neither aid the psychiatrist in his work nor enable the psychiatrist to aid the court.

It is customary to classify psychoses into two categories in terms of their presumed causal factors, or etiologies. *Organic* psychoses are those major behavior disorders for which a bodily basis, such as a brain dysfunction, has been identified. *Functional* psychoses are more or less negatively defined; this diagnosis is usually given when a clearcut physiological condition cannot be identified. The term *functional* is used to describe these disorders because the same general kind of emotional maladjustment as in neurotic reactions is believed to account for much of their etiology.

Most of the therapy directed toward psychotics tends merely to alleviate the severity of their symptoms. With a few possible exceptions, little directly effective physiological or behavioral treatment has been developed. As a result, psychiatrists and psychologists are tending more to concentrate upon therapy for the less severely disturbed, neurotic, patients and upon the *prevention* of all forms of behavior disorder. Here we review the major forms of psychological therapy and then discuss the highlights of the mental health movement in general.

There are two prototypic forms of psychological therapy in common use: psychotherapy, in which presumed personality conditions are treated, and behaviorally oriented therapies, in which the behavioral symptoms are themselves treated without regard for hypothetical underlying personality disturbance. In reviewing these two varieties of therapy we consider first two versions of individual psychotherapy, psychoanalysis as the initial and still active version and the more recently developed client-centered therapy. Then some forms of group psychotherapy are considered. Finally we discuss two of the more prominent forms of behavior therapy: therapy based upon classical Pavlovian conditioning principles, and social learning theory and behavior modification, stemming from Skinnerian operant conditioning.

Psychotherapies

PSYCHOANALYSIS. The objective of psychoanalytic therapy is to uncover the hidden, repressed bases of the client's difficulty so as to enable him to face his problems consciously. *Catharsis,* or the original "talking-out" cure discovered by Breuer and Freud, is at the heart of this procedure. It is assumed that once the repressed materials are consciously recognized there will be a release of their emotional involvement and a consequent improvement in the patient even without further more positive steps being taken by him.

Apart from the question of the relevance of the psychoanalytic technique to some disorders (it clearly fits conversion hysterical reactions nicely but is questionable for many other categories of disorder), there are many practical problems involved in its actual administration. Mainly these revolve around the fact that it is distinctly a one-to-one relationship, and is a long and continuing procedure that may require as many as five years for completion. How many clients have that much time, or that much money? Because there are only a relatively small number of authorized analysts (their own training entailing not only a personal analysis but also years of apprenticeship plus academic coursework), there are simply not enough to go around. Their charges are necessarily high (in standard analysis, $50 per hour, with hourly daily sessions lasting at least a year and preferably much longer). For these practical as well as some theoretical reasons, standard analysis has been largely superseded by various short-term versions called psychoanalytically oriented therapy.

CLIENT-CENTERED THERAPY. Client-centered therapy is also sometimes called nondirective counseling because the therapist takes a relatively more passive role than that in psychoanalysis, in which the therapist directs the course of the therapy. In fact, one of the therapist's main tasks is to reflect back to the patient, by noncommital responses and repetitions of what the client says, all the while providing him with unconditional acceptance. In this way the client is encouraged to accept, himself, what he has previously shut out and so be able to take the lead in designing his own growth.

As the client-centered movement has developed it has taken on more active facets. For example, these therapists are active in interpersonal encounters. They see themselves as precipitating client growth in a way somewhat analogous to the way a chemical catalyst works. In this sense, they are not "uncommitted." They are thus stressing active participation, empathetic communication, and even reinterpretation of client statements to highlight the latent affective core of the communication. In these ways client-centered therapy has moved closer to psychoanalytic therapy, and the gap between the two is no longer as distinct as it was at one time.

Apart from the fact that it may succeed with some types of clients with whom psychoanalysis or similar forms of directive therapy are unsuccessful, client-centered therapy has the important practical advantage of requiring much less in the way of time and effort on the part of both therapist and client. For example, the standard form of client-centered therapy usually requires between six and fifteen sessions, well below the number commonly utilized for even the briefer forms of psychoanalysis. The therapist is thus able to see a considerably greater number of clients than the psychoanalyst and thereby maximize any improvements he is able to effect.

EVALUATION OF INDIVIDUAL PSYCHOTHERAPY. In spite of the fact that almost everyone agrees that individual psychotherapy is good for *some* clients *some* of the time, there is a disturbing lack of well-controlled empirical investigations of its efficacy. Various schools offer different kinds of theoretical rationales for training individual therapists, although many agree that the effectiveness of the therapist is a function more of his own fundamental personality than of the type of therapy offered. It has been recently proposed that therapists should be trained in more than one technique, so as to be able to use whichever type of therapy seems most appropriate for the client and his problem.

GROUP THERAPIES. A major motivation behind the development of various kinds of group therapies has been the practical matter of saving time and effort. An additional and perhaps more important benefit of the group approach is that it demonstrates very clearly to the disturbed person that he is not alone in his problems; one of the major stumbling blocks to therapy and improvement generally is the feeling of isolation that many clients have and do not readily give up in response to verbal arguments alone. Further, the intensive personal interactions that are encouraged in some forms of group therapy are believed to provide participants with new insights into their problems and thereby facilitate improvement. New and more positive ways of interacting with others may be rewarded by the members of the group.

Special-interest groups, such as those concerned with therapy of alcoholics or drug addicts, have received much attention. Certain other forms of group therapy more or less follow traditional procedures of one kind or another. Prominent among these forms are the *psychodrama* procedure, in which participants are assigned roles to play in the belief that acting out will facilitate personal understanding, and family groups, in which the therapist meets with an entire family present in one place in order to uncover the dynamic interactions that may account for the adjustmental difficulties of one or more of the members of the family (usually but not always a child).

Popular attention has been given recently to a new type of group endeavor, the *sensitivity* and the *encounter* group. In these groups people with varying degrees of personal maladjustments seek to improve their self-perception and their social skills. These groups are generally directed by therapists working under the aegis of the self-actualization theories of personality. The sensitivity group is designed to sensitize participants to the emotional feelings of others, and the ways in which one's own behavior can elicit such emotional responses. Accordingly, members are encouraged to be quite frank, even to the point of deliberately anatagonizing one another.

The encounter group is similar but places more emphasis upon the failures of normal communication, as between white people and black people in contemporary society. Greater openness is thus encouraged, much as in the sensitivity group, to allow the presumed growth functions of the personality to operate. Another technique that is used to break down customary defense is the *marathon* group, which may meet continuously over an entire week end; presumably fatigue is effective in forcing the participants to abandon their usual coverups. Another way in which these defenses are put aside in encounter groups is the dispensing with clothing. The resulting *nude* groups are expected to function more effectively. Although the public response may occasionally be one of shock, disbelief, or amusement, these various groups should be regarded as serious professional endeavors. Presumably, the participant in such a group is reduced to his basic identity. With so much already revealed, he may conclude that there is very little left to hide. He is ready to be honest about himself in his communications with others.

EVALUATION OF GROUP THERAPIES. There is as yet no scientifically acceptable evaluation of the merit of group therapies. Many psychologists are concerned about the potential dangers in the group therapy process, and especially in sensitivity and encounter groups. They point out that most of us have built up our normal defense mechanisms against anxiety over a lifetime of more or less adjustive living, and that some of us are simply not ready to have these defenses rudely and suddenly removed. Group social pressure can be very strong; partly for this reason, it can be an effective therapeutic tool. Used incorrectly, the group can also be a weapon. Given the fact that there are dangers, group therapy should not be left to poorly trained leaders, as some of the many organizations now actively promoting these popular and lucrative activities seem to be doing.

It should be clear by now that psychotherapy, like hypnosis, is not something to be taken lightly. It is certainly true that some therapeutic effort is likely to be of more good than harm for many people, whose personal interactions might otherwise be simply ignored or worsen. On the other hand, there are always cases in which some improvement, and perhaps quite considerable improvement, can be found in the absence of any formal effort at therapy. This happens partly because people in trouble seek help wherever they can find it. If a person in real distress is placed on a waiting list, he simply locates help elsewhere. Our conclusion must be that psychotherapies are to be selected on the basis of careful, considered judgment, as far as possible aided by a reputable professional person, and that new and untried therapies are to be especially avoided.

Behavior Therapies

Behavior therapies share a conviction that it is more important to pay attention to the particular behaviors that are actually causing the patient trouble in his social adjustment than to attempt to treat some presumed internal state of anxiety or the like. They thus concentrate upon the "symptom" and directly violate the psychoanalytic principle that the symptom is not to be treated. That principle is based upon the presumption that if symptoms are treated and the underlying personality disorder left alone, new symptoms will simply replace the old ones as they are eliminated. The objective evidence, however, for this notion of stimulus substitutability is not very good, with the possible exception of some rather special cases, such as conversion hysteria. On the other hand, even the most objective and behaviorally oriented therapists may sometimes admit to a certain amount of displacement of "symptoms," and all such therapists will agree on the need to insure a complete therapeutic coverage of all relevant behaviors.

Although it is not always possible sharply to differentiate behaviorally oriented therapists in practice, at least two focal types can be differentiated more or less on the basis of their theoretical origin.

SOCIAL LEARNING THERAPY. As an illustration, consider the situation where a person has a severe phobic (fearful) reaction to snakes that the therapist (experimenter) wishes to remove; this happens to be a rather commonly used problem. In treating this phobia, which was severe enough to hinder the actual subjects in some of their everyday activities (walking, gardening, and the like), social learning therapists in one large study utilized for one group a film in which models interacted with a large snake and for the second group had a live model perform various activities with the snake. In these two groups the subjects were encouraged to engage in some of the feared activities themselves, such as actually touching the snake, first with a gloved hand, then with a bare hand. A third group of fearful subjects was given standard *systematic desensitization*, as developed on the basis of classical conditioning theory (see counterconditioning, Chapter 15, p. 479). These subjects were first trained to relax, then asked to imagine snakes in varying degrees of anxiety provocation. Whenever the subject reported anxiety, relaxation was again induced (by the use of tranquilizing drugs if necessary), until the situations that originally had produced strong arousal of anxiety became anxiety-free. A fourth group was a control, without special training.

The results of this experiment were that live modeling produced the strongest positive results; these subjects gave over twice as many approach responses to snakes as the other two experimental groups, whereas practically no change occurred in the controls. Moreover, a follow-up indicated that the fear of snakes had not recurred in the treated subjects, suggesting some durability for the therapy.

BEHAVIOR MODIFICATION. Behavior modification procedures have come directly out of the operant-conditioning system of Skinner. They make explicit use of response-contingent positive and negative reinforcers and disregard any internal processes. In addition to their successes with the chronic psychotic patients living in hospitals, a considerable amount of success has been enjoyed in the application of this technique to the very difficult problem of autistic children. Autistic children are psychotically withdrawn individuals who are so socially unresponsive that they do not speak. They have traditionally been almost impossible to reach by any technique, maintaining a stubborn silence and general inactivity. By concentrating on small improvements in behavior, through the shaping technique, therapists have effected striking improvement in such children, inducing them to sit quietly rather than flare up violently (e.g., bang their head or hands on the table), pay attention, and even verbalize to some extent.

EVALUATION OF BEHAVIOR THERAPIES. As is suggested by the examples used, behavior therapies have proved of greatest value in the treatment of specific symptoms like phobias. Many question the degree to which they can be made applicable to more deep-seated and complex personal difficulties (e.g., the psychopathic personality). Nevertheless, the range of their applicability is being progressively extended, and it is hard to say how far it will ultimately reach. Behavior modification techniques, for example, are being applied to toilet-training problems, feeding problems, educational problems, and an ever-widening circle of social problems. These techniques have been shown to modify clinical behaviors in well-controlled experimental demonstrations, a form of empirical verification that most other therapies have rarely bothered with, let alone achieved.

The most recent development in behavior therapy is to make the target person himself the author of his own behavior—to provide him with the information he needs to modify the contingent relationships that control his actions. It has become clear to many researchers that a possible solution to a number of ethical and technical problems might lie in

providing the individual with a behavior technology that he could apply toward his own chosen behavior change . . . we can see that no constraints are placed on *who* alters the environment to produce the desired behavior change. Given the necessary knowledge the individual can himself perform that task as well as (if not better than) an external behavior designer [Mahoney & Thoresen, 1974, p. 18].

Behavior therapy thus offers an important complement to the clinician, who is no longer restricted so exclusively to verbal techniques.

MENTAL HEALTH

Our discussion of mental health may be divided into two parts, improvement of some negative yet remediable conditions that tend to aggravate behavior disorders and the more positive steps that can be taken to improve personal adjustment.

Correctable Conditions

One of the obvious conditions that needs improvement is the operation of mental hospitals. In many ways the modern hospital, although a far cry from the days of chaining and beating, serves to strengthen rather than weaken the disturbed behavior of the patients. Physical chains have been replaced by mental ones. Institutional regimes are notoriously impersonal, putting a premium on conformity and dependence and penalizing initiative and independence. But the former characteristics are exactly what mental patients do not need, whereas the seldom encouraged latter characteristics are desperately needed by many patients if they are to climb out of the protective shells in which they are emmeshed.

Having hospital staff spend a week end as "patients" is a highly enlightening procedure that has been tried by some hospitals. The feelings of complete dependence and imprisonment that ensue give staff members a glimmer of insight into how patients must also feel when they are captured in such an institutional morass.

The shortcomings of the typical hospital were spotlighted by a recent experiment in which a number of professional health personnel faked one psychotic symptom (hearing voices) and were thereby voluntarily committed to a mental hospital. The pseudopatients made no further alteration of their condition (beyond their name, occupation, and employment circumstances), presenting all of their significant life events exactly as they had occurred. As soon as they were committed the pseudopatients ceased simulation of symptoms and after a brief period of nervousness felt they behaved normally. Nevertheless, their normality went quite undetected by hospital staff members; all but one had been initially admitted under the diagnosis of schizophrenia and were ultimately discharged as cases of "schizophrenia in remission." As the director of this experiment wryly but aptly commented, "The mentally ill are society's lepers" (Rosenhan, 1973, p. 254).

The second condition that needs correction is related to but somewhat more subtle than the weaknesses of hospital function. It concerns the basic problem of diagnostic labels. Even apart from their inaccuracy and the resistance shown by psychiatrists to change them once they are made, they suggest to patients and others alike much more of behavior inflexibility than they should. Even if they are correct—that is, the patient is really "insane," or psychotic, beyond reasonable disagreement—diagnostic labels both within and without hospitals, for neurotics as well as psychotics, so stigmatize patients as to relegate them to a kind of behavioral junkpile. They thus serve as the worst kind of "self-fulfilling prophecies." A new flexibility of attitude and orientation is perhaps the most pressing need on the part of all concerned, and reduction of the abuse and overuse of the psychiatric diagnostic system would be a great stride forward in this respect. The usual diagnostic systems have been presented in this chapter because they universally occur and the student must become familiar with them. Nevertheless, it is hoped that the reader will carry away with him at least a deep-seated concern about if not an outright rejection of the abuses of this or any other system of labeling.

Positive Steps

Here two kinds of comment can be briefly made, one social-political and the other personal. Great strides forward toward supplementing the present system of mostly state mental hospitals were taken during the mid-1960's. Among the most noteworthy achievements were the establishment of regional and community centers for quick psychiatric treatment. Not only are the state hospitals large, understaffed, and almost completely depersonalized, but they are also placed for the most part in relatively isolated locations, rendering it very inconvenient for many patients to come and go as they may need. The newer centers emphasized short-term and out-patient services, allowing patients to come just during the day or just during the night as their condition might require.

With regard to the more strictly personal matters, we have summarized some of the problems of emotional control in Chapter 15. To a very large extent, of course, these objectives are the same as those sought on mental health grounds. In summary, the appropriately "normal" personality is one that has the following three characteristics: (1) an *adequate self-concept*, especially consisting of a reasonable balance between realistic *self-esteem* and *insight* into shortcomings; (2) a substantial amount of *personal independence* and *autonomy*, permitting the kind of self-actualization that marks the normal growth of personality; and (3) an *active social role*, occupational and otherwise, to provide a groundwork for the give and take of personal interactions.

How does one develop these very desirable characteristics? In the main, unfortunately, they mostly seem to depend upon the kind of familial and larger environmental settings into which one is born. Beyond this condition, however, if an individual is aware of these objectives and willing to seek them actively there are many steps he can take. Among them are the utilization of properly trained and responsible professional mental health personnel—college counselors, for example. Carefully selected group psychotherapeutic experiences can also be valuable, again keeping in mind the need for caution with respect to the qualifications of the trainer. But above all else it is the individual's own capacity for self-assessment and his willingness to remain openminded and try to broaden his personal perspective that seem to mark the well-adjusted person in today's complex and demanding society.

Physique–Temperament Typology

The basic research on body typology described in the text was reported by Sheldon (e.g., 1954). The experiment on college women was reported by Cortes and Gatli (1964). The supporting research with children mentioned was by Davidson, McInnes, and Parnell (1957) and Walker (1962).

Demographic Determinants

The classic recent investigation of birth order was by Schachter (1959). The affiliation-need research has been reported by Atkinson, Heynes, and Veroff (1954); Staples and Walters (1961); and Dember (1964). Academic performance of first- and later-borns has been compared by Altus (1966). The psychiatric data are in Tuckman and Regan (1967), and Schachter (1964) has reported some comparisons indicating that first-borns are not as well liked as later-borns by fraternity brothers in college.

Perhaps the most impressive support for the effect of birth order has been reported by Belmont and Marolla (1973). When records for the nearly 400,000

Notes

nineteen-year-old men in the Netherlands were examined, test performance was found to vary directly with order of birth across all social classes.

Mead's famous anthropological study of sex roles was reported in her *Sex and Temperament in Three Primitive Societies* (1935). The recent example of women's perception of women is reported by Vetter (1973). Witkin et al. (1962) reported the rod-alignment study.

Assessment

Nonverbal expression has been reviewed in Fast's *Body Language* (1970). The anxiety research mentioned was reported by Nicholson (1958) and Feshbach and Loeb (1959).

Phrenology

Franz Joseph Gall, the founder and primary exponent of phrenology, wrote a number of volumes on the "science" of reading character from brain-case configurations. The final product of phrenological thought was forty-three surface areas of the brain with, as one might expect, forty-three associated mental faculties. Phrenological analysis was also extended to animals; for example, there was an area in the canine skill that was held to control the trait of loyalty to the master. Gall's chief disciple, Johann Spurzheim, was very popular and in great demand as a lecturer.

Individual Differences

The early postnatal behavior research is reported in Irwin (1930), Knop (1946), and Wolff (1959). Thomas, Chess, and Birch (1970) have described the temperamental study; Williams (1956) reviews the variety of ways in which biochemical individuality is expressed, as in the endocrine gland differences cited in the text.

Personality Theories

The standard source for presentation of personality theories is the book by Hall and Lindzey (1970); a recent review is presented in Arndt's 1974 book. For references on psychoanalysis and Freud, consult Notes, Chapter 3. The "bible" for client-centered therapy is Carl Rogers's 1951 book. His 1970 book and 1974 paper represent later expressions of his point of view. The work of Abraham Maslow, probably the second most influential self-theorist and the emphasizer of "peak" experiences, is represented in his 1968 book. George Kelly's 1955 book describes his personal construct theory.

The trait theory is best illustrated by Allport (1937). The surface-source trait dichotomy and associated factor-analytic development of theory has been emphasized by Cattell (1950). Eysenck (1960) has also developed a factor-analytic approach to personality theory.

Dollard and Miller (1950) have presented a simplified and more or less standard S-R theory of personality. Bandura (1969) is a primary source for the social learning theory approach to personality in which modeling is the key process.

Behavior Disorder

Reorganization of the ancient mental hospital was initiated by French psychologist Philipe Pinel at Salpetrière Hospital in Paris early in the nineteenth century. For example, chains were removed from the patients and medical record keeping started. William Tuke established a retreat in England in which mental patients were accorded generally humane treatment. In the U.S. Dorothea Dix led a campaign during the nineteenth century to improve hospitalization procedures. The National Committee for Mental Hygiene was founded, early in the twentieth century, by Clifford Beers. Beers had suffered from manic-depressive psychosis and recovered; his book *The Mind That Found Itself* (1908) was the first and best-known account of mental illness as seen from the perspective of a recovered patient.

The so-called medical model, the assumption that behavior disorder is a physical sickness and should be treated as such, has been most vigorously attacked by the psychiatrist Thomas Szasz (e.g., 1973). The report by Eaton and Weil (1953) describes the mental health census of the Hutterites. The similarity of hospital admission rates over a full century is indicated in reports by Goldhamer and Marshall (1949) and Dunham (1966), and the similarity over cultures by Dohrenwend and Dohrenwend (1967).

Practitioners

As an M.D., the psychiatrist is the only practitioner legally entitled to prescribe medicine. The psychiatrist therefore enjoys a number of advantages over his fellow workers in the so-called helping professions. He is typically given the highest administrative posts, a fact that is understandably annoying to many psychologists; however, there are signs that this practice, once universal, is beginning to change. Because of the possibility of physical or organic involvement in behaviorally disordered patients with uncertain causal histories, it is advisable, and often legally necessary, to have a psychiatrist (or some other M.D.) available on call in a clinic, if not on the regular staff.

In general, the psychiatrist tends to be more thoroughly trained and more extensively experienced with regard to the psychoses. However, there are relatively few psychiatrists. Other medical practitioners, who may be lacking in appropriate training and/or experience, are therefore often pressed into psychiatric service. The results of this practice frequently leave much to be desired; this is mainly because traditional medical training has typically slighted the emotional determinants and concentrated on strictly physical factors in illness.

Because of the severe shortage of trained psychiatrists, there has been a steady and increasing demand for more psychologically trained practitioners. As a matter of fact, the demand here has exceeded the supply ever since World War II, when the applied branches of psychology may be said to have come into their own.

Two types of psychological practitioner are commonly involved with behaviorally disordered patients. The *clinical psychologist* is a Ph.D. in psychology who has undergone a specialized graduate curriculum and a subsequent internship somewhat comparable to the post-M.D. residency. The clinical psychologist, because of his academic training in psychology, is generally more familiar with research techniques than the typical psychiatrist. He tends to be more trained and practiced on the neurotic than the psychotic type of disorder. He is also likely to be more of a diagnostician than the psychiatrist; this is the service that he is traditionally assumed to provide. Clinical psychologists have increasingly become directly involved in psychotherapy, however, and have achieved recognition in the sharing of this coveted activity with psychiatrists. They have also chafed under their administratively inferior role and have succeeded in effecting some changes in this respect.

The *counseling psychologist* is the second psychologically trained and oriented practitioner. His doctoral training overlaps that of the clinical psychologist to a varying degree. In general, however, the counseling psychologist tends to be more concerned with the milder forms of neurosis and with diagnostic testing. The counseling psychologist traditionally concentrates on such problems as academic and vocational, marital, and general cultural adjustment. His relationship to the clinical psychologist, and to other kinds of counselors (e.g., educational, religious) is somewhat anomalous, and it is not now clear as to what additional roles for him will be developed in the future.

The *psychiatric social worker* is trained in a school of social work, sometimes to the doctoral but more often to the master's level. His (or more properly perhaps, her, because of the majority of women involved) major service is to aid the psychiatrist or the psychologist by taking careful case histories and otherwise interacting with the patients. The fact that the social worker is likely to be in closer contact with the patients may result in his having a relatively greater direct influence than either the more remote psychiatrist or psychologist, whose roles are likely to keep them more occupied with policy matters.

Unfortunately, the same thing can be said of the least well-trained and generally least helpful of the persons concerned with patients, poorly trained and poorly paid hospital attendants or aids. Their almost constant interpersonal association with patients provides a great source of potential good, or evil in cases where personal characteristics are such as to encourage the wrong kind of interaction.

Therapies

Different systems of psychotherapy are reviewed by Bergin and Strupp (1971). Goldstein and Dean (1966) cover techniques by which the therapies can be investigated. Psychoanalytic therapy is discussed in Witenberg (1974). Client-centered therapy is described by Rogers (1951, 1970, and 1974). Jackson (1962) has described attempts to use psychotherapy on schizophrenic patients. The now largely abandoned use of brain surgery (psychosurgery) is reviewed critically by Valenstein (1973). The question of political misuse of psychiatric therapy has recently become an issue (cf. Robinson, 1973) in which this kind of radical treatment along with others has been severely criticized.

The older therapies are reviewed by Slavson (1950). Moreno (1946) is especially associated with the psychodrama technique. The newer and quite promising family therapy is described by Satir (1964), Sager and Kaplan (1972), and Minuchin (1974). Yalom (1970) summarizes the contemporary group techniques, and Maliver (1973) stresses the abuses resulting from the sudden explosion of encounter groups from 1962.

A recent review of the various behavioral therapies is by Franks and Wilson (1974). Bandura (1969) provides a very readable introduction to social learning theory and therapy. Paul and Bernstein's (1973) monograph treats systematic desensitization and similar techniques. The use of imagery and daydream techniques in behavior modification is discussed by Singer (1974). Tharp and Wetzel (1970) have applied behavior modification principles to the problem of behaviorally disordered children in their own environment. The use of token-reinforcement programs in the classroom is reviewed by O'Leary and Drabman (1971). Gray, Graubard, and Rosenberg (1974) describe an especially interesting project in which junior high school students applied the principles of behavior modification to parents and teachers as well as peers.

Self-control procedures are discussed by a collection of authors in a book edited by Goldfried and Merbaum (1973). A thorough review of the as yet unsuccessful attempts to apply behavior modification principles to the problem of control of cigarette smoking is presented by Bernstein (1969); cf. also Dunn (1973). The experiment on removal of fear by models was reported by Bandura, Blanchard, and Ritter (1969).

Mental Health

The account of the pseudopatients and their efforts to get out of the mental hospital is by Rosenhan (1973); letters provoked by his article, and his own rejoinder to them, are in *Science*, April 27, 1973, pp. 356 ff. Braginsky and Braginsky (1969, 1973) have more generally attacked the way in which professionals handle the mental health problem. Almond (1971) describes an unusual therapeutic community developed in the psychiatric ward of a general hospital. The self-governing community is marked by sharing of values, social role playing, and free and open discussion among patients and staff. This kind of therapy points in the direction that future hospital treatment for behavior disorder will most likely take. Lazarus (1969) and Sawrey and Telford (1971) focus on the various adjustmental problems of college students. Goodman's "companionship therapy" (1973), which describes the role of college students as companions to troubled children, is illustrative of the trend toward use of nonprofessionals in today's mental health movement.

This whimsical engraving by James Gillray, the British illustrator, shows in dramatic fashion an example of man's interdependence. Notice that the shock and horror expressed by the gentleman who has fallen through the ice is more than matched in the face of his companion who has suddenly been forced into a helping role.

533

his final chapter takes up phenomena that are both the most complex and the most fundamental in the study of human behavior. They are complex because of the way in which multiple variables interact in social situations. They are fundamental because few behaviors or experiences are free of social influences.

The chapter is oriented around human social interaction but touches at times on animal social relations as well. The social variables selected for discussion at the beginning are social presence, social deprivation and reinforcement, and social conformity. Social presence has been studied over a very wide range of values, from the simple presence of another human organism (which can have significant facilitatory or inhibitory effects upon performance) to the effects produced on people and animals by extremely high densities of population. Deprivation of social stimulation has been found to be an effective motivator, and presentation of social stimulation has been shown to be a potent reinforcer.

Many of the "classic" experiments in social psychology have concerned the problem of social conformity; for example, there has been intensive investigation of the role that group judgment can have on individual decision making. The most startling results have been obtained in some experiments on obedience; human subjects, following the instructions of the experimenter, proceeded to inflict what they thought to be an extremely painful and potentially very harmful electric shock upon another person although actually no shock was administered.

Group functions of various kinds are next considered, with problems of leadership, morale, and crowd behavior discussed. A central problem of social psychology, attitude and attitude change, is reviewed. The nature of persuasive communications is analyzed, and means of improving both the effectiveness of such communications and the resistance to them are examined; selected studies are described.

The last major problem treated is that of interpersonal perception and attraction. When other people are perceived some new variables are introduced into the perceptual process. A variety of explanations for various facets of person perception, especially attractability, are described.

The chapter is concluded with a brief enumeration of the social problems on which the social psychologist might be expected to work. (See also Supplements B-4, B-5, and B-7.)

Social Variables

Man is pre-eminently a social organism. He both achieves his greatest pleasures and suffers his greatest defeats at the hands of other humans. Throughout this book we have had many occasions to point to the role of social factors in various facets of individual behavior. Now we focus on the social variables themselves and outline some of the primary ways in which they have been shown to influence social interactions among men and animals.

Social interaction is readily identified. It occurs whenever one organism's behavior is significantly affected by the presence or the behavior of other organisms. Traditionally, this area of study has been the province of the special discipline of *social psychology*. Whereas psychology generally has focused on the individual, social psychology looks at the individual in relation to other individuals. Sociology concentrates generally on the groups themselves, as organizations and as institutions. Obviously there is no hard-and-fast distinction to be drawn among these interrelated disciplines but at least the broad objectives and general boundary conditions can be kept more or less distinct.

Our survey of social interaction begins by examining the effects of direct manipulation of social variables. A social variable is any condition in which some role is played by other organisms. Social variables range from the mere presence or absence of another organism to the influence that peers have on one another in a great variety of subtle as well as direct ways.

SOCIAL PRESENCE

Social Facilitation

The question of how the presence of other organisms affects behavior is one of the oldest experimental problems in social psychology. Social facilitation is usually broken down into two separate processes: audience effects and coaction effects. *Audience effects* refer to the influence that passive organisms—spectators—have on an actively performing organism; *coaction effects* refer to the influence that actively participating organisms—coactors—have on the performing individual.

In general, the data support the proposition that the performance of well-learned responses is facilitated by the presence of other organisms, either as spectators or coactors. The learning of new responses, on the other hand, is often inhibited by other organisms. An unexpected result in my own laboratory recently demonstrated this point. Male and female college students worked either alone in an experimental booth or in the presence of another subject (of the same sex). Half of the subjects in each case were active performers, attempting to learn the correct item in a series of sets of simple geometrical figures. The other half of the subjects observed a performer. (When performers and observers were in separate booths observation was by means of a display panel which indicated which responses the performer made.) All subjects were given equal opportunity to see which responses were correct and were tested regularly. The result was that all the groups showed normal improvement in test results over trials except for the women students working in the same booth (either performing or observing). Apparently the mere presence of another woman student, either as a passive (observing) or an active (performing) subject, was sufficient to inhibit the acquisition process in this experiment.

Crowding

As the effects of the human population explosion become increasingly apparent and threatening to the quality of life on the planet, social presence in its extreme form has taken on more sinister dimensions. Some of the most disturbing results have come from research with animal subjects, who are more readily manipulated in terms of population density than human subjects. In one experiment, for example, a group of four male and four female mice were placed in a small (8.5-square-foot) pen with plenty of food and water and a generally benign environment. The small initial population bred and the group prospered, all too well. As the population expanded to an ultimate total of 2,200 the quality of life deteriorated rapidly and various abnormal behaviors (e.g., indiscriminate aggression) developed. Eventually all reproduction ceased and the colony died out. There simply was not enough room for normal behavioral processes.

Regardless of the degree to which this kind of research can be meaningfully related to the human situation (and there are good reasons for thinking that human organisms have significantly more flexible adjustments to crowding), it is very probable that population control in some way will become necessary for the maintenance of anything like "normal" behavioral balance.

SOCIAL DEPRIVATION AND REINFORCEMENT

As one would expect, social stimuli make potent reinforcers. As a corollary, their deprivation is extremely motivating. In one study, for example, it was shown that the effectiveness of approval words like *good* and *fine* in discrimination learning was dependent upon the immediately preceding social conditions. Young boys learned faster with such reinforcers after being subjected to a 20-minute period of social isolation and slower after a 20-minute period during which they were abundantly supplied with social stimulation.

Crying in young children is a common behavior that is exceedingly annoying to parents and other attendants and that is under a somewhat more subtle form of social control. The crying child usually attracts attention, which often results in a cessation of the crying. A reciprocal reinforcement situation thus develops: the child is reinforced for crying (by the social attention it receives) and the adults' responding to the crying is reinforced by its cessation.

A number of experimental studies have demonstrated these relationships and the way in which crying as an operant response can be managed. In one study, for example, operant crying was reduced in four-year-old preschool children in a nursery school both by extinction (the removal of all attentive responses to it) and social reinforcement of behaviors that were incompatible with the crying.

Social Deprivation in Animals

The use of animals as subjects in social-deprivation research makes possible a degree of control of variables that is not feasible with human subjects. An excellent example of this kind of research is provided by the extensive studies of the Wisconsin Primate Laboratory, already discussed in some detail with regard to their significance for an understanding of the development of affectional relationships (Chapters 10 and 15). These investigators raised infant rhesus monkeys in varying degrees of social isolation, from mother and/or peers. They concluded that "there is a critical period somewhere between the third and sixth months of life during which social deprivation, particularly deprivation of the company of its peers, irreversibly blights the animals capacity for social adjustment" (Harlow, 1962, p. 4). Apart from the failure to mate, described earlier, socially isolated animals in general paid very little attention to other animals. Moreover, animals who had been totally deprived of social stimulation showed typical responses to extreme threat—tense crouching—when tested in the presence of another animal and failed to defend themselves from aggressive attacks. The investigators found that the period of isolation was directly proportional to the amount of socially inappropriate behavior. More extreme isolation also resulted in poorer prognosis for improvement when the opportunity for social contacts was ultimately offered.

FERAL CHILDREN. The extreme instance of human social deprivation, involving the presumed complete removal of human social stimulation for some period of time, is provided by cases of feral children. A *feral child* is a "wild" child who is discovered after an apparent period of survival and development without benefit of human society; a common presumption is that the child has been found and succored by animals, such as wolves.

Although some of the accounts of feral children make fascinating reading, their authenticity has seldom, if ever, been beyond question. The possibility of any animals, and especially wolves, actually being able to raise a human infant is too remote to merit serious consideration. Most if not all cases of feral children are believed to be the result of abandonment of unwanted children, a practice that is common in some parts of the world. A very small proportion of such children are discovered quickly enough to permit their survival. Defective children are especially prone to being abandoned. This fact is consistent with the general failure of feral children to show much learning in spite of strenuous efforts on the part of some of their discoverers. Unfortunately, there is little to be learned from feral children with regard to the role of social stimulation in development because of the impossibility of reconstructing what actually happened to them.

Social Motives

The way in which adult humans especially are motivated by social needs, such as that for affiliation, has already been described (Chapter 14, p. 433). It seems safe to assume that these various social motives develop during the give and take of social interactions, such as those just described for infants, and are expressed in a great variety of social situations, such as those described under the topics of conformity and obedience.

SOCIAL CONFORMITY

Social conformity is obviously an essential for any society. Unless some degree of conformity to social rules and practices exists, no society can function in an orderly manner. At the same time, however, excessive social conformity, and the corollary absence of individual initiative and independence of thought and action, is a threat to the quality of society as it is envisioned by many of us. Some balance between conformity and nonconformity is necessary for effective political as well as social functions.

How people conform to social expectations has long been a favorite research problem for social psychologists. In this section we examine first a set of "classic" experiments on this problem and then look at selected contemporary research. The two experimental situations in which group influences have been traditionally measured have both involved perceptual judgments.

THE AUTOKINETIC EFFECT. The autokinetic effect is the spontaneous movement of a fixed spot of light in a dark room. Subjects vary widely in the extent of such movement that they report but all report some degree of movement. In this research an individual's typical report of the amount of movement experienced was first obtained, with each subject alone in the booth. The subjects were then brought together in sets of three. Now marked changes were found in the reported movement, so that differences among the subjects decreased. It was clear that even without any evident direct influence, conformity to implicit social norms played a significant part in the overt behavior of the subjects.

A subsequent experiment on the autokinetic effect indicated the potent influence of social factors even when no face-to-face social contact occurred. The subject was instructed to wait while dark accommodation occurred. During this period he was permitted to overhear another subject (who was actually a confederate of the experimenters) make a number of movement judgments; this person then left and the real subject was brought in by himself for his turn at the task. Half of the confederate "subjects" gave distance judgments clustering around 3 inches, the other half judgments clustering around 8 inches. Subjects were clearly influenced by what they had overheard; for example, those who had overheard the larger estimates gave median judgments of 6.8 inches. It was quite clear that this kind of informational influence does not depend upon direct social contact between individuals.

Another variation upon this experimental situation has involved the manipulation of social status of the social influencer. Status-oriented persons have been shown to change their judgment substantially in accordance with their own apparent perception of the social status of the other judge. They tended to move their estimate toward those of the high-status judge (identified, say, as a college professor) and away from those of the low-status judge (the same individual, now identified as a student).

GROUP JUDGMENTS. Another series of experiments on social conformity factors has utilized more natural types of judgments (initially, simply comparing the lengths of displayed lines, later a wider variety of problems, ranging from arithmetic computations to ethical issues). In the original experiment the one true subject was seated with a small group of confederates of the experimenter—seven alleged subjects. Each person was asked to select one line from a set of three of different lengths to match a standard line, a much simpler and far more straightforward task than estimating the autokinetic movement. The true subject was asked to make his judgment next to last, so that the influence of the prior responses, all publicly made, could be assessed. After a trial or so of general agreement some of the confederate subjects began to give erroneous responses, selecting matches that were clearly wrong and placing the one true subject in considerable conflict. Under these conditions a small percentage of the subjects stoutly resisted this social pressure and continued to respond accurately; another small percentage succumbed completely to the social consensus and gave consistently similar but erroneous responses; and the majority of the subjects conformed on some but not all of the trials (one third at least on half of the trials).

A refinement of this procedure was subsequently introduced, to avoid the inefficient method of data collection (requiring seven confederates for each true subject). This technique used electronic switchboards and an (alleged) intercommunication system. Each subject was seated by himself but was told (erroneously) that the other four subjects were similarly seated and that he could see how they responded by means of lights on his own switchboard. Each switchboard did in fact present such information to the subject, but it did so by means of prerecorded tapes, tailored to suit the experimental design. The results were in general the same as had been initially found with the more cumbersome technique, but a broader set of variations was used. For example, even for simple perceptual judgments and arithmetic problems, where the true answers were readily determined, fully 30 per cent of the subjects were found to conform to the (falsified) group consensus. With insoluble, and therefore highly ambiguous, arithmetic problems, as many as 80 per cent of the subjects conformed to an illogical group answer. When social issues (e.g., free speech as a right or a privilege) were used, socially conforming responses were given by three times as many experimental subjects as control subjects tested outside the rigged situation.

Obedience

The experiments on social conformity thus far discussed have been relatively innocuous—guessing how much a point of light moves in a dark room and answering questions about problems or social issues. No one is likely to be very much upset by these procedures. Now we come to an experimental procedure that is potentially more disturbing to the subject. This experiment was designed to determine how people respond to more direct social influence. Three confederates of the experimenter and one true subject were involved in a rather elaborate design. The "cover" for the experiment was that it was intended to investigate the effects of punishment on learning in a "collective teaching" situation. The learner, actually a confederate, was trained by three teachers, two of whom were confederates and one the true subject. The teachers were instructed to shock the learner every time he made an error, and to determine among themselves how much shock to use. They were told that they could always use the same level of shock or could increase it from time to time, but in any event it could be no higher than the *lowest* level recommended by any one of them. The first two teachers, the confederates, routinely called for a 15-volt increase in shock for every error. This fact allowed the real subject, who always responded last, to control the amount of shock to be given. It was he, also, who actually administered the shock, or seemed to do so. In reality, the shock device was only a fake, made to simulate a real shocker but having no electrical power. The genuineness of the procedure was accentuated by having the learner strapped to a chair, with electrical connections attached, in an adjoining room, and having his various verbal responses (actually taped) played back to the teachers sitting before the presumed shock generator.

The responses of the learner were prearranged as follows. Beginning at 75 volts, the first sign of discomfort (a grunt) was made. When 120 volts were administered the learner shouted to the experimenter, complaining that the shocks were painful. At 135 volts he asked to be released from the experiment, and reminded the experimenter of the "heart condition" that he had casually mentioned while being strapped into the chair. The learner's discomfort increased regularly, with statements like "I can't stand the pain" and anguished screams, until at 300 volts he became silent and said no more.

In order to determine the extent to which social influence had determined the amount of shock delivered to the "subject," a comparison group was run consisting of individual teachers, with no social pressure, who were instructed to use any shock level they wished as punishment for any error. Subjects in the experiments were male volunteers, twenty to fifty years of age, who responded to a newspaper advertisement offering payment for participation in a psychological experiment.

The impressive results of the experiment are shown in Figure 17-1. It is clear that the influence of the two confederates was sufficient to push the subject into making decisions that appeared to produce not only severe discomfort and pain but also real threat of physical damage to another individual, who was merely participating in an experiment. Even after the learner cried out, reminding the experimenter of his heart condition and asking to be released, twenty-seven of the forty subjects continued to increase the intensity of the shock; in the control group only two subjects went beyond this point. Seven of the forty experimental subjects conformed to the confederates' decisions all the way to the maximum of 450 volts.

The dramatic results of this experiment were disturbing to the experimenter, who had been interested in determining the degree to which an authority figure (an experimenter) supported by social consensus (two confederates) would be able to elicit obedience to requests that seemed to violate the presumed conscience of the normal person. The experimenter commented that the results suggest that the particular kind of character produced in our society does not protect citizens from brutal and inhumane treatment imposed by a malevolent authority. The fact that adults so readily obey the commands of a single anonymous experimenter, subjecting a 50-year-old man to painful shocks even against his protests, raises the specter of the far greater harm that can be commanded of citizens by the government, with all of its power and prestige.

This last observation has been indicated, it would seem, by many subsequent events. One need only recall the many incidents of brutality in the recent Vietnam War, highlighted by the My Lai massacre. In addition there are many cases of mass murders in which willing subordinates seem to have faithfully followed the dictates of their leader.

The power of social influence to work in a positive (compassionate) as well as a negative (sadistic) direction was suggested by a follow-up experiment by the same investigator. Thirty-six of forty subjects agreed with the two confederates to cease administering shock at all, contrary to the presumed wishes of the experimenter. This more hopeful result, however, does little to negate the generally fearsome

17-1 Mean level of simulated shock administered by forty experimental subjects, under the influence of the confederate's recommendations, and by forty control subjects. The substantial difference between experimental and control curves indicates the influence of the direct social recommendations and the less obvious motivation to obey the experimenter. (Adapted from Milgram, 1964.)

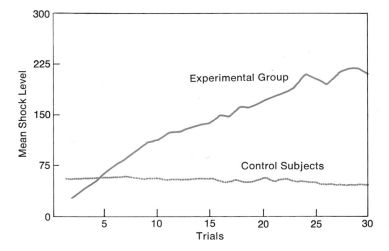

power of social influence for harm; as a matter of fact, it extends the generality of such influence by the potent social influence that can be exerted by peers as well as by figures of authority.

The powerful effect of this relatively simple way of binding an individual to authority was strikingly demonstrated in many further experiments that varied conditions along several dimensions. For example, moving the laboratory from a university building to a seedy office in the city and attributing the research to a private organization did not change the results. Some diminution of the effect, however, was achieved when the experimenter was made an "ordinary man" rather than a scientist, when the experimenter left the room so that he could not observe the shock levels selected, and when two experimenters issued contradictory instructions.

OBEDIENCE IN FIELD SITUATIONS. Obedience has been studied as a function of the level of authority represented by the uniform worn by the person (an experimenter) giving an order. In this study the uniforms used were, in increasing order of presumed status, those of a youth wearing a sports jacket, a milkman, and a private guard (resembling a policeman but without a gun). The orders given were to pick up a small bag, to put a dime in a parking meter, and to change position at a bus stop. The subjects were pedestrians in New York City who happened along and had not observed any previous encounter. Summing the results for the three different situations: the milkman was obeyed by 14 per cent of the subjects accosted, the youth by 20, and the private guard by 36 per cent.

Levels of Social Conformity

A broader view of social conformity, including all kinds of social influence, has emphasized three fundamental levels: compliance, identification, and internalization.

Compliance refers to the simplest level of social influence, in which conformity occurs only because of the direct use of positive and negative reinforcement—reward and punishment. Holding out the promise of reward and the threat of punishment, either explicitly or implicitly, is usually sufficient to motivate compliance. The key to this process is *power,* as exercised by parents, teachers, police, employers—any figures of authority who are in a position to improve or worsen one's lot in life.

Identification is the process that relates to the role that models play in social behavior. We all tend to relate to familiar and attractive people. The process of identification includes the incorporation of the values and the attitudes of these models. Conformity stemming from identification is therefore based upon one's motivation to be like someone else. The key factor in identification is the *attractiveness* of the model.

Internalization refers to the process whereby values and attitudes are accepted because of their own intrinsic worth, on the basis of one's own evaluation of them. The credibility of the source of information is the key factor in determining which of the many competing sources of information and values will be utilized as a basis for internalization. It is this process that accounts for the development of conscience (Freudian superego) as well as the more explicit sets of standards that each of us develops.

A comparison of these three levels or types of processes leading to social conformity indicates that compliance is the most superficial and most readily changed process. Withdrawal of power, as represented by reinforcement potential, can quickly terminate conformity when compliance is the sole source of that conformity. Behavior based upon identification is likely to be much more persistent, as long as the persons or groups serving as models remain attractive. Children who want to be like mother or father, and act accordingly, may develop quite different attitudes and corresponding behaviors as they grow older. Internalization represents the most longlasting level of social influence. Once we have adopted values and attitudes as our own they tend to become independent of the original source (which may have been initially effective by means of identification).

Peer Conformity

The most striking illustration of the potency of forces pushing toward social conformity, and in particular of the potency of social influence by peers, is the contemporary youth culture. To an unprecedented degree, youth today have developed and are maintaining their own culture, their own idiom, their own moral codes, their own standards of dress and speech, their own music. In all of this they appear to be not only stoutly resistant to, and at times quite contemptuous of, adult standards and traditions but also remarkably compliant to the pressures of their peers. From the point of view of social-psychological theory, contemporary youth culture thus represents a blatant rejection of compliance with adults and an exaggeration of the roles of identification and, presumably, internalization. Although all new generations tend to show resentment toward their elders as they struggle for independence, currently this resentment appears to be intensified.

Why has this dramatic cultural phenomenon occurred during the 1960's and 1970's? Social psychologists assign responsibility to several concurrent factors. Primarily, society has become excessively segregated by age. Our youth have been ready and eager for participation in adult society, but at the same time increasingly isolated from such participation. Mainly this isolation has resulted from the exceptionally long period of schooling that youth are expected to have. In clear contrast to many other societies, the period of adolescence is so prolonged as to make it one of the most prominent life periods. The consequence is that our youth, sexually and socially ready for adult society, are locked into artifical social conditions; as a result, they have turned in ever-increasing numbers to one or another of the contemporary forms of a separate youth culture.

Social Suggestibility

Social suggestibility as a form of social conformity is most clearly evidenced in the phenomena of fads and fashions. A *fad* may be identified as some particular kind of behavior that grows, usually suddenly, in popularity among a class of people and then gradually, or sometimes again suddenly, becomes less popular, sometimes disappearing completely. Card games (e.g., canasta or gin rummy), children's activities (e.g., hula hoops), and unusual actions by college students (e.g., swallowing goldfish alive) are among the many illustrations of fads in the United States. *Fashions* may be identified as fads relating to clothing and personal adornment; they are generally periodic, allegedly directed by design experts in Paris or New York.

The basis for the social suggestibility evidenced in fads and fashions is doubtless complex, but the process of identification is probably the major determinant of the massive conformity that marks faddish behavior.

Another form of social suggestibility that is much more restricted and apparently of a quite different origin should also be mentioned. This form occurs when some particular event seems to trigger off replications, often at widely scattered places throughout the world. Perhaps the best recent example of such imitation is the skyjacking problem that suddenly emerged during the late 1960's. Airplanes in flight are clearly highly susceptible to threats of violence, as the public and responsible officials were suddenly made aware. Why had these threats not been used earlier? Apparently it had not occurred to anyone, at least sufficiently to motivate actual skyjacking attempts, until the first effort was made. A similar form of imitation behavior may be seen in kidnappings and in certain acts of vandalism.

There are some behaviors that appear to be directly suggested on a more restricted, individual basis. A curious example of this kind of social suggestibility is the stimulation of yawning in one person who has just perceived someone else yawn; we hardly need to invoke either identification or instrumental value to account for this very straightforward and seemingly unintentional kind of imitation. But it does represent a rather pure illustration of how social suggestibility can operate in the absence of ulterior motivations.

The specially arranged small groups that were experimentally formed in the studies of social influence described earlier represent a somewhat unusual kind of group. Our society is composed of a great variety of organizations, more or less formally structured, in which an equally great variety of social interactions operate. In this section we first examine the nature of some of these groups, with special reference

Group Functions

to their effects on individual members, and then look at some of the research that has been performed on group functions.

TYPES OF GROUPS

Special groups have been categorized in terms of whether they deal with the whole person or with some facet of his personality. The best illustration of the former type of group is the family. In traditional Western society the family is the primary group to which each individual belongs. Not only is it the first group to which the infant belongs, it is also the most stable and most all-encompassing.

The recent weakening of traditional family structure is one of the more important of contemporary social phenomena. Fluidity in familial relationships, especially as represented by broken homes and changes in formal or informal sexual alliances, is generally believed to be a key factor in producing corresponding instability in personality development. Whereas we have long had a small number of aberrant social structures, such as the community arrangement of the Hutterites, the experimentation with various forms of communal living by contemporary youth in particular represents a much more direct and serious threat to the traditional family as a social unit. One of the more fascinating issues of contemporary times is just what will happen to the family as a group, and what viable alternatives to its traditional arrangement will emerge.

Specialty groups of various sizes and types abound in modern society. The active business or professional man, for example, may belong to an amazing array of business and/or professional, social, recreational, political, religious, and other specialized groups. The depth and scope of participation in such groups will vary widely. But in view of the strong tendency of Americans to be "joiners," special-interest groups with their related activities, such as publications and conventions, have proliferated rapidly over the past few decades. The result is that many of us are enveloped by a crazy quilt of group affiliations and are subjected to many overlapping and often incompatible demands on our time and our pocketbooks.

SOCIAL ROLES

Much of our behavior is determined by the positions that we hold in groups. Common examples of such social roles are those of mother or father in the family, employer or employee in business, professor or student in the classroom, president of a political group or secretary of a dance club. Each social or group position carries with it some more or less prescribed behavioral obligations. Once these are known for any given individual, it is possible to predict with reasonable accuracy the main outlines of his relevant behavior.

HIERARCHY OF PRIVILEGE. Most groups are organized according to some order, or hierarchy, of privilege. The highest-ranking members, such as the officers in a group with formal organization, enjoy the most privileges, whereas the lowest-ranking members pick up the crumbs. In a *caste* system, such as the traditional one in India, behavior is rigidly determined by the level of caste into which one is born. Thus the high-ranking Brahmans enjoyed many privileges accorded their caste whereas the lowly Untouchables were allowed relatively little freedom. In the much more loosely formulated *class* system, such as occurs in most Western countries, behavior is less explicitly prescribed. Moreover, mobility between social classes is relatively common, in contrast to the permanence of the caste identification; however, even with our permeable class boundaries, it is obvious that mobility is much easier for some ethnic groups than others, with black people in the United States being perhaps most seriously handicapped in this respect.

IN GROUP AND OUT GROUP. There is a remarkably powerful tendency for humans to make perceptual categorizations of other people in terms of group membership. Members of the groups to which one belongs are perceptually structured as the *in group,* whereas all others are categorized as the *out group.* This distinction will be seen as a general process of the same sort that underlies more highly formalized caste identifications. It is the basis for most of the discriminatory behavior common to complex societies, which has played so disturbing a role in the increasing racial tensions throughout the world.

LEADERSHIP

An all-round leader is more a myth than a reality. Because of the great variety of groups that require leadership it is difficult to make generalizations that apply to all types of leaders. Consider only the size dimension, for example; groups vary in size from very small, tightly knit associations to great countries such as the United States or the Soviet Union with many complex intermingled factions, or even to supranational organizations such as the United Nations, with an even more complex composition. It should be obvious that the personal characteristics required for leaders in such diverse settings vary in accordance with the variations in group structure and functions.

Various attempts have been made to define the qualities of leadership. One investigator who was involved in finding military leaders concluded that

Much effort, both scientific and otherwise, has been invested in the attempt to select young men who will turn out to be good military leaders. It is fair to say that, in contrast to the obvious success scored in recent years in the selection of people for various kinds of specific jobs, no one has yet devised a method of proven validity for selecting either military or non-military leaders [Sanford, 1952, pp. 20–21].

As group needs change, so do the demands on leadership. For example, after a period of rapid and perhaps revolutionary change there typically comes a time during which solidification of gains without further radical changes is desired; the leader tuned to this need will of course be quite different from that suited to the period of change. Thus General Dwight Eisenhower was generally considered to be well suited as president of the United States during the early 1950's when a war-weary people wanted to sit back and relax with a comfortable executive whom they could trust to maintain the status quo. Subsequently the motivation for change revived and John Kennedy was elected president with a promise to get the country moving again. Even the same group will vary its preference, from simple executive to innovative and inspirational leader.

According to some current thinking within social psychology, the most important variables in determination of leadership are (1) the personality of the leader; (2) the attitudes, needs, and problems of the followers; (3) the group itself, and particularly the interpersonal relationships that it encompasses; and (4) the situations as determined by such factors as physical settings, nature of the leadership task, and the like. The way in which these variables are perceived by group members is crucial. For example, although there seems to be some positive correlation between intelligence and effective leadership, in the last analysis people seem to prefer to be governed or led by people whom they understand.

Group Morale

Group morale, sometimes called group spirit, is one of the more important and readily identifiable products of groups. When group members identify with the group, they are likely to contribute substantially to its overall level of morale or spirit. Individual weaknesses and deficiencies, producing low individual motivation or morale, tend to be overlooked in the fusion of motivational process that marks the group. The closer the relationship between the objectives and procedures of the individual and the group, the more closely the individual tends to identify with the group; the result of such a close association is usually a greater contribution to group morale and a stronger dependence on such morale. Moreover, when a group satisfies certain of the individual's strong and otherwise unsatisfied motives (e.g., that for power), the identification process and the reciprocal give and take of motivation are likely to be even more marked.

The motivational exchange just described is typically one-sided. That is, a few individuals generally contribute a great deal to group morale, whereas much larger numbers of individuals may contribute relatively little but receive a great deal, motivationally speaking. If a chain is no stronger than its weakest link, the same statement cannot be made about group morale. Rather the motivation of the group appears to be no weaker than that generated by its more enthusiastic members; defection of some members is tolerated and group morale is likely to suffer markedly only when substantial numbers show seriously lowered motivation regarding group functions and standards.

There are both advantages and disadvantages to the way in which group morale seems to be more than the mere summation of individual motivations. A major advantage is that identification with the group permits an individual to maintain normally contradictory motivations; for example, he can justify certain of his own essentially selfish or at least self-centered motives on the grounds that they are for the common good of the group, an altruistic motive that it would otherwise be difficult to claim. Another socially desirable feature of close identification with groups is that cooperative behavior, or assistance to others that is independent of direct personal gain, is more readily elicited on the basis of group loyalties. Finally, in emergencies such as war, group loyalties can be invoked to solicit socially productive behaviors that it would be impossible to evoke on the basis of individual motivations alone.

This latter aspect of group morale suggests what is perhaps the greatest single danger of the group motivation process: the exploitation, for personal objectives or questionable group objectives, of group members by unscrupulous leadership. Leaders may disguise their true motives and shield themselves behind some overblown or even fictional group standards. Thus appeals to group unity may permit vested interests of one kind or another to achieve aims, such as personal financial profit, that the individual members would not approve if these aims were openly expressed. Those who take political statements at face value without critical scrutiny are inviting this kind of duplicity; this does not mean that politicians are the only deceivers or that all political statements are untrustworthy, but merely that politics provides a fertile field for such deception.

INTELLECTUAL FUNCTIONS OF GROUPS

Psychologists have been concerned with comparing the efficiency of individuals working on intellectual tasks when they are in groups with their performance working alone. The presumption is that cooperation among group members and mutual stimulation and criticism will result in the group's performance exceeding the total of the individuals' isolated performances.

Most of the experimental attention has been devoted to problem solving and the generation of ideas. The results are mixed. On the one hand, some clearly positive results have been reported, with group solutions definitely superior to individual solutions. On the other hand, some experiments have demonstrated that "nominal groups" (composed of individuals actually working by themselves) are superior to real groups. This result has been found, for example, in experimental tests of "brainstorming." That technique, initially advanced by an advertising executive, involves an initial period of complete freedom from criticism during which all members of the group are encouraged to propose as many ideas as they can, as rapidly as they can, without any effort to "edit" them. In spite of the lack of solid experimental support for it, brainstorming has proved popular in business, because of the strong motivation to improve the quality of ideas and the speed with which they are produced.

GROUP MOTIVATIONS: NATIONAL CHARACTER

One of the most ambitious and most interesting efforts to deal with groups has been the application of a kind of projective technique in an attempt to identify motivations characteristic of different nationalities at various times. Dominant motives of different nations have been assessed by an analysis of the art and folklore of the people. Analysis of the content of elementary school textbooks from the years 1925 and 1950 was carried out in one study involving several nations. Economic measures (e.g., the gross national product for the years between 1925 and 1950) were then also obtained. The general hypothesis under consideration was that the level of achievement motivation is correlated with the degree of achievement-centered behavior. More specifically, those countries with high achievement motivation scores in 1925 were thought to be more likely to show high levels of economic progress. This prediction was confirmed. The nations whose 1925 textbooks were full of achievement themes were found to have made the greatest economic progress in the following decades.

High need achievement in a country was found, in later research, to be associated not only with greater economic success, but also with some of the unhappy concomitants of such success: for example, behavior pathologies, such as hypertension and ulcers. Other key motives, affiliation and power, were also analyzed over many decades for seventeen different nations. Figure 17-2 shows one typical result of this analysis of elementary school textbooks in the United States from 1810 to 1950. Comparison of the shifts shown for the United States with the similar measures obtained for the Soviet Union led to some interesting suggestions. For example, the achievement motivation curve of the Soviet Union surpassed that of the United States about 1955, whereas our power motivation curve surpassed that

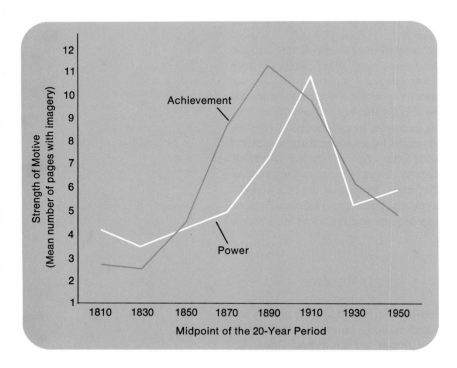

17-2 Trends in the strength of achievement and power motives for the United States from 1810 to 1950. Motive strength is inferred from content analysis of children's readers. Note how achievement reached its peak in 1890 and power 20 years later. (Adapted from Rudin, 1965.)

of the Soviet Union about a decade later—again, remember, as measured purely from an analysis of the content of the textbooks. What the latter shift portends for our use of power-oriented tactics similar to those we condemn in others, such as the totalitarian regimes, remains to be seen. But some will find confirmation of this suggestion in the increasing appearance and acceptance of violence in our culture as well as certain more specific incidents (e.g., the widespread encouragement and use of police-state tactics by a recent national administration).

It is remarkable that so much can apparently be gleaned from such a relatively simple source as elementary school textbooks. Although there are obvious risks and pitfalls in this kind of research, enough has been demonstrated to suggest the rich promise of the technique and to justify its extension into broader contexts.

COLLECTIVE BEHAVIOR

Collective behavior has been defined as relatively unorganized group behavior that originates spontaneously and depends upon interstimulation among its partic60ipants for its generally unpredictable course of development. Examples of phenomena that are included in this classification are riots, crazes, fads, mass hysteria, public revolts, protest movements, rebellions, primitive religious behavior, and reform and revolutionary movements. It should be obvious that a variety of psychological principles will be necessary to explain such behavioral diversity.

In order to provide some basis for a short treatment, the present discussion will focus on the crowd, itself a relatively broad concept. A crowd is a more or less loosely organized and generally temporary assemblage of people. Crowds are sufficiently similar to permit a number of generalizations. These will be described first through empirical or descriptive statements, followed by the presentation of selected theoretical accounts.

Empirical Generalizations

SHAPE. As crowds form they characteristically take on a circular shape. A crowd normally grows in successive layers around a circular core, which has some separation of active speakers and onlookers. As more people arrive they tend to remain on the periphery, enlarging the ring. Much milling about usually occurs, which is believed to facilitate the exchange of information, or rumor, and also to enable people to occupy positions in accordance with the role (active or passive) that they are to play. It has been suggested that the more strongly motivated persons will tend to occupy places toward the center of the circle.

BOUNDARIES. The boundaries of crowds are difficult to measure but play important roles in crowd functions. They vary in permeability, sometimes being sharply demarcated and sometimes vague and diffuse. It is at the boundary that confrontations occur between hostile groups, such as the police and a body of demonstrators. Some of the more dramatic incidents are therefore likely to occur at the boundaries rather than the core of crowds.

PHYSICAL RESTRICTIONS. Physical factors often are crucial in crowd behavior.

The width of a street, for example, determines how successful a small, active crowd can be in attempting to block passage and thereby disrupt traffic. Panic reactions (as to fire or threat of fire) are largely a function of the physical arrangements of the exits from a room or hall. Panic is unlikely when all the exits are closed and no one is permitted to leave, and when all the exits are open and everybody is given an opportunity to leave. Panic reactions have been found to set in most readily when some of the exits are open and others are blocked, creating a condition of uncertainty.

SIZE. The size of a crowd ordinarily depends on the special features that exist in its formation. Consider an unfortunately common type of incident, such as a pedestrian being knocked down by a vehicle on a busy city street. The core of a crowd typically develops quickly, composed of those individuals who happen to be close at hand when the accident occurs. The size of the crowd will normally increase up to a certain point and then stop growing. One fairly obvious explanation for the cessation of growth is that onlookers at the periphery find it increasingly difficult to see what is happening at the center, and the spread of information from the center to the periphery may not be sufficient to hold their interest. It is often difficult to estimate accurately the number of people present in larger crowds. Newspaper and police accounts are notoriously unreliable and are generally believed to be highly inflated. For example, reported estimates of the size of crowds at St. Peter's Square in Rome have run up to 1.5 million. When the square itself was measured, however, the maximum number of people that it could possibly hold was figured at less than a quarter of a million people; and this estimate assumed that people were packed, in effect, like sardines in a can—with each person occupying no more than 2 square feet.

RUMOR. Perhaps the most crucial ingredient in crowd behavior—and especially in violent crowd behavior—is the rumor. Crowd behavior characteristically depends on the passage of information in unverified and highly distorted form. One important function of rumor is that it enables uncertain individuals in a crowd to share the sentiments of the more enthusiastic and active individuals. The intensity of rumor is generally agreed to be dependent on both the level of interest in the listeners and the amount of ambiguity present. Moreover, the processes of *leveling* (shortening and simplification) and *sharpening* (exaggeration of selected points) have been applied to the passage of rumor. Their action in such situations represents a marked acceleration of the rate of change typically observed in memory (see pp. 369–370). Utilization of rapid-communication devices such as the walkie-talkie has also served to accelerate the rate at which information and rumor are passed through a crowd and removed the rumor's dependence on the physical contiguity of participating individuals.

Theories of Crowd Behavior

TRADITIONAL VIEW. The traditional theory of crowd behavior is that there is a radical change of personality among the individuals of a crowd. Actions that one would not normally perform are readily engaged in when others are so behaving. The three principal mechanisms invoked to explain this radical transformation are *anonymity*—the suspension of the responsibility of the individual, with its attendant inhibitions; *contagion*—both ideas and emotions spread from one individual to another, much in the way that an infectious disease is transmitted by pathogens transmitted from person to person; and *suggestibility*—the uncritical acceptance of demands after individual responsibility and inhibitions have been waived.

PSYCHOANALYTIC VIEW. Freud was impressed with this traditional view of crowd behavior and proceeded to revamp it within his psychoanalytic framework. The main factor in his theory was the loss of control by the superego and its replacement by the conscience of the crowd leaders.

CRITIQUE OF TRADITIONAL VIEWS. Contemporary social psychology has been critical of these traditional ideas, mainly because they were initially stated in vague and overgeneralized terms and have not been followed up by more precise and experimentally oriented empirical observations. Their potential contribution to an understanding of crowd behavior is still recognized, but not as a complete or fully satisfactory interpretation.

CONTAGION AND CONVERGENCE. Contagion remains a viable variable. It is complemented in current thinking by the simpler structural variable of *convergence*. Here the focus is on the composition of the crowd; the crowd tends to attract individuals who have some degree of predisposition toward its apparent objectives. People with such shared interests tend to converge, or come together in groups. Their shared sentiments make them easily influenced, so that the suggestibility factor is maximized. Consider a motorcycle gang or a group of adolescents assembled to hear a rock concert; there is little need to look much beyond their shared interests to explain their behavior.

The fact that crowds tend to become more homogeneous is thus differentially interpreted by contagion, which emphasizes the milling about and interchange of idea and affect, and convergence, which focuses on the composition of the group. These two factors are in no way incompatible, and both probably play an important part in certain kinds of crowd behavior.

EMERGENT NORM THEORY. The most interesting new theory of crowd behavior is *emergent norm* theory. This notion denies that crowds are really homogeneous. It holds that this feature is illusory and depends upon incomplete observation. If an apparently unruly crowd is examined carefully, according to emergent norm theory, it will be found that most individuals are not actively aggressive but are merely interested onlookers. The crowd is seen as unruly because of the conspicuous behavior of a relatively small number of its most active members.

On the positive side, this theory holds that behavioral norms emerge in each crowd and determine the kind of behavior that is regarded as appropriate and is thus accepted by all or most members even if they themselves are not actively engaged in it. The behavior of the conspicuously active minority tends to establish these norms and so sets the tone for the entire group. This point of view plays down contagion and suggestibility as crucial variables in crowd behavior and offers as primary a combination of cognitive and affective factors emerging within the group as its members strive to define their objectives. Although not yet firmly supported by experimental data, the emergent norm theory is open to empirical verification and promises to be a most useful addition to older attempts to explain these important types of behavior.

Take a Breather

PERSON PERCEPTION

What is your impression of this person?
This individual has been described as: *energetic,*

assured, talkative, cold, ironical, inquisitive, persuasive.

Please write your own evaluation of him. Turn to p. 555 when you have completed your evaluation.

Changing Attitudes

The problem of how best to change attitudes has probably been the most actively researched and discussed issue in all social psychology. We are all under a constant barrage from a wide variety of communications, ranging from the most blatant appeals to the most subtle innuendos, designed to change our attitudes on this or that matter. What are the most persuasive kinds of communications? Who are the most effective communicators? What characteristics of the audience are most important? These are some of the questions with which social psychologists have been concerned and which we will consider.

Before looking in detail at these questions, it is advisable to emphasize the dual nature of attitudes, that is, their cognitive and emotional components. Attitudes are generally more stable than opinions. They are less readily changed, because the new information that can quickly alter an opinion may operate mainly or exclusively through cognitive channels, leaving the emotional bases unaffected. But it is the emotional component that is most effective in determining our positive or negative feelings on an issue—and our disposition to act in one way or the other. Strictly cognitive appeals are therefore less likely to be effective, and a great variety of approaches to this emotional basis have been developed by such practical people as politicians and advertisers.

PERSUASIVE COMMUNICATIONS

The most common means by which attempts are made to change attitudes is the persuasive communication. Here we may review some of the more significant of the research results concerning the three elements in this kind of communication: the communicator, the message, and the audience.

The Communicator

Most of the research on the communicator has focused on the credibility characteristic. The more credible, or trustworthy, the communicator seems to be, the more weight his message is accorded. In one experiment, for example, an interaction was found between credibility of the communicator and the degree of discrepancy between his and the subjects' opinions. Subjects were given state-

552

ments about the quality of a poem that were in varying degrees discrepant from their own opinions. Attribution of this discrepant opinion to a highly credible person (in this case, T. S. Eliot, a well-known and highly respected poet) resulted in the greatest change in attitude for the most discrepant statement. The maximum change occurred for the more moderate degree of discrepancy, however, when the communicator was a person of moderate prestige and credibility (another college student).

An interesting exception to this clearly positive relationship between communicator credibility and attitude change was found in another experiment. Three speakers argued for increased leniency toward juvenile offenders. They were a judge (high credibility), a member of the audience who was not identified (neutral credibility), and a person who had been a delinquent and was now on bail after being charged with illicit drug usage (low credibility). The attitude change was measured both immediately and after a delay of three weeks.

Figure 17-3 shows these results. The delay in measurement produced a marked decrement in effectiveness of the communicators with greater credibility and a slight increment in that of the low-credibility speaker. This "sleeper effect" has been attributed to a blurring in memory of the source (communicator) and content of the message, so that the effectiveness of the credibility factor did not hold up over time.

The relationship between the communicator and the audience is another significant variable related to the credibility factor. Politicians take great pains to associate themselves with whatever audience they happen to be addressing, using vernacular and highly idiomatic language when in the presence of the "common" people, and maintaining a more kingly English when meeting with fellow politicians or, say, professional or business groups. Although the politician may sway a particular audience by appearing to have similar values as the audience or by telling them what they want to hear, he runs the risk of appearing less credible to outside observers when he uses such tactics. This is especially true if he is seen as having something to gain from his position. Thus the politician who advocates increasing highway taxes to a group of railroad men might get their votes, but if the speech is televised, the public may question his credibility because of the obvious self-interest of his position. On the other hand, if he takes a position against his own self-interest, such as advocating increased highway taxes to a group of truckers, then his credibility to outside observers may be enhanced. The audience's perception of the speaker's credibility may also be related to the finding that "accidentally overheard" communications are more persuasive than communications directed at a particular audience. We have more reason to question the possible self-interest of a speaker who is obviously trying to persuade us than one who does not even know we are listening.

The Message

There are a number of conditions most authorities seem to feel enhance the persuasiveness of the message. Putting pleasant, more or less acceptable arguments first, for example, establishes a more positive and sympathetic set, so as to soften

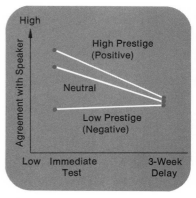

17-3 Opinion change as a function of speaker and time of test. Note that the greatest immediate effect came from the positive (high-prestige) speaker but that this difference did not persist over the three-week interval. Apparently there was a dissociation of communicator and message over this interval. (Adapted from Kelman and Hovland, 1953.)

the blow when harsher, less acceptable arguments are subsequently presented. Arousing as few counterarguments as possible is another, even more obvious procedure designed to minimize opposition and so presumably increase the effectiveness of the positive arguments. Another effective gambit is to obtain some kind of early commitment, even a simple one such as acceptance of advertising material, or better still, a free sample of some sort; this slight commitment seems to open the door to later, more serious acquiescence. Thus, in one experiment, people who had earlier signed an innocuous petition in support of safe driving agreed in significantly larger numbers (55 per cent) to having a rather ugly "Drive Carefully" sign placed in their front yard than controls who had not been so contacted (17 per cent).

The degree to which arguments opposing one's own views should be presented is another variable whose effects cannot be summarized in any simple manner. In general, it seems that one-sided presentations are most effective when made to audiences already strongly committed in favor of the position and relatively uninformed. It is considered better to offer both sides of the issues to audiences composed of unsympathetic persons, or of uncomitted but relatively intelligent and well-informed persons, or of persons who will ultimately be receiving counterarguments.

A further controversial issue involves the effectiveness of using threats, or attempting to induce fear of consequences should the audience not accept and act on the speaker's arguments. This technique is commonly adopted in advertising (social ostracism threatened, for example, if mouthwash or body odor spray is not used) and religious communications (the threat of purgatory, for example, in fundamental religion). Recent research has tended to support the common assumption that such appeals to fear are generally effective, especially when relatively low levels of anxiety are involved. When higher anxiety is initially present, however, adding additional fear may have an effect opposite to that intended, inducing greater resistance to attitude change (for example, emphasizing the threat of cancer may make an already concerned individual so acutely fearful as to prevent his submitting to the proposed medical examination).

The Audience

Some audience characteristics that make for differential susceptibility to persuasive communications have already been mentioned. Beyond these, social psychologists have concentrated on how resistance to persuasive communications develops and can be modified. It seems to be generally agreed that the most important single personal characteristic producing high resistance to attitude change is *self-esteem*. Ego strength appears to be a function of both the amount of personal success an individual has enjoyed and the manner in which he has been able to build an integrated personality. Attitudes that function as *self-protective* or *defensive devices* are especially resistant to change. Racial prejudice, for example, can become a much-needed prop that serves to bolster personality strength in extremely self-defensive individuals whose racial attitudes are extremely resistant to change.

A less personal factor is the degree to which the attitudes under fire are en-meshed in a larger set of values, such as those relating to familial, patriotic, or religious matters; attacks on superficially narrow attitudes are often blunted be-cause of the integration of those attitudes within *broader value systems,* which are much more resistant to change. Affiliation with special groups, whose attitudes and opinions are incorporated, can make a person extremely resistant to contradictory information.

One special technique is of interest as a means of increasing resistance to attitude change. This is the so-called *inoculation* procedure. It consists in exposing an individual or group to a relatively mild form of counterargument, designed to arouse sufficient defense so that when much stronger counterarguments ultimately occur they can be more stoutly resisted. The analogy is with body defenses against disease that are produced by a small amount of the pathogen; it is assumed that individuals who have never been exposed to questioning of their fundamental attitudes (e.g., their religious beliefs) may succumb to massive attacks in much the same way as they would to a sudden attack by germs to which they had never been exposed and against which they had therefore developed no immunity. When there is a sufficient degree of personal involvement, as a matter of fact, it has been demonstrated that the simple announcement of an impending attack can arouse strong resistance to change of attitudes, even in the absence of substantive argu-ments themselves.

Brainwashing

The use of coercive persuasion, or "brainwashing," by the Chinese and Russian authorities within recent years represents an extreme form of persuasive com-munication. Although there have been few, if any, authoritative reports from the Chinese or the Russians themselves concerning their techniques, studies by Western scientists have found little to substantiate the widespread fears sensational newspaper and magazine accounts have aroused in the United States. Most of the Russian "confessions" seem to have complex determining factors that are in many respects peculiar to that socio-political environment.

Breather Interpretation

PERSON PERCEPTION

In an early experiment more than 1,000 college stu-dents were given the task requested in the Breather (p. 552). They generally answered the question, "What is your impression of this person?" with remarkably complete personal descriptions. Now look back at your own answer. Was it similarly complete? Did you generate additional traits, beyond those explicitly listed? If so, were they stimulated by your reaction to your own initial efforts to prepare a complete account? How do you explain such effects of a simple list of adjectives? (See discussion on p. 559.)

A much publicized and related technique the Russian Communists have been accused of using is the psychiatric diagnosis and institutionalization of political opponents and dissidents. Although the facts of such apparent abuse of psychiatric treatment are hard to determine, some documentation has been reported in the Western press. This technique is more a direct attempt to suppress unwanted behavior than an effort to change attitudes.

The Chinese, who subjected American prisoners of war to such efforts during the 1950's, seem to use different techniques. They had a three-step process. First, they tried to "unfreeze" the attitudes of the men, by casting doubt on their standards, as of military conduct; second, they attempted to "change" the attitudes, by inducing some degree of acceptance of Chinese standards and objectives; and third, they endeavored to "refreeze" the new standards into firm attitudes. Some idea of the extent of their success is indicated by the fact that of the very great number of American prisoners held in China at that time, following the end of the Korean war, only twenty-one actually refused repatriation. Thus, although there is certainly reason to be concerned about the use of these techniques, particularly the use of such auxiliary procedures as forced isolation and drug injections, there should not be undue pessimism as to their efficacy.

When children are subjected to a complete immersion in any extremely dogmatic framework throughout their development, much more lasting effects can apparently be produced. The success of the Hitler youth movement in Nazi Germany, even to the extent that some youths were reported to have turned in their own parents for violations of the Nazi code, suggests the potency of this kind of socialization. Less dramatic but perhaps equally powerful evidence is afforded by the success of some religious organizations in indoctrinating our own youth who are concurrently exposed to alternative religious views; the strength of early emotional conditioning is reflected in the feelings of uneasiness that occur in those whose intellectual positions change as they mature.

LIFE EXPERIENCES

Use of persuasive communications is not the only way attitudes are changed. We can seek out and obtain new information on our own initiative; other new information comes our way without any attempt at influencing us, as a normal result of living in a complex environment. Given the proper emotional basis, these sources of new information can be effective in modifying both opinions and attitudes. Social psychologists have endeavored to discover some of the more important principles underlying attitude modification under the conditions of normal living. (Research involving *cognitive dissonance* is described in Chapter 7, p. 207 in relationship to its role in thinking.)

Merely suggesting that the holder of an attitude expose himself to a broader array of experiences involving the object of the attitude is not, by itself, likely to help much in the modification of prejudiced attitudes. Certainly there is no automatic reduction of a social prejudice, say, from merely encountering more of the kind of people against whom one is prejudiced. Apart from other considerations, the odds are against a radical change in attitude occurring because of the nature of the attitude itself. If one is indeed predisposed to think ill of blacks or Jews or college professors, he is almost certain to be selective in his perception of them; that is, the fact that he is prejudiced will bias his perception—he will be much more likely to notice negative features that serve to reinforce his predisposition and to ignore exceptions to it. His belief systems will then be strengthened accordingly. In this way prejudice tends to feed upon itself, growing stronger rather than weaker, unless special efforts are made to remove the blinders that it places on perceptual and thought processes. Under the proper circumstances, however, it is possible to use increased social contact to reduce prejudice, as the study next described demonstrates.

Enforced Contact

Because of its prominence as perhaps the primary social problem in the United States, antiblack prejudice among whites has been the subject of many investigations of attitude change. In one early study, the attitudes of white housewives living in biracial urban housing projects were investigated. Two of the projects were racially segregated, with white and black families in separate areas, and two projects were racially integrated, with white and black families living within the same apartment blocks. Much more relaxation of racial prejudice was found among the housewives in integrated housing when interviews were conducted. The investigators concluded that prejudice seemed to be reduced more readily when the experiences of the prejudiced persons required them to adjust their opinions of blacks as individuals and when the behavior that was inconsistent with the prejudice could not be viewed as merely conformity to a social role. The discrepant behavior must be seen as belonging to the person rather than to the situation.

In another early study, this one conducted with racially integrated boys' camp, a less optimistic result occurred. Of a total of 106 white boys, twenty-four showed substantial decreases in prejudice but twenty-seven showed increases. Individual differences, relating mainly to strong aggressive feelings in those who revealed increased prejudice, were held responsible for this result.

Shared Coping

Still another study of boys in summer camp is valuable in providing positive suggestions concerning ways in which close social contact, in the form of cooperative sharing of efforts to cope with a problem, can serve to reduce prejudice. In this study, the prejudice was deliberately induced by the experimenters on the basis of an arbitrary division of twelve-year-old boys into two groups. After cooperation was required within each group to establish a sense of group loyalty, the investigators arranged a highly competitive relationship between the groups (e.g., they delayed the arrival of one group at a social function and encouraged the group already there to take the best refreshments for themselves).

Once the rivalry between the groups was established the investigators set about to determine how it could be most effectively reduced. Their first step was to eliminate the competition and allow free mixture of the groups. They found that this procedure had little effect, except perhaps to increase the hostility of one group for the other. They then put the boys together in one single group and required cooperation (e.g., a crisis was arranged so that all the boys had to pitch in together to repair a break in the water system). After a number of such situations, in which the boys worked together in coping with common problems, the initial group prejudices were broken down.

Shared coping of this kind is found in many real-life situations in which blacks and whites work together (e.g., military service, athletic teams), and there is some reason to believe that at least the opening wedges of improved relationships are to be achieved in this way. But it is important not to be too optimistic on this issue. Deep-seated attitudes of any kind are very difficult to change. Moreover, for every situation in which cooperation is required there may be many other situations in which selective perception permits the continuation and perhaps even the enhancement of the original prejudice. Certainly merely forcing two hostile groups into closer physical proximity by itself does nothing to reduce their prejudiced attitudes. But when such groups are required to work closely together for their common good, a basis for continued modification of prejudiced attitudes is established.

New Group Affiliations

The least painful way to change attitudes is probably by forming new group affiliations. Given the degree of social mobility in American society, this factor is among the more prominent of all the ways in which attitudes are changed.

A classic study showing the effectiveness of new group affiliation in this respect was conducted on women enrolled at Bennington College during 1935 to 1939. Most of these college students came from economically privileged and politically conservative families; however, they were taught by predominantly liberal faculty members. The students' attitudes on political and social issues changed from conservative to liberal during the course of their college career. Individual interviews revealed that those seniors whose attitudes had changed in this way most strongly were motivated to be independent of their families and accepted in the liberal environment of the college. Some of the more conservative seniors, on the other hand, indicated that they had tended to isolate themselves from the college community for fear of disrupting relationships with their families.

The pervasive influence of group affiliations, by means of the social roles demanded or at least strongly suggested by the groups, should be evident to anyone who looks closely and objectively at American society. The postcollege years, for example, are most often marked by a progressive shift in the direction of social, political, and economic conservatism. A major factor in this common attitude change is probably improved financial status and a consequent move into new social and economic groups. Knowing the groups with which an individual is affiliated provides a substantial basis for estimating the kinds of attitudes that he has. Nevertheless, there are exceptions to this generalization. A follow-up study of the Bennington College women students, for example, was conducted some twenty-five years after the initial assessment. It was found that they generally maintained their strongly liberal attitudes, at least as measured by their political preferences in national elections. The investigator concluded that an important factor in this stability was the continuing reinforcement of these attitudes by husbands who were also strongly liberal in their attitudes.

The direct relationship between two (or more) individuals is fundamental to all the more complex social interactions. In this section we examine some of the research devoted to interpersonal relationships. The general problem of person perception is first discussed, after which the more specific question of personal attraction is considered.

Interpersonal Perception and Attraction

PERSON PERCEPTION

How we perceive other persons is basically a function of general perceptual mechanisms. The perceptual process is more complicated with regard to persons than with regard to objects. First, it is enormously complicated by the operation of new variables, mainly relating to social factors. Second, certain of the major determinants of perception are exaggerated and play much more active roles than they do in nonsocial perception; this discussion will focus on the more prominent of these.

VERBAL LABELS. Research has demonstrated the remarkably potent role of verbal labels in the process of forming impressions of people. This is especially true when there has been relatively little concrete observation. The breather exercise (p. 552) was designed to demonstrate this point.

In another experiment variation in a single descriptive word was found to make a surprising difference in the responses of a college class to a substitute lecturer. The class was given mimeographed sheets with a brief description of the guest lecturer. The following statement was included in the sheet given to one-half of the students: "People who know him consider him to be a rather cold person, industrious, critical, practical, and determined." The other half of the class received identical statements except for the substitution of the word *warm* for *cold* in the sentence quoted. This superficially simple variation not only produced significant differences in the way in which the lecturer was described and rated by the two groups of subjects, who were both exposed to the same lecture, but also resulted in substantial overt behavioral differences. As would be expected, the students who read the "warm" description described the lecturer in much more favorable terms (e.g., considerate, sociable, humorous, compared with self-centered, unsociable, unpopular) and participated in class discussion to a much greater degree (56 per cent participating, as compared with 32 per cent).

STEREOTYPES; SOCIAL ROLES. The operation of social roles is especially prominent among the many ways in which stereotyped preconceptions can affect interpersonal impressions. Our illustrative experiment is similar to the last one described in that again very great behavioral differences hinged upon variation in a single descriptive word. Two groups of college students from an introductory psychology class were asked to prepare a paragraph more fully describing a workingman on the basis of a very brief description. One group was given this characterization: "Works in a factory; reads a newspaper; goes to movies; average height; cracks jokes; intelligent; strong; active." The second group was given an identical description, except for the deletion of "intelligent." Subjects in the first group appeared to experience much more difficulty in forming an organized impression of this person because of the discontinuity provided by the word *intelligent*. Apparently this trait simply did not belong with the others in their stereotyped preconception of a "working man."

Most of the subjects in the first group managed to maintain their stereotype by means of one or another cognitive device. For example, the inconsistency was minimized ("He is intelligent, but doesn't possess the initiative to rise above his group") or simply denied ("He is intelligent, but not too much so, since he works in a factory").

These comments exemplify the way in which contradictory evidence is typically handled so as to maintain the integrity of one's stereotypes. An even simpler and perhaps more common technique is to regard such contradictory material as exceptional. Only when a very large number of "exceptions" accumulate is one likely to begin to question his stereotypes and perhaps ultimately revise his preconceptions.

HALO EFFECT. The halo effect, which is the unjustified influence that some salient characteristic has upon an observer's more general judgment, has already been considered with respect to thinking (Chapter 8, p. 223). It obviously plays a particularly active part in person perception. All of us tend to color our overall evaluations of other people in accordance with the way in which they fit into (or stand out from) some of our own salient interests (for example, in scholarly or athletic achievement, not to mention such commonplace matters as skin color or other physical cues). When the halo effect is combined with first impressions (the power of which is suggested by the experiments described earlier, and particularly by the one with varying "warm" and "cold" descriptions), some extremely strong and long-lasting person perceptions are formed. Fairness and accuracy in person perception requires awareness of how "halo effects" distort judgment.

ATTRIBUTION OF RESPONSIBILITY. Human observers are inclined to attribute responsibility for others' behavior in accordance with the observer's own interpretation of underlying motivations.

This factor was analyzed in an experiment in which the outcome of the action was varied. The subjects listened to tape-recorded accounts of an automobile accident involving a young driver. The car was allowed to swerve off the road and rolled down a hill. The experimental variation in the tapes was in terms of the seriousness of the consequences of the accident, ranging from death to innocent bystanders to only slight damage to the car itself. When the subjects were asked to make some judgments on the accident, the driver was held to be more responsible when the more serious consequences occurred, even though what he did was exactly the same in all the cases. This result is in accord with our expectations—we tend to assign responsibility for actions largely in terms of their consequences, even when logical support for differentiated judgment is lacking.

Why we are differentially attracted to people is a question that has intrigued scientist and layman alike. Social psychologists have come up with some answers, as suggested below, but the puzzzle is by no means solved. The role of purely physical factors (e.g., facial beauty) is obviously crucial but is difficult to pinpoint. As early as nursery school, for example, children rate physical attractiveness high in their "liking." There is apparently a kind of "chemistry" involved, and the final product is an amalgam of many different factors, which are difficult to identify. Nevertheless, some of the more crucial variables in this most complex process have been suggested and are described below.

PROXIMITY. Everyone agrees that proximity is a key factor in determination of attractiveness. It is obviously difficult to interact with people who are not close by. The extent to which the proximity variable by itself operates to produce attraction is suggested by one study of friendships within a college dormitory. Reliably more friendships were found to occur among people who lived closer together. This result is especially impressive because the distance range in the study only varied from 20 to 40 feet. Even within this restricted variation the more separated individuals apparently were less likely to form friendships.

FREQUENCY OF ASSOCIATION. Several experiments have demonstrated the efficacy of the familiarity variable, even when it is manipulated purely in terms of the number of observations. In one experiment, for example, it was arranged that pairs of strangers sit across from each other, without conversing, for varying numbers of occasions (three, six, or twelve). Statements of liking were then obtained, and the degree to which positive attraction was indicated correlated positively with the number of pairings. In another experiment subjects were simply shown photographs of strangers different numbers of times (once to twenty-five times), and again greater liking was later expressed for the persons whose photographs were more often shown and who had become in a sense more "familiar." In still another experiment an additional variable was introduced—the commitment to work with another person. When the expectation of future interaction of this kind was present, enhanced attractiveness was indicated by the subjects' ratings.

SIMILARITY. People who share attitudes and social roles are in general more attractive to each other. This commonly observed relationship appears to depend partly on the strong positive reward value of familiarity, however expressed, and partly on the absence of tensions induced by differences, which may elicit defensive postures.

How does the well-known fact that opposites can attract fit into this picture? Apparently there is a special kind of excitement—perhaps related to the more extreme appeal of the forbidden or of the unfamiliar—generated when people who are dissimilar in some respect are attracted to each other on some other basis, such as is presumably involved in "love at first sight." The results of one experiment on this general problem indicated that the greatest attraction occurred when the other person both liked and differed from the subject (in terms of expressed attitudes). Although similarity is a strong determiner of liking, dissimilarity can also be attractive when it is thus coupled with the feeling that one is liked by the dissimilar person.

RECIPROCAL ATTRACTION. People seem generally to be more attracted to persons who indicate positive feelings for them. Flattery, especially when expressed in a relatively sincere manner, is as powerful a stimulant for liking as anything. Forcing oneself to show positive feelings—even when they may not be a completely accurate reflection of one's inner state—is an excellent way to make friends and influence people.

Personal attractiveness can also be influenced by the accidents of mood and momentary self-esteem. The way in which these factors affect the attractiveness of another person is suggested by an experiment in which women college students were asked, apparently as an afterthought, to rate a young man with whom they had had a casual and presumably unplanned interaction while in the waiting room. Those subjects who had just received severely critical comments on their personality expressed substantially more liking for the young man than those who had just received complimentary comments. Thus the momentary level of one's self-esteem can apparently be a potent factor in determining the amount of attractiveness found in even a casual acquaintance.

Social Problems

No one needs to be informed about the great variety of social problems that face our society. Any comprehensive list would include such formidable problems as

1. Widespread occurrence of delinquency and crime.
2. Various facets of the so-called counterculture, such as the large-scale use of illicit drugs.
3. The pervasive cultural discrimination against minorities of various sorts—including women, who constitute a technical "majority" albeit a functional "minority."
4. The rapid changes occurring in sexual relationships, in large part occasioned by the new sexual freedom given women by the new contraceptives.
5. The consequent weakening of the family as a primary social unit, in part because of the growing disregard of formal marriage, and the concomitant experimentation with new forms of communal living.
6. The new and growing concern with environmental pollution and the quality of life on the planet Earth as a result of the sudden realization of limited natural resources, particularly of energy, and the inappropriateness of the old "pioneer" mentality.
7. The problems posed by an expanding population and the future consequences thereby indicated for the health of the economy (How will they be fed? Where will they be housed? How will the increased waste be handled?).
8. Hanging over all these questions in an ever-threatening and essentially unresolved position, the overriding question of international relations and the threat of a catastrophic nuclear war.

All these and the reactions to them constitute more than enough grist for the mill of the psychologist and other behavioral and social scientists. Obviously we cannot treat all or even many of these complex problems, but we can examine some of them and point to certain research as illustrative of what social psychology is contributing. This is done in Supplements B-4 and B-5, in which the problems of crime and aggression are treated, and in Supplement B-7 where the role of the psychologist in service to society is discussed.

Social Presence

Zajonc's 1965 paper is a good introduction to the problem of social presence. The experiment described in the text was reported by Marx, Witter, and Mueller (1972). Calhoun's research on crowding in mice is described in his 1962 report.

Social Deprivation and Reinforcement

The demonstration of the effectiveness of a brief period of social deprivation, in connection with the use of social reinforcers, was made by Gewirtz and Baer (1958). The two studies on infant crying were reported by Hart et al. (1964) and Etzel and Gewirtz (1967). The Harlow work is reviewed in Harlow and Harlow (1962). The classic study of a feral child is Itard's 1932 report on the Wild Boy of Aveyron. The chronology published by Gesell (1940) is one of the more interesting cases. Zingg (1940) reviews thirty-one of the better-reported cases.

Culture and Personality

Very readable, intriguing accounts of primitive human societies are available in Turnbull's *The Mountain People* (1972), which recounts the desocialization of the Ik, a remote tribe of nomadic hunters and gatherers, after they were forced to cease their hunting, and in Sherman and Thomas's *Hollow Folk* (1933), which describes the remarkably simplified world of some of the mountain people of our own mid-South several decades ago.

Social Conformity

The first work on the autokinetic effect was reported by Sherif (1947). Hood and Sherif (1962) performed the experiment that showed the effect of prior information on this phenomenon, and Vidulich and Kaiman (1961) the experiment demonstrating the role played by the social status of the influencer. The research on the effects of group pressure on judgments of length of line was initiated by Asch (1951) and the refinement utilizing tape-recorded intercommunications developed by Crutchfield (1955). The research showing that face-to-face social contact is most effective in producing conformity was reported by Deutsch and Gerard (1955). Kelman (1961) has advanced the theoretical analysis of conformity by levels.

Obedience

The important series of obedience studies involving alleged shock for errors were conducted and reported by Milgram, whose 1974 book is the most com-

Notes

prehensive treatment. Miller's 1972 volume also contains discussions of the ethical as well as the scientific aspects of Milgram's research.

The Deception Problem

The Milgram experiments on obedience were among the major factors in a recent and continuing controversy concerning the matter of deception in psychological experimentation. Although other fields of psychology are somewhat involved, social psychology is clearly the area of research in which deception has been most widely practiced and in which it is most vigorously claimed to be necessary for effective experimentation.

The social psychologist often feels that it is necessary to deceive subjects in order to investigate many questions that he finds important. The problem is whether any particular question is important enough to justify the deception practiced and the discomfort and possible loss of dignity that is suffered by the subjects. There is no easy answer to this problem. The American Psychological Association is wrestling with the whole issue of ethics in research and has recently completed a thorough-going revision and extension of its ethics code.

Psychology is by no means alone in wrestling with this problem. Not too long ago a federally supported medical research project was discovered to have subjected patients, without their approval, to treatment with carcinogenic (cancer-inducing) agents. The furor resulting from this and similar disclosures has resulted in new policies requiring local institutional review and approval of *any* research project involving human subjects that is submitted for federal funding. Most institutions have broadened their review process to include all human research regardless of the source of support. Although this review may be inconvenient to investigators, it is apparently necessary if human subjects are to be adequately protected from the risks imposed by the occasional researcher.

Within psychology, there have been suggestions that nondeceptive research designs can be developed to answer many of the questions that have customarily been researched by means of deception. It is doubtful that this step can satisfy all the needs of social psychology. For example, it is now very difficult to study the effects of deception itself. Nevertheless, the recent research on influences to obey and the role of social status, described in the text, is suggestive.

The ethical problem raised by the use of deception in social-psychological research is discussed by Aronson and Carlsmith (1969). Kelman (1972) has summarized the pro and con arguments and emphasized the rights of the subject. The obedience study using nurses in a nonlaboratory situation was performed by Hofling et al. (1966) and the field experiment and that varying the level of authority of the person giving the order was reported by Bickman (1971).

Youth Culture

One of the less happy facets of contemporary youth culture is its anti-intellectualism. One cannot argue with the underlying premise that science and technology have been used to abuse people, as in wars of questionable moral and legal status, destruction of the environment, and so on. But the cure for this condition lies in social and political action, rather than in the repudiation of scientific and technological procedures themselves. It is unfortunate that this extreme position has turned so many youth away from the scientific training toward which their intellectual capacity and temperament might otherwise have inclined. It is no more defensible than its polar alternative, the ultraconservative ("establishment") form of anti-intellectualism, that welcomes the technical achievements of science but not the intellectual ferment that makes them possible. That form of anti-intellectualism is represented by strong support for applied, but not fundamental science or the scientific procedures that make possible the practical products.

Another observation on the youth movement has come from a colleague:

While its impact on the surface characteristics of American life has been great, it is probably a transient phenomenon. As I see it, the impact was made possible largely by the extremely high birth rates of the 40's and 50's. There simply came to be so many young people that they were a major social, economic, and political force. If they rioted—well, you simply couldn't shoot all of them. For whatever reason, commercial or altruistic, the media catered to the new, largely humanistic, values adopted by those who were established as the spokesmen for the culture. Many assumptions were challenged, some laws and social attitudes were changed. Many people, of course, were made vastly uncomfortable by the changes but they happened anyhow. To my way of thinking, the current statistics, which indicate a declining rate of population increase, approaching zero population growth, mean that we will have an increasingly older population. Since everyone to some extent is an ex-youth, some version of the recent social changes is likely to survive—championed, I suppose, by groups such as the *Grey Panthers*. The point is that when everyone is getting older it becomes massively difficult to maintain any sort of "youth" culture. This is perhaps unfortunate for, by and large, the total effects on our society seem to have been positive [Charles Cole, personal communication, 1974].

Group Functions

Establishment of intergroup conflicts in the boys' camp situation is described by Sherif (1956) and the quick and easy production of group identification by Tajfel (1970). The loosening of normal standards for behavior under crowd or mob conditions has been labeled *deindividuation* by Festinger, Pepitone, and Newcomb (1952); the effect of this process upon aggression has been experimentally studied by Zimbardo (1970).

The advantage of group over individual problem solving was reported by Barnlund (1959). Osborn (1957) introduced the brainstorming procedure, and the negative results using it were reported by Taylor, Berry, and Block (1958) and Dunnette, Campbell, and Jaastad (1963); two factors in the advantage of nominal over real groups that have been suggested are the greater distractability of the group and the possible dominance of the group by strong and authoritarian participants. Steiner's 1972 book offers a review of group processes related to productivity. Gibb (1969) provides a comprehensive review of the leadership problem. McClelland (1961) suggested the application of motivational analysis to the problem of national character, and the follow-up study described was reported by Rudin (1965). A good introduction to social roles is provided by Bank and Biddle's 1975 paperback.

Changing Attitudes

Aronson, Turner, and Carlsmith (1963) reported the research on credibility of the communicator as related to the degree of discrepancy of the message. The experiment demonstrating the importance of the delay in measurement of attitude was performed by Kelman and Hovland (1953). Freedman and Fraser (1966) reported the experiment on placement of the careful driving sign as a function of an earlier commitment. Miller and Campbell (1959) performed the research on primacy and recency within the jury-trial setting. Support for the efficacy of threat has been reported by Leventhal and Singer (1966) and the hypothesis concerning the reversal of affectiveness at very high levels of anxiety was proposed by McGuire (1969). Higbee (1969) has reviewed the literature on the problem from 1953 to 1968. Janis and Field (1959) discuss the role of self-esteem in resistance to influence, and Katz and Stotland (1959) relate resistance to personality needs. The inoculation technique is discussed by McGuire (1969) and Tannenbaum (1967). Freedman and Sears (1965) and Apsler and Sears (1968) report on the effect of merely forewarning of an impending attack.

The term *brainwashing* was introduced by Hunter (1951) as the equivalent of the Chinese *mental cleansing*. A popular treatment of this topic is available in Brownfield (1972) and somewhat more technical treatments are given by Lifton (1961) and Schein et al. (1961). Leites and Bernaut (1954) have analyzed the Soviet confessions.

The experiment on attitude change in housewives in integrated and segregated public housing was conducted by Deutsch and Collins (1951). Mussen (1950) reported the boys' camp experiment in which both increases and decreases in prejudice were found after integrated experiences. The "shared-coping" concept was introduced by Collins (1970) and the camping experiment in which intergroup tensions were first established and then eliminated by shared coping was by Sherif (1956). The initial study of the Bennington College women was reported by Newcomb (1943) and the follow-up by Newcomb (1963).

Person Perception

A classic paper on this topic is that by Heider (1967). Asch's (1946) paper reports the experiment in which college students prepared personality descriptions from a list of descriptive terms. The experiment in which the single word *warm* was substituted for *cold* in the description of the guest lecturer was conducted by Kelley (1950). The study on the workingman and the subjects' reaction to inclusion of *intelligent* as a descriptive term was reported by Haire and Grunes (1950). Walster (1966) performed the experiment in which attribution of responsibility was found to vary with the outcome of an alleged accident. Attribution of intent is dealt with more generally in a recent paper by Kelley (1973) and in a review of the literature by Maselli and Altrochi (1969). Goffman (e.g., 1971) has reported a number of interesting interpersonal relationships from a sociological point of view.

Personal Attraction

The study of liking as a function of proximity within a college dormitory was performed by Festinger, Schachter, and Back (1950). The experiments on number of paired seatings and number of exposures to photographs were reported by Festinger, Carlsmith, and Suomi (1969) and Zajonc (1968), respectively. The commitment variable was investigated by Berscheid, Boye, and Darley (1968). Walster (1965) reported the experiment in which attraction was found to vary inversely with self-esteem. Jones, Bell, and Aronson (1971) conducted the research on similarity and dissimilarity as factors in liking. The experiment in which the flatterer was perceived as ingratiating and was disliked was done by Dickoff (1961). Jones's 1964 book and 1965 paper, "Flattery Will Get You Somewhere," show, however, that ingratiation is most often successful, in part perhaps because we tend to give the flatterer the benefit of our doubt. The study on rating of highly competent and average blunderers was reported by Aronson, Willerman, and Floyd (1966) and that on the perceived evaluations with increasing or decreasing favorability by Aronson and Linder (1965). Byrne (1971) has provided an influential paradigm for research and theorizing on personal attraction; this work is the source of the early emphasis on physical attraction mentioned in the text. A more recent review of this work is available in Huston's 1974 book.

An interesting and suggestive animal study has been reported by Pratt and Sackett (1967). They reared three groups of monkeys under varying degrees of contact with peers (none, visual and auditory contact only, and normal contact). They found that after animals of all three groups were allowed to interact freely, those from the same rearing condition showed preference for each other, even when they were completely strange to each other. This result suggests the subtle potency of obscure social behaviors in the interpersonal relationships that determine attractiveness.

Supplements

Our supplements, we hope, will be considerably more useful and attractive than the one displayed by this unfortunate individual. The illustration is from **Dr. Foote's Home Cyclopedia of Popular Medicine, Social and Sexual Science,** *published about 1880.*

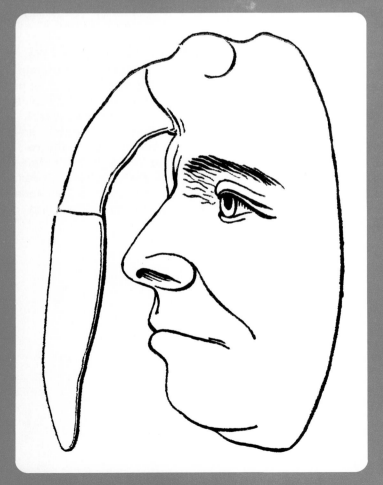

PARTY

elimiting the subject matter of as broad a science as psychology is difficult. Certain topics, however, are generally agreed to be central to the science; these core topics have been treated in the seventeen chapters of the first four parts of this book. There are many other topics of less certain status, and psychology instructors will disagree on the necessity of studying them. Some of these borderline topics have therefore been included in this part, as supplementary materials, in order to provide maximum flexibility in the assignment of test topics and in selective browsing. The sections in each of the two supplements are numbered serially, to expedite selective assignments and examinations.

The supplementary materials presented in this part are organized into major subject clusters. Supplement A, on *research methods,* describes primary procedural tools that psychologists use in collecting and processing data. Supplement B, on selectively *applied problems,* focuses on certain of the frictions in society and in interpersonal relationships that psychologists study as scientists and attempt to cope with as practitioners.

Because many of the supplemental sections deal with topics that are also discussed in the core chapters there is necessarily a certain amount of overlap among their treatments here and at earlier places in the book. This problem is aggravated by the fact that many focal topics (e.g., language, attitudes) are considered in several chapters, where their multiple relationships to core topics (e.g., thinking, learning, social interaction) can be best discussed. In any event, beyond the requirements of introductions of and transitions to topics, some redundancy can be defended on the ground that it is pedagogically useful. It is therefore hoped that the reader who remembers what he has seen once will not be unduly offended if he recognizes it again here and there in the pages that follow.

Research Methods

Measurement is a basic tool of scientific research. It is therefore fitting that we begin our discussion of research methods with a brief summary of measurement and statistics. This page from an early scientific encyclopedia illustrates the elegant measurements involved in the study of optics.

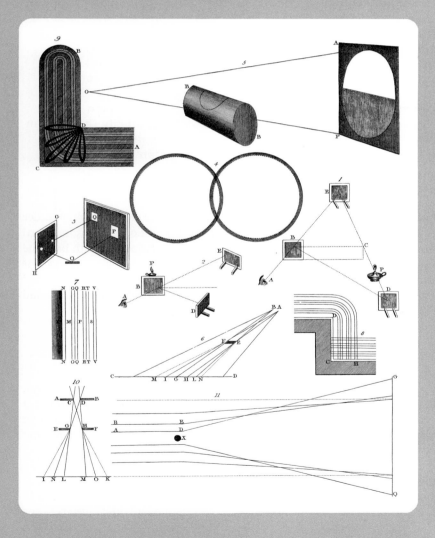

his supplement includes descriptions of some of the major methodologies that are utilized in the scientific pursuit of psychology.

The first section, on measurement and statistics, provides a general introduction to these topics. The ways in which they are used in psychology are described, with a terminal stress on certain of the pitfalls commonly associated with the misuse and misinterpretation of statistics.

A basic understanding of evolutionary theory (Charles Darwin) and the mechanisms of transmission of heredity (Gregor Mendel) is necessary for a full appreciation of contemporary research and theorizing on the interaction of hereditary and environmental influences in the determination of behavior. In section 2 we survey these two fundamental biological contributions for those who are unfamiliar with them or could use a review of them to supplement their present knowledge.

The next two sections continue the treatment of methods in experimental psychology. There are descriptions of techniques used in laboratory research on learning (section 3), and motivation (section 4).

The supplement continues (section 5) with consideration of selected research methodologies in the fields of personality (how it can be scientifically assessed), a discussion of intelligence testing (section 6), and a discussion of how public opinion can be accurately measured by polling (section 7).

1. Measurement and Statistics

The objective of this survey of measurement and statistics is *not* to show the reader *how* to "do" any particular measurement or statistical operation. Rather, in accord with the sentiments expressed in Chapter 2, it is to familiarize him with both the need for and the proper role of these numerical services, so that when he reads of such things as "ordinal scales" or the "analysis of variance" (often abbreviated "ANOVA") he will have a sufficient orientation to understand *what* is meant and *why* it is used.

MEASUREMENT

There are four fundamental types of measurement: nominal, ordinal, interval, and ratio. The first type, nominal measurement, is in some ways not really a measurement device, because it uses strictly qualitative rather than quantitative terms. But it is a necessary first step in measurement, just as it may be in identifying variables for investigations, and so is customarily included.

Nominal Measurement
Nominal measurement is some kind of classification of objects into mutually exclusive categories. Such service is necessary to separate individual instances for

purposes of identification (e.g., giving separate numbers to baseball or football players on a team). When numbers are used to represent individuals, they are not serving true numerical functions; that is, they do not indicate *how much* of anything is represented. They could be replaced by words (and as a matter of fact, athletic uniforms are now often adorned by names as well as numbers). But even here the singular advantage of economy of expression enters; for example, it is simpler to identify separate counties in a state by assigning each a number for inclusion on a state automobile license tag than it is to spell out the full name.

Ordinal Measurement

The property that is added in the ordinal measure is that of ranking, when numbers are *ordered* according to whether any one represents *more or less* of some variable ordinal measurement that is being employed. Take the example used for nominal measures in which each of the counties in a state is identified by a number. If the sequence of numbers used is determined on a systematic but essentially nonquantitative basis, say alphabetically, then the measure is nominal; however, if some quantitative ordering system is used, such as the population of each county in the last federal census, then an ordinal measurement has been achieved. The size of each county number now contains significantly more information than the identification alone; it gives us a *relative* notion of the population of the county.

PAIRED COMPARISONS. When psychological scales are prepared the special method of *paired comparisons* yields generally superior results. Suppose that one is concerned with ordering a class of students according to some attribute, say their effectiveness in oral presentation. If he tries to rank them in the natural manner by simply selecting the best, the next best, and so on, he will have difficulty in making decisions and may find himself revising his order frequently, especially if the class is large. In the paired-comparison method the rater considers only two students at any one time. Each individual is eventually compared with every other individual. In this method the difficulties in making judgments will be reduced. The improvement occurs because the rater now has only to keep any two individuals in mind for comparison at a time, and most of his judgments can be quickly made. Thus, although the paired-comparison technique may require somewhat more overall time for execution, it usually pays dividends in precision and accuracy; simply giving each of the subjects a number representing the total of his "more than" comparisons will make possible more precise ordering of the entire group.

Interval Measurement

The big question concerning ordinal measures is the *amount* of difference between successive ranks. Although the paired-comparison method just described takes a step in the direction of closing this gap, it does not go the whole way. Consider the physical measure of temperature. When one says that a particular temperature is so many degrees centigrade, we know exactly where this score stands in relation to all other temperatures that are measured in the same units. That is because each degree has the same value as any other. In other words, we have an absolute rather than merely a relative measure, and this is the essence of interval measurement.

Interval scaling in psychology is much more difficult than in physics. For such measures as IQ, where we need to have as much quantitative precision as possible, equal units are available only if certain special assumptions are made. In many instances, unfortunately, psychologists have to be content with ordinal measures where interval measures would make their professional life a great deal more comfortable.

Ratio Measurement

Psychologists may have trouble achieving interval measures, which physicists generally take for granted, but even physicists sometimes have difficulty achieving the ultimately most useful ratio measurement. Ratio measures are defined as those in which not only are the units equal but their relationships (ratios) are constant over the entire scale. In measuring time or length, for example, we can be sure that a 10-second interval is twice as long as a 5-second interval, in exactly the same way that a 60-second interval is twice as long as a 30-second interval; the same is true for various measures of physical length. This is not true, however, in such an obvious manner for temperature. It is true that 70° Fahrenheit is 1° greater than 69°, and that the difference between these two temperatures is exactly the same as that between any other two temperatures with 1° difference, because all the units are equal. But what about *ratios* of temperature? Is 70° twice as much as 35° in the same way that 10° is twice as much at 5°? No. A ratio scale requires a *zero point*, readily observed for such physical measures as time, length, weight, and volume, but not so readily available for temperature. Without a fixed zero point, as well as equal units of measurement, the relationship (ratio) of any two values at some point over the scale cannot be regarded as equivalent to the same numerical relationship at some other point on the scale.

With regard to psychology and the derivation of behavioral measures, it is not hard to see that ratio measures are for the most part unattainable. Only in some very unusual cases, such as those involving sensory function, is it possible to determine a true zero point as well as equal units of measurement and thereby apply ratio measures. Moreover, it should be noted that each successive type of measurement adds a crucial element. Thus the ratio measure, the ultimate objective of scientific quantification, has all the properties of the simpler types.

STATISTICS

Like any unfamiliar terminology or notation system, statistical formulas generally may appear much more formidable than they really are. Although statistical formulations are not designed to harass the student, it must be admitted that the mode of their presentation, deliberate or otherwise, often does have this unhappy effect. They have been developed and are used to reduce the great mass of data collected to a more manageable size and shape and thereby to facilitate their interpretation. The objective of the present discussion is to give the reader a fundamental rationale for the application of statistics and some information about the general uses of the major statistical measures. Its purpose is to familiarize him with some of the more important concepts and procedures so that he will not be completely baffled when he encounters them again and will also be in a better position to learn more about them if he ever needs to do so.

Frequency Distributions

Counting instances is the simplest and at the same time the most fundamental of all numerical operations. When counts are made of various categories, such as those in a nominal scale (say, the number of automobile license tags bearing the numeric identification of the various counties in a state), a frequency distribution can be formed. More psychologically relevant illustrations of the same principle would be to count the frequency of students falling into various personality categories on some inventory, or judged by observers to have this or that trait as the most dominant feature of their personality. Whenever the variable under investigation can itself be ordered (that is, at least ordinal data are involved) the values of the variable can themselves be used as the basis for the frequency distribution (e.g., IQ scores, ranked in categories of five or ten IQ points, or number of errors made while learning to master some task).

A simple and generally quite expressive way of portraying a frequency distribution is to prepare a graph from it. Table A-1 shows a hypothetical frequency distribution of the students in a learning experiment who made varying numbers of errors. These same data are shown graphically in Figures A-1 and A-2. Figure A-1 is a *frequency polygon*, formed by connecting the points representing the various frequencies. Figure A-2 is a *bar graph*, or histogram, presenting exactly the same

Table A-1 Frequency Distribution of Students Making Various Numbers of Errors in a Learning Experiment

Error Score	Frequency
80–89	1
70–79	0
60–69	4
50–59	10
40–49	18
30–39	12
20–29	7
10–19	2
0–9	0

A-1 Frequency polygon of the hypothetical data presented in Table A-1.

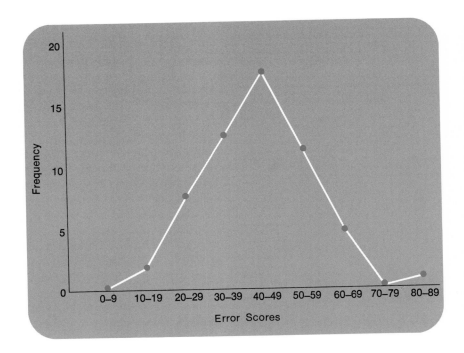

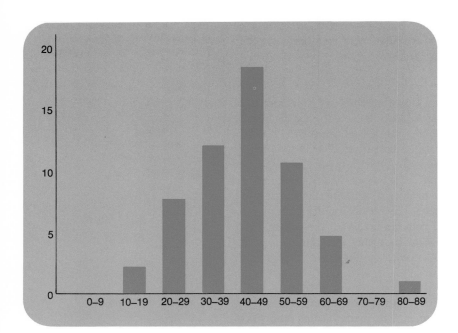

Bar graph of the hypothetical data presented in Table A-1 (and plotted also in Figure A-1).

data but in a slightly modified form. Note how much easier it is to grasp the nature of the frequency distribution from the graphs, especially the bar graph, than it is from the table.

GRAPHICAL PROCEDURES. At this point it may be well to mention one or two other technical matters concerning the way in which graphs are usually constructed. Results of experiments or other kinds of observations, and also theoretical relationships, are characteristically presented in graphical form to complement the tabular and verbal forms. Most such graphs plot the dependent variable on the *vertical ordinate,* as number of errors is plotted in Figure A-1. The independent variable is then represented by the *abscissa* (the horizontal baseline).

Let us suppose, for illustrative purposes, that we have completed an experiment in which we have measured number of trials required to memorize verbal material (dependent variable) as a function of the meaningfulness of the material (independent variable). A prose passage, as from a newspaper story, would be more meaningful than a list of unrelated English words, which in turn would usually be more meaningful than a list of words in another language. Some hypothetical results from such an experiment are shown graphically in Figure A-3. In this illustration only verbal terms are used for the independent variable, although more often in actual experimentation some kind of quantification or scaling of this variable would be provided. The means plotted would normally represent different treatment conditions, usually independent groups of subjects drawn randomly from the same general population (such as a college class) and then given differential experimental conditions, such as the three kinds of verbal materials mentioned above.

Although a large number of variations, for special purposes, may be found from time to time in graphical presentation, the type here described is the one most

576

A-3 Hypothetical relationship between number of trials required for mastery (dependent variable) and meaningfulness of material memorized (independent variable) as an illustration of graphical presentation of data.

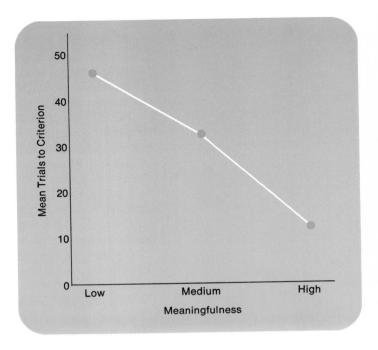

commonly used. Thus if the student will take time to fix firmly in mind the simple relationship between ordinal (vertical) presentation of the data (results) and the baseline (horizontal) representation of the independent or manipulated variable, he will be able to follow the majority of graphical presentations that he is likely to encounter.

Measures of Central Tendency

The most interesting statistic in any frequency distribution is usually a measure of its central tendency, that is, of the tendency of the scores to distribute around some central point. This statistic is customarily used as a single measure to represent the entire distribution. The most important measures of this kind are the mode, the median, and especially the arithmetic mean.

THE MODE. The mode is simply the category with the greatest frequency. Any distribution, regardless of the nature of the measures used, can generate a mode. In the illustration given in Table A-1, the score with the greatest frequency is 40–49; this is therefore the mode of that distribution. The information provided by the mode is often interesting but always limited; that is, we cannot really tell very much about the nature of the distribution from the mode alone, nor can we even tell the extent to which the mode stands out from competing categories. This information is readily available, however, from a mere glance at a bar graph (cf. Figure A-2).

THE MEDIAN. When our measures are ordinal, so that they can be distributed as shown in Table A-1, a second and generally more useful measure of central tendency can be developed. The median is the category that contains the middle score(s) of the distribution; in other words, it splits the distribution in half, right

577

down the middle. The median is a much more representative measure than the mode, especially if there is substantial skewing, or irregularity, in the distribution. Figure A-4 shows another hypothetical distribution, skewed to the left or low error side. Note that the mode in this instance would by itself provide an unrealistic idea of the total distribution, whereas the median would come closer to a fair representation.

THE MEAN. By far the most common statistic of central tendency is the arithmetic mean, the "average" as it is often carelessly called (carelessly, because *average* also refers to both mode and median). The arithmetic mean, usually abbreviated M (or expressed as *X*), is quite readily computed: the sum total of all the scores is simply divided by the number of scores. For this operation to be technically sound, however, the data must be of an interval sort; the addition of units (such as dollars or errors or IQ points) is appropriate only if this assumption can be made. Because the mean gives equal weight to each and every unit of the variable measured (thus requiring the equality of units of the interval type), it is clearly the most comprehensive of the statistics designed to represent a frequency distribution, and is also the one most often used.

Measures of Variability

Central-tendency statistics are, as already suggested, distinctly limited in the information they provide concerning any frequency distribution. They need to be complemented by some measure representing the manner in which the scores tend to cluster around the central tendency, or to put it in the more usual way, the

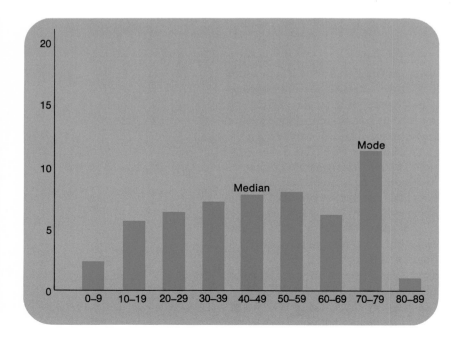

A-4 Bar graph of hypothetical distribution skewed to the left (with median and mode indicated).

manner in which scores tend to spread or disperse around the central tendency. Such statistics are called measures of variability.

THE RANGE. The simplest measure of variability is the range. It is the difference between the highest and the lowest scores, or the highest and lowest categories of scores in a frequency distribution. Obviously it provides information, albeit of a very gross sort, about the spread of scores. It is most often used, in a more or less casual manner, in nonscientific settings. Its scientific use is usually only preliminary to the use of another measure.

THE STANDARD DEVIATION. With only two scores, or categories of scores, required to determine the range, that measure is clearly one of extremely restricted value; it tells nothing at all about the nature of the vast majority of scores in the distribution. The most frequently used measure is the standard deviation (S.D. or σ). The S.D. is a sort of average indication of how much the various numbers differ among themselves. It utilizes the deviation between *each* score and the arithmetic mean, and so is both comprehensive (reflecting the contribution of all the scores) and representative of the distribution. The S.D. is computed by squaring each of these deviations, summing them, and then extracting the square root of the sum. One reason for the squaring operation is that it makes all scores positive. If the plus and minus signs are ignored in the summing process, the simpler average deviation (A.D.) can be obtained by taking the mean. However, the A.D. is not as easily handled, mathematically, as the S.D. and so is much less frequently used.

The uses of the standard deviation are surprisingly large and varied in number. Here we can mention one of them, and others will be implied in our later discussion. A *standard score* (Z) is a utilization of the standard deviation of a distribution in relation to the particular individual scores in that distribution. A standard score is the relationship between the deviation above or below the mean that any given score has compared to the S.D. for the distribution; it tells us the relative standing of the score we are interested in and so is a very useful device for the investigation of individual differences. Moreover, the standard score has the same relative meaning regardless of the kind of test used or the nature of the units involved (as long as they are interval units) and so provides a high degree of cross-measure comparability. As a result, standard scores are widely used in many areas of both applied and basic research.

PERCENTILES. Rank order of a score within a distribution of scores may also be indicated, somewhat more simply, in terms of the percentage of scores that the given score exceeds. This measure is usually given in *percentiles* (or centiles). For example, a percentile rank of 98 on a given test means that the obtained score is greater than 98 per cent of the scores on the normative group. Percentiles range from 0 to 99. Sometimes the normative group, the sample of scores against which the one obtained is being compared, will be simply those obtained within, say, a class of students, but more often, especially if the test is a well-standardized one, it will be a national group.

The Normal Curve

The "normal" curve is the most commonly found type of distribution. It is illustrated in Figure A-5. Note that the middle scores are the most frequent, with

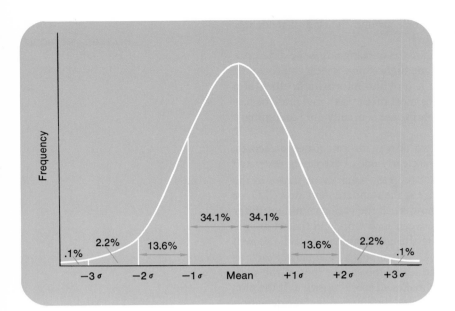

A normal distribution, showing the percentage of cases falling in successive standard deviation (Greek sigma, σ) intervals below and above the mean.

frequencies decreasing in a more or less regular fashion as either end of the distribution is approached. In other words, any particular score has about equal chances of being on one side or the other of the center, and is more likely to be toward the middle than at either end of the distribution.

It is doubtful that any reader will be unaware of the normal curve, unless in his education he has been subjected to most unusual sorts of grading procedures; the normal curve, of course, is commonly used as a basis for assigning grades in a frequency distribution of class scores. But the normal curve has both theoretical implications and practical applications that go far beyond this particular use. As a matter of fact, there is scarcely a psychological or biological measure that does not tend to be distributed normally, when appropriately random (that is, unbiased) samples are obtained; and the larger and more representative the sample, the closer the approximation to the normal curve.

One of the very useful features of the normal curve of a frequency distribution is the fact that the proportion of cases (scores) that fall varying distances above or below the mean can be designated in terms of the standard deviation. Thus a little over two thirds (68.2 per cent, to be exact, in a perfectly normal distribution) of the scores will lie between one S.D. above and below the mean, and 95 per cent of the total sample will lie within two S.D.'s of the mean. When we know the mean and the S.D. of any normal distribution therefore, we can estimate fairly closely the proportion of cases falling within any specified interval of scores. These relationships are shown in the hypothetical normal distribution in Figure A-5.

In any symmetrical distribution such as the normal curve the mean, mode, and median all tend to be closely related. If the distribution is markedly skewed, however, the median is generally the preferred measure, because it does not give the extreme scores on one side or the other undue weight.

Contingency Relationships Among Distributions

Very often in science we want to know the way in which scores on one attribute of an array of cases (most often subjects, in psychology) are related to scores on some other attribute(s) of the same cases. For example, if we have measures of both intelligence and creativity in a given school class, how are these related? Do students who score high on one measure also tend to score high on the other?

CORRELATION COEFFICIENTS. The answer to the contingency question is most often provided by means of some kind of correlation coefficient, which is a measure of the degree of contingency or closeness of relation between two distributions. The three gross types of correlation that can be obtained are illustrated in idealized form in Figure A-6. Where the relationship is positive or direct, as in (a), instances of high scores in the one distribution are associated with high scores in the other, middle scores on one distribution with middle scores on the other, and low scores on one with low scores on the other. Thus if intelligence (distribution 1) and creativity (distribution 2) were positively correlated (as they are but not to a very marked degree), highly intelligent persons would be most likely to be highly

A-6 Three kinds of contingency relationship between frequency distributions: (a) positive correlation, (b) negative correlation, (c) zero correlation.

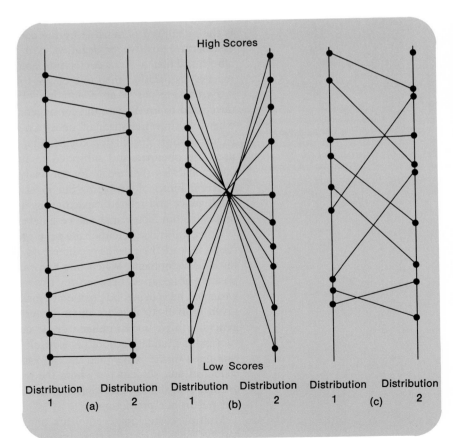

creative and persons with low intelligence would be most likely not to be very creative. Where the relationship is negative or inverse, as in (b), the opposite relationship occurs. Where there is no apparent consistent relationship, as in (c), the correlation is said to be zero. Zero correlations are generally interpreted as meaning that there is no underlying positive or negative association between the variables measured, so that only "chance" associations are reflected in the correlation coefficient.

It is very important to remember that only contingency or association, and not causal relationship, is indicated by correlations. Whether one of the two variables related is in the common-sense meaning a "cause" of the other must be determined by empirical operations of a quite different sort (e.g., experimental research) from those involved in the correlation operations.

The simplest kind of correlation coefficient is the *rank-order* (ρ or rho) measure; it is a correlation technique that can be applied to any data of ordinal or higher status, such as strictly subjective rankings of subjects. The more elaborate *product-moment* (r) correlation coefficient is much more commonly used, because it gives greater precision but it does require that the data be at least interval in nature.

The *degree* of association between any two distributions is indicated by the *size* of the correlation coefficient. The range of possible values is from 0 to 1.00, which is the maximum obtainable by the computation formulas used. The *direction* of association, positive or negative, is indicated by the sign ($+$ or $-$) of the coefficient. Thus, a $-.92$ correlation coefficient indicates a much higher (although inverse) association than one of .59 (plus signs are normally omitted).

Factor analysis is an adaptation of the correlation technique that has been developed to investigate the contingency relationships within a complex function when multiple measures of uncertain relationships to each other are available. Many separate correlation coefficients, each between a different pair of the measures, are obtained and subjected to further analysis in order to determine the commonalities that exist. Factor-analytic methods have been applied to many different kinds of problems but most intensively to the problem of measuring intelligence and related capacities; as a matter of fact, many of the special techniques within factor analysis were developed specifically for use on this problem.

Correlation coefficients have very great practical as well as theoretical significance; indeed, their use as predictive devices was probably the main reason for their initial development. When one knows that there is a high correlation (whether positive or negative) between any two variables, and has access only to one of these variables, he is in a good position to make estimates of the size of the other, for any given individual, that are much better than "chance." Thus if we know that in general a high undergraduate grade-point average is positively correlated with success in graduate school (as a result of many such contingencies having been examined in the past), then we can estimate the chances for success in graduate school of any student for whom the readily obtained undergraduate grade point average is available. The higher the correlation, the greater the confidence that we can put in our prediction.

Multiple correlation coefficients, obtained when an array of variables are related, can be even more effective, because they permit the joint calculation of the influence of more than one variable. Thus adding one or more intellectual-capacity scores to the grade point measure enables us to make better predictions of graduate school success because we have taken into account additional sources of variance in the outcome measure (or, to put it another way, additional determinants of the behavior with which we are concerned).

INFERENTIAL STATISTICS

Thus far in our review of fundamental statistical procedures we have been concerned with descriptive statistics. The frequency distribution, measures of central tendency, and measures of variability or dispersion are all descriptions of the obtained data. However, when interpretations of the data are desired, descriptive statistics are not likely to suffice. If we could always measure every single instance, or practically every instance, of the total population about which we wish to draw conclusions—for example, all the males in a given military organization, or all the females in the high schools of a particular school system—then we would not need to make inferences from our statistical measures. Only very rarely, however, are we able to obtain such complete coverage of an entire population. Our time and resources are too limited, and most of the populations about which we are concerned, especially in matters of theory, are too large. Ordinarily therefore we draw a sample of cases from a population, usually a relatively small sample, and obtain data of some sort from this sample. In order to guard against bias in our sampling we usually try to select the sample randomly, that is, by means of a mechanical system that is unlikely to have any built-in bias. We then assume that the scores obtained from the sample are representative of the population from which it has been drawn. We will ordinarily have another sample of similar subjects, who are different in some way from the first; for example, we may have given the first group of subjects a special kind of training or instructions, and the second group no special treatment (control), and we may now wish to compare them to see if the (independent) variable thus manipulated has made a difference in our dependent variable (which may involve a learning task). Suppose that we have drawn the two samples randomly from the same initial large population of, say, college students enrolled in an introductory psychology course (the most convenient type of population usually available to the college or university researcher). We assume that if both groups are treated alike they should give more or less the same results. Our question then becomes, "Can we infer any *real* differences in obtained scores as the consequence of the treatment difference we have introduced?"

The Analysis of Variance

Comparison of the results from different groups is usually conducted by use of the arithmetic means representing each group and the variability of the group scores around the means. By far the most popular and generally useful statistical tool for this purpose is the analysis of variance. The key to an understanding of what the analysis of variance does is to keep separate the notions of variability *within* one group and variability *between* groups. The analysis of variance is a statistical method that enables us to make an objective estimate as to the probability, in terms of a normal distribution of differences between means, that the actual difference between means that was obtained would occur *if* both samples had *actually* been drawn from the same population (in other words, if the experimental treatment, say, had not actually made any real difference).

RELIABILITY OF DIFFERENCES. The objective answer provided by the analysis of variance, given as an *F* value, is interpreted in terms of a *p* (for probability) measure.

The *p* value represents the number of times out of 100 cases in which a difference as large as that actually obtained between the group means can be estimated to occur "by chance," given the distributions of scores that were obtained. In other words, the *p* value tells us the chances of this large a difference occurring when there is no true difference between groups. If no real difference exists, the obtained difference is usually interpreted as having occurred from sampling variations. Since identical mean scores rarely occur, there will almost always be some difference between the groups. An objective estimate of obtained differences is therefore extremely important. Estimating the probability of a difference being a true difference is made possible by statistical techniques that utilize the variability of the scores in relation to the means. If the *p* is small, say, .01, this means that the chances are only 1 in 100 that a difference as large as that obtained between the means would have occurred "by chance"—that is, by a random selection of samples—from the *same* population.

Ordinarily, a difference at the .05 (5 per cent) level or better is required before a real difference is inferred. Such differences are then usually called *significant;* they are also sometimes called *reliable,* which to some persons is a preferable term because it more directly suggests the notion of replication, namely, the assumption that if we would repeat our experiment we are likely to obtain again a substantial difference in the same direction. Further, the term *reliable* does not have the *double meaning* of the term *significant,* which often is used to describe importance. The confidence level tells us nothing at all about the real importance (or significance, in that sense) of our results but only gives a statistical estimate of their replicability.

THE *t*-TEST. The *t*-test is another statistical procedure that estimates the probability of group differences being true differences.

Before the development of the analysis of variance, and the common use of multiple experimental treatment groups, the *t*-test was commonly applied to compare two distributions. This test can be used for small samples, up to 30 cases, but only for two means. It yields a *p* value when interpreted against the proper statistical tables, and in exactly the same way as the F-test of the analysis of variance. As a matter of fact, the *t*-test is actually the same kind of variance estimate, a special case of the more comprehensive F-test, and thus gives identical results when applied to the same data.

MULTIVARIATE ANALYSIS. Psychologists are becoming increasingly interested in experiments that involve concomitant manipulation of more than a single variable, and therefore more than just a few treatment groups. The experimental design that implements such more elaborate manipulation of variables is called multivariate analysis. Its importance stems in part from two facts in particular. First, if only limited sampling along some particular dimension is made, we are very likely to select values for which there is no difference, obtain no difference, and then quite mistakenly conclude that the variable is not an effective one; by sampling more points along each variable we utilize a more sensitive type of experimental design, and increase our chances of detecting differences. Second, the relationship of any one variable to some other may depend upon the particular level at which either (or each) variable is sampled; in other words, we may find quite different relationships, depending upon which values we happen to select. Technically, this kind of situation is referred to as an "interaction"; the analysis of variance is admirably suited to detect interactions. An interaction term can be readily computed for any combination of variables (main effects) being measured. Multivariate analysis substantially improves the opportunity to detect interactions by providing both multiple variables and multiple values along them. All of these opportunities do have a price, however; they require much more time and effort than simpler experiments, and they are also likely to produce data that are more difficult to analyze and interpret. The particular experimental design, and statistical tool, that we use must therefore be fitted to the particular task that we have. Thus there is still room, if a little circumscribed, for the modest *t*-test as well as the more sophisticated analyses of variance and the very elegant multivariate designs.

CHI-SQUARE TEST. Another test of somewhat limited applicability is the chi-square (χ^2) technique. Its big advantage is that it can be used with nominal data. The chi-square test is a measure of the probability that the *proportion* of subjects falling into one or the other of two or more categories, as compared with proportions of subjects similarly categorized from another sample, would be likely to occur by chance if the two samples were from the same population. The fundamental reasoning is similar to that in the variance tests. Of course, subjects can be categorized on the basis of their scores as well as on other bases.

THE NULL HYPOTHESIS. The statistical hypothesis that is most often tested by any use of inferential statistics is called the null hypothesis. It is so named because it assumes that there is in fact *no difference;* one then applies his F- or *t*- or chi-square value to determine the probability that the null hypothesis can be *rejected*. If the *p* value is small, the null hypothesis can be rejected; one can then interpret the results as positive support for the *experimental hypothesis,* which is really what he is interested in testing. In other words, one is able to discard, at least tentatively, on the basis of his statistical analysis, the proposition that his intergroup differences could have resulted merely from sampling variations.

Some Cautions

Inferential statistics properly applied can be a very valuable tool for experimental and other types of psychological research. Nevertheless, it has been abused, and the beginning student should be apprised of this fact. Mainly, the abuse has been in elevating the statistical technique to an unduly superior position, and making it, rather than the principles it should help produce, the objective of research.

Some examples should clarify this cautionary statement. Setting an arbitrary confidence level, regardless of the nature of the research, as a requirement for, say, publication in a professional journal, or acceptance of masters or doctoral research, seems to be a violation of the spirit if not the letter of the statistical enterprise. It is the investigator's responsibility, if statistical analyses have been used, to report these objectively. His own conclusions may of course be tempered by the nature of his statistical results, but basically it is the reader's prerogative to judge for himself the relevance of whatever p value has been attained. The relevance, as emphasized already, is really for the experimental hypothesis and the theoretical propositions.

Two common practices are especially objectionable. Each is produced by an overly submissive attitude toward orthodoxy in statistical matters. One is that the investigator so emphasizes his highly "significant" statistical indicants that he neglects to tell the reader the *direction* of the differences; perusal of reports in the most prestigious of the psychological journals will reveal more than an occasional instance of this kind of misplaced emphasis, especially during the 1960's, when the analysis of variance was perhaps in its heyday.

The second practice is less immediately irritating but more fundamentally dangerous. It consists of fitting one's experimental design to the type of statistical test available. That is, the investigator shapes his experiment more in accordance with the requirements of some statistical test than in accordance with the theoretical or empirical problem he is studying. Ideally, of course, the requirements of both the problem and the statistical analysis would be fully satisfied, but this is not always possible; some problems do not lend themselves readily to tests that yield data that can be easily subjected to standard statistical analyses.

The danger here is mainly in the stifling of initiative and creativity, particularly if the practice is accompanied by a supercilious attitude toward those who less slavishly follow the orthodox statistically oriented designs. The only justification for such a practice is the unfortunate fact that all too often experiments have been performed and data collected with no available means of analysis. But in between these two extremes there is indeed a broad middle ground where statistical analyses are applied as appropriate but are not permitted to be the major determinants of experimental design.

The fact that inferential statistics has been abused should not result in our trying to throw out the statistical baby along with its dirty bath water. Paying proper respect without being completely awed by these useful tools will pay dividends in accordance with our ability to design meaningful experiments and invent provocative theoretical interpretations.

2. Biology: Darwin and Mendel

This section describes the two overriding achievements in biology of the nineteenth century, and for that matter, two of the most significant intellectual and scientific achievements of all time. These are the detailed conceptualization of the fundamental mechanism of organic evolution by the Englishman Charles Darwin and the discovery of the fundamental mechanism of heredity by the Austrian monk Gregor Mendel.

Some indication of the enormity of these two contributions may be seen in the fact that despite great refinements in both evolutionary theory and genetics in the century since the original work, in neither case has any essential change been required. For this reason evolutionary theory and genetic transmission are presented from a historical point of view, to provide both an appreciation of the achievements of Darwin and Mendel and an understanding of the fundamental mechanisms themselves. These historical accounts also provide valuable illustrations of successful application of research methodology in biological science.

EVOLUTIONARY THEORY: CHARLES DARWIN

Charles Darwin (1809–1882) was originally trained in medicine but found its practice uncongenial (in common with a number of other prominent men in the history of psychology, notably William James and to a lesser degree, Sigmund Freud). Darwin's interest in evolutionary theory developed during his service as a naturalist on the ship *Beagle* from 1831 to 1835. His questioning of the then orthodox view of the fixity of species arose as a result of the peculiarities he observed in the distribution of slightly varied forms of animals and plants. In particular he was interested in geographically isolated animals, such as those on islands like the Galapagos chain off the west coast of South America.

Darwin observed that these animals were basically similar to their counterparts on the nearby mainland, yet were in some way conspicuously different. The appearance of distinctive differences in the same species when physically isolated did not seem logically to fit the special-creation theory, because there did not seem to be any reason for the differences in that theory. Darwin proceeded to compare this apparent result of spatial separation with what seemed to be a somewhat parallel effect of temporal separation—the differences that had been earlier observed between living species and their extinct but apparently related forms.

Pondering the basic similarities of these two types of separation, and reflecting upon some of the newer work in geology and biology, Darwin was led over a period of many years to the formalization of a new type of theory of organic evolution. Although his basic ideas with regard to natural selection were apparently initiated as early as 1838, upon his reading of a paper on population by Malthus, the formal writing did not start until 1856. Some two years later he was surprised to receive, from the geologist Alfred Russell Wallace, a manuscript with an almost identical theoretical account. He proceeded to send, jointly with Wallace, a communication on the problem to the Linnean Society, and the next year, 1859, published his landmark *On the Origin of Species by Means of Natural Selection, or the Preservation of Favoured Places in the Struggle for Life.*

Basic Principles

The crux of the Darwinian theory of organic evolution is contained within four fundamental propositions:

1. There is a great *diversity* of animal and plant forms, even within a given species or family.

2. Owing to limited food and space resources, there is a more or less continual *struggle for existence.*

3. In this struggle there is a tendency for the *best-fitted individuals* of any species to *survive.*

4. Only those individuals that survive to maturity can *reproduce,* thus *passing their best-fitting characteristics on to the next generation* and so over many generations accounting for a *gradual* (evolutionary) *change.*

No single one of these basic propositions was original with Darwin, although he was certainly the first biologist to collect such a great mass of data on similarity and dissimilarity of animal forms. The notion of the struggle for existence he found in Malthus, and Wallace at least also had the key idea of the survival of the fittest. Moreover, selective breeding—utilizing the empirical principle that animals with similar characteristics will tend to produce offspring with such characteristics—had been commonly practiced for a long time, although with no theoretical basis. But it was Darwin's genius to tie these ideas together into one unified theory with compelling evidence in its support.

Supporting Evidence

The response to Darwin's theory was not only strong but immediate, as evidenced by the fact that every one of the 1,250 copies of the first printing of *Origin of Species* was sold on the first day of its sale. The controversy evolutionary theory engendered has continued until the present time, although the central thesis was quickly accepted within scientific circles. Mainly the missing details have been debated. Most of the opposition was offered by the church.

A large number of scientific lines of evidence have been marshalled in support of the Darwinian thesis. Briefly, the most important of these are the following:

1. *Paleontological evidence.* The fossil record left in the rocks provides important support for evolutionary theory. Geologists find that the simpler forms of life are generally entombed in the oldest rock layers, those that were presumably laid down earliest; now, by means of radiocarbon dating techniques, more conclusive temporal ordering of rock layers is possible and the earlier presumptions have been confirmed. With regard to the tracing of particular lines of descent, the most impressive is probably that of the horse. There is an array of equine forms graduated progressively in size, from the earliest available fossils, approximately dog size, to the considerably larger present-day forms. This kind of evidence is certainly the most straightforward in direct support of organic evolution and is very difficult to account for on any other reasonable basis.

2. *Geographical distribution.* When the geographical distribution of different animal forms is studied, the most similar forms are generally found closer together, presumably indicating greater proximity in descent. The more radical discontinuities between animals are correlated with radical obstructions to interbreeding, such as ocean or mountain barriers for land animals. It was this kind of evidence that initially stimulated Darwin's questioning of the fixity of species position, and that was accumulated in such great volume by him.

3. *Morphological evidence.* Homologues, or structures with similar origin in

different animal species, are regarded as evidence for evolutionary theory. A great variety of such evidence exists. For one instance, whales have no hindlimbs, unlike the typical mammalian forms to which they are closely related. However, they do have the small bones similar to those which form the basis for hind limbs in other animals, and these occur in the usual mammalian location.

4. *Embryological evidence.* Embryological evidence occurs in the recapitulation of the individual development (*ontogeny*) of the evolutionary history (*phylogeny*) of the phylum. Here one fact is illustrative: Every human embryo at one stage in its development possesses a complete (but nonfunctional) set of gill arches. These subsequently turn into the ossicles, or sound-conducting bones of the ear. Their fleeting appearance in the human has no reasonable explanation other than that they are silent testimonial to some ancient ancestor that breathed in water.

5. *Physiological evidence.* Common functions exist throughout related animal forms. Here again one illustration from the many available must suffice: the fact that many of the higher organisms' biochemical functions are identical (such as bovine and human thyroid production) is quite consistent with the position that they have a common origin.

Key Questions

This brief account of the range of scientific support for evolutionary theory should not be construed to mean that Darwinism had no serious scientific opposition or questioning. On the contrary, some serious questions were quickly raised by critics. Prominent among these were two related problems. First was the question as to how similar characteristics are transmitted from one animal to its offspring, an issue by no means unique to Darwinian theory of course but needing to be resolved before the theory can be accepted as substantially complete. The second problem was the question of how the very small variations that Darwin hypothesized to accumulate over successive generations by natural selection could account for such very great differences as occur among various plants and animals within the relatively short period of time (estimated in thousands of years) then believed to have been available for such evolution to occur.

The first of these problems, that of the mechanism of hereditary transmission, was very soon to be resolved by the work of Mendel, which was initiated during the late 1850's but not generally recognized until the end of the century. The second problem, that of the small variations postulated to occur from one generation to another, was minimized when newer geological estimates of the time available for evolution to have occurred produced enormously lengthened periods of time (such as the millions of years required for the laying down and occasional erosion of the various layers in sedimentary rocks). Even more important was the discovery, almost half a century later, of the phenomenon of *mutations,* or radical changes in the genes that can account for extremely large, *discontinuous* variations in phenotype within a single generation. For example, consider the mutation that produced very short legs in sheep. This mutation happened to be an economically desirable one, because of the great saving in fencing permitted when flocks of such animals are grazed, and so was happily seized upon by English sheep breeders to make possible a new, short-legged breed of sheep. This incident indicates how selective breeding of such special characteristics can produce a radically new kind of animal in a very short time. It takes no great stretch of the imagination to recognize how such selection can also occur naturally, when mutations are favorable with regard to the environment, thus helping to increase the reasonableness of the Darwinian theory.

THE TELEOLOGY ISSUE. The most serious challenge to the church arising from Darwinian theory involved the absence of any need for an overall plan or design; the natural selection of best-fitting characteristics is all that is scientifically necessary to account for the great diversity of animal forms, and there is consequently no role left for God to play. Of course, there is also no need for assumption of God in the fixity-of-species hypothesis, or even in the special-creation version of that hypothesis. But there is the need for scientific spelling out of alternative mechanisms, such as could account for, say, the succession of cataclysmic events that some authorities postulated as responsible for speciation. Obviously, the orthodox theological assumption of a deity and the postulation of special creation are comfortably consistent hypotheses.

This issue raises the question of teleological (or purposeful) intervention in evolution itself, a problem that poses perhaps the most difficult question for many laymen to handle with regard to acceptance of Darwinism. It is therefore particularly important to spell it out in some detail. Animals (and plants) are so beautifully in accord with their environments, as Darwin's own observations among others demonstrated, that it is quite tempting to conclude that they evolved *for* such purposes. That such a purposive or directed factor in evolution is not necessary can be demonstrated on strictly logical grounds if a fully objective set of premises are adopted.

One key to a solution of this problem is to consider one's temporal orientation. Using the present vantage point in time provides one perspective. Because it is the hindsight orientation that the layman is most likely to adopt, it is to be expected that he will be impressed by the remarkable grandness of fit between organisms and their environments. However, if one adopts, rather, a futuristic perspective, and combines it with the fundamentals of Darwinian theory, a broader perspective is gained. By looking *forward*, we can better appreciate the tremendous range of possibilities for evolutionary development. What evolutionary factors are now in store for man? For other higher primates? For insects? The lines of development that will be favored cannot be predicted with confidence, because we are not in possession of a sufficient amount of information about the future. Certain lines of descent *have occurred*, however, and others have *not* (or more dramatically, some forms have evolved and survived, whereas others have become extinct). But *only* looking backward robs us of the broader perspective and so needs to be complemented if the fact that evolutionary theory does not need teleology is to be freely appreciated and accepted.

For sake of argument, at least, one should divest oneself of the premise of purposive design and focus instead on the simple Darwinian implication that *no poorly fitted organism can long survive in a highly competitive world*. Then the fact that all the surviving species do seem to be so well suited to their particular environment requires only the assumption of the natural selection of such best-fitting characteristics resulting from many successive generations in which the fittest have survived and reproduced. There are many lines of suggestive evidence in support of this assumption. For example, the natural mimicry of many forms, such as butterflies, becomes intelligible on the assumption that variations that in the history of the organism did tend to simulate dangerous animals and so discouraged natural predators have gradually been selected and indeed perfected. The remarkable adaptations found in many species, such as the butterflies shown in Figure A-7, represent the fully sharpened version of a maximally effective mimicry. These butterflies may well persist indefinitely without substantial change, assuming no appreciable environmental change. Moreover, the negative cases—both the extinction of numerous forms that have failed to adjust to environmental changes (such as the fabled dinosaur) and the more rapid dying out of the many lethal mutations— provide strong evidence for the evolutionary theory on the other side of the ledger.

The crux of the matter is the principle of *parsimony*, according to which the simplest account of some phenomenon is the most acceptable. If the facts do not demand some kind of superior or superordinate force, such as an ultimate purpose or a supreme deity, then on a strictly scientific basis any theory incorporating such a force is not supported. Of course it is still possible that such a force may exist, and also that evidence requiring this kind of concept may at some future date be brought forward. But on the basis of available evidence the insistence on this kind of scientifically unnecessary conceptualization must be recognized as a function of the a priori introduction of premises that have nothing to do with our empirical observations themselves. If the antagonists in such controversies would recognize the intrusion of this kind of external consideration into the issue, then argumentation could be more profitably focused on the proper facets of the matter, such as the premises themselves; more light and less heat should result.

BEHAVIORAL CONTINUITY. Although the evidence for organic evolution was scientifically impressive with regard to physical characteristics, that for behavioral (or mental) characteristics was not well developed during the early years of intense discussion following the appearance of *Origin of Species*. Mental discontinuity, and a clear-cut separation of man with his soul from the brute, became a rallying point for the church in particular against the proponents of Darwinism. It was Charles Darwin himself who led the attempt to remedy this defect by adducing evidence for behavioral continuity between man and the lower animals. He provided a wealth of careful behavioral observations that he interpreted as demonstrating the persistence in man of behaviors that had at one time been useful in lower animals and so had survived in evolution. Darwin's observations and theoretical interpretations centered around facial expressions. Although Darwin's own work was essentially observational and theoretical, his work stimulated both experimental and theoretical work on emotional expression as well as a strong and continuing interest in animal behavior study.

THE LAMARCKIAN ISSUE. One last evolutionary issue with close behavioral implications remains to be discussed. This is the proposition that acquired characteristics can somehow be passed on, through biological modifications of the germ plasm, to the offspring. This proposition is called the doctrine of the inheritance of acquired characteristics, or Lamarckism (so named for its foremost proponent, a

A-7 Example of mimicry in butterflies. Eyespots are common in insects and have the apparent function of frightening off insectivorous birds. The South African peacock butterfly *Automeris memusae* has the ability to cover or expose its eyespots by movement of the forewings.

French naturalist of the early nineteenth century). Darwin himself was uncertain as to whether or not to include this proposition in his own theory, and so was somewhat ambiguous on the issue. But he did at least leave the door open for it. That door has since been firmly shut, at least by the scientists in the Western world.

One of the early and best-known tests of the Lamarckian principle was the removal of the tails of many successive generations of mice without the detection of any shortening, let alone disappearance, of tails. Various behavioral experiments have been reported from time to time, but in no case has there ever been any well-substantiated and replicable evidence that the behavioral repertoire of parents can be passed on to their offspring via biological inheritance. Because geneticists now are generally agreed on the mechanisms of the transmission of characteristics, the basic principles of which we shall now summarize, little scientific interest remains in what was at one time a hotly disputed issue.

MECHANISM OF HEREDITY: GREGOR MENDEL

The fundamental principles by which hereditary characteristics are transmitted from one generation to another in all living organisms were discovered just past the midpoint of the nineteenth century by Gregor Mendel (1822–1884), an obscure Austrian monk who worked alone in his monastery garden.

Mendel's Career

The story of Mendel's outstanding work is one of the most fascinating success stories in the history of science. Mendel showed an early interest in natural science but was mainly self-taught during the years of his monastic training. He was later sent to the University of Vienna for two additional years of study in science. However, this formal education was apparently insufficient to permit him to pass the examination required for a teacher's license, although he did teach natural science in the technical secondary school at Brünn. He initiated his plant hybridizing experiments in 1856 and reported the results and his interpretations of them in 1865 to the local Natural Science society. Although this work was formally published the following year, in the transactions of the society, and was duly deposited in the major libraries throughout Europe, its great significance was generally overlooked until the year 1900. Then simultaneous and independent rediscovery of the basic Mendelian principles was made by three European botanists who in the course of their literature search found the prior publication by Mendel of almost exactly what they had just found. Mendel subsequently received, posthumously, the scientific recognition and fame that his work merited.

For centuries preceding Mendel plant hybridizers and animal breeders had been practicing the general principle that "like begets like." They had learned that if one wishes to produce a given line of plants or animals with predominant characteristics of one kind or another (such as, say, heavy beef production in cattle), the best procedure is simply to breed together animals with demonstrated high degrees of such capacity. Although some experimental work had been attempted, especially by the plant hybridizers, no one had yet been able to determine the underlying hereditary mechanism. It was this theoretical puzzle that apparently challenged Mendel so as to induce him to spend several years in patient and painstaking research with the simple and common garden pea plant.

The heart of Mendel's contribution was his ability to formulate the basic problem of heredity in a testable manner and then to develop a conceptual scheme to explain his results and predict new ones successfully. He also enjoyed a little luck, of the kind that successful scientists, like successful fishermen, seem to enjoy; in Mendel's case the luck consisted mainly of his happening to have available the garden pea. In this plant the characteristics Mendel studied show clear-cut dominance and recessive inheritance. The study of some other plant, such as the snapdragon, would have provided different sorts of data, not so readily interpretable; in the snapdragon, for example, the characteristics that Mendel was studying (e.g., plant height) show blending rather than clear dominance or recessive inheritance in the hybrid (all medium-sized plants, that is, rather than some proportion of tall and short ones).

Mendel's own evaluation of the work of his predecessors is indicated in his statement that "among all the numerous experiments made, not one has been carried out to such an extent and in such a way as to make it possible to determine the number of different forms under which the offspring of hybrids appear, or to arrange these forms with certainty according to their separate generations or definitely to ascertain their statistical relations."

Experimental Research

It was just these latter objectives that Mendel achieved with his garden pea hybridizing. He took various lines of garden peas that he had intensively bred through many generations with constant expression of one form of some character, such as tallness (in contrast to shortness) or roughness of pod (in contrast to smoothness). He proceeded to cross-breed these "pure" lines with contrasting characters, one by one, and found that invariably one or the other of the extreme expressions of the character being investigated would be found in *all* the offspring; this condition he called dominance, a term which has of course been retained.

The next step was a key one: Mendel then proceeded to develop a second generation by self-fertilization of these offspring. Now the other extreme expression (the recessive) reappeared, and always in approximately one fourth of the offspring. Mendel then proceeded to demonstrate, by careful individual cross breeding of one of the third-generation offspring, that there was really a $1:2:1$ relationship present. That is, one fourth of these plants resembled the original dominant grandparent, and one fourth resembled the original recessive grandparent; in contrast to these "pure" lines (pure or constant for that particular character) the other two fourths of the third generation plants resembled their own parents, having the ability to produce both dominant and recessive expressions of the particular character being studied (cf. Figure A-8).

Theory

From this simple empirical base Mendel was able to conceptualize the fundamental mechanism underlying heredity. The heart of his reasoning was the

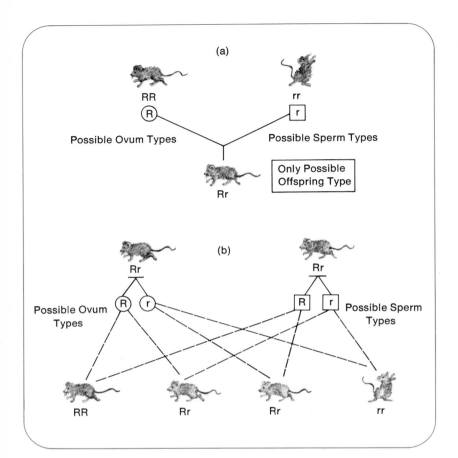

A-8 Chart showing the two-factor theory of Mendel, for the running-waltzing characteristics of mice. R = dominant running; r = recessive waltzing. Crossbreeding [panel (a)] of pure lines (RR and rr) produces hybrid offspring (Rr) that when interbred [panel (b)] produce dominant (RR), recessive (rr), and mixed (Rr) hybrid organisms in proportions 1/4, 1/4, and 2/4. [Adapted from Dunn (1932).]

assumption of two factors (now called genes) for each body character in each organism. This assumption was almost certainly suggested by the discovery of the dual potential for producing offspring of both types (that is, with either dominant or recessive characteristics) in plants that themselves showed only the dominant characteristic. Organisms that were from a pure line, with constant expression of one or the other of the two extreme values of a character, Mendel assumed to have two factors for that value; if both of these were dominant, then of course the character was expressed in dominant form. If they were both recessive, then—and only then—would the recessive character be expressed. And if the organism had one factor for each value, then it could produce either type of offspring but would itself always express the dominant value. The Mendelian theory is illustrated by the chart in Figure A-8.

Mendel proceeded to elaborate his conceptual scheme somewhat to postulate that half of the reproductive cells of an organism contain and so transmit to the next generation the factor provided by one parent, and that the other half have the factor contributed by the other parent. This proposition is called Mendel's first law, or the principle of *segregation.* Mendel's second law, or the principle of *random assortment,* held that each pair of factors operates independently of all the other factors; certain limitations to it have been found in subsequent genetic research.

Rudimentary Genetic Principles

Mendel's basic insight can be more fully described in the light of contemporary knowledge. All the cells in the body of an organism are genetically identical, except for the reproductive cells (gametes), the egg and the sperm; their differentiation into various highly specialized body parts thus depends primarily upon extracellular factors, such as the location of the embryo in which they happen to be. Somatic (bodily) cells each have a full complement of genes, with a pair of genes of each type. The genes, now known to be composed of deoxyribonucleic acid (DNA), are located on the long microscopic filaments called chromosomes in the cell nucleus. Each somatic cell contains a pair of chromosomes of the type and number characteristic of the species (e.g., four pairs for *Drosophila,* twenty-three pairs for man) with large numbers of genes linearly arranged on each chromosome. Somatic cells divide to reproduce themselves in development of the organism by a process called *mitosis,* in which each chromosome is exactly duplicated so that the chromosome (and gene) number remains the same. Reproductive cells, however, divide in a special way, by a process called *meiosis,* so that only one chromosome of each pair goes to each functional egg or sperm. It is this process that underlies the principle of segregation that Mendel described in his first law. Fusion of the egg and the sperm at conception, in sexual reproduction, restores the double-gene condition. From this single cell (the zygote) the new individual is formed by a process of normal (somatic) cell division (mitosis). At sexual maturity the meiotic process once again reduces the normal double-gene (diploid) condition to the single-gene (haploid) condition of the gametes.

Implications of Mendel's Achievement

Mendel's outstanding achievement has some important implications for contemporary science and its place in society.

First, the interplay of the empirical and the theoretical aspects of science is illustrated in nearly perfect form by this research. It is apparent that some initial insights guided Mendel's research, but the full-fledged hypothesis that he developed was the result of his thinking through the implications of his results. Moreover, the research shows in textbook clarity the effective utilization of a quantitative approach. How many equally significant scientific puzzles can still be solved by this simple kind of counting and conceptual procedure remains to be seen, but the fact that so fundamental a discovery could be made on such a basis stands as a landmark achievement in the history of science. It is especially impressive in that it was achieved entirely on the basis of conceptualization and phenotypical observations, without recourse to any of the highly refined tools that now enable biologists to probe within the organism; this point should be particularly heartening to psychologists who are necessarily obligated to work in just this fashion on most of their problems.

A second implication relates more closely to the problem of how science should be treated within the context of contemporary social problems and needs. There is an important lesson in Mendel's work. Like Darwin, Mendel provides a prime illustration of the efficacy of the so-called pure scientific approach. Here a rank amateur succeeded where a long line of professionals (e.g., plant hybridizers) had failed. But the lesson should not be misread. The proper contrast is not really between "pure" and "applied" science. Whether Mendel's work is viewed as pure in this respect (because it was apparently motivated by the challenge of a fundamental scientific problem) or applied (because it did in fact have some very obvious potential applicability) is much less important than the fact that it was carried out in the absence of any *immediate pressure* to solve the problem. In other words, Mendel was entirely uncommitted, as far as his research in plant genetics was concerned. He was free to follow his own interests. He was not overseen by any contract or grant monitor; there were probably few people who even knew what he was about. That some such monitoring is necessary in view of the increasingly large sums of money that modern research requires should not be allowed to obscure the basic fact that the more one is permitted to follow his own hunches and inclinations, the more likely he is to achieve the kind of remarkable insight so beautifully illustrated by both Darwin and Mendel.

The basic Mendelian principles of genetics apply to all forms of life that have been studied, although with certain variations in some of the simpler forms. For example, in some of the microorganisms, such as viruses and bacteria, only the haploid condition—single unpaired chromosomes—may occur. In such instances of course there is no need for meiosis, because it is this process that reduces the double-gene or diploid to the haploid condition in the higher forms of animal life.

3. Learning

This section contains information of a mainly factual sort that is generally applicable to learning experimentation. Our purpose here is to provide the basic procedural information that is necessary to a reasonably full understanding of learning research.

TYPE OF SUBJECT

Practically all behavior patterns of the "higher" organisms are subject to some modification. Practically all such behaviors can therefore be used in learning research. "Lower" animal forms, with more restricted behavioral repertoires and greater involvement of inherited patterns (cf. Figure 9-4, p. 264), show somewhat less diversity. As a practical matter, learning research has tended to concentrate both on certain animal species and on selected tasks. This concentration is at once a strength and a weakness: a strength because it tends to build up a wealth of factual information on the particular animals and tasks used, and so permits more effective research designs and interpretations, as well as facilitating the comparison of results from one laboratory to another; a weakness because it has tended to restrict research too much to such established forms and procedures and so has magnified the risk of overgeneralization.

Use of Animal Subjects

The common use of animal subjects in psychological research, and especially in learning research, is frequently criticized, and widely misunderstood. This practice therefore requires some explanation. The following discussion complements that in Chapter 2 (p. 54 ff.), where the objections to the use of animal subjects are considered.

Animal subjects are used in research for three major reasons. First, there is the interest in the animals themselves; for both theoretical and practical reasons some researchers choose to study animals. Because of the widespread use of animals (e.g., as pets and as commercial objects, such as food sources) few will find fault with this objective, at least from a practical point of view. And if we are serious about allowing freedom of inquiry we should certainly not begrudge the attention pure-scientific researchers pay to animal behavior even when we would prefer to use human subjects.

A second purpose underlying the use of animal subjects concerns the expectation that the knowledge thereby gained can be somehow applied to improve the understanding of humans. Such an application has been very effectively made in many fields (e.g., medicine) and there seems to be no good reason why at least approximately comparable applications cannot be made in psychology. This kind of application is obviously closely related to comparative psychology, but differs in that the objective is improved understanding of human psychology rather than the more generalized improvement of the understanding of the psychology of all animal forms.

It is the third objective whose appreciation is the most difficult for laymen, students of psychology, and many psychologists themselves. This objective makes the kind of subject secondary to the particular experimental or theoretical problem under investigation. In other words, whichever subject seems best to fit the needs of the investigator is used. Animal subjects are so widely used, especially in learning research, because they offer many advantages over human subjects. For example, they are more readily available, they are relatively inexpensive, and their behavior tends to be simple (at least compared to human subjects) and thus more readily manipulated and investigated.

On the negative side, there are certain problems for which animal subjects are clearly not well fitted (e.g., the "higher" mental processes). Moreover, investigators have been accused of overusing certain animal forms (mainly the most popular, in psychological research, the rat and the pigeon) simply because they are available, and so much is known about their behavior because of the great amount of prior research on them. There is obviously merit to this criticism but within recent years there has been a marked broadening of the scope of subjects in psychological investigations. The problem of generalization of result from one species to another is also frequently cited as a reason for not using animal forms, but when this criticism is leveled against animal researchers it almost always seems to be based upon an assumption of the previously mentioned objective—that knowledge of human psychology is the prime objective of our research. The question of generalizing results is one that can be resolved only through the amassing of a sufficient amount of data on a wide variety of animal forms to permit an empirical answer.

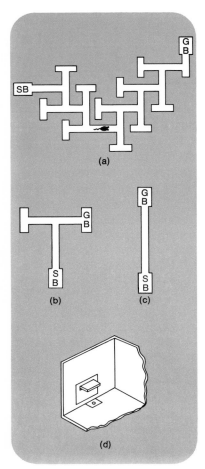

A-9 Representative pieces of
apparatus used in learning research.
Panels (a), (b), and (c) illustrate the
progressive simplification of the
maze, from a multiple-unit device
(a) through a single choice point
"T-maze" (b) to a straight runway
(c). Panel (d) shows a typical Skinner box used in operant research in
which the operation of the bar provides an incentive through the magazine opening on the floor. The ini-
tials *SB* and *GB* indicate *starting
box* and *goal box*, respectively.

The recent emphasis on biological constraints on learning, discussed in Chapter 11, is directly relevant here. But a priori answers on one side or the other of the argument are necessarily arbitrary and based upon prior assumptions for which little evidence is available.

We may conclude that there are a variety of reasons for using animal subjects in psychological research and that the investigator who prefers to use them should not be condemned on the basis of criticisms that may well be irrelevant to his objectives. Those many investigators who are primarily concerned with some particular problem and only secondarily with the kind of subjects used should at least be accorded the courtesy of having their objective understood.

PROGRESSIVE SIMPLIFICATION OF TASKS

Animal Instrumental Learning

Perhaps the most prominent trend in learning tasks during the twentieth century has been their progressive simplification, for human as well as animal forms. The earliest tasks used in animal research were relatively complex, at least by today's standards. Thorndike performed the first systematic research on animal subjects. Panel (a) of Figure 11-7 (p. 343) shows a cat in a Thorndikian "puzzle box." The experimentally naive (that is, untrained) cat has a great many responses available when placed in this kind of situation; only one, however, enables him to open the box and so obtain the reward that has been placed outside as shown in panel (b) of Figure 11-7.

Our most favored animal subject, the laboratory rat, was first used in psychological research in an even more complex type of setting. The original maze was devised around 1900, modeled after the mazelike character of Hampton Court in England. The maze was used for the rat subject because of that organism's "natural" tendencies to burrow into and follow along narrow passageways. A typical complex maze is shown in panel (a) of Figure A-9. The rat's task in the maze is to find its way to the goalbox, where an appropriate reward is placed.

Figure A-9 also shows, schematically, the progressive simplification of the multiple-unit maze. The single-stem "maze" (not really a maze any more, of course, but ordinarily so called anyway) developed next [panel (b)]. The subject is required to make a relatively short trip from start box to goal box. The T-maze has the advantage of offering only one choice point where the subject must choose to make a right or left turn. The interpretation of that choice or discrimination in terms of the various factors that are being investigated is thereby simplified; when successive discriminations are made, as in the complex multiple-unit maze, the consequences of each response can influence all responses. Other extrinsic factors, such as orientation, relationship to outside environmental cues, and the like, are confounded (that is, varied along with the independent or manipulated variable). The success of the T-maze in drawing researchers away from the more complex multiple-unit maze reflected the growing conviction that the more elementary problem of discrimination learning should be tackled before the problem of combination of such discriminations.

The next step, removal of the choice point itself, was a result of the same underlying conviction that simpler problems should be attacked first. Why does a rat proceed along the stem of the T-maze in the first place, before the choice point is even reached? It is obviously easier to answer this kind of question if one removes the choice point, leaving the starting box, stem, and goalbox components. The result was the straight runway, shown in panel (c) of Figure A-9. A further reduction in this type of apparatus also occurred, in terms of its overall length. Thus some of the earlier runways were extremely long; one experimenter even placed one of his in a corridor because it would not fit into any of the laboratory rooms. Gradually the length of the stem was reduced until it was barely longer in some cases than the start and goal segments.

Having eliminated the choice point in the maze and reduced the length of the runway, experimenters next eliminated the runway itself. This step was taken by B. F. Skinner when he devised the experimental chamber that is usually referred to as a "Skinner box." In a historical sense, the Skinner box was really more of a simplification of the original Thorndikian puzzle box (Figure 11-7, p. 343) than a further truncation of the maze or runway. Skinner's purpose was to reduce both the extraneous variation that the typical puzzle box allowed and the behavioral variability that it encouraged. These aims were achieved by production of a small sound-proofed, light-proofed chamber that contained only a single "manipulandum" (object that the subject could readily manipulate). The manipulandum most often used is a simple bar, or lever. This is shown in the cutaway view of such a chamber in panel (d) of Figure A-9. Instead of the latency measure (how soon is the response made?) or the response-duration measure (how long does it last?) Skinner used the simpler rate measure (how often is the response made during a given time period?). Response-rate data with a high degree of regularity can be produced with this kind of simplified task because of the great reduction in extraneous variables to which the subject would otherwise respond.

A Skinner (operant) box for rats is shown in Figure A-10. A similar chamber is shown in Figure A-11 for use with the pigeon, another favored laboratory subject whose use was more recently initiated by Skinner. Pigeons have a strong congenital tendency to peck and Skinner utilized this fact by replacing the bar, designed for pressing by the rat, by a transilluminated circular disk (called a key) for the pigeon to peck. Availability of grain from the feeding mechanism located at the bottom of the chamber is effected by such pecking.

Verbal Learning and Memory

On the human side of the laboratory, verbal learning procedures have also been progressively simplified, and for essentially the same reasons. Thus some of the first learning experiments involved the memorization of a long series of verbal passages, such as in a poem, or long lists of "nonsense syllables." The latter were devised by Hermann Ebbinghaus, the German experimental psychologist who initiated the systematic study of human rote learning and memory late in the nineteenth century. The nonsense syllable is simply a vowel placed between two consonants (e.g., *CUX*) that has no commonly recognized meaning in the language. Its advantage was held to be that it reduces the variability in meaning, and prior

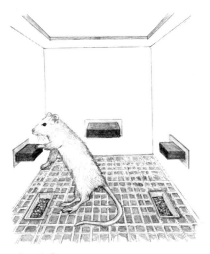

A-10   A multiple-bar operant box. The rat chooses one of the bars to press and is reinforced by means of the food magazine in the floor by the side bars.

A-11   An operant box for pigeons. Pecking the circular key produces food reinforcement (by making available the grain supply below).

learning, involved in words. Actually there is still a considerable amount of variability in the subjects' interpretations of nonsense syllables. Partly for that reason, and to permit a more objective assessment of the subjects' response to the stimuli, there has been a recent renewed trend in verbal learning research toward the use of real words for stimulus materials.

Apart from the nature of the stimulus materials, important procedural refinements have occurred. Development of the *paired-associates* research paradigm, in which stimulus and response items are separated, permitted a more efficient analysis of the elementary processes presumably involved in the formation of verbal associations. A final step in this progressive simplification has been the use of a single S–R verbal unit, such as a word or a nonsense syllable, rather than the more typical series of such units, for somewhat the same reasons as led to the use of a single choice point rather than a series of choice points in animal research. This step was taken barely a decade ago and has resulted in an acceleration of research on short-term memory (Chapter 12).

This survey has focused on a small number of very popular learning tasks, but such concentration should not be interpreted as reflecting the present state of research. It is encouraging that there is in reality a great diversity of tasks being employed, even while the older ones still maintain their popularity.

PHASES IN EXPERIMENTS

The typical learning experiment consists of a number of more or less separable phases. The following discussion most directly applies to such a typical instrumental learning experiment but is also largely applicable to the other types of behavioral experiments.

Pretraining

The pretraining phase permits the taking of necessary preliminary steps in the preparation of the subjects for the training itself. Thus human subjects are given the appropriate instructions and perhaps also otherwise prepared for the experimentation proper; for example, they might be given sample electric shocks, or have their shock thresholds determined, should this kind of unusual treatment be involved in the experiment. Emotional adaption as well as intellectual orientation to the experimenter and the total experimental situation are also accomplished during this preliminary phase.

The use of instructions with human subjects helps to shorten the pretraining phase and generally expedite the preliminary procedures. With animal subjects, on the other hand, more extended nonverbal steps are often required to set the stage for the training phase proper. Animals to be trained in a maze, for example, may be allowed a certain amount of accommodation time in the apparatus, to help them to adjust to it as well as to the total experimental situation, including the experimenter; the purpose of this procedure is to avoid having the training data contaminated with emotional reactions of various sorts.

More specific steps, having to do with, say, motivation may also be necessary.

Animal subjects are ordinarily maintained on some kind of feeding or watering schedule in advance of the experiment, so that they can be appropriately motivated by the incentives (food or water) customarily used in research. They may also need to be shown how to take the incentive in the test apparatus. This stage is usually called *magazine training* because it trains the subject to use the feeding device, which is in general similar to the magazine or cartridge-holding and emitting part of a gun. Magazine training on food incentives is a critical part of most experiments of this kind. Animal subjects that are not adequately prepared to utilize their incentives cannot be expected to make optimal use of their training opportunities; in that case the effect of the independent, manipulated variable whose influence is being investigated cannot be fairly assessed. Of course, it is sometimes true that this kind of learning, to adjust to the incentive, is made a part of the experiment proper, in which case magazine training is shifted out of its customary place in pretraining.

Training

It is in training that the primary work of the experiment is accomplished. *Acquisition* of the referent (to-be-learned) response occurs during this phase. It is at this time also that the independent variable is usually manipulated (for example, different amounts of reward, or a different arrangement of training trials may be introduced).

A variety of measures of acquisition are used. For the more complex tasks (such as memorizing a poem or learning a multiple-unit maze) the experimenter is likely to use relatively gross measures, such as number of trials required to reach some level of mastery or number of errors made per trial; in tasks involving speed, as compared with "power," the criterion of mastery is an arbitrary matter. A single error-free trial may be adopted for this purpose if the task is a difficult one; for less difficult tasks a series of successive perfect trials, say three, may be used.

When simpler tasks are involved other measures tend to be used. Thus in the T-maze or similar device the frequency of correct choices may be the basic measure of acquisition. In contemporary research the experimenter is also likely to depend on various measures of the *intensity* of the referent response. The four measures of response strength that are customary in such learning experimentation are *rate* (number of referent responses per unit time, more or less exclusively used in operant-conditioning research); *frequency* (of referent response per trial unit, more often used in instrumental learning research of a more traditional sort); *latency* of response (time elapsing between stimulus or start of trial and response); and *amplitude* of response (energy with which referent is made, as measured, say, by the degree of movement of some indicant, such as a sound-measuring device for human speech or the excursion of the bar being pressed by the rat).

Test

In experiments where the focus is upon acquisition a further test phase may not be required, because the training phase provides all the data desired. More often, however, the experimenter will wish to assess the influence of his manipulation of training variables in a further and separate phase of the experiment. In this case it is sometimes assumed that the earliest test measures are the most sensitive, perhaps because they are not "contaminated" by subsequent learning that may occur during the test itself.

One commonly used type of special test is that involving *extinction,* or the withdrawal of the customary incentive (cf. Figure 11-8, p. 349). *Resistance to extinction* is measured by the number of trials on which the trained subject continues to make the learned response in the absence of the incentive, or reinforcement. It is generally accepted as an important measure of strength of training; obviously it requires this further test phase for its measurement, in contrast to the other measures of response or training strength described.

Other commonly used test phases involve *retention* (in which the maintenance of the learned response over some time interval after acquisition is measured) and *transfer of training* (in which the manner in which the training affects some subsequent test of learning is measured). These important processes are discussed in Chapter 12.

Although the techniques briefly outlined are the most commonly used test procedures, each experimenter is likely to devise his own particular techniques for testing the effects of his training and other variables. These may involve a modification of the basic procedures or some combination of them, or be some strictly idiosyncratic procedure, depending upon the desires and the ingenuity of the experimenter.

4. Motivation

MANIPULATION OF MOTIVES

The orthodox techniques whereby motives are manipulated and measured in psychological research should be familiar to anyone interested in the problem of motivation. Independent variables are generally manipulated in one of the four following ways: (1) a goal object or incentive is *withheld* from the subject for a specified interval of time, which is typically called deprivation; (2) a *noxious* stimulus is presented to the subject; (3) the subject is offered a *symbolic* representation of some desired or noxious goal object, so as to offer promise of reward; and (4) less directly, the degree of motivation already existing in a human subject is evaluated by means of a standardized *test.*

The first two of these techniques are widely used with animal subjects especially. Food, water, and less often sexual partners have been withheld in many experimental situations, and animals are often stimulated by such noxious conditions as electric shock. With human subjects, more subtle incentives (e.g., verbal praise) or goads (e.g., verbal censure) are frequently used.

Before assuming that a particular incentive is in fact an effective one for a given subject, or class of subjects, the investigator needs to have independent evidence that it is really one that the organism will work to obtain or to avoid.

MEASUREMENT OF MOTIVES

Three categories of measurement techniques are used in research on motives.

Behavioral Measures

The simplest behavioral measure of motivation is an index of the *general activity* shown by the organism, usually an animal subject. It is assumed that the more highly motivated the subject is, the more active it will be. Activity can be measured by simply observing how much movement the subject makes, such as when it is placed on a floor marked by cross lines and a record is made of how many squares are entered within a certain time interval. More sophisticated measurement is made possible by a tilted cage (usually called a stabilimeter) that is delicately pivoted on a central axis so that any movement is detected and shown as a deflection of a recording needle, with the amount of the movement being positively correlated with the degree of deflection. The most common form of apparatus used to measure general activity in small animals is a rotating drum (squirrel cage) that permits the animal to run, with number of revolutions in some standard unit of time taken as the measure of activity.

Vigor and *persistence* of any *specific activity,* such as eating or drinking, are also widely used as a measure of the degree of motivation. With human subjects, some nonconsummatory response, such as pressing a telegraph key or turning a crank, is more likely to be used. Response rate (the number of responses performed in a given unit of time) and either responses or time to extinction (the cessation of responding, according to some criterion, such as no responses occurring in a 5-minute test session) are the two ways in which vigor and persistence of responding are most often measured.

A modification of the simple measure of vigor in some motivated behavior is to interpolate an *obstruction* or obstacle of some kind between the subject and the incentive. With rats, for example, there have been studies designed to compare various types of motivation by requiring the animal to cross an electrified grid to reach the incentive (food for hungry subjects, water for thirsty subjects, a sexually receptive partner for sexually deprived subjects, or small rat pups for a mother rat). The measure used is either the greatest amount of electrical shock that the subject will take in crossing the grid or more simply the number of times that the subject will cross with some standard shock maintained. It has even been shown that essentially the same results are obtained when no shock at all is used. That is, the strength of the subject's motivation can be measured by the number of times it bothers to cross the unelectrified grid, as well as the number of times it crosses the shocked grid, or the amount of shock that it will take and still cross the grid. The general results of this comparison in rats is that maternal drive is strongest, followed by thirst and hunger; however, the results vary with the particular deprivation periods so that accurate comparisons are not as simple as might at first appear.

The last general measurement technique is to allow the subject to make a *choice* between two or more alternatives. Dietary studies have tended to favor this technique. The results obtained with it are not always in accord with results obtained by the simpler vigor measure. An example of this kind of contradiction occurs in tests of the motivational effects of sucrose (table sugar) in water. When a preference test is used a rat will usually choose the sweeter of two incentives, regardless of their absolute values. When a vigor test is used, however, the fastest rate of licking occurs with more moderate concentrations of sucrose. This apparent paradox is resolved when one realizes that it is not possible for the rat to continue to ingest the very highest (quite syrupy) sucrose concentrations, because of insufficient salivation and similar physiological limitations. The typical subject therefore cuts off his ingestion of high concentrations of sucrose in order to allow their dilution by saliva. No such problem exists when a single incentive is offered, as in a preference test; small amounts of the stronger sucrose concentrations are then found to be distinctly preferred. Such factors as amount or volume of concentration and spacing between the offering of the incentive are thus known to be important determiners of licking or ingestion rate when this kind of incentive is offered continuously and the vigor of its intake is measured; however, amount and spacing are much less important conditions in preference testing. Interactions of this kind are common in motivational observations. They can sometimes be interpreted, as in the example just given, when we know enough about the interlocking variables.

Experimentally Based Concepts

The use of experimentation on theoretical concepts represents a refined type of behavioral measure of motivation. Here the field theorist Kurt Lewin affords an especially apt model. Lewin supervised a series of brilliantly conceived and competently executed researches while at the University of Berlin, early in his career, and a sample of these affords a nice illustration of motivational research.

One major theme ran through much of the early research, mainly doctoral dissertations, that Lewin supervised. This was the notion of the *tension system.* Briefly, a tension system is a motive that derives from an intention to carry out some act and persists until that act is finally accomplished.

The way in which this notion originated is both interesting and instructive. Lewin was impressed with the ability of the waiters in Berlin restaurants to remember exactly the amount of a given bill, until it was paid. After that they promptly reported, when asked, that they did not remember the amount. Lewin assumed that the waiter carried around with him, presumably somehow encoded within his nervous system, some motivation to collect the specific amount of money involved; this motivation was called a tension system.

Research was designed to test the implications of the tension-system concept. Two of the doctoral experiments that Lewin supervised are especially well known as tests of the tension-system notion. Lewin assumed that quasi-motives could be induced by the instructions in an experiment and that these motives would function in the same way as their real-life counterparts. In the first experiment, subjects were given a large number of simple tasks to do (such as connecting numbered dots, crossing out certain letters in prose passages, and so on); some of these they were allowed to complete and others were interrupted before completion. The hypothesis was that the uncompleted tasks would not have their underlying tension systems discharged and would therefore be more readily recalled when the subjects were later asked to name all the tasks they had performed. This prediction was confirmed; subjects consistently recalled more of the incomplete than the completed tasks. The superior recall of incomplete tasks is generally known as the *Zeigarnik effect,* named after the original graduate student investigator.

Subsequent research under Lewin's supervision involved the measurement of the tendency to resume activities that had earlier been either interrupted before completion or completed. The tension-system hypothesis was again confirmed. It was shown that individuals are more likely to resume activities that have been interrupted (and for which the underlying tension system is consequently still active) than activities they have been allowed to complete.

This research derived from everyday-life observation demonstrates Lewin's alertness in drawing ideas from his observations. His cleverness in then devising experimental tests of them to develop his theoretical notions provides a model that psychologists should attempt to imitate.

Standardized Tests

A third way of measuring motivation is by standardized tests. The same personality tests that permit manipulation of motivation—by sorting subjects into various groups on the basis of their test scores—can also be used to provide dependent or measured variables. A test commonly employed in this way would be the Manifest Anxiety Scale (MAS). The MAS permits evaluation of the individual's overall anxiety level as one aspect of his generalized motivational state. Other types of personality tests also can be used in this way. A prominent example is the projective test, in which the subject is shown some kind of ambiguous visual display and asked to describe what he sees or to make up a story about it. This procedure is called *projective* because it requires the subject to respond to an essentially unstructured stimulus. He is assumed to utilize some of his own motives in thus responding without the usual guidelines.

The best-known projective test is the Rorschach, which utilizes inkblots as test stimuli. Figure A-12 shows such a stimulus. A more popular technique is the thematic apperception test (TAT). The tester shows the subject a picture with people in ambiguous situations and asks him to make up a story from the picture. Figure A-13 is the sort of ambiguous picture used in TAT-type procedures. When one is asked to make up a story about such a picture he is assumed to draw upon fantasy materials that are representative of his stronger motivational systems. It is then possible to assess the content of such stories in terms of any particular motive of interest (e.g., achievement, affiliation, power).

The basic assumption made by both of these tests is that an individual is making free associations to a partially structured situation and will produce cues that, properly interpreted, can reveal important aspects of a person's fundamental motivations.

RELIABILITY AND VALIDITY OF TESTS

5. Personality Assessment

Reliability and validity have the same meanings for personality tests as they have for the specialized intelligence test (Supplement 6). However, they may be more

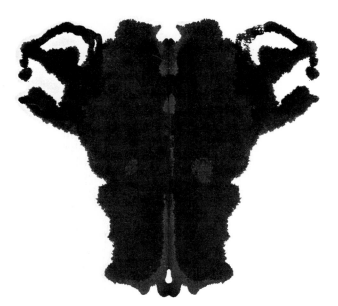

A-12 Rorschach-like inkblot.

difficult to effect for certain kinds of personality tests, especially the projective test, which is difficult to score objectively.

Simply put, reliability means consistency. The question is, "Assuming consistency in the object or event being measured, does this instrument or measure give the same or a similar result each time it is used?" Scientific progress and the development of useful technologies are heavily dependent on reliable measurement. A useful measure must also be valid; that is, it must measure to a reasonable degree what it purports to measure. An anxiety test should provide an index of anxiety just as we require our thermometers to measure temperature.

There are various ways of establishing test validity. The simplest, but also the least useful, is *face* (or content) *validity*. Experts, such as experienced clinicians, can be asked whether the test items are representative of the personality characteristic presumably being measured. Obviously this kind of demonstration of validity is not particularly reassuring; for one thing, experts can differ markedly in how they define particular traits and in which behaviors are used for identification. As a result face validity has a relatively low scientific standing.

A more satisfactory type of validity is established when direct relationships are demonstrated between the test scores and some independent, and already established, measure of the personality characteristic. This type is sometimes called *criterion validity*. In an occupational interest inventory, for example, scores supposedly indicative of interest in, say, medicine, can be validated by having successful physicians and medical researchers take the inventory and comparing their scores with those of a random selection of other persons. If medically oriented individuals do in fact score markedly higher on the medical interest aspect of the inventory, that part can be said to be valid. As a matter of fact, it is in just this way that the typical interest scale is standardized—by painstakingly sorting out items

A-13 A picture of the type used in content analysis. The subject makes up a story based on the picture. The reader may wish to try his own interpretation of this picture. What are these people doing? (Reproduced by permission of Harvard University Press.)

until patterns of scores for all the interests tested do correlate highly with the test results of selected groups of people who have already demonstrated their interest by successful participation in their occupation.

There is another illustration of criterion validity that is especially familiar to college students. This is the use of college entrance tests as predictors of later grade-point average in college. Because there is a substantial positive correlation between these measures, the entrance tests are validated as predictors of college success, at least as that is measured by grade-point average.

A third variety of validity is more theoretically oriented. *Construct validity* is demonstrated by the confirmation of the testmaker's theory about how certain personality attributes are behaviorally expressed. The test is utilized as the presumed measure of the personality attribute; it is considered to be valid, in the special sense peculiar to this particular theory, when the scores it produces bear the predicted relationship to some observed behaviors. Consider, for example, the anxiety scale that was developed from a more complex personality inventory of the sort described below; subjects who scored high in anxiety on this scale were shown, in experiments, to perform very poorly when put under severe stress in comparison both to their previous performance and the continuing performance of low-anxiety subjects. Although this kind of construct validity is extremely useful for purposes of both experimental research and test construction, it does require many assumptions as well as multiple independent confirmations with more than one criterion for an adequate demonstration. Criterion validity is simplest to establish and is usually considered to be adequate in that it permits one to use the scores for prediction and decision making.

TYPES OF MEASURES

The Interview

Interviewing is a commonplace source of nonscientific personality assessment. More technical interviewing varies along several main dimensions. Perhaps the most important of these is its degree of structure. *Informal* interviewing is relatively unstructured, leaving the course of the conversation up to the interviewer. *Formal* interviews are more structured, or standardized, with the sequence and duration of the questions determined in advance. In general, the more skillful and the better trained the interviewer, the more likely the informal mode is to be used; standardized interview formats are necessary when relatively inexperienced and only partially trained interviewers are used. A second important dimension is the purpose of the interview. *Diagnostic* interviews are designed to uncover determining variables for difficulties that the subject may be having, such as failures in school, or marriage, or on the job; *prognostic* interviews are designed to estimate the probability of success in some particular endeavor (such as parole from prison, or an academic career, or on a job in industry).

Interviewing is by far the most frequently used means of assessing personality because superficially it is so simple a process. Nevertheless, the interpersonal complexities that exist in interviewing are now better appreciated, and the results of this new attention will help to improve the process.

The Rating Scale

A more objective form of personality assessment is the rating scale. The rater judges individuals in terms of various personality attributes by assigning one person to some particular position on each of several scales representing the attributes. This enables one to record his estimates of someone else's or his own personality attributes according to the specific features listed on the scale. On some scales the responses to each item are numbered, usually from 1 to 5 or 1 to 7.

The *graphic rating scale* is often preferred because it provides an actual line for each attribute, with the rater asked to mark the estimated position of the subject somewhere along each line. In the *adjective checklist* the rater is simply asked to check each descriptive term, from a long list, that fits the subject. In effect, this form of rating reduces the scale to two points (0—not present, or 1—present) and thus loses the precision of quantification inherent in the more extended scale. It does have the advantage of being simpler and more readily completed—features that may be crucial when there are many poorly trained or weakly motivated raters and when time is short.

Perhaps the most important feature of the rating scale is the inclusion, in some forms at least, of a space in which the rater is requested to record a specific basis, in his own experience, for each attribute rated. Alternatively, the rater may be provided with a more or less extended descriptive account of exactly what is meant by each level for each of the attributes. These specifications force the rater to look more carefully at the subject's behavior and help to reduce the danger of distortion from the *halo effect*. In general, rating scales are most useful when the raters are familiar with the person and are clear as to what they are to do. When properly applied, these simple and straightforward devices can provide useful information for employers and school authorities, among others. But because there are always risks of serious intrusion of bias in ratings, they are best used as supplementary sources of information rather than as exclusive bases for decisions. Moreover, the larger the number of raters and the wider the range of their acquaintance with the subjects, the more accurate the cumulative ratings are likely to be; hence dependence upon single ratings is to be avoided as far as possible.

The Q-sort

An unusual form of rating, the Q-sort, merits special attention. The rater sorts a set of descriptive terms into a number of piles of varying degrees of applicability to the subject. He is instructed to place relatively more statements in the middle piles, more or less in accordance with the normal frequency distribution (cf. Supplement 1). The few extreme items then represent the clearly most and least descriptive.

The Q-sort technique was initially developed as a complement to factor analysis and to be used by a single subject in evaluating himself. That is, all the statements concern himself, so that his self-concept can be obtained. Moreover, the subject may be asked to sort the same items in multiple reference frameworks—for example, as he really is, as he would like to be, as he was at age twelve, as his parents would like him to be, and so on. Statistical treatments, such as factor analysis or analysis of variance, can then be applied to the data obtained from these various sortings in order to determine the more central common factors and to test specific hypotheses. The technique, used alone or with its statistical accompaniments, has proved to be a useful tool in both clinical and personality research (e.g., as a means of measuring changes in self-concept after therapy).

The Personality (Adjustment) Inventory

The personality inventory is a self-rating device designed to get a subject to provide pertinent information about himself. An early questionnaire or inventory of this sort was developed during World War I in order to enable the military quickly to screen out men who were exceptionally poor psychiatric (adjustment) risks. It was composed of relatively simple statements, such as, "Do you daydream a great deal?" It was readily scored and provided composite scores that did seem to pick out some of the men who were most poorly equipped for military duty.

The best known of the many personality inventories that have been subsequently developed is probably the *Minnesota Multiphasic Personality Inventory* (MMPI).

In its full form it consists of about 500 statements, such as "no one seems to understand me" and "I have never done anything dangerous for the thrill of it." The answers to these items (true, false, or cannot say) can be scored to provide indexes on ten psychiatric attributes (e.g., depression, paranoia), used because the inventory was initially developed in a medical context. However, it is also widely used as a means of estimating normal personality attributes on the assumption that disturbed behavior requiring psychiatric attention represents the extreme development of essentially normal tendencies that occur to some extent in everyone. Thus although the psychiatric terminology may be misleading, the MMPI has become a widely used and highly respected personality scale.

Some of the most useful items (e.g., "I work under a great deal of tension") are obviously diagnostic of at least potential behavioral difficulty. The best items are frequently obvious in their intent; therefore, subjects so inclined can "fake" their responses in accordance with their motivation to appear to be better or worse. For this reason, the validation of personality inventories is much more difficult than for intelligence tests. In response to this problem the developers of inventories have turned to subtle forms of subscales, such as the faking scale of the MMPI. It consists of a number of items the honest responder will consistently answer one way but the faker is likely to answer inconsistently. A high score on this scale thus is very suggestive of faking and the results can be interpreted accordingly.

Scoring the MMPI in terms of the ten personality dimensions produces a personality profile, that is, a graphical presentation of a person's relative standing on the set of attributes. The same thing can be done for one or more groups of subjects.

The Interest Inventory

The interest inventory is a special form of personality inventory. It is designed to uncover the central interest patterns in an individual, with special reference to occupational categories.

The interest inventory is based on a relatively high correlation between answers provided by successful persons in various occupations and the pattern of answers that produces high scores on the associated occupational scales. The initial inventory of this kind was the Strong Vocational Interest Blank. It and a small number of subsequent inventories are widely used in college settings.

The interest inventory differs markedly from the intelligence test, and to a lesser degree from the adjustment inventory, in that it has no clearly right or wrong answers. These devices are to be regarded as providing suggestions, particularly when a person is uncertain about his occupational objectives (as is characteristic of perhaps the majority of college students). Unfortunately, however, the presence of high scores in unsuspected categories or, even worse, the absence of high scores in an occupational category on which one is firmly decided frequently are taken much too seriously. Occasionally this attitude is even adopted by counselors or counselors-in-training, who should know better. The strictly suggestive nature of any interest inventory result must be emphasized if this relatively innocuous testing device is to be maximally useful and minimally dangerous.

Psychological tests are available in varied forms, ranging from the most authentic of "real-life" situations to the subtlest forms of indirect assessment. Here we shall describe a few of the more important and representative types: the behavior sample, aptitude and achievement tests, and finally the projective test. Intelligence tests are commonly categorized as distinct from "personality" tests. However, it should be noted that their separation from personality tests is completely arbitrary and done for convenience of classification rather than on any theoretical grounds, because intelligence can be regarded as one of the facets of personality.

The Behavior Sample

The most direct way to assess personality is to place the subject under the kind of environmental conditions that force him to reveal behavior modes and then simply observe how he performs. The major trouble with this direct attack is that it can be very expensive and time-consuming and can require considerable skill on the part of the testers. As a result, it is used sparingly, mainly when high-level appointments, as in business or industry, are involved.

The classic example of a behavior sample is that used by the U.S. Office of Strategic Services (OSS) in World War II. The OSS was faced with the problem of selecting men for difficult special duties, such as infiltration and sabotage behind enemy lines. It therefore needed some way of identifying those with the greatest intelligence and resourcefulness as well as tenacity and the ability to keep secrets. The problem was solved by means of an intensive behavior sample, or situation test. The candidates were put through a series of situations designed to determine the degree to which each possessed the necessary personality qualifications.

Candidates in these tests were given various difficult jobs, such as constructing a log bridge across a stream so as to move men and equipment. The candidate's assistants might have been instructed to frustrate him while his behavior was recorded by hidden observers. Later, girls at a party attempted to induce the candidate to divulge some of the information he had been instructed to keep secret. Surviving candidates seemed to do their real jobs very well and the OSS was apparently satisfied with the results of this elaborate selection system.

In more prosaic and everyday applications of the technique, behavior samples are systematically taken by observers (e.g., aggressive behavior in children at play). By far the most elaborate development of this kind of observation has been made by a group of psychologists who followed individuals throughout the entire course of their day, recording all their behavior episodes. This usage was designed strictly for research purposes, however, and was not related to any particular personality test.

Objective Tests: Aptitude and Achievement

Psychologists have devised objective tests intended to assess various special aptitudes (e.g., musical, clerical) and achievement of various sorts (e.g., reading comprehension, arithmetic). These are often paper-and-pencil procedures that have set answers and are readily scored. It is important to keep in mind that there is no such thing as an aptitude test per se; rather the aptitude test, like the intelligence test, necessarily assesses achievement. Both special and general tests of aptitude serve the purpose of predicting from the individual's performance his potential for future performance of the sort sampled by the test. The achievement test, on the contrary, is not directly concerned about the future but simply asks what level of competence the person is capable of at the present time. This may seem like a thin line—and it is—but there is considerable justification for making the distinction, in terms of the uses to which the tests are to be put.

Like all tests, aptitude and achievement tests are no better than their administration and interpretation. Tests are not magic wands that can be used to supply personality assessments on demand. All testing involves hard work, in the preparation of the testing instrument as well as its application. Aptitude tests, unfortunately, are typically found to have relatively low validity; that is, they correlate positively but not substantially with actual proficiency on the job. This fact has more serious implications for individual counseling, where a very serious error can be made if test scores are taken too literally either by counselor or counselee, than in industrial selection. Where many jobs are involved, a low but positive correlation relating scores on an aptitude test to success on the job can be valuable, and in any case it is easier to change a person's job than to undo several semesters of misdirected academic effort.

Because of the consistently low validation correlations in the early, orthodox type of aptitude test, research has been directed toward developing more precise instruments; more elaborate statistical tools such as factor analysis have been increasingly employed. Also, batteries of tests are being used more, especially when fundamental aptitudes are involved, and other kinds of personality tests (e.g., vocational interest blanks) are being considered with respect to an individual's potential for a particular occupation.

Projective Tests

The most interesting personality tests are the so-called projective tests—those that present to the subject deliberately vague and ambiguous stimuli and require that he respond, as by telling what he "sees" in a set of inkblots (Rorschach test) or making up a story about each of a set of pictures (Thematic Apperception Test— TAT). The tests are called projective because it is assumed that a subject will project much of his own personality, his conflicts and his motivations, into his responses. (See Figures A-12 and A-13, pp. 606 and 607.)

The projective tests have proved to be of some value, although perhaps not as much as initially anticipated, in clinical work, and of considerable value in research on personality. The Rorschach test has been very widely used in clinical work, although in recent years its use has somewhat declined. Mainly this has occurred because of the difficulty of scoring the responses objectively. Although the Swiss psychiatrist who developed the test and others subsequently have provided sets of scoring norms, the validity of the Rorschach technique has not been satisfactorily demonstrated. In the hands of an experienced interpreter the imaginative responses made to the series of inkblot stimuli are said to yield much revealing information about the personality of the testee. In the climate of objectivity that has recently permeated clinical psychological work, such claims have met increasing resistance.

The TAT presents the subject with a set of twenty pictures. The pictures generally show people in commonplace situations but always with a substantial degree of ambiguity of relationship. For example, one shows a seminude girl lying on a couch and a man, obviously distressed, standing nearby; sexual themes (e.g., rape, seduction, impotence, and the like) as well as illness and physical assault are commonly elicited by this particular picture.

The rationale for this test is that the fundamental themes assumed to be central in an individual's personality (e.g., hostility toward parents, aggressive tendency toward spouse, and the like) will be expressed, although perhaps in a disguised manner, in the stories told about the pictures. Again, as with the Rorschach, there is a certain difficulty in objectifying the projective data, but substantial steps in this direction have been taken. The best example is perhaps the achievement motivation research described in Chapter 14, (p. 432 ff.). Some objectivity is achieved by having judges study the protocols and count the number of achievement-related items. The same thing can be done for other personality variables, such as affiliation, motivation, aggression, and the like.

The similarity of the rationale for projective tests to psychoanalytic procedures and theories is evident. Whereas Freud preferred to analyze dreams or elicit verbal responses by having the subject free-associate, the projective test provides a somewhat more structured but still essentially open forum for the revealing of crucial information about one's personal life.

THE BINET–SIMON SCALES

6. *Intelligence Testing*

When one speaks of intelligence testing, the test that is most often meant is the individual battery first developed in the early 1900's by the French psychologist Alfred Binet, in collaboration with the physician Theodore Simon. The Binet-Simon scale that resulted was an age scale. This measure provides a composite score for each child based upon the number of items in the battery that he is able to master during the administration of the test under standardized timing and other conditions. An item is placed at, say, age five if it can be successfully performed by the average five-year-old child (in the group of children on which the test was standardized). Any child, regardless of his age, who can perform the item, is then given some credit (usually in terms of months) for age five. The child's total score, composed of all the age credits he accumulates, then determines his position on the age scale.

Binet and Simon decided on a *battery* of many different items rather than any one type because probing a child's intellectual repertoire in such different ways was more likely to provide a representative index of his *general* level of intellectual capacity than any more limited or specialized items. Thus, for example, the preschool child was asked to point out his various facial features, the school child was asked to define selected words or to use certain specified words in making up sentences.

The results of this kind of testing were reported in terms of *mental age* (MA). If the cumulative score that a given child could achieve on the battery was equal to that achieved by the average six-year-old subject, as again determined in the test *standardization,* or norm-producing work that preceded its actual use, then he was given a MA of 6 years; if his total score was equal to that of the average ten-year-old then he was assigned a MA of 10 years; and so on.

The Binet–Simon scale was eminently successful in providing a relatively objective means of estimating the relative intellectual abilities of children, particularly as these related to school success. Moreover, the results obtained with its use indicated that intelligence as it was thus measured was normally distributed in a given population, as shown by Figure A-14. Most children's scores for any given chronological age group thus clustered around the mean, the most representative MA for that particular chronological age group, with smaller numbers of children achieving high and low scores as the extremes were approached.

THE IQ

Note that chronological age (CA) was not directly used by Binet and Simon. However, it was involved in interpretation of the MA scores, because any given child was most meaningfully related to his age-mates in terms of his test scores. Also, as suggested by Figure A-14, comparisons of MA's within age groups was the most logical procedure. The direct step of relating MA and CA, to produce the intelligence quotient, or IQ, was taken by the German psychologist Stern. The IQ is a *development* score. It is simply the MA divided by the CA and then, for convenience, multiplied by 100. Thus,

$$IQ = \frac{MA}{CA} \times 100$$

It is clear that as the child achieved scores for his problem-solving ability, his store of information, and so on, that were characteristic of the average child of a higher chronological age, the MA and, therefore, the IQ increased. The advantage of using scores such as the IQ as an index of mental and chronological age is that it makes possible the direct comparison of the relative intellectual development of children of different chronological ages. Such a comparison could not be done by MA score alone. Also, the relative intellectual development of a single child over various chronological ages can be directly assessed by means of the IQ. For these reasons, the IQ index has been generally used, although the basic test scores are arranged in terms of MA units. The IQ is taken as providing an indication of relative brightness, whereas the MA indicates the level of actual achievement.

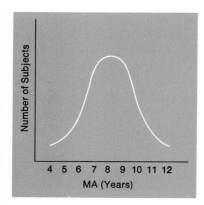

A-14 Hypothetical frequency distribution of MA scores for a group of 8-year-old children, based on an intelligence test battery.

The Binet–Simon scale proved so successful in use that it became a model for subsequent test development. In the United States the most popular revision was that first published in 1916 by L. M. Terman at Stanford University. Commonly referred to as the Stanford–Binet, this test battery was a modification of the original one, adapted for use in this country. It soon became the standard individual intelligence test. In 1937 another revision was issued by Terman and Merrill, with extension of items at each end of the CA scale and two equivalent forms (L and M) so that an individual could be retested without having to give him the same items again. The last revision as of this writing was in 1960. This latest version uses items from both the previous forms and corrects weaknesses that became evident as the 1937 revision was used. Some of the items are not well suited to the current child generation, for example. This is a persistent problem for all tests that utilize culture-dependent items. Periodic updating of items is necessary if any such test is to retain its effectiveness as a measure of ability.

Out-of-date items reduce the efficiency of tests, and are even unfair for later generations of the kind of children on whom the test was standardized and for whom it is mainly intended. The following item illustrates this kind of problem. In a subtest called Opposite Analogies, the child was given the following statement to complete: "*Snow* is white; coal is _____." Even though some bright children are able to pass this item because they grasp the concept of the analogue (i.e., snow is to white as coal is to _____), many children are puzzled by the word *coal*. They are simply not familiar with it. This vocabulary problem thus adds a new and unintended element to the difficulty of the item.

Figure A-15 shows the distribution of IQ's of the group of subjects used for standardizing the 1937 Stanford–Binet revision. The normal, or bell-shaped curve is quite evident, indicating that IQ, like MA, is "normally" distributed in the population. Most people fall around the mean, which by definition (that is, by the way the test is constructed and scored) is 100.

Limitations of the Stanford–Binet

The Stanford–Binet, as a kind of prototype of individual intelligence tests, has received the most critical attention of any of the intelligence tests in use in the United States. Its limitations are therefore reasonably well documented. It is important to keep these in mind as one studies the role of the intelligence test in both experimental–theoretical and practical applications.

Apart from the need to maintain an updated set of test items, as mentioned, there are certain inherent limitations in the Stanford–Binet battery. One of these has to do with the restricted utility of the test at either the preschool or the adult age ranges, in spite of the attempts in the revisions to extend its applicability. The original Binet–Simon scale was developed primarily for use with schoolchildren, aged five or six and up, and later forms remain most useful at this age range. As a matter of fact, as a child ages, the nature of the test itself results in a progressively lower ceiling. (That is, there is a reduction of the top scores that are possible.)

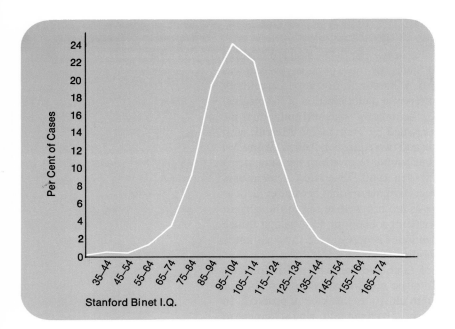

A-15 Distribution of I.Q.'s of the standardization group in the Terman-Merrill study. [From L. M. Terman and M. A. Merrill, *Measuring Intelligence* (Boston: Houghton Mifflin, 1937), p. 37. By permission of the publishers.]

Thus, a child can obtain an exceptionally high MA and therefore earn an IQ, say, of even 200 or so when he is fairly young; however, his top IQ at later ages is progressively curtailed. When used with adults, the Stanford–Binet is of even more limited value; only a gross approximation of IQ can be made. Even though "superior adult" levels have been provided, the instrument is generally useful only for the assessment of adults at relatively low levels of intellectual functioning. Because this age limitation relates to the more general question of the constancy of the IQ, further discussion will be postponed until that topic is treated in a later section.

Another basic limitation of the Stanford–Binet and most of the more widely used tests is that no attention is paid to the *why* or *how* the child answers a question in a particular way. Exclusive concern is with a single or at most a very small number of arbitrarily "correct" responses. This fact penalizes not only the child who has not had the assumed set of conventional (mainly cultural) learning experiences, but also the more inventive child. Indeed, the premium placed on the conventional response is a basic factor in the low correlation usually found between intelligence test scores and ratings of creativity. The Stanford–Binet, like practically all intelligence tests, thus implicitly "defines" intelligence in terms of cultural conformity, and so offers a useful (i.e., highly predictive) but restricted measure of intellectual functioning. Perhaps the test results are predictive of performance in "real-life" situations because the society in which the individual must function is biased in the same ways.

In defense of the Stanford–Binet and its arbitrary scoring system, it may be noted that increasing the number of "correct" answers, so as to take into account cultural and individual differences, would entail a radical increase in both the time and skill required in administering, scoring, and interpreting the test. As explained below, these factors are already sufficiently demanding as to curtail use of the test, and further increases in them would certainly reduce the test's applicability even more drastically. Nevertheless, there are clear and compelling reasons for the development of new, more open, realistically scored intelligence tests to complement conventional ones such as the Stanford–Binet and provide an alternative way of measuring intelligence.

More immediate limitations of the Stanford–Binet as it exists concern the need for well-trained and experienced test administrators and the relatively long period of time required to administer the battery (typically upwards of an hour). In view of the limited number of well-qualified test administrators and the relatively long period of time required to test each individual subject, the impossibility of applying such an individual intelligence test to the great numbers of schoolchildren in the United States becomes evident.

Administration of the Stanford–Binet

Some idea of why a well-trained tester is necessary can be obtained from a description of the general procedure used in administration of the Stanford–Binet. There is an initial period of familiarization with the child, during which the examiner attempts to establish a reasonable degree of rapport. If the child is not put at ease, his performance will be a function of inadequate motivation, poor attention, and feelings of anxiety and even fear, as well as his intellectual ability. The first few minutes that the examiner spends with the subject are therefore likely to be crucial to the success of the testing. For these and other reasons, confidence cannot be placed in results obtained by untrained and inexperienced testers.

A decision must be made as to where on the battery of items to start the examination. Probing by means of one or two sample items, such as vocabulary questions, is often the first step. The basal age, the level at which the subject is able to pass all the items, is then determined. If the tester has overestimated the general ability level of the child, he will of course need to fall back down a year or two. All the items at each succeeding year level are then tried until the child misses all the items at a particular age level. The test is concluded at this point. Partial MA credit is given for the number of items successfully passed at each year level. The cumulative MA score, with full credit assigned for the basal age level and partial thereafter, is then computed. Scoring of responses is usually accomplished at some later time because this task also requires both care and time to complete.

In addition to the various objective test procedures just described, an important part of the tester's job and another reason for the training and experience requirements, concerns the making of qualitative ("clinical"-type) observations. As a matter of fact, this part of the examiner's job may well be of equal or even greater importance than the objective facet (the MA and IQ measures themselves). This is especially likely to be true in the case of the younger and the more unusual subjects, such as those with severe emotional adjustment problems. The examiner must spend a sizable chunk of time in close contact with the subject; and, assuming adequate rapport, the interpersonal transactions that occur offer a good source for intuitive judgments concerning personality and adjustmental problems. Among other sorts of idiographic data, an individually administered test may provide the opportunity to observe and record the ways in which a given individual deals with stress and responds to problem-solving situations. Thus the various "limitations" of the individual intelligence test described above may also be regarded as advantages, because they offer opportunities to the alert and experienced testers to pick up cues and form judgments that are not possible in a group setting.

Behavioral Correlates of IQ

Because there is an inevitable selection of the more capable individuals as each academic hurdle is passed, those students who reach college tend to have higher IQ's. This remains true to a degree even with the "open admission" policies now being tried by some colleges. The result is that most college students tend to think of an individual with "average intelligence" as being approximately like the typical "average" individual they know. This belief is likely to be faulty. The true average IQ, ranging from 90 to 110 and including roughly half of the population, is much more limited in both intellectual capacity and intellectual interests than the average college student. Unless the student has had extensive experience with the lower as well as the higher half of the distribution, he is unlikely to realize the practical significance of such differences.

The relationship between IQ (as measured by the Army General Classification test, a group intelligence test) and some typical occupations is shown in Figure A-16. Although there is a considerable amount of overlapping of IQ ranges, with approximately 70 per cent of the individuals in each occupation falling within one S.D. above and below the mean IQ, it is also evident that the ranges for the highest and lowest occupations (in terms of IQ level involved) are actually fairly far apart.

EXCEPTIONAL CHILDREN

The Gifted Child

The child with a very high IQ is, unhappily, more likely to be scorned than respected in large segments of our population. Although there is some evidence that this attitude of distrust and dislike for the intellectually gifted ("brains") and for those who spend much of their time in intellectual pursuits ("eggheads") has declined over the past decade, they still are hardly treated with the respect given, say, the athletically gifted persons. Moreover, there is still abroad the myth that intellectually gifted children are more likely than average children to be deficient in other important ways, such as in emotional adjustment.

The falsity of this latter belief was clearly shown in the longitudinal study of highly gifted children who were tested in 1922. These children were selected from about one quarter of a million California schoolchildren then tested. All of them had Stanford–Binet IQs of 140 or more, with a mean of 150. As other important measures were taken on these individuals over the following years, it was observed that they tended to surpass the general population. Their intellectual ability continued at a high and productive level, as one might expect, but more impor-

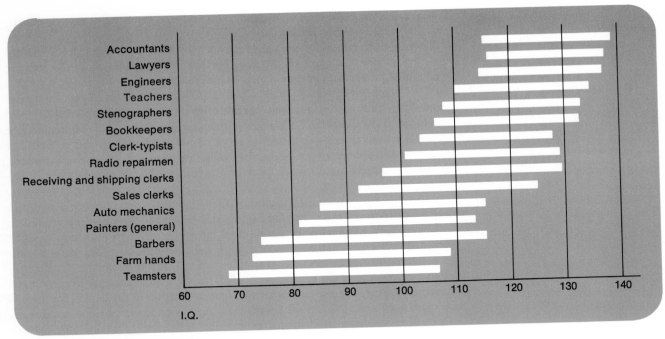

A-16 Intelligence and occupation. This graph, based on scores from the Army General Classification Test, shows the intelligence levels of fifteen occupations. Perhaps the most striking thing about these figures is the degree of overlapping, showing the wide range of occupations feasible for persons of a given IQ. (From T. W. Harrell and M. S. Harrell, Army general classification test scores for civilian occupations. *Educ. Psychol. Measmt.* 1945, 5, 229–239.)

tantly, they were not only superior in physique and health but were also successful in general adjustment to life, as indicated by lower rates of suicide, psychosis, and divorce, as well as financial status. In general, these empirical results give reason for considerable optimism rather than pessimism concerning the overall life adjustment of the intellectually gifted, and by implication the superior, children. It has been strongly indicated by this and other research that superior intellectual competence enables one to cope more effectively with stress and to maintain a generally advantageous social and economic position.

The Retarded Child

For a variety of reasons, a considerable amount of money and effort have recently been expended on the problems of retarded children. Except in the case of the most severely retarded, it has become apparent that a great deal can be done with such children, given the proper attitude on the part of their associates and correspondingly appropriately arranged working and living conditions. The major problem is to maintain a positive but not unrealistic attitude as to their potential; that potential is generally higher than one might suspect, and it is important to see that their training schedule is adjusted to take advantage of their previous experience, capacity, and motivational levels.

There are several million mentally retarded persons in the United States. Exactly how many there are can only be roughly estimated, because most of them are maintained either in their own or foster homes. Approximately one quarter of a million retarded persons are maintained in public institutions. Again, the exact figures can only be approximate because of uncertain and sometimes mixed diagnosis. (That is, not only do diagnostic standards vary, but also children may be given double diagnoses—for example, retarded and psychotic—or shifted from one diagnosis to another.) In any event, the problem is a serious one in every country, the actual dimensions of which have only recently been appreciated within our own.

Although such external and accidental factors as birth injury are often involved, most cases of mental retardation appear to be more or less directly related to genetic factors. Genetic defects have been directly implicated in certain types of retardation (e.g., mongolism, where most of the cases occur in older mothers), but more often the genetic influence is simply assumed. The inconclusive character of simply citing genealogical evidence should be evident on the basis of the prolonged treatment of the heredity–environment issue in Chapter 9; the genetic variable is in most such cases confounded with extremely poor environmental conditions. Most cases of generalized mental retardation are probably attributable to both kinds of conditions, with the proportion of influence varying from one case to another, but little in the way of concrete evidence on this issue is available.

In terms of IQ scores, the terminology now in use consists of four descriptive labels: *mild* retardation, for persons with IQ's from 55 to 69; *moderate* retardation, IQ's from 40 to 54; *severe* retardation, IQ's from 25 to 39; and *profound* retardation, IQ's below 20. These more neutral terms replace the ones formerly in use, which were *moron* (IQ's from 50 to 70), *imbecile* (IQ's from 25 to 50), and *idiot* (IQ's from 0 to 25).

Table A-2 shows the kinds of behavior potential that each of the four currently used levels of retardation may be expected to have during various ages. In interpreting or otherwise using this chart, as in all work with intelligence test scores, one must keep constantly in mind the approximate and variable character of the measurement device. It is not uncommon to find a child diagnosed as retarded, because of apparently slow learning and adjustment problems in school and low test scores, who is suddenly discovered to be partially deaf. He simply had not been able to follow instructions properly or to take advantage of school opportunities, and either he did not know or was not able to communicate to others the fact of his deafness. Such cases are becoming less frequent as more adequate testing of visual, auditory, and intellectual functioning is applied to school populations, but they still occur with sufficient frequency to justify a skeptical view of diagnostic efforts in general (which is certainly not to take the opposite point of view and condemn all testing; rather, it is more and superior analytic testing that is needed to remedy this particular problem).

Although moderately, severely, and profoundly retarded tend to get the most attention because of the more or less obvious nature of their behavior, it is really

Degree of Retardation	Characteristics
Mild	IQ: 55–69 Maximum educational potential: about sixth grade With training and supervision, capable of marginal self-support as adults Distribution: about 85 per cent of total mental retardate population: about 2 per cent of general population
Moderate	IQ: 40–54 Maximum educational potential: about second grade Can be trained in self-care and to do simple work in sheltered environment Distribution: about 10 per cent of total mental retardate population
Severe	IQ: 25–39 Maximum educational, training, and self-care capability: roughly that of average six-year-old Needs close supervision Distribution: about 5 per cent of total mental retardate population
Profound	IQ: 0–24 Maximum educational, training, and self-care capability: little or none Requires custodial or nursing care Distribution: less than 1 per cent of total mental retardate population

Adapted from J. D. Page, *Psychopathology: The Science of Understanding Deviance* (Chicago: Aldine Atherton, 1971).

the much more common mildly retarded—and even more the dull normal, with IQ's from 70 to about 80—who constitute the greater problems for society. This is because they are generally not so readily identifiable, yet they are likely to be lacking in judgment and social learning ability so that they are ready foils for the unscrupulous manipulator. Persons at these levels of intellectual functioning thus tend to swell the ranks of petty thieves, those to whom the dirtier and riskier jobs are often assigned, and prostitutes. They are useful in such capacities because their physical functions, such as those involving brute strength and sexual activity, are likely to be normal. More attention is therefore needed for them both within the family, where unfortunately the parental capacity is not likely to be very great, and the school, where if they are able to get by without becoming disciplinary problems they are likely to attract little attention from the teacher kept busy, often harassed, by other matters. Even with such added attention, it must be granted that the prospects of many of these persons finding a more socially acceptable (that is, by middle-class standards) role in society is limited because they generally come from an environment where thievery and prostitution are commonly accepted ways of life. They are therefore quite likely to be lacking in any socially "upward" motivations.

Most retarded children are born into families in which both biological and cultural legacies tend to be below normal. A sizable and unfortunate minority, however, arrive in families with middle- and upper-class social backgrounds. Most of these cases appear to be the result of adventitious conditions such as birth injury or special genetic defect. The latter factor is exemplified by the mongoloid child, with a typical IQ ranging from 30 to 50 and with a particularly happy disposition. Children of this sort constitute an especially heart-rending problem for the family into which they come because of the striking contrast between them and their siblings and parents. Often they are maintained at home, with admirable attempts made to train them there as well as possible. Sometimes they are given special schooling. They are much less likely to be sent to the kind of state institution where little effective training occurs and so can be expected to make a better adjustment to life than the less fortunate retarded children born into lower-class families with limited financial and other resources.

Given proper training and attitudes of tolerance and acceptance on the part of their associates, the mildly and moderately retarded child can make a reasonable social adjustment. The mildly retarded especially can be trained to become at least partially self-supporting. But appropriate training facilities as well as accepting social attitudes are in short supply, although both are becoming more evident as educational campaigns continue to promote acceptance and opportunity for this kind of handicapped child.

OTHER INTELLIGENCE TESTS

Among the important dimensions along which new intelligence tests have been developed are those of age, group, and performance. Some commentary on each of these dimensions and the tests that have been developed is needed.

Adult Tests

The most frequently used individual intelligence tests, now largely superseding the Stanford–Binet, are two batteries developed by Wechsler. The Wechsler Adult Intelligence Scale (WAIS) is especially valuable because it fills the void left by the inappropriateness of the Stanford–Binet for the assessment of intellective and psychomotor abilities in adults. The Wechsler Intelligence Scale for Children (WISC) is the form specifically designed to apply to children. Both of these tests are explicitly divided into verbal and performance (nonverbal) items. Separate verbal and performance IQ's are thereby obtained by comparing each subject's cumulative test score with norms for his age group. MA's are not directly computed. The obtained IQ's indicate the individual's relative performance; therefore his score is often expressed in terms of a percentile rank, which provides an index of his standing in the general population. Subjects are given progressively more difficult items until a certain number of successive items are missed. As in the Stanford–Binet, administration of the WAIS and the WISC requires a relatively high degree of training and time on the part of the examiner; because it is an individual test, it also provides the opportunity for qualitative observations to complement the objective scores.

Group Tests

Because of the time and training requirements for individual intelligence testing, a large number of *group* tests have been developed. A group test not only requires less in the way of training in administration but also permits the simultaneous testing of very large numbers of persons; it is also likely to be much more easily and quickly scored, as by machine-sorting techniques, because of the essentially objective (multiple-choice, true–false) nature of the items. Such tests are typically closely timed.

Group intelligence testing was first used on a massive scale during World War I in this country. We were faced with the need to classify as quickly and as accurately as possible the mass of raw recruits daily being inducted into the army in order to make appropriate training assignments. The result was the development by psychologists of two group tests, the Army Alpha and the Army Beta, whose widespread use survived the time of military crisis. A further development, the Army General Classification Test (AGCT), was used as a screening and classification device during World War II.

Performance Tests

The *performance* test, or the performance test item in a battery (as in the Wechsler tests), is designed to reduce the influence of strictly verbal factors in the test results. Such tests are intended to provide a more accurate estimate of fundamental intellectual abilities independent of linguistic processes than the verbal test and so make possible a fairer test for minority and disadvantaged subpopulations whose linguistic functions are substantially different from the majority of people upon whose performance the standard tests have been based. In general, performance tests indicate appreciably higher levels of intellectual functioning on the part of such persons but it cannot be safely assumed that all the handicaps associated with linguistic and other cultural differences are thereby eliminated.

The Culture-free Test

An ultimate objective of test experts is the so-called *culture-free* intelligence test. The purpose of this kind of test is to permit adequate comparisons of intelligence both across cultures and within a given society where subcultural variations are pronounced. A satisfactory form of such a test has not been devised and there are good reasons to doubt that it will ever be devised, given the pervasive nature of cultural factors in the development of the behaviors upon which intelligence tests must necessarily be based. Nevertheless, the objective is a laudable one and the research directed toward it is important. Moreover, the greater the reduction of the grosser aspects of cultural determinants in intelligence testing, the more representative test results will become. Even if a perfectly fair and culture-free testing instrument is not possible, approximations thereto can be extremely useful for both practical and theoretical purposes.

Now that we have surveyed some of the technical features of intelligence testing we can return to the hereditary–environment issue covered in Chapter 9, with particular regard to the developmental aspects of the controversy. Most of the argumentation of this sort has revolved around the issue of the constancy of the IQ as a measure of general intellectual functioning. Although much of the argumentation has been produced by extreme statements on one side or the other of the heredity-environment issue, even when these are subtracted there remains an enormous amount of problematic material over which more reasonable men may differ.

The Iowa Studies

Historically, the most famous controversy resulted from publication of a number of studies by the Iowa Child Welfare Research Station from the early 1930's. Most of these reports were of empirical investigations in which generally low-level IQ's of institutionalized children were found to show substantial, and in some cases quite spectacular, increments as a result of their placement in more intellectually stimulating environments (usually preschools or foster homes). Control groups of children remaining in the institutional setting and showing the expected constancy of IQ were usually included.

The conclusions reached by some of the Iowa researchers were in fact quite guarded with respect to the question of whether or not the increments found represented genuine IQ changes. Nevertheless, they were vigorously and often vehemently attacked. Apart from technical problems relating to statistical procedures and the like, which are almost always arguable, the basic reason for the strongly negative reaction (and in particular for the bitterness with which it occurred) was no doubt the simple fact that these data contradicted the orthodox view then held by most authorities that the IQ was primarily a function of genetically determined factors and therefore at least relatively immutable. Although the critics at the time far outnumbered the proponents of the environmental view, the controversy produced shock waves that were instrumental in stimulating much of the ensuing research on intellectual development during infancy and childhood. Moreover, contemporary thinking is probably appreciably closer to the Iowa position, especially as represented in its more moderate form, than to the genetic-determination view of that period.

One recently reported follow-up of some of this early work indicates a surprising degree of permanency of the improvement noted during the very early years. In that study, thirteen infants classified as mentally retarded were moved from an orphanage to an institution where they received care and attention from adolescent girls who were themselves retarded but able to handle this task, including cognitive stimulation to the best of their abilities. Matched controls were left in the orphanage. The transferred infants showed substantial acceleration in intelligence test scores, whereas the controls did not. Twenty-five years later the transferred subjects were re-examined and found to have maintained their intellectual improvement; all but one of the controls, on the other hand, were still classified as retarded, and showed all the typical symptoms associated with such classification.

The Preschool Years

Measures of intellectual functioning during infancy and early childhood—before formal schooling is normally started—have uniformly failed to yield estimates that predict subsequent intellectual functioning, as measured by such standard intelligence tests as the Stanford–Binet. This result raises serious questions concerning the development of intelligence during the preschool period and is therefore worth some closer attention.

A large variety of factors have been suggested as possibly related to the failure of any of the infant intelligence tests to correlate substantially with scores from standard tests administered later in childhood. Among the more promising of these, several may be mentioned. The major consideration may well be the fact that the infant has not had an opportunity to learn to do enough things to make possible an adequate estimate of his intellectual potential; in other words, his behavioral repertoire is just too skimpy to allow the kind of representative probing of a large number of behavioral functions as are involved in such tests as the Stanford–Binet. Related to this point is the difficulty of devising generally applicable test items (a procedural problem) and the large individual differences in growth patterns (a developmental problem). A somewhat different consideration relates to difficulties that examiners may have in inducing the infant, or the very young child, to perform anywhere near the extent of his true abilities; from about six months on, the infant shows awareness of strangers. Because the examiner is ordinarily a stranger (and must be, if reasonable standards of objectivity in testing are to be maintained), much variability in performance can be expected to result from the differential degree to which various infants can be persuaded to cooperate with the examiner.

In spite of these many problems, and the fact that reliable predictions of child intelligence cannot be made from infantile tests, the tests themselves have value in providing at least a gross index of the infant's overall behavioral health (mainly related to simple locomotor responses) and receptivity to stimulation. Such testing can call early attention to children who have obvious specific problems. More precise measures of intellectual and cognitive potential that can be used for intellectual predictions must await the development of new testing instruments.

The School Years

It is during the school years that the standard intelligence test makes its greatest predictive contribution, with regard to both school success in the more or less immediate future and subsequent academic and general intellectual functioning. This is, of course, hardly surprising because it was this age range, from six years or so up, that was the focal point of the initial efforts by Binet as well as most of the succeeding work on tests. Moreover, many of the assessment problems posed by the infant and very young child are at least lessened during middle and later childhood. For example, most children have by this time become accustomed to meeting and working with strangers (although accommodation periods are still necessary, as we have seen). Moreover, most children have been exposed to a wide variety of learning experiences so that they can reasonably be assumed to have had sufficient opportunity to have developed the kinds of behavior probed by the tests. Of course, the extent to which these general assumptions do not hold for any particular child or group of children determines the degree of inapplicability of the test.

With reference again to the question of constancy of the IQ, there is evidence that significant changes can occur during the period from six to ten years. One longitudinal study, over a thirty-year period, indicated that children who achieved high ratings in independent and competitive problem solving also made substantial gains in IQ over this early school period. Constant or even declining IQ's were found in children whose parental ties, with regard to emotional satisfactions particularly, remained close. These data were interpreted as support for the presumption of a critical period (the first five years of schooling) for the development of motivation to master intellectual tasks. The relationship of such motivation, and its resulting effects on IQ, to overall personality development during this period is suggested by the differential IQ changes mentioned above.

Another source of evidence concerning variability in measures of intellectual ability is the well-documented observation of a progressive deterioration in academic achievement scores of black children, relative to white, over the primary grades. This fact can of course be interpreted on the basis of an extreme hereditarian view of intelligence as the progressive unfolding of poorer genetic programming. It seems much more reasonable, however, to view such a decrement in performance as a function of the cumulative effect of a different (if not an "inferior") type of environment and, more particularly, of gradually reduced motivation to adapt to the demands of such dominant figures as teachers in the white culture. In any case, the fact of such progressive decline is further evidence against the constancy of the IQ.

In general, we may summarize present opinion on this issue by saying that most children remain in the general region of their initial IQ score, assuming appropriate testing conditions, but that quite marked changes are not uncommon. The IQ, like any other complex behavioral measure, depends upon a large number of environmental determinants; the specific nature of many is as yet unknown.

Subsequent Development

Substantial changes in IQ are of course possible, given appropriate changes in the person or in his reaction to the testing procedure. As the childhood period ends, however, the concept of IQ—a developmental index—quickly loses its significance. It was mentioned earlier that the Stanford–Binet test is of limited utility for adults, except under unusual circumstances (such as severe emotional disability, or low level of intellectual functioning). This fact follows partly from the nature of the test items but more basically from the fact that the basic intellectual functions that this kind of test measures simply do not develop much beyond the later childhood period. As a result, any developmental index cannot be expected to be of much further value. By the end of the childhood period, the average individual has mastered the basic intellectual tools and his further intellectual development will be along other lines. Adult intelligence tests are of course designed to utilize population norms based upon such other types of behaviors. An individual's scores are then more appropriately expressed in terms of the percentage of the norm population that he exceeds (percentiles, or centiles, with 50 being average) or in some similar statistical form rather than in IQ. Because of the popularity of the IQ term, however, an "IQ equivalent" is frequently used, even where the IQ itself is not at all appropriate; its real (nondevelopmental) meaning should be kept in mind.

THEORIES OF INTELLIGENCE

Thus far we have been considering mainly the methodological problems associated with intelligence testing and some of the main empirical results that have ensued from application of the tests. Theoreticians whose interest has focused on an interpretation of the nature of intelligence itself have also been active. In this section we shall review the major theories developed to "explain" intelligence, although these have tended to be more concerned with fully developed adult functions than with developmental issues.

Spearman's Two-Factor Theory

The first highly influential theory of intelligence was advanced by the British psychologist Charles Spearman. He distinguished between a general factor, *g*, which was presumed to enter into each specific behavioral function, and more specific intellectual capacities.

Spearman's interpretations were based upon the results of elaborate statistical procedures such as factor analysis, in which successive correlations are computed between test data so as to isolate statistical factors that are common to various clusters of data.

Although there has been a continuing tendency to accept the notion of "general" intelligence as the behavior potential tapped by the test batteries, Spearman's two-factor theory was not generally accepted by other theorists. Nevertheless, it served as a stimulus to continued research and theorizing and most of the subsequent work was more or less directly provoked by it.

Thurstone's Primary Mental Abilities

Spearman's theory may be regarded as occupying a position close to one end of a continuum along which degree of generality of intellectual function may be ordered for various theories. At the other end would be such views as Thorndike's, who held that intellectual functions were for the most part discrete with relatively little relationship among them (a view that is similar to his theory of transfer of training, discussed in Chapter 12). In between these two extreme positions is the view that clusters of mental abilities exist. Intelligence by this view would be neither highly general nor entirely specific, but would consist of a number of clusters of associated functions.

The best-known exponent of this type of theory is the American psychometrician L. L. Thurstone. He started with thirteen tentative factors, discarded four of these so that nine primary mental abilities remained; then, in collaboration with his wife, Thelma G. Thurstone, he further reduced the number to seven, for each of which a special test battery was prepared. The seven primary mental abilities they then envisioned were as follows: (1) *perceptual speed*, the readiness to attend

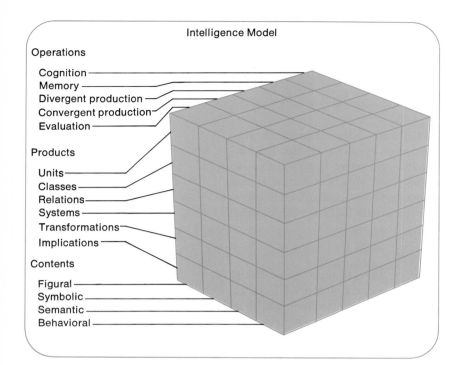

Intelligence Model

Operations

Cognition
Memory
Divergent production
Convergent production
Evaluation

Products

Units
Classes
Relations
Systems
Transformations
Implications

Contents

Figural
Symbolic
Semantic
Behavioral

A-17 A model of Guilford's theory of the structure of the intellect. (From J. P. Guilford, Intelligence: 1965 model. *American Psychologist,* 1966, **21**, Fig. 1, p. 21. By permission of the American Psychological Association and the author.)

accurately to small details in perception; (2) *spatial visualization,* the ability to organize and manipulate spatial patterns; (3) *reasoning,* the ability to understand symbolic relationships; (4) *memory,* the ability to recall previously experienced or learned materials; (5) *numerical ability,* the facility of working with numbers, as in simple arithmetic; (6) *verbal comprehension,* the facility with which one can understand words in communication and manipulate them in planning; and (7) *word fluency,* the ability to find and use words readily in communication.

Thurstone's research, like that of almost all the theoreticians in this field, involved the statistical techniques of multiple-factor analysis, many of which he himself devised.

Guilford's Structure-of-Intellect Model

The most recent of these theoretical positions, and the one that is perhaps of greatest contemporary influence, is that developed by the American psychologist J. P. Guilford. His model of intelligence is a much more complicated one. As shown in Figure A-17, it consists of three basic dimensions: *operations, contents,* and *products.* Operations are mental processes (e.g., evaluation) that work on contents (e.g., symbols) to make possible products (e.g., an implication). Of the total of 120 possible factors in intelligence (five operations multiplied by four contents multiplied by six products), a substantial number have been empirically measured.

Guilford's model has the great advantage of offering an analytic framework within which the manifold mental processes that are presumed to make up intelligence can be separately identified and related to each other. This research, like all similar work, has been enormously facilitated by the application of high-speed electronic computer systems, and as a consequence accelerated progress in this field as in so many others may be expected.

Public opinion polls of a great variety have become commonplace in American life. People are regularly asked to state their opinions on a wide range of public issues as well as on matters of more strictly personal preference, such as with regard to an array of manufactured products. Many polls are essentially research instruments and as such are likely to have indirect effects on public affairs. Others, however, in particular political polls or "straw votes," are believed to have direct and possibly profound consequences.

7. Public Opinion Polling

DANGERS OF POLLING

The kind of feedback that political poll results published in advance of an election can have on the election itself is not easy to determine. On the one hand, there is the possibility that the leader in the poll results may be hurt by a "sympathy vote" for the underdog, or by over-confidence and apathy induced by an apparent lead, especially if it is large and seems to be insurmountable. Thus Harry Truman's unexpected and largely unpredicted victory over Thomas Dewey in the presidential election of 1948 was believed by many observers to have been caused at least in part by the early polls operating in these ways, with the result that much of the public probably believed that Harry didn't have a chance—and yet voted for him in sympathy.

On the other hand, there is the possibility of the leader in the polls being substantially aided by a strong "bandwagon effect," where undecided individuals are swayed in his direction presumably by their desire to be on the winning side. Moreover, and perhaps more important, the same sentiment may operate on those who provide substantial financial donations. It is clearly to their advantage to support the winner; the influence they gain is much more likely to have significant practical effects. Consequences of this sort were widely believed to have seriously hurt Senator George McGovern in his 1972 race against President Richard Nixon, when the early polls showed him with an enormous deficit in popular support. In this election, the results closely paralleled the landslide victory consistently predicted by the polls.

The validity of these feedback influences of polls is difficult to ascertain, but there does seem to be a solid basis for concern, if, that is, one feels that people's decisions on crucial issues should be made strictly on the merits of the alternative positions. A fundamental problem with opinion polls is that many people seem to assign more value to them than they deserve. The situation is similar to that found in intelligence testing. As we have seen, the IQ is at best only a very approximate measure of general intelligence. Overevaluation of it, especially with respect to its stability, is responsible for all sorts of opinions and actions that have little real justification. Nevertheless, the IQ, if properly obtained, is probably a more stable and dependable measure than the group preferences that are commonly reported in opinion polling. In order to put the opinion poll in a more realistic perspective, therefore, some of its most important weaknesses should be spelled out.

Basic Problems

Two major types of problem confront the pollster. First, there is the problem of *whom* to poll; that is, how are the respondents selected so as to ensure that the very small sample polled is reasonably representative of the total population? Second, there is the problem of *how* to ask questions so as to obtain answers that are both valid (that is, really reflect the opinions of the respondent) and reliable (so that if repeated in the near future the same general results would be obtained).

In addition to these two sets of problems, on which the better polling organizations have worked hard and with considerable success, there are certain other weaknesses intrinsic to the polling method for which there is no real solution. There is no way, for example, for polls to predict the influence of future events, except perhaps to take additional polls (which may not always be practicable, on a time basis, if for no other reason). Thus no matter how "scientific" public opinion polls may become, they should never be accepted as final arbiters on any issues, and especially on such volatile matters as political campaigns. Nevertheless, it is worthwhile to consider the most important qualifications that the more respectable polls exhibit, because for better or worse polling promises to be a permanent feature of American life. Moreover, the more carefully operated polling services do have a remarkably high proportion of successes, especially in consideration of the extremely small size of their sample, with just enough failures to keep them honest and their users wary.

REPRESENTATIVE SAMPLING. In an effort to have each significant category of the population to be sampled adequately represented in each sample, most public opinion polls use a quota, or stratified, system of selecting individuals to be questioned. That is, the proportion of each such segment of the population (women, men, various age categories, ethnic background, educational level, and the like) to the total population is maintained within the sample.

An alternative technique, sometimes used as a spot-checking device on the stratified sample, is sampling by area. All the residents of the selected area are questioned, without exception if at all possible (in order to avoid bias that might be due to the most readily reached having markedly different opinions than the most difficult to reach). Area sampling avoids the problem of representative weighting but does introduce some new sampling problems. For example, unless the area is relatively large (say, a large town or a small city), the economic, educational, and related characteristics of one area are likely to differ from those of other areas that might have been selected but were not, so that again the basic issue of adequate representation to permit generalization of results back to whatever total population we are concerned with is likely to remain. Moreover, towns or even cities will also show regional differences among themselves. Thus the area sampling technique, although having certain advantages, shares some of the basic weaknesses of the more common stratification procedure.

Some of the sampling perils of polling are best illustrated by notable past failures. A 1936 presidential poll by a respected national magazine, the *Literary Digest*, projected results so far from the actual election returns that largely as a consequence publication of the magazine ceased shortly after the election. In this case, the main factor contributing to the exceptionally large margin of error was the fact that the survey had been done by telephone, and therefore tended to sample much too heavily from the more affluent segments of socity. Because these segments were predominantly Republican in political affiliation, the poll results substantially exaggerated the Republican vote. But telephones, which were at that time somewhat more of a luxury than they are at the present time, were not necessary to vote; and the outpouring of votes from less affluent people, largely Democratic in sympathy, defeated not only the Republican candidate but also the unfortunate magazine.

Pollsters have learned this kind of lesson well, and such a catastrophic miscalculation is unlikely to recur. There remains a substantial margin of error, even in the best of the polling procedures. Hence whenever an election is close, as several recent presidential elections have been, the sampling error may well exceed the actual difference between the candidates.

Posing the Questions. The other serious question about public opinion polling concerns the manner in which the questions are posed. On delicate social issues, when people's attitudes are ambivalent, the precise wording of the questions can be crucial. Leading questions are all too often asked by certain political officeholders in their sampling of consituents' opinions.

An early illustration of the potency of the manner of posing the question can be cited from a 1945 postwar survey concerning whether the United States should join some form of world organization. Two forms were used in separate samplings of the same population. When the subjects were asked simply if the "United States should join a world organization with police power to maintain world peace" 81 per cent responded affirmatively. When the negative option was conspicuously included, however, by the phrase "or would you like to see us stay out," only 64 per cent of the sample responded affirmatively. It is easy to see how much greater differences can be readily obtained by even grosser variations in wording and less subtle suggestions one way or the other.

Depth of Conviction. An even more troublesome, perhaps because less often recognized, source of variation in poll results concerns the *depth* of conviction expressed by the respondent. This important feature of one's opinions is rarely even considered, much less assessed, by pollsters. But polls that ignore it do so at their own risk. Related questions concern the honesty and even the insight of the respondents into their own opinions, but these are problems no poll or other survey procedure can resolve; they raise the touchy question of the correlation between verbalizations (say, intentions) and overt nonverbal behaviors.

The most clearly justifiable use of public opinion polling is in research projects of various sorts, including applied research efforts such as by political groups that seek relatively factual and objective information by which to steer their campaigns. In 1960, for example, the Democratic party attempted to assess the effects of various issues on voting behavior by a sophisticated computer simulation technique. Over 130,000 opinion poll interviews were used to generate a hypothetical cross section of the voting public. Issues were fed into the computer and the likely response of various ethnic, regional, religious, socioeconomic, and sex groupings (480 combinations in all) were simulated. However, the Democratic Party did not use the simulation technique in 1964, and its use by either party in later elections is unknown.

Informational polls in which public opinion is assessed on various public issues of current concern provide another example of the utility of opinion polling. But always the approximate and limited nature of any straw vote needs to be kept in mind and the results interpreted with due caution. In no case should society allow the use of polls to replace responsible decision making by its citizens.

Notes

Statistics

Although there are of course a good number of texts available on statistics for the behavioral sciences there is a scarcity of books that make this relatively complex topic reasonably understandable to more advanced students, let alone beginners. For a general treatment of statistics a good introductory source is Freund (1973). An especially lucid treatment of nonparametric statistics (e.g., chi-square test) can be found in Siegel (1956).

Biology: Darwin and Mendel

Charles Darwin's epochal *Origin of Species* (1859) is more readily available as a second edition (1909). Neither Darwin nor his geologist friend, Wallace, was the first to suggest the general idea of evolution. The two opposed theoretical accounts of present-day animal and plant life—special creation and gradual (evolutionary) change—had been present from at least the Greek period on, but generally the special-creation view had predominated. This view was favored within the scientific establishment as well as by theologians in the Western world (for its concurrence with the account provided in the Bible). A number of biologists in the eighteenth and early nineteenth century had suggested some kind of evolutionary theory, including Erasmus Darwin, Charles's grandfather, but the idea had little scientific support.

Darwin's great achievement consisted both in the enormous amount of data that he had amassed in support of the basic idea and the way in which he was able to coordinate these data. This more than his priority in time over Wallace is responsible for the fact that his name rather than Wallace's is associated with the doctrine, or that they are not at least jointly credited. A book of direct relevance for psychology is Darwin's *Expression of the Emotions in Man and Animals* (1872); Ekman (1973) has edited a book reviewing a century of research on facial expression stimulated by Darwin's pioneer work (cf. also Chapter 15, p. 489 ff., for a fuller discussion of this problem). Other useful volumes on the general problem of evolution and behavior have been published by Roe and Simpson (1958), Aronson et al. (1970), and Goodson (1973). Wickler's *Mimicry* (1968) in paperback is an excellent source for some remarkable evolutionary adaptations.

In the Soviet Union, biology was literally torn apart during the Stalinist era by strong official governmental support for the geneticist Lysenko, who was attempting to apply Lamarckian principles in the propagation of plants. Severe retaliatory action was taken against the geneticists who supported the more orthodox Mendelian principles. At present, this situation no longer holds, and Mendelian principles of genetics are being gradually accepted by Russian scientists.

An interesting contemporary attempt to find support for Lamarckism is Koestler's *The Midwife Toad* (1972), but this effort has been severely criticized as technically untenable (Gould, 1972).

The fascinating story of twentieth-century genetics is interestingly told in two recent historical treatments, *The Gene: A Critical History* by Carlson (1966) and *Molecular Genetics,* dealing with the more recent period of rapid progress, by Stent (1971). The three Europeans who independently discovered and appreciated the significance of Mendel's research around 1900 were Correns, Tschermak, and deVries.

Learning

Choice of subject has come to be recognized as a more important step than was formerly assumed by many researchers, because of the various restrictions on learning that have recently been emphasized (described in Chapter 11). Nevertheless, many researchers continue to prefer to use animal subjects, with their many advantages over human subjects. Animal subjects may turn out to be maximally useful in research relating to emotional learning; they seem to be susceptible to fundamental emotional conditioning without the overlay of higher intellectual functions that complicate matters in humans. This would be an ironic turn of affairs because the psychologists most closely concerned with this kind of problem —the clinical and personality specialists—tend to be most adamantly opposed to the use of animals as subjects.

A prominent aspect of the operant-conditioning procedure has been its utilization of *schedules of reinforcement.* Two major types of schedule have been developed, the *ratio* and the *interval,* to supplement continuous reinforcement (*crf*), in which every instrumental response is reinforced (rewarded). The ratio schedule reinforces the first response made after some set number of responses; that number can be fixed, producing a *fixed-ratio* schedule, or vary from one occasion to the next, producing a *variable-ratio* schedule. In the interval schedule, the first response occurring after a set period of time is reinforced; *variable-interval* and *fixed-interval* schedules are the counterparts of the similarly named ratio schedules.

Schedules of reinforcement have been most often used in training organisms in the *free-operant* situation. In this situation the subject is free to respond repeatedly, as in the typical Skinner box. This procedure contrasts with the maze or even the runway, in which *discrete trials* are used because the subject is returned to a starting point after each response.

One of the more effective techniques developed within the operant-conditioning framework has been that of *shaping*. This term refers to the selective use of reinforcement to mold a response—"shape" it—by small changes over successive occasions until the organism is responding more or less as the experimenter wishes. A common example of shaping is the demonstration of complex manipulation of gadgets by common farm animals (e.g., chickens, rabbits) in shows at county or state fairs (cf. Breland and Breland, 1966, for a discussion of this application).

Motivation

The study demonstrating that an unelectrified grid is as effective as a shocked grid in measuring motivational strength in rats was performed by Margolin and Bunch (1940). The tension-system research and rationale is described in Lewin's 1940 paper. The doctoral dissertations by Zeigarnik and Ovsiankina were published in German. Lewin's tension-system theory and the experiments performed to test it, including Zeigarnik's, are also described in Marx and Hillix (1973).

The Manifest Anxiety Scale (MAS) was devised by Taylor (1953).

A projective test need not depend upon visual stimuli. Skinner (1957) has invented a device called a verbal summator in which the ambiguous stimuli are auditory. The subject is presented with a segment of unstructured human speech and asked to record what was said. The verbal summator, according to Skinner,

consists of a phonograph or tape recorder which repeats a vague pattern of speech sounds at low intensity or against a noisy background. . . . The material sounds like fragments of natural speech heard through a wall. The responses tend to be unedited . . . because the subject remains unaware of the controlling sources and is usually convinced that he is merely repeating what he hears, although possibly with some inaccuracy [Skinner, 1957, p. 260].

Personality Assessment

An evaluation of the interview technique has been made by Matarazzo (1965). The pioneer work on the Q-sort technique was by Stephenson (1953). Butcher's 1972 book surveys the changing perspectives in objective personality assessment. It should be noted that behavior sampling is not always expensive, time-consuming, and complicated. For example, Kubancy (1973) has devised a behavior sampling code that can be used by elementary school teachers in a relatively simple and inexpensive manner.

The early personality inventory developed for military purposes was the personal Data Sheet of Woodworth developed in 1919. A comparison of delinquent and nondelinquent boys using the MMPI was made by Hathaway and Monachesi (1963). The OSS tests are described by Murray (1948). Feshbach (1970) describes the use of behavior samples in studying children's aggressive behavior. Rorschach (1942) provides the initial rationale for the inkblot projective test known by his name; there is some evidence in support of the proposition that his ten cards make possible accurate assessment of such personality attributes as ego strength by a skilled interpreter (e.g., Zubin, Eron, and Schumer, 1965). The initial development of the other major projective test, the TAT, utilizing ambiguous pictures as stimuli for stories, is described by its developer, Murray (1943).

Intelligence Testing

The longitudinal study on gifted children in California was reported by Terman (e.g., 1937). A more general treatment of the gifted child is available in Trapp and Himelstein (1962), which also treats the retarded child. The neglected role of motivation in the performance of the retarded (in contrast to the more common assumption of neurological defect) has been emphasized by Zigler (1969).

The early Iowa studies on constancy of the IQ are reviewed by Stott and Ball (1965). Skeels and Dye (1939) reported the initial improvement in IQ for the retarded children transferred from the orphanage to foster homes. The Sontag and Kagan report (1967) contains the observations made in the thirty-year longitudinal study mentioned. Hunt (1961) stresses the crucial and continuing role that environmental factors play in determining intelligence. See also the notes in Chapter 9 for further sources on this problem.

Public Opinion Polling

The research by the Democratic party was reported by Pool, Abelson, and Popkin (1964). An interesting and potentially significant recent development has been the attempt to relate physiological measures, automatically recorded as body chemistry changes by extremely sensitive new devices, to overt answers to typical polling questions. Verbal queries designed to reveal deeper sentiments have been found often to be either incomplete (subject is not able to verbalize his feelings) or inaccurate (rationalizations typically intrude, or people tell the questioner what they think they should). Collaboration of political scientists and physiologists in this new "biopolitics" program was instituted in the early 1970's at the Stony Brook campus of the State University of New York.

Applied Problems

B

All of the topics covered in this section of the supplements deal with the application of psychology to problems arising from human interaction.

This early-nineteenth-century drawing shows an example of a problem in social interaction. The gentleman on the receiving end of the fist is the innocent victim of an error in perception. The outraged owner of the small dog has reached a wrong decision about who owns the larger dog. The resulting aggressive behavioral response is based on faulty perception of the circumstances.

his final supplement contains a great variety of topics, each of which relates in some way to an adjustment required of the human organism. The supplement starts with a concise account of the intriguing concept of social traps, defined as those social situations into which one is gradually induced to enter by the prospects of quick and perhaps easy rewards, only to find later that the consequences are more deleterious than anticipated and that the trap cannot be easily escaped.

Section 2 describes the major forms of human behavior disorder, neuroses and psychoses. It is followed by a much briefer description of the related phenomenon of psychosomatic illness, in section 3.

Psychological responses to the societal problems of crime and aggression are then recounted in sections 4 and 5, respectively. A somewhat different kind of interpersonal adjustment—that of human love—is next treated, in section 6.

The last section, 7, gives further consideration to the roles that the psychologist can play as he responds to his social obligations; it ends with a consideration of some aspects of vocational choice within psychology as an example of the decisions that are faced by the student in training.

1. Social Traps

The new term *social traps* derives from the analogy that certain social situations have with fish traps. In a fish trap the unlucky organism is enticed into an apparently innocuous area by bait that promises a quick and easy meal, but once in the organism is unable to find the way out. Similarly, in many social situations, the human organism is lured into initiating behavior patterns that offer short-term rewards but that subsequently may prove to be distinctly unrewarding and perhaps even lethal, yet difficult to avoid.

Three types of social traps have been described. The first of these, personal or one-person traps, has minimal social relevance but fits the basic paradigm of early rewards and subsequent penalties. The other two types are true social processes. In the so-called missing hero variety of group trap, social misfortune develops because no single individual offers to put himself out or to take some risk. In the other type of group trap, social difficulties develop when individuals pursue their own individual ways in search of short-term benefits.

PERSONAL TRAPS

Most personal traps involve the reversal of reinforcement conditions. In other words, the short-term positive rewards gradually diminish and ultimately become long-term disadvantages. In smoking cigarettes, for example, the early rewards are social (approval of peers, feeling of identification with peers or elders, and the like) as well as intrinsically biochemical. After smoking becomes an entrenched habit, however, its long-term risks (for example, of lung cancer or other health hazards) and other disadvantages (for example, continuing expense, pollution of breathing space of others, and the like) loom increasingly larger. A similar situation occurs in many cases of drug usage, especially when addiction develops; the initial kicks and social reinforcements give way to growing regret at the insatiable demand for regular intake of increasing dosages of the drug. A basically similar picture can be painted for many other more commonplace personal habits, such as nail biting, in which initially quite innocuous behaviors develop into nuisances and may take on serious self-punishing consequences.

Although there are minor differences in the pattern of development of these various personal traps, they all seem to have one key feature: the individual is either ignorant of the ultimate negatively reinforcing consequences, like the typical fish that swims innocently into the trap, or he refuses to take them seriously enough to avoid acceptance of the short-term advantages that each offers. The latter situation is exemplified by the common feeling that "it can't happen to me" as well as by the explicit acceptance of the risks.

GROUP TRAPS: MISSING HERO

The missing hero type of social trap is best illustrated by a notorious incident, the Kitty Genovese rape-murder in New York City. A total of thirty-eight people from nearby apartments watched at one time or another during the prolonged struggle, yet not one even telephoned police. This startling incident stimulated social-psychological research in which it was found that the presence of other people inhibits individual initiative in aiding a person in distress. In one experiment, for example, undergraduate male students observed a woman fall and cry out in pain. Pairs of subjects were less likely to offer aid than single subjects, and this was especially true when the pairs were strangers.

Although public apathy and the desire not to become "involved" are most often cited as responsible for the puzzling failure of so many individuals to aid others in distress, social-psychological analysis suggests that situational variables specific to each particular incident may be more profitably examined. In terms of general factors, the tendency for each individual to look to others to take action is apparently very strong in relatively ambiguous situations in which the various roles of the active contestants are not clear; this characteristic may be responsible for much of the failure of individuals to break out of this kind of social trap and become a hero, at least of sorts.

GROUP TRAPS: COLLECTIVE HARM

The collective harm type of social trap is by far the most common and probably the most socially dangerous. It develops when a number of individuals continue to pursue their own individual aims but in so doing ultimately destroy both their own values and the gains of society. This kind of trap is especially difficult to avoid because it is insidious. It does not depend upon unethical behavior of any single individual, nor can it be resolved by the emergence of one hero or even a few heroes.

The initial illustration used to describe this kind of social trap is that of the commons, a public grazing ground characteristic of the New England village. Each individual is permitted to graze his animals freely in the commons. As long as each individual restricts the number of cattle and there are not too many individuals sharing the commons, it continues to provide a valuable benefit to all; however, as the individuals prosper and increase the number of cattle run in the commons, it eventually is overgrazed, the grass dies off, and it no longer is of value to anyone. The social trap develops because each individual pursues his own profitable way without regard for the ultimate social loss.

Laboratory Games

Psychologists have been active in designing laboratory-type games that simulate the conditions of the collective-harm variety of social trap and permit an experimental and theoretical analysis of the underlying mechanisms. Two of these games will be described as illustrative of the research that has been and can be done on this important social problem.

THE PRISONER'S DILEMMA. The prisoner's dilemma is probably the most actively researched game of its kind. The basic situation is that two prisoners have been captured by the police while committing some minor crime but are suspected of having committed more serious offenses about which they are being questioned. They are questioned and held separately. Each is given the following set of contingencies by the police (experimenter). If both confess to the more serious crime (each in a sense defecting on the other), they will both receive the standard sentence; if neither confesses (cooperation condition), they will be penalized only for the misdemeanor and will get off easily; and if one confesses and the other does not the confessor receives a reward and is released whereas the other is given a sentence twice as severe as the standard.

In this situation it is arranged that the consequences (the so-called payoff matrix) favor defecting. Suppose that a subject defects. If the other subject also defects, both receive only the standard penalty. However, if the other subject pleads innocence, the defecting subject is actually rewarded as well as set free.

The results of many experiments on the prisoner's dilemma, in which successive trials are given the same pair of subjects, is that most often subjects get locked into either continuous defecting or continuous cooperation over a series of trials. The outcome of the first few trials seems to decide which pattern is adopted. Subjects do not continue to cooperate when their partners in crime are defecting and profiting thereby; unless cooperation is quickly initiated and proves mutually profitable, it is thus not likely to develop or persist.

The analogy between these results and international relations is reasonably clear. The United States and Canada, for example, have locked-in cooperation arrangements, as reflected in their long and unfortified border, which has worked well for many years. The United States and the Soviet Union, on the other hand, have been locked into a mutually hostile and suspicious relationship, as represented by arms escalation, for over a quarter of a century, with cracks in the mutual hostility only recently having begun to appear.

THE SELL-A-DOLLAR GAME. An even more interesting version of this basic type of social trap is the recently invented Sell-a-Dollar game. It is simple enough to use as a parlor diversion. One merely offers to sell a dollar to the highest bidder, but with one unusual and essential provision—the *two* highest bidders must both pay their bids to the auctioneer. Bidding can be started at one nickel and restricted to raises of one or more nickels.

Although this may seem like a simple and foolproof activity to most participants at the outset (why should anyone pay more than its face value for a dollar?), the social trap soon becomes apparent. The first crucial stage occurs when the bidding passes 50 cents. Although at that point the auctioneer is guaranteed a profit, and the bidders may desire to block such an unreasonable outcome, at the same time they do not want to lose their 50 or more cents, so they tend to keep bidding, and thus guarantee for the auctioneer an even greater profit. The second crucial point is reached when the bidding passes $1. From then on both bidders will lose money, but one will lose $1 more than the other. Thus the motivation to cut one's loss keeps some people bidding themselves even deeper into the hole until finally (about the $4 point in one instance in which the game was experimentally attempted) the logically unreasonable bidding stops.

BREAKING OUT OF TRAPS

One of the advantages of adopting the reinforcement-type analysis of social traps is that such solutions to social problems are more readily envisioned than when causal allusions are made to genetic factors built in by evolution or to social or moralistic philosophies of one kind or another. Trying to solve social problems by appealing to good will, community spirit, or even moral scruples does not seem to work very well. On the other hand, offering people increased benefits or bringing vividly to their attention the long-range punishing consequences of behavior have been found to be effective means of changing that behavior and either preventing the development of the trap or breaking through it once it is started.

Take, for instance, the Sell-a-Dollar game described in the previous section. Suppose that when the bidding is just getting started, one bidder takes another aside and arranges a split of the profit. Such side arrangements, if they do not involve too many people and can be arranged in sufficient time, are excellent ways of preventing the sheeplike bidding that can only intensify competition and ensnare all contestants into the social trap where everybody is a loser. Such side arrangements (e.g., the ban on atmospheric testing of nuclear weapons, negotiated by the United States and the Soviet Union before the "bidding" got completely out of hand) have been cited as offering the best way of breaking out of dangerous social traps in the field of international relations.

More generally, there are various rearrangements of the reinforcement contingencies that can be made well in advance of the crucial steps in redesigning social situations. Most of our current social problems seem to have grown, like the storybook "Topsy," without any malicious intent on the part of the participants. No one, for example, planned the pollution of our environment that so suddenly became apparent to the entire nation. And everybody, certainly, is for a less polluted environment. It is only when concrete changes in the reinforcement contingencies are effectively made that such good intentions are turned into socially beneficial actions. Thus industries that pour out tons of smoky pollutants from their smokestacks will stop doing so when financial penalties are made sufficiently stiff, and children will spend time in collecting errant tin cans and old newspapers when appropriate positive rewards are offered.

Reinforcing alternative behaviors (e.g., pipe smoking as an alternative to the more dangerous cigarette smoking) is an especially effective procedure. Bringing ultimate consequences into the immediate situation (as by making small monetary payments to disadvantaged youths in job training) is another essential step. Finally, the provision of appropriate supervisory controls can help to pick up much of the social slack that otherwise permits unfettered individual actions, as in the over-grazing of the commons, to produce social harm. Even the strongest proponents of the *laissez-faire* philosophy in government have been forced to accept certain governing agencies as essential to avoid economic and social chaos in our extremely complex world with its many interacting systems of reward and punishment.

2. Behavior Disorders: Neuroses and Psychoses

Here capsule descriptions of the major forms of neuroses and psychoses are provided, along with some discussion of the causal factors (etiology) and treatments associated with the various diagnostic categories. Table B-1 presents a summary of the major forms of neurosis and psychosis that are discussed.

THE NEUROSES

Anxiety Reaction

The anxiety reaction is in one way the prototype of all neurotic reactions: it demonstrates most clearly and dramatically the existence of the anxiety that is assumed to underlie neurosis. This condition is marked by attacks of acute anxiety. They are assumed to be a pure expression of an underlying anxiety, unmarked by substitute symptoms such as characterize the other forms of neurosis.

Attacks of acute anxiety are frightening and severely debilitating experiences. They consist of increasing uneasiness, of a diffuse sort, accompanied by severe and disturbing physiological reactions (e.g., trembling, perspiring, copious sweating, irregularities in breathing, and pounding of the heart). Sedation alleviates the intensity of the reaction but obviously does nothing to relieve the precipitating conditions.

Such attacks tend to be recurrent. Chronic anxiety at a much lower level of intensity fills the interval between attacks. The catch-all term *nervous breakdown* at one time was likely to be applied particularly to anxiety reactions as well as less

Disorder	Major Symptoms
Neurosis	
Anxiety reaction	Acute anxiety including physiological reactions (e.g., trembling)
Conversion hysteria	Paralysis; loss of sensory function
Multiple personality	More than one personality organization
Obsessive–compulsive reactions	Exaggerated fear (phobia) or motor behaviors (e.g., washing hands)
Psychopathic personality	Chronic antisocial behavior, with lack of moral scruples
Behavior Problems Related to Neurosis	
Alcoholism	Progressive emotional dependence on use of alcohol
Drug addiction	Progressive emotional and/or physiological dependence on drugs
Suicidal reaction	Threatening to take and/or taking one's life
Organic Psychoses	
Senile psychosis	General deterioration of thought and behavior, especially recent memory
Alcoholism	Delerium tremors (uncontrollable convulsions with hallucinations), gradual deterioration of thought and behavior (resulting from brain damage) to death if unchecked
Paresis	Progressive deterioration of sensory and motor function (resulting from earlier untreated syphilitic infection) to vegetative condition and death
Functional Psychoses	
Schizophrenia	Withdrawal from reality; blunting of affect; marked disturbance in thought and language; delusions, hallucinations, stereotyped motor behavior
Manic–depressive (affective) reactions	Marked fluctuations in mood, ranging from severe depression to euphoria, with appropriate accompanying behaviors
Paranoia	Delusions, often logically and systematically arranged in intricate detail, but dependent on premises not accepted by other people; delusions of persecution and grandeur most common

often to other neurotic reactions. "Battle fatigue," a condition brought about by overwhelming military stresses, is another typical illustration. A "rest cure" was formerly frequently prescribed for anxiety attacks, and may even today be suggested, especially by laymen. This removal of the patient from the emotionally disturbing situation may temporarily alleviate the condition but is not likely to do so permanently; once he returns to the old environment his anxiety is likely to return. The rest treatment is thus harmful to the extent that it leaves the underlying precipitating conditions untouched.

The anxiety reaction is the most common of all the neuroses. Moreover, it is a condition that may occur in practically anyone, under sufficiently trying circumstances, at some time or other. Extreme and overt anxiety is a quite normal response to some emergency circumstances. When it becomes chronic, however, it takes on the characteristics of neurosis and requires therapeutic attention.

Conversion Hysteria

Hysteria is important not because it is commonly found, but because it shows so clearly the underlying dynamics of neurosis. Moreover, it was the type of neurotic disorder initially investigated and treated by Breuer and Freud (Chapter 3) and it is relatively well understood.

Hysteria is often referred to as *conversion* because in its pure form it represents a conversion of a fundamental personality conflict into a physical symptom. The symptoms that occur, in the absence of any organic basis, are paralysis, usually of selected musculature; loss of sensory function, such as of vision; anesthesia, again usually of selected body parts; visceral complaints, such as choking or protracted coughing; and occasionally amnesia, or memory loss, which is again selective.

The most striking aspect of the conversion reaction is its clearly instrumental function. Thus the soldier faced with anxiety-producing prospects of going into a battle may suddenly become paralyzed in his arms or legs and so unfit for battle; or the college student facing dim prospects of a different sort as final examinations approach may become blind, with equally advantageous consequences as far as avoidance of the anxiety-arousing situation is concerned.

It is important to keep in mind that conversion reactions do not represent deliberate faking or malingering; they are genuine as far as the subject is concerned, and so their obvious instrumental value does not arouse overt anxiety. Moreover, hysterical patients are surprisingly calm and collected, especially in the light of their symptoms. The soldier whose legs have suddenly become paralyzed may be amazingly cheerful.

The major problem with conversion reaction as a form of adjustment is that the symptoms may remain long after the precipitating situation has passed. For example, the soldier who escaped from his fear of front-line destruction and from his fear of being considered by his fellows as a coward may still be paralyzed after the war is over. Because the victim of a conversion reaction is convinced of the reality of his problem, it does not disappear with the change in some supposedly unrelated circumstance. That would not be realistic. The hysteric is more than an actor: he has to play his role so well that he believes it himself!

Following Freud, the treatment for conversion hysteria is generally an attempt to open up the basic conflict situation for the patient so that it can be consciously dealt with and the symptoms thereby removed. Apart from the obvious danger of precipitating too much overt anxiety if the treatment is not carefully done, there is also the problem of new symptoms developing when the old ones are relieved but the basic conflict is not really resolved. This difficulty led to the psychoanalytic notion of *stimulus substitution.* Freud felt that merely treating the symptom is not good therapy because a hysterical patient was likely to replace one symptom with another unless the underlying difficulty was effectively handled. This issue is of relevance for contemporary, behavioristically oriented therapies in which symptoms are directly treated without regard for such "deep" complications.

Classic cases of conversion hysteria have involved sensory deficit, such as that of touch. When a patient reports such an anesthesia, it typically conforms to his own expectation of what it should be, rather than to the anatomical facts. Thus a physician frequently is able to determine that a true neural deficit does not exist, strengthening the liklihood that the determinants are psychological rather than organic.

The classic paralyses and sensory deficits that once marked cases of conversion hysteria seem to have declined markedly in frequency. This decline is generally interpreted as a result of the increasing psychiatric sophistication of our population. Hysterical patients seem to be peculiarly sensitive in their symptomatology to the norms and expectations of society. Contemporary psychiatrists and psychologists are more likely to be confronted with vague visceral complaints, just as real to the patient but considerably more difficult for the professional to identify. The treatment, the uncovering of an initial traumatic experience, remains the same.

Conversion reactions probably account for the majority of various kinds of faith healings. Sudden cures, as of blindness or paralysis, are readily explained in this way. The resulting testimonials, within or without formal religious auspices, must be evaluated with this factor in mind. It should also be noted that strictly organic conditions, such as broken arms or legs, are not subject to such radical and rapid improvement.

Multiple Personality

One version of conversion reaction that seems to have caught the fancy of the public is that of so-called dual or multiple personality. The attention that these cases have received is far greater than their actual frequency would indicate; less than one hundred cases have been reported in all. Nevertheless, multiple personality is a fascinating phenomenon and neatly illustrates how fundamental dissociative processes can operate.

One of the best known of the classic cases was that of Miss Beauchamp. Four distinctly different personalities alternately appeared. These appeared to function autonomously; they were in some respects basically contradictory (e.g., a childish and hyperactive self compared with a prudish and moralistic self).

The most renowned recent case of multiple personality has been that of a young woman who underwent psychotherapy as a consequence of debilitating headaches. Known as "Eve White," she suddenly became "Eve Black" during the course of therapy. This quite different personality had apparently been active since childhood and was aware of the "normal" personality. The case was complicated by the emergence of further personalities and was portrayed in a popular motion picture under the title "Three Faces of Eve."

Table B-2 summarizes the personality differences between Eve White and Eve Black, and Figure B-1 depicts one attempt to make a psychological analysis of this interesting personality.

Much less dramatic but more common is the simpler *fugue,* in which an individual becomes at least partially amnesic and flees his past, sometimes to take

Table B-2 Personality Differences Between Eve White and Eve Black

Eve White	Eve Black
Demure, retiring, almost "saintly"	Obviously a party girl
	Shrewd, childishly vain, egocentric
Face suggests a quiet sweetness; expression in repose predominantly one of contained sadness	Face pixielike; eyes dance with mischief
Voice softly modulated, always influenced by a specifically feminine restraint	Voice a little coarsened, with echoes or implications of mirth or teasing
An industrious and able worker, competent housekeeper and a skilled cook; not colorful or glamorous; limited in spontaneity	A devotee of pranks; her repeated irresponsibilities have cruel effects on others; more heedless and unthinking, however, than deeply malicious

Adapted from Thigpen and Cleckley, 1954, pp. 141–142.

up an entirely new life. Facts of personal identification, relating to unresolved conflicts, are typically forgotten while basic skills and habits are retained. If memory of the individual's life returns, there is likely to be amnesia for the intervening activities; but the apparently spontaneous and regular alternation of entire personalities that marks the more extreme condition of multiple personality does not occur.

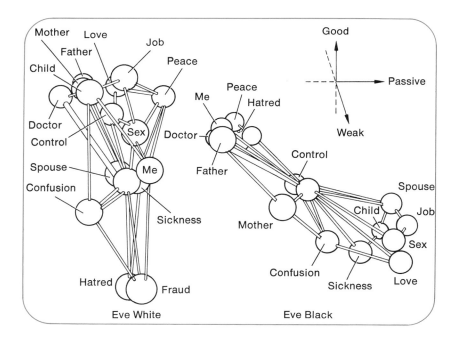

B-1 Meaning systems for Eve White and Eve Black as determined by the semantic differential (cf. Chapter 7, p. 189). The meaning systems were produced by the subject's placement of the various verbal stimuli on good-bad, strong-weak, and active-passive dimensions. It is apparent that marked differences in the ratings occurred under the two personalities. (From C. E. Osgood, and Z. Luria. A blind analysis of a case of multiple personality using the Semantic Differential. *Journal of Abnormal and Social Psychology,* 1954, **49,** 579–591.)

Obsessive-Compulsive Reactions

The obsessive-compulsive reactions are marked by persistently recurrent ideas the person seems unable to block or reject and similarly recurrent impulses toward some particular motor behavior. The ideas are usually unreasonable and recognized as such (e.g., that one is going to fail all his college courses, in spite of his having a good grade record). The motor behavior is also irrational (e.g., constant washing of one's hands, or eating or dressing in some ritualistic manner) but the person feels extremely uncomfortable unless it is performed.

The closeness of these neurotic symptoms to "normal" behavior (e.g., avoidance of stepping on each crack in a sidewalk or having some particular tune run through one's head) should point up the fact that neurotic behavior is, generally, an exaggeration of commonplace behavior. When the compulsion is itself intensified, it may turn into dangerously antisocial activity, such as pyromania (the compulsive need to set fires) or kleptomania (the compulsive need to steal).

Severe and irrational fears, known as *phobias*, are sometimes characteristic of the obsessive-compulsive patient. Practically anything can become the object of this groundless yet persistent and often overwhelming fear. The more common phobias, which in mild form are again found in many otherwise quite normal individuals, are the excessive fear of high places (acrophobia) and the fear of closed places (claustrophobia).

The fact that these particular fears have some basis in reality, that is, high places and closed places can be dangerous, helps to account for their frequent occurrence in mild form. But it is the exceptional intensity and persistence of such fears, far beyond any reasonable basis, that marks their occurrence in the neurotic person. For example, the person who has an abnormal fear of closed-in places may be unable to ride in elevators. In this respect as in so many others it is the person's own overreaction to normal conflict situations that we label neurotic when it becomes sufficiently exaggerated and abnormal. But there is no clear dividing line between normal and abnormal; extreme but still normal reactions merge gradually into mildly neurotic ones.

Character Disorder: Psychopathic Personality

Character disorders include a broad category of neurotic or near-neurotic disorder, containing a variety of diagnostic conditions. In general, individuals who are said to have a character disorder behave in a socially inappropriate manner, although often without becoming outright criminals. Moreover they do so without the usual compunction, lacking both responsibility and morality of the usual sort. In other words, their chronically inappropriate behavior is apparently due more to a lack of motivation to conform to social standards than to a lack of competence, although this may also sometimes be involved.

Because of their essentially antisocial behavior, such persons are often called *sociopaths,* as well as *psychopaths*. They are typically satisfied with themselves and ruthless in going after their objectives. Many are addicted to lying and other more subtle forms of deception. They are often adept at manipulating others to their own ends. Their ability to influence others is partly based on their own personal characteristics, as well as their lack of the usual scruples; many such individuals are

Table B-3 Characteristics of the Psychopath

Superficial charm
Intelligence
Absence of delusions and other signs of irrational thinking
Absence of anxiety and other neurotic symptoms
Unreliability; untruthfulness and insincerity
Lack of remorse, shame, or guilt
Inadequately motivated antisocial behavior (i.e., suddenly aggressive or violent, for
    little reason)
Poor judgment (self-destructively keeps making same mistakes)
Pathological egocentricity and incapacity for love; general poverty in major affective
    (emotional) reactions
Unresponsiveness in interpersonal relationships
Sex life impersonal, trivial, and poorly integrated
Lack of insight into his own behavior; failure to devise or follow a life plan

Adapted from Cleckley, 1964, p. 265.

charming and attractive, at least at first. When their essentially selfish and atypical behavior patterns become apparent, however, they experience increasing difficulty in obtaining their ends. The generally blasé attitude that they customarily exhibit may then begin to fade and overt anxiety develop. Table B-3 lists the most commonly observed characteristics of psychopathic personality.

A classic illustration of a psychopathic personality is the chronic impostor who succeeds, for a time at least, in convincing people that he is of royal blood, or a university professor, physician, or surgeon. Once uncovered, he is likely to move on—unless he has broken the law and ends up in jail. Some chronic criminals are also psychopaths, but the majority are not. Most psychopaths are less dramatic than these examples, expressing their antisocial tendencies in much milder form, and thus are not so readily detected.

The diagnosis of psychopathic personality is much easier than the treatment. As a matter of fact, the usual forms of therapy are typically ineffective. Fortunately, however, most psychopaths exhibit their peculiar behavior patterns most strongly during their youth, and as they grow older seem to settle down into less socially objectionable behavior. As with most neurotic reactions, all of us tend at one time or another to show some hint of psychopathic behavior. What distinguishes the true psychopathic personality is the chronic as well as much stronger expression of these tendencies in antisocial ways.

BEHAVIOR PROBLEMS RELATED TO NEUROSES

The problems of alcoholism, drug addiction, and suicide are listed here because they represent inappropriate means of coping with life.

Alcoholism

Although not a true neurosis in the usual sense, *alcoholism* shares some of the central features of neurosis and so may be considered here. The alcoholic is an individual who has become emotionally dependent upon frequent, excessive intake of alcoholic beverages, apparently adopting this means of coping with his conflicts. He thus becomes increasingly incapable of more realistic means of handling his problems. Ultimately, if not checked in time, he may become psychotic.

Alcoholism typically proceeds in a characteristic pattern. In the prealcoholic phase, social drinking, partly engaged in to reduce tension, changes to daily drinking, and hence solitary drinking. The step is perhaps the most crucial one. In the beginning of true alcoholism, blackouts begin and morning drinking may be engaged in as a means of coping with the hangover. Subsequent developments typically involve progressive loss of control over drinking, loss of family and job, disturbed intellectual functions, hallucinations, and ultimately psychosis.

Traditional psychotherapy, which is a relatively slow process, is not especially effective once alcoholism is well underway. The social pressures exerted by Alcoholics Anonymous seem to be the most effective therapeutic agency. The reassurance and social support from cured alcoholics made available by this mutual aid association appear to help the alcoholic learn, or relearn, more productive habits.

Alcoholism is a major health as well as social problem. It is conservatively estimated that 4 per cent of American males and 1 per cent of American females are alcoholic. Concentration on prevention of that early shift from purely social to individual and daily drinking would seem to be the most feasible way to check this scourge. Special caution seems in order for males who are concerned about their masculinity and are basically dependent, yet have inadequate control of their impulses; these are the main personality features that seem to be associated with a predisposition toward alcoholic excess.

Drug Addiction

The term *drug addiction* usually refers to involvement with heroin or some other derivative of opium, because these are the major addictive drugs. There does not seem to be a "drug personality." There are similarities to alcholism in the process by which addiction proceeds. Addicts pay an enormous psychological and social price for the momentary pleasures provided by these drugs. Physiological as well as psychological dependence on frequent "fixes" requires the user to find money to pay the exorbitant prices resulting from the illegality of these drugs. Criminal activities may be engaged in, as the addict's whole life revolves around the drug and how to obtain it with sufficient regularity to fend off the distressing withdrawal symptoms.

The enormity of this problem can be seen in this quotation:

There are more than a half million Americans who use heroin. Most are addicts who support their habit by committing crimes such as burglary, prostitution and robbery. A $40 or $50 a day heroin habit would require $150–$200 in stolen property to sustain the addict for a single day. It is estimated that half of all property crimes in New York City are committed by narcotics addicts. The cost to the nation in property losses is several billion dollars a year. The human costs are incalculable [Ognibene, 1972].

Although the ultimate course of drug addiction may be less severe than that of alcoholism, with which it is often compared, heroin addiction proceeds at a much more rapid pace than alcoholism. One is "hooked" after steady intake for just a few weeks. Moreover, the drug addict is just as resistant to treatment as the alcoholic.

Two means of treatment offer some promise. First, there is the substitution of a less addictive drug, such as methadone, which enables the patient to engage in a more nearly normal life. This procedure, however, is still controversial, in part because methadone is itself addictive. Many experts believe that complete withdrawal ("cold turkey") treatment is preferable, in spite of the fact that a very high percentage of addicts who have been "cured" this way return to the habit within a relatively short time. The second kind of treatment is the development of the Synanon movement by a group of ex-addicts, who intended to function in the manner of Alcoholics Anonymous. It remains to be seen if this group will be as effective for drug addiction as its counterpart seems to have been for alcoholism.

Suicide

Many suicides are apparently unrelated to neurosis (e.g., Japanese hari-kari, a form of cultural conformity; or the response to intractable, incurable pain). Nevertheless there is a considerable amount of overlap between the precipitating factors that produce neurosis and those that have their outcome in suicidal attempts. Among these factors are excessive shame and guilt, feelings of extreme helplessness and alienation, severe depression, and hostility.

Recent research indicates that most people provide a number of cues, such as implicit or explicit suicide threats, before they actually make an attempt on their life. Unfortunately, however, these cues are often ignored or, if noticed, not taken seriously. Attention should always be paid to such threats, especially by parents and other responsible persons, even if some persons do use such threats only as a way of manipulating others.

Another hopeful development is the recent establishment of emergency aid centers in many of the larger cities in the United States. The twenty-four-hour daily telephone monitoring provided by these centers has probably prevented many suicides and steered people in need of help to emergency medical and psychological resources.

THE ORGANIC PSYCHOSES

In a relatively small number of psychotic diagnostic categories an organic basis has been definitely implicated.

Senile Psychosis

The most important of the organic psychoses in terms of frequency is senile dementia, which results from aging and particularly from brain damage resulting from hardening of the arteries (cerebral arteriosclerosis) or hemorrhaging of the arteries in the brain (stroke). This physical impairment causes progressive deterioration in ability to think and to remember. Thus victims become increasingly unreliable in everyday functioning and require assistance in order to survive. For example, they cannot remember whether or when they took a prescribed medicine or that they just turned on the gas stove.

Almost one quarter of the first admissions to public mental hospitals fall into this category. Because there is little therapy available for this kind of patient, most senile psychotics simply while away their time in the hospital without meaningful activities and receive only perfunctory attention. Because this kind of patient tends to fill up the hospital and remain there for the remainder of his life, requiring primarily custodial care, there have been attempts to have senile psychotics placed in less expensive, more custodially oriented institutions than the mental hospital is supposed to be.

Alcoholism

Approximately 15 per cent of all first admissions to public mental hospitals are accounted for by alcoholic patients. The first distinctly abnormal stage they enter is that of *delerium tremors,* acute agitated tremors marked by fearsome hallucinatory experiences. As the disease progresses brain damage occurs, produced in part by the inadequate diet (especially lack of necessary vitamins) associated with excessive alcohol intake. Fully psychotic symptoms then begin to appear, and treatment becomes progressively hopeless until death occurs.

Organic Brain Disorder

Slightly over 5 per cent of first admissions to mental hospitals are diagnosed as having some sort of organic brain disorder, clearly a catch-all kind of classification. Although some of these cases are attributed to brain injury or severe epileptic condition, a small but homogeneous group of these is classified as *paresis,* the end product of that 5 per cent of untreated cases of syphilis in which the syphilitic agent (spirochete) attacks the central nervous system; once this occurs, as long as two or three decades after the initial infection, the patient begins to show the usual symptoms of psychosis (memory losses, judgment lapses, sensory and motor impairments) and is ultimately reduced to a purely vegetative condition before death mercifully intervenes.

THE FUNCTIONAL PSYCHOSES

Three major functional psychoses have been diagnostically defined. By far the most important of these is a broadly defined condition, schizophrenia, which has thus far thwarted the best efforts of a great variety of investigators who have attempted to discover its causes and its cures. The affective psychoses, otherwise called manic–depressive psychosis, constitute the second most important cluster of functional psychoses. Paranoia, rarely found in a pure state in hospitalized patients at least, is the third diagnostic category.

Schizophrenia

Originally called *dementia praecox,* on the mistaken assumption that it was a psychotic condition that mainly struck during youth, schizophrenia is now known to attack people at all ages and in all social and cultural settings. The term actually refers to a rather loosely related set of diagnostic categories that will probably be differentiated into finer classifications once the diverse psychotic reactions now labeled schizophrenic are better understood.

Schizophrenic reactions constitute the biggest single mental health problem. Fully one quarter of all first admissions to mental hospitals are thus classified, and approximately one half of all neuropsychiatric hospital beds are occupied by such patients. The disproportionality in these figures is accounted for by the fact that schizophrenic patients typically remain for longer periods in the hospital, and once released, are more likely to return for further treatment. They constitute about one quarter of the total number of all hospital patients at any one time in the United States.

Schizophrenic reactions are frequently marked by severe perceptual and interpretive disorder. The timeless, flat, black-and-white world of the schizophrenic contains frightening visions, in which familiar things have suddenly gone strange. The faces of his friends may suddenly become cruel. A schizophrenic girl described such an experience:

I went to my teacher and said to her, "I am afraid. . . ." She smiled gently at me. But her smile, instead of reassuring me, only increased the anxiety and confusion for I saw her teeth, white and even in the gleam of the light. Remaining all the while like themselves, soon they monopolized my entire vision as if the whole room were nothing but teeth under a remorseless light . . . [National Institute of Mental Health, 1972, p. 2].

The term *schizophrenia*, meaning literally a mental splitting, represents one of the primary features of schizophrenic behavior, the apparent split between thought and affective processes. The typical schizophrenic patient is emotionally apathetic, and is prone to display emotionality inappropriately related to his thinking, as expressed in his speech, or his situation. Associated with the blunting of emotionality is a progressive withdrawal from social contact and the patient's real environment. He seems to be living in a world of his own; when this common symptom is pronounced he is said to be *autistic* (pathologically self-centered). Delusions (intellectual distortions of reality) and hallucinations (perceptual distortions of reality) are commonly observed. Finally, extremely bizarre behavior (e.g., holding one posture for hours on end) and strange, incoherent verbal expression (e.g., frequent use of nonsense words) are found in many of the more advanced cases. In all cultures and societies such peculiar and incomprehensible behaviors have elicited fear and wonder rather than sympathy and attempted understanding.

DIAGNOSTIC CATEGORIZING. Psychiatrists have attempted to bring some order into this bewildering display of symptoms by a number of diagnostic systems. Traditionally, the *simple* schizophrenic shows progressive alienation from society and withdrawal into his own world without many of the other, bizarre behavioral symptoms; the onset of this disorder is insidious and the first clear, overt sign of undue difficulty may be the dropping out from academic or occupational activities.

The *hebephrenic* schizophrenic shows some of the more striking symptoms—heightened but inappropriate affect (e.g., loud laughter without any apparent cause), inappropriate speech (e.g., disorganized and fragmentary talk to imaginary companions), and unsystematized delusions and hallucinations (e.g., apparent visitation by God or spirits of some sort).

The *catatonic* schizophrenic is mainly characterized by extreme immobility and may sit or stand for long periods in one posture, with occasional intermittent periods of anger; that he may be perceptually and intellectually alert even during these periods of immobility and apparent complete withdrawal from the real world is suggested by his often being able to recount accurately, on later questioning or even spontaneously, exactly what was said and done by others in his presence.

The last of the orthodox diagnostic subvarieties of the disorder is the *paranoid* schizophrenic. In that condition the patient's primary symptoms are delusional. His delusions tend to be highly systematized and elaborated and are most often related to persecution (e.g., the notion that someone is after him) or grandeur (e.g., the notion that he is some exalted personage). It is not always easy to distinguish this diagnostic category from that of simple paranoia; in general, if there is any significant deterioration of personality, such as substantially reduced social interest, in addition to delusions, the patient is considered to be paranoid schizophrenic.

Few experts are really satisfied with this traditional diagnostic scheme, especially because so many patients show mixed symptomatology (and so are often simply classified as chronic-undifferentiated, a catch-all category that tells very little). Another, more dynamic way of categorizing this disorder is in terms of the onset of the symptoms. By this scheme a *reactive* schizophrenic is one whose symptoms seem to develop suddenly, and a *process* schizophrenic is one whose disorder is more insidious, perhaps extending over a period of years. The distinction is important, insofar as it can be accurately applied, because there is a substantial relationship between suddenness of onset and favorability of prognosis; that is, the quickly developing case (reactive category) appears to be most amenable to treatment and improvement. The slowly developing (process category) case is extremely resistant to treatment and less often shows spontaneous improvement (remission). Presumably this difference is related to the greater stability of thought and feeling patterns that operate over longer periods of time.

ETIOLOGY. Many now believe that schizophrenia is a mixed condition containing more than a single underlying process and that it must therefore have multiple causal (etiological) factors. Unfortunately, to date there has been little success in identifying any of such presumed causal factors. Genetic and biochemical bases have long been suspected, and are in a general way supported by data showing the much greater incidence of schizophrenia in more closely related individuals, such as identical twins as compared with fraternal twins or siblings, and the sensitivity of some of the behavioral symptoms to chemical treatment (e.g., the occasional finding of more of some chemical in the blood of schizophrenic patients than in normal patients). But there are serious problems of interpretation with all such data, and to date neither a specific genetic basis nor a specific chemical mechanism has been conclusively demonstrated to underlie the schizophrenic reactions.

Evidence for specific causal factors in the environment is little better. Nevertheless, most psychologists probably believe that a general improvement in the social environment, and a corresponding improvement in the way that individuals learn to handle stress, would result in a significant decrease in the incidence of schizophrenia, as well as of the other functional psychoses and most of the neuroses. Some suggestive support for this proposition can be found in the susceptibility of the behavioral symptoms to environmental manipulations.

In sum, the evidence thus far seems to implicate *both* heredity and environment as responsible factors in schizophrenia. The type of interaction between heredity and environment that produces schizophrenia is what researchers need to discover.

TREATMENT. In general, the prognosis for the patient labeled schizophrenic remains distressingly poor. Often a new method of treatment appears, with initially strong positive support (e.g., the drug metrazol, inducing severe shock), but invariably the effectiveness of the treatment is downgraded or even shown to be nonexistent as more thorough and better-controlled tests are applied. Some improvement in symptoms, at least, can now be effected both by chemical treatment and environmental manipulations.

The most promising of the new types of chemotherapy involves the use of the tranquilizer drugs (e.g., chlorpromazine); these chemical agents appear to reduce tensions and lower anxiety levels without significantly affecting cognitive and intellectual functions. They can thus produce quick and dramatic changes in patients' behavior on the wards and also help to shorten their stay in the hospital. They are believed to be mainly responsible for the fact that the total number of patients in mental hospitals in the United States has decreased since about 1955, although the rate of first admissions has not. But although this treatment certainly alleviates the behavioral problem, it apparently does not strike directly at the underlying determinants of the disorder.

Sensitivity of even chronic schizophrenic patients to learning and motivational factors has been demonstrated. In one interesting investigation, biochemical and learning manipulations were combined. Patients were given regular doses of insulin to reduce their blood sugar, thus inducing a potent hunger drive. The patients were offered candy incentives for performing simple tasks, which they were able to learn, and they were also able to undertake a certain amount of verbal reasoning. These subjects were then shifted to social rewards having been broken out of their chronic lethargy, and they were amenable to some improvement in social relationships.

Of greater immediate relevance, however, is the presently widespread and growing utilization of the techniques of operant conditioning (cf. Chapter 11). In the so-called token economy an entire ward of chronic schizophrenic patients may be placed in a strikingly new social setting. They are rewarded by tokens, which can be exchanged for various privileges, such as being allowed to leave the ward briefly or to see a movie, on the basis of their engaging in desired activities, such as coming promptly to meals, combing their hair, and the like. Remarkable improvements in these simple but chronically neglected behaviors have been reported in such experimental wards, and many hospitals are now beginning to take steps to make this kind of carefully controlled environment a permanent feature.

The Affective Disorders: Manic–Depressive Psychosis

In the affective psychoses, formerly more often referred to as manic–depressive psychoses to indicate the dual and cyclic character of many cases, the primary symptoms all relate to extremes of mood and emotionality. The *manic* phase shows the patient with exaggerated excitement and elation, far beyond what one might expect on the basis of any conditions in the real environment; the *depressed* phase finds him with similarly exaggerated despondency and sadness. The term *affective psychosis* has come to be preferred to the manic–depressive label because most patients alternate between one or the other of these extremes, most commonly depression, and a normal emotional state, rather than between the two extremes. Approximately 10 to 15 per cent show both phases. If there is predominant affective disturbance without significant unrelated distortions of thinking and judgment, the chances are that the psychiatric diagnosis for a newly admitted patient will be affective rather than schizophrenic. Approximately 10 per cent of first admissions to mental hospitals are accounted for by the affective diagnostic category. Because such patients typically revert to a normal condition, most of them are eventually released from the hospital.

ETIOLOGY AND TREATMENT. No agreement exists on any specific etiology for the affective psychoses, although there are some suggestions of genetic and biochemical factors being implicated, as well as behavioral circumstances (e.g., overly rigid conscience in adulthood, rejection in early childhood).

The major function of treatment is to reduce the severity of the condition and the dangers of irrevocable action, such as suicide, during the extremes of the manic and the depressed phases. During these periods contact with reality is lost and hallucinations and delusions are overtly expressed. The manic patient is a threat both to himself and others, because of his tendency toward physical acting out of his impulses; the depressed patient is mainly a risk to himself.

Drug therapy is helpful in alleviating these tempestuous swings of mood, and electroshock therapy is still being used to reduce psychotic depression (although with no clear theoretical rationale ever having been found). However, because most affective psychotics show normal remission, even in the absence of treatment, there tends to be somewhat less concern for them than for the more resistant schizophrenic patient.

Paranoia

Paranoia, or paranoid state, is relatively uncommon, mainly because if there is any evidence for personality aberrations other than the delusions themselves the diagnosis of paranoid schizophrenia is likely to be made.

The delusions of the true paranoiac are extremely systematic and often ingeniously elaborated. Once his premises are accepted, practically any event can be fitted into the delusional system (cf. Chapter 7, p. 207, for a more detailed discussion of this process). Moreover, they tend to be more effective because he is able to maintain normal social contacts. As a matter of fact, the delusions of the paranoiac are sometimes effective to a degree beyond that which might be normally anticipated, because of his intense preoccupation with them and his consequent single-minded activities. The careers of such powerful figures as the German dictator Adolf Hitler have been interpreted in this way.

Therapy is notoriously inadequate for paranoiacs. By the time this kind of patient sees a psychiatrist or psychologist his delusions are so well developed and so much a part of his personality that they defy the stoutest attempts to reshape his thinking. The milder form of delusional condition, usually called paranoid personality, is more common. Most persons with this condition remain undetected and therefore untreated. They generally live out their lives without undue disturbance, beyond the inconvenience they may cause to their relatives and associates.

3. Psychosomatic Illness

This section treats the topic of psychosomatic illness in two parts. First, we look at an influential conceptualization, the general adaptation syndrome, which is believed by many to underlie the more dramatically visible cases of psychosomatic illness. The varieties of such illness and some of the main conclusions that can be stated about them are then surveyed.

THE GENERAL ADAPTATION SYNDROME

The general adaptation syndrome is an attempt to pinpoint the course of the body's responsivity to severe and continued stress conditions. Emotions allowed to persist uncontrolled as well as all other types of stress (e.g., disease, severe wounds, chronic physical strain) are seen as the causative agents in the syndrome. Three discrete stages in the body's defense against severe stress are envisioned, as described in turn.

Alarm Reaction

In essence the first stage, the *alarm or emergency reaction*, is the pattern of autonomic reactivity described in Chapter 15 (p. 482). The alarm reaction prepares the body for immediate action. Normally, the emergency ends, with or without a successful adaptation by the subject, and the physiological changes then subside accordingly. Research with a large variety of different animals and a broad spectrum of stressors (e.g., poisons, infections, starvation, extreme temperature) has indicated that the same general pattern of physiological activity occurs in all of the cases. The similarity of the complaints that accompany many different forms of human illness is consistent with this result and the general theoretical position.

Resistance

The *stage of resistance* develops when the stress is not satisfactorily removed by the first stage, but instead persists as a direct threat to the organism. Emergency reactions of the body can be maintained for only so long. The physiological changes associated with the immediate (emotional or otherwise) reaction to the emergency disappear. In their place the organism resists the stress by developing more specialized defenses, in accordance with the nature of the stressor (the alarm or emergency reactions are undifferentiated). This process seems to be mediated by the hormonal products of the anterior pituitary (ACTH—andrenocorticotrophic hormone) and the closely related adrenal cortex (cortin). The adrenal gland actually enlarges during this period of intense secretory function; thus its increase in physical size is a reliable sign of stress. An important side effect of this differentiated reaction is that it tends to leave the organism unusually susceptible to other forms of stressors. Thus a human patient with a virus cold may be vulnerable to secondary bacterial infection, or an individual who has just satisfactorily adjusted to, say, the emotional threat posed by the loss of his job may be faced with a newly surfaced marital problem which he is poorly equipped to face.

Exhaustion

The *stage of exhaustion,* in which the organism has depleted its physiological resources and is in an extremely vulnerable condition generally follows in those cases where resistance during the second stage is not adequate and the stressor persists. As the hormonal secretions from the anterior pituitary and the adrenal cortex now begin to falter, the initial physiological reactions, which are appropriate in a temporary emergency but not a chronic situation, begin to reappear. Unless some external agent intervenes, or the stressor ceases of its own accord, death of the organism is likely to ensue.

The interaction of emotional tension with physiological depletion of the exhaustion stage is believed responsible for many of the psychosomatic disorders (e.g., ulcers, hypertension) that ravage the human organism. The development of tranquilizing drugs has helped to prevent much of this ultimate personal disaster. Tranquilizing drugs were designed to act specifically on the physiological reactivity that accompanies emotional arousal, while leaving the other physiological functions (such as the intellectual and the vegetative) essentially free to operate normally. Other sedatives are unsatisfactory for this purpose because they reduce indiscriminately all the physiological functions of an individual.

There is a price to be paid—or at least a risk to be run—in the use of tranquilizers. This risk is that, even apart from individual differences in reactivity and some side effects, the tranquilizers do nothing at all to alter the basic situation; they are strictly ameliorative agents. Thus they provide time and opportunity for positive steps to combat whatever factors were responsible for the emotional overarousal in the first place, but if too much dependence is placed on these convenient chemical agents the organism is not likely to be helped in the long run. Rather he will find himself back in the same unfortunate situation, and perhaps resorting again to the ameliorative services of the tranquilizer, thus recycling the forces that have just run their course but not really improving his basic adjustment.

PSYCHOSOMATIC DISORDERS

The psychosomatic illnesses provide the most dramatic illustrations of the power of emotionality to produce both physiological dysfunction and actual anatomical (tissue) damage. The extent to which emotional factors are substantially involved in physical symptoms is staggering; physicians themselves typically estimate that 50 to 75 per cent of their patients have primarily emotional (or psychosomatic) rather than physical disorders. Moreover, there is a wide range of psychosomatic disorder; no body system is immune from this kind of attack.

Circulatory System

Perhaps the most striking psychosomatic cases involve the circulatory system. The many idiomatic allusions to the heart—being broken-hearted, wearing one's heart on one's sleeve, the stopping or leaping of the heart in fright or joy, and the like—attest to the popular recognition of this relationship. An especially newsworthy case involved a middle-aged New York man who was severely frightened by an automobile lurching out of control toward him, until it struck a pole; within the hour he was dead from a heart attack, a victim of failure of the general adaptation syndrome. His widow sued the automobile owner for damages, on the ground that her husband's heart failure was caused by shock as a result of the driver's negligence; legal history was made when the sum of $740,000 was awarded after a court ruling that the man had been, literally, frightened to death.

Less spectacular but probably more insidiously damaging in the long run are the cases of psychosomatic hypertension ("essential hypertension"). Although the contribution of such physiological factors as cholesterol level is still in dispute, no one can really argue that emotional conditions do not play a critical and continuing role in this frequent form of circulatory ailment. The traditional psychosomatic interpretation of this common ailment (common in Western society, at least) is that it is a function of an incomplete emotional response. More specifically, the patient is supposed to show, in an anger-arousing situation, a period of rising anger, along with the physiological preparation characteristically found in attack, but no effective behavioral response made to cope with the anger. Repression of awareness of the anger reaction further aggravates the physiological dysfunction that results when vascular reactivity persists in the absence of appropriate physical activity. Hypertense patients do of course become angry on some occasions. But supposedly they are unable to express their anger sufficiently on others, such as when either authority figures or persons on whom they are dependent are involved.

Digestive System

Patients with peptic ulcer generally show a high concentration of gastric acid and pepsin in the stomach. They often give evidence of exceptional emotionality. According to medical authorities with an interest in psychosomatic disorders, when the ulcer is primarily psychosomatic in origin the patient tends to have low self-esteem and high dependency needs. Such patients also are likely to be unassertive and disinclined to show aggression. Furthermore, and more relevant to their symptoms, they have an almost continuous series of minor emergencies, produced by the contradiction between their personal feelings of low esteem and their tendency to compensate by hard work; the result is that there is a continuing tendency for gastric secretion, stimulated by the parasympathetic division of the autonomic system, which in the absence of normal food intake accumulates and presumably accounts for the ulceration. The exact manner in which the sympathetic system enters this picture is still unknown. The disorder thus is often cited as a prime example of the complex, multifactorial determination of psychosomatic illness.

Beyond this psychiatric theorizing, there is both clinical and experimental evidence for the role of emotionality in ulcer formation. Early in the last century, observations were made of a clinical patient who had a chronic fistula (opening) in his intestinal tract. The gastric mucosa and secretions could be directly observed. When this patient was fearful or angry, both increased coloration in the mucosa (lining of the intestinal tract) and increased gastric secretion were noted. More recently, essentially the same kind of result has been noted by medical researchers with subjects who also have gastric fistulas. Although there is some difference of opinion as to the precise nature of the emotions that are associated with different kinds of gastric changes, there is no question but that psychological factors are directly correlated with digestive changes.

Experimentally, ulcers have been produced in rats subjected to chronic conflict as well as monkeys in various experimental situations, such as the "executive monkey" mentioned earlier. Although again the relationship between behavioral stress and ulceration is too complex for any simple formulation, the fact of an association seems to be beyond serious question.

Another facet of digestive functioning that seems to be especially susceptible to emotional determinants is obesity. Overeating, and resulting obesity, has recently been suggested to be a consequence of the overreaction to external cues (such as the presence of food and opportunity to eat) and underreaction to the normal internal cues. Regardless of one's theoretical orientation, obesity is clearly a problem that has psychosomatic determinants as well as strictly physiological and it is currently attracting a considerable amount of experimental attention. (See also p. 426.)

Other Systems

A variety of other physiological disorders have been associated with psychosomatic origins. For example, asthmatic patients are often considered to be victims of a neurotic overdependence and their respiratory symptoms to be a function of an incomplete emotional response. Low-back pains and rheumatoid arthritis are examples of psychosomatic disorders associated with the skeletal system. Dermatitis (skin disorder) of various sorts is often similarly interpreted.

Theoretical Problems

Although the fact of an association of considerable depth and extent between emotionality and physiological dysfunction appears to be established beyond question, there are many unresolved theoretical issues related to this relationship. Perhaps the most basic theoretical problem concerns the hypothesis, early suggested by the psychoanalytic researchers of psychosomatic illness, that organic predispositions to one kind of disorder or another are responsible for *which* symptoms develop in emotionally produced illness. This hypothesis was the direct result of the common observation that the particular set of personality traits that seemed to be characteristic of any one kind of disorder (say, conflict concerning dependency needs for ulcer patients) could also be found in any number of other, "normal" persons. Why only certain individuals of those with a common personality structure seemed to develop the specific psychosomatic symptoms was thus explained. Nevertheless, the great variability ordinarily associated with these complex relationships and the fact that so many different kind of causative factors can apparently produce the same set of symptoms have made many observers understandably wary of speculative theoretical views in spite of the suggestive evidence that has been reported.

In the absence of adequate empirical support, this concept of psychosomatic specificity became progressively less appealing. However, there recently occurred a renewal of interest in the concept as the result of new research that clearly seems to demonstrate a correlation between particular psychological functions and diseases. One more specific issue that is now under consideration is whether the association is between some emotional process and disease itself, as earlier assumed, or rather between the emotional process and the organ system, more generally considered. (In other words, do persons with inadequate expression of anger tend to develop the specific symptoms of hypertension, or more generally show a tendency for circulatory disorder and perhaps also exhibit coronary symptoms?) Another related question is whether individual differences in organ susceptibility to emotional insult are responsible for the "choice of symptom" rather than predisposing personality traits. Much experimental research, with animals as well as humans, will be necessary to complement the more readily available clinical observations and speculations before definitive answers to these fundamental questions are forthcoming.

Practical Problems

Of more immediate interest is the general question of what one can do to avoid psychosomatic disorder, or emotional aggravation of physically derived diseases. Although the most effective answers to this kind of question will almost certainly come only after the appropriate theoretical issues are resolved, few people will be inclined to wait that long. In the meantime, some general suggestions can be advanced. More specific therapeutic procedures are described in Chapter 16.

First, it should be recognized that there is no magic formula to sound personal adjustment and adequate emotional control. The various suggestions for emotional control advanced earlier, in Chapter 15, represent some of the simpler, yet not always readily implemented, general admonitions. In general, it seems, personal calmness is associated with long life—and perhaps also with a personally satisfying life. The implication is that simplifying one's life can be quite helpful. How many of us actually need all of the many tasks and activities now engaged in?

All diseases, even if of strictly organic origin, have emotional concomitants, such as the patient's reactions to the fact of the disease itself, if nothing else. When disease strikes, attitudes toward the disease, and also toward attending physicians, are of prime importance. Accepting responsibility for recovery, rather than placing all the responsibility on the physician and medical treatment, is a fundamental step in the right direction. Maintaining an open avenue of communication with the physician is also of first importance, although it may not be easy in these days of limited accessibility to medical practitioners.

Finally, maintenance of appropriate motivation to improve and recover is definitely involved. Although the data are as yet admittedly skimpy and only suggestive, there does seem to be some evidence that even the incidence of cancer can be markedly influenced by emotional disturbance. In one study of 450 cancer patients, for example, almost three quarters were found to have suffered from a severe emotional trauma early in life, as compared with one tenth of the subjects in a noncancerous control group. Presumably, according to the psychosomatic interpretation, there was a renewal of early inadequate emotional responses as a result of some new crisis, such as loss of a spouse or occupational retirement, in the cancerous patients. The fact that most of the cancers developed after such a new crisis was considered evidence for the hypothesized relationship. Loss of hope and positive motivation may also be suggested as relevant factors. The problem clearly merits further careful investigation.

4. Crime

A brief treatment of any topic as complex as crime is necessarily incomplete. Rather than attempt to review the entire catalog of potential causative factors, we can summarize the main trend of results from the many investigations of psychological determinants, and then indicate some of the more promising social-psychological approaches to the problem. Although genetic conditions were at one time believed to be crucial, and from time to time are revived, solid scientific evidence in their support is lacking. The roots of crime are commonly believed to reside in poverty, and in a general sense there is much to be said for this supposition. For example, consider the following list, adapted from Rainwater (1968), of behavioral characteristics of criminals:

- High rates of school dropouts.
- Poor school accomplishment for those who do stay in.
- Difficulties in establishing stable work habits on the part of those who get jobs.
- High rates of dropping out of the labor force.
- Apathy and passive resistance in contacts with people who are "trying to help" (social workers, teachers, etc.).
- Hostility and distrust toward neighbors.
- Poor consumer skills—carelessness or ignorance in the use of money.
- High rates of mental illness.
- Marital disruptions and female-headed homes.
- Illegitimacy.
- Child abuse or indifference to children's welfare.
- Property and personal crimes.
- Drug addiction, alcoholism.
- Destructiveness and carelessness toward property, one's own and other people's.

These characteristics, which are generally disturbing to middle-class individuals who are not forced to live in such behavioral environments, are representative of the everyday life of the urban slum and ghetto. Lower-class adults have insufficient financial resources to allow them to escape living in this kind of environment, regardless of their motivation to do otherwise, and so they come to take for granted the dangers and difficulties they cannot readily escape.

In spite of their obvious general contribution, these variables do not tell the whole story. For example, few countries have done as much to abolish poverty and guarantee a minimal standard of living as Sweden, yet even there disturbing increases in crime have occurred. It seems not to be poverty or deprivation, nor the nature of the neighborhood of residence, but rather the character of the more immediate familial setting that is the most important single factor in determining whether or not delinquency will develop. Negligent parents, and especially broken homes, deprivation of affectional relationships, and especially the presence of criminal models (parents, siblings, or other relatives and associates) seem to be among the more critical determinants.

The factors listed earlier may be regarded as setting the stage for crime, rather than as directly producing it. Criminal behaviors vary widely, and when "crime" as a general phenomenon is considered, its multiple determination must be recognized. Which of the many possible determinants operate in any particular instance of criminal behavior cannot be readily decided without careful empirical study of that case.

It has been customary in certain political and social circles to depreciate the psychological determinants, such as those related to financial and other deprivations, and to extoll the virtue of the "work ethic" as a deterrent to crime. Introducing work as a motivational factor in crime reduction can yield additional understanding of the prevalence of crime. First, the common "middle-class" assumptions of morality and ethics must be divested and a more objective point of view adopted with regard to the motivational status of underprivileged children and young people in our society. What are the reasonable occupational, social, and financial expectations of many of our minority and underprivileged children? What can a young black boy, for example, anticipate in the way of occupation in a typical American city? Except for professional athletics and certain of the performing arts, success in which is possible for only a small number of the most talented and dedicated persons, access to even the ranks of skilled labor—not to mention professional and business circles—is beset by so many hurdles as to discourage all but the hardiest. Small wonder, indeed, that in a time of rapidly changing social and moral values so many people should turn to illegal pursuits, and crime should, by most indexes, reach staggering and socially unbearable proportions. The failure of responsible political and civic authorities to recognize the motivational and other psychological realities underlying this unfortunate phenomenon constitutes itself a social problem of immense proportions, and one whose solution is not readily apparent. Continuing efforts to "educate" the long-suffering public on a more sensible attitude toward the determinants of crime is a difficult task at best. Moreover, it is aggravated not only by the moralizing of shortsighted politicians, but also and more strongly by the negative emotional reactions produced in persons who are victims of criminal assaults.

CRIME AND AGGRESSION

All crimes involve some degree of aggression. Moreover, aggression and hostility are crucial factors in many forms of human misery and unhappiness in which crimes are not committed. Psychologists have therefore devoted a substantial amount of time to studying the problem of aggression, particularly with regard to the apparent increase in the level of violence in this country within recent years. The fundamental problem of aggression is treated separately next in this supplement.

CRIME AND PUNISHMENT

Simulation of Prison

One of the best ways to show people how other people live is to put them into the same environment, even if for a short time. This technique was used by a team of social psychologists who advertised for volunteers promised $15 a day to participate in an experiment on simulated prison life. Of seventy-five persons who answered the advertisement twenty-one were selected (ten for prisoner, eleven for guard roles with rotated shifts). Only those judged to be healthy, mature, emotionally stable and law abiding were selected. Most were college students attracted by the opportunity to earn money during their summer vacation. They were all warned that throughout the planned two-week session they would be subject to harassment and their privacy and civil rights violated; in short, there would be strict enforcement, just as in a typical prison situation.

The experimenters wished to reproduce in the "prisoners" the feelings regularly reported by real prisoners: frustration, powerlessness, hopelessness, and dehumanization. The only important features of prison life that were not permitted in the experiment were racism, physical brutality, indefinite period of confinement, and homosexuality.

The results were surprising even to the experimenters. The first day was relatively uneventful, but on the second day a violent rebellion erupted—the prisoners ripped off their numerical identifications and barricaded themselves inside their small cells. The guards, taunted and cursed by the prisoners even after this short period of confinement, responded with a startling show of force. They used a fire extinguisher to push the prisoners back away from the doors and broke into the cells. They then stripped the prisoners and placed the ringleaders in solitary confinement. They subsequently invented petty and inconsistent rules, which they forced the prisoners to obey, as well as requiring them to perform trivial and menial tasks (e.g., move cartons back and forth between closets) for long periods of time.

Within thirty-six hours, it was necessary to release one prisoner, who had shown fits of rage alternated with uncontrollable crying and extreme depression. Over the succeeding three days three additional prisoners were released, primarily because of extreme anxiety symptoms. A fifth prisoner was subsequently released when he developed a psychosomatic rash over his entire body shortly after his "parole" appeal was rejected by a mock parole board.

Like the prisoners, the guards developed distinctly different behavioral patterns under the pressures they experienced in the simulated prison life. Five of the guards were described as "tough but fair" whereas four were extremely hostile and cruel, persistently degrading and humiliating the prisoners. In general, the guards' most typical behavior was giving commands and the next most typical behavior was insulting the prisoners.

The objective of the experiment was to see how normal, healthy, and well-educated young men would react to the duress of prison life. The fact that even for this short period they were so radically transformed, guards as well as prisoners, is a telling testimonial to the effects we are daily wreaking on enormous numbers of our citizens who have been found guilty of a criminal offense. This experiment demonstrates the great potency of the environmental situation to break down normal behavior patterns, even in normal individuals subjected to the new conditions for a relatively short period of time. Apart from the unintended training function (prisons being generally regarded as "schools for crime"), the dehumanizing features of prison life can hardly be expected to aid in the rehabilitation process that is alleged to be a major purpose of imprisonment.

Jury Selection

Critics of our judicial system have complained that individuals from the lower classes are subject to a much more rigorous judicial system than those from the middle and upper classes. Black citizens in particular are substantially less likely to receive equitable treatment, according to this criticism. One of the ways in which bias against them is believed to operate is in the selection of juries in criminal cases.

Two social psychologists were asked to testify on this point by the defense attorney for a Black Panther who had been picked up in the vicinity of the murder of a police officer and charged with the crime. The defense attorney was interested in challenging two traditional assumptions: (1) that an unbiased jury could be obtained from the extant list of potential jurors, with wholesale exemptions of professional classes, such as ministers, teachers, lawyers, and the like, and (2) that it is possible to identify impartial jurors on the basis of their yes or no response to such questions as, "Are you prejudiced against Negroes?"

The social psychologists who testified in this case simply presented some of the results of research on attitudes that was already available. These data revealed reliably greater antiblack sentiment among whites who had the demographic characteristics of the typical potential juror (e.g., elderly, low in occupational and economic status, low in education, and active in certain religions). The poverty of the defendant and his Black Panther status were also shown to be characteristics that might be expected to elicit strong negative and prejudicial responses.

An important consequence of this testimony seemed to be that the presiding judge allowed the defense to ask potential jurors particular questions that elicited prejudicial responses (e.g., the belief that blacks are more likely to lie than whites). These questions were allowed over the objection of the prosecution to questions seeking such details and explanations of prejudices, and the claim that potential jurors should only be asked in the traditional manner if they were prejudiced.

One of the questions asked by the prosecution during cross examination on the sampling procedure involved in jury selection was:

Are we to understand from your testimony that the only way to guarantee an impartial trial for this defendant is to select a jury composed of persons who are young, who are single, who are black, who are rich, who are educated, who don't go to church, who don't believe in God, and who are opposed to the death penalty? [Rokeach and Vidmark, 1973, p. 24].

The response of the social psychologists is instructive:

it was pointed out that this would not be the conclusion that we would be willing to draw from such findings. Rather, the data suggest that a person's values and attitudes cannot help but bias him in one direction or the other and to one extent or another, and therefore, in our opinion, the best way of coming closer to the ideal of an impartial jury would be a selection procedure in which the biases of various segments of population have an equal chance of being represented, thus cancelling one another to a greater extent than is presently the case [Rokeach and Vidmark, 1973, p. 24].

This response seems to be a fair way to summarize the weakness of the status quo in this kind of situation and the need to replace what have been called fireside inductions, the transformation of common sense and culturally transmitted viewpoints into legal orthodoxy, with more scientifically based social-psychological data to be used as a base for legal actions.

Victimless Crimes

A relatively simple step that could be very helpful in the fight against crime and that requires little further research data would be to relieve the police forces of the necessity of spending so much of their time (estimated at from 30 to 50 per cent) on so-called victimless crimes (e.g., gambling, drinking, prostitution, sexual deviations such as homosexuality). If sufficient demand from the victims of real crimes such as mugging and robbery should take this direction, a surprising improvement in the efficiency of police operations might well result. But the difficulty here is that victimless crimes are really crimes against public morals. They generally involve violations of the prevalent moral code in the community and so are invested with undue amounts of motivational vigor. Perhaps the economic losses—the pinching of the "pocketbook nerve"—resulting from the continuing activities of thieves and robbers will ultimately have this consequence. In the meantime all that can be done by responsible and concerned citizens is to attempt to educate their associates and put in political office men of reasonable and enlightened views.

Aggression is one of the most natural and yet most dangerous facets of social interaction. The control of aggression is now generally recognized as constituting one of the most crucial problems with which our society must cope. Manifestations of aggression range all the way from the simplest of personal confrontations, the consequences of which may be merely mild annoyance and temporary inconvenience, to the most complex of international confrontations, the consequences of which threaten the very existence of our civilization.

5. Aggression

ORIGIN OF AGGRESSION

A great deal of attention has been accorded the problem of the origin of aggression in children, and in animal subjects, where it is feasible to employ a fuller range of experimental manipulations than can be applied to humans.

Recent research on such animals as rodents, cats, and monkeys has shown very clearly that aggression, in the form of attack by tooth or claw, is a reflexive response to strong aversive stimulation. Similar reflexive reactions can be obtained by direct stimulation of appropriate brain centers. The universality of aggressive behavior throughout animal species and its evolutionary survival role have been used as further, more theoretical, evidence for its genetic basis. Genetic controls are also suggested by the way in which breeding has markedly changed a species' aggressive predisposition, as in the case of dogs.

That aggressive reflexive responses can also be markedly modified by learning has been demonstrated. Observations on dog fighting were mentioned earlier (Chapter 9, p. 262). In general, it was found that aggressive behavior is strongly influenced by such environmental factors as isolation early in life (which tends to increase it), specific training in fighting (which also tends to increase it), and the consequences of previous fights (in which experimentally manipulated victories or defeats—produced by selection of established "winners" or "losers" for competitors—produces results in accordance with the positive or negative outcomes).

The Frustration–Aggression Hypothesis

The frustration–aggression hypothesis combines both innate determinants, as emphasized in the psychoanalytic tradition, and learning factors, as emphasized in the learning theory tradition. It was developed to apply mainly to human behavior by a Yale group of psychologists and sociologists in the late 1930's, and was initially intended to express more of an innate-determinant position. Basically, the frustration–aggression hypothesis holds that frustration (blocking of goal-directed behavior) is the prime determining factor in aggression. There is plenty of evidence in support of this proposition, but no simple relationship between frustration and aggression is to be expected. For one thing, by no means all frustration results in aggression; *frustration tolerance* develops to some degree in all children as a result of learning during the socialization process. Also, aggression can be learned and occur in the absence of frustration.

Complex interactions of aggression with age, sex, and personality variables and with child-rearing practices have been reported. The welter of interactions is so great as to defy any simple conclusion. Nevertheless, a few illustrative findings can be mentioned. There is some evidence for greater aggression with power-assertive parental practices (shouting, verbal threats as well as physical punishment) as compared to love-assertive practices (praise, reasoning, and the like). The restrictive-permissive dimension in child rearing has also been implicated; more aggression is reported to result from permissive parents, especially if they are also hostile, and less from restrictive parents, especially if they are also "warm."

The way in which the frustrated child interprets the reactions of others, such as parents and teachers, has been pointed out as a more crucial variable than the mere fact of frustration. One recent experimental study illustrates this proposition. The experiment was designed to test the hypothesis that allowing children to act out their frustration aggressively tends to reduce subsequent hostility and aggression. Third-graders were either interfered with (frustrated) or not interfered with (control) by sixth-graders who were trained as confederates of the experimenters. They were then given either social talk, aggressive play, or a "reasonable interpretation" of the behavior shown by the frustrator. The main results were that the "reasonable interpretation," surprisingly, did in fact markedly reduce both behavioral and verbal aggression directed against the frustrator. Aggressive play, however, tended to increase rather than decrease the amount of aggression shown. This result raises questions concerning the frequently assumed cathartic function of aggression, or "blowing off steam," at least as it was manipulated (verbally, in the absense of real anger) in the experiment.

Modeling

The most recent theoretical position directed toward this problem, as well as many others of like nature, is that which invokes a modeling factor within the social learning theoretical framework. Modeling has been proposed as a primary, rather than a complementary or secondary, principle. According to this position, children learn to imitate significant models in their environment. Aggression is thus the result largely of a child's observation of aggressive behavior in others, and such internal conditions as negative drive states produced from frustration do not need to be invoked.

Some of the most impressive evidence for the modeling theory comes from experimentation in which children were exposed to aggressive behavior of models. In one experiment, for example, preschool children watched a model in a discrimination task. The model was trained to exhibit a number of incidental responses, including some aggressive ones. In their own subsequent performance of the same discrimination task, 90 per cent of these children showed aggressive responding, in comparison with none of the control children, who had observed no aggression.

There seems to be little question but that modeling is an effective variable in learning of aggression as well as other behaviors, but the exact way in which such learning occurs remains to be demonstrated. It is clear, however, that allowing positive consequences (positive reinforcement, such as social acceptance) to follow aggressive behavior, however it may be produced, is an effective way of increasing it, whereas having it followed by negative consequences (such as punishment) definitely tends to suppress it.

Obviously, much research and theorizing need to be done before the dynamics of aggression and its control in children can be clearly stated. In view of the great variety of ways and social contexts in which such behavior can be developed, it is possible that no single or simple principles that can encompass all the various kinds of aggressive behavior will ever be devised.

Violence on Television

Among the many possible determinants of aggression the preoccupation with violence that marks television programs in the United States has been singled out as a major factor. The provision of so many models, practicing various forms of violence, is especially disturbing in the light of social learning theory, in which models are seen as the basis for imitative behavior.

Does violence on television programs serve to increase the level of violence in viewers, especially children, and so contribute to personal difficulties if not outright delinquency and crime? A clear-cut answer to this question is difficult to obtain, but the preponderance of the empirical evidence is that it does. In one recent study involving children under ten years of age, more aggression and more aggressive play were observed after viewing of television violence. Many studies utilizing college student subjects have suggested a similar relationship.

The fact that children's television programs typically show an even higher proportion of violence than adult programs is particularly disturbing; an analysis of prime time television programs indicated that eight of every ten plays contained some form of violence, averaging eight episodes per hour, and that children's cartoons contained six times as much violence as adult programs. Children spend an inordinate amount of time watching television. It is estimated that for a child born in the 1970's television watching will be second only to sleeping in terms of time expended up to the age of eighteen years.

There is no unanimity of opinion, however, with respect to the question of television's effects on viewers. In one field study, for example, boys exposed to aggressive content over a six-week period tended to show decreasing aggression toward their peers, whereas an opposite effect was observed in boys shown neutral television programs. This result was interpreted as evidence that observed violence serves a cathartic, or purging, role—an idea, incidentally, that can be traced as far back as Aristotle. But this exceptional result was not confirmed in a similar subsequent study performed by other investigators. Moreover, as one reviewer of the book in which it was reported has said, "We must wonder whether American society can afford to wait until common sense and humane good judgment are buttressed by unanimous consensus among social scientists about the effects of exposing our children to the corrosive effects of unending dreary hours of tawdrily commercialized brutality" (Siegel, 1973, p. 61).

PERVASIVENESS OF VIOLENCE

Television is of course not the only important source of aggression in modern society. We have already discussed the frustration–aggression theory, which holds that a natural consequence of any frustration tends to be aggression. Related notions stressing the genetic basis of aggressive behavior have also received wide circulation. But there is also much evidence for the pervasive operation of learning. Behavioral sex typing, for example, is initiated at a very early age, so that aggression is expected and accepted much more readily in boys than in girls. Aggression is more readily induced by aggressive models when both models and subjects are males.

The high level of physical punishment in some homes has also been identified as a potent source of aggression in children. It is ironic that in such instances the physical punishment of aggression fosters rather than inhibits the subsequent expression of overt aggression in children.

Beyond any specific evidence of actual violence or crime there seems to be an unnecessarily high level of violence and hostility generally present in contemporary society. It is reflected in the content of mass media other than television (e.g., magazines, newspapers). This pervasiveness of violence must play a significant role in weakening our resistance to violence and aggression generally. Moreover, the process by which we are progressively desensitized to violence is dangerously insidious. The progressive lowering of our ethical standards may thus be an even more serious by-product of the widespread existence of violence in our lives than any more direct instigation to aggression itself.

ALTERNATIVES TO AGGRESSION

Providing viable and attractive alternatives to aggression is generally agreed to be one solution to the problem of violence. But here man seems to be genetically somewhat handicapped, in that unlike many animals he does not have any built-in inhibitory mechanisms (such as the defeat postures of dogs). We must learn therefore to inhibit and control aggression. Here one useful alternative that has been suggested is empathy, or the feeling of rapport or sympathy. Exposing potential aggressors to stimuli producing empathy has been shown to reduce subsequent hostility. Perhaps other specific alternatives to aggression and hostility can be developed. With reinforcement contingencies properly arranged, we can avoid the locked-in aggressive behavior that now appears to be characteristic of so many of our interpersonal and international relationships.

Direct Alternatives

One of the most common and most obvious suggested alternatives to aggression is simply to rechannel physical activity—into competitive sports, say, as a substitute for war. Although there is probably something to that notion, its applicability is, unfortunately, extremely limited. This limitation probably arises mostly from the fact that although the young men who are so admonished traditionally do the fighting, it is older men who formulate the policies that lead to war.

PHYSICAL RELAXATION. It would be difficult to overestimate the significance of relaxation as an aid in control of emotionality and aggression. Athletic coaches have long recognized the contribution that relaxation can make to practically any aspect of physical performance—in part because such performances always have significant mental or attitudinal components. The relaxed person is far less susceptible to the minor annoyances and resentments we have been emphasizing as the building blocks of major emotional problems. Unfortunately, learning to relax the voluntary musculature is not something that anyone can undertake without special instructions, but once the know-how and the desire are present the actual procedure requires more patience than skill.

Indirect Alternatives

Apart from physical relaxation, there are a number of aids to relaxation that are frequently recommended. However, some have undesirable side effects; the use of cigarettes or alcohol or drugs for this purpose, for example, may add more problems than are solved. Moreover, many such alternatives obviously act as crutches and thus lessen the individual's intrinsic ability to cope with problems. Their short-term benefits are therefore generally believed to be more than offset by their long-term disadvantages.

Taking up hobbies or special projects is a less controversial and often more effective means many people use to reduce the tensions built up in their everyday activities. Indulgence in enjoyable activities, such as listening to music, can also have useful therapeutic effects. Finally, a small amount of humor also goes a long way toward relaxation and the avoidance as well as the reduction of unwanted emotionality. Laughter can relieve tension quickly, especially the small annoyances that so often grow into major problems.

SOCIAL CONTROLS

Any real resolution in the level of aggression at the personal or the international level must rest, ultimately, on chronically reduced levels of tension. There are numerous ways in which this desirable objective can be sought. Here we describe briefly two such ways, each taking off from adult–youth relationships but clearly having more general relevance within the context of aggression.

In general, one should encourage the operation of the various factors in emotional control that are emphasized above in his dealings with others. However, social facilitation of emotional control does involve some additional precautions. Mainly, these consist of admonitions against committing the kind of error that so many adults, especially parents and teachers, are likely to make in dealing with children and adolescents especially.

Avoiding the Attribution of Responsibility

Adolescents are especially sensitive to moral and ethical judgments, and are peculiarly prone to blame themselves for real or fancied violations of a social code. In a complex interpersonal confrontation fault is extremely difficult to pinpoint, as our earlier discussion of anger has clearly indicated (e.g., p. 471). The continuous interplay of personal interaction ensures some degree of mutual responsibility. The world may be full of "good guys" and "bad guys" as in a western movie, but only when one identifies with one side or the other.

Unfortunately, the defensiveness that is all too evident in our society seems to develop even when no overt judgment of attribution of responsibility has been made. It is therefore extremely important in dealing with subordinates especially to be scrupulously objective and avoid even the mildest hints of personal criticism and fault-finding. Standards need to be established and honored, so that violations are punished with fairness and consistency, but verbal abuse does not need to accompany such penalties. This stricture applies across all age levels and types of social interaction.

Listening

Let your child know that you are listening to him. This positive prescription is probably the most important single piece of advice that can be given parents. Finding time for children, encouraging them to express diverse opinions in an atmosphere of impersonal criticality, avoiding ridicule, sarcasm, and other forms of putting down, and accepting faults and weaknesses along with virtues and strengths —these are all more specific ways of letting a child know that you are listening to him. Once clear channels of communications are established the sound positive relationships thereby fostered can survive a formidable amount of potential conflicts. Although it is always tempting to pinpoint errors in speech or conduct— and perhaps satisfy some parental needs for emotional expression—the wise parent will overlook a great deal in order to keep the confidence of his children and thereby help them to help themselves in controlling their emotionality.

Exactly the same prescription applies equally to other types of interpersonal relationships, and again across all ages. Keeping channels of communication open—internationally, as well as interpersonally—is probably the most important step we can take toward reducing the general level of emotionality and thereby limiting aggression. Fortunately, it is also an unusually easy step to apply, and it can be a very good stepping stone to more radical means of reducing tension and preventing aggression.

With regard to its emotional (feeling) component, human love is obviously a multifaceted subjective experience that varies markedly with age and other characteristics of the subject as well as type of object and situation. Here we first dichotomize human heterosexual love into two more or less clearly separable types, the romantic myth and realistic love, with the caution that each of these two types may contain some features of the other. Because of its prominence in our society, even today as sexual mores have been and still are in an active state of flux, we pay more than the usual amount of attention to the romantic myth.

6. Human Love

THE ROMANTIC MYTH

As popularized by the motion picture industry and associated magazines of various sorts, love of the romantic myth variety has an irrational, ecstatic, and mercurial quality. It occurs, often at "first sight," between a man and a woman who are believed to be "meant for each other." The romantic myth apparently began in Europe during the Dark Ages. It rose from the courtly love patterns developed by the privileged aristocracy and was glorified in song and deed by the troubadours and the knights of that period. As initially conceived, such romantic love was deliberately kept separate from marriage, which had the dual function of sexual and economic gratification. Thus marriages were customarily arranged in advance, as by the families, so as to maximize social, economic, and political conditions; sexual satisfactions were then assumed to follow. In the meantime, the romantic love of a gentleman for a lady could be enjoyed as a pure and undefiled experience, much like seeking the Holy Grail in the Crusades, and it could be maintained apart from the dreary and tiresome problem of matrimony.

Looked at more analytically, the romantic myth can be seen as having three salient components:

FATALISM. As already suggested, there is a notion that some couples "are meant for each other." This is an important part of the peculiarly irrational quality of romantic love, as contrasted with the superficially similar irrationality of more mature heterosexual love. Interestingly, there seems to be some empirical basis for the "love at first sight" notion, although it is hard to determine how much of the support is really due to acceptance of the romantic myth itself. In any case, in one study strong first-encounter affectional interest was reported by 46 per cent of the males and 34 per cent of the females of engaged couples who were queried.

IDEALIZATION. A second component of mythical romantic love is the intense, uncritical overevaluation of the loved one. The infatuation of "puppy love" is an early version of this kind of sentiment; something of the same kind is also seen in "crushes," the intense, most often one-sided, and usually temporary emotional attachments that are often found in young people and frequently involve pairs of the same sex. Objectively, all these emotional relationships are based upon essentially irrational views of the loved one, as is evident to an outside observer.

The emotional fervor and adulation that some political or social leaders arouse in their devoted followers seems to have a basis similar to the idealization of romantic love. The similarity results mainly from the idealized image that such leaders are able to foster in their devoted followers. When the frustrated aspirations of a large group of people are focused on the real or often imagined abilities of such a leader, his feet of clay are typically overlooked.

SEXLESSNESS. Although this last component, sexlessness, was initially an integral part of the romantic-love syndrome, it has been largely if not entirely lost in our own society. During the flowering of knighthood the sexlessness of mythical romantic love from afar served to demonstrate the self-mastery of the knight and thus to maintain the truly ethereal quality of his love. Sexual gratification tends to quench passion which if unrequited holds one's romantic love true and fast to its target. The remnants at least of this general attitude can be found in the rings, pins, blazers, and so on, used to symbolize the true love of some youth in our contemporary society, corresponding to the knight's wearing the veil of his beloved into battle.

Consequences of Mythical Romantic Love

When marriages are based exclusively upon mythical romantic love their viability is likely to be extremely poor. The cardiovascular sensations associated with love are by themselves inadequate guides to lasting affectional relationships. The unrealistic expectations of so many couples, especially very young couples or those with limited educational and social backgrounds, are often based upon this romantic-love syndrome. Unless some real commonality of interests and attitudes exists, such couples are susceptible to the ravages of the very real everyday problems they face. Dirty dishes, unpaid bills, crying babies—these are among the realities of life that are not readily coped with when couples have limited resources and unrealistic attitudes. Viewing love as a panacea, as in the proposition that "love conquers all," may thus be self-defeating.

The influence of the romantic-love myth—especially the fatalistic notion that there must be "one and only one" truly matched mate—is probably more potent than its overt incidence would suggest. That is, even in those persons whose behavior and stated opinions may seem to belie acceptance of such a notion, there may often be unconscious yearnings of this type with insidious yet real behavioral significance as a result of the pervasive effect of the mass media and popular romantic themes in our society.

It is ironic that romantic love, which began as a more or less exclusive feature of the courtly life of the very affluent, should now be most prominent, and probably most devastating in its effects, among the poor and the lower middle classes of our society (witness the addiction of the working girl to the romantic magazines and movies). Also, it is probably more often among the propertied classes that marriages are arranged in advance and love sentiments expected to develop *after* marriage, perhaps a more realistic, if less romantic procedure. Of course, there are various compromises possible in which individual choice can be retained, as suggested by the features of realistic or mature heterosexual affection, to which we now turn.

MATURE LOVE

Mature or realistic heterosexual bonds in our society both contradict the assumptions of mythical romantic love and go well beyond its relatively circumscribed objectives, at least as it has been described here.

With regard to the contradictions, there is no fatalistic assumption of "one, and only one" mate; the idealization is tempered by a more realistic self-appraisal and mate appraisal; and as already indicated the sexlessness of the earlier mythical version of romantic love has been largely, if not entirely, superseded even by those otherwise addicted to the myth. Perhaps the most important of these exceptions concerns the idealization component; in mature love the mate is accepted *as is,* with weaknesses as well as strengths, faults as well as virtues, and there is a desire to maximize differences in personality between the two as sources of enrichment of the relationship rather than limitations of it.

With regard to the more extended objectives, three great clusters of functions served by the heterosexual affectional bond are evident. These focus on *social* functions (whereby the integrity of the society is maintained), *personal* functions (whereby the happiness and well-being of the individuals are served), and *biological* functions (whereby the perpetuation of the species is assured).

Social Functions

The social functions of heterosexual love mainly revolve around the primary family unit, with care and rearing of children of course a prime consideration. If the "institution" of formal marriage is forsaken, as it is being to a marked degree by the young in Western societies, then obviously some alternative method must be devised for taking care of children as they arrive. The problem is only partially alleviated by the sexual freedom permitted women by the easy effectiveness of the new oral contraceptive technique (the "pill") and by the correspondingly reduced birth rate, at least in the United States.

On a more strictly personal basis, social functions of heterosexual bonds involve the giving—and forgiving—features of mature love; tenderness toward and care of the loved one are more concrete expressions. These functions are cemented by mutuality of trust and respect, and by the willingness to make mutual commitments (sometimes aided and abetted by legal arrangements, such as "community property" laws). Commitment to and responsibility for the happiness and well-being of one's mate, and loyalty and fidelity in all phases of life, are other commonly noted criteria by which success in heterosexual affectional bonds is gauged.

Personal Functions

In general, as already suggested, there is a considerable overlap between what are here differentiated as social and personal functions; this conclusion follows from the obvious reciprocity between social and personal factors. On the one hand, the more effectively the key personal satisfactions are achieved in an interpersonal relationship, the more successfully the social functions can be served; on the other hand, it is clearly by means of social interactions that the highest personal satisfactions are achieved. Nevertheless, we can focus on the individual and his own personal needs and satisfactions, however they are managed, and describe these in their own right.

The key factor in personal happiness as a function of heterosexual alliance is apparently the companionship thus provided. This factor, along with financial and social security, seems to be most valued by many individuals. Inspiration emanating from shared experiences, and generally enhanced meaningfulness of life, are other aspects to be gained from heterosexual affectional relationships. Acceptance of the individuality of each member of the pair and serious commitment to mutual encouragement of the actualization of the potential development of each are further dividends of the maximally successful relationship.

Heterosexual satisfaction in the human is clearly a two-way street; both physical and emotional factors must be adequately involved for successful unions. It has become increasingly evident that sex education in contemporary American society is not needed for children and youths alone. Misconceptions of adults concerning intercourse are now generally regarded as sufficiently widespread to require large-scale corrective efforts of a purely informational sort. There are a very large number of incorrect sexual notions that many adults are still convinced are true (e.g., that masturbation is physically and mentally harmful, that sexual activity during menstruation is dangerous, that insufficient sexual activity in men is a cause of prostrate difficulty, that women have two physiologically distinct types of orgasm, or that penis size is an important factor in male sexual potency). Beyond misinformation, which of course contributes substantially to the emotional hang-ups so common in sexual inadequacy, there is an associated dearth of knowledge concerning purely physical techniques in intercourse. The rapid rise in recent years of sex therapy clinics is a striking demonstration that Harlow's socially isolated monkeys who were unable to develop satisfactory sexual relationships have plenty of human counterparts. Although there are many controversial aspects of this type of clinical treatment, and a very real danger of quackery developing in this socially sensitive area, there can be no doubt that many adults are in as great a need of improved physical techniques as they are of improved emotional attitudes. Certainly neither the physical nor the emotional factor is by itself sufficient for adequate sexual adjustment; both are necessary.

Biological Functions

It is typically the male who emphasizes sexual gratification, and associated aspects of physical attractiveness, as key factors in the heterosexual affectional relationship. Whether this condition will change markedly as the full fruits of increased sexual freedom and personal opportunity for women are realized cannot yet be said, but it is possible that there will be at least some change in the expressed motivations of women. In any case sexual desire for the loved one and sexual fulfilment play an obvious role in perpetuation of the species as well as constituting significant bases for enhancement of personal satisfactions.

The ease with which physical "needs" can be adjusted to situational changes is instructive. There is the report, for example, of the male anthropologist whose customary once-per-week intercourse rate was radically increased to a once-per-day rate while he was on a field trip and required to respond to the sexual demands of a native partner. He managed to adjust to the new rate without undue difficulty but was also able, although apparently with a little more difficulty, to return to his more customary weekly rate upon return to his old environment. Did his physiological need increase on the field trip? Hardly. Rather this kind of alteration can be viewed as evidence of the plasticity of the physiological substrate to the emotional variations associated with the situational changes.

The extent to which affectional factors are involved in sexual intercourse would be hard to overemphasize. The research team that has worked most intensively on an analysis and correction of physiological conditions of human intercourse and orgasm, William Masters and Virginia Johnson, quite clearly recognizes the critical involvement of emotion, over and beyond sheer physiological function. Thus in answering a query at a conference Masters is quoted as follows: "I should emphasize that I feel we have reached the investigative stage where we desperately need behavioral support. We are getting close to a physiological baseline and we are getting to the point now where I think we have a modus operandi to attack the 'what' of sexual response. It is the 'why' that needs the attacking now that some of the basic anatomic and physiologic aspects are spelled out" (1966, p. 528).

The sensitivity of the human to emotional and situational conditions in sexual performance is thus well documented. Recent experimental work with other primates has indicated the susceptibility of the physiological substrate on which sexual performance is based to emotional and situational conditions. For example, in one study of adult male rhesus monkeys reduced testosterone (male hormone) levels were found to result from physical defeat by other males; upon resumption of copulation with receptive females the testosterone levels soon returned to their earlier high levels.

As part of the "new" sexual freedom of the 1960's and 1970's in the United States and Canada at least the decision seems to have been rather clearly made by young people that heterosexual alliances are to be made with or without the benefit of formal marriage vows. When these alliances are based on affection, the trauma caused by the dissolution of such an alliance is not unlike the trauma of a divorce. A still unresolved issue in the 1970's concerns whether their married adult counterparts will engage in extramarital alliances with similar social sanction. Here again the affectional variable is seen by many as pivotal. Thus, according to many observers, as long as no permanent affectional relationships are formed, physical intimacies between adults need not have deleterious effects upon established marriages. Whether or not this radical moral position, or some similar one, will gain social approval cannot yet be said, but it is interesting that the key role of affection in matters of sexual expression and personal adjustment is so generally recognized.

Sexual Deviation

The role of emotion in "deviate" sexual expression is also of first importance. In the light of the current "gay liberation" movement, in which homosexuals of both sexes are surfacing as a group in our society for the first time and actively seeking social sanction, attention needs to be paid to this startling new social phenomenon. Granted social acceptability, which has not yet arrived, the homosexual union would seem to offer opportunity for many of the personal and social functions described above for heterosexual love relationships. To be sure, the biological function of perpetuation of the species would seem to be well beyond the capabilities of such unions.

In considering deviate forms of sexual expression it is important to recognize that the concept of deviation is primarily a statistical one. That is to say, what is deviate is simply what is not practiced on a common enough basis, with regard to sheer frequency in the population. Moral prescription is not sufficient to define deviation. Thus, keeping of mistresses, or extramarital sexual activity generally, has always been sufficiently popular in practice to avoid the stigma of deviation, even though usually morally and legally prohibited.

Cross-cultural differences, which are far greater with regard to matters of sexual expression than commonly realized in the United States, are also relevant to this discussion. Such practices as encouragement or even formalization of premarital homosexual or heterosexual behaviors or the offering of sexual intimacy with one's mate as a token of friendship are among the many examples of what to most Americans would be unusual and therefore deviate matters but are quite normal in some other cultures. The relative character of sexual deviancy must be recognized. Moreover, the richness of variety of sexual expression is apparently as great as anatomical and physiological conditions permit, and human motivation for explor-

Nonsexual Affectional Bonds

All the attention paid to the multiple problems of sexual union between adults should not make us overlook the many ways in which strictly nonsexual affectional bonds are developed among individuals of both sexes and all ages. Some of life's greatest satisfactions are to be found in the lasting friendships that we are able to establish, and one of the most potent determinants of personal inadequacy and even behavior disorder is thought to be the lack of just such relationships. Although wise parents do what they can to encourage such affectional bonds for their children, their development seems to be more a function of the total social situation in which the children are reared: neglect of this dimension of personal adjustment is possibly one of the more serious faults of our social and educational systems.

In Chapter 17 some of the general roles that social and behavioral scientists play with respect to discharging their responsibilities to society are indicated. Here, as a final problem of adjustment, we consider some of the adjustment problems faced by the psychologist with respect to his social-service interests and responsibilities. We discuss first the social responsibility of psychologists followed by some of the major patterns of social service open to behavioral scientists, and then—with special regard for the prospective graduate student—the problem of occupational decision within psychology.

7. Social-Service Roles for the Psychologist

SOCIAL RESPONSIBILITY OF BEHAVIORAL SCIENTISTS

Three Social Roles

As a result of his spectacular contribution to the war effort (in particular, the atom bomb during World War II), the theoretical physicist was thrust, much to his dismay, into the center of the political arena. No such unexpected fate is likely to be met by the behavioral scientist. By the nature of his work he has been and continues to be close to the social action. Nevertheless, we can identify three widely varying postures of involvement that the behavioral scientist can adopt with respect to the problems of society.

First, the behavioral scientist can remain relatively aloof from real problems, preferring to work within the traditional role of the *pure researcher,* whose primary motivation is simply to develop knowledge. In this position, he expresses concern for social problems as a private citizen rather than as a professional person, just like any other scientist. Such a role is probably becoming less common, although still practiced by many experimentally oriented psychologists.

Second, the psychologist can interest himself in *applied research,* with the primary objective of improving the state of directly applicable knowledge. The demand for relevance in research reflects the growing popularity of this position. Beyond the specific problems themselves, however, there is a crucial issue that is not sufficiently recognized. This is the fundamental question of *how to apply* the knowledge we already have, not to mention new knowledge as it is developed. How do we insure that vested interests (e.g., in the automobile industry) take "off the shelf" and put to work the know-how they already have but are reluctant, for one reason or another, to use? Here the psychologist occupies a central role because one key to this problem is the changing of attitudes—in responsible officials (governmental and otherwise) as well as consumers and others affected. Research on attitudes reflects this interest, but in view of the centrality of the problem a great deal more needs to be done. It is clearly foolish to continue to pile up applicable knowledge that is not going to be applied; it would be far better to concentrate research efforts more directly on improving the application process itself.

Third, the psychologist can attempt to play an active part in the determination of *policy* on social issues. If the full impact of behavioral research is to be felt, then behavioral researchers will need to have some voice in the setting of social policy. As a result they are demanding, in increasing numbers and with increasing vigor, that they be heard. This activist position is a radical departure from the traditional role of the scientist, who like the child has been expected to be seen but not heard unless requested to speak by his elders. This raises many critical questions. For example, how do we ensure that the behavioral scientist does not exceed the limits of his expertise as he strives to make his voice heard? One solution is to see that all facets of a question are represented, and interdisciplinary groups of various kinds (policy-setting as well as advisory) are becoming both popular and necessary.

PRIMARY FUNCTIONS OF THE PSYCHOLOGIST

Four focal areas cover most of the major functions served by psychologists.

Source of Ideas

One way in which the psychologist seems to be uniquely suited to assist is in the provision of new ideas about social problems. Ideally, these will be based on experimentation or theoretical work, but they need not be. The resolution of international tensions is one problem area in which a few individuals have dared to make suggestions from time to time. The fact that these seem not to have been very influential reflects more upon the state of our governmental functions than the quality of the ideas themselves. Our discussion of social traps (p. 638 ff.) indicates how fruitful suggestions can arise from psychological theory and research.

Methodology for Applying Social Programs

As already suggested, the bottleneck in many social programs is not so much the program itself, as the problem of getting it implemented. There is always a large gap between research—even applied research, let alone basic research—and its implementation in a practicable program. Traditional thinking is very difficult to break through, as social psychologists in particular know. The key role that research on attitude change can play in this respect not only justifies the high proportion of attention already paid to the problem, but actually suggests an acceleration of experimental and theoretical work.

Planning and Evaluating Social Programs

The psychologist is in a good position with respect to both of these functions because of his basic interest in human interactions and his methodological expertise (e.g., his appreciation of the need for controls). But no single discipline is able to tackle these complex problems alone. Not only are various kinds of psychologists necessary, but all such planning and evaluation will have to be interdisciplinary. The effective development of social indicators, for example, will require the joint effort of many kinds of scientists and nonscientists, each with a different point of view and background and therefore a distinct contribution to make.

Provision of Trained Manpower

Just as engineers no longer needed in the aerospace effort have been retrained to play useful roles in the solution of more pressing problems, such as those having to do with protection of the environment from pollution, so can psychologists be retrained to serve important roles in new social programs as these are developed. Fortunately, the current unemployment problem among doctorally trained psychologists has not been nearly as severe as that facing certain other professionals. For psychology, therefore, the real problem is how to arrange the training of new professionals so as to maximize the contribution of the discipline to acute social problems. The present popularity of psychology as a high school and college course provides a large reservoir of potential professionals. The strong desire of many young people to help others has in the past resulted in a disproportionately large enrollment in the clinical psychology sector of the graduate department. It should be possible to redirect many of these strongly motivated people into new social-psychological programs. These will need to be carefully planned, to ensure, for example, an adequate base in standard scientific psychology, in order to satisfy some of the questions that will be raised by stout defenders of the status quo. But although the problem of taking social action will present great difficulties, its even greater importance demands that a major effort be mounted to make psychology's contribution meaningful and effective. If such an effort is successfully implemented, we may look forward to many new ways in which scientifically trained psychologists can work with other professionals to help make life better for all of us.

With regard to some short-term but practical steps, some departments of psychology are developing formalized academic and practice-oriented programs to train psychological technicians. There is also a growing emphasis on the training of bachelor-level paraprofessionals to assume a variety of helping roles, primarily under Ph.D. supervision and in the context provided by educational institutions, community clinics, social agencies, and mental hospitals. These are some of the ways in which psychology is responding to society's growing demand for psychological services.

Some concluding comments may be helpful for those students who envision a possible career in some aspect of psychology or one of the other behavioral sciences. These comments mainly relate to the making of realistic and accurate self-appraisals before occupational goals are firmly set.

Relative Contributions of Applied and Pure Science

The following excerpt raises some general questions about the relative contributions of applied (mainly, clinical) and scientific work and points to an interesting if controversial illustration:

We can scarcely hold it against psychologists that, like other men of good will, they want to help their fellow men—either one by one in the clinic or nation by nation in, say, studies of international good will. We may agree that the world would be a better place if more men would concern themselves with personal and political problems. But we must not forget that the remedial step is necessarily a short-term measure and that it is not the only step leading to the same goal. The lively prosecution of a science of behavior, applied to the broad problem of cultural design, could have more sweeping consequences. If such a promising alternative is actually feasible, anyone who is capable of making a long-term contribution may wisely resist the effect of other consequences which, no matter how important they may be to him personally, are irrelevant to the scientific process and confine him to short-term remedial action. A classical example from another field is Albert Schweitzer. Here is a brilliant man who, for reasons we need not examine, dedicated his life to helping his fellow men—one by one. He has earned the gratitude of thousands, but we must not forget what he might have done instead. If he had worked as energetically for as many years in a laboratory of tropical medicine, he would almost certainly have made discoveries which in the long run would help—not thousands—but literally *billions* of people. . . . The young psychologist who wants above all else to help his fellow men should be made to see the tremendous potential consequences of even a small contribution to the scientific understanding of human behavior. It is possibly this understanding alone, with the improved cultural patterns which will flow from it, which will eventually alleviate the anxieties and miseries of mankind [Skinner, 1972, p. 322].

Skinner's point should not be interpreted to mean that he is arguing against the importance or, indeed, the necessity of clinical work and other forms of practice. Rather the implication is that the personal decision the young psychologist must make should lead each individual to make the optimal contributions of which he is capable. In view of the strong initial motivation of most students toward the immediate helping objective, it is especially important to point out that basic scientific work also helps, and sometimes more significantly in the long run. The greater the number of capable students who respond positively to this appeal, the better able psychology will be to provide the helping professions with a platform that is both broad and enduring.

The Pivotal Personal Question

Ultimately this issue must be decided on an individual basis. Each interested student must decide for himself whether his occupational interests lie primarily in working with *people* or in working with *ideas*. For some this is an easy choice. For many others, it is not. Furthermore, it is not even recognized by many as a difficult choice. Typically, students respond to the common motivation to help mankind by assuming that working with people is the most direct if not the only route to this achievement. For many it may be, but the decision should not be made by default, without careful consideration of the actual behaviors required in each type of work. Students frequently find that they are really more interested in the challenge of intellectual problems, including of course those related to the handling of behavioral problems, than in the actual implementation of therapeutic and similar procedures. This is a frustrating decision to come late in graduate training because of the time lost in taking unneeded course work, such as that involving technical clinical procedures, instead of more fundamental courses.

A shift from pure to applied scientific training can also be disturbing. However, it does not seem to occur as frequently, partly because so many more students start out with applied interests. Also, it can be argued that more significant positive transfer usually occurs when there is a shift from fundamental to specific training than vice versa.

In any event the need for both types of training and professional activity must be recognized, with some degree of balance necessary for optimal progress. All students should be explicitly encouraged to plan their training and their eventual professional careers with a view to a variety of alternatives, and to keep their options open as long as is reasonably possible.

Social Traps

The best single source for the research and theory on social traps is Platt's excellent 1973 paper. Hardin's 1968 article introduced and popularized the so-called tragedy of the commons, and Schelling's 1971 article on "micromotives" examined a large number of similar cases. Interpersonal traps are examined in Berne's popular 1964 book *Games People Play*. Platt (1973) credits Martin Shubik for invention of the fascinating "Sell-a-Dollar" game. The prisoner's dilemma has been studied most intensively by Rapoport (1966), and he has also pointed out the ramifications of his results to international relations (Rapoport, 1971). Experimental games are reviewed by Vinacke (1969) and by Rapoport (1973). Books by Osgood (1962) and White (1968) are somewhat more elaborate attempts by psychologists to make concrete suggestions for improving international relationships, as is the reader edited by Winnik, Moses, and Ostow (1973).

Behavior Disorders

The case of Eve White is recounted by her psychiatrists, Thigpen and Cleckley, in an article (1954) and the book *The Three Faces of Eve* (1957).

A large amount of research on neurotic reactions has utilized animal subjects. For example, Liddell (1956) applied Pavlovian classical conditioning methodology, mainly to farm animals, such as sheep and goats. Masserman (1950) developed

Notes

neurotic reactions in cats, which he proceeded to cure by a form of psychotherapy. The successful use of animal subjects in research on what many regard as uniquely human problems not only underscores the essential continuity of animal forms, behaviorally considered, but also points up the value of having such simpler forms available for research in which the experimental manipulations are necessarily noxious.

The scope of the drug addiction problem in this country is succinctly put by Ognibene (1972). Fully 90 per cent of heroin addicts who are "cured" in a hospital have returned to the habit within six months (Hunt and Odoroff, 1963). Stachink (1972) argues the case against criminal patterns for drug use; other discussions of the drug problem, with special reference to youth, are offered by Love (1971) and Wise (1971). Ball and Chambers (1970) analyze opiate addiction in a study of more than 40,000 addicts in the federal research center at Lexington, Kentucky.

Some research reported by Nichols (1963) is especially suggestive with regard to the problem of addiction. He was intrigued by the fact that physicians seem to become addicted more readily than their patients and tested the proposition that active injection of morphine is more addictive than passive. This proposition was confirmed with rat subjects; animals that worked actively to obtain the drug became addicted to it, whereas controls who received the same dosages passively did not. Morphine addiction in chimpanzees had been earlier demonstrated in a well-known study conducted by Spragg (1940).

Probably as a result of the recent increase in the frequency of depression, suicide has jumped to a relatively high standing among the major causes of death in the United States. Tenth overall, it ranks as the fifth most common cause of death in the fifteen- to twenty-four-year-old range. Fortunately, depression not only shows normal improvement, it can be effectively treated by drugs. The psychological factors in suicide and how this threat may be coped with are discussed in *The Cry for Help,* edited by Farberow and Schneidman (1961). Jackson's 1954 article, although dated with regard to statistics, still contains some useful basic information. More recent treatments are by Zusman and Davidson (1971), Lester and Lester (1971), and Choron (1972).

A famous case of childhood schizophrenia is Bettelheim's (1959) "Joey," a child who became a "machine." Interesting differences in schizophrenic symptomatology related to cultural factors are described in a report by Opler (1957); Irish schizophrenics, for example, tend to have dominating mothers, whereas Italian schizophrenics are more likely to have dominating fathers, in accordance with the respective cultures, and their symptoms can be clearly related in each instance to the underlying cultural milieu. Jackson (1962) provides a readable account of the various hypotheses concerning schizophrenia (genetic, biochemical, psychogenetic) as well as a review of the major figures in the history of our attempts to understand the disorder. An especially interesting discussion, based on personal observations, is offered by Brown (1973).

Emil Kraepelin, the nineteenth-century German psychiatrist who established the basic taxonomy that is still in use, named the disorder dementia praecox because of the apparent early deterioration, contrasted with senile dementia. Early in the twentieth century the Swiss psychiatrist Eugen Bleuler renamed the disorder schizophrenia to reflect the apparent splitting of personality into separate sets of ideas or complexes. Bleuler was also "modern" in his conception that schizophrenia is in reality a complex of different disorders that have been indiscriminately given the same name because of the fact that certain key symptoms are commonly displayed.

Schizophrenic reactions affect all ages and classes of people and are found throughout the world. A recent international study identified the most common symptoms used in diagnosis of this disorder. As reported by Carpenter, Strauss, and Bartko (1973), these were restricted affect (e.g., blank, expressionless face), poor insight, thinking aloud, poor rapport, widespread delusions, incoherent speech, providing of unreliable information, bizarre and nihilistic delusions (e.g., missing body parts reported, or even death or dissolution of the body). Negative signs, those whose appearance was found to be unlikely in the diagnosis of schizophrenia, were waking early, depressed facial expression, and elation.

Although the role of genetic factors in schizophrenia remains a lively topic, there seems now to be a general consensus that purely genetic determinants are not as important as their early main investigator, Kallman (1959), believed. In his survey of identical and fraternal twins he found that when one identical twin was diagnosed as schizophrenic (174 instances), the other was about six times as likely to be similarly diagnosed (104 instances) as was true for fraternal twins. Kallman's methodology has been criticized on many counts; more recent and less questionable treatments of the genetic factor in schizophrenia are by Rosenthal (1970) and Gottesman and Shields (1972).

The combination of a biochemical and learning approach described in the text was reported by Peters and Jenkins (1954). The explosive development of scientific interest in the biochemistry of behavior disorder over the past few years is comprehensively but technically covered by Weil-Malherbe and Szara (1971). The token economy therapy is described by Ayllon and Azrin (1968).

Psychosomatic Illness

The general adaptation syndrome is described in various works by its originator, the endocrinologist Hans Selye (e.g., 1956). Appley and Trumbull (1967) have edited a more recent book of readings on this general topic. An extremely popularized and speculative work on psychosomatic medicine is Lewis and Lewis's *Psychosomatics* (1972). Older but more technical accounts are available in Astrup (1965), MacLean (1960), and Holland and Ward (1966). These are all written from a medical or psychiatric vantage point, but more psychologically oriented and more recent treatments of psychosomatic illness are in articles by Miller (1969) and DiCara (1972). The original direct observations of gastric changes in emotionality were reported by the physician William Beaumont, in 1833. The research on ulceration from emotional stress in rats was reported by Sawrey and Weisz (1956) and Sawrey, Conger, and Turrell (1956). Schacter's 1967 essay and 1971 book focus on obesity as a psychosomatic problem. The specificity theory was initially propounded by the psychoanalyst Franz Alexander (1950), and the recent revival of interest in the concept has been stimulated by the appearance of a new book on the topic edited by Alexander, French, and Pollock (1968).

Crime

The most widely publicized recent instance of a genetic determinant in crime is the double-Y chromosome condition; a review of the evidence on this factor is available in Jarvik, Klodin, and Matsuyama (1973), who conclude that there is some factual basic implication of the factor in spite of much disagreement and a relatively small role played by this uncommon condition.

The prison simulation study was reported by Haney, Banks, and Zimbardo (1973). A methodological analysis of this situation is presented by Banuazizi and Movahedi (1975). The testimony on juror selection was reported by Rokeach and Vidmar (1973). It was Meehl (1971) who called our folk wisdom as applied to the law "fireside inductions."

Aggression

The experiment demonstrating increased aggressiveness in children after viewing aggressive compared with nonaggressive television programs was reported by Liebert and Baron (1972). Berkowitz's 1962 paper offers a comprehensive review of the problem and similar evidence from research with college students; his 1964 article also affords a broad view of the problem, including the brief historical review reaching back to Aristotle. The data on violence in television programming were reported by Gerbner (1972); a similar result was obtained by Barcus (1971). Lesser (1970) provides the estimate of time spent by children and adolescents in watching television. The Surgeon General's (1972) report on television and social behavior concludes that there is "fairly substantial experimental evidence for *short-run* causation of aggression among some children" and "much less certain evidence" for long-run manifestations. Murray (1973) and Liebert, Neale, and Davidson (1973) provide a summary of the problem and the government report. The book by Feshbach and Singer (1971) describes their field study of boys' homes in which some evidence for a cathartic effect of aggressive television content was found. Feshbach (1970) indicates the role of physical punishment in increasing aggression in children, and Feshbach's 1971 paper is a comprehensive examination of the problem of violence and aggression; it contains the suggestion of empathy as an alternative to aggression, mentioned in the text. Other books on aggression and violence are *Roots of Aggression,* edited by Berkowitz (1969), Toch's *Violent Men* (1969), Moyer's *The Physiology of Hostility* (1971), and Bandura's *Aggression: A Social Learning Analysis* (1973). The historical point of view with special regard to American violence is provided by Graham and Gurr's 1969 book. Johnson's *Aggression in Man and Animals* (1972) covers aggression over a wide spectrum of animal forms in an even-tempered and comprehensive manner. Lorenz's *On Aggression* (1966), a more controversial appraisal from an ethological point of view, is the source of the comparison of man and animals with regard to the human's lack of any built-in behavior mechanisms by means of which aggression can be inhibited. Finally, the 1972 volume of the *Nebraska Symposium on Motivation* is directed to the problem of aggression, with six contributions from a variety of perspectives.

Human Love

The discussion of romantic love leans heavily upon the unpublished materials made available by M. Nawas in his unpublished 1969 manuscript *Love: An Adventure into the Behavioral Scientist's No-Man's Land*. Data on "love at first sight" are from Burgess and Wallin (1953); *Sex and Behavior,* edited by Beach (1965), Money's *Sex Research: New Developments* (1965), and Lieberman's *Human Sexual Behavior* (1971) are useful collections of readings. The two much-discussed books by Masters and Johnson are *Human Sexual Response* (1966) and *Human Sexual Inadequacy* (1970); the former book reports their revolutionary research on the physiological nature of human sexuality, the latter book is concerned with their equally revolutionary therapy for sexual inadequacy. Discussions of the "new sexuality" in the United States are provided by Bell (1966), Bernard (1968), Miller and Siegel (1972), and Birenbaum (1970); the last essay is particularly interesting in that it emphasizes some of the negative aspects of the sexual revolution (even as seen by its proponents). Gebhart (1965) provided the anecdote on frequency of coitus mentioned in the text. Rose, Gordon, and Bernstein (1972) reported on testosterone levels in the male rhesus monkey as influenced by social stimuli. An interesting account of sexuality from a comparative ethological point of view is provided by the translation into English of Wickler's *The Sexual Code* (1972).

Social-Service Roles for the Psychologist

Smith (1973) has presented a balanced evaluation of psychology and the new social demands; Miller's (1969) paper, delivered as a presidential address to the American Psychological Association, was an earlier call for psychologists' attention to such pressing matters. Treatment in the text of the various roles that the social psychologist can play with regard to real-life programs follows Kelman's 1970 article.

A colleague has contributed this anonymous personal opinion concerning social action:

Sometimes, in the simplistic rush to "do something that will help," negative outcomes are caused. As I see it, the problem is that the majority of social-action oriented people seem to already "know" what is right. By and large, they don't believe in evaluative research as a source of relevant knowledge. This is a thing one has to guard against in running evaluative research on such things as treatment programs. A few years ago, I was doing research designed to test the relative effectiveness of providing different forms of post-treatment supportive intervention on the work adjustment of mental patients. The design was jeopardized when the hospital personnel decided that our supportive procedures were very good and began providing them to patients who had been assigned to the control (no subsequent contact) condition.

Among the many books that have been appearing to herald the increased sensitivity of behavioral science to real social problems are Varela's *Psychological Solutions to Social Problems* (1971) and collections of readings edited by Schmaltz (1971), Rossi and Williams (1972), and Hamsher and Sigall (1973).

With regard to the role of science generally in social affairs, a bibliography of nearly 4,000 references on "science for society" prepared by Bausum in 1973, is available from the American Association for the Advancement of Science for $1 per copy. Bower (1966) gives a useful social-psychological analysis of policy formation.

Abelson, P. H. The need for skepticism. *Science,* 1962, **138**(3537), 75.

Abelson, R. P., & Rosenberg, M. J. Symbolic psycho-logic: a model of attitudinal cognition. *Behavioral Science,* 1958, **3,** 1–13.

Adams, J. A. *Human memory.* New York: McGraw-Hill, 1967.

Adams, R. N. An inquiry into the nature of the family. In G. E. Dole and R. L. Carneiro (eds.), *Essays in the science of culture in honor of Leslie A. White.* New York: Crowell, 1960.

Adamson, R. E. Functional fixedness as related to problem solving: a repetition of three experiments. *Journal of Experimental Psychology,* 1952, **44,** 288–291.

Alexander, F. *Psychosomatic medicine: its principles and applications.* New York: Norton, 1950.

Alexander, F., French, T. M., & Pollock, G. H. (Eds.) *Psychosomatic specificity.* Vol. 1. Experimental study and results. Chicago: U. of Chicago Press, 1968.

Alland, A., Jr. *The human imperative.* New York: Columbia U.P., 1972.

Allport, G. W. *Personality.* New York: Holt, 1937.

Allport, G. W. *Personality: a psychological interpretation.* New York: Holt, 1937.

Almond, R. The therapeutic community. *Scientific American,* 1971, **224**(3), 34–42.

Altus, W. D. Birth order and its sequellae. *Science,* 1966, **151,** 44–49.

Anastasi, A. *Psychological testing.* (3rd Ed.) New York: Macmillan, 1968.

Andry, D. K., and Luttges, M. W. Facilitative habituation: strychnine dose effects on neural and behavioral habituation. *Agents and Action,* 1971, **1,** 103–117.

Angell, J. R. The province of functional psychology. *Psychological Review,* 1907, **14,** 61–91.

Appley, M. H., & Trumbull, R. (Eds.) *Psychological stress: issues in research.* New York: Appleton, 1967.

Apsler, R., & Sears, D. O. Warning, personal involvement, and attitude change. *Journal of Personality and Social Psychology,* 1968, **9,** 162–166.

Ardrey, R. *Territorial imperative: a personal inquiry into the animal origins of property and nations.* New York: Atheneum, 1966.

Ardrey, R. *Social contract: a personal inquiry into evolutionary sources of order and disorder.* New York: Atheneum, 1970.

Arndt, W. B., Jr. *Theories of personality.* New York: Macmillan, 1974.

Aronson, E. *The social animal.* San Francisco: Freeman, 1972.

Aronson, E., & Linder, D. Gain and loss of esteem as determinants of interpersonal attractiveness. *Journal of Experimental Social Psychology,* 1965, **1,** 156–171.

Aronson, E., & Carlsmith, J. M. Experimentation in social psychology. In G. Lindzey and E. Aronson (Eds.), *Handbook of social psychology.* Vol 2. (2nd Ed.) Reading, Mass.: Addison-Wesley, 1969.

Aronson, E., & Mills, J. The effect of severity of initiation on liking for a group. *Journal of Abnormal and Social Psychology,* 1959, **59,** 177–181.

Aronson, L. R., Tobach, E., Lehrman, D. S., & Rosenblatt, J. S. (Eds.) *Development and evolution of behavior.* San Francisco: Freeman, 1970.

Aronson, E., Turner, J., & Carlsmith, J. M. Communicator credibility and communication discrepancy as determinants of opinion change. *Journal of Abnormal and Social Psychology,* 1963, **67,** 31–36.

Aronson, E., Willerman, B., & Floyd, J. The effect of a pratfall on increasing interpersonal attractiveness. *Psychonomic Science,* 1966, **4,** 227–228.

Asch, S. E. Forming impressions of personality. *Journal of Abnormal and Social Psychology,* 1946, **41,** 258–90.

Asch, S. E. Effects of group pressure upon the modification and distortion of judgment. In H. Guetzkow (Ed.), *Groups, leadership, and men.* Pittsburgh: Carnegie Press, 1951.

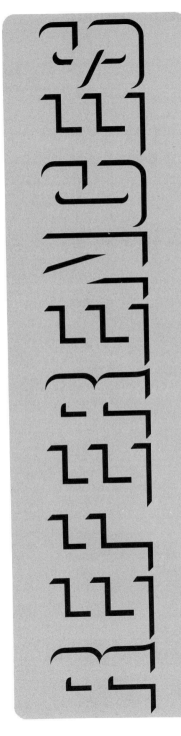

Ashley, W. R., Harper, R. S., & Runyon, D. L. The perceived size of coins in normal and hypnotically induced economic states. *American Journal of Psychology,* 1951, **64,** 564–572.

Astrup, C. *Pavlovian psychiatry—a new synthesis.* Springfield, Ill.: Bannerstone House (Thomas), 1965.

Atkinson, J. W. *An introduction to motivation.* Princeton: Van Nostrand, 1964.

Atkinson, J. W., Heyns, R. W., & Veroff, J. The effect of experimental arousal of the affiliation motive on thematic apperception. *Journal of Abnormal and Social Psychology,* 1954, **49,** 405–410.

Attneave, Fred. Multistability in perception. *Scientific American,* 1971, **225**(6), 62–71.

Ayllon, T., & Azrin, N. *The token economy: A motivational system for therapy and rehabilitation.* New York: Appleton, 1968.

Bahrick, H. P. Discriminative associative aspects of retroactive inhibition. *Quarterly Journal of Experimental Psychology,* 1970 (Nov.), **22**(4), 565–573.

Ball, J. C., & Chambers, C. D. (Eds.) *The epidemiology of opiate addiction in the United States.* Springfield, Ill.: Thomas, 1970.

Baltes, P. B., & Schaie, K. W. Aging and IQ: the myth of the twilight years. *Psychology Today,* 1974, **7,** 35–40.

Bandura, A. *Principles of behavior modification.* New York: Holt, 1969.

Bandura, A. *Aggression: a social learning analysis.* Englewood Cliffs, N.J.: Prentice-Hall, 1973.

Bandura, A., Blanchard, E. G., & Ritter, B. The relative efficacy of desensitization and modeling approaches for inducing behavioral, affective, and attitudinal changes. *Journal of Personality and Social Psychology,* 1969, **13,** 173–99.

Banuazizi, A., & Movahedi, S. Interpersonal dynamics in a simulated prison: a methodological analysis. *American Psychologist,* 1975, **30,** 152–160.

Baratz, J. C., & Shuy, R. W. (Eds.) *Teaching black children to read.* Washington, D.C.: Center for Applied Linguistics, Urban Language Series, **4,** 1969.

Barber, T. X. *Hypnosis: a scientific approach.* New York: Van Nostrand, 1969.

Barber, T., DiCara, L., Kamiya, J., Miller, N., Shapiro, D., & Stoyva, J. (Eds.) *Biofeedback and self-control 1970: an Aldine annual on the regulation of bodily processes and consciousness.* Chicago: Aldine-Atherton, 1970.

Barber, T., & Silver, M. Fact, fiction, and the experimenter bias effect. *Psychological Bulletin,* 1968, **70**(6, Pt. 2), 1–29.

Barcus, F. E. *Saturday children's television: A report of TV programming and advertising on Boston commercial television.* Boston: Action for Children's Television, 1971.

Bard, P. A diencephalic mechanism for the expression of rage with special reference to the sympathetic nervous system. *American Journal of Physiology,* 1928, **84,** 490–515.

Barnes, J. M., & Underwood, B. J. "Fate" of first-list associations in transfer-theory. *Journal of Experimental Psychology,* 1959, **58,** 97–105.

Barnlund, D. C. A comparative study of individual, majority, and group judgment. *Journal of Abnormal and Social Psychology,* 1959, **58,** 55–66.

Barron, F. Psychology of imagination. *Scientific American,* 1958, **199,** 150–156.

Barron, F., Jarvik, M. E., & Bunnell, S., Jr. The hallucinogenic drugs. *Scientific American,* 1964, **210,** 29–37.

Bartlett, F. C. *Remembering.* Cambridge: Cambridge U.P., 1932.

Baughman, E. E. *Black Americans: a psychological analysis.* New York: Academic, 1971.

Beach, F. A. Evolutionary changes in the physiological control of mating behavior of mammals. *Psychological Review,* 1947, **54,** 297–315.

Beach, F. A. (Ed.) *Sex and behavior.* New York: Wiley, 1965.

Beach, F. A. Hormonal factors controlling the differentiation, development, and display of copulatory behavior in the Ramstergig and related species. In E. Tobach, L. R. Aronson, and E. Shaw (Eds.), *The biopsychology of development.* New York: Academic, 1971.

Beers, L. *The mind that found itself.* London: Longmans, Green, 1908.

Bekesey, G. von, & Rosenblith, W. A. The mechanical properties of the ear. In S. S. Stevens (Ed.), *Handbook of experimental psychology.* New York: Wiley, 1951.

Bell, R. R. *Premarital sex in a changing society.* Englewood Cliffs, N.J.: Prentice-Hall, 1966.

Bell, R. R., & Gordon, M. (Eds.) *The social dimension of human sexuality.* Boston: Little, Brown, 1972.

Belmont, L., & Marolla, F. A. Birth order, family size and intelligence. *Science,* 1973, **182,** 1096–1101.

Benjamin, A. C. *Operationism.* Springfield, Ill.: Thomas, 1955.

Berelson, B., & Steiner, G. A. *Human behavior: an inventory of scientific findings.* New York: Harcourt, 1964.

Bergin, A. E., & Strupp, H. H. *Changing frontiers in the science of psychotherapy.* New York: Wiley, 1971.

Bergmann, G. The contribution of John B. Watson. *Psychological Review,* 1965, **63,** 265–276.

Berkowitz, L. *Aggression: a social psychological analysis.* New York: McGraw-Hill, 1962.

Berkowitz, L. *The development of motives and values in the child.* New York: Basic Books, 1964.

Berkowitz, L. (Ed.) *Roots of aggression.* New York: Atherton, 1969.

Berlyne, D. E. Recent developments in Piaget's work. *British Journal of Educational Psychology,* 1957, **27,** 1–12.

Bermant, G., & Davidson, J. M. *Biological basis of sexual behavior.* New York: Harper, 1974.

Bernard, J. L. Rapid treatment of gross obesity by operant techniques. *Psychological Reports,* 1968a, **23,** 663–666.

Bernard, J. *The sex game.* Englewood Cliffs, N.J.: Prentice-Hall, 1968b.

Bernard, L. L. *An introduction to social psychology.* New York: Holt, 1926.

Berne, E. *Games people play.* New York: Grove, 1964.

Bernstein, D. A. Modification of smoking behavior: an evaluative review. *Psychological Bulletin,* 1969, **71**(6), 418–440.

Berscheid, E., Boye, D., & Darley, J. M. Effect of forced association upon voluntary choice to associate. *Journal of Personality and Social Psychology,* 1968, **8,** 13–19.

Bettelheim, Bruno. Joey: a "mechanical boy." *Scientific American,* 1959, **200**(3), 116–127.

Bevan, W., & Steger, J. A. Free recall and abstractness of stimuli. *Science,* 1971, **172,** 597–599.

Bexton, W. H., Heron, W., & Scott, T. H. Effects of decreased variation in the sensory environment. *Canadian Journal of Psychology,* 1954, **8,** 70–76.

Biderman, A. D. Social indicators and goals. In Bauer, R. A. (Ed.), *Social indicators.* Cambridge, Mass.: M.I.T. Press, 1966.

Biederman, I. Perceiving real-world scenes. *Science,* 1972, **177,** 77–80.

Bijou, S. W., & Baer, D. M. *Child development. II. Universal state of infancy.* New York: Appleton, 1965.

Bilodeau, E. A. & Bilodeau, I. (Eds.) *Principles of skill acquisition.* New York: Academic, 1969.

Bindra, D. The problem of subjective experience: puzzlement on reading R. W. Sperry's "A modified concept of consciousness." *Psychological Review,* 1970, **77,** 581–584.

Birenbaum, A. Revolution without the revolution: sex in contemporary America. *Journal of Sex Research,* 1970, **6,** 257–267.

Black, A. H., & Prokasy, W. F. *Classical conditioning: II. Current theory and research.* New York: Appleton, 1972.

Blackburn, T. R. Sensuous-intellectual complementarity in science. *Science,* 1971, **172,** 1003–1007.

Block, R. A. The effects of instructions to forget in short-term memory. *Journal of Experimental Psychology,* 1971, **89,** 1–9.

Blough, D. S. A method for obtaining psychophysical thresholds from the pigeon. *Journal of the Experimental Analysis of Behavior,* 1958, **1,** 31–43.

Bodmer, W. F., and Cavalli-Sforza, L. L. Intelligence and race. *Scientific American,* 1970, **223,** 19–29.

Boring, E. G. *A history of experimental psychology* (2nd Ed.) New York: Appleton, 1950.

Boring, E. G. Human nature vs. sensation: William James and the psychology of the present. *American Journal of Psychology,* 1942, **55,** 310–327.

Botwinick, J. *Cognitive processes in maturity and old age.* New York: Springer, 1967.

Boulding, K. E. *The image.* Ann Arbor, Mich.: U. of Michigan Press, 1956.

Boulding, K. E. Large projects and larger questions. *Science,* 1969, **165,** 483–484.

Bourne, L. E. *Human conceptual behavior.* Boston: Allyn, 1966.

Bourne, L. E., Jr., Ekstrand, B. R., & Dominowski, R. L. *The psychology of thinking.* Englewood Cliffs, N.J.: Prentice-Hall, 1971.

Bower, G. H. Analysis of a mnemonic device. *American Scientist,* 1970, **58,** 496–510.

Bower, T. G. R. The visual world of infants. *Scientific American,* 1966, **215,** 80–97.

Bower, T. G. R. The object in the world of the infant. *Scientific American,* 1971, **225**(4), 30–38.

Bowers, K. S. Situationism in psychology: An analysis and a critique. *Psychological Review,* 1973, **80**(5), 307–333.

Bowlby, J. *Attachment and loss.* Vol. 1. *Attachment.* New York: Basic Books, 1969.

Bowlby, J. Maternal care and mental health. *World Health Organization Monograph Series,* 1951, No. 2.

690
REFERENCES

Boyd, D. A., Jr., & Nie, L. W. Congenital universal indifference to pain. *Archives of Neurology and Psychiatry,* 1949, **61,** 401–412.

Brady, J. V. Ulcers in "executive monkeys." *Scientific American,* 1958, **199,** 95–100.

Braginsky, D. D., Braginsky, B. M., & Ring, K. Methods of madness: the mental hospital as a last resort. New York: Holt, 1969.

Braginsky, D. D., & Braginsky, B. M. Psychologists: high priests of the middle class. *Psychology Today,* December, 1973, 15, 18–20, 138–142.

Brautman, E. Comparison of learning and retention of all-digit telephone numbers to prefixed and mnemonic coded numbers. *Perceptual and Motor Skills,* 1972, **36,** 267–270.

Breland, K., & Breland, M. The misbehavior of organisms. *American Psychologist,* 1961, **16**(11), 681–684.

Breland, K., & Breland, M. *Animal behavior.* New York: Macmillan, 1966.

Breuer, H., & Freud, S. *Studies in hysteria.* Boston: Beacon Press, 1961 (original edition 1895).

Bridges, K. M. B. Emotional development in early infancy. *Child Development,* 1932, **3,** 324–341.

Broadbent, D. E. *Decision and stress.* New York: Academic, 1971.

Brofenbrenner, U. Some familial antecedents of responsibility and leadership in adolescents. In L. Petrullo and B. M. Bass (Eds.), *Leadership and interpersonal behavior.* New York: Holt, 1961.

Brogden, W. J. Sensory preconditioning. *Journal of Experimental Psychology,* 1939, **25,** 323–332.

Bronson, G. W. The fear of novelty. *Psychological Bulletin,* 1968, **69,** 350–358.

Brown, J. S. Gradients of approach and avoidance responses and their relation to motivation. *Journal of Comparative and Physiological Psychology,* 1948, **41,** 450–465.

Brown, P. L., & Jenkins, H. M. Auto-shaping of the pigeon's key-peck. *Journal of the Experimental Analysis of Behavior,* 1968, **11,** 1–8.

Brown, R. *Words and things.* New York: Free Press, 1958.

Brown, R. Schizophrenia, language, and reality. *American Psychologist,* 1973, **28**(5), 395–403.

Brown, R., & Lenneberg, E. H. A study in language and cognition. *Journal of Abnormal and Social Psychology,* 1954, **49,** 454–462.

Brown, R., & McNeil, D. The "tip of the tongue" phenomenon. *Journal of Verbal Learning and Verbal Behavior,* 1966, **5,** 325–327.

Brownfield, C. A. *The brain benders: a study of the effects of isolation.* (2nd Ed.) New York: Exposition Press, 1972.

Bruce, R. W. Conditions of transfer of training. *Journal of Experimental Psychology,* 1933, **16,** 343–361.

Bruner, J. S. Nature and uses of immaturity. *American Psychologist,* 1972, **27**(8), 687–708.

Bruner, J. S., et al. *Studies in cognitive growth: a collaboration at the Center for Cognitive Studies.* New York: Wiley, 1966.

Bruner, J. S., & Goodman, C. C. Value and need as organizing factors in perception. *Journal of Abnormal Social Psychology,* 1947, **42,** 33–44.

Bruner, J. S., Goodnow, J. J., & Austin, G. A. *A study of thinking.* New York: Wiley, 1956.

Brunswik, E. *Perception and the representative design of psychological experiments.* Berkeley: U. of California Press, 1956.

Brush, R. F. (Ed.) *Aversive conditioning and learning.* New York: Academic, 1971.

Bugelski, B. R. Presentation time, total time and mediation of paired-associate learning. *Journal of Experimental Psychology,* 1962, **63,** 409–412.

Buhler, C., & Allen, M. *Introduction to humanistic psychology.* Monterey, Calif.: Brooks/Cole, 1972.

Bunch, M. E. The measurement of reminiscence. *Psychological Review,* 1938, **45,** 525–531.

Bunch, M. E. Transfer of training in the mastery of an antagonistic habit after varying intervals of time. *Journal of Comparative Psychology,* 1939, **28,** 450–456.

Bunch, M. E., & McCraven, V. Temporal course of transfer in the learning of memory material. *Journal of Comparative Psychology,* 1938, **25,** 481–496.

Burgess, E. W., & Wallin, P. *Engagement and marriage.* Philadelphia: Lippincott, 1953.

Burnham, J. C. (Ed.) *Science in America: historical selections.* New York: Holt, 1971.

Burt, C. Inheritance of general intelligence. *American Psychologist,* 1972, **27**(3), 175–190.

Burton, G. J. Evidence for non-linear response process in the human visual system from measurements on the thresholds of spatial beat frequencies. *Vision Research,* 1973, **13,** 1211–1225.

Butcher, J. N. (Ed.) *Objective personality assessment: changing perspectives.* New York: Academic, 1972.

Butter, C. *Neurophysiology: the study of the brain and behavior.* Belmont, Calif.: Brooks/Cole, 1968.

Butterfield, H. *The origins of modern science: 1300-1800.* (Rev. Ed.) New York: Macmillan, 1957.

Byrne, D. *The attraction paradigm.* New York: Academic, 1971.

Cain, W. S., & Marks, L. E. (Eds.) *Stimulus and sensation: readings in sensory psychology.* Boston: Little, Brown, 1971.

Calhoun, J. B. Population density and social pathology. *Scientific American,* 1962, **206,** 139–146.

Campbell, A., & Converse, P. E. (Eds.) *The human meaning of social change.* New York: Russell Sage Foundation, 1971.

Campbell, B. A., & Church, R. M. *Punishment and aversive behavior.* New York: Appleton, 1969.

Cannon, W. B. *Bodily changes in pain, hunger, fear and rage.* New York: Appleton, 1915.

Cannon, W. B. The James-Lange theory of emotions: a critical examination and an alternative theory. *American Journal of Psychology,* 1927, **39,** 106–124.

Carlson, E. A. *The gene: a critical history.* Philadelphia: Saunders, 1966.

Carpenter, W. T., Jr., Strauss, J. S., & Bartko, J. J. Flexible system for the diagnosis of schizophrenia: report from the WHO International Pilot Study of Schizophrenia. *Science,* 1973, **182,** 1275–1277.

Carr, A. The navigation of the green turtle. *Scientific American,* 1965, **212**(5), 79–86.

Carr, H. A. *Psychology: a study of mental activity.* New York: Longmans, 1925.

Carroll, J. B., & Casagrande, J. B. The function of language classifications in behavior. In E. E. Maccoby, T. M. Newcomb, & E. L. Hartley (Eds.), *Readings in social psychology.* New York: Holt, 1958.

Catania, A. C. Chomsky's formal analysis of natural languages: a behavioral translation. *Behaviorism,* 1972, **1**(1), 1–15.

Cattel, R. B. *The fight for our national intelligence.* London: King, 1937.

Cattell, R. B. *Personality: a systematic theoretical and factual study.* New York: McGraw-Hill, 1950.

Cermak, L. S. *Human memory.* New York: Ronald, 1972.

Chambers, J. A. *College teachers: their effect on creativity of students.* Report of U.S. Dept. of HEW, Office of Education, National Center for Educational Research and Development, 1972.

Cherry, E. C. Some experiments on the recognition of speech with one and two ears. *Journal of the Acoustical Society of America,* 1953, **25,** 975–979.

Chomsky, N. Review of B. F. Skinner's "Verbal behavior." *Language,* 1959, **35,** 26–58.

Chomsky, N. *Language and mind.* (Enlarged Ed.) New York: Harcourt, 1972.

Choron, J. *Suicide.* New York: Scribners, 1972.

Church, J. (Ed.) *Three babies.* New York: Random House, 1966.

Cleary, T. A., Humphreys, L. G., Kendrick, S. A., & Wesman, A. Educational uses of tests with disadvantaged students. *American Psychologist,* 1975, **30,** 15–41.

Cleckley, H. *The mask of sanity.* St. Louis: Mosby, 1964.

Clemente, C. G., & Sherman, M. B. Cortical synchronization and sleep patterns of acute restrained and chronic behaving cats induced by basal forebrain stimulation. *Electroencephalography and Clinical Neurophysiology,* 1963, supplement 24, 172–187.

Cofer, C. N., & Appley, M. H. *Motivation: theory and research.* New York: Wiley, 1964.

Cohen, M. R., & Nagel, E. *Introduction to logic and scientific method.* New York: Harcourt, 1934.

Cole, J. R., & Cole, S. The Ortega hypothesis. *Science,* 1972, **178,** 368–375.

Cole, M., & Bruner, J. S. Cultural differences and inferences about psychological processes. *American Psychology,* 1971, **26,** 867–876.

Conant, J. B. *On understanding science: a historical approach.* New Haven: Yale U.P., 1947.

Conger, J. J. *Adolescence and youth: psychological development in a changing world.* New York: Harper, 1973.

Cook, M. *Interpersonal perception.* Baltimore: Penguin Books, 1971.

Coover, J. E. Metapsychics and the incredulity of psychologists. In C. Murchison (Ed.), *The case for and against psychical belief.* Worcester, Mass.: Clark U.P., 1927.

Cortes, J. B., & Gatti, F. M. Physique and self-description of temperament. *Journal of Consulting Psychology,* 1965, **29,** 432–439.

Cox, F. *Psychology.* Dubuque, Iowa: Brown, 1973.

Craik, F. I. M., & Lockhart, R. S. Levels of processing. *Journal of Verbal Learning and Verbal Behavior,* 1972, **11,** 671–684.

Crombie, A. C. Early concepts of the senses and the mind. *Scientific American,* 1964, **210.**

Cronbach, L. J. *Essentials of psychological testing.* (3rd Ed.) New York: Harper, 1970.

Cronbach, L. J. Five decades of controversy over mental testing. *American Psychologist,* 1975, **30,** 1–14.

Crutchfield, R. S. Conformity and character. *American Psychologist,* 1955, **10,** 191–198.

Curtin, S. R. *Nobody ever died of old age.* Boston: Atlantic/Little, Brown, 1972.

Daniels, G. H. *Science in American society: a social history.* New York: Knopf, 1971.

Darwin, C. *Expression of emotions in man and animals.* (2nd Ed.) London: J. Murray, 1872.

Darwin, C. *The origin of species.* (2nd Ed.) London: Collier, 1909.

Davidson, M., McInnes, R., & Parnell, R. The distribution of personality traits in seven year old children: a combined psychological, psychiatric, and somatotype study. *British Journal of Educational Psychology,* 1957, **27,** 48–61.

Davis, B. D. Prospects for genetic intervention in man. *Science,* 1970, **170,** 1279–1283.

Davis, C. Results of self-selection of diets by young children. *Canadian Medical Association Journal,* 1939, **41,** 257–261.

Davis, J. C., & Okada, R. Recognition and recall of positively forgotten items. *Journal of Experimental Psychology,* 1971, **89**(1), 181–186.

Day, R. H. *Human perception.* New York: Wiley, 1969.

Day, R. Visual spatial illusions: a general explanation. *Science,* 1972, **175,** 1335–1340.

Dember, W. N. *Psychology of perception.* New York: Holt, 1960.

Dember, W. N. Birth order and need affiliation. *Journal of Abnormal and Social Psychology,* 1964, **68,** 555–557.

Dember, W. N. *Psychology of perception.* New York: Wiley, 1964.

Dember, W. N. Motivation and the cognitive revolution. *American Psychologist,* 1974, **29**(3), 161–168.

Denny, M. R. A theory of experimental extinction and its relation to a general theory. In H. H. Kendler & J. T. Spence (Eds.), *Essays in neobehaviorism.* New York: Appleton, 1971.

Dethier, V. G. A surfeit of stimuli: a paucity of receptors. *American Scientist,* 1971, **59**(6), 706–715.

Dethier, V. G., & Stellar, E. *Animal behavior.* (3rd Ed.) Englewood Cliffs, N.J.: Prentice-Hall, 1970.

Deutsch, M. *The disadvantaged child: studies of the social environment and the learning process.* New York: Basic Books, 1967.

Deutsch, M., & Collins, M. E. *Interracial housing: a psychological evaluation of a social experiment.* Minneapolis: U. of Minnesota Press, 1951.

Deutsch, M., & Gerard, H. B. A study of normative and informational social influences upon individual judgment. *Journal of Abnormal and Social Psychology,* 1955, **51,** 629–636.

DeVries, R. Conservation of generic identity in the years three to six. Doctoral dissertation, University of Chicago, 1967.

Dewey, J. The reflex arc concept in psychology. *Psychological Review,* 1896, **3,** 357–370.

DiCara, L. V. Learning mechanisms. In Frohlich, E. D. (Ed.), *Pathophysiology.* Philadelphia: Lippincott, 1972.

Dickoff, H. Reactions to evaluations by another person as a function of self-evaluation and the interaction context. Doctoral dissertation, Duke University, 1961.

Dingle, H. Migration strategies of insects. *Science,* 1972, **175,** 1327–1334.

Dixon, N. F. *Subliminal perception.* New York: McGraw-Hill, 1971.

Dixon, T. R., & Horton, D. L. (Eds.) *Verbal behavior and general behavior theory.* Englewood Cliffs, N.J.: Prentice-Hall, 1968.

Dobzhansky, T. Genetics and equality. *Science,* 1962, **137,** 113.

Dohrenwend, B. P., & Dohrenwend, B. S. Field studies of social factors in relation to three types of psychological disorders. *Journal of Abnormal Psychology,* 1967, **72,** 369–378.

Dollard, J., & Miller, N. E. *Personality and psychotherapy: an analysis in terms of learning, thinking, and culture.* New York: McGraw-Hill, 1950.

Dulany, D. E. The place of hypotheses and intentions: an analysis of verbal control in verbal conditioning. In C. W. Eriksen (Ed.), *Behavior and awareness: a symposium of research and interpretation.* Durham, N.C.: Duke U.P., 1962.

Duncan, C. P. (Ed.) *Thinking: current experimental studies.* Philadelphia: Lippincott, 1967.

Duncker, K. On problem solving. Translated by L. W. Lews from the 1935 original. *Psychological Monographs,* 1945, **58,** No. 270.

Dunham, H. W. Epidemiology of psychiatric disorders as a contribution to medical ecology. *Archives of General Psychiatry,* 1966, **14,** 1–19.

Dunlap, K. The role of eye-muscles and mouth muscles in the expression of the emotions. *Genetic Psychology Monographs,* 1927, **2,** No. 3.

Dunn, C. C. *Heredity and variation.* Midland Park, N.J.: The University Society, 1932.

Dunn, W. L., Jr., & Morris, P. *Smoking behavior: motives and incentives.* New York: Wiley, 1973.

Dunnette, M. C., Campbell, J., & Jaastad, K. The effect of group participation on brainstorming effectiveness for two industrial samples. *Journal of Applied Psychology,* 1963, **47**, 30-37.

Eaton, J. W., & Weil, R. J. The mental health of the Hutterites. *Scientific American,* 1953, **189**(6), 31-37.

Ebbinghaus, H. *Ueber das Gedachtniss.* Leipzig: Duncker and Humblot, 1885. Translated by H. Ruger & C. Bussenius, New York: Teachers College Press, 1913. Reprinted by Dover, New York, 1964.

Ebon, M. *They knew the unknown.* New York: World, 1971.

Ecclas, J. C. (Ed.) *Brain and conscious experience.* New York: Springer-Verlag, 1966.

Eisdorfer, C., & Lawton, M. P. (Eds.) *The psychology of adult development and aging.* Washington, D.C.: American Psychological Assoc., 1971.

Eisenberg, J. F., & Dillon, W. S. (Eds.) *Man and beast.* Washington: Smithsonian, 1971.

Eisenberg, L. The "human" nature of human nature. *Science,* 1972, **176**, 123-128.

Ekman, P. (Ed.) *Darwin and facial expression: a century of research in review.* New York: Academic, 1973.

Ekman, P., Sorenson, E. R., & Friesen, W. V. Pan-cultural elements in facial displays of emotion. *Science,* 1969, **164**, 86-88.

Ellenberger, H. F. *The discovery of the unconscious: the history and evolution of dynamic psychiatry.* New York: Basic Books, 1970.

Emlen, J. T., & Penney, R. L. The navigation of penguins. *Scientific American,* 1966, **215**(4), 104-113.

Epstein, W. The influence of syntactic structure on learning. *American Journal of Psychology,* 1961, **74**, 80-85.

Epstein, W. A further study of the effect of syntactic structure on learning. *American Journal of Psychology,* 1962, **75**, 121-126.

Eriksen, C. W. Figments, fantasies, and follies: a search for the subconscious mind. In C. W. Eriksen (Ed.), *Behavior and awareness: a symposium of research and interpretation.* Durham, N.C.: Duke U.P., 1962.

Erikson, E. H. *Childhood and society.* New York: Norton, 1950.

Estes, W. K. An experimental study of punishment. *Psychological Monographs,* 1944, **57** (263).

Estes, W. K. The statistical approach to learning theory. In S. Koch (Ed.), *Psychology: a study of a science.* Vol. 2. New York: McGraw-Hill, 1959.

Estes, W. K. and Skinner, B. F. Some quantitative properties of anxiety. *Journal of Experimental Psychology,* 1941, **29**, 390-400.

Etzel, B. C., & Gewirtz, J. L. Experimental modification of caretaker-maintained high-rate operant crying in a 6- and 20-week-old infant (infans tyrannotearus): extinction of crying with reinforcement of eye contact and smiling. *Journal of Experimental Child Psychology,* 1967, **5**(3), 303-317.

Eysenck, H. J. *The structure of human personality.* London: Methuen, 1960.

Eysenck, H. J. *The IQ argument: race, intelligence and education.* New York: Library, 1971.

Farberow, N. L., & Schneidman, E. S. (Eds.) *The cry for help.* New York: McGraw-Hill, 1961.

Fast, J. *Body language.* New York: M. Evans, 1970.

Fehr, F. S., & Stern, J. A. Peripheral physiological variables and emotion: The James-Lange theory revisited. *Psychological Bulletin,* 1970, **74**, 411-424.

Feigl, H. *The "mental" and the "physical": the essay and a postscript.* Minneapolis: U. of Minnesota Press, 1967.

Feleky, A. *Feelings and emotions.* New York: Pioneer, 1922.

Ferster, C. B., & Hammer, C. E. Synthesizing the components of arithmetic behavior. In W. F. Honig (Ed.), *Operant behavior: areas of research and application.* New York: Appleton, 1966.

Feshbach, S. Aggression. In P. H. Mussen (Ed.), *Carmichael's manual of child psychology.* Vol. 2. (Rev. Ed.) New York: Wiley, 1970.

Feshbach, S. Dynamics and morality of violence and aggression: some psychological considerations. *American Psychologist,* 1971, **26**(3), 281-292.

Feshbach, S., & Loeb, A. A further experimental study of a response-interference versus a drive-facilitation theory of the effect of anxiety upon learning. *Journal of Personality,* 1959, **27**, 497-506.

Feshbach, S., & Singer, R. D. *Television and aggression: an experimental field study.* San Francisco: Jossey-Bass, 1971.

Festinger, L. *A theory of cognitive dissonance.* Stanford, Calif.: Stanford U.P., 1957.

Festinger, L., Pepitone, A., & Newcomb, T. M. Some consequences of deindividuation in a group. *Journal of Abnormal and Social Psychology,* 1952, **47**, 382-389.

Festinger, L., Riecken, H. W., & Schachter, S. *When prophecy fails.* New York: Harper, 1956.

Festinger, L., Schachter, S., & Back, K. *Social pressures in informal groups: a study of human factors in housing.* New York: Harper, 1950.

Flavell, J. H. *The developmental psychology of Jean Piaget.* Princeton, N.J.: Van Nostrand, 1963.

Fletcher, R. *Instinct in man.* New York: International Universities Press, 1957.

Fouts, R. S. Use of guidance in teaching sign language to a chimpanzee (*Pan troglodytes*). *Journal of Comparative and Physiological Psychology,* 1972, **80**, 515-522.

Fouts, R. S. Acquisition and testing of gestural signs in four young chimpanzees. *Science,* 1973, **180**, 978-980.

Fox, M. W. (Ed.) *Readings in ethnology and comparative psychology.* Monterey, Calif.: Brooks/Cole, 1973.

Franks, C. M., & Wilson, G. T. (Eds.) *Behavior therapy.* New York: Brunner/Mazel, 1974.

Frederiksen, N. Toward a taxonomy of situations. *American Psychologist,* 1972, **27**, 114-123.

Freedman, J. L., & Fraser, S. C. Compliance without pressure: the foot-in-the-door technique. *Journal of Personality and Social Psychology,* 1966, **4**, 195-202.

Freedman, J. L., & Sears, D. O. Selective exposure. In Berkowitz, L. (Ed.), *Advances in experimental social psychology.* Vol. 2. New York: Academic, 1965.

Freedman, S. J., Grunebaum, H. U., & Greenblatt, M. Perceptual and cognitive changes in sensory deprivation. In P. Solomon et al. (Eds.), *Sensory deprivation.* Cambridge, Mass.: Harvard U.P., 1961.

Freud, A. The mutual influences in the development of ego and id: introduction to the discussion. *Psychoanalytic Study of the Child,* 1952, **7**, 42-50.

Freud, S. *A general introduction to psychoanalysis.* Translated by J. Riviere. Garden City, N.Y.: Doubleday, 1943.

Freund, J. E. *Modern elementary statistics.* Englewood Cliffs, N.J.: Prentice-Hall, 1973.

Friedmann, T., & Roblin, R. Gene therapy for human genetic disease? *Science,* 1972, **175**, 949-955.

Frisch, J., von. *Bees: their vision, chemical senses and language.* Ithaca, N.Y.: Cornell U.P., 1950.

Gagnon, J. H., & Simon, W. *Sexual conduct: the social sources of human sexuality.* Chicago: Aldine, 1973.

Galton, F. *Hereditary genius.* New York: Appleton, 1869.

Garcia, J., McGowan, B. K., & Green, K. F. Biological constraints on conditioning. In A. Black & W. F. Prokasy (Eds.), *Classical conditioning.* New York: Appleton, 1972.

Gardner, R. A. Probability-learning with two and three choices. *American Journal of Psychology,* 1957, **70**, 174-185.

Gardner, B. T. and Gardner, R. A. Two-way communication with an infant chimpanzee. In A. M. Schrier and F. Stollnitz (Eds.) *Behavior of non-human primates* (Vol. 4). New York: Academic Press, 1972.

Gardner, R. A., & Gardner, B. T. Teaching sign language to a chimpanzee. *Science,* 1969, **165**, 664-672.

Gebhart, P. H. *Situational factors affecting human sexual behavior.* Indiana University Institute for Sex Research, 1965.

Geldard, F. A. *The human senses.* (2nd Ed.) New York: Wiley, 1972.

Gerbner, G. Violence in television drama: trends and symbolic functions. In G. A. Comstock and E. A. Rubinstein (Eds.), *Television and social behavior.* Vol. 11 of *Media content and control.* Washington, D.C.: U.S. Government Printing Office, 1972.

Gesell, A. *Wolf child and human child.* New York: Harper, 1940.

Gesell, A., and Thompson, H. *Infant behavior, its genesis and growth.* New York: McGraw-Hill, 1934.

Gewirtz, J. L., & Baer, D. M. The effect of brief social deprivation on behaviors for a social reinforcer. *Journal of Abnormal and Social Psychology,* 1950, **56**, 49-56.

Gibb, C. A. Leadership. In Lindzey, G., and Aronson, E. (Eds.), *The handbook of social psychology.* Vol. 4. Reading, Mass.: Addison-Wesley, 1969.

Gibson, E. J., & Walk, R. D. The effect of prolonged exposure to visually presented patterns on learning to discriminate them. *Journal of Comparative and Physiological Psychology,* 1956, **49**, 239-242.

Gibson, E. J., & Walk, R. D. The visual cliff. *Scientific American,* 1960, **202**, 64-71.

Gibson, J. J. *The senses considered as perceptual systems.* Boston: Houghton, 1966.

Gilgen, A. R. (Ed.) *Contemporary scientific psychology.* New York: Academic, 1970.

Gillmor, D. S. (Ed.) *Scientific study of unidentified flying objects.* New York: Bantam, 1969.

Glaser, R. Individuals and learning: The new aptitudes. *Educational Researcher,* 1972, **1**, 5-13.

Glass, D. C. (Ed.) *Neurophysiology and emotion.* New York: Rockefeller U.P., 1967.

Gleason, K. K., & Reynierse, J. H. The behavioral

significance of pheromones in vertebrates. *Psychological Bulletin*, 1969, **71**, 58-73.

Gleitman, H. Getting animals to understand the experimenter's instructions. *Animal Learning and Behavior*, 1971, **2**(1), 1-5.

Globus, G. G. Unexpected symmetries in the "World Knot." *Science*, 1973, **180**, 1129-1136.

Glucksberg, S. Effects of verbal behavior on problem solving: labeling the functionally fixed object. Paper presented to American Psychological Association, 1964.

Glucksberg, S., & Weisberg, R. W. Verbal behavior and problem solving: some effects of labeling in a functional fixedness problem. *Journal of Experimental Psychology*, 1966, **71**, 659-664.

Goffman, E. *Relations in public: microstudies of the public order.* New York: Basic Books, 1971.

Goldfried, M. R., & Merbaum, M. (Eds.) *Behavior change through self-control.* New York: Holt, 1973.

Goldhamer, H., & Marshall, A. *Psychoses and civilization.* New York: Free Press, 1949.

Goldschmidt, R. B. Gene and Character. IV-VIII. *University of California Publications in Zoology*, 1937, **41**, 277-342.

Goldstein, A. P., & Dean, S. J. (Eds.) *The investigation of psychotherapy.* New York: Wiley, 1966.

Goodman, G. *Companionship therapy: studies in structured intimacy.* San Francisco: Jossey-Bass, 1973.

Goodson, F. E. *The evolutionary basis of modern psychology.* New York: Holt, 1973.

Goodson, F. E., & Marx, M. H. Increased resistance to audiogenic seizure in rats trained on an instrumental wheel-turning response. *Journal of Comparative and Physiological Psychology*, 1953, **46**, 225-230.

Gormezano, I., & Moore, J. W. Classical conditioning. In M. H. Marx (Ed.), *Learning: processes.* New York: Macmillan, 1969.

Gottesman, I. I., & Shields, J. *Schizophrenia and genetics: a twin study vantage point.* New York: Academic, 1972.

Gould, S. J. Zealous advocates. Review of Koestler, A., "The case of the midwife toad." *Science*, 1972, **176**, 623-625.

Goulet, L. R., & Baltes, P. B. *Life-span developmental psychology: research and theory.* New York: Academic, 1970.

Graham, H. D. and Gurr, T. R. *The history of violence in America.* New York: Bantam Books, 1969.

Grant, D. A. A preliminary model for processing information conveyed by verbal conditioned stimuli in classical conditioning. In A. H. Black and W. F. Prokasy (Eds.), *Classical conditioning. II. Current research and theory.* New York: Appleton, 1972.

Gray, F., Graubard, P. S., & Rosenberg, H. Little brother is changing you. *Psychology Today*, 1974, **7**, 42-46.

Green, D. M., & Swets, J. A. *Signal detection theory and psychophysics.* New York: Wiley, 1966.

Green, K. F., & Garcia, J. Recuperation from illness: flavor enhancement for rats. *Science*, 1971, **173**, 749-751.

Green, M., Green, R., & Carr, W. J. The hawk-goose phenomenon: a replication and an extension. *Psychonomic Science*, 1966, **4**, 185-186.

Greenough, W. T. *The nature and nurture of behavior: developmental psychobiology.* San Francisco: W. H. Freeman, 1973.

Greenspoon, J. The reinforcing effect of two spoken sounds on the frequency of two responses. *American Journal of Psychology*, 1955, **68**, 409-416.

Gregory, R. L. Visual illusions. *Scientific American*, 1968, **219**, 66-80.

Gregory, R. L. *Eye and brain.* New York: World University Library, 1966.

Gregory, R. L. *Eye and brain: the psychology of seeing.* (2nd Ed.) New York: McGraw-Hill, 1973.

Grene, M. (Ed.) *Knowing and being. Essays by Michael Polanyi.* Chicago: U. of Chicago Press, 1969.

Griffin, D. R. *Listening in the dark: the acoustic orientation of bats and men.* New Haven: Yale U.P., 1958a.

Griffin, D. R. More about bat "radar." *Scientific American*, 1958b, **199**(1), 40-44.

Guilford, J. P. *The nature of human intelligence.* New York: McGraw-Hill, 1967.

Gurr, T. R., & Graham, H. D. (Eds.) *The history of violence in America: historical and comparative perspectives.* New York: Praeger, 1969.

Guthrie, E. R. *The psychology of learning.* New York: Harper, 1935.

Guthrie, E. R. Psychological facts and psychological theory. *Psychological Bulletin*, 1946, **43**, 1-20.

Guthrie, E. R. Association by contiguity. In S. Koch (Ed.), *Psychology: a study of a science.* Vol. 2, General systematic formulations, learning and special processes. New York: McGraw-Hill, 1959.

Guthrie, E. R., & Horton, G. P. *Cats in a puzzle box.* New York: Holt, 1946.

Hailman, J. P. How an instinct is learned. *Scientific American*, 1969, **22**, 98-106.

Haire, M., & Grunes, W. F. Perceptual defenses:

processes protecting an original perception of another personality. *Human Relations,* 1950, **3,** 403–412.

Hall, C. S., & Lindzey, G. *Theories of personality.* (2nd Ed.) New York: Wiley, 1970.

Hall, E. Ethology's warning, a conversation with Nobel Prize winner Nike Tinbergen. *Psychology Today,* 1974, **7,** 65–80.

Haller, J. S., Jr. *Outcasts from evolution.* Urbana, Ill.: U. of Illinois Press, 1971.

Hamsher, J. H., & Sigall, H. *Psychology and social issues.* New York: Macmillan, 1973.

Haney, C., Banks, C., & Zimbardo, P. Interpersonal dynamics in a simulated prison. *International Journal of Criminology and Penology,* 1973, **1,** 69–97.

Hansel, C. E. M. *ESP: a scientific evaluation.* New York: Scribner, 1966.

Hardin, G. The tragedy of the commons. *Science,* 1968, **162,** 1243–1248.

Harlow, H. F. The formation of learning sets. *Psychological Review,* 1949, **56,** 51–65.

Harlow, H. F. Love in infant monkeys. *Scientific American,* 1959, **200,** 68–74.

Harlow, H. F. The heterosexual affectional system in monkeys. *American Psychologist,* 1962, **17,** 1–9.

Harlow, H. F. *Learning to love.* San Francisco: Albion, 1973.

Harlow, H. F., & Harlow, M. K. Social deprivation in monkeys. *Scientific American,* 1962, **207,** 136–146.

Harlow, H. F., McGaugh, J. L., & Thompson, R. F. *Psychology.* San Francisco: Albion, 1971.

Harper, R. *Human senses in action.* Baltimore: Williams & Wilkins, 1972.

Harris, D. B. Work and the adolescent transition to maturity. *Teachers College Record,* 1961, **63,** 146–153.

Hart, B. M., Allen, K. E., Buel, J. S., Harris, F. R., & Wolf, M. M. Effects of social reinforcement on operant crying. *Journal of Experimental Child Psychology,* 1964, **1,** 145–153.

Hartman, H. *Ego psychology and the problem of adaptation.* Translated by D. Rapaport. New York: International Universities Press, 1958.

Hartshorn, H., & May, M. A. *Studies in deceit.* New York: Macmillan, 1928.

Hasler, A. D., & Larsen, J. A. The homing salmon. *Scientific American,* 1955, **193,** 72–76.

Hathaway, S. R., & Monachesi, E. D. (Eds.) *Analyzing and predicting juvenile delinquency with the MMPI.* Minneapolis: U. of Minnesota Press, 1963.

Hebb, D. O. *Textbook of psychology.* Philadelphia: Saunders, 1972.

Hebb, D. O., Lambert, W. E., & Tucker, G. R. Language, thought and experience. *Modern Language Journal,* 1971, **55**(4), 212–222.

Hediger, H. *Wild animals in captivity.* New York: Dover, 1964.

Hefferline, R. F., & Keenan, B. Amplitude-induction gradient of a small human operant in an escape-avoidance situation. *Journal of the Experimental Analysis of Behavior,* 1961, **4,** 41–43.

Hefferline, R. F., & Perera, T. B. Proprioceptive discrimination of a covert operant without its observation by the subject. *Science,* 1963, **139,** 834–835.

Heidbreder, E. *Seven psychologies.* New York: Appleton, 1933.

Heider, F. On social cognition. *American Psychologist,* 1967, **22**(1), 25–31.

Helson, H. Current trends and issues in adaptation-level theory. *American Psychologist,* 1964, **19,** 26–38.

Helson, H., & Bevan, W. *Contemporary approaches to psychology.* Princeton, N.J.: Van Nostrand, 1967.

Henderson, N. Genetic influences on the behavior of mice can be obscured by laboratory rearing. *Journal of Comparative and Physiological Psychology,* 1970, **72,** 505–511.

Hernandez, P. R., Scherer, H., & Jouvet, M. Modification of electric activity in cochlear nucleus during "attention" in unanesthetized cats. *Science,* 1956, **123,** 331–332.

Heron, W., Doane, B. K., & Scott, T. H. Visual disturbances after prolonged perceptual isolation. *Canadian Journal of Psychology,* 1956, **10,** 13–16.

Herrnstein, R. J. I. Q. *The Atlantic,* 1971, **228**(3), 43–64.

Hess, E. H. Attitude and pupil size. *Scientific American,* 1965, **212,** 46–54.

Hess, E. H., & Polt, J. M. Pupil size as related to interest value of visual stimuli. *Science,* 1960, **132,** 349–350.

Higbee, K. L. Fifteen years of fear arousal: research on threat appeals: 1953–1968. *Psychological Bulletin,* 1969, **72**(6), 426–444.

Hilgard, E. R. What becomes of the input from the stimulus? In C. W. Eriksen (Ed.), *Behavior and awareness: a symposium of research and interpretation.* Durham, N.C.: Duke U.P., 1962.

Hilgard, E. R. *The experience of hypnosis.* New York: Harcourt, 1968.

Hilgard, E. R., Irvine, R. P., & Whipple, J. E. Rote memorization and transfer: an extension of Katona's card-trick experiments. *Journal of Experimental Psychology,* 1953, **46,** 288–292.

Hillix, W. A., & Marx, M. H. (Eds.) *Systems and theories in psychology: a reader.* St. Paul, Minn.: West, 1974.

Hinde, R. A. (Ed.) *Non-verbal communication.* New York: Cambridge U.P., 1972.

Hirsch, J. *Behavior-genetic analysis.* New York: McGraw-Hill, 1967a.

Hirsch, J. Behavior-genetic or "experimental" analysis: the challenge of science versus the lure of technology. *American Psychologist,* 1967b, **22,** 118–130.

Hofling, C. K., Bortzman, E., Dalrymple, S., Graves, N., & Pierce, C. M. An experimental study in nurse-physician relationships. *Journal of Nervous and Mental Disease,* 1966, **143,** 171–180.

Holland, B. C., & Ward, R. S. Homeostasis and psychosomatic medicine. In S. Arieti (Ed.), *American Handbook of Psychiatry.* Vol. 3. New York: Basic Books, 1966.

Honig, W. K., & James P. H. R. (Eds.) *Animal memory.* New York: Academic, 1971.

Hood, W. R., & Sherif, M. Verbal report and judgement of an unstructured stimulus. *Journal of Psychology,* 1962, **54,** 121–130.

Hubel, D. H. The visual cortex of the brain. *Scientific American,* 1963, **209,** 54–62.

Hull, C. L. *Hypnosis and suggestibility: an experimental approach.* New York: Appleton, 1933.

Hull, C. L. *Principles of behavior.* New York: Appleton, 1943.

Hull, C. L. *A behavior system.* New Haven: Yale U.P., 1952.

Hunt, G. H., & Odoroff, M. E. Follow-up study of narcotic drug addicts after hospitalization. U.S. Public Health Service Report No. 77. Washington D.C.: U.S. Government Printing Office, 1963.

Hunt, J. McV. *Intelligence and experience.* New York: Ronald, 1961.

Hunt, J. McV. *The challenge of incompetence and poverty.* Urbana: U. of Illinois Press, 1969.

Hunter, E. *Brainwashing in Red China.* New York: Vanguard, 1951.

Hunter, W. S. The delayed reaction in animals and children. *Behavior Monographs,* 1913 (6).

Hurvich, L. M., & Jameson, D. Opponent processes as a model of neural organization. *American Psychologist,* 1974, **29**(2), 80–87.

Huston, T. L. (Ed.) *Foundations of interpersonal attraction.* New York: Academic, 1974.

Hyden, H. Biochemical and molecular aspects of learning. *Proceedings of the American Philosophical Society,* 1967, **111**(6), 326–342.

Hynek, J. A. *The UFO experience.* Chicago: Regnery, 1972.

Ilg, F. L., & Ames, L. B. *Child behavior.* New York: Harper, 1955.

Irwin, F. W. *Intentional behavior and motivation: a cognitive theory.* Philadelphia: Lippincott, 1971.

Irwin, O. C. The amount and nature of activities of newborn infants under constant external stimulating conditions during the first ten days of life. *Genetic Psychology Monographs,* 1930, **8.**

Itard, J. M. G. *The wild boy of Aveyron.* Translated by G. and M. Humphrey. New York: Appleton, 1932.

Jackson, D. D. Psychotherapy for schizophrenia. *Scientific American,* 1953, **188**(1), 58–63.

Jackson, D. D. Suicide. *Scientific American,* 1954, **191,** 88–96.

Jackson, D. D. Schizophrenia. *Scientific American,* 1962, **207**(2), 65–74.

Jackson, E. W., Jr., & Kelly, E. L. Influence of suggestion and subjects' prior knowledge in research on sensory deprivation. *Science,* 1962, **135,** 211–212.

Jacobson, M. *Developmental neurobiology.* New York: Holt, 1970.

Jacobsson, E. Electrophysiology of mental activities. *American Journal of Psychology,* 1932, **44,** 677–694.

Jacobsson, E. *Progressive relaxation.* Chicago: U. of Chicago Press, 1938.

James, W. What is an emotion? *Mind,* 1884, **9,** 188–205.

James, W. *The principles of psychology.* New York: Holt, 1890. Reprinted by Dover, 1950.

Janis, I. L., & Field, P. B. Sex differences and personality factors related to persuasibility. In C. I. Hovland and I. L. Janis (Eds.), *Personality and persuasibility.* New Haven: Yale U.P., 1959.

Jarvik, L. F., Klodin, V., & Matsuyama, S. S. Human aggression and the extra Y chromosome: fact or fantasy? *American Psychologist,* 1973, **28,** 674–682.

Jencks, C. *Inequality: a reassessment of the effect of family and schooling in America.* New York: Basic Books, 1972.

Jenkins, J. G., & Dallenbach, K. M. Obliviscence during sleep and waking. *American Journal of Psychology,* 1924, **35,** 605–612.

Jensen, A. R. How much can we boost IQ and scholastic achievement? *Harvard Educational Review,* 1969a, **39**(2), 1–123.

Jensen, A. R. Reducing the heredity-environment uncertainty: a reply. *Harvard Educational Review,* 1969b, **39**(2), 449-483.

Jensen, A. R. *Educability and group differences.* New York: Harper, 1973.

Joffe, J. M., Rawson, R. A., & Mulick, J. A. Control of their environment reduces emotionality in rats. *Science,* 1973, **180,** 1383-1384.

John, E. R. Switchboard versus statistical theories of learning and memory. *Science,* 1972, **177,** 850-864.

Johnson, D. F. and Mihal, W. L. Performance of blacks and whites in computerized versus manual testing environments. *American Psychologist,* 1973, **28,** 694-699.

Johnson, D. M. *Systematic introduction to the psychology of thinking.* New York: Harper, 1972.

Johnson, R. N. *Aggression in man and animals.* Philadelphia: Saunders, 1972.

Jones, E. E. *Ingratiation.* New York: Appleton, 1964.

Jones, E. E. Flattery will get you somewhere. *Transaction,* May/June, 1965, 20-23.

Jones, E. E., Bell, L., & Aronson, E. The reciprocation of attraction from similar and dissimilar others: a study in person perception and evaluation. In C. G. McClintock (Ed.), *Experimental social psychology.* New York: Holt, 1971.

Jones, G. *Visceral learning: toward a science of self-control.* New York: Viking, 1973.

Jones, M. C., Bayley, N., Macfarlane, J. W., & Honzik, M. P. (Eds.), *The course of human development.* Waltham, Mass.: Xerox College Publishing, 1971.

Jones, N. G. B. An ethological study of some aspects of social behavior of children in nursery school. In D. Morris (Ed.), *Primate ethology.* Chicago: Aldine, 1967.

Jones, N. B. (Ed.) *Ethological studies of child behaviour.* New York: Cambridge U.P., 1972.

Jung, C. G. *Symbols of transformation.* New York: Random House, 1956.

Kagan, J. *Change and continuity in infancy.* New York: Wiley, 1971.

Kagan, J. Do infants think? *Scientific American,* 1972, **226**(3), 74-82.

Kagan, J., & Coles, R. (Eds.) *Twelve to sixteen: early adolescence.* New York: Norton, 1972.

Kagan, J., & Klein, R. E. Cross-cultural perspectives on early development. *American Psychologist,* 1973, **28**(11), 947-961.

Kahneman, D., Beatty, J., & Pollack, I. Perceptual deficit during a mental task. *Science,* 1967, **157,** 218-219.

Kallmann, F. J. The genetics of mental illness. In S. Arieti (Ed.), *American handbook of psychology.* New York: Basic Books, 1959.

Kanner, L. Judging emotions from facial expressions. *Psychological Monographs,* 1931, **41,** No. 186.

Kaplan, B. J. Malnutrition and mental deficiency. *Psychological Bulletin,* 1972, **78**(5), 321-334.

Kaplan, Helen S. *The new sex therapy: active treatment of sexual dysfunctions.* New York: Brunner/Mazel, 1974.

Karlin, J. E. All-numerical dialing: would users like it? *Bell Lab. Records,* 1958, **36,** 284-288.

Katz, D., & Stotland, E. A preliminary statement to a theory of attitude structure and change. In S. Koch (Ed.), *Psychology: a study of a science.* Vol. 3. New York: McGraw-Hill, 1959.

Kaufman, L., & Rock, I. The moon illusion. *Scientific American,* 1962, **207,** 120-130.

Kausler, D. H. *Psychology of verbal learning and memory.* New York: Academic, 1974.

Kawamura, S. The process of sub-culture progation among Japanese Macaques. *Journal of Primatology,* 1959, **2,** 43-60.

Keehn, J. G. Experimental studies of "the unconscious": operant conditioning of unconscious eyeblinking. *Behavioral Research and Therapy,* 1967, **5,** 95-102.

Keehn, J. G., Lloyd, K. E., Hibbs, M., & Johnson, D. Operant eyeblink conditioning without awareness: a preliminary report. *Psychonomic Science,* 1965, **2,** 357-358.

Kelley, H. H. The warm-cold variable in first impressions of persons. *Journal of Personality,* 1950, **18,** 431-439.

Kelley, H. H. The processes of causal attribution. *American Psychologist,* 1973, **28,** 107-128.

Kellogg, W. N. Communication and language in the home-raised chimpanzee. *Science,* 1968, **162,** 423-428.

Kelly, G. *Psychology of personal constructs.* New York: Norton, 1955.

Kelman, H. C. Processes of opinion change. *Public Opinion Quarterly,* 1961, **25,** 57-78.

Kelman, H. C. The relevance of social research to social issues: promises and pitfalls. *Sociological Review Monograph,* 1970, No. 16.

Kelman, H. C. The rights of the subject in social research: an analysis in terms of relative power and legitimacy. *American Psychologist,* 1972, **27**(11), 989-1016.

Kelman, H. C., & Hovland, C. I. "Reinstatement" of the communicator in delayed measurement of opinion change. *Journal of Abnormal and Social Psychology,* 1953, **48,** 327–335.

Kendler, H. H., & Spence, J. T. (Eds.) *Essays in neobehaviorism.* New York: Appleton, 1971.

Kennedy, E. *The new sexuality: myths, fables and hang-ups.* Garden City, N.Y.: Doubleday, 1972.

Kennedy, T. D. Verbal conditioning without awareness: the use of programmed reinforcement and recurring assessment of awareness. *Journal of Experimental Psychology,* 1970, **84,** 487–494.

Kennedy, T. D. Reinforcement frequency, task characteristics, and interval of awareness assessment as factors in verbal conditioning without awareness. *Journal of Experimental Psychology,* 1971, **88,** 103–112.

Keppel, G. Facilitation in short- and long-term retention of paired associates following distributed practice in learning. *Journal of Verbal Learning and Verbal Behavior,* 1964, **3,** 91–111.

Kimble, G. A., & Garmezy, N. *Principles of general psychology.* New York: Ronald, 1968.

Kimble, G. A., & Perlmuter, L. C. The problem of volition. *Psychological Review,* 1970, **77,** 361–384.

King, R. A. Consolidation of the neural trace in memory: investigation with one-trial avoidance conditioning and ECS. *Journal of Comparative and Physiological Psychology,* 1965, **59,** 283–284.

Kinkade, K. *A Walden II experiment: the first five years of Twin Oaks Community.* New York: Morrow, 1973.

Kinsey, A. C., Pomeroy, W. B., & Martin, C. E. *Sexual behavior in the human male.* Philadelphia: Saunders, 1948.

Kintsch, W. *Learning, memory and conceptual processes.* New York: Wiley, 1970.

Klein, G. S., Gardner, R. W., & Schlesinger, H. J. Tolerance for unrealistic experiences: a study of the generality of cognitive control. *British Journal of Psychology,* 1962, **53,** 41–55.

Kleint, H. Versuche Uber die Wahrnehmung. *Zeitscrift fur Psychologie,* 1937, **140,** 109.

Kling, J. W., & Riggs, L. A. (Eds.) *Experimental psychology.* New York: Holt, 1971.

Klinger, E. *Structure and functions of fantasy.* New York: Wiley-Interscience, 1971.

Knop, C. The dynamics of newly born babies. *Journal of Pediatrics,* 1946, **29,** 721–728.

Koestler, A. *The act of creation.* New York: Macmillan, 1964.

Koestler, A. *The case of the midwife toad.* New York: Random House, 1972.

Kohler, I. Experiments with goggles. *Scientific American,* 1962, **206,** 62–72.

Kohler, I. The formation and transformation of the perceptual world. *Psychological Issues,* 1964, **3**(12).

Köhler, W. *The mentality of apes.* New York: Harcourt, 1925.

Köhler, W. *Gestalt psychology: an introduction to the new concepts in modern psychology.* New York: Liveright, 1947.

Krech, D., Rosenzweig, M. R., & Bennett, E. L. Environmental improverishment, social isolation and changes in brain chemistry and anatomy. *Physiology and Behavior,* 1966, **1,** 99–104.

Kris, H. Notes on the development and on some current problems of psychoanalytic child psychology. *Psychoanalytic Study of the Child,* 1950, **5,** 34–62.

Kubancy, E. S., & Sloggett, B. B. Coding procedures for teachers. *Journal of Applied Behavior Analysis,* 1973, **6,** 339–344.

Kuenne, M. R. Experimental investigation of the relation of language to transposition behavior in young children. *Journal of Experimental Psychology,* 1946, **36,** 471–490.

Kuo, Zing-Yang. *The dynamics of behavior development: an epigenetic view.* New York: Random House, 1967.

Ladner, J. *Tomorrow's tomorrow.* Garden City, N.Y.: Doubleday, 1971.

Lang, P. J. Autonomic control or learning to play the internal organs. *Psychology Today,* 1970, **4**(5), 37.

Lawson, R. Schedules of irrelevant signals and maintenance of monitoring behavior. *Science,* 1959, **129,** 387–388.

Layzen, D. Heritability analyses of IQ scores: science or numerology? *Science,* 1974, **183,** 1259–1266.

Lazarus, R. S. *Patterns of adjustment and human effectiveness.* New York: McGraw-Hill, 1969.

Lee, E. S. Negro intelligence and selective migration. *American Sociological Review,* 1951, **16,** 227–233.

Leeper, R. W. Learning and the fields of perception, motivation, and personality. In S. Koch (Ed.), *Psychology: a study of a science.* Vol. 5. New York: McGraw-Hill, 1963.

Lehrman, D. S. Semantic and conceptual issues in the nature–nurture problem. In Aronson et al. (Eds.), *Development and evolution of behavior: essays in memory of T. C. Schneirla.* San Francisco: Freeman, 1970.

Leibowitz, H. W. *Visual perception.* New York: Macmillan, 1965.

Leites, N., & Bernaut, E. *Ritual of liquidation.* New York: Free Press, 1954.

Lenneberg, E. H. On explaining language. *Science,* 1969, **164,** 635-643.

Lenneberg, E. H., & Roberts, J. M. The language of experience: a study in methodology. *International Journal of American Linguistics,* 1956, **22.**

Lesser, G. W. Designing a program for broadcast television. In F. F. Korten, S. W. Cook, & J. I. Lacey (Eds.), *Psychology and the problems of society.* Washington, D.C.: American Psychological Association, 1970.

Lester, G., & Lester, D. *Suicide: the gamble with death.* Englewood Cliffs, N.J.: Prentice-Hall, 1971.

Leuba, C., Birch, L., & Appleton, J. Human problem solving during complete paralysis of the voluntary musculature. *Psychological Reports,* 1968, **22,** 849-855.

Leventhal, H., & Singer, R. P. Affect arousal and positioning of recommendations in persuasive communications. *Journal of Personality and Social Psychology,* 1966, **4,** 137-146.

Lewin, K. *A dynamic theory of personality.* New York: McGraw-Hill, 1935.

Lewin, K. *Principles of topological psychology.* New York: McGraw-Hill, 1936.

Lewin, K. Formalization and progress in psychology. *University of Iowa Studies of Child Welfare,* 1940, **16,** 9-42.

Lewis, H. R., & Lewis, M. E. *Psychosomatics: how emotions can damage your health.* New York: Viking, 1972.

Liddell, H. S. *Emotional hazards in animal and man.* Springfield, Ill.: Thomas, 1956.

Lieberman, B. (Ed.) *Human sexual behavior: a book of readings.* New York: Wiley, 1971.

Liebert, R. M., & Baron, R. A. Some immediate effects of televised violence on children's behavior. *Developmental Psychology,* 1972, **6**(3).

Liebert, R. M., Neale, J. M., & Davidson, E. S. *The early window: effects of television on children and youth.* New York: Pergamon, 1973.

Lindzey, G. and Thiessen, D. D. *Contributions to behavior-genetic analysis: the mouse as a prototype.* New York: Appleton-Century-Crofts, 1970.

Lifton, R. J. *Thought reform and the psychology of totalism.* New York: Norton, 1961.

Lloyd, A. J., & Leibrecht, B. C. Conditioning of a single motor unit. *Journal of Experimental Psychology,* 1971, **88,** 391-395.

Lockard, R. B. Reflections on the fall of comparative psychology: is there a message for us all? *American Psychologist,* 1971, **26**(2), 168-179.

Logan, F. A. Experimental psychology of animal learning and now. *American Psychologist,* 1972, **27**(2), 1055-1062.

Looft, W. R. Egocentrism and social interaction across the life span. *Psychological Bulletin,* 1972, **78,** 73-92.

Lorenz, K. *King Solomon's ring: new light on animal ways.* New York: Crowell, 1952.

Lorenz, K. *Evolution and modification of behavior.* Chicago: U. of Chicago Press, 1965.

Lorenz, K. *On aggression.* New York: Harcourt, 1966.

Lorenz, K. *Studies in animal and human behavior.* Vol. 1. Translated by R. Martin. Cambridge, Mass.: Harvard U.P., 1970.

Love, H. *Youth and the drug problem.* Springfield, Ill.: Thomas, 1971.

Luchins, A. S. Mechanization in problem solving. *Psychological Monographs,* 1942, **54,** No. 248.

Ludmerer, K. M. *Genetics and American society: a historical appraisal.* Baltimore: Johns Hopkins U.P., 1972.

Lugo, J. O., & Hershey, G. L. *Human development.* New York: Macmillan, 1974.

Luh, C. W. The conditions of retention. *Psychological Monographs,* 1922, **31.**

Luria, A. R. *The mind of a mnemonist.* Translated by L. Solotaroff. New York: Basic Books, 1968.

Luria, A. R. The functional organization of the brain. *Scientific American,* 1970, **222,** 66-78.

Luttges, M. W. *Electrophysiological dose-response effects of megimide and strychnine.* Doctoral Dissertation, University of California, Irvine, 1968.

Luttges, M. W., & McGaugh, J. L. Permanence of retrograde amnesia produced by electroconvulsive shock. *Science,* 1967, **156,** 408-410.

Lykken, D. T. The validity of the guilty knowledge technique: the effects of faking. *Journal of Applied Psychology,* 1960, **44,** 258-262.

Lykken, D. T. Psychology and the lie detector industry. *American Psychologist,* 1974, **29,** 725-738.

MacAdams, D. L. (Ed.) *Sources of color science.* Cambridge, Mass.: M.I.T. Press, 1970.

MacCorquodale, K. On Chomsky's review of Skinner's "Verbal behavior." *Journal of the Experimental Analysis of Behavior,* 1970, **13,** 83-99.

Mackworth, N. H. Originality. *American Psychologist,* 1965, **20,** 51-66.

MacLean, P. D. Psychosomatic disease and the "visceral brain." *Psychosomatic Medicine,* 1949, **2,** 338–353.

MacLean, P. D. *Psychosomatics.* In J. Field (Ed.), *Neurophysiology.* Vol. 3. Washington, D.C.: American Physiological Society, 1960.

Macnamara, J. Cognitive basis of language learning in infants. *Psychological Review,* 1972, **79,** 1–13.

Mahoney, M. J., & Thoresen, C. E. (Eds.) *Self-control: power to the person.* Monterey, Calif.: Brooks/Cole, 1974.

Maier, N. R. F. Reasoning in human. II. The solution of a problem and its appearance in consciousness. *Journal of Comparative Psychology,* 1931, **12,** 181–194.

Maliver, B. L. *The encounter game.* New York: Stein and Day, 1973.

Maltzman, I. Thinking: from a behavioristic point of view. *Psychological Review,* 1955, **62,** 275–286.

Mandler, G. Emotion. In R. Brown et al. (Eds.), *New directions in psychology.* New York: Holt, 1962.

Mandler, J. M., & Mandler, G. *Thinking: from association to Gestalt.* New York: Wiley, 1964.

Manosevitz, M., Lindzey, G. and Thiessen, D. D. *Behavioral genetics: method and research.* New York: Appleton-Century-Crofts, 1969.

Manson, W. A. and Kenney, M. D. Redirection of filial attachments in rhesus monkeys: dogs as mother surrogates. *Science,* 1974, *183,* 1209–1211.

Marañon, G. Contribution à l'étude de l'action émotive de l'adrénaline. *Revue Française d'Endocrinologie,* 1924, **2,** 301–325.

Margolin, S. E., & Bunch, M. E. The relationship between age and the strength of hunger motivation. *Comparative Psychological Monographs,* 1940, **16**(4), 1–34.

Marx, M. H. The effects of cumulative training upon retroactive inhibition and transfer. *Comparative Psychology Monographs,* 1944, **18**(2), 1–62.

Marx, M. H. Learning: processes. In M. H. Marx (Ed.), *Learning: processes.* New York: Macmillan, 1969.

Marx, M. H. (Ed.) *Learning: theories.* New York: Macmillan, 1970.

Marx, M. H., & Hillix, W. A. *Systems and theories in psychology.* (2nd Ed.) New York: McGraw-Hill, 1973.

Marx, M. H., & Tombaugh, T. N. *Motivation: psychological principles and educational implications.* San Francisco: Chandler, 1967.

Marx, M. H., & Van Spanckeren, W. J. Control of the audiogenic seizure by the rat. *Journal of Comparative and Physiological Psychology,* 1952, **45,** 170–179.

Marx, M. H., Witter, D. W., & Mueller, J. H. Interaction of sex and training method in human multiple-choice learning. *Journal of Social Psychology,* 1972, **88,** 37–42.

Maselli, M. D., & Altrocchi, J. Attribution of intent. *Psychological Bulletin,* 1969, **71,** 445–454.

Maslow, A. H. *Toward a psychology of being.* Princeton, N.J.: Van Nostrand, 1962.

Maslow, A. H. Fusions of facts and values. *American Journal of Psychoanalysis,* 1963, **23,** 117–131.

Masserman, J. H. Experimental neuroses. *Scientific American,* 1950, **182**(3), 38–43.

Masters, W. H., & Johnson, V. E. *Human sexual response.* Boston: Little, Brown, 1966.

Masters, W. H., & Johnson, V. E. *Human sexual inadequacy.* Boston: Little, Brown, 1970.

Matarazzo, J. D. The interview. In B. B. Wolman (Ed.), *Handbook of clinical psychology.* New York: McGraw-Hill, 1965.

Matin, L., & MacKinnon, G. E. Autokinetic movement: selective manipulation of directional components by image stabilization. *Science,* 1964, **143,** 147–148.

Max, L. W. Experimental study of the motor theory of consciousness. IV. Action current responses in the deaf during awakening, kinesthetic imagery and abstract thinking. *Journal of Comparative Psychology,* 1937, **24,** 301–344.

Mayr, E. The nature of the Darwinian revolution. *Science,* 1972, **176,** 981–989.

McCain, G., & Segal, E. M. *The game of science.* (2nd Ed.) Monterey, Calif.: Brooks/Cole, 1973.

McCall, R. B., Hogarty, P. S., & Hurlburt, N. Transitions in infant sensorimotor development and the prediction of childhood IQ. *American Psychologist,* 1972, **27**(8), 728–748.

McCandless, B. R. *Adolescents: behavior and development.* Hinsdale, Ill.: Dryden Press, 1970.

McClelland, D. C. *The achieving society.* Princeton, N.J.: Van Nostrand, 1961.

McClelland, D. C. Testing for competence rather than for "intelligence." *American Psychologist,* 1973, **28,** 1–14.

McConnell, R. A. ESP research at three levels of method. *Journal of Parapsychology,* 1966, **30**(3), 195–207.

McDougall, W. *An introduction to social psychology.* Boston: John W. Luce, 1923.

McGaugh, J. L. and Herz, M. *Memory consolidation,* San Francisco, Albion, 1971.

McGeoch, J. A., & Irion, A. L. *The psychology of*

human learning. New York: Longmans, Green, 1952.

McGinnies, E. Emotionality and perceptual defense. *Psychological Review,* 1949, **56,** 531-538.

McGrath, J. J. The effect of irrelevant environmental stimulation on vigilance performance. *Dissertation Abstracts,* 1961, **22**(1), 336-337.

McGrew, W. C. *An ethological study of children's behavior.* New York: Academic, 1972.

McGuigan, F. (Ed.) *Thinking: studies of covert language processes.* New York: Appleton, 1966.

McGuigan, F. J., & Schoonover, R. A. (Eds.) *The psychophysiology of thinking.* New York: Academic, 1973.

McGuire, W. J. The nature of attitudes and attitude change. In G. Lindzey & E. Aronson (Eds.), *Handbook of social psychology.* Vol. 3. (Rev. Ed.) Reading, Mass.: Addison-Wesley, 1969.

McTeer, W. *The scope of motivation: environmental, physiological, mental, social.* Monterey, Calif.: Brooks-Cole, 1972.

Mead, M. *Sex and temperament in three primitive societies.* New York: Morrow, 1935.

Meadow, A., & Parnes, S. J. Evaluation of training in creative problem solving. *Journal of Applied Psychology,* 1959, **43,** 189-194.

Meehl, P. Law and the fireside inductions: some reflections of a clinical psychologist. *Journal of Social Issues,* 1971, **27,** 65-100.

Melton, A. W. (Ed.) *Categories of human learning.* New York: Academic, 1964.

Melton, A. W., & Martin, E. (Eds.) *Coding processes in human memory.* New York: V. H. Winston, 1972.

Mendelson, J. H., Kubzansky, P. E., Liederman, P. H., Wexler, D., & Solomon, P. Physiological and psychological aspects of sensory deprivation—a case analysis. In P. Solomon et al. (Eds.), *Sensory deprivation.* Cambridge, Mass.: Harvard U.P., 1961.

Milgram, S. Behavioral study of obedience. *Journal of Abnormal and Social Psychology,* 1963, **67,** 371-378.

Milgram, S. Group pressure and action against a person. *Journal of Abnormal and Social Psychology,* 1964, **69,** 137-143.

Milgram, S. *Obedience to authority.* New York: Harper, 1974.

Miller, D. R., & Swanson, G. E. *Inner conflict and defense.* New York: Holt, 1960.

Miller, G. A., Galanter, E., & Pribram, K. H. *Plans and the structure of behavior.* New York: Holt, 1960.

Miller, G. A. Psychology as a means of promoting human welfare. *American Psychologist,* 1969, **24,** 1063-1075.

Miller, G. A., & Selfridge, J. A. Verbal context and the recall of meaningful material. *American Journal of Psychology,* 1950, **63,** 176-185.

Miller, H. L., & Siegel, P. S. *Loving: a psychological approach.* New York: Wiley, 1972.

Miller, N. E. Experimental studies of conflict. In J. McV. Hunt (Ed.), *Personality and the behavior disorders.* Vol. 1. New York: Ronald, 1944.

Miller, N. E. Studies of fear as an acquirable drive. I. Fear as motivation and fear-reduction as reinforcement in the learning of new responses. *Journal of Experimental Psychology,* 1948, **38,** 89-101.

Miller, N. E. Memory and learning. *Proceedings of the American Philosophical Society,* 1967, **111,** 315-325.

Miller, N., & Campbell, D. T. Recency and primacy in persuasion as a function of the timing of speeches and measurements. *Journal of Abnormal and Social Psychology,* 1959, **59,** 1-9.

Miller, N. E., & Dollard, J. *Social learning and imitation.* New Haven: Yale U.P., 1941.

Miller, N. E. Liberalization of basic S-R concepts: extensions to conflict behavior, motivation, and social learning. In S. Koch (Ed.), *Psychology: a study of a science.* Vol. 2. New York: McGraw-Hill, 1959.

Miller, N. E. Learning of visceral and glandular responses. *Science,* 1969, **163,** 434-445.

Miller, N. E. *Neal E. Miller: Selected papers.* Vol. 1. *Conflict, displacement learned drives and theory.* Vol. 2. *Learning and motivation and their physiological mechanisms.* Chicago: Aldine, 1971.

Miller, R., Ott, C. A., Berk, A. M., & Springer, A. D. Appetitive memory restoration after electroconvulsive shock in the rat. *Journal of Comparative and Physiological Psychology,* 1974, **4,** 717-723.

Minami, H., & Dallenbach, K. M. The effect of activity upon learning and retention in the cockroach, Periplaneta Americana. *American Journal of Psychology,* 1946, **59,** 1-58.

Minuchin, S. Families and family therapy. Cambridge, Mass.: Harvard U.P., 1974.

Mitchell, G. D. Paternalistic behavior in primates. *Psychological Bulletin,* 1969, **71,** 399-417.

Money, J. (Ed.). *Sex research: new developments.* New York: Holt, 1965.

Money, J., & Ehrhardt, A. A. *Man and woman, boy and girl: the differentiation and dimorphism of gender identity from conception to maturity.* Baltimore: Johns Hopkins U.P., 1973.

Moreno, J. L. *Psychodrama.* New York: Beacon House, 1946.

Morris, D. *The naked ape: a zoologist's study of the human animal.* New York: McGraw-Hill, 1967a.

Morris, D. (Ed.) *Primate ethology.* Chicago: Aldine, 1967b.

Morris, D. *Intimate behavior.* New York: Random House, 1971.

Morton, J. T. The distortion of syllogistic reasoning produced by personal convictions. Doctoral dissertation, Northwestern University, 1942.

Moss, C. S. *Hypnosis in perspective.* New York: McGraw-Hill, 1965.

Mowrer, O. H., & Viek, P. An experimental analogue of fear from a sense of helplessness. *Journal of Abnormal and Social Psychology,* 1948, **43,** 193–200.

Moyer, K. E. *The physiology of hostility.* Chicago: Markham, 1971.

Munn, N. L. *Handbook of psychological research on the rat.* Boston: Houghton, 1950.

Murchison, C. (Ed.) *The case for and against psychical belief.* Worcester, Mass.: Clark U.P., 1927.

Murdock, B. B. *Human memory: theory and data.* Potomac, Md.: Lawrence Erlbaum, 1974.

Murray, B. C. Reopening the question. (Review of Hynek's *UFO experience). Science,* 1972, **177,** 688–689.

Murray, H. A. *Thematic apperception test.* Cambridge, Mass.: Harvard U.P., 1943.

Murray, H. A., et al. *Assessment of men.* New York: Rinehart, 1948.

Murray, J. P. Television and violence: implications of the surgeon general's research program. *American Psychologist,* 1973, **28,** 472–478.

Mussen, P. H. Some personality and social factors related to changes in children's attitudes toward Negroes. *Journal of Abnormal and Social Psychology,* 1950, **45,** 423–441.

Myrdal, G. *The Asian drama.* Vol. 1. New York: Pantheon, 1968.

National Institute of Mental Health. *Schizophrenia: is there an answer?* Washington, D.C.: U.S. Government Printing Office, 1972.

Nauta, W. J. H. Hypothalamic regulation of sleep in rats: an experimental study. *Journal of Neurophysiology,* 1946, **9,** 285–316.

Nawas, M. Love: an adventure into the behavior scientist's no-man's land. Unpublished draft, 1969.

Neill, A. S. *"Neill, Neill, orange peel"* New York: Hart, 1972.

Newcomb, T. M. *Personality and social change: attitude formation in a student community.* New York: Dryden, 1943.

Newcomb, T. M. Persistence and regression of changed attitudes: long range studies. *Journal of Social Issues,* 1963, **19,** 3–14.

Newell, A., Shaw, J. C., & Simon, H. A. *The processes of creative thinking.* Santa Monica, Calif.: Rand Corporation, 1958.

Newell, A., & Simon, H. A. *Human problem solving.* Englewood Cliffs, N.J.: Prentice-Hall, 1972.

Newman, E. B. Effect of crowding of material in curves of forgetting. *American Journal of Psychology,* 1939, **52,** 601–609.

Newman, H. H., Freeman, F. N., & Holzinger, K. H. *Twins: a study of heredity and environment.* Chicago: U. of Chicago Press, 1937.

Nichols, J. R. A procedure which produces sustained opiate-directed behavior (morphine addiction) in the rat. *Psychological Reports,* 1963, **13**(3), 895–904.

Nichols, J. R. How opiates change behavior. *Scientific American,* 1965, **212**(2), 80–88.

Nicholson, W. M. The influence of anxiety upon learning: interference or drive increment? *Journal of Personality,* 1958, **25,** 303–319.

Nirenberg, M. W. Will society be prepared? *Science,* 1967, **157,** 633.

Nisbett, R. E., & Schacter, S. The cognitive manipulation of pain. *Journal of Experimental Social Psychology,* 1966, **2,** 227–236.

Norman, D. A. Toward a theory of memory and attention. *Psychological Review,* 1968, **75**(6), 522–536.

Norman, D. A. (Ed.) *Models of human memory.* New York: Academic, 1970.

Ognibene, P. J. Treating heroin addiction. *The New Republic,* December 23 and 30, 1972, 20–23.

Olds, J. Physiological mechanisms of reward. In M. R. Jones (Ed.), *Nebraska symposium on motivation.* Lincoln: U. of Nebraska Press, 1955.

Olds, J., & Milner, P. Positive reinforcement produced by electrical stimulation of septal area and other regions of rat brain. *Journal of Comparative and Physiological Psychology,* 1954, **47,** 419–427.

Olds, J., & Olds, M. Drives, rewards, and the brain. In *New directions in psychology.* New York: Holt, 1965.

O'Leary, K. D., & Drabman, R. Token reinforcement programs in the classroom: a review. *Psychological Bulletin,* 1971, **75**(6), 379–398.

Opler, M. K. Schizophrenia and culture. *Scientific American,* 1957, **197**(2), 103–110.

Osborn, A. F. *Applied imagination* (Rev. Ed.) New York: Scribners, 1957.

Osgood, C. E., Suci, G. J., & Tannenbaum, P. H. *The measurement of meaning.* Urbana: U. of Illinois Press, 1957.

Osgood, C. E. *Alternative to war or surrender.* Urbana: U. of Illinois Press, 1962.

Osgood, C. E. Toward a wedding of insufficiencies. In T. R. Dixon & D. L. Horton (Eds.), *Verbal behavior and general behavior theory.* Englewood Cliffs, N.J.: Prentice-Hall, 1968.

Paivio, A. *Imagery and verbal processes.* New York: Holt, 1971.

Papez, J. W. A proposed mechanism of emotion. *Archives of Neurological Psychiatry,* 1937, **38,** 725-743.

Parnes, S. J., & Meadow, A. *Evaluation of persistence of effects produced by a creative problem-solving course.* Buffalo, N.Y.: Creative Education Foundation, 1960.

Parsons, T. The school class as a social system: some of its functions in American society. *Harvard Educational Review,* 1959, **29,** 297-318.

Paul, G. L., & Bernstein, D. A. *Anxiety and clinical problems: systematic desensitization and related techniques.* Morristown, N.J.: General Learning Press, 1973.

Pavlov, I. P. *Conditioned reflexes.* Translated by G. V. Anrep. London: Oxford U.P., 1927.

Peeke, H. V. and Herz, M. J. Caudate nucleus stimulation retroactively impairs complex maze learning in the rat. *Science,* 1971, **173,** 80-82.

Penrose, L. S., & Penrose, R. Impossible objects: a special type of illusion. *British Journal of Psychology,* 1958, **49,** 31.

Perkins, F. T. Symmetry in visual recall. *American Journal of Psychology,* 1932, **44,** 473-490.

Pessah, M. A., & Roffwarg, H. P. Spontaneous middle ear activity in man: A rapid eye movement sleep phenomenon. *Science,* 1972, **178,** 773-776.

Peters, H. N. Affect and emotion. In M. H. Marx (Ed.), *Theories in contemporary psychology.* New York: Macmillan, 1963.

Peters, H. N., & Jenkins, R. L. *Psychiatric Quarterly,* 1954, **28.**

Peterson, L. R. Short-term verbal memory and learning. *Psychological Review,* 1966, **73,** 193-207.

Peterson, L. R., & Peterson, M. J. Short-term retention of individual verbal items. *Journal of Experimental Psychology,* 1959, **58,** 193-198.

Pfungst, D. *Clever Hans.* New York: Holt, 1965.

Pheiffer, C. H., Eure, S. B., & Hamilton, C. B. Reversing figures and eye movements. *American Journal of Psychology,* 1956, **69,** 452-455.

Phillips, J. L., Jr. *The origins of intellect: Piaget's theory.* San Francisco: Freeman, 1969.

Piaget, J. *Language and thought in the child.* New York: Humanities Press, 1959.

Piaget, J. The genetic approach to the psychology of thought. *Journal of Educational Psychology,* 1961, **52,** 275-281.

Pines, M. *The brain changers.* New York: Harcourt, 1973.

Platt, J. Social traps. *American Psychologist,* 1973, **28,** 641-651.

Plutchik, R. *The emotions: facts, theories and a new model.* New York: Random House, 1962.

Poincairé, H. Mathematical creation. In *The foundations of science.* Translated by G. H. Halsted. New York: Science Press, 1913.

Pool, I., Abelson, R. P., Popkin, S. L. *Candidates, issues and strategies: a computer simulation of the 1960 presidential election.* Cambridge, Mass.: M.I.T. Press, 1964.

Popenoe, J. *Inside Summerhill.* New York: Hart, 1970.

Postman, L. Retention of first-list associations as a function of the conditions of transfer. *Journal of Experimental Psychology,* 1962, **64,** 380-387.

Postman, L. Studies of learning to learn. II. Changes in transfer as a function of practice. *Journal of Verbal Learning and Verbal Behavior,* 1964, **3,** 437-447.

Postman, L. Studies of learning to learn. VI. General transfer effects in three-stage paradigms. *Journal of Verbal Learning and Verbal Behavior,* 1968, **7,** 659-664.

Postman, L. Organization and interference. *Psychological Review,* 1971, **78,** 290-302.

Pratt, C. L., & Sackett, G. P. Selection of social partners as a function of peer contact during rearing. *Science,* 1967, **155,** 1133-1135.

Premack, A. J., & Premack, D. Teaching language to an ape. *Scientific American,* 1972, **227,** 92-99.

Premack, D. Language in chimpanzee? *Science,* 1971, **172,** 808-822.

Pribram, K. H. The biology of mind: Neurobehavioral foundations. In A. R. Gilgen (Ed.), *Contemporary scientific psychology.* New York: Academic, 1970.

Price, W. J., & Bass, L. W. Scientific research and the innovate process. *Science,* 1969, **164,** 802-806.

Pritchard, R. M. A collimator stabilizing system. *Journal of Experimental Psychology,* 1961, **13,** 181-183.

Pritchard, R. M. Visual illusions viewed as stabilized retinal images. *Quarterly Journal of Experimental Psychology*, 1958, **10**, 77-81.

Pronko, N. H. *Panorama of psychology.* (2nd Ed.) Monterey, Calif.: Brooks/Cole, 1973.

Rainwater, L. Crisis of the city: poverty and deprivation. *Washington University Alumni Magazine*, 1968, 17-21.

Ranson, S. W. Somnolence caused by hypothalamic lesions in the monkey. *Archive of Neurology and Psychiatry*, 1939, **41**, 1-23.

Rapoport, A. *Two-person game theory: the essential ideas.* Ann Arbor: U. of Michigan Press, 1966.

Rapoport, A. *The big two, Soviet-American perceptions of foreign policy.* Indianapolis: Pegasus, 1971.

Rapoport, A. *Experimental games and their uses in psychology.* Morristown, N.J.: General Learning Corporation, 1973.

Razran, G. A. A quantitative study of meaning by a conditioned salivary technique (semantic conditioning). *Science*, 1939, **90**, 89-90.

Razran, G. The observable unconscious and inferable conscious in current Soviet psychophysiology: interoceptive conditioning, semantic conditioning, and the orienting reflex. *Psychological Review*, 1961, **68**, 81-147.

Razran, G. The observable unconscious and the inferable conscious in current Soviet psychophysiology. *Psychological Review*, 1961, **68**, 81-147.

Razran, G. Russian physiologists' psychology and American experimental psychology. *Psychological Bulletin*, 1965, **63**(1), 42-64.

Regan, D. *Evoked potentials in psychology: sensory physiology and clinical medicine.* New York: Wiley-Interscience, 1972.

Rheingold, H. L. The effect of environmental stimulation upon social and exploratory behaviour in the human infant. In B. M. Foss (Ed.) *Determinants of infant behaviour.* London: Methuen, 1961.

Rheingold, H. L. The social and socializing infant. In D. A. Goslin (Ed.), *Handbook of socialization theory and research.* New York: Rand McNally, 1969.

Rheingold, H. L. To rear a child. *American Psychologist*, 1973, **28**, 42-46.

Rheingold, H. L., & Eckerman, C. O. The infant separates himself from his mother. *Science*, 1968, **168**, 78-83.

Rhine, J. *Progress in parapsychology.* Durham, N.C.: Parapsychology Press, 1971.

Rice, C. E. Human echo perception. *Science*, 1967, **156**, 656-664.

Riggs, L. A., Ratliff, F., Cornsweet, J. C., & Cornsweet, T. N. The disappearance of steadily fixated visual test objects. *Journal of the Optical Society of America*, 1953, **43**, 495-501.

Robinson, D. N. Therapies: a clear and present danger. *American Psychologist*, 1973, **28**, 129-133.

Robinson, E. S. The "similarity" factor in retroaction. *American Journal of Psychology*, 1927, **39**, 297-312.

Rock, I. *An introduction to perception.* New York: Macmillan, 1975.

Roe, A., & Simpson, G. G. (Eds.) *Behavior and evolution.* New Haven, Conn.: Yale U.P., 1958.

Rogers, C. R. *Client-centered therapy: its current practice, implications and theory.* Boston: Houghton, 1951.

Rogers, C. R. *On becoming a person: a therapist's view of psychotherapy.* (2nd Ed.) Boston: Houghton, 1970.

Rogers, C. R. In retrospect: forty-six years. *American Psychologist*, 1974, **29**, 115-123.

Rogers, C. R., & Skinner, B. F. Some issues concerning the control of human behavior: A symposium. *Science*, 1956, **124**, 1057-1066.

Rogers, K. T. Optokinetic testing of cyclopean and synophthalmic fish hatchlings. *Biological Bulletin*, 1957, **112**, 241-248.

Rokeach, M., & Vidmark, N. Testimony concerning possible jury bias in a black panther murder trial. *Journal of Applied Social Psychology*, 1973, **3**(1), 19-29.

Romanes, G. J. *Animal intelligence.* London: Kegan Paul, 1886.

Rorschach, H. *Psychodiagnostics.* Berne: Hans Huber, 1942.

Rose, R. M., Gordon, T. P., & Bernstein, I. S. Plasma testosterone levels in the male Rhesus: influences of sexual and social stimuli. *Science*, 1972, **178**, 643-645.

Rosenhan, D. L. On being sane in insane places. *Science*, 1973, **179**, 250-258.

Rosenthal, R. *Experimenter effects in behavioral research.* New York: Appleton, 1966.

Rosenthal, R., & Jacobson, L. *Pygmalian in the classroom: teachers' expectation and pupil's intellectual development.* New York: Holt, 1968.

Rosenthal, D. *Genetic theory and abnormal behavior.* New York: McGraw-Hill, 1970.

Rosenzweig, M. R. Biological processes in motivation. In P. Mussen & M. R. Rosenzweig (Eds.), *Psychology: An introduction.* Lexington, Mass.: Heath, 1973.

Ross, L. E. Cognitive factors in conditioning: the

use of masking tasks in eyelid conditioning. In H. H. Kendler & J. T. Spence (Eds.), *Essays in neobehaviorism.* New York: Appleton, 1971.

Rossi, P. H., & Williams, W. (Eds.) *Evaluating social programs: theory, practice, and politics.* New York: Seminar Press, 1972.

Rubin, E. *Syncopleoede figuere.* Kobenhavn: Glydendalske Boghandel, 1915.

Rudin, S. A. The psychology of nations. *Discovery,* 1965, **26,** 22-28.

Rumbaugh, D. M., Gill, T. V., & von Glasersfeld, E. Reading and sentence completion by a chimpanzee. *Science,* 1973, **182,** 731-733.

Sager, C. J., & Kaplan, H. S. (Eds.) *Progress in group and family therapy.* New York: Brunner/Mazel, 1972.

Sanford, F. H. Research on military leadership. In J. C. Flanagan et al. (Eds.), *Psychology in the world emergency.* Pittsburgh: U. of Pittsburgh Press, 1952.

Sarton, G. *A guide to the history of science.* Waltham, Mass.: Chronica Botanica, 1952.

Satir, V. M. *Conjoint family therapy.* Palo Alto, Calif.: Science Behavior Books, 1964.

Sawrey, J. M., & Telford, C. W. *Psychology of adjustment.* (3rd Ed.) Boston: Allyn and Bacon, 1971.

Sawrey, W. L., Conger, J. J., & Turrell, E. S. An experimental investigation of the role of psychological factors in the production of gastric ulcers in rats. *Journal of Comparative and Physiological Psychology,* 1956, **49,** 457-461.

Sawrey, W. L., & Weisz, J. D. An experimental method of producing gastric ulcers. *Journal of Comparative and Physiological Psychology,* 1956, **49,** 269-270.

Scarr-Salapatek, S. Race, social class and IQ. *Science,* 1971a, **174,** 1285-1295.

Scarr-Salapatek, S. Unknowns in the IQ equation. *Science,* 1971b, **174,** 1223-1228.

Schachter, S. *The psychology of affiliation.* Stanford, Calif.: Stanford U.P., 1959.

Schachter, S. Birth order and sociometric choice. *Journal of Abnormal and Social Psychology,* 1964, **68,** 453-456.

Schachter, S. Cognitive effects on bodily functioning: Studies of obesity and eating. In D. C. Glass (Ed.), *Neurophysiology and emotion.* New York: Rockefeller U.P., 1967.

Schachter, S. *Emotion, obesity, and crime.* New York: Academic, 1971.

Schachter, S. Some extraordinary facts about obese humans and rats. *American Psychologist,* 1971, **26,** 129-144.

Schachter, S., and Latane, B. Crime, cognition and the autonomic nervous system. In D. Levine (Ed.), *Nebraska Symposium on Motivation.* Lincoln: U. of Nebraska Press, 1964, pp. 221-275.

Schachter, S., & Rodin, J. *Obese humans and rats.* Potomac, Md.: Lawrence Erlbaum, 1974.

Schachter, S., & Singer, J. E. Cognitive, social and physiological determinants of emotional state. *Psychological Review,* 1962, **69,** 379-399.

Schachter, S., and Wheeler, L. Epinephrine, chlorpromazine, and amusement. *Journal of Abnormal and Social Psychology,* 1962, **65,** 121-128.

Schaffer, H. R., & Emerson, P. E. The development of social attachments in infancy. *Monograph Society Research in Child Development,* 1964, **29**(3), 1-77.

Schaie, K. W. (Ed.). *Theory and methods of research on aging.* Morgantown: West Virginia U.P., 1968.

Schein, E. H., Schneier, I., & Barker, C. H. *Coercive persuasion.* New York: Norton, 1961.

Schelling, T. The ecology of micromotives. *Public Interest,* 1971, No. 25, 61-98.

Schildkraut, J. J., & Kety, S. S. *Biogenic amines and emotion. Science,* 1967, **156,** 21-30.

Schlaer, R. An eagle's eye: quality of the retinal image. *Science,* 1972, **176,** 920-922.

Schmaltz, L. W. (Ed.) *Scientific psychology and social concern.* New York: Harper, 1971.

Schmeck, H. M. Life crises common from 30 to 40. *St. Louis Post-Dispatch,* December 3, 1972.

Schwartz, A. G., Cook, P. R., & Harris, H. Correction of a genetic defect in a mammalian cell. *Nature New Biology,* 1971, **230,** 5-7.

Schwartz, E. Bau und Funktzion der Seitenlinie des Stresfenhechtlings (*Aplocheilus lineatus* Cuv. u. Val.). *Z. vergl. Physiol.,* 1965, **50,** 55-87.

Schwartz, G. E. Biofeedback as therapy: some theoretical and practical issues. *American Psychologist,* 1973, **28,** 666-673.

Schwartz, G. E., & Higgins, J. D. Cardiac activity preparatory to overt and covert behavior. *Science,* 1971, **173,** 1144-1145.

Scott, J. P. The process of primary socialization in canine and human infants. *Monograph Social Research in Child Development,* 1963, **28,** 1-47.

Sears, R. R., Macoby, E. E. & Levin, M. *Patterns of child rearing.* Evanston, Ill.: Row, Peterson, 1957.

Segal, S. J. *Imagery: current cognitive approaches.* New York: Academic, 1973.

Seligman, M. E. P., & Hager, J. L. (Eds.) *Biological boundaries of learning.* New York: Appleton, 1972.

Selye, H. *The stress of life.* New York: McGraw-Hill, 1956.

Severin, F. T. *Third force psychology: a humanistic orientation of the study of man.* New York: McGraw-Hill, 1971.

Shagass, C. *Evoked brain potentials in psychiatry.* New York: Plenum, 1972.

Shaw, W. A. The relation of muscular action potentials to imaginal weight lifting. *Archives of Psychology,* 1940, **247.**

Sheehan, P. W. *The function and nature of imagery.* New York: Academic, 1972.

Sheffield, F. D., Wulff, J. J., & Barker, R. Reward value of copulation without sex drive reduction. *Journal of Comparative Physiological Psychology,* 1951, **44,** 3–8.

Sheldon, W. H. *Atlas of men: a guide for somatotyping the adult male at all ages.* New York: Harper, 1954.

Sherif, M. Group influences upon the formation of norms and attitudes. In T. M. Newcomb & E. L. Hartley (Eds.), *Readings in social psychology.* New York: Holt, 1947.

Sherif, M. Experiments in group conflict. *Scientific American,* 1956, **195**(5), 54–58.

Sherif, M. Group influences upon formation of norms and attitudes. In E. E. Maccoby, T. M. Newcomb, & E. L. Hartley (Eds.), *Readings in social psychology.* (3rd Ed.) New York: Holt, 1958.

Sherman, M. C., & Sherman, I. C. *The process of human behavior.* New York: Norton, 1929.

Sherman, M., & Thomas, R. H. *Hollow folk.* New York: Crowell, 1933.

Shevrin, H., & Fritzler, D. E. Visual evoked response correlates of unconscious mental processes. *Science,* 1968, **161,** 295–298.

Sidman, M. Avoidance conditioning with brief shock and no exteroceptive warning signal. *Science,* 1953, **118,** 157–158.

Sidman, M. *Tactics of scientific research.* New York: Basic Books, 1960.

Siegel, A. E. Can we await a consensus? (Review of S. Feshbach & R. D. Singer, Television and aggression: an experimental field study.) *Contemporary Psychology,* 1973, **18,** 60–61.

Siegel, S. *Nonparametric statistics for the behavioral sciences.* New York: McGraw-Hill, 1956.

Sigel, I. E. How intelligence tests limit understanding of intelligence. *Merrill-Palmer Quarterly of Behavior and Development,* 1963, **9,** 39–56.

Simon, H. A. *The sciences of the artificial.* Cambridge, Mass.: M.I.T. Press, 1969.

Simon, H. A., & Newell, A. Human problem solving: the state of the theory in 1970. *American Psychologist,* 1971, **26,** 145–159.

Singer, J. L. *The child's world of make-believe: experimental studies of imaginative play.* New York: Academic, 1973.

Singer, J. L. *Imagery and daydream: methods in psychotherapy and behavior modification.* New York: Academic, 1974.

Singh, D. Preference for bar pressing to obtain reward over freeloading in rats and children. *Journal of Comparative and Physiological Psychology,* 1970, **73,** 320–327.

Skaggs, E. B. Further studies in retroactive inhibition. *Psychological Monographs,* 1925, **34**(8), 1–60.

Skeels, H. M., & Dye, H. B. A study of the effects of differential stimulation on mentally retarded children. *Procedures of the American Association for Mental Deficiencies,* 1939, **44,** 114–136.

Skinner, B. F. *The behavior of organisms.* New York: Appleton, 1938.

Skinner, B. F. "Superstition" in the pigeon. *Journal of Experimental Psychology,* 1948, **38,** 168–172.

Skinner, B. F. *Walden two.* New York: Macmillan, 1948.

Skinner, B. F. *Science and human behavior.* New York: Macmillan, 1953.

Skinner, B. F. A case history in scientific method. *American Psychologist,* 1956, **11,** 221–233.

Skinner, B. F. The experimental analysis of behavior. *American Scientist,* 1957, **45,** 343–371.

Skinner, B. F. *Verbal behavior.* New York: Appleton, 1957.

Skinner, B. F. Pigeons in a pelican. *American Psychologist,* 1960, **15,** 28–37.

Skinner, B. F. *The technology of teaching.* New York: Appleton, 1968.

Skinner, B. F. *Beyond freedom and dignity.* New York: Knopf, 1971.

Skinner, B. F. *Cumulative record.* (3rd Ed.) New York: Appleton, 1972.

Skinner, B. F. *About behaviorism.* New York: Knopf, 1974.

Skinner, B. F. The steep and thorny way to a science of behavior. *American Psychologist,* 1975, **30,** 42–49.

Skinner, B. F., & Ferster, C. B. *Schedules of reinforcement.* New York: Appleton, 1957.

Slavson, S. R. Group psychotherapy. *Scientific American,* 1950, **183**(6), 42–45.

Slobin, D. I. *Psycholinguistics.* Glenview, Ill.: Scott, Foresman, 1971.

Slobin, D. I. (Ed.) *The ontogenesis of grammar: a theoretical symposium.* New York: Academic, 1971.

Smith, A. G. Jupiter: the radio-active planet. *American Scientist,* 1969, **57**, 177–192.

Smith, L. T. The interanimal transfer phenomenon: a review. *Psychological Bulletin,* 1974, **81**, 1078–1095.

Smith, M. B. Is psychology relevant to new priorities? *American Psychologist,* 1973, **28**, 463–471.

Smith, E. E. Choice reaction time: an analysis of the major theoretical positions. *Psychological Bulletin,* 1968, **69**(2), 77–110.

Smith, F., & Miller, G. A. (Eds.) *The genesis of language.* Cambridge, Mass.: M.I.T. Press, 1966.

Smith, L. T., DeVietti, T. L., & Gaines, R. D. Positive inter-animal transfer with a control for arousal. *Psychological Reports,* 1973, **33**, 495–505.

Smith, S., Brown, H., Toman, J., & Goodman, L. The lack of cerebral effects of d-tubocurarine. *Anesthesiology,* 1947, **8**, 1–14.

Soal, S. G. On "Science and the supernatural." *Science,* 1956, **123**, 9–11.

Solomon, R. L., Turner, L. H., & Lessac, M. S. Some effects of delay of punishment on resistance to temptation in dogs. *Journal of Personality and Social Psychology,* 1968, **8**, 233–238.

Sontag, T., & Kagan, J. The emergence of intellectual-achievement motives. *American Journal of Orthopsychiatry,* 1967, **37**, 8–21.

Spearman, C. *The nature of intelligence and the principles of cognition.* London: Macmillan, 1923.

Spelt, D. K. The conditioning of the human fetus in utero. *Journal of Experimental Psychology,* 1948, **38**, 338–346.

Spence, K. W. The differential response in animals to stimuli varying within a single dimension. *Psychological Review,* 1937, **44**, 430–444.

Spence, K. W. *Behavior theory and conditioning.* New Haven, Conn.: Yale U.P., 1956.

Spence, K. W. *Behavior theory and learning.* Englewood Cliffs, N.J.: Prentice-Hall, 1960.

Spence, K. W. Cognitive and drive factors in the extinction of the conditioned eye blink in human subjects. *Psychological Review,* 1966, **73**, 445–458.

Sperry, R. W. Hemisphere deconnection and unity in conscious awareness. *American Psychologist,* 1968, **23**, 723–733.

Sperry, R. W. A modified concept of consciousness. *Psychological Review,* 1969, **76**, 532–536.

Sperry, R. W. An objective approach to subjective experience: further explanation of a hypothesis. *Psychological Review,* 1970, **77**, 585–590.

Spielberger, C. D. The role of awareness in verbal conditioning. In C. W. Eriksen (Ed.), *Behavior and awareness: a symposium of research and interpretation.* Durham, N.C.: Duke U.P., 1962.

Spielberger, C. D. Theoretical and epistemological issues in verbal conditioning. In S. Rosenberg (Ed.), *Directions in psycholinguistics.* New York: Macmillan, 1965.

Spielberger, C. D., & DeNike, L. D. Descriptive behaviorism versus cognitive theory in verbal operant conditioning. *Psychological Review,* 1966, **73**, 306–326.

Spinetta, J. J., & Rigler, D. The child-abusing parent: a psychological review. *Psychological Bulletin,* 1972, **77**(4), 296–304.

Spiro, M. E. *Children of the kibbutz.* Cambridge, Mass.: Harvard U.P., 1958.

Spitz, R. A. Hospitalism: an inquiry into the genesis of psychiatric conditions in early childhood. *Psychoanalytic Study of the Child,* 1945, **1**, 53–74.

Spragg, S. D. S. Morphine addiction in chimpanzees. *Comparative Psychology Monographs,* 1940, **15**, No. 7.

Spuhler, J. N. (Ed.) *Genetic diversity and human behavior.* Chicago: Aldine, 1967.

Stachnik, T. J. The case against criminal penalties for illicit drug use. *American Psychologist,* 1972, **27**(7), 637–642.

Staddon, J. E. R., & Simmelhag, V. L. The "superstition" experiment: a reexamination of its implications for the principles of adaptive behavior. *Psychological Review,* 1971, **78**, 3–43.

Standen, A. *Science is a sacred cow.* New York: Dutton, 1950.

Stanley, J. C. Predicting college success of the educationally disadvantaged. *Science,* 1971, **171**, 640–647.

Staples, F. R., & Walters, R. H. Anxiety, birth order, and susceptibility to social influence. *Journal of Abnormal and Social Psychology,* 1961, **62**, 716–719.

Stebbins, W. C. (Ed.). *Animal psychophysics.* New York: Appleton, 1970.

Steiner, I. D. *Group process and productivity.* New York: Academic, 1972.

Stent, G. S. That was the molecular biology. *Science,* 1968, **160**, 390–395.

Stent, G. S. *Molecular genetics.* San Francisco: Freeman, 1971.

Stephenson, W. *The study of behavior.* Chicago: University of Chicago Press, 1953.

Sternberg, S. High speed scanning in human memory. *Science,* 1966, **153**, 625–654.

Stevens, S. S. Psychology and the science of science. *Psychological Bulletin,* 1939, **36**, 221–263.

Stevens, S. S. The surprising simplicity of sensory metrics. *American Psychologist,* 1962, **17**(1), 29–30.

Stockard, C. R. The development of artificially produced cyclopean fish—"the magnesium embryo." *Journal of Experimental Zoology,* 1909, **6**, 285–337.

Storms, M. D., & Nisbett, R. E. Insomnia and the attribution process. *Journal of Personality and Social Psychology,* 1970, **16**, 319–328.

Stott, L. H., & Ball, R. S. Infant and preschool mental tests: review and evaluation. *Monographs of the Society for Research in Child Development,* 1965, **30**(3), 2–151.

Stratton, G. M. Vision without inversion of the retinal image. *Psychological Review,* 1897, **4**, 341–360, 463–481.

Suga, N., & Schlegel, P. Neural attenuation of responses to emitted sounds in echolocation bats. *Science,* 1972, **177**, 82–84.

Supa, M., Cotzin, M., & Dallenbach, K. M. "Facial vision": the perception of obstacles by the blind. *American Journal of Psychology,* 1944, **57**, 133–183.

Szasz, T. *The second sin.* Garden City, N.Y.: Anchor, 1973.

Taffel, C. Anxiety and the conditioning of verbal behavior. *Journal of Abnormal and Social Psychology,* 1955, **51**, 496–501.

Tajfel, H. Experiments in intergroup discrimination. *Scientific American,* 1970, **223**(5), 96–102.

Tannenbaum, P. H. The congruity principle revisited: studies in the reduction, induction, and generalization of persuasion. In L. Berkowitz (Ed.), *Advances in experimental social psychology.* Vol. 3. New York: Academic, 1967.

Tanner, J. M. Earlier maturation in man. *Scientific American,* 1968, **218**(1), 21–27.

Tart, C. T. (Ed.) *Altered states of consciousness: a book of readings.* New York: Wiley, 1969.

Tart, C. T. States of consciousness and state-specific sciences. *Science,* 1972, **176**, 1203–1210.

Taylor, D. W., Berry, P. C., & Block, C. H. Does group participation when using brainstorming facilitate or inhibit creative thinking? *Administrative Science Quarterly,* 1958, **3**, 23–47.

Taylor, J. A. A personality scale of manifest anxiety. *Journal of Abnormal and Social Psychology,* 1953, **49**, 285–290.

Terman, L. M., & Merrill, M. A. *Measuring intelligence.* Boston: Houghton, 1937.

Terrace, H. S. Stimulus control. In W. F. Honig (Ed.), *Operant behavior: areas of research and application.* New York: Appleton, 1966.

Teyler, T. J. (Ed.) *Altered states of awareness: readings from Scientific American.* San Francisco: Freeman, 1972.

Tharp, R. G., & Wetzel, R. J. *Behavior modification in the natural environment.* New York: Academic, 1969.

Thigpen, C. H., & Cleckley, H. M. A case of multiple personality. *Journal of Abnormal and Social Psychology,* 1954, **49**, 135–151.

Thigpen, C. H., & Cleckley, H. M. *The three faces of Eve.* New York: McGraw-Hill, 1957.

Thomas, A., Chess, S., & Birch, H. G. The origin of personality. *Scientific American,* 1970, **223**(2), 102–109.

Thompson, R. F. *Introduction to biopsychology.* San Francisco: Albion, 1973.

Thompson, W. R., & Melzack, R. Early environment. *Scientific American,* 1956, **194**(1), 38–42.

Thorndike, E. L. *Animal intelligence.* New York: Macmillan, 1882.

Thorndike, E. L. *Human learning.* New York: Century, 1931.

Thorndike, E. L. *Adult interests.* New York: Macmillan, 1935.

Thorndike, E. L. *Selected writings from a connectionist's psychology.* New York: Appleton, 1949.

Thorndike, E. L., & Woodworth, R. S. The influence of improvement in one mental function upon the efficiency of other functions. I and II. The estimation of magnitudes; III. Functions involving attention, observation and discrimination. *Psychological Review,* 1901, **8**, 247–261, 384–395, 553–564.

Thurstone, L. L., & Thurstone, T. G. *SRA primary mental abilities. Intermediate—ages 11–17.* Chicago: Science Research Associates, 1947.

Tiger, L., & Fox, R. *The imperial animal.* New York: Holt, 1971.

Tinbergen, N. *The study of instinct.* Oxford: Clarendon, 1951.

Tinbergen, N. The curious behavior of the stickleback. *Scientific American,* 1952, **187**, 22–26.

Tinbergen, N. *The animal in its world: field studies.* Vol. 1. Cambridge, Mass.: Harvard U.P., 1972.

Titchener, E. B. The postulates of a structural psychology. *Philosophical Review*, 1898, **7**, 449-465.

Titchener, E. B. *Textbook of psychology*. New York: Macmillan, 1910.

Toch, H. H. *Violent men*. Chicago: Aldine, 1969.

Toffler, A. *Future shock*. New York: Random House, 1970.

Tolman, E. C. *Purposive behavior in animals and man*. New York: Appleton, 1932.

Tolman, E. C. *Collected papers in psychology*. Berkeley: U. of California Press, 1951.

Tolman, E. C., & Honzik, C. H. "Insight" in rats. *University of California Publications in Psychology*, 1930, **4**, 215-232.

Tomkins, S. S., & Messick, S. (Eds.) *Computer simulation of personality*. New York: Wiley, 1963.

Tomkins, S. S. *Affects, imagery, consciousness*. Vol. 1. *The positive affects;* Vol. 2. *The negative affects*. New York: Springer, Vol. 1, 1962; Vol. 2, 1963.

Trapp, E. P., & Himelstein, P. *Readings on the exceptional child: research and theory*. New York: Appleton, 1962.

Tuckman, J., & Regan, R. A. Ordinal position and behavior problems in children. *Journal of Health and Social Behavior*, 1967, **8**, 32-39.

Tulving, E., & Donaldson, W. (Eds.) *Organization of memory*. New York: Academic, 1972.

Turnbull, C. M. *The mountain people*. New York: Simon & Schuster, 1972.

Turner, M. *Philosophy and the science of behavior*. New York: Appleton, 1967.

Tversky, A., & Kahneman, D. Judgment under uncertainty: heuristics and biases. *Science*, 1974, **185**, 1124-1131.

Uleman, J. S. Generalized verbal conditioning: some motivational and retrospective awareness effects. *Journal of Experimental Research in Personality*, 1971, **5**, 268-277.

Ulrich, R. E., Stachnik, T. J., & Mabrey, J. H. (Eds.) *Control of human behavior*. Glenview, Ill.: Scott, Foresman, 1968.

Underwood, B. J., & Schulz, R. W. *Meaningfulness and verbal learning*. Philadelphia: Lippincott, 1960.

Uttal, W. R. (Ed.) Sensory coding: selected readings. Boston: Little, Brown, 1972.

Vale, J. R. Role of behavior genetics in psychology. *American Psychologist*, 1973, **28**, 871-882.

Valenstein, E. S. *Brain control: a critical examination of brain stimulation and psychosurgery*. New York: Wiley-Interscience, 1973.

Valentine, C. W. The innate bases of fear. *Journal of Genetic Psychology*, 1930, **37**, 394-420.

Valentine, W. L., & Wickens, D. D. *Experimental foundations of general psychology*. (3rd Ed.) New York: Holt, 1949.

Vallance, T. R. Social science and social policy: amoral methodology in a matrix of values. *American Psychologist*, 1972, **27**(2), 107-113.

Vandenberg, S. G. The nature and nurture of intelligence. In D. C. Glass (Ed.), *Genetics*. New York: Rockefeller U.P. and Russell Sage Foundation, 1968.

Varela, J. A. *Psychological solutions to social problems: an introduction to social technology*. New York: Academic, 1971.

Verhave, T. The pigeon as quality control inspector. *American Psychologist*, 1966, **21**(2), 109-115.

Vetter, B. M. Studies differ on women's self perceptions. *APA Monitor*, January, 1973, **4**(1).

Vidulich, R. N., & Kaiman, I. P. The effects of information source status and dogmatism upon conformity behavior. *Journal of Abnormal and Social Psychology*, 1961, **62**, 639-642.

Vinacke, W. E. Variables in experimental games: toward a field theory. *Psychological Bulletin*, 1969, **71**(4), 293-318.

Voeks, V. W. Acquisition of S-R connections: a test of Hull's and Guthrie's theories. *Journal of Experimental Psychology*, 1954, **47**, 137-147.

Voyat, G. IQ: God-given or man-made? *Saturday Review*, May 17, 1969, 73-75, 86-87.

Walker, R. N. Body build and behavior in young children. I. Body build and nursery school teachers' ratings. *Monographs of the Society for Research in Child Development*, 1962, **27**(84).

Wallace, R. K., & Benson, H. The physiology of medication. *Scientific American*, 1972, **226**(2), 84-90.

Wallace, W. P. Review of the historical, empirical, and theoretical status of the von Restorff phenomenon. *Psychological Bulletin*, 1965, **63**(6), 410-424.

Wallace, W. P. Consistency of emission order in free recall. *Journal of Verbal Learning and Verbal Behavior*, 1970, **9**, 58-68.

Walster, E. The effect of self-esteem on romantic liking. *Journal of Experimental Social Psychology*, 1965, **1**, 184-197.

Walster, E. Assignment of responsibility for an accident. *Journal of Personality and Social Psychology*, 1966, **3**, 73-79.

Walter, W. G. *The living brain*. New York: Norton, 1953.

Ward, L. B. Reminiscence and role learning. *Psychology Monograph*, 1937, **49**(220).

Warren, N. Malnutrition and mental development. *Psychological Bulletin*, 1973, **80**, 324–328.

Warren, R. M., & Warren, R. P. Auditory illusions and confusions. *Scientific American*, 1970, **223**(6), 30–36.

Wason, P. C. Regression in reasoning? *British Journal of Psychology*, 1969, **60**, 471–480.

Wason, P. C., & Johnson-Laird, P. N. *Psychology of reasoning: structure and content.* Cambridge, Mass.: Harvard U.P., 1972.

Watson, J. *Double helix.* New York: Atheneum, 1968.

Watson, J. B. Psychology as the behaviorist views it. *Psychological Review*, 1913, **20**, 158–177.

Watson, J. B. *Psychology from the standpoint of a behaviorist.* (3rd Ed.) Philadelphia: Lippincott, 1929.

Watson, J. B. Experimental studies on the growth of the emotions. In C. Murchison (Ed.), *Psychologies of 1925.* Worcester, Mass.: Clark U.P., 1926.

Watson, J. B. *J. B. Watson.* In C. Murchison (Ed.), *A history of psychology in autobiography.* Vol. 3. Worcester, Mass.: Clark U.P., 1936.

Watson, J. B., & McDougall, E. *The battle of behaviorism.* New York: Norton, 1929.

Watson, J. B., & Rayner, R. Conditioned emotional reactions. *Journal of Experimental Psychology*, 1920, **3**, 1–14.

Watson, R. I. *The great psychologists from Aristotle to Freud.* (2nd Ed.) Philadelphia: Lippincott, 1971.

Watts, A. W. *On the taboo against knowing who you are.* New York: Collier, 1967.

Webb, B. *Sleep: an experimental approach.* New York: Macmillan, 1968.

Weil-Malherbe, H., and Szara, S. I. *The biochemistry of functional and experimental psychoses.* Springfield, Ill.: Thomas, 1971.

Weiner, B., & Reed, H. Effects of the instructional sets to remember and to forget on short-term retention: studies of rehearsal and control and retrieval inhibition (repression). *Journal of Experimental Psychology*, 1969, **79**, 226–232.

Weiss, A. P. Relation between structural and behavior psychology. *Psychological Review*, 1917, **34**, 301–317.

Wertheimer, M. Experimentelle Studien uber das Sehen von Bewegungen. *Z. Psychol.*, 1912, **61**, 161–265.

Wertheimer, M. *Productive thinking.* New York: Harper, 1945.

Wever, E. G., & Bray, C. W. Present possibilities for auditory theory. *Psychological Review*, 1930, **37**, 365–380.

Wheeler, H. (Ed.) *Beyond the punitive society.* San Francisco, Calif.: W. H. Freeman, 1973.

White, R. K. *Nobody wanted war: misperception in Vietnam and other wars.* Garden City, N.Y.: Doubleday, 1968.

White, R. W. Motivation reconsidered: the concept of competence. *Psychological Review*, 1959, **66**, 297–333.

Whorf, B. L. *Language, thought, and reality.* Cambridge, Mass.: M.I.T. Press, 1956.

Wickens, D. D. Encoding categories of words: an empirical approach to meaning. *Psychological Review*, 1970, **77**, 1–15.

Wickler, W. *Mimicry in plants and animals.* Translated by R. D. Martin. New York: McGraw-Hill, 1968.

Wickler, W. *The sexual code: the social behavior of animals and men.* Garden City, N.Y.: Doubleday, 1972.

Wilder, R. L. The role of intuition. *Science*, 1969, **156**, 605–610.

Williams, R. J. *Biochemical individuality.* New York: Wiley, 1956.

Williams, R. L. Scientific racism and IQ: the silent mugging of the black community. *Psychology Today*, May, 1974, 32–41, 101.

Wiltschko, W., & Wiltschko, R. Magnetic compass of European birds. *Science*, 1972, **176**, 62–64.

Winnik, H. Z., Moses, R., & Ostow, M. (Eds.) *Psychological bases of war.* New York: Academic, 1973.

Wise, F. *Youth and drugs.* New York: Association Press, 1971.

Witkin, H. A., Dyk, R. B., Faterson, H., Goodenough, D. R., & Karp, S. A. *Psychological differentiation.* New York: Wiley, 1962.

Wittenberg, E. G. (Ed.) *Interpersonal explorations in psychoanalysis.* New York: Basic Books, 1974.

Wittreich, W. J. The honi phenomena. *Journal of Abnormal and Social Psychology*, 1952, **64**, 418–424.

Wittreich, W. J. Visual perception and personality. 1959, **200**(4), 56–60.

Wolff, P. H. Observations on newborn infants. *Psychosomatic Medicine*, 1959, **21**, 110–118.

Wolman, B. J. (Ed.) *Handbook of general psychology.* Englewood Cliffs, N.J.: Prentice-Hall, 1973.

Wood, G. Mnemonic systems in recalls. *Journal of Educational Psychology Monograph*, 1967, **6**, Pt. 2, 1–27.

Woodward, A. E., Jr., & Bjork, R. A. The effect of forget instructions on recall of forget items. *Journal of Experimental Psychology*, 1971, **89**, 109–116.

Woodworth, R. S. *Dynamic psychology.* New York: Columbia U.P., 1918.

Woodworth, R. S. Reenforcement of perception. *American Journal of Psychology*, 1947, **60**, 119–124.

Woodworth, R. S. *Dynamics of behavior.* New York: Holt, 1958.

Wooldridge, D. E. *The machinery of the brain.* New York: McGraw-Hill, 1963.

Wooldridge, D. E. *Mechanical man: the physical basis of intelligent life.* New York: McGraw-Hill, 1968.

Worchel, P., & Dallenbach, K. M. "Facial vision": perception of obstacles by the deaf-blind. *American Journal of Psychology*, 1947, **60**, 502–553.

Worden, F. G. Attention and auditory electrophysiology. In E. Stellar & J. M. Sprague (Eds.), *Progress in physiological psychology.* Vol. 1. New York: Academic, 1966.

Wright, H. F. Observational child study. In P. H. Mussen (Ed.), *Handbook of research methods in child development.* New York: Wiley, 1960.

Wulff, F. Uber die Veranderung von Vorstellungen. *Psychologische Forschung*, 1922, **1**, 333–373.

Wundt, W. *Principles of physiological psychology* (Vols. 1–10). New York: Macmillan, 1904.

Wyckoff, L. B., Jr. The role of observing responses in discrimination learning. *Psychological Review*, 1952, **59**, 431–442.

Wylie, H. H. An experimental study of transfer of response in the white rat. *Behavior Monograph*, 1919, No. 16.

Yalom, I. D. *The theory and practice of group psychotherapy.* New York: Basic Books, 1970.

Yarrow, L. J. Research in dimensions of early maternal care. *Merrill-Palmer Quarterly*, 1963, **9**, 101–114.

Yaryan, R. B., & Festinger, L. Preparatory action and belief in the probable occurrence of future events. *Journal of Abnormal and Social Psychology*, 1961, **63**, 603–606.

Yates, F. A. *The art of memory.* Chicago: U. of Chicago Press, 1966.

Zajonc, R. B. Social facilitation. *Science*, 1965, **149**, 269–274.

Zajonc, R. B. Attitudinal effects of mere exposure. *Journal of Personality and Social Psychology*, 1968, *8*.

Zajonc, R. B. *Animal social behavior.* Morristown, N.J.: General Learning Press, 1972.

Zigler, E. Developmental versus difference theories of mental retardation and the problem of motivation. *American Journal of Mental Deficiency*, 1969, **73**(4).

Zimbardo, P. G., et al. Control of pain motivation by cognitive dissonance. *Science*, 1966, **151**(3707), 217–219.

Zimbardo, P. G. *The cognitive control of motivation: the consequences of choice and dissonance.* Glenview, Ill.: Scott, Foresman, 1969.

Zimbardo, P. G. The human choice: individuation, reason, and order versus deindividuation, impulse, and chaos. *Nebraska Symposium on Motivation, 1969*, **18**, 237–307.

Zingg, R. M. Feral man and extreme cases of social isolation. *American Journal of Psychology*, 1940, **53**, 487–517.

Zubek, J. P. *Sensory deprivation: fifteen years of research.* New York: Appleton, 1969.

Zubin, J., Eron, L. D., & Schumer, F. *An experimental approach to projective techniques.* New York: Wiley, 1965.

Zuckerman, M. Physiological measures of sexual arousal in the human. *Psychological Bulletin*, 1971, **75**, 297–329.

Zusman, J., & Davidson, D. L. *Organizing the community to prevent suicide.* Springfield, Ill.: Thomas, 1971.

aboulia Extreme inability to make decisions.

abscissa The horizontal axis of a graph, along which the independent variable (e.g., time or trials, amount of practice) is usually placed.

absolute threshold *See* threshold.

abstract Relating to conceptual categorizing of objects and events, on the basis of their properties, in contrast to real (concrete) representations of them.

accommodation Changing the curvature of the lens in accordance with the distance of seen objects so as to keep them in focus on the retina.

achievement motive Desire for effective utilization of one's ability to cope with the environment.

achievement test A test of what the subject can actually do in some activity or occupational category.

achromatic Without hue.

acoustic reflex Automatic damping response of the ear mechanism to sudden strong stimulation.

acquisition Formation of new habit or knowledge systems, as in learning experiments.

action potential Depolarization of the nerve membrane accompanying the passage of a nerve impulse.

adaptation (1) Generally, adjustment to the environment; (2) sensory change in quality or intensity of a stimulus (e.g., visual adaptation, the adjustment of the eye to the level of light).

adequate stimulus An environmental energy change that is sufficient to activate some sense organ.

adjective checklist A personality rating scale in which the judge simply checks each attribute, from a long list supplied, that he thinks applies to the subject.

adolescence The transition period immediately following puberty during which adjustment to the adult world is made.

affective tone Emotional flavor.

affiliation motive Interest in social associations, identification with a group.

afterimage The subjective experience that immediately follows the withdrawal of a stimulus (e.g., the negative visual afterimage, in which a color complementary to the stimulating color is experienced).

age norms Behavior standards for various ages that are based upon the average performance of subjects of each age category.

age scale A type of intelligence test in which items are arranged in order of difficulty, and credit for passing is assigned in age units.

aggression Attack upon persons or other objects.

alarm reaction Emergency response of the body, mainly involving the autonomic nervous system, in an acute stress situation.

alimentary system Intestinal system, serving the digestive function.

algorithm A set routine designed to find a solution to a problem, as in mathematics or computer programming, by systematic, exhaustive search.

alpha waves The electrical waves typically produced by the brain during the waking state.

amnesia Partial (selective) or total forgetting of experiences, which may either be temporary or permanent.

amniotic sac The membrane that contains both the developing embryo and its life-sustaining fluid (amniotic fluid).

analytical psychology The psychoanalytic system developed by C. G. Jung.

androgen The hormone secreted by male testes.

anorexia   Failure to eat.

anoxia   Absence of oxygen.

anterograde amnesia   Forgetting of or inability to report experiences that occur after some form of trauma, such as severe physical injury or emotional upset.

apical   At the apex, or peak.

appetitive conditioning   A form of learning in which responses that are instrumental in producing some positive incentive (e.g., food, sex object) are strengthened.

applied science   Research and interpretation utilizing scientific methodology and performed in order to obtain information that will be useful in specified ways.

approach–approach conflict   Motivational problem in which only one of two more or less equally desirable behaviors can be performed.

approach–avoidance conflict   Motivational problem in which some strongly desired behavior also entails strong undesirable consequences.

aptitude test   A test of performance designed to indicate the potential of the individual for some particular activity or occupation.

anxiety reaction   An acute form of neurosis in which generalized fear is accompanied by intense symptoms, such as palpitation, sweating, nausea.

archetype   A key concept in Jung's system of psychology; universal symbols that are inherited in the "collective unconscious" and that predispose one to particular experiences and behaviors.

ascending reticular activating system (ARAS)   Part of the reticular formation that screens sensory (afferent) impulses to the cerebral cortex and thereby has an important function in controlling attention and activation of the organism.

associationism   The general view that emphasizes the role of stimulus–response connections, or connections between ideas, in thought and behavior.

associative shifting   A descriptive interpretation of classical conditioning in which the process is viewed as an instance of replacement of an old (unconditioned) stimulus by a new (conditioned) stimulus.

atmosphere effect   The influence on judgment exercised by the context in which the judged object or person appears.

attitude   Set of beliefs and value systems about classes of people, things, or events that is inferred from an individual's spoken and other behavior.

attributes (of concepts)   Dimensions along which objects vary, forming the basis for concepts.

audience effects   Influence of spectators on a performer.

audiogenic seizure   Severe convulsive behavior followed by a comatose (unconscious) period that is readily produced in susceptible rodents by strong, high-pitched, and inescapable sound stimulation.

audiogram   The graphic record of an individual's sensitivity to sound over the entire range of auditory stimulation.

audition   Hearing.

autistic   Revolving around oneself, as in autism, a form of childhood schizophrenia in which the child does not relate normally to its environment.

autokinetic effect   The apparent movement observed in a stationary point of light in a darkened room.

autonomous   Independent, self-determining (as in *autonomous man*).

autonomic nervous system   A division of the central nervous system which services the viscera and mediates emotional responsivity; see also sympathetic and parasympathetic nervous systems, which together comprise the autonomic system.

average error (method of)   A psychophysical technique in which a subject determines the adjustment of the stimulus value.

avoidance–avoidance conflict   A motivational problem in which one of two more or less equally undesirable behaviors must be performed if some other motive is to be satisfied.

avoidance training   A kind of learning in which some instrumental response prevents the occurrence of a noxious stimulus (e.g., electric shock, verbal censure).

bar graph   A representation of numerical values in which columns are drawn vertically to show the extent of particular measures being compared.

basic anxiety   A key concept in Horney's system of psychoanalysis; the feeling of helplessness in a hostile world.

basilar membrane   The structure of the ear, within the cochlear coils, on which are located the specialized hair cells of the organ of corti.

behaviorism   A school (and system) of psychology developed by John B. Watson; the general view that stresses the role of observable (overt) behavior and minimizes mental processes.

behavior modification A therapeutic procedure, mainly developed and utilized by operant (Skinnerian) conditioners, that attempts to resolve behavioral problems by direct modification of the behavioral symptoms themselves rather than any presumed underlying internal processes.

behavior sample A form of personality test in which the subject is given an opportunity to show some actual behavior of the sort involved in the appraisal.

bilateral transfer Learning that is expressed by one side of the body, such as, say, the left hand following training of the other side (the right hand).

binaural stimulation Presentation of auditory stimulation to both ears.

binocular cues Factors that aid in depth perception and that depend on the use of both eyes.

binocular disparity *See* retinal disparity.

blastula An early stage in embryonic development in which the cells are arranged in a hollow sphere.

body language Nonverbal but expressive behavior of an organism (e.g., shrugging or slumping of the shoulders) that plays a quiet but sometimes significant role in social and interpersonal communication.

brainwashing The attempt to change fundamental attitudes and expressed opinions by concentrated forced exposures to the desired attitudes and opinions.

Cannon–Bard theory (of emotion) An interpretation of emotion in which emotional feeling is seen as a function of the dorsal thalamus and emotional expression is attributed to the hypothalamus.

cardiovascular Having to do with the circulatory system (heart and blood vessels).

caste system Rigid social placement dependent upon level of caste into which one is born.

cataract A clouding of the lens in the eye that reduces visual sensitivity.

catatonia A form of schizophrenia in which the main psychotic symptoms are exaggerated posturings.

catharsis Removal ("cleansing") of emotional tension by verbalization ("talking out") or other form of expression; a crucial process in psychoanalytic therapy.

central nervous system The brain and spinal cord.

central organizing motive (COM) Dominating interest that serves to organize and coordinate multiple behaviors.

cerebellum That part of the brain, behind and above the medulla, functioning in the control of body movements in balance and posture.

cerebral cortex The outer layer of the cerebrum, containing successive layers of gray (associative) matter, generally believed to serve in the higher mental functions.

cerebrotonia Hypothesized temperament with emphasis on intellectual functions, correlated with ectomorphic body type in Sheldon's typology.

cerebrum (cerebral hemispheres) Two large masses of brain, serving perceptual and higher mental functions, located above the brainstem.

chemotherapy Chemical treatments of disease or behavior disorder.

childhood Developmental period between infancy and adolescence, roughly from two to twelve years.

chi-square test A type of statistical analysis in which there is a computation of the probability of the obtained distributions of events in ordered categories occurring by "chance" (meaning no real difference among categories).

choice reaction time The time required to respond to one stimulus when presented with two or more stimuli.

chromosome A small stringlike body occurring in pairs in all body cells and carrying the genetic determiners, or genes.

chronological age (CA) The actual biological age of an individual expressed in months and related to his mental age (MA) for purposes of computing his relative intellectual ability, the intelligence quotient (IQ).

circular conditioning A form of learning in which an organism's self-initiated response comes to serve as a stimulus to a repetition of the same response, thus permitting its attachment to a similar response made by another person.

clairvoyance Detection of objects without using the known sensory modalities.

class system Social structure in which birth is not the sole determinant, thus permitting mobility.

classical conditioning A learning process in which an initially ineffective stimulus acquires the power of eliciting a particular response as a function of its being paired with some other stimulus initially capable of eliciting that response.

clinical validation The attempt to verify theories by adducing uncontrolled clinical observations rather than experimental data.

cloning   Asexual reproduction of genetically identical organisms.

closure   The tendency to complete experience, a concept of Gestalt psychology; for example, the visual observation of a complete circle when one with a tiny gap is actually presented.

coaction effects   Influence on behavior by actively participating organisms.

cochlea   The coiled structure in the inner ear that houses the hearing receptors.

cochlear microphonic potential   The electrical energy produced by the cochlea; evidenced by the demonstration that sounds spoken into the external ear of an anesthetized organism can be heard over a loudspeaker hooked up to the cochlea.

coding   The use of familiar items to represent unfamiliar items in memory.

coefficient of correlation   *See* correlation coefficient.

cognition   Knowledge; more specifically, those processes involved in the operation of concepts in thinking and problem solving.

cognitive control   Manipulation of one's own behavior by intellectual processes.

cognitive dissonance   Tension generated by the holding of inconsistent beliefs or cognitions, which may have contradictory implications for action.

cognitive map   (Tolman)   The organized knowledge of objects and events that an organism builds on the basis of experience.

cognitive theory   Any explanatory proposition that stresses the role of symbolic and conceptual processes as determinants of experience and behavior; typically contrasted with conditioning theory as an explanation of learning.

compensation   (psychoanalytic)   The process by which one makes up for a weakness in one function by excelling in some other.

competence   Ability to cope with the environment.

complex indicators   Behavioral cues, such as blushing or long reaction time in a word-association test, that suggest emotional involvement.

compliance   Obedience to instructions and suggestions.

compulsion   A neurotic symptom in which one feels he must carry out some act; associated with obsessions as obsessive-compulsive neurotic reaction in extreme cases.

concept   Category of properties common to a class of objects or events.

concept formation   Discovery of the dimension(s) that identify commonalities in objects. (*Synonym:* concept attainment.)

conceptualization   The use of concepts in thinking and theory construction.

conceptual object   A member of a class of objects having the essential properties that identify some particular concept.

conditioned emotional response (CER)   Emotional behavior that becomes attached to new stimuli as a result of learning.

conditioned reinforcement   The process by which a stimulus becomes a reinforcer (strengthener) for some response by association of the stimulus with a primary reinforcer (reward, such as food). (*Synonym:* secondary reinforcement.)

conditioned response (reflex)   The learned response to a stimulus (conditioned) that did not initially evoke it in classical (Pavlovian) conditioning.

conditioning   An associative or learning process in which new S–R associations are formed; generally separated into classical and operant varieties.

conduction deafness   Hearing deficit associated with a reduction of the efficiency with which sound energy is transmitted within the ear, mainly by the bones of the middle ear.

cone   A specialized receptor, found mainly in the fovea or central part of the retina, that functions in color vision.

confidence level   The degree of trust that one can have in a statistical analysis that the obtained differences are "true"—that is, that they would not occur by chance variations in the data.

conflict   State of contradictory motives, all of which cannot be satisfied.

conformity   The tendency to make oneself like others in the group.

conjunctive concept   A concept in which two or more attributes are jointly present.

connecting fiber   Nerve fiber that links sensory (afferent) and/or motor (efferent) fibers.

connectionism   The associationistic system developed by E. L. Thorndike.

conscious   (Freudian)   Relating to the level of awareness, in which the ego mainly operates.

consciousness   Subjective experience, broadly considered.

conservation   (Piaget)   Concept for an organism's ability to maintain ("conserve") the identity of an object in spite of variations in its appearance (e.g., placing a facial mask on a cat).

consolidation The hypothetical process in which memory traces, considered to be neurophysiological in nature, become stable during the period of time following registration.

conspecific Another organism of the same species.

constancy (*See* perceptual constancies.)

constant stimuli (method of) Psychophysical technique in which the subject is given in random order a set number of stimulus values, half above and half below the presumed threshold.

construct validity (test) Determination of how well a test measures what it purports to measure by means of the degree to which its scores approximate the predictions made by some special theory of personality.

consummatory motive Behavioral process whose objective is satisfaction of motive itself.

context theory of meaning (Titchener) The idea that the meaning of an object resides in the subjective experiences (e.g., images) that occur when it is perceived or imagined.

contiguity The condition of being together, a key concept in the formation of associations.

continuous reinforcement (crf) A program of reinforcement (reward) in which each instrumental response is followed by presentation of an incentive.

control (1) In experimentation, the elimination of unwanted variables (which are then said to be "controlled"); (2) more generally, management of variables, as in the statement that the objective of science is to describe, predict, and *control.*

controlled operant An instrumentally conditioned response whose rate of occurrence is restricted by the necessity of the subject's returning to a point of origin (e.g., a starting chamber in a runway or maze) before making another response.

controlled variable A factor or condition in an experimental observation whose influence has been counteracted.

convergence (social) The tendency of individuals with similar predisposition toward certain motives to assemble in a crowd.

conversion hysteria A form of neurosis in which nonorganic paralysis or anesthesia occurs, presumably as "converted" anxiety.

convoluted Deeply folded (as in the cerebral cortex).

corpus callosum Band of nerve fibers connecting the two cerebral hemispheres.

correlation coefficient A numerical index expressing the degree of correspondence between two sets of paired measures (e.g., the product-moment coefficient, designated r, ranging from zero to a maximum of 1.00, with direction of relationship indicated by $-$ for inverse or $+$ for direct).

counteraggression Personal or other attack made in response to attack.

counterconditioning Replacing an undesirable response with a more desirable but incompatible response to the same stimulus.

covert Hidden, covered, not open to direct observation.

criterion The standard the subject in a signal-detection experiment uses in judging the presence or absence of a signal (stimulus).

criterion of mastery The standard of proficiency that the experimenter establishes in a learning situation in order to measure mastery of the task.

criterion validity Determination of how well a test measures what it purports to measure in terms of the degree of correlation of its scores with some independent and well-established external measure of the same function (the criterion).

cross-sectional technique Use of groups of subjects at different ages to trace the development of some function or structure, in contrast to following the same subjects through the actual development (the longitudinal method).

cultural legacy Patterns of thinking and behavior that are inherited from one's ancestors, via social rather than biological transmission.

cumulative recorder A measuring device used in the free-operant conditioning situation whereby a pen is raised one level by every response and thus traces a cumulative curve of learning on a slowly revolving record.

curiosity motive Desire for information about some aspect of the environment.

cytology The study of cells.

dark adaptation Increase in brightness of seen objects over a period of time during which the retina adjusts to the low level of illumination.

data The results of observation, preferably recorded in numerical form.

decibel The unit of measurement of the physical intensity of sound energy, having a logarithmic relationship to a standard reference value.

decoding (memory) The translation of representational items stored in memory back to the less familiar items originally experienced, in the process of retrieval.

defense mechanism An unconscious way by which one adjusts to life.

delirium tremors An acute psychotic condition associated with chronic alcoholism in which the main symptoms are severe hallucinations and illusions accompanied by uncontrollable tremors, as of the limbs and tongue.

demography Study of the characteristics of populations, especially human ones.

dendrite That part of the neuron that receives the nerve impulse, usually short and highly branched.

denial (psychoanalytic) A defense mechanism in which one refuses to accept what others see as true motives for his behavior.

dependent variable The condition in an experiment that is measured, as a function of the independent (manipulated) variable; in psychology, some aspect of behavior.

desensitization A form of therapy in which the severity of abnormal reactions to particular stimulus situations is reduced by gradual replacement of the negative reactions with more positive ones through conditioning.

determinism The view that all events have causes.

developmental psychology The study of behavior and experience as they emerge in the young organism and change throughout its lifetime.

diagnosis Identification of a disease or disorder from its various signs and symptoms.

dichotomize To categorize into two distinct classes rather than describe on a continuum.

dichromat An individual with color-vision weakness in which either the red-green or the blue-yellow component, usually the former, is affected.

difference limen *See* threshold.

diploid Containing paired chromosomes, characteristic of the normal somatic cell that divides mitotically so as to maintain the paired condition.

discrimination Distinguishing between two or more different stimuli.

discriminative stimulus (S^D) A cue whose presence comes to serve as an occasion for making some response.

disjunctive concept A concept in which either of two or more attributes can be present, but not necessarily jointly.

displaced aggression Attack upon an individual, group, or object other than that which produced the aggression-instigating frustration.

displacement Response to an inappropriate stimulus.

displacement (psychoanalytic) A form of rechanneling of basic (libidinal) energies from socially unacceptable to socially more acceptable behaviors.

dissonance *See* cognitive dissonance.

disuse hypothesis (forgetting) The proposition that forgetting occurs, fundamentally, because of some kind of neurophysiological deterioration of the memory traces (engrams), which normally occurs progressively over long time periods in the absence of practice or rehearsal.

dizygotic twins Twins coming from separate eggs and thus no more closely related than any ordinary sibling. (*Synonym:* fraternal twins.)

DNA (deoxyribonucleic acid) Large molecules in the cell nucleus now believed to be the carriers of genetic inheritance and producers of RNA, implicated in memory.

dominant (genetic) Having the power to suppress the expression of a paired gene (called recessive) when both are present in the organism.

double alternation A discrimination learning problem in which correct performance requires the regularly alternating occurrence of the same choice on two successive trials.

double consciousness Two concurrent streams of subjective experience.

drive Motivation primarily associated with bodily deprivations (e.g., as of food, water, sex activity, air).

dualism Any philosophical view in which both mental and physical events are accepted as real.

duplicity theory The proposition that the visual receptors, the rods and the cones, have different functions; the rods serve for achromatic perception mainly under low illumination levels and for the perception of movement; the cones function for color perception and for fine details.

dynamic psychology Any psychology that stresses motivation; in particular, psychoanalysis.

echolocation Locating objects by perceiving the return of sound waves, especially cultivated by blind organisms (e.g., blind humans by special training, bats naturally).

eclectic Bringing in a variety of techniques and/or theories, regardless of their source or systematic status.

ectoderm The outer germ layer in the embryo, from which the skin, the sense organs, and the nervous system develop.

ectomorph An individual characterized by slenderness of build and sensitivity of personality in Sheldon's typology.

effector A muscle or gland activated by motor nerves.

ego (psychoanalytic) The division of the personality that is in touch with social realities and serves to delay the gratifications sought by the id.

eidetic images Extremely vivid and accurate imagery, normally visual (e.g., "photographic memory"); rare, especially in adults.

electrical stimulation of the brain (ESB) Electrical stimulation of the brain by implanted electrodes.

electroencephalogram (EEG) The graphic record of the electrical activity of the brain.

electrophysiology The use of electronic devices to study physiological functions, especially in the nervous system.

emergent The property of developing in some manner that is not predictable on the basis of prior events.

emergent norm theory Explanation of crowd behavior in terms of a behavioral norm that emerges as acceptable behavior.

emotion Disturbed or agitated state of an organism with characteristic experiential, physiological, and behavioral components.

empiricism Emphasis upon direct perceptual experience as contrasted with reason or reflection.

encoding The process by which information in a stimulus is transmitted and thereby retained during sensory transduction, in the perception and memory of meaningful materials.

endoderm The inner germ layer in the embryo from which the intestinal tract develops.

endomorph An individual characterized by fullness of build and enjoyment of sensory functions in Sheldon's typology.

engram Hypothesized neurophysiological change underlying memory. (*Synonym:* memory trace.)

epiphenomenalism The philosophic view that mental phenomena occur but as by-products of brain processes and so have no causal significance of their own.

epistemology The study of the source and the validation of knowledge; an area of philosophy.

equipotentiality principle (neurophysiology) The proposition that all parts of the brain are equally effective in contributing to the efficiency of certain higher mental functions, such as intelligence. *See also* mass action principle.

escape training A kind of learning in which some instrumental response removes the organism from noxious stimulation.

estrogen The female hormone secreted by the ovaries.

ethnocentrism The common tendency for people to use their own cultural standards as a frame of reference for all behavior, including that in other cultures, without realizing that they are doing so.

ethology Direct field observation of the natural behavior patterns of animals; a field of zoology.

etiology Study of the origins of a phenomenon, such as a disease or behavior disorder.

eugenics The science concerned with improvement of some species, particularly the human, by selective breeding designed to eliminate defective genotypes and proliferate desirable genotypes.

euthenics The science concerned with improvement of a species, particularly the human, by means of reducing environmental obstacles to desired development.

evoked potential The record of electrical discharge in the nervous system made at a point other than the locus of the stimulation.

evolution Presumed gradual changes in all living organisms that have occurred in phylogeny and are still occurring.

excitatory Activating.

exemplar Example of a concept.

experiment An observation so arranged as to make possible the clarification of the functional relationship between one or more manipulated ("independent") variables and measured ("dependent") variables, with explicit elimination of the effects of certain other ("controlled") variables.

experimental hypothesis The particular prediction about the results of an experiment that is made in advance of data collection, usually on the basis of some more or less explicit theoretical proposition.

external environment The totality of conditions outside the organism, with special reference to the effects they have on experience and behavior.

exteroceptors Receptor cells specialized to detect some form of energy from outside the organism (e.g., rods and cones for vision, hair cells for audition).

extinction A procedure used in learning experiments

in which the reinforcement previously offered after the correct instrumental response is withdrawn; alternatively, the process whereby the learned response progressively weakens and is ultimately eliminated under such nonreinforcement conditions.

extrapolation Extension of something (e.g., a curve or a conclusion) beyond its factual basis.

extrasensory perception Detection of stimuli or cognitions not based on known sensory modalities.

face validity (test) Determination of how well a test measures what it purports to measure by examination of its content. (*Synonym:* content validity.)

fact A statement or proposition accepted by some group of people at a particular time.

factor analysis Statistical methodology designed to determine the minimum number of conditions ("factors") needed to account for the pattern of intercorrelations among scores (as in tests comprising a battery).

fad Activity in which many people engage but which has a short-lived popularity.

false alarm (signal detection) Report by subject of a signal (stimulus) in a signal-detection experiment when none has actually been presented.

fatalism The belief that all events are inevitable, because they have been predetermined (or predestined).

fatigue State of weariness, as from physical or mental efforts.

fetus The later stages of a developing embryo in which body structures and functions characteristic of the adult are forming.

field theory The use of multiple correlated factors in psychological theory, based on an analogy with field forces (e.g., magnetic fields) in physics; most often associated with the work of Kurt Lewin.

filtering mechanism Screening process, with selective passage of some objects or functions, such as nerve impulses.

fixation (psychoanalytic) Retardation of normal personality development in which the objects of psychosexual attachment of an early stage (e.g., the mother) are retained.

fixed action pattern (FAP) A set form of behavior that is characteristic of a species. (*Synonym:* species-specific behavior.)

flight distance The physical distance a particular species typically allows a strange organism to approach before retreating.

flight of colors The especially vivid stream of multihued visual afterimages that typically follows momentary exposure to a very intense light stimulus.

forebrain The most anterior (forward) part of the brain, consisting mainly of the cerebrum, thalamus, and hypothalamus.

formal discipline doctrine The proposition that there are certain forms of learning or training, such as studying Latin or mathematics, that enhance many other superficially dissimilar forms of learning by a process of transfer of training.

fraternal twins *See* dizygotic twins.

free association The reporting of anything that comes into consciousness, with no restraints; a technique used in psychoanalytic therapy.

free operant An instrumentally conditioned response that the subject is able to make repeatedly, with rate of response used as the measure of learning.

free recall A type of retention test in which the subject is asked to reproduce learned materials in the absence of any cues.

frequency distribution A set of scores arranged by size and grouped into class intervals, showing the number of occurrences of each class.

frequency polygon A frequency distribution with the class-interval values connected by a continuous line, forming a polygon.

frequency theory Interpretation of hearing that stresses the role of the frequency of stimulation as the key factor in pitch sensation.

frustration The operation of blocking on-going or goal-directed behavior; also, the presumed emotional reaction to such an operation.

frustration–aggression hypothesis The proposition that all aggression is caused by frustration.

fugue Form of neurosis in which an individual becomes at least partially amnesic and disappears, to take up another life elsewhere for varying periods of time.

functional autonomy Process whereby instrumental motives become consummatory motives.

functional disorder Behavior disturbance in which there is no apparent organic (bodily) basis and which is therefore assumed to have been learned.

functional fixedness A set in which customary procedures prevent the seeing of new functions for particular objects.

functionalism A system of psychology that stresses the search for functional relationships rather than grand theories and is essentially eclectic, accepting data and techniques from various sources.

functional relationship The way in which one set of variables (dependent) varies with changes in some other set (independent) when the influence of other extraneous variables (controlled) is eliminated, as in an experiment.

fundamental frequency The basic sound-wave frequency of a vibrating body; the lowest frequency with which it vibrates.

gamete A mature reproductive cell, egg or sperm.

ganglion A cluster of nerve cell bodies located outside the central nervous system.

gastrointestinal Having to do with the structure and/or function of the intestinal tract.

gene A unit of heredity, located at some point on a chromosome, that initiates biochemical growth processes in relation to some particular body structure.

general adaptation syndrome (Selye) A conceptualization of the course of the body's continuing responsivity, focusing on emotional reactions to stress.

generalization (1) In problem solving, the discovery of a consistent rule or regularity that accounts for a variety of results; (2) in learning, the tendency for a response learned to some particular stimulus to be made to other, especially similar, stimuli.

generalized reinforcer A reinforcer (response strengthener) whose power is not restricted to any particular response but operates over a wide range of stimulus and response situations.

genotype The genetic basis in an individual for all development.

geriatrics Branch of medicine concerned with care of the aged.

germinal period The first two weeks of embryonic development, during which cellular differentiation is initiated.

gerontology The scientific study of the aged.

Gestalt psychology A school of psychology that emphasizes patterns (Gestalts) in perception and behavior (initiated by Max Wertheimer with the aid of Wolfgang Köhler and Kurt Koffka).

graphic rating scale A personality rating scale in which a line is provided for each attribute rated so that the judge can indicate exactly where on each continuum he thinks the subject belongs.

gustation Taste.

habit Strength of a behavior tendency, normally the result of reinforced practice.

habit-family hierarchy The notion of an ordered series of interacting responses that are in an organism's repertoire for coping with particular stimuli or situations (developed by C. L. Hull).

habituation The weakening of a response from repeated occurrence.

halo effect The process by which what one knows or thinks about another person affects his judgment of that person in some other respect.

haploid Containing a single chromosome of each kind, as occurs in cell division (meiotic) in eggs and sperm prior to reproduction; the normal diploid (paired) condition is then regained in the zygote formed from an egg and a sperm.

happiness A generally satisfied state of the organism, particularly if supporting verbal statements can be made (in the case of the human) consistent with expressed behaviors.

hebephrenia A form of schizophrenia in which the main psychotic symptoms are exaggerated mannerisms such as chronic giggling.

Heisenberg principle The proposition that it is impossible to measure, simultaneously and exactly, both the position and the velocity of an elementary particle; generalized as the principle of indeterminacy that is often applied to more molar problems.

heuristic A flexible method for problem solving that is adjusted by the subject to fit the situation, in contrast with the fixed routines of the algorithm.

hidden agenda Real but unstated objectives, as in a conference, political campaign, personal appeal, and so on.

hindbrain The most posterior of the three major parts of the brain, consisting of the medulla, cerebellum, and pons, and serving mainly vegetative and similar body functions.

hit (signal detection) Report by a subject of a signal (stimulus) when one has actually been presented.

hodology A special form of topological geometry in which the concept of directional forces (vectors) is added to spatial relationships (invented by field theorist Kurt Lewin).

homeostasis Maintenance of physiological balances in the body.

homologue An organ that is fundamentally like one in another organism in development and structure but that may nevertheless differ in function.

hunger Primary motive for food ingestion.

id (psychoanalytic) Part of the personality that encompasses instinctual (libidinal) impulses that unless checked push for gratification.

idea Some form of subjective experience relating to cognition.

identification The process by which one feels himself a part of a group.

idiographic With reference to a particular individual, as contrasted with generalized organisms.

idiot savant An individual who has succeeded in acquiring, by enormous amounts of practice, a prodigious memory for certain specialized subject matter (such as multiplication tables or the calendar) in spite of a generally very low intellectual ability, as evidenced both by standardized tests and common observation.

illumination The degree of light incident upon a stimulus.

illusion A false sensory experience, that is, one not in accord with the physical situation.

image A mental reproduction of a perception, in the absence of the original physical stimulus.

immediate experience Subjective experience conceived as the direct source of psychological study, by Wilhelm Wundt, contrasted with *mediate* experience, which was Wundt's way of distinguishing all other scientific study—consciousness studied as an intermediation device, to reach other phenomena.

incentive Goal object sought by an organism.

incubation stage The phase of problem solving in which an idea is formed.

independence Desire to do things for oneself.

independent variable The condition or factor in an experiment that is manipulated so as to determine its influence on some measured (dependent) variable(s).

individual psychology The psychoanalytic system developed by Alfred Adler.

infant The human organism from the neonatal stage (up to four weeks) to the age of approximately two years.

inferiority complex Adlerian term for emotional response to real or imagined deficiency.

information processing The sensory-memorial functions that occur as one's perceptual experiences are registered and maintained briefly in short-term memory before being passed into long-term memory; the emphasis is upon the informational value of experience.

inhibitory Interfering with or suppressing, as in neural function or behavior.

innate releasing mechanism (IRM) A process by which some particular stimulus produces a fixed pattern response characteristic of all members of the species.

inoculation (social) Slight exposure to new ideas designed to develop stout resistance that will later be used to combat stronger arguments.

insanity Common word for psychosis but one that is essentially without scientific standing.

insight Problem solving in which a relatively permanent and often simple solution suddenly occurs.

instinct General label for unlearned, goal-directed behavior patterns that are characteristic of all the members of a species.

instrumental conditioning Learning in which some response is strengthened as a function of its helping to satisfy a motive.

instrumental motive Behavioral objective whose primary function is to make possible satisfaction of another motive.

instrumental response Behavior that is useful as a means of obtaining some goal, thus permitting consummatory reactions such as eating.

intelligence quotient (IQ) Mental age (MA) divided by chronological age (CA), multiplied by 100, providing a relative measure of an individual's intellectual development and ability in terms of his test performance.

interaction Generally, the coming together of objects or events; statistically, the differential interrelationship among two or more variables depending upon their values and the pattern of operation of other variables.

interactionism The philosophical view, the most popular form of dualism, in which physical and mental events are both accepted as real and held to be closely interrelated.

interface Connection or junction between two or more objects or processes.

interference hypothesis (of forgetting) The proposition that most if not all forgetting is due to interference from subsequent learning (technically, *retroactive inhibition*).

internal environment Totality of conditions within the organism, with special reference to the effects they have upon experience and behavior.

internalization Acceptance of values and attitudes on the basis of their own merit, as evaluated by oneself.

interpolation Estimation of a value intermediate between two given values in an ordered series.

interposition The visual depth cue that results when

a near object blocks out part of a more distant object.

interval measurement Calibration in which all units (e.g., degrees of temperature or inches) are equal in value, making possible absolute rather than merely relative measurement.

interval schedule A program of reinforcement in which the first response made after some set period of time is rewarded.

intervening variable A hypothesized process that is inferred to mediate responses to stimuli.

intraorganismic Within an organism.

introspection Generally, the process of examining one's own consciousness; specifically, a special technique of examining and reporting subjective experiences directly, in the absence of added meaning; most emphasized by E. B. Titchener, who required long periods of concentrated practice of his students.

introspectionism The system of psychology developed by E. B. Titchener, a form of structuralism in which the whole of psychology is restricted to data available by introspection.

intuition A judgment or idea that seems to be correct to the individual but that is not made on any overt logical or factual basis.

James–Lange theory of emotion The view that it is the felt awareness of bodily changes that occur in "emotional" situations that is really the emotion.

jnd (just noticeable difference) The least change in sensation that can be detected and reported by a subject, as in a psychophysical experiment.

kinesthesis The sense of movement of muscles, tendons, and joints, by means of which postural balance and body movements are maintained.

latency period Time elapsing between a stimulus (e.g., a conditioned stimulus) and the resulting response (e.g., conditioned response); one measure of the strength of responding.

law An empirical relationship among variables that has been relatively well established; also, a proposition, usually with some theoretical or abstract content, that has received a relatively high degree of scientific acceptance.

law of effect The principle that responses are strengthened when they are followed by satisfying consequences; formulated by E. L. Thorndike and subsequently emphasized by B. F. Skinner as the principle of reinforcement.

learning Relatively enduring changes in behavior that occur with practice or experience.

leveling The tendency in memory to reduce differences so as to encompass initially diverse items under the same familiar concepts.

libido (Freudian) Drive for biological satisfaction.

light adaptation Decrease in brightness of seen objects over a period of time during which the retina adjusts to the high level of illumination.

limbic system Set of related structures in and around the midbrain that are intimately involved in motivation and emotion, in part because of the filtering of nerve impulses to and from the higher brain centers.

limbic theory of emotion The view that emotion is a function of activation of the limbic area of the brain.

limits, method of Psychophysical technique in which the subject is presented a series of stimulus values above and below the assumed threshold.

linear perspective Visual depth perception cue involving the fact that more distant objects appear to be both smaller and closer together.

linguist A specialist in language, especially the grammatical bases.

logic-tight compartmentalizing The independent maintenance of two or more separate belief systems that are logically incompatible.

longitudinal technique The method in which successive observations on the same individual organism are made as it develops, in contrast to using separate organisms of different ages for the observations.

long-term memory (LTM) Relatively permanently stored items in memory, as contrasted with the temporary storage of the short-term memory (STM) system.

magazine training Learning in which the animal subject discovers how to obtain and consume the incentive (typically food pellets) provided as reinforcers in the operant chamber (Skinner box) in learning research.

mand Skinnerian (S-R) term for a verbal command.

Manifest Anxiety Scale (MAS) A questionnaire whose items can be selectively scored to indicate the level of expressed anxiety.

manipulandum Any object or device a subject in a learning experiment is permitted to operate (e.g., a bar for a rat, a latch for a monkey, a telegraph key for a human).

mass action principle (neurophysiology) The proposition that higher mental functions, such as intelligence, depend upon the total amount of brain tissue rather than upon any particular centers. *See also* equipotentiality principle.

materialism The philosophical view that physical events constitute the fundamental and ultimate reality.

mean The arithmetical average, computed by dividing the sum of scores by their number; the most common measure of central tendency in a frequency distribution.

measurement The process of assigning numerical values to observed variables.

mechanism Process by means of which some objective is achieved or some function occurs.

median The middle score in a frequency distribution with the scores ordered by magnitude.

mediate experience *See* immediate experience.

mediated generalization Transfer between activities that is assumed to result from some covert function serving as an intermediary.

medium An individual claiming to be directed by a noncorporeal spirit or force, such as a dead person.

medulla Part of the hindbrain that mediates vital functions such as breathing and heartbeat.

meiosis Cell division that occurs in the preparation of gametes, or mature reproductive cells (eggs and sperm) in which the normal paired (diploid) number of chromosomes is reduced to a single (haploid) condition, so that only one of the two genes possessed by the parent is passed on to the offspring.

memory A generic term for the totality of retention of experience; also the process of storing and retrieving the results of experience or behavior so that the effects of learning can be demonstrated after a time interval.

memory curve The relationship between amount retained from a learning session and the time elapsing between learning and test.

memory retrieval The process of recovering memories from storage, technically called long term memory (LTM).

memory-search mechanisms Ways in which long term memory is examined in order to retrieve stored items.

memory span The number of items, such as digits, that can be held in short term memory (STM) and correctly recalled immediately after processing.

memory storage Maintenance by the organism of experienced and learned materials, retrievable on search. [*Synonym:* long-term memory (LTM).]

mental age (MA) The degree of intellectual development of an individual, as measured by the sum total of age-related test items that he is able to pass.

mesoderm The middle germ layer in the embryo, from which blood, muscle, and bone develop.

mesomorph An individual characterized by muscular build and athletic interests in Sheldon's typology.

metaphysical behaviorism A form of behaviorism in which the causal properties and even the existence of mind are denied.

methadone A drug used to allay severe withdrawal symptoms otherwise experienced when an addict is deprived of heroin.

methodological behaviorism A form of behaviorism in which psychology is viewed as necessarily depending upon behavioral expressions for all of its data; a more moderate and widely accepted view than radical or metaphysical behaviorism.

microelectrode Extremely small metal rod designed to be inserted into body tissue for the transmission or detection of electrical energy.

midbrain The central part of the brain, with centers for seeing and hearing and pathways to the forebrain.

mimicry The assumption by one species of some characteristic (such as coloration or shape) of another species; apparently has served as a protection from predators and so survived in evolution.

mind An inclusive term for all aspects of subjective experience or consciousness.

Minnesota Multiphasic Personality Inventory (MMPI) A widely used form of personality (adjustment) questionnaire from the responses to which a variety of diagnostic estimates can be made.

miss (signal detection) Report by a subject of no signal (stimulus) in a signal detection experiment when one has actually been presented.

mitosis Normal cell division in which the paired chromosomes are duplicated and recur in all daughter cells.

mob A crowd in which emotional factors play important behavior-determining roles.

modality A form or type of sensation (e.g., vision, hearing).

mode The most frequent score or class interval in a frequency distribution.

modeling Providing an example for observers to imitate; the basis for social-learning theory.

molar approach Perspective in which the focus is on the total pattern (the "big picture") rather than specific points or details.

molecular approach Perspective in which the focus is on the details and specific mechanisms of some phenomenon, in contrast to the total pattern.

monism Any philosophical view that assumes only a single kind of reality, either mental (e.g., subjective idealism) or physical (e.g., materialism).

monochromat An individual with total color weakness or blindness.

monocular cue A visual depth perception cue that operates with a single eye.

monozygotic twins Twins that have developed from the same egg and therefore have exactly the same genetic background, or genotype. (*Synonym:* identical twins.)

mood A temporary feeling tone that permeates subjective experience and behavior.

morphology The science of the structure (anatomy) of organisms.

motive Internal condition that organizes and energizes behavior in some particular direction.

motor activities Body or body part (muscle) movement.

motor set Preparing for a response by concentrating on the making of the response rather than the perception of the signal.

motor skill A more or less complex pattern of responses in which muscular coordination is a central requirement (e.g., typewriting, shooting baskets).

multiple personality Form of neurosis in which an individual alternates between two, or more, largely independent and often quite contrasting systems of personality. (*Synonyms:* split personality, dual personality.)

multivariate analysis Research design in which explicit attention is given to the simultaneous manipulation and measurement of more than single variables to permit the statistical analysis of their interactions.

mutation A suddenly appearing change in genotype, reflected by a corresponding phenotypic (bodily) change, that is passed on to offspring.

mystamus Involuntary eye movements, with alternating slow and rapid phases in opposite directions, or rapid oscillatory movements.

natural language mediator A meaningful word or phrase by means of which less familiar verbal materials can be encoded and so better remembered.

negative contrast effect Impairment of performance in a learning situation that is held to result from diminution of the incentive on the basis of its comparison with more preferred incentives also experienced.

negative eugenics The attempt to improve the genotype of a species by eliminating undesirable stock.

negative reinforcer A noxious object or event whose termination strengthens preceding responses.

negative transfer Interference exerted by the learning of some task on the subsequent learning of another task.

neonate The newly born organism, from the partunate stage (immediately after birth) to about four weeks of age.

nerve A bundle of nerve fibers.

neural deafness Hearing deficit associated with damage and malfunction within the neurological components of the ear. (*Synonym:* sensorineural deafness.)

neuron A nerve cell, the structural unit of the nervous system.

neurosis Personal maladjustment in which one is unable to cope effectively with worries, anxieties, and conflicts, causing development of some abnormal behavior symptoms; relatively less severe than psychosis in that disorientation, delusions, etc. do not occur and institutionalization is not often required.

noise (signal detection) The background variability in stimulation that is extraneous to a presented signal, and against which the presence of such a signal must be estimated by the subject.

nominal measurement The simplest form of measurement in which objects or events are merely classified into mutually exclusive categories (e.g., apples and oranges) in the absence of any true numerical calibration.

nomothetic With reference to generalized organisms, rather than particular individuals.

nondirective therapy A psychological technique in which the client is encouraged to work out his own problems with a minimum of direction from the therapist, who mainly attempts to reflect the client's own attitudes and feelings rather than impose his own; developed by Carl Rogers. (*Synonym:* client-centered therapy.)

nonsense syllable   A nonmeaningful verbal item, invented by Ebbinghaus in an effort to eliminate prior learning; now more commonly called CVC (consonant–vowel–consonant) because of the typical arrangement of the letters.

normal curve   The typical bell-shaped form of the frequency distribution in which frequencies are greatest for the middle scores or class intervals and fall off more or less regularly on both sides.

normative   Having to do with standards, as for some particular performance (e.g., vocabulary) at different ages.

normative–maturational study   An approach to the study of development that focuses on establishing behavioral standards (norms) for various stages of growth (maturation).

nucleus   A group of nerve cell bodies located within the central nervous system; also, the organizing center of the cell body, necessary for reproduction of the cell.

null hypothesis   The prediction of no differences among groups that is made for purposes of statistical analysis so that the reliability of obtained differences can be evaluated.

nurture   Environmental influence.

objective methodology   Techniques of study that depend upon observations, as of overt behaviors, in contrast to introspection and similar subjective techniques.

obsession   A neurotic symptom in which one is unable to dismiss some idea or urge; associated with compulsions in the form of obsessive-compulsive neurotic reaction in extreme cases.

occipital cortex   That part of the cerebral cortex that functions in vision, located to the rear of the cerebral hemispheres.

olfaction   Smell.

operant conditioning   Type of instrumental learning situation in which the subject emits responses and is usually permitted to respond as often as it wishes (free operant).

opponent processes theory   Interpretation of color vision that assumes the operation of three separate color systems—red-green, blue-yellow, and black-white—each consisting of paired, opposed processes.

ordinal measurement   A relatively simple form of measurement in which the measured values are ranked on a quantitative basis, so that more or less of the variable is indicated by the order of the ranking, as in the method of paired comparisons.

organic disorder   Behavior disturbance for which some bodily basis can be shown.

organism   The intact living animal, whose behavior and experience is the primary object of study in psychology.

organizer   A group of cells on the lip of the blastula that seem to determine the direction that embryonic differentiation and development take.

orienting reaction (reflex) (OR)   The nonspecific attentional response to a change in stimulation or to a novel stimulus, involving variations in sensory and visceral as well as muscular and brain-wave components.

overt   Open, as to direct observation.

overtones   Sound frequencies that result from partial vibrations of the sound-producing object, and are therefore always higher than the associated fundamental tone; *also called* partials.

paired associates   Verbal items used in S-R pairings in learning research.

paired comparisons   A technique of ordinal measurement in which a number of cases are ranked, two at a time, on some variable, permitting a cumulative score for each case in terms of how many "greater than" comparisons are achieved.

paleontology   The science of fossil remains, as found, for example, in rock layers.

papilla   A small protuberance, such as clusters of taste buds in the tongue.

paradoxical cold   The sensation of cold sometimes experienced as part of the response to high-temperature stimulation.

paradoxical sleep   REM sleep, in which the EEG pattern indicates an alert waking state, presumably reflecting dream activity, even though the subject is apparently in a state of deep sleep.

parallax   The visual depth cue that depends upon the apparent narrowing of the distance between parallel lines as the lines become more distant from the observer.

paranoia   Functional psychotic condition in which the primary symptoms are persistent and highly systematized delusions.

parapsychological phenomenon   Any event in

which behavior or experience allegedly occurs without the mediation of known behavioral processes (e.g., extrasensory perception).

parasympathetic nervous system A division of the autonomic nervous system that mainly serves to maintain vital body functions (e.g., digestion) and is generally antagonistic in function to the sympathetic divison of the autonomic nervous system.

paresis Organic psychotic condition produced by syphilitic spirochaetes' destruction of brain tissue.

parsimony The proposition that, other things being equal, the simpler of competing hypotheses is the most acceptable.

partial reinforcement extinction effect (PREE) The common finding of prolonged responding in extinction following a partial-reinforcement schedule (in which reward is not provided after every response) in training as compared with a continuous reinforcement schedule of reward.

partunate The human organism immediately after and up to several hours after birth.

pass (signal detection) Report by subject of no signal (stimulus) when none has actually been presented.

passive control A kind of observation in which the investigator does not exercise active manipulation of variables but rather waits until the desired combinations of values naturally occurs, as in the case of the astronomer who wishes to study an eclipse.

percentile A rank measure that indicates the percentage of scores exceeded in a frequency distribution by a score of any given value.

perception The meaningful awareness of the environment by means of the active interpretation of sensory signals.

perceptual constancies The various ways in which objects are perceived as the same objects in spite of marked variations in the sensory content (e.g., a plate is typically perceived as round even when the retinal patterns are various ellipses).

performance test Any test of ability or aptitude in which language factors are minimized and nonverbal responses are utilized as a means of assessing capacity.

peripheral nervous system That part of the nervous system located outside the central nervous system, including the autonomic nervous system and the nerves connecting receptors and effectors with the central nervous system.

personality The individual's unique organization of behavior; individuality.

phenomenalism Philosophical view that human knowledge is limited to the phenomena that can be experienced by the sensory system of the observer.

phenomenology The naive and untrained reporting on conscious experience, in the absence of any special training or instructions; characteristic of the Gestalt psychologists.

phenotype The body characteristics of an organism developed on the basis of its genetic potential (genotype) interacting with the environment.

pheromone A chemical stimulus produced by an organism to which other organisms, in particular conspecifics, react.

phi phenomenon Illusion of motion ("apparent movement") resulting from the successive presentation of two stationary stimuli (e.g., two lines or two lights); the experimental starting point of Gestalt psychology and the basis of many common phenomena (e.g., the stroboscope, the motion picture).

phobia Severe and irrational fear.

photopic vision Daylight vision, mediated by the cones in good illumination.

phrenology Evaluation of personality from analysis of skull configurations.

phylogeny Development of the phyla, the major divisions of plants and animals.

physiognomy Evaluation of personality by examination of facial features.

physiological zero The normal temperature of the skin, approximately 32° centigrade.

physiology Study of the functions of the organ systems of the body (e.g., digestion, circulation).

pituitary gland Endocrine gland located in the center of the head with control of growth and regulation of other endocrine glands.

place theory Interpretation of hearing that stresses the part of the cochlear membrane that is stimulated as the key factor in pitch sensation.

pleasure principle (Freud) The innate drive toward satisfaction of body needs, mainly sexual, that is presumed to be central to libido and the operating guide for the id.

polygenic With multiple genetic determination.

polygraph A recording device which measures multiple physiological variables (e.g., heart rate, blood pressure, galvanic skin response) to make possible differential evaluation of emotional responses to particular stimuli and, inferentially, the detection of "lying."

pons Portion of the hindbrain located above the

thalamus and serving to connect the cerebellum and the cerebrum.

positive contrast effect Improvement of performance in a learning situation that is held to result from enhancement of the incentive on the basis of its comparison with less preferred incentives also experienced.

positive reinforcer A satisfying object or event whose obtaining strengthens preceding responses.

positive transfer Facilitation in learning some new task as a result of prior learning.

posthypnotic suggestion The suggestion made by the hypnotist that the subject will behave in a prescribed manner after coming out of the trance; when such behavior occurs the subject is generally unaware of why he has so behaved.

power Influence on others, as exercised by parents, teachers, employers, police, and so on.

power law (Stevens) The proposition that the subjective magnitude of a sensory experience is proportional to the physical intensity of the stimulus raised to some power.

power motive (Adler) Interest in manipulating others according to one's own plans and purposes.

pragmatism The philosophic position that things should be evaluated in terms of their consequences; associated with William James.

preconscious (Freud) Memories that are not present in consciousness but are readily available.

predestination The view that there is a predetermined pattern that events must follow.

prediction A hypothesized description of the way in which specified events are expected to develop, often on the basis of some form of theoretical framework.

prejudice An emotionally based attitude about a class of people or events that is relatively fixed and resistant to change.

primary emotions The most fundamental emotional expressions: happiness, sorrow, fear, and anger.

primary motive Generally, a directly physiological drive condition, such as hunger, thirst, sex.

proactive inhibition The interfering effect upon the recall of learned materials that results from the prior learning of other materials.

probability Generally, likelihood of occurrence of some selected event; statistically, a statement of likelihood that an obtained result would occur in the absence of a presumed relationship to some determining condition.

product-moment correlation coefficient. *See* correlation coefficient.

prognosis Prediction as to the probable outcome of a disease or disorder.

projection (psychoanalytic) Attribution to others of one's own faults.

projective test An indirect test of personality in which a subject's performance in a relatively unstructured situation (e.g., making up stories from pictures) is used to make inferences about his personality.

proprioceptor A receptor in a muscle, tendon, or joint that is stimulated by body movement and mediates the sense of kinesthesis.

psychic apparatus The structural model of the mind (id, ego, superego) developed by Sigmund Freud.

psychoanalysis A therapeutic practice and a theory of personality developed by Sigmund Freud in which the sexual basis of behavior disorder and the importance of infancy and childhood determinants are stressed.

psycholinguist A specialist in the psychological aspects of language, mainly its grammatical bases and its meaningfulness.

psychology The scientific study of experience and behavior in organisms.

psychopath Neurosis in which social and moral instability is marked in the absence of any intellectual disorder. (*Synonym:* sociopath.)

psychopathology Behavior disorders.

psychophysical method A technique for measuring the relationship between psychological (sensory) function and physical (stimulus) energy.

psychophysical parallelism The philosophical view, a form of dualism, in which both physical and mental events are accepted as real and are held to be perfectly correlated in time.

psychophysics Quantitative investigation of the relationship between mental (sensory) and physical (stimulating) variables; initiated by G. Fechner.

psychosis Major behavior disorder in which disorganization of personality and behavior occurs and to which radical treatments are often applied in hospitals.

psychotherapy The use of psychological variables (e.g., personal interview, selective reinforcement and nonreinforcement) to treat behavioral problems.

public opinion poll A battery of questions concerning some topic of current interest (e.g., the functioning of the government) put to a selected sample of people in order to estimate public attitudes.

punishment Noxious stimulation applied after undesired behavior.

pure science Scientific investigation that is undertaken "for its own sake," that is, without explicit motivation to apply the results to any particular practical problem.

Purkinje effect The more rapid darkening of the long-wave end of the spectrum (e.g., reds) than the short-wave end (e.g., blues) as illumination diminishes, as at twilight, believed to result from the progressive shift from cone to rod vision.

purpose Motive or object of goal-directed behavior.

purposive behaviorism A form of behaviorism that incorporates goal direction; developed by E. C. Tolman.

pursuit rotor A special device designed to test motor (tracking) skill in which the subject must move a stylus to maintain as much contact as possible with a target spot that is moving in an irregular path on a circular plate (such as a phonograph record).

puzzle box (Thorndike) A test chamber in which an organism must learn which of a number of alternative responses is correct so as to obtain some reward.

p value The probability that a difference as large as that obtained between groups would occur as a result of random variations, in the absence of a "true" difference.

Q-sort (Stephenson) A form of rating scale in which descriptive terms are sorted into piles in accordance with the degree of their judged applicability to the subject being rated; permits a quantitative self-concept measure when one so judges himself.

radical behaviorism *See* metaphysical behaviorism.

random "Chance," meaning that unknown and essentially unmeasurable events determine some particular results, such as the toss of a coin, in the absence of any consistent bias.

random assortment (Mendel) The proposition that each pair of factors in a mating occur independently of all other factors.

range The difference between the smallest and the largest score in a frequency distribution.

rank order Relative position of various scores along some variable, using ordinal measurement so that only greater-than or less-than comparisons are possible. *See also* paired comparisons.

rapid eye movement (REM) The very rapid movements of the eye during sleep that are correlated with intense dreaming activity.

ratio measurement The most refined form of measurement in which not only are the units used equal to each other but their relationships (ratios) are also equal over the entire scale.

ratio schedule A program of reinforcement in which every *n*th response is rewarded.

rationalism The emphasis on reason or reflection in contrast to empirical (observational) procedures as a basis for conclusions.

rationalization (psychoanalytic) Defense mechanism in which socially acceptable but actually unimportant reasons are given for one's behavior.

reaction formation (psychoanalytic) The development of extreme compensatory reactions to certain of one's undesirable tendencies.

reaction time The time elapsing between the presentation of a stimulus (signal) and the making of a response.

readiness The notion that attempts to train an organism (e.g., toilet-train) will be ineffective until appropriate capacity to learn ("readiness") has developed.

reality orientation Correspondence of one's perspectives on the world with those of most other people.

reality principle (Freud) An orientation to the real world and its various social codes and restrictions that is presumed to be the basis of ego operations as these serve to check the libidinal tendencies of the id.

reasoning Type of thinking in which more or less ordered (logical) steps are used.

recall (memory) A technique of testing for retention in which the subject is required to provide a maximum number of cues and attempt to restate what he has learned.

reception paradigm In concept formation research, having the subject respond positively or negatively to each stimulus presented, with regard to whether it represents an exemplar of the target concept.

receptor Specialized body part that is sensitive to some kind of environmental energy (e.g., rods and cones for light).

recessive (genetic) Lacking the power of expression when present with a dominant paired gene.

reciprocal facilitation The activation of one process, such as muscle contraction, by the inhibition of an opposed process, such as the relaxation of a paired muscle.

recognition (memory) A technique of testing retention in which maximal cues are provided and the subject merely has to indicate whether or not each item has been previously experienced.

reduction screen A screen with a very small aperture through which only a portion of the stimulus situation, such as the texture of an object but not its surround, can be perceived.

redundancy (linguistics) A property of language by which multiple cues are provided a listener because of the essentially sequential nature of connected discourse.

reflex An automatic and fixed response of some part of the body to a particular stimulus.

reflex arc Hypothetical neural circuit consisting of stimulation of sense organ, transmission of nerve impulse to central nervous system, and response by muscle or gland.

refractory period The temporary period of neural insensitivity immediately following excitation.

registration The initial phase of information processing, in which environmental stimuli are processed ("registered") by some sensory system.

regression (psychoanalytic) Return to an earlier stage of personality development as a means of adjustment to personal problems.

reification Tendency to treat a process as a thing in theoretical explanation of events or relationships among variables.

reinforcement Generally, response strengthening; specifically, the operation in which responses are strengthened or weakened in accordance with the manipulation of their consequences (providing rewards or punishments).

relational concept A concept defined by some particular relationship between two (or more) attributes.

relearning method (memory) A technique of testing for retention in which the subject is required to repeat the learning process in the same manner as original learning, providing a savings score (per cent improvement, in terms of trials, errors, time, and the like).

releasing mechanism See innate releasing mechanism.

relevant dimension (of concepts) The characteristic

of an object that identifies a concept.

reliability (test) That property of a standardized test that enables one to obtain substantially the same score each time it is administered; self-consistency of the measuring instrument.

REM See rapid eye movement.

reminiscence An improvement in learned performance in the absence of practice over an intertest interval.

repression (psychoanalytic) Unconscious forgetting.

response-contingent Dependent upon the making of a response.

response operating characteristic (ROC) The function relating the probability of hits and false alarms for a particular level of signal in the signal detection process.

retention Memory of learned materials as measured by a test given after a time interval.

reticular activating system (RAS) Part of the reticular formation that functions selectively in the arousal of the cerebral cortex.

reticular formation Mass of nuclei and nerve fibers in the brain stem just above the spinal cord; plays an important role in attention and alertness of the organism.

retinal disparity The slight difference in images falling on the two retinas, because of the slightly different perspectives they have when both eyes look at the same object. (Synonym: binocular disparity.)

retrieval See memory retrieval.

retroactive inhibition Interference in the retention of learning produced by the interpolation of new learning between the original learning and the retention test.

retrograde amnesia Forgetting of events that occurred before some traumatic event.

retrospective falsification Distortions in memory associated with confusion of detail and relationships, and the subsequent making of incorrect connections that are not recognized as faulty.

reverie Dreamlike state of fantasy.

reversibility Piaget's concept for the ability of an organism to return in its thinking to an earlier condition, rather than simply follow the superficial transformations of an object (e.g., of a ball of clay molded into different shapes).

reward A satisfying object or event; that is, one which satisfies some ongoing motivation of the organism (e.g., food for a hungry organism).

rhodopsin Light-sensitive chemical in the rods of the retina. (*Synonym:* visual purple.)

riot Violent and disorderly behavior by a crowd.

RNA (ribonucleic acid) Complex molecules believed to play a central role in mediating memory.

ROC *See* response operating characteristic.

rod Specialized receptor cell in retina that functions in black-white vision under dim illumination.

role A set of behaviors that have been developed within society to characterize some particular social position or status (e.g., college student, professor).

Rorschach A projective personality test in which the subject tells what he sees in a series of ink-blot stimuli.

rule The principle upon which a concept is based.

Sampling Selecting scores from a large group of scores (the population).

satiation State of satisfaction of some particular motive(s).

schizophrenia The most common functional psychosis in which intellectual disorientation and confusion is accompanied by marked affective dulling and generalized social indifference; formerly known as dementia praecox.

school A group of men who share the same fundamental assumptions and theoretical predispositions toward some subject matter, such as psychology, and whose work tends therefore to show continuity.

scientific method The general procedure whereby the functional relationships among variables are determined, as far as possible under experimental (controlled) conditions of observation, and theoretically interpreted.

scotopic vision Night-time vision, mediated by the rods in dim illumination.

secondary motive Generally, a learned motive, presumably based on (that is, derivable from) some more primary motive.

secondary reinforcement Process of response strengthening in which reinforcing stimulus is initially neutral, but acquires its reinforcing property by association with some already effective stimulus.

secondary reinforcing stimulus A cue whose association with a primary (motivation-satisfying) reinforcer has lent it some temporary reinforcing power of its own. (*Synonym:* conditioned reinforcer.)

segregation (Mendel) The principle that characters in which two mated parents differ will appear separately in definite numerical ratios in the second generation (that is, in the offspring of their progeny).

selection paradigm Subjects select exemplars of the concept from among a variety shown.

self-appraisal emotions Affective judgments in which an individual evaluates himself.

semantic differential A technique utilizing factor analysis of ratings to investigate the meaningfulness to an individual of words; developed by Charles Osgood.

senile dementia Organic psychosis of old age in which the normal symptoms of aging (e.g., memory loss, disorientation) are severely exaggerated because of the physiological deterioration of the brain.

sensation Subjective experience directly resulting from adequate stimulation of receptors in a sense organ.

sense A specific class of subjective experience, produced by some form of environmental energy and mediated by cellular receptors in a specialized organ.

sensing The process of making contact with the environment by operation of one of the specialized sense organs.

sensorineural deafness *See* neural deafness.

sensory adaptation Diminution in the sensory effects of a long-continued or frequently repeated stimulus.

sensory reception Activation of a sense organ by some form of environmental energy change.

sensory set Preparation for a response by concentrating on perceiving the stimulus (signal) rather than making the response.

separation anxiety Acute fear that infants may experience when parted from their mothers.

serendipity An accidental discovery.

serial anticipation A verbal-learning research technique in which the subject is instructed to respond with the next item in a sequential list after he (or the experimenter) provides the preceding (stimulus) item.

set Orientation or readiness for some kind of behavior.

sex-linked Referring to a body characteristic whose genetic determination is mediated by genes on the sex chromosomes.

shadowing A special experimental technique in which a subject is required to attend to and repeat the auditory message being presented to one ear while a second, different message is being presented to the other ear.

shaping The operant conditioning procedure in which successively closer approximations to some desired behavior are obtained by withholding reinforcement on each trial until the organism emits a satisfactory type of response.

sharpening The tendency in memory to exaggerate prominent features, such as the size of a person's ears of the funniness of a joke.

short-term memory (STM) The holding in memory of information for a relatively brief period of time, after which forgetting will occur unless special efforts are made to retain the information, as by rehearsal, or it is passed into LTM.

Sidman avoidance schedule Avoidance training procedure in which an organism must emit an instrumental response (e.g., a bar press) at some set interval, usually in the absence of any signal, in order to prevent a noxious stimulus (e.g., electric shock).

sign An object or stimulus that is a substitute for some other object or stimulus.

sign stimulus A condition of an organism that serves as a cue for some fixed behavior of another organism that is characteristic of the species.

signal detection A process in which the subject judges on each trial whether or not a target signal was present, embedded in the extraneous stimulation called "noise."

simple reaction time Time elapsing between the presentation of a stimulus and the making of a response when only one stimulus and one response are involved.

sine wave A cyclical curve in a graph that represents the wave form of a pure tone (only the fundamental frequency included).

Skaggs–Robinson hypothesis The proposition that the amount of interference in memory varies from low to high as the similarity between the originally learned and the subsequently learned (interfering) tasks increases.

skepticism The holding back of conclusions until adequate data are available and the persistent questioning of conclusions based upon inadequate data.

Skinner box An operant-conditioning device in which some manipulandum (e.g., a bar) is provided whose operation produces reinforcers (e.g., food pellets).

social indicator A measure that is used as an indicant of the state of society with respect to some specific variable or problem (e.g., monies allocated to welfare or to the military); used in social evaluations and planning.

social variable Condition in which some role is played by other organisms.

sociology Study of the structure and function of groups of organisms.

somatic cells Cells making up parts of the body other than the reproductive organs, and therefore containing diploid (paired) chromosomes.

somatotonia Hypothesized temperament with emphasis on bodily activities, correlated with mesomorphic body type in Sheldon's typology.

somatotype Body characteristic, of a sort that is presumed to be characteristic of a large number of individuals.

sorrow Any affective state in which some type and degree of sadness is experienced.

spatial summation Cumulative neural activity resulting from multiple fibers firing at the same time.

species-specific behavior A set form of behavior characteristic of the species.

spike The action current accompanying a nervous impulse, represented by a sharp peak in the curve of negative electricity shown on recording instrument.

spinal cord That part of the central nervous system consisting of nerve fibers connecting the brain to the receptors and effectors and lying next to the backbone.

spiritistic phenomenon An event in which the influence of extraphysical forces is allegedly exerted.

spontaneous recovery Return of some partial strength of a learned (conditioned) response that has been weakened by extinction, after a rest interval without further practice or reinforcement.

standard deviation (SD, σ) A statistical index of variability, computed as the square root of the mean of the squared differences from the mean of the distribution.

standard score A converted score, based on a distribution with a mean of 0 and a standard deviation of 1.

standardization Objective determination of reliability and validity of tests.

statistics The techniques whereby numerical data are described and analyzed to permit the making of inferences about their meaning.

stereotype A fixed idea, typically based on little personal experience, which involves categories of people or organizations and which has undue influence on attitudes and behaviors.

stimulus error (Titchener) Responding to a stimulus in terms of the known properties of the stimulus rather than in terms of the physical energies per se.

stimulus generalization The tendency of an organism to make a response that has been conditioned to some particular stimulus in the presence of some new similar stimulus.

storage Maintenance of information in long-term memory (LTM) for indefinitely long periods of time in the absence of further practice or rehearsal.

stranger anxiety Fearful reactions of infants to unfamiliar people.

stream of consciousness The continuous flow of subjective experiences that marks the normal conscious state; a key concept of William James.

stroboscope A device that presents a rapid progression of different visual stimuli so as to simulate motion (e.g., the motion picture; see also phi phenomenon).

Strong Vocational Interest Blank An occupational interest test in which the subject's potential interest in multiple occupational categories can be assessed in terms of the degree to which his answers correlate with those provided by successful individuals in the various occupations.

structuralism The school (system) of psychology that considered the analysis of experience to be the primary task of psychology, using the technique of introspection developed by W. Wundt and E. B. Titchener.

subjective idealism The philosophic view that only subjective experiences really exist; a form of monism.

sublimation (psychoanalytic) Redirecting of libidinal (sexual) energies to more socially desirable channels.

suggestibility Susceptibility to social influence.

superego (psychoanalytic) A division of the personality corresponding to what is commonly labeled as "conscience," the internalized rules and regulations of society.

symbol Something that can replace or represent another object or event.

sympathetic nervous system A division of the autonomic nervous system that functions in emotional and other arousal (e.g., speeds up heart action) and is generally antagonistic in function to the parasympathetic division of the autonomic nervous system.

synapse The unidirectional junction between nerve cells; passage of the nerve impulse is always from axons to dendrites.

synesthesia A perceptual phenomenon in which stimulation in one sensory modality is experienced in a different modality (e.g., hearing sounds as colors).

tabetic Without the use of the normal afferent (feedback) stimulation from the movement of the legs, owing to destruction of the posterior column of the spinal cord; this affliction is called *tabes dorsalis* or *locomotor ataxia*.

tachistoscope A device designed to present visual materials for extremely brief time periods.

tact Skinnerian (S–R) term for verbal behavior elicited by an environmental object or event.

tactual Having to do with touch.

taste bud A bottle-shaped structure located on the tongue containing receptors for gustatory sensation.

taxis A forced movement of the body of an organism in response to some particular environmental stimulus. (*Synonym:* tropism.)

teleological The property of ascribing causal efficacy (purposiveness) to factors in the absence of any clear demonstration that their influence really preceded the allegedly purposive behavior.

teleology The view that behavior can be explained in terms of its ultimate utility.

telepathy The direct influence of one mind on another, outside known sensory channels; popularly, "mind reading."

telephone theory A simple form of the frequency theory of hearing, assuming a direct correlation of mechanical and neural frequencies (as in a telephone transmitter); now generally believed to be inadequate.

temperament The more or less chronic or consistent affective tone and emotional organization of an individual.

temporal orientation Perspective with regard to time.

temporal summation Cumulative neural activity resulting from the build-up of firing over time.

tension system (Lewin) Motive which derives from an intention to carry out some act.

texture gradient Ordered variation in the observed composition of objects as a function of varying distance.

Thematic Apperception Test (TAT) Projective personality test based on stories told as response to pictures.

theory A proposition relating variables within a circumscribed framework advanced to interpret data and serve as a basis for prediction of new data.

thinking General term for the subjective processes in which representatives of real objects and events are mentally manipulated.

thirst Primary motive for water intake.

threshold That point at which a stimulus (absolute threshold) or a change in a stimulus (difference threshold) becomes perceptible, usually identified when 50 per cent of the subjects' judgments are correct. (*Synonym:* limen.)

timbre The peculiar tonal quality of a musical instrument or other vibrating body which distinguishes its sound from other instruments with the same fundamental frequency; mainly caused by differential production of overtones.

T-maze A simplified choice device, consisting of a short runway and a single arm with right or left choices permitted, used in learning research with animals, mainly laboratory rats.

transduction The transfer of one type of energy into another, such as occurs in the sense organ (e.g., transfer of light energy to electrical energy in the eye).

transformational grammar Theoretical linguistic framework for study of the ways in which sentence parts are changed as one speaks, in the absence of any formal or explicit set of rules.

tropism A forced movement of the body of an organism in response to some particular environmental stimulus. (*Synonym:* taxis.)

t-test A statistical test applied to the means of two distributions of scores in order to permit inferences as to the reliability of the obtained difference.

two-way shuttle box Reversible training apparatus for research on aversive conditioning in which the subject is permitted to escape or avoid noxious stimulation by leaving one chamber for another, but must then return to the original chamber when the noxious stimulus occurs in the initially "safe" chamber.

unconditioned stimulus (UCS) Stimulus in classical conditioning that elicits the response (e.g., food placed on dog's tongue to produce salivation) so that it can be attached to a new (conditioned) stimulus (e.g., buzzer).

unconscious (Freudian) Level of experiences not readily recalled, in which the id mainly operates.

vacuum activity Instinctive responses emitted in absence of normal stimuli.

validity (test) The degree to which a test really measures what it purports to measure.

variable A condition or factor that is under study, preferably by manipulation, measurement, or control in an experiment.

variance The square of a standard deviation.

vertical ordinate The upright axis of a graph along which the dependent (measured) variable is usually plotted.

vestibular sense The modality that enables one to maintain posture, with respect to gravity; located in the labyrinth of the inner ear.

visceratonia Hypothesized temperament with emphasis on bodily comforts correlated with endomorphic body type in Sheldon's typology.

visual cliff Apparatus designed to study visual depth perception in young organisms, consisting of a clear plate of heavy glass under which there is variation in the distance between the floor and the glass.

volition The state of self-initiation of behavior. (*Synonym:* will.)

volley theory A modified form of frequency theory of pitch perception in which it is assumed that different nerve fibers respond in coordinated manner to account for the correlation assumed to occur between mechanical and neural frequencies.

warm-up effect The improvement during the early part of a practice period which seems to consist primarily of the subject's preparing for the responses required.

Weber–Fechner law The assumption of a logarithmic relationship between sensation and stimulus intensity.

Weber fraction The ratio between the initial intensity of a physical stimulus and the amount of change required to produce a just noticeable difference (jnd) in sensation.

willing Process of voluntary effort toward some goal.

withdrawal Social indifference; a symptom of serious behavioral maladjustment when extreme.

X-chromosome Long chromosome which when matched in the zygote with another long chromosome (forming an X) produces a female offspring.

Y-chromosome Short chromosome which when matched in the zygote with a long chromosome (forming a Y) produces a male offspring.

Zeigarnik effect The superior recall of the names of uncompleted as compared with completed tasks; the most prominent demonstration of Lewin's tension system construct.

zero point The point at which a measured variable has no value.

zygote The single-celled new organism conceived by union of the male sperm and the female egg.

INDEX